Cyclopedia
of
LITERARY
CHARACTERS

Cyclopedia

of

LITERARY
CHARACTERS

Revised Edition

Volume Three
Jonathan Wild–Peder Victorious

---

edited by
A. J. Sobczak

original editions edited by
Frank N. Magill

associate editor
Janet Alice Long

SALEM PRESS, INC.
Pasadena, California   Englewood Cliffs, New Jersey

Editor in Chief: Dawn P. Dawson
Managing Editor: Chris Moose
Project Editor: A. J. Sobczak
Acquisitions Editor: Mark Rehn
Research Supervisor: Jeffry Jensen
Research: Jun Ohnuki
Production Editor: Janet Alice Long
Layout: William Zimmerman

Library of Congress Cataloging-in-Publication Data
Cyclopedia of literary characters / edited by A. J. Sobczak ; associate editor, Janet Alice Long. — Rev. ed.
p. cm.
"This comprehensive revised edition of Cyclopedia of literary characters combines all the titles from the original Cyclopedia of literary characters and from Cyclopedia of literary characters II . . . adds character descriptions from titles included in Masterplots (revised second edition, 1996) and the Masterplots II sets covering African American literature (1994), women's literature (1995), and American fiction (supplement, 1994) . . . 3,300 titles [in all]."—Publisher's note.
Includes index
1. Literature—Stories, plots, etc. 2. Literature—Dictionaries. 3. Characters and characteristics in literature. I. Sobczak, A. J. II. Long, Janet Alice.
PN44.M3 1998
809'.927—dc21
ISBN 0-89356-438-9 (set)   97-45813
ISBN 0-89356-441-9 (vol. 3)   CIP

SECOND PRINTING
PRINTED IN THE UNITED STATES OF AMERICA

CONTENTS

CONTENTS

CONTENTS

CONTENTS

KEY TO PRONUNCIATION

As an aid to users of the *Cyclopedia of Literary Characters, Revised Edition*, guides to pronunciation have been provided for particularly difficult character names. These guides are rendered in an easy-to-use phonetic manner. Stressed syllables are indicated by small capital letters. Letters of the English language, particularly vowels, are pronounced in different ways depending on the context. Below are letters and combinations of letters used in the phonetic guides to represent various sounds, along with examples of words in which those sounds appear.

Symbols	Pronounced As In
a	answer, laugh, sample, that
ah	father, hospital
aw	awful, caught
ay	blaze, fade, waiter, weigh
ch	beach, chimp
ee	believe, cedar, leader, liter
eh	bed, head, said
ew	boot, lose
g	beg, disguise, get
i	buy, height, lie, surprise
ih	bitter, pill
j	digit, edge, jet
k	cat, kitten, hex
[n]	bon (French "silent" n)
o	cotton, hot
oh	below, coat, note, wholesome
oo	good, look
ow	couch, how
oy	boy, coin
rr (rolled r)	guerrilla (Spanish pronunciation)
s	cellar, save, scent
sh	champagne, issue, shop
uh	about, butter, enough, other
ur	birth, disturb, earth, letter
y	useful, young
z	business, zest
zh	seizure, vision

Cyclopedia
of
LITERARY
CHARACTERS

JONATHAN WILD

Author: Henry Fielding (1707-1754)
First published: 1743
Genre: Novel

Locale: England
Time: Late seventeenth century
Plot: Social satire

Jonathan Wild, a descendant of many men hanged for thievery and treason. He becomes a notorious criminal, beginning as a pickpocket while still a schoolboy. He becomes a criminal leader and gathers about him a gang of thieves who do his bidding. He shows his "greatness" as a criminal by being dishonest even to his friends and companions. His highest aim is to send his honest friend, Heartfree, to the gallows. Instead, he himself dies on the gallows, cursing humankind.

Count La Ruse, a fellow criminal with Jonathan Wild. He is a pickpocket befriended by Jonathan while in debtors' prison. He has a long career in crime that ends when he is executed by being broken on the wheel in France.

Laetitia Snap, who becomes Jonathan's wife. She keeps him at a distance for a time in order to keep her lover a secret.

She is a fitting wife for Jonathan, being herself a pickpocket and a cheat at cards. She ends up on the gallows.

Mr. Heartfree, a good man who loves his family and is honest in his dealings. He is a former schoolmate of Jonathan. He is a jeweler by trade and is ruined by Jonathan and his gang, who steal his stock, beat him terribly, and say at the same time they are his friends.

Mrs. Heartfree, an honest woman. Jonathan convinces her that her husband wants her to go with Jonathan to Holland. Jonathan mistreats her, but she returns from her extensive travels in time to save her husband from hanging after he has been framed by Jonathan. When she returns, she has a fabulous jewel, the gift of a savage chief, which restores the family's prosperity.

JORROCKS' JAUNTS AND JOLLITIES

Author: Robert Smith Surtees (1803-1864)
First published: 1838
Genre: Novel

Locale: England and Paris, France
Time: The 1830's
Plot: Wit and humor

John Jorrocks, a penny-pinching, successful Cockney grocer and tea merchant whose misadventures at numerous vacation spots outside London form the common thread of the story. Jorrocks is obsessed with fox hunting, and the thrill of the hunt is tempered only by his anxious avoidance of jumping fences and being late for supper, the prospect of either of which will cause him to give up the chase immediately. He takes extreme care with his appearance, clothing his well-fed figure in expensive or flashy pieces with a cheerful disregard for whether they flatter him or match. Accompanied by his freeloading younger friend, the Yorkshireman, Jorrocks travels to various resort towns associated with different sports. Whether deer or rabbit hunting, horse racing, gambling, or boating, his prejudices always surface: He likes only fox hunting and, as revealed in his encounters with both local inhabitants and foreign tourists, his own country and neighbors. Despite Jorrocks' efforts to keep travel costs down, events (and the Yorkshireman) frequently conspire to part him from his money. In the course of his exploits, he is pitched head first off his horse into a cesspool, arrested and convicted for trespassing by the length of his big toe, left naked after a swim when the tide takes his pants, and found sprawled under the heap of ballroom guests he knocked down during his vigorous attempt to dance. His biggest adventure is a trip to France, during which he becomes acquainted with Countess Benvolio, who generously offers to house and feed him, separates him from his traveling companion, and spends all of his money. On his final trip, he befriends and joins a boating group, less from an interest in the sport than from interest in the size of their picnic hamper. When someone hooks a fish and tips the boat, Jorrocks is hurled overboard and nearly drowns. He is nursed through the night and regains partial consciousness, though

convinced that he is already dead or at least well on his way. Calling the Yorkshireman to his side, he makes known his last wishes, revealing the location of his will and its handsome provision for his friend, especially if the young man marries Jorrocks' daughter. In spite of his condition, he manages to discuss the economic advantages of such a merger. The talk of business seems to revive him. After imparting this information in somber tones, Jorrocks suddenly orders a hearty meal and a mug of ale, admonishing the Yorkshireman to blow the foam off the ale, as it is bad for one's health. Jorrocks will survive, for the sake of his business and his belly, if for nothing else.

The Yorkshireman, a young traveling companion to Jorrocks. His philosophy is that he will provide the company as long as Jorrocks provides the cash. Throughout the story, he is known only as the Yorkshireman, except in one town, where he answers to the name of Charley Stubbs, perhaps because he runs up a large tab in a public house, then leaves his receipts, or "stubs," for Jorrocks to pay. The Yorkshireman suggests the final adventure, which is motivated by a desire for a free vacation but presented to Jorrocks, during a particularly beastly hangover, as a means of escaping his wife, who is outraged by the previous night's drunkenness. His knack for maneuvering thrifty Jorrocks to pay for the most expensive sherry and his capacity for getting Jorrocks into and out of scrapes make him an admirable trickster.

Countess Benvolio, a woman of questionable age, motives, and associates who offers her house and company to Jorrocks while he is in Paris but does not extend the invitation to his more perceptive traveling companion. The countess lives on what translates roughly from the French as Bad Boy Street. Indeed, under her direction, Jorrocks is a bad boy, lavishing money on her, dressing in even more ridiculous clothing than usual, wearing a fake mustache, and introducing himself as Colonel Jorrocks at her request. When his purse is empty, he returns to her house one day to find a rich German gentleman in his favorite chair and a bill for room and board in the countess' hand. Running into an acquaintance on the boat back to England, Jorrocks misunderstands a question about sightseeing in Paris: When asked if he has seen the Notre Dame, he admits that he did meet a very naughty dame.

— *Elizabeth Bleicher*

JOSEPH AND HIS BROTHERS
(Joseph und seine Brüder)

Author: Thomas Mann (1875-1955)
First published: 1948 (combined, in English)
Genre: Novel

Locale: Egypt and Canaan
Time: The period of Genesis
Plot: Religious

The Tales of Jacob, 1933

Joseph, one of the twelve sons of Jacob. Bright and clever, he is fascinated by the tales about his ancestors that have been handed down by his father. He is the son of his father's beloved wife, Rachel.

Jacob, Joseph's father. He tricked his own father, Isaac, into giving him the blessing of the firstborn that rightfully belonged to his brother, Esau. Because of this, he is forced to flee to his uncle, Laban, to avoid Esau's wrath.

Rachel, Joseph's mother and Jacob's beloved. Jacob is forced to work for fourteen years before he can marry her.

The Young Joseph, 1934

Joseph, a delightful companion for his father. He is more charming, graceful, and well-spoken than his older half brothers. While they labor in the fields, he learns to read. They resent him for these differences, as well as for the favors that are bestowed on him. When Jacob gives him the coat of many colors, the brothers rightly realize that this means they will be cast aside as heirs in Joseph's favor. They retaliate by planning his murder, eventually compromising by selling him into slavery.

Jacob, who worries about Joseph with his presumptuous dreams and arrogant lack of restraint in sharing them. He is unable to resist showing Joseph special favors.

Eliezer, Joseph's first teacher, a faithful servant to the family. Since the days of Abraham, there has always been a servant named Eliezer in the camp. His wisdom and knowledge of the past are so great that it is easy to confuse him with the first Eliezer, servant to Abraham. He teaches Joseph of the heavens and the stars, numbers, and the universe.

Reuben, the eldest of Jacob's sons. Although he has the most to lose by Jacob's favoritism, he does not truly resent it because he, too, is charmed by Joseph's grace and beauty. He only pretends to take part in the attack on Joseph and is devastated when he returns to save his beloved brother only to find him gone.

Joseph in Egypt, 1936

Joseph, who is now a slave. In the various roles he assumes after being sold, he wins the trust and affection of those who are in positions above him. His intelligence means that he quickly absorbs everything he is taught. He has a strong sense of religious destiny and is convinced that he is consecrated by God; thus, he believes that everything that happens to him does so because of God's plan. This is one factor that helps him to resist the seduction of Potiphar's wife.

Potiphar, a courtier in Pharaoh's court. Joseph is sold to him. Castrated in his youth, he is unable to lead the life of an ordinary man. He recognizes Joseph's talents, eventually making him overseer of all he owns.

Mont-kaw, Potiphar's overseer. He is a good man, simple but intuitive. He quickly sees Joseph's abilities and begins grooming him as his successor. While teaching Joseph, he becomes a substitute father figure to him, and the two engage in serious discussions about life and duty. When he realizes that he is ill, he enlists Joseph in a pact to serve Potiphar. This pact and the remembrance of Mont-kaw's wisdom help Joseph to resist Potiphar's wife.

Mut-em-enet, Potiphar's chief wife. Her destiny, like that of her husband, was determined by her parents when she was a young child. She was betrothed to Potiphar for political reasons. Her life is unfulfilled sexually. With little to interest her, she spends her days caring for her face and body. When she becomes aware of her fascination with Joseph, she fights those feelings. Eventually, however, her obsession overcomes her. She turns to black magic, degrading herself to win Joseph's love.

The Young Provider, 1943

Joseph, who is elevated to the highest position in the land, after accurately predicting the future for the Pharaoh, in the belief that he alone can save Egypt from famine. When his half brothers come to see him, he forgives them and is rejoined with his full brother, Benjamin, and father, Jacob.

Amenhotep, the Pharaoh, who is impressed by Joseph's ability to interpret dreams and by his religious discussions.

Reuben, the firstborn and leader of Jacob's sons. He and Benjamin alone are innocent of their brother's blood.

Judah, the most articulate of Jacob's sons. He serves as their conscience. He equates their problems in Egypt with the guilt they bear for the sin that they committed against Joseph.

— *Mary E. Mahony*

JOSEPH ANDREWS

Author: Henry Fielding (1707-1754)
First published: 1742
Genre: Novel

Locale: England
Time: Early eighteenth century
Plot: Social realism

Joseph Andrews, a simple, handsome young man of great virtue who, because of his looks and purity, becomes the erotic prey of various women. Discharged from his post as Lady Booby's footman when he fails to respond to her advances, he leaves London to return to his native Somersetshire and his true love, Fanny Goodwill. On the way he is robbed, beaten, made fun of, and nearly raped. At an inn, he meets his old tutor, Parson Adams, and together they travel home. On the way, Parson Adams rescues Fanny from a brutal ruffian. At home, however, Joseph's marriage to Fanny is thwarted by a jail term on charges brought by revengeful Lady Booby, the objections of his relatives, and the discovery that Fanny is supposedly his sister. When it turns out that he is really a son of a family named Wilson—the children had been exchanged by gypsies—the marriage takes place.

Fanny Goodwill, Joseph Andrews' attractive, virtuous sweetheart. Traveling to meet Joseph in London, after hearing that Lady Booby has dismissed him, she accompanies her lover and Parson Adams back to Somersetshire. Her adventures consist mainly of hairbreadth escapes from attackers until she is married.

Parson Abraham Adams, an earthy man who loves food, drink, and tobacco. At the same time, he is idealistic and charitable. An absent-minded tutor and the friend of Joseph and Fanny, he accompanies them home, protecting them with his fists and sharing their troubles, and at last marries them.

Lady Booby, a noblewoman torn between her pride of class and her love for her handsome young footman. After dismissing him, she returns to her Somersetshire estate and uses all her influence to prevent his marriage to Fanny.

Mrs. Slipslop, Lady Booby's housekeeper, an aggressive, misshapen woman who almost rapes Joseph and tries continually to win him over.

Pamela Booby, Joseph's sister, who tries to prevent his marriage to Fanny. Adapted from Samuel Richardson's novel *Pamela*, she exemplifies virtue based on vanity rather than, as in Fanny's case,.on natural goodness.

Squire Booby, Pamela's husband, a good man who frees Joseph from jail and accepts him as an equal. Because of class pride, however, he objects to Joseph's marriage to Fanny.

Peter Pounce, Lady Booby's steward, a stingy, uncharitable man who on one occasion saves Fanny from rape but plans to enjoy her himself.

Mr. Wilson, a kindly, intelligent man who serves as host to the penniless Joseph, Fanny, and Parson Adams. He later turns out to be Joseph's true father.

Mrs. Wilson, his wife.

The Pedlar, a good-hearted person who pays a debt for Parson Adams, saves his son from drowning, and explains the mystery of Fanny's parentage.

Mrs. Adams, the parson's good but practical wife. She objects to Joseph's marriage because she thinks it will interfere with her children's advancement.

Beau Didapper, a London fop who visits Lady Booby and tries to seduce Fanny.

Gammer and

Gaffer Andrews, Joseph and Pamela's rather fatuous parents.

A Lecherous Squire, who sets his hounds on Parson Adams, humiliates him at dinner, and tries to gain Fanny first by cunning and then by force.

A Captain, his agent, who captures Fanny at the inn and takes her off to the squire. He is stopped in time by Peter Pounce.

A Gentleman, who promises food and lodging to Joseph, Fanny, and Parson Adams but fails to make good.

A Generous Innkeeper, who promises nothing but lets the group stay at his inn without payment.

Parson Trulliber, a gluttonous, bad-tempered minister who refuses charity to Parson Adams.

Mr. Tow-Wouse, an innkeeper who is meek and stingy.

Mrs. Tow-Wouse, his vixenish wife.

Betty, their servant, who nearly ravishes Joseph while nursing him.

Mr. Scout, Lady Booby's lawyer, who throws Joseph and Fanny into jail on trumped-up charges.

JOSEPH VANCE: An Ill-Written Autobiography

Author: William De Morgan (1839-1917)
First published: 1906
Genre: Novel

Locale: England
Time: Mid-nineteenth century
Plot: Autobiographical

Joseph Vance, an honest Englishman who helps his friends and suffers sometimes for his goodness. Even his love is denied because he refuses to hurt the woman he loves by telling her that her own brother's rascality is what has put Joseph himself in a bad light.

Mr. Christopher Vance, Joseph's prodigal father. A drunkard, he is one of his son's greatest problems. He almost bankrupts himself because, while drunk, he causes a fire in the

building housing his business.

Mrs. Vance, Christopher's first wife, Joseph's mother. She dies shortly after Joseph graduates from Oxford.

Dr. Randall Thorpe, Joseph's benefactor. It is he who sends Joseph to Oxford.

Lossie Thorpe, Dr. Thorpe's oldest child, loved by Joseph. Eventually, she and Joseph spend their last days together in Italy.

Joe (Beppino) Thorpe, Dr. Thorpe's son. He is a bigamist, in one marriage using Joseph Vance's name. His son by that marriage is adopted by Joseph, whose action causes Lossie to turn against him, for she thinks he is the child's real father. Beppino is a would-be poet. He dies of typhoid fever.

Violet Thorpe, Lossie's sister.

Nolly Thorpe, Lossie's other brother.

General Desprez, a wealthy army officer, Lossie's husband. He dies before he can clear Joseph of the charges of which his wife thinks Joseph guilty.

Pheener, the Christopher Vances' maid. After her mistress' death, she marries Christopher.

Bony Macallister, Joseph's school friend. Later, he and Joseph become business partners in an engineering firm.

Janey Spencer, Joseph's wife. She loves him dearly and is drowned when she refuses to go into a lifeboat from a sinking ship after choosing to try to swim to shore with her husband.

Sibyl Perceval, an heiress who marries Beppino shortly before his death.

JOURNEY INTO FEAR

Author: Eric Ambler (1909-1998)
First published: 1940
Genre: Novel

Locale: Istanbul, Athens, and Greece
Time: January, 1940
Plot: Suspense

Graham, a brilliant engineer in charge of one of the experimental departments of a large British arms-manufacturing firm. A thin, slightly stooping man about forty years old, he is totally absorbed in his work. Quiet, likable, and naïve, he is inclined to believe the best of everyone. He is rather cool in his personal relations, and his marriage of ten years has been without passion on either side, but he is able to make himself amiable to the foreigners he encounters when traveling for his firm. He calls himself "the most harmless man alive" and is thus unwilling to believe his situation is as dangerous as it is. As the novel begins, he has been in Turkey for six weeks, investigating certain aspects of Turkish naval armaments for his firm. In the course of the novel, traveling by steamer to Italy, he becomes the victim of a Gestapo plot to disrupt the British plan to arm Turkish warships. Finally, in northern Italy, he manages to escape death at the hands of the Gestapo.

Josette Gallindo, a dancer. Slender and fair-haired, she is a sophisticated and weary woman of the world. Although she is not particularly gifted as a dancer, her dancing is theatrical and effective as a result of her sensual beauty and grace. At the beginning of the novel, she performs with her Spanish husband in an Istanbul nightclub. She meets Graham, later travels on the ship that takes him to Italy, and offers to help him escape his danger, but she is concerned less with Graham than with the financial advantages he represents. At the end of the novel, on a train to Paris, she offers herself to Graham for cash and is rejected.

Moeller, alias **Fritz Haller**, a German secret agent. An elderly man, pale and rather round-shouldered, he travels on Graham's ship to Italy as Haller, a distinguished German ar-

chaeologist, apparently a man of ideas who is too civilized to care about the usual antagonisms of people whose countries are at war with one another. Actually, he is a calculating Gestapo agent who believes only in the ideology of Nazism and has taken over the passport and identity of the real Haller, even mastering a detailed knowledge of ancient history to make his impersonation convincing. He first attempts to detain Graham and later tries to kill him to prevent him from reaching England with his knowledge of Turkish naval armaments.

Banat (bah-NAHT), a Romanian assassin, an agent for Moeller. He is a professional and "natural" killer who actually enjoys killing people and, unlike his employer, makes no pretense of serving a higher good. On the ship to Italy, Graham manages to escape death at his hands.

Kuvetli (kew-VEHT-lih), a Turkish secret agent traveling as a business representative. He is an inconspicuous small man but a devoted patriot of considerable courage who has been assigned by the Turkish secret service to travel to Italy with Graham to assist him. He tells Graham that he is willing to die for his country and does so.

Mathis (maht-EES), a French socialist. He claims to have been a socialist ever since learning in World War I that a French official who owned iron mines that had been captured by the Germans had ordered that they not be bombed. Actually, he is a "Royalist by instinct" and "a socialist by conviction" who spouts socialist slogans primarily to keep his conservative wife in line. When Graham is without real friends and is desperately seeking help, Mathis proves trustworthy.

— *Robert L. Berner*

JOURNEY TO THE CENTER OF THE EARTH
(Voyage au centre de la terre)

Author: Jules Verne (1828-1905)
First published: 1864
Genre: Novel

Locale: Hamburg, Germany; Iceland; under Earth's surface; and Stromboli, Italy
Time: The 1860's
Plot: Science fiction

Axel Lidenbrock (LEE-dehn-brok), called **Harry** in some translations, the narrator and nephew of Professor Otto Lidenbrock. Although he shares his uncle's love of geology, Axel

does not match the old man's scientific curiosity; he does not endure the hardships of discovery as willingly, preferring the comforts of home to exploring the depths of the earth. Although it is Axel who deciphers the coded message that leads to the center of the earth, he does not immediately reveal it to his uncle, fearing precisely the sort of mad dash into the earth that his uncle eventually leads. Axel's lack of a scientist's temperament is illustrated by his chronic hunger, contrasting the professor's habit of ignoring meals while involved in his research. Axel is afraid of the dangers of the voyage but hides his fear so that he will not be shown up by the brave Hans Bjelke. Axel's decision to stay with his uncle instead of turning back is a pivotal point in the novel.

Professor Otto Lidenbrock, called **Professor Hardwigg** (HAHRT-vihg) in some translations, a professor of philosophy, geology, and mineralogy at a college in Hamburg. Tall and thin, with large spectacles hiding his round eyes, fifty-year-old Lidenbrock is the archetypal scientist. He refuses to accept theories about the earth's core until he has proven them by direct observation. The negative side of his scientific character is that he sacrifices everything, including his safety and that of his companions, to his quest for knowledge, which he keeps to himself. Choleric and accustomed to giving orders, the profes-

sor has a quirk of stuttering whenever he becomes excited.

Hans Bjelke (BYEHL-keh), an Icelandic eider hunter, the expedition's guide. Built like Hercules and equally fearless, Hans wears his bright red hair to his shoulders. Calm, quiet, and unflappable in an emergency, Hans is almost invisible until danger threatens, and then he shows his resourcefulness. When Axel and the professor are at a loss as to how to replenish their water supply, Hans wordlessly breaks a hole in a rock wall, which immediately gushes water. When a volcano blows the party into the Mediterranean, Hans pulls the other two to safety.

Grauben Lidenbrock (GROW-behn), called **Gretchen** in some translations, the professor's seventeen-year-old ward and Axel's fiancée. Her character is not fully developed, existing mostly as a symbol of the pretty face to which the adventurer comes home. She appears only in the first chapter, in which she surprises Axel by approving the inner-earth expedition, and in the last chapter, where she is reunited with Axel. The two are married and move in with the professor.

— *John R. Holmes*

JOURNEY TO THE END OF THE NIGHT
(Voyage au bout de la nuit)

Author: Louis-Ferdinand Céline (Louis-Ferdinand Destouches, 1894-1961)
First published: 1932
Genre: Novel

Locale: France, Africa, and the United States
Time: During and shortly after World War I
Plot: Naturalism

Ferdinand Bardamu (fehr-dee-NAH[N] bahr-dah-MEW), a war-wounded, disillusioned, cynical neurotic and a rogue. Successively a medical student, soldier, mental patient, pimp, flea expert, Ford worker, doctor, music-hall supernumerary, and administrator of a madhouse, he undergoes experiences that would tax the strongest constitution and the sanest mind. In his restless shifting from one job to another and from one locale to another, he resembles not only the rogues of picaresque fiction but also his creator, Ferdinand Céline.

Léon Robinson (lay-OH[N]), his friend, an unscrupulous cynic who turns up, like a personal demon, everywhere Ferdinand goes. The planner of the bombing of old Madame Henrouille, he is temporarily blinded by his own bomb. He is later killed by Madelon.

Madelon (mahd-LOH[N]), an attractive young woman of easy morals. Engaged to Leon, she becomes insanely jealous when he attempts to get rid of her; and after threatening to inform the police of his murder of Madame Henrouille, she shoots him in a rage and flees.

Lola, an American Red Cross worker who becomes Ferdinand's mistress in France and who later permits him to live with her for a time after he comes to New York.

Musyne (mew-ZEEN), a dancer and prostitute, another of Ferdinand's mistresses.

Madame Hérote (ay-ROHT), a Parisian lingerie-glove-bookshop keeper and a prostitute.

Doctor Bestombes (bay-TOHMB), a psychiatrist in a mental hospital.

Roger Puta (roh-ZHAY pew-TAH), a jeweler for whom Ferdinand works before the war; during the war, he is a driver for a cabinet minister.

Lieutenant Grappa (grah-PAH), a brutal officer in charge of Topo station in Africa.

Molly, an American prostitute in Detroit; Ferdinand is briefly in love with her.

The Abbé Protiste (proh-TEEST), a priest who arranges for Léon and Madame Henrouille to set up a little business in Toulouse, showing mummies in a crypt to tourists.

Tania (tahn-YAH), a Polish friend of Ferdinand whose lover dies in Berlin.

Doctor Baryton (bah-ree-TOH[N]), a psychiatrist who operates a madhouse, becomes mad about English (which he learns from Ferdinand and from reading Macaulay), and rushes off to England and other lands, leaving the madhouse in Ferdinand's charge.

Doctor Serge Parapine (sehrzh pah-rah-PEEN), a medical researcher later employed as a staff physician at Baryton's asylum; a friend of Ferdinand.

The Henrouilles (ahn-ROO-ee), a Parisian family for whom Ferdinand performs various medical services.

Bébert (bay-BEHR), a young boy, a patient of Ferdinand, who dies of typhoid fever.

Gustave Mandamour (gew-STAHV mah[n]-dah-MEWR), a traffic policeman, a friend of Ferdinand and Leon.

Sophie (soh-FEE), a voluptuous Slovak nurse hired by Ferdinand; he is fascinated by her.

JOURNEY TO THE SKY

Author: Jamake Highwater (1942-   )
First published: 1978
Genre: Novel

Locale: Central America and southern Mexico
Time: 1839-1840
Plot: Biographical

John Lloyd Stephens, an American lawyer, diplomat, explorer, and travel writer. After practicing law for several years, the adventurous Stephens has traveled for two years in Africa, Europe, and Asia and written two well-received books on his travels. He comes across a report by Colonel Juan Galindo that mentions seeing some strange old buildings in the wilds of the Yucatán and Central America. He decides to find these ruins. He enlists his friend, Frederick Catherwood, as the expedition's artist. Equipped with an unexpected appointment as President Martin Van Buren's confidential agent to the Central American Confederation, this versatile and adaptable man sets out to find the Indian ruins. After landing in a country in the midst of civil war, then coping with treacherous terrain and a troublesome muleteer who deliberately misguides them, he and Catherwood at last find the ruins of Copan, an ancient Mayan city of worship, now overgrown with centuries of vegetation. Although beset by mosquitoes and hot weather, Stephens sets about the task of clearing idols and monuments, and Catherwood draws them. Later, he and Catherwood set out on a long trek across Central America to the ruins at Palenque. Despite bouts with malaria, mosquitoes, and other parasites, he and Catherwood manage to explore these ruins, as well as another set at Uxmal. Stephens dies in 1852 of malaria contracted while he is president of the Panama Railway Company, never having returned to the ruins he uncovered at Copan. His work there was largely forgotten until the 1940's.

Frederick Catherwood, an English architect. Officially signed as the expedition's artist, Catherwood was much more Stephens' exploring partner. After persevering with Stephens through the adventures of getting to the ruins at Copan, he continues to sketch the monuments and idols they uncover there for three weeks after Stephens has left, despite a severe bout of malaria and massive swarms of mosquitoes that force him to wear gloves while sketching the unfamiliar styles of architecture and sculpture. At Palenque, he works diligently, despite the parasites that are nesting in his foot, to sketch the strange glyphs as accurately as possible. At Uxmal, although feverish with malaria, he sketches a panorama until he drops at his easel. Catherwood makes a fortune by investing in a mine in California during the gold rush, but he dies in a shipwreck in 1854, on his way from London to New York.

Augustin, the servant hired by Stephens. He accompanies Stephens on all of his adventures through the rugged terrain of the war-torn land, until Stephens finally leaves Yucatán on a ship to Havana.

The Muleteer, the head mule driver hired by Stephens. A constant source of trouble, he several times refuses to work, demands more money, misguides the party, and once even attempts to have Stephens arrested. When, on the trip from Copan to Guatemala City, the muleteer becomes feverish, he and Stephens finally part.

Rafael Carrera, a young Indian who leads a successful conservative revolt against the Central American Confederation, defending the rights of the church. When Stephens and Catherwood leave Guatemala City, they do so with letters of protection signed by Carrera.

Francisco Morazan, the leader of the Central American Confederation troops in the area. A conscientious leader, he is considered by Stephens to be the best man in Central America.

Don Gregorio, a rich landowner in the village of Copan. A petty tyrant, he refuses hospitality to the travelers but develops a friendship with the Muleteer.

Colonel Archibald MacDonald, the British administrator of Belize. A supporter of Britain's imperial plans for Central America, he tries to undermine Stephens and Catherwood's exploration project by sending Patrick Walker and Lieutenant John Caddy to document the ruins at Palenque.

Henry Pawling, an American adventurer who joins the expedition on the road to Palenque. After Stephens and Catherwood leave Palenque, Pawling stays behind to make plaster casts of some of the ruins, which the governor of Chiapas eventually seizes, ordering Pawling to leave.

Patrick Walker and

Lieutenant John Caddy, rival British explorers sent by MacDonald to document the ruins at Palenque. Although Stephens and Catherwood hear rumors in Guatemala City that the bodies of Walker and Caddy have been found naked and drained of blood, they leave for Palenque anyway. Stephens and Catherwood find evidence at Palenque that the British explorers were there. Indeed, Walker and Caddy do publish an account of their adventures, which is quickly eclipsed by that of Stephens and Catherwood.

— *Thomas J. Cassidy*

THE JOURNEY TO THE WEST
(Hsi-yu chi)

Author: Wu Ch'eng-en (1500-c. 1582)
First published: 1592
Genre: Novel

Locale: China, India, and various mythical regions
Time: The seventh century
Plot: Fantasy

Monkey, who was born of a stone egg fecundated by the wind. He was king of the Mountain of Flowers for several hundred years, after which he set out into the world in search of knowledge that would make him immortal. Under the name

of "Aware-of-vacuity," he studied with Patriarch Subodhi for several hundred more years. Because of the tremendous magic power he had acquired, as well as his natural arrogance, he named himself "Great Sage Equal of Heaven." Permitted to live in the Kingdom of Heaven, the mischievous creature disturbed and outwitted all the divinities with his magic tricks until Buddha himself intervened and imprisoned him beneath a mountain. After five hundred years, Monkey was released through the intercession of the Bodhisattva Kuan-yin, on the condition that he become the disciple of the priest Hsuan Tsang, who was then on his way to India in quest of the Buddhist Scriptures for T'ai Tsung, the emperor of T'ang. Monkey's role now is to assist the priest against the many calamities that befall him. Although he can never overcome completely the temptation to play tricks, Monkey earns his redemption and receives the Illumination that in the end, after a successful journey to India, allows him to be received into Heaven as a Buddha.

Hsuan Tsang, a priest. Abandoned by his mother when he was born, he was rescued and brought up by the abbot of a monastery. In his old age, he was selected for his sanctity by T'ai Tsung, the emperor of T'ang, to go to India and bring back to China the Tripitaka, the sacred Scriptures of the Big Vehicle. Hsuan Tsang then received the name of Tripitaka. Tripitaka was to encounter and overcome nine great calamities to transcend his mortal condition. In spite of great devotion, he could not have accomplished his mission without the help of his four disciples, who all possess some kind of magical power. He is easily discouraged and given to tears, but his purity is his saving asset, and he is finally received into Heaven as a Buddha.

Pigsy, a lesser divinity in the Kingdom of the Jade Emperor. Chased out of Heaven for courting a Fairy maiden, he lives on earth as a demon with the face of a pig. Addicted to base pleasures of the flesh, he is given a chance to recover his former place in Heaven by the Bodhisattva Kuan-yin, who converts him and sends him to India with Tripitaka. In the end, he receives the Illumination and is admitted to Heaven as Cleanser of the Altar.

Sandy, formerly the Marshal of the Hosts of Heaven. Banished to the River of Flowing Sands for breaking a crystal cup at a celestial banquet, he lives on the flesh of human beings. He obtains his redemption by accompanying Tripitaka on his pilgrimage to India. His conduct enables him to regain a place in Heaven with the title of Golden-Bodied Arhat.

The Horse, the son of the Dragon King of the Western Ocean, condemned to death for misconduct in his father's palace. He was saved by Kuan-yin on condition that he carry Tripitaka to India. The young dragon swallows the priest's horse as the latter is trying to cross a river. Learning his mistake, he allows himself to be changed into the horse's identical image. He faithfully serves the priest and is rewarded by being made one of the eight Senior Heavenly Dragons.

T'ai Tsung, the emperor of T'ang, who died because he failed to keep his promise to save a Dragon King from execution. Brought back to life through the mediation of his minister, he is celebrating his resurrection when Kuan-yin appears and orders him to send someone to India to get the Scriptures of the Big Vehicle, then unknown in China. The emperor entrusts Hsuan Tsang with the mission. He must wait fourteen years for the priest's return.

Kuan-yin, the merciful Bodhisattva. She organizes and supervises Hsuan Tsang's pilgrimage.

Buddha, the Enlightened One. Upset by the greed, lust, and many other defects of the Chinese people, he sends Kuan-yin to China to look for a man holy enough to bring the true Scriptures from Paradise and thus set the Chinese on the way to moral reformation.

Lao Tzu, an alchemist and father of the Tao. He defeats Monkey but is unable to destroy him. Lao Tzu appears as a gruff old scholar whose lack of a sense of humor is his worst enemy.

Erh-lang, a magician, nephew of the Jade Emperor. With the help of Lao Tzu, he defeats Monkey in battle.

The Jade Emperor, the tyrant of Heaven.

The King of Crow-cock, who is killed by a magician who then assumes the king's appearance and usurps his throne. After three years, the king appears to Tripitaka in a dream and asks for help. His body is rescued by Monkey and Pigsy, then brought back to life with a "pill" borrowed from Lao Tzu.

Vaisravana, who, with the help of his son Natha, fights unsuccessfully against Monkey on behalf of the Jade Emperor.

JOURNEY'S END

Author: R. C. Sherriff (1896-1975)
First published: 1929
Genre: Drama

Locale: A battlefield in France
Time: March, 1918
Plot: Impressionistic realism

Captain Dennis Stanhope, a British officer whose three years in the front lines have made him a hard, cynical, and heavy-drinking man. Stanhope is first and foremost a soldier, however, and when his young friend is fatally wounded, he returns immediately to his duties as commanding officer.

Lieutenant Osborne, Stanhope's second in command. He is a middle-aged man who was a schoolteacher in civilian life. Osborne is anxious to keep peace in the company. He is killed, along with several other members of a raiding party sent out to capture some prisoners from whom the colonel of the regiment hopes to obtain information.

Lieutenant Raleigh, a school friend of Stanhope and the brother of Stanhope's fiancée. Raleigh worships Stanhope as a hero and can hardly recognize his old friend when he meets him in the front lines. Raleigh is a callow youth, full of vitality, who soon makes friends with Osborne. He cannot understand how the other men in the company can celebrate after Osborne and several others are killed in the raiding party. Raleigh is fatally wounded in a German attack.

Second Lieutenant Hibbert, an officer in Stanhope's company who is a malingerer and a coward. Stanhope bullies Hibbert into staying on duty after Hibbert tries to get a doctor to give him a medical excuse for being relieved from duty.

A JOVIAL CREW: Or, The Merry Beggars

Author: Richard Brome (c. 1590-c. 1652-1653)
First published: 1652
Genre: Drama

Locale: England
Time: The seventeenth century
Plot: Farce

Oldrents, a kindly country squire. Troubled by a fortune-teller's prediction that his daughters will become beggars, he becomes so melancholy and unlike his usual self that he drives them to run away with a troop of wandering beggars. At their return, his happy nature is restored.

Springlove, Oldrents' good-hearted and reliable steward. His only fault is an annual restlessness that makes him turn over his accounts to an assistant and take to the open road. He aids the squire's daughters in their runaway plan and looks after their safety. He is finally revealed as their half brother, an illegitimate son of Oldrents and the nephew of the patrico of the beggars.

Rachel and

Meriel, the squire's romantic daughters, who find begging, in reality, less pleasant than they had imagined.

Amie, a niece of Justice Clack. He tries to force her to marry Talboy. She runs away with Martin, joins the beggars, falls in love with Springlove, and is united with him in marriage when he is discovered to be Oldrents' son.

Master Talboy, Amie's jilted bridegroom.

Justice Clack, a talkative and officious country justice. His examination of the beggars in the presence of Oldrents leads to the needful disclosures and the happy ending.

The patrico, the priest of the beggars. He reveals to Oldrents that Springlove is Oldrents' son.

Hearty, a decayed gentleman, Oldrents' friend and a parasite.

Martin, Hearty's cowardly nephew, a second potential bridegroom disappointed in his hopes of winning Amie.

Oliver, the lecherous son of Justice Clack. He fails in his attempt to attack Rachel.

Vincent and

Hilliard, the lovers of the squire's daughters, who accompany them on their adventure.

THE JOY LUCK CLUB

Author: Amy Tan (1952-   )
First published: 1989
Genre: Novel

Locale: San Francisco, California; and China
Time: The 1910's, the 1940's, the 1960's, and 1987
Plot: Psychological realism

Suyuan Woo, the founder of the Joy Luck Club, which meets monthly to play mah-jongg. In fleeing from a Japanese attack in 1944, she was forced to abandon her twin infant daughters on a road outside Kweilin. She searched for them until 1949, when she immigrated to San Francisco with her second husband. Her daughter Jing-mei was born in 1951. Suyuan secretly continued looking for her other daughters until her death at the age of seventy-two, two months before the book opens.

Jing-mei (June) Woo, a thirty-six-year-old college dropout who writes advertising copy for a small ad agency in San Francisco. After her mother's death, she learns that she has two half sisters still alive in China. By setting out to meet them, she begins coming to terms with her own Chinese heritage.

Lindo Jong, Suyuan's competitive and critical best friend, who was born in 1918 in a village near Taiyuan. A marriage was arranged for her when she was two, and she joined her husband's family when she was twelve. Eventually, she tricked her mother-in-law into dissolving the marriage. After immigrating to San Francisco, she worked in a fortune cookie factory with An-mei Hsu, who introduced her to her second husband, Tin Jong. They have three children: Winston, who is killed in a car accident at the age of sixteen, Vincent, and Waverly.

Waverly Jong, a thirty-six-year-old divorcee with a five-year-old daughter, Shoshana. Waverly is a tax attorney in San Francisco. When she was nine years old, she won national attention as a chess champion. She is insecure and fears that her mother will reject her new fiancé.

An-mei Hsu, the wife of George Hsu and mother of Janice, Ruth, Rose, Matthew, Mark, Luke, and Bing. Born in 1914, she was reared by her grandmother in Ningpo until she was nine. Her mother, the widow of a respected scholar, brought disgrace on herself by becoming the third concubine of Wu Tsing, a rich merchant in Tientsin, and she eventually poisoned herself. An-mei worries that her daughter Rose will not see the choices open to her.

Rose Hsu Jordan, the third of An-mei's seven children. When she was fourteen, she saw her four-year-old brother Bing fall off a pier at a family outing and felt responsible for his death. In college, she married Ted Jordan, a dermatologist, whom she allowed to make all the decisions in their marriage. When Ted announces that he wants a divorce after fifteen years, Rose must figure out how to stand up for what she wants.

Ying-ying St. Clair, the wife of an American man who calls her "Betty." Born in 1914 in Wushi to a wealthy family, she was married at sixteen to a philanderer who abandoned her, causing her to induce the abortion of her first child. She married Clifford St. Clair in 1946, after the death of her first husband. They have a daughter, Lena, and a son who dies at birth.

Lena St. Clair, a thirty-six-year-old designer at her husband's architectural firm. After college, she married self-centered and success-oriented Harold Livotny and inspired him to start his own business. After five years of marriage, he still splits their expenses down the middle even though he makes seven times as much as she does.

— *Patricia L. Watson*

JOY OF MAN'S DESIRING
(Que ma joie demeure)

Author: Jean Giono (1895-1970)
First published: 1935
Genre: Novel

Locale: The Grémone Plateau, a French farming region
Time: The 1930's
Plot: Pastoral

Bobi, an acrobat, a stranger to the plateau and a bearer of healing and joy. Roughly thirty-five years old, he is tan and strong, with gentle, delicate hands and the language of a poet. He sees the joy of nature in plants and animals and awakens the farmers of the plateau to the beauty and joy around them. Bobi appears in the middle of the night, stays with Jourdan and Marthe (a lonely farming couple of the plateau), and speaks to them of the beauty of the stars, of the flowers and forest, of the song of birds, and of the wonder of wildlife. He represents the healer for whom Jourdan has been waiting. Jourdan takes him to visit all the other families of the plateau, and Bobi tries to transmit his joy to all. Although he loves the young Aurore, he is attracted by the womanly Josephine. When Aurore kills herself in despair, Bobi believes that all of his efforts have failed but refuses to believe that people can live without hope or joy. Leaving in the midst of a terrible storm, he is struck by lightning.

Jourdan, the first person to welcome Bobi and to respond to his love of nature. Jourdan, old before his time and lonely in spite of his loving wife, has been expecting a man to come and save them from their dreary loneliness; he fully accepts Bobi as the healer whom he has awaited so long. Jourdan plants periwinkles and narcissi and gives Bobi money to buy a stag. He scatters wheat to attract birds, and he builds a loom for Marthe and carves it lovingly with stags, does, stars, a forest, and a house—all that now brings him happiness.

Marthe, Jourdan's fifty-seven-year-old wife. She is a tall, heavy woman who seems to grow in stature and wisdom as she opens to the joys of nature and becomes a comfort to others. Her greatest joy is in seeing Jourdan grow young in his new-found joy.

Aurore, the daughter of Madame Hélène. Her father had shot himself after having opened fire on his wife and daughter in a rage of insanity. She is young, gentle, lovely, and lonely, spending much time with her mare, on horseback or with the carriage, wandering field and woods. She falls in love with Bobi when he speaks kindly to her but, succumbing to despair after seeing him with Josephine, she shoots herself in the mouth and dies.

Zulma, the daughter of Randoulet and Honorine, simple, sad, and mostly silent. She is a worry to her parents because of her lonely wanderings. Greatly attracted to the stag brought to the plateau, she comes a little closer to people, becoming less shy of their approach. Although she claims that she does not understand their language, she likes to hear them singing. When Randoulet buys five hundred sheep, Zulma finds her place as shepherdess, exults in her new role, and grows beautiful, especially in the white cloth woven from the wool of the sheep that she so happily tends.

Madame Hélène's farmer, who does not appear often but is a pivotal character in his alter-ego role. Like Bobi, he is thin, muscular, and in his mid-thirties. Unlike Bobi, he keeps to himself, reads much, and believes in the virtue of hard work. When Bobi visits him, the farmer warns Bobi that his joy is too emotional, not tempered with reason, and reflects an idyllic past rather than a realistic future. He fears that the weak will perish in Bobi's joy, and he believes that, as with his plants, a sturdier hybrid needs to be developed, one more resistant to disease. As Bobi flees the plateau, he speaks to the farmer and asks him to be the new shepherd for the people of the plateau, though one more reasonable and less passionate, ascetic rather than aesthetic.

— *Elizabeth A. Rubino*

JOY OF THE WORM

Author: Frank Sargeson (1903-1982)
First published: 1969
Genre: Novel

Locale: Rural New Zealand
Time: About 1912-1930
Plot: Tragicomedy

Jeremy Bohun, a laborer in New Zealand who becomes a county clerk, a country schoolmaster, and finally a vicar of the Church of England. The novel focuses on the mental and spiritual development of this sincere, ambitious, well-meaning protagonist from his early twenties to the approach of middle age. He is very much his father's son, having been infected with his father's passion for orotund and edifying literature in the grand manner of Edward Gibbon's *The History of the Decline and Fall of the Roman Empire* and Sir Thomas Browne's *Hydriotaphia*. Like his father, he has a strong sexual appetite, which eventually results in his fathering ten children by two different wives. His worldly progress is handicapped by an inferiority complex, also attributable to his father's influence. He is painfully aware that his father strongly favors

his brother and in fact regards him as a pale facsimile of John, who ran away from home at an early age because he could not stand his father's pedantic, overbearing personality.

James Bohun, Jeremy's father, a Methodist minister. He is already an elderly man when the novel opens, yet he is physically vigorous and vain about his appearance. He is a nonstop talker and would be regarded by most people as a bore. He is infatuated with his inexhaustible flow of second-rate opinions about the conduct of life. He is compared by the author to Miguel de Cervantes' Don Quixote. The Reverend Bohun's well-intentioned but insufferable lecturing drives his younger son clear out of New Zealand. Jeremy, however, remains close to his father. The theme of the novel has to do with the influence of heredity and environment on the development of an individual: Jeremy is gradually molded into a copy of his father and inevitably becomes a clergyman himself.

Maisie Michie, a schoolteacher who becomes Jeremy's first wife. This attractive, vivacious young woman has advanced ideas for such a puritanical environment as New Zealand prior to World War I. She and Jeremy begin sleeping together out of wedlock and get married when she discovers that she is pregnant. She is just as sensual as her husband but, like most women of the period, has been kept ignorant in matters of birth control. As a result, she produces babies at the rate of one a year. The burgeoning family puts such a financial strain on Jeremy that he begins embezzling money and eventually is forced to resign his job as county clerk. The combination of recurring pregnancies and chronic financial worries destroys Maisie's joy in living. She finally attempts to desert her family but is accidentally drowned in her departure.

Queenie Quelch, James's second wife, an attractive and good-natured woman in her mid-thirties who comes to Jeremy's father's home as a housekeeper after the death of his first wife. Queenie is another example of the restricted condition of women in New Zealand in the early part of the twentieth century. At first, she is impressed by her husband's learning and loquaciousness, but she later realizes that he is nothing but a windbag with a very ordinary mind. Her limited intelligence, her lack of education, and her stultifying provincial surroundings prevent her from realizing that there is any escape from the drudgery and monotony of being a housewife and sex object for a ruttish, insensitive old man. She dies under mysterious circumstances, and James starts thinking about finding still another wife to satisfy his lust and act as his unpaid household servant, as Jeremy does after Maisie's death.

— *Bill Delaney*

JUBIABÁ

Author: Jorge Amado (1912-   )
First published: 1935
Genre: Novel

Locale: Salvador, Bahia, Brazil, and environs
Time: The 1920's and 1930's
Plot: Political

Antônio Balduíno, also called **Baldo**, a black street-gang leader who survives successively as a beggar, singer and songwriter, professional boxer, plantation worker, circus artist, and eventually stevedore and strike leader. Antônio sees work as oppression or another kind of slavery, and from an early age he is determined never to earn money by being employed and to become famous through adventurous exploits and thereby get a ballad—an "ABC" in local parlance—written about himself. A heavy drinker, a fun-loving partygoer, and a womanizer, he is followed in the book from childhood to his mid-twenties. Many women love him, but he truly loves only one in return, a white girl, Lindinalva. She is the daughter of the rich Portuguese man who takes him in as a houseworker when Antônio's aunt (and only living relative) goes crazy. When Lindinalva dies, after asking him to look after her son, he is forced to take a job to support the boy.

Jubiabá, an old voodoo priest of the *candomblé* or *macumba* religion, a patriarch to the community on Capa-Negro Hill. He is thought to be one of only two free men there, along with Zé Camarão, and both are persecuted by the police as a result. People come to him for herbal remedies when sick as well as to have him cast spells. He is an important figure for Antônio, both as a friend and as a symbol of wisdom and independence.

Old Luísa, Antônio's aunt, who rears him alone until she goes crazy. A talker and storyteller, she cooks food and sells it downtown every night, with Antônio helping her. She often beats him for fighting and mischief but rarely hurts him, because he dodges the blows easily. She dies at the asylum after going insane when Antônio is still young.

Zé Camarão, a storyteller, singer, and *capoeira* fighter. This mulatto is an important role model for Antônio, who admires him because he is brave and a good ballad singer. He teaches Antônio the guitar and *capoeira* fighting.

Amelia, a Portuguese cook who hates Antônio, who has come to work at a rich man's house after the death of his aunt. She beats him often, declaring that black people are subhu-

man. She precipitates his running away from the house by lying that he has been ogling Lindinalva. Later, however, she takes care of Lindinalva and her son when the family is ruined.

Viriato, a deformed dwarf, part of Antônio's beggar gang and the only one of them who keeps begging into adulthood. Usually sad because he is alone in the world, he is a successful beggar but eventually drowns himself.

Gordo, Antônio's best friend, a very religious boy and man. Gordo meets Antônio when they are begging and accompanies him on most of his journeys thereafter. Often sad, he tells good stories, which always contain angels and demons, and is considered by Antônio to be a very good man. During the strike, he sees a little girl shot dead and afterward goes mad, imploring God to raise her from the dead.

Luigi, an Italian, Antônio's boxing manager and trainer who later hires him for the circus, of which he is part owner. He never understands that Antônio loses a big fight because he heard of Lindinalva's engagement the same day.

Joana, Antônio's girlfriend and a *macumba* dancer. A jealous woman, she sings Antônio's sambas with a deep, masculine voice. He leaves her for Maria dos Reis.

Maria dos Reis, a virgin whom Antônio pursues even though he knows that she is engaged to a soldier. Antônio injures and disarms the soldier in a fight and takes Maria. Eventually, she leaves Bahia with her godparents.

Rosenda Rosedá, a beautiful black dancer whom Antônio meets at the circus. Although he finds her vain and silly, he likes her, and she has a strong character to match his. Occasionally, he becomes jealous; ultimately, after winning her back from a rival, he abandons her to him.

Lindinalva Pereira, Antônio's lifelong love, the daughter of the Portuguese man who takes him in when his aunt goes mad. She is three years older than he is. Intoxicated by her beauty and personality, he is unjustly accused of ogling her. Later, Lindinalva's fiancé, Gustavo, impregnates and abandons her when the family is ruined. She eventually turns to prostitution and dies after asking Antônio to look after her son.

Gustavo Barreira, Lindinalva's fiancé and the father of Gustavinho. He is an ambitious lawyer who represents the workers in the strike and unsuccessfully attempts to get them to compromise their demands after he himself is made promises of gain from the bosses.

Gustavinho, Lindinalva's baby son by Gustavo, later adopted by Antônio.

Guisepe, an alcoholic and co-owner of the circus with Luigi. Born in Italy, he was part of a great circus there, photographs of which he keeps in his album. One night, his wife, who like him worked as a trapeze artist, fell to her death, and his decline is traced from that event.

— Philip Magnier

JUBILEE

Author: Margaret Walker (1915-　　)
First published: 1966
Genre: Novel

Locale: Georgia and Alabama
Time: The 1840's to 1870
Plot: Historical realism

Elvira (Vyry) Dutton, the protagonist, based on the author's great-grandmother, a slave on a Georgia plantation who is freed at the time of the Civil War. At the age of two, she loses her mother in childbirth. The daughter of the white plantation owner, Vyry is pale-skinned, with sandy hair and gray-blue eyes. Mistreated and beaten by her father's white wife, she develops great strength of character while retaining her capacity for compassion and for forgiveness. When her free husband is forced to leave Georgia without her and their two children, she tries to remain true to him, but at the end of the war, she marries Innis Brown. As they move westward in search of a home, she bravely endures a flood, sickness, poverty, and persecution. It is her kindness toward a pregnant white girl that brings her the support of the Greenville, Alabama, community, and a secure, permanent home for her family.

Randall Ware, a free black man, a blacksmith. A young, muscular man with coal-black skin, Ware is proud of his free birth. Having inherited money from his white guardian, he has bought property in Georgia. When he is elected to the legislature after the Civil War, he is threatened by the Ku Klux Klan and forced to sell his property and leave. When he finds Vyry in Greenville, he begs her to return to him but she decides to stay with Innis.

Innis Brown, Vyry's second husband. A former field hand, Innis is uneducated but hardworking and kindhearted. A tall man with warm brown skin and brown hair, he first befriends Vyry's two children and later saves her from marauders. After they marry, he disagrees with her only about the value of education but eventually is won over by her arguments in favor of it.

John Morris Dutton, Vyry's white father, the owner of a Georgia plantation. He is in his thirties when Vyry is born, a decent and compassionate person but politically ambitious. He leaves the running of the plantation to his spiteful wife and to a brutal overseer. Throughout his life, he refuses to admit any responsibility for his mulatto children. He does not allow Randall Ware to buy Vyry and lies to Vyry about freeing her.

After a carriage accident, he refuses to have his injured leg amputated and dies as a result.

Salina "Big Missy" Dutton, the wife of John Morris Dutton. A big-boned but lovely, dark-haired Savannah belle when she marries him, she soon makes it clear that she has no interest in sex except for necessary procreation. After producing one son and one daughter, she ceases to function as a wife, except on a social level. Her dislike of black people is intensified by her husband's frequent intimacies with slaves, and in his absence, she permits excessive cruelty toward them, herself torturing Vyry, who resembles her father. Salina is courageous in wartime, investing all of her funds in the Confederacy, even though she knows that it is failing. She dies of a stroke in 1864.

Lillian Dutton, the daughter of Salina and John. Similar in appearance to her father and to Vyry, she is sweet-tempered and gentle. In childhood, she is Vyry's playmate and mistress. Later, she marries the pacifist Kevin MacDougall, who is killed in a war that he thought senseless. After being attacked and injured by Yankees, she loses her mind and spends her later years, with her children, at the home of her aunt in Georgiana, Alabama.

Johnny Dutton, the son of Salina and John. A dark-haired, proud, and handsome man, he resembles his mother in looks and in attitude; also like her, he can be very cruel. After being graduated from West Point, he becomes an officer in the Confederate Army, is wounded in battle, and is then brought home by his black manservant. Although he falls in love, he dies suddenly before the relationship can progress to marriage.

Ed Grimes, the overseer on the Dutton estate. A short, stocky, brutal man with red hair, freckles, and little blue eyes, he has risen from his poor white beginnings to hold power over the Dutton slaves. After serving in the Confederate Army, he marries a banker's daughter and himself becomes a banker. He attempts to steal the Dutton property after it has been left to the mentally ill Lillian, but his plan is foiled by Lillian's aunt and uncle.

— Rosemary M. Canfield Reisman

JUDE THE OBSCURE

Author: Thomas Hardy (1840-1928)
First published: 1895
Genre: Novel

Locale: Wessex, England
Time: The nineteenth century
Plot: Philosophical realism

Jude Fawley, a village stonemason who is thwarted in every attempt to find success and happiness. His chief desire from the time of his youth is to become a religious scholar, but because of his sensuous temperament he is forced into an early marriage. After his first wife leaves him, he falls in love with his cousin and lives with her illegally for several years. The weight of social disapproval forces them downhill. After the tragic death of their children, his cousin leaves him also, and Jude, having turned to drink, dies a miserable death.

Arabella Donn, a country girl who tricks Jude into his first marriage. She has nothing in common with Jude and soon leaves him to go to Australia. She later returns but makes no immediate demands on him, preferring to marry another and advance her station in life. After the death of her second husband and the separation of Jude and his cousin, she tricks him into marrying her a second time. Instead of helping to brighten the last days of his life, she increases his misery and is planning her next marriage even before his death.

Sue Bridehead, Jude's cousin. Although priding herself on being a free thinker, she marries a much older man out of a sense of obligation and leaves him shortly afterward because of her revulsion toward him. She lives with Jude for several years and bears him three children. She is a strong influence on him and through her unorthodox thought becomes the primary reason for his giving up his attempts to enter the ministry. After the tragic death of her children, she undergoes a complete change in personality; now wanting to conform, she returns to her first husband.

Richard Phillotson, a village schoolmaster who instills in Jude his first desires to learn. He falls in love with Sue after she becomes his assistant and marries her in spite of obvious differences in age, thought, and belief. When she expresses her desire to live with Jude, he allows her a divorce, although it causes his own downfall. He gladly remarries her when she wants to come back to him, even though he is fully aware that she does not love him.

Little Father Time, the son of Jude and Arabella. He is a precocious child who seems to feel the weight of the world on his shoulders. Having been sent to Jude by Arabella when she married the second time, he is bothered by a sense of being unwanted and feels that he is a source of anxiety for his elders. This feeling becomes so intense that he hangs himself and the two younger children.

Drusilla Fawley, Jude's great-aunt, who raises him after the death of his parents. During his youth, she constantly warns him against ever marrying because the Fawleys have never had successful marriages.

Anny and

Sarah, friends of Arabella. They give her the idea of tricking Jude into marriage.

Mr. Donn, Arabella's father. Although he has nothing to do with the first trick on Jude, he helps Arabella carry out the second one.

Gillingham, a friend and confidant of Phillotson, whose advice Phillotson never takes.

Mrs. Edlin, a neighbor of Drusilla Fawley; she is always ready to help Jude and Sue when they need her.

Vilbert, a quack doctor. He serves as Jude's first source of disillusionment about life.

Cartlett, Arabella's second husband.

JUDITH PARIS

Author: Sir Hugh Walpole (1884-1941)
First published: 1931
Genre: Novel

Locale: England
Time: Nineteenth century
Plot: Historical

Judith Herries, later **Judith Paris**, the daughter of Francis Herries and Mirabell both of whom die on the night of her birth. After a stormy girlhood in the home of her half brother, she marries for love at seventeen. Her husband is a smuggler, a gambler, and an intriguer by turns. After his violent death, Judith goes to live in the home of a nephew and his wife. Out of pity, she gives herself to a neighbor. Now nearly forty, she finds that she is pregnant, and she goes to Paris. The expected child's father follows her, but he dies shortly after finding her. It is just after Waterloo, and a café shooting of a Prussian so unnerves Judith that she gives birth to a son at once, behind a screen. The nephew with whom she lived has committed suicide, and Judith, taking her son, goes back to live with his widow.

David Herries, who is fifty-five years older than his half sister Judith. Her girlhood is spent in his home.

William Herries, David's son. A quarrel sets him relentlessly against his brother.

Francis Herries, William's brother, with whom Judith lives after her widowhood. He shuts his eyes to his wife's infidelity, but malicious interference on the part of his nephew, acting as agent of the old feud, forces the discovery upon him. When his wife's lover escapes, Francis kills himself in futile despair.

Christabel Herries, William's wife.

Jennifer Cards, a beautiful belle. The great Herries feud begins with a quarrel between her and Christabel at a ball given by William. When Francis marries Jennifer, he becomes involved in the quarrel. Jennifer never loves her husband, and her infidelity results in Francis' suicide.

Fernyhirst, Jennifer's lover.

Walter Herries, the son of William. Intent on destroying Jennifer, he succeeds in destroying Francis.

Georges Paris, Judith's husband, with whom she leads a lonely life.

Stane, who is involved with Georges in mysterious business. After Stane causes the failure of Georges's prospects, Georges kills him and is in turn killed by Stane's father.

Warren Forster, a tiny, kindly man who has long admired Judith. She gives herself to him out of pity. He follows her to Paris and dies there.

Squire Gauntry, a tough and taciturn man. He finds the orphaned infant Judith unattended, the midwife being drunk, and takes her to his home until her half brother comes for her. She visits his place frequently as a child and is under no restrictions there. On one of her visits, she meets Georges.

Emma, Squire Gauntry's mistress and Judith's longtime

friend. Judith lives with Emma, now on the stage, in Paris.

Madame Paris, the beautiful mother of Georges. Judith meets her at Squire Gauntry's place.

Reuben Sunwood, Judith's kinsman and friend, killed in a riot incited by Walter Herries.

Adam Paris, the illegitimate son of Judith and Warren Forster.

John Herries and

Dorothy Herries, the children of Jennifer and Francis.

JULIUS CAESAR

Author: William Shakespeare (1564-1616)
First published: 1601
Genre: Drama

Locale: Rome
Time: 44 B.C.E.
Plot: Tragedy

Marcus Brutus (MAHR-kuhs BREW-tuhs), one of the leading conspirators who intend to kill Julius Caesar. Although defeated in the end, Brutus is idealistic and honorable, for he hopes to do what is best for Rome. Under Caesar, he fears, the Empire will have merely a tyrant. Something of a dreamer, he, unlike the more practical Cassius, makes a number of tactical errors, such as allowing Marcus Antonius to speak to the citizens of Rome. Finally, defeated by the forces under young Octavius and Antonius, Brutus commits suicide. He would rather accept death than be driven, caged, through the streets of Rome.

Caius Cassius (KAY-yuhs KAS-ee-uhs), another leading conspirator, one of the prime movers in the scheme. A practical man as well as a jealous one, he is a lean and ambitious person. Some of his advice to Brutus is good. He tells Brutus to have Antonius killed; failure to do this dooms the conspirators to defeat. Like Brutus, Cassius commits suicide when his forces are routed at Philippi. To the last a brave man, he has fought well and courageously.

Julius Caesar (JEWL-yuhs SEE-zur), the mighty ruler of Rome, who hopes to acquire even more power. As portrayed in the play, he is a somewhat bombastic and arrogant man, possibly even a cowardly one. From the first, he mistrusts men who, like Cassius, have "a lean and hungry look." Finally reaching for too much power, he is stabbed by a large number of conspirators led by Brutus and Cassius.

Marcus Antonius (an-TOH-nee-uhs), also known as **Mark Antony**, the close friend of Caesar. Although he denies it, he has a great ability to sway a mob and rouse them to a feverish pitch. As a result of his oratorical abilities, he, with the help of a mob, forces the conspirators to ride for their lives to escape the maddened crowd. Later, along with Octavius and Lepidus, he is to rule Rome.

Calpurnia (kal-PUR-nee-uh), Caesar's wife. Afraid because she has had frightful dreams about yawning graveyards and lions whelping in the streets, she begs her arrogant husband not to go to the capitol on the day of the assassination.

Portia (POHR-shuh), Brutus's wife. When she learns that

her husband has been forced to flee for his life, she becomes frightened for his safety. As matters worsen, she swallows hot coals and dies.

Decius Brutus (DEE-shuhs), one of the conspirators against Julius Caesar. When the others doubt that the superstitious Caesar will come to the capitol, Decius volunteers to bring him to the slaughter; he knows Caesar's vanities and will play on them until Caesar leaves the security of his house.

Publius (PUHB-lee-uhs),

Cicero (SIHS-uh-roh), and

Popilius Lena (poh-PIHL-ee-uhs LEE-nuh), three senators.

A soothsayer, who at the beginning of the play warns Caesar to beware the Ides of March. For his trouble, he is called a dreamer.

Artemidorus of Cnidos (AHR-teh-mih-DOH-ruhs of NI-dos), a teacher of rhetoric who tries to warn Caesar to beware of the conspirators led by Brutus and Cassius. Like the soothsayer, he is ignored.

Casca (KAS-kuh),

Caius Ligarius (lih-GAY-ree-uhs),

Cinna (SIHN-uh), and

Metellus Cimber (meh-TEHL-uhs SIHM-bur), the other conspirators.

Flavius (FLAY-vee-uhs) and

Marullus (ma-RUHL-uhs), tribunes who speak to the crowd at the beginning of the play.

Pindarus (PIHN-da-ruhs), Cassius' servant. At his master's orders, he runs Cassius through with a sword.

Strato (STRAY-toh), a servant and friend to Brutus. He holds Brutus' sword so that the latter can run upon it and commit suicide.

Marcus Aemilius Lepidus (ee-MIHL-ee-uhs LEHP-ih-duhs), the weakest member of the triumvirate after the deaths of Brutus and Cassius.

Lucius (LEW-shee-uhs), Brutus' servant.

Young Cato (KAY-toh),

Messala (meh-SAY-luh), and

Titinius (tih-TIHN-ee-uhs), friends of Brutus and Cassius.

JULY'S PEOPLE

Author: Nadine Gordimer (1923-   )
First published: 1981
Genre: Novel

Locale: A small settlement in rural South Africa
Time: Early 1980's
Plot: Psychological realism

Bamford (Bam) Smales, a white South African architect, married with three children. A social and political liberal, Bam

must confront his own buried fears of a true shift in the balance of black and white power when he finds himself dependent on his black houseboy, July, after the Smaleses take refuge in July's village. Cut adrift from white society, Bam sees his wife's respect for him eroding and his children assimilating easily into village life, while he himself flounders like a fish out of water in his new surroundings.

Maureen Hetherington Smales, Bam's wife, also a political liberal. It is Maureen who has dealt most closely with July during his years in their employ, yet her stay in the village brings her to an awareness of how little she has truly known July and how paternalistic is the nature of the family's relationship to him. Worn down by the strain of their situation and growing ever more resentful of Bam's helplessness, Maureen is forced to reassess the most basic assumptions of her life and is willing, by the book's conclusion, to abandon her husband and children for a chance to escape from the village.

July, also called **Mwawate** (mwah-WAH-tay), a black man who is the houseboy for the Smaleses. July has worked for many years in Johannesburg, making yearly visits to his family and his village. When a full-scale revolution breaks out in South Africa, it is July who takes charge of "his" white family, offering them sanctuary in his village. After their arrival, however, he discovers that their presence is resented by his own family and that he is trapped uncomfortably between his position of authority in the village and his long-standing position of subservience with regard to the Smaleses.

Daniel, July's assistant, a young man sympathetic to the revolution. Daniel also has worked in town, where he learned to drive, a skill that he teaches to July in the Smaleses' small truck. Daniel eventually leaves the village to join the fighting, and it seems likely that he has taken the Smaleses' only gun with him.

Martha, July's wife. Martha is resentful of the appearance of her husband's employers in their village and of the disruption that the Smaleses cause in her family's life. Martha has grown accustomed to July's long absences from the village and finds it difficult to adjust to his continual presence at home.

Gina Smales, Bam and Maureen's young daughter. Unlike her parents, Gina adjusts quickly to life in the village, falling easily into a close friendship with a young village girl.

Victor Smales, the elder of the Smaleses' two sons. Like his sister, Victor quickly adapts to village life and customs, although he displays a few initial assumptions of superiority.

Royce Smales, the family's youngest child. Along with his brother and sister, Royce is easily absorbed into village life. Both he and Victor soon begin turning quite naturally to July as a figure of almost paternal authority.

Mhani (MAH-nee), July's mother, an old village woman. Mhani (meaning "mother") is forced to surrender her hut to the Smaleses, who are the first white people with whom she has had prolonged contact. Mhani serves within the novel as a symbol of black village life that has little or no contact with white society.

The chief, the black leader in July's homeland. It is the chief who has the final say over the Smaleses' continued presence in the village. For the chief, Bam's gun is the family's primary attraction; he has been told by the white government that the black revolutionaries will usurp his power, and he hopes to defend his homeland against them.

— *Janet Lorenz*

JUMPERS

Author: Tom Stoppard (Tomas Straussler, 1937-   )
First published: 1972
Genre: Drama

Locale: England
Time: The 1970's or the future
Plot: Play of ideas

George Moore, a professor of moral philosophy (ethics) at a British university. In a department dominated by logical positivism and linguistic analysis, George, though only in his forties, is an anachronism. This circumstance is emphasized by the fact that he bears the name of a famous philosopher of the early twentieth century, G. E. Moore. George is in many respects a caricature of the abstract thinker, deeply absorbed in conceptual hair-splitting and blind to what is going on under his nose. At the core of his ramblings, there is a worthy defense of morality as something more than mere convention, but he lacks the courage of his convictions.

Dorothy (Dotty) Moore, George's beautiful wife, ten to fifteen years his junior. Dotty, once a star of musical comedy, retired prematurely after suffering a nervous breakdown during a performance. She, too, is a caricature: the bored, disillusioned neurasthenic, at once vulnerable and dangerous. When a murder occurs at a party in her flat early in the play, she apparently believes that she is the killer, though it seems unlikely that she committed the crime.

Sir Archibald (Archie) Jumper, the vice chancellor of George's university, a protean and diabolical figure. As a phi-losopher who is also an expert gymnast, he embodies the empty cleverness of much contemporary philosophy. He is also a sympathizer with the Radical Liberal Party, which as the play begins has just staged a leftist coup under the guise of an election. As a psychiatrist, he ministers sexually to Dotty. In all of his roles, he enacts the conviction that values are ad hoc, to be taken up or discarded at will.

Inspector Bones, a police detective. A self-avowed fan of Dotty, he plays the no-nonsense common man to George's educated impotence. When Archie tries to bribe him to rule the murder a suicide, he acts as the incorruptible arm of British justice, yet with some connivance on Dotty's part, he leaves shamefaced, apparently blackmailed into dropping the investigation.

Crouch, the porter, a small, stooped old man. In a comic turn, he proves to be an amateur philosopher.

The Secretary, an attractive young woman who never speaks in the course of the play. She is chiefly seen taking dictation from George. In the opening scene, she performs a striptease on a swing for the benefit of Dotty's guests.

The Archbishop of Canterbury, **Samuel Clegthorpe**,

formerly the Radical liberal spokesman for agriculture, appointed to his new post after the coup.

The Jumpers, a troupe of eight acrobats. As George explains, they are "a mixture of the more philosophical members of the university gymnastics team and the more gymnastic members of the Philosophy School." One of them, Duncan McFee, a professor of logic, is murdered during a performance at Dotty's party. His death sets the plot in motion.

— *John Wilson*

THE JUNGLE

Author: Upton Sinclair (1878-1968)
First published: 1906
Genre: Novel

Locale: The meatpacking district of Chicago, Illinois
Time: First decade of the twentieth century
Plot: Social realism

Jurgis Rudkus (YOHR-gihs RUHD-kihs), a Lithuanian immigrant overflowing with the American dream of self-made success. Jurgis arrives in the United States determined to succeed; nothing in his life works out, however. When things go against him, he vows only to work harder, and he is not given to complaining. He delays his marriage for sixteen months in order to buy a house and provide for his wife's family. When he injures his ankle in the killing beds of a meatpacking plant, he has to miss work because of his injury and is fired. He takes a lesser job in a fertilizer plant, where his pay is poor and conditions are even worse than in the meatpacking plant. His wife secretly becomes a prostitute in order to help support the family. When Jurgis learns of this, he beats Phil Connor, who encouraged her to become a prostitute. The beating results in Jurgis' imprisonment for a month. When he is released, he finds to his horror that his house has been repossessed, as has all his furniture, even though both were almost paid for. He finds his family just in time to see his wife die after a miscarriage. His small child soon drowns in rainwater on the unpaved streets of Packingtown. Utterly disenchanted, Jurgis rides the rails into the countryside, where he finds itinerant work in the fields. He sinks into a life of drinking and whoring but is soon revolted by his own depravity. He returns to Chicago and finds a job building tunnels beneath the city. Finally, when Jurgis discovers socialism, he becomes politically active, but never to the point that he really succeeds because success, in the author's eyes, is impossible for wage slaves such as Jurgis who are beholden to their capitalist employers.

Ona Lukoszaite (OW-nah lew-kah-SAHT-ee), the Lithuanian woman whom Jurgis marries and whose eleven-member family he tries to help. Ona, a quiet, ethical woman, bears the couple's first child. Because she must return to work almost immediately after childbirth, she suffers problems with her reproductive organs that plague her through the rest of her life. When Jurgis falls on hard times, Ona reluctantly becomes a prostitute in order to keep her family afloat financially. After Jurgis is imprisoned for beating her pimp, Ona is evicted from the house on which they have been making payments and finds herself in a desperate situation. By the time she and Jurgis are reunited, Ona is in the midst of a miscarriage that results in her death.

Antanas Rudkus the First (an-TAN-as), Jurgis' father, who dies shortly after Jurgis' marriage to Ona. Jurgis can provide him with only the cheapest available funeral, which nags at his soul.

Antanas Rudkus the Second, Jurgis and Ona's son, who dies in childhood by drowning in a pool of water on an ill-drained, unpaved street in Packingtown.

Marija Berczynskas (MAH-ree-ah behr-ZEHNS-kahs), Ona's cousin, who works in a bordello. She tries to get Jurgis to see that Ona's taking up prostitution was the best (perhaps the only) way to save the family, an argument that Jurgis cannot accept.

Freddie Jones, the son of a rich, capitalist meatpacker whose life convinces Jurgis that wealth results in banality, venality, family disintegration, and general unproductiveness.

Phil Connor, the man who lures Ona into prostitution, for which Jurgis beats him. While Jurgis is organizing a strike against the meatpackers, he runs into Connor and beats him a second time, resulting in a second imprisonment.

Lucas, an itinerant evangelist who is convinced that the socialist revolution will have strong roots in Christianity and in the leadership of a scientific revolutionary from Sweden named Schliemann.

— *R. Baird Shuman*

THE JUNGLE BOOKS

Author: Rudyard Kipling (1865-1936)
First published: 1894, 1895
Genre: Short fiction

Locale: India
Time: The nineteenth century
Plot: Fable

Mowgli, the boy-hero who strays away from a village in India when he is a very small child. He is pursued by Shere Khan, the tiger, but escapes when the beast misses a leap at the boy. Mowgli is reared by Mother Wolf with her own cubs and becomes a member of the jungle wolf pack. He has many adventures among the jungle animals, but when he is about seventeen years old, he realizes that he must return to the Manpack to stay.

Messua, the woman who adopts Mowgli for a time. She finally tells Mowgli that she believes he is her son who was lost in the jungle many years before.

Shere Khan, the tiger who pursues Mowgli when he is first lost in the jungle. Shere Khan shocks the other animals when he announces that he has killed a man from choice and not for food. Then follows the story of how the tiger first killed Man and was condemned to wear stripes.

Mother Wolf and

Father Wolf, who find Mowgli, give him his name, and rear him with their own cubs in the jungle.

Baloo, the bear who becomes Mowgli's teacher and instructs him in jungle lore.

Bagheera, the black panther who speaks for Mowgli's acceptance into the wolf pack and advises Mowgli to get fire to protect himself against his enemies.

Akela, the leader of the wolf pack and Mowgli's friend in many adventures.

The Bandar-Log, the monkey people, who are despised by the other jungle dwellers. They carry Mowgli off when he climbs a tree and tries to make friends with them.

Kaa, the rock python who helps to rescue Mowgli when he is carried off by the monkeys.

Gray Brother, Mowgli's brother in the wolf pack, who helps Mowgli rescue Messua and her husband when they are confined by the other villagers.

Buldeo, a village hunter, who follows Mowgli's trail when he returns to the jungle after living with Messua in the human village.

Hathi, the wise elephant, who tells the story of why the tiger has stripes.

JUNO AND THE PAYCOCK

Author: Sean O'Casey (John Casey, 1880-1964)
First published: 1925
Genre: Drama

Locale: Dublin
Time: 1922
Plot: Satire

"Captain" Jack Boyle, called the "paycock" by his wife because of his slow, consequential strut. The quintessence of impracticality, Jack needs only enough money for his daily consumption of ale or whiskey. News of an inheritance of two thousand pounds from a distant relative and the subsequent reversal, because of a legal technicality in the will, make little difference in the paycock's life. His few fleeting dreams of better conditions for the Boyle family are no discouragement to the "captain" when he learns that the money will not be forthcoming; he is drunk, he has sixpence in his pocket, and he is with "Joxer" Daly, a longtime drinking pal. That they are in an almost empty room (the unpaid-for furniture having been reclaimed) while they discuss their devotion to Ireland and the wretched state of the world is inconsequential.

Juno Boyle, his wife. Once a pretty woman, she now has a look of listless and harassed anxiety. This appearance results from a life as Jack Boyle's wife and mother of their two children. Under more favorable conditions, she probably would be handsome, active, and clever. Her lot in life is to achieve some semblance of practicality to balance her husband's insensibility.

Mary, their twenty-two-year-old daughter. Like her mother, she would be an attractive woman under better circumstances. Looking for improved circumstances leads Mary to an affair and ultimately to pregnancy; her would-be benefactor abandons her. Despite her active mind, shown in her reading and her imagination, life probably will continue to pull her back as she works futilely to go forward.

Johnny, the Boyles' son, who is as dissatisfied with family conditions as is Mary. Rebellious, Johnny fights more actively than does his sister. He has lost one arm and sustained a crippling hip injury in an Irish political demonstration. The information he gives against a member of his group shows his lack of standards and strength. When he is sought out for his informing, his cowardliness is evident as he is led out to be shot by two armed Irish Irregulars.

"Joxer" Daly, Boyle's carousing crony. His evasion of work surpasses Boyle's indifference to responsibility. His constant grinning and the twinkle in his eyes make him more amiable but no more respectable than Boyle.

Charlie Bentham, a schoolteacher who brings news of Boyle's legacy. Bentham's studiousness and wide knowledge are attractive to Mary; she sees him as the means of escaping life in the tenement. Bentham's misinterpretation of the will, depriving the Boyles of the expected money, is secondary to his abandonment of pregnant Mary.

Jerry Devine, a tenement-dweller and an active member of the Irish youth movement. Long in love with Mary, Devine still desires her after Bentham deserts her, until she tells him she is pregnant. Mary's candor is repugnant to Johnny, who berates his sister for losing an opportunity to escape to a higher scale of living.

Mrs. Maisie Madigan, a tenement-dweller and the female counterpart of Boyle and Joxer. She is as abusive of Boyle, when he cannot repay loans she made him on the strength of the inheritance, as she is exuberant in celebrating the news of the legacy with Joxer and Boyle.

"Needle" Nugent, a tailor in the tenement. To reclaim the suit Boyle orders, to be paid for when he collects his legacy, Needle snatches the suit from beside Boyle's bed.

Mrs. Tancred, a tenement neighbor of the Boyles and the mother of the boy shot after Johnny informed against him. Mrs. Tancred's lament as she goes to her son's funeral is the forecast of Juno's cry when Johnny is shot.

Irregular Mobilizers, who come for Johnny when he is to be shot.

A coal-block vendor,

a sewing-machine man, and

furniture removal men, who, in the activity of their various trades, along with the mobilizers, add to the general confusion of the final scenes of the play. Their activity spells disintegration of the Boyle household and family.

JURGEN: A Comedy of Justice

Author: James Branch Cabell (1879-1958)
First published: 1919
Genre: Novel

Locale: Poictesme, a mythical land
Time: The Middle Ages
Plot: Fantasy

Jurgen, a middle-aged pawnbroker who, searching for his lost wife, returns twenty years to the days of his youth, in which he thought himself a very clever fellow. After a year, during which he becomes a duke, a prince, a king, an emperor, and a pope, he asks to be returned to plain, practical, and moderately peaceful middle age with his wife, who is rather well suited, after all, to a man such as himself.

Adelais (Dame Lisa), his shrewish wife who, contemptuous of poetry and romance, converted a poet into a pawnbroker.

Dorothy la Désirée, his childhood sweetheart, second sister of Count Emmerick. She is Jurgen's Heart's Desire who married Heitman Michael. She also appears for a time to be Helen of Troy.

Mother Sereda (also **Aesred** and **Res Dea**), an old woman, Jurgen's godmother, who takes the color out of things and who controls Wednesdays. Her shadow follows Jurgen everywhere after she has restored to him a year of his youth, following which time she makes him the middle-aged man he is.

Queen Guenevere, with whom Jurgen has a love affair before her marriage to King Arthur. She does not recognize him after he has returned to middle age.

King Gogyrvan Gawr, her father, to whom Jurgen returns her after murdering King Thragnar.

Dame Anaïtis (The Lady of the Lake and **Queen of Cocaigne)**, a myth woman of lunar legend who instructs Jurgen in many varieties of pleasure and to whom he becomes for a while prince consort. Like Guenevere, she does not recognize the older Jurgen.

Chloris, a plump Hamadryad to whom Jurgen is husband for a time.

Queen Helen of Troy, the legendary Swan's daughter, Jurgen's (and man's) vision of supreme beauty.

Queen Dolores, Philistine ruler to whom Jurgen explains Praxagorean mathematics.

Grandfather Satan, Hell's horned and bushytailed magistrate, with whom Jurgen discusses Hell as a democracy.

St. Peter, Heaven's gatekeeper, with whom Jurgen talks over pseudo-Christian beliefs.

Koshchei the Deathless (also The Prince of Darkness), the maker of things as they are. Because Jurgen once spoke a good word for him, Koshchei disencumbers him of Dame Lisa; after a year, he restores her at Jurgen's request.

Nessus, a centaur who gives Jurgen a glittering shirt and takes him to the garden between dawn and sunrise.

Azra, Jurgen's mother, loved briefly by Coth.

Coth, Jurgen's father, whom he meets and quarrels with in Hell.

Heitman Michael, the man who married Dorothy, over whom he and Jurgen duel with swords.

Felise de Puysange, one of many women loved by Jurgen, who fathered her son.

King Thragnar, the Troll King who captured and imprisoned Guenevere. He disguises himself as Dame Lisa, and Jurgen slays him.

Dame Yolande, Jurgen kills a giant for her and with her he spends a most agreeable night after he blows out the candles.

King Smoit and

Queen Sylvia Tereu, ghosts of King Gogyrvan's grandfather and his ninth wife. According to King Smoit's story, he is also secretly the father of Coth and therefore Jurgen's grandfather.

Merlin Ambrosius, a sorcerer sent with Dame Anaïtis to fetch Guenevere for King Arthur.

Florimel, a seductive and humorously talkative vampire whom Jurgen meets and marries in Hell.

Steinvor, Jurgen's grandmother, an old woman with illusions about her children and grandchildren.

The God of Steinvor, created by Koshchei to satisfy the old woman.

JUST ABOVE MY HEAD

Author: James Baldwin (1924-1987)
First published: 1979
Genre: Novel

Locale: New York City; Birmingham, Alabama; Paris; and London
Time: The 1940's to the 1970's
Plot: Social realism

Hall Montana, a black show business promoter. Hall had served as his brother Arthur's manager until Arthur's death at the age of thirty-nine. Tall, slim, and handsome, at the age of forty-eight, two years after Arthur's death, Hall is still trying to reconcile himself to his brother's life and his death in a London pub. Hall is sensitive, reflective, reflexive, and perceptive, and in piecing together his brother's life he comes to realize more about himself and about life in general. He calls the story that he narrates "a love song to my brother."

Arthur Montana, sometimes referred to as "The Soul Emperor," a world-renowned gospel singer. An active homosexual, he has a number of affairs, principally with Crunch, a member of the Trumpets of Zion quartet, of which they were both members as teenagers; Guy Lazar, a Parisian gentleman; and Jimmy Miller, four years his junior, who became his last lover. Arthur is quiet and sensitive. Although he feels some guilt about his homosexuality, he becomes quite a realist and accepts his lifestyle. His unhappiness and heavy drinking lead to his death from a stroke in a London pub while on tour at the age of thirty-nine.

Julia Miller, a child evangelist turned model. Thirty-nine years old, slim, sleek, and beautiful, with a disarming, child-like smile, Julia was called to preach at the age of seven and remained in the pulpit until she was fourteen. Soon after her mother dies, she is seduced by her father and has a continuous affair with him until she becomes pregnant from a one-night affair with Crunch and is beaten mercilessly by her father. After losing the baby, Julia is sent to New Orleans to her grandmother. She is "discovered" while working as a waitress and becomes a top model. After a brief affair with Hall Montana, Julia goes to Africa as the mistress of an Abijan chieftain. She eventually returns to New York and purchases a house in Yonkers.

Jimmy Miller, Julia's younger brother, a pianist and Arthur Montana's last lover. Jimmy is quiet, sensitive, and precocious. Never having gotten along with his father, he is sent to his grandmother in New Orleans after his mother's death. He becomes Arthur's accompanist while Arthur is on a tour of the South during the Civil Rights movement. They later fall in love and spend many happy years together, both in America and in Europe, until Arthur's untimely death during one of their stormier episodes. Jimmy continues to wander throughout Europe, loving and missing Arthur, before finally returning to New York to the house he now shares with his sister.

Joel Miller, Julia and Jimmy's father, a common laborer who finds the monetary benefit from Julia's preaching quite to his liking and tries to persuade her to continue even after she loses her faith. After his wife's death, he rapes Julia and forces her to live in an incestuous relationship with him. When he discovers her pregnancy, he beats her savagely, causing her to miscarry. After she goes to New Orleans to her grandmother, Joel begins drinking heavily and eventually drops out of sight.

Amy Miller, Julia and Jimmy's mother and Joel's wife. Amy is shapely and elegant, as well as a fashionable dresser. She becomes ill and dies from lack of medical attention. On her deathbed, she charges Julia with the responsibility for her actions. Her death precipitates Julia's abandonment of the pulpit.

Jason "Crunch" Hogan, the guitarist for the Trumpets of Zion. Tall, slender, dark, and athletic, Crunch is a happy-go-lucky type. He is a favorite with the ladies and is Arthur's first lover. Crunch is drafted into the Korean War, but before he goes he has a brief affair with Julia Miller and presumably is the father of the child that Julia miscarries after her father's beating. After Crunch's return from Korea, he goes mad.

Alexander "Peanut" Theophilus Brown, the pianist for the Trumpets of Zion. Light-skinned, with sandy-colored hair, Peanut has poor eyesight that keeps him out of the draft. He attends Howard University and later becomes Arthur's accompanist during the time of the Civil Rights movement. After performing at a civil rights rally in Georgia, Peanut is abducted by white supremacists and is never seen again.

Red, a bass singer for the Trumpets of Zion and Crunch's cousin. Red is short, squat, and freckled. After serving a prison term for a crime that he did not commit, he is drafted into the Korean War. While in Korea, he becomes addicted to heroin. After his return to the United States, he steals from his mother to support his addiction. Eventually, he serves more time in prison for armed robbery and becomes estranged from his wife and children. After his release, Red enters a methadone treatment program and works in an antidrug organization for ghetto youth.

Paul Montana, a jazz pianist, Hall and Arthur's father. He is sensitive and loving as a father and is a loving husband. He teaches Peanut to play the piano and is instrumental in launching Arthur's career as a solo performer. He dies a few years before Arthur does.

Florence Montana, Hall and Arthur's mother. She is outspoken, down to earth, and practical. After her husband's death, she moves back home to New Orleans to live with one of her younger sisters.

Guy Lazar, a Frenchman. Arthur meets Guy Lazar during a European tour. They have an affair that lasts five days, until Arthur returns to the United States.

Clarence Webster, a music teacher. Forty-seven years old and a closet homosexual, Webster serves as impresario for the Trumpets of Zion during their first Southern tour. He is dismissed after confronting Crunch about his relationship with Arthur.

Ruth Montana, Hall's wife. Forty-two years old, big-boned, solid, and fun-loving, she lovingly helps her husband, as she always does, through the painful reconciliation period following Arthur's death.

Tony Montana, Hall Montana's son. At fifteen years of age, Tony is tall, skinny, and awkward, yet a good dancer. He is also very perceptive, and his questions regarding his Uncle Arthur's lifestyle force his father to confront many truths about Arthur's homosexuality, and more important, the fact that he loved his brother very much.

Odessa Montana, Hall Montana's daughter. Thirteen years old, tall, and with the makings of a beautiful woman, Odessa is a constant reminder of the innocence of youth.

— *Warren J. Carson*

JUSTICE

Author: John Galsworthy (1867-1933)
First published: 1910
Genre: Drama

Locale: London, England
Time: 1910
Plot: Social criticism

William Falder, a junior clerk in a law firm who raises a company check from nine to ninety pounds and is sent to prison for three years. When he is released on parole, he is apprehended by the police for not reporting to the parole authorities. He breaks away from the arresting officer and

kills himself by jumping from an office window.

Ruth Honeywell, the woman for whom Falder altered the check. He had intended to take Ruth and her two children from her brutish husband, and he needed the money for the expenses they would incur when they left London.

Robert Cokeson, a senior clerk in the firm. He supports Falder through the trial, while he is in prison, and after his release.

James and

Walter How, partners in a law firm and Falder's employers. They cause Falder's arrest, but after his release from prison they are willing to discuss taking him back into their employ.

Davis, a junior clerk first suspected of altering the check.

Hector Frome, Falder's attorney during the trial.

Harold Cleaver, the counselor for the prosecution at Falder's trial.

K

THE KALEVALA

Author: Elias Lönnrot (1802-1884)
First published: 1835
Genre: Poetry

Locale: Finland and Lapland
Time: Mythological antiquity
Plot: Saga

Kaleva, the ancestor of all heroes. Although he never appears in the poem, he is one of the unifying principles of this saga, which is put together from the Finnish folk tales of many generations.

Väinämöinen, the singer-hero, who is the Son of the Wind and the Virgin of the Air. Seeking a daughter of Louhi, the witch, for his wife, Väinämöinen is required to furnish the mother with a magic Sampo that grinds out riches. He provides the Sampo, but the daughter chooses another man for a husband. A large part of Väinämöinen's story is then concerned with his efforts to recover the Sampo and the catastrophic results of his theft.

Ilmarinen, the smith-hero and forger of the sky and of the Sampo required of Väinämöinen by Louhi. He is in love with Louhi's daughter and is chosen by her over Väinämöinen.

Lemminkäinen, a warrior-hero, who seeks as a wife a daughter of Louhi.

Joukahäinen, a young man defeated by Väinämöinen in a duel of magic songs.

Aino, Joukahäinen's sister, who is won in a song duel by Väinämöinen. She drowns herself rather than marry him.

Louhi, a witch, the ruler of Pohjola, and the mother of beautiful daughters sought as wives by Väinämöinen, Ilmarinen, and Lemminkäinen.

Kyllikki, the flower of Saari, who is abducted by Lemminkäinen.

Vipunen, a giant who swallows and disgorges Väinämöinen.

Tiera, Lemminkäinen's warrior companion.

Kullervo, a sullen, powerful slave who kills Ilmarinen's wife and ravishes his own sister. In despair, he falls on his sword.

Untamöinen, Kullervo's uncle, who carries off Kullervo's mother. When Kullervo grows up, he kills Untamöinen.

Kalervo, Kullervo's father.

Ukko, the supreme god.

Marjatta, a holy woman and virgin who gives birth to a son in a stable.

The king of Carelia, Marjatta's wise son.

KAMONGO

Author: Homer W. Smith (1895-1962)
First published: 1932
Genre: Novella

Locale: The Red Sea and the Suez Canal
Time: The 1920's
Plot: Philosophical

Joel, a thirty-year-old naturalist. He is married and teaches at a small college in the United States. Presumably, he is American, although the patina of his speech is British, sprinkled with phrases such as "jolly well." He is on a steamship bound from the eastern coast of Africa for the Suez Canal by way of the Red Sea, and he is returning from field research in Kenya. He converses at great length with an Anglican priest. His discourse on the Kamongo, a lungfish on the verge of extinction, is followed by his elaboration on Darwinian notions of evolution and his defense of scientific inquiry as superior to religious faith. He rejects the priest's suggestion that evolution is a divinely ordained progression toward perfection and insists that it is essentially a haphazard movement in an arena of chance in which many of Nature's experiments fail. The lungfish, for example, overspecialized the lung

that enabled it to survive for years at a time out of water, encased in dried mud and nurtured by its own bodily fuels; it did not become ambulatory by developing legs. Joel explains that the eel-shaped fish, with its massive-jawed, flat-toothed, snakelike head, can grow to a length of seven feet but can drown in water unless it surfaces regularly and can survive out of water only in what becomes a comatose state; as such, it is the closest living form "to the extinct link between the fishes and the first land animals" and is one of Nature's many failed experiments.

An Anglican priest, whom Joel calls "**Padre**." He is about thirty-three years old, huge, and muscular. He objects to the idea of Nature's failed experiments and argues that humans are not evolutionary beasts with specialized brains and that their innate desires for spiritual satisfaction prove the existence of a divine agent that can satisfy those desires. He agrees with Joel on the idea that life is unique and wills its own persistence in the universe, but whereas Joel sees physical characteristics as merely the debris that life, like a whirlpool, picks up in its resistance to the river of nonliving, he, the priest, identifies life's will to live as the will of God. He concedes, finally, that he himself may be an experiment, trying, in his missionary efforts, one of a number of ways of living "in order to keep alive." As he and Joel part, Joel is bemused at his concession and at his remaining secure in his faith; Joel remains satisfied with the inexplicable mystery of "the pulse of life."

Van Wernigen, who is mentioned by Joel in his conversation with the priest. He is a dentist and, as secretary to the Kenya and Uganda Scientific Society, a very competent and enthusiastic naturalist. Joel identifies him as an inspiration to himself in his own research.

Oworogwada, who is mentioned by Joel. He is a native chief with a "thirty-odd"-year-old son and a grandson. He brings Joel a Kamongo in a container of eight inches of water, in which the fish, netted and unable to surface, has drowned.

The prison superintendent, who is mentioned by Joel as having supplied a half-dozen live lungfish.

The engineer in charge of the Public Works Department, who is mentioned by Joel as having provided him with leads in his quest for lungfish.

The narrator, a third-person, unnamed, unobtrusive nonparticipant in the action. The narrator is important in providing setting and details, such as the survival of the fit Joel and priest while six others aboard the *Dumbea*, including two Lascar stokers, succumb to the oppressive heat during the first week of the two-week voyage.

— *Roy Arthur Swanson*

KANGAROO
(Kenguru)

Author: Yuz Aleshkovsky (1929-   )
First published: 1981
Genre: Novel

Locale: Moscow, Yalta, Munich, and a labor camp
Time: 1949-1956
Plot: Satire

Fan Fanych, alias **"Citizen Etcetera"** or **Newton Tarkington**, an international gangster. A crook who sustains himself by "relieving" the rich of excess funds, Fan Fanych is an iconoclast fighting to retain his individuality in the face of dehumanizing interrogation and imprisonment by Josef Stalin's Ministerstvo Vnutrennikh Del. Fanych, who is used as a guinea pig in a futuristic computer-designed crime experiment, is convicted of an imaginary crime invented by the computer and then dramatized on film: the rape and murder of Gemma, a kangaroo at the Moscow Zoo. Throughout the narrative of his exploits, from encounters with Stalin and Adolf Hitler to his imprisonment in a Soviet labor camp for the kangaroo murder, Fanych retains his spirit and irreverent wit. A dauntless antihero, Fanych outlives Stalin's regime with most of his sanity intact, free to enjoy life and to experience love.

Kidalla, a KGB investigator. Kidalla is the voice of the Soviet machine, in charge of the interrogation, trial, and imprisonment of Fan Fanych. Despite Kidalla's overt irritation over the rebellious nature of his prisoner, the reader may detect a covert bond or mutual respect that builds between this investigator and his criminal subject. Kidalla is tough and ruthless; he stops at nothing, using women, an elderly man, and an innocent kangaroo to ensure the success of the computerized crime project. After the death of Stalin, however, Kidalla mysteriously disappears.

Josef Stalin, the general secretary of the Communist Party of the Soviet Union. Stalin, as interpreted through the eyes of Fan Fanych, becomes the real criminal in the novel. The driving force behind the Soviet regime, Stalin is a merciless dictator who values his own glory above all else. Fan Fanych eavesdrops on Stalin while hiding in a secret chamber of the Livadia Palace; he overhears Stalin plot against his allies Franklin D. Roosevelt and Winston Churchill as well as sadis-

tically order the execution of an innocent shoemaker and his son. Symbolically, Fanych "hears" Stalin's foot berate the tyrant for his own miserable inhumanity, warning him that he will never find peace through the abuse of power. Stalin's death brings life to Fanych and others.

Chernyshevsky, a labor camp prisoner and party loyalist. Chernyshevsky, one of the old Bolsheviks sentenced to live out the remainder of his life in confinement, believes in the Communist Party and in Karl Marx's utopian vision despite his own personal anguish. In defiance of Fanych's reports of corruption in the state, Chernyshevsky relentlessly clings to the ideals of the revolution. He is a pathetic figure who fights valiantly for something that does not exist. The Bolshevik plays cards and argues politics with Fan Fanych in the labor camp until he is removed from prison after Stalin's death.

Professor Bolensky, a seventy-nine-year-old biologist. Bolensky, a specialist on the subject of marsupials, tutors Fanych on kangaroo behavior. Forced by Kidalla to join Fanych in confinement, the timid professor learns about sex through visits from female KGB agents as he teaches Fanych about kangaroos.

Rybkin, a zoo watchman. Under the pressure of interrogation, Rybkin accuses Fanych of the rape and murder of Gemma, the kangaroo. Fanych visits him after his liberation.

Adolf Hitler, the leader of the German National Socialist Party (Nazi Party). Hitler, on his rise to power, encounters Fan Fanych in a café and joins him for a beer. He vows to overthrow Stalin and tries to convince Fanych to join the Nazi Party.

Galya, a student of biology at the university. Young and full of life, Galya becomes the close companion of Fan Fanych after his return. The two fall in love.

— *Lisa S. Starks*

KANGAROO

Author: D. H. Lawrence (1885-1930)
First published: 1923
Genre: Novel

Locale: Sydney, Australia, and environs
Time: 1915-1922
Plot: Psychological realism

Richard Lovat Somers, a small, bearded, extremely independent British essayist and poet who has left England after having been detained there during World War I. He was harassed for his political opinions and under suspicion because of his German wife. He visits Australia with his wife, Harriet, looking for a place to settle. Through his neighbor, Jack Callcott, Richard becomes involved in a fringe political movement led by an eccentric Fascist whose code name in the secret society is Kangaroo. Aloof and distant at first and very European, Richard considers himself to be intellectually superior to the Australians whom he encounters, but he becomes friends with the Callcotts and their cousin, the taciturn Cornishman William James Trewhella, who then introduce him to Kangaroo and his national movement. Richard (autobiographically based on and drawn from a trip to Australia that the author made in 1922) is interested in Kangaroo's passion for a national brotherhood, but when asked to serve as the movement's propagandist, Richard refuses to pledge his total allegiance. As the central character, Richard observes and mediates the action.

Harriet Somers, Richard's German wife (based on Frieda Lawrence), more outgoing than her husband. She is described as fierce, handsome, and well-bred. Harriet is the first to make contact with the Callcotts, their next-door neighbors in the suburbs of Sydney. She is skeptical of Kangaroo and becomes a major obstacle in his attempt to win her husband over to the cause.

Benjamin Cooley, called **Kangaroo** because he resembles one, the forty-year-old leader of the so-called Kangaroo clubs. He aspires to become prime minister of Australia and ultimately an absolute dictator. Cooley wants to base his national movement on the notion of a "new aristocracy" and is interested in the articles that Richard has written on democracy. He wants Richard to join his cause and serve as his political theoretician. Richard interprets his movement as one based on a "benevolent tyranny." Cooley sees the tyrant as a patriarch who inspires religious loyalty among his followers. When

Cooley leads his paramilitary "Diggers" to disrupt a Labour meeting in Sydney, the violence that erupts, leaving Cooley mortally wounded, demonstrates that his motives certainly were not benevolent.

Willie Struthers, the Australian-born leader of the Socialists and Labour movement, centered in Canberra House, Sydney. He debates with Richard the socialistic and communal ideal and believes in revolution. He appeals to Richard's working-class sympathies and argues for solidarity among people. Like Cooley, Struthers attempts to recruit Richard to his cause, but Richard distrusts him.

Jack Callcott, the Somerses' neighbor, a mechanic by trade and an emblem of manly virtue. Callcott befriends Richard through their shared passion for chess. After introducing Richard to Kangaroo and the movement, Jack later suspects Richard of being a turncoat.

Victoria Callcott, Jack's wife, an attractive, friendly young woman, generous and hospitable. She invites the Somerses to visit Mullumbimby with them. She is fascinated by Harriet's worldliness and Richard's sophistication.

William James "Jaz" Trewhella, a short, stocky Cornishman who is related to the Callcotts and has settled in Australia. He possesses a quiet, discerning intelligence, and Richard befriends him as an equal. He is secretary for the coal and timber merchants union. He demonstrates more political sense than Cooley and is more individualistic than Jack Callcott.

James Sharpe, a young man from Edinburgh and "half an artist, not more," interested in music. He visits Richard in Cornwall in 1916 and takes a house on the Cornish coast. He avoids military service and, like Richard, is closely watched by the police.

John Thomas Buryan, a young Cornish farmer befriended by Richard in 1915 and 1916, before Richard is at liberty to leave England. Richard helps John Thomas with the farm work. John Thomas is the English equivalent of Jack Callcott.

— *James Michael Welsh*

KANTHAPURA

Author: Raja Rao (1908-   )
First published: 1938
Genre: Novel

Locale: Kanthapura, a village in Kara, South India
Time: Early 1930's
Plot: Folklore

Achakka, the open-minded Brahmin female narrator, who recounts the rise of Gandhian resistance to British colonial rule. Weaving Kanthapura legends and Hindu myths into her story, she documents the wisdom and daily routines of village life while recalling her own conversion to Mohandas K. (Mahatma) Gandhi's philosophy. Although she is a grandmother who survives by subsistence farming, she seems ageless in her strength and charity. As Achakka becomes increasingly involved in the resistance, she studies Vedic texts and yoga with Rangamma and participates in boycotts of foreign cloth and in

picketing against tobacco and liquor shops, during which she is beaten, along with other Gandhians. When her house, with much of Kanthapura, is burned, she goes to live in the nearby village of Kashipura.

Moorthy, a young Brahmin, the principal organizer of Gandhian resistance and the Congress Party in Kanthapura. Noble, quiet, generous, and deferent in manner, the smart and handsome deep-voiced only son drops out of the university to follow Gandhi and teach reading and writing to "untouchables." After experiencing a holy vision of the Mahatma (great soul), Moorthy distributes spinning wheels as a measure of resistance, as well as engaging in fasts and meditation. Ever admonishing Gandhians against hatred and violence, he is sorrowful but calm, and submissive but steadfast, in his leadership of nonviolent actions. Although beaten severely and imprisoned frequently, Moorthy remains loyal to Gandhian principles, despite becoming a supporter of the more pragmatic Jawaharlal Nehru in the nationalist movement.

Bhatta, the First Brahmin, or chief priest at ceremonial feasts, and primary landlord of Kanthapura. A clever, overweight opportunist, he exploits the conflict among villagers, siding with the traditionalists who oppose Gandhi's doctrine of equal treatment for untouchables because his profits are larger as a result of the cheap labor that they provide. He lobbies his cause with phony smiles of religious devotion, wearing holy ashes to enhance his image. Through frequent trips to the city of Kawar, he becomes the official legal agent of the colonial administration and the sole banker of Kanthapura, using his position to raise interest rates on mortgaged lands belonging to Gandhi's supporters. When Kanthapura is nearly destroyed in the police assaults on the resisters, the untouchables burn Bhatta's house. He sells the deeds that he holds to Bombay land speculators and moves to Kashi.

Patel Range Gowda, the primary executive officer of Kanthapura, acting as mayor, constable, and minor judge. Sturdy but fat, wealthy but charitable, smart, and aggressive, Gowda resents British intrusion into his authoritative role and sides with the Gandhians for their materialistic stability and nationalist fervor rather than for spiritual reasons. His stand results in his loss of favor with Bhatta, who essentially strips him of power. The Congress Party acknowledges his authority, a hereditary right. For accepting a minor role of leadership, the tall man is imprisoned. He returns to Kanthapura after the social upheaval and political turmoil but is rumored to have stayed only long enough to retrieve his buried jewels.

Belur Narahari Sastri, a middle-aged poet whose patron is the Maharaja of Mysore. Performing with bells on his ankles and cymbals in his hands, the singer wears a shawl given to him by the maharaja, for whom he writes an epic about the journey of the gods Rama and Sita. Their love serves as an analogy to the Gandhian struggles to achieve harmony among Hindus and Muslims and among all castes within Hinduism. Sastri's presence suggests that the nationalist movement is comparable in proportion to other legendary fights in Hinduism.

Bade Khan, a Muslim policeman whose ill-tempered grumbling and growling encourages the villagers to drive him to seek refuge on the Skeffington Coffee Estate. Short and fat, the bearded petty tyrant is particularly vindictive toward the Gandhians and brutal in his repression of those who participate in the picketing. As the violence escalates during protests, he becomes insignificant among the many policemen who are sent to Kanthapura in the attempt to quell the resistance.

Rangamma, a wealthy young Brahmin who is converted by Moorthy to Gandhi's views. Widely respected but lonely, she reads frequently and nurtures curiosity about other countries. As the resistance movement grows, she publishes a weekly political pamphlet and sponsors daily discussions on the nationalist movement, turning her home into Kanthapura's center for Congress Party activities. Bold in a traditionalist context, she refutes Bhatta's self-serving religiosity and inspires many villagers to follow Gandhi's teachings. When Moorthy is imprisoned and her father, a Vedantic teacher, dies, she continues both as organizer for the Gandhians and as Vedic interpreter and yoga teacher. Eventually, she organizes the women of Kanthapura as the Sevis, who lead nonviolent resistance marches, a role that results in her being beaten and imprisoned.

Kamalamma, Rangamma's thirty-year-old traditionalist sister. A strict adherent to the Vedic caste system, she rejects Rangamma's conversion to Gandhi's teachings and her own daughter Ratna's modern behavior and attitude. Kamalamma embodies the larger conflict within the village through her divisive stance within the family, being far more concerned with Ratna's eligibility for remarriage than with her daughter's role in the Swaraj (self-rule) movement.

Ratna, the fifteen-year-old widowed daughter of Kamalamma. Thoroughly modern in her behavior of speaking her mind and walking alone in the village, the educated, attractive niece of Rangamma follows her aunt's example by joining the resistance movement. She breaks tradition by assisting Rangamma in the teaching of the Vedic texts as justification for Gandhi's views, suffers beatings in the protest marches, and is nearly raped by a policeman. When Rangamma is imprisoned, Ratna assumes leadership of the Sevis and, eventually, also suffers imprisonment. After being released, she leaves Kanthapura to continue her activism in Bombay.

Sankar, the twenty-six-year-old secretary of the Kawar Congress Party. A saintly, ascetic widower with a young daughter, he is a lawyer of renowned integrity who embodies Gandhian ideals. He wears khadi, the homespun, symbolic cloth of resistance; eschews expensive status symbols such as the cars and fine Western-style suits that his colleagues acquire; insists on using and teaching Hindi as the nationalists' language; and renounces the use of tobacco and liquor. He contributes heavily to the Congress Party funds, and he teaches Rangamma the organizational skills of activism. When Bhatta attempts to harvest the Gandhians' crops and to auction their lands in retaliation for their refusal to pay taxes to him, Sankar organizes a massive resistance from other villages and Kawar to prevent Bhatta from succeeding in his punitive seizure of their properties.

— *Michael Loudon*

THE KARL MARX PLAY

Author: Rochelle Owens (Rochelle Bass, 1936-   )
First published: 1971 (as one-act; 1974 as two-act)
Genre: Drama

Locale: London, England
Time: The 1860's
Plot: Expressionism

Karl Heinrich Marx, a German economist, philosopher, and socialist. At home with his large family, his partner

Engels, and Leadbelly, Marx is torn in anguish between his love for his family and a passion to fulfill their needs, on one hand, and his calling to invent socialism, on the other. He is a sufferer, physically with boils and spiritually with a loss of faith and purpose, a Job in the age of science who denies his family's religion and curses Yahweh (Jehovah). Marx denies that he is a Jew and calls himself a German and a European. Engels calls him "the preacher," "a secular rabbi," "a brilliant pragmatist," and "a Jew who outgrew Judaism." Leadbelly calls him "a universal man" and, in crude, explicit language, a carnal lover of his wife Jenny. Marx's children call him "pappa." After fairly regular but assorted torment in the first two acts, Marx lets himself be prodded into his destiny.

Huddie "Leadbelly" Ledbetter, also called **Blackman** and **Herr Afrika**, an American who comes from the future to ignite Marx into going to the British Museum to sit on his boils and write *Das Kapital*, which will change the destiny of the world. Leadbelly claims that he is of "the god-people of Africa," the root base of "communalism," the real revolutionary force. Leadbelly transforms into Nelson D. Rockefeller, who substantiates what Leadbelly has been singing: He wants the milk of nursing mothers, black, yellow, and white, so that he can become strong and make money in the American way—off slaves for low wages. Leadbelly's music is evocative of the people of Africa. Although Marx prefers the plays of William Shakespeare to opera, the music and singing in the play suggest the popularity of opera in nineteenth century Europe.

Jenny von Westphalen (fon vehst-FAHL-ehn), Marx's devoted wife, a Prussian aristocrat without a thought in her head.

She calls herself a "tempting Salome" and "a wicked temptress." Marx adores her, although he had one love affair, with Lenchen. Leadbelly calls Jenny a sexy lady and the meanest woman he has even seen. She represents the domestic and romantic side in Marx's conflict.

Friedrich Engels, Marx's partner. Heir to a manufacturing fortune (ironically in Manchester, England), he shares his allowance with Marx. Engels calls himself "a good, honest revolutionary" who gives all of his energy to the goal of overthrowing tyrants, thus winning freedom and changing history.

Lenchen, the family cook, a constant reminder that there is not enough money for food, let alone anything else. In Engels' dream, she momentarily becomes Mary Burns and urges him to seek an identity apart from Marx. As Engels is about to be persuaded, she becomes Lenchen the cook again.

Elly,
Laurie,
Shirlee, and
Krista, Marx's daughters. He loves them, is proud of them, and is eager to find suitable husbands for them. They sing: "Comes the revolution, we'll don wedding dresses, and wear pretty flowers."

Baby Johann, Marx's precious son. Johann wants his father to write his book so that he can have a perfect, shiny wristwatch.

— *Frederic M. Crawford*

KASPAR

Author: Peter Handke (1942-   )
First published: 1968
Genre: Drama

Locale: Indeterminate
Time: Indeterminate
Plot: Play of ideas

Kaspar, whose name denotes a clown in German. He is described by the playwright as bearing no resemblance to any comedian; rather, he looks like Frankenstein's monster (a creature artificially imbued with life) or King Kong (a gigantic gorilla who, on film, demolished Manhattan). He starts the play by emerging from the slit in mid-curtain only after numerous fumbling attempts. The playwright's description of his appearance is precise about his costume (he has a round, wide-brimmed hat, a light-colored shirt, a colorful jacket with many metal buttons, wide pants, and clumsy shoes) and vague about his age and his height; Kaspar's "face is a mask . . . pale . . . life-like; it may have been fashioned to fit the face of the actor." Blundering about the stage, sometimes falling down, and upsetting furniture, Kaspar keeps repeating the single sentence that he knows: "I want to be a person like somebody else was once." The playwright states that Kaspar has no concept of what the sentence means. Three prompters soon begin speaking to Kaspar; they are never seen on stage. Through the course of sixty-five brief sections, Kaspar finds himself both taught and tortured by this invisible trio. He then sits quietly, struggling futilely to keep his single sentence but finding it exorcised through the pressures of other sentences with which the prompters bombard him. Taught diverse grammatical constructions, Kaspar at first distorts them surrealisti-

cally, then gradually reproduces the conformist banalities with which the prompters indoctrinate him, such as, "A place for everything and everything in its place." Kaspar begins to produce clones, five altogether, all interchangeable. He delivers a declaration of his new, self-confident persona in verse. No longer does he want to be someone else; he simply prefers keeping quiet. The five duplicate Kaspars express contentment, while the original Kaspar, speaking in a voice resembling his prompters, professes his accord with society's established values and regulations but then recognizes that learning language has trapped him into social slavery. In the brief final scene, he joins the multiple Kaspars in producing extremely grating noises with files, knives, and nails, ending with Othello's cry of disgust, "Goats and monkeys."

Three prompters, who in the original German text are called *Einsager*, a made-up word literally meaning "in-sayers," for which "indoctrinators" or "persuaders" may also be appropriate translations. They perform as Kaspar's tutors, tormentors, censors, and chorus. The playwright insists in his stage directions that they speak without undertones or overtones, irony, humor, or warmth, and that they convey to the audience the notion that they are playing at speaking, and do so with great exertion of their voices even when they speak softly.

— *Gerhard Brand*

KATE FENNIGATE

Author: Booth Tarkington (1869-1946)
First published: 1943
Genre: Novel

Locale: Middle West
Time: The twentieth century
Plot: Domestic realism

Kate Fennigate, a managing woman who knows what she wants in life and usually gets it, sometimes against great odds.

Mrs. Fennigate, her mother, interested only in eating. She dies after Kate's graduation from high school.

Mr. Fennigate, her father, interested in women and drinking. He dies during a trip to Europe with Kate.

Aunt Daisy, who takes Kate in as a household drudge. She loses her money in the stock market and later loses her mind.

Mary, Daisy's delicate daughter, whose death desolates her mother.

Ames Lanning, Mary's husband, whom Kate loves and tries to spur to success as a lawyer. After Mary's death, he marries her.

Celia, the daughter of Mary and Ames, in love with Miley Stuart.

Miley Stuart, a young engineer at the Roe Metals factory.

Mr. Roe, who employs both Kate and Ames.

Mr. Bortshleff, a lawyer who invites Ames to work with him.

Laila Capper, Kate's rich and beautiful classmate, who tries to break up Kate's marriage to Ames.

Tuke Speer, interested in Kate but persuaded by Laila to elope with her. Kate arranges for Tuke to be sent to manage Roe's New York office, thus removing the predatory Laila from Ames's presence.

KATE VAIDEN

Author: Reynolds Price (1933-   )
First published: 1986
Genre: Novel

Locale: The American South
Time: The 1930's to the 1980's
Plot: Character study

Kate Vaiden, the main character, who tells her story when she is fifty-seven years old and uncertain how many more years her cancer will allow her to live. The story, told with compelling forthrightness and in a richly idiomatic language, focuses on the dramatic events and actions that occurred between the ages of ten and twenty and that have shaped the rest of Kate's life. The first tragedy that struck was the violent death of her parents. Later and perhaps even more scarring came the death of Gaston, her high school lover, who was killed at the age of seventeen, toward the end of World War II, while still in boot camp. Restless and uncommitted, Kate eventually runs away, becomes pregnant, and then returns for a time to the kind but elderly relatives who had lovingly taken her in when she was orphaned. She gives birth to a son, but soon restlessness resumes, and she abandons the people she loves and who love her, as she feels she was abandoned. Her actions haunt her, but self-knowledge dictates her need for self-preservation, and thus she moves on whenever a place or a person confines her. In time, she manages to get an education and a good job. She settles down in Raleigh, North Carolina, and enjoys the pleasure that men can give her. A permanent relationship eludes her, sometimes by choice, sometimes not. It is only when she faces the possibility of death from cervical cancer that she knows she must find and try to make her peace with her son, Daniel Lee Vaiden, now a career Navy man. It is for him that she prepares her story, which tries to explain, not justify, a damaged and damaging life.

Noony, the black housekeeper of Kate's uncle and aunt who functions as Kate's confidant and conscience. Sensible and unsentimental, Noony gives Kate no-nonsense advice, a place to stay, and reproof when she needs it, finally offering her judgment and rejecting Kate when Kate fails to maintain contact with the people who loved and needed her most.

Dan Vaiden, Kate's father, who loves his wife passionately but discovers that he is second in her life. Tormented by pain, he kills both his wife and himself.

Frances Vaiden, Kate's mother, who cared too much for Swift, her younger nephew.

Swift Porter, an older cousin of Kate who was in love with Frances and thereby contributed to her violent death. His cruelty also was responsible for Kate running away. Much later, he makes his peace with her, answers Kate's questions about the circumstances of her parents' deaths, and helps her locate her son.

Holt Porter, Kate's uncle, who loved her as his own daughter. He is Caroline's husband.

Caroline Porter, Kate's aunt, who takes her in after Frances is killed. Reserved and undemonstrative, Caroline fails to fill the shoes of her younger sister, Kate's mother.

Walter Porter, Holt and Caroline's son, the homosexual outcast of his family. He takes Kate in and treats her with great kindness. Kate leaves him too, but Walter never holds that against her and upon his death leaves his fortune to Kate's son.

Douglas Lee, the father of Kate's son. Like Kate, Doug was orphaned; he was taken in by Walter as his ward and lover. He offers to marry Kate, but she senses problems and an absence of love. Troubled, unstable, and incapable of making genuine commitments in either love or employment, Doug commits suicide.

Whitfield Eller, a blind piano tuner who had befriended and loved Douglas Lee. For a time, he employs Kate as his driver, and he offers to marry her. Kate's heart fails to affirm what seems safe and prudent to her mind. When the ties begin to bind more strongly, she leaves Whitfield.

Tim Slaughter, the taxi driver who demonstrates a fatherly concern for Kate and takes her in for a while after she leaves Walter. Although Slaughter is eager to take care of Kate for the rest of her life, she soon moves on.

Fob, an older distant cousin of Kate who is extraordinarily fond of her and shows her much kindness and support.

— *Henry J. Baron*

THE KAYWANA TRILOGY

Author: Edgar Mittelholzer (1909-1965)
First published: 1952-1958
Genre: Novels

Locale: British Guinea
Time: 1616-1953
Plot: Historical

Children of Kaywana, 1952

Kaywana (ki-WAH-nah), the daughter of a West Indian woman and an English sailor, the mistress of both Adrian van Groenwegel and August Vyfius and the mother of children by both men. She defies the local shaman, because she believes he is poisoning her daughter. Although her daughter recovers, she kills the shaman's own daughter. She dies in a battle between the Dutch and the natives.

The Harrowing of Hubertus, 1954

Hubertus van Groenwegel, a sugar planter and slave owner born in 1727, a descendant of Kaywana, son of Adrian, husband of Rosalind Maybury, and father of several children, both legitimate and illegitimate. Although he tries to be a pious Christian, Hubertus is sorely tempted to break his marriage vows when he meets Woglinde Clackson. She is the wife of fellow planter Cranley Clackson, but they had an affair while teenagers. Now, twenty years later, she explicitly asks Hubertus to have a love affair with her. She dies of illness before completing her conquest. Hubertus then invites his widowed cousin Faustina and her sons to live at his plantation. Hubertus and Faustina have an affair just before she leaves to become Clackson's second wife; the resulting child is brought up as Graeme Clackson. Hubertus informs Rosalind of the affair, because he considers keeping it a secret to be immoral. After resigning various public offices, he becomes a serious student of philosophy and theology and reconciles his Christian beliefs and his fleshly desires. After both Rosalind and Faustina die, he takes up with an African slave and fathers a son by her.

Rosalind Maybury van Groenwegel, the English wife of Hubertus and daughter of a sugar planter. When she learns that Cranley Clackson is ill, she goes to nurse him, although she knows of Woglinde's desire for her husband. Later, she nurses Woglinde herself and takes their daughter Clara to live at Hubertus' plantation. She forgives Hubertus for his affairs, but she suspends sexual relations with him.

Kaywana Blood, 1958

Dirk van Groenwegel, another descendant of Kaywana, born in 1795, the last of the traditional van Groenwegels. He consolidates the plantation and concentrates on sugar production. His way of life is threatened by two events. First, the price of sugar falls. Second, the British government emanci-

Hendrickje van Groenwegel (hehn-DRIHK-yeh fon GREHN-vay-gehl), the great-granddaughter of Kaywana on both her father's and mother's sides, and granddaughter of an African slave. She abuses her slaves as well as those of her children whom she considers weaklings. She expresses atheistic views and has an incestuous passion for her son Adrian. Slaves hack her to death in the uprising of 1763.

Faustina van Groenwegel Clackson (fow-STEE-nah), a first cousin of Hubertus, married first to Jacques van Groenwegel and then to Cranley Clackson. After her first husband is killed in the 1763 slave revolt, she takes her family to live on Hubertus' plantation. After deciding to marry Clackson, she seduces Hubertus. They continue their love affair until she dies.

Luise van Groenwegel (lew-WEE-zeh), the third daughter of Hubertus and Rosalind, born in 1753, later the wife of Edward van Groenwegel. Although almost ten years older than her cousin Edward, she falls in love with him and pursues him. When he is only ten years old, she asks him to kiss her and place his hand on her breast. Spurning conventional suitors, she continues her advances until they finally marry, when she is twenty-nine and he is nineteen. During the Spanish-incited slave uprising of 1774, she takes a musket and helps defend her family's house while dressed in only a petticoat.

Edward van Groenwegel, an architect and painter, born in 1763 to Faustina and Jacques van Groenwegel, and husband of his cousin Luise. As a child, he is content to draw and study ants, rather than play with his brothers. As a teenager, he designs and supervises the building of a bridge on his family's plantation. After his marriage to Luise, he pursues a dual career of building and painting. While he is painting his married stepsister, Clara Clackson Hartfield, they have an affair.

pates the slaves. He keeps up the family spirit by reading old family letters. He dies in 1883, having foreseen the collapse of the sugar market.

— *Tom Feller*

KEEP THE ASPIDISTRA FLYING

Author: George Orwell (Eric Arthur Blair, 1903-1950)
First published: 1936
Genre: Novel

Locale: London, England
Time: The 1930's
Plot: Social realism

Gordon Comstock, a poet, bookseller, and writer of advertising copy who turns thirty in the course of the novel. A pale, thin man with mouse-colored, unkempt hair, he is the last male of the Comstock line, and as such he is obsessed with poverty, sterility, and decline. As a revolt against the "money-god," Gordon refuses to work for an advertising agency and instead works in bookshops, where the pay is low. His friendship with Ravelston suffers because Ravelston has more money than Gordon, and his relationship with Rosemary is hindered by Gordon's agitation concerning his poverty. He has published a short volume of poems titled *Mice* but is frustrated in his attempt to complete *London Pleasures*, the manuscript of which he finally tosses into the sewer.

Rosemary Waterlow, Gordon's girlfriend, a commercial artist who works for the New Albion advertising agency. She cares for Gordon and is kind to him, even though he mostly complains. When he pressures her to sleep with him, she agrees. When she becomes pregnant, Gordon must give up his revolt, marry Rosemary, and work for New Albion.

Philip W. H. Ravelston, the editor of the Marxist journal *Antichrist*, a friend of Gordon. He occasionally gets Gordon books to review and prints Gordon's poems in his journal. Ravelston frequently offers to loan money to Gordon—in actuality, offering a gift—but Gordon refuses as long as he can. After getting arrested for making a drunken scene, Gordon must accept Ravelston's money. Only Ravelston attends Rosemary and Gordon's wedding.

Julia Comstock, Gordon's older sister, who cannot afford to marry and will therefore become a spinster. Her future was sacrificed so that Gordon could stay in school, which makes Gordon's refusal to get a "good" job all the more irritating to his family.

Mr. Erskine, a large, slow man who, as managing director of New Albion, takes an interest in Gordon's literary abilities.

Mr. McKechnie, a dilapidated but benign Scottish bookseller. Ravelston gets Gordon a job in McKechnie's shop when Gordon refuses to work for the advertising firm.

Mr. Cheeseman, a short and parsimonious bookseller in need of an assistant. After Gordon disgraces himself by getting arrested for drunkenness, he goes to work for Mr. Cheeseman.

Mrs. Wisbeach, Gordon's landlady until the time of his arrest. She is careful to see that no one cooks in the room or brings in guests of the opposite sex.

Mrs. Meakin, also called Mother Meakin, Gordon's landlady after his arrest. She is not at all concerned with what tenants do in their rooms. Gordon's second apartment is a class below his first, and Ravelston is uncomfortable visiting him there.

Flaxman, a heavy, gregarious man who lives at Mrs. Wisbeach's house. He often asks Gordon to the pub, but Gordon never has enough money to buy a round of drinks and so will not go.

Lorenheim, also a tenant at Mrs. Wisbeach's house. Lorenheim is so lonely that he hungers for any company; Gordon tiptoes when he passes Lorenheim's door.

— John Whalen-Bridge

KEEP TIGHTLY CLOSED IN A COOL DRY PLACE

Author: Megan Terry (1932-   )
First published: 1967
Genre: Drama

Locale: A jail cell
Time: Mid-1960's
Plot: Absurdist

Jaspers, a young attorney. Disturbed by the feeling that he was becoming too much like his wife and losing his own identity and by the idea that a woman would have an influence over their two sons, he had his wife murdered. Confined to a jail cell with his two accomplices, he enlists Michaels in an effort to bully Gregory into confessing sole responsibility for the crime. When that fails, he tries to enlist Gregory in a plot to railroad Michaels. Although he is aggressive, arrogant, and quite confident that he can save himself at the expense of his accomplices, and although he wants to appear insensitive, he has an introspective side. He wonders, for example, what his wife felt when she was being murdered. In the course of the action, he metamorphoses into General Custer torturing an Indian (Gregory), a young English boy dying at Jamestown, an aggressive drag queen, his own wife, and a priest. By becoming his wife, he experiences at first hand how she felt during the murder. As the priest, he expresses doubts about his own actions and motives.

Michaels, a large, self-seeking man. Michaels served as the middleman in setting up the murder of Mrs. Jaspers. He hired Gregory and is blamed by Jaspers for selecting an incompetent. Through most of the action, Michaels sides with Jaspers in his efforts at bullying and humiliating Gregory, although he doubts that Gregory can be persuaded to accept sole responsibility for the crime. After a sexual encounter with Jaspers, however, he turns against him, stating that he cooperated with Jaspers only for the money Jaspers promised him. During the translation scenes, the characters into which Michaels changes generally are subordinates of those that Jaspers becomes.

Gregory, a good-looking, brutal young man. Gregory is the killer Michaels hired; he confessed to the plot rather than go to jail alone. He spends most of the play trying to sleep, while Jaspers attempts to rouse him. As he sleeps, he dreams of perpetrating violent rape. He resists Jaspers' attempts to force him to sign a recantation of his confession but is willing to side with Jaspers against Michaels. During the transformation scenes, Gregory often becomes characters victimized by those that Jaspers becomes.

— Philip Auslander

THE KEEPERS OF THE HOUSE

Author: Shirley Ann Grau (1929-   )
First published: 1964
Genre: Novel

Locale: Mississippi and its environs
Time: The 1960's, with flashbacks
Plot: Mythic

Abigail Howland Mason Tolliver, the narrator and protagonist, a wealthy heiress of modest beauty and intelligence. She tries to understand her family's turbulent past and present, which recapitulate anxieties of the modern South, torn by racial strife and family disintegration. Abandoned by her father and soon orphaned by her mother's death, Abigail is reared by her grandfather, William Howland, and his mulatto housekeeper, Margaret, whose light-skinned children, she learns later, are his as well. After finishing college in the East, she returns with her husband, John, to rear their children in the ancestral home. There she is reconciled with her heritage through conversations with Margaret and the spirit of her departed grandfather. She lacks rapport with Margaret's children and becomes estranged from her ambitious husband. Abigail's life reaches its climax when Margaret's son tries to ruin John's political career by revealing the secret interracial marriage in their family tree. While John is away, a mob of angry whites attacks the place. Abigail cleverly sets fire to their cars while they are busy burning her barn, and she scatters them with a few bursts of gunfire, thus keeping the house and her children safe. In the process of divorcing her husband, she learns that she has inherited most of the property in the town, and she takes revenge by using her leverage to shut down the town's economy.

William Howland, Abigail's grandfather, a strong but undemonstrative man. After the early death of his first wife, he goes into a swamp on a bet that he can find Calvin Robertson's moonshine still. He finds it but gets lost on his way back, until he comes upon a tall black woman washing clothes by the river. A strange bond immediately develops between them. He invites her to come to work for him as a housekeeper, and they live together as man and wife for thirty years, rearing three quadroon children. He is also the guiding force in Abigail's life. After she is expelled for helping two friends elope, he pulls strings to get her back into college, where he introduces her to a family friend, the young law student whom she marries.

Margaret Carmichael Howland, William's second wife, a tall, strong, and graceful woman with negroid features inherited from her mother, though her father was white. Abandoned in childhood, she is reared by her grandfather, Abner Carmichael, in a house peculiarly built to float like a boat during floods. Her lithe, free, and easy manner of speaking and moving suggests a powerful affinity with the earth, water, and nature itself. She brings life and warmth to the Howland home. Although her relationship with William is an open secret, even family members do not discover while William and Margaret are alive that they were legally married in Cleveland two months before the birth of their first child. William's death empties her life of meaning, though she lives for four more years in a new house he had bought her. She apparently takes her own life by drowning.

John Tolliver, Abigail's husband and the father of their children. His successful law practice and political career keep him away from home, and the marriage grows cold. A member of the Ku Klux Klan and the White Citizens Council, he courts segregationist votes as a candidate for governor. To the disgust of his family, he claims in a campaign speech that black people have smaller brains and thicker skulls than whites. A newspaper story about the speech spurs Margaret's son to ruin his political career by exposing the interracial marriage.

Robert Carmichael Howland, the quadroon son of William and Margaret, red-haired and fair-skinned. Like his sisters Nina and Chrissy, he was sent north to school to escape racial prejudice. He returns home to ruin Tolliver's political career by exposing his parents' interracial marriage. Abigail acknowledges him but vows to take ironic revenge on Robert by informing his white wife of his black ancestry.

Oliver, William's black servant, the only person to stay with Abigail when the Howland buildings are attacked.

— *John L. McLean*

KENILWORTH

Author: Sir Walter Scott (1771-1832)
First published: 1821
Genre: Novel

Locale: England
Time: 1575
Plot: Romance

Edmund Tressilian, an impoverished young gentleman, a friend of the earl of Sussex and an unsuccessful suitor for Amy Robsart's hand. Generous, intelligent and honorable, he seeks to free Amy from Richard Varney, whom he believes to be her paramour. When Amy, secretly the wife of the earl of Leicester, refuses to leave Cumnor Place, he tries to put his case before Queen Elizabeth. Supported by Amy's father and Sussex, he nonetheless makes a poor showing because of Varney's cleverness and his own desire to protect Amy. Accused later of cuckolding the earl of Leicester, Tressilian is forced to duel with the earl but is saved by the timely intervention of two friends. He clears himself before the queen, though too late to

save Amy from Varney's treachery.

Robert Dudley, the earl of Leicester and master of Kenilworth Castle. Rivaled only by Sussex in Elizabeth's esteem, he has the advantage of appealing to her femininity. Knowing his marriage to Amy would spoil his chance for advancement, he keeps her at Cumnor Place under Varney's supervision. Basically noble, he is also quite gullible. When he tries to tell Elizabeth of his marriage, Varney convinces him Amy has been unfaithful. In a rage, he orders Varney to kill her and fights a duel with Tressilian. On learning the truth, he reveals his marriage and tries in vain to save Amy. He suffers the loss of his wife and temporary court disfavor.

Amy Robsart, Leicester's unfortunate wife. Deeply in love with him, she wants recognition as his lawful wife but hesitates to ruin his life at court. Imprisoned at Cumnor Place, she escapes with Tressilian's servant, Wayland Smith, to Kenilworth after Varney gives her a mild dose of poison. There, she tries to see her husband and reveal her true identity, but she is deemed insane by Queen Elizabeth. Through Varney's scheme, she is sent back to Cumnor Place and tricked into falling to her death. Lovely and honorable, she is also willful and tragic.

Richard Varney, Leicester's courtier and right-hand man, a cautious, charming, clever, imaginative person who is also ambitious and unscrupulous. He is instrumental in poisoning Sussex. Facing failure in his plans to keep Amy from interfering with Leicester's advance in royal favor, he persuades his master of her infidelity. He is captured after Amy's death and commits suicide in prison.

Michael Lambourne, a swashbuckling, unprincipled man of action in Varney's service and a participant in the plans to dispose of Amy. Varney's pupil in rascality, he tries to surpass his master and is killed for his efforts.

Queen Elizabeth, an extremely shrewd and skillful ruler, adept at playing court factions against one another but still capricious and feminine. Hot-tempered, vain, and jealous, she loses her self-control when Leicester reveals his marriage, and she threatens him with execution. She eventually forgives him and restores him to royal favor.

Wayland Smith, Tressilian's hardy friend and servant. A skilled smith and alchemist, he saves Sussex from poison, helps Amy to go to Kenilworth, and prevents Leicester from killing Tressilian in a duel.

Dickie Sludge (Flibbertigibbet), Wayland's swift, ugly, clever, elfish friend. He almost causes Tressilian's death by mischievously withholding Amy's letter to Leicester, but he redeems himself by delivering it in time.

Thomas Ratcliffe, the earl of Sussex, the soldierly court opponent of Leicester. Poisoned under Varney's direction, he recovers and supports Tressilian.

Walter Raleigh, a Sussex courtier who wins Elizabeth's favor and is knighted. A friend of Tressilian, he assists at Varney's arrest.

Nicholas Blount, a soldierly, middle-aged courtier who becomes a court fool when knighted.

Dr. Demetrius Doboobie (Alasco), , a villainous alchemist and astrologer serving Leicester. Used by Varney as a poisoner, he also dies accidentally of his own poison.

Anthony Foster, the keeper of Cumnor Place, a vulgar, ugly, puritanical and miserly person who serves as Amy's jailer. After her death, he dies hiding in his gold room, unable to get out.

Janet Foster, his good-hearted daughter and Amy's maid. She aids Amy in her escape.

Sir Hugh Robsart, Amy's poor, senile father, who encourages Tressilian to free her.

Master Michael Mumblazen, Sir Hugh's overseer, a rustic, generous person who supplies Tressilian with money for the purpose of thwarting Varney.

Giles Gosling, the Cumnor innkeeper, who suggests that Tressilian put his case before Queen Elizabeth but then refuses to help Wayland.

Laurence Goldthred, a customer at Gosling's inn who wagers with Lambourne and later has his horse "borrowed" by Wayland.

Erasmus Holiday, a pretentious, pedantic schoolmaster who directs Tressilian to Wayland.

KEPLER

Author: John Banville (1945-   )
First published: 1981
Genre: Novel

Locale: Central Europe
Time: 1571-1630
Plot: Historical

Johannes Kepler (yoh-HAHN-ehs KEHP-lur), a brilliant mathematician and astronomer whose discovery that planetary bodies move in elliptical rather than circular orbits, with the sun as the focus, revolutionized philosophy and science during the seventeenth century. He is a shrewd, suspicious, and sometimes sarcastic man, frequently impatient with stupidity, but he is consistently honest and deeply compassionate toward his family and the helpless. In spite of being a German Protestant persecuted by the Catholic majority, he maintains his faith in God by finding science, especially geometry, to be a mirror of the divine plan. He views human nature optimistically by opposing Aristotle's *tabula rasa* (clean slate) model of human consciousness and proposes that all knowledge resides within the human mind and is evoked by objects in nature. He dies at the end of the novel, after many trials and setbacks, in a state of deep gratitude.

Barbara Muller Kepler, Kepler's first wife, whom he meets when she is twenty-seven years old. Carping, resentful, plump, and not very bright, she bears him six children during the course of their conjugal life; four die. She had been married twice before and outlived both husbands. She persistently chides him for not cooperating with the political and ecclesiastical authorities and modifying his philosophical principles to secure more lucrative academic positions. She dies before him and leaves him nothing in her considerable will.

Regina Ehem, Kepler's beloved stepdaughter. Of all the children, she seems to understand and love her stepfather more than the rest. She possesses a strong sense of self-sufficiency and feels a familial loyalty that the others do not. Although she and Kepler have a falling-out after her mother's death, over the contents of her will, they later come to terms with their differences.

Dr. Tycho Brahe (TEE-koh BRAH-heh), the great Danish mathematician and astronomer and Kepler's consistent supporter. Middle-aged when Kepler meets him, Brahe is brilliant, stubborn, and alcoholically self-destructive. He becomes the imperial mathematician to Emperor Rudolph and secures Kepler a semipermanent position at the court. More politically astute than Kepler, he is torn between pleasing the emperor with astronomical charts and pursuing his own scientific projects. His major conflict with Kepler is that he cannot adhere to the heliocentric Copernican model of the universe fully and proposes combining the Ptolemaic with the Copernican model, a view that offends no one.

Jobst Muller, Barbara Kepler's father. A Protestant who turned Catholic for political reasons, he is a cheerless, greedy, and well-to-do man who makes little effort to show his disappointment in his daughter's choice of a husband. A bit of a dandy, he claims noble birth and conducts prolonged negotiations in arranging Barbara's marriage and the disposition of her dowry. He dies and leaves his daughter a wealthy woman.

Susana Reuttinger, Kepler's second wife, chosen out of eleven candidates. Twenty-four years old when he meets her, she is tall and attractive but awkward. Although she is from the lower classes, she is a silent but thoughtful wife who truly loves her husband and is selflessly tender toward him. She bears him seven children, but three die in infancy. She makes his later years comfortable and secure.

Emperor Rudolph, a short, dumpy, sad-looking man who combines eagerness with detachment. He urges Kepler to draw astrological charts for him and supports him financially; he permits him to work on his astronomical research unhindered. He confesses to not liking the world and is, finally, disappointed in Kepler's findings. He becomes increasingly reclusive as his empire crumbles into religious and political wars.

Katharina Kepler, Kepler's peasant mother. Silent, cunning, and full of ancient resentments, she is accused of witchery and evoking demonic powers that she uses to punish her enemies. Highly manipulative and arrogant, she barely escapes public torture, and only her son's fame saves her from a brutal death.

Henrich Kepler, a forty-year-old epileptic and Johannes' favorite sibling. Illiterate, childlike, and unattractive, he maintains an innocent vision of the world. Having run away from home as a youth because he was brutalized by his alcoholic father, he became a street singer and beggar but finally returned home at the age of thirty-five to care for his troublesome mother.

— *Patrick Meanor*

THE KEYS OF THE KINGDOM

Author: A. J. Cronin (1896-1981)
First published: 1941
Genre: Novel

Locale: England, Scotland, and China
Time: Late nineteenth century to 1938
Plot: Religious

Francis Chisolm, the main character. He is the son of pious Catholic parents who die while he is very young, leaving him to be reared by relatives in circumstances of great poverty and personal suffering. He is rescued by his Uncle Ned and Aunt Polly, who continue his rearing and send him to the Catholic boarding school at Holywell. When his cousin, Nora, whom he loves, gives birth to an illegitimate child and commits suicide before entering a forced marriage, Chisolm decides to enter the priesthood. At seminary, he struggles to conform, but his unconventional but deep spirituality earns for him the respect of his superiors. His first appointment as a priest is as curate in a Scottish parish. His efforts to help his parishioners lead to conflict with the pastors of the first two parishes to which he is assigned. His mentor, Bishop Hamish McNabb, sends him to a missionary post in China. Arriving there in 1902, Chisolm spends the bulk of his ministry there. He humbly serves the community, Christians and non-Christians, through hard times that include an epidemic of bubonic plague and devastating civil wars. As an old man, he returns to Scotland and a small parish. He takes upon himself responsibility for rearing Nora's abandoned grandchild, Andrew. Even in his declining years, his example of simple Christian virtues and tolerance affects those who come in contact with him.

Anselm Mealey, Chisolm's childhood friend, who also enters the priesthood. Mealey is self-confident and proclaims his piety. He moves smoothly up the hierarchy of the church. As supervisor of the missions, he visits Chisolm in China. When Chisolm returns to Scotland, he finds that Mealey is now bishop of the diocese. Throughout the novel, Mealey's smoothness and success pose a contrast to Chisolm's humility and outward lack of success.

Bishop Hamish McNabb, Chisolm's friend and mentor. McNabb is headmaster of Holywell when Chisolm begins his studies there. The two recognize each other as kindred spirits and share a devotion to salmon fishing. McNabb is appointed rector of the seminary where Chisolm prepares for the priesthood. As bishop during Chisolm's early ministry, he is able to protect the young man and secure his appointment to the mission in China.

Dr. Willie Tulloch, a boyhood friend of Chisolm. He becomes a dedicated physician and an atheist. The two remain close, and Chisolm respects Tulloch for his true humanitarian concerns. Tulloch travels to China to help fight the plague and finally arrives at the mission run by Chisolm. After working ceaselessly during the outbreak, Tulloch succumbs to the disease and dies.

Nora Bannon, Chisolm's cousin. The two are very fond of each other as children and come to love each other after Chisolm is taken in by his Aunt Polly, though Bannon realizes that Polly is steering Chisolm toward the priesthood. While Chisolm is away at school, Bannon is a victim of incest and gives birth to a baby. Chisolm offers to run away with her rather than have her forced into a marriage to a family employee. Instead, she throws herself in front of a train and is killed.

Aunt Polly, the sister of Ned Bannon, who had married Chisolm's father's sister. When Ned's wife died, she became housekeeper for Ned and Ned's daughter, Nora. A devout Catholic, she sets her heart on Chisolm becoming a priest. When Chisolm is left to uncaring relatives after the death of his parents, Polly takes him away and gives him a good home. She makes sure that he receives good schooling and steers him toward the priesthood.

Mother Maria-Veronica, a member of an aristocratic German family, who has entered a religious order. She is sent with two other religious women to teach and assist at Chisolm's mission. Initially, her aristocratic hauteur makes her disdain Chisolm and look down on his simple Christianity. Eventually, his humble labors and loving personality find her approval, and they become close friends and allies.

Andrew, Nora's grandson, for whom Chisolm assumes responsibility when the priest returns to Scotland from China. Chisolm rescues him from the caring but poor couple who had taken him in when there were no relatives to help. He takes the youngster to live with him in the rectory.

Monsignor Sleeth, a self-satisfied cleric who is sent to check on the elderly Father Chisolm with the intent of removing him from his parish and dispatching him to an old priests' home. Like many others who initially scorn Chisolm for his humble demeanor and simple ideas, he too is won over by Chisolm's true Christian life.

— *Francis J. Bremer*

KIDNAPPED: Being Memoirs of the Adventures of David Balfour in the Year 1851

Author: Robert Louis Stevenson (1850-1894)
First published: 1886
Genre: Novel

Locale: Along the coast and amid the Highlands of Scotland
Time: June-August, 1751
Plot: Adventure

David Balfour, a boy in his late teens who has recently become an orphan. Having been left, as his inheritance, a letter of introduction addressed to his uncle, Ebenezer Balfour of Shaws, David decides to leave his home in Essendean in the hope that he can establish some type of relationship with his father's brother. David begins his journey with confident expectations and is somewhat taken aback when he finds that his uncle's home is in a general state of disrepair and that Ebenezer himself does not seem happy to see him. Nevertheless, David, as is his nature, soon recovers his optimistic outlook. He resolves to make the best of the situation. A short time after David's arrival at the House of Shaws, Ebenezer convinces him to join him in taking a trip to Queensferry, near the coast. It is there that David is taken aboard a ship called the *Covenant*. Once on deck, David quickly realizes that his uncle has abandoned him and that he has been kidnapped. When the *Covenant* strikes reefs along the coast, the ship sinks and David finds himself alone on a small island. In a state of despair, David nearly abandons his efforts to reach the mainland. His thoughts confused by frustration and anger, he fails to realize that he can leave the island easily at low tide. Finally, David recovers and is able to escape this predicament. He begins his return journey to the House of Shaws knowing that he must cross the wild Highlands of Scotland and reclaim his kinship as well as his inheritance.

Ebenezer Balfour, Esquire, of Shaws, David's uncle, an older man who inhabits the House of Shaws. He is a small, ugly man with a shabby appearance. Ebenezer has a poor reputation throughout the community and generally is considered to be cruel and untrustworthy. He arranges his nephew's kidnapping in an effort to keep David's portion of the family inheritance for himself.

Elias Hoseason, captain of the *Covenant*. He assists Ebenezer in the kidnapping of David. Hoseason is a large and powerfully built man who runs his ship with a firm hand. He often overlooks cruelty, and he seems to value the *Covenant* even more than the lives of his sailors.

Alan Breck Stewart, also called **Mr. Thomson** (a name given to him to protect his identity), a Scottish Highlander completely devoted to the people of his clan. Alan befriends David as a result of a mishap that occurs while the two are aboard the *Covenant*. He is a colorful character with an interesting past and an unusual sense of justice. As a deserter from the English Army, a soldier in the French Army, and a Jacobite, Alan has much to lose by guiding David on his journey through Scotland. His commitment to their friendship leads him to the conclusion that he must see David through his adventure.

Mr. Rankeillor, a lawyer in the town of Queensferry. He is a well-known and respected member of the community. Mr. Rankeillor is familiar with the arrangement between Ebenezer Balfour and Alexander Balfour, David's father. He is particularly interested in David's case. He explains the fine points, as he recalls them, to David and helps him claim his inheritance.

Mr. Campbell, the minister of Essendean, a good friend of David. He is a kindly older man who gives David advice regarding his future. He encourages David to introduce himself to his Uncle Ebenezer Balfour and gives him the letter from his father with which he can claim his kinship as well as his inheritance.

Mr. Riach, the second officer aboard the *Covenant*. He is a small man, in his late twenties or early thirties, who takes it upon himself to look after David while he is aboard the ship. Given to drink, he is unstable in his thinking. When a dispute arises, he ultimately shows loyalty to Captain Hoseason rather than to David.

— *Julie Sherrick*

THE KILLDEER

Author: James Reaney (1926-   )
First published: 1962
Genre: Drama

Locale: A small town in southwestern Ontario, Canada
Time: The 1950's or 1960's
Plot: Comedy

Mrs. Vinnie Gardner, a fussy, tyrannical, religious widow. She dominates her timid son Harry, but they nevertheless have a close and caring, if claustrophobic, relationship. A pious woman, she takes a kind of self-righteous pleasure in vicious gossip. She buys cosmetic items from Madam Fay, despite her claim that the use of cosmetics goes against her religious beliefs, because she relishes the sordid tale of adultery and murder that Madam Fay tells her during her sales call. She dies of a ruptured appendix.

Harry Gardner, Mrs. Gardner's nineteen-year-old son, who works in a bank. He loves his mother, but he has no privacy living with her. He longs to leave but is afraid of hurting his mother. He is interested in Becky, the girl who delivers eggs, but his mother insists that he marry the daughter of a wealthy banker, and he complies. Three years later, he has become a lawyer but is trapped in a loveless marriage with a wife who thinks that she owns him. He leaves her and renews his acquaintanceship with Becky, who awaits execution, having confessed to the murder of Clifford Hopkins. Harry wins an acquittal for her by discovering the true circumstances of Hopkins' death.

Becky Lorimer, later **Becky Fay**, a simple, shy country girl approximately Harry's age. She lives alone on her farm, her family having been murdered by Madam Fay's husband. Through hard work and self-sacrifice, she has kept the farm working and started a successful egg business. She feels a tender solicitude for the callow Eli Fay, Madam Fay's son, and agrees to marry him in the hope that the two of them can somehow eradicate the hatred that sprang up between their families after the disastrous affair between her father and Eli's mother. She falsely confesses to the murder of Clifford Hopkins, hoping to shield Eli from accusation. She refuses to abandon Eli, believing that he is a good man who has been poisoned by the evil influence of Hopkins.

Eli Fay, a childlike young man of nineteen who loves to play with toys and his pet rabbits. When he was twelve years old, his mother abandoned him, and his distraught father went on a homicidal rampage and then committed suicide. Traumatized by these events, he is easy prey for the evil-natured hired man, Clifford Hopkins, who reared him from that time on. A simple and weak-natured man, Eli agrees against his own wishes to marry Becky when Hopkins suggests it. He is terrified of his absent mother, fearing that she will return to punish him if he reveals what he knows about Hopkins' death. When Harry takes him in and encourages him to be a mature and responsible adult, Eli acquires the confidence to testify at Becky's retrial and to shed the childlike shell into which he has withdrawn.

Clifford Hopkins, the long-haired, bearded hired man on the Fay farm. An orphan taken in by the Fays as a boy, he has always resented his status as a hireling. His method of avenging himself on the Fays is to plant the idea of murder and suicide in Mr. Fay's mind and to corrupt the mind of young Eli, over whom he exerts a strong influence. After Eli and Becky are married, Hopkins decides that he wants Becky and her money for himself, which enrages his mistress, Madam Fay. The sullen, violent man dies not as the result of murder but of a seizure.

Madam Fay, Eli's mother, a lively, stylish cosmetics saleswoman who is consumed with hatred. In the course of a sales call on Mrs. Gardner, she reveals that she ran off with her brother-in-law, Lorimer, driving her husband so mad with anger and grief that he murdered Lorimer's wife and sons and then killed himself. An orphan herself, it was her hatred of her stepsister (Lorimer's wife), who made her feel insignificant by neither loving nor hating her, that led her to embark on the deliberately ruinous affair with Lorimer. She had been romantically involved with Hopkins since early adolescence, and it was she who mutilated his dead body, precipitating a murder charge against Becky.

Mr. Manatee, the gleefully morbid executioner. He claims that he has always wanted to be a murderer and delights in the prospect of executing the innocent Becky.

— *Catherine Swanson*

THE KILLER
(Tueur sans gages)

Author: Eugène Ionesco (1912-1994)
First published: 1958
Genre: Drama

Locale: A large city in France
Time: The twentieth century
Plot: Absurdist

Bèrenger, an average, middle-aged citizen. Usually dressed in a gray overcoat, hat, and scarf, Bèrenger is a Chaplinesque figure, muffled to reality. He yearns to live in the Radiant City. When he learns that all of its residents wish to leave because of an unknown killer, he pluckily vows to pursue him. At the end, however, Bèrenger submits to the killer because of the "vacuity of his commonplace morality, which collapses like a leaking balloon."

The Architect, the designer of the Radiant City, also police superintendent of the district and occasionally a medical practitioner. A harried civil servant who administers his departments from a pocket telephone and carries a large briefcase (symbolizing, like the other briefcases in the play, their owners' share in the evil they do not oppose), the Architect is of "ageless, bureaucratic age." He warns Mademoiselle Dany of the dangers of leaving the civil service yet is blasé about the continuing deaths.

Mademoiselle Dany, the Architect's secretary. Dany is young, blond, and beautiful. She wishes to be free of her civil service job, but after she resigns, her drowned body is found in the ornamental pool.

Edouard, Bèrenger's friend. Thin, pale, nervous, and dressed in mourning, thirty-five-year-old Edouard coughs throughout the play and is visibly ill. His right arm is slightly withered and is visibly shorter than his left. Although Edouard's spilled briefcase reveals his association with the killer, Bèrenger fails to make this recognition.

Mother Peep, a female demagogue and keeper of geese. A fat woman resembling Bèrenger's concierge, she is a satiric figure of a Fascist leader, speaking doubletalk, marching her geese in the goose step, and destroying all opposition.

Man, the lone member of the crowd who speaks for reason and the rehabilitation of the hero. Dead drunk, but in top hat and tails, the Man challenges Mother Peep and her geese and is "liquidated."

The Killer, a one-eyed dwarf who chuckles and shrugs throughout Bèrenger's final monologue. Finally, he pulls a knife and, raising it, advances chuckling toward the kneeling Bèrenger as the play ends.

— Barbara Lounsberry

THE KILLING GROUND

Author: Mary Lee Settle (1918-   )
First published: 1982
Genre: Novel

Locale: Primarily Canona, West Virginia
Time: 1960-1980
Plot: Historical realism

Hannah "Sissy" McKarkle, a writer based in New York City. Unconventional and highly intelligent, Hannah searches for truths and in so doing alienates almost everyone with whom she comes in contact. In her hometown of Canona, West Virginia, and to a large extent in her own family, Hannah is seen as an outsider and a troublemaker because she refuses to accept the restrictions that others would place on her. In this sense, she is a rebel and a lover of liberty and thus inextricably linked to other historical figures who defied popular conventions of the day. As the novel opens, Hannah has returned to her hometown to uncover the reasons for her brother Johnny's death.

John (Johnny) McKarkle, Hannah's older brother. Rich, charming, and self-absorbed, Johnny, unlike Hannah, superficially takes on the roles expected of him, from loving son to rich playboy. In so doing, he loses himself and becomes a tragic victim, a seeming sacrifice to powers beyond his control. He loves Hannah more than their parents do and virtually rears her. One night, during a fight in a jail cell, he receives a blow to the head that proves fatal.

Sally Brandon McKarkle, Hannah's mother. Hard, cold, and manipulative, she is a society lady in a coal-rich town. Mrs. McKarkle tries to cast her children according to her wishes and succeeds with Melinda and Johnny. After Johnny's death, she disowns Hannah for refusing to stay at home and tend to her.

Preston (Mooney) McKarkle, Hannah's father. An ambitious man, he leaves his family farm and achieves success running a coal mine and a law practice. He meets Sally Brandon when she is a little girl, just after her father has committed suicide. His devotion to his wife is almost fatherly, yet he fails as a father to his own children.

Ephraim McKarkle, Preston's younger brother, sixteen years Johnny's senior. A tall, plain man who is steadfast and gentle, he works the McKarkle farm. Ephraim disapproves of Hannah's choices but supports her nevertheless. As children, Hannah and Johnny spent time with Ephraim at the family farm, and Johnny comes to view him as a brother.

Rose Pagano McKarkle, Ephraim's wife. A vibrant, beautiful, passionate, and loving woman, Rose hates the cruelty of Hannah's family and helps her leave Canona after Johnny's funeral. As a young girl, Rose takes Johnny as her lover, believing that he will marry her even though she is from a lower social class.

Althea Neill, Hannah's aunt. She is eighty-three years old as the story opens. Hannah goes to Aunt Althea to find out about her family's past. Unknown to Hannah, Althea provides Jake Catlett with the means of turning his life around after he kills Johnny.

Jake Catlett, a poor hill farmer. One night in a jail-cell brawl, Jake punches Johnny so hard that Johnny falls backward and hits his head. The blow proves fatal. He later becomes a wealthy and successful coal mine operator with Althea's help.

Melinda McKarkle Cartright, Hannah's older sister. When Hannah is eleven years old, Melinda marries Spud Cartright in a wedding that her mother has orchestrated. Melinda is a younger version of her mother and pays little attention to Hannah as she grows up. After their parents have died, she cheats Hannah out of any inheritance that she might have had.

Thelma (Tel) Leftwich, Johnny's lover. A beautiful teacher, Tel has no social standing and no chance of marrying Johnny. She blames Hannah and her family for Johnny's inability to marry her, failing to see that Johnny will never marry anyone.

Candida (Candy) Pentacost, Hannah's childhood friend. She is a legislator who fights to keep coal-mining interests in check. When they are girls, Candy persuades Hannah to show a short story to her father, a newspaper editor, and he encourages her to keep writing.

Daisy Cutright,
Kitty Puss Baseheart,
Ann Randolph Potter, and
Maria Crane, Melinda's friends and symbols of all the injustices Hannah has come to hate. Hannah has known them all of her life. As the novel begins, they pick her up at her motel and take her to the gallery where she is to give a lecture.

— Aileen O'Catherine

KIM

Author: Rudyard Kipling (1865-1936)
First published: 1901
Genre: Novel

Locale: India
Time: Late nineteenth century
Plot: Adventure

Kimball O'Hara (Kim), the son of an Irish mother, who died in India when he was born, and an Irish father, who was color sergeant of the regiment called the Mavericks and who died and left Kim in the care of a half-caste woman. Kim grows up on the streets of Lahore, and his skin becomes so dark that no one can tell he is white. He attaches himself to a Tibetan lama as a chela. Kim is caught by the chaplain of the Maverick regiment, who discovers his real identity. The lama pays for Kim's education, and Kim finally distinguishes himself as a member of the British Secret Service.

A Tibetan Lama, who becomes Kim's instructor and whose ambition it is to find the holy River of the Arrow that would wash away all sin. The lama pays for Kim's schooling. After Kim's education is complete, he accompanies the lama in his wanderings, though he is really a member of the Secret Service. In the end, the lama finds his holy river, a brook on the estate of an old woman who befriends him and Kim.

Mahbub Ali, a horse trader who is really a member of the British Secret Service. Mahbub Ali is largely responsible for Kim's becoming a member of the Secret Service.

Colonel Creighton, the director of the British Secret Service, who permits Kim to resume the dress of a street boy and do Secret Service work.

Hurree Chunder Mookerjee, a babu, and also a member of the Secret Service. He is Kim's confederate in securing some valuable documents brought into India by spies for the Russians.

A KIND OF ALASKA

Author: Harold Pinter (1930-   )
First published: 1982
Genre: Drama

Locale: England
Time: The 1980's
Plot: Existentialism

Deborah, a hospital patient who has suffered from sleeping sickness (*Encephalitis lethargica*) since she was sixteen years old. She is in her mid-forties and has been asleep for twenty-nine years; hence, she does not know her age. She wakes as the play begins, and in her attempts to realize what has happened to her, she alternately thinks that she has merely overslept, that she has been awakened from the dead, that she is imprisoned or a victim of "white slavers," or that she is in a fairy tale. Unable to think or behave as a grown woman, Deborah speaks in the inflated romantic or sharply petty tones of an adolescent. Her speech is unconnected to her surroundings. She has the sexual preoccupations of an adolescent and attaches sexual meanings to her sleep, as well as to her awakening by Hornby.

Hornby, the physician who has cared for Deborah for twenty-nine years and now wakes her. He is married to Pauline and is therefore Deborah's brother-in-law. Although he seems, at first, to be a dispassionate physician who limits his talk to simple statements and queries, his personal involvement in Deborah's case is revealed as the play progresses. He views his care and awakening of Deborah in sexual terms, just as she does: He has become obsessed with her. It is Hornby who gives Deborah the most specific details of her illness and of the fate of members of her family, and he insists to her that it is the conscious ones who have suffered the most from the effects of her sickness.

Pauline, Deborah's younger sister, who is married to Hornby. She is in her early forties. She is the only member of Deborah's family who is present onstage. Initially rejected by Deborah, who cannot see her sister in the grown woman, Pauline tentatively gives facts to her sister, but she is deliberately vague: She does not mention their mother's death, their father's blindness, or their older sister Estelle's wasted life. She also describes herself as a "widow," leaving it to Hornby to reveal their marriage and the cause of its failure: his devotion to the unconscious Deborah.

— Heidi J. Holder

KINDERGARTEN

Author: Peter Rushforth (1945-   )
First published: 1979
Genre: Novel

Locale: Southwold, a small English town
Time: December 24-28, 1978
Plot: Impressionistic realism

Corrie Meeuwissen (MOY-vihs-sehn), an introspective, analytical, and extremely talented sixteen-year-old. He has written music for a Shakespeare production and is currently working on an opera. He is known to people as a polite, quiet boy who is helping his younger brothers cope with the death of their mother in a terrorist attack and the absence of their father (who is in America helping to raise money for the families of the other victims in the attack). Corrie is intensely conscious of the pressures of the outer world that destroy childhood and threaten the existence of family ties and affection. Discovering a cache of letters and photographs from Jewish parents in Nazi Germany to the headmaster of an English boarding school, Corrie reads with horrified fascination the pleas of parents desperate for a safe place to which to send their children. To him, the letters merge inextricably with his favorite fairy tales, in which children are menaced by certain evil adults, and with news reports of children held hostage by terrorists. He finishes reading the letters on his sixteenth birthday, the day on which his artist grandmother gives him a new painting and shows him for the first time a photograph of her family, whom she lost in the Holocaust. On the same day, the hostage children are released. On that day, Corrie comes to terms with his approaching maturity.

Jo Meeuwissen, Corrie's eleven-year-old brother. In one sense, Jo is like most eleven-year-olds: He litters his room with Charlie Brown cartoons, books, clothes, posters, and toys. In another sense, he is unusual: He quotes William Shakespeare, uses words from a thesaurus, and sings in German. He is also somewhat immature for his age: He frequently wets his bed. It is Jo who is most profoundly affected by his mother's death. He has nightmares about it, and on Christmas Eve he insists on going to her grave to sing. Jo is very much a child who has been prematurely robbed of childhood and innocence, a boy forced violently to confront the precariousness of life.

Matthias Meeuwissen (mah-TI-as), who is three years old and the youngest of the Meeuwissen brothers. Too young to realize the meaning of death, Matthias is the quintessential innocent child who plays football, romps with the dog, eats with gusto, and paints pictures of mythical creatures. He is unaware that life eventually will bring him painful experiences.

Lilli, the grandmother of the three boys. Once an acclaimed illustrator of children's books in prewar Germany, Lilli was one of the fortunate Jews who escaped to England, where she married a Gentile. Like her grandson Corrie, she is preoccupied with preserving the wonder of childhood and family traditions. She orchestrates an elaborately special Christmas celebration for the motherless boys, who are in her care during the holidays. During the celebration, she unveils for the boys her new collection of paintings. No longer evocations of fairy tales, these paintings are records of the Meeuwissen family in happier times.

— *E. D. Huntley*

KINDRED

Author: Octavia E. Butler (1947-   )
First published: 1979
Genre: Novel

Locale: The eastern shore of Maryland and Los Angeles, California
Time: 1815-c. 1825 and 1976
Plot: Science fiction

Edana (Dana) Franklin, the protagonist and narrator. A newly published author, Dana is a twenty-six-year-old black woman who has been married to Kevin Franklin, also an author, for four years. Dana is a modern American woman who is suddenly transported to the antebellum South. Her knowledge of medical practices allows her to help Rufus and some of the slaves.

Kevin Franklin, Dana's husband. Kevin, a white man, and Dana have a successful and mutually satisfying interracial marriage. When Kevin is transported to the past with Dana, he must pose as her master because no other relationship would be tolerated. This is as problematic for Kevin as it is for Dana.

Rufus Weylin, Dana's great-great-great-grandfather, a white plantation owner in antebellum Maryland. Rufus, by means Dana never discovers, summons Dana from the present to aid him in the past whenever his life is endangered. Rufus and Dana's relationship is based on mutual need. Rufus requires Dana's assistance in order to stay alive, and Dana must safeguard Rufus' life long enough for him to sire Dana's great-great-grandmother. Their relationship is brutally unequal, however, as Rufus is a white male slaveowner and Dana is a young black woman whom he enslaves. He resists Dana's efforts to rid him of his racism.

Tom Weylin, Rufus' father. Tom is a stereotypical white slaveowner. He is unpredictable, taking offense at the slightest infraction of his rules, and is without compassion for his slaves, beating them mercilessly when he deems it necessary. He uses female slaves sexually and discards mistresses when he tires of them. He separates families by selling fathers and children whenever he chooses.

Margaret Weylin, Rufus' mother. Margaret, who is emotionally unstable, dislikes and is jealous of Dana because of Dana's relationship with her son.

Alice Greenwood, Dana's great-great-grandmother. Rufus passionately loves the freedwoman Alice but uses her without regard for her feelings. He rapes her, beats her until she is near death after she attempts to escape with her slave husband, sells her husband, enslaves Alice, and keeps her as his mistress. Dana nurses Alice from the brink of death, helping her to regain memories that fled as a result of the trauma of her capture and her husband's torture and sale. Alice and Dana, who look much alike, have an ambivalent relationship. Although they aid each other, neither apparently likes the other. Alice forces Dana to confront her role on the plantation and challenges her loyalties to the other slaves. Alice eventually kills herself to be free of Rufus.

Sarah, the plantation cook. Sarah, a middle-aged, plump woman, appears to Dana almost as a stereotyped "Mammy," in that she looks out for the other slaves and fiercely protects the children. Sarah is a multidimensional character, an able and compassionate woman who helps Dana learn the skills she needs to survive on the plantation.

Carrie, Sarah's daughter. All of Sarah's other children are sold, but Carrie, who is inexplicably mute, is allowed to remain with Sarah as a means of preventing Sarah from attempting to escape.

Nigel, a slave child and friend of Rufus in their youth. As an adult, he exerts a slight influence over Rufus. He is Carrie's husband and the father of her children.

— *Mary E. Virginia*

KINFLICKS

Author: Lisa Alther (1944-   )
First published: 1975
Genre: Novel

Locale: Tennessee, Massachusetts, and Vermont
Time: Late 1960's to mid-1970's
Plot: Bildungsroman

Virginia Hull Babcock (Ginny) Bliss, the protagonist and narrator of half the novel. The daughter of a plant manager, she

is a popular high school girl in Hullsport, Tennessee; she is a cheerleader and girlfriend of the star athlete, with whom she has hilarious introductory sexual experiences. When she loses her virginity, however, it is to one of the tough guys, an outcast. At her father's insistence, she reluctantly enters a college in Massachusetts (Wellesley, thinly disguised as Worthley), where she comes under the influence of Miss Head, a professor of philosophy, and is introduced to the life of the mind and of artistic appreciation. During her second year, she meets Edna (Eddie) Holzer, who ridicules what Ginny has learned from Miss Head and who introduces her to lesbian sexuality. They leave college to set up an apartment in a Boston slum. They participate in anti-Vietnam War activities before moving to Stark's Bog, Vermont. Eventually, they live in an all-female commune with three other women, where they are harassed by the local young men, whose diversions are hunting and snowmobiling. After Eddie dies in a violent accident, Ginny marries Ira Bliss, the leader of the young men. They have a daughter, Wendy, but the marriage is not a success despite Ginny's efforts to act the role of a loving housewife and mother. When Hawk shows up, he convinces Ginny to participate in sexual exercises supposed to increase her spiritual awareness. They are discovered in a compromising position by Ira, who throws out Ginny. After a brief interlude in Montreal, Ginny is called back to Hullsport, where her mother is very ill. After her mother's death, she tries to commit suicide but fails; she decides to go on living, although she has no plans and no prospects.

Wesley Marshall Babcock IV, called **The Major**, Ginny's father, a tough man who tries unsuccessfully to discipline Ginny and later to force her into a conventional lifestyle. The plant he manages manufactures explosives to be used in the Vietnam War.

Mother, Ginny's mother, a pallid woman who is oversolicitous of her husband and children. When she becomes ill with a rare blood disease, she blames her children for deserting her, even though Ginny returns to be with her. Her slow death and Ginny's relationship with her are the subject of the third-person narrative that alternates with Ginny's narration. The

mother has always had an obsession with death: Her chief amusement when Ginny was young was to revise her obituary, which she did frequently. Despite the efforts of the medical profession, she dies of the blood disease.

Joe Bob Sparks, a high school athlete and Ginny's first boyfriend, later a high school coach in Hullsport.

Clem Cloyd, a partially crippled motorcycle rider who is Ginny's first lover. As an adult, he becomes a preacher in a small nondenominational church and holds a healing service for Ginny's mother.

Miss Head, a philosophy professor at Worthley College, cellist, and lover of beautiful things. She is Ginny's adviser and teacher. A lonely woman who plays the cello for amusement, always by herself, she tries to indoctrinate Ginny in the life of the mind, but the aridity of her own life drives Ginny away.

Edna (Eddie) Holzer, an illegitimate child of poor parents. She is a radical feminist, antiwar protester, and Ginny's lesbian lover. She induces Ginny to leave college and to give away most of the income Ginny receives from stock in her father's company. The women's relationship turns stormy in Vermont, and Eddie eventually dies violently.

Ira Braithwaite Bliss IV, an insurance salesman in Stark's Bog, Vermont. He also sells snowmobiles and is the leader of the young men who harass the women with whom Ginny lives. Convinced that Ginny needs only a strong man to convince her to turn her back on lesbianism, he pursues her. When Ginny's lover dies and the commune disintegrates, she agrees to marry him. They have a daughter; he takes custody of Wendy after Ginny is unfaithful to him with Hawk. At the end, he would be willing to take Ginny back, but she refuses to return.

William Hawk, a Vietnam veteran and deserter. Hawk is a fugitive whom Ginny shields and who involves her in a weirdly comic sexual experiment that leads to the end of her marriage. Hawk winds up in a veterans hospital, diagnosed as a paranoid schizophrenic.

— *John M. Muste*

THE KING

Author: Donald Barthelme (1931-1989)
First published: 1990
Genre: Novella

Locale: Great Britain
Time: Early 1940's
Plot: Alternative history

King Arthur, the legendary king of Britain, presented as still living in 1940, or perhaps returned as "the Future King" of legend. He is a shadowy character. He involves himself in the military, leaving politics to "Winston" and the propaganda machines, understanding that against the propaganda machines and the manipulativeness of modern politics not much can be done. He vaguely believes that his kingly role has outlived its usefulness and feels keenly the loss of the old romantic Round Table. In this somewhat absurdist novel, he acts in ways the legends about him would anticipate. The novella closes with a surprise. According to legend, he dies in a battle with Mordred, but in this story he rather cavalierly rewrites the legend and defeats Mordred, this time without injury to himself. He explains that he "didn't like Merlin's prophecy."

Guinevere, the queen, Arthur's wife. She plays the part of a bored and spoiled queen, in the tradition of Thomas Malory's

Le Morte D'Arthur (1485). Guinevere spends much of her time with a maidservant listening to a traitor, Lord Haw Haw, who claims that she is bad for morale because she is sleeping with Sir Launcelot. She seems to accept these accusations, even though during the time period of the book she is sleeping with the Brown Knight and not with Launcelot. She feels weary and bored and perhaps understands that the romantic role of queens is dead. She insists, however, that "all myths come from queens."

Launcelot du Lac, the chief general of King Arthur and, at one time, Guinevere's lover. The book opens with his rather random fighting for the mere thrill of it. His character seems to be defined by his first jousting with, then befriending, the Black Knight. The book ends with his dream of "the softness of Guinevere."

Sir Kay, King Arthur's aide-de-camp. He acts as a sounding board for Arthur's discussions of war and kingship. He worries a lot about Merlin's prophecies because, although he has never read them, he knows that a battle with Mordred has been foretold. He also worries about the victories of General Rommel in Africa. Later, Arthur gives him a glimpse of the prophecies about the end of the war. Arthur then rewrites them, so the end is as much as surprise to Kay as to anyone else.

Sir Roger de Ibadan, the Black Knight, a visitor from Africa. He enters the book as a jousting foe of Launcelot, but after their encounter they shake hands and become friends. There is little racial prejudice in the book. Launcelot invites the Black Knight to join "our side." Sir Roger is a vaguely passionate fellow and eventually falls in love with the female thief, Clarice. Her first love is her thieving, but she admits a certain affection for Sir Roger.

Lyonesse, the queen of Gore, a semimythical Celtic kingdom that appears in Arthurian literature. She is the wife of King Unthank. She claims that her husband does not love her and treats her badly, so she seeks comfort in the arms of Lieutenant Edward. She illustrates the dislocation of people and the dissolution of families that inevitably occur in wartime.

Lieutenant Edward, Lyonesse's lover, a twentieth century proletarian. This former plasterer is the type of commoner thrown into prominence by the war. He is a soldier freed from the bonds of duty and family, footloose and confused. He is ashamed of his common upbringing, especially after he falls in love with Lyonesse.

The Red Knight, **Sir Ironside of the Red Lands**, a communist rabble-rouser who spends his time calling Arthur a reactionary anachronism, using typical communist propaganda terminology.

The Blue Knight, who is searching for the Grail, the ultimate weapon. This ultimate weapon turns out to be a "bomb bigger than all other bombs" and is made of cobalt. He is called the blue knight because his colors are cobalt blue.

— *Robert W. Peckham*

A KING AND NO KING

Authors: Francis Beaumont (c. 1584-1616) and John Fletcher (1579-1625)
First published: 1619
Genre: Drama

Locale: Armenia and Iberia
Time: Indeterminate
Plot: Tragicomedy

Arbaces (AHR-buh-seez), the king of Iberia. He proudly proclaims his own humility and bravery after his victory over the Armenians, but he finds his self-confidence shaken by his passion for the girl he believes to be his sister. His melodramatic inner torments are relieved when he discovers that he is not the son of the previous king and is therefore free to marry Panthea.

Tigranes (tih-GRAY-neez), the king of Armenia, who is conquered and taken prisoner by Arbaces. He succumbs briefly to the charms of Panthea but recognizes the virtues of the faithful Spaconia and resolves to be constant to her.

Arane (uh-RAY-nee), the queen mother, who attempts to murder her foster son to make her daughter queen.

Gobrias (GOH-bree-uhs), the lord protector, Arbaces' father. He is forced to thwart Arane's plots until he can reveal the truth at the time when his son most welcomes it.

Panthea (PAN-thee-uh), Arane's daughter. She is distressed by her unsisterly feelings for Arbaces and accepts imprisonment to save them both from sin.

Spaconia (spa-KOH-nee-uh), an Armenian lady who follows her beloved Tigranes to Iberia. She readily forgives his brief infatuation with Panthea and agrees to become his wife.

Lygones (LI-goh-neez), her father, whose anger with his runaway daughter is mollified when he learns that she is to be Tigranes' queen.

Mardonius (mahr-DOH-nee-uhs), Arbaces' captain, the one person who dares to criticize the king to his face.

Bessus (BEH-suhs), another captain, a notorious cowardly braggart, one in the long tradition of the *milites gloriosi.*

Bacarius (ba-KAY-ree-uhs), an Iberian lord who plans a trap to deflate Bessus' pride.

KING HORN

Author: Unknown
First transcribed: c. 1225
Genre: Poetry

Locale: England and Ireland
Time: The sixth century
Plot: Sentimental

Horn, a protagonist. The son of Murri and Godhild, he is the fairest boy in the land and a paragon of competence, courage, and virtue. After the invaders of Murri's land send Horn and his twelve companions out to sea on a ship designed to sink, Horn manages to bring his crew to safety in the kingdom of Westernesse. Throughout the poem, his actions exemplify fortitude in battle, obedience to authority, and perseverance in love. Horn is incapable of evil; he is the epitome of goodness.

Murri, Horn's father and the king of Suddene, who is murdered by invaders as he rides by the sea.

Godhild, Horn's mother. After the death of her husband and the banishment of her sons, she withdraws from society and dwells alone under a rock, where she prays for the children's safety.

Athulf, Horn's brother, who resembles him, although he is not as fair. The poet says that Athulf is the best of Horn's twelve companions.

Fikenhild, Horn's antithesis, who is responsible for his exile from Westernesse. The embodiment of evil, Fikenhild is referred to as "the worst mother's child."

Aylmar, the king of Westernesse, who harbors Horn and his companions, eventually knighting them all. The poet suggests that Aylmar's kingdom is somewhat more advanced than Suddene. A steward teaches Horn how to play the harp, carve at table, and bear wine, skills Horn apparently had not acquired in his father's castle.

Rymenhild, Aylmar's daughter, who is passionately in love with Horn. She provides the impetus for Horn's application to knighthood as well as his massacre of the pagans. Rymenhild's marriage to Horn brings about the reestablishment of his family's line in Suddene.

Thurston, the king of Ireland, on whose shores Horn arrives following his exile from Westernesse. After Horn defends Ireland against numerous pagans in a battle that claims the lives of Thurston's sons, Thurston wants to make him king of the land. Instead of accepting this offer, however, Horn enlists Thurston's help in getting back to Westernesse.

Reynild, Thurston's daughter, whom he wants Horn to marry. At the end of the poem, she marries Athulf instead.

King Modi, the man whom Rymenhild marries, apparently under duress, while Horn is returning from Ireland. After Horn enters Westernesse and learns of the wedding that has just taken place, he kills Modi by throwing him over a bridge and breaking his ribs. The murder is not contrary to Horn's goodness, for the poet refers to Modi as "the boye" or "the varlet," making it clear that this character is wicked. Horn's killing of his rival is a victory of good over evil.

A palmer, who informs Horn of Rymenhild's marriage to Modi. By agreeing to exchange clothes with Horn, he makes it possible for the latter to enter the castle and claim his rightful place as the princess' beloved.

— *Rebecca Stingley Hinton*

KING JESUS

Author: Robert Graves (1895-1985)
First published: 1946
Genre: Novel

Locale: Palestine
Time: The first century A.D.
Plot: Historical

Jesus, the "wonder-worker" of Palestine, the circumstances of whose birth, development, ministry, and death are chronicled by the narrator, Agabus. He is the son of Mary, the heiress of Michal (wife of King David), and Antipater, the eldest son of Herod, to whom Mary was married secretly. He is protected by Joseph, a retired timber merchant from Emmaus. Born in Bethlehem, Jesus is taken as an infant to Leontopolis, Egypt, where during his first twelve years he learns carpentry from Joseph and the Hebrew Scriptures from Simon. Later, he marries Mary of Bethany, the sister of Martha and also an heiress of Michal. By refusing to consummate the marriage, Jesus stands for a love untouched by "the act of death." He preaches in the synagogues and in open places, always conscious of his destiny as priest, Messiah, and future king of Israel. Jesus' healings, prophetic sayings, and bold challenges to conventional interpretations of the Hebrew Scriptures lead to his condemnation by both religious and political authorities and to his crucifixion as a false king of the Jews.

Mary, or **Miriam**, a beautiful temple virgin. She is secretly married to Antipater before his death; by him, she bears her only child, Jesus. With the elderly Joseph, who accepts her as his wife, she rears Jesus in Egypt and, later, in Nazareth. Puzzled by the way in which her son is working out his royal destiny, she is present at the Crucifixion and the Resurrection.

Simon, later called **Simeon**, an Alexandrian Levite Jew, a high priest. He convinces Antipater that his future title as king of Israel would be perfected by a marriage to a descendant of Michal, one of King David's queens, and officiates at the secret marriage of Mary to Antipater just before Antipater's assassination. Later, as Simeon, he becomes Jesus' teacher in Egypt.

Joseph of Emmaus, an old timber merchant. A widower, he has been joined in his trade by his four sons. Urged by Simon, he accepts marriage to Mary but retains a small part of the bride-price until after Antipater's death, when he pays the remainder and assumes the protection of Mary and her baby, fleeing from Bethlehem to Egypt.

Herod the Great (HEHR-uhd), the king of the Jews under the protection of the Romans. He is insanely protective of his position. He arranges for the death of his descendants, including his eldest son, Antipater, and decrees the death of all children born in Bethlehem, where astrologers had predicted a future king of the Jews would appear.

Antipater (ahn-TIHP-ay-tuhr), the eldest son of Herod the Great and Queen Doris. He is secretly married to Mary and is executed soon thereafter by Herod as a potential threat to his power.

Mary the Hairdresser, the queen of the harlots, modeled on Mary Magdalene. She is the priestess of an ancient fertility cult in Hebron that celebrates the power of Eve. In a contest of wills, Jesus overcomes the power of the Female by invoking the power of God the Father. With the two other Marys, she is present at the Crucifixion and the Resurrection.

Mary of Bethany, who is married to Jesus in Hebron as his queen. She is resentful of Jesus' unwillingness to give her a child but convinces him to raise her brother Lazarus from the dead as a substitute.

Agabus the Decapolitan, the author of the narrative, begun in Egypt in A.D. 89 and finished in Rome in A.D. 93. The son of a Syrian father and a Samaritan mother, he had seen Jesus only once, as a child. From several informants, however, he has been given the secret oral traditions of Jesus' birth, life, and death; he has visited the meetings of the "Chrestians" (followers of the Chrestos, or Good Man); and into the events of Jesus' life he has woven his interests in astrology, numerology, and mythology, through which he explains why Jesus is king and why his significance has been misunderstood by his followers.

— *William L. Phillips*

KING JOHAN

Author: John Bale (1495-1563)
First published: 1538
Genre: Drama

Locale: England
Time: Early thirteenth century
Plot: Historical

England, a poor widow, persecuted by agents of the Church of Rome. She is sorely distressed at her own hardships and those of her king, which end with his defeat and ultimate death by poisoning. She is saved from her wretchedness when Verity brings in Imperial Majesty to overthrow her enemies.

King Johan, the champion of the oppressed widow and enemy of the Church of Rome. He lays aside his anger at the corrupt clergy and domination from overseas in compassion for his people. To spare them the horrors of war, he surrenders his crown to Usurped Power (Pope Innocent III) and receives it from him as a vassal of the Church. Too trusting, he shares a poisoned cup with Dissimulation and dies, lamenting the fate of his poor people.

Nobility, the king's shaky supporter. Fearful of the power of Rome, he deserts his rightful ruler. After Johan's death, Nobility is brought back into the fold by Verity.

Clergy, the king's corrupt, unwilling follower. He swears loyalty with reluctance and breaks his oath with joy. He also reforms and serves Imperial Majesty.

Civil Order, another unreliable follower. He too deserts the king in the crisis. He returns when Imperial Majesty becomes ruler.

Commonalty, the poor, blind, and ignorant child of the Widow England. His goods taken by the Church, and deprived of the Holy Scripture by the clergy, he too is found wanting and abandons his ruler.

Sedition (**Stephen Langton**), a corrupt and wittily foul-mouthed agent of the Church of Rome. Sometimes appearing as the vice Sedition itself, he also assumes the person of Stephen Langton, archbishop of Canterbury. He is an active villain throughout the play and is finally hanged by command of Imperial Majesty.

Dissimulation (**Simon of Swinsett**), another agent of the Church, also part vice and part man. Willing to accept martyrdom to remove an enemy of the Church and expecting canonization for committing murder, he shares a cup of poison with King Johan, joining his victim in death.

Private Wealth (**Cardinal Pandulphus**), a strong supporter of Usurped Power and a harsh oppressor of England and tormentor of King Johan.

Usurped Power (**Pope Innocent III**), the most powerful of Johan's enemies.

Treason, a criminal protected by benefit of clergy.

Verity, a supporter and restorer of historical truth. He rebukes the defecters and gives England a savior, Imperial Majesty.

Imperial Majesty (perhaps Henry VIII), the destroyer of the usurping powers in England. He hangs Sedition and redeems the country.

KING JOHN

Author: William Shakespeare (1564-1616)
First performed: 1623
Genre: Drama

Locale: England and France
Time: Early thirteenth century
Plot: Historical

King John, who, as a champion of opposition to the Church of Rome, is treated with a sympathy rare in English literature. John is not a clearly characterized or consistent figure. His conscience or his sense of expediency torments him when he hears that his nephew Arthur is dead by his command. He submits to Rome to save his land from France, but he dies poisoned by a monk at Swinstead Abbey before he can learn that his country is saved.

Queen Elinor, the king's mother. A strong, arrogant, and domineering woman, she guides and encourages her son and puts backbone into him. She is pleased with her blunt, illegitimate grandson, Philip the Bastard, and apparently gentle and affectionate toward her pathetic small grandson, Arthur. Her death weakens the king.

Philip the Bastard, the supposed older son of Sir Robert Faulconbridge, actually the child of King Richard the Lion-Hearted (Cœur de Lion). At Queen Elinor's suggestion, he renounces his name and inheritance and is knighted by King John, becoming Sir Richard Plantagenet. Rough, strong, and loyal, he serves his country and his king well, acting as a symbol of English manhood in exhibiting good sense and judgment as well as boldness and humor. He taunts and later kills the duke of Austria, his father's supposed slayer. He is King John's instrument in rifling the monasteries. He is honored with the final speech in the play, a brief, patriotic eulogy on England.

Constance, the widow of Geoffrey Plantagenet and mother of Arthur. Intensely emotional and ambitious for her son's career, she struggles to have him enthroned and thus indirectly causes his death. Her reaction to King Philip's desertion of her son's cause is violent. A message reaches King John that news of her son's death has caused her own "in a frenzy."

Arthur, the duke of Bretagne (breh-TAHN-y), a gentle-hearted, bewildered child. His reported execution by John's orders ruins the king. His death actually is an accident caused by an attempt to escape prison.

Robert Faulconbridge (FOH-k'n-brihj), the son of Sir Robert and Lady Faulconbridge. His father's will declares him heir and disinherits his elder brother. Eager for the property, he is willing to shame his mother and besmirch his brother to get it. His complaint to Queen Elinor and King John leads to his brother's distinguished career.

Lady Faulconbridge, the mother of the contending half brothers. She is admired by her elder son for being the mistress of Richard.

Hubert de Burgh, King John's executioner. Although he is a hard man, he is unable to have Arthur's eyes burned out or to have him killed, but, fearing the king, he reports that the boy is dead. Philip the Bastard first mistrusts him, then believes him. Hubert remains loyal to King John.

Philip, the king of France. Ambitious and untrustworthy, he shifts with every wind, seeking material advantages. He first supports Constance and Arthur, then seals an alliance with King John, then joins forces with Cardinal Pandulph to attempt John's destruction.

Lewis, the Dauphin. Eager to marry Blanch, King John's niece, he aids in cementing the alliance between the kings at Angiers, but when Cardinal Pandulph excommunicates King John, Lewis becomes a fanatical advocate of war. He leads forces of Frenchmen and disaffected Englishmen against John but finally is compelled to make peace.

Cardinal Pandulph, a legate of the pope. A shrewd and ruthless man, he foresees Arthur's death and schools Philip to use it as propaganda. When King John submits to Rome, the cardinal tries unsuccessfully to call off Lewis.

Lymoges (lih-MOHZH), the duke of Austria. A blustering, arrogant enemy of King John, he wears a lion's skin to show that he caused the death of Richard Cœur de Lion. He is too timorous to do more than bluster at Philip the Bastard's threats to hang an ass's skin on him. He is decapitated by Philip the Bastard at Angiers.

Blanch of Spain, King John's niece. A helpless pawn in power politics, she has to endure her bridegroom going to war against her uncle on her wedding day.

Prince Henry, John's son. On his father's death, he becomes King Henry III and accepts the support of both his father's loyal followers and noblemen who have defected to France.

The earl of Pembroke,
the earl of Salisbury, and
Lord Bigot, followers of the king who desert him in horror when they learn of the death of Arthur. Self-preservation drives them back to the English side, and they pledge allegiance to King Henry III.

Count Melun (meh-LEWN), a French nobleman with an English grandsire. Mortally wounded, he warns the English noblemen that Lewis intends to kill them after England is conquered.

Peter of Pomfret, a prophet who prophesies correctly that King John will resign his crown. John consigns him to Hubert with instruction that Peter be hanged at noon on the day the crown is resigned.

Chatillion (shah-tee-YOHN), the ambassador from King Philip to King John.

A citizen of Angiers, who, to avoid destruction of his city, proposes a match between Lewis and Blanch. Both kings welcome his proposal.

The earl of Essex, the nobleman who presents the disputing half brothers to King John for judgment.

James Gurney, Lady Faulconbridge's servant.

KING LEAR

Author: William Shakespeare (1564-1616)
First published: 1608
Genre: Drama

Locale: Britain
Time: The first century B.C.E.
Plot: Tragedy

Lear (leer), the king of Britain. Obstinate, arrogant, and hot-tempered, he indiscreetly plans to divide his kingdom among his daughters, giving the best and largest portion to his youngest and best-loved, Cordelia. When she refuses to flatter him with lavish and public protestations of love, he casts her off with unreasoning fury. Disillusioned and abandoned by his older daughters, he is driven to madness by his age and exposure to internal and external tempests. During his suffering, signs of unselfishness appear, and his character changes from arrogance and bitterness to love and tenderness. He is reunited with his true and loving daughter until her untimely murder parts them again.

Goneril (GON-uh-rihl), Lear's eldest daughter. Savage and blunt as a wild boar, she wears the mask of hypocritical affection to acquire a kingdom. She has contempt for her aged father, her honest sister, and her kindhearted husband. Her illicit passion for Edmund, the handsome illegitimate son of the earl of Gloucester, leads to Edmund's, Regan's, and her own death.

Regan (REE-guhn), Lear's second daughter. Treacherous in a catlike manner, she seldom initiates the action of the evil sisters but often goes a step further in cruelty. She gloats over Gloucester when his eyes are torn out and unintentionally helps him to see the light of truth. Her early widowhood gives

her some advantage over Goneril in their rivalry for Edmund, but she is poisoned by Goneril, who then commits suicide.

Cordelia (kohr-DEEL-yuh), Lear's youngest daughter. Endowed with her father's stubbornness, she refuses to flatter him as her sisters have done. In his adversity, she returns to him with love and forgiveness, restoring his sanity and redeeming him from bitterness. Her untimely death brings about Lear's death.

The earl of Kent, Lear's frank and loyal follower. Risking Lear's anger to avert his impetuous unreason, he accepts banishment as payment for truth. Like Cordelia, but even before her, he returns to aid Lear—necessarily in disguise—as the servant Caius. The impudence of Oswald arouses violent anger in him. For his master, no service is too menial or too perilous.

The earl of Gloucester, another father with good and evil children, parallel to Lear and his daughters. Having had a gay past, about which he speaks frankly and with some pride, he believes himself a man of the world and a practical politician. He is gullible and superstitious. Deceived by Edmund, he casts off his loyal, legitimate son Edgar. His loyalty to the persecuted king leads to the loss of his eyes, but his inner sight is made whole by his blinding. He dies happily reconciled to Edgar.

Edgar (in disguise, **Tom o' Bedlam**), Gloucester's legitimate son. He is forced into hiding by his credulous father and the machinations of his evil half brother. As Tom o' Bedlam, he is with the king during the tempest, and later he cares for his eyeless father both physically and spiritually. Finally, he reveals himself to Gloucester just before engaging in mortal combat with Edmund, who dies as a result of Edgar wounding him.

Edmund, Gloucester's illegitimate younger son. A Machiavellian villain governed by insatiable ambition, he attempts to destroy his half brother and his father for his own advancement. Without passion himself, he rejoices in his ability to arouse it in others, particularly Lear's two evil daughters. He has a grim and cynical sense of humor. His heartlessness is demonstrated by his plotting the murders of Lear and Cordelia, in which he is only half successful. He shows signs of repentance at the time of his death, but hardly enough to color his villainy.

The duke of Cornwall, Regan's husband. An inhuman monster, he aids in heaping hardships on the aged king and tears out Gloucester's eyes when the earl is discovered aiding the distressed monarch. His death, brought on by his cruelty, leaves Regan free to pursue Edmund as a potential husband.

The duke of Albany, Goneril's husband. Noble and kind, he is revolted by Goneril's behavior toward her father, by Gloucester's blinding, and by the murder of Cordelia. He repudiates Goneril and Regan and restores order to the kingdom.

The fool, Lear's jester, "not altogether a fool." A mixture of cleverness, bitterness, and touching loyalty, he remains with the old king in his terrible adversity. His suffering rouses Lear's pity and leads to the major change from selfish arrogance to unselfish love in the old king. The fool's end is obscure; he simply vanishes from the play. The line "My poor fool is hanged" may refer to Cordelia.

Oswald, Goneril's doglike servant. Insolent, cowardly, and evil, he is still devoted to his mistress, whom, ironically, he destroys. His last act of devotion to her is to urge his slayer to deliver a letter from her to Edmund. Because the slayer is Edgar, the letter goes to the duke of Albany as evidence of Goneril's and Edmund's falsehood.

The king of France, a suitor of Cordelia. Captivated by her character and loveliness, he marries her with only her father's curse for dowry. He sets up an invasion of England to restore the old king but is called back to France before the decisive battle, leaving the responsibility on his young queen.

The duke of Burgundy, a suitor of Cordelia. Cautious and selfish, he rejects Cordelia when he finds out that she has been cast off by her father.

The first servant of Cornwall, who, moved by Cornwall's inhuman cruelty, endeavors to save Gloucester from being blinded. Although his appearance is brief, he makes a profound impression as a character, and his action in mortally wounding Cornwall alters the course of events and leads to the overthrow of the evil forces.

An old man, Gloucester's tenant. Helping the blinded man, he delivers him to the care of the supposed mad beggar, actually Edgar.

A captain, employed by Edmund to murder Lear and Cordelia in prison. He hangs Cordelia but later is killed by the aged king, who is too late to save his beloved daughter.

A doctor, employed by Cordelia to treat her father in his illness and madness. He aids in restoring Lear to partial health.

Curan, a courtier.

THE KING MUST DIE

Author: Mary Renault (Mary Challans, 1905-1983)
First published: 1958
Genre: Novel

Locale: Greece and Crete
Time: Preclassical Greece
Plot: Historical realism

Theseus (THEE-see-uhs), the protagonist and narrator. The grandson of King Pittheus of Troizen and son of Princess Aithra, Theseus does not discover until later that he is the son of Aegeus, the king of Athens. After becoming the "king for a year" of Eleusis, Theseus journeys to Athens to reveal himself to King Aegeus. He later subdues Eleusis, vanquishing its queen; makes the isthmus safe for travelers; and allows himself to be sent to Crete as a bull-dancer. An earthquake and revolution make him king there.

Pittheus, the king of Troizen and grandfather of Theseus. Pittheus is the formative influence on Theseus when he is young, instructing him in kingship and the Greek concept of fate, called *moira*. He also reveals to Theseus the strange circumstances of his being fathered by King Aegeus of Athens.

Aithra, the princess of Troizen. She is the daughter of Pittheus, Theseus' youthful mother, and the Priestess of Mother Dia (Demeter) in Troizen. In this last capacity, she represents the remnants of the mother-worshiping religion of the earlier inhabitants of Greece.

Persephone (pur-SEH-fuh-nee), the queen of Eleusis. As the queen of a city that worships the female principle, the queen of Eleusis takes a husband yearly; he is killed in a wrestling match at the end of his year. When Theseus fights and kills one of the yearly kings, called Kerkyon, he marries the queen. Theseus undermines her rule and succeeds in exiling her from Eleusis and establishing a patriarchal power structure.

Aegeus (EE-jews), the king of Athens and father of Theseus. Worn from his many years of trying to make peace among the warring factions around Athens, Aegeus is delighted to recognize Theseus as his son. His joy is short-lived because Theseus insists on going to Crete as a bull-dancer. Aegeus later commits suicide because of a misunderstanding that Theseus died on Crete, caused by the color of Theseus' sail when he returns to Athens.

Ariadne (ar-ee-AD-nee), the princess of Crete and the "Goddess-on-Earth." Ariadne, the daughter of King Minos, falls in love with Theseus when she watches him in the bull ring and agrees to accompany him back to Athens. Theseus later abandons her on the island of Naxos during their return, and she dies during childbirth.

Asterion the Minotauros, the prince of Crete. The half

brother of Ariadne and next in line for the throne of Crete, he is the patron of Theseus' bull-dancing team but nevertheless plots against them. In addition, he is in the process of organizing a takeover of Crete when an earthquake and an uprising of the bull-dancers result in his death and the fall of the House of Minos.

Minos (MI-nuhs), the king of Crete and father of Ariadne. He is dying of leprosy and fearful of Asterion's lust for power. He asks that Theseus put him out of his misery by ritualisti-cally killing him, first exacting a promise that Theseus will protect Ariadne.

Poseidon (poh-SI-duhn), the god of bulls, horses, earthquakes, and the sea. Poseidon is Theseus' patron god and has given him the power to sense earthquakes before they occur. Early in the novel, Theseus hopes that Poseidon actually is his father.

— *Angela Hague*

THE KING OF THE GOLDEN RIVER: Or, The Black Brothers, a Legend of Syria

Author: John Ruskin (1819-1900)
First published: 1851
Genre: Novel

Locale: Stiria
Time: The legendary past
Plot: Adventure

Gluck, a good youth who, with his two brothers, owns and farms Treasure Valley in the ancient kingdom of Stiria. His brothers make Gluck work hard at the worst tasks but give him nothing. After his brothers fail to change the Golden River into gold, he tries. He succeeds because he is kind; he earns the help of the King of the Golden River, who had in turn tested each brother's mercy toward a thirsty child, an old man, and a dog. Only Gluck shared his water. All of his life, Gluck proves that he is charitable and thoughtful, even after he becomes a rich man.

Schwartz and

Hans, nicknamed the **Black Brothers**. They are stingy and mean, mistreating Gluck, killing anything that brings in no money, cheating their servants, and giving nothing to charity although they are very rich. Both the brothers, because they are evil men, fail to turn the Golden River into gold and are themselves metamorphosed into black stones.

The South-West Wind, a strange little old man befriended by Gluck when he appears at the brothers' house. Gluck gives the man shelter and offers him his own meager portion of food. When Hans and Schwartz try to throw the little man out of the house, he causes a storm to ruin the entire valley and permits no more rain to fall, so that the valley becomes a wasteland.

The King of the Golden River, who is imprisoned in a gold mug until released by Gluck. He tells Gluck how to turn the Golden River into gold by dropping holy water into it. When Gluck succeeds, the river irrigates Treasure Valley for him, making it fertile and a source of wealth.

THE KING OF THE MOUNTAINS
(Le Roi des montagnes)

Author: Edmond François About (1828-1885)
First published: 1856
Genre: Novel

Locale: Greece
Time: Mid-nineteenth century
Plot: Adventure

Hadgi-Stavros (HAHD-ji STAHV-rohs), "king of the mountains," a cruel Greek brigand. He holds people for ransom, killing them if the ransom is not paid. He shows his cruelty by torturing Hermann Schultz, even trying to roast the young German alive.

Hermann Schultz, a young German botanist doing research in the Greek mountains. Captured by the brigands, he daringly dupes them of their hostages and their ransom. He poisons the brigands with arsenic from his specimen box.

Mrs. Simons, a wealthy, arrogant Englishwoman captured by Hadgi-Stavros. She encourages Hermann with her daughter until rescued. After their rescue, she is but icily polite to the young man.

John Harris, Hermann's American friend. He keeps Photini as a hostage until the young German is released by the bandits.

Photini (foh-TEE-nee), a homely Greek girl in love with John Harris. She turns out to be the daughter of the king of the mountains.

Dmitri (DMEE-tree), a young Greek in love with Photini. He acts as Mrs. Simons' guide while on her tour of the Greek countryside, during which she is captured by the brigands.

Mary Ann Simons, the daughter of Mrs. Simons. She is loved by Hermann, although he realizes her mother will not let them marry.

Captain Pericles (PEHR-ih-kleez), a soldier in league with the brigands.

KING SOLOMON'S MINES

Author: H. Rider Haggard (1856-1925)
First published: 1885
Genre: Novel

Locale: Africa
Time: The nineteenth century
Plot: Adventure

Allan Quatermain, an English explorer and sportsman. He agrees to help Sir Henry Curtis find the latter's lost brother. He is the leader of the expedition to find the brother and, also, Solomon's treasure.

Sir Henry Curtis, Quatermain's friend and companion on the expedition.

Captain John Good, a retired army officer, Quatermain's friend and companion on the expedition.

George Neville, Sir Henry Curtis' brother, who has changed his name. Lost while hunting for King Solomon's mines, he is found and given one-third of the treasure the expedition discovers.

José Silvestre, a Portuguese explorer who, as he was dying, gave Quatermain a map showing the location of King Solomon's mines.

Ventvögel, a Hottentot hired by Quatermain for the safari. He freezes to death in the mountains during the expedition.

Umbopa, a Zulu hired by Quatermain. He is really Ignosi, hereditary chief of the Kukuana tribe. He regains his rightful place and befriends the white men.

Khiva, a Zulu hired by Quatermain. He dies saving Captain Good from an enraged elephant.

Infadoos, a native subchieftain among the Kukuanas who helps Ignosi regain his kingship of the tribe.

Twala, a hideous one-eyed giant who has usurped the kingship of the Kukuanas. He is killed by Sir Henry during a battle between his forces and the Kukuanas loyal to Ignosi.

Scragga, Twala's cruel son. He is killed with his own spear by Quatermain.

Gagool, a native sorceress who murders many of her tribesmen in a witch hunt and tries to kill the white men.

Foulata, a beautiful native woman. Saved once by the white men, she is later stabbed to death by Gagool.

THE KING, THE GREATEST ALCALDE
(El mejor alcalde, el rey)

Author: Lope de Vega Carpio (1562-1635)
First published: 1635
Genre: Drama

Locale: Spain
Time: The sixteenth century
Plot: Tragicomedy

Sancho (SAHN-choh), a poor peasant of Spain who loves an equally poor girl, Elvira. Before he can marry her, she is abducted by the feudal lord, Don Tello. Sancho goes with Nuño, her father, to the castle to say they cannot believe a nobleman guilty of such a crime. They witness the lord's evidence of outrage at such rumors, then Elvira appears to reveal his villainy. Sancho and Nuño flee to escape being beaten to death. Sancho gives in to despair in spite of Nuño's certainty that his daughter would die rather than lose her honor.

Elvira (ehl-VEE-rah), the daughter of Nuño, a poor farmer. Because she loves Sancho deeply, when their wedding is delayed she agrees to let him visit her room, for they have already taken their vows before the priest. When she opens her door, she sees that the man waiting there is Tello, not her lover. Firm in her reverence for virtue and honor, she will not yield to him, but he later forces her. Then, with her honor lost, she declares that never again will she know joy.

Don Tello de Neira (TEH-yoh deh NA-rah), the feudal lord whose consent must be obtained before the marriage of his peasants. In the case of Sancho and Elvira, he agrees to the wedding before he sees the beauty of the girl, then he lusts after her. He decrees the postponement of the wedding because he plans to force her to spend the night with him and then go to Sancho the next day. That night, he and his servants go masked to her home and take her to his castle. He is unable to force her to come willingly to him, though he keeps her prisoner for a long time. Finally, enraged, he takes her to the woods and ravishes her there.

Feliciana (feh-lee-see-AH-nah), the noble sister of Tello, who pleads with her brother to remember his good name and honor and not to stain them through lust. Although she cannot convince Tello, the king later respects her efforts and at the end promises her his protection and help in finding a worthy husband.

Nuño (NEWN-yoh), the peasant father of Elvira, who knows that his daughter is virtuous and proud. His pleas for her release have no effect on his evil overlord.

Pelayo (peh-LI-yoh), a swineherd who provides much of the humor of the play. He is preeminent among Spain's *graciosos* or clowns. He accompanies Sancho to the court of King Alfonso of Castile and takes back the king's letter ordering Tello to release Elvira. He carries news of the nobleman's disobedience and refusal back to the king and persuades him to go personally to force the lord to return the girl to her father and her sweetheart.

Alfonso VII (ahl-FOHN-soh), the king of Leon and Castile, well known for his justice to high and low and therefore the "best alcalde" or governor. When Tello disobeys his written order, he goes in disguise to the castle, uncovers the truth, and reveals his identity to his rebellious subject. He then delivers his sentence: Because Tello has dishonored Elvira, he must marry her. Following the ceremony, he will be beheaded. As his widow, Elvira will inherit half his lands and gold for her dowry when she marries Sancho. The repentant Tello finds the decision just, as he has sinned against both his own honor and the king. The peasants, in this early social drama, bless the king's wisdom as well as his actions in righting the wrongs done by the nobility to the lower class.

THE KINGDOM OF GOD
(El reino de Dios)

Authors: Gregorio Martínez Sierra (1881-1947) and María
  Martínez Sierra (1874-1974)
First published: 1922
Genre: Drama

Locale: Spain
Time: Early twentieth century
Plot: Social criticism

Sister Gracia (GRAH-see-ah), a member of the benevolent
order of St. Vincent de Paul. In the play, Sister Gracia is shown
in three stages of her devotion to the alleviation of suffering to
which she has pledged herself. At the age of nineteen, she is
assigned to a home for poverty-stricken old men. At twenty-
nine, she is assisting in a home for unwed mothers. The confusion and heartbreak there take her to the verge of collapse. Dr.
Enrique, who loves her, asks her to marry him. She refuses,
asks for a transfer, and is last seen at the age of seventy, when
she is Mother Superior in charge of an orphanage.

Gabriel (gah-bree-EHL-), formerly the valet to Sister Gracia's grandfather.

Liborio (lee-BOHR-ee-oh), a half-wit Cuban.

Trajano (trah-HAH-noh), a superannuated anarchist. He,
Gabriel, and Liborio are pensioners at the home for poverty-
stricken old men, Sister Gracia's first assignment.

Sister Manuela (mahn-WEH-lah), Mother Superior of the
old men's home.

Quica (KEE-kah), a perennial and casual offender.

Candelas (kahn-DEH-lahs), a fundamentally good and
fiercely independent girl.

Margarita (mahr-gah-REE-tah), a bitter aristocrat. She,
Quica, and Candelas are residents of the home for unwed
mothers, Sister Gracia's second assignment.

Dr. Enrique (ehn-REE-kay), a physician at the home for
unwed mothers. He loves Sister Gracia and tries to persuade
her to marry him.

Sister Cristina (krees-TEE-nah), Mother Superior at the
home for unwed mothers.

Sister Dionisia (dee-oh-NEE-see-ah), an assistant at the
orphanage, Sister Gracia's last assignment.

Juan de Dios (hwahn deh dee-OHS), an aspiring bullfighter
and former resident of the orphanage. He returns to honor
Sister Gracia with a souvenir of his first triumph in the ring.

Felipe (feh-LEE-peh), a mutinous resident of the orphanage, to whom Sister Gracia gives counsel and assurance.

Don Lorenzo (loh-REHN-soh) and

María Isabela (ee-sah-BEHL-ah), Sister Gracia's parents.

THE KINGDOM OF THIS WORLD
(El reino de este mundo)

Author: Alejo Carpentier (1904-1980)
First published: 1949
Genre: Novel

Locale: Haiti, Cuba, and Italy
Time: 1750 to after 1830
Plot: Magical Realism

Ti Noël (tee noh-EHL), a house slave and rebel. He witnesses and, at times, participates in many of the events of the
novel. He is faced with the problem of deciding whether he
should use the knowledge he has acquired during the course of
many years to answer the needs of his people. He represents an
archetypal man caught up in the eternal struggle to improve
the lot of future generations. His role is to suffer and sacrifice
himself for his fellow humans on earth, not to redeem them
for a reward in heaven.

Monsieur Lenormand de Mezy (leh-nohr-MAH[N] deh
meh-ZEE), a plantation owner and Ti Noël's master. He is
caricatured as having cheeks caked with powder and a stupid
smile. After the slave rebellion led by Bouckman, he is forced
to flee to Cuba. He functions as a representative of the oppressive presence of European culture and "civilization."

Mackandal (mah-kahn-DAHL), a fugitive slave, a rebel,
and Ti Noël's spiritual mentor. He has a deep voice and powerful torso. The first of the novel's four sections narrates his
exploits. He led an early slave uprising that used the poisoning
of livestock and people as a major tactic. He is finally captured
and burned at the stake in 1758.

Pauline Bonaparte (poh-LEEN boh-nah-PAHRT), the wife
of General Leclerc and a symbol of decadent European culture. Her frivolity, sensuality, luxury, and cowardice when the
plague strikes, followed by her renewed self-indulgence while

escorting her husband's body home to France, climax the
presentation of white decadence in contrast to the virility and
vitality of the black people.

Soliman (soh-lih-MAHN), Pauline's voodoo-practicing
black masseur. He rejects his African past, works as Henri
Christophe's valet, and travels to Rome with Christophe's wife
and daughters.

Henri Christophe (ah[n]-REE kree-STOHF), the first black
king of Haiti. He governs the country even more oppressively
than did the French settlers before him. He is heavyset, barrel-
chested, and powerful, and he wears an embroidered uniform.
The third section of the novel deals with Christophe, a hero
who becomes a tyrant. His rule is characterized not only by
oppression but also by Europeanization and the rejection of
local beliefs. The priests in his court are a parody of Christianity. The section ends with the collapse of his rule and his
loneliness, betrayal, and suicide.

Boyer (bwa-YAY), a mulatto ruler. The fourth and final part
of the novel deals with the government of Boyer (1820-1843),
which saw continued oppression but also reunification after
the collapse of Christophe's government. During his rule,
many of the old abuses are perpetuated, and there is a definite
need for a renewed struggle against tyranny.

— *Genevieve Slomski*

KINGS IN EXILE
(Les Rois en exil)

Author: Alphonse Daudet (1840-1897)
First published: 1879
Genre: Novel

Locale: Paris
Time: Nineteenth century
Plot: Political

Christian II, a rather foolish, vapid, and childish monarch who rules Illyria until he is deposed after a revolution and forced to flee to Paris with Frédérique, his queen, and Léopold, his son. He spends his exile waiting for his restoration, frequenting Parisian theaters and cafes, and selecting and rejecting mistresses. A faction working for financial gain is at the point of securing his abdication when Frédérique, in a burst of hysterical melodramatics, dissuades him. At last he does abdicate, after an invasion of Illyria launched to restore him fails, in favor of his son, who becomes King Léopold V of Illyria and Dalmatia.

Frédérique (fray-day-REEK), queen of Illyria, who actively runs the affairs of the kingdom during the period of exile. It is she who attends to financial problems, selects a tutor for the prince, and prevents the king's irrational behavior from destroying the royal family. Her platonic affair with her son's tutor, Meraut, is dignified and poignant.

Élysée Meraut (ay-lee-SAY may-ROH), the prince's tutor and a man of good taste and discretion. The warm friendship with the queen that Meraut enjoys is broken when an unfortu-

nate accident occurs while the tutor and the prince are target shooting. The prince loses the sight of one eye, and the queen, holding Meraut responsible for the incident, discharges him. Later, the queen, learning Meraut is dying, visits him, with the prince, in time to reconcile their differences.

The Duke of Rosen, a former Illyrian minister who is deposed by Christian. The duke welcomes the royal family when they arrive in Paris, uses his own funds to see that they want for nothing, and remains loyal to the monarch, even though the duke's daughter-in-law becomes Christian's mistress.

Prince Léopold (lay-oh-POHL), Christian's not particularly intelligent young son, who is Meraut's pupil.

Séphora Lévis (say-foh-RAH lay-VEE), the wife of a commoner. Christian is enamored of her, and she promises to become his mistress if he abdicates. She is never in love with Christian, but his abdication would be financially profitable to her and her husband.

Tom Lévis, Séphora's husband, an impostor who has made a fortune catering to the whims of exiled aristocrats.

THE KING'S INDIAN

Author: John Gardner (1933-1982)
First published: 1974
Genre: Novella

Locale: Boston, Nantucket, and the Atlantic and Pacific oceans
Time: Early nineteenth century
Plot: Fable

Jonathan Adams Upchurch, a nineteen-year-old Boston schoolmaster. An intellectually restless and curious young man, he is determined to save enough money to purchase a farm in Illinois, but, in an uncharacteristic moment of drunken jubilation, he buys a small sailboat and ends up on the whaling ship *Jerusalem*. Although walleyed and a lifelong landsman, he is strong and capable and soon becomes one of the ship's crew. After discovering that the *Jerusalem* is a mystery ship, Jonathan follows clues that lead only to deeper complexities. Jonathan's childhood fascination with Miranda Flint, the daughter of famed mesmerist Dr. Luther Flint, is reawakened by Augusta Dirge, the daughter of the *Jerusalem*'s captain.

Dr. Luther Flint, a famed mesmerist, a large, imposing man with a fierce mustache, an imperious manner, and a larcenous nature (he once stole the crown of the king of Sweden). Through the early years of the nineteenth century, Flint and his young daughter Miranda toured New England, baffling and mystifying audiences with their spectacular and eerie shows. It was at one of these presentations that young Jonathan Upchurch first saw them and fell under the spell of Miranda. Flint's talents for mystification make him the perfect choice to play the key role in the charade acted out on board the *Jerusalem*. He controls the ship while disguised as the blind seaman Jeremiah.

Miranda Flint, the daughter of Dr. Flint, a young blonde girl with a preternatural manner. In trances during Flint's stage shows, Miranda recounts tales of her past lives and gives detailed accounts of ancient history.

Jeremiah, the aged, blind companion of Captain Dirge. His long white hair falls to his chest, and his oracular utterings seem to rule the ship, as indeed they do, because he is actually Dr. Flint. His masked but tyrannical hold over the ship and its crew is broken only by his confrontation with Jonathan and his own destruction in a spectacular fit of spontaneous combustion.

Captain Dirge, the master of the *Jerusalem*, a large, humpbacked man always dressed in impeccable black, with long, coarse black hair streaked with gray and a bushy black beard. His obsession is to find the Vanishing Isles, a place where lost ships have been sighted in full sail and where the lines of time may merge so that the past and future meet. His long stillnesses, broken by occasional mechanical movements, hint at what he actually is: a clockwork figure controlled by Jeremiah.

Augusta Dirge, supposedly the daughter of the *Jerusalem*'s captain. She is a strikingly beautiful woman in her twenties, with hypnotic gray eyes and a sensuous yet commanding nature. She is only glimpsed by Jonathan during the initial portion of the novel but emerges to dominate his thoughts and actions. The attraction between Jonathan and Augusta is consummated near the end of the novel, when Augusta, ravaged by the mutinous crew, finally reveals herself as Miranda Flint and becomes Jonathan's at last.

Mr. Knight, the first mate of the *Jerusalem*, a tall, broad-shouldered man with a leathery face and ice-pale eyes. Although he seems to be destined to be a whaler, he is thoughtful and meditative, troubled into philosophy by the strange doings aboard the ship. He attempts to bring some reason to the *Jerusalem*, and his adherence to common decency leads to his death during the mutiny that overtakes the vessel.

Billy More, a stocky, friendly, red-haired seaman. He becomes friends with Jonathan and at one point rescues him from falling from the rigging. Like Mr. Knight, Billy More is a decent and conventional man, and like the first mate he dies in the mutiny.

Wilkins, a seaman on the *Jerusalem*, a strange character with a multitude of names: To the crew he is known as **Java Jim** and **Quicksilver Nick**; as an accomplice of Dr. Flint he goes by the name **Swami Havananda**. He is a restless, muscular man of mixed appearance, with a flat face, thick lips, and slanted eyes that are black as coals. He aids Flint in his elaborate hoax by constructing the mechanical dummy that is Captain Dirge. When the trickery is discovered, he blows out his own brains. Later, he seems to reappear, but it is only a ventriloquist trick by Flint. In a sense, Wilkins has always been nothing but an illusion of Flint's devising.

Jim Ngugi, an African harpooner. A tall, taciturn man, he seems removed from the strange events on the *Jerusalem* until the mutiny hits the ship; then he halts the slaughter and helps restore order.

Kaskiwah, an American Indian harpooner. Short and powerfully built, he seldom speaks, and even in the antarctic cold he never wears more than a buckskin shirt and trousers. Jonathan calls him "a kind of heathen saint," and it is Kaskiwah who gives Jonathan the mushrooms that reveal visions beyond reality.

Wolff, a seaman and mutineer. A didactic, humorless man with spectacles and a precise mustache, he leads the mutiny on the ship but is killed when it slips out of his control.

— *Michael Witkoski*

KINGS ROW

Author: Henry Bellamann (1882-1945)
First published: 1940
Genre: Novel

Locale: Middle West
Time: Late nineteenth century
Plot: Social criticism

Parris Mitchell, an orphan who lives in Kings Row with his German-born grandmother. He studies medicine in Vienna and becomes a staff physician in the Kings Row insane asylum. Through Louise, he discovers the tragedy caused in Kings Row by Dr. Gordon's needless operations. During an absence in Europe, he is accused of profiting from the sale of land to the hospital, but nothing comes of the charges. He broods over the many tragedies of his hometown.

Drake McHugh, Parris' friend, another orphan, an idler obsessed with women. After his guardian absconds with Drake's money inherited from his aunt and uncle, Drake gets a railroad job through Randy's father. Following an accident, Dr. Gordon amputates Drake's legs. Randy marries Drake, and Parris gives them the Tower property that he had inherited. They start a real estate business in which Parris is a silent partner. Drake dies from an illness that Parris attributes to the unnecessary amputation performed by Dr. Gordon.

Randy Monaghan, a railroad employee's daughter, who marries Drake after he loses his legs. Following Drake's death, she cares for her brother Tod.

Cassandra Tower (Cassie), Parris' friend, who gives herself to him. She is shot to death by her father, who afterward kills himself.

Dr. Tower, Cassie's father, a strange physician who commits suicide after incest with Cassie and who wills his money and property to Parris.

Elise Sandor, a newcomer to Kings Row, Parris' friend whose father buys Madame von Eln's home. Parris falls in love with her.

Jamie Wakefield, Parris' friend.

Renée, Parris' first love, who moves away from Kings Row.

Madame von Eln, Parris' grandmother.

Dr. Perdorff, Parris' piano teacher.

Dr. Gordon, a physician who amputates Drake's legs; a medical butcher, obsessed with performing surgery.

Louise Gordon, his daughter, who reveals to Parris her father's butcheries.

Dr. Nolan, Parris' superior at the asylum.

Tod Monaghan, Randy's mentally incompetent brother.

KIPPS: The Story of a Simple Soul

Author: H. G. Wells (1866-1946)
First published: 1905
Genre: Novel

Locale: England
Time: Early twentieth century
Plot: Domestic

Arthur Kipps, a simple soul who knows that there was something mysterious about his birth. Reared by an aunt and uncle, he spends a bleak childhood. After seven years of apprenticeship to a draper, he is given a position in the firm at twenty pounds a year. As a boy, he falls in love with Ann Pornick, a poor girl who goes into domestic service; later, he is enamored of a lady who teaches woodcarving in a class he attends for self-improvement. His life is radically changed when he is left a legacy of a handsome house and twelve hundred pounds a year by his paternal grandfather, who relented before his death, though he had forbidden his son to marry Kipps' mother. At once, the bewildered Kipps is petitioned by everyone for money. He buys an interest in a friend's play and is maneuvered into becoming engaged to the woodcarving teacher, who tries to change him completely and gets him to give her brother control of his money. Kipps meets his childhood sweetheart again and begins to yearn for a simpler life. They marry, and his wife is at first made unhappy by their pretentions to grandeur. His former fiancée's brother loses most of his money, however, and Kipps' now comfortable but necessarily simple life is thoroughly happy. Even after he becomes almost as rich as before with the success of his friend's play, he continues to live simply and happily.

Ann Pornick, Kipps' first love and later his wife. Seeing her as a servant in a house where he is a guest, Kipps proposes; in spite of her apprehension over the difference in their social positions, she accepts.

Helen Walsingham, a lady of whom Kipps becomes enamored. Engaged to him after his acquisition of wealth, she attempts to change his speech, dress, manners, and attitudes. Grateful at first, he becomes gloomy. Her solicitor brother speculates with Kipps' money and loses most of it.

Mr. Chitterlow, Kipps' friend, a would-be playwright. Because of Chitterlow's influence, Kipps gets drunk and stays out all night, for which he loses his job; shortly afterward, however, Kipps gets his fortune. He buys a quarter interest in Chitterlow's play, which later restores his fortune almost to its original amount.

Pornick, Ann's brother. A socialist, he is both contemptuous and jealous of Kipps' new wealth, and so he does not tell Ann of Kipps' fortune. Therefore, when Ann first sees Kipps again, her naturalness and simplicity make him yearn for the old, uncomplicated life.

KISS OF THE SPIDER WOMAN
(El beso de la mujer araña)

Author: Manuel Puig (1932-1990)
First published: 1976
Genre: Novel

Locale: Argentina
Time: 1975
Plot: Social realism

Luis Alberto Molina (lew-EES ahl-BEHR-toh moh-LEE-nah), a window dresser imprisoned for the corruption of a minor. Molina is a homosexual who views himself as a woman; he even refers to himself as a girl. He believes that in any relationship he has with a man, that man should be dominant, while Molina, as the female figure, should be passive. He has an exceptional memory for films, and he entertains and distracts Valentin by telling the story lines of romantic films that he has seen. Warmhearted and caring, Molina nurses Valentin, who becomes ill after eating the doctored prison food. Molina then cleverly prevents Valentin from eating the prison food by having the warden give Molina food as a cover for Molina's absences from the cell. Even Molina's efforts to be released from jail are not out of selfishness; he is concerned about his mother's weak heart. At the same time, he cannot betray Valentin, whom he has come to love. It is Molina's

selflessness (and perhaps his need to die as a "heroine") that leads him to sacrifice himself to Valentin's revolution.

Valentin Arregui Paz (vah-lehn-TEEN ah-RREH-gee pahs), a revolutionary who is being held indefinitely as a political prisoner. Valentin is in many ways the exact opposite of his cellmate, Molina. Valentin is a "man's man," and he believes that emotions are a weakness that, as a revolutionary committed to his cause, he cannot afford. A change occurs in his personality, however, when he finally admits that he is not pining for his equally politically committed girlfriend but, rather, that he intensely misses his former lover, Marta, who had no interest in politics, only in love. Molina's storytelling helps Valentin to become gradually less repressed, and he becomes gentler toward Molina, culminating in the kiss he gives Molina the night before Molina's release.

— *T. M. Lipman*

THE KITCHEN

Author: Arnold Wesker (1932-   )
First published: 1960
Genre: Drama

Locale: London, England
Time: The 1950's
Plot: Protest

Peter, a twenty-three-year-old cook specializing in fish. He is German but has been working for three years at the Tivoli, a London restaurant at which the play is set. He gradually assumes the dominant role in the play, mainly because of his nervous, excitable energy, which becomes manic in the end, with his smashing the kitchen's gas supply and crockery with a chopper. He is quarrelsome and jealous, with an almost hysterical laugh that suggests basic emotional instability. As the play opens, he has had a fight with Gaston; as the play progresses, his affair with Monique, which is tempestuous and frustrating, is revealed. He sees himself as "a merry fool going

into battle," but he admits that he is unable to "dream" of what he would really like in life: He can only play childish games. Peter is full of unresolved contradictions and unchanneled energies.

Hans, another German. He is on an exchange program and is four years younger than Peter. They often speak to each other in German, because Hans's English breaks down under pressure, as when he speaks with Cynthia, one of the waitresses, with whom he is infatuated. He appears to be the only cook who understands Peter and helps calm him at times. Overall, he seems happy and even cheeky.

Monique, a waitress. Although she is somewhat older than Peter, he is her lover, by whom she has become pregnant twice (the babies presumably were lost in back-street abortions). Although Peter desperately wants her to leave her husband, Monty, it becomes increasingly obvious as the play proceeds that she has no intention of doing so. Monty is able to provide her with the material comfort she craves. During the afternoon, she and Peter have another frustrating and stormy meeting, typical of their present pattern of quarrels and reconciliations. The pressure of this up-and-down relationship contributes to Peter's final act of destruction.

Paul, a young Jewish pastry cook. He and his fellow pastry cook, Raymond, together with Alfredo, counterbalance the "madmen in the kitchen" with their steady work. Paul acts as a reconciler in the various quarrels that arise. He is upset about his wife's desertion of him. During the afternoon interlude, with the kitchen at its quietest, he confronts Peter with his own dislike of Peter and his frenzy. In the only really long speech of the play, he talks of the need for solidarity among working people. His dream of harmony in the microcosm of the kitchen is only part of his (and the playwright's) dream of harmony among all workers.

Kevin, the newcomer to the kitchen. He has come from a much quieter restaurant, presumably attracted by the better pay of the Tivoli. Together with Anne, a kitchen worker, he represents the Irish in this United Nations of a kitchen. He is clearly shocked at the pace, protesting that it is impossible to do any good work at such speed and that he is physically unable to keep up with the relentless tempo. His protests draw responses from the other cooks about how they have come to terms with these problems.

Gaston,

Dimitri,

Nicholas, and

Mangolis, the four Cypriots in the play. Gaston is the oldest of them, being about forty. Unlike the others, he has lived in England for some time. As the play opens, he has been involved in a fight with Peter. Like Nicholas, he dislikes Peter, and probably all Germans. The quarrel is never resolved, adding to the personal and racial tensions of the kitchen.

The Chef, a large, middle-aged man who communicates very little during the play and exercises almost no leadership. He prefers to let his cooks sort out their own problems. Only Peter's violence at the end stirs him momentarily, revealing more than anything his contempt.

Mr. Marango, the Tivoli's owner. Together with Alfredo and the Chef, he represents the older generation who can see life only in terms of the work-money nexus. He hovers around the kitchen much of the day without contributing to its life. He is completely nonplussed by Peter's violence: He will never understand that good wages actually pay for very little.

— *David Barratt*

THE KITCHEN GOD'S WIFE

Author: Amy Tan (1952-　　)
First published: 1991
Genre: Novel

Locale: China and San Francisco, California
Time: 1921-1990
Plot: Social realism

Winnie Louie, or **Jiang Weiwei**, the protagonist and principal narrator, the daughter of a wealthy Shanghai cloth merchant and his second wife. Her mother abandons her when she is six years old. Winnie leaves her home to live on Tsunming Island for almost twelve years with her paternal uncle's family. After an arranged marriage to a young man named Wen Fu, she and her pilot-husband at first move ahead of the advancing Japanese army and then live for seven years in Kunming. Unhappy with her brutal treatment by a cruel, self-centered man, Winnie runs away, but she is picked up by the police and put in prison for more than a year because Wen Fu accuses her of being responsible for the death of their son, who was the victim of an epidemic. Later released, Winnie escapes to America, where she marries Jimmy Louie and has two children, Samuel and Pearl.

Jimmy Louie, the second husband of the protagonist. He is an American-born Chinese minister, deceased for twenty-five years at the novel's opening. He met his future wife during the first year of her marriage and a second time, seven years later, when he encouraged her to leave her abusive husband and provided the means for escape by putting her name on his passport and sending her money for an airplane ticket.

Wen Fu, a Chinese air force pilot and first husband of the protagonist. From his entrance into the story, he is depicted as a deceptive opportunist looking for a rich woman. He even uses his dead brother's credentials to obtain a place in the pilot class. He is a cruel husband and father, a womanizer, and a gambler. Fear of this man haunts Winnie for forty years after their separation, until news of his death triggers the telling of Winnie's story.

Pearl, Winnie's American daughter. Married to an American doctor, she is the mother of two daughters, Cleo and Tessa. A speech therapist in her forties, she has been diagnosed with multiple sclerosis.

Helen (Hulan), who is believed to be Winnie's sister-in-law from a previous marriage. An illiterate peasant, she manipulated her marriage to Jiaguo, Wen Fu's vice captain, who had abandoned her pregnant sister. She is Winnie's partner in a Chinese floral business in San Francisco.

Grand Auntie Du, who actually is Helen's aunt, not Winnie's. Her funeral at the beginning of the novel and her legacy to Pearl of an altar to the Kitchen God frame the novel. Although a comparatively minor character, she is involved in significant events in Winnie's life, including obtaining her release from prison.

Peanut, Winnie's cousin. A spoiled, self-centered young woman, married by her parents to a rich homosexual man, she obtains a divorce, opens a shelter for abused wives, and becomes an active communist to overthrow the feudal conditions in China that keep women in servitude.

— *Agnes A. Shields*

KLINGSOR'S LAST SUMMER
(Klingsors letzter Sommer)

Author: Hermann Hesse (1877-1962)
First published: 1920
Genre: Novella

Locale: Italy
Time: c. 1919
Plot: Bildungsroman

Klingsor (KLIHNG-zor), a famous forty-two-year-old painter born in 1877. He lives in Castagnetta in the Italian countryside. He loves the poetry of Li Po and, on occasion, calls himself **Li Po**, much as he calls his friend Hermann by the name Tu Fu. Klingsor is a heavy drinker and a womanizer. His work habits are just as intense as his carousing. The question is asked whether he is a scoundrel and profligate or a silly child. He himself feels that spirituality and sensuality are of equal value. He is aware that he lives only for the moment and that, therefore, he is not troubled by questions of mortality. Klingsor suffers from feelings presaging his impending death. Once, in a conversation, he expresses his fear that after he is gone, he and his work will be discussed in terms similar to those used for the classics. He imagines his obituary in a city newspaper to read: "outstanding painter, expressionist, great colorist, died on the sixteenth of this month." His last completed work is a self-portrait that is abstract and expressionistic. Critics well-disposed toward his work say that the portrait shows the wild and childlike man of their age: dying European man. This man is sick of vice and decadence but at the same time wants to die and is enraptured by the knowledge of his doom, submitting to his fate, beast and sage. When Klingsor is done, he locks the painting away in an unused room.

Louis the Cruel, also called **the Bird** and **the Glutton**, Klingsor's friend and also a well-known painter. Louis loves to travel and lives in railroad cars. He always leaves abruptly to go on the road again: His knapsack is his studio. He is a bon vivant, like his friend Klingsor. He has a female friend for whom he sends while he is in Castagnetta, telling her that he is dying as a means of impelling her to come to him. Louis mirrors Klingsor in his sensualism as well as in his spiritualism.

Hermann, a poet whom his friend Klingsor calls **Tu Fu**. Hermann is blond and has an astrologer friend whom he introduces to Klingsor. The latter tells Klingsor that his stars stand oddly. Hermann loves the carousel and children. Tu Fu's and Li Po's poems, of which Hermann is as fond as his friend Klingsor, tell of the transiency and death of everything except for the eternal Mother from whom humankind came.

— *Arthur Tilo Alt*

THE KNIGHT OF THE BURNING PESTLE

Author: Francis Beaumont (c. 1584-1616)
First published: 1613
Genre: Drama

Locale: England and Moldavia
Time: Early seventeenth century
Plot: Comedy

A citizen (**George**), a London grocer. He takes his wife and servant to the theater and insists that the actors include in their play the exploits of some member of his profession. He frequently comments on the progress of the action, reassures his wife, and suggests at intervals additional adventures for his hero.

Nell, his naïve wife, who is given to malapropisms. Deeply concerned for the welfare of the characters in the play, she alternately advises them, sympathizes with them, and discusses their difficulties with her devoted husband.

Ralph (or **Rafe**), their servant, well known for his histrionic talents. Encouraged by his mistress, he steps into the play within the play as George's grocer-hero, the Knight of the Burning Pestle. The knight is, like Don Quixote, an avid reader of romances, and he resolves to win honor and the favor of his lady, Susan, "the cobbler's maid in Milk Street," by rescuing distressed damsels. His heroic efforts to aid Mistress Merrythought and Humphrey are doomed to failure, but he wins, in his own view, a signal victory over the giant Barbaroso, the village barber.

Tim and

George, the knight's witty apprentices. They accompany him on his adventures, acting as his squire and his dwarf, and take great delight in using the courtly phrases their master teaches them.

Venturewell, a strong-minded, quick-tempered London merchant. He is continually infuriated by his apprentice Jasper and his daughter, who thwart his plan to marry the girl to a foolish but wealthy tradesman. Cowardly at heart, he is gulled by Jasper, who appears to him as a ghost, and he agrees at last to allow the marriage of the young couple.

Luce, his daughter. She speaks to Jasper in the extravagant language of a romantic heroine, but she participates in his schemes to deceive her father with a resourcefulness that marks her as the pert tradesman's daughter she is.

Jasper, her sweetheart, Venturewell's brash young apprentice. He also plays the romantic figure, especially when he threatens Luce with death to test her constancy. He readily dispenses with his heroics when he beats Ralph and, later, plays dead to trick his master.

Humphrey, Luce's well-meaning, rather unintelligent suitor, who inevitably finds himself at the wrong end of a cudgel, outwitted by Jasper. Even Venturewell, his staunch supporter, is turned against him in the end. He speaks in rhymed couplets that heighten the effect of his stupidity.

Merrythought, Jasper's impecunious father. He lives convinced that there will be food and drink on his table in time for his next meal and meets every experience, good or bad, with a song.

Mistress Merrythought, his shrewish wife. She refuses

her blessing to Jasper and, to spite him, leaves home with her favored younger son and the money she has saved for the child. Her husband rejoices at her departure and forces her, much to her chagrin, to sing to him before he will let her return.

Michael, her young son.

Tapster and

Host, attendants at the Bell Inn, where Ralph visits. They refuse to enter so fully into the spirit of chivalry that they will overlook the twelve shillings the knight owes them, but they gleefully propose a quest for him, an attack on the giant, "ycleped Barbaroso."

Nick, the barber, who participates willingly in the Host's game with Ralph.

The First Knight and

the Second Knight (**Sir Pockhole**), the barber's patients, "prisoners" freed by Ralph and his squire.

Pompiona, the princess of Moldavia, who appears in one of the scenes suggested by George the grocer. The knight, loyal to his Susan, refuses her offer of her hand.

William Hammerton, a pewterer.

George Greengoose, a poulterer. He and Hammerton are members of a troop of soldiers whom Ralph leads through the city, following another of George the grocer's requests.

THE KNIGHTS
(Hippês)

Author: Aristophanes (c. 450-c. 385 B.C.E.)
First performed: 424 B.C.E.
Genre: Drama

Locale: Athens
Time: Fifth century B.C.E.
Plot: Satire

Demos (DEE-mos), a personification of the Athenian people to whom all citizens owe obeisance. He is represented as a selfish, testy, and sometimes foolish old man who seems to ignore the corruption in the officials and politicians who minister to him. The play opens with Cleon, his favorite (his "servant" or his "slave"), firmly entrenched in power, ostensibly by virtue of his whining, obsequious, insolent, arrogant, and cunning qualities. Before the play is concluded, however, Demos displays his strength and craftiness (the strength and craftiness of the people themselves) in that he tolerates such knavish managers as Cleon because he can control them, because he can raise them and dash them down at will. The farcical relations of Demos and those who govern him (Cleon, succeeded by the Sausage-Seller) generate the major dramatic action of the play.

Cleon (KLEE-on), the Tanner, so called because of his ownership of a leather-processing factory. He also is called the Paphlagonian, a nickname given him to ridicule his mode of speaking (*paphlazo* means "to foam"). He assumes that his political power over Demos is secure, and he is the terror of his fellow officials. A secret oracle, however, has predicted that he will lose his position and power to one even more base than himself. Accordingly, the Sausage-Seller challenges him. They engage in vigorous debate and eventually wrestle. Cleon loses. Each displays, through the long harangue and dialogue, those mean qualities of self-interest that the playwright suggests are at the root of the political mind and that he exposes through the characters' degradation of public oratory,

infected with vulgar jargon and low metaphor.

The Sausage-Seller, **Agoracritus** (ag-oh-RAK-rih-tuhs), named for the area in which he plies his trade. He is favored by the oracle to supersede Cleon because he is a villain and trickster whose abilities (loud shrieks) make him, in the playwright's ironic view, more suitable to hold public office. After a long struggle against Cleon, his overwhelming vulgarity is crowned with success when he is installed as the governor of Demos.

Nicias (NIHSH-ee-uhs) and

Demosthenes (dih-MOS-theh-neez), two able and successful Athenian generals of opposite characters. Nicias is cautious and superstitious, whereas Demosthenes is blunt, hearty, resolute, a lover of good wine, and a religious skeptic. They appear in the opening scenes of the play, having been mistreated by Cleon, who is at the height of his power. Because of their grievances against him, they set the machinery in motion to have him deposed when they consult the oracle as to a successor.

The Chorus, the "knights" of the title. Representing the middle order of the state, they are hostile to Cleon. They consistently ridicule the senate and government of Athens, jeer at Cleon, and applaud the Sausage-Seller. Their emotional involvement and lack of perception, as well as their endorsement of change in government for the sake of change alone, define the playwright's most pointed thrust at the weakness in these citizens, a weakness that promotes corruption and dishonor in the state.

KNOW NOTHING

Author: Mary Lee Settle (1918-   )
First published: 1960
Genre: Novel

Locale: Western Virginia
Time: July 29-30, 1837; April 10-June 30, 1849; and August 10, 1856-June 3, 1861
Plot: Historical realism

Johnny Catlett, a Virginian gentleman. From a cute boy, Johnny grows into a handsome man with curly chestnut hair. Reared in a slave-owning family in which ownership and control were taken for granted, Johnny is independent and

strong-willed. Charming and courageous, he falls in love with his cousin Melinda. Because he is unwilling to commit himself, he loses her to Fish Kregg. In a fit of jealousy, he runs off to the West, where he attempts to find freedom and peace away from his dominating family. Although he attempts to shut off all of his feelings, he finds that he cannot escape from his heart or his duty and that he really is not fit for any life other than the one into which he was born. After returning to Virginia and taking over the leadership of the family after his father's death, Johnny is isolated and exhausted, with a hidden sorrow, but he remains controlled and dependable, taking his duty seriously. Attempting to maintain control during the turbulent times at the beginning of the Civil War, Johnny wonders if he is the only one who questions but does not speak. At the end, he realizes that the luxury of questioning has passed him by and, with the start of the war, that he must once again simply do his duty.

Peregrine Lacey Catlett, Johnny's father. A quiet, stern, and often bewildered man, with worried blue eyes and a light, sardonic voice, Peregrine seems fatigued and haunted by a private sadness. He regards his family as a cross he must bear. Although he is always concerned about the welfare of his slaves, as his family starts to disintegrate, he becomes frightened of losing authority and decides against freeing them. Disappointed in his eldest son, Peregrine places all the burden of the family on Johnny's shoulders, demanding that he continue playing the role of the Southern gentleman.

Melinda Lacey Kregg, Johnny's cousin. A tall, thin girl with big, black eyes, smooth raven hair, and a thin, pale face, Melinda was reared as an orphan in the Catlett household. Under the sometimes cruel rule of Cousin Annie, Melinda becomes a bitter and wild girl. Spirited, bold, and determined, she is brave, bright, and imaginative, and not outwardly frightened of anything. Having always been in love with Johnny, she futilely tries to spur him to action by flirting with Fish Kregg. Desperate to escape the Catlett household, she agrees to marry Fish. Although proud and assured, she is disturbed by Johnny's return, and her control slips. After spending one night with Johnny, in which she conceives his child, she leaves, defeated and with her spirit broken. Never recovering, she dies, still desperately in love with Johnny.

Leah Catlett, Johnny's mother. An outsider, Leah is a strict Methodist who originally finds owning slaves abhorrent. Lonely, secretive, and never very happy, she fades into the background of the Catlett household. Very self-disciplined, she is determined to maintain her control and passes on her moral judgments to Lewis. Her morals weaken, and she soon sells out, especially after she discovers how much money a slave is worth. Completely defeated, she begins to perceive the slaves as property, to be sold when necessary.

Lewis Catlett, Johnny's older brother. Shy and thin, with a dark, square face and fierce eyes, Lewis is very sensitive. Taught by his mother that owning slaves is morally wrong, he is disillusioned by his father's sin and his mother's weakness, and he never comes to terms with being a slaveowner. Isolated and solitary, he is deeply religious and becomes an abolitionist and a preacher; he eventually runs off to the North to fight with the Union Army.

Crawford "Fish" Kregg, Melinda's husband. Young, blond, and handsome, Fish is very serious and intelligent. Extremely rich, he is very sure of himself and is considered faultless and perfect, with tremendous self-discipline but absolutely no imagination. Always doing exactly what is expected of him, he is calm, even-tempered, and very stable. Lonely and aloof as a young man, he later becomes bitter and cold.

Ann Brandon Neill, a poor cousin. Once a beauty, with a straight, thin nose and auburn hair, Annie becomes old, and bitter. A poor relation, she is dominated by the Catletts and takes out her bitterness on Melinda. Made hard-bitten by life and addicted to laudanum, she marries Big Dan O'Neill, a poor Irish worker, and tries to make him into a gentleman, changing their last name to Neill. When she is widowed, she returns to the Catlett household and spends her days gossiping with Sally.

Sally Crawford Lacey, another cousin. Once an innocent, beautiful young woman, with gorgeous blonde curls, she became poor and embittered when her husband lost all of their money and shot himself. Sally, who is not a deep thinker, becomes dependent on her relations and ends up being rather catty.

— *Susan V. Myers*

KRAPP'S LAST TAPE

Author: Samuel Beckett (1906-1989)
First published: 1958
Genre: Drama

Locale: Krapp's den
Time: Mid-twentieth century
Plot: Absurdist

Krapp, the solitary character. He is a sixty-nine-year-old writer living a life filled with sadness and regret. Since reaching adulthood, Krapp has recorded on tape an annual account of personal activities. On the day on which the play's events occur, Krapp is seen listening to a recording made thirty years earlier. Even though the play has only one character, it successfully captures shifting aspects of identity and shows the younger Krapp, heard through the taped voice, filled with aspirations, becoming the cynical and bitter old man. In fact, there are few common characteristics between these two dramatized aspects of the individual. Remnants of the younger man are to be found mainly in the older Krapp's addictions to alcohol, bananas, and sexual activity. The younger Krapp's hope of sacrificing his life to become a successful writer has not been realized. The older Krapp's attention is visibly occupied in trying to recapture an experience, heard from the taped voice, of lovemaking in a punt on a lake. This incident of Krapp attempting to savor his past experiences contrasts severely with his decision to remain alone to pursue his work. The play forces together a series of opposing characteristics—companionship and solitude, life and death, love and repulsion—to demonstrate the development and division of self.

— *Ian Stuart*

THE KREUTZER SONATA
(Kreytserova sonata)

Author: Leo Tolstoy (1828-1910)
First published: 1889
Genre: Novel

Locale: Russia
Time: Late nineteenth century
Plot: Social realism

Vasyla Pozdnishef (VAHS-lyah pohz-DNIH-shehf), a Russian landed proprietor who describes the horror of marriage and the murder of his wife. The only character in the novel developed to any extent, Pozdnishef relates his macabre story to a fellow traveler on the train, who in turn relates it to the reader. The hero-villain has been brought up to avoid all moral responsibility. As a wealthy young man, he looked on women merely as the instruments of his sensual gratification. At thirty, he married and settled down to what he supposed would be an ideal and pure relationship, but instead of bliss he found only misery or "swinish carnality." From sex satiation and boredom on their honeymoon, husband and wife move to quarreling in an increasingly violent manner, to threats of separation and attempts at suicide. A new lover for Madame Pozdnishef furnishes the final straw. By this time, Pozdnishef has come to view marriage as a sham, a married woman as functionless unless she is bearing children. Trukhashevsky, the wooer, plays the violin, and Madame Pozdnishef frequently accompanies him on the piano; their music infuriates Pozdnishef. One evening, he becomes frantic while listening to the first movement of Ludwig van Beethoven's "Kreutzer Sonata"; on another occasion, finding them together, he stabs his wife with a curved Damascus dagger, while her cowardly lover flees in desperation. The entire novel is a psychological study of the effects of domestic misery, and certainly the effects are devastating. Pozdnishef himself remarks, "I'm supposed to be more or less insane." Shown in this morbid light, he is a consummate villain. Yet he is also a hero figure, in that he is the vehicle for Tolstoy's views that the physical nature of man is vile and that the ills of the world stem from his failure to triumph over the desires of his body. For many pages, Pozdnishef's conversation to his unidentified listener reads more like a formal disquisition on morality and ethics than a work of fiction. Pozdnishef remains a curious paradox. His message is straight from Tolstoy's heart, but his fanaticism and curious mannerisms estrange the reader from both him and his ideas. It is only as a tormented soul impelled to a dreadful act that Pozdnishef becomes tragically human.

Madame Pozdnishef, the beautiful daughter of an impoverished landowner. Although the reader sees her merely as a puppet manipulated for Pozdnishef's narrative, it is obvious that for several years she was a faithful and dutiful wife who bore him five children. After their relationship becomes strained, she grows peevish and moody, given to wild accusations against her husband and occasional attempts on her own life. She is moderately talented at the piano, and through a common interest in music she becomes intimate with Trukhashevsky. After she is stabbed, she is haughty until the very end, swearing that her husband is but completing the murder begun years ago.

Trukhashevsky (troo-khah-SHEHF-skihy), a semiprofessional violinist with some standing in society, the illicit lover of Madame Pozdnishef. Moist eyes, smiling red lips, and a waxed mustache make him the type of man most women call handsome. He presents himself as a gallant and talented gentleman; however, his failure to defend Madame Pozdnishef against the fury of her husband depicts his true nature.

A merchant,

A lady,

A lawyer, and

A clerk, people on the train at the beginning of the novel who discuss marriage and the place of women in society. This conversation draws Pozdnishef into his narrative.

Ivan Zakharich (ih-VAHN zah-KHAH-rihch), the doctor in attendance on Madame Pozdnishef.

KRISTIN LAVRANSDATTER

Author: Sigrid Undset (1882-1949)
First published: 1920-1922
Genre: Novel

Locale: Norway
Time: Fourteenth century
Plot: Historical realism

Lavrans Björgulfsson, the knightly landholder of a medieval manor named Jörundgaard, in Norway. A good and gentle man who strives to live his life by strict Christian standards, he particularly loves Kristin, his oldest daughter, and allows her great freedom of speech and action.

Ragnfrid Ivarsdatter, Lavrans' wife, who had inherited Jörundgaard from her father. She is a good woman who does her best to be a loving wife and mother, although she suffers pangs of conscience all of her life for loving another man before her marriage to Lavrans.

Kristin Lavransdatter, their beautiful but headstrong daughter, who is used to having her own way. When she falls in love with Erlend Nikulaussön, she breaks her troth to Simon Andréssön, a neighbor, much to her father's embarrassment. She has an affair with Erlend and later, during their betrothal, becomes pregnant. Though she begins married life under untoward circumstances, she becomes a good wife, looking after her husband's lands and other property as well as giving him many sons. She and her husband have a stormy married life, however, for the husband is as vehement and proud as his wife. Always in the background, too, is the fact that Kristin dishonored her father by her premarital behavior. Kristin works hard to provide an inheritance for her sons, especially after her husband loses his lands through treason to the crown and his family takes refuge on the manor at Jörundgaard, inherited by Kristin. After her husband's death, when her sons are old enough to fend for themselves, Kristin enters a convent. She dies there a few years later, during an epidemic of the Black Plague in 1349.

Erlend Nikulaussön, a young nobleman who falls in love with Kristin and woos her away from her betrothed. He is a handsome, violent, and contumacious man, always in some sort of scrape because he acts without thinking of the consequences. His greatest mistake is seeking to separate Norway from Sweden in the days of King Magnus VII. Charged with treason, he is found guilty and loses his lands and almost his life. Retirement to his wife's manor is galling, and so he separates from his wife to lead a lonely life on a small farm once owned by a relative, Lady Aashild. He returns to vindicate Kristin's honor when she is accused of adultery but is killed in a brawl upon his arrival.

Nikulaus Erlendssön (Naakve), the eldest son of Kristin and Erlend, a handsome, quiet person. Affected by the bickering and antagonism between his parents, he becomes a monk when he reaches manhood.

Bjorgulf Erlendssön, Kristin and Erlend's second son. He is an unfortunate child who early begins to become blind. He enters a monastery with Nikulaus, his older brother, who cares for him tenderly. Bjorgulf and Nikulaus also die of the Black Plague.

Gaute Erlendssön, the third son of Kristin and Erlend, a lover of the land and farming. He is the son who takes over Kristin's manor of Jorundgaard when he grows up.

Skule Erlendssön and

Ivar Erlendssön, the twin sons of Kristin and Erlend, adventurous boys who grow up to take service under distant kinsmen and seek their careers far from their native land. Ivar finally settles down and marries Signe Gamalsdatter, a rich young widow.

Lavrans Erlendssön, the sixth son of Kristin and Erlend. He migrates to Iceland in the service of a bishop when he grows up.

Munan Erlendssön, the seventh son of Kristin and Erlend, who dies during an epidemic while still a boy.

Erlend Erlendssön, the eighth son of Kristin and Erlend, conceived during a secret visit made by Kristin to see her husband after he had left Jörundgaard. The birth of this child, who lives but three months, causes Kristin to be wrongly accused of adultery.

Simon Andressön of Dyfrin, the young nobleman jilted by Kristin Lavransdatter when she falls in love with Erlend Nikulaussön. Simon continues to love Kristin and works on her behalf many times, even saving the life of Erlend when the latter is sentenced to die for treason. He marries Kristin's younger sister, Ramborg.

Sigrid, Simon Andressön's sister.

Arngjerd, the illegitimate daughter of Simon Andressön.

Simon Simonsson, the son of Ramborg and Simon Andressön, born after his father dies of a wound suffered while separating some brawlers.

Ramborg, the sister of Kristin. She falls in love with Simon Andressön after he has been jilted by Kristin and marries him. She is always hostile to Kristin and jealous of her.

Ulvhild, another sister of Kristin. She is crippled by a falling timber at the age of three and dies while still a young girl.

Lady Aashild, Erlend Nikulaussön's aunt and the mistress of Hangen, supposedly a witch-wife. She befriends Erlend and Kristin at the time of their marriage.

Sir Björn, Lady Aashild's husband, a strange, secretive man.

Arne Gyrdssön, a childhood playmate of Kristin who falls in love with her as he grows up. He and Kristin are falsely accused of loose sexual conduct when they are in their teens.

Bentein, a licentious young man who tries to rape Kristin and, not succeeding, spreads the false tale that she and Arne Gyrdssön have been lovers.

Sira Eirik, Bentein's grandfather, a priest.

Eline Ormsdatter, a married woman who takes Erlend Nikulaussön as her lover before he meets Kristin. Eline and Erlend have two illegitimate children. The woman, jealous of Kristin, tries to poison her. She fails and then stabs herself to death.

Ulf Haldorssön, Erlend Nikulaussön's loyal henchman for thirty-five years and a distant kinsman. Wrongly accused of fathering Kristin's eighth son, he kills a man in defense of her good name.

Jardtrud, Ulf's wife, a hate-filled and jealous woman who wrongly accuses her husband of being Kristin's lover.

Ingebjörg Filippusdatter, Kristin's friend and bed-partner during the time she spends in a convent in Oslo.

KWAKU: Or, The Man Who Could Not Keep His Mouth Shut

Author: Roy A. K. Heath (1926-   )
First published: 1982
Genre: Novel

Locale: Guyana
Time: The second half of the twentieth century
Plot: Tragedy

Kwaku Cholmondeley (KWAH-kew CHUHM-lee), the protagonist. Kwaku, an orphan reared by his uncle, becomes convinced early in life that "there was much protection in idiocy, and that intelligence was like the pimpla palm, bearer of good fruit, but afflicted by thorns." Despite his inability to keep his mouth shut and his comic posturing, Kwaku, who becomes a shoemaker, is convinced of his superiority and of his special destiny. He retains this belief throughout his marriage to Miss Gwendoline, whom he loves deeply. He eventually leaves his village to seek his fortune. Although for a

period he attains success as a healer, he ultimately fails and ends his life in terrible poverty, abused by his children.

Blossom Dean, Kwaku's lifelong friend and conscience, the village bookworm. She becomes a bus conductor and spends ten years living with a boyfriend, Wilfred Service, whom Kwaku must eventually pressure into marrying her. She is self-sufficient, loyal, and bossy. Although Kwaku is not attracted to her, he has a brief affair with her late in life. Unbeknown to Wilfred, it is Kwaku who is the father of Blossom's only child.

Miss Gwendoline, Kwaku's wife. Although theirs was an arranged marriage, it is a loving one. Miss Gwendoline, however, is skeptical of Kwaku's schemes to attain greatness and jealous of his relationships with Blossom and with his friend Mr. Barzey. Miss Gwendoline bears Kwaku eight children, for whose care she becomes single-handedly responsible upon Kwaku's departure for New Amsterdam. She partially supports the household by making and selling blood pudding. She is struck blind by a fisherman who is angry at her husband and who puts a spell on her. After this catastrophe, she loses control over the children and loses touch with reality, becoming an alcoholic.

Mr. Barzey, Kwaku's neighbor, a faith healer whom Kwaku originally befriends during Mr. Barzey's failed attempt to cure him of his gray hairs. Although somewhat senile and under the thumb of his vengeful daughter-in-law, the retiree becomes Kwaku's mentor and only male friend, teaching him how to become a photographer. Mr. Barzey, after a long struggle with his daughter-in-law, who he feels deprives him of freedom, ends up hanging himself.

Kwaku's uncle, who rears him after his mother dies and his father disappears. He has little affection for his nephew.

Philomena, Kwaku's favorite daughter, who grows to be a flirtatious teenager, much to her mother's dismay. She is ultimately disturbed by what she sees as the incestuous overtones of her relationship with her father.

Rona, Miss Gwendoline's favorite daughter. She is obedient and self-sacrificing. She becomes her mother's helper after Miss Gwendoline is blinded. Finally, however, she rebels and runs off with a lover.

— Laura Browder

L

LABRAVA

Author: Elmore Leonard (1925-   )
First published: 1983
Genre: Novel

Locale: Miami, Florida
Time: The 1980's
Plot: Detective and mystery

Joseph LaBrava, formerly an agent for the Internal Revenue Service and for the Secret Service, now a professional photographer whose work is good enough to remind experts of such great photographers as Alfred Stieglitz and Diane Arbus. He is a friend of Maurice Zola, who introduces him to Jean Shaw, a film heroine of whom Joseph had dreamed while young. Joseph and Jean have a brief affair. Joseph is responsible for foiling a plot by Richard Nobles and Cundo Rey to extort money from Jean, but he comes to the sad realization that Jean actually was the chief instigator of the scheme. She tries to convince him to ignore her part, but he resists until the end, when her promise to marry Maurice causes him to keep secret her criminal activity.

Maurice Zola, an eighty-year-old former bookie who now lives on the income from residence hotels he owns in Miami. He promotes Joseph's career as a photographer and looks after the interests of his longtime friend Jean Shaw. Unjustifiably proud of his street smarts, he is open to the clever scam that seems to be run by Richard Nobles but in fact is directed by Jean. It is Maurice's money the plotters are after. Maurice is shielded by Joseph from knowledge of Jean's role in the crimes.

Jean Shaw, a former actress who lives on money left by her third husband. In films, she always played the part of the woman who plans with her lover to kill or fleece her husband; her dark beauty was always used to portray the tragically weak woman, and she was never the heroine. In retirement, she proves to have trouble distinguishing between her film roles and her existence in the real world. When the extortion plot unravels, Joseph discovers that she and Richard, her lover, were the real plotters. In one of the novel's showdowns, Jean kills Richard. LaBrava shields her from the police, partly because of her promise to marry Maurice and partly because she is genuinely unable to distinguish real life from her film roles.

Richard Nobles, a redneck former police officer who makes a living as a security guard and a thief; he uses his security job to set up burglaries. He is Jean Shaw's lover and eagerly falls in with her plan to extort $600,000 from Maurice Zola, also welcoming the chance for vengeance on Joseph, who humiliated him. He enlists his friend Cundo Rey in the plot, expecting to cut his friend out of the profits.

Franny Kaufman, a young woman with wild hair and a subsistence job selling cosmetics to the old women who live in Zola's building. She is a talented aspiring painter who becomes Joseph's lover and part-time aide in figuring out the plot.

Cundo Rey, a Cuban who was released from prison to go to the United States as part of the Mariel boat lift. He was serving time for murder. He makes his living with con games and burglaries, and he loves his sports car more than any person. He falls in with Richard's scheme but has his own plan to get all the money for himself. Joseph is forced to kill him.

— *John M. Muste*

LADIES' HAIRDRESSER
(Damskii master)

Author: I. Grekova (Ylena Sergeyevna Ventsel', 1907-   )
First published: 1963
Genre: Novella

Locale: A large, provincial Russian city
Time: The 1960's
Plot: Social realism

Professor Marya Vladimirovna Kovaleva (vlah-dih-MIH-rov-nah koh-VAH-lyeh-vah), the director of a computer institute. A single, middle-aged woman with two sons, she is a sympathetic and competent professional who finds time to pursue her own mathematical research, to organize social and cultural events, and to run the household. An intellectual, she reads English novels for recreation. Her decision to do some-thing about her appearance takes her to a hairdressing salon, where she makes the acquaintance of an unusual hairdresser whose nonconformist attitudes arouse her curiosity and bring her back for regular visits.

Vitaly Plavnikov (vih-TAH-lee PLAV-nih-kov), a trainee hairdresser. The twenty-year-old Vitaly stands out because of his unconventional appearance and ideas, and because of his individualism in a society that stresses conformity. Reared partly in a children's home, he never finished high school as a consequence of his father's alcoholism and his stepmother's strong religious beliefs. He wants eventually, however, to go to college to study dialectical materialism. Toward this end, he has devised a rigorous plan for his own intellectual development. He is interested in Marya's advice and suggestions, so he becomes her regular hairdresser. His unusual personality is echoed in his somewhat wild appearance (he has a tuft of hair sticking up on his head), as well as in the seriousness he brings to his work. Unlike the authorities, who view hairdressing as a production-line activity, Vitaly views his job as a form of art and studies equipment, fashions, and heads with cool detachment. His attitudes lead to conflict with the authorities, who frown on his capricious treatment of clients and eventually force him to change occupations.

Galya, Marya's inefficient secretary. Marya tolerates Galya's unprofessional behavior because she has a soft spot for the attractive twenty-three-year-old and thinks of her almost as a daughter. Galya, with long, light-chestnut hair, blue eyes, a slim waist, and plump legs, is always immaculately dressed and cuts a striking appearance. She is so impressed by Marya's new hairstyle that she asks for the name of the hairdresser. Marya is happy to oblige; Galya thus meets (and eventually falls in love with) Vitaly.

Kolya and

Kostya, Marya's two sons. The twenty-two-year-old Kolya is a college senior, majoring in automation, whereas his younger brother, Kostya, a twenty-year-old sophomore, majors in computing. They live with their mother, adding to her stressful life by living, as Marya puts it, like pigs. They consume all the food in the refrigerator and create a mess but compensate with their humor and occasional thoughtful gestures.

Vyacheslav Nikolaevich Lebedev (VYA-cheh-slahv nih-koh-LA-yeh-vihch LEH-beh-dehv), Marya's deputy director. This garrulous, effeminate older man (his last name is derived from "swan") is unintentionally a hindrance to Marya's work, as his infuriating manner and appearance cause everyone to refuse granting anything for which he asks.

— *Melanie C. Hawthorne*

LADY CHATTERLEY'S LOVER

Author: D. H. Lawrence (1885-1930)
First published: 1928
Genre: Novel

Locale: The English Midlands, Venice, and London
Time: 1910-1920
Plot: Psychological realism

Sir Clifford Chatterley, the owner of an estate at Wragby in the Midlands of England. He has a considerable income from coal mines that his family has controlled for generations. His father, Sir Geoffrey, baronet of Wragby, reared him with the expectation that one of his sons would carry on the family tradition of service to England. When Clifford's older brother Herbert is killed in World War I, Clifford is encouraged by his father to marry; after a brief courtship, he marries Constance Reid. A war injury paralyzes the lower half of his body. At the age of twenty-nine, though his physical handicap is devastating, he is a handsome man, with a ruddy face and broad shoulders, and always dresses in expensive clothes. Big and strong, with a quiet, hesitating voice, he is extremely dependent on his wife, who supports his ideas and assists him in the physical functions he can no longer manage by himself. In an effort to make his mark on the world, he attempts to write short fiction and is moderately praised by critics and social commentators. This work proves to be an unsatisfactory outlet for his energies and ambitions. He had studied the technicalities of coal mining in Bonn before the war and now turns his attentions to improving coal production in his mines. Although he describes himself as a "conservative anarchist," he is interested in the working class only in terms of theoretical speculation and is very much a man of his social background. As he and his wife gradually discover the great gulf between them in terms of intellectual and temperamental matters, Clifford regresses into an almost infantile dependence on Ivy Bolton, his housekeeper; he becomes, pathetically, almost a part of the wheeled machine he uses for transportation. His hopes for an heir and his fear that Connie may leave him permanently lead him to encourage her to have contacts with other men. He sees things in an intellectual, abstract fashion, and this approach to life is instrumental in driving him and his wife apart.

Lady Constance (Connie) Reid Chatterley, Clifford's wife. Brought up in an artistic and intellectual socialist milieu, she was educated on the Continent and had a number of casual love affairs before her marriage to Clifford at the age of twenty-three. In spite of the social refinement of her background, she has the freshness and openness of a country girl and the physical traits of her Scots ancestry, including lustrous light brown hair, a ruddy complexion, a strong, athletic body, and "big, wondering eyes" that express her curiosity about and interest in the world. She has both the intelligence to understand the world and the appetite to enjoy its physical sensations, but both of these qualities have been underused during her marriage. After four years with Clifford, she has "no gleam and sparkle in the flesh" and realizes with horror that she has not had any sexually satisfying encounters for ten years. Her affair with the playwright Michaelis is sterile and isolating because she is unable to make any connection with him beyond the emptiness of his social and intellectual ideas. Although she has been living on a country estate, her contact with the natural world has been reduced and her capacity to respond to its wonders considerably diminished. Her desire to have a child, an impulse she is afraid to acknowledge, is an expression of her need to develop a relationship that is complete, a true marriage. She is not class-bound like her sister. Meeting Mellors begins a process of healing and recovery in which she moves toward a maturity with a consciousness "like a flowering wood."

Oliver Mellors, the gamekeeper at Wragby, a miner's son of about forty. Sexually active since the age of sixteen, he married a local girl, Bertha Coutts, and then discovered that they were sexually and emotionally mismatched. He studied languages at grammar school and took a job as a clerk, but then he became a blacksmith, hoping to live on a three-hundred-pound legacy with his bride. Their relationship became brutal and cruel, so he enlisted when the war started, just after their only child was born. The army gave him the opportunity to continue his education. When he was sure that his wife had taken up with another man, he left the army and returned to England to work as a gamekeeper. Although weakened by pneumonia while abroad, he is still strong, agile, tall, and wiry; with warm blue eyes and dark hair, he has a figure of "exquisite, delicate manliness," projecting an image of youthful freshness when at his ease but seeming much older and slightly stooped when tired or worried. In essence, he has become a member of the upper classes in manner and educational background, though he despises the established methods of dealing with business and commerce. He has not divorced his wife because he does not want to mix with the authorities in any way, and he often speaks articulately in the Derby dialect as a gesture of defiance or rebellion, although he has a full command of standard English. His ability to conduct conversations on conceptual matters with real depth is in contrast to the stale intellectualism of the conversations at Wragby among Clifford's acquaintances. He is most comfortable in the natural world, whose subtle beauty he understands and appreciates. Although he claims he is not unhappy to be done with passion for a woman, he is glad of his response to Lady Chatterley. He believes in being warmhearted with other people, but his disappointments have led him to build some formidable defenses. He is a semisocialist but not a subversive, and he is willing to stake everything on love. He recognizes that Connie Chatterley is the first woman who combines all the qualities he admires, and he is willing to risk further pain and disappointment to live with her.

Michaelis (Mick), a minor playwright and family friend of the Chatterleys, with whom Connie has a brief, unsatisfying, and empty affair.

Duncan Forbes, an unmarried modern artist who is enamored of Connie Chatterley. He is something of an idealist who claims kinship with the working class and paints in a modernist style. Mellors thinks his work is "cruel and repellent" but respects Forbes's sincerity of commitment. Forbes's spiritual impotence parallels that of Michaelis and limits his possibilities for growth.

Tommy Dukes, a brigadier general in the army and an old friend of Clifford. His contempt for a purely mental existence, his disdain for systematic, coldly rational thinking, and his belief in bodily awareness are ironically undercut by his background and training, which leave him, like other "modern" men, trapped in the intellectualism he criticizes and cut off from the sensory and emotional experiences for which he longs.

Hilda Reid, Constance's sister. Very sure of herself and confident of the rightness of her opinions on everything, she is an attractive woman with "golden, glowing skin" and a "naturally strong, warm physique" who has "a very hell of a will of her own." Her husband is divorcing her, and she is "off" men. She despises Mellors and is blind to his virtues, trapped by preposterous ideas about class status. She is genuinely concerned about her sister and helps to arrange some of the details of Connie's life.

Ivy Bolton, the Chatterleys' housekeeper, widowed in her early twenties when her husband is killed in a mining accident. She thinks all men are "big babies." She becomes Clifford's nursemaid and then a kind of half mistress and half foster mother to him. She likes contact with the upper classes and knows when to give in to a man. She sympathizes with Connie and provides many of the things Clifford needs, although her attention encourages his regression toward infantilism as well as his industrial ambition.

— *Leon Lewis*

THE LADY FOR RANSOM

Author: Alfred Duggan (1903-1964)
First published: 1953
Genre: Novel

Locale: Italy and the eastern Roman Empire
Time: The 1060's and 1070's
Plot: Historical

Roger fitzOdo, a cheeky, pragmatic young man adrift in chaotic eleventh century Italy. Fleeing marauders who killed his parents, he begs to join a company of Norman knights. Roussel de Balliol, their commander, takes him in knowing that the boy's skills with horses and metalwork will be useful. From that moment on, Roger honors and serves Messer Roussel as his lord and hero. Roger, who learned Greek from his mother, becomes the company's official translator when it goes to Asia. This completes his acceptance as a trusted member of Roussel's household. He also explains local politics and mores to the Frankish knights, whose feudal outlook is very different from the bureaucratic and commerce-centered Roman mentality. During the years the company fights in Asia, Roger matures and learns the arts of war. Although more slightly built than the full-blooded Normans and not of noble birth, he finally is deemed a knight. He then wears chain mail

and rides into battle at his commander's side. Roger also negotiates with Turks and Roman factions when Roussel is absent or too dispirited to do so. As narrator of the novel, Roger seldom second-guesses his lord's decisions, but he is a sharp observer of human nature and all levels of politics, and he comments on the foibles of those around him. Roger becomes a monk after Messer Roussel is assassinated and his troop breaks up.

Messer Roussel de Balliol, the leader of a group of Norman knights who seek fame and fortune in Italy's local wars. When the Roman emperor offers to hire them as mercenaries, Roussel eagerly agrees. Over the next decade, Roussel leads his company to many victories in the eastern empire. The greatest is at Zompi, where his 530 men prevail over 3,000 led by the recently proclaimed Caesar, John Ducas. By this time, Roussel is pitted against factions in the empire's internal struggles as often as against the Turks. Tall, red-headed, and perpetually sunburned, Roussel is instantly recognizable in Mediterranean lands. Amid the chaos of the Roman empire in the late eleventh century, he often becomes the sole authority on its fringes. He is a fair overlord when he takes over towns, asking only food and supplies for his men, rather than imposing ruinous taxes. Roussel's leadership and bravery inspire other warriors to join him. His eventual goal is to found a Frankish state in the east. After his capture by Turks and subsequent trial by ordeal on a trumped-up charge of treason, he gives up this ambition and loyally supports Alexius Comnenus, the domestic of Asia and Europe, until poisoned by a eunuch who serves another commander.

Lady Matilda de Balliol, Messer Roussel's wife, a tall, rawboned woman. The daughter of a Lombard noble, she married the Norman knight after her father's town fell to his band. It was a marriage of convenience on both sides, but Matilda and Roussel come to love and respect each other. Matilda travels with Roussel's band. She rides a warhorse and takes part in Roussel's councils, along with his other advisers. Her advice usually is practical and often is prescient about opposing leaders' hidden intentions. Despite the book's title, Lady Matilda is never held for ransom. She does ransom Roussel and his men when they are captured by Turks, using ineptly applied makeup and light chatter to disorient their captors during the bargaining. Matilda is as much concerned with honor as her husband is; she feels responsible for all members of the company, both knights and their dependents. She bears and rears three children during the troop's campaigns. Matilda shares Roussel's dream of providing for the children's futures by establishing their own Norman realm in Asia, but when this becomes impossible, she does not despair. Instead, she takes shelter in a convent during Roussel's descent from power. There, she assesses the political situation while seemingly involved in the ladylike pastimes of embroidery and gossip.

Alexius Comnenus, a cousin of Emperor Michael and the domestic, or commander, of the empire's armies of Asia and Europe. Alexius survives the maze of Byzantine politics through his tactical skills and balanced judgment. When Roussel is tried for rebellion, he arranges matters so that the Norman is not blinded and is held in a relatively decent prison until he can be released. Alexius later becomes emperor and leads a long struggle against the Turks.

— *Emily Alward*

THE LADY FROM THE SEA
(Fruen fra havet)

Author: Henrik Ibsen (1828-1906)
First published: 1888
Genre: Drama

Locale: A small town in northern Norway
Time: The nineteenth century
Plot: Psychological realism

Ellida Wangel, a woman dominated by the sea. She feels stifled in her new home after she marries and goes away from the sea to live in the mountains. She feels strangely drawn to a sailor who had known and loved her years earlier. When he appears again, she feels his hold over her, as well as feeling the conflicting hold of her husband. Left to her own choice, she stays with her husband. She feels that she has retained her sanity by being able to make a choice for herself.

Dr. Wangel, Ellida's husband, a physician. He tries to understand the strains on his wife's mind and gives her a verbal release from her vows so that she can decide for herself whether to go with her former suitor or remain with her husband.

Boletta and

Hilda Wangel, Dr. Wangel's daughters by his first wife. They find their stepmother a difficult person with whom to make friends.

Arnholm, Boletta's former tutor and another early sweetheart of Ellida. She refused in the past to marry Arnholm because, she said, she already was betrothed.

The stranger, a sailor who has a powerful psychological hold over Ellida because he makes her think she has been betrothed to him in a strange ceremony by the sea. He has murdered a man and is a fugitive from justice. Ellida finally decides to stay with her husband and breaks the hold the stranger has over her mind.

Lyngstrand, a traveling sculptor who stops at the Wangels' house. His story of a sailor and his wife reawakens in Ellida's mind memory of the sailor who had betrothed himself to her years earlier.

LADY INTO FOX

Author: David Garnett (1892-1981)
First published: 1922
Genre: Novel

Locale: England
Time: 1880
Plot: Fantasy

Mr. Richard Tebrick, a young Englishman who finds he has married a vixen. His worry over her and her cubs and his jealousy of her mate make him seem a madman not only to his neighbors but even occasionally to himself. When he and his wife are attacked by dogs who kill her, Mr. Tebrick loses his reason. He recovers, however, and lives many years.

Silvia Fox Tebrick, his wife, a beautiful country girl with hazel eyes, reddish-brown hair, and brownish, freckled skin who, in her twenty-third year, turns into a small, bright-red fox. Though she can no longer speak, she communicates by looks and signs, and she understands her husband as she did before. At first retaining in part her womanly nature, she gradually becomes more foxlike in eating and in other habits. When released, she disappears, mates with a dog-fox, and later lets her cubs play with their godfather, Mr. Tebrick.

Nanny Cork, Silvia's old nurse, who becomes the Tebricks' housekeeper. She accepts Silvia's transformation as if it were nothing unusual and continues her interest in Silvia's welfare.

Askew, a jockey hired by Mr. Tebrick to follow the fox hunts and report on the animals killed.

Sorel,

Kaspar,

Selwyn,

Esther, and

Angelica, Silvia's cubs. Angelica, who greatly resembles her mother, is Mr. Tebrick's favorite.

The Reverend Canon Fox, Silvia's uncle, a clergyman who visits Mr. Tebrick and thinks him insane.

James, the Tebrick gardener and groom.

Polly, Mrs. Cork's grandaughter, who enjoys playing with Mrs. Tebrick until the vixen leaves to seek a mate.

Simon, Mrs. Cork's son.

LADY MACBETH OF THE MTSENSK DISTRICT
("Ledi Makbet Mtsenskogo uezda")

Author: Nikolai Leskov (1831-1895)
First published: 1865
Genre: Short fiction

Locale: Mtsensk District, Russia
Time: Mid-nineteenth century
Plot: Realism

Katerina L'vovna Izmaylova (kah-teh-RIH-nah LVOV-nah ihz-MAY-loh-vah), the wife and, later, the widow of Zinovy Borisovich Izmaylov. She was born into a poor family, and she married at the age of twenty-four largely to improve her material circumstances. She is described as highly attractive, if not beautiful; her straight, thin nose, sparkling dark eyes, and black hair seem to accentuate the more direct appeal imparted by her fine white neck, firm breasts, and gracefully rounded shoulders. After five years as his wife, she has begun chafing at the dullness of life with Zinovy; she succumbs to Sergey's charms and then entices him to continue their passionate though potentially very scandalous love affair. It is she who resolves to kill the three people who might create difficulties for them; once her mind is set on murder, she acts with a cold-blooded efficiency that even Sergey, as her accomplice, finds disconcerting. She apparently is susceptible to remorse only unconsciously, as when she dreams of a large sleek cat that has the voice and the accusatory features of her murdered father-in-law. Although she is capable of intense sensual yearnings, she is also, until the last, loyal to Sergey. She exhibits unflinching stoicism when, confronted with the evidence of her crimes, she confesses calmly and then is flogged before being sent into penal exile. By this time, she has conceived and given birth to a child, which she relinquishes without protest or second thought; however, when Sergey's attention wanders to other women and he openly taunts her with his affection for Sonetka, she plunges her rival into the Volga river and then drowns herself.

Sergey (sehr-GAY), a clerk who works on the Izmaylovs' property and who becomes Katerina's lover. His brash but ingratiating manner arouses Katerina's interest; he is also a handsome fellow, with ruddy features and long, black, curly hair that she finds particularly appealing. Although there are some hints that previously he may have carried on with other women, he is able to convince Katerina of his devotion to her. He displays some resentment of social privilege. When Katerina's father-in-law obtains from Sergey an admission that he has had sexual relations with Katerina, he submits to a severe lashing as a form of chastisement. He takes a somewhat less active part than Katerina in the murder of her husband and of young Fedya; in both instances, he restrains them while his

lover administers the fatal blows. On the other hand, once he realizes that Fedya would be able to claim much of the Izmaylovs' estate, it is Sergey who insists that they do away with the young boy. Sergey may be affected by stirrings of conscience, and he is easily swayed by religious appeals. A priest induces him to confess by emphasizing repentance and the final judgment. Once Sergey has confessed, he implicates Katerina without any reservations; it is his testimony that initiates proceedings against her. He feels no particular compunction in jettisoning Katerina for other lovers, and he bluntly informs her that, once she has fallen from a more elevated social station and become a convict like him, he has no special need for her. After a tawdry affair with Fiona, he precipitates the final crisis by taking warm woolen stockings Katerina has brought for him and presenting them, amid open displays of affection, to Sonetka, his most recent paramour.

Boris Timofeyevich Izmaylov (tih-moh-FEH-yeh-vihch ihz-MAY-lov), the father of Zinovy, a man nearly eighty years old. He happens to be present during his son's absence, and he sees Sergey surreptitiously leaving Katerina's bedchamber; he then asks the young man pointedly what he has been doing with his daughter-in-law. He administers punishment by whipping Sergey and then locking him in a storeroom. When Katerina finds out, she demands that Boris release him. That night, he eats pickled mushrooms and kasha that Katerina has prepared; she has added a white powder used on rats, and Boris dies in a manner that outwardly resembles food poisoning.

Zinovy Borisovich Izmaylov (zih-NOH-vee boh-RIH-soh-vihch), Katerina's husband. He is more than fifty years old. Earlier, he had been widowed after a marriage of twenty years. He and his father would rise at dawn and then attend to business among local merchants. After being away for some time, he hears rumors of Katerina's illicit love affair and returns home abruptly. When, instead of denying his accusations, Katerina parades Sergey in front of him, Zinovy fumes, rages, and slaps her face; Katerina takes him by the throat, has Sergey hold him down, and then beats him on the head with a candlestick before they throttle him to make sure that he is dead.

Fyodor Ignat'yevich Lyamin (FYOH-dohr ih-GNAH-tyeh-vihch LYA-mihn), or **Fedya**, a young nephew of Boris' cousin.

Because funds to start the family business had been provided by way of this distant relative, he would stand to share in the capital. He is brought to the district by his aunt. He comes down briefly with chicken pox and reads lives of the saints with devoted interest. He is frightened enough to scream when Sergey appears; however, evidently according to plan, it is Katerina who smothers him with a pillow, after Sergey has pinioned his arms and legs.

Fiona (FYOH-nah), a female convict, formerly a soldier's wife, described as beautiful and tall, with thick black hair and dreamy eyes. She seems willing to give in to any man, and others regard her as cheap and common. She is Sergey's first lover in exile.

Sonetka (SOH-neht-kah), another convict, a blond woman of seventeen. Her sharp features and delicate rosy skin seemingly correspond to her reputedly passionate nature, though she does not yield herself easily to male blandishments. She responds to Sergey's amorous attentions but evidently is not aware of Katerina's jealousy.

— *J. R. Broadus*

THE LADY OF THE LAKE

Author: Sir Walter Scott (1771-1832)
First published: 1810
Genre: Poetry

Locale: The Scottish Highlands
Time: The sixteenth century
Plot: Historical

Ellen Douglas, who, with her rebel father, hides from the king near Loch Katrine in the Highlands. Befriended by James Fitz-James, a powerful nobleman, she is instrumental in bringing the rebel clans and the king's forces together. In the end, her marriage to Malcolm Graeme is blessed by the monarch.

James of Douglas, Ellen's father, who once was a powerful nobleman but who now is in rebellion against the king. Finally, because he can no longer agree with one of his powerful leaders, he gives himself up to the royal court. He finally is restored to favor.

Roderick Dhu, a rebel Highland chief who befriends Ellen and her father but whose ruthless military tactics Ellen abhors. Dhu, in the guise of a guard, fights a duel with James Fitz-James and is overcome. The rebel and loyal forces do not fight, but Dhu, in prison, dies thinking his clans fought a glorious battle.

James Fitz-James, a nobleman, friendly to Ellen, who at the poem's end is discovered to be the king.

Allan-Bane, a minstrel in the service of James of Douglas who is faithful to that nobleman even while he hides with his forces in the Highlands. The minstrel is also a prophet and seer of sorts, and he knows that matters between the clans and the king will end well. It is Allan-Bane who, as a kindly gesture, gives the dying Roderick Dhu the impression that the clans fought bravely against the king.

Malcolm Graeme, a young rebel nobleman who was once the object of an attack by Dhu's forces after Ellen had refused Dhu's suit because she and Malcolm were in love. Finally, with the king's blessing, he marries Ellen.

LADY WINDERMERE'S FAN

Author: Oscar Wilde (1854-1900)
First published: 1893
Genre: Drama

Locale: London, England
Time: The nineteenth century
Plot: Comedy of manners

Lady Margaret Windermere, a proper woman. After discovering that her husband is giving money to Mrs. Erlynne, she doubts his assertions that the relationship is honorable. Angry that he insists on inviting Mrs. Erlynne to their ball, Lady Windermere threatens to strike Mrs. Erlynne with her fan if she appears, but Lady Windermere loses her nerve and drops the fan instead. Put in a reckless mood, Lady Windermere accepts the attentions of Lord Darlington, a man-about-town, and agrees to run off with him. Mrs. Erlynne intercepts Lady Windermere's letter to her husband and follows her. At the expense of her own reputation, Mrs. Erlynne saves that of Lady Windermere. From that time on, Lady Windermere defends Mrs. Erlynne and calls her a good woman, though she does not understand Mrs. Erlynne's motives.

Mrs. Erlynne, who years ago left her husband and daughter to run away with another man. Her daughter is Lady Windermere, whom she saves from similar ignominy. She does not reveal the relationship to Lady Windermere, not wishing to destroy her illusions.

Lord Windermere, the husband of Lady Windermere. He is helping Mrs. Erlynne, whom he admires, to regain the approval of society, and hence he insists that she be invited to the ball. Mrs. Erlynne takes the blame when Lady Windermere's fan is found in Lord Darlington's rooms. Lord Windermere is furious about this and thinks she has betrayed his confidence.

The duchess of Berwick, who informs Lady Windermere of a rumored affair between Mrs. Erlynne and Lord Windermere.

Lord Augustus Lorton, the disreputable brother of the duchess of Berwick. He breaks his engagement with Mrs. Erlynne when she takes Lady Windermere's blame. Later, he accepts her explanation that his own interests took her to Lord Darlington's rooms, and the engagement is renewed.

Lord Darlington, a man-about-town. He persuades Lady Windermere to run away with him. Mrs. Erlynne pursues Lady Windermere to his rooms and, reminding her of her duty to her child, persuades her to go back to her husband.

THE LADY WITH THE DOG
("Dama s sobachkoi")

Author: Anton Chekhov (1860-1904)
First published: 1899
Genre: Short fiction

Locale: Yalta and Moscow
Time: The 1890's
Plot: Psychological realism

Dmitrii Dmitrich Gurov (DMIH-tree DMIH-trihch GEW-rov), a Moscow banker. A married man approaching middle age, Dmitrii is a property owner, the father of three children, and an amateur singer who once had aspirations to join a private opera company. He is also a veteran adulterer. While vacationing by himself at Yalta, he intends to continue his infidelity if the opportunity presents itself. He is, however, clearly aware that each new affair soon palls, although the prospect of inevitable boredom over his conquests and his disgust over each affair's messy ending do not dissuade him from striking up an acquaintance with Anna, who seems to be easy prey. His shallow and cynical attitude toward women (to whom he refers as the "lower breed") is in part the result of his bitterness over marriage to a severe, intellectual woman whom he wed while still at the university. His round of activities, both at the seaside resort and in Moscow, is characterized by cynicism and boredom and by the spurious pleasures of card games at his clubs and sophisticated chatter at social gatherings. His immersion in the old pleasures proves useless, however, in disguising the fact that he has fallen deeply in love with Anna. As their affair lengthens and becomes increasingly serious, Dmitrii's trifling, pleasure-obsessed existence grows tragic.

Anna Sergeevna von Diederitz (AHN-nah sehr-GEH-yehv-nah von DIH-deh-rihtz), a young married woman. Anna, a sensitive and morally conscientious but inexperienced young woman, has been married for two years to a minor provincial official whom she detests. Her affair with Dmitrii is cataclysmic for her; she sees herself as a "fallen woman" and becomes despondent. She feels, moreover, that she has deceived not only her husband but herself as well. Her visit to Yalta is the result of frustration occasioned by the sameness of her life. Driven by curiosity, by the urge "to live," she has convinced her husband that she suffers from an undefined illness and thus needs the rest that Yalta affords. Initially, her lovemaking with Dmitrii prompts her to self-disgust, a disgust she feels that Dmitrii shares; in her own eyes, she has become petty and despicable. At the same time, her love for Dmitrii deepens, and when he later appears in her provincial town, she recognizes that she and Dmitrii are doomed by their emotions. Anna perceives her own ambivalence; she realizes that even while she despises herself for her infidelity and is made miserable by a potentially tragic future, she is thrilled by the richer life she secretly shares with Dmitrii.

— *John Steven Childs*

THE LADY'S NOT FOR BURNING

Author: Christopher Fry (1907-   )
First published: 1949
Genre: Drama

Locale: Cool Clary, a small market town
Time: c. 1400
Plot: Comedy

Thomas Mendip, a discharged soldier who wants to be hanged. He is part egoist and part misanthrope. So that he will be hanged, he claims to have killed old Skipps. After he is tortured to make him stop confessing, he falls in love with Jennet Jourdemayne. His love for her makes him decide to escape from jail and go on living.

Jennet Jourdemayne, a beautiful girl accused of being a witch so that her property can be confiscated by the town. She is accused of turning old Skipps into a dog. When her supposed victim turns up, she is allowed to escape with Thomas, leaving her property confiscate. She learns that love and fancy have a place in life.

Skipps, an old rag and bone man, supposedly turned into a dog by Jennet Jourdemayne. Thomas claims to have killed him. He turns up hale and hearty.

Hebble Tyson, the mayor of Cool Clary. He wants to confiscate Jennet's property and is bothered by Thomas' attempts

to be hanged. His problem is solved when Jennet and Thomas fall in love and escape from jail.

Richard, an orphan and the mayor's clerk. He loves Alizon Eliot and marries her.

Alizon Eliot, a handsome young woman betrothed to Humphrey Devize. She loves Richard and on the night of her betrothal party elopes with him.

Humphrey Devize, the mayor's nephew. He decides that he does not really want to marry Alizon, though he and his brothers had fought over her. He tries to seduce Janet by offering to help her escape. She refuses him.

Nicholas Devize, Humphrey's brother. He thinks for a while that the stars have decreed that he shall marry Alizon. After his brother decides he does not want to marry her, Nicholas decides that he does not want to marry her either.

Margaret Devize, the sister of the mayor. She is Humphrey and Nicholas' mother.

LAFCADIO'S ADVENTURES
(Les Caves du Vatican)

Author: André Gide (1869-1951)
First published: 1914
Genre: Novel

Locale: France and Italy
Time: The 1890's, during the pontificate of Leo XIII
Plot: Satire

Lafcadio Wluiki (laf-KAH-dee-oh lew-KEE), a charming nineteen-year-old, born a bastard, whose natural father turns out to be the dying Count Juste-Agénor de Baraglioul. Lafcadio is a free spirit, deliberately eschewing any kind of bond or constraint. His spirit of adventure and his obsession with the possibilities of his own nature lead him to test himself in a gamelike fashion, by pushing out of a speeding train, without any specific reason, Amédée Fleurissoire, whom he had never met before. This paradigmatic expression of the "gratuitous act" affects the lives of most of the characters. At the end, torn between conflicting tendencies, he tears away from Geneviève's arms and seems ready to plunge into the unpredictable drifts of life.

Julius de Baraglioul (zhew-LYEWS deh bah-rah-GLYEWL), a pompous, narrow-minded, pious writer of mediocre novels. He is Lafcadio's half brother. His ultimate goal is to be elected to the French Academy. At one point, having realized that his writing system distorts reality, he undergoes an allegedly radical metamorphosis, sets up to attack logic and consistency, and conceives a young hero who will perform a "gratuitous act." Faced with the reality of an unmotivated crime, namely Amédée's murder, he refutes it with vehemence and is driven back to his old, narrow ideological system, his boldness surfacing only on paper. Through Julius, the author caricatures the figure of the novelist and calls into question the process of writing itself.

Juste-Agénor de Baraglioul (zhewst ah-gay-NOHR), a wealthy aristocrat, the father of Julius and Lafcadio. He never openly reveals that he is Lafcadio's natural father, but he summons Lafcadio before dying and bequeaths him part of his fortune.

Marguerite de Baraglioul (mahr-geh-REET), Julius' wife, a surly, religious, middle-aged woman who complains about everything.

Geneviève de Baraglioul (zheh-neh-VYEHV), the daughter of Julius and Marguerite, a beautiful, innocent, young volunteer nurse who falls in love with Lafcadio (her half uncle) and gives herself to him after his gratuitous murder of Amédée. She does not succeed, however, in making him reintegrate the world of conventional morality. She is a parody of the romantic heroine.

Anthime Armand-Dubois (ahn-TEEM ahr-MAH[N]-dew-BWAH), not only a pragmatic scientist but also a vehemently anticlerical, atheistic Freemason, suffering from acute sciatica. He is Julius' brother-in-law. Converted to an ardent faith by a

dream in which he is visited by the Virgin Mary, he is simultaneously cured from his sciatica and socially and financially ruined by the Freemasonry. The rumor that the pope residing in the Vatican is a false one restores him to his previous atheism and brings back his crippling disease.

Véronique (vay-roh-NEEK), Anthime's pious wife, the sister of Marguerite and Arnica. She is a good-natured woman who puts up with her husband's bad disposition with great patience.

Amédée Fleurissoire (ah-may-DAY flew-ree-SWAHR), Julius' brother-in-law, united in an unconsummated marriage to Arnica Péterat. He is a pious, chaste, gullible, and ludicrous character who turns out to be the principal victim of Protos' swindle. As soon as he hears the rumor that the real pope has been kidnapped and imprisoned in the castle Sant'Angelo, he sets out for Rome to attempt to deliver him. His falling prey to bedbugs in Marseilles, fleas in Toulon, and mosquitoes in Genoa constitutes the ironic prologue to his fatal involvement with Protos' underground society. His senseless death epitomizes the absurdity of his whole life.

Arnica (ahr-nee-KAH), Amédée's wife, the youngest sister of Marguerite and Véronique. After having suffered the rejection of her family and the mockery of her classmates, she kindles the love of two very close friends, Fleurissoire and Blafaphas. Almost by chance, she chooses Amédée, who, in turn, promises his friend never to exercise his conjugal rights.

Protos, also known as **Defouqueblize** (deh-fohk-BLEEZ), a former schoolmate of Lafcadio. He is a mysterious, fascinating, and highly resourceful character who revels in disguising himself and assuming various identities so as better to manipulate his victims. He is the mastermind of a vast swindle undertaken by a secret society, the "Mille-Pattes," which collects funds to deliver the real pope, allegedly imprisoned in the cellars of the Vatican. His recourse to histrionic effects is counterbalanced by the excessive credulity of his dupes. At the end, he is arrested, not because of his swindle but for Lafcadio's gratuitous crime, after Carola's denunciation.

Carola Venitequa (veh-nee-tay-KAH), a prostitute with a big heart whose very name suggests sexual availability. Protos' former mistress, she lives with Lafcadio for a while, returns to Protos, initiates Amédée to the pleasures of love, and is subjected to Julius' clumsy advances. At the end, she denounces Protos to the police, believing that he was responsible for Amédée's murder, and ends up being strangled by him.

— *Marie-Denise Boros Azzi*

THE LAIS OF MARIE DE FRANCE

Author: Marie de France (c. 1150-c. 1190)
First transcribed: c. 1167
Genre: Poetry

Locale: Largely Brittany
Time: Primarily the reign of King Arthur
Plot: Romance

Guigemar (geeg-MAHR), a handsome Breton knight unequaled in valor but indifferent to love. During a hunting party, he is injured when an arrow rebounds from his prey, a strange white doe with a stag's horns. The deer predicts that Guigemar will be healed only when he has suffered for love; this prediction comes true when the knight, transported by a ghost ship, falls in love with a married lady. Even after the lady's escape from a jealous old husband, Guigemar is obliged to do battle

with the baron Meriaduc, who had given her shelter and who planned to keep her for himself.

Lanval (lahn-VAHL), a knight from Brittany in the service of King Arthur of England. Lanval is overlooked when lavish gifts are bestowed by the king. Saddened, as well as alienated from the other knights, who are jealous of his physical beauty and chivalric prowess, he is magically visited by a beautiful and wealthy maiden. With the enchanted damsel as his secret invisible lover, Lanval is able to live in luxury. Accused of homosexuality by Arthur's queen, whose advances he had spurned, Lanval is saved from the Round Table's harsh judgment when the maiden herself appears in King Arthur's court and bears her lover off on horseback to the idyllic island of Avalon.

Le Fresne (leh FREHZ-neh), whose name means "the ash tree," the twin sister of La Codre and legitimate daughter of a rich Breton knight. Abandoned at birth by her mother and left in an ash tree at the door of an abbey, Le Fresne is reared by the abbess. She becomes the mistress of the noble Gurun, who cherishes her and takes her to live with him. Faithful and loving, Le Fresne continues to serve Gurun, even assisting in preparations for his marriage to another woman. Her virtue is rewarded when the mother of the bride recognizes her abandoned twin child in Le Fresne and repents of her deception. Upon annulment of the marriage of her newly found sister, Le Fresne weds her beloved Gurun.

Milun (mee-LO[N]), a highly esteemed knight from South Wales, the lover of a noble damsel by whom he has an illegitimate son. To save the honor of his beloved, Milun agrees to send his infant son to be reared in secrecy by the mother's sister in northern England. Although another nobleman is chosen as a husband for the girl, Milun is able to communicate with her for twenty years by means of a messenger swan. Learning that a young Welsh knight has established a reputation on the Continent that rivals his own, Milun hastens to challenge the young upstart. During the joust, Milun is unhorsed. Recognizing a signet ring on his opponent's finger, Milun is reunited with his son. They return together to Wales. Finding his beloved a widow, Milun is united in marriage with his lady by their son.

Eliduc (eh-lee-DEWK), a worthy knight of Brittany, slandered by his peers and exiled by the king. Promising fidelity to his wife, Eliduc leaves for England in search of mercenary work. Engaged in the service of a powerful nobleman, Eliduc distinguishes himself as a clever military leader and attracts the romantic attention of the man's daughter. Eliduc responds to her love and soon cannot bear to be separated from her. Returning to his native land, Eliduc loses his newly beloved on board ship; she dies of grief after learning that Eliduc is married. Leaving her body in a small chapel near his castle, the mourning Eliduc shows no joy in reunion with his wife, preferring to spend time in the chapel lamenting his deceased lover. When his wife discovers the truth and through the magical power of a red flower revives her rival, Eliduc builds a convent and allows his wife to take the veil. After many years of wedded bliss, Eliduc builds a monastery, places his second wife in the convent, and devotes himself to God.

Equitan (eh-kee-TAHEN), a king of Brittany, respected by his people. He begins a foolish love affair with his loyal seneschal's wife, who soon wishes to do away with her husband so that she can become queen. Equitan acquiesces to her scheme, but both he and his mistress fall victim to their own murderous plot.

Bisclavret (bihs-klah-VRAY), a Breton baron who secretly becomes a werewolf three days each week. (His name means "werewolf" in the Breton language.) Coaxed by his wife into revealing the secret of his whereabouts, Bisclavret is left permanently in the werewolf stage when she and her lover, a neighbor, confiscate his human clothing. Though in a savage state, Bisclavret befriends the king during the course of a royal hunting party in the area. Bisclavret takes advantage of his position as the king's pet beast to avenge himself, attacking the neighbor at a festival and later biting off his wife's nose. He is restored to his human state when the wife confesses all to the king and returns the stolen clothing.

Yonec (yoh-NEHK), the illegitimate son of Muldumarec and a beautiful lady married to a rich but very old Breton nobleman. Muldumarec, who flew into his beloved's room in the form of a bird, impaled himself on iron spikes placed on the lady's window by the suspicious husband. Before expiring, he predicted that his death would one day be avenged by his as yet unborn son. Shortly after he is dubbed a knight, Yonec, wielding his father's sword, fulfills the prophecy.

Tristan (tree-STAHN), the estranged nephew of King Marc of Cornwall and lover of Marc's wife (Queen Iseult, unnamed by the author), exiled by the jealous uncle to his native Wales. Tristan enjoys a brief amorous encounter with his beloved when she responds to a prearranged signal from him.

La Codre (kohdr), the twin sister of Le Fresne. She is married to Gurun but is replaced as his wife by his mistress, La Codre's newly discovered sister, Le Fresne. She is later married to a rich nobleman.

Gurun, (gew-RO[N]), a nobleman from the city of Dol in Brittany. He is the lover, then husband, of Le Fresne.

Muldumarec (mewl-dew-MAH-rehk), the father of Yonec. The victim of a jealous husband, he was impaled on iron spikes when, transformed into a bird, he flew into the room of his beloved. His death was avenged when his son Yonec slew the murderer.

King Marc, a Cornish king, the husband of Queen Iseult and uncle of the queen's lover, Tristan. Angered by the infidelity of his queen and nephew, both of whom he genuinely loves, he banishes Tristan from Cornwall. The two will later be reconciled.

Guildeluec (geel-deh-LEWEHK), Eliduc's wife. When her husband returns from exile with the body of his dead mistress, Guildeluec resuscitates her, lovingly relinquishes her own position as wife, and establishes a religious order.

Guilliadun (geel-yah-DO[N]), the English mistress of Eliduc, ignorant of the fact that he is married. She learns the truth from a sailor aboard the ship taking her to Eliduc's homeland and dies from the trauma and grief. Resuscitated by a miraculous red flower placed in her mouth by Eliduc's wife, she becomes Eliduc's second wife, as the first withdraws to a convent. After years of almsgiving, she becomes a nun.

— *Judith L. Barban*

LALLA ROOKH: An Oriental Romance

Author: Thomas Moore (1779-1852)
First published: 1817
Genre: Poetry

Locale: India
Time: c. 1700
Plot: Love

Lalla Rookh (**Tulip Cheek**), Emperor Aurungzebe's daughter, promised to King Aliris. She sets forth by caravan for Cashmere, where she is to meet and marry her betrothed. Among the servants in the bridal entourage is the poet Feramorz, with whom Lalla Rookh falls in love. Wishing to present her heart undefiled to her bridegroom, she banishes the poet from her presence, only to learn to her joy on her arrival in Cashmere that Feramorz is Aliris, disguised for the purpose of winning her love.

Aliris, the young king of Bucharia. To win the love of his betrothed, Lalla Rookh, he disguises himself as the poet Feramorz and accompanies the bridal caravan to Cashmere. With his beauty and the charms of his music and poetry, Feramorz wins the love of the bride-to-be. When the caravan arrives in Cashmere, he reveals himself as King Aliris, disguised.

Fadladeen, the chamberlain of the harem and a bumptious know-all. As protector of Lalla Rookh in the bridal caravan, he delivers opinions on all subjects and persons, especially on the poet Feramorz, whose beautiful love poems he attacks with a particular vehemence as he analyzes them from every possible angle. When he finally learns Feramorz's true identity as King Aliris, he recants and proclaims the king the greatest poet of all time.

Aurungzebe, the emperor of Delhi and Lalla Rookh's father.

Abdalla, the recently abdicated king of Lesser Bucharia and the father of young King Aliris.

THE LAMB
(L'Agneau)

Author: François Mauriac (1885-1970)
First published: 1954
Genre: Novel

Locale: Larjuzon, a country home outside Paris
Time: 1921
Plot: Fable

Xavier Dartigelonghue (zhah-VYAY dahr-teezh-LOHNG), a middle-class young man intending to enter a seminary in Paris. Sensitive and intelligent, he is interested in human nature and, by aspiring to the priesthood, hopes to touch the lives of others. On the train to Paris, he meets Jean de Mirbel, who is separating from his wife, Michèle. Through a series of questions on the value of the priesthood, Jean intensifies Xavier's self-doubts about his vocation and convinces him to return to his home in Larjuzon. This temptation, forcing Xavier to reconsider his plans, is followed by sensual conflict. Attracted by Dominique's beauty and kindness, he replaces spiritual vocation with passionate desire. Her departure requires renunciation of this love; a higher love for the orphan Roland impels him to make a sacrifice that enables him to perceive the earthly presence of Christ. Through self-sacrifice, he restores dignity to Roland's life. By recognizing the force of divine grace that sustains his suffering, Xavier resists the third temptation of earthly pleasure proposed by a cynical priest. Financially and psychologically, Xavier ensures Roland's well-being, but on returning to Jean's villa on bicycle, he is killed by the car driven by Jean. In dying, Xavier becomes an instrument of divine grace and, like Christ, endures self-sacrifice that leads to self-knowledge and the actualization of love.

Jean de Mirbel (zhah[n] deh meer-BEHL), a landowner in the Landes, near Bordeaux. A handsome but bitter man, he suffers from an impotent relationship with his wife, Michèle, and seeks separation from her. Worldly, self-centered, and calculating, he exploits and twists for his own demonic purposes Xavier's intentions to become a priest. His cruelty extends to verbal and physical abuse of the orphan Roland, whom he intends to return to public assistance. After learning of Xavier's intention to entrust Roland to Dominique, Jean is frustrated in his desire to hurt. To prevent Roland's escape, he rushes to the rectory and accidentally kills Xavier. Through Xavier's death, Jean learns shame and remorse; now requiring the support of others, he returns to Michèle and seeks reconciliation.

Michèle de Mirbel (mee-SHEHL), Jean's wife. A large-boned, strong woman, she suffers from loneliness and depression in an unfulfilling marriage, which Jean wants to dissolve. Fearful and anxious, she hopes to keep the marriage intact and, therefore, acquiesces to Jean's demands. In assuming responsibility for Roland, she knows and experiences love; however, weak in resolve and uncommitted in principle, she agrees with Jean to return the child to the orphanage. The love that is unanswered as wife and mother then extends to Xavier. She becomes jealous of Dominique, who enjoys a reciprocal relationship with Xavier and who also directs her attentions to Roland. Xavier's death eases her tensions between unrequited love and emotional weakness: By consoling Jean after Xavier's accident, she restores her marriage.

Brigitte Pian (bree-ZHEET pee-AH[N]) Michèle's stepmother. A pallid, elderly lady with yellowish-white hair, she wears black-tinted glasses to hide her eyes and wrinkles. She practices Catholicism devoutly but schemes to injure others. After discovering the relationship between Xavier and Dominique, she informs Xavier's parents of his desire to disobey their wishes and instructs her secretary, Dominique, to leave with her for Bordeaux. She shatters their love, and, through her efforts, Xavier's parents present their son with an ultimatum: He must turn to the study of law or be disinherited. After Xavier's death, she offers Masses. She uses the accident to accuse Jean of murder and Xavier of suicide.

Dominique (doh-mee-NEEK), Madame Pian's secretary. She is a withdrawn young lady who needs income and is, therefore, controlled by Madame Pian. Her innocent, considerate nature draws her to Roland, who is physically and verbally abused. Despite her affection for Roland and her passionate love for Xavier, she obeys Madame Pian's command to leave the Mirbels' villa. She assumes custody of Roland, however, and uses 150,000 francs inherited from Xavier's will to accommodate earthly pressures of survival with spiritual impulses of love.

Roland, an orphan placed in the Mirbels' custody. A victim of physical and psychological abuse, he is frightened of Jean but becomes resigned to his situation and to his return to the orphanage. Through Roland's presence, Xavier discovers the resources of compassion and the means to actualize love.

Curé de Baluzac (koo-RAY deh bah-lew-ZAK) a cynical, materialistic priest. Although he discourages Xavier from en-

tering the priesthood, he serves as an intermediary, allowing Xavier to bring Roland to Dominique at the rectory. At the end, he continues to celebrate Mass, but he prefers earthly pleasures.

— *Donald Gilman*

LANARK: A Life in Four Books

Author: Alasdair Gray (1934-   )
First published: 1981
Genre: Novel

Locale: Glasgow and imaginary worlds
Time: Probably mid-twentieth century and later
Plot: Metafiction

Lanark, the protagonist. Nondescript in his physical appearance, he is remarkable for his emotional reserve. His manner suggests at once mystery and transparent personality. At the novel's opening, he finds himself in a railroad car, without memory of his past. Drifting through the almost continually dark and damp streets of a half-wasted city called Unthank, he learns how to acquire funds through a public welfare agency that, despite its procedural formality, seems to dispense monies arbitrarily. Determined to witness each day's brief moment of sunlight on the horizon, he often sits alone in the rain on the small balcony of a club called The Elite. Lanark eventually is drawn into one of the club's cliques, the one formed around Sludden. At Sludden's suggestion, he attempts to provide a purposeful center to his existence by becoming a writer. Disturbed by a scaly patch of skin on his arm, which increases in size as he scratches it, he discovers that the woman he has been pursuing, Rima, bears this affliction over much of her body. After he makes love to her unsatisfactorily, she pushes him out of her apartment. Shortly afterward, he wakes to find that his entire arm has become dragonlike. After being sucked down a tunnel, he wakes, cured of his affliction, in an underground utopia of bright artificial lights called the Institute. There, he becomes a doctor in much the same illogical way as he earlier became a writer. Later, he meets Rima again and cures her, and they escape back to Unthank. Rima leaves Lanark for Sludden, who has become a sort of managing director of the city. Against his instincts, Lanark accepts the post of provost and travels to an international conference at which the fate of Unthank will be decided. With his moods swinging between fatigued bewilderment and inflated self-importance, he allows several beautiful young women to get him drunk, is arrested for urinating off a bridge, and misses most of the conference. Recognizing that his political naïveté has served Sludden's Machiavellian schemes, he returns to Unthank in disgrace, witnesses the eventual destruction of the city by fire and flood, and, without protest, accepts the announcement of his impending execution.

Duncan Thaw, Lanark's alter ego, a neurotic art student in Glasgow. Born into a lower-middle-class family shortly before the outbreak of World War II, he escapes the German bombing of Glasgow with his mother and his sister, Ruth. Eventually, they join his father, who is working as the personnel director of a munitions plant. From an early age, Duncan is subject to attacks of asthma and outbreaks of eczema. As he matures, he recognizes that his physical ailments have become a neurotic defense mechanism against his dismal environs and his own unnaturally constrained personality. Pressured by his parents to do well in school, he excels in art and in English but barely

gets by in mathematics. He seems destined for a secure but dull career as a librarian when, by fortuitous circumstance, he is offered a fellowship to the Art School. There, he antagonizes several instructors with his self-assured willfulness, but, because of his obvious talent and his friendship with the registrar, he is granted unusual privileges, such as being permitted to pursue his own projects in a loft near the school instead of attending regular classes. Haunted by his unrequited infatuation for Kate Caldwell, a girl he knew in secondary school, he pursues a relationship with Marjory Laidlaw, a fellow student at the Art School. Tortured by her alternating friendliness and clear avoidance of physical intimacy with him, he intends to break off with her decisively but ends up doing so very lamely. Unable to complete an overly large, overly ambitious painting of the canal system between Glasgow and the surrounding countryside, he becomes delusional and, in a nightmarish sequence out of the writings of Fyodor Dostoevski, imagines murdering Marjory. All Duncan's expectations of great success eventually are wrecked as his eccentricities and careless remarks detract from his work. Ultimately, Duncan travels north, intending to visit his father, who has retired to the countryside. When he peeks through the window of his father's residence, however, he cannot bear to disturb his father's apparent contentment. Duncan ends up on a desolate seashore, where he strips off his clothes and walks into the water.

Rima, Lanark's companion and the mother of his child. Hardened by the purposeless nature of her existence in Unthank, she is saved from a fatally complete transformation into a dragon by Lanark's insistent devotion, which, in effect, gives her a reason for living. She soon grows tired of his strict adherence to his principles, however, and leaves him, explaining that he simply does not need her enough. Ironically, she chooses to live with Sludden.

Sludden, a lascivious schemer who charms others in such a way that they accept the inevitability of his using them. Politically as astute as he is unprincipled, he transforms himself from a coffeehouse radical to a self-aggrandizing figure in the establishment. He understands his hypocrisy only to the extent of being able to profit from it politically. In the end, he sacrifices Unthank to his personal ambitions. His serene domesticity with Rima and Alexander (Lanark's son) is clearly a trite posture.

Professor Ozenfant, a research scientist at the Institute who eventually becomes its director and a powerful international figure. His hypocrisy is more polished and, for that reason, more dangerous than Sludden's. His love of music and his smooth managerial style are simply the ironic manifestations of a completely amoral self-assurance about the realization of his ambitions for power.

Duncan Thaw, Sr., Duncan's father. Although he succeeds financially during the war, he lacks the educational qualifications for anything but menial work after the war. Devoted to his wife, he exhausts himself caring for her during her long and, eventually, fatal illness. Despite Duncan Sr.'s seemingly perverse inability to focus himself, he sacrifices his own comfort to his son's ambitions as an artist. Finally, however, he recognizes that Duncan Jr. is taking advantage of his good-heartedness and retires to the countryside to find some peace from family responsibilities.

Marjory Laidlaw, the daughter of a college professor. She is attracted to Duncan Thaw more out of a compassionate interest in the emotional sensitivity and turmoil that underlie his talent than out of any passionate interest in him, romantically or sexually. She contrives to bring others along on their dates and avoids situations in which she will be clearly alone with him. Naïvely good-hearted, she apparently does not recognize the degree to which her limited but genuine interest tortures him.

— *Martin Kich*

LANCELOT: Or, The Knight of the Cart
(Lancelot: Ou, Le Chevalier à la charrette)

Author: Chrétien de Troyes (c. 1150-c. 1190)
First transcribed: c. 1168
Genre: Poetry

Locale: Britain
Time: The sixth century
Plot: Romance

Lancelot, the best knight in the world and the lover of the queen. He is a warrior but has some peculiarities that undermine him, and they all stem from his love. He is prone to contemplate rather than take action. Seeing an attempted rape, he debates whether to intervene; caught between love and honor, he debates whether to leap into the cart to save Guenevere. More seriously, perhaps, he is forever swooning whenever he thinks of Guenevere. At one point, he finds a comb in which is a single strand of her hair, and he nearly falls off his horse. At another point, he is so wrapped up in thoughts of her that he does not hear another knight's challenge. It is only when the knight knocks him from his horse into a river that he is shaken from his reverie.

Guenevere, the queen of Logres, the most beautiful lady in the kingdom. In accordance with the dictates of courtly love, she is also somewhat fickle. She is Lancelot's inspiration—without her, his prowess would come to naught. When he finally meets her in Meleagant's castle, having rescued her and all the prisoners, she turns her back on him and walks out of the room without so much as speaking to him. She later explains that this was because he hesitated before getting into the cart and therefore must have considered his honor more important than his love. Her genuine affection for him is revealed, however, in her suicidal attitude when she believes him dead, though toward the end of the poem, she once more demonstrates her power over him by sending him word that he is to lose a tournament rather than win it. By obeying her command in this instance, Lancelot reassures her that, contrary to his earlier behavior, he now values her love more than his own honor.

Meleagant, the utterly detestable son of the king of Gorre. He abducts Guenevere at the beginning of the poem. He re-fuses to take advice, even when that consists of a statement of the obvious. When his father, King Bademagu, advises him not to fight Lancelot, his response is scorn. He says that he will not kneel before Lancelot and pay him homage, comments that also reveal his arrogance. He is also a coward, locking Lancelot in prison so that he cannot be present for the combat at the end of the poem. Meleagant is a static character, a stock villain who shows no development during the course of the plot.

Arthur, the king of Logres (Britain), a very weak character, as he is almost nowhere else in Arthurian literature. When Meleagant announces that he has taken many of his knights prisoner, Arthur's response is to lament the fact that he can do nothing to remedy the situation. A cuckold must always be portrayed as weak because the reader's sympathy should be with the lovers, but here such weakness is taken to an extreme: Readers may wonder how Arthur ever became king.

Gawain, a knight of the Round Table, usually considered the best of King Arthur's knights. When he sets out to rescue the queen, therefore, readers believe he is going to be the hero. He is clearly unfit for the quest, as his contrast with Lancelot shows. He thinks logically, whereas Lancelot is driven by love. Gawain utterly refuses to get into the cart because he has thought of the repercussions such an act might have on his reputation, whereas Lancelot, almost heedless of this, leaps straight in.

Bademagu, the king of Gorre, Meleagant's father. Although he is essentially virtuous, behaving courteously toward Guenevere, and is full of praise for Lancelot, he does not attempt to prevent his son from indulging in evil behavior.

— *C. M. Adderley*

LARGO DESOLATO

Author: Václav Havel (1936-   )
First published: 1985
Genre: Drama

Locale: Prague, Czechoslovakia
Time: Late 1970's or early 1980's
Plot: Absurdist

Professor Leopold Nettles, the protagonist, a philosopher and the writer of a book that contains a paragraph that the authorities deem subversive. He seems most concerned about his bodily functions, and he paces his apartment like a wild animal in a cage. He is unable to write and is handicapped by the constant pressure of impending imprisonment. Most of the time, he drinks rum and takes pills while waiting to be taken away. He claims to be a coward who lacks human integrity and doubts himself capable of love. He quotes from things he has said as if he is some other person, and he quotes what Bertram has told him he is. In short, he is not himself but only a hollow shell who remains, although he resents it, a prisoner to everyone else's expectations of who he is. He is a symbol of truth and conviction to the outside world. Leopold is also the playwright's literary analogy to himself.

Edward, a friend of Leopold who empathizes with Leopold's situation and encourages him to go out or at least to keep the window open. Edward's genuine interest, however, is in Suzana. He disengages himself from Leopold at Suzana's entrance, speaking with her in the kitchen and taking her first to the movies and later to a dinner dance. Edward represents opportunists who sympathize but will not be personally inconvenienced.

Suzana, Leopold's wife. She lives with Leopold and shops for him but is continually angry at him. She emphasizes the impracticality of Leopold's existence: She assures him that he cannot eat an egg with a silver spoon and that he does not know how to wash a pot. In addition, her behavior suggests that she even has to sleep with another man. She does not want Leopold to recant and live a normal life, yet she wishes a normal life for herself: She goes to the movies and a dinner dance with Edward.

First Sidney and
Second Sidney, two men who are virtually indistinguishable from each other, except that one smokes and the other drinks. They are proletarians who work in a paper mill; they represent the common and silent majority. Basically inarticulate, they think of Leopold as their spokesperson. They expect him to take their stand and supply him with plenty of paper to expedite their expectations. Each one, ironically, asks for nothing for himself, but something for the other.

Lucy, Leopold's mistress. She wants to "unblock" Leopold by giving him love. Leopold feels physical attraction toward her but is impotent with her and unable to protect her from the police. She encourages Leopold to write something new and is taken away by the secret police slaves, to Leopold's shame, covered only in a bedspread.

Bertram, one of the more intelligent citizens. He berates Leopold for not answering letters and for retaining only the role of the philosopher and not actually being one anymore.

First Chap and
Second Chap, two men who are virtually indistinguishable from each other and who represent the military police. They tell Leopold that he will not have to go to jail if he will deny that he was the person who wrote the subversive paragraph. Although Leopold, because of the political situation, is not any longer the same person who wrote that essay, there is a certain ironic validity to their charge. The expectations of others that he is brave, courageous, and forthright force him to lie to the police, claiming that indeed he is himself. Leopold's concern about when he will be taken in as a prisoner continues.

First Man and
Second Man, two men who follow orders and take Lucy away in a bedspread. Both represent slaves who have capitulated to the regime and do not think for themselves.

Marguerite, a young and silly graduate student who has read all of Leopold's books and fancies herself to be in love with the man as well as his ideas. She wants the same things from him that Lucy does (and perhaps that Suzana did). She represents and underlines the silly, irrepressible romantic feelings that people have for political martyrs. Lucy's feelings that these people are heroes are assurance that political martyrs— even those who, such as Leopold, have lost the courage of their convictions—will continue to meet the psychological demands of the times despite their personal toll.

— *Marjorie J. Oberlander*

THE LAST ATHENIAN
(Den siste Athenaren)

Author: Viktor Rydberg (1828-1895)
First published: 1859
Genre: Novel

Locale: Athens
Time: The fourth century
Plot: Historical

Chrysanteus (krih-SAHN-tee-uhs), an archon of Athens and its richest citizen. A pagan, he believes in Plato's philosophy of moderation and reason, as opposed to the Christian philosophy. He is forced to flee to the mountains and there is killed by the forces of Domitius.

Hermione (hur-MI-oh-nee), Chrysanteus' daughter and also a believer in the pagan philosophy. She is captured by Domitius' forces and is forcibly baptized a Christian. Rather than live under these conditions, she kills herself.

Peter, bishop of Athens. He is a sworn enemy of Chrysanteus and also of the Athanasian Christians. He connives to obtain Chrysanteus' wealth in order to buy the bishopric of Rome. He is poisoned by his fellow priests on orders of the Athanasians.

Charmides (KAHR-mih-deez), Hermione's betrothed. He is used by Bishop Peter in his fight against paganism and Chrysanteus. He is killed by a young Jew who discovers that Charmides has seduced his betrothed, the daughter of a Jew to whom Charmides owed a large amount of money.

Clemens (KLEH-mehns), Chrysanteus' long-lost son, who was reared as a Christian. He is returned to his father's pagan household but is so fanatic a Christian that he leaves and becomes a hermit, living in a cave outside Athens.

Annaeus Domitius (a-NEE-uhs doh-MIH-see-uhs), the Roman proconsul in Athens, who tries to keep to a middle-of-the-road policy and not sympathize with any of the religious factions in the city.

THE LAST CHRONICLE OF BARSET

Author: Anthony Trollope (1815-1882)
First published: 1867
Genre: Novel

Locale: Barsetshire, England
Time: Mid-nineteenth century
Plot: Domestic realism

The Reverend Josiah Crawley, perpetual curate of Hogglestock, a poor parish. He is frequently unable to pay his bills from his meager living, and Dean Arabin often gives him money he is shy about taking. On one occasion, he pays a butcher's bill with a stolen check and is brought before a magistrate's court. The court decides on a full trial, for Crawley's explanation is vague and contradictory. In addition, Mrs. Proudie attempts to have him removed from his living. Finally, John Eames reaches Mrs. Arabin, traveling in Europe, who completely exonerates Crawley and explains the stolen check. Crawley later receives the more profitable living of St. Ewold's.

Grace Crawley, his daughter, in love with Major Henry Grantly. When Mr. Crawley is accused, Henry Grantly feels he must stick by Grace and, despite the fierce objection of his father, he proposes to her. Grace nobly refuses, but, after her father is cleared, she marries Henry.

Mrs. Mary Crawley, the self-sacrificing wife of Mr. Crawley, who copes extremely well with his intransigence and eccentricity.

Bishop Thomas Proudie, bishop of Barchester, a weak man who is harassed by his wife until he agrees to bring Mr. Crawley before a clerical commission.

Mrs. Proudie, wife of the bishop, who believes it her mission to uphold the honor of the Church. She persecutes Crawley and shames her husband by insisting on attending all his conferences. She dies of a heart attack.

Major Henry Grantly, a retired officer and widower with a small daughter. When his father opposes his plans to marry Grace Crawley, he is ready to sell his lodge and move to France.

Archdeacon Theophilus Grantly, archdeacon and wealthy ecclesiastical power in Barchester. He opposes his son's marriage to Grace Crawley.

Susan Grantly, his wife, who tries to keep peace between husband and son.

Francis Arabin, dean of Barchester Cathedral, who has always befriended the Crawleys.

Eleanor Arabin, his wife, whose generosity in stuffing an additional twenty pounds into the envelope for Mr. Crawley inadvertently precipitates the events of the novel. When she hears of the trouble, she immediately returns to give evidence.

Lilian Dale (Lily), a friend of Grace Crawley previously jilted by Adolphus Crosbie. Although Crosbie's wife, Lady Alexandrina, has died, Lily still refuses to allow Crosbie to court her again.

John Eames, now private secretary to Sir Raffle Buffle and the cousin of Grace Crawley. At his own expense, he goes to Italy to find Mrs. Arabin. Although in love with Lily, he barely extricates himself from the clutches of Madalina Demolines.

Bernard Dale, the heir of the squire of Allington, Lily's cousin, who becomes engaged to Emily Dunstable.

Emily Dunstable, cousin of Mrs. Martha Dunstable Thorne, a wealthy heiress.

Mrs. Martha Dunstable Thorne, a jolly social woman who tries to give Henry Grantly the courage to remain loyal to Grace.

Dr. Thomas Thorne, her husband, who sides with the Crawleys.

Christopher Dale, the squire of Allington, who is extremely fond of Grace Crawley.

Mrs. Mary Dale, Lily's mother, who invites Grace to stay at Allington after the magistrate's hearing.

Lady Julia de Guest, the constant benefactor of John Eames.

Lady Lufton, an aristocrat who constantly opposes Mrs. Proudie and defends the Crawleys.

Mr. Soames, Lord Lufton's business agent, who thought he had dropped the check at Hogglestock parsonage.

Adolphus Crosbie, now a widower, in debt to Gagebee, who would like to marry Lily Dale.

Lady Dumbello, the marchioness of Hartletop, also known as **Griselda Grantly**, daughter of the archdeacon, who sides with her father in objecting to Henry's marriage to Grace.

The Reverend Septimus Harding the aged father of Eleanor Arabin, with whom he lives, and Susan Grantly. A warm old man, he requests, on his deathbed, that Crawley be given the living at St. Ewold's.

Edith Grantly, daughter of Major Henry Grantly.

Mr. Thomas Toogood, the lawyer who defends Mr. Crawley.

The Reverend Caleb Trumble, the clergyman Mrs. Proudie sends to take over Mr. Crawley's parish.

The Reverend Dr. Mortimer Tempest, a rural dean and vicar of Silverbridge. He leads the clerical commission investigating the case and thinks that Crawley should be judged by the court before the Church decides about his living.

Miss Madalina Demolines, a young London lady who plots to marry John Eames and writes an anonymous note to Lily Dale.

Lady Demolines, willingly a partner in her daughter's schemes.

Sir Raffle Buffle, the pompous chairman of the Income Tax Office.

Mr. Fletcher, the butcher who received the stolen check.

Mr. Quiverful, a member of the clerical commission and warden of Hiram's Hospital. Mrs. Proudie appoints him to the commission.

The Reverend Caleb Oriel, rector of Greshamsbury and a member of the clerical commission.

The Reverend Mark Robarts, vicar of Framley, a member of the clerical commission.

Mr. Kissing, a silly secretary in the Income Tax Office.

Mr. Peter Bangles, a wine merchant who finally marries Madalina Demolines.

THE LAST DAYS OF POMPEII

Author: Edward Bulwer-Lytton (1803-1873)
First published: 1834
Genre: Novel

Locale: Pompeii
Time: 79 C.E.
Plot: Historical

Glaucus (GLOH-kuhs), a Glaucus, handsome and popular Greek. He is saved from death in the arena by the eruption of Vesuvius; he is saved from death after the eruption by the blind flower girl Nydia.

Clodius (KLOH-dee-uhs), a foppish Roman of Pompeii and a friend of Glaucus.

Nydia (NIH-dee-uh), a blind flower girl from Greece who is hopelessly in love with Glaucus. Through her ability to move in the darkness, she is able to guide Glaucus and Ione to safety aboard a small ship. Then she drowns herself.

Burbo (BUR-boh), a wine seller and the owner of Nydia.

Arbaces (AHR-buh-seez), priest of Isis, who prays for the return of Egypt's power. Meanwhile, he tries to turn his ward Apaecides into a priest and to marry the boy's sister, Ione. He stabs Apaecides and puts the blame on Glaucus, who is then condemned to the arena.

Apaecides (uh-PEE-sih-deez), the ward of Arbaces, converted to Christianity by an earthquake.

Ione (i-OH-nee), a lovely Neapolitan girl, seen and loved by Glaucus.

Diomed (DI-oh-mehd), a wealthy freedman.

Julia (JEWL-yuh), his daughter, in love with Glaucus.

A priest, a witness to the innocence of Glaucus but held prisoner by Arbaces.

Sallust (SA-luhst), a friend of Glaucus, but too drunk to answer Nydia's letter for help. Finally, his appeal to the praetor at the arena causes the crowd to demand that Arbaces be thrown to the lion; before this can take place, however, the fatal earthquake begins.

THE LAST GENTLEMAN

Author: Walker Percy (1916-1990)
First published: 1966
Genre: Novel

Locale: New York City, the South, and the Southwest
Time: Mid-1960's
Plot: Comic realism

Williston Bibb (Will) Barrett, a twenty-five-year-old humidification engineer at Macy's. He is a likable young man from the South who experiences occasional spells of amnesia and disorientation. He worries about his mental health as well as his lack of purpose in life. After two years at Princeton University and five years of unsuccessful psychoanalysis, Barrett is ready to leave New York City when the opportunity arises after his meeting with the Vaught family. Barrett is a seeker after meaning who has lived a life of mere possibility until now, but he thinks he has found the beginning of a commitment when he believes himself to be in love with Kitty Vaught. His more important discoveries come, however, when he is hired as a companion for Jamie Vaught, Kitty's sixteen-year-old brother, who is terminally ill with leukemia. Barrett is the type of metaphysical seeker who is described in the philosophical works of such existentialist philosophers as Søren Kierkegaard and Albert Camus. His name pays homage to American scholar William Barrett, whose *Irrational Man* (1958), a study of existentialism, influenced the author.

Chandler Vaught, a genial millionaire from Alabama who made his money from a gigantic car dealership. Now an elderly man, Vaught is amiable but lacks intellect and self-awareness. He feels disappointed about the behavior of his talented children, each of whom he gives $100,000 on his or her twenty-first birthday. His older son, Sutter, has abandoned a promising medical practice to become an assistant coroner, and his older daughter, Val, has become a member of a religious order. He hopes for better things from Kitty and Jamie, who, because of his illness, will receive his gift at the age of sixteen. Vaught hires Barrett to be Jamie's companion.

Kitty Vaught, a pretty young woman of twenty-one who has received both a good education at expensive preparatory schools and many years of ballet training. She lacks experience with men and a clear purpose in life. Currently, she is a protégée of Rita Vaught, the worldly divorced wife of Sutter; however, Kitty finds Barrett's infatuation with her flattering and confusing. Barrett persuades her to go home with the family instead of touring Europe with Rita. When Kitty joins Jamie and Barrett as students at the university, she begins to acquire the characteristics of a typical college coed.

Rita Vaught, the former wife of Sutter Vaught. Rita is the secretary to a major foundation and an enthusiast of Southwest American Indian and Mexican Indian art. A handsome and experienced woman of thirty, she has made the Vaughts a kind of surrogate family, and Mr. and Mrs. Vaught consider her more responsible than their own children. She is the first to inform Barrett of the true nature of Jamie's terminal illness. Her attempt to bribe Barrett to abandon his interest in Kitty backfires. Her friendship with Kitty may conceal a lesbian interest in the ingenuous Southern girl. She has moved Kitty into her apartment, leaves notes and poems for Kitty at a secret site in Central Park, and plans to take Kitty to Europe for a grand tour. Barrett's appearance threatens to disrupt this relationship.

Jamie Vaught, the younger son of Chandler Vaught, stricken with a terminal case of leukemia at the age of sixteen. A brilliant student in science and mathematics, he has been hospitalized for several weeks, since the time when he was preparing for his secondary school graduation. Jamie tries to live intensely, because he has begun to perceive, without being told, that his life may be short. His meeting with Barrett seems to provide Jamie with new energy, and, after Barrett is hired to be a tutor and companion for him, they attend college classes and take trips together. Their final journey occurs when Sutter,

Jamie's brother, takes Jamie to New Mexico, and the concerned family sends Barrett to follow them. Almost by choice, Jamie dies in the presence of Barrett and Sutter, the two most honest and morally aware people in the novel (except perhaps for his sister, Val).

Valentine (Val) Vaught, the elder daughter of Chandler Vaught. Unlike Kitty, she has chosen a purpose in life: Much to her father's disappointment, she has joined a Roman Catholic order and chosen a vocation as a teacher and social worker among impoverished African Americans in Tyree County, Alabama. A plumpish woman with a pale complexion, Val likes Barrett immediately and attributes some of her social conscience to a speech she once heard his late father deliver. Val places a charge on Barrett to make sure that Jamie will know about the means of Christian salvation when he dies.

Sutter Vaught, the cynical elder son of Chandler Vaught, a medical doctor who has abandoned a promising practice to become an assistant coroner. A thin and abrasive man, Sutter has become more alienated from conventional behavior since his marriage to Rita ended. He has returned to occasional bouts of excessive drinking and womanizing, and he ironically refers to himself as a pornographer in his notebook, which Barrett discovers and reads on his journey to the Southwest. Sutter's private observations, however, treat pornography as a means of analyzing the malaise of the twentieth century. One of his amusements is shooting holes in the walls of his room in the family mansion in Alabama, using his personal pistol. Sutter regards his former profession of medicine with contempt; however, he treats every form of social untruth with disdain, much like the alienated seekers in existentialist fiction. Jamie greatly admires Sutter, and Barrett comes to believe that Sutter is one of the few people he knows who will tell the truth in almost any situation. Sutter precipitates the closing events of the novel by yielding to Jamie's request and taking him away from home and college to New Mexico, where Jamie dies in the presence of Sutter and Barrett.

— *Edgar L. Chapman*

THE LAST MEETING OF THE KNIGHTS OF THE WHITE MAGNOLIA

Author: Preston Jones (1936-1979)
First published: 1976
Genre: Drama

Locale: Bradleyville, Texas
Time: 1962
Plot: Comedy

Ramsey (Ramsey-Eyes) Washington Blankenship, the elderly black custodian of the Cattleman's Hotel. He is an obliging, amiable widower who finds the mumbo jumbo of the Knights of the White Magnolia more amusing than threatening. At seventy-five years of age, he is set in his ways and content with his simple life. He lacks racial bitterness, despite the fact that the Knights, excepting Colonel Kinkaid, treat him with contempt. Although slow and shuffling, he is not the ignorant and illiterate fool they take him to be. In the breakup of the last meeting of the Knights, it is Ramsey-Eyes who remains serenely dignified and triumphant.

Rufe Phelps, a refinery worker. Like most of the Knights, he is narrowly provincial, low-class, and poorly educated. At fifty-five years of age, married but childless, he values the socializing and sense of tradition afforded by the organization. He and Olin Potts, friendly enemies, wage a continual verbal battle. They enter arguing over horseshoes and set the mood for the eventual brawl and collapse of the order. Rufe is also the sponsor of Lonnie Roy McNeil, whose prospective membership infuriates Colonel Kinkaid and adds to the bickering.

Olin Potts, a cotton farmer. Like Rufe, and one year older, he is married but childless. Besides entering into spirited arguments with Rufe, he serves as the group's genealogist. He is able to outline the lineage of nearly anyone in Bradleyville, Texas, but is abysmally misinformed about world events. He and Rufe exit as they entered, arguing over trivial things.

Red Grover, the owner of Red's Place, a small bar and package store. Although a longtime resident of Bradleyville, he remains an outsider, having come from Mississippi. At the age of forty-eight, he is a cynical, bitter bachelor who finds little good in anything. Habitually sarcastic and abrasive, he is arrogant toward Ramsey-Eyes, but his special target is the alcoholic Skip Hampton, whom he despises. The hostility between the two finally erupts into physical violence, ensuring the demise of the chapter.

L. D. Alexander, a supermarket manager and Imperial Wizard of the Knights. Married, with a small family, at forty-nine years of age he has achieved nominal middle-class status. A firm believer in white supremacy, he has the most at stake in keeping the fraternal order united, but all of his efforts to maintain decorum and soothe ruffled egos fail. In the end, even he must face the inevitable.

Colonel J. C. Kinkaid, the owner of the Cattleman's Hotel and a retired U.S. Army officer. At the age of seventy-five, he is an invalid confined to a wheelchair. World War I wounds and shell shock have contributed to his mental disorientation, making him seem hopelessly senile. He endlessly reminisces about his military experiences and often seems unable to relate to current realities. There remain in him vestiges of dignity and honor lacking in the others, and he provides the group a degree of respectability. Although gruff and cantankerous, he is kind to Ramsey-Eyes and values him as a loyal servant, unlike Red Grover, who uses Ramsey-Eyes as a scapegoat. The strain of the bickering and verbal abuse take their toll on him, and his lapse into a comatose state forces the play's climax.

Skip Hampton, a service station attendant. At thirty-one years of age, he already is the town lush. A Korean War veteran who never saw action except in his alcohol-fueled imagination, he seems to resent Colonel Kinkaid, a certified hero; however, he is more pathetic than mean. His alcoholism makes him whine and plead, which infuriates Red Grover. Their disruptive behavior climaxes when Skip attacks Red with what appears to be a knife and Red smashes him in the stomach with a whiskey bottle.

Lonnie Roy McNeil, a pipe fitter and candidate for membership in the Knights. Friendly and eager to join, he is both naïve and simpleminded, a very young twenty-one. After surviving the ordeal of initiation, when all propriety is lost and the meeting begins to turn into a free-for-all, he panics and bolts, never to be seen again.

Milo Crawford, a feed store clerk. At twenty-six years of age, he is shackled to a domineering and demanding mother who is jealous of anything that threatens her hold over him.

Because he is very thin-skinned and defensive about his situation, he is a natural target for the barbs of Red Grover and the rest. In the fray that ends the meeting, even L. D. Alexander insults Milo's mother, sending him off in an indignant huff.

— *John W. Fiero*

THE LAST OF SUMMER

Author: Kate O'Brien (1897-1974)
First published: 1943
Genre: Novel

Locale: Ireland
Time: 1939
Plot: Naturalism

Hannah Kernahans, a strong-willed Irishwoman who seeks to order the world to suit herself. She binds her eldest son to her and, refusing to let him go, uses whatever means she must to hold him. As a young woman, she had been jilted by a suitor who discovered her iron will. She married the suitor's brother but always claimed that it was she who changed her mind.

Tom Kernahans, Hannah's son, who is tied to her. He believes that she is always right, always unselfish, and always serving his best interests. When he breaks off with the woman he loves, he fails to realize that he is doing what his mother planned for him to do for her own selfish interests. Nor does he realize that his mother will not let him marry anyone else. Tom is weak, rather than stupid.

Angèle Maury, Hannah's niece, an actress who is in love with Tom. She is the daughter of the man who jilted Hannah, and the woman fiercely resents the girl. Angèle is torn between her love for Tom, which keeps her in Ireland, and her love for her mother's country, France, which is threatened by war with Nazi Germany. Tom makes the decision for her, and she returns to France.

Martin Kernahans, Tom's brother, a self-reliant, widely traveled student. He is also in love with Angèle, who goes to France with him after Tom, thinking Angèle loves his brother, has released her from their engagement. Martin goes to France because he feels a duty to help protect Europe from the Nazis.

Norrie O'Byrne, a woman who loves Tom deeply. She is used by Tom's mother as bait in getting Tom to break his engagement with Angèle.

THE LAST OF THE BARONS

Author: Edward Bulwer-Lytton (1803-1873)
First published: 1843
Genre: Novel

Locale: England
Time: 1467-1471
Plot: Historical

Marmaduke Nevile, a noble whose father fought for Lancaster. He comes to London to seek service with Warwick.

Nicholas Alwyn, a younger son of a good family, who fights to restore King Edward. He captures Nevile in battle.

Lord Montagu, Warwick's brother, who, as a Yorkist, refuses help to Nevile.

The Earl of Warwick, the kingmaker, who takes Nevile into his household. Insulted by Edward IV, he puts Henry VI on the throne. He is killed at the battle of Barnet.

Isabella, Warwick's haughty older daughter.

Anne, his gentle younger daughter. When lecherous King Edward comes to her bedroom, Warner and Nevile save her.

Edward IV, King of England, deposed by the insulted Warwick.

Henry VI, put on the throne by Warwick but removed by a coalition of the rich merchants and the Yorkists.

William de Hastings, a royal chamberlain to Edward IV. He is in love with Sibyll.

Adam Warner, an alchemist who is working on a model of a steam engine. He and Sibyll are killed during the Wars of the Roses.

Sibyll Warner, his daughter, rescued by Nevile from a crowd. Later, when he is wounded by robbers, she cures him.

The Duchess of Bedford, a patroness of science and of Warner.

Katherine de Bonville, Warwick's sister, who secretly marries Hastings after her husband's death.

THE LAST OF THE JUST
(Le Dernier des Justes)

Author: André Schwarz-Bart (1928-   )
First published: 1959
Genre: Novel

Locale: Poland, Germany, and France
Time: Early 1900's to 1943
Plot: Bildungsroman

Ernie Levy, a furrier's apprentice and one of the thirty-six Just Men. Born in Germany, this second son of Benjamin and Leah Levy studied secular subjects as well as Hebrew and the

Talmud. He is intelligent, sensitive, and loving, so he quickly understands, though at first rejects, the need for martyrdom that pervades the history of the Levys and the Just Men. At the end of 1938, after Nazi persecution erupts, Ernie and his family emigrate to Paris, and he soon enlists in the French army. Following France's defeat and his demobilization, he leads a hidden existence until he is recognized as Jewish. He returns to Paris at the age of twenty, an Unknown Just, an Inconsolable. There, he falls in love with Golda Engelbaum. After she is taken in a Nazi raid, he joins her in the internment camp. In October, 1943, he volunteers to accompany her and a group of children to Auschwitz to console them in their fear and death. In the gas chamber, while comforting them, he addresses a final prayer.

Mordecai Levy, a retired itinerant peddler. He is Ernie's grandfather and the keeper of Levy tradition. In his young adulthood in Poland, he was tall, handsome, full of cheer and humor, and eager to conquer new worlds. After his marriage to Judith Ackerman, whom he dearly loves, he became henpecked, except in matters concerning Ernie's Jewish education.

Judith Levy, a housewife. As a young woman, she was the beautiful daughter of a well-to-do baker, strong-willed, impatient, sensible, and smart. In Germany, she is able to adapt to her new life as she grows in stature and influence, ultimately becoming Mother Judith, the protector of the clan. She and the other Levys all die in a concentration camp.

Benjamin Levy, a tailor. Ernie's father is bright and introspective, wondering about the nature of God and the origin of evil. After surviving a pogrom, he moves first to Berlin and then to Stillenstadt, where he sets up a tailor's shop and marries Leah Blumenthal, with whom he has four children. Like his father before him and his son after him, Benjamin refuses to accept his Just Man status.

Leah Levy, a housewife. Leah is a pleasant young woman, thin and tiny, in awe of her formidable mother-in-law. She desperately seeks reassurance of her own importance in her husband's eyes. Not until their death in the camps, however, does she understand the depth of his feelings.

Golda Engelbaum, Ernie's fiancée. She is a vivacious, pretty, red-haired young woman who, despite her limp and the constant Nazi roundups of Jews, lives to the fullest, perhaps resigned but not bitter. A gay and fantastic storyteller, she is a fine contrast to the serious and thoughtful Ernie. It is after a liberating walk through Paris without the infamous yellow star that they make love in his garret and she becomes his "wife." Later, she is interned at a transit camp and shipped to Auschwitz to die.

Julius Kremer, a schoolteacher. In his thirty-two years of teaching in Stillenstadt, Kremer most enjoys speaking of the civic consciousness presented in the works of Friedrich von Schiller. Because he speaks against Nazi terror, he is accused of loving Jews; because he encourages the budding romance between the Jewish Ernie Levy and the gentile Ilse Bruckner, he is dismissed.

Ilse Bruckner, a pupil. Ilse, a young classmate of Ernie, is a delicate, blond girl, flirtatious but cruel with Ernie, whom she likes for his beatific weakness yet despises for his Jewishness.

The narrator, a friend of Ernie. He writes of Ernie's ancestry in a detached manner at first and comments objectively about universal political cowardice vis-à-vis persecutions of Jews. He soon wearies of so much pain and suffering. Angry with God for abandoning His people, he feels the presence of the six million tormented Jewish souls. He writes the novel to bear witness.

— *Pierre L. Horn*

THE LAST OF THE MOHICANS

Author: James Fenimore Cooper (1789-1851)
First published: 1826
Genre: Novel

Locale: Northern New York State
Time: 1757
Plot: Adventure

Natty Bumppo, called **Hawkeye**, the hardy, noble frontier scout in his prime during the French and Indian Wars. Traveling with his Indian companions, Chingachgook and his son Uncas, in Upper New York, he befriends an English soldier, a Connecticut singing master, and their two female charges. When the travelers are ambushed by hostile Huron warriors, he leaves the party to get help, in turn ambushes their captors with the aid of Chingachgook and Uncas, and leads the group to Fort William Henry, besieged by the French. In the massacre of English that takes place after the garrison is forced to surrender, the girls are captured again by Indians. Hawkeye assists once more in the escape of one of the girls; however, a renegade Huron chief, Magua, claims the other as his reluctant wife. In the ensuing fighting, the girl and Hawkeye's friend, the noble young Uncas, are killed. Hawkeye shoots Magua in return. In the end, he and Chingachgook return sorrowfully to the wilderness.

Chingachgook (chihn-GACH-gook), a courageous, loyal Mohican chief, Hawkeye's inseparable friend. An implacable enemy of the Hurons, he is decorated like a figure of Death.

Left to protect the English colonel after the massacre, he joins the final battle with intense ferocity, only to see his son die. His grief is relieved somewhat by Hawkeye's companionship.

Uncas (UHN-kuhs), Chingachgook's stalwart son, the last of the Mohicans. A young and handsome chieftain, he falls in love with Cora Munro while protecting her and proves invaluable in tracking her after she has been captured. When a Delaware chief awards her to Uncas' rival, Magua, he follows them and is killed avenging her murder.

Major Duncan Heyward, the young English officer in charge of escorting the Munro girls from Fort Edward to Fort William Henry. Brave, good-looking and clever, he falls in love with Alice Munro and eventually succeeds in rescuing her from the Hurons. He finally marries her with Colonel Munro's blessing.

Magua (MA-gyew-uh), "Le Renard Subtil," the handsome renegade Huron chief. Both cunning and malicious, he seeks to avenge himself on Colonel Munro by turning his spirited daughter Cora into a servile squaw. Twice thwarted by Hawkeye and his companions, he wins Cora by putting his case before Tamenund, a Delaware chieftain. This victory, however, is short-lived. Cora is killed by another Huron, and Magua, after killing Uncas, is shot by Hawkeye.

Cora Munro, the colonel's beautiful older daughter. She is independent, equal to every situation, and bears up well under the strain of a capture, a massacre, and the threat of marrying Magua. Her love for Uncas, however, remains unrequited when she is carried off by Magua and then stabbed.

Alice Munro, the colonel's younger daughter, a pale, immature, but lovely half sister of Cora. Frail and clinging, she excites Heyward's protective feelings during their adventures, and he marries her.

Colonel Munro, the able but unsuccessful defender of Fort William Henry and the affectionate father of Cora and Alice. After surrendering to the French, he is forced to watch helplessly the slaughter of the men, women, and children from the fort. His sorrow is doubled when Cora is killed.

David Gamut, a mild, ungainly singing master who accompanies Heyward and the Munro girls. His schoolbook piety contrasts with Hawkeye's natural pantheism. A rather ineffective person, he is nevertheless useful to Hawkeye, for the Hurons believe him insane and let him pass without trouble.

The Marquis de Montcalm, the skilled, enterprising general who captures Fort William Henry and then allows the defeated English to be massacred by savage Hurons.

Tamenund (ta-meh-NUHND), the old Delaware chief who foolishly decides to give Cora to Magua.

Hard Heart, the Delaware chief whom Magua flatters to gain Cora.

General Webb, the incompetent commander of Fort Edward, who refuses to aid Colonel Munro against the French.

A Huron chief, who calls on Heyward, who is impersonating a witch doctor, to cure a relative; he is duped when his captives are released.

LAST OF THE RED HOT LOVERS

Author: Neil Simon (1927-   )
First published: 1970
Genre: Drama

Locale: An apartment in New York City
Time: 1969-1970
Plot: Comedy

Barney Cashman, the forty-seven-year-old owner of a New York seafood restaurant, who is facing a severe midlife crisis. He describes himself as a "nice" man with a "nice" wife, living a "nice," but completely uneventful, life. He has been faithful to his wife during their twenty-three-year marriage, but he has had fantasies. Determined to experience for one afternoon a memorable romantic episode before he dies, he overcomes his timidity and arranges a tryst with an attractive woman who has been a patron at his restaurant. Neither this encounter (act 1), nor the two that follow (acts 2 and 3), are successful, however, so Barney ends as he began, a "nice," thoroughly moral, man.

Elaine Navazio, a somewhat coarse woman in her late thirties who believes, when she accepts Barney's invitation to meet him at his mother's apartment, that he wants only a quick sexual encounter. She is totally unimpressed by his attempts to make anything more than that of their meeting. She says that she indulges in extramarital sexual encounters because they make her feel alive, and she has no sympathy for Barney's needs. She leaves, sarcastically wishing him luck in his quest

for the "impossible dream" and hoping there is a cigarette machine in the lobby.

Bobbi Michele, a twenty-seven-year-old unemployed entertainer who visits Barney to repay twenty dollars that he loaned to her to pay an accompanist who assisted her during an audition. She is an offbeat representative of the "new morality" of the 1960's who regales Barney with her wild stories of coast-to-coast sexual encounters, real and imagined, and persuades her straitlaced friend to join her in getting high on marijuana.

Jeanette Fisher, a contemporary of Barney and a family friend, a very depressed lady who has decided to repay her husband's confession of infidelity by having an affair with Barney. She tells him that she does not find him physically attractive, however, and rambles about the immorality that she finds rampant in society. They argue about whether there are any "decent" people left in the world, and after Barney has pretended to stalk her in an effort to show her some "indecencies," she leaves, chastened, to forgive her husband, Mel.

— *Edythe M. McGovern*

THE LAST OF THE VIKINGS
(Den siste viking)

Author: Johan Bojer (1872-1959)
First published: 1921
Genre: Novel

Locale: Norway
Time: Early nineteenth century
Plot: Regional

Khristaver Myran, a Lofoten fisherman, owner of the *Seal*. He goes into debt to buy his boat but brings her through a difficult fishing season with success. His career makes him feel a veritable son of the Vikings of old.

Lars, Khristàver's son. He dreams of being a Viking. On his first trip to the fishing grounds, he proves himself a man at work and play.

Elezeus Hylla, a crew member of the *Seal*, brother-in-law to Khristàver. He dies of exposure on the fishing expedition.

Kaneles Gomon, a boyish member of the crew. He is vain of his yellow mustache. When the vessel overturns, he is the only man lost.

Arnt Awson, a landlubber who makes his first trip to sea as a fisherman on the *Seal*.

Henry Rabben, a crewman who is vain of his beard.
Peter Suzansa, owner and captain of the *Sea-fire*.
Andreas Ekra, owner and captain of the *Storm-bird*
Jacob Damnit-all-with-a-limp, owner and captain of the

Sea-bird. He rescues the crew of the *Seal* when their vessel overturns.

The Inspector, a government official who enforces the fishing regulations at the fishing grounds.

THE LAST OF THE WINE

Author: Mary Renault (Mary Challans, 1905-1983)
First published: 1956
Genre: Novel

Locale: Athens and the Aegean Sea
Time: 430-402 B.C.E.
Plot: Historical

Alexias, the son of Myron and the central character and narrator. He is dedicated to the Platonic principle of achieving physical and spiritual excellence. He transcends being merely "typical" in his dedication to his ideal and his dedication to his lover-mentor, Lysis. He constantly strives to be honorable as a man and a citizen, but he is willing to sacrifice his honor for the welfare of his family by posing for a sculptor during the siege of Athens. He is sensitive to the difficulties his stepmother faces and tries to be patient and understanding with his father. His patriotism, religious devotion, and commitment to the ideal of excellence are exemplary.

Myron, Alexias' father, an urbane Athenian gentleman. As a moderate in his political views, he genuinely labors to attain good government in Athens and to provide for his family. He can be stubborn and insensitive, especially in his relationship with Alexias, but fundamentally he is a good man dedicated to family and duty.

Lysis, a handsome and sophisticated moral mentor to Alexias. Myron approves him as a lover for his son. The Alexias-Lysis bond is an illustration of the ideal homosexual relationship in which the moral and physical well-being of the beloved supersedes a merely lustful gratification. He is generous to Alexias in his triumph at the Isthmian Games and proves his commitment to Alexias when he tries to support Alexias during the last battle to free Athens, even though he himself is fatally wounded.

Sokrates (SOK-ruh-teez), a moral guide and teacher to Alexias and Lysis. He constantly strives to help his pupils toward their goal of becoming excellent men and citizens, and he risks his own safety to adhere to his principles. He rebukes the powerful Kritias for his lust but guides Alexias to accept Lysis as his lover. He symbolizes Athenian civilization.

Xenophon (ZEHN-uh-fon), Alexias' schoolmate and friend, spartan in his views and character. He is practical, conservative, and soldierly. Alexias calls him an "old-style Athenian knight," because he is so disciplined and rigorously trained. His embracing of the Spartans as allies later in life comes as no surprise. He is loyal and trustworthy.

Kritias, a subverter of Sokrates' teaching. He is less concerned with achieving "goodness" than with advancing himself. He is attracted to the beautiful boy Alexias and tries to seduce him in his own household during Myron's banquet. His unwelcome attentions to Alexias draw Sokrates' scorn. His oratorical skills inflame the citizens to accept tyranny over a more democratic rule. Although once a pupil of Sokrates, he has rejected the quest for inner perfection and masks his crudeness and falsity under the guise of a dedicated politician.

Alkibiades, a flamboyant, controversial politician and general who uses his charisma to charm Athenians. Although he is viewed as "the Goddess's [Athene's] favorite son," he has wandered from the teachings of Sokrates. As both historical figure and character in the novel, he is enigmatic; his most exciting ventures dwindle into failures. Although he is a brilliant strategist with intensely loyal followers, his campaigns are thwarted or his advice is ignored. He is apparently disloyal to Athens but no more committed to the Spartans and Persians who give him refuge.

Plato, a brooding friend to Alexias who joins him as a disciple of Sokrates. He is willing to surrender his aristocratic position to serve Athens but rejects trusting government to the "mob." He reveals his essential kindness when he helps Alexias tend to the injured Lysis at the Isthmian Games.

— *Elizabeth R. Nelson*

THE LAST PICTURE SHOW

Author: Larry McMurtry (1936-   )
First published: 1966
Genre: Novel

Locale: Primarily the fictional West Texas town of Thalia
Time: Mid-1950's
Plot: Comic realism

Sonny Crawford, a teenager who, having no supportive parents or other relatives, lives in a rooming house in Thalia, Texas, and earns a living delivering bottled gas to rural customers. He is reasonably intelligent, though vulnerable and unsophisticated. During his senior year in high school, he terminates a relationship with Charlene Duggs, who has allowed him limited liberties with her body; covets Jacy Farrow, the beautiful, rich girlfriend of Duane; and is seduced by Ruth Popper, the withdrawn, sensitive wife of the high school football coach. After months of seeing Ruth Popper almost daily,

Sonny is easily drawn into a summer romance with Jacy, who has dropped Duane and needs a temporary diversion. Finally, with the closing of the cinema and with Sam's and Billy's deaths, the destruction of Sonny's world is complete. Feeling lost and alone, he returns to Ruth Popper.

Duane Moore, Sonny's best friend, who is also on his own, financially and otherwise. Duane has more appeal for girls than Sonny because of his athletic prowess: His position on the high school football team is in the backfield, whereas Sonny plays in the line. Duane's dreams are bigger than Sonny's.

Madly in love with Jacy Farrow, he assumes that they will be married one day, despite the objections of Jacy's parents. Devastated and confused when Jacy drops him after their senior trip, Duane leaves Thalia temporarily to work in the oil fields of West Texas. He hopes that Jacy will miss him and relent. On a return visit, he injures Sonny in a fight, sees the futility of a reconciliation with Jacy, and eventually enlists in the Army. Duane will not, it seems, be content to live out his life in the North Central Texas village of Thalia.

Sam the Lion, a man in his sixties who takes an interest in Sonny and Duane. Sam owns the local film theater (picture show), café, and pool hall. Most of his time is spent in the pool hall, where he is most in touch with the boys. Sam has a tragic past but has come to terms with it and made a meaningful life for himself in Thalia. He is a source of comfort and emotional support not only for Sonny and Duane but also for Billy, who has become his ward. Sam's long-term affair with Lois Farrow has been her salvation as well.

Herman Popper, Thalia's high school football coach. A big, crude, foulmouthed man, Popper is a latent homosexual. He is totally insensitive to the needs of his wife, Ruth, whom he uses to satisfy his occasional need to dominate a female sexually. Clearly out of fear of his own suppressed feelings, he is quick to publicly accuse other men of suspected deviant behavior. He is incompetent as a coach and as a teacher.

Ruth Popper, a forty-year-old woman unhappily married for twenty years to Herman Popper. Her affair with Sonny Crawford brings her to life. Though devastated when he abandons her in favor of Jacy, she takes Sonny back when he realizes his need for her. Ruth knows that some risks must be taken if she is to have any measure of fulfillment.

Jacy Farrow, a shallow, self-focused high school student. Jacy is the spoiled yet emotionally deprived only child of Lois and Gene Farrow. She is concerned primarily with her looks and with maintaining and enhancing her popularity. She uses Duane and Sonny, among others, as if they are no more human than the stuffed toys in her bedroom. She is a young woman of almost no real substance.

Lois Farrow, the attractive mother of Jacy and an object of physical interest to various men in town. Lois and her husband, Jacy's father, are among the Texans made newly rich by oil. Money notwithstanding, the couple is not happy together. Lois is in love with Sam the Lion, who adores her but will not allow her to divorce her husband for him. Lois seduces Sonny as compensation for his having been cheated of his wedding night with Jacy.

Genevieve, a waitress at Sam's café. Often working the night shift, she is available as a sympathetic listener to Sonny and to Duane when they are most alone and in need of a friend: in the early hours of the morning. Sonny is physically attracted to her but does not reveal his feelings. In his will, Sam leaves Genevieve the café.

Billy, a retarded youth who lives with and is taken care of by Sam. Billy is also generally protected by Sonny and Duane, though they anger Sam by allowing Billy to be the object of a prank. Billy spends his time sweeping the pool hall, the cinema, and the local streets. His daily viewing of the current film gives him his major pleasure, and he, like many others, suffers when the picture show finally closes. He dies in a tragic accident.

— *P. R. Lannert*

THE LAST PURITAN: A Memoir in the Form of a Novel

Author: George Santayana (1863-1952)
First published: 1935
Genre: Novel

Locale: Connecticut, Massachusetts, and England
Time: Early twentieth century
Plot: Social realism

Oliver Alden, a young man who despises human weakness. He is a puritan in spite of himself. He is not prudish or a prig; he simply and truly believes that one must do one's duty, whether it is pleasant or unpleasant. He does not really believe in love, because it is illogical and unreasonable at times; for this reason, he is rejected by the two women to whom, out of a sense of duty, he proposes. At the end of his life, he provides in his will for all the people to whom he feels responsible, but he leaves the largest sum to his mother because he feels it is his duty to do so.

Peter Alden, Oliver's father, who spends most of his life wandering about the world. He marries the daughter of a psychiatrist because the psychiatrist tells him that what he needs to cure his mostly imaginary ills are a home and a wife. He commits suicide in order to free Oliver of a sense of duty toward him.

Harriet Alden, Oliver's mother. She does not allow Oliver to play with other children, because they might be vulgar or dirty, and she allows Oliver no exposure to the frivolities of life.

Fraulein Irma Schlote, Oliver's governess, who gives Oliver a love of nature and of the German language and brings a little light into his childhood.

Jim Darnley, Oliver's closest friend, who is worldly and sophisticated and has no sense of duty whatever. He is killed in the war, adding his wife and child to Oliver's list of responsibilities.

Rose Darnley, Jim's sister, one of the women to whom Oliver proposes. She refuses him because she knows that he is proposing because he feels it is his duty to marry and have children.

Mario Van de Weyer, Oliver's cousin, a romantic young man who lives off his rich relatives. Oliver is greatly puzzled by the fact that Mario does not mind sponging off others. Mario is a happy-go-lucky fellow who immediately enlists when the war breaks out.

Edith Van de Weyer, also Oliver's cousin, to whom he proposes marriage. She refuses him because he forgets to say anything about loving her in his proposal, and she wants more than mere duty in marriage.

Bobby, Jim's illegitimate son, for whom Oliver provides in his will.

THE LAST TEMPTATION OF CHRIST
(Ho teleutaios peirasmos)

Author: Nikos Kazantzakis (1883-1957)
First published: 1955
Genre: Novel

Locale: Israel
Time: First century C.E.
Plot: Psychological realism

Jesus, a carpenter and cross-maker, the son of Mary and the carpenter Joseph. A troubled youth, full of fear and rebelliousness, and tormented by "vulture claws" seemingly sent from God, he is also possessed by a strong pity for humanity. Continually tempted to be something other than who he really is, he grows as he journeys from home to the monastery, where he loses much of his guilt, and turns to preaching love to the people. Later, his trials and visions in the desert convince him that the rotten tree of the world must be felled by ax and fire. Eventually, he becomes obsessed by death, knowing that his own is necessary. When he awakes from his final nightmare of a compromised life and finds himself on the cross, he is filled with a hero's joy.

Judas Iscariot, a blacksmith. Committed to the cause of Israel and a member of the fierce Zealots, he can kill and, in fact, is commissioned to kill Jesus. He hesitates because he suspects that Jesus may be the One. A man of action who challenges and finally comes to love the man of contemplation, Jesus, he is the only disciple with the necessary endurance to assist the Messiah in his sacrificial death.

Mary, the wife of Joseph of Nazareth and the mother of Jesus. Past her youth, she continually grieves because of the agitation her paralytic husband and possessed son cause her. Preoccupied with her own pain, she prays that her son live a normal life and be a family man, not a saint.

Joseph, a carpenter. Paralyzed since his wedding day, he has spent each day since in convulsive, sputtering efforts to pronounce the syllables of God's name: A-do-na-i. His strangled impotence, a powerfully drawn symbol of Israel, torments the youthful Jesus.

Zebedee, a fisherman, the father of John and Jacob. He is called "old stuff-pockets" by his "adopted sons" and neighbors. He fears the poor and despises the young cross-maker. A landowner and town elder, he subscribes to a simplistic pragmatism. He is obedient to the law but impatient with ideas of sharing wealth. His house becomes the staging area for Jesus and his disciples as they plan their campaigns. Gradually, his heart is softened and his mind "lightly intoxicated" by Jesus' teachings.

Mary Magdalene, Jesus' childhood playmate and adolescent sweetheart. Her fall into harlotry, Jesus believes, is his fault. Like Jesus, she begins in rebellion but comes to understand something of his mission, and they are reconciled.

Simeon, a rabbi. He is another struggler, seeking to understand the seven levels of scriptural meaning. Promised by God that he will see the Son of Man in his lifetime, he watches over Jesus from infancy, knowing that his is a life of "nothing but miracles" but baffled as to its direction.

Peter, the son of Old Jonah and brother of Andrew. He responds to Jesus' call, despite his uncertainties, finding his ordinary life as a fisherman suffocating. Frustrated by his own indecisiveness, he nevertheless makes it possible for Jesus to elucidate the mystery of their mission precisely because, in his confusion, he asks many questions. It is Peter who sees visions and understands that the New Law is salvation for all the world, not for Israel alone.

Matthew, a customs officer and publican. Brought into the group of disciples by Jesus, he feels the heavy responsibility of recording for future generations the words and miracles of his holy man, and he hears the rustle of an angel's wings at his right hand, guiding his words. Both Matthew and Jesus himself resist the angel's version until Jesus pauses to reflect that humankind's truth could be what God calls lies.

The guardian angel, a figure who appears to Jesus as he hangs on the cross. Later, taking the form of a small black person, this figure guides Jesus into a life of domestic contentment.

Tiny old men, shrunken disciples who return, at the culmination of the final dream sequence, wounded and dispirited, to denounce Jesus for betraying them and to remind him of what he had taught them: That life was made for wings.

— *Rebecca R. Butler*

THE LAST TYCOON

Author: F. Scott Fitzgerald (1896-1940)
First published: 1941
Genre: Novel

Locale: Hollywood, California
Time: The 1930's
Plot: Social realism

Monroe Stahr, a brilliant, young film producer, as much interested in the artistic value of motion pictures as in making money. Having lost his wife whom he had loved deeply, he now courts death through overwork. He is extremely interested in the welfare of his employees, although he is not always appreciated by them. His short but passionate affair with Kathleen seems to be at the center of this unfinished novel.

Kathleen Moore, Stahr's mistress, who reminds him of his dead wife. She later marries another man out of a sense of obligation but continues her affair with Stahr.

Pat Brady, Stahr's partner. Interested only in making money, Brady is a cold and calculating man. He often opposes Stahr's policies although he understands almost nothing of the technical end of the industry.

Cecilia Brady, Pat's daughter, the narrator of the story. She falls in love with Stahr, but he pays no attention to her. After an affair with another man, she suffers a complete breakdown; she relates the story from a tuberculosis sanatorium.

Wylie Whyte, a screenwriter who tries to marry Cecilia and thus gain her father's influence.

Pete Zavras, a cameraman whom Stahr helps to find work. He later helps Stahr when Kathleen's husband finds out she is having an affair.

Schwartz, a ruined producer who commits suicide.

THE LATE GEORGE APLEY: A Novel in the Form of a Memoir

Author: John Phillips Marquand (1893-1960)
First published: 1937
Genre: Novel

Locale: Boston, Massachusetts
Time: Late nineteenth and early twentieth centuries
Plot: Naturalism

George William Apley, a proper Bostonian carefully trained since childhood to be a respectable member of Boston Brahmin society. Though as a college student he belittled the Brahmin pride of family, he acquired it himself as he matured, and later he attempted to pass it on to his children. Undistinguished academically at Harvard, he had been active in campus affairs and a member of a select club. Unfit for active business, he derived his income from investments and from his father's substantial legacy. Though he admired Ralph Waldo Emerson's writings, he never became an Emersonian nonconformist; in fact, he believed that the individual in society must submit to the common will. Like his father and his Uncle William, he was a generous giver to worthy causes.

John Apley, his son, who stirred George's heart with pride over his war service, including a wound, and who later married a woman of good family. It was John who requested the writing of his father's life story.

Eleanor Apley, George's daughter. She greatly disappointed George by marrying a journalist.

Catharine Bosworth Apley, his wife, whose marriage to George was unexciting but successful. According to his sister Amelia, George simply let Catherine and her family dominate him.

Mr. Willing, George Apley's biographer, staid, polished, and politely dull. Like George himself, Mr. Willing is snobbish, for he is also a Brahmin. In accordance with John's request, he includes along with George's commendable characteristics and actions some derogatory and unsavory details in his life, but he attempts to excuse these as minor aberrations in an essentially admirable man.

Mary Monahan, an attractive girl whose love affair with George ended when George's parents removed him from such a lower-class association.

William Apley, George's uncle, a wealthy businessman who spent little on himself and scorned ostentation but who was secretly a generous philanthropist. He controlled the Apley mills and opposed labor unions. When he was more than eighty years old, he shocked the family by marrying his nurse.

Amelia Apley, George's sister. She was more independent and forceful than George.

O'Reilly, a lawyer who tricked George into a scandal.

Horatio Apley, holder of a diplomatic post in Rome.

Thomas Apley and

Elizabeth Hancock Apley, George's parents.

Miss Prentiss, the young nurse whom Uncle William married.

Newcomb Simmings, Amelia Apley's husband.

Louise Hogarth Apley, John's wife. She is a divorcee, but when George learns that she is from a fine family, he is satisfied with her.

William Budd, Eleanor's husband.

THE LATE MATTIA PASCAL
(Il fu Mattia Pascal)

Author: Luigi Pirandello (1867-1936)
First published: 1904
Genre: Novel

Locale: Italy
Time: Early twentieth century
Plot: Psychological realism

Mattia Pascal (maht-TEE-ah PAHS-kahl), a young Italian who undergoes the experience of living two different lives. Forced into an unhappy marriage with Romilda Pescatore, he flees on impulse and in Monte Carlo makes a sizable coup at the gaming tables. On his way home, he hears that the body of a dead man has been identified by his wife as his own. Thus he is free to become another man, and he decides that this man will be called **Adriano Meis** (ahd-REE-ah-noh mayees). A large portion of the novel concerns the failure of "Adriano" to achieve a sense of identity. As "Adriano," Mattia is both a legal and psychological nonentity, but his anomalous position can be corrected only by assuming the hardly more real identity of the "late Mattia Pascal." Returning to his village after staging a fake suicide, he learns that Romilda has married again. Not wishing to create new problems in this domestic situation, he settles down to a quiet, retiring life. Mattia's chief quality as the teller of his own story is ironical detachment from both of his identities.

Batty Malagna (mah-LAHN-nyah), the cheating steward of Mattia's widowed mother. He is chiefly responsible for thrusting Mattia into his unhappy marriage.

Signora Marianna Dondi-Pescatore (DOHN-dee-pehs-kah-TOH-ray), the old harridan who becomes Mattia's mother-in-law. Having driven Mattia away on his adventures, she is dismayed and alarmed by his return after he has been presumed dead.

Romilda Pescatore, Mattia's wife and after his supposed death the wife of his best friend, Gerolamo Pomino. She is a beautiful woman of no moral integrity, and in spite of the law and her marriage vows, she has no desire to take up with Mattia after his reappearance.

Don Eligio Pellegrinotto (eh-lee-JEE-oh pehl-leh-gree-NOHT-toh), an aged priest and librarian who encourages Mattia to write the account of his startling adventures.

Roberto Pascal, Mattia's brother. He marries well and has no desire to help either his widowed mother or Mattia. After Mattia's reappearance, he underlines the legal problems facing a man who has been legally declared dead.

The Cavaliere Tito Lenzi (TEE-toh LEHN-zee), a chance acquaintance of "Adriano." The fantasies of the older man and his useless learning warn Mattia of the emptiness of a rootless life.

Adriana Paleari (pah-leh-AH-ree), a virtuous and devout Roman woman. She is attracted to Mattia but cannot understand the ambiguousness of his position. Not knowing that it is impossible for Mattia to go to the police because of his false identity, she is dumbfounded when he refuses to prosecute her brother-in-law for theft.

Anselmo Paleari, Adriana's father and Mattia Pascal's landlord. A confirmed spiritualist, he is behind the séances that lead to Mattia's final catastrophe in his life as "Adriano Meis."

Terenzio Papiano (teh-rehn-ZEE-oh pah-pee-AH-noh), Adriana's scoundrelly brother-in-law. He robs Mattia to get the money he needs to repay the dowry of his dead wife.

Silvia Caporale (kah-poh-RAH-lay), a middle-aged Roman music teacher. She is the confidant of Adriana and tries, by persuasion and séance, to bring Mattia to the point of proposing marriage.

The Marquis Giglio d'Auletta (jee-LYEE-oh dah-ew-LEHT-tah), Terenzio Papiano's employer. He hopes to refound the Kingdom of the Two Sicilies.

Pepita Pantagoda (peh-PEE-tah pahn-tah-GOH-dah), the granddaughter of the Marquis Giglio d'Auletta. Her vanity almost involves Mattia in a duel.

Manuel Bernaldez (mahn-WEHL behr-NAHL-dehs), a Spanish painter. He paints a portrait of Pepita's dog and threatens to fight a duel with Mattia.

Francesco Meis, a supposed relative of Adriano Meis. Meeting him frightens Mattia Pascal.

LAUGHING BOY

Author: Oliver La Farge (1901-1963)
First published: 1929
Genre: Novel

Locale: Arizona and New Mexico
Time: 1915
Plot: Regional

Laughing Boy, also called **Sings Before Spears**, a youthful, talented Navajo Indian from a Southwestern reservation. Because he has not been exposed to white society and schooling, he is known as a "blanket Indian." His primary interests are crafting jewelry, raising sheep, and racing horses. An outdoor type, he is a man of action rather than of words. In contests with friends and foes, he is cheerful, highly competitive, and usually successful. He knows and respects tribal culture and mores and has the capacity for deep romantic love.

Slim Girl, also called **Came with War**, a young, beautiful, and energetic Indian woman of mixed Navajo and Apache descent. She is somewhat extroverted, highly intelligent, bold, wily, and cheerful. Having been sent to a white school as a child, she is divided between cultures in conflict. First loving and then marrying Laughing Boy, she perceives him as a means of fulfilling her dream of returning to the reservation. Having experienced unhappiness and misfortune in white culture, she learns all that she can about her Indian heritage from Laughing Boy.

Jesting Squaw's son, a young Navajo friend of Laughing Boy who shares his exuberance, high spirits, and competitive activities. Like Laughing Boy, he is a reservation or blanket Indian. His profound sense of guilt over breaking a tribal taboo reflects the degree of his dedication to Navajo culture.

Two Bows, Laughing Boy's father, a Navajo craftsman of middle age, a man of dignity, taciturnity, and reserve. A talented jewelry maker himself, he has taught the art to his son and offers him encouragement and generous praise. In large

measure, he represents a masculine ideal among reservation Indians.

Red Man, a treacherous, vengeful young Navajo, an introverted and malcontent villain. His loss of Slim Girl to Laughing Boy arouses his jealous anger and spirit of revenge.

Yellow Singer, an elderly Navajo who lives on the fringe of white society and has been thoroughly corrupted by it. Although usually intoxicated, he recalls the Indian ceremonies and performs the marriage rite for Slim Girl and Laughing Boy.

Killed a Navajo, Laughing Boy's uncle, a middle-aged reservation Indian. A stickler for Indian customs, he lives in a hogan. During Laughing Boy's visit to the reservation, he attempts unsuccessfully to dissuade him from marrying Slim Girl.

Narrow Nose, an inexperienced American trading post owner who becomes an object of scorn to the Navajo. He lacks both patience and understanding; thus, the Indians' haggling, sharp dealing, and occasional thievery exasperate him.

George, an American rancher from the East who lives near the reservation. He takes Slim Girl for his mistress, not knowing that she cares only for the money he provides. Ironically, he has genuine affection for her and attempts to persuade her to adopt American ways. The relationship is broken when Laughing Boy, having discovered it, wounds him with an arrow.

— *Stanley Archer*

LAUGHTER IN THE DARK
(Kamera obskura)

Author: Vladimir Nabokov (1899-1977)
First published: 1932
Genre: Novel

Locale: Berlin, the south of France, and Switzerland
Time: Late 1920's or early 1930's
Plot: Love

Albert Albinus, an independently wealthy German art collector and art critic. This shy, scholarly, middle-aged family man lives a staid upper-middle-class existence but has always longed for a passionate love affair. He foolishly falls in love with a trollop half his age whose treachery causes him to lose his wife, his daughter, his eyesight, much money, and finally his life. He is a well-meaning, good-natured victim of his repressed libido. Most of the story is told through his point of view.

Margot Peters, an usherette who becomes Albinus' mistress. Although only eighteen years old and looking more like sixteen, she has grown up in a tough environment and has had considerable worldly experience. She has been a prostitute and a kept woman. She is beautiful and bursting with sex appeal, however, which is why she captivates Albinus. She has no affection for him but tries to get him to divorce his wife and marry her. Her fierce motivation to escape from her sordid lower-class background, to live in luxury, and to have a film career provides the main impetus for the action in the novel. She is the personification of the adage that beauty is only skin deep.

Axel Rex, a talented but improvident painter and cartoonist. He is about the same age as Albinus and shares his artistic tastes; otherwise, his character is diametrically opposite. He is ruthless and sadistic; however, he has the ability to charm most people, including Albinus. Although Rex is described as strikingly ugly, with hollow cheeks, thick lips, and dull white skin, he appeals to women like Margot because of his uninhibited animal nature. They are soulmates: His external ugliness mirrors her internal ugliness. Being more clever and daring than Margot, he provides leadership in duping Albinus and cheating him out of his money. When Albinus loses his eyesight in an auto accident, Rex takes malicious delight in moving into his home and making love to Margot in front of the blind man. This hateful but fascinating character provides a new twist to the old story of the infatuated middle-aged lover's downfall.

Paul, Albinus' brother-in-law, a fat, unimaginative, highly conventional man who is devoted to his sister and her family and is there for dinner practically every night. After Albinus deserts Elizabeth, he acts as her protector and adviser. He also tries to be a father to his young niece. He is infuriated by his brother-in-law's behavior but eventually rescues him from the clutches of the unscrupulous Margot and Axel Rex.

Elizabeth Albinus, Albinus' wife, a good homemaker and mother but cool, refined, and uninspiring as a sexual partner. She is the hapless victim of Albinus' infidelity; however, her bland personality makes it understandable that he might be drawn into an affair with a more passionate woman.

Irma Albinus, the eight-year-old daughter of Albert and Elizabeth. She dies of pneumonia indirectly as a result of her father's desertion. Although her death makes him feel consumed with guilt, he still cannot break free of Margot and return to his bereaved wife, as he knows he should.

— *Bill Delaney*

LAVENGRO: The Scholar—The Gypsy—The Priest

Author: George Henry Borrow (1803-1881)
First published: 1851
Genre: Novel

Locale: England, Scotland, and Ireland
Time: The nineteenth century
Plot: Autobiographical

George, the narrator, who is called "Lavengro," the Zingary gypsy word for "word master" or "philologist." In this romance of circumstantial incidents and philosophical conversations, George is in search of something in which to believe. As a child, he moves about with his family. Apprenticed to a lawyer, he is convinced that authorship is his calling. Always mindful of his surroundings—nature, people, things—George goes through the strain of establishing himself in London, getting some of his writing accepted, and leaving the city to become a gypsy. His circumstantial relationships with various associates constitute the theme that no man is an island. George passes through the stages of scholar, writer, and tinker.

Lavengro's Father, an army officer. His influence on his son is manifest in two ways. The father's gift of books, including *Robinson Crusoe*, to his young son turns George's interest to reading. George's escapade in fighting can be traced to his early recollection of his father's having fought for an hour with a swarthy individual, Big Ben Brain. Typical of the barrier between father and his sensitive child is the father's lack of understanding of his second son's interests and his preference for George's older brother.

John, George's older brother, an artist.

Jasper Petulengro, George's gypsy friend. From childhood, George and Mr. Petulengro meet intermittently. Their first meeting is in a gypsy camp near George's home, when he attracts the young Jasper with a de-fanged viper. At successive meetings, Mr. Petulengro offers George a home with the gypsies, avenges his mother-in-law's death by fighting with George, and teaches George to make horseshoes so that he may sustain himself on the road.

Isopel Berners (Belle), George's companion in the gypsy camp when he turns tinker. The handsome young woman is the illegitimate child of a gypsy mother and a noble father. At their first meeting, Belle instructs George in defending himself against a gypsy with whom she is roaming and who wants to steal George's tinker supplies. George and Belle's platonic relationship is the essence of beauty as they sustain themselves by peddling George's wares. She is also in search of something beyond her present condition. They live fully as they converse in the dingle with the various passers-by who stop to discuss religions, nationalities, words, and dreams of far-off places.

Mrs. Herne, also **Hearne**, Petulengro's mother-in-law, who takes a violent dislike to George. Biding her time, some years later Mrs. Herne gives him poisoned food. Seeing that he is not going to die, the old crone jabs at his face, attempting to blind him. Unsuccessful, she commits suicide because of her loss of face resulting from her failed attempts at murder.

Peter Williams, a Welsh evangelist. He happens by at the time of George's poisoning and sees George restored to health. Hearing Peter's harangue of self-condemnation for having sinned against the Holy Ghost, George gives his benefactor a new view of himself and his evangelistic work. Believing in his own goodness, Peter goes back to Wales to continue preaching the gospel.

Winifred, his wife, whose compassion toward her husband and his guilt feelings is supported by George's attitudes. The Williamses try to get George to travel and work with them in their evangelism, but the young tinker declines their offer in order to continue his own search for truth.

Francis Ardry, George's associate in London. A young man of means being groomed for Parliament, he shows George, in his period as a writer, the night spots of London.

Glorious John, a wealthy Armenian publisher in London and George's friend. After a long period of conversations on writing, translating, and relationships among peoples, George loses his friend through philosophizing that had he the Armenian's wealth, he would fight the Persians in their oppression of the Armenians. This chance remark provokes Glorious John's unceremonious departure for his home country.

The Apple Woman, an old vendor at London Bridge. A rare book owned by the apple woman plays a big part in the story. Given to George, who will exchange the book for a Bible, the book is stolen. The theft and the grand price the thief unwittingly receives for the rare volume is a lesson, from the thief, to George in his subsequent bartering.

The Flaming Tinman, a tinker who accosts George to take his tinker supplies from him. Called "the Blazing Bosville" by Belle, the Tinman, a bully of the roads, has driven other tinkers out of business. George's defiance of the Tinman is abetted by Belle, who leaves the company of the Tinman and Moll, his wife, to stay with George.

Jack Slingsby, the tinker whom George bought out as he starts on the last stage of his search. Slingsby has been forced out of business by the threats of the Tinman.

The Man in Black, a patron of the public house near George and Belle's dingle, who comes to the camp at night to talk.

LAWD TODAY

Author: Richard Wright (1908-1960)
First published: 1963
Genre: Novel

Locale: The South Side of Chicago
Time: The 1930's
Plot: Naturalism

Jake Jackson, a Chicago post office employee. A relatively young, round-faced, dark-skinned black man, Jake is angry, frustrated, and full of contradictions. He left Mississippi to escape the racial prejudice there, but he does not find his desired personal freedom and affirmation in Chicago. Although he is a Republican admirer of successful whites such as John D. Rockefeller and is contemptuous of the poor, he is deeply in debt and retains his job only as the result of political payoffs. At one moment, he sentimentalizes about the beneficence of whites, but at the next, he floods over with anger at their meanness. His hatred of anti-American radicals gives way to his feeling that Uncle Sam holds back his black nephews. Jake is a detestable man in many ways, but he is also a man trapped by racism, economic depression, and a failed marriage. As one day in the life of Jake Jackson ends, he lies bleeding in a drunken sleep.

Lil Jackson, Jake's wife. Lil, a good-natured woman, is fully alive only when Jake is away. She married him at the age of seventeen, when, according to Jake, she tricked him by claiming to be pregnant. Later, she did become pregnant, and he tricked her into an abortion, which led to the "female problems" that prevent her from having sex. Lil, trapped like Jake in a dead-end, bleak existence, tells him as he wakes on Abraham Lincoln's birthday that she has a tumor and needs an expensive operation. He spends most of their money on his own appearance and entertainment. Verbally and physically abused by Jake, she reports him to the post office. After he beats her again that night and she cuts him, the novel

closes with Lil saying to herself, "Lawd, I wish I was dead."

Albert (Al) Johnson, another post office employee. Al, a fat and dark-skinned African American, works hard, saves his money, and is the least depressed of the four friends. He is secure in his belief that he will amount to something someday.

Robert (Bob) Madison, another post office employee. Bob's apartment provides the friends with the setting for their bridge games. He spends the day in pain from untreated gonorrhea and is the focus of the friendly banter of his pals. He is divorced and complains about the alimony payments he must make. He and his friends spend most of their leisure and work time together, chatting about sex, racial mores, sports, the meaning of life and death, and their dreams of the future.

Nathan "Slim" Williams, another post office employee, the fourth of the close friends. Slim is a tall, slender womanizer who suffers from tuberculosis. His work at the post office is killing him, but he is trapped by lack of money and cannot leave. Slim and his three friends are rather naïve men who can quickly convince themselves that Father Divine, the black religious leader of the 1930's, may really be God, that whites are humane and smart, and that black people have only themselves to blame for their problems. They are also aware of racial oppression and white hypocrisy, and they are conscious that they live in a warped world that imposes its ambiguities and contradictions on them.

Doc Higgins, an older man who runs a barbershop. He shares Jake's dismissal of Duke's communism and his acceptance of the capitalist philosophy of self-help. He has influence in corrupt local politics.

Duke, an idealistic young man who tries to convince Doc that the problem of unemployment cannot be solved by self-help. He, like Doc, appears in a minor role to comment on

race, politics, and the Great Depression. Their comments, taking place on Lincoln's birthday, contrast the promise of slave emancipation with the reality of racist suppression and warping of black lives.

— *William E. Pemberton*

THE LAY OF IGOR'S CAMPAIGN
(Slovo o polku Igoreve)

Author: Unknown
First published: c. 1187
Genre: Poetry

Locale: The Russian steppes
Time: Late twelfth century
Plot: Romance

Prince Igor Svyatoslavich (ee-GOHR svya-toh-SLAH-vihch), the ruler of the city of Novgorod-Seversk. He leads his troops against the Polovetsians in 1185. He is the grandson of Oleg, prince of Chernigov, and the son of Svyatoslav of Chernigov. Although he is the title character, Igor's stature as a hero is sometimes questioned, but his courage is never in doubt. He foolishly ignores the bad omen of the solar eclipse in assaulting the Polovetsians, but the initial encounter is successful. Igor refers to his troops as "friends" and "brothers," and he is likened to a "mother bird." When Igor's troops are defeated by the heathens, Russia is left open to their raids, and the poet suggests that Igor's "willfulness" cost them the battle. When Igor escapes with the aid of a Polovetsian named Ovlur, he is compared to an ermine, a white duck, a gray wolf, and a falcon, and his return is celebrated. The poet says that as it is hard for the body to exist without a head, so it is difficult for Russia without Igor.

Prince Vsevolod Svyatoslavich (VSEH-voh-lod), Igor's brother, known as the **Wild Ox**. He is perhaps even hungrier for glory than is Igor. He stands "at the head of all,/ Flinging arrows at the enemy" and striking them down with his sword. His golden helmet flashes among the Polovetsian troops, and he appears to be reckless in his daring. Their defeat comes when the brothers are parted during the battle, and the poet says that Vsevolod, too, is guilty of "willfulness." The real Vsevolod from history also managed to escape, but no mention is made of that in the poem.

Yaroslavna (yah-roh-SLAHV-nah), Igor's wife, who in her lament for her lost husband offers some of the best poetic passages in the tale, which is often described as a "prose

poem." (The Russian *slovo*, or word, usually is translated as "lay" or "song.") In her lament, she weeps and appeals to God. The way the tale is structured, the poet makes it seem that her prayers have been answered, for the next section concerns Igor's escape.

Boyan, a bard or minstrel of the past whose poetic powers were so great that he was regarded as a wizard. He never directly appears in the poem but is mentioned several times. Hailed as the "nightingale of olden times," Boyan is represented as both poet and wise man, and he is invoked in both the introductory and concluding sections of the tale, so that he serves a function similar to that of the traditional muse.

Oleg Svyatoslavich, the prince of Chernigov and grandfather of Igor and Vsevolod. He is mentioned briefly after the initial victory but is associated with civil war and discontent. His function might be to set the stage for the impending disaster.

Svyatoslav (svya-toh-SLAHV), the grand prince of Kiev and cousin of Igor and Vsevolod. He appears in two sizable passages after the defeat, first to tell of a nightmare and then to pronounce the so-called Golden Word. The dream concerns the lost "falcons," Igor and Vsevolod, to whom he addresses the Golden Word, to the effect that they went into battle too soon and therefore failed to achieve glory even as they turned his hair gray with worry. Primarily, he laments the evils of the time and reflects on other Russian princes who have contributed to civil strife and left the motherland vulnerable to pagan invasion.

— *Ron McFarland*

THE LAY OF THE LAST MINSTREL

Author: Sir Walter Scott (1771-1832)
First published: 1805
Genre: Poetry

Locale: The Scottish border
Time: Mid-sixteenth century
Plot: Historical

Sir William of Deloraine, a knight who has served the lord of Branksome. When Branksome is killed in a battle against the English, Deloraine remains faithful to the memory of his leader and stays on to serve Lady Buccleuch, Branksome's widow. Returning from a mission to get a magic book, Deloraine fights Lord Cranstoun, Branksome's former enemy who is in love with Branksome's daughter. Deloraine falls wounded. He recovers and lives to see harmony restored between the Scots and the English.

Lady Buccleuch, Lord Branksome's widow, the daughter of a magician. Spirits tell her that Branksome Castle is doomed unless pride dies and frees love. Lady Buccleuch does not heed the spirits at first. Finally, however, when Deloraine's life may be lost and when her son may be taken from her, she relents. Her change of heart, shown by the blessing she gives to the love of her daughter Margaret for Lord Cranstoun, the late Lord Branksome's enemy, brings peace to Branksome Castle and the Scottish border.

Lord Cranstoun, a knight who fought against Lord Branksome but who loves Margaret, Branksome's daughter. Cranstoun, having wounded Deloraine, makes amends by donning Deloraine's armor and fighting, as that knight, against an English champion. When he wins, the English forces retire, Lady Buccleuch blesses his suit for Margaret's hand, and Deloraine has leisure for his wounds to heal.

The Dwarf, an evil magician devoted to Lord Cranstoun. The Dwarf causes mischief at Branksome Castle by posing as the Master of Buccleuch. At a banquet, the Dwarf is killed by a thunderbolt, and in the eerie light Deloraine sees the form of the dead wizard, Michael Scott, whose book Lady Buccleuch had sent Deloraine to bring from Melrose Abbey.

The ghost of Michael Scott, a wraith whose activities complicate the lives of those who live at Branksome Castle. At the end, Branksome's knights make pilgrimages to pray for rest for Michael Scott's soul.

Margaret, Lady Buccleuch's daughter and Cranstoun's beloved.

The Master of Buccleuch, Lady Buccleuch's son, a small boy.

LAZARILLO DE TORMES
(La vida de Lazarillo de Tormes y de sus fortunas y adversidades)

Author: Unknown
First published: 1553
Genre: Novel

Locale: Spain
Time: The sixteenth century
Plot: Picaresque

Lazarillo de Tormes (lah-sah-REE-yoh deh TOHR-mehs), so named because he was born in a mill over the River Tormes. Bereaved at an early age by the death of his father, Lazarillo is given by his impoverished mother to his first master, a blind beggar whose cruelty is precisely the kind of education the unfortunate lad needs to remove his naïvete and prepare him to exist in a cruel world that promises only hardships for him. Treated cruelly, Lazarillo learns all the tricks of providing himself with food and drink. Becoming sharp and witty, although keeping his good nature, he develops the ability to please people and impress them. He is a kindhearted, generous lad, though his environment might well train him in the opposite direction. He is what may be best described as one of nature's gentlemen. Given an opportunity by a kindly chaplain, Lazarillo settles down to an honest career as a water carrier. A diligent worker, he saves enough money to become respectable. Another friend, the archpriest of St. Savior's Church in Toledo, provides Lazarillo with an opportunity to marry an honest and hardworking woman who gives her husband no trouble, though gossip, until silenced by Lazarillo, tries to make out that the young woman is the archpriest's mistress. By his wit, competence, and industry, Lazarillo thrives and becomes a government inspector of wines at Toledo, a post that provides him with comfort and self-respect, if not affluence or great honor.

Antonia Pérez Goncales (ahn-TOH-nyah PEH-rehs gohn-SAH-lehs), Lazarillo's mother. A good but poor woman, she faces adversity following the death of her husband. To help her keep alive and provide for her small son, she takes a Moorish lover, by whom she has a dark-skinned child. After her lover's conviction for theft, she is thrown upon her own meager resources, at which time she tries to provide for Lazarillo by putting him in the service of a blind beggar.

Thome Goncales (TOH-meh), Lazarillo's father, a miller. Convicted of fraud and theft, he enters military service and is killed shortly thereafter in a battle with the Moors, while Lazarillo is a small child.

The Zayde (SI-deh), a stable master for the comendador de la Magdalena. He is a Moor who becomes the lover of Lazarillo's mother. Being a poor man, the Zayde steals to provide for his mistress and the two children, Lazarillo and his half brother. His thievery discovered, the unhappy man is punished brutally and forbidden to see his adopted family.

The Blind Beggar, Lazarillo's first master. He treats Lazarillo cruelly from the first, beating the boy and starving him. He is a clever man who imparts his knowledge of human nature to the boy. No better master could have been found to acquaint Lazarillo with the rigors of life for a poor boy in sixteenth century Spain, though Lazarillo realizes this fact only later in life; as a boy, he becomes bitter toward the man.

The Penurious Priest, Lazarillo's second master, who also starves the lad and keeps up a battle for months to prevent his acolyte from stealing either food or money; he has little success against the ingenious Lazarillo.

The Proud Squire, Lazarillo's third master. A man of honor, he starves himself rather than admit he is without money. Lazarillo joins him in the expectation of finding a rich master, only to learn he must beg on behalf of his master as well as for himself. Eventually the squire, besieged by creditors, disappears.

The Friar, Lazarillo's fourth master, who is so busy and walks so far each day that Lazarillo leaves him after a few days.

The Seller of Papal Indulgences, a hypocritical pardoner who knows, like Geoffrey Chaucer's famous Pardoner, all the tricks to part poor Christians from their money. He is a fraud in every way, but he has little effect on the quite honest Lazarillo.

The Chaplain, Lazarillo's sixth master and first real benefactor. He gives Lazarillo work as his water carrier, enters into a partnership with the lad, and provides Lazarillo with a mule and the other necessities of his work.

The Archpriest of St. Savior's Church, a good and benevolent clergyman who helps Lazarillo to preferment and becomes his friend. He introduces Lazarillo to his future wife.

Lazarillo's Wife, a former servant of the archpriest. She gives birth to Lazarillo's child, a daughter.

LAZARUS LAUGHED

Author: Eugene O'Neill (1888-1953)
First published: 1927
Genre: Drama

Locale: Bethany, Athens, and Rome
Time: c. A.D. 30
Plot: Mythic

Lazarus of Bethany (LA-zuh-ruhs), a man raised from the dead by Jesus. Tall and powerful, Lazarus is about fifty years of age, with graying hair and a heavy beard, as the play begins. Having been freed from the fear of death by the power of the miracle, Lazarus shows this higher awareness by being the only character who wears no mask. He has a broad, noble forehead and deep, black eyes, and he radiates a mystic light. He is also rejuvenated as the play proceeds: When he is taken as a prisoner to Athens some months after the miracle of his resurrection, he appears to be less than thirty-five years old; months later, in Rome, he appears twenty-five. Encountering Caligula and Tiberius Caesar, Lazarus tries in vain to convey to them and to others the message that there is no death. He has a hypnotic, triumphant, infectious laugh that can be seen in his eyes as much as it can be heard in his voice. When he is burned alive at the stake at the end of the play, he is gagged so as to stop the sound of his all-knowing laugh.

Miriam, Lazarus' wife. She is slender and delicate, and she ages as the play proceeds. Her mask is pale, marblelike, and suggestive of all women. She recognizes the evil in the Roman world and asks Lazarus to take her home to Bethany. Sensing the eventual death of Lazarus in Rome, Miriam begins to mourn the passing of his laughter, which she feels is like a son to her. She dies after eating a poisoned peach given to her by Pompeia. Lazarus, momentarily lonely after Miriam's death, is nevertheless able to laugh his triumphant laugh.

Tiberius Caesar (ti-BEE-ree-uhs SEE-zuhr), the emperor of Rome. Although he is seventy-six years old and corpulent, Tiberius is tall and still possesses muscular strength. His mask is blotchy and purple, suggesting both his imperial standing and his sickness resulting from age and debauchery. Terrified of death, he seeks from Lazarus the secret of youth. Eventually, he partly resigns himself to death and is ready to die laughing with Lazarus. Soon after, Tiberius is strangled by Caligula.

Gaius Caligula (GAY-uhs kuh-LIHG-yuh-luh), the future emperor of Rome. Twenty-one years old at the time of the play, Caligula is bony and nearly malformed with his incongruous wide shoulders and apelike, wiry legs. His mask emphasizes his wrinkled forehead, troubled eyes, and hollow temples. A power seeker, he accompanies Lazarus from Athens to Rome and is obsessed with his laughter and his message of triumph over death. Caligula strangles Tiberius in a fit of jealous rage and permits the final death of Lazarus to emphasize the power of Caesar over death.

Pompeia (pom-PEE-uh), a Roman noblewoman and the favorite mistress of Tiberius. Her mask shows blood, lust, dissipation, and evil beauty. Thinking Lazarus to be a strange sort of magician, she bets Caligula a night of passion against a string of pearls that Lazarus will not laugh at her, then kills Miriam to induce Lazarus' grief.

— *Glenn Hopp*

LEAF STORM
(La hojarasca)

Author: Gabriel García Márquez (1928-   )
First published: 1955
Genre: Novella

Locale: Macondo, an imaginary town in Colombia
Time: Late nineteenth and early twentieth centuries
Plot: Magical Realism

The Doctor, a resident of Macondo for a quarter century, a grass eater, an insomniac, and a suicide by hanging. The Doctor is variously perceived as lustful and vulgar, without pity, hardened, animal-like, and already dead before death. He is the focus of interior monologues emanating from the Colonel, Isabel, and the Child. He is possibly French, and his name is never known, although he lives as a guest in the Colonel's home for eight years. He practices medicine in Macondo until the banana company arrives and his patients drift away. When the company and its "leaf storm" of humanity depart, a night of rebellion brings Macondo back to his door, but the Doctor refuses to treat wounded men, saying that he has "forgotten" his profession. This denial makes the community long to see his death and physical decay for the next ten years.

The Colonel, a retired military officer. Unconventional and independent, the Colonel goes his own way. He feels pity and sorrow for the Doctor's isolation. As the novella ends, the Colonel is about to fulfill his sacred promise to bury the Doctor.

Isabel (EE-sah-behl), the daughter of the Colonel, an abandoned wife and mother of the Child. At thirty years of age, she is a woman wounded by departures: her mother's death in childbirth, the loss of Meme, Martín's disappearance, and Adelaida's self-effacement. Longing to abide by convention and the town's judgment of the Doctor, Isabel fears the result of her father's promise, which she perceives as intolerable.

The Child, Isabel's son. Almost eleven years old, the boy conveys the astonished and colorful perceptions of one who does not fully understand what he sees. Closeted in the dead man's room with his mother and grandfather, the Child presents a grotesque portrait of the hanged Doctor.

Meme (MEH-meh), the Colonel's Indian foster child and servant, and the Doctor's mistress and servant. Meme creates for Isabel a legendary past in her account of the nineteenth century journey to Macondo. Once happy and friendly, Meme comes to live what Isabel sees as a sterile and anonymous life. As the Doctor's unloved mistress, Meme suffers at least one abortion; the Doctor suggests that a second pregnancy may be the result of Meme's loose character. She vanishes about eleven years before the Doctor's death; the town suspects that the Doctor murdered her.

The Mayor, the representative of the town, who attempts to delay the burial and fulfill the community's desire for the Doctor to remain unburied; he is, however, equally interested in a bribe.

Martín (mahr-TEEN), Isabel's husband. They were married eleven years before the novel's events, Martín vanished two years later with the Colonel's signed notes as financial backing. He remains a neat, vague figure to Isabel.

Adelaida (ah-dehl-EH-dah), the Colonel's second wife, Isabel's stepmother. The Colonel portrays his wife as a once-dominant and vigorous figure who is now sterile, eaten up with religion and superstition. For Adelaida, the Doctor is a test from God, intended to teach prudence.

The Pup, a priest. The Pup is a mirror image of the Doctor, who is disturbed by the idea of a present or absent God. A mysterious resemblance and the coincidence of their arrival in Macondo on the same day connect the two men. The Pup's strong grip on the town allows him to protect and save the Doctor after he denies treatment to injured men.

— *Marlene Youmans*

THE LEAN LANDS
(Las tierras flacas)

Author: Agustín Yáñez (1904-1980)
First published: 1962
Genre: Novel

Locale: Tierra Santo, in Jalisco, Mexico
Time: Early 1920's
Plot: Allegory

Epifanio Trujillo (eh-pee-FAH-nee-oh trew-HEE-yoh), an imperious landowner and patriarch, the father of approximately one hundred children by various mistresses. He has spent his life accumulating land, cattle, women, and children. Fat and lethargic in his old age, he comes under the complete domination of his daughter, Plácida. Because he failed to specify how his estate would be divided, he witnesses his heirs struggle among themselves for supremacy. His obsession with Teófila and his pursuit of her sewing machine leads to their destruction. After his death, his lands come under the control of the one son who had renounced his name, Jacob Gallo.

Miguel Arcángel Trujillo (mee-GEHL ahr-KAHN-hehl), also called **Jacob Gallo** (GAH-yoh), the son of Epifanio Trujillo and Sara Gallo. He married against his father's wishes, adopted his mother's name, and sought his fortune elsewhere. Returning to his father's domain as a wealthy landowner in his own right, he is determined to use his wealth and knowledge to bring progress to the lean lands. He wins the support of the peasants with proposals to dig new wells and provide fertilizers, better seed, and breeding animals. He outwits his half brothers and sister, acquires control of his father's estate, and becomes the new authority in the lean lands.

Plácida Trujillo (PLAH-see-dah), the daughter of Don Epifanio and mistress of his house. As prudish as her father was licentious, she is coldhearted and cruel. Jacob Gallo saves her from the fury of the mob that burned down her father's house. While in his custody, she repeatedly tries to commit suicide. In the end, she distributes her family's property to the peasants and becomes the servant and understudy of the good witch, Matiana.

Jesús Trujillo (heh-SEWS), also called **the Sneak** and **Snake in the Grass**, the son of Don Epifanio. He cloaks his evil intentions with fine manners and sweet talk. In the hope of winning his father's favor, he takes brutal measures to steal the deceased Teófila's sewing machine for Don Epifanio. He instigates the mutilation of Matiana, anticipating that it would result in the fall of Jacob Gallo and allow him to acquire complete control over his father's estate. Instead, the peasants rise up to destroy the Trujillos. Jesús escapes the mob's fury but is later apprehended by Jacob's men and brought to trial.

Felipe Trujillo (feh-LEE-peh), known as **the Bully**. His father, Don Epifanio, hoped that he would become the strong-man and defender of the Trujillo name and fortune. To prevent Jesús from winning his father's favor and gaining advantage over him in the struggle for the inheritance, Felipe seizes Teófila's sewing machine from Jesús. He takes advantage of the peasants' belief in its miraculous powers by charging them for praying before it. After Matiana is blinded by Jesús' hired thugs, the enraged peasants hang him and return Teófila's sewing machine to her parents.

Rómulo Garabito (ROH-mew-loh gahr-ah-BEE-toh), a poor and fatalistic peasant who is the grandson of Teódulo Garabito and the father of Teófila. He closely identifies himself with the land and yearns for his grandfather's time, when a true spirit of community reigned among the inhabitants of the lean lands. Don Epifanio gives him the choice of giving up his deceased daughter's sewing machine or surrendering his farm to pay off his debts. Rómulo is saved from this dilemma by Jacob Gallo, who presents Don Epifanio with a new sewing machine for his birthday. Although he finds himself loosely allied with the Gallos, he does not believe in progress and fears that the innovations introduced by Jacob Gallo will result in greater oppression.

Teófila Garabito (teh-OH-fee-lah), the saintly daughter of Rómulo. Beautiful, intelligent, and virtuous, she convinces her father that she could earn money for the family with a sewing machine. Don Epifanio is obsessed with her and hoped to marry her. When she dies of meningitis at the age of twenty, her parents are certain that God has rescued her from Don Epifanio. The destruction of the Trujillos through her sewing machine is considered to be her most important miracle.

Matiana (mah-tee-AH-nah), an old midwife with a reputation for being a witch. She assists at births, illnesses, deaths, and all other emergencies and provides herbal remedies, prayers, and spells. She serves as mediator between the peasants and the supernatural, using her mental powers to execute justice in favor of the weak. Her mutilation at the hands of Jesús' hired thugs precipitates the peasant uprising that destroys the power of the Trujillos.

— *Evelyn Toft*

LEAR

Author: Edward Bond (1934-   )
First published: 1972
Genre: Drama

Locale: England
Time: Unspecified
Plot: Allegory

Lear, the king of England, now in his old age. Lear's enterprise to protect his lands from attack by the dukes of North and Cornwall is near completion. By constructing a wall around his kingdom, Lear is shown as a strong and politically effective leader. His failure, however, is that in keeping enemies out, Lear also traps within the country various internal destructive forces. Consequently, civil war breaks out, and Lear is driven from his own kingdom. Wandering in the wilderness, he returns to an almost childlike state, shrugging off responsibility for the society he created. Captured by the new government, Lear begins to learn, for the first time, the kind of king and father he has been. Strict and authoritarian, but with the best of intentions, Lear has been overprotective, suffocating his daughters' individuality and causing them to respond viciously to the world. Now, as their prisoner, Lear is made "politically ineffective" by the removal of his eyes. Lear's blinding symbolically begins his growth in understanding, and he begins to see that the only way forward is a peaceful one. Lear is shot attempting to destroy the wall, which represents the severe and annihilating man Lear was as both a parent and a king.

Bodice, Lear's daughter. Ambitious, intelligent, organized, and dangerous, Bodice, like her sister, craves political power. Unlike Fontanelle, however, Bodice is not easily fooled. She marries North expecting nothing and so is not surprised at discovering that her husband's bravery is far from genuine. Having taken joint control of the country, she discovers the limitations of power and fails to achieve the success and fulfillment she desires. Bodice emerges as an isolated and lonely woman.

Fontanelle, Lear's daughter. Fontanelle's psychological scars, caused by a lonely childhood without a mother and living surrounded by the death of soldiers in war, go deeper than those of her sister. Fontanelle, a scheming but not particularly intelligent woman, is searching for the love and security always denied her. She does not find it through her acquisition of power, her marriage to Cornwall, the torture of Lear's chief adviser, Warrington, or her countless romantic affairs.

Duke of North, Bodice's husband. North is a foolish character who is simply a pawn in the political game played by Lear's daughters. According to his wife, North is impotent and a coward afraid of war.

Duke of Cornwall, Fontanelle's husband. Like North, Cornwall is fraudulent, deceiving Fontanelle into marrying him by sending the letters and pictures of others. Cornwall, described by Fontanelle as a "frightened little boy," like North is afraid of fighting.

The Gravedigger's Boy, a thoughtful and compassionate man. His farm serves as a model of self-sufficiency, demonstrating how it is possible to survive in spite of the political world in which he lives. Generous to Warrington and Lear, providing both with food and Lear with a place to stay, the Gravedigger's Boy has an ignorance of politics that leads to his death. His ghost returns to provide Lear with hope of an escape from reality. Lear's gradual insight into the cause of suffering, however, means that the vision Lear has of the boy fades: The Gravedigger's Boy dies for a second time.

Cordelia, the Gravedigger's Boy's Wife, a happily married and pregnant farmer's wife. From the beginning of the play, Cordelia is concerned about her husband's philanthropic nature. The arrival of Lear also causes her great concern. Cordelia's fears for their well-being are justified by the arrival of the soldiers, the murder of her husband, and her own rape and subsequent miscarriage. As a result of this incident, Cordelia becomes openly aggressive, determined to wage war on those responsible for shattering her life. Cordelia, along with her new husband, John, lead an army against the forces of Bodice and Fontanelle. Having successfully acquired control of the state, she sets about creating the society of which Lear could only dream. Unfortunately for Cordelia, in doing so she repeats the mistakes of Lear.

John the Carpenter, a character who demonstrates integrity and bravery. Despite his love for Cordelia, John respects her marriage to the Gravedigger's Boy and settles for simply visiting her at the farm. One such occasion is the time of the soldiers' attack. John saves Cordelia, murders the aggressors, and subsequently marries her. Together, they attack the armies of Bodice and Fontanelle. John is unrelenting in his attitude toward Lear's daughters, apparently unconcerned by the pain and suffering he causes.

— *Ian Stuart*

THE LEARNING TREE

Author: Gordon Parks (1912-   )
First published: 1963
Genre: Novel

Locale: A small town in Kansas
Time: Mid-1920's
Plot: Domestic realism

Newton Buchanan Winger, the protagonist, a boy of twelve. He experiences momentous encounters of life, including death, violent and otherwise, and love, both sexual and familial. The youngest in a large, close-knit family, Newt grows both physically and emotionally. At the end, when he leaves the Midwest town of his birth for a new home in Minnesota, his mother's dream of him going on to better things seemingly is fulfilled.

Sarah Winger, Newt's mother, a housekeeper for a white judge. She is the keystone of the Winger family. Although increasingly suffering from the heart condition that eventually kills her, Sarah leads her family and is, for an African American in the 1920s, a respected person in town. Sarah's hopes crystallize around Newt, who shows both intellectual ability and artistic promise.

Jack Winger, Sarah's husband and Newt's father. He is hardworking and well-intentioned but does not always understand or sympathize with Newt's interests or Sarah's ambitions for Newt. A struggling farmer willing to do whatever work is necessary to keep his family together, Jack is an honorable figure in Cherokee Flats. He is well aware that Sarah is the dominant figure of their household.

Arcella Jefferson, Newt's first love. Newt and Arcella fall in love, sit together in the segregated movie house, exchange presents, and talk about their future life together. Arcella abandons Newt and becomes pregnant by a young white man, Chauncey Cavanaugh. Her family is forced to leave town in disgrace.

Jefferson Cavanaugh, a judge and the pillar of the community in Cherokee Flats. Cavanaugh, a white man, is the employer of Sarah Winger and the father of Chauncey. A figure of both power and responsibility, the judge epitomizes the social and political establishment. Cavanaugh does not merely represent the white forces in town. After his mother deserted him, he was reared in the Winger home and thus shows less bigotry and prejudice than did many whites in America during the 1920s.

Marcus Savage, a slightly older contemporary of Newt. His violent nature leads him first to a reformatory, then to a series of confrontations with Newt, and finally to his death. Marcus, whose father, Booker, commits the murder that is one of the centerpieces of the novel, is a victim both of his own nature and of the environment created by his broken home and the wider white-dominated society. Although Marcus attempts to murder Newt, the latter sympathizes with Marcus as a victim in a world in which racial prejudice is a reality.

— *Eugene S. Larson*

LEAVE IT TO PSMITH

Author: P. G. Wodehouse (1881-1975)
First published: 1923
Genre: Novel

Locale: Primarily Blandings Castle
Time: Late Edwardian era
Plot: Wit and humor

Ronald Eustace Psmith, a clever, charming aristocrat who has left the family fish business to seek employment. Very tall and very thin, Psmith (the *p* is silent) is a solemn young man who wears a top hat, morning coat, and monocle. He travels to Blandings Castle by train with Lord Emsworth, who has mistaken Psmith for Ralston McTodd, a fashionable poet invited to Blandings by Lady Constance, Lord Emsworth's sister. Psmith encourages the mistaken identity because he knows that Eve Halliday, a pretty girl he has just met and with whom he has fallen in love, is also going to Blandings, to catalog Lord Emsworth's library. While traveling to Blandings, Psmith is approached by Freddie Threepwood, Lord Emsworth's son, and asked if he will steal Lady Constance's diamond necklace. Because Psmith knows and likes the Jacksons, whom the theft will benefit, he agrees to help in this scheme. After many comic complications, Psmith finally obtains the necklace and Eve's love. He accepts a position as Lord Emsworth's private secretary.

Eve Halliday, the young, attractive heroine. Eve is retained to catalog the library at Blandings and finds herself attracted to Psmith. She soon learns from a girlfriend, however, that he is not Ralston McTodd, the poet, as he claims. She proceeds cautiously until she discovers his real identity and motivation.

Clarence, the ninth earl of Emsworth, owner of Blandings Castle. Somewhat doddering and constantly preoccupied with his cherished flowers, Lord Emsworth is also prone to misplace his glasses. Lunching at his club one day with poet Ralston McTodd, whom he sees only dimly without his glasses, Lord Emsworth chatters on about his running battle with his gardener over the proper care of his flowers, a monologue that both bores and enrages his guest. McTodd gratefully slips away from Lord Emsworth at his first chance and drops his plans to visit Blandings that week at Lady Constance's invitation. Soon after finding his glasses, Lord Emsworth mis-takes Psmith for McTodd and takes him to Blandings as the poet.

Lady Constance Keeble, Lord Emsworth's sister. Angry that her stepdaughter Phyllis has married against her wishes, Lady Constance refuses to help Phyllis and her husband, Mike Jackson, purchase a small house in the country. Lady Constance's tightfistedness prompts her husband, Joe Keeble, and her nephew Freddie to plot with Psmith to steal her diamond necklace, sell it, and use part of the profits to set up the Jacksons in their new home.

The Honorable Freddie Threepwood, Lord Emsworth's son. Freddie, a carefree, empty-headed young man, hits on the idea to steal his aunt's necklace, but both he and his uncle realize that he lacks the ingenuity to work out the details. After seeing an advertisement placed by Psmith in a London newspaper offering his services for any endeavor (even criminal), Freddie recruits him to carry out the mission. Freddie seeks a thousand pounds of the money they will realize from selling the necklace to pay off racetrack losses and to begin a bookmaking operation.

Rupert Baxter, Lord Emsworth's private secretary. The coldly efficient Baxter is immediately suspicious of Psmith when his signature does not match that of McTodd. Baxter tries to block Psmith's efforts to steal Lady Constance's necklace by hiring a private detective to stay at Blandings posing as Susan, the new parlormaid. When the necklace is stolen during a poetry reading given by Psmith, Baxter guesses correctly that it has been hidden in a flowerpot in the garden. Early one morning, he sneaks outside to investigate but is accidentally locked out. To get back in the house, Baxter tries to wake someone in the nearest bedroom by tossing the flowerpots one by one through an open window. It happens to be the window of Lord Emsworth, who, with some prompting from Psmith, decides that Baxter has gone insane and dismisses him.

Edward Cootes and

Liz, an American gangster and his partner, who is the brains of their operation. They arrive separately at Blandings, having also heard about Lady Constance's valuable necklace. They team up to steal it and have a final showdown over the necklace with Psmith and Eve in a ramshackle cottage on the grounds at Blandings. When Freddie clumsily stumbles upstairs and sends one of his legs crashing through the ceiling, Psmith in the confusion is able to get the necklace from the gangsters.

— Glenn Hopp

LEAVING HOME

Author: Lionel G. Garcia (1935-   )
First published: 1985
Genre: Novel

Locale: Southern California
Time: Early 1940's
Plot: Psychological realism

Adolfo, a poverty-stricken former major-league baseball pitcher who ruins his career with alcohol. Adolfo realizes that he has made no plans for his future, so he decides to see if Isabel, the only woman he has truly loved, will let him move in with her. She refuses him. Adolfo's insecurity is evident in his attempts to appear to be the winner in arguments with his cousin Maria and in his making himself the hero of every baseball story he tells. Adolfo is also insecure about his ability to perform sexually, a problem he never had in younger years. Adding to his insecurity is the cruelty of people telling him that his mouth resembles a rectum whenever he is not wearing his dentures. Although poverty prevents him from improving his appearance, Adolfo is concerned about how he looks. Adolfo has a good sense of humor and wants to be liked by everyone; open dislike crushes him. He loves telling baseball and war stories, but people at the boarding house where he lives start to avoid him so they will not have to hear another story. After his various love affairs fail to lead to true love, Adolfo's search for stability leads him back to Maria's house, where he is happy.

Maria, an emotional yet strong woman who is able to overcome adversity. Maria manages to overcome being jilted by the man she was in love with, the father of one of her children. She carries, delivers, and keeps her illegitimate daughter, also named Maria, despite what others might think. She does, however, experience emotional problems during the pregnancy. Maria loves her family deeply and does not want them to move away from home. She sees no need to seek riches. Maria has a strong belief in God but also believes in witchcraft. She begins to lose her faith in God when her son, Arnoldo, is killed. By the end of the novel, Maria is unhappy, empty, and bitter. She brightens when she learns that her cousin Adolfo will move back in with her.

Carmen, a strong-willed young woman determined to make something of her life. Carmen is Maria's favorite child but feels no regret when she leaves her mother to move to San Diego to find a job. Carmen works hard, a trait inherited from her mother, and enjoys doing things for others. While she is in a sanitarium being treated for tuberculosis, she helps the orderlies with the other patients and decides to become a nurse. She enters the Navy for training and gets a job at a naval hospital, then later is made an officer. By the end of the novel, Carmen has become engaged to a naval officer and achieved almost all of her goals.

Isabel, Adolfo's former lover. Isabel, like Maria, is left alone by the father of her child, Adolfo. Isabel, however, is not as strong as Maria. Beaten almost to death by her father, Isabel is sent to live with relatives until her baby is born. Isabel is kind and considerate. She takes Carmen in and helps her find a job. When Carmen gets sick, Isabel looks after her. Even though she still has feelings for Adolfo, Isabel tells him that she cannot forgive him for the pain he has caused her.

The Professor (Manuel Garcia), Adolfo's sidekick. The Professor is a small man who feels inferior to Adolfo, even though he finished high school and has taught elementary school. He is willing to take risks and stands up for himself.

THE LEFT HAND OF DARKNESS

Author: Ursula K. Le Guin (1929-   )
First published: 1969
Genre: Novel

Locale: The planet Gethen/Winter
Time: The future
Plot: Science fiction

Genly Ai (GEHN-lee AY-ee), an envoy to the planet Gethen from the Ekumen, a league of planets. Not yet thirty years old, dark-skinned, and somewhat taller and stronger than the native Gethenians, Ai is occasionally impatient, quick to despair and to rejoice, somewhat of an innocent, and not always aware of the motives of others. Ai's mission is to prepare the way for Gethenians to join the Ekumen, offering opportunities for "communication, trade, treaty, and alliance, nothing else." He begins his stay on Gethen in Karhide, a country loosely run by a monarch and his council. Betrayed, as he believes, by the prime minister, Therem Harth rem ir Estraven, he travels to Orgoreyn, a country tightly controlled by the Commensal, the thirty-three heads of its districts. There, he is truly betrayed and sent to a work camp, from which Estraven rescues him. The two cross the vast northern expanse of ice back to Karhide, a difficult journey during which they become friends.

Therem Harth rem ir Estraven (THAYR-ehm hahrth rehm ihr ehs-TRAY-vehn), the "King's Ear," or prime minister of Karhide. Stocky and dark, with a layer of fat to protect against the constant cold of Gethen, he has black eyes and sleek hair.

Estraven is an androgyne, neither man nor woman but both, as are all Gethenians. A cautious, authoritative, methodical, far-seeing person, Estraven is the first to believe Ai and perceive the importance of his mission. When Estraven falls from favor with the monarch (for suggesting that Karhide join the Ekumen) and is exiled, he travels to Orgoreyn and attempts to prepare the way for Ai there. Estraven's preparation and steadfastness play a large part in the success of the journey over the ice, and his understanding of the politics of both Karhide and Orgoreyn lead to the eventual success of Ai's mission. Estraven is killed as he attempts to cross back from Karhide to Orgoreyn and safety.

Argaven XV (ahr-GAH-vehn), the monarch of Karhide. Insane, as have been all the kings of Karhide, Argaven perceives only the threat to his own power in Ai's mission and exiles Estraven as a traitor as a result of Estraven's counsel to join the Ekumen. He nevertheless later receives Ai's ship, thus tacitly agreeing to join the league of planets, to save face for his country.

Pemmer Harge rem ir Tibe (PEHM-muhr HAHR-geh rehm ihr TEE-beh), Argaven's cousin. Tibe becomes prime minister after Estraven's exile and then regent when the king becomes pregnant. Tibe thrives on intrigue and power and attempts to unify Karhide by talking of "pride of country and love of the parentland," trying to achieve unity of fear and anger against the "other." It is on Tibe's orders that Estraven is shot.

Faxe the Weaver (fahks), a Foreteller. A Weaver is the focal point of a Handdarata foretelling group; thus, Faxe practices a philosophical discipline and has the ability to interpret (or weave) as a whole the individual forces of a foretelling group to provide answers to questions about the future. Tall, slim, beautiful, and extremely intelligent and wise, Faxe answers Ai's question about whether Gethen will become a member of the Ekumen. Later, Faxe is elected by his district to the king's council, where he becomes a member of the opposition, a counterweight to the power of the prime minister.

Yegey (YAY-gay), a member of the Commensal, or one of the thirty-three rulers of the country of Orgoreyn. Ai describes him as a "delicate, dapper, drawling fellow with keen eyes." Yegey is a member of the Open Trade faction, which favors an alliance with the Ekumen. When his faction looks likely to lose in its efforts to bring about this alliance, he condones Ai's arrest to maintain his own power.

Obsle (OB-sleh), another of the Commensal and a member of the Open Trade faction. Although he has no manners and is rather frumpy, he is perhaps the most far-seeing commensal. He, too, condones Ai's arrest.

Vanake Slose (VAH-neh-keh slohz), an idealistic, religious Open Trade Commensal who sees Ai and the Ekumen as the fulfillment of religious prophecy.

Shusgis (SHEHS-gihs), a wealthy Commensal who is also a member of the Sarf, or secret police. His geniality and kindness serve his own purposes, and he betrays his guest, Ai.

— *Karen M. Cleveland*

THE LEFT-HANDED WOMAN
(Die linkshändige Frau)

Author: Peter Handke (1942-   )
First published: 1976
Genre: Novel

Locale: An unnamed city in West Germany
Time: Winter, 1975-Spring, 1976
Plot: Philosophical realism

Marianne, referred to as **the Woman**, a thirty-year-old translator of French and a suburban housewife in an unnamed West German city. She, her husband, Bruno, and their child live in a bungalow on a hill overlooking the city. Marianne is lonely, as are the other characters of the novel. In spite of that, she suggests to Bruno that he leave her after he has returned from a business trip. There appears to be no specific reason for her suggestion. Marianne translates from the French that the ideal man is someone who loves her for what she is and will become. The idea that her husband leave her comes to her as an "illumination." Whether this separation is permanent is not known.

Bruno, a sales manager for a porcelain firm. He has brown eyes that can observe without being observed. After his return from a business trip to Finland, where he did not know the language and felt very lonely, he says to Marianne that he felt that they were bound to each other but that he could now exist without her. After spending the night in a nearby hotel where they had gone for dinner, Marianne tells him that he should go to live with Franziska. Bruno does so. After a fight with the actor at Marianne's impromptu party, where Bruno accused the actor of wanting to be his wife's lover, he and the actor play Ping-Pong together and are the last to leave the party. They leave together.

Stefan, referred to as **the Child**, Bruno and Marianne's eight-year-old son. He writes an essay for school that seems to be a parable of the novel's theme. It is titled "My Idea for a Better Life." Everyone would live on islands, he would have no more than four friends, and all the people he did not know would disappear. Stefan spends much time with his friend Jürgen and occasionally goes on outings with his mother.

The Father, Marianne's father, an unhappy elderly man who is color-blind. He lives with a female companion. He comes to visit Marianne after receiving a letter from Franziska. He recognizes a film actor in a department store and tells him that he can improve by starting to risk himself while acting.

Franziska, Stefan's schoolteacher and Marianne's friend. She and Bruno live together at Marianne's suggestion. She tries unsuccessfully to get Marianne to join a women's group.

The actor, an unemployed, flabby man. He meets Marianne and her father after they have had their picture taken. He is criticized by Marianne's father for holding back, for trying to be a personality instead of giving of himself totally. He contrives to meet Marianne in a café.

Ernst, referred to as **the publisher**, a corpulent man about fifty years old. He is Marianne's employer after Bruno leaves her. She had worked for Ernst a long time earlier. He appears with champagne at her door, then makes a pass at her. Ernst says to Marianne that she is entering a long period of loneliness, which she takes as a threat.

The chauffeur, Ernst's driver. He attends Marianne's party and makes a sketch of her company.

The salesgirl, a woman who sells Marianne a sweater for her husband and who attends Marianne's party. She has a child, who is kept in a back room during working hours.

Jürgen, Stefan's playmate and schoolmate.

— *Arthur Tilo Alt*

THE LEGEND OF GOOD WOMEN

Author: Geoffrey Chaucer (c. 1343-1400)
First transcribed: 1380-1386
Genre: Poetry

Locale: Indeterminate
Time: Indeterminate
Plot: Mythic

Chaucer (CHAW-sur), a dreamer. In a vision, he is denounced by Cupid for heresy against the laws of love for writing and translating disparaging remarks about womankind.

Cupid, the god of love. In a dream, he accuses Chaucer, the dreamer, of heresy against love's laws.

Alceste (al-SEHST), the wife of Admetus and the companion of Cupid in Chaucer's dream. She suggests that Chaucer win Cupid's forgiveness by writing a legend of wives and maidens forever true in love.

Cleopatra (klee-oh-PA-truh), the queen of Egypt, whose love of Antony is so great that, on his death, she causes herself to be bitten by a poisonous serpent.

Antony, Cleopatra's beloved.

Thisbe (THIHZ-beh), the daughter of a lord of Babylon. She is loved by Pyramus, who, mistakenly thinking her dead, commits suicide. She finds his body and, in her grief, joins him in death.

Pyramus (PIHR-a-muhs), the son of a lord of Babylon and Thisbe's beloved.

Dido (DIH-doh), the queen of Carthage. According to Chaucer, Aeneas wins Dido's love, seduces her, and when he has grown weary of her, invents a vision that gives him an excuse to leave her. In her grief, she stabs herself.

Aeneas (ee-NEE-uhs), Dido's betrayer.

Hypsipyle (hihp-SIHP-ih-lee), the queen of Lemnos. She marries Jason and dies of a broken heart when he leaves her.

Medea (mee-DEE-uh), a princess of Colchis. She marries Jason, who leaves her for Creusa.

Jason, the betrayer of Hypsipyle and Medea.

Creusa (kreh-EW-suh), the daughter of Kreon, the king of Corinth, for whom Jason betrays Medea.

Lucretia (lew-KREE-shuh), the chaste, devoted wife of Colatyne (Collatinus). When she is ravished by Tarquinius (Tarquin), she takes her own life so that her husband will not have to bear the shame.

Colatyne (or **Collatinus**), Lucretia's husband.

Tarquinius (tahr-KWIHN-ee-uhs), also called **Tarquin**, Lucretia's ravisher.

Ariadne (ar-ee-AD-nee), the daughter of King Minos. Taken from Crete by Theseus, she is deserted on their way to Athens.

Theseus (THEE-see-uhs), a prince of Athens, Ariadne's betrayer.

Philomela (fihl-oh-MEE-lah), a princess of Athens ravished by her brother-in-law, Tereus.

Tereus (TEE-ree-uhs), a lord of Thrace, Philomela's ravisher.

Progne (PROG-nee), Tereus' wife, Philomela's sister.

Phyllis, a Greek maiden betrayed by Demophon, who promises marriage and instead sails away.

Demophon (DEE-mo-fon), Theseus' son, Phyllis' betrayer.

Ypermistra or **Hypermnestra** (hi-purm-NEHS-truh), one of the fifty daughters of Danao (Danaus), the king of Egypt. She is urged by her father to kill her bridegroom, Lino, but, out of pity, she cannot and warns him to escape. He does so, leaving her to her fate.

Lino, Ypermistra's bridegroom.

Danao, Ypermistra's father.

THE LEGEND OF SLEEPY HOLLOW

Author: Washington Irving (1783-1859)
First published: 1820
Genre: Short fiction

Locale: Tarry Town, New York
Time: The 1780's
Plot: Folklore

Ichabod Crane, the itinerant schoolteacher of Sleepy Hollow, less a character than a caricature, grotesque in his physical appearance. He is very tall, with narrow shoulders and long arms that dangle out of his sleeves; his feet are so large that they might have served as shovels. He has a small flat head, with large ears and a long snipe nose. The teller of the story, Diedrich Knickerbocker, says that to see him striding in profile across a hilltop on a windy day with his clothes fluttering around him, one might take him for "the genius of famine descended on the earth." Ichabod's most basic characteristic is his great hunger; Knickerbocker says he has the dilating power

of an anaconda and seems able to swallow up everything placed before him. A shrewd New Englander in the midst of simple Dutch farmers, Ichabod wants to swallow up the land that belongs to Katrina Van Tassel's father. His downfall is the result of his other appetite—his willingness to "swallow," or believe, everything about the marvelous and the supernatural. Because of his gullible appetite for the marvelous, he is frightened away from Katrina and Sleepy Hollow by Brom Bones, who pretends to be the legendary Headless Horseman.

Katrina Van Tassel, the only child of a wealthy Dutch farmer. At the age of eighteen, she is seen by the always hungry Ichabod as "plump as a partridge" and as ripe and rosy-cheeked as one of her father's peaches. Wearing a charming combination of Old and New World clothing, Katrina is a bit of a flirt who has the "prettiest foot and ankle in the county." She is so deliciously irresistible to Ichabod that he wants to swallow her (and her father's farm).

Baltus Van Tassel, Katrina's father, a wealthy, thriving, contented Dutch farmer, satisfied with his wealth but not proud of it.

Abraham Van Brunt, called **Brom Bones**, a strong and broad-shouldered man who is the hero of the countryside. He is famed for his horsemanship, his physical strength, and his love of tricks and merriment. He is always ready for a fight or a frolic. He is the leader of a small band of young men who look up to him as their model and with whom he rides throughout the countryside playing pranks and getting into brawls. He is also a suitor for the hand of Katrina and is jealous when she pays too much attention to Ichabod. His knowledge of Ichabod's gullibility enables him to play the part of the Headless Horseman and frighten the greedy pedagogue away.

Diedrich Knickerbocker, an old gentleman, familiar with the history of old Dutch New York, who tells the story of Ichabod's encounter with the Headless Horseman.

The Headless Horseman, the spirit of a Hessian soldier, a legendary figure said to haunt Sleepy Hollow. Brom Bones dresses up as the Headless Horseman and frightens Ichabod so badly that he leaves the area and never returns.

— *Charles E. May*

THE LEGEND OF THE GLORIOUS ADVENTURES OF TYL ULENSPIEGEL IN THE LAND OF FLANDERS AND ELSEWHERE
(La Légende et les aventures héroïques, joyeuses et glorieuses d'Ulenspiegel et de Lamme Goedzak au pays de Flanders et ailleurs)

Author: Charles de Coster (1827-1879)
First published: 1867
Genre: Novel

Locale: The Low Countries
Time: The sixteenth century
Plot: Historical

Tyl Ulenspiegel, a young Fleming who seeks revenge upon the Spanish for the mistreatment of his parents. He wanders far, fighting the Spanish and looking for the Seven, who will save his land. He finds the Seven in a vision. Tyl appears dead and is buried, but he later rises from his grave to be the spirit of the new Flanders freed from the grip of the Spanish.

Katheline, a midwife who brings Tyl Ulenspiegel into the world. She is the first to see him, in a vision, as the spirit of his native Flanders. Tortured as a witch, she goes mad. A later witch's trial by water causes her death.

Nele, Katheline's illegitimate daughter. She is Ulenspiegel's childhood playmate and, later, his wife. She goes in search of her wandering lover, saves him from the gallows, and marries him. She becomes the spirit of the heart of Flanders after it is freed from Spanish domination.

Claes, Tyl Ulenspiegel's father. He is tortured and put to death by the Inquisition.

Soetkin, Tyl Ulenspiegel's mother. She dies of grief over her husband's death and the tortures inflicted upon her by the Inquisition.

Hans Dudzeele, Katheline's lover. He steals Claes' money from Soetkin and kills his accomplice. Denounced as a witch by mad Katheline, who did not realize what she was doing, he is tortured and put to slow death by fire.

Lamme Goedzak, Tyl Ulenspiegel's companion in his wanderings. He is a fat buffoon seeking his wife, who has become a nun. He drowns in food and drink his sorrow over losing her. Eventually, they are reunited.

The Seven, the Seven Deadly Sins, seen in a vision by Ulenspiegel. With the freeing of Flanders from the Spanish, they become seven virtues: Pride, Gluttony, Idleness, Avarice, Anger, Envy, and Lust become Noble Spirit, Appetite, Reverie, Economy, Vivacity, Emulation, and Love, respectively.

Philip, king of Spain and symbol to Tyl Ulenspiegel of the Spanish domination of Flanders.

Prince William of Orange, with whose forces Tyl Ulenspiegel fights against King Philip and the Inquisition.

LEGEND OF THE MOOR'S LEGACY

Author: Washington Irving (1783-1859)
First published: 1832
Genre: Short fiction

Locale: Granada, Spain
Time: The seventeenth century
Plot: Folklore

Pedro Gil (PEH-droh heel), called **Peregil** (peh-reh-HEEL), a poor local water carrier and native of Galicia. A happy, honest, and amiable fellow, Peregil labors with his beloved donkey to support his nagging wife and hungry children. Compassionate toward all creatures, he discovers a sick Moor lying beside the road. Risking persecution by authorities for aiding a Moor, Peregil straps the man to his donkey and returns home. Defying his wife's orders to abandon the Moor, Peregil attempts to nurse the man. Before the Moor dies, he offers Peregil a small sandalwood box as a reward for his kindness. Fearing that he will be charged with murder and robbery, Peregil slips out into the night to bury the Moor. On his return, he is accosted by the alguazil (warrant officer) and taken to the Alcalde (judge). Truthfully relaying the incident, Peregil is released but must relinquish his donkey to pay the cost of the inquiry. During an argument with his wife, the sandalwood box falls to the floor. Peregil discovers a scroll written in Arabic and a yellow wax taper. He takes the scroll to a Mussulman (Moor) who sells trinkets in the market. They agree to read the scroll outside the Tower of the Seven Floors, hoping to find the legendary enchanted treasure. When the floor opens, the two men fill their pockets with precious metals and agree to keep their discovery a secret. Unable to keep the secret, honest Peregil tells his wife about his good fortune. When Peregil's wife flaunts her new wealth, he is arrested again, along with the Mussulman. After Peregil recounts his tale, the Alcalde, the barber, and the alguazil force Peregil and the Mussulman to return and open the tower vault. When the three men exhibit excess greed, the Moor blows out the taper and the vault closes, trapping the three men forever. Recovering his donkey, Peregil moves his family to Portugal and assumes the role of the wealthy Don Pedro Gil.

Pedrillo Pedrugo (peh-DREE-yoh peh-DREW-goh), a meddlesome barber and neighbor. A gossip and snitch, Pedrillo spies Peregil with the Moor. Pedrillo follows Peregil to the Moor's burial site and reports the incident to his client, the Alcalde. Pedrillo, who is rumored to have slept with one eye open, catches a glance of Peregil's wife's new diamond ornament. He rushes to the Alcalde to report his observation. Going along to the tower with the Alcalde and the alguazil, Pedrillo is entombed within the walls of the vault.

The Alcalde (ahl-KAHL-deh), a greedy judge who manipulates the law for monetary gain. Concluding that Peregil murdered and robbed the Moor, the Alcalde promises to ignore the incident if Peregil gives the judge his acquired riches. Realizing that Peregil is really a Good Samaritan, the Alcalde dismisses Peregil after confiscating his donkey. Following the tattling barber's second report about Peregil's newly acquired riches, Alcalde demands that Peregil and the Moor reopen the tower. The Alcalde carries out so much gold that the weight is too much for Peregil's poor donkey to bear. Still unsatisfied with the amount of gold and ignoring the wise Moor's advice on the ills of avarice, Alcalde reenters the vault for more treasure. The Moor blows out the taper, closing off the entrance and trapping the greedy judge forever.

The Moor, or Mussulman, a reasonable, levelheaded, and shrewd businessman. Agreeing to help Peregil, the Moor reads the scroll and opens the tower. Never exhibiting greed, the Moor respects the legendary treasure and takes only what he needs. Forced to reopen the vault, the Moor warns Alcalde that the men had enough wealth for any reasonable man. Ignoring the Moor's warning, the Alcalde returns to carry out another coffer, and the Moor buries him, along with the barber and the alguazil. The Moor returns to Africa to live in his native city, Tangiers.

Peregil's wife, a lazy, gossiping spendthrift. She nags more than she nurtures. She does not support Peregil's compassion and belittles his kindness when he brings the Moor home. Constantly complaining about her impoverished condition, she enhances Peregil's guilt. Consequently, he reveals his secret and indulges her with ornaments. After promising to keep the secret, only a day passes before she flaunts her new wealth and gossips about a new future, causing Pedrillo's suspicions. Once in Portugal, Peregil's wife adorns herself in lace and jewels and maintains the role of the fashionable Señora Gil.

The alguazil (ahl-gwah-SEEL), a warrant officer, the Alcalde's henchman. He is entombed in the tower with the Alcalde and the barber.

Mateo (mah-TEH-oh), a gossiping squire who narrates the legend.

— *Patricia T. Cheves*

LEGS

Author: William Kennedy (1928-   )
First published: 1975
Genre: Novel

Locale: Albany, New York
Time: The 1920's and 1930's
Plot: Regional

John Thomas "Legs" Diamond, a ruthless gangster and bootlegger. Brutal and ambitious, yet possessing a certain raw style, Diamond symbolizes the mood and energy of the years of Prohibition. Initially a second-rate thug, Diamond wages a violent war on competing bootleggers and builds an underworld empire that makes him one of the most famous—and most feared—figures of the decade. Diamond is also a man of rapacious appetites, with a wife, a mistress, and a taste for the high life. The air of power and magnetism that he exudes draws Marcus Gorman into his inner circle.

Marcus Gorman, a rising young attorney from Albany, New York. Gorman serves as the book's narrator, drawing the reader into Diamond's violent world even as he himself is pulled into it. Marcus begins as a respectable outsider, with a law practice and political ambitions. He finds himself unable to resist the twisted magnetism of Diamond's outlaw life. He is hired by Diamond, ostensibly for legal representation, but soon realizes that his ties to the gangster will sometimes require activities on both sides of the law. Fascinated by the contradictions and sheer animal energy of the criminal he comes to know as a friend, Marcus abandons what he terms "the moral gold standard" in his own life and casts his lot with Diamond.

Marion "Kiki" Roberts, a showgirl who is Diamond's mistress, described by Marcus as the most beautiful woman he has ever seen. Kiki is devoted to Diamond, who keeps her, protected by bodyguards, close to wherever he is staying. Theirs is a passionately physical relationship, and Kiki bitterly resents Diamond's time with his wife. For many years, Kiki refuses to allow herself to believe the stories she hears of her lover's brutality toward his enemies, loyally accepting only Diamond's version of his actions.

Alice Diamond, Diamond's wife. Alice, too, is fiercely devoted to Diamond and is deeply angry over his affair with Kiki. Contrary to Marcus' expectations, she is outspoken and assertive. A warm, amply proportioned woman, she is a regular churchgoer, despite the irregular nature of her life with her husband.

Murray "The Goose" Pucinski, one of Diamond's henchmen. Murray the Goose is a sadistic killer whose enthusiasm for his work results in the unplanned death of one of Diamond's rivals. This event places the gangster in jeopardy and leads to his later decision to use Murray as a scapegoat in his dealings with Jimmy Biondo.

Jimmy Biondo, a gangster and one of Diamond's chief rivals. Diamond alternately battles and forms shaky alliances with Biondo throughout the story.

Charlie Northrup, a onetime friend of Diamond, now Jimmy Biondo's brother-in-law. Northrup is a small-time racketeer and bootlegger whose defiance and ties to Biondo earn for him Diamond's enmity.

Joe "Speed" Fogarty, one of Diamond's henchmen. Fogarty is an uncomplicated, garden-variety thug. Affable and loyal to his employer, he bears an uncanny resemblance to Diamond's dead brother.

Jesse Franklin, a middle-aged black man. Jesse is employed by Diamond as a moonshiner. It is through his account that Marcus first learns the true fate of Charlie Northrup.

— *Janet Lorenz*

LENZ
(Lenz: Eine Reliquie von Georg Büchner)

Author: Georg Büchner (1813-1837)
First published: 1839
Genre: Short fiction

Locale: The Vosges Mountains near Strasbourg, France
Time: Late January and early February, 1778
Plot: Biographical

Jacob Michael Reinhold Lenz, a talented poet of the German Storm and Stress movement. At the age of twenty-seven, Lenz is no longer able to write and has gone to the small town of Waldbach, hoping to ease his mental suffering, which verges on insanity. His alternating mood swings and strange behavior reveal a deeply troubled personality. Physically, Lenz is shy and blond, with a child's face and generally unkempt clothes. As a writer, he opposes idealism and insists instead on a reality portrayed so that the reader responds emotionally. At the beginning of this prose fragment, Lenz is desperate to save himself from the abyss of madness. Amid the normal, everyday activities of the village and with the soothing company of Oberlin, he finds a certain amount of peace and is able to fit into society. His tenuous hold on sanity is soon upset by the thought that he might have to leave Waldbach, and he begins to show increasing symptoms of mental breakdown: He suffers tremendous guilt and a religious crisis; he uses self-inflicted pain to combat the cold, dead feeling inside; he creates strange pranks in his mind and makes horrible faces; he talks to himself constantly to dispel an intense loneliness; and finally, when his attacks begin to occur during the day as well as at night, he attempts suicide.

Johann Friedrich Oberlin, a Pietist pastor in the Alsatian town of Waldbach in Steinthal. Extremely well liked and trusted by the townspeople, Oberlin easily offers advice, prayer, consolation, and instruction. At the age of thirty-eight, he is married and quite comfortable and satisfied as a family man and pastor of a small town. Generous and compassionate, he willingly takes Lenz in and cares for him, without knowing about his situation. Such action corresponds to Oberlin's view of God's will, that he help the less fortunate. He also enjoys Lenz's company and comes to care deeply about him. He exudes an inner peace and attempts to give Lenz a refuge. Because he becomes so important to Lenz, he precipitates a serious crisis when he supports Kaufmann's opinion that Lenz should obey his father and return home.

Christopher Kaufmann, a friend of many of the Storm and Stress poets. He had taken Lenz into his home for several months before Lenz went to Waldbach. A rather prosaic figure, he is a supporter of the idealist period in literature, which was then popular. His arrival at Oberlin's home with his fiancée triggers a psychological crisis when he tells Lenz about Lenz's father's letters demanding that Lenz return home and stop wasting his time in Waldbach. Kaufmann complicates the problem by taking Oberlin away from Lenz at this critical time to go to Switzerland with him.

Madame Oberlin, Pastor Oberlin's wife. She is in many ways a reflection of Oberlin himself, gentle and compassionate, accepting Lenz as he is and asking no questions about the past. When his condition becomes evident, she prays for him and substitutes as a good listener while her husband is in Switzerland.

Sebastian Scheidecker (SHI-dehk-uhr), a schoolmaster at Bellefosse. He befriended Lenz before this period in his life and comes, at Oberlin's request, to take Lenz to Strasbourg when suicide attempts make it impossible for Lenz to remain in Waldbach.

— *Susan L. Piepke*

THE LEOPARD
(Il gattopardo)

Author: Giuseppe Tomasi di Lampedusa (1896-1957)
First published: 1958
Genre: Novel

Locale: Sicily
Time: 1860-1910
Plot: Historical

Don Fabrizio Corbera (fah-BREEZ-zee-oh kohr-BEH-rah), the prince of Salina, around whom the novel and its themes revolve. Fabrizio represents the old Sicilian aristocracy, which, as the story begins, is under siege. The Italian

Risorgimento, the movement for Italian unity, is about to defeat the Bourbon monarchy that controls Naples and Sicily. By 1870, ten years after the novel's story begins, Italy is one kingdom, with Rome as its capital. Fabrizio, who is forty-five years old as the story begins, looks on his advancing age and the passing old order of the country with mixed feelings. His personal life is full of disillusionment, but he is aware of the need for political and social compromise. He envies his nephew's lust for his bride but sadly realizes that the marriage is a financial and social necessity. Through most of his adult life, Fabrizio has been similarly torn between personal disappointment and an attempt to transcend personal preoccupations, and he has studied the stars for answers. Eventually, Fabrizio is able to welcome death as a release. He realizes that life will go on without him and that his concerns with the past essentially have been futile.

Tancredi Falconeri (tahn-KREH-dee fahl-koh-NEH-ree), Fabrizio's handsome, dashing nephew, who represents the spirit of compromise that will build the new Italy from its fragmented, aristocratic past. Tancredi joined Garibaldi's army and marries Angelica Sedara for similar reasons, knowing that the old Sicily is passing, that his family needs money, and that acceptance of change is better than futile resistance.

Don Calogero Sedara (kah-loh-JEHR-oh say-DAH-rah), the mayor of Donnafugata, where Fabrizio owns property. Don Calogero is crude and uncultured but wealthy and ambi-

tious. He is aware that his own social origins, from the poor peasantry, represent the ascendancy in modern Italy, and he is eager to manipulate Fabrizio for personal gain.

Angelica Sedara (ahn-jehl-EE-kah), Don Calogero's beautiful daughter, who falls in love with Tancredi. Although she loves Tancredi, Angelica clearly sees what is to be gained from a union with the house of Salina; she has no illusions about love's fragility.

Aimone Chevalley di Monterzuolo (I-moh-neh keh-VAHL-lay dee mohn-tehr-zew-oh-loh), a representative of the Piedmontese government of unification. He asks Fabrizio to serve as a senator in the new kingdom under Victor Emmanuel. Fabrizio refuses, arguing that progress in Sicily is unlikely because Sicilians are obsessed with the past and their visions of past glory. Chevalley protests, believing that the new government can solve Sicily's problems and move Italy into the future.

Concetta Corbera (kohn-CHEHT-tah), Fabrizio's strongest daughter. Her life is embittered by her loss of Tancredi to Angelica Sedara. Concetta and her sisters, Carolina and Caterina, have tried to perpetuate a Christian spirit at the family villa well into the twentieth century, but as the novel ends, Concetta breaks with the past she wanted to preserve. The Salina family line seems at an end.

— *Gordon Walters*

LEOPARDS AND·LILIES

Author: Alfred Duggan (1903-1964)
First published: 1954
Genre: Novel

Locale: Southern England
Time: 1215-1252
Plot: Historical

Margaret FitzGerold, the daughter of Warin FitzGerold, chamberlain to King John. When she first appears, she is a girl of thirteen, immediately promised in marriage by her father to the son of a powerful neighbor. Her story from then on is an account of her struggle to assert her independence and authority in a world in which a woman, especially a noblewoman or heiress, must at all times be the property of one man or another, to be married off at the will of her current protector, whether this is her father or (once her father is dead) King John himself. Margaret's first marriage does not last long, but by the time her sickly first husband dies, England has been plunged into civil war between the king and his barons. In this confusion, Margaret suffers a severe social degradation, being married to Falkes de Brealte, a Norman knight of low birth but a successful mercenary soldier and captain of the king's crossbows. Margaret is half attracted and half repelled by him. She compromises, assisting him as long as he is rising in the social scale but deserting him in the end and claiming that her marriage to him eight years earlier was forced and therefore should be declared void. Sadly for her, her desertion at this point is condemned even by Falkes's enemies. After she has died alone and friendless, it is revealed that her appeal for annulment of marriage was rejected by the pope. Readers know that her marriage was in a sense compelled, even though she made no effort to escape from it while her husband was successful. Her tragedy is that of a strong, if selfish, character,

condemned by a world that is as selfish as herself, but more calculating and without her errors of timing.

Falkes de Brealte, the captain of the king's crossbows. Falkes owes his name to his boyhood killing of a fully armored knight while armed only with a scythe. A Norman by birth, he has no position in English society except that which he can win by violence and professional competence. His marriage to Margaret is a payoff by King John for loyal service, and it gives Falkes a chance at achieving not only wealth but also security. For a while, in the civil wars that follow John's compelled granting of the Magna Carta, Falkes continues to rise, helped by the good sense of his wife. She counsels the raid on St. Albans Abbey, though she also sends Falkes back to be flogged by the monks in penance for his deed. At the battle of Lincoln, he plays a dominant role in the king's victory. Once King John is dead, Falkes's violent ways become less successful. His last castle, Bedford, eventually is stormed by his enemies, now loyal to the boy-king Henry, and Falkes loses all of his possessions and is sent into exile. He is still accompanied, however, by men who remain loyal to him against all self-interest. His likable and straightforward villainy is set against his wife's strong will but cold heart.

King John, a totally unscrupulous monarch set on imposing his will on a rebellious country. He is killed in the end by his own gluttony.

William the Marshal, an old hero and famous fighter in single combats, eventually regent of England in the place of the nine-year-old King Henry, successor to John. The marshal's romantic passion for chivalry and courtesy is contrasted with Falkes's professionalism and is shown to be merely the effect of greater wealth and security.

Sir Reginald Croc, a mercenary knight in Falkes's service. He is killed at the battle of Lincoln, without support from the noble knights of his own side, for thrusting himself into a battle between gentlemen.

Sir William de Brealte, Falkes's legitimate half brother, totally devoted to Falkes's service but as incompetent as he is brave. His mistakes lead to the fall of the castle of Bedford, as well as the capture of Margaret, while Falkes is absent. Sir William is hanged without mercy as another interloper and ruffian, a fate unthinkable for more gentlemanly enemies of the king and the marshal.

— T. A. Shippey

LESS THAN ANGELS

Author: Barbara Pym (Mary Crampton, 1913-1980)
First published: 1955
Genre: Novel

Locale: London, its suburbs, and the English countryside
Time: The 1950's
Plot: Fiction of manners

Catherine Oliphant, a writer of stories and articles for women's magazines. A short, slender woman, thirty-one years old, she is a keen observer of everyday life, more perceptive in her reading of the nuances of social behavior than are many of the anthropologists who figure in the story. She is witty, whimsical, self-deprecating, and unconventional. In her fiction, she manipulates romantic clichés with ironic detachment, yet she nurtures such fancies herself. As the novel begins, she is awaiting the return of her lover, Tom Mallow, who has been in Africa for nearly two years. Later, after Tom leaves her, she develops an interest in Alaric Lydgate, a fellow outsider.

Tom Mallow, an anthropologist. Handsome, vain, self-absorbed, and unfailingly attractive to women, the twenty-nine-year-old Tom is the last scion of a once-prominent family with a rundown estate in Shropshire. He returns from Africa with a nearly completed dissertation and no real belief in his work. After jilting Catherine for a young student, Deirdre Swan, he goes back to Africa, where he is killed by accident when police fire into a crowd to suppress a riot.

Professor Felix Byron Mainwaring, an eminent anthropologist. A cultured man from a privileged background, he is conscious of his distinction. In retirement, he has turned to fund-raising, using his considerable charm to establish in London an anthropological library and research center. The irony is that he has entirely lost his passion for the actual practice of anthropology.

Minnie Foresight, a wealthy widow whom Mainwaring has persuaded to endow the center and from whom he expects additional funds to provide research grants for promising students.

Esther Clovis, who is currently Mainwaring's administrative assistant at the library and research center, a middle-aged woman with a long-established and near-religious devotion to anthropology.

Gertrude Lydgate, an anthropologist and linguist specializing in African languages. As the novel begins, she has recently become the housemate of Esther Clovis, whose fervor for anthropology she shares.

Father Gemini, a Roman Catholic priest and an anthropologist, a sometime collaborator with Gertrude Lydgate. Sur-

reptitiously, he prevails on Foresight to give to him the money ticketed for Mainwaring's grants to use for a project of his own.

Digby Fox, an anthropology student in his third year at the university, hopeful of receiving a grant from Mainwaring's center. After Tom's death, Digby receives Tom's fellowship and, apparently, inherits his relationship with Deirdre Swan as well.

Mark Penfold, another third-year anthropology student, Digby's constant companion. After the fiasco of the research grants, the cynical Mark abandons anthropology for business: He has a job lined up in the firm of his fiancée's father.

Jean-Pierre le Rossignol, an anthropology student from France. His reductionism and his French condescension render him hilariously incompetent as an interpreter of English customs.

Deirdre Swan, a nineteen-year-old anthropology student who lives with her mother, her mother's sister, and her older brother in a suburb north of London. Her commitment to her chosen field of study is minimal, but she is wholehearted in her commitment to Tom. She perceives him as a romantic ideal, never seeing him clearly. After his death, she refuses to dramatize their love, and it is clear that she is ready to get on with her life.

Alaric Lydgate, Gertrude Lydgate's brother and the Swans' next-door neighbor, an anthropologist recently removed from the Colonial Service in Africa. He regards himself as a failure and is oppressed by the trunkfuls of field notes that he has never "written up." He enjoys a minor reputation as a merciless reviewer in anthropological journals. Craggy-featured and eccentric, he finds in Catherine a kindred spirit; at her urging, he consigns all of his notes to a liberating bonfire, much to the horror of his sister and Miss Clovis.

Elaine, Tom's first love, from Shropshire, a woman of his own class and still attached to him. She takes great interest in raising golden retrievers. After Tom's death, she goes to London with his sister for lunch with Catherine and Deirdre; the lunch is a civil but surreal meeting of the women in Tom's life.

— John Wilson

THE LESSON
(La Leçon)

Author: Eugène Ionesco (1912-1994)
First published: 1954
Genre: Drama

Locale: Europe
Time: The 1930's
Plot: Absurdist

The professor, between fifty and sixty years old, who tutors individual pupils for their "total doctorate" examinations. During a session with a young female student, he is meek at first. He becomes more intense and authoritarian as the lesson advances. Eventually, he becomes irrationally, even absurdly, angry; disallowing any interruptions of his barrage on philology, the old man grows increasingly excited. First, he attacks the student using language as a tool of dominance, power, deception, and, in the end, violent cruelty. Finally, he loses all patience and sinks into a homicidal mania. He aids the maid in disposing of the student's body.

The pupil, an eighteen-year-old woman wearing a gray student's smock with a small white collar and carrying a student's bookbag. A new student of this professor, the young lady is hopeful of passing a "total doctorate" exam and has engaged the professor as a tutor. As the lesson progresses, she displays an absurd lack of elementary knowledge, such as the capital of France and the seasons of the year; she can add and multiply but is unable to subtract. Faced with what appears to be a remorseless and ominous personal attack, this pupil develops a toothache that eventually spreads over her entire body. Midway through the lesson, she unexpectedly musters enough courage and composure to defy the professor— without success. Reduced to an aching helplessness, the young woman becomes the pathetic victim of the domineering and maniacal professor as her body falls, "flopping into an immodest position in the chair."

The maid, also called **Marie**, a stout woman between forty-five and fifty years old, wearing an appropriate apron and peasant's cap. She is proper, detached, and resigned but watchful. On one occasion, she interrupts the lesson to warn the professor to remain calm; on another, she interrupts to warn him against moving the lesson into the realm of philology: "Arithmetic leads to philology, and philology leads to crime," she scolds. The maid seems slightly annoyed at the results of the professor's stabbing session and calmly complains about the number of students (this is the fortieth) that he has victimized this way, because she is obliged to aid in the disposal of the bodies. Like the professor, she wears a swastika-like armband during the removal of the pupil's body. With no other apparent concern and in her original attire, she ushers in yet another pupil.

— *Cynthia Jane Whitney*

A LESSON BEFORE DYING

Author: Ernest J. Gaines (1933-   )
First published: 1993
Genre: Novel

Locale: A small Cajun community in Louisiana
Time: Sometime after World War II
Plot: Social realism

Grant Wiggins, who grew up in the "quarters" and has returned from a California university to teach "reading, writing, and 'rithmetic" in the plantation school. As a first-person narrator in a plot progression that is both bitter and humorous, Grant is not altogether admirable. Struggling with individual and communal concerns, he behaves from a perspective of superiority. In tragic and comedic episodes, he exhibits an ironic detachment that is neither naïve nor dispassionate but perplexingly veiled. His self-deprecatory and contemptuous voice disguises skepticism and uncertainty. Only reluctantly does he attempt the role of secular priest to a convicted man.

Jefferson, a reluctant participant in a liquor store shootout in which three persons are killed: Brother and Bear (the robbers) and Alcee Grope (the white owner). As the lone survivor, Jefferson is accused of planning the robbery and of murder. At his trial, the defense attorney contends that Jefferson is incapable of premeditated murder even though he behaved "like a fool" or "a cornered animal." To the outrage of Jefferson's godmother and significant others in the "quarters," the lawyer further argues, "Why, I could just as soon put a hog in the electric chair as this." Jefferson is sentenced by a panel of twelve white men to death by electrocution. Enduring the drab conditions of incarceration, Jefferson achieves self-awareness when he is encouraged by his former teacher, Grant Wiggins, to write his thoughts. As a result, after responding detachedly to his godmother and Grant for months and literally wallowing in home-prepared food, Jefferson speaks eloquently, in his diary, of his humanity.

Aunt Lou, Grant's God-fearing aunt, who is challenged to rise above private agitation to confront a brutal character assault. She possesses attributes of the author's maternal aunt, Miss Augusteen Jefferson. Aunt Lou and Miss Emma Glenn, as elders, provide the bedrock of family life that sustains the "quarters." Through Jefferson's months of suffering, Aunt Lou's adaptability serves as a contrast to Grant's lackluster vacillation. Behaving as a role model, however imperfectly, Aunt Lou does not succumb to past fears and immobility when a resident of the "quarters" is defamed. Her wish is that Jefferson meet his execution like a man, not the unthinking "hog" he was called by the white lawyer.

Miss Emma Glenn, the godmother of the accused man. She persuades Grant to impart something of himself (as a teacher and symbol) to Jefferson in an effort to prove the lawyer wrong. Miss Emma moves through the trial episodes and the world of the narrative with a calm and control that seem always on the verge of eruption. Through Miss Emma, Jefferson becomes a concern of the entire community— "quarters" occupants, the Bayonne residents, even Grant's students in the church school.

— Bettye J. Williams

A LESSON FROM ALOES

Author: Athol Fugard (1932-   )
First published: 1981
Genre: Drama

Locale: Port Elizabeth, South Africa
Time: Autumn, 1963
Plot: Representational

Piet Bezuidenhout (peet be-ZI-dehn-howt), a native Afrikaner (of Dutch descent and white), originally a farmer, later a bus driver, and now in his mid-forties and retired. He lives with his wife, Gladys, in Algoa Park, Port Elizabeth, South Africa. In his quiet life of retirement, Piet takes long walks into the veld to collect and classify aloes—hardy, cactuslike plants that can survive in an arid and hostile environment. Spectacled and studious, gentle, and sensitive, Piet is a lover of words, ready at a moment's notice to recite the works of his favorite English poets. Piet was recently very active in local politics, vigorously opposing the South African policy of apartheid. After police repression destroyed the Liberal Party, however, Piet retired from his political activism. He nevertheless remains a moderately hopeful man, convinced that social injustices can be remedied and that the world can be made a better place.

Steve Daniels, a bricklayer, a mason, a former political activist, and Piet's closest friend in the struggle against apartheid. Forty-two years old and Coloured (of mixed racial blood), Steve has just been released from jail and is no longer willing to fight for social change in South Africa. Deeply humiliated by his arrest and interrogation, as well as still under a banning order that makes it impossible for him and his family to live in South Africa, Steve is now frustrated, defeated, and pessimistic about South African politics. The government is forcing him to leave his homeland, and Steve is bitter about having to move to England. When he arrives at Piet's home for a farewell dinner party, he is initially playful and friendly with his best friend, but ultimately his bitter pessimism clashes with Piet's quiet and restrained hopefulness.

Gladys Bezuidenhout, Piet's wife, born in South Africa of English parents, also in her mid-forties. A recent victim of a nervous breakdown, Gladys is withdrawn, apprehensive, and bitter. She still nurses the indignity she felt when the police raided their house and confiscated her personal diaries and still is traumatized by the electric-shock therapy treatments she received in the hospital. During the period of Piet's activism, Gladys had been indifferent about South African politics. Now, she is angered and frightened by Piet's allusions to the political situation. Steve's farewell visit precipitates another breakdown as she accuses Piet of being the informant who caused Steve's arrest. At the end of the play, she volunteers to return to the asylum for more treatments and rest.

— Terry Nienhuis

LET ME BREATHE THUNDER

Author: William Attaway (1911-1986)
First published: 1939
Genre: Novel

Locale: Northwestern United States
Time: The 1930's
Plot: Naturalism

Ed, the narrator, a white man in his twenties. Ed, a migrant worker, is quiet, reflective, and loyal to his buddy Step. He tells nothing about his family or background. He killed steers in St. Louis, Missouri, and rides the rails from job to job.

Step, a white man in his twenties. He is an impetuous leader with red hair and a quick temper. A former fighter, he seems cold on the outside but hides a sensitive soul. Little is revealed concerning his background. He works hard, drinks hard, fights hard, and has little respect for women, yet is very responsible in taking care of an abandoned nine-year-old boy.

Hi Boy, a nine-year-old Mexican boy abandoned by his family in a Southwestern town called La Cruces. He gives away the last of his money when he meets Step and Ed. Hi Boy shoots a rifle. His name comes from the phrase he often speaks.

Sampson, the owner of Four Mile Farm, an apple and sheep ranch in Yakima Valley. He hires Ed and Step. He is a kind, lonely man, a widower with one daughter. He speaks Spanish and urges Hi Boy to live with him. His four sons died in World War I, and his wife died of grief soon afterward.

Anna Sampson, a blond teenage girl who likes film magazines and romance. She falls in love with Step and tries to get him to stay on the farm. Her final attempt to acquire independence results in tragedy.

Mag, a fifty-three-year-old black woman. She is a former prostitute who now owns a brothel, a house, and land in Yakima. Mag is tough but kind and affectionate to Ed, Hi Boy, and her old friend Step. Mag loves a special handmade four-barrel shotgun but cannot shoot.

Cooper, Mag's companion, a "high yellow" black man with failing health who has a wild past. His struggle with Anna and Mag creates the climax of the novel.

— Stephen F. Soitos

LET THE CIRCLE BE UNBROKEN

Author: Mildred D. Taylor (1943-   )
First published: 1981
Genre: Novel

Locale: Rural Mississippi
Time: The 1930's
Plot: Social realism

Cassie Logan, one of four children in the Logan family. Cassie is old enough to understand segregation and what it means to be black in the South during the 1930's. She has an inquiring mind and wishes to learn more about the Mississippi constitution. Proud of her race, she despises her mulatto cousin, Suzella, who thinks of herself as white. The execution of her friend T. J., her brother Stacey's running away from home, racial hostility in her neighborhood, and the reality of the Depression take their toll on her emotionally. Her parents' nurturing of pride and self-respect and her close family ties, however, help Cassie to survive.

David Logan, called **Papa**, Cassie's father. Papa is an old-fashioned disciplinarian but a hardworking and considerate father. He tries to support his family on their small farm, but the Agricultural Adjustment Administration (AAA) and the exploitation of poor farmers by powerful white landowners make his cotton cultivation a constant struggle against poverty. He is forced to seek employment out of town to survive. He continually foils the plans of Harlan Granger, who is determined to annex his property through deception.

Harlan Granger, the most powerful of four major white landowners in the county. He thrives in an environment of segregation and prejudice, gets practically anything he wants from the sheriff's office, and is hated by the poor sharecroppers in the county. He is envious of the Logans' four-hundred-acre property and attempts to annex it to his six-thousand-acre estate.

T. J. Avery, a young black friend of the Logans. T. J. is tried and executed for the shooting death of a local merchant, even though the murder was committed by a white boy.

Wade Jamison, T. J.'s white attorney and legal counsel of the Logans. Jamison tries to secure a lesser charge against T. J. during the trial, but the all-white jury scorns Jamison, witnesses stereotype him as a "nigger lawyer," and the judge treats him disrespectfully. Later, he succeeds in securing the release of Stacey Logan and Moe Turner.

Suzella Rankin, a light-skinned second cousin of the Logans, from New York. Her white mother and black father are separated. She goes to Mississippi to stay with "family" for a while but is despised because she identifies herself with her mother's white heritage. She worsens relations between herself and the Logans by befriending white boys in the neighborhood, but later she is loved by the family.

Stacey Logan, the eldest son in the Logan family. Stacey is devastated by the execution of his friend T. J. and becomes more depressed when Papa leaves home in search of work. At the age of fourteen, he and Moe Turner, a friend, run away to find work on a Louisiana cane field, leaving the Logans to undertake a long search before they find the boys in detention.

Mama, Cassie's mother. She was born in the Mississippi delta region to a sharecropper. At the age of nineteen, she began teaching in Spokane County and married David Logan. She lost her teaching job because she supported a boycott against the Wallaces, who ran the store on the Granger plantation. Mama assists students with evening lessons, works hard to help sustain the family, and runs the farm in Papa's absence.

— *N. Samuel Murrell*

LET THE DEAD BURY THEIR DEAD

Author: Randall Kenan (1963-   )
First published: 1992
Genre: Short fiction

Locale: Tims Creek, North Carolina
Time: Primarily the twentieth century
Plot: Occult

Clarence Pickett, a young boy in "Clarence and the Dead." At the age of three, he begins to pass on advice from dead residents of the town to living ones, usually concerning people and details the young boy could have no way of knowing.

John Edgar Stokes, an old black man from the story "Things of This World." He has a showdown with some local white bigots shortly before his death.

Henrietta Williams, an older black woman in "The Foundations of the Earth." After her grandson's death, she invites her grandson's male lover to stay with her for a few days.

Aaron Streeter, a spoiled and self-conscious man in the story "Cornsilk." He dwells on and fantasizes over a brief incestuous relationship that he had with his half sister, Jamonica, years earlier.

Mabel Pearsall, a spiritually and physically tired schoolteacher who, in the story "The Strange and Tragic Ballad of Mabel Pearsall," becomes obsessed with the idea that a young

child she sometimes babysits is her husband's illegitimate offspring.

Booker T. Washington, a fictionalized version of the influential black educator. In the story "This Far," he visits Tims Creek in 1915, shortly before his death, trying to find connections to some old friends.

Dean Williams, a white homosexual man hired to seduce and help blackmail a wealthy black man in the story "Run, Mourner, Run."

Lena Walker, a recently widowed middle-aged black woman in the story "What Are Days?" She has a brief, passionate affair with a teenage boy who later seems to disappear.

The Reverend Barden, a minister in "Ragnarok! The Day the Gods Die." He delivers a eulogy for a young woman with whom he had a sexual affair.

Ida Perry, the widow of the deceased judge "Butch" Perry. She begins to be haunted by the spirit of a young black male whom her husband beat to death many years earlier.

Reginald Kain, the imaginary editor of the title story, a fictional oral history of a slave revolt.

Pharaoh, also known as **Menes**. In the title story, he leads a possibly apocryphal slave revolt that results in the founding of a settlement that eventually became Tims Creek.

— *Thomas J. Cassidy*

LETTER TO LORD LISZT
(Brief an Lord Liszt)

Author: Martin Walser (1927-   )
First published: 1982
Genre: Novel

Locale: Southwestern Germany, near Lake Constance
Time: Mid-June in the early 1980's
Plot: Social realism

Franz Horn, a middle-aged business executive in the Chemnitz Denture corporation. An ineffectual but highly conscientious bureaucrat, he is in charge of the company's personnel, taxes, and properties. He possesses a photographic memory, in which he documents the alcoholic shortcomings of his most serious rival, Liszt. Most of the novel consists of a letter—with nineteen postscripts—to Liszt, in which he reveals his authentic feelings of disgust toward him. A lonely and suicidal but highly sensitive man, Horn had planned to abandon the company and join its primary rival, Stierle Dentures, but Stierle's suicide and subsequent events stopped him. Horn is pathologically suspicious of Liszt and is torn between admiration for his great talents and repulsion at his crass manipulation of his underlings. He decides at the novel's conclusion not to send the letter and departs, after downing three bottles of wine, for his mother's name-day celebration.

Arthur Thiele (TEE-leh), the middle-aged head of the Chemnitz Denture and Fin Star corporation. Wealthy, self-reliant, and handsome, Thiele is the envy of both Horn and Liszt. He is completely relaxed in the world and enjoys all the privileges his wealth offers him. He saves Horn's life after Horn's suicide attempt yet keeps him employed. He is an inveterate womanizer and performs every action with an ease and assurance that drives Horn to despair. Wherever he goes, he is at center stage because of his charisma.

Dr. Horst Liszt (lihst), a tall, attractive, brilliant alcoholic whose fall within the company is inevitable. Liszt is the major rival of Horn, yet he is also his closest friend. He is well dressed and highly articulate but at heart a manipulative seeker of power and privilege. Liszt possesses all the qualities that Horn lacks. In a letter that initially had been intended as a note of apology for a drunken argument on the feast of the Ascension, Horn declares him the most accomplished monster he has ever encountered.

Dr. Rudolf Ryynänen (ree-NAY-nehn), an up-and-coming young business executive. Ryynänen is an Austro-Finn who was discovered in Helsinki by Thiele. He has brought into the company his major area of expertise, the surfboard business, and has increased the profits of the company enormously. His innovative business practices have put both Horn and Liszt out

of any serious running for executive advancement within the company, and he is highly resented by both men.

Benedikt Stierle (SHTEER-leh), the middle-aged president of Chemnitz's chief rival in the denture business. The novel opens with the announcement of his suicide and the burning of his company's plant on the eve of Horn's decision to leave his job and join Stierle. Those events eradicate Horn's plan to improve his professional status.

Klothilde Horn (kloh-TIHL-deh), Horn's seventy-six-year-old mother. She is a highly controlling matriarchal figure who is very much in charge of Horn and his family. A former waitress, she is so secretive that she refuses to tell him the identity of his real father, permitting him to believe that Vater Willi is his father. At the end of the novel, Horn leaves for the celebration of her name day.

Hilde Horn, Franz Horn's attractive wife. She is an excellent wife and mother of two daughters, as well as being an amateur singer who teaches singing to talented local students. She, too, has an excellent memory. She quarrels with Franz over his pathological hoarding instinct. Their marriage has been resuscitated since Franz's suicide attempt, but they never talk about it.

Vater Willi (FAH-tehr VIHL-lee), ostensibly Franz Horn's father but actually his stepfather. He is dead before the novel begins. Horn recalls him as a down-to-earth, dyspeptic bricklayer, a kind man who spent his weekends smoking, drinking, and playing cards.

Mrs. Brass, Horn's secretary, who has been a member of the staff of Chemnitz Denture from its inception. She is an attractive middle-aged woman who wears her blond hair pulled back into a severe bun. She spends most of her time either sighing or complaining but is overly solicitous of Horn's well-being. The major gossip of the office, she treats all subordinates with a withering frostiness.

Erna Zentgraf (TSEHNT-grahf), Liszt's secretary, a highly loyal woman who takes great pains to cover up her boss's progressive alcoholism. She is an excellent amateur singer and a student of Hilde Horn. She sings wherever she is and enthusiastically expresses her gratitude for the gifts that life has given her.

— *Patrick Meanor*

LETTERS FROM THE UNDERWORLD
(Zapiski iz podpolya)

Author: Fyodor Dostoevski (1821-1881)
First published: 1864
Genre: Novel

Locale: St. Petersburg, Russia
Time: Mid-nineteenth century
Plot: Impressionistic realism

The narrator, the "I" of the treatise, a man convinced of his own depravity. A theorist addressing imaginary listeners, his readers, he declares that he will tell only the truth. Ugly in face and misshapen in body, though with an intelligent, even practiced alertness, he was for many years morbidly shy and grotesque in his vices. A government clerk of a mean and vindictive disposition, he declares that he would devote his life to idleness and the creation of beauty could he live again. As it is, he will continue in the same vein, acutely conscious of his intellectual prowess, aware of the pleasure he finds in humiliating himself painfully. He knows himself a pretender (even this autobiographical sketch is in jest), but he is now incapable of feeling. He describes incidents that show his lack of acumen, his inability to love or take action, his despicable indulgence in self-pity, and his consciously depraved behavior. He presents his bookishness, his intense self-consciousness, his inability to follow a line of action, and his masochistic-sadistic impulses as examples of humankind's perverse nature, which refuses the attainment of perfection or even the striving for it.

Liza (LIH-zuh), a peasant girl come to St. Petersburg, an inexperienced prostitute. As the victim of the narrator's determined debauch, the rather handsome, strong, contemplative Liza finds in the man's drunken meanderings a kind of solace. Accepting his admonitions as to the life she is beginning, she goes to see him because she believes that he offers her hope and love. Although his own surroundings are even more distasteful than hers, she insists on unburdening her feeling of love for him. Taking advantage of her tender feelings, he makes love to her and then tells her spitefully that he has no feelings except the desire to wield power, to hold another soul in his hands. Humiliated, she throws back the money he disdainfully gives her and leaves him.

Anton Antonitch Syetotchkin (ahn-TOHN ahn-TOHN-ihch seh-TOHCH-kihn), the narrator's immediate superior in a government office, a kind man with a pleasant family and a generous disposition and the one person the narrator seems to respect. Anton lends the young clerk advances on his salary and welcomes the lonely and bookish young man into his home. Evenings spent listening to discussions of conservative politics and mundane affairs cause the young man to postpone his burning desire to embrace humankind, a desire that is as false as his other emotions.

Simonov (sih-MYOH-nof), the narrator's school friend, a pleasant person who lends him money and occasionally entertains the self-conscious clerk. Simonov allows the narrator to come with other student friends to a farewell party for a mutual friend. Later, he becomes embarrassed at the fellow's boorish behavior but lends him money to continue the debauch at a brothel.

Zverkov (zvehr-KOHF), an army officer who owns two hundred serfs and is much respected in consequence. Because he is a hale fellow, an amusing storyteller, and a man about town, the narrator resents him. Zverkov, instead of taking offense at the insulting manner of his former schoolmate, declares that such a low person cannot insult him. This haughtiness, coupled with his bragging stories of conquest, infuriates but tantalizes the narrator, who abases and humiliates himself purposely before his old friends.

LETTING GO

Author: Philip Roth (1933-   )
First published: 1962
Genre: Novel

Locale: Chicago, New York, Iowa, and Pennsylvania
Time: The 1950's
Plot: Satire

Gabriel (Gabe) Wallach, a young instructor of English at the University of Chicago. He had studied creative writing at the University of Iowa, where he met a fellow graduate student, Paul Herz. He becomes heavily involved in Paul's complicated life with Libby DeWitt, the woman Paul eventually marries. Gabe finds Paul a job as an instructor at the University of Chicago, and their involvements deepen. Gabe's life is complicated by devotion to his widowed father, his affair with Martha Reganhart, his encounters with his department chairman and his wife, and his love-hate relationship with the Herzes.

Paul Herz, Gabe's friend and colleague at the University of Chicago. Poor, hardworking, and not especially witty or intelligent, he has an affair with Libby DeWitt, a student whom he later marries. He has aspirations to become a writer, but eventually, under pressure of poverty and family responsibilities, he decides to become a schoolteacher instead.

Elizabeth (Libby) DeWitt, a student who becomes Paul's wife. She was reared as a Catholic but later decides to convert and be as good a Jewish wife to Paul as possible. Early in their relationship, she becomes pregnant and reluctantly agrees to an abortion. Later, wanting a child but unable for health reasons to risk conceiving another one, she persuades Paul to adopt a baby. The baby, Rachel, is found through Gabe's help,

but adoption is difficult and almost fails. In a strange, almost perverse way, Gabe is attracted to Libby, but he resists the temptation to become her lover, realizing that such a relationship might be disastrous for her as well as for Paul.

Martha Reganhart, a divorcée and mother of two children who becomes Gabe's mistress after they meet in a restaurant, where she is waiting on tables. Gabe is attracted not only by her beauty but also by her crazy household and her determination to make something out of her life despite the handicaps of her upbringing and bad marriage. The relationship falters, however, when Gabe finds himself unable to make a full commitment to her and her children.

Marge Howells, a woman from Kenosha, Wisconsin, with whom Gabe has an affair in Iowa. She falls in love with Gabe, who from the outset recognizes that the relationship cannot last. He lets it continue rather than face the alternatives of loneliness and the absence of sex in his life, but he eventually breaks it off, using a visit to his father in New York as the occasion.

Theresa Haug, a waitress who works with Martha Reganhart. She is separated from her husband and becomes pregnant with an unwanted baby. It is her child that Gabe arranges for the Herzes to adopt, but the arrangement becomes complicated when Theresa's husband, Harry Bigoness, balks.

Sid Jaffe, a lawyer, Martha's longtime suitor, whom she does not love enough to marry, although he has been consistently kind to her and her children. After her breakup with Gabe, she finally agrees to marry him.

Asher Herz, Paul's bachelor uncle, whose independent lifestyle is in direct contrast to Paul's. Before marrying Libby, Paul considers a life like Asher's and is almost persuaded by its attractions.

John Spigliano, Gabe's department chairman at the University of Chicago, through whom he meets Martha Reganhart, one of John's older students. He is married to Pat; they have two children and like to throw parties. At their Christmas party, after walking out on Martha, Gabe flirts brazenly with one of his female colleagues, Peggy Moberly, after watching Paul and Libby furtively embracing.

— *Jay L. Halio*

THE LIAR
(Le Menteur)

Author: Pierre Corneille (1606-1684)
First published: 1644
Genre: Drama

Locale: Paris, France
Time: The seventeenth century
Plot: Farce

Dorante (doh-RAHNT), a young student who has recently arrived in Paris to get a social education. A brazen liar, he accommodates himself so well to his new situation that he captivates Clarice, Lucrèce, and their companions with accounts of his heroic exploits in war and his extraordinary amatory adventures in Paris. Enmeshed more and more in a web of lies, mistaken identities, and the like, he finally marries Lucrèce, whom he swears he has loved all along.

Géronte (zhay-ROHNT), Dorante's father, who comes to Paris to arrange a marriage for his son. He is duped into believing that Dorante has been forced to marry a woman to save her honor. When he learns of the deception, he swears he will never again help his rogue of a son, but he docilely arranges for his marriage to Lucrèce nevertheless.

Lucrèce (lew-KREHS), a shy and virtuous girl who finally marries Dorante, who captivated her with his first lies on his arrival in Paris.

Clarice (klah-REES), a young girl betrothed to Alcippe, and a friend of Lucrèce.

Alcippe (ahl-SEEP), Dorante's friend and the jealous lover of Clarice, whom he finally marries after they all become extricated from the web of Dorante's lies.

Cliton (klee-TOH[N]), Dorante's valet and mentor in Paris, who is hired because of his military and amatory connections.

Philiste (fee-LEEST), a friend of Dorante and Alcippe.

Sabine (sah-BEEN), Lucrèce's maid and Dorante's fellow liar.

LIBER AMORIS: Or, The New Pygmalion

Author: William Hazlitt (1778-1830)
First published: 1823
Genre: Novel

Locale: London and Scotland
Time: 1820-1822
Plot: Autobiographical

H. (William Hazlitt), a writer and lover. The author is writing an account of his own foolish passion for a young girl, S. (Sarah Walker), whom he meets in a boardinghouse owned by her father, M.W. (Micaiah Walker). Aware, in his heart, that the girl allows him more liberties than her show of demureness would justify, he is nevertheless romantic enough to endow her with an innocence and good intent that cause him to keep trying to persuade her to marry him. As he inevitably must, he finally learns that reality and one's own image of it are not necessarily the same.

S. (Sarah Walker), a young girl loved by H., in her late teens when she meets the writer. She sits on his lap day after

day exchanging kisses with him. She fails, however, to appreciate his elaborate protestations of love and can answer only that her regard can go no further than friendship. When she is caught playing the same game with another, her lover is forced to realize that his love is not what she seems.

C.P. (Peter George Patmore), William Hazlitt's friend, to whom he writes about his love for Sarah Walker.

J.S.K. (James Sheridan Knowles), William Hazlitt's friend, to whom the closing letters of *Liber Amoris* are addressed.

M.W. (Micaiah Walker), William Hazlitt's landlord, the father of Sarah Walker.

LIBRA

Author: Don DeLillo (1936-   )
First published: 1988
Genre: Novel

Locale: The United States, Japan, and the Soviet Union
Time: Primarily the 1950's and 1960's
Plot: Postmodernism

Lee Harvey Oswald, John F. Kennedy's assassin. Dyslexic and fatherless, the emotionally insecure Oswald—reared by a neurotic mother and frequently uprooted while growing up—is a misfit, a "solitary," who exists at the very margins

(social, economic, and psychological) of American life. Even as he exacerbates his own social isolation, he fantasizes about belonging, about having a "destiny" and a part to play in history. He drifts across America, following first his mother, then his brother, a Marine. He joins the Navy, is assigned to a U-2 base in Japan, and is befriended by local communists. Back in the United States, he convinces himself that he will be happy if he can live in the Soviet Union. He defects and marries Marina, a Soviet. He comes to feel again that things would be all right if only he could live somewhere else; he sets his sights first on Texas, then on Cuba. Back in the United States, he becomes an object of interest to both the Federal Bureau of Investigation (FBI) and the Central Intelligence Agency (CIA). Their very different interests fuel both his sense of importance and his paranoia. Oswald drifts from one marginal job to another, physically abuses his wife, and becomes involved in both right- and left-wing activities; he is a Libran, "sitting on the scales, ready to be tilted either way." In the plot to kill Kennedy, Oswald's desires and the plotters' needs intersect. Once caught, Oswald comes to believe, cheerfully, that he has found his life's true purpose, his destiny: to sit in a cell—a room of his own—and think and write about the assassination.

Nicholas Branch, a retired senior CIA analyst. He is in his fifteenth year working on contract with the CIA to write the secret history of the assassination. In this sense, Branch, in his room, with his computer and boxes and shelves of endlessly expanding materials, picks up where Oswald left off in 1963. Working in an area of research he sees as marked by ambiguity and error, by political bias, and by systematic fantasy, Branch wonders how to approach this kind of data and how to distinguish history from paranoia and coincidence from conspiracy. Paranoia proves contagious, however: The more material Branch receives, the more he wonders how much is being withheld.

Walter "Win" Everett, Jr., an embittered fifty-one-year-old CIA agent forced into semiretirement following the Bay of Pigs debacle. Exiled to Texas Women's College, he plots his revenge, a plan that will excite and shock the exile community and the whole country. His plan is an assassination attempt on the president, a "spectacular miss" that will lead to Fidel Castro but that will also expose earlier CIA attempts on Castro's life. At a still deeper level, the plan will be penetrable by only a select few at the CIA. In furtherance of his plan, he decides to create a fictional assassin. Discovering that his fiction already exists in the real world, as Oswald, proves disconcerting and suggests how little control Everett has over his own plot.

Laurence Parmenter, who is, like Everett, a CIA "true believer" and Bay of Pigs veteran. Unlike Everett, Parmenter is a gentleman spy, educated at the finest schools. His anti-Castro anticommunism is linked to opportunities for personal profit. He serves as an intermediary between Everett and Mackey.

Guy Bannister, a sixty-three-year-old former FBI agent. Pushed out of government service, he runs a detective agency in New Orleans that is a front for channeling CIA money to local anti-Castro forces.

David Ferrie, a forty-five-year-old former airline pilot who was discharged for sexual misconduct. He suffers from a disease that has made him completely hairless and interested in the occult, pseudoscience, anticommunism, and young boys.

George de Mohrenschildt, an oft-married "multinational man" with divided loyalties and a penchant for turning spying into personal profit. At a gathering of Russian émigrés, he befriends Oswald, whom he then encourages to meet with the CIA and inadvertently gives the idea of assassinating Edwin Walker.

Major General Edwin A. Walker, a controversial far-right political activist. Oswald shoots at him but misses, the bullet changing course when it nicks a window frame. Walker rails against communism, fluoridation, integration, and the income tax.

Theodore J. Mackey, also known as **T-Jay**, a CIA operative born **Joseph Michael Norniak** and assigned this pseudonym. Like Everett, he refused to sign a letter of reprimand concerning his unauthorized activities following the Bay of Pigs operation and was demoted to training novices. Mackey trusts no one, not even Everett, whose plan he modifies (and betrays). Instead of a spectacular miss in the assassination attempt, Mackey opts for a direct hit.

Carmine Latta, a New Orleans mobster who controlled one-third of the Cuban drug trade before Castro took power in Cuba and who now supplies cash (via Ferrie) to the exiles in return for gambling concessions after Castro is deposed. He offers to take care of Jack Ruby's financial problems in exchange for Ruby killing Oswald.

Marina Oswald, Oswald's Russian wife.

Jack Ruby, the owner of a Dallas strip club. He is protective of the girls he exploits but unsure about his own sexuality. He accepts Carmine Latta's offer and shoots Oswald.

Marguerite Oswald, Oswald's mother, who was married three times: once widowed, once abandoned, and once divorced. She has a fantasy of family life. Grievance is her most characteristic mode of address.

— *Robert A. Morace*

LIE DOWN IN DARKNESS

Author: William Styron (1925-   )
First published: 1951
Genre: Novel

Locale: Virginia and New York City
Time: The 1920's through 1945
Plot: Psychological realism

Peyton Loftis, the youngest daughter of Helen and Milton Loftis. She is emotionally scarred by her mother's continuous rejection and her father's smothering love and indulgence. At her sixteenth birthday party, Peyton, encouraged by her father, drinks alcohol and infuriates her mother. When Helen attempts to make Peyton leave the party, Peyton proclaims her hatred for her mother. Later that evening, Peyton becomes aware of her father's infidelity, causing further distress. She soon leaves home for college, and her subsequent attempts to return lead only to further estrangement. She eventually leaves school for New York City, where she meets and marries Harry Miller. The wedding—Peyton's last attempt to return home and win her mother's approval—ends with Peyton and Milton both becoming drunk, Peyton telling Milton to stop smothering her, and Helen declaring that she despises Peyton. Peyton and Harry leave for their honeymoon, but their marriage already is doomed. Seemingly incapable of love and yet insanely jealous of Harry's perceived indiscretions, Peyton begins sleeping with other men. She returns to Harry, simultaneously blaming him and begging his forgiveness. Harry leaves her, and Peyton's letters to her father reveal the depths of her despair. She kills herself by jumping naked from a building in New York, and her body is left unclaimed and buried in Potter's Field until Harry rescues it.

Milton Loftis, a lawyer in Port Warwick, Virginia, whose career is stagnant and whose family life is miserable. He is constantly put down by his wife, Helen, who assumes moral superiority and who maintains financial control of the family by means of a substantial inheritance. Milton turns to alcohol and eventually to Dolly Bonner to find solace. He virtually ignores his eldest daughter, Maudie, but is lovingly obsessed with Peyton and constantly tries to serve as mediator between her and Helen. Although Milton behaves miserably when Maudie is critically ill, wandering drunk through Charlottesville while she is in surgery, Maudie's death brings a temporary reconciliation with Helen. Events at Peyton's wedding, however, bring not only another split with Helen but also conflict with Peyton, who screams at him to stop smothering her. Milton's subsequent contacts with Peyton are through letters, and he is devastated when he receives word of her death. Helen rejects his attempts at reconciliation and even refuses to go in the same car with him to Peyton's funeral. At the novel's end, with Peyton reburied in Port Warwick, Milton is ready to leave Dolly but has no sense of purpose or direction.

Helen Peyton Loftis, Milton's wife, who dotes entirely on the handicapped eldest daughter, Maudie, and bitterly resents the hold that Peyton has over Milton. She constantly rejects Peyton's attempts to win her love. Following Maudie's death, Helen irrationally blames Peyton for it. She reconciles with Milton, however. After Peyton announces her desire to return home for her wedding, Helen throws herself into plans for it. At the wedding, she becomes angry and once again rejects Peyton. Despite counseling from Carey Carr, Helen is unable to find meaning in her life or to feel love. Following Peyton's death, she rejects Milton's attempt at reconciliation and steels herself to face life alone.

Maudie Loftis, the physically handicapped and mentally retarded daughter of Helen and Milton who becomes the sole object of her mother's affection. The night before leaving for college, Peyton attempts to assist Maudie but allows her to fall. Although Maudie receives only a slight bruise and is undisturbed by the fall, Helen viciously attacks Peyton. Helen later suggests that the fall contributed to Maudie's death.

Dolly Bonner, Milton's mistress, who is devastated when Milton returns to Helen after Maudie's death. She readily accepts him back after the Loftises fight at Peyton's wedding. Eagerly anticipating Milton's impending divorce, Dolly is crushed when she realizes, at Peyton's funeral, that she is losing Milton again, probably permanently.

Carey Carr, the Episcopal rector at Helen's church to whom Helen turns in her despair. Strongly attracted to Helen, Carey listens and seeks to comfort her but is unable to offer any real help. His own belief in God is so uncertain that he can only mildly protest when Helen angrily asserts that God does not exist.

Harry Miller, a Jewish artist whom Peyton meets in New York and marries. He loves Peyton and attempts to help her but is so tormented by her unfaithfulness and her unfounded attacks on him that he leaves her. When Harry learns of Peyton's death, he has her body exhumed from Potter's Field and shipped to Port Warwick for reburial.

— *Verbie Lovorn Prevost*

A LIE OF THE MIND

Author: Sam Shepard (Samuel Shepard Rogers, 1943-   )
First published: 1986
Genre: Drama

Locale: Oklahoma and Montana
Time: The 1970's or 1980's
Plot: Psychological realism

Jake, the violent and jealous husband of Beth. This combination of traits has kept him in trouble with the law and with his wife's family. He has come to his brother, Frankie, for help after beating his wife—as he believes, to death—because of an affair he assumes Beth to have had while taking part in a community play. Jake tries to avoid responsibility for his actions by pretending to be insane, a ruse seen through by his sister Sally, who helped Jake use the same tactic to escape blame in the death of their father. Jake is not mentally stable, and his psychological condition deteriorates quickly as a result of his mother's care and of tracking Frankie to Beth's family's farm in Montana, where Jake believes his brother to be stealing his wife.

Beth, Jake's wife, a pretty young woman whose brain has been damaged by the brutal beating inflicted on her by Jake, who left her for dead. She is recovering physically, but she functions mentally like a child. She has moments when she is disturbingly lucid. Following Frankie's arrival at the farm, Beth transfers her love for Jake onto Frankie.

Frankie, Jake's younger brother, who, because of his concern for Beth, has gone to her family's farm in Montana to corroborate Jake's story of having killed Beth. While trying to get around Mike's guarding of Beth, Frankie is mistaken for a deer and shot in the leg by Baylor, Beth's father. Because Baylor does not want the sheriff to know of the shooting, Frankie's wound is not treated by anyone but Beth, who tries to answer Frankie's questions.

Sally, Jake's younger sister, who refuses to live in the same house with him and so leaves when Frankie brings Jake to the farm. She is bothered by Jake's lack of responsibility for his actions and refuses to become a part of a scheme to keep him out of trouble for beating Beth. She has protected Jake from the blame in their father's death, but she refuses to protect him again.

Lorraine, Jake's mother. She mothers him more than she mothers her other children. She works to deny any blame for Jake and even goes as far as suggesting that he find another woman and forget about Beth. Her solution to Jake's troubles is the same one to which she was subjected by Jake's alcoholic father, who packed up when trouble arose; thus, she is helping to continue and condone a cycle of abuse.

Baylor, Beth's father. He is a man concerned about himself, not his family. His refusal to attend Beth's wedding and the shack in which he lives during deer season are symbols of his self-absorption. He has few kind words for his wife or his children and views the trip to see Beth in the hospital as a good chance to sell mules.

Meg, Beth's mother, a woman whose attempts to understand Baylor's withdrawal from her and from their family have drained her of any desire to make sense of the world. Instead, she tries to block out unpleasant events. She is forced, however, to deal with her daughter's injuries in a somewhat productive manner. Meg is, in many ways, more of an invalid than is Beth.

Mike, a young man whose desire to protect his sister from any more harm consumes him. He blames not only Jake for Beth's injuries but also Jake's entire family. When Frankie arrives seeking information about Beth's condition, Mike threatens Frankie. The violence lurking in Mike is later used to subdue and torture Jake when he arrives, although Mike later releases Jake when he realizes that no member of his family is taking much notice of the defense of the family's honor that he has undertaken.

— *Eric H. Hobson*

A LIFE

Author: Hugh Leonard (John Keyes Byrne, 1926-   )
First published: 1980
Genre: Drama

Locale: A small town near Dublin, Ireland
Time: The 1970's
Plot: Psychological realism

Drumm (Desmond Drumm), a sixty-four-year-old Irish civil servant on the verge of retirement. Crusty, intellectual, and snobbish, with a biting wit, he clearly regards himself as better than everyone he knows. He is married to a woman he does not respect, childless, and separated from his community by his exacting standards for intellect and work; he is almost totally isolated. News that he has only six months to live prompts Drumm to attempt a healing of old wounds and a final assessment of his life. That final accounting primarily involves his relationship with his wife and with two childhood friends.

Desmond (Desmond Drumm), a twenty-four-year-old, Drumm's younger self. Desmond is in love with Mary and eager to believe that he can make her live up to what is "best" in her, encouraging her to take her studies more seriously and to avoid the dances and frivolity she loves. The seeds of his later arrogance are evident in his scornful attitude toward Lar. His fellow students' nickname for him, "Mammy Cough-Bottle," hints at the later difficulty he will have getting along with his community.

Dolly Drumm, Drumm's sixty-year-old, long-suffering wife, who loves him dearly but is desperately afraid of angering him. She is more aware of his scorn for her and more wounded by it, than she reveals. She smooths over his every harshness with deliberate cheerfulness and continues to hope for a better future.

Dorothy, Dolly's younger self, a twenty-year-old student in a technical training program. She has been attracted to Desmond since the first time she saw him, and she is closer to him in interests than is Mary, but Desmond is blind to her virtues and marries her only when he loses Mary. He gets a better wife than he deserves.

Mary Kearns, the woman Drumm once loved, now sixty years old. Outspoken, humorous, good-humored, and "more

physical than intellectual," she is nevertheless wiser than Desmond by far. Married to a man the world regards as worthless, she has not only put up with him but also sensed his worth and his warmth. While drunk, her husband accidentally backed a car into her, so she limps slightly, but she is unresentful and accepts the situation as an accident for which her husband should not be blamed. She is not, however, a saint, and when Drumm hurts her husband, she knows exactly how to strike back. Eventually, she gives Drumm the honest accounting of his life's credits and debits for which he has asked.

Mibs, the young Mary, twenty years old. Pretty, lively, and gay, she is no scholar and has no wish to be one. She is attracted to Desmond but chooses Lar instead (despite her parents' preferences) because, even at the age of twenty, she senses that Desmond would seek to shape her every thought and action, whereas Lar will leave a bit of her for herself.

Kearns (Larry Kearns), Mary's sixty-four-year-old husband. He "messes everything up," cannot keep a job, and is overly fond of drinking. He is physical whereas Drumm is intellectual and popular whereas Drumm is friendless. He is also warmhearted and generous, and he is unwounded by most of Drumm's jibes because he is incapable of suspecting ill will in anyone, having none himself. It is largely his contrasting personality that makes Drumm realize that "instead of friends, I've had standards," and the two characters illuminate each other.

Lar (Larry Kearns), Kearns' younger self, who is twenty-four years old. Already too fond of idleness and drink, he wins Mary because he is warm and funny, whereas Desmond is cold and sardonic. His acceptance of and pleasure in the physical side of life includes, but is not limited to, sex. An abundance of goodwill makes him want everyone to be happy.

— *Helen Lojek*

THE LIFE AND DEATH OF MR. BADMAN

Author: John Bunyan (1628-1688)
First published: 1680
Genre: Novel

Locale: Unspecified
Time: Anytime
Plot: Religious

Mr. Badman, a sinner lately dead and the subject of a dialogue that makes up this story, which is, in a sense, a companion piece to the author's *The Pilgrim's Progress*. The very epitome of evil, Mr. Badman is used, in a conversation between Mr. Wiseman and Mr. Attentive, as a model of what happens to the unrepentent sinner as he makes his heedless way through life. His evil-doing begins while he is yet a child; one sin begets another until the sinner's corruption is complete. The author expects his reader to rejoice in the punishment Mr. Badman so richly deserves.

Mr. Wiseman, the author's spokesman, who relates to Mr.

Attentive the story of the late Mr. Badman's evil life. Each sinful episode related by Mr. Wiseman brings forth from him or his listener a kind of sermon or the recitation of a series of edifying examples designed to prove the author's point to his readers.

Mr. Attentive, the listener to, and commentator on, Mr. Wiseman's account of Mr. Badman's wicked career.

Courteous Reader, who is addressed by the author as a probable sinner. He is asked seriously to consider Mr. Badman's life and to decide whether or not he is following him on the road to destruction.

THE LIFE AND EXTRAORDINARY ADVENTURES OF PRIVATE IVAN CHONKIN
and PRETENDER TO THE THRONE
(Zhizn' i neobychainye priklyucheniya soldata Ivana Chonkina *and* Pretendent na prestol)

Author: Vladimir Voinovich (1932-   )
First published: 1975 and 1979
Genre: Novel

Locale: Krasnoye, Russia
Time: 1941
Plot: Satire

The Life and Extraordinary Adventures of Private Ivan Chonkin, 1975

Ivan Chonkin (ee-VAN CHON-keen), a simple Russian soldier sent to the village of Krasnoye to guard a small military plane. Short and puny, bowlegged and lop-eared, he is ill-suited for any role outside of his world, from which he is snatched away and thrust into a situation that almost costs him his life. Instead of living a normal life he desires, he becomes the center of attention and the unwitting opponent of an entire state apparatus. He remains oblivious to all the commotion.

Nyura Belyashova (NYEW-rah bee-LYAH-shoh-vah), the postmistress and Chonkin's lover. A simple, unmarried woman, she is a perfect partner for Chonkin. Only slightly better educated and on the receiving end of cruel jokes, she is unwanted and unloved by anyone else except for her cow and pig. Chonkin's love seem to be Nyura's compensation for years of emptiness and loneliness.

Pretender to the Throne, 1979

Ivan Chonkin, who continues to be the center of attention and of frantic attempts by officials to deal with him. In the end, he fades into the oblivion from which he came, leaving Nyura and everybody else as bewildered as when he came on the scene.

Nyura Belyashova, who, like Chonkin, is unable to understand why people are not allowed to enjoy their happiness. She expresses her bewilderment during her efforts to save her lover. Their plight marks the depth of dehumanization to which Soviet citizens often were subjected.

Ivan Golubev, who refuses to allow harvesting in the rain and is accused of sabotage. He is brave enough to resign from the Communist Party, thus proving that even under dangerous

Ivan Golubev (EE-van goh-LEWB-yehv), a local manager of the collective farm. Although he has more common sense than other functionaries, he still plods through his routine as long as his sense of propriety is not disturbed.

Captain Milyaga (mee-LYAH-gah), the head of the local NKVD (the precursor to the KGB). Milyaga is merciless in peaceful times but cowardly when the going gets tough. Caught in a bizarre turn of events, he becomes a victim of his incompetence and lack of common sense, and he is coldly disposed of by equally incompetent and nonsensical comrades.

Kuzma Gladishev (kew-ZMAH gla-DEE-shehv), a pseudo-scientist raising hybrid potato-tomato plants. By pursuing a nonsensical project, he embodies the type of scientist during Stalin's reign whose work was based primarily on loyalty to the Party. He comes across as ludicrous and worthless.

circumstances a person can preserve his dignity and defy his fellow citizens' prevailing submissive attitude.

Lieutenant Filippov (fee-LEE-pohv), Milyaga's replacement. Though expected to be of the same mold, he displays some conscience and humanness. Although he believes that he is only executing orders from above, he suggests that Chonkin be freed because he has committed no crime. He is still bothered by Chonkin's confession, albeit made under duress. He is at times ashamed of his work but, after all, somebody has to do it. His ambivalence brings on a persecution mania. He decides to help Nyura in her efforts to free Chonkin, but before he can do so, he is arrested as an enemy agent.

Pavel Evpraksein (PAHV-yehl yehv-PRAK-sin), a prosecutor at Chonkin's trial, a farcical example of Soviet justice. Cold-blooded and cruel toward "the enemies of the state," he sees himself as a murderer when drunk. He believes that humans are like wolves to their fellows and cannot get along without punishment, that everyone is guilty of something sooner or later, and that if the Party accuses a person of wrongdoing, he or she should admit guilt. After procuring Chonkin's death sentence, Evpraksein commits suicide, leaving a note saying, "Please consider my life invalid."

Boris Ermolkin (uhr-MOHL-keen), the editor of the local newspaper, lacking in integrity but not in sycophancy, and with a false understanding of his profession. Afraid of the truth, he hides behind professional idiosyncrasies, making sure that Stalin's name is mentioned in each article at least twelve times. He would kill his three-and-a-half-year-old son if the Party so ordered. Not held in high esteem even by his comrades, he dies after being kicked in the head by a horse.

— *Vasa D. Mihailovich*

THE LIFE AND OPINIONS OF KATER MURR
(Lebensansichten des Katers Murr, nebst fragmentarischer Biographie des Kapellmeisters Johannes Kreisler in zufälligen Makulaturblättern)

Author: E. T. A. Hoffmann (1776-1822)
First published: 1819-1821
Genre: Novel

Locale: Germany
Time: Late eighteenth and early nineteenth centuries
Plot: Bildungsroman

Kater Murr (KAH-tehr mewr), a literary tomcat. After being adopted by Master Abraham, he uses his extraordinary intelligence to learn to read and write. His literary masterpiece is his autobiography, written on the back of discarded leaves that happen to contain Kreisler's biography. His death brings a premature end to his memoirs after two volumes. In his egotistical view of himself, Murr is a genius. He feels no embarrassment at expecting future generations of cats to idolize him, and he holds nothing back about the follies of his adolescence, including outbreaks of lovesickness and a brief fling at membership in a cat fraternity.

Johannes Kreisler (yoh-HAHN-nehs KRIZ-lehr), the Kapellmeister (resident composer) of Prince Irenäus' unofficial court at Sieghartshof. About thirty years old, he has dark hair and eyes that give him a soulful look. Kreisler is an eccentric, extremely changeable person with contradictory emotions: At any moment, extreme melancholy may give way to extreme sarcasm. His character was formed by a childhood made desolate by the deaths, a few years apart, of his mother and aunt, and desertion by his father. Kept out of school by the musician uncle who reared him, he learned from various tutors, the most capricious of whom was his piano teacher, Abraham Liscov. Kreisler pursues music until his late teens, with brief interruptions for a diplomatic career. He has become Kapellmeister to the grand duke when the demands of the court become especially humiliating, causing him to run off to Master Abraham in Sieghartshof. Kreisler's love of music is closely intermingled with love of a more romantic sort, for his singing pupil Julia Benzon. He believes that true musicians reach out spiritually to their beloved. After the mysterious affair of Prince Hektor (in which Kreisler stabs the prince's adjutant in self-defense and is very nearly killed), Kreisler keeps in touch with Master Abraham by letter. He has escaped the court to seek refuge in an abbey filled with music-loving monks. Kreisler appears to have attained peace until the appearance of Father Cyprianus brings long-simmering intrigues to bear on him. At the urging of Master Abraham, he goes back to the court, only to find that Julia is to be married.

Master Abraham Liscov (LIHS-kohf), a magician, organ builder, and unofficial counselor to Fürst Irenäus. He is a small, thin man with snow-white hair and coal-black eyebrows, fond of making elaborate artificial devices and playing tricks on people. Having begun his career as a piano tuner, organ builder, and music teacher, he turns up briefly in Italy, as a magician. In Naples, he becomes associated with the conjurer Severino, taking over his Invisible Maiden trick and even his name after the old man's death. There, he becomes involved with the sinister Prince Hektor and with the psychic Chiara, who returns to Germany as Master Abraham's wife before disappearing mysteriously. Now, he serves as "Master of Pleasures" and ironical expert in magic to Fürst Irenäus (as well as a counterforce to Rätin Benzon).

Fürst Irenäus (fewrst ih-rehn-AY-ews), the owner of the court at Sieghartshof. A kindly, cultured, and mildly eccentric aristocrat who has become a wealthy private citizen by losing his tiny princedom through purchase rather than war, Irenäus continues to hold court in his palace of Sieghartshof.

Rätin Benzon (RAY-tihn BEHNT-zohn), a witty, worldly, and intelligent woman in her middle thirties who wishes to pull the strings of the puppets in Irenäus' court. She and the Fürst once had a secret affair, resulting in a child. Having greatly influenced Hedwiga's spiritual development, she is now trying to find a good husband for her daughter Julia and to neutralize what she sees as Master Abraham's opposing plans.

Julia Benzon, the Rätin's daughter. With a voice as beautiful as her face and spirit, she is Kreisler's distant beloved. Eventually, the Rätin marries her to Prince Ignaz, Hedwiga's emotionally retarded brother.

Princess Hedwiga (HEHD-vee-gah), Irenäus' daughter. She is haunted by memories of the mad painter Leonard Ettlinger, who attempted to murder her and then died insane from hopeless love for her mother, the Fürstin. Because she finds an uncanny resemblance to Ettlinger in Kreisler, she at first fears the musician as a madman. Only later does she become reconciled to him. Her betrothal to Prince Hektor is an ominous development, as it intensifies her trances and fainting spells.

— *Paul Kistel*

THE LIFE AND OPINIONS OF TRISTRAM SHANDY, GENT.

Author: Laurence Sterne (1713-1768)
First published: 1759-1767
Genre: Novel

Locale: Shandy Hall in England
Time: 1718-1766
Plot: Wit and humor

Tristram Shandy, the narrator and ostensible hero of this literary farrago devoted to some details of his early life, his father's opinions and eccentricities, his uncle's passion for the reenactment of Marlborough's military campaigns, and assorted oddities of mind and conduct. His mother having incurred some time before the expense of a needless trip to London for a lying-in, Tristram, according to the terms of his parents' marriage contract, is born at Shandy Hall on November 5, 1718. Various misfortunes befall him early in life: a broken nose, crushed by the doctor's forceps at birth; the wrong name, Tristram instead of Trismegistus, when he is christened by a stupid young curate; and the loss of his member, a heavy sash having fallen while he was relieving himself through an open window. Although he is crushed by these irreparable incidents of damage, his father still insists that the boy have a proper education, and to this end Mr. Shandy writes a "Tristra-paedia" in imitation of the "Cyro-paedia" designed for the training of Cyrus the Great, as set forth in the pages of Xenophon. Except for a few scattered hints, the reader learns almost nothing about Tristram's later life. Sterne devotes most of the novel to reporting humorous incidents and the sayings of the other characters.

Walter Shandy, Tristram's father, a crotchety retired turkey merchant who possesses an immense stock of obscure information acquired by reading old books collected by his ancestors. As the result of his reading, he takes delight in lengthy discussions on unimportant topics. A man of acute sensibilities, alert to the minor pricks and vexations of life, he has developed a droll but sharp manner of peevishness, but he is so open and generous in all other ways that his friends are seldom offended by his sharpness of tongue. He suffers from sciatica as well as loquacity.

Mrs. Shandy, a good-natured but rather stupid woman. Typical is her interruption of the moment of Tristram's conception on the first Sunday of March, 1718, to ask her husband if he has remembered to wind the clock. "I dare say" and "I suppose not" in response to Mr. Shandy are her most brilliant remarks in conversation.

Toby Shandy, called **My Uncle Toby**, a retired army captain who had been wounded in the groin during the siege of Namur in 1698. Now retired to the country, he spends most of his time amid a large and complicated series of miniature fortifications and military emplacements on the bowling green behind Shandy Hall. There he follows with all the interest and enthusiasm of actual conflict the military campaigns of the duke of Marlborough on the Continent. Occasionally forced into conversations with his brother, as on the night of Tristram's birth, he escapes the flood of Mr. Shandy's discourse by whistling "Lillibullero" to himself. Completely innocent on the subjects of women and sex, he is pursued by a neighbor, the Widow Wadman, whose intentions are matrimonial and whose campaign on the old soldier's heart is as strategically planned as his own miniature battles.

Widow Wadman, a buxom woman who lays siege to Uncle Toby's bachelor life and begs him to show her the exact spot where he was wounded. Eventually, he indicates on a map the location of Namur. Her question kills her chance of a proposal when Corporal Trim tells his embarrassed master what the widow really wants to know.

Corporal Trim, the faithful and loquacious servant of Uncle Toby. He helps his master enact mimic battles on the bowling green.

Susannah, a vain and careless maid. Supposed to tell the curate to christen the sickly baby Trismegistus, after the minor philosopher admired by Mr. Shandy, she arrives on the scene so out of breath that she can say only that the name is Tris-something, and the curate decides that the child is to be called Tristram. He is pleased because that is his own name.

Parson Yorick, a mercurial and eccentric clergyman completely innocent of the ways of the wicked world. He is in the habit of speaking his mind plainly, often to the discomfiture or resentment of the man toward whom his remarks are directed. Once a lover of fine horses, he rides about the countryside on a nag that would disgrace Don Quixote. The reason is that his good horses were always spavined or wind-broken by anxious fathers who borrowed the animals to ride for a midwife.

Dr. Slop, a squat, bungling country doctor, the author of a book on midwifery. For a fee of five guineas, this "man-midwife" sits in the back parlor of Shandy Hall and listens to Mr. Shandy hold forth on various topics, including a treatise on oaths, while a midwife is attending Mrs. Shandy upstairs. When he is called in to assist at the birth, he permanently flattens Tristram's nose with his forceps.

Obadiah, the outdoors servant at Shandy Hall, an awkward, good-natured fellow.

Jonathan, Mr. Shandy's dull-witted coachman.

Le Fever, a poor lieutenant who falls sick while traveling to rejoin his regiment in Flanders. When Corporal Trim, who has visited the dying man at the village inn, reports to Uncle Toby that the poor fellow will never march again, the old soldier is so moved that he swears one of his rare oaths while declaring that Le Fever shall not die. The recording angel, making a note of the oath, drops a tear on the word and blots it out forever.

Tom, Corporal Trim's brother, who marries the widow of a Jew in Lisbon.

A Negress, a friend of Tom Trim, who motivates a discussion on slavery.

Mrs. Bridget, Widow Wadman's maid, ambitious to marry Corporal Trim.

Eugenius, the friend and adviser of Parson Yorick. He witnesses the clergyman's dying moments.

Master Bobby Shandy, Tristram's older brother, whose death at an early age is reported. His sudden death gives Corporal Trim a good opportunity to provide the servants of Shandy Hall with a dramatic illustration—he drops his hat—of human mortality, the fact that a person can be here one moment and gone the next. Trim's action causes Susannah,

who has been thinking of the gown that may become hers when her mistress goes into mourning, to burst into tears.

LIFE & TIMES OF MICHAEL K

Author: J. M. Coetzee (1940-   )
First published: 1983
Genre: Novel

Locale: Cape Town, South Africa, and the adjacent country-side
Time: The 1980's
Plot: Allegory

Michael K, a thirty-one-year-old black South African, homeless, propertyless, deformed by a harelip curled like a snail's foot, and slow of mind. Brought up at Huis Norenius, a school for poor and abandoned children, Michael K lives a life of solitude and isolation, working as a gardener for the city of Cape Town and eventually taking to the war-ravaged country-side in a continuous and unsuccessful effort to find a sanctuary. A gardener at an abandoned farmhouse in the country, a wanderer in the mountains, a prisoner in relocation or rehabilitation camps, and finally an ailing migrant along the roads and the seashore, Michael K has no money, no papers, no friends, no family, and no place, even among the armies of the homeless and the destitute. Having lived a life in cages, he wishes only to be left alone to plant the pumpkin seeds he carries in a small packet—his sole possession.

Anna K, Michael's mother, formerly a domestic for a retired hosiery manufacturer and his wife living at Sea Point on the Atlantic Ocean. A dying, dropsical woman, Anna K suffers from gross swelling of the arms, legs, and belly. She wishes to leave Cape Town and return to her birthplace at Prince Albert, a considerable distance away, but her son is unable to get the necessary passes or railway tickets from the authorities. They set out together, Michael pushing his mother in a rudely converted wheelbarrow, but she dies en route, at the hospital in Stellenbosch.

Visagie's grandson, a pale, plump army deserter. Finding Michael K at his grandfather's run-down and abandoned farm, Visagie's grandson assumes that Michael K had been hired to watch over the place. Anemic and weakhearted, the grandson wishes to live hidden away at the farm until the war's end, and he attempts to transform Michael into a body-servant. The grandson is soon abandoned by Michael K, who, sent on a shopping mission into Prince Albert, buries in a tin can the forty rand in notes given to him for the purpose and wanders away.

Robert, an internee of the Jakkelsdrif Relocation Camp, where Michael K is taken after he is arrested by the police. A man with a large family, Robert befriends the malnourished and ailing Michael, teaching him the ways of the camps and how to survive the long day-trips to the railways or surround-

ing farms, where the male internees are taken to work for subsistence wages.

The guard, who is stationed at the Jakkelsdrif Relocation Camp. A diabetic white soldier who would desert if given the chance, the guard makes it clear that he would shoot Michael K should he try to escape the camp. Over time, the guard begins to show Michael K some kindness, passing food to him through the wire mesh of the camp fence. After three internees go missing the night of a huge fire in neighboring Prince Albert, the guard himself is interned for incompetence and is later stabbed in a fight.

Captain Oosthuizen, a member of the Prince Albert Police Department who recognizes and arrests Michael K after he escapes from Jakkelsdrif, calling him, mistakenly, Michaels.

The doctor, a sympathetic white medical officer at the Kenilworth rehabilitation camp, the narrator of one major section of the novel. The doctor is fascinated and frustrated by Michael, who seems to have no sense of self, no needs, no desires, and no interest in becoming healthy. When the police wish to interrogate Michael K about his encounters with black guerrilla fighters, the doctor intercedes, claiming that Michael K is in no condition to undergo such harsh treatment, let alone make the arduous journey to the site of the interrogation. The doctor genuinely wants to know Michael's story, but he has no way of penetrating to the truth and will never know it.

Noel, the chief medical officer at Kenilworth, a sixty-year-old man under orders to release prisoners from the infirmary when they are well enough to return to the camp's regimen of hard labor. A decent, soft man, like the doctor he takes an interest in Michael K and allows him to stay on in the infirmary.

Felicity, a nurse at Kenilworth.

December, a robust and cheerful vagabond who befriends Michael K at Sea Point, where Michael goes after he escapes from Kenilworth. Declaring that "tomorrow you will be a new man," December gives Michael K food, shelter, and his sister in a generous effort to provide the obviously dying Michael perhaps his only moment of sexual pleasure.

— *Michael Zeitlin*

LIFE BEFORE MAN

Author: Margaret Atwood (1939-   )
First published: 1979
Genre: Novel

Locale: Toronto, Ontario, Canada
Time: October 29, 1976-August 18, 1978
Plot: Domestic realism

Elizabeth Schoenhof (SHEHN-hohf), the thirty-nine-year-old protagonist, who works in special projects in a Toronto

museum of natural history. Elizabeth desperately needs to be in control, of her own life as well as the lives of others. As the daughter of a chronically alcoholic mother and a frequently absent father, she had to become streetwise at an early age. When her former lover Chris kills himself, her world begins to unravel. Still, the other characters continue to orbit around Elizabeth, which is a tribute to her very real strength. For some years, she and Nate have had an open marriage, but they no longer have a sexual relationship themselves, although they confide in each other about their separate affairs. At the end, she lets Nate go to live with his current lover, Lesje, and is trying to find happiness in her new arrangement. Elizabeth is clearly the central character in the tangled sexual skein that makes up the novel, which is a mildly acidic portrait of modern marriage.

Nate Schoenhof, her thirty-four-year-old husband, trained as a lawyer. A man with little backbone and with less moral sense, Nate "dropped out" from the world of lawyering because he wanted his life to be "honest." He has recently been a woodworker making toys at home, but he sometimes seems more the child for whom the toys have been made, especially in his relationship with Elizabeth. He sees himself as persecuted by three generations of women—his mother and his daughters included—but reality is that Nate is ineffectual and indecisive, and Elizabeth must dismiss him in the end when he cannot make up his own mind about what he wants to do.

Lesje (LEHS-yeh), Nate's new lover, an assistant paleontologist at the same museum where Elizabeth works. She became interested in dinosaurs as a child and never lost that interest; she now prepares dinosaur and other fossil exhibits at the museum. Lesje is the complete opposite of Elizabeth—frightened, insecure, and unable to deal with other people's anger or desperation—and her life is lived in reaction to Eliza-

beth's. When Elizabeth dismisses Nate and he moves in with Lesje, Lesje is not sure her life has improved. She is now pregnant and yearns for the simpler life she had earlier with William.

Chris, Elizabeth's former lover, who killed himself after Elizabeth ended their affair, when he wanted more from it than she was willing to give. Chris had also worked in the museum where Elizabeth and Lesje hold their jobs. It is his shotgun suicide that moves the action of the novel forward.

Martha, Nate's most recent former lover, a secretary at the legal firm where he once worked. She is attractive but lacks self-respect and is easily hurt by his absences.

William, the man with whom Lesje is living at the opening of the novel. He is involved in pollution research and tends to take Lesje for granted. He comes from London, Ontario, unlike the other main characters, who grew up in Toronto, and he appears naïve in comparison to them. Elizabeth sleeps with William once but finds no pleasure in it. Like the other men in the novel, William seems a dinosaur in some dark prehistory of "life before man," that is, before the beginnings of what the author would like to see as truly civilized human sexual relations.

Janet and

Nancy, Nate and Elizabeth's young daughters.

Auntie Muriel, the miserly woman who reared Elizabeth and her sister after their alcoholic mother died. When her aunt is dying in the hospital, Elizabeth can only comfort and forgive her. It fits Elizabeth's character perfectly that so few people know about her background.

— *David Peck*

LIFE IN LONDON

Author: Pierce Egan (1772-1849)
First published: 1821
Genre: Novel

Locale: London
Time: Early nineteenth century
Plot: Picaresque

Corinthian Tom, the scion of a wealthy British family. He is a young chap anxious to experience life. Under the tutelage of Bob Logic, he explores all the facets of London life by getting into scrapes and out of them. He is accompanied part of the time by his cousin, Jerry Hawthorn.

Bob Logic, a onetime law student in London. He is a merry chap who always has a joke. He is Corinthian Tom's mentor after Tom's parents die. He ends up in debtor's prison.

Corinthian Kate (Catherine), a beautiful and talented courtesan, one of the most desired in London. She becomes Corinthian Tom's mistress.

Jerry Hawthorn, Tom's country cousin. He comes to London to learn about life in the city. He is a likable young chap.

He has to leave the life of London when he falls ill.

Doctor Pleas'em, favorite doctor of the gay young blades of London.

Mr. Primefit, a most accomplished tailor. He is popular because he does not press his customers for payment.

Miss Satire, a fashionable woman attracted to Jerry.

Lady Wanton, Miss Satire's sister, a lively woman who first embarrasses Jerry and then, disguised as a nun, flirts with him.

The Duchess of Hearts, a fashionable, beautiful woman who strikes Jerry dumb with her beauty.

Trifle, the skinniest dandy in the city.

Sue, a friend of Corinthian Kate. She is attracted to Jerry.

LIFE IN THE IRON MILLS: Or, The Korl Woman

Author: Rebecca Harding Davis (1831-1910)
First published: 1861
Genre: Novella

Locale: An industrial town
Time: Mid-nineteenth century
Plot: Social realism

The narrator, an unnamed individual of unspecified gender, obviously a member of the privileged class. For some

reason, this person has settled in a working-class area of a mill town, in the house where the two protagonists of the story once lived. He or she owns the statue of the "korl woman."

Hugh Wolfe, a nineteen-year-old iron mill furnace tender. Born into poverty and a mill worker since childhood, he is undernourished and tubercular. Because he does not indulge in vicious pastimes, he is considered effeminate by his fellow workers. His kindness has earned him the love of his cousin Deborah and the young Janey. When upper-class visitors to the mill praise his skill at carving, Hugh thinks that a better life might be possible, and he keeps the stolen money Deborah gives him. Arrested for the theft and sentenced to prison, he commits suicide.

Deborah, Hugh's cousin, a cotton mill worker. She is called "the hunchback" because of her deformity. Her love for Hugh is the central truth in her life. To help him, she steals a pocketbook from the wealthy Mitchell. As Hugh's supposed accessory, she receives only a short prison sentence. After her release, she is taken in by a Quaker woman and spends the rest of her life in a mountain settlement.

Janey, a young Irish girl. She is important primarily as the focus of Hugh's dreams. Although he knows that she will soon lose her health and her beauty, he imagines having enough money to make a decent life with her. Meanwhile, he is her protector.

Young Kirby, the son of the man who owns the iron mill where Hugh works. He despises and fears his employees, whom he views as subhuman, and believes that his only responsibility to them is to make sure that they are paid.

Mitchell, young Kirby's brother-in-law. A wealthy dilettante, he has no convictions and sees the world as a place constructed solely for his amusement. Mitchell refuses to help Hugh fulfill his artistic ambitions and later prosecutes him for the theft of his pocketbook.

Doctor May, a friend of young Kirby. A sentimentalist, he thinks that by speaking kindly to Hugh, he is fulfilling his duty to humanity. He refuses to give Hugh financial backing. Reading of Hugh's sentence, he is offended by what he terms the young man's ingratitude.

— *Rosemary M. Canfield Reisman*

LIFE IS A DREAM
(La vida es sueño)

Author: Pedro Calderón de la Barca (1600-1681)
First published: 1636
Genre: Drama

Locale: Poland
Time: The sixteenth century
Plot: Melodrama

Segismundo (say-hees-MEWN-doh), the heir to the throne of Poland, who has been imprisoned in a tower on the Russian frontier because horrible portents at his birth and later predictions by astrologers have convinced his father, King Basilio, that the boy will grow into a monster who will destroy the land. Finally, because the king sees his land split over the matter of succession, Segismundo is drugged and transported from his prison to the court of Warsaw. There, uncouth and inexperienced, he behaves boorishly. He accuses the court of wronging him and scorns his father's explanations thus: "What man is so foolish as to lay on the disinterested stars the responsibility for his own actions?" Impossible as a king, he is again drugged and returned to his tower, where he is told it was all a dream. Later liberated by an army recruited by Rosaura, in revenge on the ambitious Astolfo, he thinks he is still dreaming. He wonders why he should strive in a dream for something that disappears upon waking. On that account, he will not accept the throne when his followers overthrow King Basilio. He treats everybody kindly and generously, marries Estrella, and forces Astolfo to keep his promise and marry Rosaura.

Rosaura (rroh-SAH-ew-rah), a Russian woman traveling with her servant Fife to the court of Warsaw to seek the Pole who had promised to marry her. Crossing the Russian-Polish boundary, disguised as a man for protection against bandits, she loses her horse and her way. She finds and sympathizes with a young man, chained to the doorway of a tower and bemoaning his fate. He warns her to flee, which she does, after giving him the sword she has been carrying.

Clotaldo (kloh-TAHL-doh), a Polish general and guardian of the imprisoned Segismundo. He captures Rosaura and Fife but sends them on their way. He recognizes the sword as one he had left in Russia with a noblewoman with whom he had been in love, and he supposes the disguised Rosaura is his own son. Duty to his king, however, seals his lips. When Segismundo returns to his own tower prison from his unfortunate experiences in Warsaw, Clotaldo assures the prince that life is a dream and that in dreams men's evil thoughts and ambitions are unchecked. Awake, one can control one's passions and behave like a sane individual. Later, when Segismundo gets a second chance, Clotaldo is unharmed because of his earlier advice.

King Basilio (bah-SEE-lyoh), the father of Segismundo, faced with the problem of succession to the Polish throne. Claimants are Astolfo, his nephew, and Estrella, his niece; their rival supporters form political factions that will disrupt the country in civil war. Calling an assembly, King Basilio announces that his son, who supposedly died with his mother, is really alive. With the consent of the claimants, he will send for the prince and see what sort of king he might make.

Astolfo (ahs-TOHL-foh), one claimant for the Polish throne. While in Russia, he had contracted matrimony with Rosaura, but now he wants to marry Estrella so that he can be sure of becoming king of Poland. When Segismundo awakes from his drugged sleep, he manhandles Astolfo for daring to touch the attractive Estrella.

Estrella (ehs-TRAY-lyah), a princess whom Segismundo embraces, to the consternation of the courtiers. Eventually, after his second visit to the court, during which he acts with proper dignity because of his conviction that life is a dream, Estrella becomes his queen.

Fife (FEE-fay), the *gracioso*, or comic servant, of Rosaura, who adds humor and philosophy to the comedy.

LIFE IS ELSEWHERE
(La Vie est ailleurs)

Author: Milan Kundera (1929-   )
First published: 1973
Genre: Novel

Locale: Prague, Czechoslovakia
Time: The 1930's through the early 1950's
Plot: Satire

Jaromil, a young lyric poet. Jaromil was born into overwhelming, devoted, mother love. This devotion is a boon to his childhood but becomes increasingly odious as he grows older. It is his bad fortune to support this love wonderfully. He is a precious boy, pretty rather than handsome, and he has, for his one talent, the dainty art of lyric poetry. His genius is feminine (no one could understand the masculine and feminine humors quite so vividly as a lyric poet), and he wants, with the furious insecurity of youth, to become a man. He works at this, awkwardly, with the help of his two adult loves. One is a redheaded shop girl, for whom he conceives a great passion, and the other is the Czechoslovak Communist revolution. This leads Jaromil to great cruelty. Besides the injustice he does to his own art, making it serve the revolution, he betrays to the revolution both the brother of his redheaded lover (who has the benefit of his omnivorous jealousy) and the modern artist who had first recognized his talent and served as his mentor. He does not live long enough to regret these actions. In the tradition of lyric poets, he stands ridiculously on his dignity. Having been humiliated in public, he ignores a cold night and catches his death of fever. In the weakness of approaching death, he clings to the one certainty of his life: the love of his mother.

Jaromil's mother, called **Maman**, an insincere woman who is acted on more than she acts and thus is treated somewhat brutally by the world. To secure some consolation from life, she has settled all of her own hopes on her son. Having mistaken the daring of her first romantic abandon for a great passion, she becomes pregnant. She lives, sometimes proudly, sometimes self-pityingly, through her loveless (and, after Jaromil, childless) marriage, her own unsettling affair with Jaromil's radical modern art instructor, the loss of her comfortable prerevolution bourgeois life, and Jaromil's love affairs. Always, she comes back to her one true occupation, her love for her son. Consequently, she faces the greatest disappointment of her life when he dies in early youth. He does not do so without professing (it is almost a deathbed confession) his most tender affection for her.

The redheaded girl, Jaromil's young lover. She is a homely, talkative, uncomplicated, and proletarian young woman. She is not temperamentally suited to his poet's muse. He wants to make a grand leap into the absolute at every opportunity, whereas she is earthbound and makes everything mundane by her unpretentious manner. Jaromil's energetic poetic revisionism is equal to this challenge. He builds up a consuming passion for her and wills to absolve every defect he sees in her, if only she will submit to his tyrannical affections with gratitude. She herself is sexually uncomplicated, breezily bisexual, and naturally promiscuous. She responds to the strength of his ardor for her and reins in her own nature. In doing so, she makes a fateful mistake. She tells an innocent lie, which works on Jaromil's jealousy so that he ends up denouncing her favorite brother to the police; brother and sister are both sent to prison. She is, after his own talent, Jaromil's chief victim.

Jaromil's father, an engineer. He is a philandering, soccer-playing, earthbound spirit; in short, he is whatever his wife wishes he would not be and everything Jaromil wishes that he himself could be. His influence over his son is slight, both because his son inherited almost no characteristics from him and because of his own early death. He nevertheless remains an idol to his son. Having conceived his son offhandedly, he is reconciled to marrying his lover when her family presents him with what is, in effect, a substantial dowry. This dowry makes his place in the world; secure in his place, he abides by his marriage, grudgingly and apathetically. When he dies, during a Nazi attack on a Jewish ghetto, it is thought that he had been a martyr of the resistance. Later, it is revealed that he had died keeping a rendezvous with his Jewish lover.

The artist, Jaromil's mentor. He is a modern artist and expects art to be unpredictable, to consist of the random, coming as it does from the great stream of the human subconscious touching certain individual lives. For him, to be an artist is to answer the call of freedom. To be an artist is to stand against the horrors of modern life, the petty inhumanities of industrial society, and the great inhumanities of modern war. He encourages Jaromil to think of himself as one of the elect, touched by a random muse, with a talent that has little to do with himself and that opens up possibilities beyond himself. He indulges his autocratic nature in an affair with Jaromil's mother, making her into his own arbitrary creation, driving her, finally, to a nervous breakdown. He follows his love of freedom into the time of the revolution, which causes his fall. The revolution demands that art serve the tastes of the proletariat and supply the needs of agitprop. He has followed his urge to be utterly modern into the time when the modern has rejected him, and no one is so avid for this new modernity as his protégé, Jaromil. He is eventually forced from his teaching and made to be a construction worker.

— *Fritz Monsma*

THE LIFE OF AN AMOROUS MAN
(Kōshoku ichidai otoko)

Author: Ihara Saikaku (Hirayama Tōgogo, 1642-1693)
First published: 1683
Genre: Novel

Locale: Japan
Time: Early seventeenth century
Plot: Picaresque

Yonosuke, "Man of the World," the son of a wealthy playboy businessman and a courtesan of the pleasure quarter in Kyoto who settle down into domesticity after marriage. Precocious concerning love and sex, Yonosuke has his calligraphy teacher copy down his first love letter at the age of seven. As a teenager, he engages in numerous escapades in his search for pleasures of the flesh. Finally, his father disowns him when he is nineteen years old. For the next fifteen years, Yonosuke engages in a variety of occupations, such as salmon peddler, Shinto priest, wandering singer and actor, male prostitute, manager of male prostitutes, and attendant of rich businessmen. The money he earns is quickly frittered away drinking and visiting women of the pleasure quarter. Although physically attractive, well educated, and personally charming, Yonosuke is not always successful in his quest for love and is several times rejected, is beaten by outraged husbands, and once ends up in jail. After almost dying in a shipwreck, he learns that his father has died and that his mother wants him at home. He returns to become head of his family and receives a gift of twenty-five thousand kan of silver from his mother to do with as he wishes. He immediately decides to use the money to ransom all the courtesans in Japan's pleasure quarters that he finds appealing. Yonosuke marries after being accepted back into his family, but domestic life does not long satisfy him, and soon he resumes his travels throughout the country to visit brothels and pleasure houses. He is a likable rake and is frequently generous to women and servants. He is knowledgeable about the customs, manners, and ranking of the world of the demimonde and often makes fools of courtesans and their masters who do not behave properly. By the time he is fifty-four years old, he had made love to 3,742 women and 725 boys and has a museum full of mementos of lovers he has abandoned all over Japan. Gray-headed and emaciated at the age of sixty (a time of rebirth in Japan), he builds a ship, the *Yoshiiro-maru* (its name means "lust"), to set sail with six male drinking companions for an island inhabited only by women. Yonosuke is the model playboy of the merchant class during Japan's feudal age, a hero of the new urban culture that was emerging in Japan in the seventeenth century. Only occasionally is he stricken with remorse for his deeds, and his penitent mood never lasts long.

— *Joseph Laker*

THE LIFE OF MAN
(Zhizn' cheloveka)

Author: Leonid Andreyev (1871-1919)
First published: 1907
Genre: Drama

Locale: Russia
Time: Early twentieth century
Plot: Allegory

Someone in gray, called **He**, a figure who serves onstage as a narrator. He introduces the work during the prologue and at intervals provides commentary on the stages of the man's life. During his appearances, this character remains apart from the others, who do not seem aware of his presence. He is taller than an ordinary man and is dressed in a hat and broad gray smock that shroud him in gloomy darkness except for his massive, weighty chin, nose, and cheekbones. His lips are often tightly pursed, and his eyes remain hidden. He speaks in a cold but solemn voice, uninflected by compassion or human concern; he is described as resembling one who is paid to read from the book of fate on an hourly basis.

The man's father, a character who appears briefly during the first act. He seems affected by extreme weariness, which set in during his wife's prolonged struggle to give birth to their son. Remorse for the suffering she has endured is offset by the father's delight in their son's clear physical resemblance to him. During this time, the father evidently is prone to conflicting and wildly oscillating feelings; in reflecting on some of his own shortcomings, he resolves to provide moral guidance by preventing his son from torturing animals or associating with unworthy friends.

The man, who is shown during five periods of his life. By the second act, he has married; he has become an architect, but he is chronically out of work, and he lives in grinding abject poverty. Subsequently, he is favored by fortune, and his material wishes are fulfilled to the extent that he is able to stage a lavish ball in his elegantly appointed mansion. Later, his station in life has declined to the point that his once-magnificent house has become dark and empty. In early manhood, his wants and aspirations had centered on fine food, clothing, and other hallmarks of worldly success; eventually, his most intensely felt yearnings concern questions of life itself. In some flights of fantasy, he is inclined to portray himself as a valiant solitary knight engaged in combat with harsh, unrelenting fate; toward the end, he bitterly denounces the arbitrary injustice of his lot. When his son is wantonly attacked and struck in the head by a stone, then lies in the throes of death, the man summons forth bittersweet memories of the young man's childhood joys. After praying, he inveighs against God, the Devil, or fate as he curses his life, with all of its hopes and sorrows. At the end, ragged, gray, and bowed with age, he is surrounded by leering, mocking revelers in a tavern before he utters anguished cries of helpless defiance and abruptly dies.

The wife, a figure who is described on her first appearance as very pretty, delicate, and graceful. She seems to grow old at about the same rate as her husband. Although, toward the end, she has become markedly gray and wrinkled, she scarcely has cause to doubt her husband's continuing attachment to her. She has great regard for his talents as an architect; on many matters, her feelings seem to complement those of the man. When he is hungry and dejected, she commiserates with him, and early in their life she shares in his fond expectations of fame and prosperity. Whatever differences there may be arise when their son is about to die; she prays to God in a plaintive entreaty and reproaches her husband for an excess of pride when, in more pointed tones, he requests the Almighty to spare their son's life. They seem united in grief when the young man's final moments pass. It becomes known later that the wife has preceded her husband in death.

— *J. R. Broadus*

THE LIFE OF MARIANNE
(La Vie de Marianne)

Author: Marivaux (Pierre Carlet de Chamblain Marivaux, 1688-1763), completed by Marie-Jeanne Riccoboni
First published: 1731-1741
Genre: Novel

Locale: France
Time: Late seventeenth century
Plot: Fiction of manners

Marianne (mahr-YAHN), the countess of ———, a virtuous orphan. Orphaned as an infant, she is put in the care of a kind woman who dies when Marianne is fifteen years old. Her second benefactor, M. de Climal, offers to set her up in an apartment. She proudly rejects this proposal. She takes up residence in a nearby convent, where she is sought out by a young man who becomes attracted to her appearance when he sees her on the street. He turns out to be M. de Valville, with whom she falls in love and whom she plans to marry until he becomes infatuated with Mlle Varthon and jilts his fiancée.

M. de Valville (deh vahl-VEEL), a young man attracted to Marianne when he sees her on the street. He seeks her out and becomes engaged to her, only to become infatuated with Mlle Varthon, for whom he jilts Marianne.

M. de Climal (deh klee-MAHL), Marianne's benefactor in Paris. He arranges for her lodging with Mme Dutour and later, with protestations of undying love, offers to set her up in an apartment. His offer sends Marianne off to a convent.

Mme de Valville, M. de Valville's mother and Marianne's loving benefactress at the convent until her death, which leaves the girl alone in the world.

Mlle Varthon (vahr-TOH[N]), a young woman who attracts M. de Valville away from Marianne.

Mlle de Tervire (deh tehr-VEER), a nun who tries to comfort Marianne by telling her the story of her own life.

Mme Dutour (dew-TEWR), a shopkeeper, Marianne's landlady, provided by M. de Climal.

LIFE WITH FATHER

Author: Clarence Day, Jr. (1874-1935)
First published: 1935
Genre: Novel

Locale: New York City
Time: Late nineteenth century
Plot: Short fiction

Clarence Day, Sr., a domestic tyrant, critical, quick-tempered, and eccentric, who dominates his family, but not completely. Father ("Clare" to his wife) is a loud groaner when he himself is ill, but he has little sympathy with others' illnesses. Since he is a systematic businessman, he cannot understand his wife's dislike of figures and the keeping of household accounts. Companionable and popular with his chosen friends, he is dictatorial toward people he does not like. He enjoys his family despite all the complaints he makes about them.

Mrs. Clarence (Vinnie) Day, his wife, who puts up with Father's tantrums, sometimes ignoring them, at other times countering with scorn and illogic to exasperate and often defeat her noisy mate.

Clarence Day, Jr., the narrator, the nearsighted oldest son, who as a child suffers the misfortune of the name Clarence, vainly tries to play the violin, and is alternately entertained and frightened by Father's many explosions.

Margaret, cook in the Day household for twenty-six years.

George and

Julian, younger brothers of Clarence, Jr.

Herr M., Clarence Jr.'s violin teacher.

Cousin Julie, Mrs. Day's favorite niece, who lives with the Days after finishing school.

Miss Edna Gulick, conductor of a current-events class attended by Mrs. Day.

Delia, a temporary cook who is quickly dismissed after Father complains about her.

LIGEIA

Author: Edgar Allan Poe (1809-1849)
First published: 1838
Genre: Short fiction

Locale: Germany and England
Time: Early nineteenth century
Plot: Gothic

The Narrator, a learned man enslaved to the memory of a woman whose powerful will once triumphed over death itself to return to him. Half insane through grief after Ligeia's death, and addicted to opium, he nevertheless remarries. Forgetful of Ligeia for a month, he abandons himself to Lady Rowena; but memory returns, and love turns to hatred and loathing. He witnesses (or so he believes) the dropping of poison into some wine he gives Rowena when she is ill. After Rowena's death, he is awed by the rising of her corpse, which he recognizes not as that of Rowena but of his lost Ligeia.

Ligeia, his first wife, a beautiful woman of rare learning and musically eloquent voice. Tall and slender, she is quietly majestic whether in repose or walking with "incomprehensible lightness and elasticity." Her features are "strange" rather than classically regular: the skin pale, forehead broad, luxuriously curly hair glossy and black. Her nose is slightly aquiline; when her short upper lip and her voluptuous under one part in a radiant smile, her teeth gleam brilliantly. Her eyes are most notable: unusually large and luminously black, with long and jetty lashes and slightly irregular black brows. Though Ligeia is outwardly calm and speaks in a low, distinct, and melodious voice, a passionately intense will shows in the fierce energy of her wild words. Her knowledge of classical and modern European languages leads her (and her worshiping husband) into extensive metaphysical investigations. When Ligeia falls ill, her wild eyes blaze, her skin turns waxen, and the veins in her forehead swell and sink. With her dying breath she murmurs that humans submit to death only through feebleness of will. When Lady Rowena later dies, Ligeia, through the power of her will, returns from death and enters the body of her successor.

Lady Rowena Trevanion, the second wife, fair-haired and blue-eyed. She falls ill and slowly dies, wasting away while she becomes increasingly irritable and fearful, her fear being increased by mysterious sounds and sights. (Her illness may be compared to that which for five years tortured and finally killed Virginia Poe, the author's young wife.)

LIGHT

Author: Eva Figes (1932-   )
First published: 1983
Genre: Novel

Locale: Giverny, France
Time: A summer day in 1900
Plot: Prose poem

Claude Monet (klohd moh-NAY), an Impressionist painter and architect of the gardens at Giverny. Grizzled but vigorous, Claude retains his appetite for life and light. He seduces, tracks, and hunts his quarry of light through the day. A delicate perceiver, Claude believes that sight is born again each day and that people live in a luminous bath of light. The serpents in his lovely gardens of blossom and water are machines, progress, and even war. As creator of his own Eden, Claude rules his gardens and his household, peopled by less powerful beings who are careful to bow to his moods.

Alice Raingo Hoschédé (ray[n]-GOH oh-shay-DAY), Claude's second wife. Old in spirit and appearance, Alice is oppressed by a sense of sin and punishment. Her life stopped with the death of her daughter Suzanne a year earlier; now she feels that the walls between past and present, visible and invisible, are collapsing. Claude thinks that his second wife has always harbored complex and unhappy feelings, but she finds that some vital link with her husband was never forged. The two are in part divided by shadows from the past—Suzanne; Claude's first wife, Camille; and the memory of Alice's bankrupt first husband. During a year of mourning, much of the management of the domestic household has passed to Alice's daughter Marthe.

Marthe Hoschédé (mahrt), Alice's elder daughter. Like the biblical Martha, Marthe is a solid domestic support in her household. Her virtues are hearth ones: a sense of duty, practicality, dependability, and responsibility. Solid and thick in appearance, Marthe sees herself as a woman who has never come first with another person. Claude relies on her to run the household and stay with her mother, and much of the care of Suzanne's children falls to her as well. Theodore Butler's proposal of marriage allows her a measure of happiness; her sister Suzanne's children will become her own.

Lily Butler, Alice's granddaughter, the daughter of Suzanne and Theodore Butler. In this young child is found the mysterious and marvelous sensibility of the artist. To her, the house is fascinating and old, full of secrets. She wonders at the humblest garden scenes—drops on a spider's web, drifting petals, precious colors in pebbles.

Germaine Hoschédé (zhehr-MEHN), Alice's younger daughter. Germaine spends the day in a flush of anticipation and fear, all of her thoughts absorbed by a suitor's proposal of marriage. Although she asks her mother to intercede with her stepfather, the proposal is dismissed by Claude, who sees neither money nor prospects in this young man who longs to invent machines for the future. By evening, it is the plain stay-at-home elder sister, Marthe, who is to be married. Through her pain, Germaine dimly grasps a subtle shift in family relationships. She will continue as before, a "passenger" on a "ship" under Claude's command.

Michel Monet (mee-SHEHL), the son of Claude and Camille. Withdrawn and quiet, Michel suffers from his father's talent. He has the painter's sensibility but not his ability. Stifled and almost paralyzed by his father's genius, he is unable to speak of his father save in the third person. Gripped by the magic and authority of his father's paintings, Michel is unable to conceive of any other activity in life worth undertaking.

Octave Mirbeau (ohk-TAHV meer-BOH), a writer and friend of the family. The notorious and witty Mirbeau is a mixture of elements, at one moment sardonic and amusing, at another kind and sympathetic. Both political and religious topics unleash his mocking, but behind his lively front lies considerable unhappiness resulting from marital problems. He shares with Claude a passion for gardening.

Anatole Toussaint (ah-nah-TOHL tew-SAY[N]), a parish priest. The Abbe Toussaint is a complex figure, a priest who has faced black doubt and who believes in evolution and botanical experimentation. His manner is nervous and diffident, his appearance bony and simian. Another gardening enthusiast, Toussaint finds joy in his connection with Claude, although in his pleasure he forgets to offer consolation to Alice.

Theodore Butler, an American painter and father of Jimmy and Lily. Once flamboyant and playful, Claude's stepson-in-law has aged and grown thin since his wife's death. He is marked by the sorrow of Suzanne's loss and by the realization of his own limitations as a painter. Theodore proposes to Marthe as a means to remain in Claude Monet's vital sphere of activity and to provide a mother for his children.

Jean-Pierre Hoschédé (zhah[n]-PYEHR), Alice's son. On the verge of the great world, about to continue his studies, Jean-Pierre is full of excitement. He longs to join the world's bustle and progress.

Jimmy Butler, the son of Suzanne and Theodore. Adventurous within a small boy's limits, Jimmy dreams of tigers and Ohio. He has begun to fasten his affections on his Aunt Marthe.

— Marlene Youmans

LIGHT IN AUGUST

Author: William Faulkner (1897-1962)
First published: 1932
Genre: Novel

Locale: Mississippi
Time: 1930
Plot: Psychological realism

Joe Christmas, a mulatto. Placed in an orphan home by his demented grandfather, he is to lead a tortured life of social isolation, as he belongs neither to the white nor to the black race; in fact, he prefers this kind of existence. After staying with the fanatical Calvin McEachern during his boyhood, Joe knocks his foster father unconscious and strikes out on his own, rejecting any friendly overtures. At last, he is driven to his final desperate act: He kills his benefactress, Joanna Burden, and faces death at the hands of merciless Percy Grimm.

Joanna Burden, Joe Christmas' mistress, the descendant of a New England family. Rejected by many of her neighbors, she is the friend of blacks and interested in improving their lot. In her efforts to make Joe useful to the world, she also tries to possess and dominate him sexually, and so meets her death.

Calvin McEachern, Joe's foster father. A ruthless, unrelenting religious fundamentalist, McEachern, without real animosity, often beats the boy savagely for trifling misdemeanors and tells him to repent. He demands that "the Almighty be as magnanimous as himself."

Eupheus Hines (Doc), Joe Christmas' grandfather. A hot-tempered little man, he is often in fights. When he learns that his daughter Milly has a mulatto lover, the fiery old man kills him. Later, he allows Milly to die in childbirth, unaided by a doctor. Soon after her death, he places the baby in an orphanage. Years later, learning of Joe's imprisonment, Doc Hines demands that his grandson be lynched. Prior to this time, the old man has devoted much effort to preaching to bemused blacks about white supremacy.

Gail Hightower, a minister. Most of Hightower's life has been devoted to a dream. Long before, his grandfather had died while serving with a troop of Confederate cavalry. Because of his grandfather, he becomes obsessed with the Civil War. Now an outcast, he has driven his wife to her death because of this obsession; in the process, he is forced from his church by his outraged congregation.

Joe Brown (Lucas Burch), Lena Grove's lover and the unwilling father of her child. A loudmouthed, weak man, he deserts Lena and finds work in another town. After meeting Joe Christmas, he becomes a bootlegger and lives with Joe in a cabin behind Joanna Burden's house. When Christmas is captured, Brown, hoping for a large reward, tells the sheriff that Joe has murdered Miss Burden. Unable to face responsibilities, he hops a freight train in order to avoid Lena.

Lena Grove, a country girl seduced and deserted by Joe Brown. Ostensibly, this simple-hearted, fecund young woman pursues her lover because he is the father of her child; actually, she continues looking for him so that she can see different parts of the South.

Milly Hines, Doc Hines's daughter. She dies in childbirth because her enraged father refuses to let a doctor deliver her mulatto child.

Byron Bunch, a worker at the sawmill. Although he loves Lena, this good man helps her look for Joe Brown.

Mrs. Hines, Joe Christmas' grandmother. Always loving Joe, she tries to get Hightower to say that Joe was elsewhere when the murder was committed.

Mrs. McEachern, Calvin McEachern's long-suffering, patient wife. Like the other women, she is rebuffed when she tries to help Joe Christmas.

Percy Grimm, a brutal National Guard captain. He hunts Joe down after the latter escapes from a deputy. Not satisfied with shooting Christmas, Grimm also mutilates the injured man.

LIGHTNING
(Mukashigatari inazuma-byōshi)

Author: Santō Kyōden (1761-1816)
First published: 1806
Genre: Novel

Locale: Japan
Time: The fifteenth century
Plot: Family

Sasaki Katsura, a young man, the elder son of a feudal lord and his late first wife. After a period of dissipation, Katsura, with the help of loyal friends and retainers, successfully foils a plot to prevent him from being named as his father's heir.

Sasaki Sadakuni, Katsura's father, a feudal lord of Yamato Province. For a time, he is deceived by the plot against Katsura. When the plot is revealed, however, he forgives Katsura and makes him his heir.

Kumode no Kata (Lady Spider), the present wife of Sadakuni and a plotter against Katsura. She wants her own son to be Sadakuni's heir.

Sasaki Hanagata, the twelve-year-old son of Lady Spider and Sadakuni.

Ichō no Mae (Lady Ginkgo), Katsura's wife. Persecuted and abducted by her husband's enemies, she is rescued and finally reunited with her husband.

Tsukiwaka (Young-moon), the young son of Katsura and Lady Ginkgo. He is saved from attempted kidnapping and at last is restored to his parents.

Fuwa Dōken (Road-dog), steward to the House of Sasaki. He is the chief villain, Lady Spider's co-plotter. Foiled in his attempts to discredit Katsura and to murder Lady Ginkgo and Young-moon, he is imprisoned after his plot is exposed.

Fuwa Banzaemon, Katsura's retainer and the son of Road-dog. He promotes Katsura's infatuation with a dancing girl whom he himself loves. Discharged, he commits a murder and hides out in the brothels of Kyoto.

Fujinami (Wisteria-wave), the dancing girl loved by Katsura and Banzaemon. She is killed by a loyal retainer of Katsura.

Sasara Sampachirō, Katsura's loyal retainer. Having killed Wisteria-wave, he rescues Young-moon and goes into hiding under the name of Namuemon. Later he saves Young-moon's life by beheading his own blind son and identifying the head as that of Young-moon.

Kuritaro (Chestnut-son), Sampachirō's blind son, sacrificed by his father in order to save the life of Young-moon.

Kaede (Maple), Sampachirō's daughter, who is haunted by serpents. Having sold herself for a treasured painting previously stolen by a disloyal retainer of the House of Sasaki, she is cured of her affliction by the magical power of the painting.

Hasebe Unroku, a disloyal retainer. He steals the magic painting and disappears. Later, he is recognized as the perpetrator of a six-year-old robbery. Sampachirō forces him to commit suicide to expiate his sins.

Nagoya Sansaburō, a loyal retainer. Unsuccessful in his early efforts to reform Katsura, he engineers Young-moon's escape. It is he who finally locates Banzaemon and his gang.

Nagoya Saburozaemon, Sansaburō's father, killed by Banzaemon.

Yuasa Matahei, a painter, the brother of Wisteria-wave. Impressed by Sampachirō's loyalty and learning that Sampachirō aided his wife when she was robbed six years before, he takes only symbolic revenge for the killing of Wisteria-wave: He assaults Sampachirō's hat instead of his head.

Umezu Kamon (Good-gate), a hero-recluse. He rescues Lady Ginkgo from death at the hands of Road-dog. He is instrumental in restoring Katsura to his father's favor.

Sarujiro (Monkey-son), a street preacher and Sansaburō's son. He saves Katsura's life at a temple festival.

Shikazō (Deer), Sansaburō's faithful servant, who helps him search for Banzaemon.

Ashikaga Yoshimasa, under whose shogunship Sadakuni lives.

Hamana, the governor general with whose connivance Road-dog plans to take over his lord's domain.

Katsumoto, the new governor general, who backs Katsura in his attempts to return to paternal favor.

LIKE ONE OF THE FAMILY: Conversations from a Domestic's Life

Author: Alice Childress (1920-1994)
First published: 1956
Genre: Novel

Locale: New York City
Time: The 1950's
Plot: Social realism

Mildred Johnson, a thirty-two-year-old African American woman, originally from the South, now living in a three-room apartment in New York City and earning her living doing housework for white families. Her character is developed in a series of one-sided conversations, primarily with her friend Marge. Many of these conversations concern Mildred's experiences as a day maid in a variety of white homes. Mildred encounters many stereotypical assumptions about African Americans in these homes, but her responses are not what one would expect of a domestic servant in the mid-1950's. In the first conversation, from which the book takes its name, Mrs. C. has been holding forth to a friend on Mildred being "like one of the family." After delivering a litany of the ways in which she is not "like the family," Mildred notes that after having worked herself into a sweat all day, "I do not feel like no weekend house guest. I feel like a servant." She then asks her speechless employer for a raise. At other times, she is less direct but no less effective. In "The Pocketbook Game," she holds her peace "for months" as Mrs. E. keeps her handbag close to her whenever Mildred is in her apartment. She finally has her opportunity when Mrs. E. sends her on an errand. Mildred reports to Marge that she had waited in the hall a few minutes, then frantically rushed back into the apartment to get her own purse. When the embarrassed Mrs. E. says that she hopes Mildred does not think Mrs. E. distrusts her, the sassy Mildred cuts her off, saying that she understands, " 'cause if I paid anybody as little as you pay me, I'd hold my pocketbook, too." Mildred's interests and assertiveness are not limited to her job and her employers. A number of her one-sided conversations with Marge focus on civil rights, especially the integration of schools in the South and the resulting violence and tension. Perhaps the most memorable of these is "Let's Face It," in which Mildred gets the better of a visiting Southern racist whom she calls "Mr. Alabama." When her employer's best efforts to keep this houseguest away from Mildred fail, Mr. Alabama regales Mildred with concerns about the efforts at desegregation and with tales of the "really fine Nigras" he has known. Mildred astounds Mr. Alabama by sitting down with him, whispering what she would do to his "Uncle Toms," given the chance, and then delivering her message, "Yes, we're gonna go to the schools, ride the buses, eat in the restaurants, work on all kinds of jobs, sit in the railroad stations, and do all the things that free people are supposed to have the right to do." Some conversations deal poignantly with Mildred's personal life. "Dance with Me, Henry" focuses on Mildred's hurt and loneliness when friends at a party ignore her in favor of "glama-rama chicks." "All About Miss Tubman" is Mildred's conversation with nine children from her apartment building, in which she tells them stories of Harriet Tubman. She becomes so upset with the children's lack of knowledge about black history and their inability to believe that the black heroine she describes could exist that Marge has to intervene and calm her down. The final conversation, "Men in Your Life," describes the unsatisfactory relationship between Mildred's friend Tessie and her boorish husband, Clarence. Mildred's observations about this relationship and her unpleasant date with Clarence's "cheap" brother Wallace lead her to decide that she will marry her friend Eddie even though he is a poor salesman without the economic stability of men like Clarence and Wallace. This is not a surprising conclusion because Mildred, a sassy black woman, is not ashamed of or worried by poverty or hard work.

Marge, Mildred's friend and best listener. She lives in the same building, and her apartment is a regular stopping place for Mildred. She is supportive of Mildred even though Mildred sometimes takes advantage of her. Marge is no pushover, and their relationship at times seems more necessary for Mildred than for Marge.

— Elsie Galbreath Haley

LIKE WATER FOR CHOCOLATE: A Novel in Monthly Installments
with Recipes, Romances, and Home Remedies
(Como agua para chocolate)

Author: Laura Esquivel (1950-   )
First published: 1989
Genre: Novel

Locale: Near Piedras Negras, Mexico
Time: The 1910's to the early 1930's
Plot: Love

Tita de la Garza (TEE-tah), the youngest daughter in a ranch-owning family. The rules of her tradition-bound family dictate that the youngest daughter remain single and care for her mother until the latter dies; therefore, Tita grows up in the kitchen, learning about life and cooking from the ranch's Indian cook, Nacha. Her childhood sweetheart marries her older sister Rosaura so that he can be near Tita, but Tita's vengeful mother regularly punishes the lovers for their clandestine meetings. Tita rebels against her fate through the marvelous recipes she prepares, which provoke magical reactions. After the deaths of her mother and her sister, Tita and her lover, Pedro, are united in a passion so intense that they perish in its blaze. Tita is immortalized in her diary and recipe book, in which she had written all of her recipes and the events surrounding their preparation.

Mamá Elena (mah-MAH eh-LEH-nah), Tita's tyrannical mother, widowed with three daughters. Her attempts to prevent an adulterous relationship between Tita and Pedro occupy much of Mamá Elena's destructive attention. Fearless in her cruelty, she even intimidates the captain of a marauding band of revolutionary soldiers, thus preserving the ranch's inhabitants and livestock from attack. Later, she becomes paralyzed from a spinal injury she suffers when a group of bandits try unsuccessfully to rape her. She is then forced to rely on Tita to cook for her. Needlessly suspicious that Tita is poisoning her food, Mamá Elena soon dies from an overdose of the emetic she takes to counteract the food's supposed noxious effects. She continues to plague Tita and Pedro from beyond the grave. After Mamá Elena's death, Tita discovers her secret past: Her mother had enjoyed an affair with a mulatto man who fathered Tita's sister Gertrudis. When her family discovered Mamá Elena's relationship, they forced her into marriage with a white man and had the mulatto murdered when the affair continued.

Rosaura de la Garza (rroh-SOW-rah), Tita's older sister, who marries Pedro Muzquiz at Mamá Elena's suggestion. Rosaura lives her life according to her mother's dictates, attempting to maintain the respect and admiration of the cream of society. Jealous of his love for Tita, Rosaura tries unsuccessfully to impress Pedro with her cooking. Rosaura cannot even produce milk to nurse her son and daughter. Her attitude toward cooking and her knowledge of Pedro's undying love for Tita are manifested in Rosaura's obesity and flatulence.

Gertrudis de la Garza (hehr-TREW-dees), Tita's rebellious older sister, fathered by Mamá Elena's mulatto lover. Loyal and sympathetic to her sister Tita and a great fan of her sister's culinary talents, Gertrudis is so overwhelmed by passion after eating one of Tita's special dishes that she abandons her family and rides off on horseback with a revolutionary soldier. Unable to satisfy her lust with him, she tames her sexual appetite as a prostitute until the soldier returns and marries her. She lives happily, eventually becomes a general in the revolutionary army, and visits the ranch with her soldiers after Mamá Elena's death.

Pedro Muzquiz (mews-KEES), Tita's childhood sweetheart, who marries her sister Rosaura to remain near Tita. After her death, Mamá Elena whirls into him in the form of a firecracker, nearly burning him to death, but he recovers under Tita's care. When Rosaura dies, he is finally freely united with Tita, and his ecstasy is so overwhelming that it proves fatal.

John Brown, the de la Garzas' family doctor from Texas. A widower with a young son, he visits the de la Garza ranch when Rosaura gives birth. He admires Tita. When she suffers a nervous breakdown, he rescues her and cares for her in his home and later proposes marriage. They become engaged, but when Tita breaks off the relationship, he bows out amicably. He later returns to the ranch happily to celebrate his son Alex's marriage to Rosaura's daughter Esperanza.

Nacha (NAH-chah), the de la Garzas' Indian cook. One of a long line of expert cooks, she rears Tita from childhood in the kitchen and teaches her secrets to Tita, even whispering recipes to her from beyond the grave. On the day of Rosaura's wedding, after tasting the wedding cake icing in which Tita has shed tears, Nacha dies, overcome with grief and loneliness for the fiancé whom Mamá Elena had forbidden her to marry.

LILIOM: A Legend in Seven Scenes

Author: Ferenc Molnár (1878-1952)
First published: 1909
Genre: Drama

Locale: Budapest
Time: Early twentieth century
Plot: Fantasy

Mrs. Muskat, the owner of a merry-go-round in Budapest.
Liliom, her successful barker, discharged for flirting with Julie, whom he eventually marries. He refuses to go back to Mrs. Muskat because he has plans to rob a factory paymaster.

When caught, he stabs himself and dies. In a vision, after sixteen years of purification by fire, he returns to Earth to find himself idealized by his wife and his daughter.

Julie, a country girl who marries Liliom.

Louise, their daughter. She has been taught by Julie to idolize her father. When he returns from death for a day after sixteen years and strikes Louise in irritation, she says the blow felt tender, like a caress.

Marie, Julie's friend, who is lured by Wolf's uniform and marries him.

Wolf, a porter.

Mrs. Hollunder, Julie's aunt, who runs a photograph gallery.

Ficsur, who encourages Liliom to steal a knife from the Hollunder kitchen and hold up the cashier.

Linzman, the factory paymaster whom Liliom plans to rob. Having already paid off the workers, he has no money when Liliom accosts him.

Two policemen, who carry the dying Liliom to the photographer's shop and later figure as heavenly police in his vision.

THE LIME WORKS
(Das Kalkwerk)

Author: Thomas Bernhard (1931-1989)
First published: 1970
Genre: Novel

Locale: An abandoned lime works near Sicking, Upper Austria
Time: c. 1970
Plot: Philosophical realism

Konrad, an eccentric scientist who is working on the definitive scientific treatise on the sense of hearing. He is a highly intelligent and sensitive man in late middle age. Konrad lives in an abandoned lime works in Upper Austria with his handicapped wife. He subjects her to endless experiments in which he forces her to make ever more subtle aural discriminations. She torments him by constantly making requests that interrupt his train of thought. He is obsessed with writing his great work, which he claims to have worked out in his head, but remains unable to put anything down on paper. One day, he loses his mind and kills his wife with the rifle that is strapped to her wheelchair. He is found by the police several days later, nearly frozen and cowering in a manure pit. He is awaiting trial for her murder.

Konrad's wife, a woman who is handicapped and confined to a wheelchair. In late middle age, she is forced to serve as a subject in her husband's ongoing experiments on the sense of hearing.

The narrator, an unnamed local insurance salesman who is gathering information on the Konrad couple. He interviews the local people and the police, but much of what he gathers as evidence is merely hearsay and rumor.

Fro and

Wieser, two local estate managers who provide much of the information concerning the Konrads to the narrator. They often report what they have heard from others.

— *Thomas F. Barry*

LINCOLN

Author: Gore Vidal (1925-   )
First published: 1984
Genre: Novel

Locale: Washington, D.C.
Time: 1861-1865
Plot: Historical

Abraham Lincoln, the sixteenth president of the United States. The Lincoln portrayed here, nicknamed "The Tycoon" by close associates in the White House, is a complex man. Not only is he the Lincoln usually portrayed in biographies—the jesting, self-deprecating backwoods sage—but he also is a complex, calculating man of genius with an acutely accurate awareness of what the American people support. Thought to be a country bumpkin by such cabinet members as Salmon Chase and William Seward prior to his arrival at the White House, he soon amazes them with his wily command of politics and situations. His love and concern for the Union soldiers fighting the battles of the Civil War is as deep as the love he shows for his eccentric wife, Mary, and his children.

Mary Todd Lincoln, Lincoln's wife, nearly as complex a character as her husband. An opinionated and strong-willed woman who often clashes with her husband's associates, Mary is distinctly a liability to Abraham's political fortunes. He deflects criticism of her, loyally supporting her bad moods and extravagant spending to the end of his life.

John Hay, President Lincoln's Harvard-trained personal secretary and confidant. A good-natured, often high-spirited young man, as well as an aesthete in a White House filled with philistines, Hay is portrayed as an invaluable source of political insights for Lincoln as well as a much-needed admirer, friend, adviser, and sounding board.

William Seward, the handsome U.S. secretary of state under Lincoln and Lincoln's onetime political opponent. Seward is a rather self-congratulatory, pompous individual, with a penchant for speaking his mind on many subjects. A formidable presence on the Lincoln cabinet and a capable overseer of the war effort, Seward initially believed the Southern states ought to be allowed to go their own way without Northern interference. Under pressure from Lincoln, he changed his mind.

Salmon P. Chase, the U.S. secretary of the Treasury. Known as the radical abolitionist of President Lincoln's cabinet, Chase feared that the president was too ordinary a politician for the demands of his position. He came to realize, much to his chagrin, what a knowledgeable, wily leader Lincoln really was. A bachelor father, he devotes his affection to his twenty-three-year-old daughter, Kate, and she reciprocates that love.

Edwin Stanton, the U.S. secretary of war. Stanton, large in stature and firm of opinion, is a balding, bespectacled strategist who has the habit of sneering at others' ideas. Although not fond of Lincoln, Stanton works hard for him and for the Union war effort.

David Herold, a dull-witted, uncouth young hooligan and self-confessed enemy of both the Union cause and President Lincoln. Drifting around the brothels of Washington, D.C.,

and environs, he searches for a way to kill the president. He joins with a group of coconspirators, the chief of whom is John Wilkes Booth. Booth has the brains and instincts Herold lacks, so it is he rather than Herold who assassinates Lincoln.

John Wilkes Booth, the assassin of President Lincoln. This Southern actor is portrayed as a shadowy, hate-filled figure who stalks his sworn enemy to avenge the South's defeat in the Civil War. Self-consciously theatrical, Booth comes across as an often ludicrously affected man hamstrung at times by his own ineptitude.

— *John D. Raymer*

LINDEN HILLS

Author: Gloria Naylor (1950-)
First published: 1985
Genre: Novel

Locale: A suburb of a northern city
Time: Early 1980's
Plot: Social realism

Willie Mason, an idealistic twenty-year-old African American poet who lives in a slum bordering the exclusive black neighborhood of Linden Hills. He survives by working odd jobs. Willie left school after completing the ninth grade, believing that he needed to live among the people in order to write, and he takes pride in memorizing and reciting poetry. Willie is intelligent and widely read but rather naïve, and he questions whether he has chosen the right path in life. When he joins his friend Lester to work in Linden Hills for money to spend at Christmas, he discovers the terrible price that people must pay to live there. Willie decides that he will never become part of the soulless society there.

Lester Tilson, Willie's friend, also twenty years old, a poet, and a dropout. He lives with his mother and sister in the first house in Linden Hills, one filled with discord. Lester scorns the materialism of Linden Hills, yet he accepts its comforts. He serves as Willie's cynical guide and companion as they work their way street by street to the bottom of the Hills and the home of Luther Nedeed.

Luther Nedeed, a wealthy fifth-generation mortician and head of the Tupelo Realty Corporation, which owns all the land in Linden Hills and leases property for a thousand years and a day. He is a carbon copy of his forefathers, all of whom were named Luther and were, like him, short, "frog-eyed," and very dark. A baleful and enigmatic figure, he seems to control life and death in the Hills. Ironically, although he believes in the importance of family, he destroys many people, including his wife and son.

Willa Prescott Nedeed, Luther's wife. She is known only as "Mrs. Nedeed" until the final chapter. Unlike the earlier generations of nameless Nedeed wives, selected for their pale skin, Willa is brown-skinned. Like the others, however, she exists only to produce an heir. When she gives birth to a pale son, Luther refuses to recognize him, though the child resembles him in all other respects. Eventually, he locks Willa and their son in the basement, where the child dies. At first grief-stricken and paralyzed, Willa struggles to reclaim her identity and becomes a force with which to reckon.

— *Joanne McCarthy*

THE LINE OF THE SUN

Author: Judith Ortiz Cofer (1952-)
First published: 1989
Genre: Novel

Locale: Salud, Puerto Rico, and Paterson, New Jersey
Time: The 1930's-1960's
Plot: Bildungsroman

Marisol (MAH-ree-sohl), the protagonist and first-person narrator. Her story actually begins years before her birth, with the recalling of episodes involving her uncle Gusmán, her grandparents, and her father and mother. These events lead up to her birth and growth into a young woman. She admits at the end of the novel to having created parts of the story from her imagination. Her interpretation of events and imaginary additions clearly reflect the development of her own character.

Gusmán (gews-MAHN), Marisol's uncle. The story begins with his childhood. Other members of the family have considered Gusmán reckless and wild from birth. From being an uncontrollable child, he grows into an unconventional adult with the life's goal of finding the disreputable spiritist Rosa.

His real and invented history and finally his heroic actions at the time of tragedy in Paterson are catalytic to Marisol's understanding of her dual culture and the self she creates through her writing.

Ramona, Marisol's mother. She first appears as the older sister of Gusmán. Her courtship and her marriage to Rafael in Salud are traced forward to Marisol's birth. She remains the constant link to Marisol's island culture. Ramona never assimilates into American life, first re-creating her homeland within the structure of El Building and later succumbing to her life as a "prisoner," isolated from the community she loves by a home in the suburbs. She eventually returns to Salud after her husband's death.

Rafael Santacruz, Marisol's father. He is blond and fair-skinned, and when he wears his Navy uniform, Marisol describes him as looking like an American sailor. Stationed at the Brooklyn Navy yard, he chooses to locate the family in Paterson as a safer alternative to New York City. He assimilates easily into affluent America and attempts to separate his family from its Latin culture. He is unable to effect much change because his visits with the family are so short. He sees that the children receive their education at Saint Jerome's, where they are the only Puerto Rican students.

Rosa, a spiritist, or medium, called **La Cabra** (she-goat) by those who suspect her of wrongdoing. She is sought for potions and predictions of the future. Mamá Cielo takes Gusmán to Rosa to have his demons exorcised; ironically, he becomes possessed by his love for her. She has a daughter, Sarita, who much later becomes a religious zealot back in Puerto Rico and whom Gusmán eventually marries.

— *Vicki Due Hendricks*

THE LION AND THE JEWEL

Author: Wole Soyinka (1934-   )
First published: 1963
Genre: Drama

Locale: Ilujinle, a village in western Nigeria
Time: The 1950's
Plot: Comedy

Baroka (bah-ROH-kah), the "Bale" of Ilujinle, the "Lion" in the title of the play. This village chief is sixty-two years old, very proud, deceptive, and cunning. His attempt to win the village belle, Sidi, through deception is the central focus of the play. The Bale manipulates the other characters by feigning sexual impotence.

Sidi (SEE-dee), the village belle, about eighteen years old, very pretty and coquettish. She distracts the young schoolteacher, Lakunle, attracts a traveling photographer who wants her picture to be in a magazine, and passively flirts with the Bale, unaware of the Bale's vast experience in romance. Sidi is tricked into making love with the Bale at the end of the comedy.

Lakunle (lah-KEWN-lay), a young, "modern," and stylishly dressed liberal. He is in fact a conservative who pretends to be interested in social revolution; his real concern is for Sidi or any other available young woman in the village.

Lakunle's supposed platonic love for Sidi is no match for the Bale's cunning and experience, and Lakunle proves to be a poor adversary.

Sadiku (sah-DEE-kew), the primary wife of the Bale. One of her principal jobs is to woo younger wives for the Bale. She convinces Sidi that the young woman should marry the Bale by telling her that the Bale is old and that Sidi will have the honor of being the senior wife of the new Bale.

The favorite, the Bale's present young woman. She tries to please him, but she is informed by the Bale that she has no time to improve her affection because he is taking a new wife. She represents another conquest by the Bale.

The surveyor, an outsider who is planning to build a road through the village. He is easily bought off by the Bale, who offers gifts if he will build the road in another place, thus preserving the land and the traditions of his people.

— *Robert J. Willis*

THE LION OF FLANDERS
(De leeuw van Vlaanderen)

Author: Hendrik Conscience (1812-1883)
First published: 1838
Genre: Novel

Locale: Flanders
Time: 1298-1305
Plot: Historical

Philip the Fair, king of France. With his treasury almost depleted, he eyes the rich cities of Flanders for possible revenue. When the Flemish burghers refuse to pay the taxes levied by the king, he brings his armies against them. He encounters such stubborn resistance that he finally is forced to give up his efforts to subdue the fiercely independent people of Flanders.

Joanna of Navarre, queen of France, whose hatred of the Flemings causes King Philip to dishonor himself and to make an enemy of his brother, Charles de Valois.

Count Guy of Flanders, a vassal of Philip the Fair. A victim of Philip's displeasure, he finds himself the king's prisoner and, at the same time, the rallying point of the party supporting Flemish independence. He dies in prison before the peace treaty with France is signed.

Count Robert de Bethune, called the **Lion of Flanders**. He is the son of Count Guy of Flanders. Imprisoned with his father by Philip the Fair, he is released for a time when Adolf of Niewland takes his place. During his freedom, he rallies the forces of Flanders and finally leads them to victory against the

French. Returning to prison, he is freed after the signing of the peace treaty and becomes the ruler of Flanders.

Adolf of Niewland, a Flemish knight who goes to prison as a hostage for Count Robert de Bethune. He is the protector and, later, the husband of Lady Matilda.

Peter Deconinck, the dean of the cloth-workers' guild at Bruges, and

Jan Breydel, the dean of the butchers' guild, who are knighted by Count Robert de Bethune for their services in the cause of Flemish independence.

Lady Matilda, Count Robert de Bethune's daughter and later the bride of Adolf of Niewland.

Philippa, Count Guy of Flanders' daughter, who is imprisoned and poisoned by the French.

Sir Diederik die Vos, called **The Fox**, a Flemish noble who has escaped from prison in France. Disguised as a friar, he brings word from Count Robert de Bethune that Count Robert's jailer would free him temporarily if someone would take his place.

Lord Guy, the younger brother of Count Robert de Bethune.

Count Robert d'Artois, leader of the French forces defeated at Courtrai.

Charles de Valois, King Philip's brother, who is betrayed by the king when he tries to effect a reconciliation between the Flemish nobles and King Philip.

THE LITIGANTS
(Les Plaideurs)

Author: Jean Racine (1639-1699)
First published: 1669
Genre: Drama

Locale: Normandy, France
Time: The seventeenth century
Plot: Satire

Dandin (dah[n]-DA[N]), a judge, presented in scenes designed to ridicule lawyers. Because of his eccentric behavior, he is regarded by his family as mad and in need of being watched day and night. Insisting on going to court, he tries every means of escape until, finally, his son Leandre suggests that he preside at the trial of Citron, a dog accused of eating a chicken. When Leandre's marriage contract is produced, the judge acquits Citron as a welcoming present to the bride, Isabelle.

Leandre (lay-AHNDR), Dandin's son. While attempting to keep a watchful eye on his eccentric father, he is engaged in an attempt to communicate with Isabelle. Disguised as a police commissioner, he tricks her into declaring her love for him and tricks her father, Chicanneau, into signing a marriage contract between the lovers.

L'Intime (l'an-TEEM), a secretary persuaded by Leandre to disguise himself as a process server and deliver a note to Isabelle. He gets a thrashing from her father, Chicanneau, for his pains.

Chicanneau (shee-kah-NOH), a litigant and the father of Isabelle. Under the impression that he is signing a police report, he puts his signature to a marriage contract between his daughter and Leandre.

Isabelle (ee-zah-BEHL), Chicanneau's daughter, who marries Leandre.

Petit Jean (peh-TEE zhahn), a porter set to keep watch over Judge Dandin.

La Comtesse, a litigant.

Citron (see-TROH[N]), a dog tried by Judge Dandin, with Petit Jean and L'Intime acting as lawyers.

Le Souffleur (sewf-LEWR), the prompter.

LITTLE BIG MAN

Author: Thomas Berger (1924-   )
First published: 1964
Genre: Novel

Locale: Western United States
Time: 1852-1876 and 1952-1953
Plot: Picaresque

Jack Crabb, later called **Little Big Man**, an adventurer, pioneer, and adopted Indian, the only Caucasian survivor of the Battle of the Little Bighorn. Short, slender, red-haired, and fair-skinned, and always feeling undersized, the intrepid Jack relies on slyness and trickery to survive in his violent, tumultuous world. At about the age of ten, Jack is abducted from a wagon train in Nebraska Territory by a Northern Cheyenne tribe, and he spends the next five years with the Cheyenne, eventually becoming "Little Big Man," a brave of the tribe. Jack's values and outlook on life are shaped by his years among the Cheyenne. He feels sympathy for the Indians and their harmonious but difficult life in the natural world, but he also reflects the cynical realism of American adventurers and pioneers bent on conquering and possessing traditional Indian territory. At 111 years of age, Jack narrates the novel as an interview and thus serves as the novel's unifying figure as well as its hero.

Old Lodge Skins, the chief of the Cheyenne tribe that abducts and then adopts Jack Crabb. He is Jack's mentor. Robust, battle-scarred, and leather-skinned, Old Lodge Skins is elderly when Jack first sees him. When he dies gloriously on a mountaintop, almost twenty-five years later, Old Lodge Skins, who is by then perhaps ninety years old, offers a joyous death-chant to commemorate his long, vital life. Old Lodge Skins becomes Jack's acknowledged spiritual mentor, a sage

of an ancient, vanishing race who teaches Jack to accept all that befalls him as the mixed but necessary blessings of human existence.

General George Armstrong Custer, the flamboyant leader of the U.S. Seventh Cavalry, destined to perish at the Battle of the Little Bighorn in June, 1876. With his long blond hair and dashing manner, Custer is egotistical, cruel, and ambitious. He is also undeniably heroic, and Jack acknowledges Custer's authority and leadership as he watches Custer die, undaunted, at the Little Bighorn. Perplexing and loathsome to Jack, Custer is the opposite of and adversary to Old Lodge Skins and the Indians' way of life.

James Butler "Wild Bill" Hickok, a gunfighter and gambler, an uneasy friend to Jack Crabb. A "Wild West" figure, Hickok has curly blond hair and mustache, stands more than six feet tall, and possesses the Western hero's slim waist and broad chest. Hickok becomes Jack's friend and competing gambler in Kansas City, and he instructs Jack in the ways of "gun-handling." His pearl-handled revolvers jutting dramatically from his silk waist-sash, Hickok blusters his way through life, ever vigilant and ever fearful of surprise attack. Shrewd and mistrustful, Hickok charms and dazzles hangers-on and intimidates or kills adversaries. Like General Custer, Hickok is mythologized in his own lifetime. He is shot fatally in the back on August 2, 1876.

Mrs. Pendrake, a minister's wife and briefly Jack Crabb's legally adoptive mother, the only woman Jack ever truly loves. Mrs. Pendrake is fair-complected, a beautiful young woman with long, dark blonde hair and blue eyes. The first "civilized" Caucasian woman Jack has encountered in five years, she exhibits the cold, well-mannered ways of idle middle-class women. Jack runs away from the Pendrake home after discovering Mrs. Pendrake's involvement in an adulterous relationship. The unrequited love that Mrs. Pendrake inspires in Jack is, in his own words, "the real tragedy" of his life.

Caroline Crabb, Jack's older sister. Caroline, six feet tall, with a head of flaming red hair, dresses like a man and works at a traditionally male occupation, that of mule-team driver. She falls in love, unsuccessfully, with several men. Surfacing at several points in the novel, Caroline is a romantic at heart, in spite of her male appearance and occupation. At one point, she rescues Jack from a barroom beating. In her early forties, emotionally fatigued and physically worn down, Caroline lapses into permanent delusion, and Jack places her in an asylum. She is Jack's only link to his immediate family.

Younger Bear, a Cheyenne brave of Old Lodge Skins's clan, Jack's adversary throughout the novel. Tall and physically powerful, Younger Bear is a ferocious warrior but is overly intense, vain, and self-centered. His discontentment and pathological quest for numerous scalps overshadow his physical prowess and bravery. Always envious of Jack and resentful of Old Lodge Skins's preference for Jack (as Little Big Man), the quixotic Younger Bear nevertheless saves Jack's life at the Battle of the Little Bighorn to fulfill an oath.

Little Horse, another Cheyenne friend to Jack, a *heemaneh* (homosexual) who is drawn to women's roles and tribal artistic functions rather than to a brave's combat role. From the time that Jack is one of the tribe's children, along with Younger Bear and other boys, Little Horse shows little inclination toward male hunting and war-making roles. When Jack reunites with Old Lodge Skins's band, he finds that Little Horse has declared himself a *heemaneh*, has dressed in women's decorative robes, and is tending to the domestic needs of Younger Bear, who has taken in Little Horse as one of his "wives." Little Horse is killed in a massacre prior to the Battle of the Little Bighorn.

Amelia, a young prostitute whom Jack encounters in a Kansas City brothel. She claims to be Jack's niece. Short, slight, and pale, the auburn-haired Amelia gratefully accommodates Jack's happy delusion and is "rescued" to a life of pampered ease and comfort. She stays in a boarding school while Jack leaves for the seasonal buffalo hunt. Amelia quickly learns a lady's deportment, speech, and dress. Eventually, she marries a lawyer who is the son of a state senator, thus completing her transformation from prostitute to respectable married woman.

Lavender, a freeman whom Jack first meets as the Pendrakes' yardman. Lavender leaves the Pendrakes and Missouri and joins a band of Hunkpapa Sioux, who accept him as a "Black White Man." Lavender always feels sad, out of place, and restless, with no clear identity. At the same time, he is perceptive, intelligent, and sensitive. When he reunites with Jack prior to the battle at the Little Bighorn, Lavender is a scout-interpreter for one of General Custer's field officers. Once again feeling like a man with no cultural identity, Lavender anguishes over being Custer's agent, a role he fears is unsympathetic to his adopted Sioux band. Empathizing with Lavender's identity confusion, Jack grieves Lavender's death and scalping at the hands of a Sioux brave who recognizes him at the Battle of the Little Bighorn.

— *David W. Pitre*

THE LITTLE CLAY CART
(Mrcchakatika)

Author: Unknown, attributed to Sudraka (fl. 100 B.C.E.)
First performed: Between the second and sixth centuries B.C.E.
Genre: Drama

Locale: The ancient city of Ujjayini
Time: The fifth century B.C.E.
Plot: Tragicomedy

Chārudatta, a wise and honorable young Brāhmana left impoverished after spending his fortune for the welfare of others. In love with and loved by Vasantasenā, he is falsely accused of her murder and condemned to die. As he is being prepared for execution, Vasantasenā appears just in time to identify the true murderer and save her lover's life. Chārudatta's fortune is restored, and he is made an official at court by the new and just king, Āryaka.

Vasantasenā, a wealthy courtesan who is in love with Chārudatta. When she goes to the park to meet her lover, she is set upon by Samsthānaka, who chokes her and leaves her for dead. She is rescued by a Buddhist monk. While Chārudatta is being falsely accused and tried for her murder, she is being nursed back to health. She appears at the place of execution in time to save her lover's life.

Samsthānaka, King Pālaka's brother-in-law. Enamored of Vasantasenā and madly jealous of her attentions to Chārudatta,

he chokes her, leaves her for dead, and accuses his rival of the murder.

Āryaka, a captive prince freed through the efforts of Sarvilaka and Chārudatta. He later deposes King Pālaka and restores to Chārudatta his fortune and his rightful place in the world.

Sarvilaka, a thieving Brāhmana, Prince Āryaka's friend and liberator. He steals the jewels left by Vasantasenā in Chārudatta's care and buys his bride, Madanikā, with them.

Madanikā, Vasantasenā's slave and confidant, whom Sarvilaka purchases as his bride.

Rohasena, Chārudatta's son, to whom Vasantasenā gives a little gold cart to replace a clay one, which is all his father is able to afford.

Maitreya, a poor Brāhmana, Chārudatta's friend and confidant.

Pālaka, the unjust king deposed by Prince Āryaka.

LITTLE DORRIT

Author: Charles Dickens (1812-1870)
First published: 1855-1857
Genre: Novel

Locale: England
Time: The 1820's
Plot: Social realism

William Dorrit, a quiet, shy, self-contained man so long imprisoned for debt that he has become known to all as the "Father of the Marshalsea." Never able to understand the complexity of business details that reduced him to bankruptcy, he accepts his fate and "testimonials," as he calls small gifts of money given him by visitors to the prison, with the same equanimity. His wife and two children had joined him in prison, where a third child, their daughter Amy, had been born; and Mrs. Dorrit had died there. Over the Dorrit family hangs the shadow of some great but mysterious wrong. When it is discovered that Mr. Dorrit is the heir at law to an unclaimed fortune, he leaves the prison and begins a life of extravagance and display on the fringes of society. His mind, weakened by twenty-five years of imprisonment, slowly deteriorates. He dies, in a palace in Rome, believing he is back in the Marshalsea.

Amy Dorrit, called **Little Dorrit** because she is the youngest child of the family, born in the Marshalsea Prison. After her mother's death, she becomes the stay and protector of the family, ministering to the needs of her gentle father, her sister Fanny, and her brother Tip. A seamstress, she sews for Mrs. Clennam, who has suppressed the codicil to a will that gave Little Dorrit an inheritance of two thousand guineas. Little Dorrit is never at ease surrounded by the splendor and wealth of the Dorrits once they are freed from the Marshalsea, and she returns to the prison to nurse Arthur Clennam after his confinement there. The wrongs done to both are eventually righted, and they marry.

Fanny Dorrit, Mr. Dorrit's older daughter. A ballet dancer, she is able to make her way into society, and she marries Edmund Sparkler.

Edward Dorrit, nicknamed **Tip**, a ne'er-do-well and spendthrift for whom, before their restoration to affluence, Little Dorrit secures a variety of jobs, none of which he holds very long.

Frederick Dorrit, Mr. Dorrit's brother, also a bankrupt. After losing his money, he gave up bathing and supported himself by playing a clarinet in a theater orchestra. He had taken in and cared for Arthur Clennam's real mother. He remains simple in tastes and heart.

Mrs. Clennam, a stern, implacable, cold-hearted woman, an invalid who for years has managed from her sickbed the English branch of her husband's business. She has kept from Arthur Clennam the knowledge that he is the son of a woman whom his father had loved but never married, and she has withheld Little Dorrit's rightful inheritance. Threatened with exposure by M. Blandois, who is trying to blackmail her, she confesses the wrong to Little Dorrit and is forgiven.

Arthur Clennam, the son of the woman his father put aside when he married Mrs. Clennam. For twenty years, he has lived with his father in China. After Mr. Clennam's death, he returns to England, bringing with him his father's last bequest, an old watch inscribed with the letters DNF (Do Not Forget). On his arrival, he is attracted to Little Dorrit, who is partly a servant and partly a friend in the Clennam household. Arthur incurs Mrs. Clennam's displeasure when he withdraws from the family business and goes into partnership with Daniel Doyce, an engineer and inventor. Ruined when Mr. Merdle's involved financial structure collapses, he is imprisoned in the Marshalsea. There, during an illness, he is nursed by Little Dorrit. They marry after his release.

M. Blandois, alias **Rigaud**, "a cruel gentleman with slender white hands." Condemned to death for the murder of his wife, he escapes from the prison in Marseilles and makes his way to England, where, having gained knowledge of Mrs. Clennam's deceptions and frauds, he attempts to blackmail her. He is killed when the rickety Clennam house collapses, burying him in the ruins.

Daniel Doyce, the engineer who becomes Arthur Clennam's partner. Because he has been successful during a business trip abroad, he is able to free Arthur from the Marshalsea and to assure the future prosperity of the firm of Doyce and Clennam.

Mrs. Flora Finching, Arthur Clennam's first love. Now widowed, she is still artless, sentimental, and gushingly foolish in her conversation. She lives with her father, Christopher Casby.

Christopher Casby, Flora Finching's father, the miserly landlord of Bleeding Heart Yard. A complete hypocrite, he poses as a benefactor and philanthropist while his agent forces his tenants into greater poverty. To those unaware of his true nature, he is known as "The Last of the Patriarchs."

Mr. Pancks, Mr. Casby's agent and rent collector, who finally rebels against his skinflint employer and publicly humiliates him. He advises Arthur Clennam to invest in Mr. Merdle's financial enterprises and thus helps to bring about Arthur's bankruptcy.

Mr. Merdle, a financial wizard. His bankruptcy ruins many investors, and he commits suicide by bleeding himself with a penknife.

Mrs. Merdle, his wife, Edmund Sparkler's mother.

Edmund Sparkler, the son of Mrs. Merdle and her first husband, an army officer stationed for a time in North America. It is reported that Edmund's brains were frozen when he was born during a great Canadian frost. Claiming that Fanny Dorrit is a "doosed fine gal," he marries her.

Mr. Meagles, a benevolent, sentimental retired banker who mistakenly prides himself on the fact that he is a practical man.

Mrs. Meagles, his homely but cheerful wife, a perfect partner in the marriage.

Minnie Meagles, their daughter, familiarly called **Pet**. Fair and mild of temper, like her parents, she marries Henry Gowan.

Henry Gowan, a young artist who marries Minnie Meagles. He is a distant connection of the Barnacle family.

Mrs. Gowan, his mother, somewhat aloof in manner because she is proud of her family connections.

Mrs. General, a wealthy widow who becomes the social mentor of the Dorrit family after they have become wealthy. Mr. Dorrit proposes to her shortly before his death.

Jeremiah Flintwinch, at one time Mrs. Clennam's servant, later her rascally partner in her deceptions and acts of fraud.

Affery Flintwinch, Mrs. Clennam's maid, whom Flintwinch married against her will. She is gentle and submissive to Mrs. Clennam, abused by her husband.

Ephraim Flintwinch, Jeremiah's brother and confederate.

Harriet Beadle (Tattycoram), a foundling taken in by Mr. Meagles. A headstrong girl, she runs away from her benefactors and seeks the protection of Miss Wade. Later, she recovers the papers that gave M. Blandois his hold over Mrs. Clennam and returns to service with the Meagles family.

Miss Wade, a strange, tormented, unhappy woman who persuades Tattycoram to desert Mr. and Mrs. Meagles. She gains possession of the documents with which Mr. Blandois is trying to blackmail Mrs. Clennam.

Lord Decimus Tite Barnacle, a pompous official high in the Circumlocution Office of the government.

Tite Barnacle, an official of the Circumlocution Office involved in the circumstances of Mr. Dorrit's bankruptcy. Arthur Clennam interviews him while trying to secure Mr. Dorrit's release from the Marshalsea Prison.

Clarence Barnacle, called **Barnacle, Junior**, Tite Barnacle's son, a fatuous clerk in the Circumlocution Office.

Ferdinand Barnacle, Lord Barnacle's private secretary, an airy, sprightly young man.

John Baptist Cavalletto, an Italian smuggler imprisoned with M. Blandois, then called Rigaud, in Marseilles. He later enters the employ of Arthur Clennam and is instrumental in tracking down Blandois.

John Chivery, the turnkey of the Marshalsea Prison.

John Chivery, Jr., his son, in love with Little Dorrit.

Bob, another turnkey of the Marshalsea, Little Dorrit's godfather.

Mr. Cripples, a schoolmaster who offers instruction to children of the prisoners confined in the Marshalsea.

Dr. Haggage, the brandy-drinking debtor who officiates at the birth of Little Dorrit.

Mrs. Bangham, a chairwoman, nurse, and messenger between the outer world and prisoners in the Marshalsea.

Mr. Plornish, a plasterer, one of Mr. Casby's tenants in Bleeding Heart Yard.

Mrs. Plornish, his wife, a friend of Little Dorrit.

John Nandy, Mrs. Plornish's father, considered by his daughter a "sweet singer."

Maggy, Mrs. Bangham's granddaughter, Little Dorrit's friend. "Never to be older than ten," she is blind in one eye and partly bald as the result of fever. She helps to care for the Plornish children.

Mrs. Tickit, housekeeper to the Meagles family.

Lord Lancaster Stiltstalking, an austere superannuated politician maintained by the Circumlocution Office in diplomatic posts abroad.

Mr. Rugg, Mr. Pancks's landlord, an accountant and debt collector.

Anastasia Rugg, his daughter, the owner of a modest property acquired through a breach-of-promise suit.

THE LITTLE FOXES

Author: Lillian Hellman (1905-1984)
First published: 1939
Genre: Drama

Locale: The Deep South
Time: 1900
Plot: Social realism

Regina Giddens, a conniving and grasping woman. Eager for her share in the profits of a proposed cotton mill, she contrives to get her fatally ill husband, Horace, home from the hospital to be worked on by her family to supply her share of the needed investment. When he refuses to have anything to do with the project, she cruelly taunts him with her contempt and refuses him his medicine when he feels the onset of a fatal attack.

Benjamin and

Oscar Hubbard, Regina Giddens' conniving and grasping brothers. Lacking Regina's share of the investment needed for the construction of the cotton mill, they descend on the fatally ill Horace Giddens in an attempt to persuade him to put up the money. When he refuses to have anything to do with the venture, they "borrow" his bonds and go off to complete the deal.

Horace Giddens, Regina Giddens' honest, fatally ill husband. Sick of his scheming wife and her grasping family, he refuses to invest in the projected cotton mill. When he learns of the theft of his bonds by Benjamin and Oscar Hubbard, he ties Regina's hands by planning a will that makes her the beneficiary of the bonds. He dies when she deprives him of his medicine.

Alexandra, the daughter of Regina and Horace Giddens. Sickened by the treatment given her father by her mother and her uncles, she leaves Regina and the Hubbards after Horace's death.

Birdie Hubbard, Oscar Hubbard's wife, who longs for a return to the refinements of a bygone day.

Leo Hubbard, Oscar Hubbard's son, an ally in the theft of Horace Giddens' bonds.

THE LITTLE GIRLS

Author: Elizabeth Bowen (1899-1973)
First published: 1964
Genre: Novel

Locale: Somerset and London, England
Time: Late 1950's or early 1960's, and 1914
Plot: Psychological realism

Dinah Piggott Delacroix (dee-NAH deh-lah-KRWAH), nicknamed **Dicey** as a child, the protagonist, a well-to-do English widow and grandmother. She is still slim and attractive, looking younger than her years (sixtyish); she is as spontaneous, willful, and imaginative as a child. Preoccupied with retaining the past, she is collecting treasured objects from her current friends to bury in a time capsule when she recalls the cache of secret treasures she and two eleven-year-old school friends buried some fifty years earlier, just before World War I. She impulsively seeks out those school friends through newspaper advertisements as a means of finding the box and exploring its contents. Although the box is discovered to be empty, by forcing the women (and herself) to confront their buried pasts in reminiscences, Dinah helps them to resolve their emotional problems and herself to grow up. A conflict with Clare brings the imaginative Dinah more respect for the individuality of others and for the passage of time in the world of reality.

Clare Burkin-Jones, nicknamed **Mumbo** as a child, the daughter of a handsome army major and his pedestrian wife. As a child, she was drawn to poetry and loved Dinah's beautiful and artistically sensitive mother, as did the father whom she adored and whose death in the war she has never been able to accept. A large woman who wears tailored suits and a turban, she has resumed her father's name after an unhappy marriage and now operates a successful chain of gift shops, having denied her youthful literary gifts to deal with emotionally safer opaque objects instead. The antithesis to Dinah's childish

buoyancy and trust in chance, she is a rather cynical rationalist with a strong sense of the role of choice and personal responsibility in life. Her jealousy of Dinah and cruelty to her on the last day the children saw one another are resolved when she finally expresses a love and respect for Dinah and her more affirmative perspective on life.

Sheila Beaker Artworth, nicknamed **Sheikie** as a child, a chic, appearance-conscious, childless matron who never left Southstone, where the three women lived as children. She married a local realtor and settled into a life of provincial respectability, although with a tendency to drink to escape her sense of unfulfillment. She has had a love affair, but the man died, not realizing how much the inarticulate Sheila loved him. As a child, she was high-spirited and talented, an unselfconscious dancer whose bodily movements were her means of self-expression, but she no longer dances. Reliving the past helps her to regain the self-esteem she has lost through failing as a lover, a begetter, and a dancer, and she has begun to refuse drinks and once again to gesture like a dancer before the novel ends.

Major Frank Wilkins, Dinah's neighbor, close friend, and companion. He is also sixtyish and still slim and handsome but generally more adult. He warns her that one cannot go back in time with impunity and, after Dinah's quarrel with Clare, makes Clare realize how much she once meant and still means to Dinah.

— Harriet Blodgett

THE LITTLE HOTEL

Author: Christina Stead (1902-1983)
First published: 1973
Genre: Novel

Locale: Switzerland
Time: The postwar 1940's
Plot: Social realism

Madame Bonnard, the narrator, the wife of Roger and mother of Olivier. At the age of twenty-six, she runs the Hotel-Swiss-Touring, a fourth-class establishment. She is gossipy and sometimes friendly with her hotel guests, especially the "permanent" guests. She suspects her best friend, Julie, of trying to have an affair with Roger, and she judges Julie to be jealous and malicious.

Roger, her husband, who spies on the guests, usually discreetly. He chain-smokes and makes sure that he has a night out now and then. Although it is against Swiss law, he searches the belongings of Miss Abbey-Chillard, who has not paid her bill, and finds enough money to settle her account.

Mrs. Lilia Trollope, the character whose story is most fully explored, an Englishwoman who is divorced from her husband and living with Robert Wilkins under the pretext that he is her cousin. Lilia's central conflict is that Robert will not marry her, although he lives off her money, claiming to manage it for her. She also complains of having nothing to do and of being ignored: Robert reads the newspaper at meals instead of talking to her. Mrs. Powell, an American racist, suspects Lilia of being Eurasian (Lilia's mother was a Dutch-Javanese), and the narrator says that the Wilkinses do not want their blood mixed with that of a half-caste. Lilia is friendly with Madame Blaise, although she suspects the Blaises of somehow wanting to harm her. She is kind to Miss Abbey-Chillard, despite Robert's

annoyance, and gives her money to go to Zermatt to die with her friends. Lilia is religious, often going to church to pray to her saints for guidance. Her central decision, which the Princess Bili helps Lilia make, is to leave Robert and to return to England and her grown children. Even in leaving Robert, however, Lilia says that she has had a true love.

Mr. Robert Wilkins, a retired man who follows the stock market and currency fluctuations. He lives with Lilia Trollope and has control of her money, as well as power of attorney over her. Robert says that he is a natural bachelor and does not want to be responsible for anyone else. When his sister comes to visit, Robert tells Lilia to make believe that she does not know him. Robert believes that Lilia will never leave him because she would be terrified to live on her own. When she does leave, he vows to keep her capital and to tell her to come abroad again.

Madame Blaise, Lilia's closest friend for most of the novel, a rich woman married to a doctor who brings her drugs when he visits every second weekend. Wilkins says that she also takes drugs that the doctor does not supply. Tall and heavy, with blue eyes and straight white hair, Madame Blaise is called rude and selfish. She would prefer that her son in America die rather than get married. The money that she has sequestered in America probably originally belonged to Nazis. She tells Lilia that she is afraid that if she goes back with the doctor to their house in Basel, she will die, a prediction that comes true.

Dr. Blaise, a sinister man who passes around to his friends photographs of deformed patients who are naked. He is a brisk, elderly, dark-haired man. When Wilkins, Mrs. Trollope, and the Blaises go out to dinner together, the doctor runs up the bill that Wilkins will have to pay and calls him a little rubber salesman. He ensures that Madame Blaise will come home by refusing to bring her any more "medicine." Madame Blaise accuses her husband of having married her for her money. Soon after her death, he marries the ugly, surly housekeeper Ermyntrud to inherit Madame Blaise's money.

Princess Bili di Rovino, a rich old American widow of an Italian prince. She plans to travel to Argentina to have an operation that will make her young again. In her sixties, with bright yellow hair and blue eyes, the princess plans to marry a thirty-three-year-old Spaniard, but he eventually decides that he wants a younger woman. She takes with her to restaurants her pet Sealyham terrier, Angel, who she claims can sing. Although she is eccentric and vain, the princess is kind to Lilia and tries to get Wilkins to marry her. She tells Lilia to refuse to bring out any more money from England until Wilkins agrees to marriage.

The Mayor of B., a high-ranking official of a Belgian city who has come to Switzerland for treatment for a nervous breakdown. Almost completely a comic character, the mayor has only one serious theme, his aversion to Germans, which brings denials of allegiance from all the Swiss-Germans working at the hotel. The mayor writes many numbered documents, and he continually buys champagne, which he drinks with the servants. Serious trouble ensues only when the mayor takes to going out naked except for a hat and a muffler.

Miss Abbey-Chillard, a tall, thin Englishwoman, an invalid whom Lilia befriends. She specializes in being pathetic, complaining that any help she is given is not quite right.

Mrs. Powell, a partly deaf, old American woman who campaigns to get rid of Mrs. Trollope and objects to black guests eating in the dining room.

Clara, the lively Swiss-German housekeeper. She has a cheerful red and yellow face.

Luisa, the Italian maid, who has a tubercular sister. Luisa is emotional and tries to teach the guests Italian.

Charlie, the porter, a Frenchman who in his earlier days sailed all over the world. He has a bad police record, the result of his fondness for young girls.

— *Kate M. Begnal*

LITTLE HOUSE ON THE PRAIRIE

Author: Laura Ingalls Wilder (1867-1957)
First published: 1935
Genre: Novel

Locale: The prairie lands of Kansas and the Dakota Territory
Time: The 1870's
Plot: Historical realism

Laura Ingalls, the five-year-old narrator, the second daughter of Charles and Caroline Ingalls. Laura, the author's autobiographical self, is high-spirited and inquisitive, and she has inherited her father's storytelling ability. She describes the pioneering experience and her own thoughts and feelings in detail.

Charles Ingalls, the father of Laura, Mary, and Carrie Ingalls. Reared on the frontier, he is a great woodsman and hunter. He is renowned for his fiddling and his entertaining stories and songs. A kind and fun-loving man, he becomes restless and moves his family west in search of open land and economic opportunity.

Caroline Quiner Ingalls, the girls' mother. Descended from Scots and with family roots in New England, she, like her husband, is a product of the American frontier. Quiet and capable, she is able to make a cozy home for her family under the most primitive circumstances. She is an educated and well-bred woman who has passed along to her daughters a quiet respect for others, along with a great love of books.

Mary Ingalls, Laura's older sister. A bright, responsible girl, Mary is calmer in spirit than Laura. Mary is always

obedient and immaculately groomed. Her altruism is sometimes a source of irritation and envy for Laura, who nevertheless loves her fair-haired sister dearly.

Baby Carrie Ingalls, Laura and Mary's infant sister. Too young to participate fully in the family's pioneer adventures, she is mainly a focus of loving concern and responsibility for the two older girls and their parents.

Jack, the Ingalls' brave bulldog. Jack trots beneath the Ingalls' covered wagon on the long journey to Kansas. At one point, it appears that he has drowned in a treacherous river crossing. The entire family is greatly saddened by his loss. One evening, miles away, the tired dog miraculously reappears. Jack continues on with the Ingalls and remains a fearless protector of the family and a loyal friend to Laura.

Pet and

Patty, the family's mustangs. Named by Mary and Laura, these strong and gentle wagon horses are vital to the success of the Ingalls family's endeavor and figure into many of the stories Laura shares with the reader.

— *Cynthia Breslin Beres*

THE LITTLE MINISTER

Author: Sir James M. Barrie (1860-1937)
First published: 1891
Genre: Novel

Locale: The village of Thrums, in Scotland
Time: Mid-nineteenth century
Plot: Sentimental

Gavin Dishart, the little minister of Auld Licht Parish, in Thrums. He falls in love with Babbie, a girl he believes to be a

gypsy but who is actually the ward of Lord Rintoul. Their path of love is strewn with difficulties, but the sincere and able young minister wins out and marries Babbie, at first in a gypsy camp and, later, in a church. He and his wife live happily afterward, parents of a little daughter who learns their story from her grandfather.

Mr. Gavin Ogilvy, a schoolmaster. He is really Gavin Dishart's father. When his wife's first husband returns, Mr. Ogilvy disappears from her life, thinking he can thus make happy the woman he loves. Eventually he tells Gavin the story, but he never lets his identity be known to Gavin's mother.

Babbie, a girl whom Lord Rintoul was expected to marry. In an attempt to help rebellious weavers escape the law, she disguises herself as a gypsy. While disguised, she claims to be the little minister's wife at one time. Although at first she laughs at the minister, she falls in love with him. After some harrowing adventures, she and Gavin are married.

Margaret Dishart, Gavin's mother. She marries Mr. Ogilvy, thinking her first husband has been lost at sea. When

the first husband returns, Mr. Ogilvy disappears to save her embarrassment, and she never sees him again.

Lord Rintoul, a local aristocrat. Planning to marry Babbie himself, he tries unsuccessfully to prevent her marriage to the little minister at the gypsy camp.

Rob Dow, a man rescued from drink by the minister. He tries to protect the minister from Babbie, whom he believes to be a witch. He leaps to his death to save the minister from drowning during a flood.

Nanny Webster, a penniless old woman in Gavin's parish. Babbie thwarts the minister's attempt to send the old lady to the poorhouse.

Dr. McQueen, who helps Gavin in his attempt to send Nanny to the poorhouse.

Micah, Rob's little son.

Adam Dishart, Margaret's first husband, for a time believed lost at sea. He eventually returns home to claim his wife.

LITTLE WOMEN

Author: Louisa May Alcott (1832-1888)
First published: 1868-1869
Genre: Novel

Locale: A New England village, New York City, and Italy
Time: The nineteenth century
Plot: Didactic

Meg March, the oldest of the March girls, a plump governess to unruly neighborhood children. She marries John Brooke.

Jo March, a tall, awkward, tomboyish girl who likes to write and to devise plays and entertainments for her sisters. In character and personality, she corresponds to the author. She resents Meg's interest in John but later is happy to have him as a brother-in-law. She writes and sells stories and becomes a governess for Mrs. Kirke in New York. Proposed to by Laurie, she rejects him. She later marries Professor Bhaer, with whom she establishes a boys' school at Plumfield, Aunt March's old home.

Beth March, a gentle homebody helpful to Mrs. March in keeping house. She contracts scarlet fever, from which she never fully recovers. She dies during the spring after Jo's return from New York.

Amy March, a curly-haired dreamer who aspires to be a famous artist. She is a companion of Aunt Carrol on a European trip. She marries Laurie.

Mrs. March (Marmee), the kindly, understanding, lovable mother of the four March girls.

Mr. March, her husband, an army chaplain in the Civil War who becomes ill while away but who later returns well and happy.

Theodore Lawrence (Laurie), a young neighbor who joins the March family circle. He falls in love with Jo, but after his rejection by her he transfers his feelings to Amy, whom he marries.

Professor Bhaer, a tutor in love with Jo, whom he marries.

Mr. Lawrence, the wealthy, indulgent grandfather of Laurie.

Aunt March, a wealthy, irascible relative who wills her home to Jo.

John Brooke, Laurie's tutor, who falls in love with and marries Meg.

Aunt Carrol, a relative of the Marches.

Mrs. Kirke, a New York boardinghouse keeper.

Daisy and
Demi, Meg's children.

LIVES OF GIRLS AND WOMEN

Author: Alice Munro (1931-   )
First published: 1971
Genre: Novel

Locale: Jubilee, a small town in southwestern Ontario
Time: Approximately the 1950's
Plot: Bildungsroman

Del Jordan, the protagonist and narrator, who lives in Jubilee, a small town in Ontario, Canada. Each of the eight chapters of this "autobiographical" novel presents a new stage in Del's coming-of-age. She begins the story as a curious child, becomes an academically successful but not very popular student, takes a lover, and becomes a writer. As the chapters unfold, she confronts for the first time the idea of death, gradually recognizes the complexity of her relationship with her mother, desires passionately but ultimately rejects religious affiliation, and engages in initial sexual experiments that

are as awkward as her first genuine romance is fulfilling. Finally, she makes the painful decision to leave Jubilee and to abandon conventional small-town life in favor of the independent life of a writer. Although Del emerges as both a witty and a highly intelligent woman, it is an unyielding sense of independence that most characterizes her. Each chapter of the book demonstrates her reluctance to be constrained by traditional interpretations both of the world and of womanhood, a reluctance that often evokes pathos because it is coupled with her keen sympathy for those who accept such interpretations.

She discovers in the course of writing her first novel, based loosely on her experiences in Jubilee, that whatever truth she captures about the people and their town ultimately is itself an interpretation; it is, however, hers.

Ada (Addie) Morrison Jordan, Del's mother. She is a middle-aged, intelligent woman who yearns for more culture and freedom than the traditional, small-town world of Jubilee can provide. She makes attempts at broadening her horizons by joining Great Books clubs and by selling encyclopedias. Her emphasis on education as the way to escape from Jubilee certainly influences Del. Despite her unconventional rejection of religion and her avid faith in the future liberation of women, she remains steadfastly traditional in her views concerning sex, possibly because she views any attachment to a man as ultimately destructive of a woman's potential to live her own life.

Garnet French, Del's first, genuine love, a handsome, poor, Baptist backwoodsman. He was a drinker and troublemaker before being changed by time spent in jail and by religion. He now hopes to become a minister. Although his intelligence is no match for Del's, Garnet nevertheless attracts Del because of his raw sexuality, and it is with Garnet that Del first experiences real sexual fulfillment. Despite her deep attachment to him, however, she is forced to declare her independence when Garnet attempts to "baptize" her in the local river, revealing both his deep-seated wish that she become a Baptist and his resentment that she is not like him.

Uncle Benny, an eccentric, illiterate backwoodsman, thirty-seven years old, who is no relation to anyone in Jubilee but who is called Uncle Benny by all. He works for Del's father, who raises silver foxes on a nearby farm. When Del is still a child, Uncle Benny shows her, through his unconventional, often chaotic behavior, that human beings can and do live in a variety of ways. His unconventional activities include arranging by mail to allow a woman and her child, sight unseen, to share his dilapidated shack on the Flats Road; the results are disastrous.

Naomi, a plump, pretty girl, Del's closest friend and confidante throughout adolescence. Together they wonder and worry about sex, sharing their teenage fantasies and romanticizing about future lovers. Despite the influence of Del's independent personality, Naomi wishes for and ends up finally with a "normal," traditional life, becoming pregnant by and marrying a man she does not love, then looking forward to a future as a suburban housewife.

Elinor Farris, the director of the yearly Jubilee junior high operetta. A native of Jubilee, she is middle-aged and unmarried. She devotes herself fanatically to the annual operetta, perhaps because her sexual life is so unfulfilling. She drowns in the local river, possibly a suicide.

Uncle Craig, Del's aging, stout, and half-blind uncle whose passion in life is to compile a complete, objective history of Jubilee. His death shows Del that humans are mortal, subjective creatures and suggests that compiling such histories may in fact be impossible.

Jerry Storey, an extremely intelligent though unattractive student in Del's high school. His chief interest is science. Jerry and Del become intimate because they are intellectual companions; however, their adolescent experiments with sex are highly unsuccessful.

Art Chamberlain, a local radio newscaster and World War II veteran. Women find him humorous and attractive. Because of her youth, Del initially thinks his passes at her are erotic, but she quickly becomes aware of the more perverse side of his, and human, sexuality.

Fern Dogherty, a boarder in the Jordan household. An overweight woman in her thirties, she failed in her attempt to become an opera singer. She has an affair with Art Chamberlain until he leaves Jubilee.

Marion Sherriff, a stocky, alienated, seventeen-year-old girl who commits suicide, possibly because she is pregnant out of wedlock. Del bases the central character of her first novel on Marion.

— *Matthew K. Davis*

THE LIVING

Author: Annie Dillard (1945-   )
First published: 1992
Genre: Novel

Locale: Whatcom and the Bellingham Bay area in Washington
Time: 1855-1897
Plot: Historical realism

Clare Fishburn, who arrives in Washington with his family in 1855, at the age of five. He grows up in the developing settlement of Whatcom and works at various jobs, including high school teacher and real estate agent. He marries June Randall, his neighbor Minta Honer's sister, and they have three children. Clare finds happiness in all aspects of his life and is always enthusiastic. Even when Beal Obenchain threatens him with death, he still enjoys life to the fullest.

Ada Fishburn Tawes, who makes the overland journey from Missouri to Whatcom by covered wagon with her sons and husband. Her husband, Rooney, dies from asphyxiation while digging a well. She later marries Norval Tawes, a Methodist minister whom she outlives. Her religious faith is strong. She remains in the Whatcom area for the rest of her life.

Glee Fishburn, Clare's younger brother. He marries Grace, the niece of a Seattle madam. He works as a fisherman in

Whatcom, rears several children, and falls out of love with his wife, preferring to stay on his boat and fish.

June Randall Fishburn, a Baltimore debutante. She gives up the chance to marry well in Baltimore and instead settles in Whatcom with her husband, Clare Fishburn. More practical than her pious sister Minta, she rears three children and remains steadfastly supportive of Clare, even after they lose their fortune in the panic of 1893.

John Ireland Sharp, who loses his parents and all four siblings when they drown in Bellingham Bay. Adopted by Axel and Martha Obenchain, he excels in the local school, attends Oberlin Academy in Ohio, teaches school in New York City, and returns to Whatcom as principal of its high school. Dreamy and melancholy, he supports socialist causes but loses faith in their efficacy. He prefers solitude to society.

Pearl Rush, the daughter of Whatcom's first settlers, touted as the village's most beautiful young woman. She marries John Ireland Sharp, and they rear several sons. She is far more materially acquisitive than her intellectual husband.

Beal Obenchain, a foster brother to John Ireland Sharp, a violent and cruel bully. As an adult, he lives a hermit's life in a hollowed tree stump near the beach, supporting himself by doing odd jobs. He considers himself intellectually superior to all of Whatcom and devises strange and cruel schemes, including threatening Clare Fishburn with death.

Minta Randall Honer, the daughter of a prominent Maryland senator. She marries Eustace Honer in Baltimore and moves with him to Whatcom. They have three children. Eustace dies by drowning in a logjam, and the two younger children die in a house fire. She moves to nearby Goshen with her surviving son, Hugh, and becomes a successful farmer and beloved foster mother to three half-Indian children.

Hugh Honer, who grows up lonely but strong. He studies science at the University of Washington and courts Vinnie Fishburn, the daughter of Glee and Grace. He later studies medicine at Johns Hopkins and plans to return to Whatcom to marry Vinnie and settle there.

— *Ann A. Merrill*

LIVING

Author: Henry Green (Henry Vincent Yorke, 1905-1973)
First published: 1929
Genre: Novel

Locale: Birmingham and Liverpool, England
Time: Early twentieth century
Plot: Neorealism

Lily Gates, a woman in her twenties who takes care of three working-class men. Attractive, blonde, and bright, Lily wants desperately to break out of the boredom of her daily domestic chores. A romantic by nature who lost her mother as a child, she makes the most of her banal life. She falls in love with the romantic Bert Jones and elopes with him to Liverpool, where, unable to find his parents, he abandons her on the street. She returns home full of guilt and takes up her domestic duties as before. She resigns herself to living without love in Birmingham.

Joe Gates, the father of Lily and a worker in the Dupret Foundry, a cynical, manipulative, selfish man in his sixties who tries to avoid work. He lives in the household of Mr. Craigan, his best friend, with his daughter and Mr. Dale. To advance himself at work, he befriends the notorious informer, Mr. Tupe, and spends drunken evenings with him. He threatens to blackmail his closest friend, Mr. Craigan, loses his job, and spends his remaining years in an alcoholic haze.

Mr. Craigan, the head of the household and a master moulder at the foundry. He is in his mid-sixties and is a confirmed bachelor. Although he is not a relative, Lily Gates calls him Grandad. He provides a home for Lily, Joe Gates, and the young Mr. Dale. He uses his control benignly and is terrified of being abandoned by everyone in his old age even though he has put money away for his retirement years. He spends his nonworking hours listening to classical music and rereading the novels of Charles Dickens. Although he is highly respected at work by everyone, he is retired early because of his age.

Jim Dale, an extremely attractive man in his twenties who works at the foundry. He is in love with Lily but is unable to articulate his feelings, though he regularly accompanies her to the cinema. He moves out when Lily elopes with Bert Jones, because the house would be unbearable without her.

Bert Jones, a foundry worker in his mid-twenties. He falls in love with Lily Gates and promises to take her to Canada or Australia when he secures the funds from his parents. Impetuously, he elopes with Lily to Liverpool; however, after failing to locate his wandering family, he abandons her on the street and disappears forever.

Mr. Dupret, the owner of the foundry, a man in his mid-sixties. He is an arrogant, stubborn, and contrary man who goes out of his way to punish anyone who tries to usurp his power. He refuses to change any of his costly operating procedures. He is habitually unfaithful to his wife and condescending toward his son, but loyal to the older employees. He dies toward the end of the novel.

Richard Dupret, the naïve and awkward son of the owner of the company. Unable to get his father to take him seriously, he desperately wants to assert his authority. He succeeds in firing some of the less productive employees in the company after his father's death.

Mr. Bridges, the manager of the foundry, in his mid-sixties. A company man, he harshly enforces the disciplinary rules. Neurotically insecure, he indulges in complex power struggles with other bureaucrats and is deeply disturbed by anyone not following the chain of command. He loses his job because he is too old and cannot relinquish his antiquated managerial practices.

Mr. Tarver, an engineer in his thirties. Seeing the waste in the foundry and the injustice done to the employees by the elder Mr. Dupret and Mr. Bridges, he attempts to correct the situation. Ambitious and somewhat manipulative, he succeeds in impressing Richard Dupret with his modernistic views on improving production.

Mr. Tupe, a common laborer at the foundry, in his sixties. An informer, he tells the management everything that the workers are doing. A betrayer of his friends, he loses his job because of his age and spends his retirement begging for drinking money.

— *Patrick Meanor*

LIZA OF LAMBETH

Author: W. Somerset Maugham (1874-1965)
First published: 1897
Genre: Novel

Locale: England
Time: Late nineteenth century
Plot: Naturalism

Liza Kemp, a working girl of Lambeth who lives a brutal life in that depressing borough. She works in a factory and gives most of her wages to a drunken mother who never speaks civilly to anyone. Spurning a faithful lover, Liza accepts a married man who has five children. After many unpleasant events, such as a thorough beating at the hands of her lover's wife, Liza dies of a miscarriage for which her lover is responsible.

Jim Blakeston, Liza's married lover, who is typical of the brutish lower-class husband. He beats his wife, drinks too much, and is fond of but neglectful of his children. Liza's death depresses him, but no one doubts that his shoddy life will go on about as usual without her.

Tom, a young man of Liza's class whose love for her is honest. When her neighbors turn against Liza, Tom remains faithful. Though knowing she is to bear Jim's child, he wants to marry her. His concern for her is the one genuinely kind emotion in the novel.

Sally, Liza's friend, who is typical of the young girl who marries a brutish husband but has too much pride to disclose that he abuses her.

Mrs. Blakeston, Jim's wife, who gives Liza a fatal beating for stealing her husband.

THE LIZARD'S TAIL
(Cola de lagartija)

Author: Luisa Valenzuela (1938-   )
First published: 1983
Genre: Novel

Locale: Argentina
Time: The 1970's and early 1980's
Plot: Social morality

The Sorcerer, the protagonist and main narrator, known also as **the witchdoc** and by several other names. A cabinet minister in the presidency of the Generalissimo, he held even more power when Madam President, the Generalissimo's widow, succeeded to the presidency. He supervised state terror under these regimes. The Sorcerer is a paranoid megalomaniac, living in a continuing delusion of his own divinity and feeling completely self-sufficient. He has a third testicle, which he regards as his twin sister, Estrella. Under the government of the military presidents who succeed Madam President, the Sorcerer creates a kingdom of his own and decides to extend his absolute selfhood by having a son with Estrella, a child to be called I. His final legacy, after the explosion that interrupts the gestation, is a thin line of blood running from his remains to the capital. The Sorcerer's life story is a representation of the life of José López Rega, who was a minister in General Juan Perón's return to the Argentine presidency (1973-1974) and who virtually ran Argentina for a time during the succeeding presidency (1974-1976) of Isabelita Perón, the general's widow. López Rega was a practitioner of the occult and the leader of a death squad known as the Argentine Anticommunist Association.

Luisa Valenzuela (lew-EE-sah vahl-ehn-SWEH-lah), a novelist with dark, curly hair, like the author of *The Lizard's Tail.* Valenzuela is also a narrator and a minor participant in the events of the novel. She is writing a fictionalized biography of the Sorcerer and competes with him, because he is also writing a novel. She is associated with the resistance to authoritarian rule and is concerned about the novelist's role in politics. Unable to kill off the Sorcerer through writing, she formally removes herself from the text toward the end but returns in the final episode to comment with her friend Navoni on the arrival of the line of blood in the capital. They decide that it is not the river of blood needed to end the rule of the generals.

The Egret, a tall, handsome, young, blond eunuch. He received his nickname from the Sorcerer, who selects him as his aide-de-camp. The Sorcerer uses the Egret for sexual purposes but also reviles him as his dog. The Egret is unfailingly loyal to his master and helps him to prepare the gestation of his son.

Estrella (ehs-TREH-yah), the Sorcerer's third testicle, whom he considers his twin sister. Estrella becomes pregnant with the Sorcerer's child and grows to watermelon size. The Sorcerer takes on female bodily characteristics during the pregnancy, in complete union with his sister.

The Dead Woman, a representation of Evita Perón, the charismatic wife of Juan Perón during his first period as president of Argentina from 1946 through her death in 1952. The Sorcerer did not know her then but has conserved her forefinger and now passes himself off as her High Priest. He foments a morbid pseudoreligious cult similar to the real-life Argentine cult of Evita and tapes the Egret's high-pitched voice bearing the Dead Woman's message of support for her High Priest against his enemies.

The Generalissimo, a representation of Juan Perón, seen in the novel at the point that the Dead Woman's well-preserved body, like the historical Evita's, is returned to Argentina in the 1970's from its hiding place abroad. The Generalissimo is not only a decisive leader but also a devoted worshiper of the Dead Woman.

Madam President, a representation of President María Estela Martínez de Perón, who was known as Isabelita, although like all contemporary historical personages, she is not named in the novel. The Sorcerer calls her **the Intruder**, because she replaced the venerated Dead Woman as the Generalissimo's wife. The Sorcerer has sexual relations with her as part of his control over her.

The Machi (MAH-chee), an old Indian witch of a mushroom cult whom the Sorcerer brought from the south to a secret site near the capital to teach him and then to guard his hallucinogenic mushrooms. He has abandoned her but returns to the labyrinthine sanctuary where the mushrooms are kept and encounters her alive but so shrunken that she seems to be only a heap of bones and rags. The Sorcerer has her bones made into a soup, which he drinks at an Aztec-like ceremony. The Machi's revenge is that her soup upsets him and knocks him out for two days and nights.

Alfredo Navoni (ahl-FREH-doh nah-VOH-nee), a political dissident and activist who is a friend and former lover of Luisa. Navoni encourages her to continue writing her biography of the Sorcerer when fear deters her, and she helps him with his activities. They briefly rekindle their love affair.

— *John Deredita*

LOCAL ANAESTHETIC
(Örtlich betäubt)

Author: Günter Grass (1927-   )
First published: 1969
Genre: Novel

Locale: West Berlin
Time: 1967
Plot: Social realism

Eberhard Starusch (AY-behr-hahrt SHTAH-rewsh), nicknamed **Hardy**. He is the grown-up Störtebeker, a character from *The Tin Drum* (1961) who had been the wartime leader of a Danzig youth gang, the Dusters. Starusch, at the time of this story, is a forty-year-old teacher of German and history. Despite the aggressive look of his forcefully protruding chin, Starusch, who describes himself as a liberal Marxist, is inclined to compromise. His life is boring and uncommitted. He even avoids the painful consequences of dental work through frequent doses of anesthetic. While having bridgework done, he daydreams about his life and carries on a discussion with his dentist. Starusch claims to have been an engineer, who, when rejected by his fiancée, returned to school with money she gave him in compensation and earned a teacher's certificate. He discusses with the dentist his attempt to dissuade his student, Philipp Scherbaum, from acting on his values in a provocative way.

The dentist, a rationalist disciple of the Stoic Seneca who treats and counsels both Starusch and Philipp Scherbaum. He is a staunch supporter of science and reality. The anesthetizing television, which he uses to distract his patients, is the medium that prompts Starusch's confused outpouring of present predicament, memory, and fantasy.

Philipp "Flip" Scherbaum (SHEHR-bowm), Starusch's favorite student, a talented seventeen-year-old who is deeply concerned about acting in response to his values. An uncompromising idealist, Philipp is appalled by the napalming of civilians in Vietnam and decides to douse his dachshund, Max, with gasoline and to set him on fire in front of Hotel Kempinski's café, which would be packed with cake-eating women. Starusch employs dialogue to delay and eventually to undermine Philipp's action. Philipp begins to doubt his original impulse and to consider modifications and alternatives. To the disgust of his radical girlfriend, Vero Lewand, he eventually decides that the act, lacking spontaneity and purity, would be without value. He accepts the editorship of the school paper and more and more pursues a path of reformism and compromise.

Veronica (Vero) Lewand (LAY-vahnd), the thin and nasal seventeen-year-old radical student and girlfriend of Scherbaum. She continually wears absinthe-green tights. She has embraced extreme radicalism with religious fervor and proclaims it didactically through her nose. She denounces any form of reformism or compromise with reaction but is willing to use an offer of sex or threat of blackmail to deter Starusch from interfering in Scherbaum's planned immolation of his dog.

Irmgard Seifert (ZI-fehrt), a thirty-nine-year-old fellow teacher and friend of Starusch who speaks in proclamations and is nicknamed the "arch angel." Seifert, a self-righteous champion of civic morality and anti-authoritarianism, is overwhelmed with guilt and self-incrimination when she discovers letters she had written in 1945 as a seventeen-year-old squad leader in the Nazi League of German Girls. She had conveniently forgotten ordering teenage boys to defend their refugee camp to the death against the enemy and demanding that the Nazi authorities take action against a recalcitrant peasant. Totally self-absorbed, she, in her guilt, is unable to think or talk of anything or anyone else. Starusch, whom she regards as insufficiently sensitive and committed, eventually frees her of her guilt by burning the letters. Both partially overcome their lack of commitment and inaction by agreeing to a seemingly interminable engagement.

Sieglinde (Linde) Krings (zeeh-LIHN-deh krihngz), Starusch's thin, rigid, and goatlike former fiancée. Krings, whose father was a prisoner of war in Russia, is the apparent heiress to the Krings Cement Works. Starusch, a promising engineer, was hired by Linde and became her fiancé. She tired of his boring pedantry and ended the engagement after two and a half years. The dentist claims that the whole story of Linde is a fabrication. Undeterred, Starusch insists on the veracity of his version and cannot free himself from the memory of Linde, against whom he has concocted murderous fantasies of revenge.

Field Marshal General Ferdinand Krings, a former commander on the Eastern Front who directed one losing action after another and won the hatred of his men by demanding futile resistance. He returned home after being released from a Russian prison camp in 1956. Having lost his own battles, he was determined to re-create battles lost by others and to win them himself. To his dismay, he was defeated by his daughter, Linde. Rather than shoot himself, he decided to go into politics.

Heinz Schlottau (hints SHLAHT-tow), an electrician at the Krings Cement Company who had served under Ferdinand Krings. He re-created, for Krings, the lay of battles in a sandbox with lights and switches. He traded information on Krings' troop dispositions to Linde for sex. In Starusch's fantasies, after Linde broke her engagement with Starusch, she married Schlottau. The dentist claims that Starusch, if he had ever been an engineer, had an affair with Schlottau's wife, which wrecked his engagement and cost him his job.

— *Bernard A. Cook*

THE LOCUSTS HAVE NO KING

Author: Dawn Powell (1897-1965)
First published: 1948
Genre: Novel

Locale: Manhattan
Time: 1948
Plot: Satire

Frederick Olliver, the protagonist, a writer of thoughtful essays about literary subjects who supplements his meager income by teaching and hack editorial work. Following seven years of work, he publishes a book on a medieval topic that wins him acclaim and relative fame. Up to this point, Frederick has been overshadowed by the success of the playwright Lyle Gaynor, his married mistress. His jealousy of Lyle's comparative brilliance and her apparent treatment of him as a pathetic failure lead Frederick into a painful affair with the dumb, vivacious, and unfaithful Dodo Brennan. When he can meet Lyle as an equal, he begins reevaluating his love life and returns to her. Frederick is prepared for mature love not by literary success but by the pain and humiliation he experiences in being torn between two very different women.

Lyle Gaynor, the cowriter of popular Broadway plays with her husband, Allan. She does almost all the work. The lack of passion and understanding in her marriage drives Lyle to Frederick. His affair with Dodo infuriates her, and she finds comfort with Edwin Stalk before Allan's departure throws her into even greater confusion. Lyle regards success in her career and romantic happiness as equals but does not understand why the latter is more difficult to achieve.

Dodo Brennan, a young woman from Baltimore who goes to Manhattan to seek romantic adventure. It is unclear why she

is attracted to Frederick, though he helps her find work in the New York office of a movie studio. The coquettish Dodo infuriates Frederick by openly flirting with other men and by ridiculing him in public. Her temptation of Frederick ends when she is named in a divorce suit filed by the wife of her longtime friend, Larry Glay, an advertising man.

Murray Cahill, Frederick's roommate of seven years. Murray is Frederick's opposite, spending night after night lurching from bar to bar, yet he mirrors his friend's romantic turmoil. Murray keeps fluctuating among Judy Dahl (his artist girlfriend), his estranged wife, and an endless assortment of other female admirers before deciding to settle down after Judy becomes pregnant.

Allan Gaynor, an actor who became a playwright after a crippling accident. The bitter yet flamboyant Allan convinces people that he collaborates with his wife on their plays, but his contributions consist primarily of complaining that Lyle is behind schedule on their work. He rarely leaves their apartment yet still manages to ensnare adoring young women. After he is stabbed by his building's janitor, whose wife he seduced, Allan shocks Lyle by running off to Hollywood with his latest protégée.

— Michael Adams

LOITERING WITH INTENT

Author: Muriel Spark (1918-   )
First published: 1981
Genre: Novel

Locale: London, England
Time: 1949-1950
Plot: Comic realism

Fleur Talbot, a novelist about twenty-five years old. She has an appetite for living and observing. She thinks how good it is to be a woman and an artist in the middle of the twentieth century. She completes her first novel, *Warrender Chase*, while working as a secretary to Sir Quentin Oliver, transcribing, improving, and even adding to the memoirs of his society, the Autobiographical Association. Her inventions sometimes turn out to be true, and the members like them. Although she recognizes that her job might influence her novel, she is astonished when Sir Quentin quotes from it. She suspects that he has her proofs and then finds her manuscript missing. She then steals the autobiographies (Sir Quentin has them stolen back) and later finds her manuscript. Pages torn from Sir Quentin's diary enable her to expose him. Just before her novel is published (to great success), however, a policeman almost charges her with "loitering with intent," a phrase that describes her activity as an artist. She becomes a successful novelist and lives in Paris.

Sir Quentin Oliver, a baronet of about sixty who is the founder and leader of the Autobiographical Association. He attended Eton and Trinity College, Cambridge, and is of slight build, with white hair. He habitually holds his hands with the fingertips touching. His snobbery, based on title and rank

alone, is boundless, as is his appetite for power over the association, the members of which trust him with their secrets. When he realizes that Fleur is suspicious, he takes over the rewriting, has Dottie steal Fleur's manuscript, and obtains Fleur's page proofs. He embellishes the autobiographies with her material. His diary shows that he has driven Lady Bernice to suicide. Fleur uncovers his scheme, which includes drugging the members, and he flees. Like Fleur's fictional hero, he dies in a car crash.

Lady Bernice "Bucks" Gilbert, an acquaintance of Sir Quentin. She gives a lavish party because Sir Quentin claims that she has no friends. Afterward, she calls her guests, but no one returns her calls. She then believes that Sir Quentin's allegation is true and commits suicide.

Lady Edwina Oliver, Sir Quentin's ninety-two-year-old mother, an incontinent invalid said to be insane. Tall and thin, she has wild eyes, talonlike painted nails, four greenish teeth, and a voice that croaks and shrieks. She dresses garishly in old black gowns and beads and is hated by Beryl Tims. Fleur likes and befriends her. Far from being crazy, she understands her son well. She gives his diary to Fleur, enabling Fleur to expose Sir Quentin. She is his heir and burns the autobiographies. She dies later, at the age of ninety-eight.

Beryl Tims, Sir Quentin's divorced housekeeper, who aspires to be his wife. She has an upper-class accent and is stupid, greedy, and "beautifully awful." She simpers provocatively around Sir Quentin and may be "high priestess" at his "rites." She burns Fleur's proofs but gets no settlement from Sir Quentin. She ends up managing Maisie Young's restaurant.

Dottie, Leslie's wife, the lover of Revisson Doe, Fleur's friend, and Fleur's successor as secretary to Sir Quentin. Dottie is large, sweet-faced, and religious; she is also smarter than Beryl. She resents and criticizes Fleur. After joining the association, she tells Sir Quentin that Fleur suspects him, steals Fleur's manuscript, and demands the return of his papers. She escapes Sir Quentin and, after many marriages and divorces, lives near Fleur in Paris.

Leslie, Dottie's husband, about thirty, the lover of Fleur and later of Gray Mauser. Tall, blonde, and youthful, he calls himself a critic but really is a lawyer's clerk. He is jealous and critical of Fleur; nevertheless, he has an affair with her, which angers Dottie less than his homosexual liaison with Gray Mauser. His novel *Two Ways* is not as successful as *Warrender Chase*.

Solly Mendelsohn, a reporter. A large man, he limps from a war injury and is foulmouthed. He helps Fleur with Edwina, finds Fleur a publisher, absconds with Sir Quentin's papers, and keeps copies of Fleur's novel in safety. Fleur mourns his death.

Revisson Doe, a sixty-six-year-old publisher. He promises to publish *Warrender Chase* but reneges after receiving Sir Quentin's threats and has the type of her novel destroyed. Fleur recognizes his hairless head at Dottie's window.

— *George Soule*

LOLITA

Author: Vladimir Nabokov (1899-1977)
First published: 1955
Genre: Novel

Locale: France and numerous small American towns
Time: Primarily the late 1940's and early 1950's
Plot: Satire

Humbert Humbert, the novel's middle-aged, Central European narrator, who "writes" the book as his confession while in a prison cell awaiting trial for murder. After his sudden death of coronary thrombosis a few days before the trial's scheduled start, his book is "edited" by John Ray, Jr., presumably a professor of psychology. Humbert's name is fictitious and often distorted in the text, rendered as Humbug, Humbird, Humburger, Hamburg, or Homberg. Born in 1910 in Paris, he is the son of a Continental European father (with Swiss, French, and Austrian genes) who owned a luxury hotel on the Riviera and of a beautiful English mother who is killed by a lightning bolt when the boy is three years old. Humbert traces his sexual obsession for girls between the ages of nine and fourteen—his term for them is "nymphets"—to a case of interrupted coitus he suffered when, at the age of thirteen, he and a certain Annabel Leigh had their romance forever aborted by her early death.

Lolita Haze, also called Dolores, Dolly, Lo, and Lolly, a twelve-year-old whose mother Humbert marries. She becomes his capricious child-mistress after her mother's death. She is a gum-chewing, Coke-swilling, comic-book-addicted schoolgirl who exploits Humbert's obsession with her and is largely insensitive to his feelings. Vexed by his possessiveness, she runs off with playwright Clare Quilty, who turns out to be impotent and even more perverted than Humbert. At the age of sixteen, she marries a plain, dull, poor mechanic who quickly impregnates her. While Lolita is a "nymphet," Humbert raves about her chestnut hair, supple limbs, honey-hued shoulders, and slim hips. After she has married and grown beyond nymphet age, he deplores her "washed-out gray eyes" and "rope-veined, narrow hands." The "editor's" preface informs the reader that Lolita died giving birth to a stillborn girl.

Clare Quilty, an American dramatist whose most popular play is *The Little Nymph* and who is a year younger than Humbert. The clever Quilty pursues Humbert and Lolita throughout their cross-country wandering and induces the girl to leave her stepfather. Humbert confronts Quilty toward the novel's end, killing him in an orgy of bloodletting, pumping dozens of bullets into the playwright.

Charlotte Haze, Lolita's mother and Humbert's second wife. She is a conventionally middle-class, humorless, religious widow whose lust for him repels Humbert. He shudders over her plump thighs, coral lips, and bountiful breasts. After their marriage, she fawns over him. Then, however, she reads his secret diary and discovers his passion for her daughter, whom she detests. Rushing frantically out of the house, Charlotte is killed by a passing car.

Valeria, Humbert's first wife, who abandons him for a White Russian former colonel who has been reduced to driving a taxi in Paris.

Rita, a drunken divorcée twice Lolita's age but very slight and thin. She becomes Humbert's complaisant companion for the two years he spends searching for Lolita.

Richard (Dick) Schiller, Lolita's husband, a simple, poor, hard-of-hearing, out-of-work mechanic.

— *Gerhard Brand*

THE LONE RANGER AND TONTO FISTFIGHT IN HEAVEN

Author: Sherman Alexie (1966-   )
First published: 1993
Genre: Short fiction

Locale: The Spokane Indian Reservation, Wellpinit, Washington
Time: The 1960's through the 1980's
Plot: Comic realism

Victor, a member of the Spokane tribe living on the reservation. At the age of five, he snuggles between his drunk parents to sleep. He is a gifted fancydancer at the age of nine and plays high school basketball. He surprises tribal members by playing the music of Béla Bartók at a barbecue. He is sporadically employed and drinks at times. His romances are not successful. He is a generous person and often apologetic. He retrieves his father's ashes from Phoenix and notes that he can have a reunion with his high school classmates any weekend at the local bar. His needs are simple; primarily what he wants out of life is a fair trade.

Victor's father, a protester of the Vietnam War who spent time in Walla Walla, Washington, and was at Woodstock when Jimi Hendrix played the national anthem. He takes his children to visit Hendrix's gravesite and survives a serious motorcycle accident. He maintains that his wife is extremely beautiful. An absentee father, he travels around the country and dies in Phoenix.

Victor's mother, who met her husband at a Spokane party and accepts his chronic absence from their marital life. She loves her husband in a steadfast way and weeps when he is found dead, even though they no longer lived together.

Thomas Builds-the-Fire, a childhood friend of Victor and Junior who is a consummate storyteller and self-proclaimed visionary. At the age of ten, he shares use of a bicycle with Victor; five years later, Victor deliberately beats him while drunk. He accompanies Victor to Phoenix and worries about killing the lone animal in Nevada on the return trip. His story-telling abilities have been evident since his youth, but there is not the audience for them that he believes should exist.

Junior Polatkin, who is educated at a white school and lives off the reservation for a time. As a child, he is tormented by non-Indian peers. He is academically advanced, however, doing junior high school spelling in the second grade. A juvenile diabetic, his ketoacidosis is mistaken for drunkenness. After being named valedictorian of his farm school, he attends college. He has a non-Indian girlfriend in Seattle; they fight frequently and break up. He fathers a son and has parental visitation rights.

Norma Many Horses, a powerful woman. She is self-sufficient, as handy on the back of a horse as on a basketball court, and considered to be a problem-solver. She works as a sports reporter for the local paper. She is an excellent dancer and acts as moral arbiter for tribal issues. Her fry-bread is legendary, and she is married to James Many Horses, for whom she cares while he is in the later stages of terminal cancer.

James Many Horses, Norma's husband. He is willing to ride in reverse in Simon's car to retrieve Norma from the Powwow Tavern. He has a humorous attitude about life and his illness. He has been a jokester since his childhood.

Julius Windmaker, a young reservation basketball hero who began drinking Sterno before graduating from high school. This caused him to lose his athletic edge.

— *Cherelyn Bush*

THE LONELY LONDONERS

Author: Samuel Selvon (1923-1994)
First published: 1956
Genre: Novel

Locale: London, England
Time: Mid-1950's
Plot: Comic realism

Moses Aloetta, a factory worker on the night shift, a dialect-speaking Trinidadian immigrant who arrives several years before the large influx of West Indians into England. He is softhearted despite himself, generous, and relatively responsible. Newer immigrants often contact him for help in getting settled. Having confronted the problems of racism and low status in securing lodging and employment himself, he is knowing, weary, and tolerant, initiating others in the ways of survival in London but concerned that black people not be seen as social parasites. A wry observer of the passing scene, he has an active sex life but decides never to marry. Often lonely, miserable, homesick, and ambivalent about life in the metropolis, he is sustained, and sustains others, by maintaining close contact with a circle of fellow West Indian exiles for whom he is a natural, though unofficial, leader and father-confessor. Worried about the future and his lack of progress, with a sense of impermanence but little to return to in the Caribbean, he nevertheless preserves his calypsonian sense of humor and essential delight in life.

Henry Oliver, called **Galahad**, a Trinidadian immigrant befriended by Moses. An electrician at home, he acts brash and overconfident but soon turns to Moses for guidance. Determined to avoid going on the dole, he finds night work in a factory. Arriving in winter wearing only a tropical suit over his pajamas and with only a toothbrush for luggage, he is an eccentric who sweats in the cold and freezes in the summer; he later acquires a large wardrobe and takes elaborate care of his appearance. At first wounded and puzzled by British color prejudice, he is gradually swept along by the excitement of his encounters with English girls and the romance of finally living in a great and famous city.

Captain (Cap), an unemployed Nigerian immigrant and former roommate of Moses, who thinks that Cap gives black people a bad name. Sent to England to study law, Cap spends all of his time and money womanizing and has his allowance canceled. Innocent-faced, ingratiating, irresponsible, and amoral, he refuses to work, preferring to live off his many white girlfriends and other, mainly West Indian, acquaintances. Occasionally having to trap and eat seagulls to get by, he is a cheerful if slightly mad survivor, "doing nothing, having nothing, owing everybody, and yet . . . living on and on . . . with women left and right."

Tolroy, a frugal Jamaican factory worker who saves his money to send for his mother but, to his annoyance and dismay, unexpectedly ends up with five relatives, including Tanty Bessy, who reared him as a child.

Tanty Bessy, Tolroy's aunt, an old Jamaican woman who moves to London with her relatives. Though boisterous, loud-voiced, gossipy, and indiscreet, she is generous and warm-hearted. Having cared for many of the children in her extended family, she continues her role of housekeeper and custodian of family values, criticizing black men, including Tolroy, for preferring white women. Unintimidated by her new surroundings, she becomes a well-known personality in her working-class community and teaches a local merchant to grant credit West Indian-style.

Lewis, a Jamaican factory worker married to Tolroy's sister Agnes. Gullible and jealous, he is encouraged by Moses to think that Agnes is unfaithful and beats the innocent woman until she leaves him.

Daniel, a West Indian friend of Moses who enjoys showing that black men can have culture and sophisticated tastes by taking lower-class English girls to concerts and the ballet. Generous and protective of women, he is exploited by Cap.

Bartholomew, a light-skinned Trinidadian clerk who unsuccessfully tries to distance himself from his black compatriots and pass himself off as a South American. Pretentious, penurious, jealous, and insecure, he loses the only white girl he ever had and then searches for her obsessively.

Big City, a Trinidadian with an English wife, no job, and an uncertain source of income.

Five Past Twelve, a very dark Barbadian truck driver and friend of Moses. Fond of drink, marijuana, women, and parties, he delights in acting badly at Harris' functions.

Harris, a well-mannered black Jamaican who organizes dances, knows the socially prominent, and attempts to copy their speech and dress, thus inviting the derision of some of his West Indian acquaintances.

— *Douglas Rollins*

THE LONELY PASSION OF JUDITH HEARNE

Author: Brian Moore (1921-   )
First published: 1955
Genre: Novel

Locale: Belfast, Northern Ireland
Time: Early 1950's
Plot: Social realism

Judith Hearne, a forty-year-old, unmarried, poor, and plain woman without family. She lives at Mrs. Henry (May) Rice's boardinghouse, the latest in a series of increasingly shabby residences in Belfast. Her meager income as a piano teacher is steadily dwindling as suspicion about her secret bouts of drinking increases. Judith's façade of middle-class gentility, imposed by an aunt tyrannical even in death and by her Roman Catholic training, is beginning to show cracks. Lonely and without the experience of love—familial, romantic, or religious—Judith is unable to assess the feelings of others toward her; hence, her disastrous misreading of James Madden's motives and her imposition on her pitying friend Moira O'Neill. The dashing of her hopes for marriage marks the beginning of her final descent into uncontrolled alcoholism, a descent speeded by the loss of her religious faith and by her ejection from Mrs. Rice's after a noisy two-day binge. Committed to Earnscliffe Home, a place she has always instinctively loathed, Judith is nursed by nuns of the church that has failed her. Their care is professional and largely impersonal, though kind enough. In her bare white room, Judith is consigned to a living death, a victim of Irish society, in which, despite strong middle-class morality and the dominance of the church, a single woman without family, friends, or faith can slip through the cracks, unmourned.

James Madden, the fiftyish brother of Mrs. Rice and an unpaying tenant in her boardinghouse. Recently returned to Ireland after thirty undistinguished years in the United States, Madden fits into neither the New World nor the Old. A big talker and drinker, Madden has a flashy façade that masks his sense of failure. Lamed in a tram accident in New York, he is currently frittering on drink the ten thousand dollars in compensation he received, despite confident talk of investing it in a business. Madden, a widower, is alienated from his one daughter, Sheila, because she is a middle-class American married to a man Madden detests and fears. Prompted by loneliness and a sense of injury, he rapes Mary, the lush sixteen-year-old maid in the Rice household. His flattering attention to Judith is at first prompted by her willingness to soothe his

bruised ego, then by his misperception that she has money he could invest in a vaguely defined restaurant venture. He does not realize the devastation he precipitates in her when he incredulously rejects her suggestion that they marry.

Moira O'Neill, the middle-aged wife of Professor Owen O'Neill, a mother of four. She has a happy and materially very comfortable family life. Moira has always had support and luck, which have enabled her to rise above her humble beginnings. Perhaps out of guilt and certainly out of pity, Moira sustains Judith's acquaintance since youth with her husband's family, tolerating Judith's weekly visits, her boring conversations, and her inroads into the family's sherry and food. Perhaps she does not realize that the golden circle of O'Neill family life cruelly points up Judith's solitude. Ironically, the O'Neills' sense of charity propels Judith, after her breakdown, into Earnscliffe, the place she most fears.

Bernard Rice, the son of landlady May Rice. Nearing thirty, he is a talented poet of intelligence and spiteful wit. Indolent and obese, he allows himself to be kept and babied by his doting mother. His self-indulgence extends to a sexual dalliance with the helpless servant Mary. To avenge himself on his uncle, James Madden, and to keep from his mother the guilty secret he and James share in their mutual violation of Mary, Bernard lays the way for Judith's slide into overt alcoholism when he leads her to believe that James admires and wishes to marry her. Bernard, a cynic, is fully aware of the purposelessness of his own life.

Father Francis Xavier Quigley, the parish priest of St. Malabar Church. An imposing figure, he has a keen sense of the power he wields over his parishioners but no real compassion for them. Despite Judith's repeated pleas for his help as her faith wavers, he recoils from her and comes nowhere near to understanding the despair and anguish behind her attack on the tabernacle in the church. Even after her breakdown and confinement at Earnscliffe, his concern for her rises only out of his reluctant sense of his priestly duty.

— *Jill Rollins*

LONESOME DOVE

Author: Larry McMurtry (1936-   )
First published: 1985
Genre: Novel

Locale: The Great Plains of the United States
Time: Late nineteenth century
Plot: Western

Augustus McCrae, a former Texas Ranger (with his friend Woodrow F. Call) and co-owner of the Hat Creek Cattle Company of Lonesome Dove, Texas, also with Woodrow. He decides to take their cattle herd to the richer grazing lands in the northern plains at about the time that railroads have made such cattle drives a thing of the past. Augustus convinces Woodrow and several of his other friends to make this romantic trek with him. Augustus is garrulous but affable, and just when it seems that he might be no more than a windbag, he demonstrates his intelligence and trail skills by bravely rescuing Lorena Wood from the evil Indian Blue Duck, the villain of the story. Augustus begins the drive in part to see, once more, the love of his life, Clara Allen, who lives along the route of the cattle drive.

Woodrow F. Call, Augustus' partner, who is as taciturn and grim as Augustus is warm and friendly. He is the father, by a prostitute, of Newt, one of the boys on the drive. He never acknowledges this fact but symbolically recognizes Newt as his son by giving Newt control of the cattle ranch the men establish in Montana. He must leave the ranch to return to Lonesome Dove with the body of Augustus, who is fatally wounded in an Indian attack. Woodrow, who hides his dark side from himself, learns the most about his own life and how the world has changed around him during this final journey.

Jake Spoon, a former Texas Ranger and an old friend of Augustus and Woodrow. He arrives in Lonesome Dove on the run from an Arkansas sheriff. He is the first to suggest the idea of the cattle drive, hoping that if he is on the move, he will escape capture. He falls in with a gang of robbers and meets a tragic fate at the hands of his old friends. He serves to show how the gunplay and trickery at which Woodrow and Augustus are skilled must be kept under control lest they turn malevolent.

Newt, a teenage trailhand and unrecognized son of Woodrow. Augustus tells Newt who his father is. His role in the story gradually grows larger as he changes from a green kid to a young man who accepts and understands the responsibilities of adulthood. He remains bitter because Woodrow will not embrace him as his own.

Josh Deets, a loyal and able black trailhand and longtime friend of Augustus, Woodrow, and Jake. He rode with Augustus and Woodrow when they were Rangers and is one of the key wranglers on the cattle drive. In one of the most shocking incidents in the novel, he is killed suddenly by a hostile Indian.

Clara Allen, Augustus' former lover, who has made a new life for herself on the plains. Her husband, disabled from a horse kick, dies, and she operates her farm more efficiently than he did. Strong, intelligent, and independent, she is one of the most admirable figures in the story.

Lorena Wood, a beautiful blonde prostitute in Lonesome Dove and the girlfriend of Jake Spoon. She goes on the cattle drive because Jake has promised to break off from the drive and take her to San Francisco. Instead, she is kidnapped and sold into slavery by Blue Duck. Augustus rescues her, and she winds up living on Clara's farm.

Blue Duck, an Indian raider, a longtime enemy of Augustus and Woodrow who dogs the cattle drive and creates trouble. He meets his end when he crosses paths with Woodrow.

July Johnson, the inept sheriff who is after Jake Spoon. He leads a group of drifters who fall in with him as he trails Jake, but he is the only one of his group to escape massacre at the hands of Blue Duck. He also makes his way to Clara's farm, where he finds his child. The baby was abandoned by his wife, Elmira, who passed through on her way to a reunion with her reprobate lover, Dee Boot, who is hanged shortly after they reconnect. She is later killed by Indians. Clara convinces July to stay at her ranch and take care of his child.

— James Baird

A LONG AND HAPPY LIFE

Author: Reynolds Price (1933-   )
First published: 1962
Genre: Novel

Locale: A rural North Carolina community
Time: July to December, 1957
Plot: Domestic realism

Rosacoke Mustian, a woman about twenty years old who must make important decisions when she discovers that she is pregnant. The father of the child, Wesley Beavers, has offered to marry her, but she fears the very thought of childbirth because her friend, Mildred Sutton, died during the birth of her child Sledge. Rosacoke's participation in the church Christmas pageant as the Virgin Mary reassures her and gives her the strength to determine her future. She decides to marry Wesley.

Wesley Beavers, Rosacoke's boyfriend and the father of the child she is carrying. Wesley, who is twenty-four years old, has been seeing Rosacoke for three years, all the while sleeping with other women. It is not until he learns of her pregnancy that he decides to settle down and marry her, more out of a sense of honor than because he loves her.

Emma Mustian, Rosacoke's mother. A widow who has survived many ordeals, she serves as a role model for her daughter.

Milo Mustian, Rosacoke's older brother. The death of Milo's son Horatio Mustian II also gives Rosacoke pause when she contemplates motherhood.

Sissie Mustian, Milo's wife. As the mother of four children who is carrying her fifth, Horatio Mustian II, she offers a model of what Rosacoke might expect if she marries Wesley.

Horatio (Rato) Mustian, Rosacoke's younger brother, a private in the Army. Like his deceased father, he appears to have little religion and few morals. He goes home shortly before Christmas to relate his experiences in the military. While in the Army, he forgets how to pray.

Mildred Sutton, Rosacoke's African American friend. Like Rosacoke, she became pregnant out of wedlock. She died giving birth to her son Sledge before the opening of the novel.

Sledge Sutton, Mildred's child, the son of Sammy Ransom.

Isaac Alston, the oldest member of the community.

Horatio Mustian II, Milo's child, who dies.

LONG DAY'S JOURNEY INTO NIGHT

Author: Eugene O'Neill (1888-1953)
First published: 1956
Genre: Drama

Locale: The Tyrones' summer house, New London, Connecticut
Time: 1912
Plot: Psychological realism

James Tyrone, who is sixty-five years old but looks ten years younger. This strikingly handsome, vital man is based on the playwright's father, James Tyrone, a popular actor. Of Irish peasant stock, this character has never been sick and is impatient with those who are, like his wife and younger son. Because of his poverty-stricken youth, he is incredibly stingy, compulsively turning off light bulbs and reluctant to pay for anything except the cheapest goods and services, except when he is investing in land. His stinginess has brought on the play's central tragedy, the morphine addiction of his wife, for whom he called a quack doctor rather than getting qualified medical help when she was sick after bearing her younger son. Now that the son has tuberculosis, James wants to send him to the cheap state sanatorium rather than pay for decent medical services. Although he loves his family, he is the victim of his own ingrained compulsions. They have damaged him as well: He was a promising Shakespearean actor and thinks he could have become a great actor but squandered his talent by buying the rights to a potboiler play in which he performed for a generation to secure a comfortable income. Consequently, he is a disappointed man who drowns his frustrations in drink.

Mary Cavan Tyrone, his wife, fifty-four years old. Her figure still is young and graceful, but her once beautiful face is thin and pale, her hair is white, and her hands are disfigured by rheumatism. She was educated by nuns in a Catholic school and wanted to become a nun herself. Instead, she met James Tyrone, fell in love, married him, and became addicted to morphine prescribed by an inexpensive doctor. Her hope to be a concert pianist was ruined by her rheumatic hands. As the play opens, she has been home for two months from a sanatorium, where she supposedly became free from her addiction, but the fear that her younger son's illness may be tuberculosis rather than a recurrence of malaria and that her husband will be too stingy to pay for proper medical care for Edmund causes her to relapse. The long day's journey is her gradual retreat into addiction until, at midnight, she is insane from drowning herself in the drug.

James (Jamie) Tyrone, Jr., their older son. Although he is only thirty-three years old, he is ravaged by dissipation. Generally, he is cynical, though he can have a beguiling charm that makes him attractive to women and popular with men. Like his father, he is an actor, but he lacks his father's vitality and squanders his talent on alcohol and prostitutes. Like his brother Edmund, he is fond of quoting decadent poetry. A manic-depressive, like the rest of his family, he has a love-hate relationship with them. In a moment of truth, he confesses to Edmund that he loves him but will try to destroy him by setting a horrible example and warns Edmund to break free of him.

Edmund Tyrone, the younger son, twenty-three years old, tall, thin, and wiry, with large dark eyes, a hypersensitive mouth, a thin Irish face, and a nervous sensibility. He is a portrait of the playwright as a young man. As the play opens, he is in ill health. The crisis is in part brought about by the discovery that he has tuberculosis and must go to a sanatorium. He has been a common seaman and has subsequently lived a bohemian life as an occasional actor and poet. His father complains of his left-wing politics and his morbid taste for decadent literature but admits grudgingly that he has a genuine touch of the poet. Hero-worshiping his dissolute older brother, Edmund has been imitating Jamie's dissipation. It is possible that the enforced stay in a sanatorium will turn his life around and help him become a serious artist.

Cathleen, the hired girl, in her early twenties, "a buxom Irish peasant" with black hair and reddish cheeks, described as "amiable, ignorant, clumsy." A minor character, she provides some exposition and serves occasionally as someone to whom Edmund or Mary can talk before the other members of the family arrive.

— *Robert E. Morsberger*

THE LONG DREAM

Author: Richard Wright (1908-1960)
First published: 1958
Genre: Novel

Locale: Mississippi
Time: Late 1930's and the 1940's
Plot: Bildungsroman

Rex "Fishbelly" Tucker, a young black man, the central character. When the story opens, Fish is five years old, the only son of Tyree Tucker, the leading black person in Clintonville,

Mississippi, which has a population of ten thousand blacks and fifteen thousand whites. Fish comes to understand that he lives in a twisted society that makes it wrong to be black. At about the age of six, he spits at his image in the mirror and exclaims, "nigger." At the age of twelve, he is initiated into manhood when an older friend is brutally beaten, castrated, and lynched because of his involvement with a white woman. Fish's father, an undertaker, and Dr. Bruce, the town's black physician, keep Fish with them as they examine the mutilated young man's body. At the age of sixteen, Fish joins Tyree in business and watches as his father is dragged into conflict with the white power structure and is killed. Fish has information that threatens these same whites and is jailed for two years. As the book ends, he is on an airplane to Paris to join a black friend.

Tyree Tucker, Fish's father, an undertaker who owns rental property, including brothels and a bar. Tyree is the power broker between the black community and the local white establishment. When his sympathetic but uncomprehending white lawyer refers to Tyree as corrupt, the black man explodes with anger, saying that such words do not apply to black-white relations: He does what whites make him do if he wants to protect his family and provide a good life for them. His life presents a puzzle to Fish. Tyree looks down on the town's poor black population; he touches members of the lower class only when they are dead and only for money, he says. He humbles himself before whites, however, throwing himself in tears on the mercy of the white police chief and others. Fish hates his father as he sees him crawl before white people, but Fish also comes to understand Tyree's desperate need to educate him to reality. Tyree makes Fish face racism, something church leaders, teachers, and other adults had hidden from the boy. Tyree forces Fish to see that there are two worlds, the warped and disturbed dream world of the blacks that is controlled by the distant and dangerous real world of the whites. As Tyree works over the lynched man's body, he tells Fish that his job is to bury black dreams. Tyree is killed after exposing the corruption of the town's white officials.

Emma Tucker, Fish's mother. Emma, a good woman, is ineffectual in shaping Fish's life. When white people lynch Chris Sims, she has only the church to offer to Fish as a support and as protection.

Chris Sims, a twenty-four-year-old hotel employee. Chris is lynched by whites when a white woman who has enticed him into an affair becomes frightened and accuses him of rape.

Gladys, a beautiful, light-skinned mulatto prostitute at the Grove. Fish falls in love with her, which forces him to confront his attitude toward color and his fascination with white women. She burns to death in the Grove fire, just as Fish begins to earn enough to take her out of the trade.

Dr. Bruce, a fifty-year-old black physician and partner of Tyree. He works on Chris Sims's mutilated body. Dr. Bruce escapes after the Grove fire, going north with Gloria Mason.

Gloria Mason, Tyree's mistress. Gloria is a beautiful mulatto who confuses Fish because she talks and acts like a white person. He has no standards by which to judge her. She turns proof of police corruption over to Fish, and she flees to the North with Dr. Bruce.

Gerald Cantley, Clintonville's police chief. Tyree pays him graft and buries the people he murders, in return for being allowed to manage the black population of Clintonville and to run various illegal operations.

— *William E. Pemberton*

THE LONG GOODBYE

Author: Raymond Chandler (1888-1959)
First published: 1953
Genre: Novel

Locale: Los Angeles, California, and its suburbs
Time: The 1950's
Plot: Detective and mystery

Philip Marlowe, a Los Angeles private detective who befriends Terry Lennox, a gentle drunk with good manners. When Lennox comes to Marlowe for help, the detective drives him across the border into Mexico, unaware that earlier that night, Lennox's rich and promiscuous wife, Sylvia, had been brutally murdered. Later, Marlowe is drawn into the rich social world dominated by Sylvia's father, Harlan Potter, when Eileen Wade asks him to help her writer husband, Roger Wade. As Marlowe tries to understand and help Roger Wade, an alcoholic, he finds himself trying to find the murderer of Sylvia Lennox. With the help of detective Bernie Ohls, Marlowe discovers the truth.

Terry Lennox, a war hero and a drunkard. He marries Sylvia Lennox for the second time, knowing what kind of woman she is. After Marlowe has taken him across the border, he flies to a remote Mexican village, from which he writes Marlowe a suicide note. Harlan Potter's lawyer confirms his death, and everyone but Marlowe believes he killed his wife.

Roger Wade, a writer of popular historical romances who drinks too much. Marlowe believes that Wade is drinking to forget some terrible experience, but before Wade reveals what it is, he apparently commits suicide. Marlowe believes that his suicide, like Terry Lennox's, was phony.

Eileen Wade, an incredibly beautiful woman who tries to get Marlowe involved in the problems of her marriage. He finds her behavior strange and inexplicable, as when she apparently mistakes him for a former lover and tries to seduce him. She had been, Marlowe discovers, the wartime wife of Terry Lennox and later murdered Sylvia, whom she blamed for what became of Terry. When Marlowe reveals that he will try to prove that she murdered Sylvia Lennox and Roger Wade, Eileen commits suicide.

Harlan Potter, the father of Sylvia Lennox and Linda Loring. He owns newspapers and is worth more than $100 million. He uses threats and the promise of helping Marlowe's business to try to get Marlowe to stop investigating the death of his daughter, Sylvia. His privacy is worth more to him than anything else in life, and he has the money and power to preserve it.

Sylvia Lennox, a beautiful, spoiled, and rich woman who uses men for her amusement. She has been married six times, twice to Terry Lennox. No one is surprised when she is murdered, because a number of people would have had strong reasons to kill her.

Linda Loring, Sylvia's sister. Also beautiful, she is otherwise unlike her sister, remaining faithful to her suspicious and nasty doctor husband until the end. She leaves him to spend the night with Marlowe before departing for Paris, where she will obtain a divorce and begin a new life.

Bernie Ohls, a sheriff's deputy, an old friend of Marlowe. He helps Marlowe with information about the police investigation of Sylvia Lennox's death and argues with Marlowe about the state of American society.

— *John M. Muste*

THE LONG JOURNEY
(Den lange rejse)

Author: Johannes V. Jensen (1873-1950)
First published: 1908-1922
Genre: Novels

Locale: Northern Europe
Time: Prehistoric to historic
Plot: Epic

Fyr, a man living before the glacial age. He brings fire from a volcano and learns to use it for personal warmth, for cooking, and as a god. A band of human beings gathers about him, and he teaches them many primitive arts. Fyr is made a sacrifice to the fire god he created, and he is cooked and eaten by his people.

Carl, a typical man of the glacial age. An outcast for letting his tribe's fire go out, he flees to the north and learns to live with the cold, protecting himself against the elements in the early Stone Age.

Mam, Carl's mate, who brings new ideas, such as using vegetables for food and keeping a permanent home.

White Bear, a late Stone Age man. He becomes an outcast after killing a priest in a dispute over a woman. Becoming a builder of boats, he travels over the seas. He also learns to tame horses and use them with a chariot.

May, White Bear's mate. While her husband and son are at sea, she and her daughters take care of the crops and animals.

Wolf, White Bear's son. He learns how to sit astride a horse and becomes a nomad.

Norna Gest, a strange mortal who lives so long as he keeps a partially burned candle. He brings techniques of smelting and forging metals. He also becomes a wandering skald. He helps create a bronze bull to serve as an idol for the Jutlanders.

Gro, Norna Gest's mother.

Tole, a leader in Jutland who, with Norna Gest's help, casts a bronze idol.

Christopher Columbus, who is portrayed as carrying man's long journey from Europe to the West Indies.

Cortés, the European who defeats the Stone Age people of Mexico and thus extends man's journey from Europe to the American continent.

Charles Darwin, a modern man whose new weapon is science.

THE LONG NIGHT

Author: Andrew Lytle (1902-1995)
First published: 1936
Genre: Novel

Locale: Alabama, Mississippi, and Tennessee
Time: 1857-1862
Plot: Historical

Lawrence McIvor, the narrator of part 1; William McIvor's son, to whom Pleasant McIvor, his uncle, tells a strange story of revenge and war.

Cameron (Cam) McIvor, his grandfather, an Alabama planter; good-natured except when drunk or angry, when he is dangerous and fearless. Having discovered Tyson Lovell's unscrupulous operations, he is murdered on Lovell's orders.

Pleasant McIvor, Cameron's favorite son; powerfully built, daring, wily, and determined avenger of his father's death. He kills off Lovell's gang one after another, first with aid, then by himself, until in the war he gives up his vengeance-seeking. He will kill no more—privately or as a soldier—and he deserts.

William McIvor, Pleasant's older brother. Tall, spare, quiet, and scholarly, he is different from the other McIvors. He dies of gangrene from war wounds.

Levi McIvor, Pleasant's younger brother and close companion. He dies after attending William in his illness.

Eli McIvor, Pleasant's uncle, killed at Shiloh.

Tyson Lovell, a wealthy landowner and leader of a gang of slave speculators and mule stealers. To get rid of Cameron, he gets him declared an outlaw and then arranges his murder. Found by Pleasant two years later, he is knocked out with a pistol butt before Pleasant flees Lovell's trap.

Lieutenant Roswell Ellis, Pleasant's friend. He dies of wounds received in an action the danger of which had not been reported by Pleasant, who had been busy seeking his private vengeance.

Albert Sydney Johnston, a Confederate general killed at Shiloh.

Job Caruthers, a young bully shot to death by Cameron.

Mebane Caruthers, Job's twin, who helps him get revenge for a well-deserved beating by Cameron. Mebane is wounded by Cameron, brings suit, and almost ruins him financially.

Penter Wilton and

Jeems Wilton, brothers who, after a quarrel with Cameron, hold him in bed while he is killed. Penter is later dragged to death by his horse, and Jeems is shot to death.

Fox, the murderer of Cameron.

Bob Pritchard, a McIvor kinsman and avenger trapped and killed by Botterall's posse.

Sheriff Lem Botterall, an enemy who is trampled to death by a wild stallion lashed by Pleasant.

Judge Lawson Wilton, a district attorney, Lovell's tool, killed after telling of the plot that resulted in Cameron's murder.

Armistead McIvor, Judge Wilton's killer. Armistead is later a Confederate colonel.

Dee Day and

Damon, two gang members stabbed to death by Pleasant.

Awsumb, a gang member stalked but not attacked by Pleasant, who decides he has had enough of vengeance.

THE LONG VOYAGE
(Le Grand Voyage)

Author: Jorge Semprun (1923-)
First published: 1963
Genre: Novel

Locale: France and Germany
Time: 1936-1945
Plot: Historical realism

Manuel (mahn-WEHL), also called **Gérard** (zhay-RAHR), a twenty-one-year-old member of the French resistance and formerly a philosophy student in Paris. Manuel is a Spanish Red who fled to France after Francisco Franco's victory in Spain. He is lucid, courageous, and a firm believer in humankind's capacity for goodness and human solidarity, despite the horrors he witnesses in German concentration camps. As the novel begins, Manuel is traveling across Germany in a cattle car with other prisoners of war. The narrative then recounts his experience of the journey, his activities in the resistance before his arrest, the brutality of his existence in the camps, and finally his meditations after the war is over on the meaning of both his own sufferings and those of the other victims of the Nazis.

The guy from Semur (seh-MEWR), Manuel's companion and soul mate on the train ride, also a young resistance fighter whose courage and dignity sustain him through most of the journey. Poorly educated and an inexperienced provincial, the guy from Semur nevertheless makes judgments that are remarkably sound. As the journey progresses, Manuel's respect and admiration for him grows. Despite his courage and resolve, his fragile constitution cannot stand up to the rigors of the "long voyage," and he dies of apparent heart failure shortly before the train arrives at the camp.

Hans Frieberg (FREE-behrg), a German Jewish émigré in Paris. He is a philosophy student and Manuel's friend. During the occupation, he joins the resistance because he does not want to die passively simply because he is a Jew. A member of the "Tabou" resistance network, he dies when the group's hideout is overrun by the Gestapo.

Michel (mee-SHEHL), the third of the group of student friends that includes Manuel and Hans. Michel also joins the resistance, operating under the name of Jacques. Like Manuel, he survives the war. At the novel's end, he accompanies Manuel on a journey to discover precisely what has become of Hans.

Dr. Haas, the Gestapo officer who arrests Manuel. He is characterized by his dapper appearance, his gold teeth, and his brutality.

Ramaillet (rah-mi-YAY), a black marketeer who is Manuel's cell mate at the prison at Auxerres, where Manuel is sent before being deported to Germany. He is the epitome of the small-minded, selfish individual who seeks to profit from the war. Although he regularly receives packages containing food in prison, he refuses to share them with his cell mates, preferring to wait until the latter are asleep to satisfy his hunger. When confronted with his selfishness, he speaks of the "injustice" of having to share with others who have nothing to offer in return.

Haroux (ah-REW), one of Manuel's fellow prisoners in the concentration camp; he also survives the war. He is cheerful, imperturbable, and proud of being French. Although he is still relatively young, his health has been destroyed by the rigors of camp existence. His hair is prematurely white, and his heart is severely weakened. After the war, he is disillusioned with his homeland when French authorities refuse to offer financial assistance to Manuel because he is Spanish.

Ilse Koch (EEL-zeh kosh), the wife of the concentration camp commandant. She is a short, squat woman with cold eyes and short hair. She takes prisoners as lovers; after their execution, she has their skin turned into lampshades.

Sigrid (see-GRIHD), a beautiful, green-eyed German girl, a model by profession and an acquaintance of Manuel after the war. Although he is attracted to her, Manuel finds it difficult to overlook the fact that she is German. Like many of her compatriots, she claims to be ignorant of what transpired in the death camps, preferring to live a hedonistic existence in the present.

— *Richard J. Golsan*

THE LONGEST JOURNEY

Author: E. M. Forster (1879-1970)
First published: 1907
Genre: Novel

Locale: England
Time: Early twentieth century
Plot: Social realism

Frederick (Rickie) Elliot, a sensitive young man. After a childhood made lonely and unhappy by his lameness and the loveless relationship between his father and mother, he finds a certain contentment as a student at Cambridge. During his engagement to Agnes Pembroke, he learns that Stephen Wonham is his half brother. When Rickie's marriage turns out to be an empty gesture, his flight with Stephen marks the beginning of his soul's regeneration, until he is killed in an effort to save Stephen's life.

Agnes Pembroke, Rickie Elliot's old friend, who marries him after the death of her fiancé, Gerald Dawes. She forces him into a dull and conventional life. Finally, in her effort to alienate him from his half brother, Stephen Wonham, she loses him when he and Stephen go away together.

Herbert Pembroke, Agnes Pembroke's brother, with whom she and Rickie Elliot live after their marriage.

Stephen Wonham, Rickie Elliot's half brother. When he learns of his relationship to Rickie, he goes to him and Agnes hoping for love and a home, but he is refused both. Later, he persuades Rickie to turn his back on Agnes' domination and go away with him.

Stewart Ansell, Rickie Elliot's Cambridge friend, who opposes his marriage to Agnes Pembroke and later persuades him to accept Stephen Wonham.

Mrs. Emily Failing, Rickie Elliot's domineering aunt.

Gerald Dawes, Agnes Pembroke's fiancé, who is killed before their marriage.

LOOK AT ME

Author: Anita Brookner (1928-   )
First published: 1983
Genre: Novel

Locale: London, England
Time: The 1980's
Plot: Satire

Frances Hinton, an aspiring writer who works in the reference library of a medical research institute. Healthy, practical, quiet, and calm, Frances is also modestly attractive. An observer rather than a participant in life, Frances is weighed down spiritually by responsibilities taken on too early in life, at the time of her mother's illness and eventual death. An orphan now, Frances feels herself claustrophobically locked into an existence heading nowhere. In search of excitement, she is drawn into the glittering life of the Frasers. Before long, her dreams of life with them, and of life with James Anstey, are dashed when Alix Fraser senses an independent streak in her and tires of her. Frances takes up her writing again, attempting to turn her pain into something amusing.

Nick Fraser, a doctor doing research at the institute. Tall, handsome, athletic, well-connected, and socially charming, Nick has everything going for him. His visits to the reference library enchant the employees, and he receives special treatment because the women are all half in love with him. Although he is working on the subject of depression, Nick is half of a lively, thoughtless couple that takes up Frances for a while, then drops her.

Alix Fraser, Nick Fraser's wife. Tall and fair, not beautiful but with an aura of power that commands attention, and possessing a wonderful mouth and an even better laugh, Alix is Nick's perfect complement. As careless and brilliant as he is, Alix is somewhat more cruel and blatant. For diversion, she takes Frances into her circle, calling her Fanny (a name Frances hates). She manipulates Frances and then disregards her when James Anstey and Maria become even more amusing.

James Anstey, the other doctor doing research at the institute. Attractive, divorced, and living with his mother, James is meticulous about his work and quiet enough to pale beside the likes of Nick Fraser. Taken up by the Frasers, James becomes Frances' escort and eventual beau. James decides to rent the Frasers' spare bedroom. When Frances falls out of favor with Alix, James is content to align himself further with the Frasers

and Maria, at the expense of Frances.

Olivia Benedict, a coworker of Frances at the medical institute library and her closest friend, crippled from a long-ago car accident. She admires Nick and is silently critical of Alix. Olivia and her quiet, moral life provide an ironic opposite to the glittering Frasers.

David Benedict, Olivia's brother, a doctor. He was responsible for getting jobs for Frances and Olivia at the institute. It was long assumed by Frances' mother and by David's parents that David eventually would be Frances' mate.

Maria, a handsome, high-boned northern Italian woman. She is a neighbor and friend to the Frasers, especially Alix, and a regular at their dinner outings. She takes Frances' place in the foursome, apparently paired with James Anstey.

Dr. Leventhal, a librarian and the supervisor of Frances and Olivia. He is the sole support of his widowed sister, with whom he lives.

Dr. Simek, a foreign library patron who is researching the history of the treatment of melancholia. He becomes ill with the flu, and Frances visits him at Dr. Leventhal's request.

Mrs. Halloran, another library patron, an eccentric who is researching the influence of the planet Saturn on behavior anomalies. Her attempts to engage Dr. Simek in conversation provide comic relief in the quiet medical institute library.

Miss Morpeth, a retired librarian living in a Kensington flat. She was Frances' predecessor at the institute library and is visited once a month by Frances. The obligatory visits annoy Miss Morpeth, and one Sunday she speaks angrily to Frances. This display of bald truthfulness is one catalyst that drives Frances to want the Frasers' company.

Nancy Mulvaney, an elderly housekeeper who previously worked for Frances' mother, Beatrice, and now works for Frances. Her shuffling, ghostly presence often makes Frances uncomfortable, but she provides needed solace after the shock of Frances' last meal with the Frasers, James Anstey, and Maria.

— *Patricia Clark*

LOOK BACK IN ANGER

Author: John Osborne (1929-1994)
First published: 1957
Genre: Drama

Locale: A city in the English Midlands
Time: The 1950's
Plot: Protest drama

Jimmy Porter, a twenty-five-year-old man who lives in Britain's industrial midlands. An educated, well-read individual, Jimmy works in a factory, tends a sweet-stall he is trying to buy, and issues diatribes about British society, which he feels has denied him opportunity simply because of his working-class background. Jimmy prides himself on his honesty, but he can be cruel, as is seen in his verbal attacks on his wife, Alison, and on his friend Cliff Lewis, who lives with them. Jimmy excuses himself for mistreating Alison by insisting that she is too possessive and that she cannot understand him because she has never suffered, as he suffered when, at the age of ten, he had to watch his father die. Because he insists on complete loyalty, he feels betrayed when his wife does not accompany him to the deathbed of a friend's mother, yet he does not see anything wrong with his having an affair with Helena, his wife's friend. The egocentric Jimmy seems incapable of empathizing with his wife, even when she grieves over losing their baby. He takes her back only after she has completely abased herself to him.

Alison Porter, Jimmy's wife. A woman of upper-middle-class background, she is perceptive enough to understand that her husband resents everything in her that reminds him of the social differences between them. After three years of marriage, she is miserable. The only way that she can survive Jimmy's constant verbal attacks on her and on her family is to conceal her feelings and remain silent. Although she says that Jimmy is the only man she has ever loved, Alison so yearns for peace that, with the encouragement of her friend Helena, she finally leaves him without telling him that she is pregnant. After losing the baby, she returns to Jimmy, begs his forgiveness for betraying him, and promises that because she has experienced suffering, she can now be the kind of wife he wants and needs.

Cliff Lewis, a friend of Jimmy, also from the working classes. A gentle person, he does not have Jimmy's fire or his

wit, but he also lacks his cruelty. Cliff is genuinely fond of Alison. He shows his appreciation for her housekeeping efforts, and he tries to defend her from Jimmy's verbal abuse. It is he, not Jimmy, who bandages Alison's arm after she burns it. Of all the characters in the play, Cliff seems to understand best what other people are feeling. Even when Helena thinks that she hates Jimmy, Cliff guesses that she really desires him, and he alone sees through her attempts to break up the marriage. Because he so dislikes Helena, Cliff moves out when he senses that she is moving in.

Helena Charles, a beautiful, elegant actress, a friend of Alison and a member of her social circle. Helena comes to spend a few days with the Porters, but, finding herself increasingly attracted to Jimmy, she stays on, intent on driving a wedge between Jimmy and Alison. As Alison's confidant, Helena urges her to face up to Jimmy or to leave him; meanwhile, she increases the pressure by wiring Alison's father to come for her. When Alison walks out, Helena remains, becoming Jimmy's mistress and his housekeeper. By the time Alison comes back, Helena has realized that the affair is finished, and with her usual dignity she goes on her way.

Colonel Redfern, Alison's father, a good-looking man of sixty who has returned to England after spending forty years in the army, primarily in India. When Alison became involved with Jimmy, the colonel did not oppose his wife in her efforts to break up the match. When he arrives to pick up Alison, he admits that he should have taken a stronger stand and even confesses a liking for Jimmy, who has the energy both the colonel and Alison lack. In his generosity and his decency, the colonel symbolizes the best of the old order. His appearance in the play, so unlike Jimmy's caricature of him, casts doubt on Jimmy's clever but stereotype-based pronouncements.

— Rosemary M. Canfield Reisman

LOOK HOMEWARD, ANGEL: A Story of the Buried Life

Author: Thomas Wolfe (1900-1938)
First published: 1929
Genre: Novel

Locale: North Carolina
Time: 1900-early 1920's
Plot: Impressionistic realism

Eugene Gant, a shy, imaginative, awkward boy. The youngest child in a tumultuous family, with a wastrel father and a penny-pinching mother, he passes through childhood alone and misunderstood, for there is no family affection. He is precocious, with an insatiable appetite for books. He hates his mother's penuriousness, the family jealousies, and the waste of all their lives, yet is fascinated by the drunken magniloquence of his father. His salvation is the private school he is allowed to attend, for the Leonards, who operate it, develop and shape his mania for reading. At fifteen, he enters the state university, where he is considered a freak although he does brilliantly in his studies. He has his first bitter love affair with Laura James during that summer. In his sophomore year, he

becomes something of a campus personality. The great tragedy of these years is the death of his brother Ben, who had loved him in his own strange fashion. Just before he leaves for Harvard for graduate study, his brother Luke asks him to sign a release of his future inheritance on the excuse that he has had his share of their parent's estate in extra schooling. Knowing that he is being tricked by his grasping and jealous family, he signs so that he can break away from them forever.

Oliver Gant, his father, a stonecutter from Pennsylvania who has wandered to North Carolina and married there. Hating his wife and her miserly attitude, he is drunken and promiscuous, yet fascinating to his children because of his wild generosities and his alcoholic rhetoric. He is the exact opposite of his wife: She has an overpowering urge to acquire property and he wants none of it. He will not go with her when she moves to another house so that she can take in boarders. Their entire marriage has been an unending war, but she wins at last, for his failing health forces him to live with her.

Eliza Gant, Oliver's wife and Eugene's mother, the daughter of a family named Pentland from the mountains. They have all grown prosperous through financial acumen and native thrift. Eliza has an instinctive feeling for the future value of real estate and an almost insane penuriousness; she acquires land until she is a wealthy woman. She alienates Eugene with her stinginess, which will never allow her to enjoy the money that she has accumulated. She is rocklike in her immobility, absorbed in her passion for money and her endless, involved reminiscences.

Ben Gant, their son, silent and withdrawn yet capable of deep affection for Eugene. He dies of pneumonia because his mother will not call a reliable doctor in time. His is a wasted life, for he was endowed with potentialities that were never realized.

Steve Gant, another son. He is a braggart and wastrel, with all of his father's worst qualities but none of his charm.

Luke Gant, another son. He is a comic figure, stuttering, generous, and ineffectual.

Helen Gant, a daughter. She has her father's expansive nature and takes his side against her mother. She is the only member of the family who can handle the father when he is drunk.

Daisy Gant, another daughter. She is a pretty but colorless girl who plays little part in the family drama.

Margaret Leonard, wife of the principal of the private school that Eugene attends. She directs his haphazard reading so as to develop the best in his mind; she really takes the place of the mother who has had no time for him.

Laura James, a young girl five years older than Eugene who is spending the summer at Eliza's boarding house. Eugene falls in love with her and she with him. When she returns home, however, she writes that she is to marry a man to whom she has been engaged for a year.

LOOKING BACKWARD: 2000-1887

Author: Edward Bellamy (1850-1898)
First published: 1888
Genre: Novel

Locale: Boston, Massachusetts
Time: 1887 and 2000
Plot: Utopian

Julian West, a young Bostonian who, sleeping under hypnosis in his sound-proofed cellar, goes forward into the year 2000 to find himself in a socialistic United States where government controls everything and everyone is happy, healthy, and well-off. Julian is delighted with this new world and falls in love with a young woman of the time. They marry and plan a secure, happy life in the twenty-first century.

Dr. Leete, Julian's host in the year 2000. He is a doctor who, like everyone else at the time, has retired at forty-five. He likes Julian and enjoys showing him the brave new world of the year 2000.

Edith Leete, the great-granddaughter of Julian's nineteenth century sweetheart. She falls in love with Julian through the love letters he wrote to his sweetheart in the 1880's. She readily agrees to marry Julian, who has found security as a college lecturer in history.

Edith Bartlett, Julian's sweetheart in the nineteenth century. She saved his letters and passed them on to posterity after his mysterious disappearance.

Dr. Pillsbury, a quack who performs the hypnosis that allows Julian to sleep from 1887 to 2000. He administers the treatment to relieve the young man's chronic insomnia.

Mr. Bartlett, Edith Bartlett's father and Julian's host during his last evening spent in the year 1887.

LOOKOUT CARTRIDGE

Author: Joseph McElroy (1930-   )
First published: 1974
Genre: Novel

Locale: London, Corsica, Stonehenge, the Hebrides, and New York City
Time: 1971
Plot: Suspense

Cartwright, an American investor, living in London, who has become involved in the production of an avant-garde film about life in contemporary England. A moderately successful businessman with a wife and two teenage children, he sees the film as a means of adding a new dimension to his life. When most of the film is stolen before filming is complete, Cartwright becomes obsessed with discovering who stole it and why. Following a variety of clues, some of which lead to dead ends, he travels back and forth across the Atlantic Ocean. His quest leads him into a labyrinth of characters and their motivations: filmmakers, international businessmen, smug-

glers, gangsters, and terrorists. Everyone seems somehow related to a conspiracy that may be exposed by something in the film. Cartwright jeopardizes not only his own life but also the lives of family and friends in his pursuit of the answers.

Virginia (Jenny) Cartwright, his seventeen-year-old daughter. Jenny is an intelligent, attractive, and intrepid girl who learns of the conspiracy through her relationship with a young American man. On her own, she seeks out clues and travels internationally in an attempt to protect her father. Even the mistaken idea that she has been murdered does not stop him.

Dagger DiGorro, Cartwright's friend and collaborator on the film. DiGorro was the technician and cowriter/codirector, but Cartwright discovers that he may have been involved in the destruction of the film. DiGorro needs money and operates on the fringe of the law, as a smuggler or in the black market.

Paul Flint, an idealistic young American. Paul and his brothers, Jack and Gene, are members of a radical organization that is adopting terrorist tactics to achieve their utopian goals. Paul's face apparently has been captured on film at some of the locations. Afraid that he will be identified, he and his colleagues want to destroy the film. Paul, in rejection of the terrorist plans, is leaving the group.

Claire, a young secretary in the film company. She is DiGorro's niece and the first person Cartwright goes to see in New York to get information. Her connection to the conspiracy is circumstantial and unwitting. She looks so much like Jenny

that even Cartwright fleetingly mistakes her for his daughter. Eventually, she is killed by mistake, with Jenny as the intended victim.

Sub, a longtime friend of Cartwright. A decent man being divorced by his wife, Sub lives with his two young children in New York. Cartwright stays in Sub's apartment while he is there; thus, Sub and his children are also endangered. Sub may be the only adult in the novel completely innocent of any connection to the conspiracy.

Incremona, a killer who is the apparent ringleader of a set of gangsters. He is a shadowy figure who embodies the immediate threat of the conspiracy. Cartwright finally kills him by dropping a television set on him from Sub's apartment window. His death completes the action of the novel, even if it does not answer all of Cartwright's questions.

— *William J. McDonald*

LOOT

Author: Joe Orton (1933-1967)
First published: 1967
Genre: Drama

Locale: England
Time: The 1960's
Plot: Absurdist

Fay McMahon, a nurse to Mrs. Mary McLeavy, who died three days before the action of the play. Fay is a femme fatale, a mercenary who will do anything for money. She convinced Mrs. McLeavy to change her will, leaving everything to Fay. Her seven husbands in the past decade all died violently, and she has poisoned her patient. When she learns that Hal and Dennis have robbed a bank, she demands a third of the spoils and decides to marry Dennis now that he is rich.

McLeavy, Fay's employer, a devout Catholic. A self-proclaimed good man, he insists that his wife was precious to him, but he has devoted most of his attention to his roses. He at first refuses to believe that his son is a bank robber, then wants to disown him, and finally is willing to testify against him. He respects authority and tries to cooperate with Truscott's investigation, only to be arrested for making derogatory remarks about the police.

Hal McLeavy, the only child of the McLeavys. Burdened by Catholic guilt, he worries about committing some unforgivable sin yet deflowers virgins and steals from slot machines. He hopes to use the proceeds from the robbery to open an

extravagant brothel. His upbringing makes him incapable of lying, and he readily confesses to Fay and Truscott.

Dennis, Hal's young friend, an undertaker's assistant. A ladies' man who has impregnated five young women, he longs for the experience a woman such as Fay can offer. In charge of the funeral, he switches the stolen money and Mrs. McLeavy's body between the coffin and a wardrobe in the McLeavy house. Dennis saves the coffin when a fiery accident occurs on the way to the funeral, and he also eliminates the evidence (the deceased's stomach) of Fay's poisoning.

Truscott, a police inspector. Flamboyant and sneaky, he investigates both the bank robbery and the poisoning while pretending to be from the water board. He assaults Dennis for denying knowledge of the theft and beats Hal for telling the truth. Truscott has followed Fay's crimes for years and traps her into a confession. After tormenting the suspects, he accepts a bribe of 25 percent and arrests McLeavy, the only innocent person around.

— *Michael Adams*

LORD JIM

Author: Joseph Conrad (Jósef Teodor Konrad Nałęcz Korzeniowski, 1857-1924)
First published: 1900
Genre: Novel

Locale: Ports and islands of the East
Time: Late nineteenth century
Plot: Psychological realism

Jim, a British seaman and chief mate of the *Patna*. When the ship seems to be sinking after striking a submerged derelict, he jumps into a lifeboat at the urging of his fellow officers, who have already abandoned the ship and her passengers. The *Patna*, however, does not sink; it is discovered by a French gunboat and towed to port. Jim and his three companions are sighted and brought to port separately. After the ensuing investigation, Jim spends the remainder of his life trying to regain his heroic conception of himself and to prove to men that it

was not "he" who jumped. Finally, on the island of Patusan, he earns from the natives the title of "Lord Jim" and faces his death in a heroic manner.

Marlow, an intelligent sea captain and "insatiably curious psychological observer" who sympathizes with Jim and aids him. Narrating most of the story, he says Jim is "one of us," meaning, perhaps, that he is neither maliciously evil nor excessively good.

Captain Brierly, the "unimpeachable professional seaman" and a nautical assessor at the inquiry into the desertion of the *Patna*. He identifies himself with Jim in some strange way. Awakened, perhaps, to humankind's vulnerability, he commits suicide on his next voyage.

The French Lieutenant, an unimaginatively brave man who stays aboard the *Patna* for thirty hours while she is being towed to port. He never thinks that he has been heroic.

Stein, a trader who is also a naturalist and a moral philosopher. He gives Jim a chance to have his dream of rehabilitation come true by making him the agent for his enterprises on the island of Patusan.

Chester, a loathsome creature who has been everything but a pirate. He offers Jim a job that would exile him on a guano island for life because, as he says, Jim "is no earthly good for anything else." He mistakes Jim for one of his own kind.

Cornelius, the former unsuccessful agent for Stein on Patusan. He resents Jim and finally aids Brown in causing Jim's destruction.

Gentleman Brown, a renegade who with a cutthroat crew lands on Patusan to get supplies but remains to rob and plunder. In sympathy, not understanding Brown's deceit, Jim makes a pact with him. Brown's deception results in Jim's death.

Doramin, the leader of Patusan natives with whom Jim makes friends. When Doramin's son is killed because of Jim's misjudgment, Doramin is bound by honor to kill Jim.

Dain Waris, Doramin's son and Jim's friend, killed treacherously by Brown. By his error in judgment, Jim is responsible for his friend's death.

The Rajah, the ruler of the natives on Patusan; he unsuccessfully opposes Jim.

Tamb' Itam, the faithful servant of Jim on Patusan.

Kossim, the confidant of the Rajah.

Sherif Ali, a wandering stranger, an Arab half-breed, who invites tribes from the interior to form a third force on Patusan.

The Captain, the German skipper of the *Patna*, who abandoned his ship and its load of passengers without remorse.

The Chief Engineer, who swears that he saw the ship go down.

The Second Engineer, who also seems to have no remorse for abandoning the ship.

Captain O'Brien, a large, noisy old man who says that abandoning the *Patna* was a disgrace.

Captain Jones, the first mate serving under Captain Brierly. He finds it hard to explain Brierly's suicide, all the more because he did not like Brierly while the man was alive.

Captain Robinson, an old renegade who has done almost everything from opium smuggling to stealing. Chester takes him in on the guano deal because Robinson has some money.

Jewel, Jim's native wife on Patusan. She finds it difficult to understand his ideals.

LORD OF THE FLIES

Author: William Golding (1911-1993)
First published: 1954
Genre: Novel

Locale: A previously uninhabited tropical island
Time: Unspecified
Plot: Fable

Ralph, a British schoolboy who is the boys' chief until Jack weans them away and turns Ralph into their prey. Ralph is the chief spokesman for civilized values in the novel. It is Ralph who finds the conch shell that comes to symbolize order and Ralph who advocates building shelter and keeping a fire going. The son of a naval officer, Ralph is dedicated to duty and the hope of eventual rescue. For Ralph, keeping a fire going is almost an obsession, and it is ironic that the fire set at the end of the novel to drive him out of hiding attracts the ship that lands to rescue the boys. At times, however, Ralph is tempted by the allure of barbarism, a conflict apparent early in the novel when he encounters Piggy. First taunting Piggy, then regretting his behavior, he foreshadows his later hesitancy in asserting the values he initially represents. In fact, Ralph is toying with the idea of giving in and joining Jack's band when he learns that Jack is planning to kill him.

Jack Merridew, another schoolboy, Ralph's antagonist. Jack is a charismatic leader unable to accept a subservient role in the society created by the boys. He revels in the hunt and the power it confers on him, and he relishes the anarchy accorded the group by the absence of adult supervision. Jack uses fear, ritual, and violence to secure the blind obedience of the other boys. For Jack, superior strength and weaponry, not rules, agreements, and elections, confer leadership. Early in the novel, he lashes out at Piggy, breaking his glasses. It is as if he realizes that Piggy provides the intellectual foundation for

Ralph's leadership and that, without Piggy, Ralph would be malleable.

Piggy, the intellectual of the group, an overweight, near-sighted, asthmatic boy. Piggy is an object of ridicule, suffering the group's taunts and its contempt. He relies on Ralph for protection but also functions as Ralph's adviser, refusing to let him forget that survival depends on rules and order. The breaking of Piggy's spectacles—one lens at a time—symbolizes the breaking of the last link to civilized values, and Piggy's death represents barbarism and evil triumphant. Moments before his death, Piggy seizes the conch (which, along with Piggy and his spectacles, is smashed by a boulder) and demands that the boys choose between rules and killing, between law and "breaking things up."

Simon, a strange, introverted boy. Early on, Simon seems aware that something is amiss and withdraws to meditate in a secret hiding place. In a critical scene, he confronts the head of the pig (Jack's offering to "the beast") and struggles with the realization that civilization and its trappings are but a flimsy veil thrown over human depravity. Simon discovers the dead parachutist and returns to reveal the true identity of the beast, but he is killed by the frenzied, chanting hunters.

Sam and

Eric, twins whom the boys call "Samneric." They are Ralph's last followers, loyal to the end. Only when captured by Jack and his hunters and subjected to torture do they switch sides. Even then, they warn Ralph of the fate Jack has in mind for him. They are later forced to reveal Ralph's hiding place.

Roger, one of Jack's first followers. It is Roger who tips the boulder that crushes Piggy. Although the act itself is a product of a "delirious abandonment" born of the violence and excite-ment of the moment (Ralph and Jack fighting), it confers on Roger the status of executioner, a role he seems to accept and even relish.

— *Ron Carter*

THE LORD OF THE RINGS

Author: J. R. R. Tolkien (1892-1973)
First published: 1954-1955
Genre: Novel

Locale: Middle-earth
Time: The Third Age
Plot: Fantasy

Frodo Baggins, the principal protagonist. Frodo is a hobbit, a member of a diminutive, peace-loving race that inhabits the Shire, a rural area in the northwest of Middle-earth. From his Uncle Bilbo, Frodo inherits a magic ring that confers the power of invisibility upon its wearer. Although he at first regards it as merely a useful toy, he comes to learn that it is in fact the Ruling Ring, an enormously powerful talisman created and lost by Sauron, the malevolent Dark Lord, ages before. Should Sauron recover the Ring, he will become powerful enough to plunge Middle-earth into an age of darkness. The Ring is a potent weapon that enables its wearer to control the wills of others, but it is inherently evil, inevitably corrupting its possessors. Rather than attempt to use it to defeat Sauron, therefore, Frodo seeks to destroy it. This, however, can be done only where the Ring was made: in the volcanic fires of Mount Doom, in the heart of Sauron's kingdom. Pursued by Sauron's emissaries—including monsters such as Orcs, Trolls, and the terrifying Ringwraiths—Frodo and a handful of companions undertake the apparently hopeless quest of carrying the Ring to Mount Doom. Along the way, Frodo bears the colossal burden of the Ring, which exerts an inexorable pressure upon his mind and spirit. He yields to its temptation only when he is on the point of accomplishing his quest, claiming the Ring for himself as he stands by the fiery fissures of Mount Doom. He is saved at the last moment by Gollum, who bites the Ring—and a finger—from Frodo's hand and falls into the abyss, destroying the Ring and vanquishing Sauron. A small, unassuming member of an obscure race, Frodo is outwardly ordinary, an unlikely hero in a titanic struggle for world supremacy, yet his simplicity and essential goodness give him the ability to resist the Ring's pull far longer than a seemingly more powerful character could. Although he is terribly worn, Frodo is ennobled by his long ordeal. A somewhat bourgeois and self-interested country squire at the story's beginning, he becomes a saintlike figure by its conclusion.

Samwise (Sam) Gamgee, Frodo's faithful servant and companion, who accompanies him for the duration of the quest. Like Frodo, Sam begins the story as a cheerful but simple character and unlikely hero; he too gains in dignity and stature over the course of the tale. Although he leaves the Shire as a working-class gardener's son, he returns vastly broadened by his adventures. He becomes the mayor of Hobbiton, the Shire's principal community.

Meriadoc (Merry) Brandybuck, a young hobbit, one of Frodo's companions. Merry earns renown by helping to kill the chief Ringwraith during the major battle of the War of the Ring. Upon returning, he leads the hobbits in freeing the Shire, which has fallen under the control of a band of evil men.

Peregrin (Pippin) Took, another of Frodo's companions, also a young hobbit. In Gondor, Pippin helps to save the life of the Lord Faramir; in the climactic battle, he kills a huge Troll and is nearly killed himself.

Gandalf, also known as **Mithrandir**, a wizard, an old-looking but seemingly ageless man with various magical skills, notably a control over fires and lights. Accompanying Frodo and the others, he is pulled into an abyss by a powerful demon and apparently killed. He returns from death with heightened powers, and it becomes clear that he is in fact an angelic emissary sent to Middle-earth to oppose the forces of darkness. The leader of the resistance to Sauron, Gandalf is the principal architect of the allied victory in the War of the Ring.

Aragorn, initially known to the hobbits only as **Strider**, a wandering man expert in the ways of the wild. After Frodo, Sam, Merry, and Pippin flee the Shire with the Ringwraiths in pursuit, Aragorn leads the terrified hobbits through the northern wilderness to the safety of Rivendell. There, they learn that he is in fact the heir of the ancient kings of Middle-earth. After Gandalf's fall, Aragorn again leads Frodo and his companions on the quest to destroy the Ring. His lineage is revealed to the world when he arrives in Gondor, the principal kingdom of the southwest and the chief bulwark against Sauron's forces. Although Gandalf is the spiritual leader and grand strategist of the allied campaign, Aragorn becomes its military and tactical head. After Sauron's defeat, he is crowned under the name King Elessar, and he works to restore the former glory of his kingdom.

Gimli, a Dwarf, one of a race of short, tough people expert in mining and metalwork and noted for their use of axes in battle. Gimli is one of the nine members of the company that sets out from Rivendell on the quest to destroy the Ring.

Legolas, an Elf, a member of an ancient race of tall, beautiful, and supremely talented people who live in near-perfect harmony with nature. An expert bowman, he is another member of the company. Although Elves and Dwarves are historical enemies, he and Gimli become close friends.

Boromir, a nobleman of Gondor who joins the company in Rivendell. A valiant, powerful warrior, he nevertheless is unable to resist the corrupting force of the Ring, which he wants to use as a weapon against Sauron. Boromir's attempt to take the Ring from Frodo by force leads to the splitting of the fellowship. When Frodo flees from him, he repents; shortly thereafter, he is killed defending Merry and Pippin from a band of Orcs.

Gollum, also known as **Smeágol**, a pathetic, shriveled, formerly hobbitlike creature who long possessed the Ring, which has driven him insane. Consumed by desire for it, he pursues Frodo to the summit of Mount Doom, where he seizes the Ring but falls to his death. A tormented being, he is perhaps the most complex and interesting character in the book. After Frodo and Sam leave the rest of the company, they capture Gollum, who promises to act as their guide on the journey to Mount Doom. Along the way, Gollum grows to love and respect Frodo, and he is nearly redeemed; sadly, Sam inadvertently interferes at the critical moment. Gollum then betrays the hobbits by leading them to Shelob's lair.

Sauron, also known as **The Dark Lord**, an enormously powerful, malevolent spirit who rules over the desolate land of Mordor in the southeast of Middle-earth. He lost the Ring, which contains much of his power, in an epic battle ages earlier. Having rebuilt his armies of Orcs and Trolls into a force of overwhelming strength, he initiates a frantic search for the Ring—the only weapon that could defeat him—before launching a campaign of conquest. Sauron personifies the ruthless will to power, but his strength is also his weakness: He cannot comprehend that anyone in possession of the Ring would not use it to dominate others. He is thus blind to the central point of the allied strategy and fails to defend against the Ring's destruction.

The Ringwraiths, also known as the **Black Riders**, Sauron's chief servants. Ghostly and terrifying spirits of men, they are invisible unless clothed, and they are able to sense the Ring's presence. Dressed in black and riding black horses, they pursue the hobbits from the Shire to Rivendell. Later, mounted on huge, predatory flying reptiles, they reappear to daunt the allied troops.

Elrond, the half-human, half-Elf ruler of Rivendell, the northern haven where the representatives of the "free peoples" (Elves, Dwarves, men, and hobbits) meet to discuss the fate of the Ring. Elrond takes little direct part in the War of the Ring, but his wisdom is revered by all; it is his advice that convinces the council to seek the Ring's destruction.

Galadriel, an Elf queen who rules the forest realm of Lothlórien, where the company of the Ring takes refuge after Gandalf's fall. Wise, powerful, and supremely beautiful, she rejects Frodo's offer to give her the Ring, recognizing that it would turn her into a tyrant.

Celeborn, Galadriel's husband, an Elf king.

Théoden, the elderly king of Rohan, a broad realm of grassy plains to the north of Gondor. Rohan, which is renowned for its horses and its cavalry, is Gondor's traditional ally. In his dotage, however, Théoden has fallen under the sway of Wormtongue, an evil counselor in the pay of the treacherous wizard Saruman. When war threatens, therefore, Théoden at first seeks to remain neutral. Gandalf visits Rohan and exposes Wormtongue's treachery; reinvigorated, Théoden leads his troops heroically. He is killed at the climactic moment of the war's greatest battle.

Éomer, Théoden's nephew, who becomes king of Rohan after Théoden's death. A mighty warrior, he becomes Aragorn's friend and steadfast ally.

Éowyn, Éomer's sister. Distraught over her unrequited love for Aragorn, she disguises herself as a man and rides to battle with Rohan's army. With the aid of Merry, she kills the chief Ringwraith, but she is badly wounded. While convalescing, she falls in love with Faramir, whom she marries after the war's end.

Treebeard, also known as **Fangorn**, the chief of the Ents, large, ancient, physically powerful treelike beings who care for the forests of Middle-earth. After meeting Merry and Pippin, who have fled into his forest to escape Orcs, Treebeard decides to lead the Ents to battle against his treacherous neighbor Saruman.

Quickbeam, also known as **Bregalad**, a young, talkative Ent who befriends Merry and Pippin.

Saruman, a wizard who resembles Gandalf in appearance and power but who has forsaken the side of right. Abandoning his role as a leader of the free peoples, he creates his own army of Orcs and enters into league with Sauron, but he betrays his ally by continuing to seek the Ring for himself. His armies are defeated by the forces of Rohan, and his fortress is smashed by the Ents; he is thus left stranded in his impregnable tower, reviled by all. He reappears late in the story as **Sharkey**, the leader of the ruffians who devastate the Shire in Frodo's absence. After his men are defeated by the hobbits, he is killed by Wormtongue, his former servant.

Wormtongue, also known as **Gríma**, Théoden's corrupt counselor and an agent of Saruman. When Saruman scorns him before a mob of angry hobbits, Wormtongue cuts the wizard's throat, and he is in turn killed by the crowd.

Faramir, Boromir's younger brother, a nobleman of Gondor. He assists Frodo and Sam on their journey and is later wounded in battle. After his recovery, Aragorn appoints him lord over one of Gondor's provinces, and he marries Éowyn.

Denethor, the father of Boromir and Faramir. A proud, bitter man, he is the last in the long line of regents who have ruled Gondor since the disappearance of the last king. He resents the coming of Aragorn, whom he sees as an uncouth pretender come to supplant him. Eventually, jealousy and despair drive him mad. When he believes that Sauron is about to overcome Gondor, he burns himself to death; he attempts to burn his wounded son Faramir as well, but he is stopped by Pippin and Beregond.

Beregond, a soldier of Gondor and a member of Denethor's personal guard. He earns Denethor's hatred by resisting the order to burn Faramir, an act for which Aragorn later rewards him.

Bergil, Beregond's son, a boy who acts as Pippin's guide to Gondor's capital.

Tom Bombadil, a clownish but mysterious and powerful being who twice rescues the hobbits soon after they leave the Shire. Reputed to be the oldest being in Middle-earth, he is able to control the forces of nature within the bounds of his own small territory.

Goldberry, Tom Bombadil's wife, a river sprite.

Barliman Butterbur, the proprietor of the Prancing Pony, an inn in the village of Bree where the hobbits find shelter during their flight to Rivendell.

Bill Ferny, an evil, sullen resident of Bree who assists the Ringwraiths.

Glorfindel, an Elf lord who helps the hobbits on the last stage of the journey to Rivendell.

Gwaihir, the chief of a race of giant talking eagles. Early in the narrative, Gwaihir helps Gandalf escape from Saruman's prison; later, he and his relatives save Frodo and Sam from the eruption of Mount Doom.

Arwen Undómiel, Elrond's daughter, who renounces immortality—the birthright of the Elves—to marry Aragorn.

Shadowfax, Gandalf's horse, the fastest in Middle-earth.

Prince Imrahil, a nobleman of Gondor.

Ghân-buri-Ghân, the chief of a race of wild men who inhabit the wilderness between Gondor and Rohan.

Shelob, a huge, ancient spider to whose lair Gollum leads Frodo and Sam.

Bilbo Baggins, Frodo's uncle, whose finding of the Ring is recounted in Tolkien's earlier *The Hobbit* (1938). Bilbo appears only briefly in *The Lord of the Rings*.

Farmer Maggot, a prosperous hobbit who assists Frodo.

Fredegar (Fatty) Bolger, a likable but somewhat timid hobbit who declines to accompany Frodo.

Hamfast (Gaffer) Gamgee, Sam's father, a retired gardener and village oracle.

Rose (Rosie) Cotton, Sam's sweetheart, who later becomes his wife.

Lobelia Sackville-Baggins, Bilbo's cousin by marriage, a cantankerous, disagreeable relative who seeks Frodo's property. She redeems herself by her spirited resistance of the ruffians who occupy the Shire.

Lotho Sackville-Baggins, Lobelia's worthless son, who conspires with Saruman to take over the Shire. Installed as a puppet ruler, he loses control of the ruffians and is murdered by Wormtongue.

Círdan, a mystical, visionary Elf who is the keeper of the Grey Havens, the gateway to the immortal lands of the Elves across the western sea. At the story's conclusion, Frodo, Bilbo, Gandalf, Elrond, and Galadriel board a ship at the Grey Havens and leave Middle-earth forever.

LORNA DOONE: A Romance of Exmoor

Author: R. D. Blackmore (1825-1900)
First published: 1869
Genre: Novel

Locale: England
Time: Late seventeenth century
Plot: Adventure

John Ridd, the narrator and courageous hero. His hatred of the outlaw Doone clan is at variance with his love for beautiful Lorna Doone. At last, after many adventures, including the vanquishing of the Doones, he marries Lorna.

Sir Ensor Doone, the head of the Doone clan, loved by Lorna. Dying, he gives his blessing to her and John Ridd.

Lorna Doone, Sir Ensor's ward. Captured by the Doones when a small child, she turns out to be an heiress, Lady Dugal. In love with John Ridd and hating the savage members of the Doone clan, she bravely resists the Doones' tyrannical efforts to marry her to Carver Doone.

Carver Doone, Sir Ensor's son and the most villainous of the Doones. The actual murderer of John Ridd's father, he is finally slain by John.

Annie Ridd, John's sister.

Tom Faggus, a highwayman and John Ridd's cousin. Annie's love for Tom involves John in his concerns, almost resulting in John's execution.

Jeremy Stickles, the king's messenger. Saved by John Ridd from death at the hands of the Doones, he is later able to rescue John from execution.

Reuben Huckaback, John Ridd's great-uncle, who is also a victim of robbery by the Doones.

Ruth, the granddaughter of Huckaback, who wants John Ridd to marry her.

John Fry, who, at the start of the novel, is sent to bring John Ridd home from school. Returning, they discover that the Doones have murdered John Ridd's father.

Lord Alan Brandir, Lorna's relative, whose brutal murder by Carver Doone is instrumental in causing her to hate the clan.

THE LOSER
(A cinkos)

Author: George Konrád (1933-   )
First published: 1980
Genre: Novel

Locale: Budapest and other areas in Hungary
Time: The 1980's
Plot: Psychological realism

T, a dedicated Hungarian Communist. A man in his fifties, he has fought all of his life for a just society. Rejecting the hierarchical system of his family, he risked his life to fight the Nazis, only to be distrusted by his supposed Soviet brothers. In the postwar reorganization, during the brief uprising crushed by the Soviets, and in the following decades, he has gained influence only to lose it because of his intellectual honesty. He has suffered arrest, imprisonment, and torture, and at last been released, only to be once again confined. At the beginning of the novel, he is freed from a mental institution but no longer feels at home in the outside world.

T's wife, a translator. Seventeen years younger than T, she is small and almost childlike, a bright, exuberant creature. During twenty years of marriage to him, she has kept her capacity for joy and hope. When T becomes incapable of giving himself to her emotionally, however, she leaves him for a young lover.

Dani, T's younger brother. A dark-bearded, charming man, he has always been mercurial, infatuated with danger but essentially selfish, willing to inform on others, even his brother, to save himself. When his girlfriend blocks his attempt to escape to the West, in frustration he turns on her, killing her and then eventually hanging himself.

Teri, Dani's girlfriend. A girl with a fair complexion, an appealing mouth, and an insatiable sexual appetite, she is unprincipled and disloyal. Because she cannot bear to lose her power over Dani, she informs on him. He chokes her to death.

T's grandfather, the owner of a hardware store. A small but forceful man, he is respected for his sincere piety, his generous and forgiving nature, and his courage. His home, where T and Dani were reared, was full of kindness and love.

T's grandmother, the mother of a large family. From the time of her marriage, she would flout tradition, for example, refusing to cut off her luxuriant red hair. Tenderly and joyfully sensual, she is adored by her pious husband. In temperament, she is much like T's wife.

T's mother, the daughter of a landowner. Given to her Jewish husband because of his wealth, she was a cold, bitter woman and a defiant shoplifter. While still young, she died of cancer.

T's father, a large, lusty, red-haired man who died at the age of fifty-five in pursuit of a young woman. Like T's grandparents, he symbolizes a richer, warmer life than is possible under Communism.

Sophie, an art teacher, T's mistress, and his fellow revolutionary. A sensitive woman, she fears arrest and torture. When the Nazis try to break T by torturing her in front of him, he chooses to let her suffer rather than betray his companions; thus, he begins his long process of emotional death. After she is taken to Auschwitz, Sophie kills herself.

V., a Hungarian Communist. A cheery man, he is above all a survivor. Taken to the Soviet Union, he becomes a Soviet colonel; returning to Hungary, he establishes a sound economy, avoids trouble during the difficult decades when T is so often in prison, and finally becomes the general manager of a coal mine.

G., a Jewish tailor and a dedicated Communist. A small, balding man with a skimpy mustache, he is so ordinary in appearance that he is an ideal spy. After the war, when he is haphazardly appointed police chief, he seizes power and, with his torture chamber, becomes the most feared man in the new society. Eventually, he arrests and tortures almost all of his former companions, including T. At one point, however, he is imprisoned.

R., a Communist whom T befriended when they were both in Moscow. He depends on G. for his power, although he despises and fears him. Eventually, he is blamed by the Soviets for excessive murders and is himself taken to the Soviet Union and killed.

— *Rosemary M. Canfield Reisman*

LOSING BATTLES

Author: Eudora Welty (1909-   )
First published: 1970
Genre: Novel

Locale: The rural Mississippi hill country
Time: The 1930's
Plot: Pastoral

Granny Vaughn, the frail and indomitable matriarch whose birthday is the occasion for the family reunion. As small as a boy, she sits enthroned on her rocker, from which she fixes her slit eyes on her well-wishers and tells them just how they measure up or fall short. She claims to be one hundred years old, although she is actually ninety, and she has been saving one family secret for this day when the family history is retold.

Jack Renfro, Granny's great-grandson and the hope of the family. He is small in stature, unfailingly cheerful, and pleased to do his best to live up to his family's expectations and take a starring role in the family legend. Escaping from Parchman to be on time for the reunion, Jack unknowingly plays the Good Samaritan to Judge Moody, who sent him to prison. Then, crediting the judge with saving the life of his baby daughter, Jack brings the Moodys home to the family circle.

Beulah Renfro, the mother of Jack and four other children, Granny's only granddaughter. She is an energetic cook, gardener, and talker, feeding everyone and explaining everything. She protects Granny and draws her authority from the older woman's while mediating the family stories to the benefit of her favorites. Much as she resents Judge Moody for sending Jack to prison, she cannot refuse him and his wife a meal and a place to sleep.

Gloria Short Renfro, a freckled redhead, a passionate wife to Jack and devoted mother to Lady May, intent on leaving Jack's family behind. She came to Banner to learn from and take the place of Miss Julia Mortimer but fell in love, married, and left teaching, much to the family's approval. When she leaps in the road to save her baby girl, Judge Moody drives his Buick up steep Banner Top, where it hangs over an abrupt drop. As the long day and night of storytelling wears on, the mystery of this orphan's parentage is unraveled.

Miss Julia Percival Mortimer, an imposing figure and unforgettable teacher. Of missionary stock, she had challenged the generations of Banner students to quit worshiping themselves quite so wholeheartedly and became the mortal enemy in the Vaughn-Beecham legend. Judge Moody, a former pupil himself, received a summons from her; he arrives after her death but in time to defend her memory before the chroniclers at the reunion. Her funeral brings other loyal former students, great and small, from far and wide.

Miss Lexie Renfro, the witchlike old-maid sister of Ralph Renfro, Beulah's husband. She claims to have worshiped Miss Julia as her student, but her own matter-of-fact account of tying Miss Julia into her bed and denying her books and pencils, while serving as her nurse companion, chills both Gloria and Granny.

Nathan Beecham, the eldest of Beulah's brothers. His long hair is streaked with white, his face is brown and wrinkled, and he has only one hand. A wanderer who places wooden signs warning of God's wrath throughout the countryside, he returns in time for the reunion, standing the whole while behind Granny's chair.

Curly Stovall, a large man with small eyes, the local storekeeper and Jack's antagonist. It was Curly who took the heirloom ring from Jack's younger sister Ella Fay, provoking Jack to stuff Curly into his own floor model coffin and appropriate the broken store safe. Curly brought charges in response, resulting in Jack being sent to prison.

Curtis,

Dolphus,

Percy, and

Noah Webster Beecham, collectively known as the Beecham brother, who along with their wives serve as the chorus for the day's surprises and for the well-known but ever-changing family history.

Brother Bethune, a man carrying a well-worn Bible and a loaded gun. He arrives at the reunion to stand in for the late departed Grandpa, although everyone knows that he will not be up to the task. His job is to bless the gathering, recite the family history, and forgive Jack.

Willy Trimble, the local handyman. He spells his name "Willy Trimble?" because Miss Julia Mortimer told him not to. He is the one who discovers her body, and he has built her a coffin (she taught him how to use a saw), but it is rejected by those in charge.

— *Rebecca R. Butler*

THE LOST FLYING BOAT

Author: Alan Sillitoe (1928-   )
First published: 1983
Genre: Novel

Locale: South Africa, the skies over the oceans of the Southern Hemisphere, and Antarctica
Time: c. 1950
Plot: Adventure

"Sparks" Adcock, the narrator, a wireless radio operator on a mysterious flying boat expedition. The youngest and newest member of the crew, the confused twenty-seven-year-old Adcock, still in love with his wife despite their failed marriage, is a listener and observer by nature and is eminently suited to his profession. Suspicious and wary of everyone, and doubtful of the legality and safety of the expedition, the inwardly disturbed Adcock retires to the peaceful refuge of his wireless station to analyze the expedition and its crew. Devoted to a life of communication, he finds Captain Bennett's orders of radio silence and the sending of false messages difficult to obey. He occasionally defies these orders. This defiance adds to his excitement about the illegality of it all and foreshadows his ultimate act of defiance, the murder of Captain Bennett. The only surviving member of the crew, Adcock realizes that the communication to which he had devoted his life had, in reality, gotten him nowhere.

Captain Bennett, the pilot of the flying boat *Aldebaran* and leader of an expedition to recover lost gold in the Kerguelen Islands. A taciturn, autocratic perfectionist, the over-forty, gray-haired, cigar-smoking Bennett is a preoccupied, tired, and lonely man. An excellent pilot who is happiest when in the air, he is suspicious of everyone and paranoid about his crew's loyalty. Determined to retrieve the gold and convinced that it will buy the freedom he seeks, he becomes more and more desperate as he realizes that he will never be free of his troubled conscience or of the crime that began his odyssey. His desperation builds as more and more members of his crew are

lost and climaxes when he chooses to shoot his only friend rather than give up the gold. Shot twice by Adcock, he manages to make an emergency landing of his flying boat, thus saving Adcock's life.

Nash, the chief gunner of the expedition and Captain Bennett's only friend. A large, dark man suffering from an incontinent bladder, his wife and family deserted him while he was in jail prior to joining the expedition. Intelligent, diplomatic, and even-tempered, he is also pragmatic, organized, and full of practical knowledge. Although he does not fully trust Captain Bennett, he does support him, rationalizes his actions, and is extremely loyal to him. Nash acts as a buffer between Captain Bennett and the rest of the crew, but that loyalty seems unappreciated, as Captain Bennett shoots him while he is attempting to toss the gold overboard.

Rose, the navigator and second in command of the flying boat. A rather quiet, serious man, badly scarred on one side of his face, he seems to be accustomed to living with his disfigurement. Later, however, he suggests that he is not happy futilely trying to live with it anymore and plans on having it fixed after the expedition. Both physically and emotionally cut off from the rest of the crew, he becomes more and more suspicious of Captain Bennett and of his plans for the crew and the cargo. He convinces himself that he and the expedition are doomed, then commits suicide by shooting himself through the heart with Adcock's gun.

— *Susan V. Myers*

THE LOST HONOR OF KATHARINA BLUM: Or, How Violence Develops and Where It Can Lead
(Die verlorene Ehre der Katharina Blum: Oder, Wie Gewalt entstehen und wohin sie führen kann)

Author: Heinrich Böll (1917-1985)
First published: 1974
Genre: Novel

Locale: An unnamed German city
Time: February 20-24, 1974
Plot: Social realism

Katharina Blum (ka-tah-REE-nah blewm), a twenty-seven-year-old certified housekeeper who has been in charge of the Blorna household for four years. Katharina is a very private and proper person and an almost compulsive worker

bent on improving herself. When she meets a fugitive, Ludwig Götten, at a party, she immediately falls in love with him. After he spends the night with her in her condominium apartment, Katharina tells him how to avoid the police by crawling through the heating ducts, which, along with the whole complex, had been designed by her employer, Trude Blorna. She subsequently expresses no regret over her murder of the sensationalist reporter Werner Tötges and looks forward to life with Götten at the end of their eight-year prison terms.

Erwin Beizmenne (EHR-veen BITS-mehn-neh), the chief crime commissioner. After Götten's escape, Beizmenne, through a series of insensitive interrogations, attempts to establish a connection between Katharina and Götten's crimes.

Werner Tötges (VEHR-nehr TEHT-gehs), a reporter for the sensationalist *News*. Tötges, disgracefully attacking Katharina's character and honor, accuses her of involvement in Götten's crimes. Katharina, distraught by the viciousness and lack of integrity of this man who has destroyed her privacy and reputation, invites him to her once-beloved apartment, purportedly for an interview, and shoots him.

Ludwig Götten (LEWT-vihg GEH-tehn), a twenty-six-year-old army deserter who absconds with army funds. Götten, who is accused of being a radical bank robber and murderer, is under police surveillance when he meets Katharina. He is later wounded when apprehended by the police. He affirms Katharina's innocence.

Hubert Blorna (BLOHR-nah), a forty-two-year-old corporate attorney. Katharina works for Blorna and his wife, Trude. Blorna and his wife depend on Katharina to bring order to their household and lives. Blorna, who is in love with Katharina, agrees to serve as a lawyer not only for her but for Götten as well. He is distraught over the course of events and, in his despondency, neglects his appearance and physical hygiene. The scandal has undermined his association with Lüding and Sträubleder Investments and has left him and his wife in serious financial difficulties.

Trude Blorna (TREW-deh), an architect and the wife of Hubert Blorna. Trude Blorna is an outspoken person whose student radicalism is capitalized on by Werner Tötges, who refers to her as "Trude the Red." The architectural firm with which she is associated attempts to dismiss her because of the Blum scandal, and she is blacklisted by firms that believe that her reputed radicalism and association with Katharina will alienate potential customers.

Alois Sträubleder (AH-loh-ees STROYB-leh-dehr), an influential businessman who is Hubert Blorna's friend and client. Sträubleder, a married man with four children, had made a pass at Trude Blorna and is infatuated with Katharina. Although Katharina did not respond to his interest, he had driven her home from a party at the Blornas' home and forced his way into her apartment. He is the mysterious "gentlemen visitor" remembered by neighbors. Sträubleder, in futile expectation, had given Katharina a key to his country place and a valuable

ring. He desperately sought Blorna's assistance to avoid any implication in Katharina's police troubles.

Else Woltersheim (EHL-zeh VOHL-tehrs-him), Katharina's godmother, friend, and confidant. A former home economics instructor who now runs a catering business, the forty-four-year-old woman had encouraged Katharina to better herself. She attempts to provide moral support to Katharina during her ordeal.

Konrad Beiters (BI-tehrz), a textile agent and intimate friend of Else Woltersheim. Beiters is a congenial fifty-six-year-old former Nazi. He stands by Katharina and Else when Katharina is accused of consorting with and assisting a violent criminal. It is with Beiters' gun, which Katharina had taken without his knowledge, that Tötges is shot.

Walter Moeding (MEH-dihng), a crime commissioner, Beizmenne's assistant. Moeding is a friendly policeman who takes pity on Katharina and treats her kindly. Katharina goes to his apartment to confess her murder of Tötges.

Adolf Schönner (AY-dolf SHEH-nehr), a press photographer for the *News*. Schönner is found murdered in a wooded area on Ash Wednesday. His murder is at first falsely ascribed to Katharina.

Hertha Scheumel (SHOY-mehl), a salesgirl and distant cousin of Katharina. She is a seventeen-year-old blond who dresses in flashy clothes. She picks up Götten at Café Polkt and takes him to a party at Else Woltersheim's apartment.

Karl, an undercover police agent who had been shadowing Götten. Karl, disguised as a carnival reveler in a sheikh's costume, made a point of dancing with Hertha's friend, Claudia Sterm, and invited himself to accompany them and Götten to Woltersheim's party. He informed the police on the outside when Götten and Katharina left the party together.

Wilhelm Brettloh (BREHT-loh), Katharina's former husband. After six months, Katharina left Brettloh, a conservative and sycophantic textile worker, toward whom she had developed a tremendous aversion. Brettloh is not surprised that Katharina's irreligious and ambitious nature has led her to consort with a criminal.

Mr. Fehnern (FAY-nehrn), a certified accountant for whom Katharina worked after her divorce. Before he was sent to prison for embezzlement and forgery, Fehnern made it possible for her to complete an adult education course to become a certified housekeeper.

Mrs. Blum, Katharina's elderly mother, confined in a rest home. She is recovering from cancer surgery when her death is precipitated by an importune, and subsequently distorted, interview by Tötges.

— *Bernard A. Cook*

LOST HORIZON

Author: James Hilton (1900-1954)
First published: 1933
Genre: Novel

Locale: Tibet
Time: 1931
Plot: Adventure

Hugh Conway, a charming, brilliant man—tall, bronzed, with short brown hair and blue eyes—who is a veteran of ten years of unspectacular work in the British Consular Service. He is found by his friend Rutherford in a mission hospital

suffering from fatigue. He relates how he was kidnapped and flown to Shangri-La, a peaceful lamasery in the high Himalayas, where the ancient and wise High Lama hoped to preserve a record of the culture of Western civilization against its total destruction by modern warfare. When the aged High Lama knew he was about to die, he asked Conway to succeed him as High Lama. Though tempted to accept, Conway decided it was his duty to accompany his kidnapped companions back to civilization when the opportunity to leave arose. Before Rutherford hears the rest of the story, Conway disappears from the hospital, apparently drawn back to the tranquillity of Shangri-La.

Rutherford, his friend and former schoolmate, who finds Conway suffering from fatigue and amnesia in a mission hospital in China.

Henry Barnard, a large, fleshy man with a hard-bitten face who is wanted for fraud and embezzlement in the United States. He is satisfied to stay in Shangri-La and enjoy the pleasant life there.

Miss Roberta Brinklow, a missionary, neither young nor pretty, who plans to convert the lamas and the tribesmen in the valley of Shangri-La.

Captain Mallison, another British consul, young, pink-cheeked, intelligent, excitable. He is anxious to leave Shangri-La and turn Barnard over to British authorities, and he is later insistent upon taking Lo-Tsen with him. Rutherford is unable to learn what happened to Mallison.

Chang, a Chinese lama who meets Conway and his friends near their wrecked plane and conducts them to Shangri-La.

Father Perrault, the High Lama, a very intelligent, scholarly man two hundred and fifty years old. Formerly a Capuchin friar, he adopts the Buddhist faith and establishes the lamasery of Shangri-La. He adds guests from time to time but permits none to leave.

Lo-Tsen, a beautiful Chinese girl with whom Mallison falls in love and who accompanies Conway and Mallison when they leave Shangri-La. In reality sixty-five years old, she quickly loses her youth and beauty outside the charmed lamasery and becomes a bent, withered old woman. She brings Conway to the mission hospital.

Briac, a Frenchman who was once a pupil of Frédéric Chopin and who plays for Conway some of the composer's unpublished music.

LOST ILLUSIONS
(Illusions perdues)

Author: Honoré de Balzac (1799-1850)
First published: 1837-1843
Genre: Novel

Locale: Angoulême, France
Time: Early nineteenth century
Plot: Naturalism

David Séchard (dah-VEED say-SHAHR), a naïve printer who is the victim of knavery throughout his life. Even his avaricious father cheats him when he sells the son his business. David's friendship for Lucien Chardon, his brother-in-law, also costs him a great deal. David spends his time working on a new process for making paper and eventually loses his business. All turns out well in the end, as Lucien Chardon sends him a large sum of money and David's father dies leaving him well off.

Lucien Chardon (lew-SYAH[N] shahr-DOH[N]), an unscrupulous but attractive poet, David's brother-in-law. His escapades help to disgrace his sister and her husband and to ruin them financially for a time. After an affair with an aristocratic woman ends in his being found in her bedroom, he goes to Paris to lead a dissolute life as a journalist and man-about-town, living at the expense of David and Eve and an actress who is his mistress.

Eve Chardon, Lucien's sister, who marries David Séchard. She lavishes love and money on her scapegrace brother. After her husband becomes involved with his paper-making process, she tries vainly to save his printing business by taking over its management.

Mme de Bargeton (deh bahr-zheh-TOH[N]), Lucien's first mistress. When her affair with him is discovered, she takes him to Paris, where she later leaves him penniless. She becomes the wife of the comte du Châtelet.

M. de Bargeton, elderly first husband of Mme Bargeton. Despite his age, he fights a duel in defense of his wife's honor.

M. Petit-Claud (peh-TEE-kloh), an unscrupulous lawyer who helps David's business rivals, even though David is his client.

The Cointet Brothers (kwahn-TAY), David's business rivals in the printing business. They cheat him out of his paper-making invention and his print shop.

Coralie (koh-rah-LEE), an actress who becomes Lucien's mistress.

M. Séchard, David's avaricious father. He refuses to help his son financially to keep him out of debtors' prison.

A Spanish priest, who hires Lucien to act as a front in his unscrupulous dealings.

A LOST LADY

Author: Willa Cather (1873-1947)
First published: 1923
Genre: Novel

Locale: Nebraska
Time: Late nineteenth and early twentieth centuries
Plot: Domestic realism

Marian Forrester, the charming, lovely wife of Captain Daniel Forrester, a contractor during the great railroad-building period in the West. She is shown first in her home in Sweet Water, Colorado, where she sheds the warm radiance of her personality on all about her, from the railway and mining aristocracy who come visiting in their private cars to the village boys who go fishing in the creek running through the Forrester property. One of these is Niel Herbert, an impressionable adolescent through whose eyes, as he grows in years and understanding, the story of her decline is presented. The flaw in Mrs. Forrester's character is the fact that she possesses no inner resources of her own. As long as she can draw on her husband's quiet strength, she is her gay, gracious self. But when a series of misfortunes strike the old railroader—a fall from a horse, a bank failure, a crippling stroke—she finds herself tied to a semi-invalid, trapped in a dwindling community no longer important on the Burlington line, and she becomes desperate. Unable to face neglect or hardship, she finds escape in love affairs and drink, and in the end surrenders herself as well as her business affairs to Ivy Peters, an unscrupulous shyster lawyer of the new generation in the West. Eventually, Niel Herbert hears that she has died in the Argentine as the wife of an English rancher named Henry Collins. Mrs. Forrester is one of Willa Cather's most complex characters, a figure requiring great insight and skill to reveal clearly the reasons for her degradation and the contradictory, ambiguous elements in her nature that make her both a woman of grace and poise and a person capable of coarseness and lust in her pursuit of virile younger men. The picture of her deterioration is linked subtly with the declining importance of Sweet Water as a frontier town and the passing of the Old West into a newer and less heroic age.

Captain Daniel Forrester, a builder whose great dream had been to see the railroads spanning the continent. A reserved, silent man, he has been a doer rather than a sayer, as unimpeachable in his honor as he is punctilious in courtesy. After a fall from his horse, he retires to his Sweet Water home with his younger wife. When a Denver bank fails, he assumes a moral obligation and uses his private fortune to satisfy its depositors. A short time later, he suffers a stroke from which he never fully recovers. Courteous, considerate, honorable, he never reveals his knowledge of his wife's infidelities. His death leaves her finally lost without his patience and strength to sustain her bright but brittle charm. The passing of Captain Forrester shows a way of life that was once great and spacious giving place to a new way that is tawdry, petty, and crude.

Niel Herbert, the sensitive, perceptive young man from whose point of view much of Mrs. Forrester's story is presented. His attitude toward her is one of boyish adoration until he accidentally learns of her affair with Frank Ellinger. As he grows older, he thinks of her more and more in relation to her husband, the dignified, noble old man whom he sees as the embodiment of the imagination and enterprise that went into

the building of the West. After reading law for a time in his uncle's office, Niel eventually goes to study architecture at the Massachusetts Institute of Technology.

Francis Bosworth Ellinger, called Frank, a bachelor of forty with a reputation for being fast and dangerous; he had on one occasion driven publicly through Denver with a pretty prostitute. He is a frequent visitor at the Forrester home. During one of these visits, while Captain Forrester is in Denver, Niel Herbert goes out early in the morning to pick a bunch of wild roses for Mrs. Forrester. As he is about to put them outside the French window of her bedroom, he hears Frank's voice inside. Niel's discovery that she has a lover ends his admiration for Mrs. Forrester and his loyalty to an ideal, though she continues to fascinate and puzzle him. Mrs. Forrester becomes hysterical when she reads the account of Frank's marriage to Constance Ogden, and she creates a town scandal by attempting to telephone him while he is on his honeymoon.

Ivy Peters, so nicknamed because of his red, puffy skin, a shrewd, ruthless young man who gets ahead in the world by carrying on a tricky law practice. He becomes Mrs. Forrester's lover and persuades her to turn her business affairs over to him; he eventually comes into possession of the Forrester home. He represents the new generation, taking the profits without any of the risks, despised by Judge Pommeroy.

Judge Pommeroy, Niel Herbert's uncle. When Niel's father decides to leave Sweet Water for work in Denver, the boy remains behind to read law in his uncle's office. The judge has been Captain Forrester's friend for twenty years and has attended to all his business affairs since the captain's illness without a fee. After her husband's death, Mrs. Forrester sends an order asking the judge to turn all money and securities over to Ivy Peters and to give an account of his transactions. Judge Pommeroy is hurt and offended.

Constance Ogden, a rather pretty but spoiled and determined young woman who wants to marry Frank Ellinger and does so, with her mother's clever assistance.

Orville Ogden, a businessman from Denver and Captain Forrester's friend. He becomes concerned for Mrs. Forrester's future when he stops over in Sweet Water and learns that she is no longer Judge Pommeroy's client.

Mrs. Ogden, his homely, affected, but shrewd wife. Her concern is to get her daughter Constance married.

THE LOST LANGUAGE OF CRANES

Author: David Leavitt (1961-   )
First published: 1986
Genre: Novel

Locale: New York City
Time: The 1980's
Plot: Family

Philip Benjamin, a twenty-five-year-old gay man who works as an editor of romance novels. A solitary only child, Philip had lost himself in Derek Moulthorp's children's fantasies. At the beginning of the novel, Philip is in love with Eliot, who, by coincidence, is Moulthorp's foster son. At Philip's request, Eliot takes Philip to dinner at Moulthorp's apartment. Philip questions Moulthorp's partner, Geoffrey, about Eliot's deceased parents. Believing that Philip has invaded his privacy, Eliot stops returning his calls. Eliot's openness about his own sexuality, however, prompts Philip to tell his parents, with

whom he has a rather distant relationship, that he is gay. His mother rejects him, but Philip and his father communicate honestly for the first time. Although Philip believes that he will never recover from losing Eliot, he and a college friend, Brad, ultimately become lovers.

Owen Benjamin, Philip's father, the dean of admissions at the Harte School, a private school for rich boys. At the outset, Owen faces two crises. First, he and his wife, Rose, must either purchase or vacate the rent-controlled apartment in which they have lived for many years. Second, Owen is no longer content with anonymous encounters in a pornographic movie theater or with hiding his homosexuality from his wife. When Philip "comes out" to his parents, Owen questions his son, hoping to find a model for an openly gay lifestyle. Owen invites to dinner Winston Penn, a coach at Harte whom he incorrectly believes is gay. Owen tells Philip that he is inviting Penn for his son's benefit, but Owen is himself infatuated with his colleague. After watching Owen flirt with Penn at dinner, Rose asks her husband to leave. Owen takes refuge at Philip's apartment, uncertain whether his separation from his wife will be permanent.

Rose Benjamin, Philip's mother, a copy editor for a literary publishing house. She edited Derek Moulthorpe's novels and introduced them to her son. Although she has had affairs with other men, she accepts her polite but uncommunicative relationship with Owen. When their building goes co-op, Rose is profoundly distressed by having to choose between leaving the apartment that has been home for many years or using their life savings on a down payment. When she learns that both her son and husband are gay, Rose, overburdened already, rejects them both.

Eliot Abrams, an independently wealthy young man who dabbles in freelance graphic design. When his parents were killed in an automobile accident, Eliot was adopted by Derek Moulthorp and his lover, Geoffrey. Accepting his foster parents' homosexuality as the norm, Eliot suffers none of Philip's sexual confusion. He is increasingly burdened by Philip's dependency and eagerness to please. When Philip questions Geoffrey about Eliot's parents, Eliot stops returning Philip's calls. Eliot goes to Europe and begins an affair with a young Frenchman.

Jerene Parks, a six-foot-tall black woman who is Eliot's roommate. Jerene is the adopted daughter of a black couple who have achieved a lonely affluence and impress upon their daughter the importance of preserving appearances. When Jerene tells them that she is a lesbian, they cease communicating with her. During research for her doctoral dissertation on lost languages, Jerene discovers "the crane child," a neglected boy who created a private language to communicate with the cranes at a nearby construction project. This story becomes for her a metaphor for the way people model their identities on a chosen love object. Having found a measure of self-acceptance, Jerene leaves graduate school. She begins a relationship with Laura, a neurotically fearful but devoted young woman. Jerene volunteers for the Gay Hotline and talks anonymously to Owen when he calls, distraught, to discuss his own and his son's homosexuality.

Derek Moulthorpe, a writer of children's fantasies and Eliot's foster father. When Eliot and Philip come to dinner, Moulthorpe cooks a meal with all blue foods. Afterward, at Philip's suggestion, Derek and Geoffrey, his partner of many years, accompany the young men to their favorite gay bar. Feeling old, they leave quickly.

Brad Robinson, a college friend of Philip who fantasizes about glamorous actors but has had few actual relationships. Brad's analysis of Eliot's selfish behavior helps the grieving Philip to put his lover's rejection in perspective. Brad and Philip's long friendship culminates in an honest, mutually supportive love relationship.

Winston Penn, a handsome lacrosse coach at the Harte School. During dinner at the Benjamins' apartment, Winston takes the family turmoil in stride. Penn plans eventually to return to Austin to get a Ph.D. and marry his fiancée, Nancy.

— *Wendy Bousfield*

THE LOST STEPS
(Los pasos perdidos)

Author: Alejo Carpentier (1904-1980)
First published: 1953
Genre: Novel

Locale: An unnamed U.S. city, a South American city, and the South American jungle
Time: Late 1940's
Plot: Psychological realism

The narrator, a composer and music theoretician now writing for films and advertisements. Despising his job, bored with a marriage that is only a convenience, and unable to create anything worthwhile, he is terrified at the prospect of a vacation, which will force him to confront the sterility of his existence. Luckily, an old friend, the curator of a museum, offers him a reprieve by asking him to travel to South America to acquire some primitive instruments. The six-week journey completely changes the narrator's life. As he travels into an increasingly primitive environment, his own modern alienation gradually slips away until he feels at one with his world. He begins to compose again and finds a woman whom he admires and loves; he vows to remain forever in the primitive settlement where he has found peace. Compelled, however, by outside forces and the pressure of his music, he does leave but insists that he will return immediately. In the city, he is delayed by legal and financial difficulties. When he finally does return, he finds the doors to his happy life closed. He ruefully then starts another journey back to civilization, realizing that an artist must travel with time, not against it.

Mouche (muhsh), an astrologist, the narrator's French mistress. Priding herself on her artistic sensibilities and modern and progressive ideas, Mouche has intellectual pretensions and superficiality that are stripped away by the authenticity of the jungle. Unable to tolerate her any longer, the narrator takes advantage of her illness to send her away.

Rosario (rroh-SAHR-ee-oh), the narrator's ideal of the true woman. She is near death when she is rescued in the Andes. The narrator's admiration of her courage changes to passion as he continually compares the earthy mestiza woman to the polished, civilized Mouche. Rosario cannot comprehend his need to write music. When he leaves, she uses this music as an excuse to marry someone else.

Ruth, an actress and star of a long-running Broadway play, the narrator's wife. Ruth and her husband see each other only on Sunday mornings. When he does not return from his trip, she claims he is lost in the jungle and stages his rescue as a gigantic publicity stunt. Enraged by his request for a divorce, she frustrates his efforts to get back to Rosario.

Fray Pedro de Henestrosa (PEH-droh deh ehn-ehs-TROH-sah), a Capuchin friar and martyr who is admired for his courage and willingness to help others. Knowing that it means certain death, he undertakes a mission to the lands of savage Indians. They kill him and horribly mutilate his body as a warning to others.

El Adelantado (ah-deh-lahn-TAH-doh), a man who has founded his own city. While prospecting for gold, he became lost in the wilderness and stumbled across a primitive Indian settlement. Recovering from a leg wound, he begins to develop a sense of solidarity with the people, until he eventually identifies himself completely with them. He uses his gold to better their living conditions and, marrying within their tribe, soon becomes their leader.

Yannes, a Greek diamond hunter and lover of *The Odyssey*. His overwhelming ambition is to find the beautiful stones that will enable him to build a templelike house by the sea.

The curator, the narrator's friend and former employer. An admirer of the narrator's theories on the origin of primitive music, he gives him the task of finding some primitive instruments for his museum.

Marcos, El Adelantado's son. Against his father's wishes, he had once left the settlement and gone to seek his fortune in the city. Humiliated and mistreated, he returned home filled with resentment and scorn for everything he had seen in the outside world.

Simon, a shoemaker, now turned itinerant river merchant, who tries to help the narrator find his way back to the lost village.

— *Charlene E. Suscavage*

THE LOST WEEKEND

Author: Charles Reginald Jackson (1903-1968)
First published: 1944
Genre: Novel

Locale: New York City
Time: October, 1936
Plot: Psychological realism

Don Birnam, an unsuccessful writer who becomes an alcoholic. Even though his friends and relatives try to help him, he has no wish to overcome his alcoholism. When sent to a rest farm for a cure, he manages to find liquor there. He is left alone one weekend; to get liquor, he takes the housekeeper's money, tries to steal a purse in a restaurant, and finally manages to borrow some money. He is hospitalized for a few hours; upon his release, he immediately goes to get more whiskey to satisfy his need.

Wick Birnam, Don's brother. He tries to help Don break away from alcohol in every way he can. Wick is spending a

weekend in the country when his brother has his nightmarish experiences.

Helen, Don's friend, who tries with Wick to help the alcoholic. She even takes Don to her apartment. When she does, he steals her fur coat and pawns it for a few dollars for whiskey.

Gloria, a hostess at Sam's Bar. She agrees to go on a date with Don after he tells her a fiction about having a frigid wife and several children. He forgets the appointment.

Bim, a male nurse in the alcoholic ward of a hospital where Don is taken after he loses consciousness.

LOUIS LAMBERT

Author: Honoré de Balzac (1799-1850)
First published: 1832
Genre: Novel

Locale: Vendôme, France
Time: 1811-1824
Plot: Philosophical realism

Louis Lambert (lwee lahm-BEHR), called **Pythagoras** by his schoolmates, a sensitive young philosophy student at a private secondary school. He is an intellectual prodigy subject to flights of mysticism, resembling a youthful Balzac. As he enters boarding school at the age of fourteen, he is slight but powerful and dark-haired, with a pronounced forehead and striking eyes. He is tanned and healthy, but after only a few months of a rigid school regime, he becomes pale, sickly, and depressed. Having been accustomed to guiding his own education, he cannot adapt to being told what to study and when and misses the outdoors and his freedom. Reserved and retiring, Lambert is reluctant to participate in classes and recreational activities and consequently is treated as lazy, recalcitrant, and antisocial by faculty and fellow students. Derisively nicknamed Pythagoras, he succeeds in acquiring only one friend, the narrator. After leaving school, he spends three years in

Paris, engaging in scientific studies, but he is alone and destitute. Lambert's attempts to formulate a unifying theory of the universe, one that would account for spiritual phenomena as well as for matter and motion, lead him to further social isolation, intellectual isolation, and finally a cataleptic state, interpreted by most as insanity. His love for Pauline de Villenoix, rather than drawing him out of himself, seems to hasten his degeneration and early demise at the age of twenty-eight.

The narrator, nicknamed **the Poet**, Lambert's only school chum, a dreamy, romantic reader and writer of poetry, somewhat resembling Balzac as a young man. Later, he writes books, including the account of the companion he admired so greatly. He claims only to begin to grasp at the age of thirty the ideas expounded by Lambert at fourteen. Losing contact after school, he does not see Lambert again until a chance meeting with Lambert's uncle, who relates the tale of his engagement to Mlle de Villenoix, his catalepsy on the eve of their wedding, and his continued incapacity. Visiting Lambert and noting all that the uncle and Pauline tell him, and reading Lambert's notes and letters, the narrator reconstructs the story, suspecting that what the uncle names madness is precipitated by passionate love and might be, as Pauline believes, a form of premature entrance into the spiritual realm. Despite promises to return, the narrator comes back only to visit Lambert's grave, fearful that the influence of Lambert's ideas and magnetic personality might lead him far from ordinary social living into the dangers of metaphysical speculation.

Pauline de Villenoix (poh-LEEN deh veel-NWAH), Lambert's fiancée, the embodiment of his ideal of an angel. Beautiful, charming, meditative, and heir to her grandfather's fortune, she is refused admittance to aristocratic circles because of her illegitimate birth and Jewish ancestry. She loves Lambert and, after great effort, persuades her uncle (her legal guardian), who had hoped to arrange a more prestigious alliance, to approve their marriage. When Lambert falls into a state of catalepsy just before the projected wedding, she takes him to her estate, where she devotedly cares for him until his death three years later. Refusing to believe him insane, considering him only transcended to a higher world, she looks forward to the day when she can join him in the spiritual realm after death. She will allow God his intellect if she can claim his heart.

— Elizabeth A. Rubino

LOVE AND SALT WATER

Author: Ethel Wilson (1888-1980)
First published: 1956
Genre: Novel

Locale: British Columbia, at sea, and Saskatoon, Saskatchewan
Time: 1930-1950
Plot: Social realism

Ellen "Gypsy" Cuppy, a young woman who grows to maturity in the course of the novel. The small, dark, bright-eyed younger daughter of the Cuppy family, Ellen possesses an intelligence, imagination, and independence that allow her to look critically at society and the people with whom she comes in contact. At the age of sixteen, after her mother's sudden death, she takes a cruise to London with her father, which strains their relationship. Ellen then returns to Canada, joins the Canadian navy as a Wren, and, after the war, works at an office job in Vancouver. During this time, she breaks off an engagement to Huw Peake, the stepbrother of Morgan Peake, who she finally realizes is bad-tempered. Later, in Saskatoon, she falls in love with George Gordon, a Montreal businessman whose love for her perseveres even after a boating accident, for which she is primarily responsible, severely disfigures her face.

Nora Cuppy, Ellen's older sister, tall, fair, and beautiful. The unimaginative and passive Nora marries Morgan Peake, who is nineteen years her senior, and gives birth to three sons; the first dies in infancy and the second is born with Down syndrome and is institutionalized. The third son, Johnny, is smothered by his overbearing and possessive mother. When Nora does allow her son out of her sight, he nearly drowns in Active Pass, and Ellen, who tries to save him, receives the disfigurement that changes her life.

Frank Cuppy, Ellen and Nora's father, employed in the oil business. Tall, good-looking, and successful, Frank is an absentee husband and father whose work often takes him to Mexico and Persia. Although he prefers the world of business and is often distracted in the company of his family, he loves his wife and daughters and is continuously focusing on a future when the girls will be grown and Susan can accompany him on his business travels. After Susan's death, Frank marries Nicola Gracey, whom he meets on a cruise taken to help him get over the death of his wife.

Susan Cuppy, Ellen and Nora's mother, Frank's wife. A small, imaginative woman, Susan is happy with her family, although she longs to accompany her husband on his travels. Because Frank is apart from her for nearly two-thirds of their married life, she becomes close to Ellen, who has her same dreamy personality. Susan dies early in the novel, on her younger daughter's birthday.

Morgan Peake, a well-known lawyer and member of Parliament. Less attractive than the members of the Cuppy family, Morgan is dark and plump and only a few years younger than Frank Cuppy. Although his superb mind and judgment are emphasized over his enigmatic and unemotional personality, Morgan is devoted to Nora and to their second son, whom he continues to visit after everyone else in the family has forgotten him.

Johnny Peake, Nora and Morgan's small son. Although Johnny has been sheltered from life by his mother, he still possesses a childlike joy and independence when under his Aunt Ellen's care. His desire to see a seal causes Ellen to take the boat into dangerous waters, the result of which is nearly fatal for both of them. Johnny is honest to the point of cruelty at the novel's end, when he comments on the ugliness of Ellen's scarred face.

George Gordon, a Montreal businessman who is a suitor to Ellen. A kind, proud man who diverted his energies into business and books after his first wife left him, George initially sees Ellen once a year when he goes to Saskatoon on business. After falling in love, he continues to court her, even after Ellen states her refusal to marry, and thus be controlled by, anyone.

Huw Peake, Ellen's fiancé, an apprentice in his stepbrother's office. A bad-tempered and morose young man, Huw is finally recognized by Ellen and Morgan as having a faulty character; they both initially think that his behavior is the result of having been a prisoner of war for more than three years.

Nicola Gracey, an agreeable woman on the cruise ship whom Frank Cuppy later marries.

— Cassandra Kircher

LOVE FOR LOVE

Author: William Congreve (1670-1729)
First published: 1695
Genre: Drama

Locale: London, England
Time: The seventeenth century
Plot: Comedy of manners

Valentine Legend, a young would-be playwright. He loves Angelica. He is also in debt, having wasted his money in high living. Although he falls into disfavor with his father, Sir Sampson Legend, he redeems himself and eventually marries Angelica.

Sir Sampson Legend, who decides to disinherit his son Valentine, a wastrel. His plan fails when Valentine feigns madness.

Angelica, a beautiful young woman loved by Valentine. She is both wealthy and clever. Loving Valentine, she puts up with his temporary faults and finally marries him.

Jeremy, Valentine's clever but knavish servant.

Trapland, a lecherous, elderly scrivener, one of Valentine's creditors.

Scandal, Valentine's friend. He plays upon Foresight's belief in astrology to prevent a marriage between Ben Legend and Prue Foresight. He also flirts with Mrs. Foresight, a young woman married to an old man.

Ben Legend, Valentine's young brother, who stands to inherit Sir Sampson's estate if Valentine is cut off.

Foresight, a foolish old man who believes in astrology and has a young wife. He is Angelica's uncle. He realizes at last that he is really an old fool and admits it.

Prue Foresight, his countrified daughter. She dislikes Ben, whom her father wants her to marry. Although she is fascinated by Tattle, who almost succeeds in seducing her, she ends up wanting to marry Robin, a butler.

Mrs. Foresight, Foresight's young, flirtatious wife.

Mistress Frail, Mrs. Foresight's sister. She wants to marry a rich man, but she is finally tricked into marrying Tattle.

Tattle, a talkative young dandy. He is tricked into marrying Mistress Frail.

Buckram, a lawyer working for Sir Sampson.

Robin, a butler who is in love with Prue.

LOVE FOR LYDIA

Author: H. E. Bates (1905-1974)
First published: 1952
Genre: Novel

Locale: Evensford, in the English Midlands
Time: 1929-1931
Plot: Love

Richardson, the protagonist and narrator, nineteen years old. At the beginning of the story, he is naïvely dissatisfied with his position at the local newspaper and longs for a life of effete leisure that his middle-class family is unable to provide. He meets Lydia Aspen and abandons his job so that he can escort her to local dances and outings with his, later their, friends. It is Richardson who introduces Lydia to the social whirl of which he is fond, yet it is she who helps him to realize the deadly futility of this kind of life. After a brief absence, Richardson returns to Evensford and Lydia with open eyes. Through his experiences, he is able to identify not only his real needs and desires but also what is real and important in his life.

Lydia Aspen, the youngest member of a local aristocratic family. The sheltered Lydia quickly embraces the round of parties, dances, and fetes that life at the Aspen house affords. She is a free spirit whose thirst for new experiences seems to know no bounds. Lydia eventually falls prey to her own physical and emotional abandonment, however, only to be saved by the devotion of Richardson and Blackie Johnson to their quixotic mistress.

Tom Holland, a young farmer and a friend of Richardson. Stolidly loyal, Tom falls under Lydia's spell and, despite his misgivings, betrays his friendship with Richardson. Tom later provides Richardson with sanctuary when life without Lydia's exclusive love no longer seems bearable, and it is Tom who finally shows him the terrible price that must be paid for betrayal.

Nancy Holland, Tom's sister. Hopelessly in love with Richardson, Nancy vainly waits for him to come to his senses and marry her. Her devotion to Richardson and her love of her family contrast to the flightiness and vengefulness of Lydia.

Alex Sanderson, Richardson's friend. A debonair man-about-town, Alex is horrified when his infatuation with Lydia shows him how shallow a person he has become. In a fit of alcoholic remorse, he throws himself off a bridge. Alex's death awakens Richardson to the perfidy of Lydia's love.

Blackie Johnson, a mechanic and taxi driver. He becomes Lydia's faithful slave, seeking to do nothing but grant her every whim. Blackie remains a dark and frightening person to all the characters except Lydia, who regards him as an interesting and friendly pup whom she can manipulate with flirtation and money.

— *Jennifer L. Wyatt*

LOVE IN A WOOD: Or, St. James's Park

Author: William Wycherley (1641?-1715)
First published: 1672
Genre: Drama

Locale: London, England
Time: The seventeenth century
Plot: Comedy of manners

Lady Flippant, a widow in search of a husband. Although temporarily enamored of Mr. Dapperwit, to whom she makes advances, she has her eye on Sir Simon Addleplot, whom she intends all along to marry and finally does.

Alderman Gripe, an elderly usurer, Lady Flippant's brother. Enamored of Lucy, he is brought to her by Mrs. Joyner. He frightens the girl with his hasty attentions and is forced to pay five hundred pounds in hush money to her mother, Mrs. Crossbite. He later marries Lucy to get even with his son-in-law, Dapperwit.

Mr. Dapperwit, a witless fop. Enamored of Lucy, he is tricked into marrying the six-months-pregnant Mistress Martha.

Mistress Martha, Alderman Gripe's daughter. Finding herself six months pregnant, she succeeds in marrying Dapperwit.

Lucy, Mrs. Crossbite's daughter, who is in love with Dapperwit. She marries Alderman Gripe in revenge for Dapperwit's marriage to his daughter, Mistress Martha.

Sir Simon Addleplot, a fortune hunter. In pursuit of Mistress Martha, he must finally be satisfied with Lady Flippant.

Mrs. Crossbite, a procuress and Lucy's mother. She blackmails Alderman Gripe and maneuvers him into marrying her daughter.

Mrs. Joyner, a matchmaker and procuress engaged in finding a husband for Mrs. Flippant, in finding a wife for Sir Simon Addleplot, and in procuring Lucy for Alderman Gripe.

Mr. Ranger, a young man-about-town engaged to Lydia.

Mr. Vincent, Mr. Ranger's friend and confidant.

Lydia, Mr. Ranger's cousin and his betrothed.

Mr. Valentine, a young gallant betrothed to Christina.

Christina, a young woman in love with Mr. Valentine.

LOVE IN THE RUINS: The Adventures of a Bad Catholic at a Time Near the End of the World

Author: Walker Percy (1916-1990)
First published: 1971
Genre: Novel

Locale: Louisiana
Time: 1983, with a coda in 1988
Plot: Social satire

Dr. Thomas More, the narrator, a psychiatrist in Paradise Estates, Louisiana. By his own admission, this forty-five-year-old man loves "women best, music and science next, whiskey next, God fourth, and my fellow man hardly at all." His life is complicated by his two most prominent qualities: his heart full of love and his good mind. Because of his wife's adultery, his daughter's death, his guilt over his affair with his neighbor's daughter, and his conviction that the world is going to end, this bad Catholic is afflicted with alcoholism and troublesome mood swings. His personal problems land him in a mental hospital, where he is both a patient and a member of the staff. When his plans for revolutionizing psychiatry through his mood-altering invention—the lapsometer—fall through, he returns to his life as a practicing psychiatrist, forsakes his philandering, chaotic lifestyle, and marries his nurse, Ellen Oglethorpe.

Ellen Oglethorpe, More's nurse, a beautiful but tyrannical Georgia Presbyterian who believes not in God but in doing what is right. When she threatens to leave and become Art Immelmann's traveling secretary, More pulls her off the plane, marries her, and regains some stability in his life.

Miss Marva, More's mother, a psychic. Unlike her son, she is on good terms with the world. When a group of black revolutionaries called the Bantus take over 99 percent of Paradise Estates, she nevertheless flourishes by selling "astrological real estate" to the Bantus.

Eukie, Miss Marva's black servant. She calls More a "treasure," but he insists that he is good for nothing but serving cocktails to his wife's bridge club.

Art Immelmann, an insidious stranger who poses as the liaison officer between the National Institutes of Mental Health (NIMH) and the Ford, Carnegie, and Rockefeller Foundations. He talks More into signing over the rights to the lapsometer to him and then uses the invention to increase tensions among people. After adding the lapsometer to the Maryland arsenal, he promises that More will win the Nobel Prize.

Lola Rhoades, an accomplished cellist, twenty years old, one of More's girlfriends. Foolish, impetuous, and gallant, she saves More's life when he has an attack of "brain hives" in a grassy bunker by fetching her brother to help him. The six-foot-tall beauty saves More's life a second time by shooting at a Bantu who is holding a gun on him.

Dr. George "Dusty" Rhoades, More's neighbor and Lola's father. Rhoades, who is president of the American Christian Proctological Association, is also an arch conservative and bigot. He strongly disapproves of More's conduct with his daughter. He saves More's life after his attack of "brain hives" by injecting him with epinephrine.

Moira Schaffner, a secretary at the Love Clinic, another one of More's girlfriends. A poor girl who supported herself by working for the civil service and for the NIMH before coming to Paradise, she makes More jealous because of her attraction to Dr. Buddy Brown. Along with Ellen and Lola, she hides out with More in the abandoned motel during the riots.

Dr. Buddy Brown, a doctor at the Love Clinic. Not only does he contend with More for Moira's affections, but he also disagrees with More's belief that Mr. Ives is not insane enough to be committed to the Happy Isles Separation Center (the innocuous name of which is a euphemism for euthanasia).

Mr. Ives, a mute and possibly senile psychopath. After working for the Hartford Insurance Company, Mr. Ives loses his wife, retires to the woods in Louisiana, and then moves to Tampa, Florida, where he spends his time digging for the fountain of youth. Dr. More keeps him from being sent to the Happy Isles.

Dr. Kenneth Stryker, the chief of staff at the Love Clinic. He is a tall man who emphasizes propriety, even to the point of dressing like a funeral director. He is completely devoid of moral scruples.

Dr. Helga Heine, a Bavarian gynecologist and assistant to Dr. Stryker. She makes love to Dr. Stryker after observing the lovemaking of two of their patients.

Father Kev Kevin, a former priest, now a Love Clinic counselor. He implements some of the findings of the article that More had intended to send to the journal *Brain*, but he completely misinterprets their meaning.

Father Rinaldo Smith, a priest who ministers to a small congregation, performing the traditional rites of the Roman Catholic Church. For a time, he is More's fellow patient in a psychiatric ward, where in his disturbed state he reveals a prophetic vision of the spiritual condition of America.

Doris, More's wealthy former wife. Reared as an Episcopalian and accustomed to Virginian gentility, she is embittered by the death of their daughter, Samantha. Increasingly absorbed in Eastern mysticism, she leaves More, telling him that she is going "in search of myself."

Alistair Fuchs-Forbes, Doris' British lover, a hypocritical guru. He tells More that he shares More's hatred of materialism, even though he is primarily interested in Doris' money. Ironically, he gets Doris, but she leaves her money to More.

Victor Charles, More's stammering former servant who worked for more than twenty years for him and his mother. One of the leaders of the Bantu movement, he eventually runs for Congress and asks More to act as his campaign manager.

Colley, an encephalographer, electronic wizard, black belt in karate, and graduate of the New York University medical school. More refers to him as a "black Leonardo."

Charlie Parker, a Paradise golf professional and self-proclaimed nonconformist. Even though he and his wife try to revive Choctaw customs and camp near a Confederate salt mine, his conservative side becomes apparent in his angry verbal attacks against the rioters who burn the golf course.

Leroy Ledbetter, a seventh-generation Anglo-Saxon American and a friend of More. He and More are part owners of the Paradise Bowling Lanes. Leroy destroys his business when he refuses to give a lane to a black couple from Tougaloo and thereby incites a riot.

— *Alan Brown*

LOVE IN THE TIME OF CHOLERA
(El Amor en los tiempos del cólera)

Author: Gabriel García Márquez (1928-   )
First published: 1985
Genre: Novel

Locale: Colombia
Time: Late nineteenth and early twentieth centuries
Plot: Love

Florentino Ariza (flohr-ehn-TEE-noh ah-REE-sah), a man completely devoted to romantic passion. He is the illegitimate son of a philandering father and a resourceful single mother. While still an adolescent, he falls madly in love with Fermina Daza. When she rejects him after the two have made plans to marry, he sets out on a solitary quest to win back Fermina. He even writes and publishes a book, *Lover's Companion*, in celebration of his undying love for Fermina. He tries to improve his social status by quitting his job as a telegraph messenger and going to work for his uncle and the Riverboat Company of the Caribbean. He eventually becomes president of the company. He is consumed by his passionate love for Fermina. At times, because of this passion, he becomes physically sick; at other times, he seems driven nearly to madness, particularly when she rejects him and he engages in sexual affairs to try to forget his love for her. Everything Florentino does must be understood in terms of his love for Fermina. His determination to win her back and consummate their love is fraught with pitfalls, including his own physical decrepitude (he becomes bald, breaks his leg, and is left lame) and the violent deaths of two of his former mistresses. Ultimately, he is rewarded for his persistent love.

Fermina Daza (fehr-MEE-nah DAH-zah), the daughter of a mule dealer, a strong-willed woman who submits neither to her father's domination nor to Florentino's early attempts to make her his wife. Although she rejects Florentino, she remains in love with him for the more than fifty years that she is married to Dr. Juvenal Urbino, whom she marries because he is of a higher social class. In fact, she judges her husband in comparison with Florentino, finding Urbino passionless and even unmanly. She spends the night after her husband dies thinking not of him but of Florentino. Clearly, she has always loved Florentino; in fact, she is consumed by her love for

Florentino, though she does not fully realize this until the final chapter of the novel.

Dr. Juvenal Urbino (HEW-vehn-ahl ewr-BEE-noh), a prominent doctor who studied in Paris and has devoted his life to fighting cholera. Although he has a passion for finding a cure for cholera, he is clearly passionless in human relationships. Considering that his marriage with Fermina is something of a failure, one might conclude that he has misdirected his passion for most of his life. He is redeemed from this shortcoming during his dying moments, when he finally confesses his deep love for his wife.

Jeremiah de Saint-Amour, a seemingly minor character who introduces the theme of unrequited love. Like Florentino, this Caribbean refugee has lived his life for love. Although he is Dr. Urbino's most sympathetic chess companion (Dr. Urbino considers him a friend), he is also an escaped fugitive who at one time ate human flesh. Saint-Amour therefore also introduces the conflict between appearance and reality. He commits suicide in the first chapter because he loved life and his secret Haitian mistress with such passion that he thought he could not survive old age and decay.

Lotario Thugat (loh-TAHR-ee-oh TEW-gaht), Florentino's employer at the telegraph office and also, more significantly, the one who introduces Florentino into the world of earthly passion by taking him to houses of prostitution.

Rosalba (rohs-AHL-bah), possibly the name of the woman who takes Florentino's virginity and fully initiates him into the world of earthly passion. From his brief experience with Rosalba, Florentino learns that sexual passion can temporarily replace the love he feels for Fermina.

América Vicuña (ah-MEHR-ee-kah vee-KEWN-yah), a fourteen-year-old girl who represents the final sexual conquest for the now aging Florentino, who is still trying to get over being rejected by Fermina. In love with Florentino, she commits suicide after Florentino rejects her and returns to Fermina. She acts as something of a counterpart to Jeremiah de Saint-Amour: Both end their lives as a result of unrequited love.

Lorenzo Daza, Fermina's father, a former mule trader who, it is alleged in a local scandal sheet, has engaged in illegal trafficking of firearms and the sale of other contraband. Because he has social aspirations for his daughter, he prevents

her marriage to Florentino, who at the time of the engagement is a telegraph messenger. He is expelled from the country when his shady business deals are revealed.

Tránsito Ariza (TRAHN-see-toh), Florentino's mother, who fully understands the ways of human passion and thus is of great help to her son when he falls hopelessly in love with Fermina. As owner of a pawnshop, she takes in jewelry owned by wealthier ladies to help pay for her son's wedding.

— *Richard Logsdon*

LOVE MEDICINE

Author: Louise Erdrich (1954-   )
First published: 1984
Genre: Novel

Locale: A North Dakota Indian reservation and nearby towns
Time: 1934-1984
Plot: Social

Marie Lazarre Kashpaw, the wife of Nector Kashpaw. A loving and long-suffering woman, biological mother of five children and mother substitute to numerous others not her own, she is a kind of maternal ideal. She rears June and Lipsha Morrissey. Nector, when he meets her in 1934, calls her "a skinny white girl . . . pale as birch." In her youth, she enters the Sacred Heart Convent as a means of escaping the reservation, but she later leaves. She marries and tolerates her husband's infidelity, never giving up hope that she can have him exclusively. To that end, as an old woman she resorts to love medicine.

Nector Kashpaw, formerly a film actor and later tribal chairman on a Chippewa reservation in North Dakota. A man of divided impulses and loyalties, he loves his wife, Marie, but also has a passion for his first love, Lulu Nanapush Lamartine. His vacillations are both serious and comic. His wife claims credit for his political success, having nominated him as tribal chairman and kept him sober enough to do the job, and he cannot control his attraction to Lulu. As an old man, he chokes to death on Lipsha Morrissey's love medicine.

Lulu Nanapush Lamartine, a strong and willful woman, the object of many men's desire, and the mother of eight children, including Gerry Nanapush. Her many sexual affairs and her political clashes with the tribal council make her something of an outcast. She has a lifelong love for Nector Kashpaw that is less a secret than she thinks. Her narrative in the penultimate chapter pulls together many of the novel's threads.

June Morrissey Kashpaw, the wife of Marie Kashpaw's son Gordie. She dies in a blizzard on Easter morning, 1981, and becomes a focus in the memories of many characters by the strength of her influence on the Kashpaw, Morrissey, and Nanapush families.

Gerry Nanapush, a leader in the American Indian Movement. His fugitive status with the federal authorities makes

him a heroic figure, and his connection with June Morrissey Kashpaw produces Lipsha. He reveals his paternity to Lipsha on the way to the Canadian border for his final escape.

Lipsha Morrissey, a latter-day medicine man, June's unacknowledged son, brought up by Marie and Nector Kashpaw. A gentle, naïve man, Lipsha plays the wise fool: "God's been going deaf," he says, "[Indian Gods] will do a favor if you ask them right." His actions and observations bring to light many themes of love. He concocts a love potion for Nector at the request of Marie.

Albertine Johnson, a nurse and later a medical school student. An intelligent and sensitive young woman, she sees the poverty of reservation life and the self-destructiveness of both men and women there. Her career ambitions do not end her love for them; her life is hope.

Henry Lamartine, Jr., a Vietnam veteran, the son of Lulu but not of Henry. His sexual encounter with his then-fifteen-year-old cousin Albertine shows how ravaged he is by his life as a soldier and a Native American. He drowns himself in front of his brother Lyman Lamartine.

Lyman Lamartine, another of Lulu's sons, the half brother of Henry. He tries hard but unsuccessfully to help his brother out of his post-Vietnam trauma. They share a red convertible and long summer drives, including a trip to Alaska.

Sister Leopolda, a nun in the Sacred Heart Convent. Her possessiveness and cruelty toward the young Marie constitute a unique variation on the theme of love.

Gordie Kashpaw, the son of Marie and Nector. After the death of his wife, June, he is consumed by grief and guilt and turns to alcohol. He identifies a road-killed deer as June herself, confesses to her murder, and then wanders through an apple orchard, weeping, in another improvisation in the theme of love.

— *Kerry Ahearn*

THE LOVE SUICIDES AT SONEZAKI
(Sonezaki Shinjū)

Author: Chikamatsu Monzaemon (Sugimori Nobumori, 1653-1725)
First performed: 1703
Genre: Drama

Locale: Osaka, Japan
Time: The eighteenth century
Plot: Love

Gihei, a wealthy Japanese man from the country who wants to spend an evening in Osaka with O Hatsu, a famous geisha; she refuses him. Later, he abducts her for a while.

O Hatsu, a famous geisha, in love with a poor young man. To save the honor of Tokubei, she commits suicide, so that his traitorous friend cannot use her lover's money to ransom her.

Tokubei, a poor young man in love with O Hatsu. He refuses to marry an heiress, but he lends the dowry money to his friend, who refuses to return it so that it can be re-turned to the family of the girl Tokubei refuses to marry. To save his honor, Tokubei commits suicide, as does his beloved O Hatsu.

Kyuemon, Tokubei's uncle and employer. He tries to ar-range Tokubei's marriage with an heiress. Too late, he learns of his nephew's friend's evil ways. When he finds his nephew, Tokubei already has committed suicide.

Kuheiji, Tokubei's evil friend. In addition to taking the young man's money, Kuheiji plots to ransom O Hatsu and keep her for himself. His plan fails when she dies.

THE LOVED AND THE LOST

Author: Morley Callaghan (1903-1990)
First published: 1951
Genre: Novel

Locale: Montreal, Canada
Time: Late 1940's
Plot: Social

James McAlpine, a former Navy lieutenant commander and a history professor at the University of Toronto in his early thirties. A magazine article he writes, titled "The Independent Man," leads Joseph Carver to invite him to Montreal to write a triweekly column for the *Sun*. In Montreal, the normally prag-matic and conventional Jim comes under the spell of Peggy Sanderson, and his desire to understand, protect, reform, and possess her becomes an obsession that overshadows both his initial attraction to Catherine Carver and his wish to achieve status among Montreal's English-speaking elite. He believes that his final betrayal of Peggy, when he leaves her alone on the night of her greatest crisis, makes him responsible for her murder.

Peggy Sanderson, the daughter of an Ontario United Church minister. Though in her mid-twenties, she looks far younger; she is petite, fair, childlike in appearance, and inno-cent in demeanor. That seeming innocence is belied by her free-spirited disregard for propriety. In particular, she seeks out friendships with some of Montreal's black jazz musicians in the face of racial and social taboos. Whether she is a slut in search of forbidden excitement or an enlightened humanist transformed by her childhood friendship with the one black family in her town is the mystery that obsesses Jim McAlpine and that earns for Peggy the contempt of whites and the uneasy resentment of blacks. Her flirtation with the forbidden leads inevitably to her rape and murder at the hands of a criminal who could be any one of the many men, white and black, that she both repelled and attracted.

Joseph Carver, the wealthy elderly publisher of the Mon-treal *Sun* newspaper. A secure member of Montreal's English elite, Carver enjoys his power and status. Although he pro-fesses to admire independent thinking, he attempts to impose his values on his inferiors, both business and social. His initial admiration for Jim McAlpine turns to bewilderment when Jim does not conform.

Catherine Carver, a beautiful, cultivated twenty-seven-year-old divorcee and daughter of Joseph Carver. Admired and envied in her Junior League circle, Catherine is nevertheless unsure and lonely after the breakup of her disastrous, short marriage. Attracted by his seeming strength of character, she falls in love with Jim but is quickly disappointed, recognizing soon that her love is not reciprocated. Identifying Jim as the artist of the unsigned drawing of Peggy that appears in news-paper accounts of her murder, Catherine agrees with her father to contact the police and link Jim with Peggy.

Chuck Foley, an account executive and latent poet in his thirties who introduces Jim to Peggy. The red-haired Foley, separated from his wife, is saved from complete cynicism by his enduring friendship with Jim and his longing to reen-counter the idealism of his youth. He introduces Jim to the initially congenial companionship of the Chalet Restaurant bar. He does his best to disillusion Jim about Peggy, without success.

Walter Malone, an embittered middle-aged editorial writer, big, gray-haired, and a drinker. Attracted to Peggy and assuming that her supposed sexual license will extend to him, he tries to make love to her. When she rejects him, he is furious and vengeful. In a jazz club located on St. Antoine Street in Montreal's black district, he tries once again to force himself on her, precipitating a violent melee that involves both blacks and whites and brings all the latent conflict into the open. It is early the next morning that Peggy is raped and murdered, crimes for which Malone has both motive and capa-bility.

Wolgast, a big, bald, immigrant Polish Jew, half owner of the Chalet Restaurant bar. He confides to Jim his dream of achieving a comfortable place in Canadian society. At first protective of Peggy, Wolgast threatens her physically after she brings a black companion into the bar and jeopardizes his bar's standing in the largely white community.

Ron Wilson, a black trumpet player presumed to be Peggy's latest paramour. His marriage is shaky, and both his and his wife's hostility find an outlet in the violence directed at Peggy in the jazz club.

Milton Rogers, a friend of Foley, a photographer, and a jazz aficionado. His enthusiasm for a new jazz singer leads Jim, Foley, and Wolgast to the club where, that night, the climactic brawl occurs.

— *Jill Rollins*

THE LOVED ONE: An Anglo-American Tragedy

Author: Evelyn Waugh (1903-1966)
First published: 1948
Genre: Novel

Locale: Hollywood and Los Angeles, California
Time: Late 1940's
Plot: Satire

Dennis Barlow, an English dilettante who has traveled to Southern California. His only book of poetry, written while he was in the British Air Force during World War II, received strong reviews and several awards, but the paper shortage took the book out of print. Curious, pragmatic, and a "man of sensibility rather than sentiment," the twenty-eight-year-old Barlow goes to Hollywood to help write the life of Percy Shelley for films. Unable to write the sort of script required by Megalopolitan Studios, he is dismissed from his job, moves in with Sir Francis Hinsley, and begins work at The Happier Hunting Ground, a pet mortuary, where his new employer, Mr. Schultz, finds him congenial and reverent. Barlow, fascinated by the American way of death at The Happier Hunting Ground and at Whispering Glades, courts Aimee Thanatogenos, an employee at Whispering Glades, with poetry plagiarized from the *Oxford Book of English Verse*. Aimee, unlike Mr. Schultz, finds Dennis irreverent of things that should be sacred, such as citizenship and social conscience. After Aimee's suicide, Mr. Joyboy prompts Barlow to cremate the corpse at The Happier Hunting Ground before Barlow returns to England. At the conclusion of the novel, Barlow is waiting for Aimee's corpse to burn.

Aimee Thanatogenos (ay-MAY tha-na-TO-geh-nohs), the fiancée of both Barlow and Mr. Joyboy and assistant to Mr. Joyboy at Whispering Glades, a cemetery in the Hollywood Hills. Aimee, who was graduated from the university in 1943 with beauticraft as her first subject, has no family and few friends, lives alone, and loves her work at Whispering Glades, "her true home." She has dark, straight hair and eyes that are "greenish and remote, with a rich glint of lunacy." Considering herself an artist of sorts and a "handmaid to the morticians," Aimee works "like a nun, intently, serenely, methodically." She presents herself to the world dressed and scented in obedience to advertisements. When Aimee cannot resolve her dilemma of being engaged simultaneously to Barlow and Mr. Joyboy, she takes an elevator to the top story of Whispering Glades, goes to Mr. Joyboy's workroom, injects herself with cyanide, and covers herself with a sheet, thus leading to Mr. Joyboy's discovery of her corpse.

Mr. Joyboy, the chief cosmetician and embalmer at Whispering Glades. An expert on facial expressions on corpses, Mr. Joyboy enjoys great popularity at Whispering Glades and in the funeral industry. He is unmarried and is regarded by every female employee at Whispering Glades as debonnaire and as a figure of romance. In addition to being a Rotarian and a Knight of Pythias, Mr. Joyboy is a regular contributor to *The Casket*, a mortuary publication. He is an intimate of Dr. Kenworthy. By the standards of motion-picture studios, Mr. Joyboy is not handsome. Tall but unathletic, he has scant eyebrows and invisible eyelashes. His hair, though neat, is sparse, and his hands are fleshy. His best feature is his teeth, and even they are not perfect: They seem too large for his mouth. Mr. Joyboy lives with his mother in a shabby home. He is saving his money for a house and children, and he believes "anything

spent inconspicuously, anything spent on Mom" is "money down the drain." Mr. Joyboy's jealousy leads him to expose to Aimee two facts about Barlow that she cannot tolerate: that he is employed at The Happier Hunting Ground and that he plagiarized the poems he gave her. After these revelations, Aimee consents to marry Mr. Joyboy. To save his reputation after Aimee's suicide, Mr. Joyboy gets Barlow to cremate Aimee's corpse and pays for Barlow's first-class travel to England.

Sir Ambrose Abercrombie, the leader of the English expatriate colony in Hollywood. Sir Ambrose, the guardian of the British image in Hollywood, is not quite sixty years old, dresses in conservative British attire complete with monocle, and heads the Cricket Club. At the beginning of the novel, he pays Sir Francis a visit concerning Barlow's disgraceful job at The Happier Hunting Ground. Later, Sir Ambrose supervises Barlow's arrangements at Whispering Glades for Sir Francis' funeral. Finally, it is Sir Ambrose who gives Barlow a check from the Cricket Club to return to England (tourist class) so that Barlow will not disgrace them by becoming a nonsectarian minister.

Sir Francis Hinsley, a screenwriter at Megalopolitan Studios and former president of the Cricket Club. Sir Francis, who has worked for Megalopolitan Studios for twenty-five years, has a "weak, sensitive, intelligent face, blurred somewhat by soft living and long boredom." He follows the conservative dress of Sir Ambrose, complete with monocle, and refrains from reading Barlow's poetry because, as he says of himself, he has never been "much good at anything new." When Barlow loses his job at Megalopolitan Studios, Sir Francis takes him in, regarding Barlow as "a young man of genius, the hope of English poetry." Stigmatized by Barlow's new job at The Happier Hunting Ground and no longer of legitimate service to Megalopolitan Studios, Sir Francis is fired, after which he commits suicide, hanging himself from the rafters in his home with his suspenders. Barlow meets Aimee while he is making funeral arrangements for Sir Francis.

Guru Brahmin, actually three contributors to an advice-to-the-lovelorn column for a newspaper, the chief correspondent being Mr. Slump. The column, formerly called "Aunt Lydia's Post Bag," is now called "The Wisdom of the Guru Brahmin." Mr. Slump, a gloomy man given to drinking whiskey and smoking, deals with the letters to Guru Brahmin that require private answers. It is he, therefore, who answers the numerous letters from Aimee Thanatogenos regarding her dilemma with Barlow and Mr. Joyboy. In the course of the novel, Mr. Slump's condition deteriorates until he appears at work illshaven and scarcely sober. The night after he is fired, Aimee traces him by telephone to Mooney's Saloon to get advice. Mr. Slump suggests that she jump from a top-floor window.

Dr. Wilbur Kenworthy, called **The Dreamer**, the founder of the commercialized Whispering Glades Memorial Park, a racially segregated cemetery. Fear of disgracing Whispering Glades and Mr. Kenworthy and, thereby, ruining his own reputation drives Mr. Joyboy to seek Barlow's help in covering up the death of Aimee Thanatogenos.

Mr. Schultz, the owner of The Happier Hunting Ground, a pet cemetery in Southern California. He is a pragmatic realist, concerned with profits and resentful that people will spend more money burying relatives they hate than burying pets they love. Because he finds Barlow congenial and reverent, he encourages Barlow to stay on at The Happier Hunting Ground.

Mrs. Joyboy, Mr. Joyboy's mother. She has small angry eyes, frizzy hair, and a shapeless body; she wears pince-nez on a very thick nose and wears positively insulting clothes. Resentful of being moved away from the East to Hollywood, where everything is too expensive, Mrs. Joyboy dotes on her aged, almost naked parrot Sambo and watches political commentaries on television. Sambo's death gives Mr. Joyboy the opportunity to arrange the parrot's open-casket funeral at The Happier Hunting Ground and to invite Aimee to the ceremony, where she sees Barlow presiding. Mr. Joyboy cannot leave his mother to be with Aimee on the night of her suicide because his mother's new bird has just arrived.

Juanita del Pablo, a star at Megalopolitan Studios. Sir Francis Hinsley has the job of re-creating her image because the Catholic League of Decency has put pressure on Megalopolitan Studios to clean up its films. Sir Francis' failure with this task contributes, in part, to his dismissal from Megalopolitan Studios. Sir Ambrose arranges to have her sing at Sir Francis' funeral.

The Reverend Errol Bartholomew, a nonsectarian bishop. After he reads the service for the Alsatian's funeral service at The Happier Hunting Ground, Barlow talks to him and decides to become a nonsectarian minister so that his class will be at least as high as a mortician's.

— *Carol Franks*

THE LOVER
(L'Amant)

Author: Marguerite Duras (1914-1996)
First published: 1984
Genre: Novel

Locale: Indochina and France
Time: Late 1920's through the 1940's
Plot: New Novel

The narrator, an older French woman. Now a successful writer in France, the narrator reminisces about her childhood and adolescence in Indochina, focusing on an image that appears to be central to her identity, an image of herself dressed in gold lamé high heels, a silk dress with a very low neckline, and a man's fedora. As she crosses a branch of the Mekong River, she is watched by a Chinese millionaire in his black chauffeur-driven limousine. Although she is only fifteen and he is twelve years older, she becomes his mistress, accepting money and elegant dinners at expensive restaurants for herself and her impoverished family. They accept his generosity but humiliate him, refusing to acknowledge him because he is Chinese. Even the narrator denies the depth of her feelings when she is confronted by her mother. Although marriage is of no interest to her, he awakens her sensibility and desire, her love of lovemaking. After finishing high school, she leaves Saigon for France to continue her education, thus ending the one-and-a-half-year relationship with her Chinese lover.

The narrator's lover, a wealthy Chinese heir. Attracted to the young girl he sees standing by the rail on the ferry, he offers her a ride to her boarding school. They become lovers, frequenting his apartment in Cholon, where he awakens her sexual desire. Their relationship cannot last because he is Chinese and she is white. His rich father is adamantly opposed to any future union, and the son, weak and timid, will not oppose him and risk being disinherited. After the narrator's departure for France, he marries a young, well-to-do Chinese woman, the marriage arranged ten years earlier by their families. As he reveals years later, he never loses his love for the narrator.

The narrator's mother, a schoolteacher. Verging on despair and madness, she, after the death of her husband, rears her three children on her salary as a headmistress of a girls' school in Sadec. In an effort to combat their constant poverty, she invests her savings in land that, to their dismay, is flooded annually by salt water let in by the crumbling dikes.

The narrator's older brother, a gambler. Cruel and insensitive, he steals from his mother, his sister, and even the housekeeper to support his opium and gambling habits. He is sent away from the family home on several occasions to protect the other children. Finally, at the age of fifty, when there is nothing left for him to take, he holds his first job, as a messenger for a marine insurance company. He keeps the job until his death fifteen years later. When he dies, he is buried, at his mother's previous request, with her in the same grave.

The narrator's younger brother, an accountant's clerk in Saigon. Intimidated and tormented by his older brother, he is loved by his sister, two years younger than he. At the age of twenty-seven, he dies of bronchial pneumonia during the Japanese occupation of World War II. His sister is devastated to discover that someone she thought should be immortal could die. His death spurs the narrator to attempt suicide.

— *Barbara Wiedemann*

LOVERS AND TYRANTS

Author: Francine du Plessix Gray (1930-   )
First published: 1976
Genre: Novel

Locale: Paris, St. Tropez, and Brittany, France; New York City; rural Massachusetts; the American Southwest; and Las Vegas, Nevada
Time: 1935 to the early 1970's
Plot: Bildungsroman

Stephanie, the protagonist and first-person narrator. She is ignored initially by her "flapper" mother, a beautiful Russian émigré who turns her over to a Russian émigré governess. Later, her father, an impoverished aristocrat, is killed in World War II. Stephanie is thus rendered insecure about love. She behaves as a "good girl" to win the love of her mother and her husband, but she finds that all of her various "lovers" are also "tyrants" who limit her freedom and potential. Her life and the novel are about her struggle to reconcile the opposed values of stable love and freedom.

Lydia Romanovna Mishanskaya (Mishka), Stephanie's governess from the time she is four years old until she is nine. She is the first "tyrant" in Stephanie's eyes. She is a strict, emotionally repressed, unmarried woman whose hypochondria and needy love make Stephanie dependent and fearful.

Stephanie's father, a conservative French viscount who is living in Paris and is estranged from Stephanie's mother. He is a pilot who is killed early in World War II. This news is withheld from Stephanie, who is unable until much later to grieve properly for the distant parent she idolized.

Stephanie's mother, a beautiful Russian who escaped to Paris in the 1920's. She is obsessed with social class, status, and achievement. Initially bored by Stephanie as a small child, she becomes an attentive mother in New York City after their escape from German-occupied Paris. She is a tyrant in the mind of Stephanie, who finds it hard to please her.

Joan Riley, a student at Stephanie's exclusive girls' school in New York City. Like Stephanie, she is a newcomer from an undistinguished background. She shares with Stephanie a love of opera and art. She is Stephanie's first real friend.

Louis Bonaparte, an impoverished Frenchman with whom Stephanie has a torrid affair during her first year in Paris after her graduation from college. Louis' pedigree, summed up in his famous name, is pleasing to Stephanie's mother. Louis tyrannizes Stephanie by relating solely to her.

Paul, Stephanie's lover since college. She initially rejected him but ultimately marries him. He is reserved and withdrawn, preferring country life and complete order. He is an excellent husband but cannot fulfill Stephanie's desire for growth, change, and conversation.

Aunt Charlotte, one of many French relatives of Stephanie living in Brittany. Stephanie finally comes to terms with the group as an adult, when she visits her father's grave.

Gregory Hillsman, a Jesuit who leaves the order but continues to act as Stephanie's confessor and spiritual adviser.

Elijah Stewart, a childlike photographer in his early twenties. Stephanie travels with him around the American Southwest. He is a homosexual but has an affair with Stephanie, who by this time has left her husband after undergoing surgery for possibly terminal cancer.

— *Andrew F. Macdonald*

LOVE'S LABOUR'S LOST

Author: William Shakespeare (1564-1616)
First published: 1598
Genre: Drama

Locale: Navarre, Spain
Time: The sixteenth century
Plot: Comedy of manners

Berowne (beh-REWN), a witty, sophisticated young lord in the court of King Ferdinand of Navarre. Although he joins his monarch's idealistic academy, he warns his companions of the folly of study for its own sake and advises them to seek wisdom in the contemplation of feminine beauty. He delights in words, exchanging puns and rhymes with his friends and waxing rhapsodic when he falls in love. He meets his match in Rosaline and swears that he will henceforth woo with "rustic yeas and honest kersey noes." She orders him to temper his ironic wit with sympathy; he must spend the next year jesting in hospitals.

Rosaline (ROHZ-uh-lin), one of the charming ladies in waiting to the princess of France. Clever and sparkling, she whets her mind in verbal battles with Boyet and spars endlessly with Berowne, who is continually overcome by her wit. She is the first of William Shakespeare's bright, confident heroines, the prototype for Beatrice, Viola, Portia, and Rosalind.

Ferdinand, the king of Navarre, an idealistic young ruler who intends to win everlasting fame by establishing a Platonic academy devoted to study and ascetic living. The appearance of the princess of France on a diplomatic mission quickly disperses his noble goals as he and his lords promptly fall in love and turn their attention to sonnets, masques, and gifts. Brought suddenly to Earth by the news of the death of the princess' father, he affirms the seriousness of his love and promises to spend a year in a hermitage, as his lady requests, to prove the depth of his affection.

The princess of France, a dignified young woman who remains aware of her serious responsibilities while she delights in jesting with Boyet, her ladies, and the hunters, and in teasing the lovesick lords.

Longaville (LONG-uh-vihl) and

Dumaine (dew-MAYN), Ferdinand's courtiers. They fall in love with Katharine and Maria when their king succumbs to the charms of the girls' mistress, the princess. Both are quick-witted young men and eloquently poetic lovers, a little bewildered by the wit and independence of their ladies.

Katharine and

Maria, the princess' ladies, who gleefully torment their lovers with endless repartee, although they admit their romantic inclinations within their own circle.

Boyet (boy-EHT), a sharp-tongued courtier who accompanies the princess to Navarre and passes his time exchanging bawdy quips with her ladies.

Don Adriano de Armado (ah-dree-AH-noh deh ahr-MAH-doh), a boastful Spanish soldier, a descendant of the braggart of the *commedia dell'arte* productions. He fancies himself a gallant courtier and amuses the lords and ladies with his fantastic phraseology and his elaborate dress, which only temporarily hides the fact that he is too poor to own a shirt. He embroiders his affair with the country wench, Jaquenetta, and almost convinces himself that it is a *grande amour* in the tradition of King Cophetua and the Beggar Maid of the old ballads.

Costard (KOS-turd), a rustic clown. He is fascinated by all the extravagant language he hears and takes great pleasure in using the long words of Armado and Berowne and the Latinisms of Holofernes and Sir Nathaniel.

Moth, Don Adriano's impudent page, who impishly taunts his master.

Holofernes (hol-uh-FUR-neez), the village schoolmaster, an incurable pedant. He prides himself on the excellence of his Latin and the precision of his pronunciation.

Sir Nathaniel, the curate, who admires Holofernes and joins him in snubbing their less learned fellow citizens, such as Costard and Dull, for their ignorance.

Dull, the constable. He can make no sense of the Latinate effusions of Holofernes and Sir Nathaniel and clings to his facts.

Jaquenetta (jak-eh-NEHT-uh), a country girl who is much admired by Don Adriano.

LOVING

Author: Henry Green (Henry Vincent Yorke, 1905-1973)
First published: 1945
Genre: Novel

Locale: Ireland
Time: During World War II
Plot: Domestic

Mrs. Tennant, the owner of a mansion in Ireland. She is a vague woman. Though she loses a valuable ring, she does not blame her servants, for she realizes she is forgetful.

Charley Raunce, Mrs. Tennant's English footman, who aspires to be the butler. Immediately upon the death of old Eldon, the longtime butler, Raunce acquires the household account book, secures Mrs. Tennant's agreement, and assumes the butler's authority in the servants' quarters. He loves Edith, one of the maids, and finds that she loves him too. He is content to remain in Ireland, safe from service in World War II, until he realizes that he is missing out on the excitement and satisfaction of aiding in the war effort. He decides to return to England, and he and Edith elope.

Edith, an upstairs maid in love with Raunce. It is she who twice finds Mrs. Tennant's ring and sees to its return. She elopes with Raunce to England.

Kate, another upstairs maid.

Mrs. Burch, the caustic housekeeper, in charge of Edith and Kate.

Mrs. Jack Tennant, Mrs. Tennant's daughter-in-law. Her love affair with Captain Davenport scandalizes the servants' quarters.

Captain Davenport, one of Mrs. Tennant's neighbors. He is found one morning by Edith in bed with Mrs. Jack Tennant.

Albert, Raunce's assistant. He leaves Mrs. Tennant's service because he thinks his employer suspects he might have stolen the ring that disappears. He returns to England and becomes an aerial gunner.

Jack Tennant, Mrs. Tennant's son, on military duty in England. When his mother and wife leave Ireland to visit him, the servants are upset at being left on their own in the mansion and almost desert their duties.

THE LOWER DEPTHS
(Na dne)

Author: Maxim Gorky (Aleksey Maksimovich Peshkov, 1868-1936)
First published: 1902
Genre: Drama

Locale: Russia
Time: Late nineteenth century
Plot: Naturalism

Mikhail Kostilyoff (mih-hah-IHL kohs-tih-LYOHF), the greedy and corrupt landlord of the flophouse in which the characters live and the action takes place. Suspicious of his wife, he trails her constantly. A superstitious hypocrite, he says pious platitudes and then raises the rent on Kleshtch, an impoverished tenant. He cowers before Pepel, to whom he owes money for stolen goods, and he bullies his sister-in-law, Natasha. No one misses him in the slightest when he is killed during a brawl.

Vassilisa Karpovna (vah-sih-LIH-sah kahr-POHV-nah), his wife, a malicious woman who cuckolds Kostilyoff in an affair with Pepel. Plotting her husband's death, she tries to involve Pepel by offering him Natasha. She is intensely jealous of Natasha, however, and whips the girl at every opportunity. When her husband is killed, Vassilisa readily turns Pepel over to the police, but both Pepel and Natasha accuse her of complicity in the crime, and she sits in jail as the play closes.

Natasha (nah-TAH-shah), Vassilisa's sister, a decent, pretty girl who is little more than a servant in Kostilyoff's flophouse.

She yearns for dignity but despairs at her hopeless position. When Pepel offers to take her away, she is hesitant. Natasha later gets the impression that Kostilyoff's death was premeditated by Pepel, and she goes into a fit of hysterics. She disappears after her release from the hospital where she was taken after being beaten by Vassilisa.

Vaska Pepel (VAHS-kah PEH-pehl), called **Vassily** (vah-SIH-lih), a young thief burdened by his past and his relationship with Vassilisa. He hopes to overcome his squalor by beginning a new life with Natasha. Vaska is clever and spirited, and although he rejects Vassilisa's murderous proposal, his good qualities come to nothing when he angrily knocks Kostilyoff down during a brawl that starts after Vassilisa savagely beats Natasha.

Luka (LOO-kah), an old traveler without a passport. A gentle, compassionate liar, he comforts the others by subscribing to their pathetic dreams of wholeness and dignity. Recognizing the savagery of truth, Luka prefers the misleading aspects of the imagination. In some measure, everyone is touched by his presence, but few are changed by it. In the confusion that surrounds Kostilyoff's death, Luka disappears.

Satine (sah-TIHN), a cynical young cardsharp and jailbird. At once shrewd and easygoing, Satine provides the final comment on Luka's personality and influence. Men like Luka, he says, are significant only because people are weak and need lies; nevertheless, he admits that Luka served as a kind of purgative.

Andrei Kleshtch (an-DRAY klehshch), a down-and-out locksmith who holds his fellows in contempt. Unable to bear his wife's dying, he goes out to get drunk. After her death, he succumbs to fits of anger and torpor, but he ends by achieving fellowship with the other tenants.

Anna Kleshtch (AHN-nah), his wife. On the verge of death, she cannot accept the notion of a just afterlife. Luka tries to comfort her before she dies.

The actor, a nameless, alcoholic, and verbose man who dreams of taking the cure. He gets encouragement from Luka, but after Luka disappears, he is unable to maintain his self-respect. In the end, he hangs himself.

The baron, a poseur and cardsharp who pathetically boasts of his family's past wealth and nobility. He obtains satisfaction by ridiculing the dreams of Nastya, the prostitute who supports him.

Nastya (NAH-styah), a prostitute who reads sentimentally romantic novels, wishes for a fatal love affair, respects Luka's compassion, and adds to the general bickering in the tenement.

Bubnoff (boob-NOHF), an ill-natured capmaker, ignorant and sardonic, who has made a place for himself in the loose camaraderie of the flophouse.

Abram Miedviedieff (ah-BRAHM mehd-VEH-dehf), Vassilisa's uncle, a mediocre, seedily respectable policeman who pesters Luka about his passport, hopes to arrest Vaska Pepel for thievery, and explains away such matters as the gossip about Vassilisa and Vaska, Kostilyoff's activities as a receiver of stolen goods, and Vassilisa's cruel treatment of Natasha by saying that these are family affairs. He leaves the police and takes to drink after his marriage to Kvashnya, a street vendor.

Kvashnya (kvah-shnyah), a sharp-tongued, boisterous seller of dumplings and meat pies. In her rough way, she is kind to Anna and tries to give food to the dying woman. Although she claims that she was overjoyed when her first husband died and that she will not be bothered with another, she marries Miedviedieff, the policeman, and bullies him with tongue-lashings and beatings.

Alyoshka (a-LYEW-shkah), a reckless, happy-go-lucky young shoemaker. When he is drunk, he lies down in the middle of the street and plays gay tunes on his concertina.

Hassan (HAHS-ahn), a Tatar porter. His hand is crushed while he is at work, and he is afraid that amputation may be necessary.

Krivoy Zob (krih-VOY zohb), Hassan's friend and fellow porter.

LOYALTIES

Author: John Galsworthy (1867-1933)
First published: 1922
Genre: Drama

Locale: London, England
Time: Early 1920's
Plot: Social criticism

Captain Ronald Dancy, D.S.O., retired, an officer who thrived on the excitement of war and languishes on the placidity of peace. After creating his own excitement with horses and women, he gets himself into trouble by stealing some money from a house guest while he himself is a guest. His friends stand by him against the accusation of the man who has lost the money. In the end, however, it is clear that he is guilty. When the police come to arrest him, he goes to his room and shoots himself.

Ferdinand de Levis, a prosperous Jew who has risen to wealth by degrees, having started very modestly. He sells for a thousand pounds a horse Dancy has given him, and Dancy steals the money. De Levis is unpopular with the set at the house where he and Dancy are guests. He shows poor form by openly accusing Dancy of theft before his friends. When Dancy drops his suit for defamation of character against

de Levis, the latter is willing to let bygones be bygones.

Mabel Dancy, Dancy's wife, who is loyal to him even after she discovers that he is a thief.

Jacob Twisden, Dancy's attorney, who is tough and straightforward. He discovers that Dancy did indeed take the money and advises him to drop his suit against de Levis.

Charles Winsor, Dancy and de Levis' host at Meldon Court, where the theft takes place.

Paolio Ricardos, an Italian wine merchant whose daughter has been intimate with Dancy. Ricardos threatens to expose Dancy if he does not provide for the daughter. To get the money to pay Ricardos, Dancy steals the thousand pounds from de Levis.

General Canynge, Dancy's superior officer. When it becomes apparent that Dancy has stolen the money, he offers Dancy a billet in the Spanish war.

LU ANN HAMPTON LAVERTY OBERLANDER

Author: Preston Jones (1936-1979)
First published: 1976
Genre: Drama

Locale: Bradleyville, West Texas
Time: 1953, 1963, and 1973
Plot: Naturalism

Lu Ann Hampton Laverty Oberlander, a typical but especially pretty and popular girl at the high school in Bradleyville, Texas. Although Lu Ann later becomes a hairdresser, as a

teenager, she hates school and cannot wait to get out of school and preferably out of the state. She has no concrete plans for marriage or a career, however, and is mainly interested in having fun. After her brother, Skip Hampton, introduces her to his army buddy Dale Laverty, Lu Ann marries him, hoping for a more exciting life. They move to San Angelo and then to Snyder, but then she is left alone in their trailer house for weeks at a time while he is out on the road. After Dale leaves Lu Ann and their daughter, Charmaine, Lu Ann moves back to Bradleyville to live with her mother. She works as a hairdresser until she meets Corky in Red Grover's bar. They are married only a short time before Corky is killed in an accident, leaving Lu Ann a widow in her late thirties. She ends up once again living in her mother's house but now cares for her invalid mother, despite others' suggestions that the old woman be put in a hospital. Driving a Howdy Wagon in Big Spring, Lu Ann dwells on her happier past but exhibits no self-pity or regrets.

Skip Hampton, Lu Ann's older brother, a gas station attendant and veteran of the Korean War. Despite the fact that Skip never got closer than sixty miles to the front, he boasts about his bravery in battle. Always looking for an easy and quick way to become rich as a young man, Skip spends much of his time drinking. He never marries and lives with his mother and his sister. Skip attempts suicide by cutting his throat with a broken beer bottle in Red Grover's bar. At the age of forty-four, he is already a gray-haired, shaky man, one whom Lu Ann cannot trust with pocket money for fear he will spend it on alcohol.

Billy Bob Wortman, Lu Ann's high school boyfriend, later a successful preacher in Kansas City. Tall and lanky, Billy Bob was a star on the high school basketball team but discovered that he was not good enough to play in college. Billy Bob is devoutly religious and a bit too straitlaced for Lu Ann. He visits Lu Ann and her mother in 1973.

Dale Laverty, a truck driver, Lu Ann's first husband and the father of Charmaine Laverty. Dale served with Skip in the Korean War. His goal is to drive a truck, find a wife, and live in a house trailer so that he can feel free to move at any time. When he comes home drunk one night, Lu Ann throws him out, and he never comes back.

Corky Oberlander, a surveyor for the highway department. As part of his position, Corky inspects dirt, a job he takes very seriously. He picks up Lu Ann at Red Grover's bar and later becomes her second husband. He is killed in a collision between his truck and a road machine.

Claudine Hampton, a practical nurse, Lu Ann and Skip's mother. In the first act, she is a heavyset woman in her early forties, and her hair is grayish blonde; by the third act, it is totally white. She frequently warns Lu Ann that her high school days will be the happiest years of her life. She worries about Lu Ann's lack of plans for the future, but she worries more about Skip's drinking. During the final act, Claudine is a stroke victim, paralyzed, confined to a wheelchair, and unable to speak. She is patiently cared for at home by Lu Ann.

Charmaine Laverty, the daughter of Lu Ann and her first husband, Dale Laverty. Spoiled and shallow, she is disrespectful to her mother and her uncle.

— *Lou Thompson*

LUCIEN LEUWEN

Author: Stendhal (Marie-Henri Beyle, 1783-1842)
First published: 1855, 1894
Genre: Novel

Locale: France
Time: The 1830's
Plot: Psychological

Lucien Leuwen (lew-SYAH[N] lew-VAH[N]), the hero of this unfinished novel. The son of a rich banker, he is expelled from school for expressing mild republican leanings, and he becomes an officer in a regiment of lancers going to maintain order at Nancy. There he falls in love with a wealthy, aristocratic widow, but he is tricked into leaving her. Obtaining a government post in Paris through his father's influence, he is successful until he is disillusioned because of a love affair. On his father's death, he insists on full payment to creditors and salvages only a modest income for himself and his mother. Given an embassy appointment, he is only mildly melancholy for his lost love.

Bathilde de Chasteller (bah-TEELD deh shas-tehl-LAY), a beautiful, aristocratic widow, Lucien's true love. The aristo-

cratic young men of the town are afraid that he will marry her and take her and her money away.

Dr. du Poirier (dew pwahr-YAY), a physician and the leader of the monarchist set in Nancy. He tricks Lucien into leaving Bathilde by making him think that her several days' illness is confinement to childbed.

Monsieur Leuwen, Lucien's father. Charming and wealthy, he is ambitious both for his son and for himself. Powerful enough to dictate who shall be in the Cabinet, he arranges to have a fatuous man given a post in exchange for his wife's becoming Lucien's mistress.

Madame Grandet (grahn-DAY), a beautiful and ambitious woman. "Bought" for Lucien, she comes to love him. Learning the truth, however, he is greatly upset and leaves Paris.

LUCINDA BRAYFORD

Author: Martin Boyd (1893-1972)
First published: 1946
Genre: Novel

Locale: Melbourne, London, and southern France
Time: Mid-1800's to the 1940's
Plot: Family

Lucinda Brayford, a rich "Anglo-Australian" from Melbourne. Lucinda's story begins when, as a beautiful and fatuous young woman in snobbish Melbourne society, she en-

snares and marries an English nobleman. As the years pass and the events of the twentieth century bear on her, Lucinda evolves from a foolish romantic into a pragmatist but loses none of the snobbishness and false values that have shaped her pointless life. Lucinda's doings form the core of the novel, and all the other characters revolve around her.

Hugo Brayford, Lucinda's husband, an English gentleman. Hugo emerges as a stereotypical British aristocrat: handsome and gallant, shallow and idle, doing nothing except hunting and socializing. His long-standing affair with another woman and the war injury that leaves his face deformed strongly affect the way Lucinda's outlook on life develops.

Frederick Vane, Lucinda's father, a successful Australian businessman. The brusque, middle-aged, nondescript Vane typifies upstart colonials as seen through British eyes. His obsession with money and social climbing help to determine not only Lucinda's loveless marriage but also her questionable values.

Julie Vane, Frederick's wife and Lucinda's mother. A social climber who doggedly sets out to re-create British social life in Australia, Julie is an attractive, likable, and sometimes comic woman as she exhibits her Anglo-Australian snobbery and pretensions. She helps to send her daughter on a false course that leaves Lucinda unfulfilled as a woman.

Arthur Brayford, Hugo's eldest brother. Although he holds the family title, Arthur lacks his brother's surface charm and looks. He develops into one of the few characters to appear sure of himself, seem satisfied with what he has made of his life, and assume responsibility for others—all in opposition to Lucinda's selfishness and disillusionment.

Paul Brayford, Hugo's elder brother. Paul, eccentric and tedious as a young man, even more so when older, is generally undistinguished and somewhat crabbed in appearance. His interminable pronouncements on the superiority of the British aristocracy, on art, and on the downfall of Western civilization serve to highlight Lucinda's moral and spiritual disintegration.

Marian Brayford, Arthur's wife. Like her husband, she typifies the British gentry who live anachronistic lives on their decaying estates. Marian, a plain woman in appearance, is solid, outspoken, and confident of her place as the lady of the manor. She is the antithesis to the would-be aristocrat Lucinda.

Tony, an early admirer of Lucinda. In his twenties when Lucinda develops a crush on him, Tony—pretentious, arty, frivolous, and almost pretty in appearance—is soon banished by her parents, who consider him unsuitable as a potential husband. Years later, he reappears in Lucinda's life, an aging and feckless provincial from Australia on the grand tour of Europe.

Pat Lanfranc, Lucinda's lover. He is a good-looking young army officer from an Irish family and is far more sensitive than Lucinda's husband. When Hugo dies, Pat refuses to marry Lucinda, thus all but extinguishing her illusions.

Stephen, Lucinda's son. Possessing a romantic sensibility and a delicate nature, he can face neither the failure of his marriage nor the rigors of service in World War II. He mopes about, fades, then dies in his early twenties. Although devastated by his death, Lucinda manages to rekindle—at least for the moment—her own flagging sense of life as she listens to the King's Chapel choir that her son loved.

— *Robert L. Ross*

THE LUCK OF GINGER COFFEY

Author: Brian Moore (1921-   )
First published: 1960
Genre: Novel

Locale: Montreal, Canada
Time: January, 1956
Plot: Domestic realism

James Francis "Ginger" Coffey, an unemployed Irish immigrant to Canada. A large, red-haired, thirty-nine-year-old with a full mustache, he is a well-meaning but unrealistically optimistic ne'er-do-well who affects the jaunty appearance of a Dublin squire, exuding charm and blarney. Essentially good at heart but without personal insight, he is irresponsible and thoughtless, habitually evading the truth, rationalizing away his shortcomings, and blaming others for his failures. Having left Ireland and a series of disappointing jobs, he settles in Montreal, expecting to find fame and fortune despite his general lack of qualifications. After a few months, his initial scheme fails, and he finds himself without money or job prospects and in the middle of a marital crisis, the result of fifteen years of inflated dreams, empty promises, and chronic prevarication. Caught in his own web of exaggerations, half-truths, and lies, he is forced to swallow his pride, confront the reality of his existence, and reevaluate his relationships with his wife and daughter. Circumstances and his conscious attempts to be more realistic, responsible, and self-sacrificing result in a clearer view of himself and his possibilities, as well as a reconciliation with his estranged wife.

Veronica (Vera) Coffey, Ginger's wife. A tall, dark-haired, attractive thirty-five-year-old, she is angry at Ginger and tired of being let down and taken for granted. Flattered and tempted by Gerry's offer of love and a new life, she leaves Ginger, finds a job, changes her hairstyle, and assumes a new attitude of independence. Concerned for her daughter Paulie, she maintains contact with Ginger. When Gerry refuses to help Ginger avoid a possible prison sentence, she is shocked; questioning the nature of Gerry's desire for her, she decides that she could not love him and returns to the chastened Ginger.

Pauline (Paulie) Coffey, Ginger's fourteen-year-old daughter. By turns selfish or loving, and oblivious or caring, Pauline is in a difficult period of transition. With loyalties divided between her quarreling parents and wanting to pursue her own interests free of supervision, she chooses to live with her overworked father. When Ginger disapproves of her behavior and choice of friends, she threatens to run off with her disreputable-looking older boyfriend, Bruno. Their recognition of her obvious potential for trouble helps reunite her parents.

Gerald (Gerry) Grosvenor, a successful political cartoonist and Veronica's would-be lover. A tall, neat, talkative, and popular thirty-year-old, he is the Coffeys' closest acquaintance in Canada and has been secretly in love with Veronica since their first meeting. He helps Ginger (who thinks of him as adolescent) get a job at the *Tribune* and later challenges him with his emotional and wholehearted fight to win Veronica.

G. E. MacGregor, the managing editor of the *Tribune*. A pale, thin, tough, tyrannical old Scot, he is feared and disliked by his employees, especially his nonunionized and exploited proofreaders. Quick to detect the falsehoods of others, he makes promises he has no intention of keeping.

Warren K. Wilson, an itinerant worker, a former delivery-man for the Tiny Ones diaper service. Approaching middle age, he is an avid follower of correspondence courses on self-improvement and dreams of a glamorous life as a magazine photographer.

William O'Brien (Billy) Davis, a proofreader at the *Tribune*. A white-goateed, frail, seventy-two-year-old who emigrated from Ireland at the age of twenty, he is ill and living in poverty, trying to subsist on a low-paying job that he is about to lose.

Fox, a proofreader at the *Tribune*, in charge of the night shift. Physically handicapped, intelligent, and cynical, he leads Coffey and the others on drinking bouts, despite having been a vagrant institutionalized for alcoholism a few years earlier.

A. K. Brott, the president of Tiny Ones diaper service. A testy, intense, hardworking entrepreneur, he believes in Ginger and offers to make him his personal assistant, thus renewing Ginger's faith in Canada and himself.

Stanley Mountain, the delivery depot manager for Tiny Ones. A fat, white-haired former Royal Canadian Air Force transport officer, he tries to maintain a military-type operation at the diaper service.

Michel Beaulieu, the five-year-old son of Ginger's landlord. He often seeks out Ginger for companionship and affection, which he returns when Ginger feels most alone.

— *Douglas Rollins*

LUCKY JIM

Author: Kingsley Amis (1922-1995)
First published: 1954
Genre: Novel

Locale: An English provincial college
Time: Shortly after World War II
Plot: Social satire

James (Jim) Dixon, a first-year lecturer in history at an English provincial college. Jim comes from a lower-middle-class background, which puts him at a disadvantage with the comparatively well-to-do Professor Welch, upon whom he is dependent for renewal of his lecturing contract for another year. Jim has little interest in his subject, medieval history. Instead, he likes attractive women and drinking, interests that are genuine and unpretentious but unlikely to gain him employment.

Margaret Peel, a sour, neurotic senior lecturer at the same college who is involved with Jim. The relationship is not a happy one. Margaret uses her emotional instability as a means of blackmailing Jim and others into meeting her needs, even going so far as to fake a suicide attempt. She seems to be incapable of acting spontaneously, and in this and many other regards she is shown to be in direct contrast to Christine Callaghan.

Professor "Neddy" Welch, the inane but menacing figure who represents everything about the arts that Jim both fears and detests. His dominant trait is obliviousness, which sometimes results in actions that appear to be malicious. His interests in music and folk culture may be mere poses intended to establish status, and he behaves as if he were at a prestigious school such as Oxford rather than the second-rate provincial college where he actually teaches. Welch is pedantic, absent-minded, and clumsy around machinery, but also cunning. He holds Jim's future in his hands and proposes Jim for the "Merrie England" speech at the college festival, a proposal that he knows Jim dare not refuse.

Bertrand Welch, Professor Welch's son, a painter. Bertrand shares many faults with his father but exercises them more aggressively. He dresses and acts the part of the bohemian artist (even to the point of wearing a beret) but is actually a bully and a shameless social climber, pretending to carry on an affair with Christine in the hope of landing a job with her uncle, Julius Gore-Urquhart. Like his father, he is a living rebuke to the cultural values he claims to hold.

Julius Gore-Urquhart, a well-to-do patron of the arts and an astute judge of character. Gore-Urquhart is looking for a private secretary but realizes immediately that Bertrand Welch will not do. Instead, he chooses Jim. Although Jim lacks the qualifications for the job, he also lacks what Gore-Urquhart calls the "disqualifications." Gore-Urquhart is not above speeding the development of certain situations and is partly responsible for Jim's drunkenness during his disastrous "Merrie England" speech.

Christine Callaghan, Julius Gore-Urquhart's niece, an attractive, unpretentious young woman. Jim is attracted to her immediately not only because of her looks but also because she clearly does not share the sham values of the Welches. Her defining moment comes when she good-naturedly helps Jim hide damage, caused by his smoking in bed, to bedclothes and furniture in the Welch home. In contrast, Margaret uses the situation to manipulate Jim even further.

— *Grove Koger*

LUCY

Author: Jamaica Kincaid (Elaine Potter Richardson, 1949-   )
First published: 1990
Genre: Novel

Locale: An unnamed city in the United States
Time: Late 1960's
Plot: Psychological realism

Lucy Josephine Potter, the protagonist, a young woman who has left her home in the West Indies to work as a live-in child care provider at the home of Mariah and Lewis. She finds the United States to be very different from her former home and experiences homesickness at first. Although she takes excellent care of Lewis and Mariah's four little girls, she is restless, rebellious, and intent on acquiring her independence by separating herself from her mother, both physically and emotionally. She cannot forgive her mother for denying her the ambitious future her parents planned for her brothers. Even though Lucy has intimate relations with men, she does not allow herself to fall in love with any of them.

Mariah, Lucy's employer, an attractive, wealthy white woman who genuinely likes Lucy but does not understand her. She tries to make friends with Lucy and does not comprehend the barrier their separate histories place between them. Mariah has always had a pampered, easy life, so she expects happiness. Believing that her husband Lewis loves her, she does not handle the disintegration of her marriage very well, nor does she realize the cause of it.

Lewis, Mariah's husband, a wealthy lawyer. He falls in love with his wife's best friend, Dinah. Kind to Lucy and the children, he manipulates Mariah into believing that she has asked for the divorce.

Dinah, Mariah's envious best friend and Lewis' lover. She treats Lucy with condescension.

Peggy, Lucy's best friend, a woman of Irish extraction who lives with her parents and works at the motor vehicle registry. Peggy and Lucy seem to have nothing in common, but their friendship is strong. Peggy introduces Lucy to Paul, although Peggy disapproves of him. Eventually, Peggy and Lucy share an apartment.

Hugh, Dinah's twenty-two-year-old brother, who has traveled to Africa and Asia. He is Lucy's lover during the summer when the family vacations at Mariah's old summer home. Because of his experience in other countries, he appeals to Lucy, although she does not love him.

Paul, an artist with whom Lucy has an affair. He helps her find employment after she leaves her child care job. Lucy is fond of him but desires no commitment. He finally becomes Peggy's lover.

Maude Quick, one of Lucy's prudish, mean-spirited relatives. She lives in the United States and brings news of Lucy's father's death. Lucy has always intensely disliked her because she has been held up as a role model for Lucy.

Louisa,

Jane,

May, and

Miriam, Mariah and Lewis' children. Lucy is fond of all the girls, but Miriam is her favorite.

Timothy Simon, a photographer who aspires to greatness in his field but who forces himself to photograph food for the cooking sections of magazines in order to make a living. He hires Lucy as his receptionist.

Lucy's mother, who appears only in Lucy's memories but nevertheless continues to influence Lucy's thoughts and behavior. She has a strong personality, loves her daughter, and does not understand why Lucy refuses to answer her letters.

— *Cheri Louise Ross*

LUCY GAYHEART

Author: Willa Cather (1873-1947)
First published: 1935
Genre: Novel

Locale: Haverford, Nebraska, and Chicago, Illinois
Time: Christmas, 1901, to Winter, 1902-1903, and 1927
Plot: Psychological realism

Lucy Gayheart, a music student in Chicago. She is a bright, willful, and talented young pianist, the darling of her hometown of Haverford, Nebraska. She is particularly prized by her father, Jacob Gayheart, and the heir to the local bank, Howard Gordon. While studying music under her mentor, Paul Auerbach, Lucy attends a recital by Clement Sebastian, a concert singer. Later, while working with Clement, Lucy falls in love with him, as both a man and an artist. Pleased and surprised to learn that he shares her feelings, although he has a wife in England, she lies to Howard Gordon that she and Sebastian have been lovers. In late spring, Sebastian leaves for a tour of Europe, and Lucy is devastated in September to hear that he has died in a boating accident. She returns to Haverford depressed, amid much curiosity and gossip, but tells no one her tale. Barely tolerated by her older sister, Pauline Gayheart, she is completely scorned by Howard Gordon, who has married another woman. After an argument with Pauline in the middle of winter, she walks down to an old ice-skating area, unaware that while she was away in Chicago, the riverbed shifted and that the area is no longer safe for skating. The ice breaks, she falls in, her feet get caught on a log, and she drowns.

Howard Gordon, the son of a Haverford banker and a businessman in his own right. Wealthy, strong-willed, handsome, and accustomed to getting his own way, he decides—as he and Lucy are leaving Haverford after Christmas—that he will marry her. When he meets her in Chicago for the opera season, he proposes to her. Lucy refuses, exaggerating the nature of her relationship with Sebastian, and he walks out on her. Several weeks later, he marries Harriet Arkwright, a young heiress whom he had been courting but whom he does not love. When Lucy returns to Haverford, he ignores her as a means of punishing her, though he still feels deeply in love with her. He refuses to give her a ride when he passes her on his sleigh on a bitterly cold day and does not tell her that the old skating area is unsafe. Twenty-five years later, when Lucy's father dies, Howard is a successful businessman in his fifties, stuck in a loveless marriage. He still misses Lucy and still blames himself, though he has come to terms with his actions to some degree. Having held the mortgage on Jacob Gayheart's property, he becomes its sole owner. He leases it to a teller, Milton Chase, rent-free, with strict instructions that nothing must happen to a cement sidewalk in which Lucy left three footprints when she was a girl and

Howard had just moved to Haverford.

Clement Sebastian, a concert singer. Talented, middle-aged, and married to a wife in England, he finds himself falling in love with his young rehearsal accompanist, Lucy. He dies in a boating accident when his professional accompanist, James Mockford, grabs onto him in panic and takes them both down.

Pauline Gayheart, Lucy's unmarried older sister. Not unmusical herself, she was forced to be practical by her father's impractical nature and her mother's death. Pauline reared her sister, Lucy. It is as a result of a fight about money matters with Pauline, who is impatient with her sister's flightiness and self-absorption, that Lucy leaves to go skating and drowns. Pauline dies twenty years after Lucy and five years before their father.

Jacob Gayheart, a local watchmaker and band leader in Haverford. Happy and good-natured, but impractical, he doted on his daughter Lucy and encouraged her musical ability. Toward the end of his life, he becomes a fast friend and chess companion of Howard Gordon.

Paul Auerbach, Lucy's music teacher in Chicago. Less of a romantic than Sebastian, he tries to encourage Lucy to marry Howard Gordon. Lucy has intentions of returning to Chicago to give piano lessons for him when she dies.

James Mockford, Sebastian's professional accompanist, born poor. He is an ambitious man. Sebastian makes plans to replace him. It was as a result of treatment to his bad hip that a position as Sebastian's rehearsal accompanist opened up. Lucy views him as a grotesque, almost evil—if talented—man. Mockford grabs Sebastian in a headlock after their boat capsizes, drowning them both.

— *Thomas J. Cassidy*

THE LUSIADS
(Os Lusíadas)

Author: Luís de Camões (c. 1524-1580)
First published: 1572
Genre: Poetry

Locale: Europe, Africa, and Asia
Time: The fifteenth century
Plot: Epic

Vasco da Gama (VAHS-koh dah GAH-mah), a Portuguese sailor and explorer. He is chosen to head the expedition that first rounds Africa's Cape of Good Hope to find a sea route to Asia.

Jove (johv), the chief of the gods. He announces that the Fates have decreed that the Portuguese expedition shall succeed in its mission.

Venus, a goddess friendly to the Portuguese. She takes their side against Bacchus and helps them in their adventures. She saves them from storms and ambushes and provides them with a resting place on their way home. She gives da Gama a vision of Portugal's future greatness.

Mars, a god who sides with Venus on the side of the Portuguese.

Bacchus (BAK-uhs), the patron god of Asia. He tries to prevent the Portuguese from success in their expedition. He enlists the aid of Neptune in his efforts against them.

Veloso (veh-LOH-soh), one of da Gama's men. He explores part of Africa before rejoining the expedition.

The Spirit of the Cape of Good Hope, who appears to da Gama. The spirit says he was once a Titan named Adamastor. He has been made into a range of mountains forming the Cape of Good Hope for his pursuit of a nymph.

The king of Mombassa, an African monarch to whom da Gama relates his adventures and the history of Portugal up to that time.

The emperor of Malabar, an Asiatic monarch who welcomes the Portuguese to Asia and arranges for them to trade their goods for spices and other Oriental products.

Mercury, a god who guides the Portuguese to Mombassa.

Neptune, the god of the sea who, at the request of Bacchus, sends storms to destroy the ships of the Portuguese. Venus saves the ships.

THE LUTE
(Pi-pa ji)

Author: Gao Ming (c. 1303-c. 1370)
First published: 1367
Genre: Drama

Locale: Honan Province, China
Time: c. 200
Plot: Opera

Ts'ai Jung, a young scholar and native of Ch'en-liu. Recently married to a local girl, he is summoned to appear in Lo-yang to take the imperial examinations for the doctorate, or *chin-shih* degree. He goes, leaving his wife and elderly parents under the watchful eye of a neighbor, Grandfather Chang. In acquiring the degree, he ranks first, a superb feat. As a result, the emperor orders him to marry the prime minister's daughter and to take residence at the official's house. Unable to return to his first wife and to his parents, he remains ignorant that their area has fallen victim to famine. His first wife makes heroic efforts to care for her husband's parents until they eventually die of age and their sufferings. She then finds her husband and his second wife in Lo-yang, and she joins them in a happy trio. The fictional character of Ts'ai Jung was modeled on the historical scholar-official Ts'ai Yung, who as a youth was distinguished for his devotion to his parents and his love of study.

Chao Wu-niang, Ts'ai Jung's first wife. A native of Ch'en-liu, she is a beauty as well as a woman of the highest character. She is also the most important character in the drama and its real protagonist. Strong-minded and relatively independent, she is perfectly obedient to the Confucian rules for her behavior and has a filial heart. When her husband is far away from home for a number of years and famine strikes her area, she overcomes severe adversity to feed and minister to her aged in-laws. Before her husband left for the capital, she did not hesitate to remonstrate respectfully when she thought him wrong. She is not afraid to break the Confucian rules under certain circumstances to keep her in-laws alive. When they die, she buries them, although she requires financial help. Afterward, she journeys unchaperoned the many miles to the capital to find her husband. When she learns that he has taken a second wife, that does not faze her; she happily joins them to form a trio. The emperor commends them for their filial conduct.

Chang Ta-kung, a neighbor of the Ts'ai family in Ch'en-liu. After Father Ts'ai urges his son to seek a government career through the imperial examinations at Lo-yang, Chang agrees with the old man that the best form of filial piety is to bring fame and fortune to one's parents through success in the examinations and an official career. He tries to persuade young Ts'ai to do as his father wishes and promises to take care of the family while Ts'ai is absent. During the famine, Wu-niang does everything in her power to help her in-laws; however, after she obtains official grain for Ts'ai's parents, it is stolen from her. Chang intervenes and offers the family half of the grain he had obtained. When Mother Ts'ai dies, Chang pays her funeral expenses. When Father Ts'ai dies, Wu-niang again has no money. She cuts her hair and goes into the street to sell it. When she can find no buyer, Chang pays the father's funeral expenses. He is an exemplary good neighbor.

Father Ts'ai and

Mother Ts'ai, middle-class parents of modest means who have educated a brilliant son for an official career. When he is summoned to the capital to compete in the imperial examinations, he has the opportunity to become a *chin-shih* and thus be qualified to become a government official. Although he thinks that his filial piety requires him to give up such an ambition to remain in the presence of his aged parents, he finds that Father Ts'ai has a completely different idea. The son complies with

his father's wishes. In the absence of their son, the Ts'ais as well as Wu-niang suffer so terribly that their views change. Mother Ts'ai blames her husband for sending their son away to satisfy his own ambition. He, in turn, is disillusioned to the extent that when he becomes terminally ill, he bequeaths his staff to Chang Ta-kung and requests him to beat his son should he return home. Even Wu-niang questions the ethics of her husband's decision.

Mr. Niu, the prime minister (*Shou-hsiang*) of the realm and second father-in-law to Ts'ai Jung. Niu is proud of his wealth and power. He is also arrogant, straitlaced, autocratic, and bullheaded. Knowing that Niu's daughter has declared to her father that she will not marry any man other than a first winner in the imperial examinations, the emperor suggests that Niu marry his daughter to Ts'ai. The minister sends a matchmaker to negotiate the marriage with the young man. He declines the offer on the grounds that he is already married. The minister is enraged at Ts'ai's "impudence." Ts'ai responds by petitioning the emperor to allow him to decline the marriage and to resign his civil service position. His petition is denied. He is ordered to prepare for the wedding and to live with his new wife in her father's household.

Mistress Niu (Niu Hsiao-chieh), the prime minister's daughter, who becomes Ts'ai's second wife. She is a lover of nature's beauty and is romantically inclined. Highly disciplined, she is morally correct and is strict with the servants, but she is not lacking in sympathy with those who are less fortunate. She truly loves Ts'ai and is upset at Ts'ai's distress and depression. When she discovers her husband's secret, she chastises him for deserting his parents and wife. She proposes that they go together to visit his family in Ch'en-liu. When the prime minister learns what they propose to do, he is furious that they would use their time to help such poor and humble people. He soon realizes that his outburst was wrong. He decides to have the Ts'ai family brought to the capital and sends a messenger to Ch'en-liu to fetch them. Ts'ai's parents are dead by then, and Wu-niang has arrived at Lo-yang and become Mistress Niu's maid. When Mistress Niu learns that her maid is actually her husband's first wife, she realizes that he had too much integrity to divorce her. Eventually, the three live in harmony.

— *Richard P. Benton*

LUTHER

Author: John Osborne (1929-1994)
First published: 1961
Genre: Drama

Locale: Germany
Time: 1506-1530
Plot: Historical

Martin Luther, a brilliant university scholar, capable of considerable worldly success as a lawyer or political adviser to the powerful. He chooses instead to join the Roman Catholic order of the Eremites of St. Augustine. Physically unprepossessing, he is subject to severe attacks of constipation, which he attributes to his spiritual difficulties—also manifested in feverish nightmares—and deep depression. His spiritual excesses and complaints seem to other members of his order something of a joke, but he is deeply respected for his learning and his contribution to the reputation of the University of

Wittenberg, where he teaches. He is not satisfied by scholarship and is constantly questioning his own spiritual worth and the public practices of the Catholic Church. He is also a dangerously persuasive orator.

Hans, Martin's father, a miner, proud of his son's gifts but outspoken in his disappointment in Luther's choice of the church when so much could have been made of his gifts in the lay world. Although uneducated, he is not stupid, and he becomes a part owner of the mine in which he works. He is talkative, unawed by the clergy, and, though rather vulgar in argument, somewhat persuasive.

Brother Weinand, a monk friendly to Luther but determined to break him of his dramatic sense of sin. Educated in Latin and Greek but bearing his learning modestly, he recognizes the unusual intellectual gifts of Luther. He possesses a beautiful singing voice.

Lucas, Hans's miner friend, who often accompanies him in visiting Luther at the monastery. A sensible man, he is somewhat disappointed in Luther, having hoped that Luther might marry his daughter; he is therefore able to understand Hans's chagrin yet assuage Hans's anger at his son's folly.

John Tetzel, a Dominican famed for his persuasive oratory and his sale of indulgences to the public. He is in his late middle age, silver-haired, sophisticated, oratorically shrewd, and, on occasion, startlingly rude and witty. His success in taking enormous sums from an ignorant public precipitates Luther's public attack, and Tetzel is not loath to do something about it. Despite his vows, he takes a handsome salary for his services and supports a woman and two children.

Johann von Staupitz, the vicar general of the Augustinian Order, a man who, in late middle age, is quiet, gentle-voiced, and thoughtful. He respects Luther's gifts and understands his criticisms of the excesses of Roman Catholicism, but he knows the dangers of attacking the powers of the church. He advises, directs, and warns Luther in a straightforward and understanding manner.

Thomas de Vio, known as **Catejan**, the cardinal of San Sisto and general of the Dominican Order, a theologian and papal legate in Germany. Fifty years old, shrewd, tough, and capable of considerable political guile, he is often charming, but when Luther proves stubborn, he is quick to reveal an ability to be threatening.

The Knight, a professional soldier, tired, depressed, filthy, and weary of the military repercussions of the revolution sparked by Luther. He is aware of the implications of Luther's attack for the political world and scornful of Luther's refusal to support the peasants in their attempt to throw off their oppressors.

Katherine von Bora, a former nun, Luther's wife. She is in her twenties, big-boned, pleasant-looking, a good cook, and a thrifty housekeeper. She is the mother of Luther's child, Hans, and is a comfort to Luther in his times of travail.

— *Charles Pullen*

LYDIE BREEZE

Author: John Guare (1938-   )
First published: 1982
Genre: Drama

Locale: Nantucket Island
Time: 1895
Plot: Mythic

Lydie Hickman, the fifteen-year-old daughter of Joshua Hickman and Lydie Breeze Hickman. Highly sensitive and theatrical, Lydie has comically flighty ways that do not quite hide the emotional maelstrom underlying her adolescent psyche. Obsessed with her mother's suicide and embarrassed by her father's stint in prison, Lydie is worried that she will never become a woman because she has not yet begun to menstruate. She claims that she hates men in general and her father in particular, but in reality she yearns for adulthood, the attention of men, and a normal relationship with her father.

Joshua Hickman, Lydie's father, the widower of Lydie Breeze, a tired, broken man in his mid-fifties. Joshua fought in the Civil War, and after the war he attempted to form a utopian community with his wife and his best friends, Dan Grady and Amos Marsh. He now does little but drink rye whiskey and swim far out into the Atlantic Ocean. He is back from the prison term he served for accidentally killing Dan in a petty, drunken fight.

Jeremiah Grady, a highly successful actor and Dan Grady's son. In his late twenties, Jeremiah is unyieldingly serious and histrionic, partly because of the torment he feels over his difficult past and partly because his manner reflects a lifelong habit of adopting a role to compensate for being unsure of himself. At the age of thirteen, Jeremiah witnessed his father's death and was then seduced by Lydie Breeze, who infected Jeremiah with the syphilis Dan Grady had given her. Jeremiah travels from England to Nantucket to avenge his father's death but instead comes to a peace with his past and drowns himself with Beaty, his lover from adolescence.

Beaty, an Irish serving girl in her early thirties. She works for the Hickmans but is, in effect, a surrogate mother for Lydie Hickman. Feisty, independent, protective, and outwardly hostile toward men, Beaty has an enormous influence on the impressionable Lydie, fomenting the young girl's distrust of men. As a fifteen-year-old girl working for the Hickmans, Beaty was starved for affection and yearned for the kind of male attention commanded by Lydie Breeze. She gave her virginity to the equally young Jeremiah and contracted syphilis.

Gussie Hickman, Lydie's older sister, twenty-two years old, the secretary and mistress of Senator Amos Mason, an aspirant to the presidency of the United States. Gussie affects refinement, dressing in fine clothes and dropping names and places encountered during her travels, but betrays her antecedents with a coarse vocabulary. She chain-smokes and wheezes comically with severe asthma. Endearingly irreverent and verbally clever, she is also superficially addicted to the spotlights of power and prestige.

Jude Emerson, a young man close to Lydie's age who captures and bands birds for the federal government. He falls in love with Lydie.

Lucian Rock, an inventor who is going to Europe to sell his high-speed industrial sewing machine. Intense, poetic, and nattily dressed, Lucian takes Gussie to Europe after her romance with Amos Mason fails.

— *Terry Nienhuis*

LYSISTRATA
(Lysistratē)

Author: Aristophanes (c. 450-c. 385 B.C.E.)
First performed: 411 B.C.E.
Genre: Drama

Locale: Athens
Time: The period of the Peloponnesian War, fifth century B.C.E.
Plot: Satire

Lysistrata (li-SIHS-trah-tah), an idealistic Athenian woman who is not content to stand submissively by and witness the obvious waste that war brings to the land. In her effort to bring a permanent peace to Greece, she demonstrates qualities that mark her as one of the archetypal revolutionaries: relentless fervor, cunning, and intractability. In addition to the traits of a revolutionary, Lysistrata possesses a healthy supply of inimitable wit and humor, qualities lacking in the ordinary stage conception of a revolutionary. She reasons and persuades the women of Greece to cast their lots with her so that by simply refusing the men sexual satisfaction she can bring them to her terms: abolition of war and the relinquishment of the treasury to women. Amid the rollicking ribaldry, Lysistrata's plan to seize and occupy the Acropolis of Athens with her army of celibate women weathers a storm of protest, succeeds, and wrecks the framework of a society dominated by men.

Cleonice (klee-oh-NI-see), a lusty Athenian friend of Lysistrata. At first reluctant to go along with so devastating and sacrificing a plan, she eventually is browbeaten by Lysistrata into accepting the challenge to save Greece from the total ruin of war. She partakes of the solemn oath, binding herself to refrain from sharing the marriage bed with her husband. Constantly on hand, Cleonice adds much zest with ribald commentary and turns out to be one of Lysistrata's main supporters.

Myrrhine (mih-REE-nee), one of Lysistrata's captains, representing Anagyra. Just as the idealism of Lysistrata is wearing thin and the torment of self-denial is weakening the ranks of the women, Myrrhine's husband appears. Acting under orders from Lysistrata, she subjects him to unendurable, teasing torture. This episode is not only one of the play's funniest but also the point at which Lysistrata's strategy turns toward success.

Lampito (LAM-pih-toh), a woman of Sparta who agrees to participate in Lysistrata's plan. Her loyalty and resourcefulness bring success in that land. Lampito, typical of the Athenian's concept of Spartan women, is athletic, bold, and well-proportioned. A key figure throughout the play, she steps forward at the very inception of Lysistrata's plan to be the major seconding voice. Her example ensures the revolt of the women.

Cinesias (sih-NEE-see-uhs), the husband of Myrrhine. Exhibiting all symptoms of lust, he begs his wife to return to him.

A child, the infant son of Myrrhine and Cinesias, brought by his father in an attempt to bribe his mother into deserting the women's cause.

A magistrate, a pompous representative of law and order who seeks to treat the revolutionaries as silly housewives to be spanked and sent to their kitchens. Much to his chagrin, he discovers them in no mood to be so treated. After seeing his force of Scythian policemen rebuffed, and after being defeated completely by Lysistrata's determined female logic, he becomes the echo and image of the playwright's laughter at the ineffectuality of the law when pitted against organized femininity.

A Chorus of old men, who head the first unsuccessful attempt to dislodge the women from the Acropolis. They toil uphill with smoke faggots and engage in much humorous comment on the character of women in general. Their efforts are confined mostly to threats and ineffectual maneuvering as the women prove too much for them.

A Chorus of women, antagonists of the old men. The women establish a swift rapport with them, not only making their smoke faggots useless by soaking them but also besting them in a verbal exchange of ridicule and insult.

A Spartan herald, also suffering the pangs of thwarted love.

Spartan envoys, with whom the Athenian women conclude a treaty of peace.

M

M. C. HIGGINS, THE GREAT

Author: Virginia Hamilton (1936-)
First published: 1974
Genre: Novel

Locale: Near Harenton, Ohio, in the Cumberland Mountains
Time: The 1970's
Plot: Social realism

Mayo Cornelius (M. C.) Higgins, a black teenager. The eldest child in his family, M. C. has a strong sense of responsibility. He worries about the younger children, whom he supervises when his parents are at work; about his mother, whom he adores; and about his father, toward whom his feelings are ambivalent, combining respect and concern with anger. M. C. is athletic, a superb swimmer and a wrestler who will soon be able to defeat his father in their periodic tests of strength. He knows woodcraft and mountain lore. He also knows how to think for himself; despite his father's warnings, he has chosen a best friend from the feared Killburn clan.

Banina Higgins, M. C.'s mother, a beautiful and talented woman, the real center of the Higgins household. Banina

works as a housecleaner an hour's walk from her home. She is especially close to M. C.

Jones Higgins, M. C.'s father, a day laborer. A complex man, Jones is strict with his children, yet loving and playful. Born and reared in the mountains, Jones is determined to pass along to his children both his knowledge of nature and his love of the place where his family has lived for generations.

Ben Killburn, M. C.'s best friend, a member of an inbred family that, because of its reputed supernatural powers, is unjustly feared by other mountain people. Ben is loyal, quiet, and thoughtful. M. C. is influenced deeply by Ben's idealism and by his sense of the sacredness of nature.

— *Rosemary M. Canfield Reisman*

MA RAINEY'S BLACK BOTTOM

Author: August Wilson (1945-)
First published: 1985
Genre: Drama

Locale: A recording studio in Chicago, Illinois
Time: March, 1927
Plot: Psychological realism

Levee, the trumpet player in the band of black musicians that accompanies blues singer Ma Rainey. Not well educated but stylish, flamboyant, brash, energetic, and ambitious, Levee is in his early thirties and is the youngest of the musicians. Scorning the conservative musical style favored by Ma Rainey, Levee plays in a new, improvisational jazz style and dreams about forming his own band. He offers his own arrangements and songs to Sturdyvant, the white owner of the run-down Chicago recording studio, but Ma insists on her own arrangements. Anxious to please Sturdyvant but insistent that he is not cowed by whites, Levee is a study in growing anger and frustration, quarreling constantly with Ma and the rest of his fellow musicians during the recording session that constitutes the action of the play. Levee's frustration culminates in his fatal stabbing of Toledo, another member of the band.

Ma Rainey, the most popular black blues singer of her day, called the Mother of the Blues. A short, heavy woman, dressed opulently in a full-length fur coat, matching hat, emerald-green dress, matching headband, and several strands of pearls, Ma carries herself with a royal air, but, like any black person in Chicago in the 1920's, she is a second-class citizen. She is

unable, for example, to get a white cab driver to take her to the recording studio. Consciously playing the prima donna, she makes arbitrary demands of her white manager and the white studio owner as a way of compensating for her ultimate powerlessness. She appears unaware that her style of music is falling out of favor.

Toledo, the band's piano player and the only member of the band who can read. In his middle fifties, Toledo is self-taught and the most educated and philosophical of the musicians. He lectures the confused and apathetic band members on African history.

Sturdyvant, the white owner of the recording studio, concerned mainly with profit and insensitive to black performers, preferring to deal with them as little as possible.

Irvin, Ma Rainey's white manager, tall, corpulent, and proud of his knowledge of and ability to deal with African Americans. Irvin attempts to keep Ma and Sturdyvant satisfied at the same time but usually fails to satisfy either one.

Cutler, the leader of the band, the guitar and trombone player, and the most sensible of the musicians. In his middle fifties, Cutler is cautious and even unimaginative personally and musically. He is not introspective but tries at all times to defuse hostilities and keep everyone's attention on the business at hand.

Slow Drag, the bass player in the band, in his middle fifties, deceptively intelligent but bored by life. Sporting a large, wicked smile, Slow Drag plays with startling ease, gracefully incorporating underlying African rhythms in his music.

Dussie Mae, Ma's lesbian lover, a young, dark-skinned, sensual black woman, dressed provocatively in a fur jacket and a skin-tight canary-yellow dress.

Sylvester, Ma's nephew, a huge, black Arkansas country boy. Dressed uncomfortably in a new suit and coat, Sylvester stutters in almost every sentence he speaks. Ma has brought him to the recording session to do the voice introduction to her song, "Ma Rainey's Black Bottom."

A policeman, who brings Ma to the recording studio to check her identity after the automobile accident and the fight with the taxi driver.

— *Terry Nienhuis*

THE MABINOGION

Author: Unknown
First transcribed: The twelfth and thirteenth centuries
Genre: Novel

Locale: Arthurian Britain, primarily Wales
Time: The Middle Ages
Plot: Folklore

Pwyll (PEW-uhl), prince of Dyved. To redeem himself after an attempt to steal a deer, he agrees to change places and appearances with the chieftain who has caught him in the act and to slay the chieftain's enemy after a year's time. His contract fulfilled, he returns home, where he sees the beautiful lady Rhiannon ride by, subdues her suitor, and marries her.

Rhiannon (REE-ah-non), Pwyll's wife.

Pryderi (prih-DEH-ree), the son of Pwyll and Rhiannon.

Kicva (KIHK-vah), Pryderi's wife.

Bendigeid Vran (behn-DIH-geed vran), the son of Llyr and king of the Island of the Mighty. While making war on the Irish because of their treatment of Matholwch and Branwen, he is killed by a poisoned arrow.

Branwen, Bendigeid Vran's sister, who is given in marriage to Matholwch. She dies of sorrow when her brother is killed in battle.

Matholwch (mah-THOH-lewkh), king of Ireland, Branwen's husband.

Manawydan (mah-now-IH-dan), Bendigeid Vran's brother. With Pryderi, another survivor of the Irish war, he settles on land that is magically desolated until it is learned that the source of the curse is a churchman avenging an ancient insult.

King Math, the son of Mathonwy.

Goewin (GEE-wihn), King Math's footmaiden, raped by Gwydion and Gilvaethwy.

Gwydion (GWIH-dih-yon), King Math's warrior, and

Gilvaethwy (gihl-VAY-thew), his brother, turned by King Math into animals for three years as punishment for their rape of Goewin.

Llew Llaw Gyffes (tlih tlow GIH-fehs), Gwydion's favorite son, for whom King Math creates an elfwife, Blodeuwedd.

Blodeuwedd (blon-DEW-wehth), Llew Llaw Gyffe's elfwife. For her faithlessness, she is turned into an owl.

Macsen Wledig (WLEH-dihg), the emperor of Rome, who dreams of a beautiful maiden and, after a long search, finds her just as she appeared in the dream.

Lludd (tlihth), king of Britain. His people ravaged by three plagues, he seeks the help of his brother, Llevelys, who offers three successful remedies.

Llevelys (tleh-VEH-lihs), Lludd's wise brother, king of France.

Kilhwch (KIH-lewkh), King Arthur's knight. By dint of cunning, magic, and the help of his fellow knights, he wins Olwen from Ysbaddaden.

Olwen (OHL-wehn), Ysbaddaden's beautiful daughter, who is won by Kilhwch.

Ysbaddaden (ihs-bah-THAH-dehn), a crafty giant, Olwen's father.

King Arthur, the legendary British leader.

Rhonabwy (roh-NAH-bew), a dreamer who, in sleep, finds himself in King Arthur's court.

Owain (OH-win), a knight. He overcomes the Knight of the Fountain, marries his widow, and assumes his title.

Peredur (peh-REH-dihr), a matchless knight at King Arthur's court.

Gerint (GEH-rihnt), King Arthur's knight. Spending more time with his wife than in knightly pursuits, he finds himself obliged to prove to his people his strength and valor.

Enid, Gerint's wife.

MAC FLECKNOE

Author: John Dryden (1631-1700)
First published: 1682
Genre: Poetry

Locale: London, England
Time: Late 1670's
Plot: Mock-heroic

Flecknoe, the monarch of dullness, who is prepared to abdicate and does so in the course of the action. His character is derived from that of Richard Flecknoe, an obscure seventeenth century English poet known for his insipid verses, for publishing his works at his own expense, and for his modest claims about them. His two dramas that were produced proved to be failures on stage. Like Shadwell, he was also a lute

player. In the satire, Flecknoe fills the role of both monarch and prophet, the prophetic role being appropriate because the real Flecknoe was a Catholic priest. His speeches, which consist of more than 120 verses, show him to be good-humored and enthusiastic about his decision to abdicate and his hopes for Shadwell's reign. His undisguised and energetic delight in praising inferior literary talent, low genres, and coarse humor lend an air of gaiety to the satire. Far from attacking superior dramatists such as Ben Jonson, he dismisses them as irrelevant to his purpose. As often happens to characters in Shadwell's works, he becomes a victim of farce, falling through a trap door at the conclusion.

Shadwell, the successor to Flecknoe, designated "Mac" (son of) Flecknoe. He is modeled on Thomas Shadwell, a successful Restoration dramatist and rival of Dryden. Although his poetry generally was regarded as inferior, his comedies enjoyed a favorable reception in the theater. In the satire, he delivers no speeches, but he is described at length by Flecknoe. His action is limited to his arriving at the throne of dullness, taking his oath, and being crowned. The poem emphasizes his humble origins in Norwich, his stupidity, his obesity, and his numerous shortcomings as a writer. It describes his past experiences at public spectacles and his lute playing as indications of his lack of genuine creativity. Unlike Flecknoe, who is energetic despite his approaching death, Shadwell is portrayed as indolent and lethargic.

Herringman, a captain of the guard at the coronation. The reference is to Henry Herringman, a London publisher and bookseller who had published works by Dryden, Shadwell, and Flecknoe. His role is only ceremonial.

Sir Formal Trifle, a fop known for his inflated oratory. The character is borrowed from Shadwell's *The Virtuoso* (1676). In the poem, he is cited as a proper model for Shadwell's style.

The character suggests that when Shadwell abandons his usual dullness for serious portrayal of emotion, he achieves only pomposity and grandiloquence.

Johnson, a dramatist known for his standard of excellence. The character is a fictive representation of Ben Jonson, the Elizabethan and Jacobean master of comedy, whom Shadwell admired and emulated. Although Jonson wrote comedies of humor similar to those of Shadwell, Jonson represents the ideal of wit, the antithesis of Shadwell's dullness. Shadwell is warned not to link himself with Jonson on the basis that both men were obese. Despite Shadwell's claims of being a successor to Jonson, the poem depicts Jonson as hostile to him and insists that the true lineage is from Flecknoe.

Fletcher, a reference to John Fletcher, the dramatist. With Jonson, Fletcher serves to establish the implied standard for playwriting. In Dryden's day, Fletcher was perceived as a master of tragedy because of his ability to portray strong emotion.

Ancient Dekker, a minor prophet. The allusion is to Thomas Dekker, an Elizabethan dramatist and author of domestic comedies about middle-class life. Because he wrote about middle-class manners and morals, he is placed among the host of inferior poets. Dryden gives him one of the brief prophetic roles in the poem, as one who predicted Shadwell's rise to monarch of dullness.

— *Stanley Archer*

MACBETH

Author: William Shakespeare (1564-1616)
First published: 1623
Genre: Drama

Locale: Scotland
Time: The eleventh century
Plot: Tragedy

Macbeth (mak-BEHTH), thane of Glamis, later thane of Cawdor and king of Scotland. A brave and successful military leader, and potentially a good and great man, he wins general admiration as well as the particular gratitude of King Duncan, his kinsman. Meeting the Three Weird Sisters, he succumbs to their tempting prophecies, but he also needs the urging of his wife to become a traitor, a murderer, and a usurper. He is gifted, or cursed, with a powerful and vivid imagination and with fiery, poetic language. Gaining power, he grows more ruthless, until finally he loses even the vestiges of humanity. He dies desperately, cheated by the ambiguous prophecies, in full realization of the worthlessness of the fruits of his ambition.

Lady Macbeth, the strong-willed, persuasive, and charming wife of Macbeth. Ambitious for her husband's glory, she finds herself unable to kill King Duncan in his sleep because he resembles her father. As Macbeth becomes more inhuman, she becomes remorseful and breaks under the strain. In her sleepwalking, she relives the events of the night of the king's murder and tries to wash her hands clean of imaginary bloodstains.

Banquo (BAN-kwoh), Macbeth's fellow commander. A man of noble character, seemingly unmoved by the prophecy of the Three Weird Sisters that he will beget kings, he is not completely innocent. He does not disclose his suspicions of Macbeth, and he accepts a place in Macbeth's court. After being murdered by Macbeth's assassins, Banquo appears at a

ceremonial banquet. His blood-spattered ghost, visible only to Macbeth, unnerves the king completely. In the final vision shown to Macbeth by the Three Weird Sisters, Banquo and his line of kings appear.

The Three Weird Sisters, three witches, sinister hags who seem more closely allied to the Norns or Fates than to conventional witches. They make prophetic statements to Macbeth that are true but deceptive. Their prophecy of his becoming thane of Cawdor is fulfilled immediately, tempting him to take direct action to carry out the second prophecy, that he shall be king. They lull him into false security by telling him that he has nothing to fear until Birnam Wood comes to Dunsinane and that he cannot be killed by any man born of woman.

Macduff (mak-DUHF), thane of Fife. He and Lennox arrive at Macbeth's castle just after the murder of King Duncan, and Macduff discovers the body. A brave but prudent man, he flees Scotland and offers his help to Malcolm. Underestimating the villainy of Macbeth's character, he is thunderstruck at hearing of the atrocious murder of his wife and children. He becomes a steel-hearted avenger. Before killing Macbeth, he deprives him of his last symbol of security, for as a cesarean child he was not actually born of woman. He presents Macbeth's head to Malcolm and proclaims the young prince king of Scotland.

Duncan, the king of Scotland. Gentle and trusting, he shows great kindness to Macbeth. His murder by Macbeth is therefore almost incredibly fiendish.

Malcolm (MAL-kuhm), King Duncan's eldest son. Far more cautious and shrewd than his father, he leaves for England to escape possible assassination. He is reluctant to give his trust to Macduff but finally, realizing his loyalty, accepts his aid in taking the throne of Scotland.

Donalbain (DON-ahl-bahn), King Duncan's younger son. After consulting with Malcolm, he agrees to take a separate path, going to Ireland so that the potential heirs to the throne would not be accessible to a common assassination.

Fleance (FLEE-ahns), the son of Banquo. He escapes the murderers who kill his father and lives to haunt Macbeth with the Three Weird Sisters' prophecy that kings will spring from Banquo's line.

Ross, a nobleman of Scotland. He is Duncan's messenger to Macbeth, bringing him word of his new title, thane of Cawdor. He also bears news to his kinswoman, Lady Macduff, of her husband's departure from Scotland. His third office as messenger is to carry word to Macduff of the destruction of his entire family. He fights in Malcolm's army against Macbeth.

Lennox, a nobleman of Scotland. He is Macduff's companion when the latter brings the message to King Duncan at Macbeth's castle. He also deserts Macbeth and joins forces with Malcolm.

Lady Macduff, a victim of Macbeth's most horrible atrocity. She is human and pathetic.

Macduff's son, a brave and precocious child. He faces Macbeth's hired murderers without flinching and dies calling to his mother to save herself.

Siward (SEE-wurd), the earl of Northumberland, the general of the English forces supporting Malcolm. He is the type of the noble father accepting stoically the death of a heroic son.

Young Siward, the general's courageous son. He dies fighting Macbeth hand to hand.

A Scottish doctor, called in to minister to Lady Macbeth. He witnesses her sleepwalking in which she relives the night of the murder.

A gentlewoman, an attendant to Lady Macbeth. She is with the doctor and observes Lady Macbeth during the sleepwalking scene.

A sergeant (also called captain in the folio text), a wounded survivor of the battle at the beginning of the play. He reports to King Duncan the heroism of Macbeth and Banquo.

A porter, a comical drunkard. Roused by the knocking on the castle door, he pretends to be the gatekeeper of Hell and imagines various candidates clamoring for admission. The audience, knowing of Duncan's murder, can realize how ironically near the truth is the idea of the castle as Hell.

Hecate (HEHK-eh-tee), the patroness of the Witches. It is generally accepted among Shakespearean scholars that Hecate is an addition to the play by another author, perhaps Thomas Middleton.

A messenger, who brings word that Birnam Wood apparently is moving. His message destroys one of Macbeth's illusions of safety.

Seyton, an officer attending Macbeth. He brings word of Lady Macbeth's death.

Menteith,

Angus, and

Caithness, Scottish noblemen who join Malcolm against Macbeth.

THE MACGUFFIN

Author: Stanley Elkin (1930-1995)
First published: 1991
Genre: Novel

Locale: An unnamed city in the American Midwest
Time: The 1990's
Plot: Psychological realism

Robert Druff, also called Bob and Bobbo, the city commissioner of streets. At the age of fifty-eight, wearing his ill-fitting clothes and suffering from heart disease, a collapsed lung, and poor circulation, Druff finds himself "on the downhill side of destiny." He swallows Valium to calm himself and chews coca leaves to create a sense of "restored obsession," the antidote to what he otherwise experiences as a vaguely defined loss of force (a strange malady given that Druff never had much force to lose). Alternately overbearing and self-deprecating, ridiculing others and feeling ridiculous, he recognizes his own inconsequence. He is understandably disappointed by his "bozo itinerary" and "pointless odyssey"— his cruising for potholes and reviewing of streets he superintends yet barely knows. Frequently invoking the Marlon Brando line from *On the Waterfront*, "I could have been a contender," but realizing that it rings rather hollow, he constructs an increasingly involved and fantastic plot that is at once playful and paranoid. Druff has the starring role as detective/victim.

Rose Helen Druff, his wife of thirty-six years. They met while at college; the fact that her hip problem made her "a relatively presentable cripple" did little to assuage "her savage resentment," which led to a suicide attempt that in turn led Druff to propose marriage. She later saves him "from the humiliation of his body" following heart surgery. He cannot save his now deaf "Miss Kitty" (one of Druff's many allusions to television shows and films, in this case the television Western *Gunsmoke*) from her worst fear, that even though she wears her hearing aids to bed, she will burn to death in her sleep because the batteries will run down and she will be unable to hear the smoke alarm.

Michael Druff, sometimes called Mikey, their son. Even though he is thirty years old, he still lives with his parents. Despite his manic weight lifting, he is fearful and craven, like his father. Mikey's largely fantasized relationship with Su'ad al Najaf provides Druff with an important element in his own Hitchcock-like fantasy.

Su'ad al Najaf, called **Suzy**, a Lebanese graduate student who is fatally injured while crossing a city street. Her death, coupled with her Middle Eastern background and Mikey's having known her, lead Druff to concoct a fantastic plot around the Oriental rugs Su'ad was smuggling, using them as the MacGuffin, the Hitchcockian device to set the plot in motion.

Margaret Glorio, a forty-four-year-old free-lance buyer for local department stores. Druff picks her up—"hijacks" her—at Toober's Restaurant. Although he comes on strong, she has sex with him but refuses to become his mistress. Margaret is the one who tells Druff that Su'ad is a rug smuggler.

MacGuffin, film director Alfred Hitchcock's term for the narrative pretext, or riddle, that appears to motivate and integrate a film's incidents. In Druff's fantasy, the MacGuffin takes on a life of its own, in effect becoming a character in its own right. It is the "spirit of narrative in his life" for whom Druff functions as little more than raw material.

Charles, a driver from whom Druff, while hitchhiking one morning, catches a ride. They carry on a conversation that pleasantly surprises Druff because it does not sound like dialogue in a book. Soon, however, Druff does start sounding like someone in a book (not a very good one at that), and Charles is more than happy to get rid of him.

— Robert A. Morace

MACHO!

Author: Victor Villaseñor (1940-   )
First published: 1973
Genre: Novel

Locale: Mexico and California
Time: Late 1960's
Plot: Bildungsroman

Roberto Garcia (rroh-BEHR-toh gahr-SEE-ah), the eldest child in a large family of poor farmers, natives of a rural village in Michoacan, Mexico. Because of his father's drinking, Roberto, not yet eighteen when the story begins, must provide for his mother and the other children by doing most of the farm labor. His maturity, strength, and intelligence are immediately evident. Roberto embodies the best of the Spanish male/macho tradition: He silently accepts his father's condition and does his work for him; he competently oversees the older men with whom he works, offering no excuses for anything; and he tactfully deals with those who challenge him—but fights when necessary. Roberto's struggle between tradition and change quickly becomes the novel's central conflict. Roberto meets every test with honor, and, in the process, shows that a real man, while honor-bound, may choose not only how he honors his traditions but also how he may change them.

Juan Aguilar (hwahn ah-gee-LAHR), the most experienced and most dominant of the village *norteños*, who travel north across the Mexican border illegally each year to work seasonally on U.S. farms. Like most *norteños*, Juan returns to the village each year to squander his earnings. Prematurely old, Juan is feeling the effects of his hard and dissolute life; thus, mostly out of predatory self-interest, he asks Roberto to accompany him north. Although the extent to which Juan will exploit Roberto remains uncertain, Juan sees in Roberto an image of the son he never had and gradually develops a genuine sense of responsibility for him. Ironically, it is often Roberto who protects Juan on their travels.

Pedro, Juan's *norteño* companion of the past ten years and Roberto's sworn enemy, because he humiliated Roberto's father. Roberto exacts a measure of revenge, and Pedro literally loses face midway through the novel, but their differences remain unresolved.

Esperanza (ehs-pehr-RAHN-sah), the eldest, at sixteen, of Roberto's younger siblings. Her desire for improvement, coupled with her natural intelligence and resourcefulness, has allowed her to transcend the educational constraints normally imposed on women of her village. She supports and encourages Roberto's efforts to challenge tradition whenever it impedes progress. Despite his belief that Esperanza is too idealistic and too hopeful, Roberto is closer to her than to anyone else in his family.

Don Carlos Villanueva (vee-yah-new-EH-vah), Roberto's *patrón*, the aged owner of the land Roberto and the others work. The don was the first in the local community to see that the volcanic dust of a newly formed volcano had improved the soil. With his erect bearing and intelligence, his love of horse racing, and his success without compromise, Don Carlos represents the finest of old Spanish Mexico.

Gloria Sanchez (SAHN-chehs), the potential romantic interest who is most similar to Esperanza. Although Roberto and Gloria are greatly attracted to each other, Gloria's Americanized and outspoken personality naturally clashes with Roberto's traditional values of hard work and stoicism. Their cultural conflict makes it difficult for a relationship to develop.

Lydia Sanchez, Gloria's much less studious younger sister. Lydia has not seriously evaluated Roberto's or Gloria's values. Although both sisters are physically attracted to Roberto, Lydia, unencumbered by ideology, has the advantage when it comes to developing a romantic relationship.

Antonio, the aging former foreman, who chooses Roberto as his successor. Antonio represents the Mexican male traditions of hard work and deceptively clever resourcefulness. He is a respected older worker, though a minor stock character.

Pablo Reyes (RREH-yehs), the eldest of the thirteen Reyes brothers. Together, Pablo and his brothers personify the age-old Mexican tradition of violence and revenge. When the Reyes brothers retaliate in ambush for a humiliation, the resulting deaths initiate a *norteños*-Reyes feud.

MACHO CAMACHO'S BEAT
(La guaracha del Macho Camacho)

Author: Luis Rafael Sánchez (1936-   )
First published: 1976
Genre: Novel

Locale: San Juan, Puerto Rico
Time: Early 1970's
Plot: Social satire

The Heathen Chinky, also called **The Mother**, a woman who has been used sexually since she was five years old. Her brother was killed in the Korean War, and her mother died of grief shortly thereafter. When her husband deserted her for a Chicano woman, he left her alone with her encephalitic, retarded son. She prostitutes herself to pay for the boy's food and medical expenses and calculates the price of her material wants in terms of the number of tricks she will have to turn. At the suggestion of the Old Man, she has taken to leaving her child in a nearby park for a beneficial "sun bath" while she meets him. Ironically, she is waiting for the senator's arrival when her child is hit and killed by the car driven by his son, Benny.

Senator Vincente Reinosa (veen-SEHN-teh rra-NOH-sah), called **The Old Man**, a Puerto Rican politician. Reinosa prides himself on supporting the U.S. involvement in Vietnam and on his coining of the phrase "Yankee this is home" in response to the "Yankee go home" sentiments of the nationalist movement for independence. He has an inflated sense of his sexual prowess, classing himself within a great tradition beginning with Don Juan and coming down to him through Ricardo Montalbán and other Latin lovers. The senator's wife allows him in her bed only on rare occasions, and she is quick to make the sign of the cross immediately thereafter. His relations with his son are limited to providing material goods and immunity from the law. While he waits in traffic, creating inane campaign slogans ("Vince is a prince and easy to convince"), his son, Benny, kills the child of his mistress.

Graciela Alcántara y López de Montefrío (grah-see-EH-lah ahl-KAHN-tah-rah ee LOH-pehs deh mohn-teh-FREE-oh), Reinosa's wife. Having been sheltered from the world of men by her widowed mother and sent off to finishing school in Switzerland, she remains ignorant of sexual matters until the day of her wedding. She has since become resigned to this fact of life with the attitude of a Christian martyr. Her relations with her son are limited to admonishing him to keep his friends' motorcycles out of her garden and to prodding him to observe the social graces. She does not care for native Puerto Rican artists who depict the sordid reality around her; she claims that she was not born to look at ugly things. She will not be able to avoid the reality of her life for long. While her son is out on the street mourning the fact that the Kid's brains have stained the door of his Ferrari, Graciela discovers to her dismay that even her posh psychiatrist has become enchanted by Macho Camacho's vulgar *guaracha*.

Benny, the son of the senator and Graciela. Benny is a lazy and reluctant university student and a budding terrorist. He is responsible for plotting and carrying out with his friends the firebombing of the office of a local nationalist group, causing at least one death. His father has presented him with a brand-new Ferrari, which becomes the object of Benny's sexual fantasies; he masturbates in his bed each night with visions of the car dancing in his head. When Benny kills the Kid, his only regret is that the door of his Ferrari is dirtied with the child's blood and brains.

Doña Chon (DOH-nyah chohn), the Heathen Chinky's friend and neighbor. Doña Chon is enormously overweight and is constantly conjuring up some traditional Creole concoction in her kitchen. She pours forth platitudes and prayers as she pontificates on the problems of the world. She is genuinely kind; she shows concern for the welfare of the Kid; and she mourns deeply the unjustifiably long imprisonment of her daughter Tutú on a minor drug charge. It is because Doña Chon is delayed at the office of her daughter's inept attorney that she is unable to reach the child in time to take him home safely.

The Kid, the encephalitic and mentally retarded son of the Heathen Chinky. He consumes three lizards and innumerable flies per day and lives in a constant puddle of vomit and drool. He is tortured mercilessly by the neighborhood children when he is left in the park, and he is killed as he runs away from his own reflection in a broken mirror.

MCTEAGUE: A Story of San Francisco

Author: Frank Norris (1870-1902)
First published: 1899
Genre: Novel

Locale: San Francisco, and Death Valley, California
Time: The 1890's
Plot: Naturalism

McTeague (Mac), a massive, slow-witted man with a blond mustache and enormously strong hands. An unlicensed dentist, McTeague sometimes pulls teeth with his bare hands. He snoozes away Sunday afternoons in his dentist chair until he meets Trina Sieppe, the cousin and fiancée of his friend, Marcus Schouler. His friend sees that McTeague and Trina are attracted and with fairly good grace accepts the situation. Many of McTeague's violent and even repulsive qualities are highlighted by incidents in the novel. At an outing, Marcus and McTeague wrestle; Marcus, envious and angry, bites off McTeague's ear lobe; the dentist, in turn, breaks Marcus' arm. In adversity, McTeague's brutality is intensified by drink. Sadistically, he bites his wife's fingers until they are infected and have to be amputated. Adversity can only intensify his desperation, and one is not surprised when he beats his wife to death and then flees the consequences. In the middle of the desert, he is met by his former friend, now a member of the sheriff's posse; again a violent struggle is the only response McTeague can give. He kills his friend, but not before Marcus has handcuffed them together under the boiling sun. McTeague's death, like his life, is brutish. Readers have considered McTeague's career, as related by Norris, a triumph of realistic description.

Marcus Schouler, who lives above McTeague's dental office. The two men are friends. Smaller than McTeague but gifted with more intelligence, Marcus broods over the loss of his fiancée and her prize money and is petty enough to report McTeague to the authorities for practicing without a license. By fate or by sheer perversity, he binds his enemy to his own corpse with handcuffs; the two face eternity only hours apart.

Trina Sieppe, McTeague's wife, trained to be a thrifty housewife by her Swiss parents. She overdevelops this trait after she wins five thousand dollars in a lottery. She spends every spare moment carving small wooden Noah's Ark animals for her uncle's "import" business. Although counting coins is her only joy, she does buy a huge gold tooth as a sign for her husband's dental office. Sexually subservient to her husband's physical strength, she cannot protect herself from his drunken fury when he bites her finger tips. Her character shows only vestigial kindness, and her miserliness leads to her death.

Grannis, an aged English bookbinder, comforted each night by the delicate sounds of his neighbor's teatray on the opposite side of a partition. The tray belongs to the seamstress next door.

Miss Parker, a genteel dressmaker. She responds with fluttering heart when she hears Grannis and his supper tray. They marry.

Zerkov, a junk dealer.

Maria Macapa, a maid who collects junk for Zerkov. She raves about "gold dishes" once owned by her family. These ravings lead Zerkov to marry Maria. A head blow ends her aberration, however, and in frustration, Zerkov kills her.

Papa Sieppe and

Mamma Sieppe, Trina's parents, elderly Swiss immigrants.

MACUNAÍMA
(Macunaíma, o Herói Sem Nenhum Caracter)

Author: Mário de Andrade (1893-1945)
First published: 1928
Genre: Novel

Locale: Brazil
Time: Early twentieth century
Plot: Comic realism

Macunaíma (ma-kew-nah-EE-mah), the mock hero. He is lazy, selfish, and abusive, a liar whose main interests are women and money. Even as a child, he shows an incredible capacity to metamorphose himself into different appearances to fulfill his needs and desires. After killing his mother unintentionally—she had been changed into a deer by an evil force—Macunaíma, along with his two brothers and Iriqui, mourns for a month. They then leave their homeland. On their way, they encounter Ci, the Mother of the Forest, who is raped by Macunaíma with the help of his two brothers. As a consequence, he becomes the Emperor of the Dense Jungle. Later, in a fight against a lake monster, he loses the magical amulet, called Muiraquitã, that Ci gave to him. The stone accidentally comes into Venceslau's possession, and this event precipitates the hero's journey to São Paulo to recover it. After several failed attempts, he kills his enemy and recovers the magical stone. Back in the forest, Macunaíma falls victim to Vei's rancor: The hero dives into the lake to find a siren that Vei has promised to him and instead is attacked and crippled by piranhas. Once again, he loses the Muiraquitã. Ultimately, because he is bored with life, the hero is transformed into the constellation Ursa Major.

Maanape (mah-ah-NAH-peh), Macunaíma's elder brother. He is a sorcerer and uses his knowledge and power to cure Macunaíma of the many diseases acquired by the latter in São Paulo. He also uses his abilities to bring his brother back to life following the first fight with Venceslau.

Jiguê (zhee-GEH), Macunaíma's witless brother. He is the permanent victim of his brother's tricks, and Macunaíma repeatedly steals his women. Jiguê's loyalty to Macunaíma motivates him to follow his brother to São Paulo. When they return to the forest, Jiguê, fed up with his brother's mockeries, decides to take vengeance on him but fails, being defeated again by Macunaíma's guile. Finally, Jiguê is changed into a leprous shadow.

Ci (see), the Mother of the Forest. She is the queen of the Icamiabas, an Amazonian-like society formed solely of women. Ci, raped by Macunaíma, gives birth to a child who soon dies. Once the mourning period is over, she gives a magical green stone, shaped like an alligator, to Macunaíma, and then she transforms herself into a star in the sky.

Venceslau Pietro Pietra (vehn-sehs-LOW pee-EH-troh pee-EH-trah), the man-eating giant Piaimã. He is the villain. By obtaining the Muiraquitã, he becomes a rich landowner and establishes himself in São Paulo. Macunaíma decides to recover his amulet from Venceslau's hands, and, after several attempts, he is able to destroy the giant by throwing him in a boiling pot of macaroni.

Vei (va), the sun, represented as a female entity. At the beginning, she protects the hero, but in return for her kindness, she receives his ingratitude. Macunaíma, instead of accepting one of Vei's daughters as his wife, would rather seduce a Portuguese fisherwoman. Vei takes vengeance on him by injuring his private parts with heat rays and leading him to the treacherous arms of a siren.

— *Daniel Altamiranda*

MADAME BOVARY

Author: Gustave Flaubert (1821-1880)
First published: 1857
Genre: Novel

Locale: France
Time: Mid-nineteenth century
Plot: Psychological realism

Emma Bovary (boh-vah-REE), a sentimental young woman whose foolishly romantic ideas on life and love cause her to become dissatisfied with her humdrum husband and the circumstances of her married life. Her feelings of disillusionment lead her first into two desperate, hopeless love affairs and

then to an agonizing and ugly death from arsenic poisoning. Filled with fiery, indefinite conceptions of love, which she is capable of translating only into gaudy bourgeois displays of materialism, she is unable to reconcile herself to a life of tedium as the wife of a country doctor. In her attempt to escape into a more exciting world of passion and dream, she drifts into shabby, sordid affairs with Rodolphe Bourlanger and Léon Dupuis. The first of these lovers, an older man, dominates the affair; the second, inexperienced and young, is dominated. Because Emma brings to both of these affairs little more than an insubstantial and frantic desire to escape her dull husband and the monotony of her life, the eventual collapse of her romantic dreams, the folly of her passionate surrender to passion and intrigue, and her death, brought on by false, empty pride, are inevitable.

Charles Bovary (shahrl), Emma's well-meaning but docile and mediocre medical husband. An unimaginative clod without intelligence or insight, he is unable to understand, console, or satisfy the terrible needs of his wife. Every move he makes to become a more important figure in her sight is frustrated by his inadequacy as a lover and a doctor, for he is as much a failure in his practice as he is in his relations with Emma. Her suicide leaves him grief-stricken and financially ruined as the result of her extravagance. Soon after her death, he discovers in the secret drawer of her desk the love letters sent her by Rodolphe and Léon, and he learns of her infidelity for the first time. When he dies, the sum of twelve francs and seventy-five centimes is his only legacy to his small daughter.

Rodolphe Bourlanger (roh-DOHLF bewr-lahn-ZHAY), Emma Bovary's first lover. A well-to-do bachelor and the owner of the Château La Huchette, he is a shrewd, suave, and brittle man with considerable knowledge of women and a taste for intrigue. Sensing the relationship between Emma and her husband, he makes friends with the Bovarys, sends them gifts of venison and fowls, and invites them to the chateau. On the pretext of concern for Emma's health, he suggests that they go riding together. He finds Emma so easy a conquest that after a short time he begins to neglect her, partly out of boredom, partly because he cannot see in himself the Byronic image Emma has created in her imagination; she never sees Rodolphe as the loutish, vulgar man he is. After he writes her a letter of farewell, on the pretext that he is going on a long journey, Emma suffers a serious attack of brain fever.

Léon Dupuis (lay-OH[N] dew-PWEE), a young law clerk infatuated by Emma Bovary but without the courage to declare himself or to possess her. With him, she indulges herself in a progressively lascivious manner in her attempt to capture the excitement and passion of the romantic love she desires. Léon, because he lacks depth and maturity, merely intensifies Emma's growing estrangement from her everyday world. When Léon, who never realizes the encouragement Emma offers him, goes off to continue his studies in Paris, she is filled with rage, hate, and unfulfilled desire, and a short time later she turns to Rodolphe Bourlanger. After that affair, she meets Léon once more in Rouen, and they become lovers. Oppressed by debts, living only for sensation, and realizing that she is pulling Léon down to her own degraded level, Emma ends the affair by committing suicide.

Monsieur Lheureux (lewr-REH), an unscrupulous, corrupt draper and moneylender who makes Emma the victim of his unsavory business deals by driving her deeper and deeper into debt. Her inability to repay the exorbitant loans he has made her in secret forces the issue of suicide upon her as her only escape from her baseless world.

Monsieur Homais (oh-MAY), a chemist, presented in a masterpiece of ironic characterization. A speaker in clichés, the possessor of a wholly trite "Scientific Outlook" on society, he regards himself as a modern man and a thinker. His pomposity and astoundingly superficial ideals become one of the remarkable facets of the novel, as Flaubert sketches the hypocrisy and mediocrity of Charles Bovary's friend. Homais epitomizes the small-town promoter, raconteur, and self-styled liberal.

Hippolyte Tautain (ee-poh-LEET toh-TEH[N]), a mentally retarded, clubfooted boy operated on by Charles Bovary at the insistence of M. Homais, who wishes to bring greater glory to the region by proving the merits of a new surgical device. Bovary's crude handling of the operation and the malpractice involved in the use of the device cause the boy to lose his leg. The episode provides Flaubert with an excellent commentary on both Homais and Bovary.

Théodore Rouault (tay-oh-DOHR rew-AHL), Emma Bovary's father, a farmer. Charles Bovary first meets Emma when he is summoned to set Rouault's broken leg.

Berthe Bovary (behrt), the neglected young daughter of Emma and Charles Bovary. Orphaned and left without an inheritance, she is sent to live with her father's mother. When that woman dies, the child is turned over to the care of an aunt, who puts her to work in a cotton-spinning factory.

Captain Binet (bee-NAY), the tax collector in the town of Yonville-l'Abbaye.

Justin (zhews-TA[N]), the assistant in the shop of Mr. Homais. Emma persuades her young admirer to admit her to the room where poisons are kept. There, before horrified Justin can stop her, she secures a quantity of arsenic and eats it.

Madame Veuve Lefrançois (vehv leh-frah[n]-SWAH), the proprietress of the inn in Yonville-l'Abbaye. Hippolyte Tautain is the hostler at her establishment.

Félicité (fay-lee-see-TAY), the Bovarys' maid.

Héloïse Bovary (ayl-WAHZ), Charles Bovary's first wife, a woman much older than he, who had deceived the Bovarys as to the amount of property she owned. Her death following a severe hemorrhage frees Charles from his nagging, domineering wife, and soon afterward he marries young Emma Rouault.

MADEMOISELLE DE MAUPIN

Author: Théophile Gautier (1811-1872)
First published: 1835-1836
Genre: Novel

Locale: France
Time: Early nineteenth century
Plot: Sentimental

M. d'Albert (dahl-BEHR), a young aesthete, handsome, well-educated, and worldly, who has dreamed of and who seeks an ideal woman. Though Rosette provides for a while an education in love's delights, she cannot cure his moods of dreamy longing. Théodore both fascinates and troubles d'Albert, who (to Silvio) admits loving a man but a man who is almost certainly a woman in disguise. He is joyously surprised by Madelaine-Rosalind's offer of a night of love, is transported by the wonderful love itself, and is left astonished at Théodore's disappearance.

Rosette, his mistress, a pretty and charming young woman prescribed by De C——— as a cure for d'Albert's vaporish idealism. She is intelligent, witty, and capricious. From the beginning, she stirs d'Albert sexually and, becoming his mistress, delights him with a variety of pleasures. But these soon pall, and she struggles to conquer his boredom and his return to wistful dreaming. Simultaneously in love with the elusive Théodore, Rosette is saddened to learn that the disguised Isnabel is apparently Théodore's mistress.

Théodore de Sérannes (tay-oh-DOHR deh say-RAHN), in reality Mademoiselle Madelaine de Maupin. In disguise, Madelaine appears to be an extremely handsome young man, an accomplished conversationalist, horseman, and swordsman. Believing she could never, as a woman, discover the true nature of men, she has (posing as a man) somewhat bitterly observed their perfidy and shams when they thought themselves safe from exposure. After the smitten d'Albert has learned her secret, Madelaine (in costume as William Shake-

speare's Rosalind) appears in d'Albert's room and grants him one night of perfect love. Also, after leaving d'Albert's room, she spends a mysteriously lengthy visit with Rosette. She then goes out of the life of both Rosette and d'Albert forever, leaving each to comfort and love the other as best they may. As for herself, Madelaine confesses to Graciosa that a bisexual element in her nature prevents her from ever completely loving anyone, man or woman. Though in part modeled upon Shakespeare's Rosalind, whom she plays in an amateur production of *As You Like It*, Madelaine is, especially in her sensuality, a very different woman.

De C———, a man of the world, d'Albert's friend who introduces him to Rosette.

Madame de Thémines (deh tay-MEEN), a fashionable madam and a former intimate of De C———.

Isnabel (eez-nah-BEHL), Théodore's page, in reality a young woman whose sex is secretly discovered by Rosette after a riding accident.

Silvio (seel-VYOH), d'Albert's friend to whom he writes long confessional letters.

Graciosa (grah-SYOH-sah), Madelaine's epistolary confidante.

THE MADMAN AND THE NUN: Or, There Is Nothing Bad Which Could Not Turn into Something Worse
(Wariat i zakonnica: Czyli, Nie ma złego, co by na jeszcze gorsze nie wyszło)

Author: Stanisław Ignacy Witkiewicz (1885-1939)
First published: 1925
Genre: Drama

Locale: Central Europe
Time: The 1920's
Plot: Surrealism

Alexander Walpurg, a mad poet confined in an insane asylum. The twenty-nine-year-old Walpurg embodies the romantic conception of the poet as reflected in his model, German poet Heinrich von Kleist. His life has been in total service to his art and has been lived on the edge, filled with excesses in drink, drugs, sex, and violence. Walpurg represents the romantic stereotype of the poet physically as well, with his dark complexion, brooding good looks, slender figure, and disheveled beard and mustache. Walpurg views the creative process as a power that compels him to create and views his madness as a symptom of the highly explosive and unpredictable creative surge that propels him to rebel against social conformity.

Sister Anna, whose real name is **Alina**, a young nun assisting in the psychiatric ward where Walpurg is confined. Sister Anna entered the convent when her lover abandoned her under the influence of Walpurg's poetry, which they used to read together. Believing that she can save Walpurg from despair, she takes off her nun's habit and large cross on a chain and releases Walpurg from his straitjacket, revealing in their subsequent lovemaking an ardent and passionate temperament. She is a very pretty light blonde with a twenty-two-year-old's naïveté and vulnerability.

Dr. Jan Bidello, a non-Freudian psychiatrist and one of the doctors working on Walpurg's case. Bidello distrusts psychoanalysis, having no confidence in its therapeutic value. He believes that people who have become insane cannot be cured but only subdued through drugs, confinement, and straitjackets. He is sarcastic and dictatorial in manner. When Grün suggests that Walpurg be released from his straitjacket, Bidello

protests that there is no honor among madmen, a theory soon verified when Walpurg stabs him in the temple with a pencil, thereby killing him. In the final *coup de théâtre*, Bidello returns as a gallant man-about-town and whisks off the dead Walpurg and Sister Anna to a new, pleasurable life, meanwhile cautioning Grün to analyze himself quite thoroughly.

Dr. Ephraim Grün, a psychoanalyst of the Freudian school. Grün is in many respects a caricature of the excesses of psychoanalysis, reflected in his uncritical discussion of the resolution of complexes, the sexual drive, guilt feelings, and the role of the subconscious. His diagnosis of Walpurg's madness shows its root in a twin sister complex, with the killing of Bidello forming the resolution of that complex. When Walpurg hangs himself despite Grün's assertions that he is cured, Grün feels a new complex coming on but can no longer identify it. Reduced to speaking psychobabble, Grün is confined in Walpurg's cell.

Sister Barbara, the mother superior of the convent. Sixty years old, Sister Barbara has the demeanor of an aristocratic matron. She is a strict authoritarian and exercises her power over Sister Anna by using the will of God as her justification. When Sister Anna's love affair is discovered, Sister Barbara's reaction reveals her to be a bigoted, class-conscious, vindictive woman.

Professor Ernest Walldorff, the director of the psychiatric ward. A minor character, he appears in the last scene to shift his allegiance from psychiatry to brain surgery. Walldorff projects the caricature image of the mad scientist as he shuts Grün into Walpurg's cell and throws away the key.

Alfred and

Paphnatius, two attendants dressed in hospital uniforms. Alfred is bald with a black beard, whereas Paphnatius has red hair and beard. Both represent soulless automatons who exe- cute whatever is commanded with jerky and mechanical movements.

— Christine Kiebuzinska

MADMEN AND SPECIALISTS

Author: Wole Soyinka (1934-   )
First published: 1971
Genre: Drama

Locale: Indeterminate, but similar to Nigeria after the 1967- 1969 civil war
Time: Indeterminate
Plot: Mythic

Dr. Bero, also called **The Specialist**, a medical doctor returning from service in a civil war analogous to the Biafran secession from Nigeria (1967-1970) but generalized by its echoes of similar conflicts such as the 1960-1964 Katangan conflict in the Congo (now Zaire). Bero began service as a doctor but found that he had a talent for intelligence work and has since become the head of intelligence, in which position he acquired the nickname "The Specialist." He claims to have eaten and enjoyed human flesh, particularly testicles. He has sent four spies, masquerading as beggars, to watch his father, the Old Man, whom he has had confined in the basement surgery of their house. Against his father's metaphysical proc- lamations of the new deity As, Bero claims to understand the nature of real (temporal) power. Bero's four spies are former disciples of the Old Man. When the Old Man recaptures their allegiance and is at the point of "operating" on one of them, Bero appears and shoots him.

The Old Man, Bero's father, also a medical doctor. He likes his regular arguments with the Priest. During the last of these, he submits that cannibalism should be made legal. Shortly thereafter, he follows his son to war and is given charge of convalescent patients, whom he converts to the partly obscurantist, partly cynical cult of As. His comments on cannibalism threaten to bring severe legal reprisals. His son rescues him and has him taken home to be confined in the surgery. At his first opportunity, he reasserts his control over the beggars. He is shot by Bero as he attempts to cut open the Cripple and sample his flesh.

Aafaa (ah-AH-fah), one of the four mendicants, subject to St. Vitus' Dance. He is the most voluble of the four, often leading them in elaborate charades. His comments, even to Bero, are often satirical and challenging, and Bero finds it necessary to remind him who employs him and his fellows. He, Goyi, and the Blind Man help the Old Man prepare the Cripple for his "operation."

Iya Agba, one of two old women. She and her companion are herbalists who have accumulated generations of knowl- edge. They have shared their secrets generously with Bero's sister but now fear that Bero may misuse them. In the climactic scene, as Bero shoots the Old Man, Iya Agba sets fire to her entire collection of herbs and mixtures.

Si Bero, Bero's sister. While waiting for her father and brother to return, she has studied so diligently under the two old women that she knows all that they know. They do not find this dangerous, in spite of Bero, because they know her to be a good person. She is unaware of the Old Man's presence and is overjoyed to see her brother. Her joy turns quickly to appre- hension when she perceives how he has changed.

The Priest, a longtime friend of the Old Man. He consis- tently refuses Si Bero's compound to treat a long-standing ailment; although she says it is the very same compound, he does not trust it to be as well made as her father's. After his first shock at the Old Man's comment on cannibalism, he decides that it was only an arguing point. When Bero implies that he has eaten human flesh, the Priest is shocked anew, and he employs a transparent pretext to refuse a dinner invitation.

The Blind Man, another mendicant. He is distinguished from the others by his long, rambling speech toward the end of the play, in which he both represents and parodies the motives of different parties in the civil war.

Iya Mate (mah-TEH), the second old woman. She is more cautious than Iya Agba, whom she allows to take the lead in destroying the storeroom of herbal secrets.

Goyi and

The Cripple, the other two mendicants. Goyi is bent for- ward by an ever-present back brace, and the Cripple drags himself along on his knees.

— James L. Hodge

THE MADRAS HOUSE

Author: Harley Granville-Barker (1877-1946)
First published: 1911
Genre: Drama

Locale: London, England
Time: Early twentieth century
Plot: Social criticism

Henry Huxtable, the respectable, middle-class part owner of the Madras House.

Katherine Huxtable, the respectable, middle-class wife of Henry Huxtable.

Constantine Madras, Katherine Huxtable's black sheep brother and part owner of the Madras House. To escape En- glish priggishness, he had retreated some years before to Ara- bia, where he reportedly lived as the master of a harem. Upon his return to England on business concerning the Madras House, he is a threat to the Huxtable idea of respectability and decency. When it is revealed that he is the father of Marion Yates's unborn child, he expects her meekly to receive his assistance. When she refuses, he is disturbed by her lack of feminine docility and returns to his Arabian household.

Philip Madras, Constantine Madras' son. When he learns that his wife, Jessica, is about to fall in love with Major Hippisly Thomas, he recognizes her for the first time as a person. To please her, he gives up his interest in the Madras House in the hope that they can work together for the good of society.

Marion Yates, an employee at the Madras House and the mother of Constantine Madras' unborn child.

Jessica Madras, Philip Madras' wife. Feeling herself regarded with indifference by her husband, she is about to fall in love with Major Hippisly Thomas. When she finally is recognized by Philip as a person as well as a wife, she unites with him in an endeavor to be useful to society.

Eustace Perrin State, an American, a prospective buyer of the Madras House.

Major Hippisly Thomas, Philip Madras' best friend.

Amelia Madras, Constantine Madras' wife, whom he leaves for life in Arabia.

Mr. Brigstock and

Miss Chancellor, employees of the Madras House.

THE MADWOMAN OF CHAILLOT
(La Folle de Chaillot)

Author: Jean Giraudoux (1882-1944)
First published: 1945
Genre: Drama

Locale: The Chaillot district of Paris
Time: A little before noon in the spring of next year
Plot: Parable

Countess Aurelia (oh-ray-LYAH), the **Madwoman of Chaillot** (shah-YOH). Living eternally in the moment when her life was loveliest, and as champion of beauty and of the gentle people of Paris, she is confronted, at a sidewalk café, with the brutal forces of materialism in the form of a syndicate preparing to drill for oil beneath the streets. Realizing that justice, as it is ordinarily understood, will be powerless against the destroyers of beauty, she forms and carries out, with the help of her gentle friends, a plan to annihilate the financiers. With the materialists gone, all the manifestations of spring return to the world. The Madwoman is thanked by all for saving humanity from its exploiters.

Mme Constance (koh[n]-STAHNS), the **Madwoman of Passy** (pah-SEE),

Mlle Gabrielle (gay-BRYEHL), the **Madwoman of St. Sulpice**, and

Mme Josephine (zhoh-zay-FEEN), the **Madwoman of la Concorde** (koh[n]-KOHRD), Countess Aurelia's gentle compatriots, who form a tribunal for a fair trial of the materialists, whom they find guilty on all charges.

The Ragpicker, one of the gentle people. He agrees to speak for the defense at the trial of the materialists.

The President,
the Baron,
the Broker, and

the Prospector, the representatives of the forces of materialism, the destroyers of beauty and the enemies of humanity. Armed with a plan for drilling for oil beneath the streets of Paris, they oppose Countess Aurelia and her gentle friends, the champions of beauty and humanity. The financiers eventually are tried by a court of gentle ones, found guilty, and condemned to extermination. Lured to Countess Aurelia's by the promise of oil, they follow one another like sheep through a door that they are led to believe opens the way to the treasure. In reality, they are headed for the sewers of Paris, never to return.

Pierre (pyehr), a young assassin hired by the materialists to bomb the city architect, who is opposed to the drilling of oil beneath the streets. When the young man finds himself unable to carry out his task, he plans to jump in the river but is rescued and convinced by Countess Aurelia that life is worth living.

The Sewer Man, Countess Aurelia's gentle friend who shows her a secret door to the sewers of Paris through which the materialists are led, never to return.

The Waiter,
the Little Man,
the Street Singer,
the Flower Girl, and
the Shoe Lace Peddlar, free, gentle people of Paris.

THE MAGAZINE NOVELS OF PAULINE HOPKINS

Author: Pauline Hopkins (1859-1930)
First published: 1988
Genre: Novels

Locale: United States
Time: The latter half of the nineteenth century
Plot: Social realism

Hagar's Daughter: A Story of Southern Caste Prejudice, 1901-1902

Hagar, a beautiful woman first married to Ellis Enson, then to John Bowen. Until St. Clair Enson breaks the news, Hagar is unaware of her African American heritage. She and Ellis have a daughter; after she believes Ellis to be dead, Hagar attempts to take her own life and that of her daughter. She eventually learns that the child she and Bowen have reared is her own daughter. After Bowen's death, she remarries Enson.

Jewel, the title character, adopted by Bowen and his first wife. She loves her stepmother, Hagar, but does not learn that Hagar is in fact her natural mother and that she is part African American until after she marries Cuthbert Sumner. Jewel dies of Roman fever at the age of twenty-one.

Ellis Enson, a Southern aristocrat, Hagar's first husband. He is attacked and left for dead. Believing his wife and daughter to be dead, he changes his name and becomes a famous detective.

St. Clair Enson, the major villain. He masterminds a scheme to get rich by marrying Jewel. He changes his name to Colonel Benson and later kills his mistress, Elise Bradford.

Cuthbert Sumner, a Northern aristocrat framed for the murder of Elise Bradford. He marries Jewel, unaware of her African American heritage. Detective Henson clears him of the murder charge.

Aurelia Madison, a participant in the scheme to defraud the Bowens.

Winona: A Tale of Negro Life in the South and Southwest, 1902

Winona, the daughter of White Eagle and a runaway slave. She falls in love with Maxwell, becomes an heiress, and marries him.

Judah, a strong, handsome African American who loves Winona. Judah is instrumental in solving the mystery of the missing heir.

White Eagle, an English aristocrat who is falsely convicted of murder. He flees to America but is killed by Colonel Titus to keep him and his daughter from inheriting a fortune.

Colonel Titus, the indirect heir who kills White Eagle and kidnaps Winona and Judah, forcing them to work as slaves.

Warren Maxwell, a handsome, unprejudiced, twenty-eight-year-old English lawyer. He is sent to America to find the missing heir. He is nearly killed by proslavery forces but is saved. He marries Winona and takes her to England.

John Brown, the historical personage, known for abolitionist actions.

Of One Blood: Or, The Hidden Self, 1902-1903

Reuel Briggs, a medical student who keeps his African American heritage a secret. He marries Dianthe Lusk. After her death, he learns that she and Aubrey Livingston are his siblings. He becomes **King Ergamenes** of the lost city of Telassar in Africa.

Aubrey Livingston, the false friend of Briggs. He plots Briggs's death, commits two murders, and kills himself.

Dianthe Lusk, a beautiful, talented singer with the Fisk University choir. She marries Briggs. When tricked into believing that he is dead, she marries Livingston, who poisons her.

Ai, a high priest of the lost civilization of Telassar.

— *Cheri Louise Ross*

MAGGIE: A Girl of the Streets

Author: Stephen Crane (1871-1900)
First published: 1893
Genre: Novel

Locale: New York City
Time: Late nineteenth century
Plot: Naturalism

Maggie, a girl who has grown up in the slums of New York. Although surrounded by corruption of all sorts throughout her youth, she has remained uncontaminated by it. When she falls in love with Pete, a friend of her brother, her moral deterioration begins. After she has lived with him, her family, who are anything but models of decorum, will have nothing to do with her. She turns to prostitution but finds it hard to support herself; eventually, she commits suicide.

Jimmy, Maggie's brother. After his father's death, he goes to work to support Maggie and their mother. He quickly falls into the normal patterns of life for men of his class, has a succession of affairs, and fathers several illegitimate children.

When Maggie tries to return home after her affair with Pete, he is highly indignant and will do nothing to help her.

Pete, Jimmy's friend and Maggie's lover. After seducing Maggie, he quickly tires of her and turns her out. Thereafter, he denies any responsibility toward her.

The Mother, a woman given to drink and constant haranguing with her husband and children. When Maggie and Jimmy were small, she left them to shift for themselves most of the time, but it is she who assumes an attitude of outraged virtue when Maggie tries to return home. After her daughter's death, she is inconsolable.

THE MAGIC MOUNTAIN
(Der Zauberberg)

Author: Thomas Mann (1875-1955)
First published: 1924
Genre: Novel

Locale: Davos, Switzerland
Time: 1907-1914
Plot: Philosophical

Hans Castorp (hahns KAHS-tohrp), a young German of middle-class and commercial background. He is a sedate, sensible, correct young man, appreciative of good living, but without particular ambition or aspiration. This spiritual lack, Mann suggests, is allied to physical illness. About to enter a shipbuilding firm, Hans goes to make a three-week visit at the International Sanatorium Berghof, where his cousin is a patient. There, he learns that he himself has contracted tuberculosis, and he spends seven years at the sanatorium. Spiritually unattached to his own time and place, he resigns himself rather easily to his new role as an inmate of the "magic mountain," where the spiritual conflicts and defects of modern Europe are polarized and where time and place are allied to eternity and infinity. His experience takes on the significance of a spiritual journey. He is exposed to a threadbare version of Western liberalism and rationalism (in the person of Settembrini); to the lure of irrational desire (in the person of Madame Chauchat); to Catholic absolutism and mysticism (in the person of Naphta, whose arguments with Settembrini make up a large part of the second portion of the novel). Finally (in the person of Mynheer Peeperkorn), he feels the attraction of a strong, vital personality that makes the intellectual strife of Settembrini and Naphta sound quite hollow. Lost in a snowstorm that quickly becomes a symbol of his passage through uncharted spiritual regions, Hans attains a vision of an earthly paradise and of blood sacrifice—the two opposed forces life has revealed to him—and he achieves a further revelation of the importance of goodness and love. Ironically, after he returns to the sanatorium, he forgets; the vision has literally led him beyond himself and his capacity. He now dabbles in spiritualism and, in a famous passage, also soothes himself with romantic music that, he feels, contains at its heart the death wish. It is a snatch of this music that Hans has on his lips when, at the conclusion of the novel, he is glimpsed on a battlefield of World War I.

Ludovico Settembrini (lew-doh-FEE-koh seh-tehm-BREE-nee), an Italian humanist, man of letters, apostle of reason, progress, equality, and the brotherhood of man, as well as a fiery Italian nationalist. His case is incurable; no longer able to return to the land of action (a fact that has obvious symbolic connotations), he spends his energy in hollow eloquence and in ineffectual writing for the International League for the Organization of Progress.

Leo Naphta (LAY-oh NAHF-tah), an apostate Jew converted to Catholicism, educated by the Jesuits, brilliant in his defense of the immaterial, the spiritual, the authoritarian, the medieval. He gets the better of Settembrini in his many arguments with the Italian, but it becomes clear that Naphta's rigidity is essentially a form of death. Toward the end of the novel, having goaded Settembrini into a duel, Naphta turns his gun on himself.

Clavdia Chauchat (KLAHF-dee-ah koh-SHAH), a Russian, married but refusing to carry a ring on her finger, wandering about Europe from sanatorium to sanatorium. Her manners are in many ways the antithesis of what Hans has learned to accept as ladylike; but that very difference seems to attract him once he has begun to lose his ties with Hamburg, and on a carnival night, they consummate the passion she has aroused in him. She leaves the sanatorium for a time but returns in the company of Mynheer Peeperkorn.

Mynheer Peeperkorn (MEEN-hayr PAY-pur-kohrn), an enormously wealthy, burly ex-planter. He is inarticulate (thus enforcing the difference between him, on one hand, and Set-tembrini and Naphta, on the other), but exudes a strength of personality that engages the respect of Hans, who allies himself with the Dutchman. But Peeperkorn, feeling the approach of impotence, kills himself (another facet of nineteenth century individualism gone).

Joachim Ziemssen (YOH-ahkh-ihm ZEEM-sehn), Hans's cousin, soldierly, courteous, brave. A foil to Hans, he refuses to yield to the magic of the mountain, keeps track of time, chafes to return to the flatland so that he can pursue his career as a soldier. Though in love with an inmate, Marusja, he, unlike Castorp, refuses to yield to his passion. Finally, he insists on leaving, though he is not fully cured. He is gloriously happy for a while but returns to the sanatorium to die.

Marusja (mah-ROOS-yah), a pretty young Russian girl, silently adored by Joachim Ziemssen.

Hofrat Behrens (HOHF-raht BAY-rehns), the chief medical officer at the sanatorium. His wife had died there some years before, and he stayed on when he found himself tainted with the disease. He is a mixture of melancholy and forced jocularity.

Dr. Krokowski (kroh-KOF-skee), a foil to Behrens. If Behrens represents the medical point of view, Krokowski represents the psychoanalytical.

Frau Stöhr, a middle-aged woman who irks Castorp at the dinner table by her boring conversation, yet he welcomes her gossip about Clavdia Chauchat.

Miss Robinson, an elderly English woman and table companion of Castorp.

Fräulein Engelhart (ANG-ehl-hahrt), a school mistress from Konigsberg, another table companion of Castorp.

Dr. Leo Blumenkohl (BLEW-mehn-kohl), a physician from Odessa. The advanced stage of his illness causes him to be the quietest person at Castorp's table.

Herr Albin (AHL-been), a patient who, unable to take his illness philosophically, creates excitement by demonstrating suicidal intentions.

Tous Les Deux (tew lay doo), an old Mexican woman known by this name because her conversation consists of only a few French phrases that always contain the words "tous les deux."

Sister Berta (BAYR-tah), formerly **Alfreda Schildknecht** (ahl-FRAY-dah SHIHLD-knasht), a talkative nurse who tries to explain her frustrations to reluctant Hans Castorp and Joachim Ziemssen.

Adriatica von Mylendonk (ah-dree-AH-tih-kah fon MEE-lehn-donk), the director of the sanatorium, who surprises Castorp by her businesslike manner.

THE MAGICIAN OF LUBLIN
(Der Kuntsnmakher fun Lublin)

Author: Isaac Bashevis Singer (1904-1991)
First published: 1959
Genre: Novel

Locale: Poland
Time: Late nineteenth century
Plot: Psychological realism

Yasha Mazur, a traveling acrobat and juggler, the protagonist. He is a short man, broad-shouldered, lean, blue-eyed, and clean-shaven, with a narrow chin and a short Slavic nose. He is forty years old but looks ten years younger. Yasha is considered rich by local standards. He is an escape artist and can pick any lock. He is Jewish but agnostic. He visits his wife only on high holidays. The rest of the time, he travels with his show and visits his three mistresses. Yasha is entirely self-taught, and his mother died when he was seven years old. He has many personalities, because there is always another role to play for his mistresses: religious, heretical, good or evil, false, and sincere. Although he is ready to renounce his religion, he cherishes and venerates any page torn from a holy book.

Esther, Yasha's wife of twenty years. She is forty years old, religious, small, and dark, with a youthful face. She is loyal and devoted to Yasha. She is unable to bear children and is distressed by this inability. She insists on maintaining a Jewish household, and Yasha does not interfere. Although she knows about her husband's infidelity, she tries to dissuade him from immuring himself. She takes up sewing to support herself and him.

Magda Zbarski, Yasha's assistant and mistress. She is in her late twenties, swarthy, and flat-chested. She lives with her mother Elzbieta and brother Bolek. Through Yasha, she is her family's sole support. Yasha sleeps with her in Elzbieta's house, and Elzbeita calls him "son." Magda, jealous and desperate over Yasha's womanizing and his neglect of her, commits suicide.

Zeftel Lekach, the relatively young wife of the convicted thief Leibush, who escaped from prison but did not return to her. She is supported by a "pension" from a local gang of thieves. She is a plain peasant woman devoted to Yasha. She sells her belongings and moves to Warsaw to be near Yasha

and to escape the boredom and drudgery of life in Piask. She falls into the hands of Herman, a pimp, and his sister, Rytza Miltz, who trade in girls to be lured to Buenos Aires as prostitutes. Herman divorces his wife and marries Zeftel. She and Herman operate one of the biggest brothels in Buenos Aires.

Emilia Chrabotzky, once the well-to-do wife of a professor, now impoverished, widowed, and Yasha's mistress. She is Polish, a Catholic, and pretty. She lives in Warsaw with her fourteen-year-old daughter, Halina. She refuses any physical relationship with Yasha until they are married. After Yasha leaves her, she marries a widowed professor. She writes Yasha a long letter after he has become famous and respected as a holy man. Among other things, she reports that Halina has been cured of her ailments.

Kazimierz Zaruski, a wealthy usurer and miser. His servant-maid and Yadwiga, Emilia's former servant-maid, know each other. He keeps his money in a big box in his rooms. He is asleep when Yasha enters his apartment to rob him. Yasha leaves behind a wadded sheet of paper that he had torn out of his notebook. It contains the names and addresses of prospective burglary victims as well as Emilia's name and address.

— *Arthur Tilo Alt*

THE MAGNIFICENT AMBERSONS

Author: Booth Tarkington (1869-1946)
First published: 1918
Genre: Novel

Locale: A midwestern city
Time: 1873 to early in the twentieth century
Plot: Social realism

George Amberson Minafer, the protagonist, the only offspring of Isabel Amberson's marriage to Wilbur Minafer. During his childhood, when the Ambersons dominate their Midland town, George is spoiled by his mother, becoming a source of irritation to the community. His contempt for those who are not of his own class makes the townspeople yearn for his downfall. He is proud of his status and his powerful family. He falls in love with Lucy Morgan when he is a college student and at his social peak. George, unlike Lucy's father, Eugene Morgan, is without a profession. Closely linked with the past, he has reigned over the community like a despotic feudal lord. He fails to see the significance of the rising industrial tide and the concomitant decline of his family's fortune until it is too late. George hates the automobile, as the most visible exponent of progress, and its local manufacturer, Eugene Morgan. George later bars Morgan from his widowed mother's life. Declining property values, bad investments, and family greed eventually leave George destitute and the sole supporter of his aunt, Fanny Minafer. Ironically, an automobile accident that sends him to the hospital reunites George with Lucy, who still loves him, and Eugene, who forgives him.

Lucy Morgan, the daughter of Eugene Morgan and George's love interest. Small in stature and possessing a lively wit, she is nevertheless formidable and self-reliant. Having accompanied her peripatetic father on his journeys from an early age, Lucy has an independence that makes her more than a match for George Minafer. Despite enormous pressure from George, she refuses to betroth herself to him as long as he refrains from working for a living. She is thoroughly imbued

with the values of her father, a thriving automobile manufacturer. The only thing she concedes to George's repeated overtures is a kind of quasi engagement. Her strength of will is such that she refuses to acknowledge her depth of feeling for George even when he tells her that they are parting for good. Although she regrets the grime and decay that are associated with the industrialization of the city, she is firmly committed to the future, moving with her father to successively newer homes that are increasingly distant from the inner city. She finally accepts George at the end of the novel, after he has lost his fortune and must work for a living.

Isabel Amberson Minafer, George's mother and the object of Eugene Morgan's affection. After Isabel marries the taciturn businessman Wilbur Minafer, she compensates by slavishly devoting herself to her son George. The depth of her love can be measured by the fact that after she is widowed, she allows George to bar former fiancé Eugene Morgan from her life. Even after her death, she apparently communicates to Eugene through a psychic and asks him to help her son.

Eugene Morgan, Lucy's father and the embodiment of the future in the novel. As a debt-ridden young lawyer, Eugene inadvertently sacrifices his engagement to Isabel through a drinking mishap on the Amberson estate. He returns twenty years later to rebuild the relationship and to make his fortune in the automobile industry. Self-confident and sharing Lucy's keen sense of humor, he prophesies the success of his machines and the decline of the inner city. He is the classic self-made man, and his rise parallels the fall of the house of Amberson.

Fanny Minafer, George's aunt and sister to Wilbur Minafer. As a young woman, Fanny loved Eugene Morgan, and his return twenty years later rekindles her affection. Indeed, throughout most of the novel she schemes to capture her long-sought prize and escape unmarried old age. When Fanny tells George about local gossip concerning Isabel and Eugene, he ends the relationship. George continually torments her about her unmarried status; ironically, she must rely on him when the Amberson estate dissipates.

George Amberson, Isabel's brother and George's namesake. He is the novel's philosopher. Although he is abysmal as an investor—he contributes as much as anyone to the loss of the family fortune—his is the story's most consistently intelligent voice. He foresees the passing of the Ambersons, and he counsels his nephew to ignore the gossip about Isabel and Eugene. After the loss of the family fortune, he accepts a consulship and leaves town.

— Cliff Prewencki

MAGNIFICENT OBSESSION

Author: Lloyd C. Douglas (1877-1951)
First published: 1929
Genre: Novel

Locale: Detroit, Michigan, and Europe
Time: Early twentieth century
Plot: Domestic realism

Dr. Wayne Hudson, an eminent brain surgeon who dies from drowning when the inhalator that might have saved his life is used to resuscitate a wealthy playboy. Somewhat of a mystic, the doctor is a generous philanthropist, but he hides his good deeds; he thinks his great ability as a surgeon is a gift that comes from doing unknown good for other people.

Joyce Hudson, the doctor's daughter.

Helen Brent Hudson, Joyce Hudson's school friend who becomes Dr. Hudson's second wife. After she is a widow, Robert Merrick makes her the recipient of some of his philanthropy and then falls in love with her. In Rome, her life is saved after a train wreck by Dr. Merrick, who keeps his identity a secret. She discovers at last that she loves Merrick, and the two are to be married.

Nancy Ashford, superintendent of the Hudson Clinic. She has been in love with Dr. Hudson. She tells Robert Merrick he ought to try to take Dr. Hudson's place.

Robert Merrick, a rich playboy who becomes a doctor in order to take the place of Dr. Hudson, a famous brain surgeon whose life is lost when an inhalator is used for young Merrick. Merrick tries the doctor's theory of philanthropy, deriving power from hidden good deeds. He finds that it is indeed a secret to a successful life, and thus Merrick succeeds in becoming a famous brain surgeon himself. He marries Dr. Hudson's widow.

Dawson, a fellow medical student aided financially by Merrick so that the young man can finish medical school. This philanthropic act inspires Merrick and convinces him that he can follow in Dr. Hudson's footsteps.

THE MAGUS

Author: John Fowles (1926-   )
First published: 1965; revised, 1977
Genre: Novel

Locale: England and Greece
Time: 1953
Plot: Psychological realism

Nicholas Urfe, a young Oxford graduate who mistakes himself for a poet and takes a job teaching English at the Lord Byron School for boys on the island of Phraxos, Greece. An only child of deceased middle-class parents, in his mid-twenties, he is honest and perceptive but an Oxford dandy and a self-centered existentialist who exploits the affections of women. He goes to Greece because he is bored, needs a new mystery, and is not ready to marry Alison Kelly, his latest romantic interest. On the lonely island, he is disillusioned to discover that he is inauthentic and not a poet after all. He becomes depressed to the brink of suicide but falls in love with Greece, with his role in a masque (or psychodrama) conducted by the mysterious Maurice Conchis, and with Lily, an ideal woman who plays several roles in the masque. Conchis shapes his consciousness, making him suffer and learn. In the course of his experiences, Nicholas compares himself to Adam, Narcissus, Icarus, Candide, Theseus, Eumenides, and Orpheus. In the end, he is "disintoxicated" by the idealized Lily and returns to England, where he seeks to reconcile with Alison as his true love, his "reality" and standard by which to live.

Alison Kelly, a young Australian woman living in London who falls in love with Nicholas. An independent yet waiflike girl in her early twenties, she has a thin boyish figure, a deep tan, long hair that is bleached almost blonde, truth-seeking gray eyes in a hard face, and a salty directness. She is not beautiful, often not even pretty, but has a natural warmth and aura of sexuality. She has had an abortion and has not been happy since, and she is breaking off an affair. To Nicholas, she seems intensely vital, daring, bluntly honest, and somewhat crude. Although she is an expert coaxer and handler of men, she cannot induce him to marry her and goes off to become an air hostess. She is hurt so badly by him that she conspires in the masque of Conchis and pretends to have committed suicide, then later reveals that she is alive after all but makes him wait more than three months before giving him a chance to talk to her. At the end, it remains uncertain whether she will ever forgive him.

Maurice Conchis, a powerful rich old illusionist, or Magus, with a villa on the island of Phraxos. He is the godfather of Lily and Rose. Brown as old leather, short, and nearly bald, he is sixty to seventy years old, with intensely dark simian eyes that seem not quite human. He resembles Pablo Picasso and is also compared to Prospero, Svengali, Mohandas K. (Mahatma) Gandhi, Johann Sebastian Bach, Hades, Zeus, and God. His mother was Greek. During the German occupation in World War II, he was mayor of the village on Phraxos and survived being shot by a firing squad. At present, he has a heart condition and may die at any time. He seems to have business interests all over the world and is a connoisseur of art, a musician, a medical doctor, a hypnotist, and a sort of novelist, creating with real people. Every year, he draws a teacher at the Lord Byron School into a psychodrama, or "godgame," that tests and may build character. He teaches Nicholas the meanings of freedom, hazard, responsible individualism, and the smile of wisdom.

Lily, a rich and cultivated young Englishwoman who plays several roles in the godgame of her godfather, Conchis. Beau-tiful, elegant, cool, aloof, highly cultured, multilingual, and extremely intelligent, she is everything the more normal Alison is not. She has very white skin; long, silky blonde hair; a Botticelli face; cool hyacinth eyes with tilted corners; and a Mona Lisa smile. As Artemis, Isis, Astarte, and Kali in the psychodrama, she is a goddess; as Lily Montgomery, she is a pure and genteel lady of the Edwardian period; as Julie Holmes, she is a contemporary liberated woman; and as Dr. Vanessa Maxwell, she is an "advanced" psychologist who reduces Nicholas to a negative case study. In her disintoxication of Nicholas, she makes love in front of him with her actual lover, a black American named Joe.

Rose, Lily's twin sister, who acts with her in the psychodrama, for a while in the role of June Holmes. Nicholas differentiates between the twins by noting that Lily has a scar on her wrist and that Rose has a much more modern face.

— *Michael Hollister*

THE MAHABHARATA
(Mahābhārata)

Author: Unknown
First transcribed: c. 400 B.C.E.-200 C.E.
Genre: Poetry

Locale: Northern India
Time: Antiquity
Plot: Epic

Krishna (KREESH-nuh), an incarnation (avatar) of the god Vishnu. Krishna rules the Yadavas, on the northwestern coast of India. He is a close friend of Arjuna. In the great war between the Kauravas (KOW-ruh-vuhs) and the Pandavas (PAHN-duh-vuhs), Krishna acts as Arjuna's charioteer. When Arjuna feels reluctance to fight and kill his cousins, Krishna convinces him to fight, teaches him basic truths about the universe, and reveals his divine glory. This extended scene is related in the *Bhagavad Gita*, a major Hindu scripture. In the battle, Krishna does not fight; instead, he encourages and assists Arjuna.

Dhritarashtra (dree-tuh-RASH-truh), who would be king except that being born blind disqualifies him. He eventually does rule because of the death of his brother, Pandu. He has one hundred sons, born in an unusual manner. His sons are known as the Kauravas. His weakness as king is shown in his inability to resist the evil plans of his eldest son, Duryodhana. Dhritarashtra permits the dice game in which Duryodhana wins everything from Yudhishthira, including the other four Pandavas. Dhritarashtra also cannot avert the war in which his sons are all killed.

Pandu (PAHN-dew), Dhritarashtra's brother. Because of a curse, he cannot lie with his wives, Kunti (KEWN-tee) and Madri (MAH-dree). He dies early in the epic, when he finally lies with Madri. His wives have sons by several gods. These sons (except for Karna) are known as the Pandavas.

Yudhishthira (yew-DEESH-tee-ruh), the oldest son of Pandu and the rightful ruler. His actual father is the god of rightness and truth, Dharma. Yudhishthira is committed to truth and justice, but he cannot resist Duryodhana's challenge to a dice game. He is clearly cheated during the gaming but will not stop until he has lost all of his possessions, himself, his brothers, and their common wife, Draupadi.

Bhima (BIH-muh), the second son of Kunti. His father is Vayu (VAH-yew), the god of the wind. Because of the wind's great strength, Bhima is the strongest man in the world. He is not especially bright, but he is good-hearted. He also has an enormous appetite for food and drink. Being Vayu's son, Bhima is a half brother to Hanuman, a monkey god from another Indian epic, *The Ramayana*. Both Bhima and Hanuman can change size.

Arjuna (UHR-jewn-uh), the third son of Kunti. His father is Indra (EEN-druh), a warrior god. Because of his father, Arjuna is a great warrior, especially as an archer. He has the ability to shoot thousands of arrows nearly simultaneously. Arjuna leads the Pandavas in many ways. After Yudhishthira's loss at dice, the Pandavas must spend thirteen years in exile and a fourteenth in disguise. Arjuna is transformed, by a curse, into a dancing girl during this year.

Nakula (NAH-kool-uh) and
Sahadeva (suh-huh-DAY-vuh), the last two Pandavas, sons of Madri by the Asvins (UHSH-veens), twin gods associated with healing and horses. They do not play as large a role as the sons of Kunti.

Karna (KAHR-nuh), Kunti's first son. His father is Surya (SUHR-yuh), the sun god. Born with natural armor, Karna is abandoned by his mother. When he finally comes into contact with her and his brothers, he is very hostile. Karna becomes an ally of Duryodhana. As a warrior, he seems the equal of Arjuna.

Draupadi (DROW-puh-dee), the common wife of the Pandavas. This unusual arrangement results from Kunti telling Arjuna that he must share with his brothers. When Yudhishthira loses her in the dice game, Kunti protests cleverly that, having lost himself already, Yudhishthira cannot lose her.

Duryodhana (dewr-YOH-duh-nuh), the first son of Dhritarashtra. He seeks to take the kingship from Yudhishthira. Early in the epic, he plots to burn the Pandavas alive in their house. When this plot fails, Duryodhana plans the dice game. He seeks to find and kill the Pandavas during their exile. He is dishonorable and unjust, the opposite of Yudhish-thira.

Sakuni (SHAH-kew-nee), Duryodhana's maternal uncle. He actually throws the dice against Yudhishthira, gloating as he wins each throw. Sakuni plots with Duryodhana to destroy the Pandavas.

Bhishma (BIHSH-muh), the grandfather of both the Kauravas and the Pandavas. While fighting for the Kauravas, he knows that the Pandavas have right on their side.

Drona (DROH-nuh), the martial arts teacher of both the Pandavas and the Kauravas. Like Bhishma, he sympathizes with the Pandavas but fights for the Kauravas.

— *Gene Doty*

THE MAID OF HONOUR

Author: Philip Massinger (1583-1640)
First published: 1632
Genre: Drama

Locale: Palermo and Siena, Italy
Time: The Renaissance
Plot: Tragicomedy

Camiola (ka-mee-OH-lah), the "Maid of Honour." Although she is deeply in love with Bertoldo, she refuses to marry him because of his vow of celibacy as a Knight of Malta. In spite of his faithlessness in accepting the love of Aurelia, Camiola forgives him, ransoms him, and wins him back to his knightly vows. She herself weds the church as a nun.

Roberto (roh-BEHR-toh), the king of Sicily. He is a just, reasonable, and peaceful monarch but is unwisely overindulgent to his evil favorite, Fulgentio. Camiola finally persuades him to renounce Fulgentio.

Bertoldo (behr-TOHL-doh), the half brother of the king. Eager for glory in battle, he disregards the king's wishes and joins Duke Ferdinand in an unjust war on Siena. After being captured, he accepts the love of his captor, Duchess Aurelia, moved more by ambition than by desire. Shame heaped on him by Camiola leads to his repentance.

Fulgentio (fewl-JEHN-tee-oh), the king's unworthy favorite. Arrogant, selfish, and unprincipled, he first tries to force

Camiola to marry him, then tries to blacken her name. For this he is banished.

Sylli (SEE-lee), an absurd suitor for Camiola's hand. He is convinced that she loves him to distraction until the moment that she announces her entrance into the convent.

Adorni (ah-DOHR-nee), a faithful, self-sacrificing youth in love with Camiola. Although he fails to win her, she endows him with a large fortune when she renounces the world.

Ferdinand, the duke of Urbin. Angry at being rejected by Aurelia, he attacks her land and suffers defeat.

Aurelia (oh-REE-lee-ah), the duchess of Siena. A proud and passionate woman, she conceives a violent infatuation for her prisoner Bertoldo.

Gonzaga (gohn-ZAH-gah), the Sienese general, a Knight of Malta. Recognizing his prisoner Bertoldo as a Knight of Malta fighting in an unjust cause, he degrades him and dismisses him from the order.

Astutio (ahs-TEWT-ee-oh), an ambassador to Siena from King Roberto.

THE MAIDS
(Les Bonnes)

Author: Jean Genet (1910-1986)
First published: 1948
Genre: Drama

Locale: An elegant feminine bedroom
Time: Indeterminate, possibly in the early twentieth century
Plot: Surrealism

Solange (soh-LAHNZH), a maid between thirty and thirty-five years of age. She is a bitter, violent, frustrated young woman who tends to dominate her sister Claire, who is also a maid. In many respects, the two sisters are similar, even interchangeable. They both deeply resent the humiliating and subservient position they have been allotted by society. They are nothing; they have no real being, except that Madame, their mistress, makes them. Envious of each other, as well as of Madame, they passionately hate and love each other just as they passionately hate and love Madame, that love-hate relationship being colored with erotic overtones. Alienated from the real world by social prejudices, each time Madame goes out, they escape their tawdry existence by playing a game, setting up a dream world. In this ritual, each in turn impersonates Madame and her relationship with her lover, while the other plays the part of the other sister she is not, as the maid she is. During that ceremonial game, they both speak in a falsely exalted, deliberately artificial, declamatory language,

in which they throw harsh insults at each other, acting out all of their anger and frustration at each other as well as at Madame. When the real Madame arrives onstage, they interrupt the game, but far from reintegrating reality, they continue to act. Now, however, they play the roles of obedient and faithful servants. Solange seems harder than Claire, whom she tries to dominate; however, she is in fact more cowardly than her sister. She did not have the courage to write the letters of denunciation that sent Monsieur, Madame's lover, to jail. She kept Monsieur's letters to Madame because she was in love with him. At the end, after Madame's departure, she pushes the "ceremony" to its logical conclusion by giving Claire the cup of poisoned tea that they had prepared for Madame. She will then become Solange Lemercier, the murderess. Through the ritual, she at last will have attained a reality of her own.

Claire, Madame's maid and Solange's younger sister. Sharing Solange's degrading predicament and most of her emotions, she seems gentler yet more perfidious. She, too, must resort to living in a fantasy world to escape her sordid life. When the curtain rises, she plays at impersonating her mistress, exaggerating the latter's gestures and language, making her look like a haughty shrew. Every night, she parades on the balcony, wrapped in drapes or in a bedspread, saluting like a queen the

multitude below her. After Madame has left to join her lover, she decides to resume the ceremony and to play it to the bitter end by drinking the poisoned tea destined for Madame, in a solemn ritual that will put an end to the sisters' humiliation and allow them to achieve their final deliverance.

Madame, a kept woman of about twenty-five living on the fringes of society. She is as alienated from the real world as her maids. Dressed in gaudy attire, she lives out a fantasy with Monsieur, her lover, painting a glowing picture of her alleged martyrdom and heroism. She plans to follow her lover to Siberia, devoting her life to him. She will not drink the poisoned tea Claire brings her, in an exalted renunciation of all earthly matters. As soon as she hears that Monsieur is free, she runs out to drink champagne with him. She is kind to her maids, giving them her old clothes and the flowers that she does not want. She loves them as disposable objects, smothering them under her affected kindness. She is onstage only for a brief time, but she still remains a powerful force, ever present in her absence, during the whole play. Lacking a personal name, she is a symbol, a function, directly responsible for the maids' sordid predicament.

Monsieur, Madame's lover, who is never seen by the audience but who stands in the center of Madame's life. In this bourgeois atmosphere, he is the only one ennobled by prison, the victim of Claire's anonymous false accusations.

— *Marie-Denise Boros Azzi*

THE MAID'S TRAGEDY

Authors: Francis Beaumont (c. 1584-1616) and John Fletcher (1579-1625)
First published: 1619
Genre: Drama

Locale: Rhodes
Time: Antiquity
Plot: Tragedy

The king of Rhodes, who is to all appearances a just, if undistinguished, ruler. He is, in fact, a man who does not scruple to use those around him ruthlessly for his own ends. He brings bloody death upon himself by his dishonoring of Evadne and by his despicable treatment of Amintor, a courtier.

Evadne (eh-VAD-nee), a noblewoman, mistress to the king, who arranges her marriage to Amintor. She shows herself almost completely self-centered in the opening scenes, in which she coldly reveals her duplicity to her husband and tells him that she is simply using him to conceal her relationship with the king. The force with which she vows to be his wife in name only suggests the strength of character that makes her a tragic figure. Confronted by her brother with the dishonor she has brought upon herself, her husband, and her family, she recoils in horror from the hell in which she has placed herself, begs forgiveness of Amintor, and resolves to "redeem one minute of my age or, like another Niobe . . . weep till I am water." She finds this redemption in tying the king to his bed and stabbing him to death as she accuses him of villainy. When she returns to her husband, she feels herself purged, free at last to offer herself as his wife. Death is the only recourse left to her when Amintor, horrified by the slaying of an anointed king, repulses her.

Amintor (eh-MIHN-tohr), Evadne's ill-used husband. He is, from the moment of his marriage, conscience-stricken by his betrayal of Aspatia, to whom he had been betrothed. He attempts to justify himself by reflecting that he acted on the king's orders, but he recognizes simultaneously that the king had no control over his will; he could have refused the bride who was offered to him. Shocked by Evadne's wedding-night declaration, he plays the part of happy husband badly, but his reverence for royal blood restrains him from avenging his honor with violence and ultimately causes his final repudiation of his wife. Some pity for her lingers in him, however, and he turns, too late, to try to prevent her suicide. He kills himself beside the body of Aspatia, whom he had slain unintentionally.

Melantius (meh-LAN-shee-uhs), Evadne's brother, a valiant soldier. Devoted to his friend Amintor, he persuades him to explain the reason for his strange fits of misery. Unlike Amintor, he feels no allegiance to an unjust monarch, and he plots the killing, which is carried out by Evadne, while playing on the king's overconfidence to attain his ends.

Aspatia (eh-SPAY-shuh), Amintor's betrothed, who grieves constantly after his marriage to Evadne and sings sad songs of faithful maidens and false lovers. She longs for death and finally finds it at the moment when she least desires it, when she hears from Amintor that he still loves her. She had come to him disguised as a boy and deliberately provoked him to a duel; he wounded her mortally before he realized who she was.

Calianax (ka-lih-A-nuhks), her father, a cowardly, testy old man. He was a longtime enemy of Melantius, who used his distrust to advance his plot against the king.

Lysippus (li-SIH-puhs), the king's brother and successor. Recognizing the justice of Melantius' cause, he pardons him and his followers, who hold the key military positions in the city.

Diphilus (DI-fih-luhs), Melantius' brother and fellow conspirator.

Cleon (KLEE-on) and

Strato (STRAY-toh), nobles in the court of Rhodes.

Diagoras (di-A-guh-ruhs), the doorkeeper in the king's banqueting hall.

Dula (DEW-luh), Evadne's witty lady-in-waiting.

Antiphila (an-TIH-fih-luh) and

Olympias (oh-LIHM-pee-uhs), Aspatia's devoted maids.

Two gentlemen, servants of the king who watch Evadne enter his bedchamber and plan to enjoy themselves. They discover their master's body and fear that they will be accused of his murder.

MAIN STREET: The Story of Carol Kennicott

Author: Sinclair Lewis (1885-1951)
First published: 1920
Genre: Novel

Locale: A small midwestern town
Time: c. 1910-1920
Plot: Social satire

Carol Kennicott, an idealistic girl eager to reform the world. Interested in sociology and civic improvement, she longs to transform the ugliness of midwestern America into something more beautiful. Having married Dr. Will Kennicott, she moves to his home in Gopher Prairie, Minnesota, a hideous small town indistinguishable from hundreds of similar communities. There, she shocks and angers the townspeople by her criticisms and by her attempts to combat the local smugness. To its citizens, Gopher Prairie is perfection; they can see no need for change. To her, it is an ugly, gossipy, narrow-minded village, sunk in dullness and self-satisfaction. Her efforts to change the town fail, and she drifts into a mild flirtation with Erik Valborg, a Swedish tailor with artistic yearnings. Frightened by the village gossip, she and her husband take a trip to California; but on her return, she realizes that she must get away from both her husband and Gopher Prairie. After some argument, she and her small son leave for Washington, where she stays for more than a year. The flight is a failure, for she finds Washington only an agglomeration of the small towns in America. She returns to Gopher Prairie, realizing that it is her home. Her crusade has failed; she can only hope that her children will accomplish what she has been unable to do.

Dr. Will Kennicott, Carol's husband, a successful physician in Gopher Prairie. Though he loves Carol, he is dull and unimaginative, unable to enter her world or to understand her longings. He is the typical self-satisfied citizen of a small town.

Guy Pollock, a lawyer. Though sensitive and intellectual, he is the victim of the "village virus" that has deprived him of all initiative. At first, he appears to Carol as the most hopeful person in town, but he disappoints her with his timidity and conventionalism.

Vida Sherwin, a teacher at the high school. Though better educated, she is as satisfied with the Gopher Prairie standards as are the other citizens. She marries Raymond Wutherspoon.

Raymond Wutherspoon, a sales clerk in the Bon Ton Store. A pallid, silly man, he marries Vida Sherwin. He goes to France during World War I and returns as a major.

Erik Valborg, a tailor in Gopher Prairie, the son of a Swedish farmer. Handsome and aesthetically inclined, he attracts Carol, and they have a mild flirtation. Gossip drives him from the town; he goes to Minneapolis and is last seen playing small parts in the movies.

Bea Sorenson, a farm girl who comes to Gopher Prairie to find work. She is as much fascinated by the town as Carol is repelled. She becomes the Kennicotts' hired girl and Carol's only real friend. She marries Miles Bjornstam and has a son. She and the little boy both die of typhoid fever.

Miles Bjornstam, the village handyman and radical, one of the few genuine people in Gopher Prairie and one of the few who understand Carol. He marries Bea Sorenson; when she and their child die, he leaves the town.

Mrs. Bogart, the Kennicotts' neighbor. She is the epitome of village narrow-mindedness.

Sam Clark, a hardware dealer and solid citizen.

Percy Bresnahan, born in Gopher Prairie but now a successful automobile manufacturer in Boston. He visits his home for occasional fishing trips and stoutly maintains that it is God's country. Heavy-handed, jocular, and thoroughly standardized, he is the forerunner of George F. Babbitt.

James Blauser, known as "Honest Jim." A professional hustler and promoter, he is hired to start a campaign for a Greater Gopher Prairie. Not much is accomplished.

Hugh, Will and Carol's first child, on whom she lavishes her attention.

MAJOR BARBARA

Author: George Bernard Shaw (1856-1950)
First published: 1907
Genre: Drama

Locale: London and Middlesex
Time: January, 1906
Plot: Play of ideas

Sir Andrew Undershaft, a munitions tycoon. Believing that poverty is the root of all discontent and, consequently, a threat to capitalism, he uses his power and wealth in an attempt to eliminate it. In a war of ideas with his daughter Barbara, he proves that a donation from a dealer in death—namely, himself—will buy the good graces of the Salvation Army. He then proceeds to fill the void created by her disillusionment by converting her to his own creed.

Barbara, Sir Andrew's daughter. As a major in the Salvation Army, she exercises her moral fervor in the cause of winning the souls of the poor to the kingdom of God. When her father proves to her that a donation from his deplored and destructive profession can win the favor of the Army, she

becomes converted to his creed that it is useless to attempt the salvation of souls until the souls' destroyer, poverty, has been eliminated.

Adolphus Cusins, a professor of Greek, Barbara's suitor. His intellect, added to Sir Andrew's power and Barbara's moral fervor, completes the trinity that Sir Andrew believes will be the salvation of society.

Lady Britomart Undershaft, Sir Andrew's domineering wife, who abhors what she calls her husband's immorality, though she does not hesitate to capitalize on it.

Stephen Undershaft, Sir Andrew's painfully conventional son.

Sarah Undershaft, Sir Andrew's younger daughter.

Charles Lomax, Sarah Undershaft's vacuous suitor.
Snobby Price,
Rummy Mitchens,

Peter Shirley, and
Bill Walker, frequenters of the Salvation Army headquarters.

THE MAKEPEACE EXPERIMENT
(Lubimow)

Author: Andrei Sinyavsky (as Abram Tertz, 1925-1997)
First published: 1963
Genre: Novel

Locale: Lyubimov, a fictitious small Russian town
Time: Early 1960's
Plot: Satire

Leonard (Lenny) Makepeace, also known as **Leonid Tikhomirov** (leh-oh-NIHD tih-khoh MIH-rov), a young bicycle repairman in the fictitious Russian city of Lyubimov. Lenny's father was a cobbler who perished in World War II. His mother dotes on him, trying continually to fatten his lean, narrow-chested frame with cottage cheese. Lenny becomes obsessed with coming to power in Lyubimov because he thinks this will please Serafima Petrovna, the attractive local language teacher. He obtains power by the use of "mental magnetism," a skill he acquired by reading a book written by Samson Samsonovich Proferansov, the philanthropist ancestor of Savely Kuzmich Proferansov, a Lyubimov librarian. After taking power, Lenny enforces a hypnotic utopia on the citizens of Lyubimov, protecting the city from outside authorities by means of a sort of mental camouflage. Lenny's utopia embodies a naïve idealism, well-meaning but at variance with the many frailties of human nature. In the end, his control erodes, and he even commands certain unappreciative citizens to die in the interest of a public welfare that he defines. His friends and supporters desert him as the outside authorities retake the city by force. Lenny sneaks out of the city and into obscurity by hitching a ride on a freight train.

Savely Kuzmich Proferansov (sah-VYEH-lee kewz-MIHKH proh-feh-RAN-sov), the Lyubimov municipal librarian and the intermittent narrator of the novel's events. A widower with a bald spot and a grown daughter, Savely befriends Lenny Makepeace, suggesting that Lenny involve himself in reading as solace for Serafima Petrovna's lack of affection. When Lenny's reading results in his taking control of the city, Savely is elevated to become his official historiographer. Savely's writing, however, is openly influenced by the will of his disembodied ancestor, Samson Samsonovich Proferansov, who dictates much of its content. When Lenny's utopia falls apart, Savely is able to survive by ingratiating himself with the former leader, Semyon Gavrilovich Tishchenko.

Samson Samsonovich Proferansov, the disembodied spirit of a nineteenth century nobleman and philanthropist, a friend and correspondent of Antoine Lavoisier and Leo Tolstoy, and a sojourner to mystic India. He first appears to his descendant, Savely Kuzmich Proferansov, in the human form of a professor sent to investigate the finding of a "skeleton of a monk with boar's tusks instead of teeth." It is he who directs Savely to write down events concerning the city's history, and it is he who meddles in these events by making his book, *The Magnet of the Soul*, available for Lenny Makepeace to read.

Serafima Petrovna Kozlova (seh-rah-FIH-mah peh-TROHV-nah KOH-zloh-vah), a beautiful language teacher in Lyubimov who is admired by many of the male inhabitants of the city. She tells Lenny Makepeace that she will have him only if he lays the city of Lyubimov at her feet. Lenny's subsequent mental power over the city's inhabitants includes Serafima, who is made to show constant adoration for him. She and Lenny are married, but the marriage is never consummated. In a moment of mental freedom, she denies Savely Kuzmich's prejudicial contention that she is a "Jewess" but admits to Lenny's consternation that she has been married before, that she has a daughter living elsewhere, and that she has had affairs with several local men, including Dr. Linde. She eventually flees the city and Lenny, taking with her the money with which he had wallpapered her room.

Dr. Linde, a local physician with an ash-blond moustache who tells Lenny Makepeace about his having spotted a live prehistoric pterodactyl near Lyubimov. His pterodactyl is later encountered by government troops trying to find their way to Lyubimov through Lenny's mental camouflage. Dr. Linde becomes Lenny's chief medical officer but is demoted to hospital orderly after Lenny finds out about his affair with Serafima Petrovna. In the end, he refuses to run away with Serafima, choosing instead to seek favor with Semyon Gavrilovich Tishchenko.

Vitaly Kochetov (vih-TAH-lee koh-cheh-TOV), a government agent, a minor character referred to as Vitya in an earlier novel. He manages to infiltrate Lyubimov despite Lenny Makepeace's security system. Overhearing Lenny's intentions, he becomes Lenny's staunch supporter and friend. Like Dr. Linde, he refuses to run away with Serafima Petrovna, and he is killed confronting a government tank.

Semyon Gavrilovich Tishchenko (sehm-YON gahv-RIH-loh-vihch TIH-shchehn-koh), the secretary of the Lyubimov Party Committee, the town leader who is mentally forced to surrender his power to Lenny Makepeace. He retires to the riverbank and bides his time by fishing. As Lenny's control of Lyubimov diminishes, various citizens come to make their peace with him. After Lenny's departure, he is restored to a secondary position of power.

Lenny's mother, an aging widow who continually asks her son to "have a little cottage cheese." When she asks Lenny not to tear down the local monastery, he forces her to mouth the words "There is no God." In the end, she requests a priest to perform a service for the welfare of her son.

— *Lee B. Croft*

THE MAKING OF AMERICANS: Being a History of a Family's Progress

Author: Gertrude Stein (1874-1946)
First published: 1925
Genre: Novel

Locale: Bridgepoint (Baltimore) and Gossols (Oakland)
Time: Sixty years, probably in the late nineteenth and early twentieth centuries
Plot: Psychological realism

Henry Dehning, a rich merchant. Although he is of medium height, his facial features denote strength: a firm chin, a strong, curved nose, and coarse, bushy eyebrows. These are matched by square shoulders and a stocky body, both of which belie his agility in movement and gentle temper. He is of immigrant parents and is a self-made man. In his business dealings, he is firm, careful, practical, and basically honest. In love, he does not mind feeling owned; in fact, he likes somewhat aggressive women. As a successful patriarch, he likes giving kindly advice, which tends to be sprinkled with Old World wisdom despite his many years spent in America.

Jenny Dehning, Henry Dehning's wife. She is a fair woman, heavy but attractive. She has a healthy, prosperous look about her. Her pride in her husband's success does not prevent her from upbraiding him for his lapses in social niceties. She is usually cheerful, but at times she can be crude, harsh, aggressive, and filled with her own importance.

Julia Dehning, the eldest daughter of Henry and Jenny Dehning. Fair like her mother, she radiates the energy, vigor, and daring that come from a pampered existence. Her father adores her. From her grandparents' tradition, she inherited a need for romance and passion. She thinks that she has a taste for adventure and the more refined experiences of life, which is what attracts her to Alfred Hersland; however, the core of her being is not really adventurous or passionate. Like her father, a part of Julia resists learning or change.

David Hersland, a successful businessman. He is a big man, with small, brown, piercing eyes covered by long, rough eyebrows. He inherited his mother's strength, which helped make him a success. His father, however, was a weak and uncertain man, and because of this mixture of traits, he begins projects with vigor but often has trouble completing them. He can also be quite impatient and irritable. Although he devotes much thought to his children's education, he ignores his wife.

Fanny Hissen, David Hersland's wife, small and mild-mannered. From a well-to-do family, she lives a rather isolated life after moving to Gossols with David. Understandably, her world centers on her family life. She is never really important to her husband, and as their children grow older, she diminishes in importance to them. Despite her mild demeanor, she carries a streak of stubbornness that sometimes turns her into a peevishly domineering mother and employer.

Martha Hersland, the eldest child of David Hersland. She is somewhat attractive, small, and has blue eyes and a pleasant manner. She resembles her father in that she likes to feel important and is competitive. Unlike him, however, she can usually finish what she begins. Her assertive demeanor hides a lack of intelligence that prevents her from really understanding life. She marries Phillip Redfern, but the marriage is an unhappy one. After his death, she returns home to her father.

Alfred Hersland, the son of David Hersland. Well dressed, with strong, attractive features, he carries himself with a certain dignity and grace and thinks that he has a passion and strength for living, like his father. He desires the distinction of someone who cares about elegance and beauty in art and living. In actuality, however, he cannot sense things deeply or learn from experience. He is never either completely a success or completely a failure in life.

— *Ruth Hsu*

THE MAKIOKA SISTERS
(Sasameyuki)

Author: Jun'ichirō Tanizaki (1886-1965)
First published: 1943-1948
Genre: Novel

Locale: The Kobe-Osaka district and Tokyo
Time: 1938-1941
Plot: Social realism

Yukiko, the third of the four sisters, still unmarried at the age of thirty. She is a slender, delicate-looking beauty whose dress, appearance, and manner are thoroughly Japanese and suggest a sheltered maiden of old. She graduated from a ladies' seminary with honors in English and understands Western music better than she does Japanese music. Her shy, gentle manner masks a complex, intelligent, and critical nature. She is too reserved to talk frankly, and her overt docility causes much confusion and embarrassment to those seeking a good husband for her. She loves children and is especially attached to her niece, Etsuko.

Taeko, nicknamed **Koi-san** (which means "small daughter"), the youngest of the sisters, in her mid-twenties, but the most worldly and independent. Stylish Western clothes suit her firm, plump body and round face, but, paradoxically, she studies traditional Japanese dance and uses her artistic talents to create dolls to sell and to exhibit. Lively and gay, but also practical, she saves her earnings and is determined to be a financially independent professional woman. Impatient to get married but forced by Japanese custom to wait until Yukiko is married, Taeko exhibits willful behavior that complicates her sisters' lives.

Sachiko, the second sister, in her thirties. She is the mistress of the Ashiya branch of the family. In appearance the healthiest of the sisters but actually the weakest physically, she falls between the extremes of her younger sisters in style and outlook; she wears Western clothes in the summer and Japanese clothes the rest of the year and is very emotional. Her father's favorite, she still has something of the spoiled child about her, but she is devoted to her sisters and labors on their behalf, using her social position to help Taeko sell dolls and to search actively for a husband for Yukiko.

Teinosuke, an accountant. He took the Makioka name when he married Sachiko. Although he is a commercial-school graduate, he is interested in international politics and literature, and he writes poetry. In contrast to his brother-in-law, he is boyish and outgoing and actively seeks to help his sisters-in-law.

Mrs. Itani, the owner of a beauty shop that the sisters frequent. An enterprising, practical woman who supports a bedridden husband and who put a brother through medical school and a daughter through a university education, she is considered unladylike for speaking her mind directly. Her genuine friendliness, however, makes her inoffensive. She perceives that the Makiokas still rely on their former glory and need to be prodded; hence, she is very active in marriage negotiations for Yukiko.

Tsuruko, the eldest sister and mistress of the main house in Osaka. She is the tallest of the sisters and has the sturdiest build. The most conservatively educated, she is also the least adventurous. The mother of six children and an industrious housewife, she is much less secure than she appears to be. She sometimes rehearses conversations and can take several hours to write one letter. She and her husband respond deliberately and cautiously to all marriage proposals for Yukiko.

Tatsuo, a banker. He took the Makioka name when he married Tsuruko. An austere, retiring man who takes his responsibility as head of the family very seriously, he nevertheless sells the family shop and, after one humiliating experience as a marriage go-between for Yukiko, confines his efforts to the final stages of a marriage negotiation.

Etsuko, Sachiko's six-year-old daughter. Plump, rosy-cheeked, and lively, she is, like her mother, much weaker physically than she appears to be and requires much care, especially from her favorite aunt, Yukiko.

O-Haru, a maid. She started working in Sachiko's household when she was fourteen years old and, even after five years' service, is a slovenly, lazy person. Despite her poor grooming habits and her preference for talk over work, she has a good reputation because she is generous and likable. As a servant, she is the messenger involved in family affairs.

Okubata, also called **Kei-boy**, the pampered younger son of a wealthy, respectable family. His attempted elopement with Taeko when she was nineteen causes some concern in Yukiko's marriage negotiations. Although Taeko recognizes that Okubata is a spendthrift who cares more about the crease in his trousers than about her welfare, she remains attached to him.

Itakura, a professional photographer. He studied photography in Hollywood for several years before returning to Japan, in his late twenties, to open a studio. He meets Taeko when she hires him to prepare advertising copy. They are attracted to each other despite the difference in class.

Mimaki Minoru, a charming man of forty-four who has lived abroad for several years, studied physics and aeronautics, and is now known as an architect, though he is currently unemployed. Knowledgeable, sociable, and witty, he also drinks heavily and spends freely. His connection to a noble and wealthy family makes him a good catch for Yukiko.

Miyoshi, a bartender. Taeko's affair with him leads to her pregnancy. Although the baby dies at birth, Taeko moves in with him.

— *Shakuntala Jayaswal*

MALCOLM

Author: James Purdy (1923-   )
First published: 1959
Genre: Novel

Locale: An unidentified American city
Time: Mid-twentieth century
Plot: Surrealism

Malcolm, a fifteen-year-old who sits for months on a bench in front of a palatial hotel. When Mr. Cox finds Malcolm and suggests that the lad visit some addresses he knows, Malcolm makes the visits and hopes at times to find a new home, because his father has disappeared. Malcolm begins a journal and includes the conversations he hears at the addresses. Malcolm's misunderstandings of many of the words he hears in the depraved society to which Mr. Cox introduces him provide much of the humor in the surrealistic novel. Malcolm eventually marries an older woman named Melba. When he scuffles with a man he believes to be his father, he cuts his head on the marble bathroom floor. The injury forces him to stay in bed. His hair turns snow white. He contracts a cold and pneumonia and informs Melba that he has also suffered the bite of a dog. When Melba informs Malcolm that he is dying, Malcolm requests to see Madame Girard. Madame Girard comes quickly, but Malcolm does not seem to recognize her. It is Madame Girard who provides Malcolm's funeral.

Mr. Cox, the most famous astrologer and the greatest walker of his period and the source of most of the addresses Malcolm visits. Mr. Cox is also a pederast; Malcolm mistak-

enly believes this word means that he is a star gazer. After Malcolm's death, the reader is told, a young man follows through on twenty-five addresses supplied by Mr. Cox.

Melba, the popular singing star who proposes marriage to Malcolm upon their first meeting. This older woman immediately sends her first husband, Gus, to "mature" Malcolm before the wedding, which is to occur a week later. Malcolm becomes Melba's third husband. When Melba discovers that Malcolm is dying, she leaves and never returns. Melba marries her Cuban valet and is happy for five years. She eventually retires from her singing career.

Gus, the motorcyclist who takes Malcolm to Melba. Gus, Melba's first husband, helps Malcolm to mature before the wedding by taking him to a tattoo boutique and to a prostitute. The next morning, Malcolm finds Gus dead in the house of prostitution.

Kermit and
Laureen Raphaelson, the residents of the second address that Malcolm visits. Laureen is a large, plump woman, whereas Kermit is a very short man. Kermit tells Malcolm that Mr. Cox convinced Laureen, after their marriage, to go out

with others for a fee. Kermit eventually leaves his unfaithful wife and marries a retired film star. Laureen later marries Girard Girard.

Girard Girard, the third addressee that Mr. Cox gives to Malcolm. This unfaithful husband, poet, billionaire, and explorer later leaves his wife to marry Laureen Raphaelson.

Madame Girard, the wife of the third addressee. Girard leaves her, and she becomes the companion of a biochemist. She does not marry the biochemist, however, because of her devotion to her name.

Malcolm's father, who abandons Malcolm, appears in a restaurant after Malcolm's marriage, tries to ignore his son, and calls Malcolm a pederast.

Eloisa Brace, the female artist who invites Malcolm to move in. Eloisa begins to paint Malcolm and takes a check for $10,000 from Madame Girard for the unfinished portrait. When Eloisa's husband, Jerome, tells her that she would not take the money if she were truly a serious artist, Eloisa eats the check. When an anonymous donor—probably Girard Girard—later provides her with a pension, she loses all of her talent. Eloisa and Jerome become active in social concerns.

Jerome Brace, Eloisa's husband, a famous burglar who has been convicted, and author of the book titled *They Could Have Me Back*. Jerome becomes a social activist.

Estel Blanc, an undertaker, the first person Malcolm visits. This inhospitable man tells Malcolm to return in twenty years and gives Malcolm a second address, that of Kermit and Laureen Raphaelson. Later, Estel becomes the entrepreneur of a small opera company.

Cori Naldi, who sings during Malcolm's visit to Blanc's establishment. She becomes the permanent star of Blanc's opera company.

Professor Robinolte, the expert who tattoos Malcolm and Gus and promises to send Malcolm a birthday card and a Christmas card each year.

Madame Rosita, the owner of the house of prostitution that Gus and Malcolm visit. Madame Rosita compliments Malcolm on his performance during his visit and gives him a shaving mug with pictures of George Washington and the first American flag.

— *Anita P. Davis*

THE MALCONTENT

Author: John Marston (1576-1634)
First published: 1604
Genre: Drama

Locale: Genoa, Italy
Time: The thirteenth century
Plot: Tragicomedy

Giovanni Altofronto (jee-oh-VAHN-nee AHL-toh-FROHN-toh), the deposed duke of Genoa. Disguised as **Malevole** (mah-LEH-voh-leh), the Malcontent, he hurls insults at the dissolute courtiers and ladies around him while he inwardly laments the misfortunes that have forced him to play this role. His feigned eccentricity enables him to learn of the court intrigues and eventually to engineer the recovery of his dukedom.

Celso (CHEHL-soh), Altofronto's friend and his spy at the usurper's court.

Pietro Jacomo (pee-EH-troh JAH-coh-moh), the usurper duke. He dotes on his faithless young wife and pampers his adopted heir, Mendoza, until Malevole tells him of their disloyalty and helps him avenge this dishonor. Chastened by the recognition of his own blindness to others, he gratefully relinquishes his title to the rightful duke.

Mendoza (mehn-DOH-zah), his ambitious protégé, the duchess' lover. His ruthless plans to destroy all those who stand between him and the dukedom are foiled only by Malevole's intervention.

Ferneze (fehr-NEH-zay), a handsome, unprincipled courtier, Mendoza's rival for the favors of the duchess.

Aurelia (ah-ew-REH-lee-ah), Jacomo's young wife, who succumbs to both Mendoza and Ferneze. She repents when she believes her husband has committed suicide, and she is happily reunited with him after Malevole has exposed Mendoza's treachery.

Maria, Altofronto's virtuous wife. She repulses Mendoza's advances, preferring death to disloyalty to her husband.

Bilioso (bee-lee-OH-soh), a foolish old courtier, regularly deceived by his young wife. Malevole taunts him for his fluctuating allegiance to each new claimant to the dukedom.

Maquerelle (mah-kew-REHL-lay), Aurelia's aging lady in waiting. She aids and abets the duchess and her ladies in their infidelities.

Emilia and

Biancha (BEE-ahn-kah), the duchess' attendants.

THE MALTESE FALCON

Author: Dashiell Hammett (1894-1961)
First published: 1930
Genre: Novel

Locale: San Francisco, California
Time: 1928
Plot: Detective and mystery

Sam Spade, a tall, blond, pleasantly satanic-looking, hard-boiled private detective suspected of having killed Thursby and of having also killed Miles Archer in order to marry Iva. He at last learns how he has been used in the plot to get the Maltese falcon; he discovers the murderers of Miles and Thursby, and he turns Brigid over to the police.

Brigid O'Shaughnessy, his tall, attractive, auburn-haired, deceitful client, who first masquerades as a Miss Wonderly, then shoots Miles, double-crosses her associates, and finally attempts in vain to seduce Sam into letting her go free of a murder charge.

Casper Gutman, her fat, tough employer, who is attempting to get hold of the Maltese falcon. He is shot by Wilmer Cook.

Wilmer Cook, Gutman's young bodyguard, murderer of Thursby, Jacobi, and Gutman.

Joel Cairo, Gutman's dark-skinned, flashily dressed one-time agent.

Miles Archer, Spade's middle-aged partner, solidly built, wide-shouldered, red-faced. He is shot and killed by Brigid.

Floyd Thursby, Brigid's murdered accomplice.

Iva Archer, Miles's wife, a voluptuous, still pretty blonde in her thirties; in love with Sam.

Kemidov, a Russian in Constantinople who has substituted a lead imitation for the genuine Maltese falcon.

Jacobi, captain of the ship *La Paloma*; killed by Wilmer.

Effie Perine, Sam's lanky, boyish-faced, suntanned secretary.

Rhea Gutman, daughter of Gutman.

MAMA

Author: Terry McMillan (1951-   )
First published: 1987
Genre: Novel

Locale: Point Haven, Michigan; Los Angeles, California; and New York City
Time: 1964-1984
Plot: Social realism

Mildred Peacock, a black mother of five. Mildred struggles to rear her children during the turbulent 1960's and 1970's. She has a great capacity for living, and many of her actions reveal her unflinching desire to help her children live as fully as possible. In addition, Mildred wants to love and be loved. After becoming pregnant when she is seventeen, she marries her child's father, Crook Peacock, who brings little love to her life; she has four more children by him, and he abuses her physically and emotionally. Mildred takes his abuse for ten years before she divorces him. As a single mother and a high school dropout, Mildred does whatever she can to pay her rent and utilities and put food on the table for her children. She works on an assembly line before she is laid off, and she even works briefly as a prostitute to keep her children from starving. Mildred even swallows her pride and applies for and receives government aid. For Mildred, rearing children is not everything. She tries to find love in the arms of a number of men, eventually marrying two more times. Life in Point Haven, Michigan, is difficult as Mildred struggles to make ends meet. After her oldest daughter moves to Los Angeles, Mildred moves there too; her children's lives continue to be important to her, and she continues to have financial problems. Mildred often drinks too much, and after the thrill of Los Angeles fades and her children are grown, she returns to Point Haven. When she realizes she is getting old and that the sort of love she wanted is not going to enter her life, she gives up drinking, comes to love her old sagging self, and accepts the fact that she has triumphed, at least in one area, for all of her children are healthy and relatively happy adults.

Freda, Mildred's oldest daughter. When the novel begins, Freda is ten years old, and she thinks it is her responsibility to help Mildred rear the children, which means that Freda is the one to create order out of the chaos of Mildred's life. Freda is a younger version of Mildred. Even as a child, she is depicted as plotting and scheming. Freda smokes cigarettes, secures a part-time job, and vows at an early age to escape the moving, eviction notices, and bills that encircle her mother's life. She is almost raped when she is a young teen by one of Mildred's boyfriends, and she keeps this pain from her mother for many years, though the pain plagues her relationships with men and has something to do with her own adult alcoholism. Freda takes the steps that Mildred has been unable to take and leaves Point Haven, going to Los Angeles, where she secures a job, attends college, and becomes involved in the Black Power and feminist movements of the early 1970's. Freda helps Mildred and the rest of her family move to Los Angeles. Freda does so well in college that she is offered a scholarship to attend Stanford University, where she meets Delbert and has her first serious and long-term relationship. Delbert introduces Freda to cocaine and other drugs. She gives up cocaine but becomes a puppet to alcohol. On her thirtieth birthday, when she looks in the mirror and sees her mother's worn and tired face, she calls the local Alcoholics Anonymous chapter and takes charge of her life.

Curly Mae, Mildred's sister-in-law and best friend. Curly Mae suffers from low self-esteem, in part as a result of her husband's neglect. During her marriage, her husband asks her to work as a prostitute, and she agrees. Like Mildred, Curly Mae drinks too much, and her drinking takes its toll; she has her first stroke while in her early forties and her second one a few years later. More than anything, however, Curly Mae is the listening ear that Mildred needs.

— *Charles P. Toombs*

MAMA DAY

Author: Gloria Naylor (1950-   )
First published: 1988
Genre: Novel

Locale: The island of Willow Springs, off the coast of South Carolina and Georgia, and New York City
Time: Primarily the 1980's, but going back to 1799
Plot: Psychological realism

Miranda (Mama) Day, the elderly matriarch of the Day clan and unofficial ruler of Willow Springs. Linked to Sapphira Wade, her ancestor, in terms of possessing intuition, herbal knowledge, and magic, she is a conjure woman with the power to destroy and to heal. As midwife and healer, she has medicinal powers superior to those of medical doctors.

Abigail Day, Miranda's sister and soulmate, grandmother to Ophelia. Abigail and Miranda know each other's minds and write joint letters to Ophelia.

Ophelia (Cocoa) Day, who, despite the title of the novel, is the protagonist and one of the narrators in the novel. She is Miranda's spiritual descendant as Miranda is Sapphira's. She leaves Willow Springs to make her fortune in New York City, where she meets and marries George Andrews. She returns to Willow Springs for two weeks every August. The novel primarily concerns the events that occur when she brings George home one summer.

George Andrews, a successful engineer with heart trouble. When Ophelia is sick, he is the means by which she is saved, though he loses his life in the process. Although he is dead, he is the other narrator in the novel, and his love not only saves his wife but also enables him to communicate with her.

Sapphira Wade, an African American slave and wife to Bascombe Wade, whose plantation consisted of Willow Springs. She persuaded him to free his slaves and deed his property to them, and she was responsible for his death when he would not free her. The mother of seven sons, she is a legend on the island.

Ruby, Miranda's adversary, a jealous, murderous "mountain" of a woman who uses magic to kill Frances so that she can marry Junior Lee. When he shows an interest in Ophelia, Ruby uses nightshade and a spell to almost kill her. Miranda destroys her and her home with lightning.

Bernice Duvall, Ambush's wife, so desperate to have a child that she resorts to quackery and pills. Miranda saves her life and takes her to the "other place," one associated with Sapphira, to ensure her pregnancy. Her son is known first as Chick, a term related to his appearance and the ritual Miranda performs to help Bernice get pregnant, and then as Little Caesar. He dies in the storm at the end of the novel.

Dr. Buzzard, whose real name is **Rainbow Simpson**, a bootlegger, gambler, and herbalist with pretensions of possessing magic. Unlike Ruby, he knows better than to challenge Miranda's magic.

Mrs. Jackson, an administrator and mentor to George at the Wallace P. Andrews Shelter for Boys. Her consistency, sympathy, and fairness help mold George's character. He is guided by her declaration that only the present has potential.

Dr. Smithfield, a local physician who has confidence in Miranda's medical knowledge and who works with her on Bernice.

— Thomas L. Erskine

THE MAMBO KINGS PLAY SONGS OF LOVE

Author: Oscar Hijuelos (1951-   )
First published: 1989
Genre: Novel

Locale: New York City
Time: The 1950's to the 1980's
Plot: Historical realism

Cesar Castillo (SEH-sahr kahs-TEE-yoh), the novel's protagonist, born and reared in a poor family in Oriente, the eastern section of Cuba. During his childhood, Cesar suffers the violence of his abusive father. In Oriente, Cesar marries Luisa, with whom he has a daughter, Mariela. Their marriage is rather unstable, and after several separations, Cesar finally leaves Luisa permanently and goes to Havana. In 1949, Cesar decides to immigrate to New York City with his brother, Nestor, in the hope of succeeding as a musician. Once in the United States, Cesar and Nestor form the Mambo Kings, an orchestra that enjoys moderate success in dance halls and theaters. Cesar's greatest accomplishment in show business is his appearance on an episode of *I Love Lucy* in 1955. Soon after, however, Nestor is killed in a car accident. This event changes Cesar's personality; he is transformed from an apparently happy fellow into a sad, alcoholic man who tries to become more like his late brother. As Cesar becomes older and less attractive, his already low self-esteem (only temporarily bolstered by his extreme good looks) begins to worsen, and his life sinks into a series of escapes that finally ends in a melancholic remembrance of his past experiences.

Nestor Castillo, the younger of the two Castillo brothers. He spends most of his life mourning for a lost love named María back in Cuba. Although he is mainly a follower of his brother, Cesar, it is Nestor who composes "Beautiful María of My Soul," the most popular song of the Mambo Kings' repertoire. In spite of his melancholia, Nestor manages to marry a girl named Delores in New York, and they have two children, Eugenio and Leticia. Nestor tries to overcome his sadness and be a good husband and father, but he is unable to overcome his basically unhappy disposition.

Eugenio Castillo (eh-ew-HEHN-ee-oh), Nestor and Delores' son. Eugenio appears in the novel as a sort of alter ego of the author; his role in the story itself is secondary. Eugenio becomes important to the plot only after his father's death, when he becomes closer to his uncle Cesar. Nevertheless, Eugenio is an important element in the book, because he narrates the prologue and epilogue. In the epilogue, moreover, Eugenio becomes the main character of a brief narrative sequence set in Los Angeles, in which he goes to meet Desi Arnaz after Cesar's death.

Delores Castillo, Nestor's wife. Delores is an interesting woman who, unlike Nestor and Cesar, is eager to study and attend school. She firmly believes that her role as a mother and wife is not in conflict with her impulse to learn from books. This interest in studying is one of the main causes of her marital problems, but she manages most of the time to do what she wants without provoking a major break with Nestor. After Nestor's death, she remarries, to a quiet man who is tolerant of her aspirations.

Desi Arnaz (DEH-seeh ahr-NAHS), a real-life musician from Oriente who became the best-known Cuban entertainer in the United States. In *The Mambo Kings Play Songs of Love*, the fictional Desi invites Cesar and Nestor to appear on his television show. Years later, both Desi and Eugenio recall the past and express sorrow for a life that does not give any meaning to the act of dying.

MAN AND SUPERMAN: A Comedy and a Philosophy

Author: George Bernard Shaw (1856-1950)
First published: 1903
Genre: Drama

Locale: England and Spain
Time: c. 1900
Plot: Play of ideas

Ann Whitefield, a good-looking and vital young woman. At the urging of the Life Force, which is striving toward the eventual creation of the Superman, she is a liar, a coquette, a bully, and a hypocrite. She is also charming enough to get away with it all. Her flagrant violations of the romantic idea of the woman's role in courtship enable her to entrap Jack Tanner.

John (Jack) Tanner, a big, bearded, and wealthy young man with an Olympian manner but a saving sense of humor. Tanner is the dramatically unconventional author of *The Revolutionist's Handbook*. With no illusions about Ann or any other woman, he wants to preserve his freedom from them all. Tanner tries to flee to a Muhammadan country where men are protected. Ann tracks him down and captures him in Spain. Realizing that all of Nature is conspiring against his independence, Tanner reluctantly submits to the marriage.

Octavius Robinson, a young man who wants to write a great play. Handsome, sincere, romantic, and naïve, he is in love with Ann, who calls him "Ricky-ticky-tavy." She pities him for idealizing women and predicts that he will remain a bachelor.

Violet Robinson, Octavius' intelligent and exquisitely pretty sister. Violet is found to be pregnant. She finally reveals that she is secretly married, but she will not name her husband. Violet, as purposeful and predatory as Ann, is more direct in her methods.

Hector Malone, Junior, an American gentleman of twenty-four. Manly and moral but romantic, Hector has married Violet, but at her insistence he does not acknowledge the marriage.

Hector Malone, Senior, an Irishman who has made himself a billionaire in America. Violently prejudiced against the English middle class, he calls on Violet and threatens to disinherit his son if he marries her. When it is inadvertently revealed that they already are married, Violet charms and bullies Hector, Senior, into accepting her. Her husband dramatically gives up his inheritance, but Violet promises to make him change his mind.

Henry Straker, Tanner's chauffeur, a presentable young Cockney socialist who is afflicted with pride of class. Straker warns Tanner that Ann is after him.

Mendoza (mehn-DOH-zah), a tall, witty London Jew who had formerly been a waiter. Disappointed in his love for Straker's sister Louisa, Mendoza has set up as leader of a troop of bandits who specialize in robbing motorists passing through the Spanish Sierras. He captures Tanner and Straker as they flee from Ann. Tanner takes a liking to Mendoza and tells the soldiers sent to capture the bandits that Mendoza's men are his escorts.

Roebuck Ramsden, an elderly gentleman who prides himself on his progressive ideas. He is appointed Ann's guardian along with Jack Tanner, whom he detests.

Rhoda Whitefield, Ann's younger sister. Ann keeps Rhoda and Tanner apart, lest Rhoda snare him.

Mrs. Whitefield, the mother of Ann and Rhoda. A faded, squeaking woman, she is the scapegoat for Ann's willful actions.

Susan Ramsden, Roebuck's daughter, a hard-headed woman who represents the narrowest sort of conventionality.

Don Juan Tenorio (hwahn teh-NOH-ryoh), the legendary lover. While Jack Tanner is Mendoza's captive, he dreams of Don Juan in Hell. Don Juan, who is much like Tanner, is bored by the petty chatter of Hell's society and decides to pursue the contemplative life in Heaven.

Don Gonzalo (gohn-ZAH-loh), who is much like Roebuck Ramsden. In life, Don Gonzalo, a soldier, had been killed by Don Juan in a duel. He appears in the form of the marble statue that drags Don Giovanni to Hell at the end of Mozart's opera. Bored with Heaven, Don Gonzalo takes up residence in Hell.

The Devil, who resembles Mendoza. He is a moralist, a wit, a romantic, and a reformer.

Doña Ana de Ulloa (AH-nah deh ew-LYOH-ah), who resembles Ann Whitefield. Ana personifies the female vessel through which the Life Force strives toward its ultimate goal, the Superman. Everything else must be subordinated to that end; thus woman, by her nature, must be a stealthy and cunning predator.

A MAN FOR ALL SEASONS

Author: Robert Bolt (1924-1995)
First published: 1960
Genre: Drama

Locale: London, England, and its environs
Time: 1530-1535
Plot: Historical

Sir Thomas More, an author, humanist, and lawyer who begins the play as a member of the King's Council and rises to become lord chancellor of England. In his late forties, More is witty yet devout, a loyal Englishman yet a committed member of the Catholic Church. Respected throughout Europe for his intellectual and moral integrity, More dooms himself by refusing to accept Henry's break with Rome over the king's divorce and remarriage. By not submitting to pressure or fear, More

becomes first a prisoner of his king and finally a martyr for his conscience and his beliefs.

Alice More, Sir Thomas' wife. Also in her late forties, she is a solid, no-nonsense woman from a merchant family, and her interests are considerably less intellectual than her husband's; she has never learned to read or write. Although she clearly loves Thomas, she is baffled and often infuriated by his stubborn stand on the question of the divorce and religious allegiance to Rome. In the end, however, she accepts his position and even his self-imposed death because of her great love and respect for him.

Margaret (Meg) More, the daughter of Sir Thomas and Alice, in her middle twenties and remarkably well educated for a young woman of her time. She has the plain honesty of her mother tempered by the intellectual subtlety of her father. More clearly loves his Meg, as he calls her, above everything else in this world, and his greatest torment is to be separated from her by his imprisonment.

William Roper, Margaret's suitor and later her husband, a young man in his early thirties who is highly opinionated and equally indiscreet in religious and political matters. Although his beliefs change several times during the drama, he is passionately devoted to each of them in sequence, from his initial fanatic Protestantism to his final staunch Catholicism. Roper's fervent but mutable convictions are contrasted to More's quiet but steadfast faith.

Henry VIII, the king of England. In his late thirties when the play begins, he is talented, attractive, and ambitious. He craves both power to do what he pleases and the approval of More; when he cannot have both, he does not hesitate to use flattery, force, or threats, and he ends up resorting to imprisonment and execution of More. A self-conscious character, Henry moves through the play in a larger-than-life fashion; the monarch's actions are not restrained by the rules of logic or laws that govern other men. At times, his actions seem those of an intelligent but petulant child—but a child with enormous power.

Thomas Cardinal Wolsey, prince of the church and lord chancellor of England, an aged, fat man clothed in expensive robes and surrounded by the trappings of power, with a powerful intellect undiminished by time but an equally enormous ambition frustrated by his inability to please his royal master in the service that matters: securing a divorce. The son of a butcher, Wolsey has risen in the king's service through ability and intelligence, but when he fails to secure the divorce, he falls from favor, and only his death, on November 29, 1530, saves him from a trial for treason.

Thomas Cromwell, secretary to the cardinal. Like Wolsey, Cromwell comes from humble origins and has risen as a result of relentless intelligence and ambition, but he lacks even Wolsey's rudimentary scruples. In his late thirties, Cromwell starts as Wolsey's secretary and advances steadily, shifting his allegiance to the king after Wolsey's fall. Having forsaken his own moral integrity to acquire power and position, he cannot understand More, who would gladly renounce these worldly goods rather than betray his own moral values.

Richard Rich, a young man in his early thirties who wants to make his way in the world but whose moral character is unequal to either his ambition or his intellect. He would prefer to be a protégé of More but accepts other positions as they occur, ending as a creature of Cromwell. In the end, his perjured testimony serves as the pretext to convict More of treason.

Thomas Cranmer, the archbishop of Canterbury. In his late forties, Cranmer is More's contemporary solely in age. He participates willingly in the trial to condemn More and follows Cromwell's lead.

Thomas Howard, the duke of Norfolk and earl marshal of England, a member of the first rank of the nobility. His life and actions are predicated on loyal and usually unquestioning service to his king. He is a friend of More and attempts to persuade him to accept the changing situation in England. At the end, Howard remains true to his king and serves on the tribunal that condemns his friend.

Chapuys, the Spanish ambassador, a professional diplomat in his sixties. His sole concern is to guard the interests of his own royal master.

The Common Man, a fellow in late middle age who appears throughout the play to set the scene, explain the situation, and provide commentary on the unfolding events.

— *Michael Witkoski*

MAN IN THE HOLOCENE
(Der Mensch erscheint im Holozän)

Author: Max Frisch (1911-1991)
First published: 1979
Genre: Novel

Locale: Ticino, a Swiss canton near Italy
Time: The 1970's
Plot: Psychological realism

Geiser (GI-zehr), a retired businessman who lives alone in a house in a village high in the Swiss Alps. His wife died years before the action of the novel. He is seventy-three years old and is beginning to experience symptoms of senility. The novel begins during the last few days of a severe storm that has caused some minor landslides in the area. The roadways are blocked, and there have been some disruptions of telephone and electrical service. Geiser passes the time building a pagoda out of crisp bread and reading encyclopedia articles about thunder and lightning. He gradually becomes more involved with his encyclopedia readings and obsessively peruses pieces on weather, the local geography and its history of landslides, the age of the dinosaurs, and the vast eras of geological time. Geiser is very concerned with the possibility that he may be losing his memory as a result of senility and thus starts to read articles about the symptoms of aging. He makes lists of various items as a test of his memory, such as types of thunder, the supplies in his kitchen, and the contents of his deep freezer. He takes notes on his reading at first but then abandons that and cuts out the encyclopedia articles instead. He tacks them up on the walls of his house, which soon become completely covered. When neighbors come by to bring him soup, he refuses to answer the doorbell. At one point, in a state of disorientation, he kills his pet cat and roasts it in the fireplace. Geiser decides to hike over the mountain pass into the next valley, a dangerous journey for a man his age. He gets lost several times. Exhausted and unable to make the trip, he returns home. Having suffered a mild stroke, he falls down the stairs and injures himself slightly. Telephone service has been restored, and his telephone rings periodically—presumably his daughter calling—but he refuses to answer it. He begins to remember a climb he made with his brother some fifty years earlier, on the Matterhorn. With the roadway cleared, his daughter arrives to check on him; it is likely that she will have to commit him to a home for the aged.

— *Thomas F. Barry*

THE MAN OF FEELING

Author: Henry Mackenzie (1745-1831)
First published: 1771
Genre: Novel

Locale: England
Time: Mid-eighteenth century
Plot: Sentimental

Mr. Harley, the man of feeling. Being an extremely virtuous man, he believes that all human beings are like himself. He has many disappointments and some genuine trouble because he believes people are essentially good. He is unambitious for money, and he is unambitious in love. When he finds that the woman he loves is affianced to a wealthy man, he is heartbroken, although he has never declared his love. Because of his feelings on the matter, he becomes physically ill and dies.

Miss Walton, a rich heiress of a higher station in life than Mr. Harley. It is for her that he pines away and dies. She belatedly comes to love him, tells him so on his deathbed, and breaks off her engagement to the man of her father's choice. She remains single after Harley's death.

Miss Atkins, a London prostitute who wishes to return to her family. With Harley's help, she is reunited with her father. When Harley first meets her, he takes her to a brothel for food, since the poor girl has done so poorly in her profession as to be hungry and penniless.

Mr. Atkins, the prostitute's father, a retired army officer. Through Harley, he and his daughter are reconciled.

Mr. Edwards, a farmer who loses his lands because of the Enclosure Acts and then, though an old man, enters the army to take his son's place so that the son, who has been seized by a press gang, may remain at home to care for his wife and children. Harley promises the old man a farm on his estates.

Miss Harley, Harley's maiden aunt. She rears Harley after the deaths of his parents and inculcates him with virtue.

THE MAN OF MODE: Or, Sir Fopling Flutter

Author: Sir George Etherege (1635?-1691)
First published: 1676
Genre: Drama

Locale: London, England
Time: The 1670's
Plot: Comedy of manners

Dorimant, a London dandy with a great reputation as a lover. He brutally casts off one mistress for another. He masquerades part of the time as Courtage to hide his identity from Lady Woodvill, Harriet's mother. As Courtage, he wins Lady Woodvill's admiration, as a means of acquiring her consent to marry her daughter.

Sir Fopling Flutter, a foolish fop. He dresses, acts, and speaks foolishly.

Lady Loveit, Dorimant's mistress. Tired of her, he tries to escape from the entanglement with her. She complains bitterly to Bellinda, not knowing that she is supplanted in Dorimant's affections by Bellinda.

Bellinda, a beautiful woman who succeeds Lady Loveit as Dorimant's mistress. She is as amoral as Lady Loveit and Dorimant. She does not mind Dorimant marrying Harriet as long as her love affair with him remains a secret.

Harriet, a beautiful, wealthy girl from the country. She is attracted to Dorimant, but she is the girl Old Bellair wants his son to marry. She is uninterested in marrying young Bellair and he is uninterested in marrying her. She is finally permitted to marry Dorimant.

Bellair, a London dandy and a friend of Dorimant. He wishes to marry Emilia, rather than Harriet, the woman his father has chosen for him. He marries Emilia without his father's knowledge.

Old Bellair, Bellair's father. He falls in love with Emilia, whom his son loves, and wants to marry her himself.

Lady Townley, young Bellair's aunt. Bellair hopes she can help him win his father's consent to marry Emilia.

Lady Woodvill, Harriet's mother. She is eager for a marriage between her daughter and Bellair. Her main interest is in keeping her daughter from being seduced by Dorimant.

Emilia, a young woman whom Bellair hopes to marry. Old Bellair is also smitten and wants to marry her, not knowing of his son's intentions. She and Bellair marry secretly before Old Bellair can intervene.

THE MAN WHO CAME TO DINNER

Authors: George S. Kaufman (1889-1961) and Moss Hart (1904-1961)
First published: 1939
Genre: Drama

Locale: Mesalia, Ohio
Time: The 1930's
Plot: Comedy

Sheridan Whiteside, a middle-aged, Falstaffian-girthed celebrity. He is a critic, lecturer, and radio personality, the intimate friend of anyone worth knowing. He is an egomaniac who "would see his mother burned at the stake if that was the only way he could light his cigarette." His cruel wit and penchant for aggressive repartee make him a great comic character, insofar as humor often depends on other people's misery or discomfort. That he is obviously impossible to live with is amply demonstrated when he disrupts, through his presence, a conservative upper-middle-class household in a small town in Ohio. Most of the time, he acts the consummate tyrant, but a few isolated acts of genuine kindness make him human, although not redeemable. For all of his sins, he remains disdainfully unrepentant.

Maggie Cutler, Whiteside's private secretary and chief interference runner for the past ten years. In her thirties, she is sarcastic and cynical, and she knows where the bodies are buried. After she meets Bert Jefferson and goes ice skating with him, she decides that the fast lane with Whiteside is infinitely less preferable than conventional delights of domesticity. The fear of losing a good secretary prompts Whiteside to try to destroy the relationship, but her seriousness about her love induces him to help her achieve her goal.

Lorraine Sheldon, a bitchy actress, young and beautiful, the vicious epitome of the glamorous, brainless, superficial superstar. Whiteside lures her to Ohio by telling her that Jefferson's play has a marvelous part for her. She thus unwittingly lets herself be used to break up the romance between Jefferson and Maggie. Seducing a man for benefit is, for her, all in a day's work.

Professor Metz, "a strange-looking little man in his fifties," an entomologist who once lived for two years in a cave with nothing but plant lice. He is the first of three eccentrics to visit Whiteside during his convalescence. He brings the great man a present of a colony of ten thousand roaches.

Beverly Carlton, a Noël Cowardish character who dashes around the world composing and writing plays and being devastatingly charming. His latest comedy, he says, is the best since Molière. He breezes in to visit Whiteside and wish him a "Merry Christmas." He stays about a quarter of an hour, using part of the time to regale him with a number from his new revue. Maggie enlists him in an attempt to lure Jefferson away from Lorraine Sheldon, trying to counter Whiteside's attempt to break up her romance.

Banjo, a famous Hollywood comedian, a grown-up adolescent. He is as loony offscreen as on—the Marx brothers all wrapped into one—but he good-heartedly allows himself to be the means by which Maggie can retrieve her happiness.

Bert Jefferson, the owner and editor of the Mesalia *Journal*. He is "an interesting-looking young man in his early thirties" who has written a producible play. He naïvely and ambitiously allows himself to be lured by the chance of making it to the big time, even if it means the sacrifice of personal happiness.

Dr. Bradley, Whiteside's doctor while Whiteside is in Mesalia. He diagnoses Whiteside's injuries by looking at the wrong X rays. He is also a late-blooming author who tries to get Whiteside to read his book, *Forty Years an Ohio Doctor*.

Miss Preen, a spinsterish nurse who attends Whiteside. A humorless prude, she becomes the constant butt of his insults and name-calling, to which she reacts with routine indignation.

The Stanleys, the family in whose house Whiteside stays during his recovery from a hip injury. The offspring get along well with Whiteside and take his advice to leave home and establish their independence: the son to travel around the world taking photographs; the daughter to elope with a union organizer.

— *Wm. Laird Kleine-Ahlbrandt*

THE MAN WHO CRIED I AM

Author: John A. Williams (1925-   )
First published: 1967
Genre: Novel

Locale: New York City; Washington, D.C.; Amsterdam; Paris, and Lagos, Nigeria
Time: Primarily the 1960's
Plot: Social realism

Maxwell (Max) Reddick, a black novelist and journalist in his forties. Max struggles relentlessly against the forces of prejudice that would prevent him and other black people from achieving a place in American life and letters. After an assignment in the Army during World War II, he goes to Harlem and lives in poverty while writing his first novel. Although many liberals offer help, none of their promises or jobs ever materializes. Living in Europe, he at first believes that there is less racism there, but he becomes more aware of it when he marries a Dutch girl, Margrit. He travels to Africa and sees at first hand the corruption that is encouraged by whites and all too willingly carried on by black people. Later, Max hears of the death of Harry Ames and receives the message about the King Alfred Plan to control black people in America. He also discovers that he is suffering from terminal cancer. Soon afterward, he dies fighting two black CIA agents. He has passed on the material

given him by Harry to Minister Q., but the minister also is assassinated, so there is no one left who can expose this conspiracy against black people.

Harry Ames, an expatriate black novelist modeled on Richard Wright. Ames was one of the earliest black novelists and spent some time in the Communist Party in the 1930's and 1940's. He leaves the Communist Party in the 1940's and struggles to continue as a novelist. He befriends Max Reddick, although there is a natural rivalry among the fellow writers. He perceives a great opportunity when the Lykeion Foundation offers him a fellowship and a year in Athens; however, the offer is withdrawn when it is discovered that he has a white wife. He becomes dissatisfied with the failure of the foundation and the failure of other white people and groups to deliver on their promises, and he takes refuge from hate and misunderstanding in Europe. Although Europe is less racist, Harry is cut off from his roots and never matches his early success. In place of creation, he becomes interested in Africa and politics. Through an African diplomat, Jaja Enzkwu, he discovers an international conspiracy called the Alliance Blanc dedicated to exploiting the African nations and preventing them from uniting. The contribution of the United States, the King Alfred Plan, anticipates arresting and relocating all black people in the country. When Harry learns of the conspiracy against black people, he sends Michelle, his lover, with a copy of the plan for Reddick. Soon afterward, he is assassinated.

Margrit Westoever (Maggie) Reddick, the Dutch wife of Max. She is blonde, beautiful, and in love with Max, but she can do little to help him in his struggle.

Charlotte Ames, Harry's wife. Their marriage is not a happy one, although she does help Harry financially and encourages him in his writing. She is white and finds an interracial marriage easier in Europe than in America.

Marion Dawes, a young black novelist in Europe who is modeled on James Baldwin. He receives critical and financial support from whites because he is a homosexual. He sees Harry Ames as a father figure whom he must defeat before he can succeed.

Jaja Enzkwu (JAY-jay EENZ-kew), a diplomat for an African country. He discovers the Alliance Blanc and the King Alfred Plan. He is assassinated soon after informing Harry Ames of the conspiracy.

Paul Durrell, a black leader modeled on Martin Luther King, Jr. Reddick fears that Durrell's flaws and timidity will harm the black cause.

Minister Q., a Black Power advocate who is modeled on Malcolm X. He is shot down soon after receiving news of the King Alfred Plan.

Bernard Zutkin, a literary critic who has some influence in publishing circles.

Roger Wilkinson, a black expatriate writer who is also a CIA agent. He kills Max Reddick at the end of the novel.

— *James Sullivan*

THE MAN WHO KILLED THE DEER

Author: Frank Waters (1902-1995)
First published: 1942
Genre: Novel

Locale: The Pueblo Indian Reservation, near Taos, New Mexico
Time: Late 1930's, before the outbreak of World War II
Plot: Social realism

Martiniano, a young American Indian, part Pueblo and part Apache, tall, broad-shouldered, strong, and capable. Forced, as a boy, to attend a U.S. government boarding school, he returns as a man to his pueblo (village). Spiritually lost, he finds comfort neither in the ways of the white man nor in those of the Indian. For his failure to conform to the Pueblo traditions, he is considered a rebel and is forced to live in a hut outside the compound. After he kills a deer on government land after the close of hunting season, he is fined and humiliated. This action seems to precipitate more and more acts that provoke punishment by the pueblo leadership. He struggles with the injustice of being punished by the pueblo for behavior that he was taught at the white man's school. He imagines that the deer he killed is still alive and is taunting him. He sees the deer as the symbol of his troubles. He becomes even more depressed when he discovers that his bride, Flowers Playing, seems to possess special powers over the wild deer that roam the area. He hopes that, by joining Manuel Rena's secret peyote cult, he will begin to develop a faith, but the cult is discovered and must be abandoned. With the birth of his son, he begins to find peace and to understand the beauty of the ways of his ancestors and of the necessity of being a part of their tradition, meanwhile acknowledging the inevitable encroachment of the modern world.

Flowers Playing, an American Indian woman, part Ute and part Arapahoe. She is first seen by Martiniano when she is among a group of visiting Plains Indian dancers. He is enchanted with her wild grace and her striking beauty. The two are married and have a good initial year together, though they are ostracized from the pueblo society. An emotional barrier develops between them as a result of Martiniano's sense of guilt and frustration, and he blames the deer that he has killed for having destroyed his wife's love for him. Gradually, as they look forward to the birth of their child, the couple's relationship is restored.

Palemon, the closest friend of Martiniano. Much like Martiniano in appearance, he is slightly older than his friend. One night, he responds to a mysterious inner summons that leads him into the mountains. There he finds Martiniano in a state of semiconsciousness, having been injured by the government agent who had discovered him hunting out of season. Palemon saves Martiniano's life and continues to be his only friend among the pueblo members, providing support and wise counsel whenever needed.

Rodolfo Byers, a white man who owns the trading post nearest the pueblo. When Martiniano is assessed a fine of $150 for killing a deer out of season, Byers quietly pays the fine. He also provides credit at his trading post so that Martiniano can purchase items necessary to grow corn on his small plot of land. Byers takes Martiniano and Flowers Playing on a buying trip for the trading post, during which he assures Martiniano that each man has some special burden, such as the deer that haunts Martiniano, and that the burden will pass.

Manuel Rena, the leader of the peyote cult. Rena is a member of the pueblo, but, unlike most, he is a rich man, having fertile land, good horses, and a large herd of sheep. A big, handsome man, he wears polished leather boots and the finest of blankets from Mexico. Rena convinces Martiniano that Father Peyote will give him strength and faith. Martiniano, seeking an alternative to the Indian ways and to the domination of the mercenary Catholic priest, joins the cult.

— *P. R. Lannert*

THE MAN WHO LOVED CHILDREN

Author: Christina Stead (1902-1983)
First published: 1940
Genre: Novel

Locale: Washington, D.C., Baltimore, Annapolis, Harpers Ferry, and Singapore
Time: 1936-1940
Plot: Family

Samuel Clemens (Sam) Pollit, a husband and father. A man in his late thirties or early forties, he is a bureaucrat by profession and a moralist by nature. His real interest is in having children and playing with them. Whatever happens to him, from losing his job to losing his wife, Sam takes it as one more proof of the world's persecution of moral superiority. At the end of the novel, he has learned nothing: He will continue to wear out women and children in his service.

Henrietta Collyer (Henny) Pollit, Sam's second wife. A tall, slender society girl when she married Sam, she has been driven to physical and emotional exhaustion by his demands for sexual gratification and regular production of babies. She is filled with hatred: hatred of her husband, of her stepdaughter, of the rundown house in Baltimore to which he eventually moves her, and of her debt-burdened life. After she has been spurned by her lover, she drinks poison and dies.

Louisa (Louie, Looloo) Pollit, Sam's daughter by his first wife. At the beginning of the novel, she is a large, fat, and clumsy eleven-year-old. Mocked and teased by her father, as well as criticized and insulted by the stepmother whom she loves, Louisa is saddled with much of the housework. Because she is talented and bright, it is clear that if she leaves home Louisa can succeed. Her father, however, says that he will never let her go. After planning to kill her parents and actually mixing the poison for Henrietta, Louisa runs away from home.

Ernest (Ernie) Pollit, Henrietta's oldest son. A shrewd, quiet boy who is ten years old at the beginning of the novel, he is very close to his mother. Ernie loves money above all other things. When he discovers that Henrietta has stolen his savings, he is brokenhearted, and he hangs a representation of himself. Still determined to make money, he plans to leave

school to do so.

Evelyn (Evie, Little Womey) Pollit, the only daughter of Sam and Henrietta. A good, happy, and obedient child, she is destined to be a beauty like her mother. When the novel ends, she is approaching her teenage years, and it is clear that Sam will expect her to take the place of Henrietta and Louisa as a household slave.

Tommy Pollit, a four-year-old son of Sam and Henrietta. A handsome boy with dark eyes, curly hair, and a grin that women cannot resist, he survives the emotional turmoil of the household by clinging to Henrietta and Louisa. When Louisa leaves, she has no doubt that Tommy will be taken in by an aunt.

Bert Anderson, Henrietta's lover. A vulgar, lusty man who works in Washington for the Internal Revenue Service, he makes Henrietta feel young and beautiful again. After she tells him that Sam has received an anonymous note about their affair, he fears damage to his career and breaks off their relationship. Even though he sees her desperation, he leaves her waiting for him in a bar, making it clear to her that she has been only a diversion. This incident helps drive her toward suicide.

Miss Aiden, a teacher at Annapolis High School. A tall, golden-haired, good-natured woman who is devoted to her students, she becomes Louisa's first love. When she comes to dinner with the family on Sam's birthday, she sees their poverty and the atmosphere of hatred and desperation. By telling Louisa that one day she will be famous, Miss Aiden gives her the courage to leave home.

— *Rosemary M. Canfield Reisman*

THE MAN WHO WAS THURSDAY: A Nightmare

Author: G. K. Chesterton (1874-1936)
First published: 1908
Genre: Novel

Locale: London, England
Time: Early twentieth century
Plot: Allegory

Lucian Gregory, an anarchist and a poet. He hopes to be elected as Thursday on the Central Anarchist Council but is disappointed. In the long run, he turns out to be the only intellectual anarchist.

Sunday, the chairman of the Central Anarchist Council. He turns out to be a wealthy Scotland Yard official in charge of efforts to unearth anarchists. He gives a party on his estate and turns up dressed as a symbol of the Christian Sabbath.

Gabriel Syme, a poet who believes in order. Gregory takes him to the meeting of the Central Anarchist Council. Though he is a police spy, Syme is elected to be Thursday, the post his friend wanted.

The Marquis de St. Eustache, a dapper man who is Wednesday on the Central Anarchist Council. He is sent by the

anarchists to kill the czar of Russia and the president of France, but he turns out to be another police spy for Scotland Yard.

Bull, who is Saturday on the Central Anarchist Council and is also a police spy.

Gogol, who is Tuesday on the Central Anarchist Council and is also a police spy.

Professor de Worms, who is Friday on the Central Anarchist Council. He turns out to be a young actor disguised as the professor in order to act as a spy on the anarchists for Scotland Yard.

The Secretary, who is Monday on the Central Anarchist Council. He also is a spy for Scotland Yard.

THE MAN WHO WATCHED THE TRAINS GO BY
(L'Homme qui regardait passer les trains)

Author: Georges Simenon (1903-1989)
First published: 1938
Genre: Novel

Locale: Groningen, Amsterdam, and Paris
Time: The 1930's
Plot: Psychological realism

Kees Popinga (poh-peen-GAH), a forty-year-old man who is proud of his family, possessions, and responsible position as managing clerk for Julius De Coster and Son, Ship Chandlers. He is a model citizen of Groningen, Holland. He changes radically, however, into the man referred to in Paris newspapers as the "Madman from the Zuider Zee" and the "Thug from Amsterdam" as a result of an unexpected meeting with his employer. De Coster tells Kees that he no longer has a job, that the firm is bankrupt, and that he himself is leaving town. These events, along with a vague longing for a change, prompt Kees to give up his respectable way of life. He finds that he enjoys reading about himself as a criminal. When police arrest unruly customers at a café where Kees waits for Jeanne, he hides in the lavatory. From that time on, he identifies himself with the criminal world. Having rejected the values that previously had ordered his life, Kees believes that he is free to do whatever he wants with impunity. As a result of his exploits, Kees is convinced that he is a superior person, and he wants others to recognize this. Newspaper articles continue to refer to him as a maniac. One of his letters directing the police to the car thieves' base of operation results in the thieves agreeing to help the police find him. Kees realizes that he must severely restrict his behavior, the very thing he considers abhorrent, to remain free. In the end, he is sent to an insane asylum in Amsterdam. Ironically, Kees is institutionalized for trying to free himself from bourgeois values.

Mums, Kees Popinga's wife, an amiable and dignified woman who is devoted to her family. Shocked by Kees's abandonment, she believes that his behavior is a result of a fit of madness or loss of memory. To support her family, she finds work at the Van Jonghe biscuit factory. After Kees is institutionalized, she visits him regularly.

Julius De Coster (zhew-LYEWS deh koh-STEHR), a man nearly sixty years of age who heads the firm of Julius De Coster and Son, Ship Chandlers. At a chance meeting with Kees Popinga, he confesses that his family's supposedly reputable firm always has been involved in fraudulent activities. Because the firm is bankrupt, he decides to fake suicide and leave Groningen. He advises Kees to give up his respectable life and begin again on a new plane.

Jeanne Rozier (zhahn roh-ZYAY), a prostitute and a car thief's mistress. She tries to help Kees by introducing him to her criminal friends after she learns that he is a murderer.

Pamela Mackinsen, Julius De Coster's mistress, a cabaret dancer whom Kees Popinga murders.

— *Frank Ardolino*

THE MAN WHO WOULD BE KING

Author: Rudyard Kipling (1865-1936)
First published: 1888
Genre: Short fiction

Locale: India and Afghanistan
Time: Late nineteenth century
Plot: Allegory

An unnamed newspaperman, who serves as the narrator. It is probable that this character is the author himself. With a journalist's sixth sense, he allows himself to become involved in the adventures of Daniel Dravot and Peachey Carnehan. Against his better judgment, he helps them prepare to seize control of the kingdom of Kafiristan. With his books and maps, he provides them with the information they need. Three years later, when Carnehan returns more dead than alive, the narrator persuades the horribly crippled man to tell his fantastic story, although it exhausts his last bit of strength. Out of a spirit of charity and pity, the narrator arranges for Carnehan's care, only to learn that his friend died two days after telling his tale of wonder and terror.

Peachey Carnehan, a vagabond adventurer who risks his life to become one of the rulers of Kafiristan, a mystical kingdom that supposedly forms part of Afghanistan. Although he is a big man, he involves the narrator in his scheme by persuasion and not by intimidation. Although committed to their plan, Carnehan is far more cautious than Dravot and is determined to remain true to their contract, which forbids consuming liquor or becoming involved with women. Seemingly more interested in the business of governing and the mystic nature of kingship than in personal gain, Carnehan is disturbed by his friend's intoxication with power, but he never wavers in his loyalty to Dravot, despite the latter's fatal mistakes. Carnehan is an opportunist who exploits both people and events. He plays repeatedly on the naïveté of his subjects and uses his knowledge of masonic rituals to help Dravot control the leaders of Kafiristan. He is also a brave man who endures not only physical pain but also excruciating mental torture on behalf of his associate. Against all odds, he makes his way back to the narrator so that he can tell his story to a sympathetic listener before he dies. Crippled by the people whom he sought to rule and whom he deceived, Carnehan never surrenders his spirit or ceases to scheme. Only death puts an end to his career.

Daniel Dravot, a dreamer and soldier of fortune, the companion of Carnehan and the mastermind behind their attempt to seize the tiny kingdom of Kafiristan. Physically intimidating, this red-bearded giant ignores all warnings in his effort to follow his dream of power and wealth. Using modern weapons, he imposes his will on the superstitious people of Kafiristan, and although he brings them peace and a modest prosperity, he does not hesitate to exploit them. Rich beyond his expectations and endowed with almost godlike power, he decides to break his contract with Carnehan by taking a wife. His subjects turn on Dravot, who proves himself to be a lustful human and not a deity. Attempting to escape his rebellious kingdom, Dravot is captured, but he is allowed to die like a monarch, proud and defiant to the end.

— *Clifton W. Potter, Jr.*

THE MAN WITH THE GOLDEN ARM

Author: Nelson Algren (Nelson Ahlgren Abraham, 1909-1981)
First published: 1949
Genre: Novel

Locale: Chicago, Illinois
Time: 1946-1948
Plot: Social realism

Francis Majcinek (mi-CHEE-nehk), a card dealer known to everyone in his westside Chicago neighborhood as **Frankie Machine**. Twenty-nine years old, with shaggy blond hair, buffalo eyes, and a square face, Frankie has such a steady, machinelike talent for dealing cards that he can boast that he has the touch; he is the man with the golden arm. Frankie also uses his arm for shooting up morphine, a habit he developed during World War II to relieve the pain of shrapnel lodged in his liver. Honorably discharged from the Army with a Purple Heart and a Good Conduct Medal, Frankie hopes to find a job as a jazz drummer. His addiction to drugs, his unhappy marriage, and his tendency toward criminal activities (for example, he gets caught trying to steal electric irons from a department store and serves nine months in jail) prevent him from realizing his ambitions. In a moment of anger and desperation, he kills Louie Fomorowski. As the police close in on him, Frankie hangs himself in a lonely hotel room.

Sophie "Zosh" Majcinek, Frankie's wife. She is twenty-six years old, with pale eyes and ash-blonde hair in pin curls, unhappily confined to a wheelchair as the result of an automobile accident that occurred while Frankie was driving while intoxicated. Zosh and Frankie have known each other since childhood but have never really trusted each other. They quarreled before they were married, they quarreled on their wedding night, and they have quarreled ever since, excepting the thirty-six months when Frankie was in the Army. Once a sharp dresser and a fine dancer, Zosh now sits home all day, complaining and asking Frankie to wheel her around the apartment. When Frankie finally moves out, Zosh goes insane. In the end, she is confined to a mental institution, rocking herself on a cot, uttering not a word to anyone.

Molly Novotny, a nightclub hostess in love with Frankie. In her early twenties—though looking more like thirty, with a careworn, heart-shaped face, dark hair, and dark eyes—Molly earns a percentage of every drink she hustles in the early morning hours at the Club Safari. She lives downstairs from Frankie and Zosh, supporting not only herself but also Drunkie John, an alcoholic close to forty who abuses her both physically and mentally. Wanting to care for someone, Molly falls in love with Frankie, bestowing on him her tenderness, compassion, and pity. After Frankie is jailed for theft, she leaves the neighborhood and finds work as a stripper in a black nightclub. When Frankie later needs a place to hide from the law, Molly takes him in. For a brief moment, they make plans for a happy future together. Drunkie John alerts the police to Frankie's whereabouts, however, and their dreams are over.

Solly "Sparrow" Saltskin, a small-time hustler and devoted friend of Frankie. The jittery, bespectacled Sparrow thrives on petty crime and gambling, including dog-stealing, window-peeping, and burglary; it is his idea to shoplift the electric irons, but Frankie is the one who gets caught. More than anyone else, Sparrow admires Frankie, but, under the unrelenting interrogation of Captain Bednar, he confesses to having witnessed the murder of Louie Fomorowski.

Louie Fomorowski, known as **Nifty Louie**, a flashily dressed, pale-faced former junkie who has kicked the habit and now deals drugs, dispensing the hits of morphine Frankie craves. When Frankie and Sparrow take Louie's lucky silver dollar in a card game, Louie angrily tries to get it back from them but makes the mistake of insulting Frankie, who responds with a crushing blow that snaps Louie's neck.

Captain Bednar, known as **Record Head**, the weary commander of the local police station house. Sitting at the same scarred desk for twenty years, Captain Bednar has been recording the crimes in the neighborhood, retaining in his unforgiving memory the perpetrator of every misdemeanor long since forgotten by everyone else. With the unsolved murder of Louie Fomorowski relentlessly weighing on him, Captain Bednar forces Sparrow to implicate Frankie in the crime. In the end, it is Bednar who feels more lost, more alone, and ultimately more guilty than anyone else.

— *James I. Deutsch*

THE MAN WITHOUT A COUNTRY

Author: Edward Everett Hale (1822-1909)
First published: 1863
Genre: Short fiction

Locale: The United States and the high seas
Time: The nineteenth century
Plot: Historical

Philip Nolan, a brash young American army officer who becomes involved in Aaron Burr's conspiracy against the United States. At his court-martial, in a show of bravado, the young man curses his country. As a result, he is sentenced to serve out his life aboard naval vessels, never seeing the United States or hearing it mentioned. Even his books and periodicals are excised of all allusions to his country. Through the years, Nolan is transferred from one navy vessel to another, always wearing an army uniform with plain buttons, thus acquiring the nickname of "Plain Buttons." As time passes, authorities in the Navy and in Washington forget Nolan, but he is still passed from one ship to another, never allowed within a hundred miles of the American coast. As the years pass his unconcern, worn bravely at first, fades away, as he wanders the seas an official expatriate—countryless, friendless, even nameless. As he finally lies dying, an old man, the captain of his current prison ship tells Nolan what has happened in the fifty-six years since Nolan left the country—omitting, for the dying man's sake, only the Civil War.

Colonel Morgan, the army officer conducting the court-martial that sends Philip Nolan to his years of wandering over the sea.

THE MAN WITHOUT QUALITIES
(Der Mann ohne Eigenschaften)

Author: Robert Musil (1880-1942)
First published: 1930-1943
Genre: Novel

Locale: Kakania, a fictionalized Austro-Hungarian Empire
Time: 1913-1914
Plot: Social morality

Ulrich (EWL-reekh), the man without qualities, a handsome and unattached thirty-year-old. He has taken a vacation from life, letting the events of the external world move him without motivation in any direction. An "officer" without military commission, through the intercession (or intervention) of his domineering father, he drifts into a leadership role in the planning of the Collateral Campaign, a celebration of two anniversaries important to the Austro-Hungarian political profile. Ulrich is the ultimate "observer" character who becomes the receptacle for the longings and projects of those around him. His only action is passive reaction, a novelistic device that allows the author to paint the portraits of the other characters by how they are reflected in Ulrich. He refuses to treat life as a series of opportunities and choices, as the other characters do, but rather allows the strivings and struggles of others to affect his actions in whatever way they will. Simultaneously "not open to wooing" and eminently obtainable by everyone, he constitutes the narrative perspective without speaking in the first person.

Walter (VAHL-tehr), Ulrich's friend, a second-rate musical talent. He is suspicious, paranoiac, small-minded, and territorial, especially in his marriage. Middle-aged and lacking the fire and talent of his hero, Richard Wagner, he wants to give his wife, Clarisse, a child, but she refuses, on the grounds that he is imperfect and undeserving of passing on his mediocrity to offspring. By weighing his own achievements against the great Wagner, Walter diminishes his own accomplishments and guarantees his unhappiness. He watches helplessly as his wife deteriorates into madness.

Clarisse (klah-RIH-seh), Walter's wife and fellow musician. Overwhelmed with the "musicality" of a recent murder and the accused murderer, she gradually loses her sanity in the vise of her obsessions, which include a disgust for her own husband and a strong desire to have a child by Ulrich. The fierceness underneath her cultured and well-bred exterior is reflected in the social turmoil around her, disguised in ballets, operas, symphonies, and other "cultural" pursuits. A female embodiment of the Wagnerian principles of perfection and greatness, she fails to reconcile the facts of her own life with her ambitions, paralleling a comparison of herself and her ideal to the aesthetic dialectic between the ideal of music and its actual physical manifestation.

Herr Dr. Paul Arnheim (AHRN-him), a handsome man in his early forties, a man of business and finance "coming to power," with a "capacious memory." Upright and military in posture (partly a product of a zealous Austrian patriotism), self-possessed, assured, and Machiavellian, he is both conscious of the meaninglessness of superficial activities toward the betterment of humanity and able to manipulate the emotional palette of the other characters, especially women, toward his own ends. He is less successful with Ulrich, because he can find no character traits to exploit. Accustomed to getting his way through carefully constructed "friendships," he is frustrated by Ulrich's "impolite" indifference to his offers of companionship and social prominence. He finds a contradiction between his almost intuitive ability to make money (a practice that sometimes "gets us into situations that are not quite in good style") and the incipient greatness of accomplishment that seems to elude him despite his business successes.

Diotima (dee-o-TIH-mah), a beautiful and rich woman in her mid-thirties. She is socially prominent and is the organizational force behind the absurd Collateral Campaign, the ultimate social fund-raising event in Vienna at the verge of the Great War. She spends her time preparing for the planning of the Collateral Campaign and lying in bed trying to choose a lover among Arnheim, the financier, Count Leinsdorf, the nobleman, and Ulrich, the indifferent and therefore desirable object of conquest.

Bonadea (boh-nah-DEH-ah), a married but unfaithful woman in her mid-thirties, with a sensual and primitive core underneath a sophisticated veneer. She seduces Ulrich by taking advantage of his passivity and represents the natural, organic, sexual underlife of the glittering Vienna society. Her impassioned devices for being with Ulrich are disguised to herself as noble impulses toward good. Her involvement with the Moosbrugger case is nothing more than a way of endearing herself to Ulrich, whom she perceives as vitally interested in the criminal's fate.

Agathe (ah-GAH-teh), Ulrich's twin sister, separated from him at birth and reared in an entirely different environment, yet so much like him that there is a sexual bond between them. Beautiful in a crystalline, remote sense, she represents the spiritual, existential, intellectual, and emotional commitments that Ulrich avoids while being attracted to them. Her high-mindedness and almost regal bearing are undercut by a petty crime of forgery she committed at her father's death. Appearing only in the third volume, she is an unfinished character; the author died before completing the book.

General Stumm von Bordwehr (shtewm fon BOHRD-vehr), a man for whom regulation and rule are the essential identifiers of order on Earth, a parody of the naïve military mind stumbling through a philosophical labyrinth quite beyond its capacity. He is captivated by his discovery that libraries are set out in some organized taxonomy, a realization of almost transcendental significance to him. His goal in life is to bring order to society in all of its forms, "to get the civilian mind into proper order."

Moosbrugger (MOHZ-brew-gehr), the "musical" murderer of a prostitute, in whose crime the characters see a poetic and philosophical metaphor. His case is raised to a *cause célèbre* by the attentions of high society. Clarisse goes insane trying to connect Moosbrugger to her own sense of the aesthetic. He is instinctive rather than intellectual and, as such, stands for the primitive "doer" in a world of "thinkers." He murders the prostitute because she clings to him, demanding that he manifest some sort of personality or character. In this respect, he is the sinister *Doppelgänger* of Ulrich.

Count Leinsdorf (LINZ-dohrf), the highest-ranking character who actually participates in the book's plot. Naïve about the forces of racial and regional unrest in his country, and thinking in terms of a unified Europe impossible to achieve, he represents the hierarchy of the Austro-Hungarian monarchy about to collapse from the weight of modern political realities. Ignorant of music and attaching no importance to literature, he holds his title and is referred to as "His Highness" purely from claims of primogeniture, without any notion of the obligations of nobility toward its subjects.

Rachel and

Soliman (SOH-lih-mahn), servants to Diotima and Arnheim, respectively. They serve as spies, messengers, and informal advisers to their employers. They reduce their high-flown rationalizations to the simple and universal workings of sexual attraction. Far from controlling their desires with social conventions, they succumb "to wild urge to commit violent escapades." Soliman, a "blackamoor," seduces Rachel, wearing Diotima's cast-off lingerie, in her room while the upper society talks in the chambers below. Their flirtations and affairs are a mirror image of the ostensibly more respectable affairs of their masters. As sounding boards for their master and mistress, they allow the narrative to include the uncensored thoughts of the main characters.

— *Thomas J. Taylor*

MANCHILD IN THE PROMISED LAND

Author: Claude Brown (1937-   )
First published: 1965
Genre: Novel

Locale: Harlem, New York
Time: The 1940's to 1960
Plot: Social criticism

Claude Brown, referred to as "**Sonny**" throughout most of the book, the first-person narrator and voice of the author. Sonny is a young black child at the opening of the novel, and this is his story of growth and survival in the streets of Harlem. His youth corresponds to the era of drugs, violence, and racial unrest in Harlem, and he learns quite young that survival depends on one's ability to fight everything and everyone. Unhappy under the roof of his abusive father and complacent mother, Sonny considers the streets of Harlem his home, and fear is his constant companion. Before reaching his teen years, Sonny has been shot, arrested, and sent to two reformatories, and he has experimented with various drugs, including heroin. As he matures, he witnesses the tragic self-destruction of most of his childhood friends, and he realizes that in order to escape poverty, addiction, and early death he must leave Harlem through the only avenue open to him: education. At the end of the novel, Sonny has left New York to obtain a college degree.

Mr. Papenek, the administrator of Wiltwyck School for Boys. During Sonny's stay at Wiltwyck, Mr. Papenek encourages Sonny to continue his education to escape Harlem street life. He is the first adult to recognize a potential in Sonny to rise above the traditional expectations of a black child from Harlem. Sonny is impressed with Mr. Papenek's ability to command respect through his intellect rather than his physical strength.

Sugar, a young black girl who grows up with Sonny. Throughout her childhood, Sugar develops a crush on Sonny, even though Sonny considers her too homely to be his girlfriend. As she matures, she grows into a beautiful woman, and her crush on Sonny fades, though they continue to share a strong bond. Despite her beauty, Sugar becomes one of the tragic statistics of Harlem. Having no economic, social, or educational resources, Sugar turns to prostitution and becomes addicted to drugs. The last time Sonny sees Sugar, she is in a heroin-induced stupor. Her senseless fall is one of several motivating factors behind Sonny's determination to leave Harlem.

Pimp, Sonny's younger brother. Pimp looks upon Sonny as a role model, though Sonny constantly encourages Pimp to avoid his mistakes on the street. Pimp, more than any other person, owns Sonny's heart, and Sonny devotes much of his young adulthood after leaving Harlem to helping Pimp make his way. In spite of these efforts, however, Pimp falls victim to heroin addiction and eventually is jailed for committing armed robbery to support his habit.

Danny, Sonny's friend and mentor in the streets. Slightly older than Sonny, Danny saves Sonny from various dangerous situations. Danny, himself a heroin addict, reinforces Sonny's fear of heroin addiction and constantly reminds him of the endless waste ahead of him should be succumb to the plague. Danny is one of Sonny's few friends who survive heroin addiction. At the end of the novel, Danny has turned to Christianity and family life.

— *Penelope A. LeFew*

THE MANDELBAUM GATE

Author: Muriel Spark (1918-   )
First published: 1965
Genre: Novel

Locale: Israel and Jordan
Time: Summer, 1961
Plot: Parody

Freddy Hamilton, a career diplomat in his mid-forties who is currently assigned to the British consulate in Jerusalem, Israel. Polite, urbane, a lifelong bachelor, and an envoy of old-fashioned charm and gentility, he has the reserve of the model representative: He straddles the fence, making concessions to both sides, committing himself only to maintaining the status quo. His career of service abroad is itself an evasion. He has never been able to stand up to his manipulative mother, and his routine weekly letters home attempt to cajole her into some semblance of normality. Similarly, he is a popular houseguest because he offends nobody, either by commission or by omission; he even composes thank-you notes in formal verse. He is being typically diplomatic about Barbara's predicament when she suddenly cites what the apocalypse predicts about the lukewarm: that they will be expelled. Perhaps as a result, he appoints himself as her guardian and protector when she gets into real political trouble. Strangely, he does this in a kind of trance; later, he cannot recall everything that happens during this adventure.

Barbara Vaughan, who is nearly thirty years old, a single teacher in an English boarding school. She is in Jerusalem to meet her fiancé, an archaeologist working at Qumram in Jordan. Half English country gentry, half London Jewish, and a convert to Catholicism, she is attempting to escape from her former companion and oldest friend, the headmistress of her school. She is honest, intelligent, unfashionably passionate, and committed to her faith. Her falling in love so late in life had come as a surprise; she had almost reconciled herself to life as an unmarried woman, sharing a home with her friend Ricky. She then met Harry Clegg on vacation the previous summer, and the two immediately fell into an impassioned affair. Returning to school afterward, she found herself unable to confess herself to Ricky, and the courtship had continued by mail. At term's end, Barbara felt that she had to see Harry, so she evaded Ricky and went to the Holy Land. There, she runs into a snag: Harry is in Jordan, on the other side of the Mandelbaum Gate dividing the city into Israeli and Jordanian sectors. In the current state of tension, the Jordanians are imprisoning all Jews as spies, and she is Jewish by their norms. Despite Freddy's warning, she determines to see the holy places of her faith and to join Harry, even though the church has so far refused to approve their betrothal, on the grounds that a former marriage of his may have been valid.

Yusif (Joe) Ramdez, a sixty-year-old man known as **the Agent** because he operates a travel agency, a life insurance agency, and a detective agency, as well as trafficking in intelligence, all in Jordan. On one hand, Ramdez is a Middle Eastern tout, the know-it-all guide common in fiction but here raised to a higher power. On the other hand, he represents a real evil, for he thrives on the kinds of misunderstandings endemic in politically tense situations. He profits from the kind of danger into which Barbara has put herself, and his spy ring has penetrated the British consulate.

Abdul Ramdez, Joe's thirty-four-year-old (but appearing younger) son and his representative in Israel. While supposedly giving lessons in Arabic to Freddy, Abdul keeps trying to sell him a life insurance policy and simultaneously pick up any intelligence leads. He resembles his father in being a pathological liar and also in his intelligence. Disillusioned about politics at an early age, he has learned to counterfeit poses as a means of acquiring information; unlike his father, he does not believe in any cause beyond his own profit.

Suzi Ramdez, Joe's thirty-year-old daughter. Like her brother, she is a subagent. Although possessing all the intelligence and craftiness of her father and brother, she is handicapped by the inferior situation into which Arab women are forced by their male-dominant culture. Despite these disadvantages, Suzi manages to acquire independence by seizing the opportunities created in the disorientation of the time and by superseding tradition. Sharing much of the political skepticism of Abdul, she engineers a plan to keep Barbara safe in Jordan, even to the extent of circumventing her father.

Edith (Ricky) Rickward, Barbara's thirty-year-old headmistress and oldest friend. Six years of companionship have created a close bond between the two women, but Barbara finds it fairly easy to break away to pursue her relationship with Harry, probably because she subconsciously resents Ricky's manipulative tactics. Ricky is determined, however, to prevent the liaison and follows Barbara to the Holy Land. A consummate intellectual and conventional liberated woman, she acts as if sex did not exist. Having discovered it, Barbara can no longer maintain this pretense.

Michael Aaronson, Barbara's thirty-year-old cousin. She confides in him, working out in conversation with him the position on which she finally acts.

Alexandros, a fifty-year-old Arab Catholic from Lebanon, a dealer in antiquities, curios, and information on the Jordanian side of the city. An honest, responsible businessman in a corrupt city, he assists Freddy in his efforts to protect Barbara. Suzi is his mistress.

Ruth Gardnor, the thirty-year-old wife of one of the members of the British consulate and a Jordanian spy.

— *James L. Livingston*

MANETTE SALOMON

Authors: Edmond de Goncourt (1822-1896) and Jules de Goncourt (1830-1870)
First published: 1867
Genre: Novel

Locale: Paris, France
Time: The nineteenth century
Plot: Naturalism

Manette Salomon (mah-NEHT sah-loh-MOH[N]), a Jewish model, Naz de Coriolis' mistress. With her frank, ignorant nature and exotic Jewishness, she delights her lover, but when she becomes famous as the subject of his successful painting, there grows in her a pride that causes her to change. Mistaken for Coriolis' wife, she finds this status attractive. When she becomes a mother, her greed for success comes to the fore, and she gradually gains ascendancy over her lover. When they are married, the fulfillment of her ambition spells the death of his creativity.

Naz de Coriolis (nahz deh kohr-yoh-LEES), a young painter who vows never to wed because he believes marriage and fatherhood destroy the artist's creativity. Fascinated by Manette Salomon's physical perfection and exotic Jewishness, he takes her as a model and his mistress. When fame and motherhood arouse her pride and ambition, he has not the strength to struggle against either her domination over him or the resulting death of his creativity.

Anatole Bazoche (ah-nah-TOHL bah-ZOHSH), a painter, Naz de Coriolis' close friend, who is alienated from him by Manette. A true bohemian to the last, Anatole, never a "success," retains his freedom.

Chassagnol (shah-sah-NYOHL), a painter alienated from Naz de Coriolis by Manette.

Garnotelle (gahr-noh-TEHL), a mediocre but successful painter after whom Manette insists Naz de Coriolis model himself.

Crescent (kreh-SAH[N]), a painter, and

Mme Crescent, his wife, who befriend Manette but become cool toward her when they learn that she is Jewish.

MANFRED

Author: George Gordon, Lord Byron (1788-1824)
First published: 1817
Genre: Drama

Locale: The Alps
Time: Indeterminate
Plot: Poetic

Manfred, a magician who summons the spirits of the universe, asking them for knowledge and oblivion. Although he contemplates suicide, mourning his limited powers, he is saved by a chamois hunter. He continues to raise other spirits and refuses the help of the church. Because he does not give his loyalty to the church or the powers of evil, he dies conquered by nothing but death.

The Spirit of Air, who asks Manfred what he wants to forget, a question the magician cannot answer.

The Spirit of Interior Fire,
the Spirit of Ocean,
the Spirit of Earth,
the Spirit of Exterior Fire, and
the Spirit of Night, spirits summoned by Manfred.

The Spirit of Manfred's Destiny, summoned by Manfred. It takes on the bodily shape of a beautiful woman who eludes the magician's embrace.

The Chamois Hunter, who saves Manfred from death. Seeing Manfred preparing to leap to his death on the Jungfrau Mountain, the hunter prevents the suicide. He feels sorry for Manfred but cannot help the magician solve his problems.

The Witch of the Alps, summoned by Manfred. She offers to share the beauties of nature with the magician and to aid him, if he agrees to obey her. She departs when Manfred refuses.

The Abbot of St. Maurice, who tries to save Manfred's soul for God but fails.

Astarte, whom Manfred has wronged. She is summoned from her tomb at Manfred's request by spirits in the Hall of Arimanes. She prophesies that his despair will end the next day. Death fulfills her prophecy.

MANHATTAN TRANSFER

Author: John Dos Passos (1896-1970)
First published: 1925
Genre: Novel

Locale: New York City
Time: The 1910's and 1920's
Plot: Impressionistic realism

Ellen Thatcher, the character who helps keep together the amorphous plot of the novel. She is an actress who lives through chaotic times, America just before and after World War I. She becomes a success as an actress, a failure as a woman. She is married three times, but never to the one man she loves.

Jimmy Herf, an arrival from Europe who comes to New York with his widowed mother; she dies shortly after their arrival. He is unhappy and tries to find himself. He works on a newspaper before the war and does Red Cross work with Ellen in Europe during the hostilities. He and Ellen marry and have a child, but they drift apart. Still confused but happy, he leaves New York.

George Baldwin, a cautious, intelligent lawyer and a ruthless, self-centered opportunist. He steers a shrewd course through New York City politics, but proves his emotional immaturity in his affairs with women. He is Ellen's third husband, whom she marries not out of love but because of apathy.

Joe Harland, Herf's blacksheep relative who, having won and lost several fortunes in Wall Street, finally settles for a job as a night watchman in order to earn whiskey money.

Gus McNiel, a milkman who, through the good work done by George Baldwin, wins a financial settlement after he has been run over by a train. Baldwin's professional and personal lives are involved with McNiel. Baldwin, who helps McNiel rise to political power, does not hesitate to seduce McNiel's wife Nellie when he has the chance.

Stan Emery, a drunken college boy who is finally expelled from the school he attends. He is the only man Ellen ever loves. His drinking goes from bad to worse, and while drunk he marries a slattern named Pearline. Filled with self-disgust, he finally sets fire to his apartment and perishes in the flames. Ellen had become pregnant by him, but after his death she has an abortion.

Joe O'Keefe, a young labor organizer who comes back from the war with a syphilitic infection and a grudge against big business.

Emile and

Congo, two young Frenchmen who come to New York to seek their fortunes. Emile finds his in the arms of a widowed Frenchwoman who owns a delicatessen; Congo makes a fortune as a successful bootlegger.

Jeff Merivale and

Emily Merivale, Herf's wealthy uncle and aunt and also his legal guardians.

Susie Thatcher and

Ed Thatcher, Ellen's parents. Susie dies, a neurotic, while Ellen is a child. Ed works hard to support his daughter and provides for her until she leaves home for a career on the stage.

John Oglethorpe, Ellen's first husband, who is a competent but lazy homosexual actor.

Harry Goldweiser, a wealthy Broadway producer who loves Ellen. Ellen never loves him, though she treats him kindly because her career depends on his influence.

Ruth Prynne, a young actress who is a friend of Ellen and John Oglethorpe and Jimmy Herf.

Cecily Baldwin, Baldwin's socially prominent wife, from whom he obtains a divorce in order to marry Ellen.

MANHUNT
(El acoso)

Author: Alejo Carpentier (1904-1980)
First published: 1956
Genre: Novel

Locale: Havana, Cuba
Time: Early 1930's
Plot: Psychological

The unnamed protagonist, referred to mainly as **the hunted**, a university student and a member of a terrorist group. A boy imitating macho types, he comes from the province to turbulent Havana at the end of General Gerardo Machado's dictatorship (1933) to study architecture and the charms of the prostitute Estrella. He takes residence with his old wet nurse but soon gets swept away by the political turmoil. He joins the Communist Party but abandons it for "direct" action. He participates in the execution of his friend and role model, who has betrayed an important plan. Later, he sees the revolutionary terrorism degenerate into killings for a price, though justified by the same rhetoric. After a murder he has arranged, he is betrayed by Estrella and is arrested by the police. The hint of torture makes him betray his comrades. When he is released, he himself becomes hunted by the survivors. After rediscovering God, he wanders through Havana and remembers different episodes of his life. Thrown out of every possible shelter and fleeing from his pursuers, he ends up in the concert hall, where Beethoven's *Eroica* symphony is being performed, precisely the music he heard when he was in hiding with the wet nurse. In too much of a rush to wait for a ticket, he leaves the alleged false banknote with the ticket taker. During the performance, guided by the music, he reviews the key events of his life. After the performance, he tries to hide in the concert hall but is executed by his comrades the night of Easter Sunday.

Estrella (ehs-TREH-yah), a young prostitute (her name means "star" in Spanish), a "friend" of various characters of the novel. To avoid harassment, she betrays the protagonist to the police. When he returns to see her the night he is on the run, his confession shows her the awful consequences of her betrayal. She betrays him again when the taxi driver makes a fuss about the allegedly false banknote. When the ticket taker appears with the same bill, she gets irritated and throws him out.

An old black woman, the protagonist's former wet nurse. She tries to keep a motherly eye on the young student, but to no avail. She shelters him when he returns, hunted by his comrades, but falls ill and dies shortly thereafter.

The niece, who takes care of the old woman during her illness and fusses about the quantities of food she eats.

The ticket taker, a student of music working at the concert hall. For weeks, he has been preparing for the concert, listening to a recording of *Eroica* and reading books about the symphony. The banknote that the unknown "concert fan" gives him is too tempting, however, and he leaves for Estrella's arms. He finds her unexpectedly irritated, however, and is rejected because of the supposedly counterfeit bill. Infuriated with himself, he manages to return for the finale of the symphony. When the death is investigated by the police, he gives the bill to the policeman.

The traitor, another university student, a comrade of the protagonist and his macho model.

The scholarship holder, another university student and the protagonist's friend from the province. He introduces the protagonist to Estrella.

The policeman, who investigates the murder and keeps the banknote because there is nothing wrong with it.

— Emil Volek

MANON LESCAUT
(Histoire du chevalier des Grieux et de Manon Lescaut)

Author: Abbé Prévost (Antoine-François Prévost d'Exiles, 1697-1763)
First published: 1731; revised, 1753
Genre: Novel

Locale: France and New Orleans
Time: 1700
Plot: Sentimental

The Chevalier des Grieux (day gree-YEW), a student of philosophy at Amiens. He becomes a seminary student, a card cheat, and finally, returning from New Orleans after Manon's death, a priest.

Tiberge (tee-BEHRZH), a fellow student who urges des Grieux to forget Manon by studying religion at the Seminary of Saint-Supplice. He follows des Grieux to America and persuades him to return to France.

The Father of des Grieux, who gets his son released from jail but will not help Manon.

Manon Lescaut (mah-NOH[N] lehs-KOH), a pretty courtesan who attracts des Grieux. She also bestows her attentions on M. de B——— and later on M. de G——— M———, at the suggestion of her brother. She dies an exile in New Orleans.

M. Lescaut, of the Royal guards, the unscrupulous brother of Manon. He is killed by a man whose fortune he won at cards.

M. de B———, who is in love with Manon.

M. de G——— M———, a wealthy old man duped and robbed by des Grieux and Manon.

M. de G——— M——— Jr., the son, who comes to avenge his father but is won over by the charms of Manon.

M. de T———, who helps dupe young G——— M———. He is arrested by the police.

The Governor of New Orleans, who forbids the marriage of Manon and the chevalier because his nephew, Synnelet, loves her.

M. Synnelet (see-neh-LAY), who fights a duel with des Grieux over Manon in New Orleans.

A MAN'S BLESSING
(A ciascuno il suo)

Author: Leonardo Sciascia (1921-1989)
First published: 1966
Genre: Novel

Locale: A village in western Sicily, near Agrigento
Time: August, 1964-September, 1965
Plot: Detective and mystery

Professor Paolo Laurana (pah-OH-loh lahew-RAH-nah), a middle-aged teacher of Italian literature and history. He is a resident of a small Sicilian village, unnamed in the story. When two prominent citizens of the town are murdered mysteriously, Laurana takes up the investigation on his own. A scholar and a longtime bachelor, he is attracted to Signora Roscio, the widow of one of the murdered men. He pursues clues that lead him to Palermo, where he learns that Dr. Roscio was about to reveal a scandal about a prominent citizen of the region. Laurana, a bit timid but curious, pursues the clues until he falls victim to the murderer of the two men.

Dean Rosello, the dean of the church of Sant'Anna in the town, a scrupulous churchman who is the uncle of the murdered Dr. Roscio's widow, Luisa. Luisa was reared in Dean Rosello's house, as was his nephew Rosello, who is now a lawyer. It is in the dean's sacristy that Laurana sees the edition of the newspaper *L'osservatore Romano* containing the word *Unicuique* and confirms his suspicions that the death threat sent to the pharmacist, the murdered Manno, was cut from this paper. Rosello, a down-to-earth clergyman beloved by his parish, dislikes his nephew the lawyer, whom he considers unscrupulous.

Rosello, a lawyer, the nephew of Dean Rosello and cousin of Luisa, the widow of the late Dr. Roscio. An unscrupulous manipulator, he is considered by the rector of Sant'Anna to be a fool but a clever one. His power is immense, though not evident to all. Rosello is rumored to have been caught in bed with Luisa. Laurana discovers all this information in his investigations and actually meets Rosello one day in the company of a known Mafia assassin. Rosello pretends to be Laurana's helper in his investigations, though in the end, Rosello's purpose is to find out how much Laurana knows.

Dr. Roscio (ROHS-kee-oh), a prominent physician in the town who went hunting with his friend, the pharmacist Manno, and was murdered by persons unknown. Laurana uncovers the fact that Dr. Roscio had caught his wife in bed with Rosello the lawyer and then proceeded to gather a dossier on Rosello's illegal activities. He then went to a Communist deputy in Palermo and said that he had a file on a prominent man in his community. Dr. Roscio asked if the deputy would reveal the dossier and call for an investigation, if given the file. The deputy agreed, but Dr. Roscio was murdered before he could hand over the dossier.

Signora Luisa Roscio, the widow of Dr. Roscio and niece of Dean Rosello, a voluptuous young woman in her prime. She and her cousin Rosello, the lawyer, conspire to murder Laurana, who has uncovered the background of the murder of Dr. Roscio and the pharmacist Manno. She tricks Laurana into believing that she is sincerely interested in convicting her cousin Rosello and makes an appointment with Laurana to give him more details of a diary of her husband's she allegedly has found. The appointment is actually an appointment with death for Laurana.

— Philip Brantingham

MAN'S FATE
(La Condition humaine)

Author: André Malraux (1901-1976)
First published: 1933
Genre: Novel

Locale: Shanghai, China
Time: 1927
Plot: Social realism

Ch'en (shehn), a Chinese terrorist dedicated to the revolution. In an attempt to kill Chiang Kai-shek with a bomb, he blows himself up but fails in his mission.

Kyo (kyoh), a communist organizer of French and Japanese parentage. He is tormented by thoughts of his wife's freely confessed adultery. Arrested by König, he kills himself with a cyanide tablet given him by Katov.

Gisors (zhee-SOHR), Kyo's old French father, who resembles an ascetic abbot. After the revolutionary plot fails, he returns to Japan to teach painting.

May, Kyo's sensual German wife, a physician with advanced views on marriage relationships. The communist plot having failed and Kyo being dead, she goes to Moscow to practice medicine.

Baron de Clappique (deh klah-PEEK), a French adventurer and unscrupulous businessman; König's friend who permits Kyo to be arrested instead of warning him to hide. The baron, in disguise, escapes China on a French ship.

Katov (kah-TOHV), an experienced Russian revolutionist and former convict. His kindly face, mischievous eyes, and upturned nose do not reveal his coldly murderous nature. Arrested by König, he generously gives Kyo the cyanide tablet he has provided for himself, and he is executed.

Hemmelrich (ay-mehl-REEK), a cowardly German revolutionist whose wife and child are killed in the destruction of his shop by Chiang's police, who later shoot Hemmelrich.

Ferral (feh-RAHL), a French businessman who decides to support Chiang. Angered by Valérie's duplicity, he releases forty birds and a kangaroo in her room. He returns to France on the liner that also takes the baron.

König (koo-NEEG), chief of Chiang's police, who foils the communist plot and executes the revolutionary group.

Chiang Kai-shek (shyahng kay-chehk), leader of the Blue forces.

Valérie (vah-lay-REE), Ferral's deceitful mistress.

MAN'S HOPE
(L'Espoir)

Author: André Malraux (1901-1976)
First published: 1937
Genre: Novel

Locale: Spain
Time: 1936-1937
Plot: Adventure

Manuel (mahn-WEHL), a sound engineer in the film industry when the novel opens. He is a handsome, jovial, and idealistic young man whose political convictions have led him to join the Communist Party. When the Spanish Civil War breaks out, he becomes a soldier in the Republican army, and because of his leadership qualities, he quickly climbs through the ranks to become a high-ranking officer. Generous and outgoing at the outset of the novel, Manuel becomes increasingly detached as the realities of command force him to make brutal and occasionally inhuman decisions in the name of efficiency. An able and courageous commander at the novel's end, he has lost some of his humanity.

Colonel Magnin (mah-NYEEN), a French aviator, volunteer for the Spanish Republic, and head of the Republic's International Squadron. Tall, mustachioed, and philosophical by nature, Magnin is a shrewd observer of people and an excellent judge of character. He combines a passion for flying with an idealistic devotion to the cause of the Republic and the principles of individual liberty and social justice for which it stands. Although it is his responsibility to mold a motley assortment of foreign volunteers and mercenaries into an effective fighting force, he is skeptical of those like the communists who are obsessed with discipline.

Garcia (gahr-SEE-ah), the head of the Spanish intelligence service. He is a corpulent, robust, and good-natured man who, in Magnin's view, gives the impression of being a wealthy landowner. An anthropologist before the war and a famous intellectual, Garcia is a man of extraordinary culture and learning. As the author's principal mouthpiece within the novel, Garcia provides an overview of the meaning of the struggle, analyzes the role of the intellectual in revolutionary politics, and addresses with great insight the metaphysical and moral quandaries inevitably brought by war.

Captain Hernandez (ehr-NAHN-dehs), a career army officer who remains loyal to the Republic when Francisco Franco launches his uprising. He is a severe, uncompromising idealist whose inflexibility ultimately destroys him. Although he recognizes that the brutal expediency and efficiency of the communists are necessary to defeat the fascists, Hernandez refuses to sacrifice his personal principles to the cause of victory. He is given to making noble and chivalric gestures that seem hopelessly outdated in a modern, mechanized war. Ultimately disillusioned, Hernandez is captured by the fascists during the Republican retreat from Toledo and is executed along with the other prisoners. Although a sympathetic and admirable character, Hernandez is held up as a negative example in the novel because his overly rigorous idealism ultimately serves no one and in fact plays into the hands of the fascists.

Colonel Ximenes (hee-MEHN-ehs), the Civil Guard commander in Barcelona and, like Hernandez, a career officer who remains loyal to the Republic, despite his conservative and traditionalist views. Unlike Hernandez, Ximenes understands that one's personal beliefs and values must be sacrificed in the short run for the sake of victory over the fascists. Thus, during the struggle for Barcelona, Ximenes willingly fights alongside the anarchists, the traditional enemies of the Civil Guard, to save the city from falling into the hands of Franco's supporters.

Puig (pweeg), a dashing, enthusiastic anarchist leader in Barcelona. He cuts a romantic figure, in his leather jacket and turban, during the fighting. Despite important philosophical and temperamental differences, Puig and his comrade-in-arms Colonel Ximenes share an admiration for courage and a belief in the fraternity of those fighting for the Republic that transcends social and political differences. Puig has no patience and can conceive of the struggle only in terms of an immediate victory. In keeping with this "apocalyptic" stance, he dies while driving a car full speed into a barricade set up by the fascists.

Slade, a tough young American journalist whose reports on important events in the war such as the bombing of Madrid are quoted verbatim in the novel. His reports confirm his strong support of the Republic and underscore the brutality of the fascists' tactics and their utter contempt for human life.

Giovanni Scali (jee-oh-VAH-nee SKAH-lee), an Italian art historian who serves as a volunteer in the international air squadron and acts as second in command to Magnin. He is a diminutive, curly-haired man who is both sensitive and intelligent. Scali believes in the value of the individual and the individual's creative potential but insists that the greatness of people lies in their capacity to act collectively to achieve a common goal. The international air squadron therefore is greater than the individual members who compose it.

Alvear (ahl-veh-AHR), an aging Spanish art dealer and the father of pilot Jaime Alvear. He questions the value of the Republic's struggle against Franco. He does not believe that social and economic reform alleviate suffering or improve what he describes as the "quality of man." In a conversation with Scali, he claims that art is superior to life because the latter is ephemeral and full of suffering, whereas art is eternal and a source of comfort and fulfillment.

The Negus (NEH-gews), one of the leaders of the anarchists and a former deckhand in Barcelona. He is a skilled saboteur and guerrilla fighter who accompanies Puig in his suicidal assault on the Fascist barricade. When the war drags on, he loses interest but continues to fight because he enjoys his work as a saboteur.

— *Richard J. Golsan*

MANSFIELD PARK

Author: Jane Austen (1775-1817)
First published: 1814
Genre: Novel

Locale: Northamptonshire, England
Time: Early nineteenth century
Plot: Domestic realism

Fanny Price, the heroine of the novel. Brought up by the Bertrams at Mansfield Park, she is timid and self-effacing and is constantly reminded by her Aunt Norris of her position as a poor relation. She has always loved Edmund Bertram, the second son. Henry Crawford falls in love with her and proposes, but she refuses him, for she considers him shallow and worldly. Thus she angers Sir Thomas Bertram, who feels that she has thrown away her best chance for marriage. Later, when both Bertram daughters disgrace themselves, Sir Thomas understands Fanny's real worth. Edmund, who had thought himself in love with Mary Crawford, is shocked by her attitude toward his sisters' behavior and realizes that he actually loves Fanny. They are married at the end of the novel.

Sir Thomas Bertram, a wealthy baronet, the owner of Mansfield Park. He is dignified, reserved, fundamentally kind and just, but too remote from his children to understand them. Though fond of Fanny Price, he is angered by her refusal to marry Henry Crawford; however, when his daughters disgrace him, he realizes that Fanny has a better judgment of people than he and is happy when she marries his younger son.

Lady Bertram, his wife, the spoiled beauty of her family. She is an indolent, self-indulgent, good-natured woman.

Mrs. Norris, her sister, the widow of a clergyman. A stingy, ill-tempered busybody, she is unbearably severe to her poor niece, Fanny Price, but lavish in her flattery of the rich Bertrams. Her flattery does much to ruin the characters of the Bertram daughters. After Maria Bertram's divorce, Mrs. Norris goes to live with her.

Mrs. Price, the third sister, Fanny's mother. She has made the worst marriage, her husband being a lieutenant of marines without fortune or connections. They have nine children and live on the edge of poverty.

Lieutenant Price, her husband, a marine officer disabled for active service. He is uncouth but good-natured.

William Price, their son, in the Royal Navy. The favorite of his sister Fanny, he gets his promotion through the Crawfords' friendship with her.

Tom Bertram, the older son of Sir Thomas. He is headstrong, worldly, and idle, but a severe illness sobers him.

Edmund Bertram, the second son, a serious young man who desires to take holy orders. He fancies himself in love with Mary Crawford until, disgusted by her cynical attitude toward the clergy and by her easy acceptance of his sisters' conduct, he becomes aware that he really loves Fanny Price. They are married and live near Mansfield Park.

Maria Bertram, the older daughter, spoiled and selfish. She marries wealthy Mr. Rushworth but tires of him, runs off with Henry Crawford, and is irretrievably disgraced.

Julia Bertram, the second daughter, equally spoiled. She elopes with Mr. Yates and by so doing cuts herself off from her family.

Henry Crawford, a wealthy young man who flirts with Maria Bertram. He falls in love with Fanny Price, but she refuses him, and he elopes with Maria. They separate after a few months.

Mary Crawford, his sister. She is cynical and worldly but attracts Edmund Bertram. He is disillusioned and repelled when she takes his sisters' conduct so casually.

Mr. Rushworth, the rich but brainless husband of Maria Bertram, whom she deserts for Henry Crawford.

Mr. Yates, a fashionable young man who visits Mansfield Park and eventually elopes with Julia Bertram. The marriage greatly displeases her father.

THE MANSION

Author: William Faulkner (1897-1962)
First published: 1959
Genre: Novel

Locale: Mississippi
Time: 1908-1948
Plot: Social realism

Mink (M. C.) Snopes, the central character. He is a child-sized man who lives by his own code, trusting "Old Moster" not to play tricks on him. Mink's code lets him accept self-caused trouble. He is patient, humble, tenacious, hardworking, focused, thoughtful about things, and a strict rule keeper. His thoughts pepper the novel, and most of them read like poetry. Against all odds, he is pardoned after thirty-eight years in the Parchman prison. He manages to get a gun in Memphis and go to Jefferson to kill Flem. After the murder, he remains free.

Linda Snopes Kohl, Eula Varner Snopes's daughter by Hoake McCarron. Linda despises Flem. She marries a communist Jewish sculptor and goes to Spain to fight in the war. He dies in a plane crash, and she is deafened by an exploding bomb. Back in Jefferson, she creates problems by trying to educate black children. She works in the Pascagoula Shipyards near the end of the war. At home again, despising Flem, she manipulates Gavin, getting him to petition for Mink Snopes's release from Parchman. She helps Mink escape after Flem's murder. A Jaguar she ordered as soon as she knew Gavin could secure Mink's pardon is delivered the day of Flem's funeral. She dismisses Gavin's disillusionment and leaves him to put a marker on Flem's grave.

Gavin Stevens, an idealistic patsy for Linda to the bitter end, as he had been for Linda's mother. He sees her as innocent until the end of the book, and he is unable to see her as manipulative. While getting Mink out of prison, he believes Linda has no notion that Mink would kill Flem or that he, himself, would feel professionally soiled and personally responsible if Mink did, because he got the pardon knowing Mink would do just that. On the day of Flem's funeral, he realizes that Linda knew all those things and had used him. At the book's end, he continues executing tasks she assigns.

Vladimir Kyrilytch (V. K.) Ratliff, Faulkner's voice of reason. He knows Linda will involve Gavin in something bad and spends the novel watchdogging him. He discovers that Mink sidestepped Gavin's ploy to keep him out of Mississippi

and calls to give warning, realizing that Linda's use of Gavin to instigate Flem's murder is the "bad" he had feared. He tries to help Gavin cope with lost illusions. The two search out Mink and give him money Linda left him.

Montgomery Ward Snopes, a chief force in the novel who sets the stage for Flem's murder. He had a pornography business on the side and might have done time in federal prison, but Flem wanted him in Parchman and framed him with bootlegged whiskey planted in his shop. Before leaving for prison, Montgomery gives Reba Rivers, madam of a Memphis brothel, $40 of Flem's money to send, anonymously, to Mink. Mink had $3.75 of that left when pardoned; without it, he could not have bought the pistol. At Parchman, Flem tells him to trick Mink into escaping and getting caught. Montgomery has mink wear a girl's dress, telling him it is Flem's idea. Mink kills Flem over that dress. After serving two years, Montgomery moves to California and gets rich making pornographic films.

Flem Snopes, who, by framing Montgomery Ward Snopes on charges of possession of bootlegged whiskey, makes sure Mink stays at Parchman twenty extra years. He has Montgomery trick Mink into an attempted escape and then have him captured. Flem is virtually a flat character, never more so than when he sits staring at Mink, fumbling with a gun until it fires.

Charles "Chick" Mallison, Gavin's nephew. He learns, in the course of the book, that though he loved his father, Gavin had been the chief influence on his life. Although Chick narrates a few chapters of the novel, his role is that of sounding board for Gavin and Ratliff. Through the course of the novel, he takes Gavin's advice and continues in law school past the time he wanted to join the Air Force, but he does manage to fly in the war, not as a pilot but as guard of a case containing locations of bomb sites. After the war, he helps Gavin handle a few typical political problems in Jefferson.

— *Jo Culbertson Davis*

A MANUAL FOR MANUEL
(Libro de Manuel)

Author: Julio Cortázar (1914-1984)
First published: 1973
Genre: Novel

Locale: Paris and Buenos Aires
Time: 1969-1972
Plot: Social morality

Andrés Fava (ahn-DREHS FAH-vah), the main narrator, an Argentine intellectual living in Paris. He is connected to the members, though not much to the activities, of a principally

Latin American activist group, the Screwery, that operates there. Andrés tenaciously clings to his world of ideas and aesthetics, erotic freedom, and phonograph records but also harbors an underlying urge to be a man of action. This urge is expressed in a dream he has had, in which an unknown Cuban gives him a message. Andrés cannot remember the dream message until he makes a kind of personal commitment to activism by going to join the members of the Screwery at Verrières, the suburb where they are holding a kidnapped Latin American police official. The message proves to be simple: "Wake up." Andrés does so more through this show of solidarity than through his intense erotic experiences with Ludmilla and Francine, in which he also was seeking illumination.

The one I told you, always designated by this expression, never by name, an Argentine writer who is quietly chronicling the activities of the Screwery, with which he is peripherally involved. His narrative, together with the clippings and other documentary materials collected by Susana for her son Manuel, seems to correspond to the novel, so the one I told you can be seen as a surrogate author. Throughout, he worries about the disjunct quality of his narrative and its multiple perspectives—aspects of *A Manual for Manuel* itself. The one I told you is present at the Verrières shootout and appears to die there—many plot details are left hanging—because subsequently Andrés is organizing the writer's somewhat chaotic notes and jottings.

Marcos, the Argentine head of the Screwery, a curly-haired, dedicated revolutionary who is also something of an intellectual. Under Marcos' direction, the members of the Screwery create small provocations in Parisian public places, aimed at raising consciousness among ordinary citizens. They also undertake a complex international operation, the kidnapping of a police official. Marcos is resolute, and he can be tender with someone he loves, such as Ludmilla. He apparently dies at the Verrières shootout.

Ludmilla, an actress of Polish descent who has been Andrés' lover and who begins a relationship with Marcos shortly before the kidnapping. Both men call her Polonette, or little Polish girl. She is more intuitive and less structured and conceptual than these men; her imagination inspires them both. Aware of Andrés' parallel relationship with Francine, Ludmilla is quicker than he to recognize that their own relationship is at an end. She moves on naturally and unresentfully to Marcos and to involvement in the Screwery. Ludmilla wishes to learn about Latin American politics and activism, and Marcos patiently begins to teach her. She is a survivor of the events at Verrières.

Susana, an Argentine member of the Screwery, married to Patricio. They are the parents of the infant Manuel. Susana is putting together a scrapbook of political clippings that is to serve as a kind of primer for Manuel. A translator for UNESCO, Susana often translates the French clippings for the benefit of Fernando, who has recently arrived in France.

Patricio (pah-TREE-syoh), Manuel's father and Susana's husband, an active member of the Screwery, which often gathers at his and Susana's apartment. Susana and Patricio's relative domesticity contrasts somewhat with the more bohemian lifestyle of Andrés and some of the others. He and Susana survive Verrières.

Manuel, the son of Susana and Patricio, an energetic infant who keeps his parents and the members of the Screwery busy attending to his needs and steering him away from household hazards. Manuel is to be the recipient of the documentary collage that his mother and other Screwery members are assembling, and to which Andrés adds all the narrative fragments written by the one I told you.

Lonstein, an Argentine who works at the morgue but cultivates intellectual interests and occasionally writes a poem. His friends call him the little rabbi. He practices solitude, celibacy, and onanism and expounds his theory and practice of the latter in a conversation with the one I told you. Lonstein speaks in a unique patois featuring portmanteau words, Argentine slang, and hispanicized French expressions. Apolitical and removed from the activities of the Screwery, he has reservations about the authoritarian tendency of revolutionaries. At the end of the novel, Lonstein is at the morgue cleaning the corpse of an unspecified friend—whether it is Marcos, the one I told you, or Andrés is unclear.

Francine, Andrés' French lover, a well-organized, university-trained woman who owns a bookshop and lives in a well-appointed apartment. Despite her Gallic rationality and her awareness of his attachment to Ludmilla, she is patient with Andrés' search for himself, perhaps even after he has in effect raped her at a hotel where they spend the night of the kidnapping alone together.

Gómez, a Panamanian member of the Screwery who is considered to be a conventional, unimaginative Marxist militant by intellectuals in the group. He is the lover of Monique, a French member of the group. Gómez is an avid stamp collector. He is last seen in jail after the Verrières incident, undaunted and pleased with the relative success of the operation.

Oscar Lemos, an Argentine who flies from Buenos Aires to Paris with counterfeit money to be used for the expenses of the kidnapping. With the kind of subversive humor typical of the Screwery, Oscar poses as a veterinarian and brings a live turquoise-colored penguin and several armadillos, purportedly for donation to a French zoo but really to distract attention from the containers of falsified bills.

Gladis, an Argentine flight attendant who accompanies her lover Oscar to Paris on one of her Aerolineas Argentinas flights. Gladis is forced to abandon her job because of her complicity in Oscar's elaborate ruse. She and Oscar appear to escape from Verrières and are last seen on their flight home to Buenos Aires.

Heredia (eh-REH-dyah), a witty Brazilian member of the Screwery who has spent time in London and returns for the kidnapping, then is imprisoned with Gómez after the events at Verrières.

Lucien Verneuil, a French member of the Screwery. He participates in both the group's antic disruptions of Parisian street life and the kidnapping. He volunteers his mother's country home for the sequestering of the police official at a time when she is traveling. Despite his association with the Screwery, Verneuil has something of the conventional French attitude toward Latin American volatility, and he is more authoritarian in outlook than some of his companions. He is wounded at Verrières.

Roland, a French member of the Screwery, similar in characteristics to Lucien Verneuil.

Fernando, a Chilean who has just arrived in Paris and is a friend of Patricio and Susana. He is not a member of the Screwery. Fernando has a slight speech impediment that causes him to pronounce the sound of *w* as that of *v*.

The Vip (beep), the Screwery's name for the portly Latin American police official in charge of international antiterrorist operations whom they kidnap and hold in exchange for a number of political prisoners to be freed from Latin American jails. He is called **Beto** (BAY-toh) by his wife and **Don Gualberto** (gwahl-BAYR-toh) by his subordinates. The Vip is freed at Verrières by the secret and regular police.

The Vipess, the Vip's conventional, foolish, loquacious wife.

Higinio (ee-HEE-nyoh), a Latin American secret police official entrusted with protecting the Vip. Higinio is called the Gi-ant by the Screwery, whose code name for the secret police is the ants. He is ruthless: At Verrières, he is prepared to have the Vip shot to ensure that the kidnappers will be charged with the maximum offense.

— *John Deredita*

MARAT/SADE

Author: Peter Weiss (1916-1982)
First published: 1964
Genre: Drama

Locale: Charenton asylum, near Paris
Time: July 13, 1808, and July 13, 1793
Plot: Social morality

Marquis de Sade (mahr-KEE deh sahd), a French writer and libertine. While Sade, at the age of sixty-eight, is confined at Charenton asylum for his nontraditional views on sex and violence, he stages a play about Marat's death, which took place on the same date fifteen years earlier. He both directs the actors—the asylum's inmates, who are either mentally disturbed or confined for political reasons—and participates in the action. In his conversations with Marat, Sade expresses a certain amount of sympathy for the goals of the French Revolution, but he also shows himself as Marat's philosophical opponent by professing an extreme form of individualism and strong faith in the power of subjective imagination.

Jean-Paul Marat (zhah[n]-pohl mah-RA), a French physician and revolutionary leader. He is forty-nine years of age and spends many hours sitting in the bathtub to cool his skin, which is afflicted by an illness. Like the historical figure he represents, the actor playing Marat at Charenton suffers from paranoia and undergoes hydrotherapy. Although he is a strong advocate of the revolution, Marat has a vision of a just society directed toward the future. He is, nevertheless, perceived as the revolution's central catalyst in the public eye because of his inflammatory speeches and articles, and he is killed by Corday in his bathtub on the eve of Bastille Day.

Charlotte Corday (shahr-LOHT kohr-DAY), an attractive virgin, twenty-four years old. Because her role at Charenton is played by an inmate suffering from sleeping sickness, she must often be awakened and supported in her movements by two sister-nurses. As in the case of the historical figure, she repeatedly appears at Marat's door before she is admitted by his mistress and finds the opportunity to thrust her dagger into his chest.

Jacques Roux (zhahk rew), a former priest turned social radical. The inmate playing his role at Charenton has a history similar to that of the historical figure, which is the reason the asylum guards have tied together his shirt sleeves, as a way of restricting his movements. Roux calls for immediate violence and for the takeover of shops and factories by the people of France and thus functions as the alter ego of Marat, whose radicalism is restricted by both his illness and his political prudence. Roux repeatedly interrupts the play within the play with his call for radical action, and he has the last word during

the uprising of the inmates with which the play ends, as he shouts his call for a political decision into the audience.

Duperret (dew-peh-RAY), a deputy of the Girondists, the more conservative wing of the French revolutionary parliament. He dresses in the ostentatious manner of an *incroyable* and is played at Charenton by an erotomaniac. In contrast to the platonic love of the historical figure, the actor in the play constantly makes sexual advances toward Corday, who completely disregards them. He also is out of place because of his reactionary political and social views.

Simonne Evrard (see-MUHN eh-VRAHR), Marat's mistress. The actress playing Simonne at Charenton wears both a hospital uniform and a housewife's apron, and she constantly wrings a cloth in her hands when she is not in the process of changing Marat's head bandage. She sees her task as trying to persuade Marat to refrain from future political activities (including writing) and to keep him shielded from the public, although she fails during Corday's third visit.

Coulmier (kewl-MEEAY), the asylum director. He is dressed in elegant clothes and carries a walking stick. Coulmier throws out Napoleonic phrases and sees (or tries to see) no connection between the events in Sade's play and his own time, thus repeatedly admonishing the marquis to stick to the previously censured text.

The Herald, a man who wears a harlequin's smock over his hospital shirt and a two-pointed cap with bells and spangles. Playing the roles of both narrator and stage manager, the Herald often interrupts and comments on the action of the interior play. His views express both an ironic distance from the historical events and a warning against their recurrence in the present.

Kokol,

Polpoch,

Cucurucu, and

Rossignol, collectively known as **the Four Singers**, who are dressed grotesquely, representing partly comedians and partly figures of the Parisian mob. Although they hail both Marat, for his political views and actions, and Sade, for his advocation of complete sexual freedom, they participate in the glorification of Napoleon as much as they do in the revolt of the inmates of Charenton at the end of the play.

— *Helmut F. Pfanner*

THE MARBLE FAUN: Or, The Romance of Monte Beni

Author: Nathaniel Hawthorne (1804-1864)
First published: 1860
Genre: Novel

Locale: Rome, Italy
Time: Mid-nineteenth century
Plot: Psychological realism

Donatello, in reality the Count of *Monte Beni*, at first a naïve young man who seems to be almost dim-witted, with little formal education and almost no intellectual, moral, or emotional depth. He appears almost a creature out of the mythical past, a faun out of his time and place associating with the painters and sculptors of an artists' colony in nineteenth century Rome. Feeling a kinship with nature and its inhabitants, he is truly happy only in the woods and gardens. He falls in love with Miriam Schaefer, a beautiful but mysterious young painter. One night, at her unspoken behest, Donatello murders a man. This crime brings about a change in the young Italian nobleman, who for a time retires to his ancestral home in Tuscany. He finds that he is no longer akin to nature, but in exchange for this loss, he acquires new depth of soul under the torment of his crime and awakes to moral values. In the garb of a penitent, he returns to Rome, where he is reunited briefly with his beloved during the carnival season. At the end of that time, he is seized by the authorities and imprisoned.

Miriam Schaefer, an exotically beautiful young woman of wealth who appears mysteriously among the people of an artist colony in Rome. She is also a painter, and her life is haunted by a man who appears to be an artist's model. He seems to have a strange hold over the girl and causes her great uneasiness. Miriam's lover, Donatello, rids her of the presence of this troublesome man by throwing him from the famous Tarpeian Rock. Because her eyes had commanded Donatello to commit the crime, Miriam feels as guilty as if the act had been her own. Also, she feels a bond with her companion-accomplice as strong as marriage ties. She, like Donatello, suffers the pangs of conscience fiercely. She and her lover, reunited after his return from a period of retirement in Tuscany, find a brief period of happiness before he is committed to prison. Miriam, who goes free, is really a member of an aristocratic Italian family and was at one time engaged to marry the man who haunted her. Her real name is never mentioned.

Brother Antonio, a Capuchin monk, the man who haunts and hounds Miriam Schaefer until he is murdered by Donatello. Having shown himself to be of great merit, at least on the surface, he is granted unusual freedom by his order, a freedom he uses in order to dog the girl's footsteps. Once her fiancé, he had committed a crime in which Miriam, though innocent, was implicated.

Hilda, a pretty, virtuous American girl studying painting in Rome. Because she is Miriam's friend, she becomes involved in the intrigue surrounding Miriam. She witnesses the midnight murder committed by Donatello, and at Miriam's request, she delivers a strange parcel that causes her to be held in a convent as a possible accessory to the crime. Hilda is much affected by the terrible deed she witnesses, even though she has no guilt. The weight of her knowledge drives the overly sensitive girl to lose all interest in her work. Though she is faithful to and proud of her Puritan heritage, she becomes so disturbed that she enters a confessional in St. Peter's Cathedral and tells her story to a priest. In the end, her experiences cause her to love Kenyon, a young American in love with her.

Kenyon, a young American sculptor working in Rome. He loves Hilda and is one of the little circle of friends surrounding Miriam Schaefer. He brings Donatello and Miriam together again after they have suffered alone following the murder of Brother Antonio by Donatello. Kenyon's love for Hilda is eventually rewarded, for she comes to love him, and they are married. Once after their marriage, they encounter Miriam, who both blesses and repulses them silently. They do not disturb her expiation and grief.

MARBOT: A Biography
(Marbot: Eine Biographie)

Author: Wolfgang Hildesheimer (1916-1991)
First published: 1981
Genre: Novel

Locale: England, Germany, Switzerland, France, and Italy
Time: 1801-1830
Plot: Historical realism

Sir Andrew Marbot, a reserved and independent British aristocrat, aesthete, and art theorist. Despite extensive, seemingly authentic documentation from sources credited to a great number of European artists, writers, and thinkers at the beginning of the nineteenth century, Marbot is a fictitious character. A portrait, painted by Eugene Delacroix in 1827 and included in the novel, shows Marbot as a twenty-six-year-old attractive young man. His controlled posture and the skeptical expression around his mouth seem intended to make him appear distant and determined. His bushy, barely tamed black hair and his large, expressive eyes with slightly drooping lids give him a touch of melancholy. The full lips and the weak chin seem to suggest a strong sensuality. His biographer describes him as an

inconspicuous and very private person. He was born in 1801 as the oldest of three children and grew up on his parents' estate, Marbot Hall, in the north of Northumberland, England. Because there was considerable wealth in the family, Andrew lived without financial worries and never trained for a specific profession. There is evidence that he would have liked to be a painter but lacked the "gift of creation." He could have chosen the life of an eccentric like Lord Byron but has a distaste for public display and makes efforts to remain within the confines of convention. He is, however, by no means a conformist. In his work as well as in his life, he is fiercely independent, and it is his independence in judgment that earns for him a place in the history of art criticism. It is also this radical independence, together with a coolness of composure, that leads to his undramatic suicide. Beyond this seemingly cool and detached attitude, however, is an unplumbed depth of feeling, conviction, and passion. His suicide, which he views as the only logical solution to "a future full of necessary repetition," demonstrates the radical determination of which he is capable. This determination is juxtaposed to his incestuous relationship with his mother. He manages to sever the relationship after several years, has two brief love affairs, and lives with Anna Maria Baiardi, but he is never able to forget; his lifelong occupation with art has to be understood as a sublimation of his forbidden drives. This Oedipal relationship, together with a natural insight into people, enables Marbot to analyze paintings from a psychological viewpoint anticipating twentieth century aesthetics.

The narrator-biographer, an unnamed art historian and dedicated scholar devoted to securing a place for Marbot in the history of art criticism. The fact that the novel is presented as a real biography attributes a special importance to the narrator-biographer. Because academic convention requires that all available sources, documents, and dates speak for themselves, the biographer remains anonymous. Because the biographer is at the same time the creator of the fictitious biography, however, he might be construed as the main character. He has invented the main character as well as his life story and has selected the sources. In addition, he analyzes, translates, and sets the tone. He is a knowledgeable, sympathetic, open-minded, devoted, and partial interpreter of his main character.

Lady Catherine, Marbot's mother. She was born in 1781 as the only child of Lord and Lady Claverton and married Sir Francis Marbot in 1799. She had three children and lost her husband after twenty-one years of marriage as a result of a hunting accident. She is a deeply religious person who suffered extremely in her incestuous relationship with her oldest son. After her separation from Andrew, she confesses her sin to Father van Rossum and dies of a broken heart in 1832, two years after the death of her son.

Father Gerard van Rossum, a Dutch Jesuit and Marbot's tutor. He was born in 1766 and served first the Clavertons and then the Marbots as family chaplain and tutor. He is an enlightened and tolerant educator to Andrew and an understanding and compassionate spiritual guide to Lady Catherine. Despite his knowledge of the incestuous relationship, he continues the correspondence with his former pupil. After Andrew's death, he collects, edits, and publishes his notes and letters and by doing so preserves Marbot's work for future generations.

— *Jochen Richter*

MARCHING ON

Author: James Boyd (1888-1944)
First published: 1927
Genre: Novel

Locale: North Carolina
Time: The Civil War period
Plot: Historical

James Fraser, a North Carolina farm boy, awkward, uncouth, sensitive, and proud. He is ambitious to rise in life. His experience as a railroad worker in Wilmington and his Civil War service, including a long internment as a prisoner of war, mature him. His dedication to his beliefs and his determination to endure life's hardships enable him to regard himself as humanly equal to those whom he had once looked upon as his superiors. James may be thought of as an illustration of what Thomas Jefferson in a letter to John Adams called a "true aristocrat," the grounds of whose aristocracy are "virtue and talents."

Stewart Prevost, a rich planter's daughter loved by James. Appreciative of his desire to better himself, she offers him money to help him do so. Less conscious than James of the difference in social and financial status between them, she loves him and is willing to marry him.

Colonel Prevost, her father. Although he is courteous and friendly to the Fraser family, he gives the impression that he considers them beneath himself and his daughter, and he at first opposes a continuation of the relationship between Stewart and James. Later, convinced of James's true worth, he is happy to have Stewart marry a Fraser.

Charles Prevost, Stewart's brother, a Confederate captain under whom James serves. After Charles is killed, James shoots the killers.

MARDI, AND A VOYAGE THITHER

Author: Herman Melville (1819-1891)
First published: 1849
Genre: Novel

Locale: Islands of the Western Pacific
Time: Mid-nineteenth century
Plot: Allegory

The narrator, a young American sailor in the South Seas who, with a companion, jumps ship and leaves in a small boat for hospitable islands. At sea, he meets a blonde native girl named Yillah. The party is welcomed to an island by a group of natives who call the narrator "Taji," thinking he is that god reincarnated. The narrator falls in love with Yillah. When she mysteriously disappears, he wanders the seas, visiting many islands, looking for her. His quest is to no avail.

Yillah, the narrator's sweetheart, the symbol of good in the novel.

Hautia, a dark native queen who is Yillah's rival for the narrator's love. Though the narrator finds her attractive, he refuses the favors she offers him.

Jarl, a sailor aboard the *Arcturion* who, with the narrator, leaves the whaling vessel and travels among the islands of the South Seas.

Samoa, a native whom Jarl and the narrator find hiding in a derelict ship. The sailors befriend him, and he accompanies them on their travels.

Media, a native king who mistakes the narrator for the god Taji and offers him the hospitality of the island.

Babbalanja, a wise man in Media's court who tells the narrator that having lost Yillah, he will never again find her.

King Donjalolo, monarch of the island of Juam, who moves from place to place on his island home in order to escape reality.

Yoomy, the minstrel-poet of King Media's court.

MARIA CHAPDELAINE: A Romance of French Canada

Author: Louis Hémon (1880-1913)
First published: 1916
Genre: Novel

Locale: Northern Quebec
Time: Early twentieth century
Plot: Regional

Maria Chapdelaine (mahr-YAH shahp-deh-LEHN), a French-Canadian farm girl. After the death of the man she loves, Maria looks upon the northland as a hostile country and almost accepts Lorenzo Surprenant as a husband, knowing he will take her to an easier life in a city in the United States. She finally decides, however, that she can, like her mother, be a good pioneer wife. She then accepts Eutrope Gagnon, a farmer like her father, as her husband.

Samuel Chapdelaine, Maria's father. He moves his family many times, for he wants always to be away from neighbors and civilization. He is a hardworking man.

Mrs. Chapdelaine, Maria's mother. Her death, which she faces as steadfastly as she does life, convinces Maria to remain in the north and marry a farmer.

François Paradis (frah[n]-SWAH pah-rah-DEE), a young fur trader who falls in love with Maria. He dies of exposure while traveling on foot across the wastes of northern Quebec to visit Maria at Christmastime.

Eutrope Gagnon (yew-TROHP gahn-YOHN), a pioneering farmer and suitor for Maria's hand. He is an honest, hardworking young man. He can say little for himself, but his earnestness wins Maria.

Lorenzo Surprenant (loh-rehn-ZOH sewr-preh-NA[N]), a suitor for Maria's hand. He works in factories in the United States and tries to convince Maria that life as his wife will be easier for her than life as a farmer's wife in Quebec.

MARIA MAGDALENA

Author: Friedrich Hebbel (1813-1863)
First published: 1844
Genre: Drama

Locale: Germany
Time: The nineteenth century
Plot: Domestic realism

Clara, a young girl who, to prove her love, gives herself physically to the man she loves. She is crushed when he does not want to marry her and seizes as his excuse the fact that Clara's brother has been accused of theft. Feeling that her pregnancy and its disgrace may drive her father to suicide, Clara thinks of killing herself. The arrival of an old suitor who still wants to marry her only puts off the action for a time. Clara drowns herself in the household well.

Leonard, Clara's lover and fiancé. He is a selfish, calculating young man. As a means of getting a job, he courts the mayor's daughter. Finding that the girl loves him, he throws over Clara, despite her pregnancy, and marries his new love. Leonard is killed in a duel by the secretary, a suitor who loves Clara.

The secretary, a childhood sweetheart of Clara. He wants to marry her, though she is pregnant by Leonard. He vows to fight a duel with Leonard, does so, and is fatally wounded.

Karl, Clara's brother. Because of his unsavory reputation, he is accused of theft and thus gives Leonard an excuse to break off with Clara. Later, Karl is cleared of any guilt.

Anthony, Clara's father. He is a simpleminded cabinetmaker who does not understand what happens to his family. The secretary, dying, accuses Anthony of Clara's death because of his pride and weakness. Anthony, unable to comprehend the mysteries of life, fails to see how he can be at all responsible for his daughter's suicide.

Anthony's wife, Clara's mother. She is a respectable, Godfearing woman who wishes only the best for her family. The accusations leveled against her son are enough of a shock to kill her.

MARIUS THE EPICUREAN: His Sensations and Ideas

Author: Walter Pater (1839-1894)
First published: 1885
Genre: Novel

Locale: The Roman Empire
Time: The second century
Plot: Philosophical

Marius, a young Roman of intellectual power living in the reign of Marcus Aurelius. As a young man, influenced by life on a country estate, he becomes an idealist of strong convictions, but his mother's death turns him into a skeptic. From skepticism he later turns to Oriental mysticism and the early Greek philosophers. After reading the writings of Aristippus of Cyrene, he becomes an epicurean, seeking sensory experiences that will lead him to wisdom and an appreciation of the universe. He is finally converted to Christianity before his death.

Flavian, Marius' schoolmate and friend. He influences Marius to read literature and philosophy. He also encourages Marius to become a poet. His death from the plague is a great shock to Marius.

Marcus Aurelius, the Roman emperor, a patron of art and learning. He appoints Marius to be his secretary and editor.

Cornelius, an officer in the famous Twelfth Legion. He becomes Marius' friend and acquaints Marius with the people of Rome and the city itself. Because he is a Christian and a happy man, he becomes an influence on Marius' life and thinking. Under Cornelius' and Cecelia's influence, Marius turns to Christianity.

Cecilia, a calm, happy Christian woman. She is a friend of Cornelius and becomes Marius' friend too, helping him to discover the beauty of Christian religion and thought.

Galen, the famous Roman physician under whose influence Marius comes for a time as a young man.

MARKED BY FIRE

Author: Joyce Carol Thomas (1938-   )
First published: 1982
Genre: Novel

Locale: Ponca City, Oklahoma
Time: 1951-1971
Plot: Bildungsroman

Abyssinia (Abby) Jackson, a girl believed to hold special gifts because she was born in a cotton field during a tornado, in the midst of fire and water. Abby grows up as a favored child, surrounded by love, in Ponca City's black community. Adults watch her small adventures with pride, even as they feel free to rebuke her for daydreaming or her raids on vegetable gardens. Abby reads the newspaper to elderly neighbors and sings at important church events. Her early childhood is almost idyllic, but in 1961 multiple tragedies shake her world and jeopardize her health. Her father leaves town in despair when a tornado destroys his barber shop. Abby aids Trembling Sally, a woman caught up in the same tornado; the woman blames Abby for her troubles and swears to make her suffer. Abby also is raped and beaten by Brother Jacobs, a dairyman. Bedfast and speechless for many months after the rape, she recovers her voice only when attacked by a swarm of wasps. Her beautiful singing voice does not return until she is an adult, although she always hears songs in her head. Abby graduates from high school with honors. She abandons plans to attend medical school when she agrees to become Ponca City's new herb doctor and healer of troubled people.

Mother Barker, Abby's godmother, a folk-medicine healer who was the midwife at Abby's birth. She takes a special interest in the young woman. She gives Abby her secret recipe for pound cake, hovers with medicines and benevolent rituals during her long convalescence, and finally picks Abby as her successor in the healing arts. Mother Barker is a practical woman whose remedies are an important resource for her clients, but she also serves as an opinion maker and shows a touch of mysticism in her symbolic warnings about future events.

Strong Jackson, Abby's father, owner of the Better Way Barbershop, which functions as a meeting place for Ponca City's black males. A lively, balding man known for his jokes, Strong has a prickly pride that is damaged when the tornado levels his shop. Stunned, he leaves town on a bus the same evening, but he never forgets Abby or his wife, Patience, and he comes back to them four years later. By chance or divine providence, he gets off the train and walks past the river just as the crazed Trembling Sally is holding Abby under its waters. He rescues his daughter and returns home with her. From that time on, his hard work, steady presence, and determination to rebuild his barbershop help heal Abby's psychic wounds.

Patience Jackson, Abby's hardworking mother. Patience has no particular skills except domestic ones, and she has to earn a living in the cotton fields, but her gentle nature hides a fierce protectiveness. When Brother Jackson, who raped Abby, is set to be released from the penitentiary, she makes sure the townsfolk know she is sitting guard by her front window with a shotgun.

Trembling Sally, a woman who get the shakes and then loses her senses when she is caught up in a tornado. She harasses and frightens all the neighborhood children but nurses a special enmity toward Abby. Sally probably put the wasp's nest in Abby's bedroom; she tries to drown her and eventually dies by fire when she sets ablaze the house where Abby is staying with Lily Norene's orphaned children.

Lily Norene, a perky girl with a "high yellow" complexion and a good but unspectacular school record. She is Abby's best friend. After high school, Lily Norene marries, quickly has five children, and becomes the victim of vicious beatings by her husband. Ignoring Abby's advice to leave him, she stays. She dies of a stroke caused by too many blows to her head.

— Emily Alward

MARKET HARBOROUGH: Or, How Mr. Sawyer Went to the Shires

Author: George J. Whyte-Melville (1821-1878)
First published: 1861
Genre: Novel

Locale: England
Time: The nineteenth century
Plot: Sport

John Standish Sawyer, a country gentleman who, deciding that fox hunting is poor in his own country, goes to Market Harborough. There he meets other ardent fox hunters and falls in love with the parson's daughter, who is also devoted to fox hunting. A steeplechase is held, and though Sawyer rides a fine race, he takes a fall near the end of the course and breaks his collarbone. The parson's daughter decides then to marry him. After the marriage, she makes him give up hunting. He is soon observed reading a book about hunting; he will be back with the hounds before long.

The Honorable Crasher, Sawyer's friend and hunting companion at Market Harborough.

Isaac, Sawyer's groom and horse handler. He tricks the Honorable Crasher into buying, for a large sum, a handsome but worthless horse belonging to Sawyer. With the money from the sale, Sawyer buys a horse good enough to enable him to make a fine showing in the steeplechase.

Tiptop, the Honorable Crasher's groom. He is tricked by Isaac's substitution of horses in a test run into giving his master a glowing report of Sawyer's worthless horse.

Cecilia Dove, the pretty and coquettish daughter of the parson. She marries Sawyer.

Mr. Dove, the parson, an ardent fox hunter.

MARMION: A Tale of Flodden Field

Author: Sir Walter Scott (1771-1832)
First published: 1808
Genre: Poetry

Locale: The Scottish border
Time: Early sixteenth century
Plot: Historical

Lord Marmion, an English nobleman whose reputation as a fine, brave knight is spotless. He is sent by the English king to try to persuade the Scots to stop raiding the border. Actually, he had declared his love for a young nun, Constance de Beverley, who renounced her vows, left the convent, and followed him. He then met a young heiress and abandoned Constance. He has fought a duel with the knight who loves the heiress, Clare, and left his adversary for dead. He is mortally wounded in battle and on his deathbed repents all of his sins.

Ralph de Wilton, Marmion's foe in the duel, who is now disguised as a palmer. He loved Clare but was betrayed by Marmion with some forged papers attesting to the fact that de Wilton was not true to the king. He is finally restored to his title and lands and wins the hand of Clare.

Clare Fitz-Clare, a young novice nun who has joined the convent rather than marry Marmion after the man she really loves, de Wilton, is believed to be fatally wounded. She is finally able to marry de Wilton with the king's blessing.

Constance de Beverley, a nun who broke her vows, fled the convent, and followed Marmion for three years as a page boy. She has the papers forged by Marmion to discredit de Wilton, and she begs the abbess to get them to the king so that Clare will not be forced to marry Marmion. The ecclesiastical court puts her to death.

Archibald Douglas, a Scottish nobleman who is charged with Marmion's safe conduct while he is in Scotland, and with the safekeeping of the nuns.

THE MARQUISE OF O———
(Die Marquise von O———)

Author: Heinrich von Kleist (1777-1811)
First published: 1808
Genre: Novella

Locale: The northern Italian town of M———
Time: Early nineteenth century
Plot: Psychological

Giulietta (jee-ew-LEE-eht-tah), the Marquise of O———, a widow from a distinguished family and the mother of two children. A woman of unblemished reputation, Giulietta has lived with her parents since the death of her husband three years earlier, caring for them and rearing her children. She loved her husband very much and, although still young, has decided not to remarry. She enjoys a quiet life devoted to art, reading, and her domestic duties. Her world suddenly becomes incomprehensible to her as she begins to suffer the physical changes associated with pregnancy. Knowing that she has not had relations with a man since her husband died, she is devastated when both a doctor and a midwife diagnose her pregnancy. Cast out by her family, she finds an inner strength to gather her children and go to her own estate to rear them alone. Realizing that it would be impossible to convince anyone of her innocence, she heroically submits to this inexplicable turn of events. An announcement in the newspapers declares that she will marry the father if he will identify himself. After an initial shock of horror and rejection, she consents to a marriage and is eventually reconciled to her new husband.

Count F———, a Russian officer, a lieutenant colonel in the Rifle Corps in the Russian forces. He is a man of excellent family and character who prevents a group of soldiers from assaulting Giulietta during the Russian attack on the citadel at M———. After she falls unconscious, however, he assaults her himself, with the result that she becomes pregnant. He suffers greatly from guilt and tries to make amends by marrying her before her condition becomes evident. His haste surprises the family and Giulietta, who have no idea what has taken place and therefore put him off. Sent away on orders, he returns to discover Giulietta's situation and persists in trying to right the wrong he has done. Responding to her advertisement for the father of her child, he endures humiliation before her parents and agrees to a marriage in name only. Through his generosity, exemplary conduct, and love, he eventually wins Giulietta's consent to a real marriage.

Colonel Lorenzo G———, the commandant of the citadel at M——— and the father of Giulietta. Colonel G——— is a loving father to Giulietta, but he reacts with great severity to her apparent transgression, refusing to listen to her protestations of innocence and throwing her out of the house. His violent temper and stubbornness seem to stand in the way of resolving the situation. An extremely tearful and emotional reconciliation scene eventually does take place, however, and he stands with Giulietta to face the man who responds to her advertisement. He arranges the resulting wedding.

Colonel G———'s wife, Giulietta's mother. Although she loves her daughter very much, she cannot accept Giulietta's innocence at first because the whole situation seems impossible. Her strength of character and love are revealed when she defies her husband's will and goes to Giulietta. By resorting to a deception, she becomes convinced of her daughter's innocence and begs her forgiveness. Bringing Giulietta back to the family home, she brings about a reconciliation with the colonel as well.

Giulietta's brother, whose role is to carry out the commandant's orders without question. Believing his sister guilty, he is the one who angrily informs her that she must leave her children behind and get out of their parents' house immediately. When she defies him, taking her children with her, he does not have the strength of conviction to stop her.

The doctor and

The midwife, whose function is to confirm the reality of Giulietta's pregnancy.

General K———, the count's uncle, who verifies the count's family background. He represents part of the objective evidence of the count's good character and appropriate social standing.

— *Susan L. Piepke*

THE MARRIAGE
(El casamiento)

Author: Witold Gombrowicz (1904-1969)
First published: 1948
Genre: Drama

Locale: France and Poland
Time: The interwar period and during World War II
Plot: Absurdist

Henry, a son and a prince. As a Polish soldier in World War II fighting in France, Henry dreams of his lost family and family estate in Poland. Despite his resistance, Henry is swept away to the dream constructed in interwar Poland. In his dream, he finds that each of his acts and gestures results in an action that is irrevocable. Thus, when he kneels in front of his father to honor him, this act designates his father as king and Henry as prince. As prince, Henry is propelled to participate in an honorable marriage to his former betrothed, Molly, now a prostitute. He wavers in indecision. Through an equally insignificant gesture, he finds that he has dethroned his father and becomes a dictator king demanding that everyone honor his bride-to-be, Molly. Despite these despotic acts, he is never convinced of the truth of his assertions and demands evidence by way of the suicide of his friend Johnny as an act of submission to Henry's will. He finds himself still imprisoned by doubts because of the double bind in the existential quandary of being both the subject and object of social form. Ultimately, the inability to become the real self emerges as the real tragedy of Henry's submission to social forms and judgments.

Johnny, Henry's friend and a courtier. Johnny is both Henry's companion in France and guide to Henry's dream-constructed reality. In the course of Henry's projection into the inner dream of the king's court, Johnny fades from his role as friend and becomes a courtier. When Henry demands that Johnny kill himself in response to his demand for an act that will prove the strength of his will over others, Johnny's death brings about the collision of the reality of their friendship and his simultaneous desire to deform Johnny as subject to his will. As a character, Johnny is not individualized but merely projects those qualities ascribed to him by Henry's dream.

Frank, Henry's father, an innkeeper and king. In the first stages of Henry's dream, Frank appears as the slovenly innkeeper of a cheap roadside inn in whom Henry ultimately recognizes his father. After Henry makes this recognition, Frank demands absolute obedience; when his authority is threatened by the jeering Drunkard, he is suddenly projected to his role as king because of Henry's act of tribute. As king,

Frank is vacillating and terror-stricken lest someone dethrone him. When Henry, in his attempts to calm Frank, dethrones him by touching him, Frank is reduced to the role of a deposed king and prisoner. Like Johnny, Frank is the projection of Henry's dream, and consequently his actions emerge out of Henry's dream-state.

Katherine, Henry's mother, Frank's wife, and queen. In her role as innkeeper's wife, Katherine is apologetic. As Henry's mother, she reinforces the father's demands for total obedience. Her role in the play is much like her husband's, to show the consequences of Henry's thoughts and gestures as he attempts to create a reality entirely subject to his will.

Molly, a servant and Henry's betrothed. Henry recognizes Molly, his former betrothed, in the slovenly scullery maid at the inn. Suspicions are raised about her virtue, and Henry, to prove the validity of his desires, demands that a wedding take place so that he can alter reality to serve his will and thereby prove that Molly is pure and virtuous. She too is a projection of Henry's dream and subject to Henry's thinking of her as his pure betrothed and simultaneously a deceiving slut who is capable of betraying him with his best friend, Johnny. Consequently, she projects these double qualities as a character and does not exist in her own right.

The Drunkard, a grotesque, foulmouthed figure. The Drunkard's pointing finger serves to undermine the construction of Henry's reality. His function in the play is to show the impossibility of creating a reality entirely subject to one's will; his pointing finger has the capacity to create doubts, to undermine, and ultimately to destroy Henry's creation of a kingdom and marriage entirely subject to his will.

Drunkards, followers of the Drunkard who, with their presence, reinforce the Drunkard's pointed finger.

Court dignitaries, creations of Henry's dream-constructed kingdom. As characters, their actions shift in response to Henry's doubts; thus, at times they fully support Henry's belief in the purity of Molly, and at other times they whisper and spread rumors about the farce of Henry's imminent marriage.

— *Christine Kiebuzinska*

MARRIAGE À LA MODE

Author: John Dryden (1631-1700)
First published: 1673
Genre: Drama

Locale: Sicily
Time: The seventeenth century
Plot: Comedy of manners

Palamede (pah-lah-MEH-dee), a courtier. Ordered by his father to marry Melantha, he becomes attracted to and declares his love for Rhodophil's wife, Doralice. Later, when Doralice becomes reconciled with her husband, Palamede woos Melantha, and they agree to marry.

Rhodophil (ROH-doh-fihl), the captain of the King's Guard. Married to Doralice, he desires Melantha. When Palamede's father insists that his son marry Melantha at once, Rhodophil and Doralice are reconciled, and each man pledges to respect the other's wife.

Doralice (doh-rah-lees), Rhodophil's wife, desired by Palamede.

Melantha (meh-LAN-thuh), Palamede's intended, desired by Rhodophil.

Polydamus (po-lee-DAM-uhs), the usurper of the throne of Sicily. In search of his long-lost son, he is convinced by Hermogenes that Leonidas is, indeed, his heir, and he accepts the youth as his own along with Palmyra, the boy's foster sister. Later, it is revealed that Leonidas is, in reality, the heir

of the rightful king, and Polydamus is forced to give up the throne to him. The usurper is then forgiven by the new king, to whom he gives Palmyra, now revealed as his own daughter, in marriage.

Hermogenes (hurm-AH-jeh-neez), a fisherman who raises Leonidas and Palmyra as his own.

Leonidas (lee-o-NIH-duhs), the son of the rightful king of Sicily, who is brought up as Hermogenes' child. His identity is finally revealed, and he wins back the throne from Polydamus.

Palmyra (pahl-MIHR-ah), Polydamus' daughter, who is brought up as Hermogenes' child. After her identity is made known, she marries the now rightful king, Leonidas.

Argaleon (AHR-gah-LEE-ohn), Polydamus' favorite, who attempts to marry Palmyra and have Leonidas banished.

Amalthea (am-al-THEE-ah), Argaleon's sister, who is in love with Leonidas.

Philotis (fihl-OH-tihs), Melantha's maid.

Eubulus (EE-ew-bew-luhs), a former governor who reveals to Palmyra that Leonidas is the son of the rightful king.

THE MARRIAGE OF FIGARO
(La Folle Journée: Ou, Le Mariage de Figaro)

Author: Pierre-Augustin Caron de Beaumarchais (1732-1799)
First published: 1784
Genre: Drama

Locale: Seville, Spain
Time: The 1780's
Plot: Comedy

Figaro (FEE-gah-roh), a valet to Count Almaviva. In Beaumarchais' earlier comedy *The Barber of Seville* (1775), Figaro had helped the young count to marry Rosine. With the passage of time, however, the count has begun to treat Figaro rather badly, and Figaro fears that the count may assert his nonexistent "lord's right" to sleep with Figaro's fiancée, Suzanne. Figaro is quite willing to assist the count in his amorous adventures with women other than the countess, but he draws a line when it concerns Suzanne. Although he loves Suzanne, Figaro is tormented by jealousy. In his famous monologue in act V, Figaro laments both the allegation of Suzanne's infidelity, which is based on misinformation, and the corruptive power of the nobility. Throughout this comedy, Figaro expresses both subservience to his master and a desire to free himself from the count's oppressive power over his life. Fortuitous events prevent unsympathetic characters from achieving their evil designs, and Figaro and Suzanne are married at the end of act V.

Suzanne, a maid to Countess Almaviva and the fiancée of Figaro. She truly loves Figaro but regrets that Figaro and the count tend to take women for granted. She and the countess decide to teach Figaro and the count a lesson. Suzanne and the countess trade places and clothing. When the count is with the woman he believes to be Suzanne, he actually is with his wife. By switching roles and deceiving both Figaro and the count, the women achieve their goal of teaching their men to pay more respect to them.

Count Almaviva (ahl-mah-VEE-vah), an Andalusian nobleman who had married Rosine in act V of *The Barber of Seville*. In the earlier play, the count was a sympathetic and considerate suitor, but here he is insensitive and exploitative. He does not hide his interest in other women from his wife and thus humiliates her in front of others. The count does his best to prevent Suzanne from marrying Figaro, but his attempts to separate them fail when his wife disguises herself as Suzanne and allows her husband to court her. She plays her role so well that both the count and the jealous Figaro believe her to be Suzanne. Once his error is made public, the humiliated count has no choice but to permit Suzanne's marriage to Figaro and to reaffirm his love for the countess.

Countess Almaviva, the wife of Count Almaviva. She is portrayed as a very lonely but dignified woman. She resents her husband's rakish behavior, but she does not want other women to learn that the count is now more attracted to younger women. With the assistance of her maid Suzanne and the count's young page Chérubin, she tricks her husband into realizing that her mature love for him is more meaningful than his lust for more physically attractive women. She is a psychologically profound character who seeks to reconcile her search for happiness through married love with her desire to maintain her high social standing.

Chérubin (SHAY-rew-ban), the count's male page. The role of Chérubin traditionally is played by a young actress. Having a woman play the role of Chérubin makes it more believable when the countess has Chérubin dress as a woman in order to attract the attention of the lascivious count.

Bridoison, a judge with a noticeable speech defect whose main role is to come on stage for the planned marriage of Figaro and Suzanne. His final comments end the play and underline the central role of chance in the count's failure to frustrate the search for happiness by Suzanne, Figaro, and the countess.

Dr. Bártholo (BAHR-toh-loh), the former guardian of the countess. He seeks revenge on the count and on Figaro.

Marceline (mahrs-eh-LAYN), the elderly housekeeper, a creditor of Figaro. She demands repayment or marriage. She eventually discovers that he is her son, by Dr. Bártholo.

— *Edmund J. Campion*

MARSE CHAN

Author: Thomas Nelson Page (1853-1922)
First published: 1884
Genre: Short fiction

Locale: Virginia
Time: The Civil War period
Plot: Regional

Marse Chan, a young Virginia gentleman, loyal to his family and to his state in the Civil War, during which he becomes a captain. His love for Anne never ceases, even though she rejects him following the duel with her father. He is killed leading a regimental charge. When he dies, he has next to his heart the letter of penitence and love that Anne wrote after her father agreed not to stand any longer between the lovers.

Anne Chamberlin, his pretty sweetheart, sorrel-haired and dark-eyed. Proud and unforgiving after her father's duel, she rejects Marse Chan's attempt at reconciliation before he leaves for the war. Her heart and thoughts remain with him, and when she dies not long before the fall of Richmond, she is buried next to Marse Chan.

Sam, Marse Chan's servant, a slave given to Mr. Channing's baby son to be his lifetime body servant. He is Marse Chan's boyhood playmate, his idolizing servant at college and during the war, and the driver who takes his body home for burial. Sam is the prototype of the loyal slave in romantic Southern fiction who regards his relationship to his master not as bondage but as loving service to a kindly and wholly admirable superior.

Mr. Channing, Marse Chan's father, a plantation owner and, like his son, a model Southern gentleman.

Colonel Chamberlin, Anne's father, the owner of a neighboring plantation. A Democrat, he is angered at being defeated in a Congressional election won by Mr. Channing, a Whig. The colonel's hurt pride causes the feud that separates the two families.

Maria, a slave sold by Colonel Chamberlin and bought by Mr. Channing. The purchase of Maria and several other slaves leads to two lawsuits by the colonel, who loses both of them. Humiliated in a duel with Marse Chan over his insulting remarks about Mr. Channing, he holds a grudge until he hears of Marse Chan's defense of the Chamberlin name in a fight with Ronny.

Mrs. Channing, Mr. Channing's wife.

Mr. Ronny, a lieutenant under Marse Chan, who knocks him down for making improper remarks about Anne and her father.

Ham Fisher, a black carriage driver rescued from a burning barn by Mr. Channing, who is permanently blinded as a result.

Miss Lucy Chamberlin, Colonel Chamberlin's sister and housekeeper.

Mr. Hall, a schoolmaster.

THE MARTIAN CHRONICLES

Author: Ray Bradbury (1920-   )
First published: 1950
Genre: Novel

Locale: Mars and the United States
Time: 1999-2026
Plot: Science fiction

John Spender, an astronaut, a member of the fourth expedition to Mars. In "June 2001: And the Moon Be Still as Bright," he is overwhelmed by the deaths of the Martians, accidentally caused when the third expedition infected them with chicken pox. He realizes that Earth people will exploit and destroy Mars, making it into another intolerable Earth. He tries to prevent colonization by stopping his own crewmates and kills several of them in the process. He explains his thoughts to Captain Wilder, but then rather than running away, he allows himself to be found and killed because he realizes that his cause is doomed. The crew buries him as they think a Martian would be buried.

Captain Wilder, an astronaut, the leader of the fourth expedition to Mars. He and his crew find the Martians dead of

chicken pox and the planet little more than a museum. He understands that Spender is trying to save Mars from the destruction that humans will bring, and he knows that instead of creating a new life on Mars, the people of Earth will only bring with them the evil that they are trying to escape. Not satisfied with staying on the new planet and watching what will happen, he leaves to take command of a ship going to the outer planets. In "April 2026: The Long Years," he stops at Mars on his return to Earth many years after war has destroyed most life on Earth and finds Hathaway living alone with a family he has created. Hathaway, now an old man, dies during the reunion, and the captain and his crew leave Mars to go back to Earth to see if any life remains.

Sam Parkhill, an astronaut, a member of the fourth expedition. He sees Mars as a planet ripe for the picking, and he takes considerable joy in destroying Martian monuments. When Spender starts killing crew members, he is the first to want to hunt Spender down, and he is determined to shoot him in the head. Captain Wilder prevents this killing and eventually knocks Sam's teeth out after Spender's death when Sam uses the crystal towers of the deserted city for target practice. In "November 2005: The Off Season," Sam brings his wife to Mars and sets up a hot dog stand on one of the highways, hoping to cash in on the boom of business he thinks will come when the fleet of colonization rockets arrives. The last of the Martians, knowing telepathically what is happening on Earth, arrive to give him the deed to the planet, but he kills many of them and flees in panic. Finally, they convince him that their intentions are peaceful, and they give him the deed. He thinks that he will at last be a rich man, but on that night war breaks out on Earth, and he and his wife see it catch fire in the night sky.

Hathaway, an astronaut, a member of the fourth expedition. He brings his family to Mars and settles there. In "April 2026: The Long Years," when war breaks out on Earth and everyone is recalled from Mars, he and his family are up in the hills and are left behind, becoming the last humans on Mars of which he is aware. When his family dies, he creates machines in their images and eventually forgets that they are machines. He creates a lighted city around them and becomes content in the illusion that he is not alone. He dies shortly after Captain Wilder returns and is buried on Mars near the graves of his human family. The androids he creates remain behind to live on the Mars he has created for them.

— *C. D. Akerley*

MARTIN CHUZZLEWIT

Author: Charles Dickens (1812-1870)
First published: 1844; serial form, 1843-1844
Genre: Novel

Locale: England and America
Time: Early nineteenth century
Plot: Social realism

Martin Chuzzlewit (Senior), a rich, eccentric old man descended from a long family line noted for selfishness. He dislikes his fawning relatives and suspects that everyone about him is after his fortune. After quarreling with and disinheriting his grandson and namesake, whom he had intended to make his heir, he goes to live with Seth Pecksniff in order to test the motives of that self-styled architect and arch-hypocrite. Having tested young Martin Chuzzlewit by turning him loose to fend for himself in the world and having witnessed many proofs of Pecksniff's duplicity and hypocrisy, he rights the wrongs done to his grandson and abandons Pecksniff to his downward career of drunkenness and beggary.

Martin Chuzzlewit, the title character, a rather wayward and selfish young man brought up in expectation of becoming his grandfather's heir. The two quarrel when Martin falls in love with Mary Graham, his grandfather's companion and ward, and the old man turns his grandson out of the house. Hoping to become an architect, young Martin studies for a time with Seth Pecksniff, a relative, but after a few hints dropped by old Martin, the young man is rebuffed by Pecksniff. With Mark Tapley, a young hostler, he goes to America. Martin's reactions during this journey show Dickens' singular bias against the "uncivilized" areas, customs, and citizens of the United States. After his return to England, Martin seeks an interview with his grandfather, but Pecksniff, with whom the old man is living, turns the humbled young man from his door. Comforted only by the love of Mary Graham, he returns to London. Old Martin Chuzzlewit, no longer the senile man he had seemed to be while residing with Pecksniff, appears in London soon afterward, is reunited with his grandson, and gives his blessing to the marriage of young Martin and Mary Graham.

Anthony Chuzzlewit, old Martin Chuzzlewit's brother, a miserly man of cunning and suspicious nature.

Jonas Chuzzlewit, Anthony Chuzzlewit's son. Eager to inherit his father's wealth, he attempts to poison the old man, but his scheme is discovered beforehand by his father and Chuffey, a faithful clerk. Because old Anthony dies of a broken heart a short time later, Jonas believes himself a murderer. He marries Mercy Pecksniff and treats her brutally. Later, he becomes convinced that Montague Tigg, a flashy speculator, has learned his secret. Desperate because Tigg demands hush money, Jonas murders him. His guilt is revealed and he is arrested, but he poisons himself while waiting for a coach to take him off to prison.

George Chuzzlewit, a corpulent bachelor.

Mary Graham, old Martin Chuzzlewit's ward, a young woman of great integrity and sweetness. Although his great hope is that she and young Martin Chuzzlewit will fall in love and marry, he tests the young people by telling Mary that she will receive nothing after he is dead and by disinheriting his grandson. Mary remains faithful in her devotion to young Martin through all his hardships and tribulations. They are finally reunited with old Martin's blessing.

Seth Pecksniff, old Martin Chuzzlewit's cousin, an architect and land surveyor who has never built anything, though he receives large premiums from those who study under him. Young Martin Chuzzlewit becomes one of his apprentices, but Pecksniff turns him away to please the young man's grandfather and to ensure his own advancement. In all of his dealings, he is completely self-seeking; he performs no generous act, shows no generous motives. Servile, false, conniving, he is a complete hypocrite and a monster of selfishness. He becomes a drunkard and a writer of begging letters to his prosperous relatives.

Charity Pecksniff, called **Cherry**, his older daughter. Deserted by Augustus Moddle, her betrothed, she becomes her father's ill-tempered companion in his later years.

Mercy Pecksniff, called **Merry**, a vain, selfish woman who marries her cousin, Jonas Chuzzlewit, partly to spite her sister. The cruel treatment she receives at his hands transforms her into "a model of uncomplaining endurance and self-denying affection." Old Martin Chuzzlewit provides for her after her husband's death.

John Westlock, an apprentice to Seth Pecksniff, who sees through his master, quarrels with him, and leaves him. His departure leaves room for Martin Chuzzlewit in the Pecksniff household. Always a good friend of Tom Pinch, he falls in love with and marries Tom's sister Ruth. His suspicions of Jonas Chuzzlewit's behavior lead also to the discovery of Tigg's murder and the attempted murder of old Anthony Chuzzlewit.

Tom Pinch, Pecksniff's meek, overworked assistant. Left by his grandmother in Pecksniff's care, he is too trusting and too much burdened by a needless sense of obligation to see his master in his true light. Friendship with John Westlock and Martin Chuzzlewit teach him confidence, however, and when Pecksniff forces his attentions on Mary Graham, Tom sees Pecksniff for the hypocrite he is. When Pecksniff discharges him, he is hired by an unknown patron, old Martin Chuzzlewit, to catalog a library; with the money thus earned he is able to support his sister Ruth.

Ruth Pinch, a governess, Tom Pinch's loyal sister. She marries John Westlock.

Mark Tapley, the merry, self-reliant hostler at the Blue Dragon Inn in Wiltshire. Eager to see more of the world, he goes with Martin Chuzzlewit to America, where they are swindled by land speculators and disillusioned by all that they see and hear. After his return, he marries Mrs. Lupin, the landlady of the Blue Dragon, and renames the inn the Jolly Tapley, a name that he considers "wery new, conwivial, and expressive."

Mrs. Lupin, landlady of the Blue Dragon Inn, a buxom, beaming widow, later Mrs. Mark Tapley. When they meet after Mark's return to England, he kisses her often and heartily, but insists that he is really kissing his country after having lived "among the patriots."

Montague Tigg, also known as **Tigg Montague, Esq.**, director of the Anglo-Bengalee Disinterested Loan and Life Insurance Company and a swindler. Having learned of Jonas Chuzzlewit's attempt to poison his father, he blackmails Jonas into buying his worthless stock and persuading Pecksniff to invest his funds as well. Jonas kills him. When news of his death reaches London, another partner, David Crimple, makes off with all the funds.

David Crimple, a former pawnbroker and tapster and secretary of the Anglo-Bengalee Disinterested Loan and Life Insurance Company. His theft of the company funds ruins Pecksniff, who had invested in the enterprise on the advice of Jonas Chuzzlewit.

Dr. John Jobling, a physician employed by Montague Tigg as medical inspector for the insurance company.

Nadgett, Tom Pinch's landlord in London, employed by Montague Tigg as an investigator. He follows his employer and Jonas Chuzzlewit into the country and sees only Jonas returning. Acting on this knowledge, he unmasks Jonas as Tigg's murderer.

Chuffey, Anthony Chuzzlewit's devoted clerk. Old, deaf, and almost blind, he is also shrewd, and he helps to save his employer from Jonas Chuzzlewit's attempt to poison his father.

Sairey Gamp, a Cockney midwife and nurse who displays the same zest at a lying-in or a laying-out. She is fat, husky-voiced, moist-eyed, red-nosed, and over-fond of drink, so that she is always surrounded by the odor of spirits. Her fabrications she credits to her completely imaginary friend, Mrs. Harris. She is one of Dickens' great comic characters.

Chevy Slyme, a distant relative of old Martin Chuzzlewit, a dubious character who is "always waiting around the corner." He is a friend of Jonas Chuzzlewit and Montague Tigg.

Mr. Spottletoe, another relative of old Martin Chuzzlewit, also eager for a share of his relative's fortune.

Mrs. Spottletoe, his wife, a woman of a "poetical constitution."

Lewsome, a young surgeon. Under obligations to Jonas Chuzzlewit, he sells Jonas the drugs with which the son makes an attempt on his father's life. After Anthony Chuzzlewit's death, he confesses to John Westlock his part in the affair and thus helps bring Jonas to justice.

Paul Sweedlepipe, a hairdresser and bird fancier, Sairey Gamp's landlord.

Mrs. Betsey Prig, a Cockney day nurse and Sairey Gamp's bosom friend, with whom she often nurses "turn and turn about." They finally quarrel because Betsey dares to doubt the existence of Mrs. Harris.

Mrs. M. Todgers, landlady of the Commercial Boarding House, at which the Pecksniffs stay while in London.

Mr. Jinkins, the oldest resident at Mrs. Todgers' boarding-house. His recreation is identifying carriages driving in the parks on Sundays.

Augustus Moddle, a young gentleman living at Mrs. Todgers' boardinghouse. He is at first smitten by Mercy Pecksniff, but after her marriage to Jonas Chuzzlewit, he becomes, rather helplessly, engaged to her sister Charity. On the eve of the wedding, he runs away, leaving behind a letter in which he announces his departure for Van Dieman's Land and his determination never to be taken alive if Charity pursues him.

Bailey, the "boots" at Mrs. Todgers' boardinghouse. He eventually becomes Mr. Sweedlepipe's assistant.

Mr. Fips, the lawyer through whom old Martin Chuzzlewit engages Tom Pinch to catalog a library.

Mr. Mould, an undertaker whose countenance always seems caught between a look of melancholy and a satisfied smirk.

Mrs. Mould, his wife.

The Misses Mould, their daughters, two plump sisters with cheeks like ripe peaches.

Tacker, Mr. Mould's chief mourner.

Sophia, a girl taught by Ruth Pinch. Mrs. Todgers calls her "a syrup."

Wolf and
Pip, friends and confederates of Montague Tigg.

The Hon. Elijah Pogram, a bombastic congressman whom Martin Chuzzlewit meets in New York.

Zephaniah Scadder, a land speculator who, representing the Eden Land Corporation, sells Martin Chuzzlewit fifty acres of land in the backwoods community named Eden.

Major Pawkins, a New York politician who boasts that he is a man of the people.

Mrs. Pawkins, his wife and keeper of a boardinghouse.

Mr. Bevan, a kindhearted citizen of Massachusetts who lends Martin Chuzzlewit the money for his return passage to England.

General Fladdock, an American militia officer and a snob.

Lafayette Kettle, a loud-voiced American, secretary of the Watertoast Association of United Sympathizers.

General Cyrus Choke, an officer of the militia, a member of the Eden Land Corporation and the Watertoast Association of United Sympathizers.

Colonel Diver, editor of the New York *Rowdy Journal*.

Jefferson Brick, war correspondent of the *Rowdy Journal*.

Mrs. Brick, his wife, an American "matron."

Cicero, a New York truckman, formerly a slave.

Captain Kedgick, landlord of the National Hotel in New York, in whose hostelry Martin Chuzzlewit stays during his visit to the United States.

Professor Mullit, an American educator, the author of many pamphlets written under the name of Suturb.

Mr. Norris, a wealthy, sentimental abolitionist.

Mrs. Norris, his faded wife.

Miss Toppit, an American woman of literary pretensions.

Mrs. Hominy, another American literary light.

THE MARTYRED

Author: Richard E. Kim (1932-   )
First published: 1964
Genre: Novel

Locale: Korea
Time: 1950-1951
Plot: Existentialism

Captain Lee, a history instructor at a Seoul university who joins the Korean army after the Communist invasion of Seoul. When United Nations forces conquer the North Korean capital of Pyongyang, Lee is sent there with Army Political Intelligence to discover what really happened to fourteen Christian ministers arrested by the Communist secret police. A detached, intellectual observer, he interviews Mr. Shin, one of the two surviving clergymen, to determine the truth. Lee, whose parents were Christian, is an atheist who believes only in truth. Unlike his commander, Colonel Chang, he resists shaping the truth to serve a purpose. Gradually, he becomes Mr. Shin's ally and protector.

Mr. Shin, one of the fourteen Christian ministers imprisoned by the Communists a week before the Korean War began. Colonel Chang suspects Shin of betraying his fellow ministers in exchange for his life. Although Shin denies that he saw the twelve murdered ministers after their arrest, he was in fact present at their death. When the investigation uncovers conflicting evidence, Shin says that he is guarding truth that others may not want to hear. He lies about the details of the ministers' deaths and the fact that some weakened under torture and betrayed the others because he believes that the persecuted Christians of Pyongyang need to believe in this martyrdom. Like Lee, Shin can no longer believe in God, but he loves his people. Although he is innocent, he identifies himself as a traitor and praises the martyrs' courage. He bears his loss of faith silently. Shin sacrifices himself for those who need the hope he gives them. He ignores his own fragile health to help incoming refugees, refusing to flee the city when the United Nations troops withdraw. After he is presumed dead, strange stories are told of his appearance in many provinces of Korea.

Indoe Park, Lee's friend and fellow history instructor, now a Marine. Ten years ago, Park abandoned his boyhood Christianity; his father, the minister of Pyongyang's Central Presbyterian Church, disowned him. The father was one of the twelve executed ministers. Park has been sent to Pyongyang to represent the families of the victims at a memorial service, but he has really come to see Shin. In spite of his anger at his father's fanaticism, Park hopes to discover that his father weakened and had doubts, as he does. Shin tells him the truth, that at the end his father refused to pray to an unjust God. Shin also asks Park to pretend to believe for the sake of the suffering people. Park offers himself as the returning prodigal son that the church elders need. When he dies in battle, he is given a Christian burial.

Colonel Chang, the chief of Army Political Intelligence and Lee's commanding officer. A cynic, Chang wants to exploit the murdered churchmen for propaganda purposes. He argues that truth can be buried and still be the truth. Lee, Shin, Park, and Chaplain Koh resist him. Requesting another assignment, Chang goes underground to establish an intelligence network before the Chinese Communists can attack Pyongyang. He arranges for newspaper articles praising the martyrs, telling people what he thinks is necessary for them to know. There is kindness in his intentions, even though he does not seem to understand the notion of sacrifice for others. Chang dies heroically in a raid, leaving behind money to buy Bibles for the refugees.

Chaplain Koh, now a military man but previously a Pyongyang minister who disappeared abruptly. He is thought to be a Communist informer, but people do not see him clearly. He is no coward, having worked for Chang before he was kidnapped for his own safety. One of his parishioners was the informer, but Koh protects the informer's memory for the sake of the man's father. Koh is asked to return to his church and is forgiven. When he learns of the United Nations retreat, he refuses to go south to Seoul, choosing to resign from the Army rather than leave Pyongyang. He will not betray the faith of his parishioners, and he risks his life to help refugees. Eventually, his followers smuggle him out of the city. In the South, he leads a church in a crowded refugee camp.

Major Minn, a Korean army doctor who cannot bring himself to abandon his dying patients during the retreat from Pyongyang. He is not trying to be brave, he says, just decent. His fate is unknown.

Mr. Hann, the other surviving minister, a young friend of Mr. Shin. He is an innocent who goes mad after Shin confesses his own lack of belief in God.

— *Joanne McCarthy*

MARU

Author: Bessie Head (1937-1986)
First published: 1971
Genre: Novel

Locale: Botswana
Time: Mid-twentieth century
Plot: Social

Maru (MAH-rew), an African tribal leader soon to be installed as hereditary Paramount chief in the village of Dilepe, Botswana. Adhering to the gods within him rather than to any external source of personal feeling, he is prompted to marry a woman of Bushman origin, an "untouchable" in the eyes of his fellow tribespeople. To do so, however, he must renounce his chieftainship, even though he is more just and wise a ruler than the brother who will take his place. With three trusted companions and his bride, the younger Margaret Cadmore, he travels a thousand miles away to start a new life as a subsistence farmer.

Moleka (moh-LAY-kah), the second most powerful man in Dilepe. He and Maru are close friends but then become bitter enemies and rivals for the love of the younger Margaret Cadmore. With the help of his spies, Maru maneuvers Moleka into a marriage with Dikeledi, even though Moleka loves Margaret.

Margaret Cadmore (younger), an orphan and a light-skinned woman of the Masarwa tribe, reared by and named for a missionary. She becomes a schoolteacher in the village of Dilepe. When she first arrives in Dilepe, she is subjected to the same racial humiliation and ridicule as she was in her childhood. Treated as an outcast, she once again becomes a victim of racial oppression. Margaret is also an artist and chooses themes from ordinary events in the village. She initially falls in love with Moleka, but as a result of Maru's powers of persuasion, she marries Maru and begins to learn to love him.

Margaret Cadmore (older), a white missionary to Africa. She finds the dead body of a woman and a live baby girl on the side of the road. After giving orders to bury the mother, she takes in the baby, gives the girl her own name, and provides for her education. She is described as a woman who lived without love. Because she felt that she had missed something in life, she was often irritable and impatient. She also learned to draw on her own inner resources.

Dikeledi (dee-kay-LAY-dee), Maru's sister and a teacher at the school where the younger Margaret Cadmore teaches. Margaret's openness about her tribal heritage, despite the ridicule it engenders, wins the respect, admiration, and friendship of Dikeledi. When she learns that Margaret is a painter, Dikeledi brings Margaret a parcel full of artist's supplies and encourages her to experiment with all the materials. Dikeledi is involved in a painful love affair with the womanizer Moleka and becomes pregnant with his child. She marries him after Maru's forceful interventions.

— *Genevieve Slomski*

MARY
(Mashenka)

Author: Vladimir Nabokov (1899-1977)
First published: 1926
Genre: Novel

Locale: Berlin, Germany
Time: 1924
Plot: Ironic

Lev Glebovich Ganin (GLEH-boh-vihch GAH-nihn), the alias of a twenty-four-year-old Russian émigré who lives in a Berlin pension with several other émigrés. Bored with a dreary love affair with a woman named Lyudmila, Ganin discovers that a fellow boarder's wife, a woman named Mary who is due to arrive in Berlin from Russia in just a few days' time, is actually his own first love. Breaking off his current affair, he spends the next few days dreaming about the romance he shared with Mary as a youth and about the difficult conditions of their separation. Stimulated by these memories, he decides to intercept Mary at the station and to resume his romance with her. He succeeds in getting Mary's husband, Alfyorov, hopelessly drunk on the eve of Mary's arrival, but as he sets out to meet her train, he realizes that there is no need to renew their acquaintance, because the image of Mary that he had been reviving in his mind is the only Mary that truly matters. As the novel ends, he boards a train and leaves Berlin for the south.

Aleksey Ivanovich Alfyorov (ah-lehk-SAY ee-VAH-noh-vihch alf-YOH-rov), Ganin's garrulous neighbor in the pension. Smug and self-absorbed, Alfyorov waxes eloquently about his admiration for German efficiency and his love for his wife. His essential boorishness emerges when he becomes drunk on the eve of his wife's arrival. He is easily duped when Ganin resets his alarm clock so that he will sleep through Mary's arrival.

Anton Sergeevich Podtyagin (sehr-GEH-yeh-vihch pod-TYA-gihn), an elderly Russian poet who lives in the pension with Ganin. A sympathetic figure, Podtyagin wrote a poem that linked Ganin and Mary. He now seeks in desperation to leave Berlin for a new life in Paris, but after a series of mishaps prevents him from making his scheduled departure, he falls ill. At the end of the novel, it appears that he may die.

Klara, a twenty-six-year-old Russian woman who also lives in Ganin's pension. Troubled over the fact that she is getting older and has not found a romantic attachment in her life, she focuses her thoughts on the mysterious Ganin, but he does not let her become closely acquainted with his true nature and even allows her to suspect that he may be capable of thievery. His relationship with her friend Lyudmila is also an early source of discomfort for her. He remains an enigma to her until he leaves the pension at the end of the novel.

Lyudmila Rubanski (lyuhd-MIH-lah rew-BAHN-skee), Ganin's lover at the outset of the novel, a twenty-five-year-old woman who has become repugnant to him because of the thorough triteness of her opinions and the artificiality of her behavior with him.

Kolin (KOH-lihn) and

Gornotsvetov (gohr-noh-TSVEH-tov), two ballet dancers who live together in a room in Ganin's pension. They hold the party at which Alfyorov becomes drunk on the eve of his wife's arrival.

Mary, the enchanting woman whom Ganin loved as a teenager. Although she lives a rich life in Ganin's recollections, she never appears in the present-day setting of the novel.

Lydia Nikolaevna Dorn (nih-koh-LA-yehv-nah), the widow of a German businessman and the landlady of Ganin's pension.

— *Julian W. Connolly*

MARY BARTON

Author: Elizabeth Gaskell (1810-1865)
First published: 1848
Genre: Novel

Locale: Manchester, England
Time: Mid-nineteenth century
Plot: Social realism

Mary Barton, the protagonist. By the end of the novel, Mary represents an ideal of Victorian femininity. Much of the novel traces Mary's development toward this ideal as it comes into conflict with the reality of her social standing. Mary is the ambitious daughter of a laborer. Her prescribed social role is to remain at home, running the household, but she fantasizes about a marriage that would cross class boundaries and allow her to become a lady. She constructs these fantasies around her thoughts about her aunt Esther, who ran away with a soldier. Mary imagines her as being well off when, in fact, Esther has become a prostitute. Mary's ambition makes her scorn the attentions of a young man from her own class, Jem Wilson. Her involvement with Henry Carson, the son of a factory owner, leads to tragedy when Carson is murdered and Jem is arrested for the crime.

John Barton, Mary's father, who is almost as important a character as Mary. Unlike his friend George Wilson, John is a working man whose tribulations, especially the death of his young son Tom from undernourishment, have embittered him. After the death of his wife, John sinks further into an isolating cynicism. He does not give enough attention to rearing Mary and is overindulgent with her. His despair over their class standing feeds Mary's ambition.

Margaret Jennings, Mary's best friend. She is the model for proper behavior against which Mary is contrasted. She lives with and cares for her grandfather, Job Legh, whose behavior acts as a positive contrast to that of John Barton. Margaret, like Mary, is a seamstress, but she does not go out to work. Her long hours of sewing eventually make her blind, but she and her grandfather are saved from penury by Margaret's

singing. As her singing takes her away from Manchester, her good influence on Mary abates.

Jem Wilson, the son of George Wilson. Early in the novel, Jem's heroism is highlighted as he rescues his father and another workman from a fire at the Carson Mill. Jem is a self-made man who improved his class status through education as an engineer. He loves Mary from childhood and eventually confronts Henry Carson, not to vie with him for Mary but to demand that Carson marry her or leave her alone. His self-sacrificing nature is displayed again at his trial, at which he refuses to reveal John Barton's guilt, even to save himself, for fear of what this might do to Mary.

Henry Carson, the only son of the owner of the Carson Mill. He is spoiled and irresponsible. His treatment of the factory owners, unlike his father's, comes not from ignorance of their poverty but from contempt for their lack of refinement. He begins to flirt with Mary because she is attractive and appears easily swayed by wealth. Eventually, he realizes that he loves her, but his confession of love makes it clear that he saw her initially as only a conquest.

Mr. Carson, Henry's father. His actions at the mill toward the workers are described as similar to those of a neglectful parent. When his son is killed, he becomes a figure of vengeance, using all of his power to ensure a speedy trial and execution. After hearing John Barton's deathbed confession, Mr. Carson is able to reform his relationship with the lower classes, fulfilling what the author clearly sees as the proper role of beneficent patron.

— *Jasmine Yong Hall*

MARY OLIVIER: A Life

Author: May Sinclair (1863-1946)
First published: 1919
Genre: Novel

Locale: Essex and Yorkshire, England
Time: 1865-1910
Plot: Impressionistic realism

Mary Olivier (oh-lee-VYAY), the protagonist, whose search for happiness is the story of her life and the theme of the novel. Treated with indifference by her mother, she yearns for love but always loses the object of her affections. A bright girl with an independent mind, she is expelled from school for her religious unorthodoxy. Later, she is jilted by Maurice Jourdain because she is too intensely intellectual

for a woman. In middle age, she finds a satisfying relationship with the scholar Richard Nicholson but rejects him so that she can care for her mother. At that point, she realizes that happiness does not depend on others but instead lies within herself.

Emilius Olivier (eh-mee-LYEWS), Mary's father, an impressive man with a red-brown beard and mustache. He is jealous of his wife's love for her sons and bullies them until he can get them out of the house. He is occasionally kind to Mary only because her mother does not love her. After getting drunk and disgracing the family at the home of the local squire, he is forced to relocate the family in an isolated Yorkshire village. He dies of apoplexy.

Caroline Olivier, Mary's mother, a soft, pretty woman with brown hair. She struggles to protect her beloved sons from her tyrannical husband. In old age, she has a stroke. Having lost all of her sons, she is now dependent on the daughter whom she has always kept at a distance. Two years after Mary has given up her lover, Caroline dies.

Mark Olivier, Caroline's favorite son and the special target of Emilius' spite. Even in childhood, he is protective of Mary. After joining the army, he goes to India, where he dies of heart failure.

Daniel Olivier, another of the Olivier sons. Thwarted in every desire, including his love for Effie Draper, he is placed in an office job, which he hates and from which he is eventually fired for drinking. Even though he could have returned to that position, he goes to Canada and thus escapes his family.

Rodney (Roddy) Olivier, another of Mary's brothers and her childhood playmate. Although he loves the sea, he is in fragile health because of a boyhood attack of rheumatic fever and thus cannot take a job that requires physical exertion. He is sent to Canada to work on a farm. When he returns to England, he dies.

Jeremy (Jimmy) Parsonby, Mary's first love, a serious boy with blue eyes and dark hair. He is eight years older than Mary. Because of some disgraceful action, he is sent to Australia. Although she is only thirteen years old when he leaves, she never forgets him or recovers from her sense of loss.

Maurice Jourdain (moh-REES zhewr-DEH[N]), Mary's fiancé, a man with black eyes and sallow skin. At first, he appears to encourage Mary's intellectual development, even offering to pay for her schooling. After they are engaged (several years after their first meeting), however, he becomes unhappy with her independence of mind and jilts her.

Mr. Sutcliffe, a tall, handsome squire. He falls in love with the seventeen-year-old Mary despite the fact that he is married. Because of his feelings, he moves to the Continent, where he dies.

Richard Nicholson, Sutcliffe's nephew, a tall, thin man with dark eyes and hair. He is a classics scholar. When Mary meets him, he is forty-five years old, and she is thirty-nine. After she takes a position as his secretary, he discovers her talent as a poet and a translator. Although they fall in love, she refuses his proposal because she must care for her bedridden mother. When her mother dies, Mary is free, but, unfortunately, Richard has already planned to marry a woman who has loved him for many years. The marriage is unhappy.

— *Rosemary M. Canfield Reisman*

MASKS
(Onnamen)

Author: Fumiko Enchi (1905-1986)
First published: 1958
Genre: Novel

Locale: Kyoto and Tokyo, Japan
Time: Mid-1950's
Plot: Social

Mieko Toganō, the daughter of the head priest at a temple in Shinshu and the wife of a banker. She is also a prostitute, a poet, and a teacher of poetry. She bore twins, a mentally retarded girl, Harumé, and a beloved son, Akio. When Mieko appears, her slow and grave gestures refer to another landscape that can be seen only with her metaphysical eye. The subtexts of the novel create the emotional ambience of Mieko's character, both remote and involved at the same time. Mieko is compared to a large blossoming tree with a voice floating toward Ibuki and Mikamé and having a wordless communication and complicity in crime with Yasuko. It is difficult to plumb the depth of Mieko's heart. There is nothing more tragic than her immobility, which compares to that of a mountain lake whose waters are rushing beneath the surface toward a waterfall. The secret workings of her mind resemble flowers in a garden at nighttime, filling the darkness with perfumes; her masklike face indicates features but does not identify her as an individual. Her language, conduct, and posture reveal uncanny sensitivity to the slightest nuances of behavior. Despite apparent physical inertia, she evinces gestures of dignity and grandeur. She is in the grip of primeval powers that direct her amorous affairs and those of others. Her delight in poetry and calligraphy, fashion, and a garden with a miniature pond, reflecting the perception of beauty, shifts to a melancholy consciousness of the transience of human life.

Akio Toganō, Mieko's beloved son, who died in a ski accident on Mount Fuji. He seems to reappear in masks and dreams and to be born again thanks to Mieko's strategies.

Tsuneo Ibuki, a professor of Japanese Heian literature. He is married to Sadako and is the father of a three-year-old daughter. He falls in love with Yasuko.

Toyoki Mikamé, an expert of psychology and folklore. A bachelor in love with Yasuko, Toyoki observes communication with spirits that depart this life and float ceaselessly through the atmosphere, share the space around the living, and become alive in various masks and costumes and in dreams.

Yasuko Toganō, Akio's widow of a year. She is described as a flowerlike beauty who has just opened her petals. Her study of Heian spirit possession is a continuation of her dead husband's research. Long after Akio's death, Yasuko sees him in her dreams, in which she stabs him in his eyes and kills him. From that moment on, she feels that her body no longer belongs to Akio but rather to Mieko. Harumé, who is possessed by dog spirits, bites and draws blood from Yasuko. Yasuko consents with Mieko to switch places in bed with Harumé when Ibuki comes to spend the night with Yasuko.

Harumé Toganō, Akio's twin sister, who is severely mentally retarded. She does not really know what is going on when in bed with Ibuki. Ibuki does not immediately realize that the even-featured face, with closed eyelids relaxed as camellia petals, is not that of Yasuko. In bed with Ibuki, Harumé resembles the *zo-no-onna* mask, from the Nō drama, with Akio's features. Harumé bears a child but dies at its birth. The child is brought up with an old nurse at the Shrine of the Fields. When Ibuki visits there and sees his and Harumé's child, he has the impression that his friend Akio has emerged from death. Harumé's child has Akio's features.

— *Marlies Kronegger*

THE MASTER AND MARGARITA
(Master i Margarita)

Author: Mikhail Bulgakov (1891-1940)
First published: 1966-1967
Genre: Novel

Locale: First century Jerusalem and postrevolutionary Moscow
Time: The years 30 and 1920
Plot: Satire

The Master, an unnamed Muscovite who, after winning a lottery, retires to a basement apartment to write a novel about Pontius Pilate. Devastated when it is rejected by scornful editors, he attempts to burn the manuscript. The Master finds refuge in a mental hospital, where he meets Ivan and continues to imagine ancient Yershalayim. He is retrieved from the hospital by Woland, at the request of Margarita.

Margarita, the wife of a wealthy factory owner who falls in love with the Master and visits him clandestinely in his basement rooms. She fervently believes in his novel and attempts, unsuccessfully, to get editors to publish it. After the Master's disappearance, she is summoned by Azazello and flies off, naked, on a broom to apartment number 50 at 302-b Sadovaya Street in Moscow, where she serves as hostess of Satan's spring ball of the full moon.

Woland, also known as **Satan**, **Messire**, and the **Devil**, who shows up, in the guise of a German professor, in Moscow's Patriarchs' Pond Park. The magic show that he and his cohorts perform at the Variety Theater, in which the emcee is beheaded and money and clothing materialize, ends in pandemonium. Woland takes over Berlioz's apartment as his headquarters. There, he stages a satanic ball attended by a wide range of guests, living and deceased.

Ivan Nikolayevich Ponyrev (nih-koh-LA-yeh-vihch POH-nih-rehv), a young writer who uses the pen name **Ivan Homeless**. He is commissioned to write an antireligious poem about Jesus. His hysterical account of the supernatural mischief of Woland and his cohorts to fellow writers at the Griboyedov House causes him to be hospitalized and diagnosed as schizophrenic. After meeting the Master in an adjoining room, he listens to his story and becomes his literary disciple.

Yeshua Ha-Nozri, an accused rabble-rouser from Galilee. He is a solitary and timorous figure unsure of his calling. Resentful of Matthu Levi, he asks him to burn his manuscript. He is put to an agonizing death on Bald Mountain on the outskirts of Yershalayim.

Matthu Levi, a former tax collector who becomes Yeshua's self-appointed and sole disciple and maintains a chronicle of his master's life. Bitter over Yeshua's torturous execution, he attempts, unsuccessfully, to shorten his prolonged agony. He is offered a position by the guilt-wracked Pilate.

Pontius Pilate, also known as **Hegemon**, the Fifth Roman Procurator of Judea. He suffers from severe headaches and from weariness with the onerous duties of his office. He reluctantly accedes to the necessity of executing Yeshua.

Yehudah of Kerioth, a young man who informs the authorities about Yeshua's seditious statements. Lured to a romantic rendezvous, he is robbed and murdered.

Koroviev (koh-ROV-yehv), also known as **Fagot**, who introduces himself as Woland's interpreter. He is Satan's chief assistant and is an important participant in the bizarre events at apartment 50 and at the Variety Theater.

Azazello, one of Woland's assistants. He summons Margarita to apartment 50 and instructs her in how to fly.

Behemoth, also known as **Tom**, one of Woland's assistants. He has the form of a huge tomcat. Ivan Homeless chases him onto a streetcar and throughout Moscow. Behemoth is an active instigator of much of the supernatural mischief in the Variety Theater and apartment 50.

Hella, a naked witch who embarrasses the bar manager at the Variety Theater and who shows up at the satanic ball in apartment 50.

Mikhail Alexandrovich Berlioz (ah-lehk-SAN-droh-vihch), an unimaginative cultural commissar, chairman of the board of the writers' association, MASSOLIT. He is skeptical of the supernatural. He meets with Ivan in Patriarchs' Pond Park to discuss revisions in Ivan's antireligious poem about Jesus. While there, he also encounters Woland, who accurately predicts his imminent beheading by a streetcar.

Styopa Likhodeyev (STYOH-pah lih-khoh-DEH-yehv), the director of the Variety Theater. He shares apartment number 50 with Berlioz. The day after Berlioz's death, he is visited by Woland and his cohorts, who mysteriously transport him to Yalta and commandeer his apartment for their own diabolical activities.

Professor Stravinsky, the director of a mental hospital on the outskirts of Moscow, to which an increasing number of characters are consigned. He diagnoses Ivan Homeless as schizophrenic.

Grigory Danilovich Rimsky (grih-GOH-ree dah-NIH-loh-vihch RIHM-skee), the financial manager of the Variety Theater. Forced to assume responsibility after Likhodeyev's mysterious disappearance, he becomes terrified by Woland's supernatural mischief and flees to Leningrad.

Ivan Savelievich Varenukha (sah-VEH-lyeh-vihch vah-REH-new-khah), the house manager of the Variety Theater. Assigned by Rimsky to investigate the telegrams that they have been receiving from Likhodeyev in Yalta, he becomes the terrified victim of supernatural acts.

Arkady Apollonovich Sempleyarov (ahr-KAH-dee ah-poh-LOH-noh-vihch sehm-pleh-YA-rov), a pompous Soviet commissar. In the audience at the Variety Theater during Woland's magic show, he vocally demands a complete exposé. Woland responds by exposing him as an adulterous liar.

Nikanor Ivanovich Bosoy (nih-kah-NOHR ee-VAH-noh-vihch boh-SOY), the house chairman of 302-b Sadovaya

Street. After Berlioz's death, he receives thirty-two applications for his rooms. A generous bribe makes him partial to Woland, until Koroviev alerts the police to the foreign currency that has mysteriously materialized in his possession.

Latunsky (lah-TEWN-skee), a powerful Moscow literary critic. Margarita wreaks revenge on him for his devastating

attack on the Master's novel by destroying his apartment.

Aphranius, the head of the Roman secret service in Judea. He provides Pontius Pilate with information and disinformation about seditious plots involving Yeshua and arranges for the assassination of Yehuda.

— *Steven G. Kellman*

THE MASTER BUILDER
(Bygmester Solness)

Author: Henrik Ibsen (1828-1906)
First published: 1892
Genre: Drama

Locale: Norway
Time: The nineteenth century
Plot: Psychological realism

Halvard Solness, the master builder. Although he is no longer young, he is evidently attractive to women: His wife, Aline, his bookkeeper, Kaia Fosli, and Hilda Wangel, a young woman from a nearby village who had seen him only once ten years earlier, are all in love with him. Solness became successful after a tragedy, the death of his infant twin sons, caused him to turn from building churches to building houses. He has achieved success through working for Knut Brovik, whom he surpassed, put down, and now employs. He has two fears: fear of the younger generation, which will treat him as he has treated Brovik, and fear of heights. The fear of heights interferes with his hanging a wreath on the tower of each new building, a task he now delegates to a workman. When vivacious Hilda Wangel appears to collect "the kingdom" that he promised her ten years earlier after he had hung his last wreath on the church tower in her village, Solness is at last overpowered by her stronger personality. Through Hilda's influence, he approves plans designed by the young architect Ragnar Brovik and climbs a scaffolding to place a wreath on a new house. Both courses mean oblivion for him. He falls into a quarry and is crushed.

Hilda Wangel, a fanciful young woman from the village of Lysanger. Little more than a child at the time, Hilda had fallen in love with Solness when he hung a wreath on the church tower in Lysanger. He has remained her hero. She is a charming young woman, filled with a quality the playwright calls "joy in life." When Solness falls into the quarry, Hilda is exalted. She cries, "But he mounted right to the top. And I heard harps in the air. . . . My—my Master Builder!"

Aline Solness, Halvard's wife, a quiet, hopeless woman, once beautiful. Aline's life purpose ended because of a fire that destroyed her family home, in which she and Halvard lived, because her twin baby boys died soon afterward. Through a sense of duty, she insisted on nursing the babies when she was

ill from the excitement of the fire, and they died as a result. Halvard says that Aline had a talent "for building up children's souls in perfect balance, and in noble and beautiful forms." She keeps three nurseries in their present house, and their new home is to contain three empty nurseries. Aline is naturally jealous of Kaia and Hilda, although she and Hilda come to like each other. Knowing her husband's fear of heights, she tries to prevent his fatal climb. She faints when he falls at the conclusion of the play.

Knut Brovik, formerly an independent architect, now employed in Solness' office. Old, ill, and dying, Brovik lives only for his son, an aspiring architect. His one wish is that he might see Ragnar a success. Because Solness never approves anything that Ragnar does, Brovik has come to doubt his son's talent. He pleads with Solness to let Ragnar have the commission for a villa, plans for which he has already drawn. Although Brovik gave Solness his start in architecture, Solness, knowing Ragnar's talent, will not give Brovik any encouragement. Brovik is dead when Hilda finally persuades Solness to approve Ragnar's plans for the villa.

Kaia Fosli, Knut Brovik's niece, Solness' bookkeeper, engaged to marry Ragnar. Kaia is a quiet girl in love with Solness. Solness employs her to keep Ragnar, who is very much in love with her, in his employ, and hence in subjection.

Ragnar Brovik, a talented young man employed by Solness as a draftsman. Ragnar represents the younger generation that Solness fears will displace him. Ragnar does not realize his ability until he learns from Hilda that Solness employs Kaia not because he cares for her at all but because he fears Ragnar's talent and wants to keep it hidden.

Dr. Herdal, a physician concerned about Halvard and Aline. He serves as an audience for both Halvard and Aline and thus is a vehicle for expressing their personalities.

"MASTER HAROLD" . . . AND THE BOYS

Author: Athol Fugard (1932-   )
First published: 1982
Genre: Drama

Locale: St. George's Park Tea Room, Port Elizabeth, South Africa
Time: 1950
Plot: Political realism

Sam, a black South African man in his forties. Sam has worked for many years for a white family and is a trusted presence in their lives. A figure of dignity and wisdom, he has become in many ways a surrogate father for the family's

young son, Hally, whose real father is an alcoholic. Sam's genuine affection for the boy is tempered by a sense of self-worth that will not allow him to accept humiliating treatment from Hally as long as their relationship is a friendship not defined by the restrictions of apartheid. When Hally's actions alter the tone of that relationship, Sam becomes a symbol of the humanity of black South Africa, forced into a position of subservience by an inhumane social system.

Harold (Hally), a white, seventeen-year-old South African boy. Hally's parents own the tearoom where Sam and Willie work and where the play's action is set. A student, Hally enjoys showing off his knowledge to Willie and Sam, already displaying an air of superiority and condescension although the three enjoy an easy familiarity. Hally is also unhappy and confused, and he looks to Sam for the male guidance that his own father has failed to provide. His resentment toward his father, however, gradually becomes refocused on Sam as Hally assuages his own feelings of humiliation by insisting that Sam

treat him as his superior. Halley's actions toward his longtime friend create an irreparable rift in what has been one of the central relationships in his young life.

Willie Malopo, a black man about Sam's age, employed in the tearoom owned by Hally's parents. Less thoughtful and reflective than Sam, Willie is also less deeply involved in the lives of Hally and his parents. His relationship with Hally falls within the traditional boundaries of that between a black South African and the son of his white employers, and it becomes symbolic within the story of the type of relationship that Sam and Hally have so far transcended as the play opens and into which they will fall by its close.

— *Janet Lorenz*

THE MASTER OF BALLANTRAE

Author: Robert Louis Stevenson (1850-1894)
First published: 1889
Genre: Novel

Locale: Scotland, India, France, and America
Time: Mid-eighteenth century
Plot: Adventure

James Durie, the master of Ballantrae. Reported dead after the Battle of Culloden, he escapes to America, then goes to France, where he makes heavy financial demands on his brother Henry, now the heir to Durrisdeer, over a period of seven years. As Mr. Bally, James returns to Scotland, where he and Henry fight a duel. James apparently is killed, though his body disappears. Severely wounded, he is rescued by smugglers and taken to India, where he makes a fortune and acquires a native servant, Secundra Dass. When James again returns to Durrisdeer, Henry and his family flee to New York but are followed by James. In America, Henry decides to get rid of his evil brother permanently, but Secundra Dass overhears plans for James's murder and shortly thereafter reports that his master has died. Henry, determined to satisfy himself that James is really dead, comes upon his brother's grave just as Secundra Dass is exhuming James, who has not died but has been placed in a state of suspended animation by Secundra Dass as a means of tricking Henry. When Henry sees his brother's eyes flutter open after a week underground, he drops dead of shock. Despite many hours of strenuous effort, Secundra Dass is unable to revive James fully because of the cold temperature; at last, the brothers, deadly enemies, are buried in the same grave.

Henry Durie, James's younger brother, who remains at Durrisdeer. After James's reported death, Henry, now the heir, marries Alison. Plagued almost constantly by his very much

alive brother James, Henry finally flees to America with his family, but his relentless brother pursues him. Hated and hating, the two brothers, after a macabre graveside scene, are placed in the same grave in the remote American wilderness.

Lord Durrisdeer, the father of James and Henry. A canny Scot, he protects his estate by having one son on each side in the Stuart uprising.

Alison Graeme, a wealthy relative betrothed to James. After the report of his death, she marries Henry, though she still loves James. When James returns to Durrisdeer for the first time, Alison seems to prefer his company to that of her husband.

Ephraim Mackellar, the factor of Durrisdeer, loyal to Henry. He narrates most of the story.

Colonel Francis Burke, who first brings word that James is alive and in France. James demands that money be sent to him.

Captain Teach, a pirate who captures James and Burke, and whose treasure James steals.

Jacob Chew, an Indian trader of New York with whom James makes a wilderness expedition.

Secundra Dass, a servant acquired by James in India. He returns to Scotland with James, then accompanies his master to America. Attempting to trick Henry, he places James in a state of suspended animation, then is unable to revive him.

THE MASTER OF GO
(Meijin)

Author: Yasunari Kawabata (1899-1972)
First published: 1942-1954
Genre: Novel

Locale: Tokyo and Itō, Japan
Time: 1938-1940
Plot: Livre à clef

Shūsai, the master of Go and the emblem of a transition between the past aristocratic order and the new, more democratic era. Shūsai has devoted his life to the game of Go, losing himself in the artistry of play. At the age of sixty-five, he agrees to a retirement match with Otaké, a strenuous five-

month game that further weakens the fragile old man. A move by Otaké that seems to take unfair advantage of the rules angers the master, and, shortly thereafter, he makes an error that costs him the game. A year later, the master dies.

Otaké, the challenger. The nervous and aggressive young

Otaké lacks the master's love of game-playing for its own sake. He reluctantly accepts a shorter timetable to accommodate the ailing master, and he threatens to forfeit the match when the modified schedule prevents him from attending to his sick child. Otaké's lack of concern for the spirit of artistic play, further revealed by his opportunistic move, signals the triumph of the materialistic modern age.

Uragami, the narrator. As a newspaper reporter, Uragami faithfully reports the progress of the match with a sensitivity to detail. As the narrator of the novel, however, he often recounts events by association rather than chronological sequence. Although he lacks the dedication and stamina of either contestant, he admires the master's devotion to the aesthetics of the game, and he convinces Otaké not to spoil the match by forfeiting it over a dispute.

— *Steven L. Hale*

THE MASTER OF THE MILL

Author: Frederick Philip Grove (Felix Paul Greve, 1879-1948)
First published: 1944
Genre: Novel

Locale: Langholm, in Canada
Time: 1882-1939
Plot: Family

Senator Samuel Clark, a brilliant engineer and millionaire mill owner. The senator is making sense of his life and preparing for death. He remembers designing the first great mill. He later learns that his father financed it with money obtained from insurance fraud. Sam, taking over, dispatches his father's blackmailer to England and anonymously reimburses the insurance company. The senator has never loved power, industry, or money but has possessed all three and is forced by his position to become the agent of change in industry, thus increasing his power and fortune. Sam is interested in culture, philanthropy, and the well-being of his workers. Both his father and his son (whom Sam outlives) are apostles of industrial capitalism; between them is Sam the idealist, who is mastered by the mill. Although he is the titular head of the giant monopoly and faceless corporation that the mill engenders, it is in fact self-sustaining. Sam's private life is also marked by defeat. His marriage to Maud Carter was based on shared aesthetic interests, but she despised both mill and miller. Maud Dolittle, Sam's sales manager and vice president, understands both. As a widower, however, Sam realizes his feeling for her too late. He treats his daughter, Ruth, with hostile indifference because his wife died at her birth. His son, Edmund, who is out of sympathy with his father's views, ousts him from control. The old man's only consolation is his rapport with the third Maud, his widowed daughter-in-law. His will leaves her in control of the mill and puts his money into a charitable foundation for the unemployed. In death as in life, Sam's chief concern was for the human victims of the industrial developments he had, however unwillingly, promoted.

Rudyard Clark, Sam's father, a working man and founder of the Clark fortune. A ruthless Victorian capitalist, he paid blackmail for the crime that enabled him to rebuild the mill and then maintained control of it by ensuring that the services on which it depended were provided by his own companies. The profits from the mill thus could be routed from the public company to the private ones. With his money, he built a mansion for his son's wife. Injured by machinery, he dies mysteriously in the company of his blackmailer.

Edmund Clark, the son of Sam Clark and Maud Carter, a flying ace and financier. Edmund returns from the war determined to make the mill a monopoly, a private company, and totally automated. In pursuit of these goals, he eliminates other shareholders, discovers that his grandfather was an arsonist, wrests control from his father, and provokes the strike in which he is killed. Edmund believes that advancing technology will provide a work-free Eden for laborers and power for an elite who will control the machines.

Maud Dolittle, a brilliant businesswoman and Sam's right hand. Edmund's mistress and eventually his wife's friend, she contributes to the narrative.

Ruth Clark, Sam's daughter. She avoids sexual involvement and fortune hunters by marrying a very old French marquis.

Odette Charlebois, Sam's housekeeper. A surrogate mother to his children, she also contributes to the narrative.

Lady Clark, formerly **Maud Fanshawe**, the beautiful youngest daughter of a poor but brilliant university president. She is the wife (later widow) of Sir Edmund, inheritor of the mansion and the mill, and collector of the Clarks' history. Needing a rich husband, Maud married Edmund because of the understanding they shared and her comprehension of and assistance in his schemes. Now she provides a home for Edmund's dying father, Sam.

— *Jocelyn Creigh Cass*

THE MASTERS

Author: C. P. Snow (1905-1980)
First published: 1951
Genre: Novel

Locale: Cambridge, England
Time: Mid-twentieth century
Plot: Psychological realism

Lewis Eliot, a junior faculty member at the unidentified college—similar to Cambridge University in England—where the story takes place. He comes from a rather poor family and has managed to advance in society. The story of the election of a master at the college is told from his point of view. He throws his support to Jago and remains loyal to him to the end of the affair.

Paul Jago, a senior faculty member and candidate for the position of master. He is ambitious, mercurial, and very quick to seek the position of master. His affability and humane spirit win him the early support of many, but some crucial flaws in his character eventually erode his standing. He has not published any work of substantial scholarship. He is temperamental and given to excessive bursts of emotion. His marriage has not been ideal, and some doubt that his wife has the ability or social skills necessary to support him successfully in the position of master. Eventually, these matters cause strategic support to shift away from Jago, and he loses the election. He takes the loss very hard but still is able to be reconciled to the man who defeats him.

Ronald Nightingale, a scientist on the faculty, somewhat of a misfit. He showed promise early but never lived up to the expectations everyone had of him. He has not made any great contributions to the sciences and will not. As a result, he is bitter and spiteful. He first supports Jago but soon changes his choice to Crawford. After becoming a supporter of Crawford, he begins to gossip and to threaten and cajole others within the college. He circulates flyers demeaning the character of Jago and Jago's wife until Crawford asks him to desist. He remains loyal to Crawford to the end of the story.

Arthur Brown, a senior faculty member who supports Jago. He is described as being a politician by nature. Throughout the novel, he is the organizer and prime mover of the party that supports Jago. Not particularly ambitious himself, he loves to wield power and influence and is an expert at political maneuvering. Like Calvert, he produced fruitful scholarship early in his career but has done little since. He is happy and comfortable in his position at the college.

Roy Calvert, a faculty member and friend of Eliot. He is a good teacher but has done little scholarship. He is similar to Brown in many ways: content, not ambitious, conservative, and quite active in the political workings of the college. He lacks, however, the skill and drive of Brown and tends to be impatient, sometimes overbearing and domineering. It is he who forces Jago and Crawford to cast votes so that there will be a majority and an outsider will not be brought in to fill the position of master. As the novel progresses, he begins to see Jago's faults, and his support for him wavers. As the election draws closer, he proposes a new candidate. When the other faculty members will not go along with him, he switches his support to Crawford.

Maurice Gay, an elderly faculty member who is eccentric and perhaps a bit senile. He is an expert on "Saga-men," the heroes of ancient Norse and Icelandic legend. His pomposity makes him a comic but likable character. Later in the book, he becomes important to the election by shifting his support away from Crawford to Jago.

Alice Jago, Paul Jago's wife, an unattractive, pretentious, graceless woman who has always been an embarrassment to her husband. Though ambitious, she does not have the social acumen necessary to be the wife of the master, a fact that different faculty members begin to recognize. As the novel progresses, she suffers deeply from the gossip and slander generated against her by Nightingale and others.

— *David W. Landrum*

MASTRO-DON GESUALDO

Author: Giovanni Verga (1840-1922)
First published: 1889
Genre: Novel

Locale: San Giovanni, Sicily
Time: First half of the nineteenth century
Plot: Social

Gesualdo Motta (geh-sew-AHL-doh MOHT-tah), an ambitious peasant whose business acumen has made him into a rich landowner. Desiring gentility along with his riches, he marries Donna Bianca Trao, but the marriage succeeds only in widening the gaps on both sides of his world, leaving him hated by the peasantry, scorned by the gentry, and used by all for the wealth he had hoped would bring him satisfaction.

Bianca Trao (bee-AHN-kah trah-oh), a poor gentlewoman who marries Gesualdo Motta in the hope that his riches will ease the financial burdens of her family.

Isabella Motta (ee-zah-BEHL-lah), the daughter of Bianca Trao and Gesualdo Motta, who gradually grows away from the peasant Motta and eventually becomes completely a Trao. She is given in marriage to the duke di Leyra.

The duke di Leyra, Isabella Motta's extravagant husband, who soon runs through her dowry and then despoils Gesualdo Motta of his property.

Don Diego and
Don Ferdinando Trao, Bianca Trao's brothers.

Santo (SAHN-toh) and
Speranza Motta (speh-RAHN-zah), Gesualdo's brother and sister.

Fortunato Burgio (fohr-tew-NAH-toh bur-JEE-oh), Speranza Motta's husband.

Nunzio Motta (NEWN-zee-oh), Gesualdo Motta's father.

Baron Ninì Rubiera (nee-NEE rew-bee-EH-rah), Bianca Trao's cousin and her lover before her marriage to Gesualdo Motta, to whom Ninì eventually goes hopelessly in debt.

Baroness Rubiera, Ninì's mother, who refuses to allow her son to marry the fortuneless Bianca Trao.

Diodata (dee-oh-DAH-tah), Gesualdo Motta's faithful, humble servant and mistress, who is married off to Nani l'Orbo.

Nani l'Orbo (NAH-nee LOHR-boh), Gesualdo Motta's servant, married to Diodata. He blackmails his master, the father of Diodata's children, for support and property.

Baron Zacco (ZAHK-koh), a Trao relative and, when it suits his purposes, an ally of Gesualdo Motta.

Don Filippo Margarone (mahr-gah-ROH-neh), the local political leader.

Fifì Margarone, Don Filippo Margarone's daughter, the choice of Baroness Rubiera as a bride for her son Ninì.

Signora Aglae (AHG-lyay), an actress for whom Ninì goes in debt to Gesualdo Motta.

Madame Giuseppina Alosi (jee-ew-sehp-PEE-nah ah-LOH-see), a widow married for her wealth by Baron Ninì Rubiera.

Donna Sarina (sah-REE-nah) or **Cirmena** (cheer-MEH-nah), a poor Trao relative, the sole family representative at Bianca Trao's wedding to Gesualdo Motta.

Corrado la Gurna (kohr-RAH-doh), Donna Cirmena Trao's nephew, loved by Isabella Motta.

Lupi (LEW-pee), a priest.

Master Titta (TEET-tah), a barber who intercepts a note Ninì has written to Signora Aglae and gives it to Fifi, who then breaks her engagement to Ninì.

THE MATCHMAKER

Author: Thornton Wilder (1897-1975)
First published: 1956
Genre: Drama

Locale: Yonkers and New York City
Time: The 1880's
Plot: Comedy

Dolly Gallagher Levi, a friend of Vandergelder's late wife, living in a sort of impoverished elegance as a matchmaker. Of an uncertain age and possessing considerable charm, she also offers music lessons and physical therapy. A meddlesome busybody and fun-loving schemer, she would like New York to be more like Vienna, from which her late husband Ephraim had come. After skillfully pulling a number of strings, she finally gets her wish to become the second Mrs. Vandergelder, with the aim of using her husband's money to spread joy in the world.

Horace Vandergelder, the merchant of Yonkers (the title of the 1938 version of this play), a wealthy sexagenarian, described as the most influential citizen of Yonkers—where, it is said, nothing ever happens. He is the president of the Hudson River Provision Dealers' Recreational, Musical, and Burial Society. This irritable, vain, shrewd, foppish, complacent, mildly misanthropic, and rather curmudgeonly man is called Wolf-trap by his employees. Having been widowed, he is eager to remarry. At the end, he proves soft-hearted enough to facilitate three marriages, including his own.

Cornelius Hackl, the hardworking longtime chief clerk, thirty-three years old, in Vandergelder's hay, feed, provision, and hardware business. An inhibited Presbyterian who never learned to dance, he closes the store in his master's absence and goes to New York in search of adventures. Having experienced women only as customers, he begins to enjoy their perceived mysteriousness and to live up to the matchmaker's preposterous pretense that he is a man about town. He winds up as the business partner of Vandergelder and the husband of Mrs. Molloy.

Irene Molloy, a milliner who hates hats. She is nostalgic for her late husband, Peter, because he was so good at marital fights. She believes that Vandergelder would be a fitting replacement. Starved for adventure, she finally marries Hackl, her male counterpart in this respect.

Flora Van Huysen, a prosperous New York spinster of fifty, florid and sentimental. Vandergelder wants her to detain his niece and her boyfriend and keep them from eloping, but this rather literal-minded lady is opposed to keeping young lovers apart and thus works at cross purposes with the merchant. It is at her home that everyone finally gathers. After some confusion caused by the bumbling Flora, her imperturbability and old-fashioned common sense contribute to the unraveling of the tangled skein.

Malachi Stack, a man of fifty with a checkered background who claims to have had about fifty different employers. Vandergelder hires him as an apprentice and immediately sends him to New York to help him win a wife and prevent the elopement of his niece and her beau. The worldly-wise and rather sardonic Stack tends toward dishonesty and drink, but he believes in limiting himself to one vice at a time.

Barnaby Tucker, Vandergelder's seventeen-year-old junior clerk. He goes along with Hackl as his sidekick and receives his first kiss, from Mrs. Molloy. He has the last word in the play, wishing the audience the right amount of adventure.

Ermengarde, Vandergelder's niece and his only relative. A pretty girl of twenty-four, she finally gets her uncle's consent to marry Ambrose Kemper, an artist.

— *Harry Zohn*

MAUD MARTHA

Author: Gwendolyn Brooks (1917-   )
First published: 1953
Genre: Novel

Locale: The South Side of Chicago, Illinois
Time: The 1930's and the 1940's
Plot: Psychological realism

Maud Martha Brown Phillips, the protagonist. She is the daughter of Belva and Abraham Brown, reared with her older sister Helen and brother Harry in Cottage Grove, a neighborhood on Chicago's South Side. She is first seen at the age of seven. Maud perceives herself as ordinary and not beautiful, with her dark coloring and nappy hair. She desires to be cherished and dreams of an exciting life in New York City. Helen warns her to stop reading books if she ever wants to get a boyfriend. Maud Martha eventually marries Paul Phillips

and moves to a dingy kitchenette apartment on the third floor of a graystone building. There they read together. She loses herself in *Of Human Bondage* while he falls asleep with *Sex in the Married Life*. After the birth of their daughter Paulette, Maud settles for a life that is clearly less than she had hoped for, in a listless marriage and living in a shabby apartment in a quirky neighborhood, but she remains determined to survive life's indignities.

Paul Phillips, a grocery clerk, Maud's insensitive husband.

He is interested in her at first because she is an incorruptible virgin. He cannot concede defeat so "allows" Maud to steal him away from the city's nightlife, beautiful "high yellow" (light-skinned) women, fancy clothes, and impressive cars. He retains his obsession with the social whirl, however, cultivating an invitation to the Foxy Cats Club Ball and barely hiding his desire to leave his wife at home. After his efforts at social climbing fail, he makes little attempt to be a good husband. Lacking the sensitivity and patience to respect Maud's fondness for family holiday celebrations, he makes her put their daughter to bed and invites his beer-drinking friends over for Christmas.

Belva Brown, Maud's fussy and domineering mother. She is alternately kind and harsh with her daughter. Although she provides a solid home for her three children, never forgetting a birthday and making each holiday a special memory, she is a thorn in Maud's side, almost fainting at the birth of her first grandchild and unfavorably comparing Maud to Helen even after they are grown.

Helen Brown, Maud's older and prettier sister. Despite being less intelligent than her sister, Helen is the family's favorite. She scolds Maud for losing herself in books. Seldom sympathetic to others, she hates the "hulk of rotten wood" they call home and uses her beauty to marry a doctor, whom she does not love but who can give her a different and more comfortable life.

Abraham Brown, Maud's father, who has worked as a janitor all his life. He loves his old house and worries constantly about Helen's well-being, never realizing how hurt and slighted Maud feels.

David McKemster, Maud's former boyfriend. He aspires to leave his humble neighborhood to go to the university. After Maud is married, she accidentally meets him at a lecture, but he is cool to her when he spots his white intellectual friends from college.

Paulette Phillips, Maud and Paul's daughter. Her innocent child's voice finally enables Maud to face and break the silence she has constructed for herself.

— *Carol F. Bender*

MAURICE

Author: E. M. Forster (1879-1970)
First published: 1971
Genre: Novel

Locale: Cambridge, London, and Clive Durham's country estate, Penge
Time: 1903-1913
Plot: Bildungsroman

Maurice Hall, a healthy and handsome, though indifferent, student (at Sunnington and later at Cambridge) who becomes a successful London stockbroker. Conventional, respectable, and suburban, imaginatively slow and intellectually muddled, he begins in a state of vague sexual uneasiness and, by means of his largely platonic relationship with Clive Durham and a fully consummated relationship with Alec Scudder, develops a clear recognition and acceptance of his own homosexuality. Having fought his way to this understanding of his essential nature, he defies class, family, and sexual constraints to establish a mature and satisfying relationship with Alec. They go off to build a life together in the greenwood.

Clive Durham, a Cambridge classics scholar who becomes an aspiring politician. As a slight, attractive blond undergraduate, he makes Maurice aware of his sexual inclinations. They discover and confess their love for each other and spend three years together, traveling to Italy and keeping company regularly in London. At Clive's insistence, the relationship is kept free of any physical passion and made to burn with an idealized sort of Hellenic spirituality. After an illness and a period of self-disgust on a solitary trip to Greece, Clive turns his interests to women, renouncing Maurice, marrying Lady Anne Wood, and setting up as a country squire at Penge, the family seat. Although now apparently "normal," he is still unable to face up to the reality of the body or to regard sex as anything but dark and shameful.

Alec Scudder, a gamekeeper at Penge, the Durham estate. A butcher's boy, vital, frank, and resourceful, he had planned to immigrate to Argentina until he met Maurice at Penge. He responds to Maurice's heartsick cry for a friend when, half-asleep, the young, miserable stockbroker calls out the window,

"Come." Alec does come, spending the night and convincing Maurice that the body can educate the spirit and that the two can come together lastingly. He writes Maurice, shows his independence through a pretense of blackmail, and ultimately sacrifices his future in Argentina for the uncertain future of a life with this man from an entirely different class and background.

Mrs. Hall, Maurice's mother. A widow since the early death of Maurice's father, she is a rather faceless embodiment of conventional suburban society. Her son must confront and ultimately rejects her comfortably orthodox views on education, politics, marriage, and family.

Ada Hall, Maurice's eldest younger sister and, for a time, his rival for Clive's affection. She inherits a fortune from her grandfather, Mr. Grace, and goes on to marry Arthur Chapman, one of Maurice's old school friends.

Dr. Barry, a neighbor of the Halls. He is a retired physician, at once cynical and chivalric. He is the protective yet predatory male to whom Maurice first confesses his sexual dilemma. Barry dismisses Maurice's problem as rubbish and goes on to indict the unspeakable vice of homosexuality while suggesting that venereal disease and prostitution are quite acceptable, even a badge of manhood.

Mrs. Durham, Clive's mother, a widow whose class snobbery is both appalling and ironic, because the family estate is virtually collapsing around her. Her chief aim is to see Clive suitably married and elected to Parliament.

Risley, a bright and flamboyant Cambridge undergraduate whom Maurice meets at a dean's tea. He is tall, dark, and affected, and his bohemian otherness attracts Maurice, while his clear homosexual mannerisms frighten him. Risley later recommends to Maurice a hypnotist with a 50 percent cure rate for cases of "congenital homosexuality."

Mr. Lasker Jones, a hypnotist, vaguely American and chillingly cool, to whom Maurice applies for a "cure." At first, Jones recommends exercise and strolling about with a gun, but after seeing Alec's letter, he advises that the young men go off

to France or Italy, where homosexuality is not against the law.

Mr. Borenius, the new rector at Penge, brought by Clive's wife, Anne. His chief concerns are to get Alec confirmed in the church and to see him married before the young man emigrates.

— *Thomas J. Campbell*

MAX HAVELAAR

Author: Multatuli (Edward Douwes Dekker, 1820-1887)
First published: 1860
Genre: Novel

Locale: Java
Time: 1857
Plot: Satire

Max Havelaar, a Dutch colonial administrator. An idealist who is deeply concerned with justice for all, he arrives in Java to find conditions among the Javanese laborers worse than he had anticipated. Finding that the Dutch, who rule through the Javanese nobility, have acquiesced in the plundering and mistreatment of the laborers by their native masters, he attempts by persuasion and example to improve the situation while he gathers information for a report to his superiors. When his report is complete, he presents it to one indifferent official after another until he finds himself relieved of his job and forsaken by the government he has served.

Radhen Adhipatti Karta Natta Negara, the native regent of Lebak. A relatively poor man with a large family and appearances to keep up, he extorts, under Dutch protection, goods and services from his people. When Max Havelaar lodges an official protest against him, the Javanese is upheld by the Dutch, who denounce Havelaar for his pains.

Tine, Max Havelaar's devoted wife and champion.

Mr. Verbrugge, the controller serving under Max Havelaar. Although he is well aware of the exploitation of the Javanese by the Dutch, he is afraid to risk the security of his job by trying to fight against the complacent colonial administration.

Mr. Slimering, a Dutch colonial official with whom Max Havelaar lodges a protest against the injustices suffered by the Javenese laborers. Slimering denounces the protest in favor of the corrupt native chiefs.

Saïdyah, a young Javanese whose story is used as an example of colonial injustice. His father loses his possessions by extortion, and his betrothed is murdered by Dutch troops; Saïdyah himself is killed later.

Batavus Drystubble, a Dutch coffee broker of Amsterdam. He does not believe that the Javanese are mistreated.

Shawlman, Batavus Drystubble's schoolmate, a writer who brings to him the manuscript of the story of Max Havelaar.

THE MAYOR OF CASTERBRIDGE: The Life and Death of a Man of Character

Author: Thomas Hardy (1840-1928)
First published: 1886
Genre: Novel

Locale: Wessex, England
Time: The nineteenth century
Plot: Psychological realism

Michael Henchard, the mayor of Casterbridge and a prosperous corn merchant. In his youth, while drunk, he had sold his wife and child to a seaman. Years later, this information becomes known in Casterbridge; as a result, Henchard is ruined. Too stern and unyielding to resume his friendship with Donald Farfrae, his former manager, the headstrong ex-mayor faces declining fortune. Finally, he is forced to declare bankruptcy and is publicly humiliated during the visit of royalty. At last, broken in spirit, he takes refuge in a shack and dies practically friendless.

Susan Henchard-Newson, Henchard's wife. A plain, simple woman, she finally tires of her husband's repeated threats to sell her to the highest bidder. When he offers her for sale, she throws her wedding ring at him and leaves with the sailor Newson, her baby in her arms. Years later, thinking Newson drowned, she returns and remarries Henchard.

Elizabeth-Jane Newson, Henchard's attractive stepdaughter. A proper young woman, she is attracted to the personable young Farfrae. After the death of Lucetta, she marries the young corn merchant.

Donald Farfrae, a corn merchant in Casterbridge and Henchard's thriving business competitor. At first Henchard's good friend and manager, he gradually drifts apart from the mayor when the latter becomes jealous of the young man's capability and popularity. The estrangement, however, helps to bring Farfrae increasing prosperity. He captures much of the grain market and, against his will, gradually takes away much of his former employer's business. When Farfrae marries Lucetta, the break between the two men is complete.

Lucetta Templeman, a woman Henchard had known as Lucetta Le Sueur, later Farfrae's wife. An attractive but aging coquette, she intended to marry Henchard until she encountered the handsome Farfrae. After meeting him, she decides that she does not care to see Henchard again, even though the latter was once her lover. Her marriage to Farfrae goes smoothly until Jopp reads some love letters, which Lucetta had sent to Henchard, aloud to the denizens of Mixen Lane. Learning she is exposed as a loose woman, she has a miscarriage and dies.

Richard Newson, a bluff, hearty sailor. In his youth, he had bought Henchard's wife and child. The ex-mayor's destruction is complete when the sailor comes to Casterbridge to claim his daughter, Elizabeth-Jane.

Jopp, a surly former employee of Henchard. Snubbed by Lucetta, he gets his revenge when he has the chance to read her love letters aloud in the Three Mariners Inn and takes part in a parade that exposes her to the people.

Abel Whittle, Henchard's simple-minded employee. Although abused by his former employer, Abel, remembering how good the sick man had been to Abel's mother, takes care of him in his final illness.

THE MAYOR OF ZALAMEA
(El alcalde de Zalamea)

Author: Pedro Calderón de la Barca (1600-1681)
First published: 1651
Genre: Drama

Locale: Zalamea, Spain
Time: The sixteenth century
Plot: Tragedy

Pedro Crespo (PEH-droh KREHS-poh), a farmer of Zalamea whose story was first told in a play by Lope de Vega. He is a candidate for mayor in the approaching elections. Because he is wealthy, his house is selected as lodgings for Captain Ataide, who is leading his troops to Guadalupe. Although he is a commoner, he is a proud and independent man.

Juan Crespo (hwahn), his son, who wants his father to refuse hospitality to the Spanish soldiers. Later, he suspects the trickery of Captain Ataide and is almost killed for drawing a sword against him in defense of his sister. Saved by the arrival of Don Lope, Juan decides to enlist under his banner and march away with him.

Isabel (EE-sah-behl), the daughter of Pedro Crespo. Upon the arrival of the soldiers, she hides in the attic, where she is discovered by Captain Ataide, who kidnaps her. After his death, she enters a nunnery.

Inés (ee-NEHS), Isabel's cousin, who hides with her in the Crespo attic.

Don Álvaro de Ataide (AHL-vah-roh deh ah-TI-deh), a captain and the leader of a company of soldiers billeted in Zalamea. Curious about Isabel's beauty, of which he has heard, he schemes to see her. After his troops leave Zalamea, he sneaks back to the village and with the help of Rebolledo abducts her and violates her. She is rescued too late by her brother. When Crespo, now mayor, orders the captain to make amends by marrying Isabel, Ataide refuses with the declaration that she is beneath him. Crespo orders him jailed. In jail, he is slain by an unidentified assailant.

Rebolledo (rreh-boh-YEH-doh), a military veteran who, in return for permission to operate official troop gambling, helps Captain Ataide in his schemes. Learning from a servant about Isabel's hiding place, he fakes a quarrel with the captain and, fleeing, leads him to the attic where Isabel and Inés are hiding. Later, he helps kidnap Isabel and ties up Crespo when he attempts to rescue his daughter.

A sergeant, also ordered by Captain Ataide to aid in the abduction plot.

Chispa (CHEES-pah), Rebolledo's mistress, who accompanies the troops and encourages them by singing marching songs. She disguises herself as a man to help Rebolledo seize Isabel.

Don Lope de Figueroa (LOH-peh deh fee-gehr-OH-ah), the commander of a Spanish regiment, who has an eye for pretty girls but a wounded leg that makes them safe with him. He turns the captain out of Crespo's house and lodges there himself. He wins Crespo's friendship by protecting him, as well as Isabel's pity by displaying his battle wounds.

Philip II, the king of Spain, who is on his way to Portugal with his army. He does not arrive in Zalamea in time to free Captain Ataide, who already has been garroted in his cell. When he does arrive in the village, however, the king declares the punishment just and appoints Crespo perpetual mayor of Zalamea.

Don Mendo (MEHN-doh), a down-at-the-heels squire who yearns for Isabel.

Nuño (NEWN-yoh), Don Mendo's picaresque servant.

MEAN SPIRIT

Author: Linda Hogan (1947-   )
First published: 1990
Genre: Novel

Locale: Watona, Oklahoma
Time: Early 1920's
Plot: Magical Realism

Belle Graycloud, a tribal leader of the Osage people and matriarch of the Graycloud family. She lives with her family on a farm in Watona, Oklahoma, is well schooled in tribal medicine, and keeps bees. Her peaceful life is disrupted when white businessmen swindle Indians out of their oil-rich land and murder them. Belle makes a courageous stand against the local authorities at Sorrow Cave, where she protests the shooting of sacred bats by townspeople. When John Hale and his partners discover oil on her land, she is shot by Jess Gold and left for dead. She survives, and the Indian community stages a mock funeral to protect her. Belle goes into hiding among the elusive Hill people. She later returns to her family just before Hale is convicted of theft and murder.

Moses Graycloud, Belle's husband and Osage elder. Although quiet and less flamboyant than his wife, Moses is an outspoken leader. When government officials try to cheat him and other Indians out of their government allotments, Moses bravely objects, but to no avail. As a result of his reduced income, Moses must sell his prize horse and other items to support his family. When sacred eagles are slaughtered for their feathers, Moses writes letters of protest to President Warren Harding and also informs him of the murders of oil-rich Indians. He staunchly supports Belle at Sorrow Cave. When his house is bombed, Moses kills his brother-in-law, who is a member of Hale's gang.

Michael Horse, a seer and keeper of the eternal fire of the Osage tribe. He is the last person in the territory to live in a tepee but one of the first to own a car. Michael is the tribal historian and keeps a personal diary as well. His quest to capture Benoit's horse, Redshirt, leads him to the Hill settlement, where he continues his work on the history of his people.

Grace Blanket, one of the Hill Indians who descends to Watona to live among the whites. Oil is discovered on her land, and she becomes the richest Indian in the territory. Her wealth makes her a target for white swindlers who eventually murder her.

Nola, Grace's beautiful thirteen-year-old daughter. She lives with the Grayclouds after her mother's death. She is protected by four Hill Indians, one of whom is presumed to be her father. Nola inherits her mother's wealth and marries Will Forest, the son of her guardian. Pregnant by Will and fearful that he might kill her for her inheritance, Nola shoots her husband, escapes to the Hill people, and there gives birth to a daughter.

Stace Red Hawk, a Sioux and a government investigator working to uncover the identity of those who are murdering Indians in Watona. He masterminds Belle's fake funeral and works to expose Hale's illegal schemes. Finally, he quits his government post and follows his calling as a medicine man.

Lettie Graycloud, Moses and Belle's beautiful older daughter. She is the mistress and eventual wife of Benoit. She and Benoit marry while he is incarcerated, and they are allowed a wedding night in a local hotel under armed guard. After Benoit's death, Lettie becomes more active in tribal affairs.

Benoit, a handsome French Indian who is the husband of Sara Blanket and, after Sara's murder, Lettie Graycloud. He is arrested on suspicion of murdering his wife and is held for several months but never formally charged. The day after he marries Lettie, Benoit is found hanged in his cell, his death presumed a suicide.

John Hale, a white businessman and oil magnate. Hale is the ringleader of a group of white men who attempt to swindle the Indians out of their oil-laden land. His technique is to convince them to sign an insurance policy, appointing him as the beneficiary. He then arranges their deaths and collects the insurance money. He eventually is caught, tried, and sent to prison.

Jess Gold, the sheriff of Watona. He is attracted to Lettie Graycloud and dates her before her marriage to Benoit. He also opposes Belle when she defends Sorrow Cave. After Belle is shot, Gold is found near her body, suffering from convulsions resulting from repeated stings by Belle's bees. He dies a short time later. When Hale is tried, it is revealed that Gold was a key member of Hale's group and Belle's attempted murderer.

Louise Graycloud, Belle and Moses' second daughter, who rejects her Indian heritage. After the murders and the suffering of her family, she returns to Indian ways.

Floyd Graycloud, Louise's white husband, who takes Louise's surname and embraces the Indian culture.

Ben Graycloud and

Rena Graycloud, Floyd and Louise's children.

— Pegge Bochynski

MEASURE FOR MEASURE

Author: William Shakespeare (1564-1616)
First published: 1623
Genre: Drama

Locale: Vienna
Time: The sixteenth century
Plot: Tragicomedy

Angelo (AN-jeh-loh), a Viennese nobleman, the duke's deputy, a man who is cold, arrogant, and unbending in the knowledge of his own virtuous life. He refuses to look with sympathy on the offense of Claudio and stands firm for justice untempered with mercy. He is shocked to find himself tempted by Isabella, but he dismisses all moral scruples and attempts to seduce her, promising to free her brother if she will yield to him. Once he thinks he has had his will, he orders Claudio's execution to take place. Faced with the duke's knowledge of his behavior, he, still in character, asks death as the fitting recompense for his sins; mercy is still no part of his character, although it is that quality, meted out by the duke in accord with the pleas of Isabella and Mariana, that ultimately saves him.

Vincentio (veen-CHEHN-see-oh), the duke of Vienna, a rather ambiguous figure who acts at times as a force of divine destiny in the lives of his subjects. He has wavered in the enforcement of his state's unjust laws. Pretending to go on a trip to Poland, he leaves the government in Angelo's hands to try to remedy this laxity as well as to test Angelo's "pale and cloistered virtue." He moves quietly to counteract the effects of Angelo's strict law enforcement on Isabella, Claudio, and Mariana.

Isabella (eez-eh-BEHL-ah), a young noblewoman who emerges from the nunnery where she is a postulant to try to save the life of her condemned brother. Her moral standards, like Angelo's, are absolute; she is appalled to find herself faced with two equally dreadful alternatives: to watch her brother die, knowing that it is in her power to save him, or to surrender herself to Angelo. She cannot entirely comprehend Claudio's passionate desire to live, no matter what the cost. Virtue is, for her, more alive than life itself, and she cannot help feeling a certain sense of justice in his condemnation, although she would save him if she could do so without causing her own damnation. She learns, as Angelo does not, to value mercy, and she is able at the end of the play to join Mariana on her knees to plead for the deputy's life.

Claudio (KLOH-dee-oh), Isabella's brother, condemned to death for getting his fiancée with child. He finds small consolation in the duke's description of death, and he makes a passionate defense of life, describing the horrors of the unknown.

Escalus (EHS-keh-luhs), a wise old Viennese counselor, left by the duke as Angelo's adviser. He deals humorously and sympathetically with the rather incoherent testimony of Elbow, the volunteer constable.

Mariana (mah-ree-AH-nah), a young woman betrothed to Angelo and legally his wife when he rejected her because of difficulties over her dowry. She agrees, at the duke's request, to take Isabella's place in the garden house where Angelo had arranged to meet her. Claiming Angelo as her husband at the duke's reentry into the city, she asks mercy for his betrayal of Claudio and Isabella.

Lucio (LEW-shee-oh), a dissolute young man who brags of his desertion of his mistress and gives the disguised duke bits of malicious gossip about himself. He is sentenced, for his boasting and his slander, to marry the prostitute he has abandoned.

Mrs. Overdone, a bawd.

Pompey, her servant.

Juliet, Claudio's fiancée, who is cared for by the disguised duke.

Elbow, a clownish volunteer constable whose malapropisms make enforcement of the law more than difficult.

Francisca (fran-SIHS-kuh), a nun of the order Isabella is entering.

Froth, a laconic patron of Mrs. Overdone's establishment.

Provost (PROV-uhst), an officer of the state who pities Claudio and helps the duke save him, thus disobeying Angelo's orders.

Abhorson, the hangman, a man of rather macabre humor.

Barnardine, a long-term prisoner freed by the merciful duke.

Friar Thomas and

Friar Peter, religious men who aid the duke.

A MEASURE OF TIME

Author: Rosa Guy (1928-   )
First published: 1983
Genre: Novel

Locale: Montgomery, Alabama; Cleveland, Ohio; and New York City, particularly Harlem
Time: The 1920's to the 1950's
Plot: Bildungsroman

Dorine Davis, a saucy, free-spirited, hardheaded woman who plays both sides of the law. Reared by her grandmother, Dorine is hired out to do housework. At the age of ten, she is sent to work for a white man, Master Norton, who sexually molests her. Her family's inability to protect her makes Dorine realize that she must make her own way. She saves her money earned from housecleaning and performing sexual favors, a financial pattern she establishes in youth and follows as a young adult in Cleveland; only when she moves to New York City with her boyfriend, Sonny, does she hope to free herself by their making a life together. With the failure of this scheme, however, Dorine turns to a life of professional shoplifting, or "boosting," confidence tricks, and nightclub management. Always a self-proclaimed "doer" rather than a "dreamer," she ends up in wistful reverie over Harlem in its heyday and her youth.

Sonny, a natural hustler and Dorine's great love. He meets her in Cleveland when he is twenty-five and she is fourteen. For a time, he is Dorine's lover and pimp, but Sonny soon makes it clear that he cannot be domesticated. All shiny surface, Sonny pops in and out of Dorine's life; unknown to him, he has already fathered a son by her. When he dies from a heart attack, Sonny is eulogized as "Mr. Harlem."

Big H, a "bookish" club owner and numbers racketeer and Dorine's second major love interest. A West Indian by heritage, Big H is an economic force in Harlem and the political and intellectual confidant of W. E. B. Du Bois. Attracting the attention of the Dutch Schultz gang, Big H is kidnapped and held for ransom; after his return, he is never quite the same, and the "kingdom" of Harlem is taken over by white mobsters.

Harry Brisbane, a failed West Indian restaurateur who is Dorine's third love. After the closing of his café, The Rising Sun, Harry finds himself pursued by Dorine. He is gratified to discover that Dorine is illiterate, and he is happy for a time to be her teacher, accountant, and chauffeur. Miffed by his economic idealism, however, Dorine forces Harry to confront the illegal source of their income by making him witness one of her thefts. Dorine and he fight more and more; eventually, Harry is committed to a mental hospital, where he dies.

— *S. Thomas Mack*

MEDEA
(Mēdeia)

Author: Euripides (c. 485-406 B.C.E.)
First performed: 431 B.C.E.
Genre: Drama

Locale: Corinth
Time: Antiquity
Plot: Tragedy

Medea (mih-DEE-uh), a princess of Colchis and the wife of Jason. Medea had aided Jason in avoiding the traps laid for him by her father, King Aeetes of Colchis, while regaining the Golden Fleece. Fleeing with Jason, she had murdered her own brother to aid in the escape. In Jason's hereditary kingdom of Iolcus, where they first settled but where Pelias, Jason's uncle, had cheated him of his rights, Medea tricked the daughters of

Pelias into murdering their father. For this deed, Medea, Jason, and their two children were exiled. The play is set in Corinth, where they went after leaving Iolcus and where Jason has put Medea aside so that he can marry Glauce, the daughter of Creon, the king of Corinth. It is at this point that the action of the play begins. The dramatic development, centering around Medea, is perhaps the finest example in Greek drama of character development. Medea changes from a woman overwhelmed with sorrow at her husband's desertion to a woman dominated by a fury of revenge in which every other feeling, even love for her children, is sacrificed to a desire to hurt Jason. The opening situation of the play concerns a sympathetic presentation of the sorrowful plight of Medea. She has given up home and position for Jason and can belong to no other except through him; these facts are conveyed by the nurse before Medea appears. Medea cries out violently against Jason before she appears and foreshadows the destruction of the children. When she appears, she is proud but courteous and self-possessed. She expresses her ills as those of all women, but greater, and she asks the Chorus not to betray her if she finds the means of vengeance. They promise secrecy. Creon appears to pronounce a sentence of exile on Medea and the children because he is afraid of her power as a sorceress. She is able only to convince him to grant her a one-day respite. When Creon leaves, Medea reveals her more barbaric and violent side in a terrible speech in which she decides to poison Creon and his daughter. At the appearance of Jason, Medea reveals her full fury as a betrayed mistress and becomes less sympathetic. Blinded by jealousy, she exhibits passion unchecked and untamed. Aegeus, the king of Athens, suddenly appears and promises refuge to Medea if she can make her way to his city alone. Assured of a place of refuge, she calls Jason to her and, feigning sweetness and repentance, forgives him, asking only that he obtain a pardon for the children through the princess, his wife. She then gives them a poisoned robe and a golden crown to present to the princess, and they leave. When the children return, the struggle between Medea's love for them and her passion for revenge reaches a height in a speech in which the latter triumphs. A messenger enters with news of the death of the princess and Creon, and Medea enters the house. Immediately, the screams of the children are heard.

Jason enters and Medea appears above the house, in a chariot supplied by her grandfather Helios, god of the sun, with the bodies of her children. She has destroyed the house of Jason, and her revenge is complete.

Jason, the king of Iolcus, the incarnation of a moderation and wisdom that are negative, not rooted in emotion. He is presented first as the faithless husband and is unreservedly condemned by the Chorus and servants. He loves neither Medea nor Creon's daughter. His only passion is his love for his children, which arouses some sympathy for him.

The two children of Medea and Jason, silent except for their offstage screams as they are murdered. They are central to the plot as Medea's only successful means of revenge against Jason.

Creon (KREE-on), the king of Corinth. His sentence of exile expresses the fear of Medea's power as a sorceress.

Aegeus (EE-jews), the king of Athens, who offers Medea a place of refuge. His appearance is a coincidence, but it provides a glimpse of Medea as she was before the disaster, a princess renowned for wisdom. The scene also emphasizes the child-motive: Aegeus had gone to Delphi because he is childless, and thus he already is in the position in which Jason is left at the end of the play.

A nurse, Medea's devoted servant. Desperately anxious, she identifies herself completely with the cause of her mistress. She speaks the prologue.

A Chorus of Corinthian women, sympathetic to the suffering of Medea. They swear secrecy to her revenge, though they realize the horror of the means.

The tutor to Medea's children, a good and faithful slave. He clearly condemns Jason's conduct.

A messenger, who brings the news of the death of Creon and his daughter.

A MEDITATION
(Una meditación)

Author: Juan Benet (1927-1993)
First published: 1970
Genre: Novel

Locale: Región and elsewhere in northwestern Spain
Time: The 1920's to the 1960's
Plot: Antistory

The narrator, the main character, a member of a conservative family and observer of the history of Región during the 1920's and the 1930's, a crucial period during which Región, as a microcosm of Spain, is preparing for a civil war. He relies on memory to present, again and again, some facts and characters that change and become distorted by time.

Mary, the cousin of the narrator. She is the only member of his clan who crosses the boundary that separates his family from the house of the Ruan family, another powerful clan of Región. Mary weds Julian, the instructor of the Ruan children. Julian is a republican who goes into exile after the Spanish Civil War. In the United States, Mary divorces Julian and marries a physician, with whom she goes back to Región, where she lives for a while with her former family, with the Ruan family, and at their new home. After Mary's death, the house is abandoned by her husband.

Emilio Ruiz (eh-MEE-lee-oh rrew-EES), the fiancé of Mary's eldest sister. A rich landowner and the owner of a mine,

he is a conservative who becomes—without marrying Mary's sister—the leader of her conservative family. He succeeds in alienating Mary and her new husband.

Jorge Ruan (HOHR-heh RREW-ahn), the elder of the Ruan family, who cares for Mary when she comes back and is abandoned by her family.

Enrique Ruan (ehn-REE-keh), a poet who dies at the end of the Spanish Civil War. A small gathering of friends makes a pilgrimage to the Ruans' family dwelling to put a stone there in memory of him.

Muerte (MWEHR-teh), the owner of an inn that doubles as a brothel, where Emilio Ruiz stays when he visits his mine.

Provocación (proh-voh-kah-see-OHN), a daughter of Anhelo and sister of Perturbación—or Persecución, as she is also called on occasion. Provocación is a prostitute in Barcelona who comes to the inn to spend her summer vacation and stay with her sister.

Cayetano Corral (ki-yeh-TAH-noh), a member of another

Región family and friend of the narrator. He ends up in a solitary house trying to repair a clock.

Carlos Bonaval (boh-nah-VAHL), a member of another Región family, supposedly an enemy clan of the narrator's family because one of its members is alleged to have stolen the formula of a liquor that was the pride of the narrator's family.

The Numa (NEW-mah), the mythical guardian or vigilante of the region. People feel protected under his shadow. He kills trespassers and, although nobody has seen him, maintains order in his domain and enforces a strict law against all intruders.

— *Jaime Ferran*

MEEK HERITAGE
(Hurskas kurjuus)

Author: Frans Eemil Sillanpää (1888-1964)
First published: 1919
Genre: Novel

Locale: Finland
Time: 1857-1917
Plot: Impressionistic realism

Jussi Toivola (JUHS-see toy-VOH-lah), also called **Juha** and **Janne**, the shy, inept, simpleminded, and disreputable hero. More a victim than a master of his circumstances, Jussi is swept along through his life and changes names as frequently as he changes dwellings. A Finnish peasant, he is born of a minor landholder and a third wife. His childhood is uneventful, broken only by his father's cruelty and games on Pig Hill. He is still a youth when his father dies. He and his mother go to live with her brother, a well-to-do landholder. After his mother's death, he herds cattle until he is thrown out by his uncle for his part in a practical joke. As a young man, he takes up logging for seven years under a peculiar but kindly boss. Later, he becomes a farmhand, marries a serving girl, and sets up as a crofter with an acre of his own. He has five children and achieves marginal prosperity. His horse then dies, his eldest son virtually kills a younger brother and moves away, his wife dies of a mysterious ailment, and his eldest daughter leaves home and drowns herself soon afterward. Jussi, now a poor old man, becomes known as a rabble-rouser. Taking part in a Socialist revolution, he is left to guard a landowner who is killed during the looting. When the Socialists are defeated, he is arrested, judged, and shot. His wastrel life ends in a common grave with other revolutionaries.

Rina Toivola, Jussi's wife, a loose, easygoing farm girl. She sleeps across from him when he comes to work as a farmhand at Pirjola. One evening, she lets him sleep with her because she needs a husband for her illegitimate child. She is a lax housekeeper for Jussi but bears five children. Worn out and embittered from years of poverty, drudgery, and family misfortune, she dies attended by her eldest daughter.

Benjamin Nikila (NIH-kih-lah), Jussi's father. Old and prurient, he marries a servant girl who bears him Jussi. An adept tobacco chewer and wife beater, he initiates Jussi into the harshness of life. Having mortgaged his home during a famine, he dies before the place is taken.

Kalle Toivola (KAHL-leh), Rina's strange, illegitimate son. After crippling his brother, he moves to the city and becomes a cabbie. He joins the Socialists, sends his father newspapers,

and leads a group during a Socialist uprising.

Hilda Toivola, Jussi's eldest daughter, a spiritless girl in whom childishness and old age are sadly mixed. After watching her mother die and being sent to serve a well-to-do family, she drowns herself.

Ville Toivola (VIHL-leh), Jussi's liveliest son. He is injured by Kalle and never recovers.

Lempi and

Martin, Jussi's youngest children. Neglected and waiflike, they are forced to fend for themselves. They are found crying and helpless after Jussi's arrest.

Maja Nikila (MAH-zhah), Jussi's gentle mother. Thinking to improve her station as a servant girl, she marries Benjamin and bears him a son. She is rewarded finally with nothing but a hard and weary death.

Keinonen (ki-NOH-nehn), the puzzling gang boss of the lumberjacks under whom Jussi works. He sees that Jussi keeps his pay from the greedy Toivolas. After his death, Jussi becomes a farmhand.

Kalle and

Emma Tuorila (tew-ohr-IHL-ah), the uncle and aunt with whom Jussi goes to live after his father's death. Never welcome in their home, he is thrown out after a practical joke by one of his friends.

Gustav Toivola, the friend who plays the joke and then turns on Jussi when he comes to stay at Toivola.

Mina Toivola, Gustav's avaricious, shrewish mother, who tries to cheat Jussi of wages earned as a lumberjack.

The master of Pirjola (pur-JOH-luh), the tough, prosperous farmer for whom Jussi works after his foresting job. He dislikes Jussi but lends him money.

Rinne (RIHN-nuh), the Socialist organizer in Jussi's community.

Pa Ollila (ohl-LI-lah), the landowner who collects on Benjamin's unpaid mortgage.

Lovisa (loh-VEE-sah), the bullying cupperwoman who assists Jussi's birth.

Manda, a high-spirited farm girl whom Jussi once liked.

THE MEETING AT TELGTE
(Das Treffen in Telgte)

Author: Günter Grass (1927-   )
First published: 1979
Genre: Novel

Locale: The town of Telgte in Westphalia, Germany
Time: May, 1647
Plot: Historical

Simon Dach (dahkh), a professor of poetry in Königsberg (Germany) and an important poet in his own right. He organizes the meeting of poets in 1647, originally to be held in Osnabrück but forced to be held in the small village of Telgte because Osnabrück is full of soldiers. Dach, a moderate but decisive man, has decided to gather German poets from all over Europe to hold a disputation and conference. In reality, this meeting never took place. The novel commemorates the founding of the postwar German literary group, Group 47. Dach represents the founder of Group 47, Hans Werner Richter.

Christoffel Gelnhausen (gehln-HOW-zehn), who is modeled after German satirist Hans Jakob Christoffel von Grimmelshausen, who wrote the famous picaresque novel *Simplicissimus* (1668). In the novel, Gelnhausen (taking his name from the town where Grimmelshausen was born) is an imperial officer who helps the gathered poets move to Telgte and who considers himself somewhat of a poet and thinker. He is portrayed as a bit of a buffoon and a windbag.

Heinrich Albert (HIN-rihkh), a composer and organist, friend of Simon Dach, and leading figure in the circle of poets in Königsberg. He arrives at Telgte with his friend, Heinrich Schütz, who is considered the best church composer of his time. Albert introduces Schütz to the poets; Schütz comes merely to listen to the poets read and dispute.

Libuschka (lih-BEWSH-kah), also known as **Courage**, the landlady at the Bridge Tavern, the inn in Telgte where the poets and writers find refuge. A buxom and hearty person, she enjoys the company of the poets and herself is able to quote often from their works. She and Gelnhausen are closely allied. Her nickname of Courage (supposedly she is the original for Bertolt Brecht's Mother Courage) comes from her experiences during the Thirty Years' War, which is now coming to an end. She has also been mentioned in Grimmelshausen's book *Life Story of the Archtraitress and Rowdy Courasche*.

Philipp von Zesen (fon TSEH-zehn), a prominent poet and novelist, one of the few professional writers of his time able to live by his pen. A somewhat testy and nervous person, he takes part in the discussions at the tavern as one who is interested in purifying the German language. He is the most excitable one at the meeting and the noisiest.

Paul Gerhardt (GEHR-hahrt), a Lutheran minister, renowned as a hymnist (many of his hymns are still in use). He joins the meeting as a religious poet and is constantly angered by the bawdiness of some of the poets. He is a good friend of Dach and Albert. When the meeting ends, he goes off with them.

Andreas Gryphius (ahn-DRAY-ahs GRI-fee-uhs), a poet and dramatist, one of the most famous German poets of the seventeenth century. A skeptic and a brilliant scholar, he traveled all over Europe searching for work. Gryphius, who was a Lutheran, also wrote hymns that are still sung today. At the meeting, Gryphius is both moody and witty. He reads from his dramas in a stentorian voice and impresses many with his sincere expression; others are put to sleep by his reading. Gryphius deplores the weakness and frailty of human beings.

— *Philip Brantingham*

MELMOTH THE WANDERER

Author: Charles Robert Maturin (1780-1824)
First published: 1820
Genre: Novel

Locale: Ireland
Time: Early nineteenth century
Plot: Gothic

John Melmoth, a young Irishman who inherits his uncle's property, including a portrait of an early ancestor, which he is directed to destroy. He discovers a manuscript that tells about Melmoth the Wanderer, who visits John. Then a shipwrecked Spaniard tells of visitations of Melmoth the Wanderer. The Wanderer appears to John to tell him that he has finished his earthly pilgrimage of a century and a half. John hears strange noises in the night, and the next morning, his dread kinsman is gone.

John Melmoth's Uncle, who, though not a superstitious man, believes a stranger has been lurking about his house. He dies and leaves his property to his nephew with instructions to destroy a hidden portrait of an earlier John Melmoth.

Melmoth the Wanderer, a seventeenth century ancestor of young John Melmoth, also named John. He is doomed to wander the earth for a century and a half while trying to seduce souls to Satan. He wins not one soul in that time. Finally, he returns to his home in Ireland. He ends his life by plunging, or being thrown, over a cliff.

Mr. Stanton, an Englishman who leaves a manuscript telling the strange story of Melmoth the Wanderer. Stanton met the Wanderer in Spain, angered him, and was cursed. Because of the curse, Stanton was confined in Bedlam as a madman; he was visited by the Wanderer, who offered to secure Stanton's release from the asylum if Stanton would sell his soul to Satan. Stanton refused.

Alonzo Moncada, a Spaniard shipwrecked near the Melmoth home. While imprisoned by the Inquisition, he was approached by the Wanderer, who offered freedom in exchange for Moncada's soul. Moncada refused, but he later escaped prison anyway.

An Old Jewish Doctor, who makes a study of the history of the Wanderer. He tells Moncada about the daughter of Don Francisco di Aliaga, who was shipwrecked as an infant and grew up on an uninhabited island where she was visited by the Wanderer and fell in love with him. After she was found and returned home, the Wanderer visited her again, and they were married in a Satanic ceremony. Found out, she was turned over to the Inquisition. She died shortly after giving birth to the Wanderer's child. Her dying words expressed the hope that both she and the Wanderer would enter Heaven.

THE MEMBER OF THE WEDDING

Author: Carson McCullers (1917-1967)
First published: 1946
Genre: Drama

Locale: Georgia
Time: August, 1945
Plot: Impressionistic realism

Frankie Addams, a confident yet naïve tomboy. The twelve-year-old is conscious of her height (five feet, six inches) and has had her hair shaved off, though it has grown to resemble a boy's. She is uneasy about her developing sensuality, her family relationships, and social behavior, especially among adults, servants, and other adolescents. Recently, she has been evicted from a movie house for booing a romantic film and has been rejected as a member of a local girls' club. The motherless blonde girl decides to become a member of her brother's wedding party in an attempt to end her loneliness and to become someone of consequence. She is dreamy and restless, and she lives in fantasy.

Berenice Sadie Brown, a stout, motherly black cook. First married at the age of thirteen, she has had four husbands in her forty-five years and is a philosophical observer of the community about her, both black and white. She has a flat face and one blue glass eye that sometimes bothers her (at which times she removes it and uses a black eye-patch); nevertheless, she does not seem to be a grotesque, for her motherly role and characteristics are dominant. She alone has authority with Frankie and tells her that she must grow up; she is regarded by the black community as its matriarch.

Royal Addams, Frankie's widowed father. A small-town jeweler, he is a deliberate and absentminded man of about forty-five, set in his ways and old-fashioned in look and manner. He is conservative in outlook, unmindful of his responsibility for Frankie's social and personal development; he has never spanked her. He has allowed Berenice to be his surrogate as a parent. He spends long hours at his store, and when he is home, he does not seem to hear much of what Frankie says to him.

Jarvis Addams, Frankie's brother, a good-looking twenty-one-year-old soldier. He is somewhat embarrassed because he has brought his fiancée, Janice, to be married at his home and Frankie does not understand the proprieties of a wedding.

Janice Williams, Jarvis' fiancée, a pretty, fresh-looking girl of between eighteen and nineteen. She has a pleasing personality and is sensitive to Frankie's sense of alienation; she assures Frankie that she and Jarvis love her and want her to visit them after their wedding trip. She is eager to be accepted by her new family.

T. T. Williams, a friend of Berenice. A large and pompous-looking black man of about fifty, he dresses like a church deacon, wearing a black suit and a red emblem in his lapel. He is timid and overly polite, having experienced the worst aspects of race relations, yet he is a guardian of Berenice's foster brother, Honey Camden Brown, and collects donations for the funeral of Sis Laura, the vegetable vendor who dies.

Honey Camden Brown, Berenice's foster brother. A slender, limber black man of about twenty, he is a foil to T. T. Williams: He is light brown in skin color; wears bright, fashionable clothes; and is either brusque or speaks in a manner that combines hostility and teasing. His having been "left out" of society has made him mean, Berenice thinks. Only reluctantly does he "yes, sir" Royal Addams; he is tired of being called a nigger. When he is refused service, he draws a razor, then is hunted down. Ironically, he declares that he is happy now because he is free of a sense of inferiority, but he is caught and hangs himself in jail.

John Henry "Candy" West, Frankie's seven-year-old cousin. He is a delicate, active boy who wears gold-rimmed spectacles that give him the look of a judge. He is sunburned, fair-haired, and usually barefoot. Although he is much younger than Frankie, he is in many ways more mature; he is certainly more realistic and more perspicacious about matters of race, class, and status. His death from meningitis the same week that Honey commits suicide affects Frankie: She senses his presence, "solemn-looking and ghost gray," but also senses her loss, which she tries to compensate for by befriending Barney MacKean.

— *Marian B. McLeod*

MEMED, MY HAWK
(İnce Memed)

Author: Yashar Kemal (Yaşar Kemal Gökçeli, 1922-   )
First published: 1955
Genre: Novel

Locale: Turkey
Time: Probably the 1940's
Plot: Folklore

İnce Memed, or Slim Memed, a young man who is eighteen years old when he takes up his calling. During the difficult early years of his life, when he experienced beatings and privations, he became physically stunted and somewhat gnarled; he never grew to his full height. He has developed into a hardened, bitter young man who nevertheless can manage an ironically cheerful smile much of the time. He falls deeply in love with Hatçe, and his attachment to her leads to a violent confrontation with Abdi Ağa and his minions. Memed becomes an outlaw, but of a special sort; rather than subjecting innocent wayfarers to suffering and indignities, he decides to avenge acts of oppression and injustice Abdi has perpetrated. Toward the end, he rejoins Hatçe and marries her. She is killed in a gun battle. In a final act of bold defiance, he rides up to his rival's house and shoots Abdi dead.

Deuneh, Memed's mother. She grows wheat and is compelled, at a rate more unfavorable than that imposed on others, to turn three-fourths of her crop over to Abdi. When Memed and Hatçe run away from the authorities, Abdi and Veli trample Deuneh to death.

Hatçe, a young woman. After an adolescent courtship, she becomes Memed's lover. At about the age of sixteen, she leaves Veli, her nominal betrothed, behind; when fighting erupts, she is captured by Abdi's men and accused, falsely, of murder. After Memed rescues her from captivity, she remains with him and becomes his wife. She gives birth to his infant son but later is killed during an armed confrontation.

Abdi Ağa, a powerful local landowner. He has a long, sharp face; small, calculating eyes; and pink cheeks, as well as whiskers that have brought him the disparaging epithet of "goat beard" among the villagers. He is unusually cruel and grasping even by the standards of such potentates. He demands rental in kind that reduces his tenants to penury, and he feels few qualms about beating and kicking those who will not yield easily to his demands. He is also capable of craven manipulations to bring about the perversion of justice; he recruits witnesses who will perjure themselves in an effort to show that Hatçe, whom he holds in prison, actually killed his nephew. He hires various desperados and unsavory characters for the purpose of reducing Memed to submission. He is taken by surprise when his youthful opponent finally kills him.

Veli, Abdi's nephew. Hatçe's parents are induced to offer Hatçe to Veli in marriage, but Memed kills Veli before the marriage can take place.

Mad Durdu, a well-known bandit. He is relatively young, but his features seem twisted with the wrinkles and long reddish scar that are the most distinctive parts of his appearance. Durdu takes an unseemly delight in forcing travelers to undress, and he imposes this treatment indiscriminately on those who are unfortunate enough to encounter him. Memed joins him for a time, but later he and others rebel against this practice. Durdu dies ignominiously during a conflict elsewhere.

Sergeant Recep, a man over fifty years old. Although much about his past is murky, it is known that he has operated as a bandit for some time. Memed meets him with Durdu. Later, Recep assists the young outlaw in various ways, until he dies from wounds received in one encounter.

Kerimoğlu, a nomad leader. He receives Durdu hospitably but protests when he is robbed and told to turn over his own underwear. Memed comes to his support, and they force Durdu to back down.

Ali Safa Bey, a former lawyer who has given up his practice. He is adept at obtaining title to land through underhanded pretexts, and he later becomes associated with Abdi Ağa in various schemes.

Kalaycı Osman, a local outlaw who has connections with Ali Safa Bey. His main claim to infamy is the murder of some forty men, including the killing of his own cousin on the man's wedding night. Abdi Ağa enlists him during his campaign against Memed, but Kalaycı Osman is mortally wounded instead.

İraz, a woman whom Hatçe addresses as an aunt. She is imprisoned as a result of Abdi's machinations, but she assists in Hatçe's escape from her captors, and she aids Memed during the later fighting with Abdi's men. She proves to be stalwart and courageous under difficult conditions.

Sergeant Asım, a local police officer. Because during an earlier clash Memed had spared his life, he will not accept the outlaw's surrender when the child of Memed and Hatçe is born.

— *J. R. Broadus*

MEMENTO MORI

Author: Muriel Spark (1918-　　)
First published: 1959
Genre: Novel

Locale: London, England
Time: The 1950's
Plot: Psychological realism

Dame Lettie Colston, an elderly pioneer penal reformer and Godfrey Colston's sister. She resents the caregiving she and Godfrey must provide for Godfrey's wife, Charmian. Recently, Dame Lettie has begun to receive phone calls from an anonymous man who tells her, "Remember, you must die." The police can find no leads. She becomes increasingly agitated, fearful, and even obsessed. At the home of retired police inspector Henry Mortimer, she meets with others who have received similar calls, but nothing is settled. Dame Lettie remains terrified and refuses to leave her house. Through a bizarre series of circumstances, someone breaks into her house, steals jewelry, and bludgeons Dame Lettie to death when she confronts him.

Godfrey Colston, a former chairman of Colston Breweries and Dame Lettie's brother. Many years ago, he had an affair with Lisa Brooke. His wife, Charmian, is recovering from a stroke. His housekeeper, Mrs. Pettigrew, blackmails him when she uncovers the secret of his affair. When he learns that Charmian also carried on an affair, he no longer fears Mrs. Pettigrew's threats.

Charmian Colston, Godfrey's wife. She is a famous novelist (also known as **Charmian Piper**) now suffering episodes of dementia after a stroke. For several years after her marriage to Godfrey, she carried on an affair with Guy Leet. As the story progresses, her mental capacity is restored. She decides to move to a nursing home rather than stay with Godfrey.

Jean Taylor, a companion for many years to Charmian. She enjoyed her years with Charmian, surrounded by a rich cultural and aesthetic life. Now Jean is one of the twelve residents in Maud Long Medical Ward, a long-term care facility. Jean suffers from the advanced stages of arthritis, but she is sound of mind. She never married, although many years ago she was in love with Alec Warner. Jean is the confidante of Dame Lettie Colston, who often visits her and shares her fears about a mysterious caller. Jean offers several penetrating insights about the state of old age.

Mabel Pettigrew, the elderly housekeeper for Dame Lettie Colston and her brother Godfrey. Mrs. Pettigrew is a selfish and scheming woman. She blackmailed her former employer, Lisa Brooke, and forced her to bequeath her entire estate to her. When the will is contested by Miss Brooke's brother and family, Mrs. Pettigrew begins to blackmail her new employer, Godfrey Colston. That plan backfires, but eventually she inherits Lisa Brooke's estate and enjoys a comfortable old age.

Alec Warner, a former sociologist and, since his seventieth birthday, an amateur gerontologist. In his youth, he had an affair with Jean Taylor, but he gave her up because she was from a lower social class. He became engaged to Dame Lettie, but they were incompatible and never married. He spends his time compiling detailed records on the physical condition, behaviors, and attitudes of many of his old friends. He often visits Olive Mannering, who provides him with information based on her contacts with old people. Coming home one night, he discovers that his apartment has caught fire. All of his records are consumed in the flames.

Guy Leet, a poet and former lover of Charmian Piper. He secretly married Lisa Brooke in order to put an end to Lisa's blackmailing of Charmian. Lisa knew of Charmian and Guy's affair. Now he is an arthritic old man hunched over two canes. It appears that he stands to inherit Lisa's estate, but eventually his claim is denied when it is learned that Lisa Brooke already had been married to another man.

Percy Mannering, a former poet. He loves to argue with Guy Leet over issues of poetry and poetic reputations. When he receives a phone call from the mysterious caller, he is exhilarated and inspired to write a sonnet. He ends his days in a nursing home.

Olive Mannering, a granddaughter of poet Percy Mannering. She is sympathetic toward Godfrey Colston's son Eric, who is estranged from his parents. She is also one of Alec Warner's contacts, providing him with information for his gerontological research. Olive marries newly widowed Ronald Sidebottome, and she faithfully visits her grandfather, Percy, when he is admitted to a nursing home.

Henry Mortimer, a retired chief inspector of police. He meets with the principal characters after many of them have been contacted by the mystery caller. He tries to defuse their irrational fears. After they leave, he admits that he has been receiving the same calls himself, but his caller has a woman's voice.

— *Robert E. Yahnke*

MEMOIRS OF A CAVALIER: Or, A Military Journal of the Wars in Germany, and the Wars in England, from the Year 1632 to the Year 1648

Author: Daniel Defoe (1660-1731)
First published: 1720
Genre: Novel

Locale: England and the Continent
Time: 1630-1648
Plot: Adventure

The Cavalier, the second son of a landed gentleman. As a student at Oxford, he realizes that he has no taste for the academic life, the law, the Church, or medicine, and he receives his father's permission to travel on the Continent. With his companion, Captain Fielding, he observes or takes part in campaigns in Germany, where he witnesses the terrible siege of Magdeburg; in Sweden, where he serves in the Swedish forces and is a special attendant to the king; and in Holland, where he observes the Dutch in their fight against the Spanish. Returning to England, he enters the service of Charles I against the Scots and serves the royalist cause in the English Civil War. With the royalist defeat, he retires, content to have

served king, country, and honor to the best of his ability.

Captain Fielding, the Cavalier's friend and traveling companion.

Sir John Hepburn, the Cavalier's friend in the Swedish forces.

Gustavus Adolphus, the king of Sweden, to whom the Cavalier becomes a special attendant, serving sometimes as his emissary. The king loses his life in the battle of Lützen.

Charles I, the king of England, who is served by the Cavalier in his campaign against the Scots and in the English Civil War.

MEMOIRS OF A FOX-HUNTING MAN

Author: Siegfried Sassoon (1886-1967)
First published: 1928
Genre: Novel

Locale: England and France
Time: 1895-1916
Plot: Social

George Sherston, an orphan. He is reared by his aunt. His skill with horses gains him entry into high society, a life he cannot afford. He also excels as a cricket player. World War I finds him refusing a commission because he distrusts his ability. After serving in the cavalry, he ends up as an infantry officer fighting bravely but angrily as he sees his friends killed. This character is a thinly veiled portrait of the author.

Aunt Evelyn, who rears George. She buys him his first pony when he is nine years old and later sells a ring to buy him a jumper, Cockbird.

Tom Dixon, Evelyn's groom and George's riding teacher, who is killed in George's infantry company in France.

Mr. Star, George's incompetent tutor.

Mr. Pennett, George Sherston's penurious and unsympathetic trustee.

Denis Milden, George's boyhood friend and later Master of the Ringwell Hounds and the Packlestone Hunt.

Stephen Colwood, an excellent horseman killed in France during the war.

Nigel Croplady, a wealthy braggart. He is defeated by George, with Stephen's encouragement, in the Colonel's Cup Race.

Captain Huxtable, a neighbor who gets George an infantry commission.

Dick Tiltwood, a young soldier in George's company. He is killed in the trenches.

MEMOIRS OF A MIDGET

Author: Walter de la Mare (1873-1956)
First published: 1921
Genre: Novel

Locale: England
Time: Late nineteenth century
Plot: Fantasy

Miss M., a pretty midget. Reared in seclusion, she first goes into the world after her parents die, when she is eighteen years old. She finds that some people accept her as a person and that others look upon her as a mere curiosity. In financial straits, she hires herself out to a circus and has several unfortunate experiences. Through a legacy, she finally becomes financially independent and settles down with Mrs. Bowater as her housekeeper. One night, she disappears mysteriously and is never seen again.

Mrs. Monnerie, a wealthy woman who becomes Miss M.'s patroness. She treats the midget like a little child and, when her use for the midget is over, discards the tiny girl for a new favorite. She gives Miss M. the nickname of Midgetina.

Mrs. Bowater, Miss M.'s erstwhile landlady. A stern woman, she nevertheless shows great affection for the midget. When Miss M. gains financial independence, Mrs. Bowater becomes her housekeeper.

Mr. Anon, a dwarf. He becomes Miss M.'s friend and falls in love with her. To save her embarrassment before her friends and acquaintances, he takes her place in a pony-riding act and is mortally injured by a fall from a pony.

Fanny Bowater, Mrs. Bowater's daughter and for a time Miss M.'s friend. Becoming a favorite of Mrs. Monnerie, she replaces Miss M.

Lady Pollacke, a true friend of Miss M. She tries to help the midget find a place for herself in the world.

Sir Walter Pollacke, Lady Pollacke's husband. Like his wife, he tries to help the midget. He becomes her guardian and financial adviser.

Percy Maudlen, a languid, ill-mannered young man, Mrs. Monnerie's nephew. Miss M. dislikes him.

Susan Monnerie, a niece of Mrs. Monnerie. She is a friend to Miss M.

Lord B., Mrs. Monnerie's father.

MEMOIRS OF A PHYSICIAN
(Mémoires d'un médecin)

Authors: Alexandre Dumas, *père* (1802-1870), with Auguste Maquet (1813-1888)
First published: 1846-1848
Genre: Novel

Locale: Paris and its environs
Time: The eighteenth century
Plot: Historical

Joseph Balsamo (zhoh-SEHF bahl-sah-MOH), the **Count de Fenix** (deh fay-NEEKS), a revolutionary and practitioner of magic. Involved in machinations at the court of Louis XV, he is able, through sorcery, to gather information to further the plots in which he becomes engaged.

Lorenza Feliciani (loh-REHN-zah feh-lee-SYAH-nee), Joseph Balsamo's wife and the unwilling medium for his sorcery until her death at the hands of Althotas.

Madame Jeanne du Barry (zhahn dew bah-REE), the favorite of Louis XV and the ally of the duc de Richelieu and Joseph Balsamo in an attempt to unseat M. de Choiseul as the king's minister.

Armand (ahr-MAH[N]), **duc de Richelieu** (dewk deh reesh-LYEW), a political opportunist who, with the aid of Madame du Barry and compromising information gotten through the sorceries of Joseph Balsamo, forces Louis XV to dismiss his minister, M. de Choiseul.

M. de Choiseul (deh shwah-ZEWL), Louis XV's minister, who is dismissed on the strength of information gathered through the necromancy of Joseph Balsamo.

Althotas (ahl-toh-TAS), Joseph Balsamo's instructor in

magic. He kills Lorenza Feliciani by drawing from her the blood needed for an elixir of youth. When the vial containing the liquid is broken, he sets fire to his manuscripts and perishes with them in the flames.

Andrée (ahn-DRAY), a young girl saved from the violence of the mob and, later, hypnotized by Joseph Balsamo and forced to give information useful to his sinister purposes. She finally retires to a convent.

Baron de Taverney (deh tah-vehr-NAY), Andrée's impoverished father.

Philippe (fee-LEEP), Andrée's brother.

Gilbert (zheel-BEHR), a young proletarian in love with Andrée, whom he has rescued from mob violence.

Louis XV (lwee), king of France.

Jean Jacques Rousseau (zhahn zhahk rew-SOH), the philosopher.

M. de Sartines (deh sahr-TEEN), the lieutenant of police.

The Duchess of Grammont (grah-MOH[N]), M. de Choiseul's sister.

Nicole (nee-KOHL), Andrée's maid.

Marat (mah-RAH), a surgeon.

MEMOIRS OF AN INFANTRY OFFICER

Author: Siegfried Sassoon (1886-1967)
First published: 1930
Genre: Novel

Locale: France and England
Time: 1916-1917
Plot: Social

George Sherston, who is transformed from "a fox-hunting man" to an officer in World War I. He is ordered to plan a raid for his soldiers without taking part in the fighting. Later, an attack of enteritis removes him from dangerous duty. Finally, however, he gets into the Battle of Arras and is wounded. Back in England, he writes a critical letter to his superiors. He expects to be court-martialed, but they refuse to take the letter seriously. When he resignedly recants, he is sent back to the battlefield.

Aunt Evelyn, who reared the orphan George and now thinks him safe in the transport service. She upsets him with her worry about his safety.

Colonel Kinjack, who believes Sherston is cracking up following the Battle of the Somme and has him assigned to an army school.

Tyrrell, a pacifist philosopher who helps Sherston compose his defiant letter to Colonel Kinjack.

Major O'Brien, a friend of Sherston and a casualty in a minor raid that is exaggerated in the London papers.

Kendle, who is killed at Sherston's side by a sniper.

David Cromlech, an iconoclast and fellow fighter at the Somme. He persuades Sherston to retract his critical statements by pointing out that otherwise he will be put into an insane asylum for the duration.

MEMOIRS OF HADRIAN
(Mémoires d'Hadrien)

Author: Marguerite Yourcenar (Marguerite de Crayencour, 1903-1987)
First published: 1951
Genre: Novel

Locale: Rome and the Roman Empire
Time: Second century A.D.
Plot: Historical realism

Hadrian (HAY-dree-uhn), formally known as **Publius Aelius Hadrianus**, the Roman emperor. Knowing that his death is fast approaching, Hadrian sets down in the most truthful manner possible the important events of his sixty years, along with his meditations on politics, the arts, and the world. Beginning with his Roman schooling, he sees the beauty of philosophy, grammar, and poetry, and their applicability to human affairs. In Rome, he learns Greek and is thus opened to another world and what he sees as an almost perfect mode of thinking and being. He climbs the judicial and military ladder, always learning from even the most mediocre tasks and duties the reasons why and the manner in which people act and behave, as well as developing his own commanding and governing style. The diversity of his aptitudes, an intuitive touch during difficult negotiations, his battlefield skill, personal self-discipline, and interest in barbarian cultures and religions all bring him to the attention of his cousin, Emperor Trajan. Hadrian supremely believes in life and, therefore, in change and movement; open to all situations and human possibilities, he is always ready to react. Following Trajan's death and his accession to the throne at the age of forty, he desires to establish or maintain the Roman order in the world by means of a mix of intelligent compromises, commercial treaties and nonaggression pacts, all-out war, and negotiated peace. His only passion has been for Antinous, a handsome Greco-Asian youth who makes him completely happy, perhaps for the first time. Feeling constricted in this relationship, however, he seeks ways to leave Antinous. When the young man commits suicide, the emperor creates an almost megalomaniacal cult by building cities, temples, and statues in his favorite's memory. No longer charmed by easy pleasures, he also falls into long lapses of melancholy as he turns to thoughts of immortality, interrupted by fits of exasperation, impatience, and anger. During the four-year Jewish rebellion against the Romans in Judaea, Hadrian is confronted with the unsettling discovery that not all countries regard the civilizing influences of Greece and Rome as necessary or even as useful. He is further astonished to realize that other modes of living exist and that there are other relationships with God that reject

his conception of the perfect society, even if this rejection means annihilation and dispersal. It is during the Middle Eastern campaign that he suffers his first heart seizure. The rapid deterioration of his health renders the selection of his successor highly pressing. Having settled on Antoninus, he can live his final days in appeasement.

Antinous (an-TIHN-uh-wuhs), a Bythinian adolescent. Naïve in his innocence and attractive to Hadrian because of his beauty and accented speech, he instills in Hadrian a renewed vitality as both participate in the pursuit of arts and letters. Seeing in the emperor a god and a master, he is concerned with the notion of sacrifice and suicide. When he senses Hadrian's interest waning, he kills himself in a ritual, even religious, act, one in which he finds a secret satisfaction and perhaps a hidden pride. Through his own death, he hopes to prolong Hadrian's life by having the remainder of his earthly years added to the emperor's.

Trajan (TRAY-juhn), formally known as **Marcus Ulpius Traianus**, the previous Roman emperor. Indecisive and bearing a grudge against Hadrian, he waits literally until his dying breath to adopt him and thereby make him the new ruler of an empire threatened on all sides and on the verge of economic collapse after ten years of useless wars.

Plotina, Trajan's wife and an ally of Hadrian. Even before she may have forged her husband's testament naming Hadrian his heir, she is a close, devoted friend of Hadrian, with whom she shares a love for literature, philosophy, and the arts. She also willingly offered support during his professional rise, including his marriage to Sabina, the emperor's grandniece.

Antoninus (an-tuh-NI-nuhs), a virtuous senator and administrator. He is adopted by Hadrian in order to make him emperor, with the order that he, in turn, take Marcus Aurelius as his adopted son.

Sabina, Hadrian's long-suffering wife. Married to a neglectful man, she quickly becomes bitter and shrewish, preferring to live at her country home rather than in the imperial palace. That she often tries to encourage his enemies shows her obvious hatred for him.

— *Pierre L. Horn*

THE MEMORANDUM
(Vyrozumění)

Author: Václav Havel (1936-)
First published: 1966
Genre: Drama

Locale: Prague
Time: Unspecified, post-World War II
Plot: Satire

Josef Gross, the managing director of an anonymous administrative department in a large bureaucratic organization. Stymied by the paralyzing amount of paperwork required by the bureaucracy to effect even the smallest actions, he authorizes the purchase of a new mail register without going through the proper channels. Manipulated by the conniving deputy director for taking this initiative, he gradually becomes enmeshed in a bureaucratic nightmare, in which he will be perceived as guilty of illegal conduct no matter what course of action he chooses. A major source of frustration during this process is his struggle to stem the introduction of a new bureaucratic language called "Ptydepe." Ostensibly intended to make office communications more accurate and precise, this nonsensical artificial language represents the supreme symbol of a faceless, insensitive bureaucratic order with instructions that have the effect of dehumanizing individuals and reducing them to mindless automatons. Outsmarted by his deputy, Gross is coerced first into changing jobs with the deputy and then into resigning because of his hostile attitude toward Ptydepe. After a short stint as the "staff watcher," whose duties consist of monitoring the actions and words of the staff from a secret vantage point, Gross is restored to his original post by the collapse of the pro-Ptydepe movement. Having been returned to his position, however, Gross finds that his authority is essentially a matter of form and not of substance. As the play closes, he finds himself unable to help the sole member of his organization who had shown kindness to him, a secretary named Maria.

Jan Ballas, Gross's manipulative deputy director. Having introduced Ptydepe into the organization surreptitiously, Ballas succeeds in blackmailing Gross to resign from his position, yet he too discovers that power is a fleeting illusion. When Ptydepe proves to be an utter failure, Ballas hands over the reins of power to Gross but continues to use the twin levers of coercion and zeal to remain firmly entrenched in the bureaucracy.

Maria, a secretary at the translation center. Her faithful devotion to the regulations introduced by others finally gives way to simpler and deeper emotions of kindness and sympathy for her harassed superior Gross. After she helps Gross by illegally translating an official memorandum denouncing Ptydepe, she is forced to leave the office staff. Gross feels too cowed by the weight of the bureaucracy to resist her dismissal.

George, the original staff watcher whose position Gross temporarily occupies. He denounces Maria after he overhears her making the unauthorized translation.

Mark Lear, a teacher of Ptydepe. Obsessed with the language and its strange rules, Lear tries to instruct his hapless pupils in the nuances of Ptydepe. A stern instructor, he dismisses anyone who makes a mistake. As a consequence, he eventually ends up teaching to an empty classroom.

Otto Small, the head of the translation center. He will not translate any document written in Ptydepe without authorization from Dr. Savant, the Ptydepe expert. He and Dr. Savant spend much of their time discussing food and women.

Alex Savant, the staff Ptydepe expert. He will not authorize any translation without proper registration documents from Helena, the chair of the translation center.

Helena, the chair of the translation center. She will not issue any registration documents unless a staff member has a memorandum already translated from Ptydepe; thus, the vicious circle of bureaucratic paralysis closes.

— Julian W. Connolly

MEN AND ANGELS

Author: Mary Gordon (1949-)
First published: 1985
Genre: Novel

Locale: Selby, a small college town in Massachusetts
Time: The 1980's
Plot: Family

Laura Post, the dangerously neurotic twenty-two-year-old nanny to the two Foster children. Born to a mother who disliked her from her birth, Laura has spent her short life seeking love. Her mother's withering contempt for Laura and undisguised pleasure in Laura's sister have left Laura emotionally crippled, unable to recognize love or to give it. In her late adolescence, Laura turned to religion and came to believe that she had been visited by the Holy Spirit. She now believes that the Spirit directs her every move and that it has sent her to the house of Anne Foster. In her constant Bible reading, Laura sees God only as a power of wrath and destruction.

Anne Foster, who in her late thirties is a deeply loving mother to her two children and is deeply in love with her husband. She also is driven by her desire to use her intellect and her knowledge of art history. While her husband spends an academic term in France, Anne works at preparing a catalog for a major showing of the paintings of Caroline Watson. The project requires her to hire a live-in baby-sitter. She employs Laura even though she dislikes her (and dislikes herself for feeling that dislike). Like Laura, Anne was born to a mother who preferred her sister, but with the aid of her father's love she has emerged as a joyous, loving woman whose lack of self-confidence is masked by her strong intelligence. Anne is interested in the career of Caroline Watson (a fictional painter modeled somewhat on Mary Cassatt) partly because she likes Watson's paintings but also as a result of her feminist sympathies.

Jane Watson, a medievalist in her seventies, the beloved daughter-in-law of the long-dead painter Carolyn Watson. She now possesses her mother-in-law's letters and diaries, materials that Anne needs to see in order to prepare the catalog. Although Jane can be a dragon, she immediately recognizes the intelligent sensitivity Anne brings to the catalog project. Jane was married to Carolyn's ineffectual son Stephen, but she and Carolyn callously disregarded his needs as they indulged their friendship. Long after Stephen's death, Jane's remorse made her seek forgiveness in Christianity. Jane says of Laura that she has missed the central message of the Gospels—the immensity of God's love for humans.

Michael Foster, Anne's husband, a scholar of nineteenth century French literature. He and Anne had planned to spend his academic leave together in France with their children, but he saw that she longed to accept the catalog assignment and did not want her to miss that opportunity. He loves his wife and children deeply.

Benedict (Ben) Hardy, a London gallery owner who is Jane's lover and Anne's longtime mentor. Years ago, Ben introduced Anne to serious study of art history. He helped get her the assignment of writing the Watson catalog and introduced her to Jane. He is a favorite of Sarah and Peter, the Foster children.

Hélène, Michael's friend and academic mentor. She is self-serving and self-centered. She dislikes Anne and constantly finds ways to belittle her. While Michael is in France, she maliciously suggests to Anne that he has taken on a lover there. It is she who introduces Laura to Anne.

Ed Corcoran, an electrician who is rewiring Anne's house. Anne is drawn to this man, who loves his son the way she loves hers and who treats his difficult brain-damaged wife with care and respect.

— Ann D. Garbett

MEN OF MAIZE
(Hombres de maíz)

Author: Miguel Ángel Asturias (1899-1974)
First published: 1949
Genre: Novel

Locale: Guatemala
Time: The twentieth century
Plot: Social morality

Gaspár Ilóm (GAHS-pahr ee-LOHM), an Indian guerrilla leader poisoned by the Machojóns. He fought against the maize growers, who were destroying the forests. The Indians believed that he rose from the dead to continue to curse those who burn down the forest to cultivate maize as a cash crop instead of treating it as a sacred food.

Piojosa Grande (pee-oh-HOH-sah GRAHN-deh), the "Great Fleabag," the wife of Gaspár Ilóm. She tried unsuccessfully to escape the massacre of her husband's men with their son. According to Indian lore, she is the rain and her son is the maize.

Tomás Machojón (toh-MAHS mah-choh-HOHN), an elderly landowner and maize grower. He believes himself and his son to be under the curse of the firefly wizards for having poisoned Gaspár Ilóm. He makes his peons burn land in the hope that he will see his dead son in the fires. In a fit of madness, he sets the maize fields ablaze. He is consumed in the fire, along with his wife, his men, and his hacienda.

Machojón, the son of Tomás Machojón who died in a fire on his journey to claim the hand of Candelario Reinosa. The peons claim that he appears in the flames whenever the forest is burned to clear the land to plant maize.

Candelario Reinosa (kahn-dehl-LAHR-ee-oh rra-NOH-sah), Machojón's sweetheart. She was convinced that Machojón tried to visit her at night but could not see her.

Colonel Gonzalo "Chalo" Godoy (gohn-SAHL-loh CHAH-loh goh-DOY), the foulmouthed, blue-eyed commander of the Mounted Patrol. The Indians believed that he was cursed by the firefly wizards for having led the massacre of Gaspár Ilóm's men. He died seven years after the massacre in a forest fire that the Indians believe was caused by the Deer of the Seventh Fire.

Goyo Yic (GOH-yoh yeek), an elderly blind Indian beggar abandoned by his wife, María Tecún. After an operation restores his sight, he searches relentlessly for his family, hoping

that he can recognize María Tecún by her voice, because he has never seen her. When he and Domingo Revolorio drink all the liquor they have to sell at a fair, they are arrested and imprisoned on an island off the coast. There, Goyo Yic meets his son and María Tecún. After he and his son are released from prison, he returns with them to their village, Pisigüilito. According to Indian legend, a blind Goyo Yic searched for his family. Upon hearing María Tecún's voice, his sight was restored; he then saw her turn into stone on a ridge that bears her name.

María Tecún (teh-KEWN), the freckled, red-haired wife of Goyo Yic, saved by Goyo Yic when the rest of her family was slaughtered. Not wanting any more children, she abandons her husband. She is reunited with him many years later, when she comes to visit their son in prison. Indian lore maintains that a witchcraft spell makes her leave her husband and turns her into stone.

Dionisio "Nicho" Aquino (dee-oh-NEE-see-oh NEE-choh ah-KEE-noh), the postman of San Miguel Acatán. He neglects his postal duties to search for his missing wife. While searching for her, he experiences being guided through a cave into a fantastic subterranean world by an old man who claims to be a firefly wizard. There, he meets the coyote, who is his *nagual*, or animal protector, and sees Gaspár Ilóm among the Invincible Ones. He realizes that his wife died by falling into a water hole. A fugitive from justice for failing to deliver the town's mail to the capital, he finds work in a hotel on the coast. Through his dealings with the prisoners on the island, he meets Goyo Yic and María Tecún and returns with them to Pisigüilito.

Hilario Sacayón (ee-LAHR-ee-oh sah-kah-YOHN), a mule driver and inventor of stories that become a part of Indian lore. Charged with the task of finding the missing postman, he fails, although he thought he saw Nicho Aquino in the form of a coyote on María Tecún Ridge.

The Deer of the Seventh Fire, who also is identified as the curer and the firefly wizard. When a deer is killed by Gaudencio Tecún, the curer also dies because the deer was the curer's *nagual*. Indian legend holds that it avenged the death of Gaspár Ilóm and the destruction of the land by killing Godoy and destroying the Machojóns.

— *Evelyn Toft*

THE MENAECHMI
(Menaechmi)

Author: Plautus (c. 255-184 B.C.E.)
First performed: The second century B.C.E.
Genre: Drama

Locale: Epidamnum, a city of Macedonia
Time: The third century B.C.E.
Plot: Farce

Menaechmus of Epidamnum (meh-NEEK-muhs of eh-pih-DAM-nuhm), an identical twin. When Menaechmus was a child, Moschus, his father, had taken him to Tarentum on a trading expedition. After the boy wandered away from his father and became lost, he was found and adopted by a citizen of Epidamnum, a city in Asia Minor noted for its sinfulness. By the time the play opens, Menaechmus has married and inherited his foster father's considerable estate. He also has taken up with a courtesan, Erotium. He gives her a robe he has stolen from his wife's closet.

Menaechmus Sosicles (SOS-ih-kleez), the other twin. Proud, witty, and hot-tempered like his brother, Sosicles comes to Epidamnum searching for his long-lost brother. His appearance in the city precipitates a series of comic encounters based on mistaken identity. At last, the two Menaechmi come face to face, and there is a happy reunion. Menaechmus of Epidamnum agrees to sell all his goods, including his wife, and return to Sicily with his brother.

Messenio (meh-SEE-nee-oh), Sosicles' servant. Messenio does everything faithfully and well because he dislikes being beaten. He rescues Menaechmus, whom he mistakes for his master, from four servants who are carrying him off. Menaechmus "frees" him in gratitude. Later, when the twins are reunited, Messenio is freed in earnest and made Menaechmus' auctioneer.

Peniculus (pee-NIH-kuh-luhs), Menaechmus' parasite. A spiteful, gluttonous, and ungrateful hanger-on, Peniculus, seeing Sosicles coming from Erotium's house, thinks Menaechmus has cheated him of a meal. He tells Menaechmus' wife that her husband has stolen her robe, only to learn that the wife will not reward him for his treachery.

The wife of Menaechmus of Epidamnum, a nagging, possessive woman with a passion for keeping her husband under her control. She mistakes Sosicles for her husband, argues with him about her robe, which Sosicles is carrying, and calls on her father to take her home.

An old man, Menaechmus' father-in-law, who chides both his daughter and Menaechmus for their faults. When he mistakes Sosicles for Menaechmus, Sosicles pretends madness as a means of escape. The old man sends a physician and four servants to restrain the madman. They lay hold of a very bewildered Menaechmus but are driven off by Messenio.

Erotium (eh-ROH-shee-uhm), a rather simple-minded courtesan. She entertains Sosicles, mistakes him for Menaechmus, and gives him the stolen robe to take to a tailor. When the real Menaechmus calls and disclaims knowledge of the robe, Erotium thinks he is trying to cheat her and bars him from the house.

An old physician, who is called in by Menaechmus' father-in-law to diagnose Sosicles' supposed madness.

Cylindrus (sih-LIHN-druhs), Erotium's cook, who mistakes Sosicles for Menaechmus and leads him to Erotium's house.

THE MERCHANT OF VENICE

Author: William Shakespeare (1564-1616)
First published: 1600
Genre: Drama

Locale: Venice
Time: The sixteenth century
Plot: Tragicomedy

Shylock (SHI-lok), a rich Jewish moneylender. He hates Antonio for often lending money at lower interest than the usurer demands; hence, when Antonio wishes to borrow three thousand ducats to help Bassanio, Shylock prepares a trap. Seemingly in jest, he persuades Antonio to sign a bond stating that, should the loan not be repaid within three months, a pound of flesh from any part of his body will be forfeited to Shylock. Next, Shylock has bad news when he learns that his daughter, Jessica, has eloped with Lorenzo, taking with her much of his money. He gets good news when he learns that Antonio's ships have been lost at sea. Antonio being ruined and the loan due, Shylock brings the case before the duke. He refuses Bassanio's offer of six thousand ducats and demands his pound of flesh. Portia, Bassanio's wife, disguised as a lawyer, claims that Shylock must have the flesh but can take not a single drop of blood with it. Further, she maintains that Shylock, an alien, has threatened the life of a Venetian; therefore, half of his fortune goes to Antonio, the other half to the state. Shylock is allowed to keep half for Jessica and Lorenzo if he will become a Christian. The character of Shylock has become one of the most controversial in Shakespearean drama. Is he a villain or a tragic figure? Does the author intend the audience to regard him as an example of Jewish malevolence or to sympathize with him as a persecuted man?

Portia (POHR-shuh), an heiress whose father had stipulated in his will that any suitor must win her by choosing from among three caskets of gold, silver, and lead the one containing her portrait. The prince of Morocco and the prince of

Aragon choose respectively the gold and the silver caskets and find only mocking messages; Bassanio, whom she loves, selects the lead casket and wins her. Learning of Antonio's misfortune, she offers her dowry to buy off Shylock and goes to Venice disguised as a lawyer. When Shylock refuses the money and rejects her plea for mercy, she outwits him by arguing that he is entitled to a pound of Antonio's flesh but cannot shed any blood in obtaining it, thus saving Antonio and ruining Shylock.

Antonio (an-TOH-nee-oh), the merchant of Venice. Rich and generous, he wishes to aid his impecunious friend Bassanio to woo Portia. Having no ready money, he borrows three thousand ducats from Shylock. His ships are apparently lost at sea, and he is saved from death only by Portia's cleverness. At the end of the play, he learns that some of his ships have returned and that he is not ruined.

Bassanio (ba-SAH-nee-oh), a friend of Antonio, in need of money to woo Portia. To help him, Antonio concludes his almost fatal bargain with Shylock. Bassanio chooses the right casket at Portia's home and thus is able to marry her.

Gratiano (GRAY-shee-AH-noh), a friend of Bassanio. He marries Nerissa, Portia's waiting woman.

Nerissa (neh-RIHS-uh), Portia's clever waiting woman. She marries Gratiano.

Jessica, the daughter of Shylock. She elopes with Lorenzo, taking with her much of Shylock's money and jewels. Her marriage is a heavy blow to her father.

Lorenzo (loh-REHN-zoh), a Venetian who marries Jessica.

The prince of Morocco, a tawny Moor, one of Portia's suitors. He chooses the gold casket, in which he finds a skull and some mocking verses.

The prince of Aragon, another of Portia's wooers. He chooses the silver casket, in which he finds the portrait of a blinking idiot.

Tubal (TEW-buhl), a Jew and a friend of Shylock.

Launcelot Gobbo (LOHN-seh-lot GOB-boh), a clown, Shylock's comic servant. Hating his master, he changes to the service of Bassanio. He acts as a messenger between Jessica and Lorenzo.

Old Gobbo, Launcelot's father, who is "sandblind."

MERIDIAN

Author: Alice Walker (1944-   )
First published: 1976
Genre: Novel

Locale: New York City, Georgia, Mississippi, and Alabama
Time: The 1960's, during the Civil Rights movement
Plot: Social morality

Meridian Hill, a black civil rights worker. A thin woman with a dark thick braid and reddish-brown skin, she is neither pretty nor homely but is at her most beautiful when sad. Meridian comes from a poor but respectable family in the South. She becomes pregnant while still in high school and soon finds herself with a husband and a son she cannot love. Her only satisfaction comes from working with civil rights workers registering voters, a campaign she joins in 1960 after the workers' headquarters is bombed. A college scholarship enables her to break away from her miserable life; she simply gives her baby away and leaves. An honors student in college, she works hard to earn the money to stay in school and struggles with her attempts to define herself. A passionate love for another civil rights worker, Truman Held, ends unhappily, and she does not form satisfying friendships. Meridian joins a militant revolutionary group but leaves it when she discovers that she cannot say with conviction that she would kill for the revolution. Instead, she returns to the South to work with and for her people, becoming a daring and eccentric civil rights worker as she moves from town to town, attempting to find her place within the Civil Rights movement and the world. By the end of the novel, a never-specified illness and her own self-neglect have left her with sallow skin, glassy yellow eyes, and a nearly bald head covered with a cap, yet she uses all of her energy to work for her people. She never finds a totally satisfying life for herself, but she serves as an anchoring point for the lives of those she touches.

Truman Held, an artist and civil rights worker. A handsome man with olive skin, black eyes, a neat beard and mustache, and the regal-looking nose of an Ethiopian warrior, Truman is vain about his looks and pretentious in his mannerisms. As a lover, he is selfish, interested only in his own pleasure. Meridian falls in love with him, but he is not attracted to strong women, and he does not return her love. Instead, he marries Lynne Rabinowitz, a white woman, and together they move to Mississippi to work in the Civil Rights movement. Truman's greatest struggle is an internal one: Can he be loyal both to the movement and to his white wife? He finds that he cannot and begins to hate Lynne for her whiteness. Over the years, he periodically runs back to Meridian, feeling a bond to her that he cannot ignore or explain.

Lynne Rabinowitz, a white woman from a wealthy suburb who joins the Civil Rights movement and marries Truman Held. Thin, with dark eyes, she comes to Meridian's black college as an exchange student and falls in love with Truman. In the beginning, she thinks of poor black people as a form of art, but her contributions to the Civil Rights movement are real. She is intelligent and unrestrained and is a popular and hard worker in the movement, which she serves as long as she is permitted; eventually, she is forced out by black workers who resent her. When she is raped by one of them, she becomes embittered about the movement and begins to hate black people in general and Truman in particular. Abandoned by her husband, disowned by her parents, and rejected by the movement, she returns to New York City to live on welfare and forms a bond of friendship with Meridian. That bond is not completed, however, until Lynne's daughter by Truman, Camara, is abused and killed and both women put Truman out of their lives.

Anne-Marion Coles, a black revolutionary and Meridian's first friend in college. A round and brash woman, she is the first among her peers to cut her hair in a "natural." Anne-Marion is an honors student with a temper, always ready for an argument. She joins the Civil Rights movement because she wants black people to have the same opportunities to be wealthy and exploitive as whites have. She and Meridian find themselves on opposing sides of various conflicts: Anne-Marion participates in a college riot that Meridian will not join, and she is one of the revolutionaries who urge Meridian to declare her willingness to kill. Finally, she ends the friendship, because she cares deeply for Meridian but cannot save her. Ten years later, she still cannot forgive Meridian for not being more militant, and she continues to write long, angry letters to her. She cannot forgive Meridian, but neither can she let her go.

— *Cynthia A. Bily*

THE MERRY-GO-ROUND IN THE SEA

Author: Randolph Stow (1935-   )
First published: 1965
Genre: Novel

Locale: Geraldton, Western Australia, and its environs
Time: 1942
Plot: Bildungsroman

Rob Coram, a six-year-old when his cousin Rick, whom he idolizes, is sent from their small town in Western Australia to fight in World War II. Rob is alive to his senses and grows up registering the colors, smells, and sounds of his small town and the differing sensations in the farm life of his grandparents. He learns about sex from young friends and about the war from the newspaper and from the foreign boats and immigrants coming into Geraldton, the harbor town where he lives. His most perplexing experience of war comes from studying his distraught cousin Rick when Rick returns home from Malaya. As Rob grows older after the end of the war, aging from ten to thirteen, he comes to hate killing animals. Although his perceptions change from those of a child to those of an adolescent, he remains sensitive, poetic, and reflective. His goal is to swim to the wrecked ship off the coast, which is to him the mysterious merry-go-round in the sea.

Rick Maplestead, the handsome, blond-haired, blue-eyed cousin of Rob Coram. He fights for Australia in World War II. Rick leaves home a cheery optimist but is humiliated, starved, and degraded in a prisoner of war camp in Malaya. When he returns to Geraldton, skinny and sick, he disappoints Rob and the family as the months pass because of his constant negative outlook and his unwillingness to develop a goal or to fit in. He is emotionally troubled; he curses and criticizes his country and makes a failure of an attempted romantic relationship with Jane Wexford. He continues his friendship with his young cousin Rob, preferring the simpler world of childhood to the more complex and disappointing world of adulthood. Ultimately, however, neither family nor homeland satisfies him. The novel ends with Rick bidding good-bye to both his cousin and his country.

Hugh Mackay, Rick's friend. He ships off with him to war and is captured with Rick and made a prisoner in the same camp in Malaya. Hugh becomes very discouraged and ill as a captive and almost dies; however, he survives and returns to Geraldton with Rick. Rick held up better in war, but Hugh is the better-adjusted survivor in peacetime. Hugh gets a law degree, buys a house in the suburbs, and dreams of golf. He becomes the model of adjustment and mediocrity that Rick despises.

Jane Wexford, Rick's attractive girlfriend. Jane is well meaning, but she has had no experience that could have prepared her to deal with the moody and malcontent Rick. Loving him, yet unable to satisfy him or hold him to her, Jane tries to kill herself but fails at the attempt. Instead of winning Rick back, Jane's attempted suicide and her obvious misery convince him never to see her again.

— *Ray Willbanks*

THE MERRY WIVES OF WINDSOR

Author: William Shakespeare (1564-1616)
First published: 1602
Genre: Drama

Locale: England
Time: The sixteenth century
Plot: Comedy

Sir John Falstaff (FOHL-staf), the jovial, rotund friend of Prince Hal in *Henry IV*, who comes with his hangers-on to Windsor and amuses himself by wooing the respectable ladies of two merchants. Twice gulled by the "merry wives," beaten and dumped into the Thames from a laundry basket, he tries a third time to succeed in his amorous designs and plans a rendezvous in the woods. He is discovered there by his friends wearing a buck's head and lying face down for fear of the fairies and elves who have been pinching him. He accepts this last deception in good humor and confesses that he was rather dubious about the authenticity of the spirits who visited him.

Mistress Page and

Mistress Ford, the brisk, practical ladies on whom Falstaff practices his romantic arts. Incensed as much by his identical letter to each of them as by his presumption in writing, they outwit the fat knight at every turn and firmly convince their husbands of their fidelity.

Thomas Page, Mistress Page's husband, a well-to-do burgher dwelling at Windsor. He trusts his wife's ability to withstand Falstaff's advances, although he follows his more suspicious friend Ford when he sets out to search for the knight at his own home. He disapproves of Fenton's suit for his daughter's hand, fearing the young man's high social standing, and arranges Anne's elopement with Slender. He is, however, quickly pacified when she announces her marriage to Fenton.

Ford, Page's jealous friend. He disguises himself as Brook to ferret out Falstaff's plans, and he instigates the searches that precipitate the knight's unexpected bath in the Thames and his thorough thrashing.

Mistress Quickly, an old busybody, Dr. Caius' nurse and housekeeper. She supposes herself Anne Page's confidante and tries to use her influence to marry the girl to her master. She is much distressed by young William Page's Latin lessons, for she is sure that his exercises contain improper language.

Sir Hugh Evans, the Welsh parson, a pedantic scholar whose "correctness" is made more ridiculous by his heavy accent. Duped by the host into challenging Dr. Caius to a duel, he quickly and surreptitiously convinces his adversary that friendship is preferable to fighting. He joins the final plot against Falstaff and, dressed as a satyr, leads the "elves" and "fairies" to the knight.

Dr. Caius (keez), a French doctor, a rather stupid man and one of Anne Page's suitors. His ignorance of the English language provides much amusement for his companions.

Justice Shallow, a foolish old country squire who is determined to sue Falstaff for injuries to his men, his property, and his pride. He avidly pursues his scheme for wedding his nephew to Mistress Anne Page and her handsome dowry.

Slender, Shallow's rather simple-minded nephew. He is willing to acquiesce in his uncle's wishes. Having little notion of the proper methods of courtship, he confesses his indifference to Anne and wishes privately that he had his book of songs and sonnets to help him woo her.

Simple, Slender's aptly named servant, who is almost as literal-minded as his master.

Anne Page, an attractive, intelligent young woman. She quickly assesses the defects of character in the prospective husbands put forth by each of her parents and resourcefully arranges her elopement with Fenton.

Fenton, Anne's sweetheart, a well-born, sensible young man and a persistent suitor.

Pistol,

Nym, and

Bardolph, Falstaff's disreputable cronies, who cozen Shallow, Slender, and the host and direct a steady barrage of insults and jests at the fat knight.

The host of the Garter, a loquacious taverner. He jokes with Falstaff and amuses himself by setting up a duel between Dr. Caius and Sir Hugh. He assists in most of the deceptions and plots afoot in Windsor, abetting Ford's disguise, Dr. Caius' courtship, and Fenton's elopement. He is forced to take some of his own medicine when Bardolph, Nym, and Pistol make off with three of his horses.

William Page, Anne's younger brother, Sir Hugh's apt pupil in Latin.

Robin, Falstaff's page, who carries messages to Mistress Ford and Mistress Page.

THE MESSENGER

Author: Charles Wright (1932-   )
First published: 1963
Genre: Novel

Locale: New York City
Time: The late 1950's and early 1960's
Plot: Psychological realism

Charlie Stevenson, the protagonist, an introspective twenty-nine-year-old African American veteran of the Korean War. He lives in the subterranean junkie world of New York City. Although he works as a messenger for a service in Rockefeller Center, his passion is for reading great literature with the hope of one day producing his own written works. Born in Sedalia, a small Missouri town, he was reared by his maternal grandparents after his mother died; his father had abandoned the family earlier. Charlie has spent his life since the age of fourteen wandering across America in search of a home.

Shirley, the woman Charlie once hoped to marry. Her optimism about life is in contrast to Charlie's sense of despair about living in the squalor of New York City. Shirley invites Charlie to find pleasure in the city by picnicking with him under the boardwalk of Coney Island and by encouraging him to leave his apartment and his wine-soaked existence. She also encourages him to return to Greenwich Village, where he had once found fellow artistic spirits and other intellectuals, but Charlie refuses.

Troy Lamb, a man of Scottish and German descent, one of Charlie's oldest friends in Manhattan. A promising intellectual, Troy has studied philosophy and anthropology at prestigious universities. A fellowship has allowed him to take his wife, Susan Mantle, to study with him in Africa. For all of his interest in African and African American culture, Troy sometimes reminds Charlie, through inadvertent signals, that there will always be signs or gestures of racial discrimination. On

first seeing Charlie, Troy's young son calls Charlie a "nigger," a remark that leaves Charlie wary of Troy throughout the novel.

Maxine, a precocious seven-year-old who lives in the same tenement as Charlie. She is a bright spot in the lonely man's life. Charlie takes her on "dates" to the Statue of Liberty and encourages her artistic impulses. After she draws some abstract pictures, he takes her to the Museum of Modern Art to look at abstract masterpieces. As was the case with Shirley, Maxine's presence provides a warm contrast to the cold world of economic hardship that Charlie experiences as an outsider in the grownup world.

Claudia, or **The Grand Duchess**, the most prominent of an outrageous cast of secondary characters who populate this novel. Claudia is a male "drag queen" who sells himself for kicks and for profit on the streets of New York. Although Claudia's lifestyle is bizarre, his wild sense of humor, musicality, and general high spirits often provide a stay against Charlie's loneliness and despair.

Ruby Stonewall, Charlie's cousin, a promising blues singer in Missouri before she lost her singing voice. After a series of setbacks—her husband leaves her, her son dies of influenza, and she ends a painful relationship with a white man in Kansas City—Ruby feels defeated in life. In Kansas City, however, Ruby takes a job as a chambermaid and counsels Charlie on how to live with compassion, pride, and self-acceptance in a segregated society.

Grandma, the maternal grandmother who reared Charlie in

a small Missouri town in the 1940's and 1950's. Her world-weary grandson visits her in the fall of 1958. Grandma's decline reminds Charlie that the innocence of his past is no longer available to him. She dies during Charlie's visit home,

leaving him with only the depression of the here and now in his yellowing room on West Forty-Ninth Street in the heart of Manhattan.

— *Daniel Charles Morris*

MESSER MARCO POLO

Author: Donn Byrne (Brian Oswald Donn-Byrne, 1889-1928)
First published: 1921
Genre: Novel

Locale: Venice and China
Time: The thirteenth century
Plot: Exotic

Marco Polo, the famous Venetian traveler. Told by a Chinese sea captain of the beauty of Golden Bells, he falls in love with his image of her. He imagines it his duty to convert the Chinese princess to Christianity. After he goes to China, the girl is his only convert. She and Marco fall in love and are happily married for three years; then Golden Bells dies. Marco stays with Kubla Khan for fourteen more years, but finally jealousy in the emperor's court forces him to leave. He will not go, however, until Golden Bells appears in a vision and pleads with him not to remain and risk his life. He departs sadly from China, the land of his beloved.

Golden Bells, the daughter of Kubla Khan, emperor of China. Told of Marco Polo's plight on the wide desert, she asks the court magician to save the young man and bring him to her father's court. She falls in love with Marco Polo, and the two live happily married for three years until her death. Al-

though she becomes Marco Polo's only convert to Christianity, she cannot believe what she is told of sin; she does not wish to be convinced that feminine beauty is sinful.

Nicholas and

Matthew Polo, Marco Polo's father and uncle, respectively. They take young Marco with them to China, ostensibly as a Christian missionary sent by the pope.

Kubla Khan, the emperor of China. It is at his request that Marco Polo, as a Christian missionary, goes to China.

Li Po, the court poet at the court of Kubla Khan. He is friendly to Golden Bells and to Marco Polo.

Sanang, the court magician of Kubla Khan. He effects the rescue of Marco Polo from the desert at Golden Bells' request. Later, it is he who furnishes Marco Polo with a vision of the long-dead Golden Bells.

THE METAMORPHOSES

Author: Ovid (Publius Ovidius Naso, 43 B.C.E.-17 C.E.)
First transcribed: Before 8 C.E.
Genre: Poetry

Locale: Realms of the gods, Greece, and the Roman Empire
Time: Indeterminate
Plot: Mythic

Jove, the Thunderer, god of the sky. He appears in two guises: as king of Mount Olympus and as habitual seducer of nymphs and young girls. As ruler, he is so offended by the evil excesses of the men of the Iron Age, especially Lycaon, that he transforms Lycaon into a wolf and cleanses the earth with a great flood. As seducer, he is unable both to restrain his passion for Io, Europa, Callisto, Semele, and others and to protect them from the jealous ire of his wife, Juno.

Apollo, also known as **Phoebus** (FEE-buhs), the god of the sun. He also exhibits two natures. In his sterner guise, he is both the driver of the great sun chariot, the reins of which he is disastrously persuaded to hand over to his son Phaeton, and the avenger of Latona, his mother, who had been insulted by Niobe. He often also appears as a frustrated lover of both boys and girls, unable to win the affections of Daphne and losing those of Ciparissus and Hyacinthus.

Juno, the goddess of marriage and childbirth, the queen of Mount Olympus, and the jealous wife of Jove. She appears throughout the work, intent on punishing the hapless victims of Jove's lust.

Bacchus (BA-kuhs), the god of wine and founder of the Bacchanalian mysteries. He is quick to reward those who follow him and to loose vengeance on those, such as Pentheus and the daughters of Minyas, who deny his divinity.

Diana, the goddess of the moon and the hunt. She jealously guards the virgins in her troupe, expelling any like Callisto

who, willingly or not, lose their virginity. Fiercely protective of her own privacy, she not only transforms Actaeon into a deer when he stumbles upon her bathing but allows his dogs to tear him apart.

Minerva (muh-NUR-vuh), also called **Pallas** (PA-luhs), the goddess of wisdom and craftsmanship. She appears as the zealous protector of her own honor and the honor of the gods. Those who disobey her commands or challenge her authority are dealt with summarily. She transforms Arachne, who challenged her to a weaving contest, into a spider.

Venus, the goddess of love and beauty. She embodies erotic desire in her own relationships with Mars and Adonis, in her inciting Cupid to awaken passion in others, and in her indulgence of such votaries as Pygmalion.

Io (I-oh), a nymph, who is representative of the young females ravished by the gods. Reluctant to succumb to Jove's advances, she is transformed into a white cow in a vain attempt to avert the wrath of Juno, who first puts her under the harsh guardianship of Argos and then has her tormented by the Furies. She ends up in Egypt, where she regains her human form. Ovid claims she is worshiped there under the name of Isis.

Cadmus, the founder of Thebes. He is one of the legendary kings, like Minos and Aegeus, whose fate is entwined with the whims of the gods. Aided by Apollo and Pallas, and tormented by Juno, he and his wife eventually are transformed into serpents, closing the circle of his career, which began with the slaying of the serpent of Mars.

Perseus (PUR-see-uhs), the heroic son of Jove and Danaë. Like Hercules, he inherits his suprahuman qualities from his divine parent, but he is also aided in his quests by his patron, Pallas. Her cunning helps him to defeat the Gorgon Medusa. Single-minded in his pursuits, he rescues and marries Andromeda and defeats his enemies by judicious display of the Gorgon's head.

Medea (muh-DEE-uh), an enchantress. She is less the jealous wife, tormented into slaying her children, than the epitome of the dangerous sorceress, devotee of Hecate, who uses her magical powers first to aid and then to destroy Jason. Thwarted in her attempt to poison Theseus, she disappears into a cloud as dark as her night magic.

Pythagoras (pih-THA-gur-uhs), a philosopher, an exile from Samos. He took up residence around 530 B.C. in Crotona, in southern Italy, where he founded a movement with religious, political, and philosophical aims. Ovid depicts the philosopher through a long discourse in which Pythagoras advocates vegetarianism and teaches the doctrines of the transmigration of souls and the eternal mutation of all natural things.

Julius Caesar, a descendant of Venus through the line of Aeneas' son Iulus. He is elevated to godhead after his assassination. Ovid praises Caesar most for being the father (adoptive) of the great Augustus, "the best of men to right his father's cause," who is a ruler destined to outshine his father as Theseus did Aegeus and Agamemnon did Atreus.

— *Jane Anderson Jones*

THE METAMORPHOSIS
(Die Verwandlung)

Author: Franz Kafka (1883-1924)
First published: 1915
Genre: Novella

Locale: Prague
Time: The 1910's
Plot: Allegory

Gregor Samsa, a young traveling salesman who awakes one morning to find himself transformed into a hideous vermin. Self-effacing to the point of suicide, he dutifully leaves the family apartment early every day for a job he hates so that he can pay off his father's debts. Incapacitated by his new physical form and scorned by his mother, father, and sister, he expires of his own volition.

Grete Samsa, Gregor's younger sister, an aspiring violinist whose studies at a musical conservatory Gregor hopes to be able to finance. After the metamorphosis, she shows some compassion for her deformed brother but eventually comes to share her parents' belief that all would be best if Gregor disappeared.

Mr. Samsa, Gregor's father, a stern disciplinarian who violently attacks Gregor when his deformed son dares venture out of his room. Following a business failure, Mr. Samsa sits around the apartment reading the newspaper while Gregor is off at work earning money to pay off his debts. After Gregor's metamorphosis, he gets a job as a bank guard.

Anna Samsa, Gregor's mother. Following Gregor's metamorphosis, she gets a job making underwear. She acquiesces to her husband's insistence that Gregor must disappear.

The Chief Clerk, Gregor's immediate boss at the sales firm. When, after five years of exemplary service, Gregor once fails to catch the five o'clock train to work, the Chief Clerk immediately rushes to Gregor's apartment to demand an explanation.

Three Lodgers, unnamed and indistinguishable men. Each sports an identical full beard. The Samsas provide them room and board when Gregor is no longer able to bring in a salary. They voice their disgust at the sight of Gregor. After his death, they are peremptorily evicted by his newly assertive father.

Charwoman, an old widow who adopts a matter-of-fact attitude toward her responsibility of cleaning up after the verminous Gregor. After discovering and disposing of his dead body, she is dismissed from employment by the Samsas.

— *Steven G. Kellman*

METAPHYSICS OF A TWO-HEADED CALF: A Tropical Australian Play in Three Acts
(Metafizyka dwugłowego cielęcia)

Author: Stanisław Ignacy Witkiewicz (1885-1939)
First published: 1962
Genre: Drama

Locale: British New Guinea and Australia
Time: The 1920's
Plot: Surrealism

Patricianello (pah-TREE-chee-ah-NEHL-loh), the sixteen-year-old son of Lady Leocadia Clay. Although his name implies that he is a little lordling, Patricianello is also the calf of the play's title. He attempts the creation of self in the face of shifting, ambiguous relationships and the instability and uncertainty of colonialism in the tropics. In the first act, he is seen playing with cardboard cubes on the floor while dressed in red tights. He is told to dress properly. In each succeeding act, he is more and more constricted by convention. Patricianello's uncertainty about his parentage and identity is manipu-

lated by his putative real and spiritual fathers as they attempt to ply him into their own image by gagging him and packing him off, thereby negating his quest for self and freedom.

Lady Leocadia Clay (leh-oh-KAH-dee-ah), Patricianello's mother, Sir Robert's wife, and Mikulin's mistress. She is forty-eight years old, with gray hair but shapely legs and a seductive manner. To Patricianello, she is a restrictive old mother, unlike the young beautiful mother of his dreams. Lady Leocadia has a propensity for sentimentality, exhibited when she and Mikulin recount their former love and when she views Sir

Robert's body. It is revealed that in a night of abandon she also became Ludwig's mistress. Ultimately, her love life puts Patricianello's parentage into question. As a result, after her death Patricianello's putative fathers fight over Patricianello's future.

Sir Robert Clay, the governor of New Guinea, assumed to have died from the tropical disease Kala-Azar while on an expedition to hunt for bugs for his collection. Sir Robert's body is brought in at the end of the first act. The *coup de théâtre* in the third act finds him reappearing wearing tails and a fur coat. He too claims Patricianello as his son and assists the others in packing him off. The last scene finds him calling for his car to go to the club for a game of bridge.

Professor Edward Mikulin-Pechbauer, a famous bacteriologist and Lady Leocadia's lover. Mikulin's last name has connotations of bad luck, and in general he presents a caricature of the scientist in his mad pursuit for a new serum for the dreaded Kala-Azar disease. He is as ruthless in his love life as he is in his scientific experiments. He inoculates Lady Leocadia with the Kala-Azar disease to test the efficacy of his serum. Choked by the Hooded Figure in the second act, he returns in the third-act *coup de théâtre* as one of Patricianello's putative fathers, determined to mold Patricianello into his own image.

Ludwig, Prince von and zu Turm und Parvis, the handsome, blond, thirty-year-old nephew of Lady Leocadia. A whip-cracking, self-assured cynical young man, he is one of Patricianello's spiritual fathers. He wants to whip Patricianello into shape by tempting him with his own sister, Mirabella.

Mirabella Parvis, Ludwig's eighteen-year-old, very pretty, chestnut-haired sister. She is the temptress of the play who, in her second-act dance, seduces Jack Rivers, Mikulin, the Hooded Figure, and Patricianello. Like Patricianello, Mirabella is manipulated by others, and her beauty is used by Ludwig for his own ends. Her desire for love and a simple life

are thwarted by the machinations of others, and when Patricianello is packed off, she is killed by the governor as she and the twin-image Patricianello look forward to the future.

King, the chief of the Aparura clan. He is a gigantic Papuan with frizzy black hair and black skin who appears in his native half-naked dress in the first act. The action of the play presents the increasing confinement and corruption of the King as he appears in a business suit and ultimately tails while tossing off gin and tonics, one after another.

Jack Rivers, the president of the Gold Stock Exchange of Kalgoorlie, Western Australia. An entrepreneur, Rivers makes a deal with Ludwig to skim off the profits from a phony mine. As Mirabella's lover, he promises to share Mirabella with Patricianello as well as to teach him how to love her.

Hooded Figure, an embodiment of Kala-Azar. Appearing in the second-act deathbed scene of Lady Leocadia, he is a tall, sinister figure in a brown coat that hangs down to the ground, with a hood over his head. In the final *coup de théâtre*, he sheds his coat and hood to reveal a twin-image Patricianello, dressed in tails as a young man about town. The Hooded Figure in turn is also packed off by Sir Robert Clay, thereby thwarting the Hooded Figure's happiness with Mirabella.

Old Hag, a hunchbacked, incredibly old, grotesque figure in gray rags who may be connected to Mirabella, because Ludwig pays her for her "niece." She reappears in the final act behind the wheel of the car carrying Mikulin, Lady Leocadia, and the King.

Six Papuans, the gigantic black subjects of the King.

Four Sailors, who are dressed in white and carry the body of Sir Robert Clay.

Six Porters, who appear wearing green aprons. Two of them pack off Patricianello while the others carry out the trunk with the Hooded Figure.

— *Christine Kiebuzinska*

MICAH CLARKE

Author: Sir Arthur Conan Doyle (1859-1930)
First published: 1889
Genre: Novel

Locale: England
Time: Late seventeenth century
Plot: Historical

Micah Clarke, a young English Puritan who enlists in the forces of the duke of Monmouth when that nobleman makes his bid for the English throne in 1685. A strong, able, and honest man, Clarke becomes a captain of infantry, goes on various missions for the usurper, and is captured when Monmouth is defeated. He is ransomed by his friend Decimus Saxon and goes to the Continent to be a mercenary soldier.

Reuben Lockarby, Clarke's close friend. Although himself a strong Anglican, he joins Clarke out of friendship as a member of Monmouth's forces. He becomes a captain of infantry.

Decimus Saxon, a mercenary soldier who becomes a colonel under the duke of Monmouth. He enlists Clarke in the pretender's cause. He rescues Clarke by ransoming him with money taken from the duke of Beaufort by blackmail.

Sir Gervas, a London dandy who has gone through his fortune. He joins Clarke and his friends as a follower of Monmouth.

Sir Jacob Clancy, a hermit who lost his estates through helping Charles II regain the English throne. He sends money and a warning to the duke of Monmouth by the hand of Clarke.

The duke of Monmouth, the leader of the Protestant insurrection against James II. His forces are defeated, and he is captured and beheaded.

Stephen Timewell, a wealthy wool merchant and mayor of Taunton. As an anti-Catholic, he helps the duke of Monmouth in the preparations to unseat James II.

Ruth Timewell, Stephen's daughter, who is courted by Reuben.

The duke of Beaufort, the lord of Wales, who agrees to support Monmouth if Monmouth's forces can get to Bristol. En route there, they are intercepted by the king's army at Sedgemoor and defeated.

Joseph Clarke, Micah Clarke's father, a Puritan. He is a veteran of the English civil war of the 1640's, in which he fought under Oliver Cromwell.

MICHAEL AND HIS LOST ANGEL

Author: Henry Arthur Jones (1851-1929)
First published: 1896
Genre: Drama

Locale: England and Italy
Time: The nineteenth century
Plot: Social realism

The Reverend Michael Feversham, a stern, conscientious vicar at Cleveheddon. He is full of moral fervor and has strong moral convictions, reinforced by his belief that his dead mother is his guardian angel. He learns through his attraction to Audrie Lesden what temptations of the flesh can be, and he commits adultery with her. He finally makes a public confession, as he had forced Rose Gibbard to do, and leaves his parish. He almost loses his faith but turns to Catholicism in the hope that he can be saved.

Rose Gibbard, a woman in the parish who commits adultery and bears a child. She is forced by the vicar to make a public confession because he believes that is the only way she can be absolved of sin. Later, she is sent to an Anglican religious house.

Andrew Gibbard, Rose's father and the parish clerk. Although he knows Michael is conscientious, he cannot forgive the vicar for making Rose confess publicly. He has only scorn for the vicar until the clergyman makes a public confession of his own sin.

Audrie Lesden, a wealthy, attractive woman reputed to be a widow. She is attracted to Michael, but she is torn between wanting to be worthy of him and having worldly pleasures. She arranges to be left alone on an island overnight with him and takes him for her lover. She leaves the town for a while when her husband is heard from, but she returns after he is dead. Then the vicar tells her he cannot love her honorably. She dies loving the vicar, saying she will be his guardian angel.

Sir Lyolf Feversham, a relative of the vicar. He tries to warn the vicar away from entanglements with Audrie.

Father Hilary, a Roman Catholic priest to whom the Anglican vicar turns for spiritual help when his original faith cannot sustain him.

MICKELSSON'S GHOSTS

Author: John Gardner (1933-1982)
First published: 1982
Genre: Novel

Locale: Binghamton, New York, and Susquehanna, Pennsylvania
Time: 1980-1981
Plot: Psychological realism

Peter J. Mickelsson, the novel's center of consciousness, an internationally known professor of philosophy specializing in ethics. He has recently left Providence, Rhode Island, and his wife to take a position at the State University of New York at Binghamton in the hopes of putting his life back in order. Having suffered one nervous breakdown, Mickelsson appears on the verge of another as he struggles with his wife's long-distance demands, the Internal Revenue Service, alcohol, and his own stalled career. Essentially an idealist, he wears his newly donned armor of irony and cynicism rather self-consciously as he tries to overcome feelings of guilt and responsibility for his mounting personal and professional failures. The division within his personality becomes steadily more pronounced as he divides his time, mind, and energies between the university and rural Susquehanna, Pennsylvania; between the classes he teaches (badly, he believes) and the farmhouse he has recently bought and is in the process of renovating; between a beautiful colleague, Jessica Stark, and a local prostitute, Donnie Matthews; between Friedrich Nietzsche and Martin Luther; between reality and hallucination; and ultimately between faith and hope on one hand and despair on the other. As he grows increasingly detached from others, both geographically and emotionally, he becomes progressively but uneasily amoral in his actions. He is finally saved by his own self-questioning, by the faith that others continue to have in him, by his willingness to cry out and to pray— even though prayer runs counter to the evidence of the rational, existential mind—and finally by what may be telepathy or simply luck.

Ellen, Mickelsson's wife, whose faith in Mickelsson turns to bitterness, buttressed by her acceptance of the fashionable view that she is Mickelsson's victim. Instead of struggling against the world, she gives in to it, drawing support from her work in modern theater.

Leslie, Mickelsson's daughter. She lives with her mother but bears no grudge against her father.

Mark, Mickelsson's son, an idealist actively involved in protecting the environment. Ironically, Mickelsson's land and the area around it turn out to be chemically contaminated as a result of the illegal dumping of toxic waste.

Mickelsson's father, a farmer and expert amateur carpenter who represents for Mickelsson the wholeness, selflessness, and nobility of character he has lost in his own life. The father appears only in Mickelsson's memories.

Dr. Rifkin, the Providence psychiatrist whose remarks Mickelsson often recalls from their sessions together—sessions he now continues in his mind. He does not find Rifkin's psychiatric explanations convincing.

Finney, the Providence lawyer who is handling Mickelsson's divorce. Jovially cynical, he finds his client's guilt and generosity unrealistic and oddly humorous.

John Pearson, Mickelsson's taciturn neighbor. A dowser and former dairy farmer, he accepts the world's strangeness in the same way that he has accepted his wife's death from cancer one year earlier.

Owen Thomas, the friendly owner of a Susquehanna hardware store. Like many of the other townspeople, he seems to trust Mickelsson instinctively.

Donnie Matthews, a blonde, buxom teenage prostitute with whom Mickelsson has an affair. Claiming to be pregnant with his child, she extorts fifteen thousand dollars from him. She phones Mickelsson much later in the novel to say that she threw the money in the ocean (Mickelsson had stolen it), had an abortion (against Mickelsson's wishes, though he now approves), and has decided to lead a very different life, thanks to his influence and example.

Jessica Stark, the only member of the university's sociology department who is not a Marxist. Tall, beautiful, intelligent, and widowed, she has an affair with Mickelsson. Despite his thinking of her as his salvation and despite her attempts to help him put his life in order, he abandons Jessica when her Marxist colleagues try to oust her from the department. It is to her, however, that Mickelsson goes at the end of the novel to escape madness by rejoining the human community.

Michael Nugent, a lonely and rather demanding student who tries to befriend and model himself on Mickelsson. He sees himself as a clown, as someone who is not entirely human but only pretends to be. His death, at first assumed to be a suicide, proves to be a murder.

Professor Warren, Nugent's chemistry instructor and "friend," a former Mormon. His suspicions about chemical contamination cause him to become interested in the house Mickelsson now owns, a house believed to be connected to the Mormon founder, Joseph Smith. Lawler murders Warren because he mistakenly believes that Warren is trying to find evidence that will discredit Smith.

Alan Blassenheim, the brightest and most idealistic of Mickelsson's students. His idealism does not prevent him from jilting his girlfriend, Brenda Winburn.

Brenda Winburn, a member of the university swim team and, until her affair with Alan Blassenheim, the class nihilist. She thinks of Mickelsson's class as a kind of church and thus an alternative to a world made in the image of her bickering parents. Jilted by her boyfriend, she gets drunk and turns to Mickelsson for help.

Charles Lepatofsky, the wife of Tim's cousin. The short, fat, cheerful man sells Mickelsson a Jeep. It is his four- or five-year-old daughter, Lily, who hears Mickelsson's prayer and therefore saves his life.

The fat man, who is nearly blind. He lives in the same building as Donnie. In 1965, he stole from a bank the money that Mickelsson in turn steals from him. During the break-in, the fat man suffers a fatal heart attack.

Theodosia Sprague and

Caleb Sprague, the brother and sister who previously owned Mickelsson's farmhouse. Mickelsson either sees or imagines their ghosts. Caleb murdered their child; she in turn murdered him and was subsequently hanged for the crime.

Tacky Tinklepaugh, a Susquehanna policeman. In his fifties, he is poorly paid, a heavy drinker, and cynical but also heroic. He believes in maintaining a balance among human beings and between humankind and nature. Although he suspects that Mickelsson may have been responsible for the fat man's death, he chooses not to make an arrest.

Edward Lawler, a specialist in medieval philosophy who is entirely devoted to his work. Distressed by Ludwig Wittgenstein's views on the purpose and nature of philosophy in the modern world, he sets out to preserve the letter of idealism (as a fiction, anyway) even as he violates its spirit. Having no family and no friends, he is also a religious fanatic—one of a secret band of Mormon killers, the Danites, or Sons of Dan—and is responsible for the deaths of Nugent and Warren. He forces Mickelsson at gunpoint to tear his house apart to find the evidence Mickelsson knows does not exist but that Lawler fears will discredit Mormonism's sacred texts. His plan is foiled, and he is arrested.

Tim Booker, a young real estate agent who arranges the sale of Dr. Bauer's farmhouse to Mickelsson. A former medic in Vietnam, Tim rides a motorcycle, practices witchcraft (white magic), and is a closet environmentalist. He introduces Mickelsson to his "cousin," Donnie Matthews, and to Lepatofsky.

— Robert A. Morace

MIDAQ ALLEY
(Zuqaq al-Midaqq)

Author: Naguib Mahfouz (1911-   )
First published: 1947
Genre: Novel

Locale: Cairo, Egypt
Time: Early 1940's
Plot: Historical realism

Hamida (hah-MEE-dah), a resident of Cairo's Midaq Alley, a beautiful young woman and foster daughter of Umm Hamida, who serves as her matchmaker. Hamida, ever devoted to material possessions, agrees to marry Abbas Hilu, a barber, who falls desperately in love with her and leaves Midaq Alley to work for the British so that he can save money to buy Hamida everything she desires. Having sealed their engagement, he has no sooner left than Salim Alwan, a rich store owner, leaves his wife with the intention of marrying Hamida. Viewing this union as a means of quickly gaining wealth and position, Hamida, with Umm Hamida's connivance, proceeds to make plans for her wedding to Salim, completely ignoring her commitment to Abbas. Before they can be married, Salim

dies unexpectedly of a heart attack, leaving Hamida desolate. Soon afterward, however, Ibrahim Faraj begins his pursuit of Hamida, and they run away together, with the expectation on Hamida's part that they will marry soon. Ibrahim has other ideas, setting Hamida up in his elegant apartment, which is essentially a school for prostitutes, and turning her into a wealthy, successful prostitute with a large following among the British and American servicemen stationed in Egypt during World War II. When a much richer Abbas returns from his work with the British, Hamida, desperate to escape the enslavement Ibrahim has imposed upon her, persuades Abbas to kill him. Before the planned murder, Abbas finds Hamida in a bar surrounded by soldiers. After she rejects him, he throws a glass at her, cutting her face, and is attacked and killed by the soldiers.

Abbas Hilu (ah-BAHS HEE-lew), a simple barber who, infatuated by the beautiful Hamida, becomes engaged to her and leaves Cairo's Midaq Alley, where he has spent much of his life, to work for the British, who are stationed outside Cairo during World War II. Although Hamida betrays Abbas, shunning him at times after she has promised to marry him, Abbas retains his feelings for her. He is about to avenge her honor by killing Ibrahim Faraj at her suggestion. He enters the bar where he plans to commit the murder but finds Hamida there surrounded by amorous soldiers. Infuriated at Hamida's rejection of him when she sees him, Abbas throws a beer glass at her, cutting her flawless face. The soldiers turn on Abbas and kill him before he has the opportunity to murder Ibrahim.

Salim Alwan (sah-LEEM AHL-wahn), a rich, successful businessman who owns a large retail store. Salim, impassioned by Hamida's great beauty, divorces his wife and plans to marry Hamida, who, already engaged to Abbas Hilu, overlooks that commitment in order to gain the wealth and security Salim can offer her. Salim, however, dies of a heart attack before the two are joined, leaving Hamida desolate.

Ibrahim Faraj (ee-brah-HEEM FAH-rahzh), a pimp who lures Hamida into his plush apartment, leading her to expect that they will soon marry. It becomes apparent, however, that Ibrahim wants only to train Hamida to be a prostitute who will work for him and enrich him further.

Umm Hamida (EWM hah-MEE-dah), Hamida's foster mother, who conspires with her daughter to negate her engagement to Abbas Hilu in order to marry Salim Alwan for his money. When these plans are shattered by Salim's death, Umm Hamida again encourages Hamida to snatch the golden ring rather than honor her commitment to marry Abbas.

Radwan Husaini (RAHD-wahn hew-SAY-nee), a holy man, devoutly Muslim, whom Umm Hamida and Hamida consult regarding Hamida's proposed marriage to Salim Alwan. Although Radwan advises them against this marriage, they completely ignore his advice.

Kirsha (KEER-shah), owner of a coffeehouse where people from Midaq Alley gather.

Husain Kirsha (hew-SAYN), son of the coffeehouse owner, a close friend and confidant of Abbas Hilu.

— *R. Baird Shuman*

MID-CHANNEL

Author: Arthur Wing Pinero (1855-1934)
First published: 1910
Genre: Drama

Locale: London, England
Time: Early twentieth century
Plot: Psychological realism

Zoe Blundell, an attractive, elegant woman in her late thirties. Convinced that after fourteen years of marriage, her husband Theodore is as tired of her as she is irritated with him, Zoe avoids him as much as possible, going out every night with her male friends. At first, she is enthusiastic about a second honeymoon in Paris; however, she quarrels with her husband about his choice of a hotel. After he leaves her, Zoe goes to the Continent on her own. During the final weeks of her stay there, she is joined by Ferris, who becomes her lover. Back in London, she learns from Ethel that Ferris had virtually proposed marriage to her. Blaming herself, Zoe tells Ferris to forget about her and to marry the younger woman. When Theodore rejects her, however, Zoe changes her mind and decides to marry Ferris after all. At his apartment, she learns that he has just formalized his engagement to Ethel. Realizing that he will be miserable if he marries her instead, she declines the offer he has been forced to make and leaps from the balcony, killing herself.

Theodore Blundell, her husband, a forty-six-year-old stockbroker. His love for Zoe has dwindled into affection, unexpressed admiration, and frequent irritation. He is obtuse about women in general and his wife in particular. Theodore cannot see how much she craves attention and praise from him, and he has no inkling of how desperate she is. At Mottram's suggestion, he tries to pay her compliments and even agrees to take her to Paris. He spoils everything, however, by insisting that they stay at an inferior hotel. A quarrel ensues, and he walks out. Theodore is soon snapped up by a woman in her twenties. Eventually, he gets rid of her, intending to return to Zoe. Though she is willing to forgive Theodore for his infidelity, when Zoe admits that she, too, has been unfaithful, her husband says that he will never again live under the same roof with her. Theodore then offers to give his wife a divorce provided that Ferris agrees to marry her. He descends on Ferris and secures the young man's word of honor that he will marry Zoe.

The Honorable Peter Mottram, Theodore's partner, a polished, middle-aged man, one of Zoe's followers. Although he is a confirmed bachelor, he has observed much about human nature. He warns both Theodore and Zoe that midway in a marriage there often is a difficult passage, and he does his best to bring them back together. When Theodore goes to Ferris, Mottram accompanies him, to prevent his jealous friend from attacking Zoe's lover. After she kills herself, Mottram remembers that she had mentioned suicide to him as a way out of her misery.

Leonard Ferris, another of Zoe's followers. A man of independent means, he is an extremely eligible bachelor. Urged by his aunt to marry and settle down, he has been paying court to Ethel, but he is still obsessed with Zoe. After being with her in Italy, he has once again decided to marry Zoe, instead of Ethel. When Zoe turns him away, he tears up the pictures of them together on the trip and becomes formally engaged to Ethel. A few moments later, while Ethel and her mother are still in his apartment, he has to deal with a hysterical Zoe, who demands that he marry her. Although he agrees, promising somehow to get out of his engagement, he seems relieved when Zoe declines his offer. With his usual inability to face issues squarely, he refuses to take any responsibility for her death and declares it an accident.

Alice Annerly, Theodore's mistress, a young, pretty woman who is gifted at flattering older men. She is also very practical. When Theodore rejects her suggestion that he marry her, she negotiates with him and obtains a sizable sum for ending their relationship.

Ethel Drayson Pierpoint, a pretty young woman of twenty-five who looks to Zoe for good advice, generally about her relationship with Ferris. Ethel's sincere love for Ferris is shown when she takes him back without any questions after his trip abroad and his subsequent neglect of her.

Mrs. Pierpoint, her mother, a pleasant woman who likes Ferris and approves of the marriage.

— Rosemary M. Canfield Reisman

THE MIDDLE AGE OF MRS. ELIOT

Author: Angus Wilson (1913-1991)
First published: 1958
Genre: Novel

Locale: London, an Eastern capital, and southern England
Time: The 1950's
Plot: Psychological realism

Meg Eliot, a wealthy forty-three-year-old society matron. Striking in appearance, with large brown eyes, laugh lines, and thick, graying yellow hair, Meg occupies her time with her collection of porcelain and with charitable works in which her wealth and confidence allow her dominance. Insecure as a child, she values the luxury her husband provides and trusts all financial matters to him. As the novel opens, she is about to accompany him on a trip around the world. After his death on that trip, she is left relatively poor and learns that, without wealth and a husband, her world is circumscribed and her dominance over people rejected. Analyzing her marriage, she realizes that there, too, she had been manipulative. After training to be a secretary, she suffers a physical and emotional breakdown and is sheltered by her long-estranged brother David at his nursery, Andredaswood, in Sussex. Returning to health and a more authentic sense of confidence, she reenters the world, taking a series of jobs that will allow her to understand life as it is, not as, in her wealth and security, she had once fantasized it to be.

Bill Eliot, a successful barrister, fifty-five years old. With his drink-flushed, coarse, and sensual face and his overweight body, Bill is a conventionally masculine man. For Meg's sake, he has sacrificed an interesting career in criminal law for a more profitable corporate practice that affords them the style of life Meg craves. They have spent all he has made. Worried about his health and Meg's future, Bill has become a compulsive gambler. At the Srem Panh airport in Badai, he intervenes to prevent the assassination of a Badai minister whom he had admired at the airport and is himself killed, leaving his financial affairs chaotic.

David Parker, Meg's estranged older brother. David, a pacifist during World War II, is casual in appearance, with thick, prematurely gray hair and a distaste for conventional clothing and for Meg and Bill's feckless and worldly life. Rejecting a junior fellowship at Oxford, he has formed a chaste emotional and business partnership with Gordon Paget, the man he loves. An agnostic, he nevertheless espouses a Quaker-like quietism and has disciplined himself to a detached compassion for human life. Despite Gordon's terminal illness and death, David must care for Meg after her collapse; in the stress of the two situations, he moves toward greater emotional involvement, finally wanting to keep Meg at Andredaswood

even though she insists on returning to work and to a larger world.

Lady Viola Pirie, a friend of Meg. Stern, with a square gray face, she lives a lonely life in a flat that she shares with her son Tom, with whom she is obsessively concerned. She offers Meg a room until Meg's attempts to help Tom are misinterpreted as sexual overtures by the young man and until Meg rejects Viola's strongly felt belief that a woman is nothing without a man.

Tom Pirie, about twenty-two years old, the bearded and grubby son of Viola. Emotionally immature and clumsy, with a tendency to spit as he talks, Tom aspires to authorship, expecting his first book to be successful but lacking talent and intelligence. Because his mother will not permit him to do women's work at home and he will do no other, he is spoiled and selfish. When Meg attempts to reorganize his life, he perceives her as sexually starved, a once grande dame now to be cut down to size.

Poll Robson, a dumpy, middle-aged friend of Meg. Moon-faced, with lifeless blue eyes, she once studied art with Meg but now drinks too much, picks up acquaintances at pubs and clubs, borrows money, and fantasizes an aristocratic background. She believes that this way of life is the only one possible for women of their age and background who lack money.

Jill Stokes, Meg's oldest friend. Once beautiful, she now is a bitter widow with a frozen smile. Like Meg, she loved her husband; unlike Meg, she is obsessed with the past to the degree that she will not accept a son-in-law who cannot share her obsession and, consequently, has alienated herself from her beloved daughter and granddaughter. She offers quarters to Meg but asks her to leave when Meg tries to mediate these strained relationships.

Else Bode, the housekeeper, shopper, clerk, and secretary for David and Gordon. With sapphire eyes and wrinkled, papery skin, she is an emaciated, governess-like refugee from Adolf Hitler's Germany. Her strongest emotion is self-effacing love for David and Gordon, but she is jealous of Meg's assertiveness and of David's ability to attract love. Her virtues are her devotion and courage; her weakness is the passive aggression that contrasts with Meg's desire to participate actively in life.

— Betty Richardson

THE MIDDLE GROUND

Author: Margaret Drabble (1939-   )
First published: 1980
Genre: Novel

Locale: England
Time: Late 1970's
Plot: Psychological realism

Kate Armstrong, a thirty-one-year-old mother, divorcée, and successful writer of articles about women and the underprivileged. A brown-haired woman from a middle-class background, Kate is going through a midlife crisis in both her private and professional lives. Up to this point, she had been energetic, successful, witty, and lucky. She postponed a career to take care of her family, then returned to journalism when her children entered school. Her husband, Stuart, an unsuccessful artist, became envious of her success and began having affairs, and she divorced him. When the book opens, she is depressed, restless, self-absorbed, and frantically trying to balance the responsibilities she feels toward her parents, her children, her friends, and herself. Her house, as busy as a bus station, serves as a metaphor for her life of turmoil. The book ends with Kate realizing that she does have some control over her life and finally coming to terms with herself.

Hugo Mainwaring, Kate's friend, a writer on international affairs. A worldly man with a Cambridge education, Hugo is quiet and reserved, yet often the mediator in social situations. During an assignment in Eritrea, he lost half of his arm while saving a child's life. At the beginning of the novel, he is experiencing a midlife crisis caused in part by a failed marriage, a son recently brain damaged by an overdose of anesthetic during a routine operation, and boredom. By the novel's end, he, too, has made some changes by expressing his fondness for Kate and agreeing to be fitted for an artificial limb.

Ted Stennett, a specialist in tropical disease and epidemics, Evelyn's husband and Kate's lover. Aggressive, ambitious, competitive, and talkative, Ted is passionately interested in and successful at his profession. These same qualities, when transferred to his personal life, lead him to pursue a string of women successfully, despite his physical unattractiveness. At the novel's end, Ted places his disillusionment with marriage and fatherhood in perspective as he reflects on the negative repercussions of his past womanizing.

Evelyn Stennett, a full-time social worker, Ted's wife, and Kate's friend. Well-bred, well-educated, and serious, Evelyn works hard helping those who are less fortunate than herself. Her personal life is marred by a socially maladjusted son, who abuses drugs and alcohol and engages in skinhead behavior, and a husband whose womanizing she chooses to ignore. Toward the novel's end, she is seriously injured in a domestic conflict while visiting one of her clients. Her eventual release from the hospital inspires Kate to organize the party that concludes the novel.

Peter Armstrong, Kate's brother, an office worker turned machine tester. At the age of forty, Peter experiences a transformation that results in his becoming what Kate calls "normal." Kate suspects, however, that he is responsible for anonymous letters to her criticizing the views she presents in her journalism.

Judith Street, an art historian, Hugo's former wife. An intelligent, independent, well-educated woman, she falls apart after her son suffers permanent brain damage. Kate and Judith do not get along.

Nancy Mainwaring, Hugo's mother, a manager of an art gallery. An elderly, stylish woman, she alternately neglected and smothered her son while he was growing up.

— *Cassandra Kircher*

THE MIDDLE OF THE JOURNEY

Author: Lionel Trilling (1905-1975)
First published: 1947
Genre: Novel

Locale: Connecticut
Time: Mid-1930's
Plot: Political

John Laskell, an urban affairs expert. At the age of thirty-three, this sensitive, introspective, scholarly man has just had a brush with death from scarlet fever and as a result is undergoing a somewhat premature midlife crisis. He finds himself reevaluating everything that he formerly believed, especially his left-wing politics, which had brought him into contact with many American communists and fellow travelers during the Great Depression. At the invitation of his friends, the Crooms, he goes to spend six weeks recuperating in rural Connecticut. While he is experiencing his transformation from the idealistic illusions of youth to the skeptical conservatism of middle age, he perceives most of the people he encounters as living symbols of the subtle changes taking place in American political thought at that critical point in history.

Gifford Maxim, a former member of the Communist Party who has just defected and is now anti-Communist. Maxim is described as a brilliant intellectual with the body of a wrestler. He and Laskell attended college together. Maxim has worked as a secret agent for the Communist Party, receiving orders directly from Moscow, and hints that he has been involved in espionage and other crimes. He is afraid that he will be murdered because he knows too much. Laskell is disgusted with Maxim for his apparent cowardice and betrayal of principles; he helps him establish a new life, however, by getting him a job with an innocuous liberal journal.

Nancy Croom, a young housewife and mother. She and her husband, Arthur, represent typical middle-class communist sympathizers of the period. Although they are not card-carrying members of that party, they have lost faith in traditional religion and believe that, instead of waiting for "pie in the sky," humankind should unite under socialism, as expounded by Karl Marx, and make the present world as nearly perfect as possible. Nancy is outraged when she learns of Maxim's defection. She and her husband both serve as spokespersons for the opposition to Maxim's new viewpoint. They also represent the foolish middle-class intellectuals' belief in the innate nobility of the working class, which is shattered by the events that transpire.

Arthur Croom, a young professor of economics who shares his wife's illusions about communism and the desirability of a dictatorship of the proletariat.

Duck Caldwell, the Crooms' handyman. In keeping with their politics, the Crooms have many illusions about this local representative of the working class. They think that he is authentic, talented, and independent, a diamond in the rough. His actual behavior shows him to be lazy, cruel, lecherous, and a drunkard. At the climax of the novel, he accidentally kills his daughter, Susan, by brutally slapping her across the face at a public gathering. He avoids going to prison only because his wife had never told him of the child's potentially fatal heart defect.

Emily Caldwell, Duck's wife, another representative of the proletariat. Unlike her husband, she has artistic and intellectual pretensions. She has bad taste, no discipline, and little strength of character. She and Laskell have a brief affair. Although he sympathizes with her, he finds that he cannot love or respect her.

Susan Caldwell, the daughter of Duck and Emily. This eleven-year-old girl has been infected by her mother's cultural aspirations and hopes to go to Vassar or Smith. She and Laskell become friendly on the basis of their shared interest in literature. Her tragic death shocks everyone into a new perspective of reality.

— *Bill Delaney*

MIDDLE PASSAGE

Author: Charles Johnson (1948-   )
First published: 1990
Genre: Novel

Locale: On board a slave ship
Time: 1830
Plot: Bildungsroman

Rutherford Calhoun, the novel's first-person narrator. Calhoun, a well-educated and pleasure-seeking slave, is manumitted at the age of twenty-one. Angered by his brother's refusal of their master's wealth, Calhoun leaves rural Illinois for New Orleans, where he survives on charm, thievery, and lies. When Boston schoolteacher Isadora Bailey, aided by black underworld king Papa Zeringue, attempts to force Calhoun into marriage, he stows away on the *Republic*, a slave ship about to sail to Africa. His shipmates are divided into many factions, and Calhoun, as always guided by his own best interests, pledges allegiance to them all. Thus he vows loyalty to Captain Falcon, to the mutiny-bound crew, and finally to the African captives, the Allmuseri. Amid wild storms, cruel treatment of the black captives, the slaves' rebellion, a life-threatening illness, and a dark-night-of-the-soul experience, Calhoun, a philosopher as well as a trickster, examines the dualistic and hierarchical view of reality by which he and America live. Gradually, this experience gives him a new vision, one of interdependence and compassion. When the ship sinks, Calhoun is rescued by Papa Zeringue and Isadora Bailey, from whom he fled at his journey's beginning. Calhoun's conversion is complete. With Isadora Bailey now his wife, he sets off for Illinois to reunite with his brother.

— *Francine Dempsey*

MIDDLEMARCH: A Study of Provincial Life

Author: George Eliot (Mary Ann Evans, 1819-1880)
First published: 1871-1872
Genre: Novel

Locale: England
Time: The nineteenth century
Plot: Psychological realism

Dorothea "Dodo" Brooke, the sensitive and well-bred heroine, who, in her desire to devote herself to something meaningful, marries an arid clerical scholar, Edward Casaubon. After Casaubon's death, Dorothea, against the advice of friends and family, marries Will Ladislaw, an impulsive artist anad political thinker. Dorothea also befriends the progressive young doctor of Middlemarch, Tertius Lydgate.

The Reverend Edward Casaubon, the clergyman at Lowick, near Middlemarch. Casaubon is a gloomy, severe, unimaginative, and unsuccessful scholar who soon destroys Dorothea's enthusiasm. He is so jealous of Dorothea's friendship with his cousin, Will Ladislaw, that he adds a codicil to his will depriving Dorothea of his property should she marry his younger relative.

Will Ladislaw, Casaubon's young cousin, whose English heritage is mixed with alien Polish blood. Ladislaw is forceful, imaginative, energetic, and unconventional. An artist and a liberal, he represents an appropriate object of devotion for Dorothea, although many in Middlemarch are shocked by his views. After marrying Dorothea, he becomes a member of Parliament.

Celia "Kitty" Brooke, Dorothea's younger sister, a calm and placid young lady. She has none of Dorothea's aspirations, but she is affectionate. She marries Sir James Chettam, a staid landowner.

Sir James Chettam, the owner of Freshitt Hall. A conservative gentleman, Sir James loves first Dorothea, then Celia, whom he happily weds.

Dr. Tertius Lydgate, a young doctor who comes to Middlemarch to establish a new hospital along progressive lines and to pursue scientific research. His noble career is destroyed by his improvident marriage and consequent debts.

Rosamond Vincy Lydgate, the beautiful, spoiled, and selfish daugher of the mayor of Middlemarch. Once married, she insists on living in a style that her husband, Dr. Lydgate, cannot afford.

Mr. Arthur Brooke, of Tipton Grange, the genial, rambling, and ineffectual uncle of Dorothea and Celia. His vague benevolence leads him to run for Parliament; he is soundly beaten.

Fred Vincy, Rosamond's brother, equally spoiled but less selfish. Although Fred gets into debt as a student and rebels against his family's plans to establish him as a respectable vicar, he later reforms, becomes an industrious farmer, and marries Mary Garth.

Mary Garth, the level-headed, competent daughter of a large, old-fashioned family securely tied to the land. She takes care of her aged, ailing relative, Peter Featherstone, before she marries Fred Vincy, her childhood sweetheart.

Mr. Walter Vincy, the mayor of Middlemarch and a prosperous manufacturer. Mr. Vincy, who loves comfort and genial company, is neither wise nor sympathetic in dealing with the problems his children face.

Mrs. Lucy Vincy, his wife, a warm, sentimental woman who spoils her children and has vast pretentions to social gentility. She objects to Fred's relationship with the simple, commonplace Garths.

Mr. Nicholas Bulstrode, the enormously pious, evangelical, wealthy banker of Middlemarch. Bulstrode uses his public morality and his money to control events in Middlemarch; however, the questionable connections and the shady early marriage that built up his fortune are eventually revealed.

Mrs. Harriet Vincy Bulstrode, his wife and the sister of Mayor Vincy. Although she seems to care only for social prestige, she loyally supports her husband after his disgrace.

Peter Featherstone, the wealthy, aged owner of Stone Court. He tries to give his fortune to Mary Garth while she is nursing him during his final illness, but she refuses. His capricious will, cutting off all his grasping relatives, brings to Middlemarch strangers who precipitate Bulstrode's disgrace.

The Reverend Camden Farebrother, the vicar of St. Botolph's, a genial and casual clergyman. An expert whist-player and a friend of Lydgate, he is also, unsuccessfully, in love with Mary Garth.

The Reverend Humphrey Cadwallader, of Freshitt and Tipton, another genial clergyman who is particularly fond of fishing.

Mrs. Elinor Cadwallader, his wife, a talkative woman always acquainted with the latest scandal.

Caleb Garth, Mary's father, a stalwart and honest surveyor, land agent, and unsuccessful builder. He pays Fred Vincy's debts.

Susan Garth, his loyal, devoted wife, who educates her children with scholarly care and insight.

Mrs. Selina Plymdale, a Middlemarch gossip, friendly with the Vincys and the Bulstrodes.

Ned Plymdale, her son, a disappointed suitor of Rosamond Vincy.

Borthrop Trumbull, a florid auctioneer and cousin to old Featherstone.

John Raffles, an old reprobate and blackmailer who enters Middlemarch because he has married the mother of Feather-

stone's unexpected heir and periodically appears to get money. Just before he dies, he reveals Bulstrode's sordid past.

Joshua Rigg, an enigmatic man who inherits Featherstone's house and money. He must adopt Featherstone's name as well.

Mr. Tyke, an evangelical clergyman, supported by Bulstrode and Lydgate for the post of chaplain at the new hospital.

Naumann, a German artist and a friend of Will Ladislaw.

Mrs. Jane Waule, the widowed, avaricious sister of Peter Featherstone.

Solomon Featherstone, her wealthy and equally avaricious brother.

Jonah Featherstone, another of Peter's disappointed brothers.

Mrs. Martha Cranch, a poor sister of Peter Featherstone, also neglected in his will.

Tom Cranch, her unintelligent and unenterprising son.

Ben Garth, the active, athletic son of the Garths.

Letty Garth, the Garths' very bright younger daughter.

Alfred Garth, the son for whose engineering career the Garths are saving the money they use to pay Fred Vincy's debts.

Christy Garth, the Garths' oldest son, who becomes a scholar and tutor.

Mrs. Farebrother, the mother of the Reverend Mr. Camden.

Miss Henrietta Noble, her pious, understanding sister.

Miss Winifred Farebrother, Camden's sister, who idolizes him.

The Dowager Lady Chettam, Sir James's stiff and formal mother.

Arthur Chettam, the child of Sir James and Celia.

Sir Godwin Lydgate, of Quallingham in the north of England, Lydgate's distant and distinguished cousin. Rosamond appeals to him for money but is denied.

Tantripp, Dorothea's faithful and understanding maid.

Mme Laure, a French actress whom Lydgate once loved.

Dr. Sprague and

Dr. Minchin, conservative Middlemarch physicians.

Mr. Wrench, at first physician to the Vincys, replaced by the more competent and progressive Lydgate.

Mr. Standish, the local lawyer who represents Peter Featherstone.

Mr. Mawmsey, a Middlemarch grocer.

Mrs. Mawmsey, his wife, a Middlemarch gossip.

Harry Toller, a local brewer.

Miss Sophy Toller, his daughter, who finally marries Ned Plymdale.

Edwin Larcher, a local businessman.

Mrs. Larcher, his wife, a local gossip.

Mr. Bambridge, a horse dealer who swindles Fred Vincy.

Mr. Horrock, his friend.

Mr. Hawley, a local citizen who frequently comments on people and events.

Mr. Chichely, another local citizen.

Dagley, an insolent farmer on Arthur Brooke's land.

Pinkerton, Mr. Brooke's political opponent in the election for Parliament.

MIDNIGHT'S CHILDREN

Author: Salman Rushdie (1947-   )
First published: 1981
Genre: Novel

Locale: India and Pakistan
Time: 1947-1977, with flashbacks
Plot: Magical Realism

Saleem Sinai, the narrator, nicknamed **Snotnose**, **Sniffer**, **Stainface**, and **Baldy**, a thirty-year-old Muslim Indian. He was born at midnight on India's independence day, August 15, 1947. Saleem sees his personal history and the history of the other thousand children born in the first hour of independence as intimately connected to the future of all of India. He is the apparent son of a wealthy Muslim merchant in Bombay, but it was later discovered that he was switched at birth with Shiva, another of midnight's children. Saleem believes that by using the power of his enormous but sensitive nose, he will become the leader of the magically talented midnight's children, who can change the world. After going through many trying and fantastic experiences, which occasion the deaths of most of his family and contemporaries, Saleem composes his memoirs in anticipation of his own end.

Shiva, Saleem's rival and the other infant exchanged at birth, named after the Hindu god of procreation and destruction. Also one of midnight's children, Shiva personifies power and violence. His knees are his magical characteristic, knees that can squeeze the life out of any person. After Saleem discovers his own background, he fears that Shiva will discover his and attempt to replace Saleem and punish him for the deception. Shiva, an organizer of a youthful street gang in Bombay when young, joins the military and succeeds ruthlessly, becoming India's most famous war hero. He ultimately exposes his fellow midnight's children, all of whom are subsequently sterilized by the Indian government. Shiva already has fathered many illegitimate children, however, including one by Parvati, whom Saleem accepts as his son.

Parvati-the-witch, who was born only seven seconds after midnight and is another of midnight's children. Her abilities are in conjuring and sorcery. She is in love with Saleem, but he resists her because of his desires for Jamila, his sister. To overcome Saleem's objections to marriage, Parvati seduces and becomes pregnant by Shiva. She marries Saleem and takes the name **Laylah Sinai**. She dies in a government-sponsored riot led by Shiva.

Aadam Sinai, the son of Parvati and Shiva, born at midnight in 1975, coinciding with a state of emergency proclaimed by the Indian government. Aadam is born with elephant-sized ears, and Saleem sees him as the new midnight's child.

Padma, Saleem's plump and illiterate housekeeper. It is she to whom Saleem tells his tale after he discovers her working in Mary Pereira's pickle factory. Padma doubts much of what Saleem has to say but is fascinated by his seemingly super-natural history. She wishes to marry Saleem, but he resists because of his impotence.

Mary Pereira, a Christian Indian, a midwife, and Saleem's nurse. Because of her love for an Indian radical, she switches Saleem and Shiva at birth, thus bringing Saleem into the Aziz-Sinai family, both fulfilling a prophecy by a soothsayer and also misleading everyone. After confessing her crime many years later, Mary eventually reappears in a factory manufacturing pickle chutney, and it is there that Saleem composes his memoirs.

Aadam Aziz, Saleem's supposed grandfather and family patriarch from Kashmir. A medical doctor trained in Germany, Aziz falls in love with Naseem Ghani, a young Indian woman, by examining various parts of her body over a long period of time through a hole in a sheet.

Naseem Ghani, Saleem's supposed grandmother and wife of Aadam Aziz. Known as the Reverend Mother, Naseem Aziz becomes the family matriarch, eventually eclipsing even her husband. She dies, along with many others among Saleem's family, in Pakistan during the Indo-Pakistani war of 1965.

Alia Aziz, Saleem's supposed mother. Dark-complected in a society that admires fairness, she was first married to a poet, Nadir Khan. The marriage was not consummated. She then married Ahmed Sinai, who changed her name to Amina Sinai. She, too, dies in Pakistan.

Ahmed Sinai, Saleem's supposed father, a Muslim businessman in Bombay. Something of a dreamer and ultimately ineffective, he drowns his disappointments in drink.

William Methwold, an Englishman whose distant ancestor and namesake founded Bombay. Gifted with thick, black, center-parted, and brilliantined hair, he seduces the wife of a street singer, thus becoming the father of Saleem. Methwold sold his Bombay estate to Ahmed Sinai, turning over the property on August 15, 1947, India's independence day and the birthday of midnight's children.

Jamila Sinai, the **Brass Monkey**, Saleem's supposed sister. A tomboy when young, after the family moves to Muslim Pakistan, she becomes a popular singer of religious and nationalistic songs known as **Jamila Singer**. Saleem falls in love with her, but his passion is not reciprocated.

Wee Willie Winkle, an Indian street singer, the supposed father of Shiva. Vanita, his wife, was seduced by Methwold and died giving birth to Saleem, who was immediately switched with Shiva by Mary Pereira.

— *Eugene S. Larson*

A MIDSUMMER NIGHT'S DREAM

Author: William Shakespeare (1564-1616)
First published: 1600
Genre: Drama

Locale: Athens
Time: Antiquity
Plot: Comedy

Theseus (THEE-see-uhs), the duke of Athens, a wise, temperate ruler. Although he mistrusts the fantasy and imagination of "lunatics, lovers, and poets," he can perceive with good humor the love and duty inspiring the abortive dramatic efforts of his subjects, and he tries to teach his bride and queen, Hippolyta, the value of their good intentions.

Hippolyta (hih-POL-ih-tuh), Theseus' bride, the queen of the Amazons, the maiden warriors whom he has conquered. She is a woman of regal dignity, less willing than her lord to be tolerant of the faults of Peter Quince's play, although she is more ready than he to believe the lovers' description of their night in the forest.

Titania (tih-TAY-nee-uh), the imperious queen of the fairies. She feuds with her husband Oberon over her "little changeling boy," whom the king wants as his page. Enchanted by Oberon's flower, "love in idleness," she becomes enamored of Bottom the Weaver in his ass's head and dotes on him until her husband takes pity on her and frees her from the spell. She is quickly reconciled with him, and they join in blessing the marriage of Theseus and Hippolyta, their favorites among mortals.

Oberon (OH-beh-ron), the king of the fairies, who gleefully plots with Puck to cast a spell on the fairy queen and take away her changeling. Once he has stolen the child, he repents his mischief and frees Titania from her ridiculous dotage. He teases her for her fondness for Theseus and is, in return, forced to confess his own affection for Hippolyta.

Puck, the merry, mischievous elf, Robin Goodfellow, of English folk legend. He is Oberon's servant. He brings about the confusion of the young Athenians on Midsummer Eve as he tries to carry out Oberon's wishes; the king has taken pity on Helena and hopes to turn Demetrius' scorn for her into love. Puck simply enchants the first Athenian he sees, Lysander, and with great amusement watches the confusion that follows, commenting, "Lord, what fools these mortals be!"

Hermia (HEHR-mee-uh), a bright, bold young Athenian maiden. She defies her father and flees into the Athenian wood to elope with her beloved Lysander. She shows herself to be a small spitfire when she finds Demetrius and Lysander, through Puck's machinations, suddenly rivaling each other for Helena's affection rather than hers.

Helena (HEHL-eh-nuh), a maiden who mournfully follows Demetrius, spaniel-like, in spite of the scorn with which he repulses her affection. When she suddenly finds both Demetrius and Lysander at her feet, she can only believe that they are teasing her.

Demetrius (deh-MEE-tree-uhs), a rather fickle Athenian youth. He deserts his first love, Helena, to win the approval of Hermia's father for marriage with her, but he cannot win Hermia herself. His affections are returned, by Oberon's herb, to Helena, and he is wed to her on his duke's marriage day.

Lysander (lih-SAN-dur), Hermia's sweetheart, who plans their elopement to escape Theseus' decree that the girl must follow her father's will or enter a nunnery. He brashly argues with Demetrius, first over Hermia, then over Helena, before he is happily wed to his first love.

Nick Bottom, a good-natured craftsman and weaver. He is so enthralled by the prospect of Quince's play, *Pyramus and Thisbe*, that he longs to play all the other parts in addition to his assigned role of the hero. He is supremely complacent as Titania's paramour and takes for granted the services of the fairies who scratch the ass's ears placed on his head by Puck. He marvels at his "most rare vision" after his release from the fairy spell.

Peter Quince, a carpenter, director of the infamous play of "tragical mirth" presented in honor of Theseus' wedding. Completely well-meaning, he illustrates, as he mangles his prologue, the "love and tongue-tied simplicity" of which Theseus speaks.

Snug, a joiner,

Snout, a tinker,

Flute, a bellows-maker, and

Starveling, a tailor, the other craftsmen-actors who portray, respectively, Lion, Wall, Thisbe, and Moonshine.

Egeus (ee-JEE-uhs), Hermia's father. He is determined that his daughter will marry Demetrius, not Lysander, whom she loves.

Philostrate (FIH-los-trayt), Theseus' master of the revels.

Peaseblossom,

Cobweb,

Moth, and

Mustardseed, Titania's fairy attendants who wait on Bottom.

THE MIGHTY AND THEIR FALL

Author: Ivy Compton-Burnett (1884-1969)
First published: 1961
Genre: Novel

Locale: An unnamed town in England
Time: Mid-twentieth century
Plot: Domestic realism

Ninian Middleton, the father in an upper-class English family. A self-righteous widower who deeply loves his mother and children, he decides to take a new wife and provide his children with a stepmother. When he learns that his daughter Lavinia has taken immoral steps to prevent the marriage, he reacts harshly to her, not by banishing her from the family but by putting her in circumstances in which the act of hiding a letter from his fiancée will never be forgotten and, therefore, never really forgiven. Ninian subsequently makes a similar mistake when his sick brother, Ransom, asks him to burn a will. His own transgression in this situation makes it possible to reconcile with his daughter.

Lavinia Middleton, the eldest daughter of Ninian. She hopes to save her father from the mistake of what she sees as an ill-begotten second marriage. She hides a letter written to her father from his fiancée, and when this act is exposed, she seems unconcerned about being forgiven by other family members. When she inherits money from her uncle Ransom, she announces that she will marry another uncle, Hugo, despite the shadings of incest and the difference in age. Given almost entirely to selfish desires after her first act of villainy, Lavinia never recovers from being tainted, although she does become reconciled with other family members who reveal themselves to be as bad as she is.

Selina Middleton, Ninian's mother. Selina acts as the matriarch of the family. She is the embodiment of English stuffiness and womanhood until she is caught in a heinous lie: In order to prevent the marriage of Lavinia and her own adopted son Hugo, Selina claims that Hugo is in fact a blood member of the family, an illegitimate half brother of Ninian. When Hugo discovers the truth and reveals it, Selina is exposed as a liar before her family. She acts to control events from beyond the grave—to prevent the marriage of Lavinia and Hugo—by leaving Hugo most of her own money at her death. When this occurs, Hugo abandons his intentions to marry Lavinia, as Selina had anticipated.

Ransom Middleton, a long-absent brother of Ninian. Something of the stereotypical wicked uncle, Ransom returns home to die. He assumes a relationship with Lavinia after she is exposed for hiding the letter to her father. Ransom shares a kinship with Lavinia for her misdeed; upon his death, he leaves Lavinia most of his estate.

Hugo Middleton, the adopted son of Selina and her late husband. The only character in the novel who acts from purely selfish motives, Hugo never claims to be doing evil for the sake of achieving a greater good. He would marry Lavinia for her money; when the need for money is removed, he decides not to marry her while openly acknowledging that he prefers the free ways of being a bachelor.

Teresa Chilton, fiancée to Ninian and later stepmother to the children of the family. Teresa acts honorably on all counts. When she realizes that she will not be received warmly in the household by family members, particularly the children, she offers to release Ninian from the engagement.

— *Carl Singleton*

MIGUEL STREET

Author: V. S. Naipaul (1932-   )
First published: 1959
Genre: Novel

Locale: Trinidad
Time: Late 1930's to late 1940's
Plot: Comic realism

The narrator, an adult recounting his life as a boy living on Miguel Street with his widowed mother. He gives an observant, intelligent, and sensitive yet naïve child's view of the street's eccentric personalities, often imparting sympathy when the street denies it. An early admirer of Hat, he becomes more critical with age and leaves Trinidad at the age of eighteen to study abroad.

Hat, a keeper of cows and a gambler. In appearance and affected mannerisms, he is like a dark-brown, early-middle-aged Rex Harrison. He enjoys life and imbues simple things with mystery. A keen observer with an ironic sense of humor and sympathy for the least fortunate, he is the wise arbiter, conscience, and spokesman for the street, which changes irrevocably when Hat is imprisoned for beating his unfaithful female companion.

Bogart, a would-be tailor. Appearing languorous and bored, with small, sleepy eyes, he tries to assume the mannerisms and personality of Humphrey Bogart. He mysteriously disappears from time to time and eventually is arrested for bigamy. He left a childless marriage "feeling sad and small" and later was forced to marry a woman he made pregnant. Hat says Bogart returned to the street "to be a man among we men."

Popo, a carpenter who eschews making objects of utility for the never-finished "thing without a name." Supported by his wife, Emelda, he relishes life's simple pleasures and is friendly to the young narrator, who thinks him to be a philosopher. Not accepted by the street until Emelda deserts him and he becomes drunken and aggressive, Popo is arrested for theft soon after she returns. After his release from prison, he is a hero on the street but is changed temperamentally, turning to practical carpentry and driving away the narrator.

George, an unemployed resident of Miguel Street but never one of the gang. Short, fat, gray-mustached, and sadistic, he often brutally beats his children and wife, who tends cows. When his frail wife dies, possibly as a result of a beating, he sells the cows, turns his house into a brothel, and marries off his pathetic daughter Dolly. Competition kills his business, and George dies a sad, unlamented man.

Elias, George's son, a student of Titus Hoyt. Despite frequent cruel beatings, he is understanding and forgiving of his father. Thought by his neighbors to be bright and a model for other boys, he wants to be a doctor, but after a series of failures, he gradually lowers his expectations and finds work driving a scavenging cart.

Man-man, an unemployed madman who takes all day to cover the street with one chalked word and controls his dog's bowels to gain advantage and income. A self-declared new messiah who stages his own crucifixion, he is confined by the authorities after cursing those he invited to stone him.

B. Wordsworth, a gentle poet who claims to be writing one line a month on his great projected poem. He befriends the narrator, introducing him to the beauty and mystery of life and telling him a tragic story of lost love, a story he recants when near death.

Big Foot, a holder of many jobs and a well-known prankster and comedian. He is widely feared as a bully until he reveals his weakness by crying after losing a boxing match.

Morgan, who is ignored as a pyrotechnicist and unsuccessful as a self-deprecating comedian. He is given to violent rages of frustration. This small, birdlike father of ten finally gets laughs when publicly humiliated by his six-foot wife and achieves wide recognition when he burns down his own house in a spectacular fireworks display.

Titus Hoyt, the headmaster of his own school. Interested, despite their resistance, in the improvement of the neighborhood boys, he writes fraudulent letters of self-promotion to the newspaper.

Laura, the mother of eight children by seven fathers. Happy and vivacious, she grieves when her eldest daughter, Lorna, becomes pregnant and thinks it just as well when Lorna commits suicide.

Eddoes, a scavenging-cart driver who is meticulous about cleanliness and his appearance. He is proud of his job, his junk collection, and the child he rears, mistakenly convinced that she is his own.

Mrs. Hereira, a wealthy doctor's wife who gives up everything for the love of the drunken and brutal Toni. Despairing of Toni's improvement and fearing for her life, she returns to her husband.

Bhakcu, the narrator's uncle, a large man who cannot resist tinkering with (and usually damaging) motor vehicles. A Brahmin, he sings the *Rāmāyāna* and beats his fat wife with an oiled cricket bat that she maintains.

Bolo, a sixty-year-old carter and barber who distrusts newspapers and feels cheated by everyone. Finally winning a sweepstakes, he tears up the ticket in disbelief and becomes a recluse.

Edward, Hat's brother, a primitive artist and worker for the United States military. Another Miguel Street eccentric, he becomes very Americanized but leaves Trinidad for Aruba or Curaçao when his formerly childless wife runs off with an American soldier and becomes pregnant.

— *Douglas Rollins*

THE MIKADO: Or, The Town of Titipu

Author: W. S. Gilbert (1836-1911)
First published: 1885
Genre: Drama

Locale: Titipu, Japan
Time: The Middle Ages
Plot: Satire

The Mikado of Japan, a humane monarch who desires to let the punishment fit the crime. To steady the young men of his kingdom, he has made flirting a capital crime. Without being in the least angry, he can calmly order a lawbreaker to be boiled in oil. All cheerfully bow to his will except Katisha, his daughter-in-law elect.

Nanki-Poo, the son of the Mikado. Loving Yum-Yum, he flees the court disguised as a second trombone to escape from his elderly fiancée, Katisha. He is willing to sacrifice his life for a month of marriage with Yum-Yum but unhesitatingly gives her up when he finds that she will have to be buried alive after his execution. After being declared dead by affidavit—a death that imperils the lives of the executioner and his accomplices—he refuses to return to life unless Ko-Ko marries Katisha. After she is safely married, he returns to life, receives his father's blessing, and faces a life of married bliss with Yum-Yum.

Ko-Ko, the chicken-hearted Lord High Executioner of Titipu. Appointed to his position by his fellow townsmen because he could not execute anybody else until he had executed himself, he is troubled by a command from the Mikado that an execution take place immediately. Loving himself with a tenderer passion than he loves Yum-Yum, his ward and affianced bride, he consents to let Nanki-Poo marry her for a month if he will allow himself to be executed at the end of that time. Unable to bring himself to kill anybody, he decides that an affidavit of Nanki-Poo's death will be as good as an execution. Faced with a choice of boiling in oil for encompassing the death of the heir apparent or of marrying Katisha, he reluctantly chooses the latter and saves his life.

Pooh-Bah, the self-important Lord High Everything Else. An extremely haughty individual of pre-Adamite ancestry, he humiliates himself by accepting the salaries of all the offices he holds and by taking bribes, which he styles "insults."

Katisha, an elderly lady of appalling aspect. Being an acquired taste, appealing only to connoisseurs, she has worked hard to teach Nanki-Poo to love her. Enraged at his desertion, she seeks revenge. When she thinks Nanki-Poo is dead, she marries Ko-Ko. On learning of his deception, she gives way to frightful fury but finally decides to make the best of her bargain.

Yum-Yum, Ko-Ko's ward, engaged to him. A child of nature, she takes after her mother and rejoices in her loveliness. She loves Nanki-Poo but is unwilling to pay for a month of marital bliss with her life. She becomes the emperor's daughter-in-law elect.

Pitti-Sing, Yum-Yum's sister. She testifies to Nanki-Poo's fictional death.

Peep-Bo, Yum-Yum's other sister, the third of the three maids from school.

Pish-Tush, a noble lord. With Pooh-Bah, he attempts to persuade Ko-Ko to execute himself.

THE MILL ON THE FLOSS

Author: George Eliot (Mary Ann Evans, 1819-1880)
First published: 1860
Genre: Novel

Locale: England
Time: The nineteenth century
Plot: Domestic realism

Maggie Tulliver, the impetuous and generous young heroine. Regarded as wild and gypsy-like by most of her respectable relatives, the sensitive and imaginative Maggie does not fit into the provincial society in and near St. Ogg's on the River Floss. She worships her brother Tom, who judges her harshly and thinks her unreliable. She loves Philip Wakem, the crippled son of her father's worst enemy, but must promise never to see him. Despite her feeling for Philip and her love for her cousin, Lucy Deane, Maggie is strongly attracted to her cousin's fiancé, Stephen Guest. Stephen persuades her to go boating, but they neglect their destination and are forced to spend the night on a freighter that rescues them. Almost everyone in St. Ogg's, her brother included, thinks Maggie responsible and regards her as an evil and designing woman. In the final scene, during a flood, Maggie takes a boat to rescue Tom, who is at the family mill. The two are reconciled before the raging river drowns them.

Tom Tulliver, Maggie's brother. Although never quick at school, Tom assumes financial responsibility for the family when he is only sixteen, after the father has lost his mill and home through a series of lawsuits. Tom pledges to follow his father in having nothing to do with the Wakem family. He works hard and, through his industry and careful investments in partnership with Bob Jakin, pays off his father's debts and eventually gets the mill back. Somewhat priggish, Tom judges others severely, but he is also generous to his mother and sister.

Edward Tulliver, the father of Maggie and Tom and the owner of Dorlcote Mill, near St. Ogg's on the River Floss. An emotional and hot-tempered man, Tulliver engages in several lawsuits that, in combination with other financial reverses, cause him to lose his mill. Tulliver must swallow his pride and work in the mill as the hated Wakem's manager. When Tom finally earns the money to pay off his father's debts, Tulliver meets Wakem and thrashes him. The exertion produces Tulliver's second stroke, and he dies. He is always partial to his clever and imaginative daughter Maggie.

Mrs. Elizabeth Tulliver (Bessy), Edward's wife, proud of her birth as a Dodson and grieved that her husband's temper and improvidence cause her to lose her home and furnishings. She is dependent on the advice and opinions of her more prosperous sisters. Her pleading visit to Wakem inadvertently causes him to plan to buy the mill when Tulliver is bankrupt. Regarding Maggie as wild and unladylike, she is partial to her son Tom.

Philip Wakem, a lawyer's son, humpbacked as the result of a childhood accident. An excellent scholar and a talented artist, he loves Maggie from the time he first meets her, for she does not judge him by his infirmity. He hopes to marry Maggie despite family objections and her temporary attraction to Stephen Guest.

Lucy Deane, Maggie's blonde and pretty cousin. She and Maggie go to boarding school together and become great friends. Maggie confesses her feeling for Philip Wakem to Lucy. At the end, Lucy understands that Maggie was essentially blameless in the boating escapade with Stephen Guest, and she forgives Maggie. She marries Stephen after Maggie is dead.

Stephen Guest, the handsome son of the wealthiest and most socially prominent family in St. Ogg's. Although engaged to Lucy, he is so attracted to Maggie that he pleads with her to marry him. After the boating trip, when Maggie is in disgrace, he goes off to Holland.

Mrs. Jane Glegg, the sister of Mrs. Tulliver. She is wealthy, parsimonious, and the proudest of the Dodson sisters. Although she dislikes Maggie, she defends her after the episode with Stephen Guest.

Mrs. Sophy Pullet, another of the Dodson sisters. She is wealthy and sentimental, crying copiously at every misfortune.

Mrs. Susan Deane, another Dodson sister, the pale and ailing mother of Lucy. She and Tulliver die about the same time.

Mr. Deane, her husband, who has worked his way up in the prosperous firm of Guest and Co., bankers, ship owners, and tradesmen. Although rather pompous about his achievements, he helps Tom get established in his firm.

Mrs. Gritty Moss, Mr. Tulliver's sister, a kind, poor woman with eight children. She has Maggie's ardent nature, although she lacks her niece's intelligence.

Mr. Moss, her husband, an unsuccessful farmer.

Mr. Glegg, husband of Jane Glegg, a wealthy, retired, prudent gentleman who had made a fortune in the wool business.

Mr. Pullet, husband of Sophy Pullet, a tiny, wealthy gentleman farmer who sucks lozenges throughout all family discussions.

Bob Jakin, Tom Tulliver's boyhood friend. He becomes Tom's partner in numerous investments.

John Wakem, the father of Philip and a lawyer in St. Ogg's. Although he does not hate Mr. Tulliver initially, Tulliver's frequent insults cause him to enjoy the family's downfall. His love for his son, however, later leads him to approve of the possibility of Philip's marrying Maggie.

The Reverend Walter Stelling, the owner of King's Lorton, the school attended by Tom Tulliver and Philip Wakem. He regards Tom as hopelessly stupid.

Luke Moggs, the head miller at Dorlcote Mill, fond of Maggie and entirely loyal to the Tullivers.

Mr. Riley, a local auctioneer, surveyor, and engineer, who dies leaving Mr. Tulliver with his debts.

The Reverend Dr. Kenn, rector of St. Ogg's, a clergyman sympathetic toward Maggie.

Mrs. Kenn, his wife, who runs a charity bazaar in St. Ogg's.

Mr. Poulter, the village schoolmaster.

Mr. Pivart, the owner of land near Dorlcote Mill who wishes to irrigate his land and is sued unsuccessfully by Mr. Tulliver.

Mr. Dix, another gentleman unsuccessfully sued by Mr. Tulliver.

Mr. Furley, the gentleman who owns the mortgage on Mr. Tulliver's land and transfers it to lawyer Wakem.

Mr. Gore, a scheming lawyer.

Mr. Jetsome, the young manager of the mill under Wakem after Tulliver dies. While drunk, he is pitched off his horse and severely injured.

Prissy Jakin, Bob Jakin's tiny "Dutch doll" wife.

Mrs. Jakin, Bob's massive mother.

THE MILL ON THE PO
(Il mulino del Po)

Author: Riccardo Bacchelli (1891-1895)
First published: 1938-1940
Genre: Novel

Locale: The region of the Po River, near Ferrera, Italy
Time: 1812-1872
Plot: Historical

Lazzaro Scacerni (lahz-ZAH-roh ska-CHEHR-nee), owner of St. Michael's mill on the Po River. He builds the mill with money inherited from a dying captain he met in Napoleon

Bonaparte's Russian campaign. Although illiterate, he creates a good business and maintains his mill through the adversities of flood, war, and political upheaval. He hates the smugglers in the neighborhood who use his beloved mill as a rendezvous, and he is outraged when his own son becomes involved in smuggling grain to the Austrian enemy in the 1840's.

Giuseppe Scacerni (jee-ew-SEHP-peh), the cowardly and crafty son of Lazzaro. He cares nothing for his father's mill and trade except its profits. He takes a part in selling grain to his country's enemies. He forces Cecilia to marry him through threats: If she marries him, he agrees he will not inform the authorities that his father possesses concealed firearms. When Giuseppe's son dies while fighting with Garibaldi, he loses his reason, and he is at last confined in a madhouse.

Dosolina Scacerni (doh-soh-LEE-nah), wife of the miller Lazzaro. Although Lazzaro is attractive to women and makes many conquests, he chooses this poor but delicately beautiful girl to be his wife. She is twenty years his junior. In 1855, she dies of cholera. Lazzaro follows her in death the next day.

Cecilia Scacerni, an orphan befriended, when a child, by Lazzaro. Her parents' mill is washed up on the shore of the river near St. Michael's mill during a flood. Lazzaro reestablishes her mill and cares for her as he would his own daughter. She sacrifices her own happiness to save her benefactor from prison by marrying Giuseppe. She is the last of the Scacerni family left to tend St. Michael's mill.

Beffa, a helper at the mill who incurs Lazzaro's wrath by declaring that the miller has been cuckolded. He is a tool of the smugglers who operate near the mill. He is killed in a gang feud.

Raguseo (rah-GEW-seh-oh), leader of the gang of smugglers who rendezvous at St. Michael's mill. He threatens to harm the miller when Beffa is fired from his job as the miller's helper. Like Beffa, he is killed when a feud breaks out in the gang.

Lazzarino Scacerni (lahz-zah-REE-noh), the son of Giuseppe and Cecilia. Vigorous and intelligent like his grandfather and a joy to both his parents, he is killed while fighting as a volunteer with Garibaldi.

THE MIMIC MEN

Author: V. S. Naipaul (1932-   )
First published: 1967
Genre: Novel

Locale: The Caribbean and London
Time: The 1930's, 1940's, and 1960's
Plot: Psychological realism

Ranjit Ralph Kripal Singh, the protagonist and narrator, a politician in exile. The son of a poor schoolteacher and a woman from a wealthy family, Singh is a member of the Indian minority on the Caribbean island of Isabella. Intelligent and sensitive, he feels alienated during his childhood, during his university years in London, and during his later years as a real estate developer and a politician on his native island. Banished after a coup, at the age of forty he is finished, a purposeless exile living in a lower-middle-class area of London.

Sandra Singh, Ralph's wife. A tall, big-boned, large-breasted woman with an ill-tempered expression on her face, she has cut herself off from her lower-class London family and is attempting to move upward in society by getting a degree from the well-known school where Ralph is enrolled. She fails her qualifying examination twice, however, and then changes course, persuades Ralph to marry her, and goes to Isabella with him. There, although she tries to adopt the manners of the wealthy, she cannot keep up the pretense; soon, she is publicly mocked and snubbed. After numerous infidelities, she leaves Singh and moves to Miami.

Cecil, Ralph's uncle and schoolmate. A young brother of Ralph's mother, he is aggressive and flamboyant, even as a child. He inherits the bottling works on which the family fortune is based, but he soon loses his money and his license. Brandishing his Luger, he tyrannizes Isabella residents and almost certainly is the person who shoots Ralph's father and his common-law wife.

Kripalsingh, later **Gurudeva**, Ralph's father. A poor schoolteacher for whom a brilliant future was once predicted, he lapses into irritability as one misadventure follows another. Deserting his family, he becomes the leader of a protest movement and then a prophet who lives in the hills and fathers at least one other son. Eventually, he is killed, probably by Cecil.

"Champ" Deschampsneufs (day-SHAH-noof), a schoolmate of Ralph. A member of Isabella's most aristocratic family, he becomes a friend of Ralph despite the difference in their social positions. After working in a bank, he moves to Quebec, where he paints and dabbles in the Hindu religion.

Wendy Deschampsneufs, Champ's younger sister. A small and ugly but vivacious woman, she first becomes a friend of Sandra and then suddenly drops her. Later, she is a central force in the political movement led by Ralph and Ethelbert Browne. After a few months, she becomes bored and joins her brother in Quebec.

Ethelbert Browne, a black schoolmate of Ralph. As a boy, he is skinny, nervous, and insecure, with a mirthless smile and a wart on his chin. He is embarrassed when Ralph visits his home; as a result, their friendship breaks up until after both young men have gone to school in London and returned to Isabella. A feverish talker and a journalist, Browne becomes a folk leader and attains power along with Ralph. Lacking the skills of a politician, however, he also falls.

— *Rosemary M. Canfield Reisman*

THE MINISTRY OF FEAR

Author: Graham Greene (1904-1991)
First published: 1943
Genre: Novel

Locale: London, England, and its environs
Time: During World War II
Plot: Psychological realism

Arthur Rowe, a middle-aged Englishman living through World War II in London. He is a lonely widower, having killed his wife to prevent her living in pain. By accident, he comes into possession of secret films taken by Nazi agents, and he immediately becomes the object of their search. He suffers amnesia when injured in a bombing raid and is unable for a time to remember anything beyond his youth. He finds himself confined in a nursing home that is a front for Nazi activities. He escapes and, aided by counter-intelligence agents, uncovers the Nazi activities. He regains his memory at the same time. Meanwhile, he has fallen in love with Anna Hilfe, sister of the spy group's leader.

Mr. Jones, a private detective. He is hired by Rowe, who wants to know why someone wants to kill him. Jones disappears, and his employer turns the case over to counter-intelligence.

Anna Hilfe, a young Austrian refugee. She informs Rowe that Nazi agents are after him. Though her brother is a Nazi spy, she helps Rowe uncover the enemy activities because she has fallen in love with the Englishman.

Willi Hilfe, an Austrian refugee, Anna's brother. He helps Rowe "escape" when a man is supposedly murdered. Hilfe turns out to be the head of a Nazi fifth-column group operating in England. He commits suicide when he is found out.

Dr. Forester, head of the nursing home in which Rowe finds himself. Forester, an enemy agent, is killed by one of the hospital attendants.

MINNA VON BARNHELM: Or, The Soldier's Fortune
(Minna von Barnhelm: Oder, Das Soldatenglück)

Author: Gotthold Ephraim Lessing (1729-1781)
First published: 1767
Genre: Drama

Locale: Germany
Time: The eighteenth century
Plot: Comedy

Minna von Barnhelm (MIH-nah fon BAHRN-hehlm), a charming and beautiful young heiress betrothed to a former Prussian officer, Major Tellheim. Hearing no word from him after the peace, she sets out resolutely with her maid Franziska to find the major. Stopping at an inn, the two women are given the quarters of Tellheim, whom the landlord has dispossessed for nonpayment of rent. Minna learns of Tellheim's misfortune and, so that his pride will not stand in their way, she pretends to have lost her own fortune too. After many misunderstandings, word is received that Tellheim's commission and property have been restored. The lovers are soon reconciled.

Major von Tellheim (TEHL-him), a gallant and brave soldier recently discharged from the army, wounded and under shadow of suspicion for double dealing. As much as he loves Minna, he has purposely broken off communications with her to clear his good name, restore his health, and regain his fortune. Never one to accept charity, he rejects the repayment of a loan by the widow of a comrade-in-arms, the offer of financial help from his old sergeant, and the sympathy as well as the fortune of his fiancée. On the other hand, his own generosity, in advancing war taxes for a destitute principality and borrowing large funds for what he was led to believe is a destitute Minna, is forthright and sincere. Eventually, his name is cleared and his property restored. He and Minna then plan their wedding.

Just (yewst), the major's humorous, loyal servant. He defends his master against insults from the landlord and does all he can to ease the major's financial difficulties.

Franziska (fran-TSIHS-kah), Minna's resourceful maid and confidante. She joins her mistress in the intrigue designed to mollify the major's pride. In the process, she finds a husband for herself.

Sergeant Paul Werner (VEHR-nehr), Tellheim's loyal sergeant. He places all of his resources at the disposal of the major, even offering to raise money by selling his farm. When the major's problems finally are resolved, Werner becomes engaged to Franziska.

Lieutenant Riccault de la Marlinière (rih-KOHL duh lah mahr-lee-NYEHR), a mercenary and a gambler. Welcomed because he brings the news that Major Tellheim's good name and commission will soon be restored, he proves to be a scoundrel who manages to gain sympathy and money from Minna for his illicit gambling enterprises.

The landlord, a greedy, prying innkeeper. He dispossesses Tellheim and rents his room to Minna when the major falls behind in his rent.

Count von Bruchsal (BREWKH-zahl), Minna's uncle, who controls her wealth. He arrives in time to give the reconciled lovers his blessing.

A MINOR APOCALYPSE
(Mała apokalipsa)

Author: Tadeusz Konwicki (1926-   )
First published: 1979
Genre: Novel

Locale: Poland
Time: The not-too-distant future
Plot: Political

Konwicki (kohn-WIHTS-kih), the narrator. Konwicki is a famous middle-aged writer living in the Polish capital. Like the actual Tadeusz Konwicki, the narrator is an astute observer of the disintegration of Polish culture and its near-total (in this grim fantasy) subjugation to the Russian giant to its east.

Unlike the defiant author, however, the fictional Konwicki is, in his own eyes, an aging, largely passive figure whose best work quite likely is behind him. He abhors the suffocating Russian influence and bemoans the ineffectuality that marks Polish institutions, but he is unsure what part he can or should play in protesting conditions. Thus, when revolutionary friends give him the honor of martyring himself (by burning himself to death) for the cause, his principal reaction is indecision. The very structure of his day-long odyssey around Warsaw (circular and rambling), which composes the bulk of the novel, reflects his indecisiveness, which results not only from cowardice and cynicism (can his martyrdom possibly make any difference?) but also hope. If Konwicki did not have hope that his martyrdom might make some genuine difference, his decision would be an easy one: He would decline the honor. His decision at the end, to go through with the self-immolation, is the best clue to Konwicki's character.

Hubert, a Polish dissident. For his visit to Konwicki, Hubert dresses in his best suit and sports a cane and a "sinister-looking" briefcase. Once, in the past, Hubert had attempted to hang himself because of attacks from his political enemies, but at present he seems a bit too well-fed and complacent for a radical. He is willing to let Konwicki martyr himself, although it is doubtful that Hubert is himself any longer capable of such action. Still, he seems to have some genuine affection for Konwicki and is bothered to the point of physical collapse by Konwicki's objections to Hubert's cheerful suggestion that he martyr himself.

Rysio (REW-syoh), Hubert's companion. Konwicki remembers Rysio as an energetic blond god in his younger days, but in the present Rysio is a dull, uninspired writer who, politically, is little more than a hanger-on.

Nadezhda (nah-DEHZH-dah), also called **Hope**, a dissident. Nadezhda gives Konwicki specific instructions for carrying out his martyrdom. More important, being from Russia,

Nadezhda affords Konwicki, through his conversations with her, the opportunity to address any number of issues concerning Russian-Polish relations. More important still, being a beautiful woman, Nadezhda evokes from Konwicki pangs of lust, reminding him of his humanity and how much potential beauty and pleasure he is giving up by his martyrdom.

Tadzio Skorko, a young man from the provinces. Tadzio accompanies Konwicki during much of his rambling around Warsaw. He seems at first an almost pathetically and naïvely ardent admirer of the famous writer. Strangely enough, this impression is not entirely eroded when Konwicki discovers that Tadzio is really a police informer.

George, Ryzio's brother, a propaganda head. George represents the Pole who has "sold out" to the other side. He is intelligent enough to know that his position is not entirely ethical, yet, like a good bureaucrat, he is energetic in defense of himself and the bureaucracy that he represents.

Kobialka (koh-bee-AHL-kah), Konwicki's neighbor. Kobialka demonstrates for the hesitant Konwicki that even in the ineffectual society of fallen Poland one can take a stand. He in effect martyrs himself by removing his clothes on television and attacking the Polish-Russian system.

The chief, a member of the secret police. Along with his assistants, this torturer is not the maniacal, mustache-twirling villain of grade-B films but is typical of the Eastern European view of the bureaucracy. Even in the middle of torturing Konwicki, the secret police officers are all slightly bored, rather friendly, and generally ineffectual, like the bureaucracy they represent, less evil than banal.

— *Dennis Vannatta*

MINTY ALLEY

Author: C. L. R. James (1901-1989)
First published: 1936
Genre: Novel

Locale: A working-class neighborhood in Trinidad
Time: The 1930's
Plot: Social realism

Haynes, a bookstore clerk. A sheltered, solitary, middle-class, black bachelor of twenty, he has recently lost his beloved, widowed mother, a headmistress who had controlled and planned his life. Left with only his small income, timid, naïve, and dependent on his servant Ella, he enters a period of initiation when he takes a room in a lower-class compound in Minty Alley. Initially an interested observer and always a privileged and respected outsider, he is gradually drawn into the conflicts, intrigues, and passions of the yard inhabitants. He is sought for his advice and is expected to be an arbiter of disputes. His relationship with Maisie aids in his transformation.

Ella, Haynes's servant. Good-natured, selfless, and dedicated to Haynes's welfare, she is dubious about his living among the socially inferior people of Minty Alley. Perspicacious and wise in the ways of the yard, she keeps Haynes informed and protected, jealously preparing his food and cleaning for him until ill health forces her to leave.

Mrs. Alice Rouse, Haynes's landlord, a baker. A short, stout, handsome, brown-skinned woman of about forty-five, she is struggling to make a living and maintain her dignity while providing employment and support for her rebellious niece Maisie and for her paramour of seventeen years, Benoit.

She is strong-willed, religious, hardworking, and independent, having left an unfaithful husband many years earlier. Betrayed by Benoit and her friend, Nurse Jackson; taunted by Maisie; and beset by financial problems, she becomes increasingly emotional, calling on the power of both conventional and folk religion (obeah) to regain her man and punish her tormentors. When Benoit is ill and abandoned by his wife, Mrs. Rouse is loyal and forgiving, but all she can do for him is arrange his funeral and pay the expenses.

McCarthy Benoit, Mrs. Rouse's common-law husband and a helper in the bakery. A large, very dark Afro-East Indian of about forty, he is a selfish, compulsive womanizer with few scruples about exploiting and then hurting, shaming, and deserting Mrs. Rouse. He marries Nurse Jackson because she appears white and can provide him with gifts and money. Although he is confident of his sexual powers and a braggart, he sometimes practices obeah to help obtain his ends. He declines quickly after his marriage, quarreling with the nurse, who abandons him after he suffers a series of strokes. He eventually dies of a stroke.

Maisie, Mrs. Rouse's niece and Haynes's mistress. Barely seventeen years old, big, strong, and very attractive, she is a vivacious, manipulative, and sarcastic girl who is in full rebellion against Mrs. Rouse, the aunt who has reared her. Lying and stealing when she pleases, she takes malicious pleasure in stirring up trouble and puncturing what she sees as pretensions in her aunt and others. Confident, amused, independent, and unsentimental, she becomes Haynes's first friend and sexual partner without demands or further expectations. Forced by her aunt to leave the yard, she boldly carries out her plan to go to America, where she hopes to work for a high salary.

Nurse Jackson, a roomer and friend of Mrs. Rouse. Short, very thin, and nearly white in complexion, with long, silky hair, she is dishonest, coldly calculating, and manipulative. A brutal woman with a questionable past, she has at least one illegitimate child, whom she alternately pampers and viciously beats. In her late thirties and initially a source of brightness, good humor, and some luxury in the yard, she steals Benoit from Mrs. Rouse and publicly humiliates her. She dominates

the unemployed Benoit after their marriage and deserts him when he becomes ill, claiming his infidelity. Convicted of stealing from her employers, she eventually moves to America with her son.

Miss Atwell, a roomer and friend of Mrs. Rouse. Nearing fifty, very small, with a lined face and keen, alert eyes, she is no longer visited or supported by the man who kept her, and she fears seizure by the bailiff. A good-hearted supporter of Mrs. Rouse, she is a constant, if tiresome, source of information for Haynes.

Philomen, Mrs. Rouse's faithful East Indian servant. Fat, brown, and pleasant-looking, she is smiling and good-natured despite the demands on her. After nine years, she is forced to leave the yard when Mrs. Rouse believes the obeah man who tells her that Indians are the source of all of her troubles.

— *Douglas Rollins*

MIRACLE OF THE ROSE
(Miracle de la rose)

Author: Jean Genet (1910-1986)
First published: 1946; revised, 1951
Genre: Novel

Locale: A boys' reformatory at Mettray and the Fontevrault Prison
Time: The twentieth century
Plot: Psychological

Jean Genet (zhah[n] zheh-NAY), a defensive, thirty-year-old Fontevrault "lifer" with repeated burglary convictions who sees himself as a character in a dream, a living skeleton, and a dead man irrevocably locked within the restrictions of prison life. In his inverted moral order, he covets infamous acts of brutality so that he can attain the spiritual heights of Harcamone, a rapist-murderer, and thus achieve his own death by decapitation as the epitome of beauty. The thin, lightly muscled, slow-moving narrator masks his fears by assuming an offensive, angry posture and consciously appears humorless to avoid losing control of himself through laughter. First entering Mettray for having stabbed out the eye of a child, Genet idolizes "big shots" who have descended further than he. At Fontevrault, Genet reveres both Harcamone, a God figure, and Bulkaen, the hand of God. The narrator's violent, repressed desires find sexual outlets in his memories of thievery, his fantasies, his eruptive attacks, and his need to participate in other inmates' orgasms.

Bulkaen (bewl-KA[N]), also known as **Robert**, **Pierrot** (pyeh-ROH), **Jewel**, and **Rocky's girl**, a twenty-two-year-old, green-eyed, blond, tattooed Fontevrault inmate who is the immediate sexual and spiritual focus of the narrator's longing. A proud, icy, vindictive thief who disguises the anguish of feeling abandoned with lies and manipulations, Bulkaen both inspires the narrator to passion and, according to Genet, shatters his life. Although he initiates contact, Pierrot contemptuously rejects the narrator's first advances but eventually allows Genet to kiss him and becomes his "kid." As the instrument of God, Bulkaen reveals the narrator's fate. After his death, he is internalized by Genet as the priest who aids the narrator's psychic support of Harcamone.

Harcamone (ahr-kah-MUH[N]), a rapist-murderer who escapes life imprisonment by severing the carotid artery of the least offensive prison guard and being sentenced to the guillotine. He has achieved the pinnacle of glory to the narrator and

is the source of the miracles Genet witnesses. Harcamone is a small-boned and impassive, but mournful, celibate. He has transcended his slight foreign accent, his limp, and his hand wrapped in white gauze. He is the distant, haunting focus of Genet's attention, the illumined superbeing that the narrator aspires to be but believes that he cannot be. Harcamone's concentration is on his impending death.

Divers (dee-VEHR), also called **Riton-la-Noie** (ree-TOH[N]-lah-NWAH), who is eight years older than the narrator and a bisexual "big shot." He "marries" Genet at Mettray and consummates the marriage fifteen years later at Fontevrault. Although top-heavy with well-developed shoulders, Divers appears physically proportionate because of his graceful carriage. Divers, who is syphilitic, masks a profound internal despair with audacity and shiftiness. As a Fontevrault trusty, Divers enjoys prison routine and manipulates within the system. The narrator holds Divers responsible for Harcamone's execution because he is the informant whose information led to Harcamone's fourth conviction.

Botchako (boht-shah-KOH), also called **the Bandit**, an epileptic who is known as the prison's worst bully. He is Bulkaen's lover and has a boxer's physique, deep-set eyes, and a hoarse voice. He is so filled with repressed rage that once he initiates a physical assault, he is unable to stop the attack. Botchako's intimacy with Bulkaen arouses the narrator's jealousy and increases the passion in his sexual relationship with Divers. The Bandit offers the narrator his friendship; he is humiliated, however, by the narrator's rejection, for which Genet feels continual guilt. Botchako cuts the trapdoor through which he and Bulkaen attempt escape. As a result, Bulkaen is machine-gunned to death immediately, and Botchako dies three days later. To the narrator, Botchako has both prevented his sexual fulfillment with Bulkaen and activated their spiritual union.

Villeroy (veel-RWAH), a blond man two years older than

the narrator, a murderer (patricide) who is second-in-command of Mettray's Family B and Genet's "big shot." By creating a trapdoor in the dormitory so that he can meet his lover outside the reformatory, returning hours later to the narrator's bed, Villeroy catalyzes in Genet his initial awareness of a continuum of male intimacy and of his place in that continuum. Villeroy is transferred to another Mettray Family after he kicks to death the head of Family B.

Rocky, also called **René** (reh-NAY), a Fontevrault infirmary attendant, Bulkaen's former partner in burglary and his current "big shot." Tall and strong, Rocky does not outwardly evidence either his caring for Bulkaen or his hurt at the narrator's rejection of his offer to share a cigarette butt, an offer of friendship. He is a pragmatist whom the narrator bribes for phenobarbital so that he can become closer to Bulkaen through the disciplinary cell. Rocky's departure is the stimulus for Bulkaen to request that the narrator write him a love poem.

Van Roy, a bully and traitor who buys the narrator from Villeroy for three months' cheese ration and one month later gives him to Divers. He arranges the Mettray "big shot" humiliation of Bulkaen that the narrator later accepts as a means to descend closer to Harcamone. Van Roy receives an early discharge from Mettray by betraying the escape plans of his fellow "big shots."

— *Kathleen Mills*

THE MIRACLE WORKER

Author: William Gibson (1914-   )
First published: 1959
Genre: Drama

Locale: Tuscumbia, Alabama, and Boston, Massachusetts
Time: The 1880's
Plot: Psychological realism

Annie Sullivan, the teacher of the deaf and blind child Helen Keller. Annie, herself blind during her childhood years, comes to the Keller household at the age of twenty to attempt to teach language to seven-year-old Helen. Her brash self-confidence is a pose covering her deep fear of possible failure in her first position. The clashes of wills between herself and Helen and between herself and the child's father pique her Irish temper enough to help her through the difficult first months as she attempts merely to discipline Helen into obedience and calm. With tireless perseverance, she repeats the manual alphabet into Helen's hand, spelling out the name of every object the child can touch and hoping that the child's keen mind will somehow make the connection between the words spelled and the objects felt.

Captain Arthur Keller, a retired Civil War officer who edits a town newspaper in Tuscumbia, Alabama. He is a haughty man in his mid-fifties, apparently accustomed during his military career to instant and unquestioning obedience to his every whim. Disappointment at the seeming cowardice of his teenage son and the terrible physical affliction of his small daughter gnaw at his heart, causing him to be irascible and sharply demanding at times with his family. Underneath, he is a concerned and loving father and husband. He is especially frustrated in his efforts to dominate Annie Sullivan, Helen's teacher, finding her persistence and inner courage more than a match for his chauvinism.

Kate Keller, the young second wife of Captain Keller and mother of Helen. For more than five years, she has tried unsuccessfully to cope with Helen's random destructive movements and angry tantrums. With a new baby in the family, she realizes the desperate need to teach Helen self-control. With gentle persuasion and a sure instinct for her husband's temperament, Kate manages to persuade her husband to hire An-

nie as a teacher and to let her have her way with Helen.

Helen Keller, a child of seven who lost both sight and hearing as a result of high fever during a babyhood illness. Locked inside the dark cage of her body, she is unable to communicate her simplest wants and needs to others except through violent tantrums and howls resembling those of a hurt animal. She has become a tyrant in her home and a menace to her infant sister. As a last effort to control her, Captain Keller hires a young governess, Annie Sullivan, to teach her simple human conduct. Helen's yearning for knowledge leads her far beyond behavior control to the discovery of language and all that this discovery opens to her in terms of life and love.

James Keller, Helen's teenage half brother. Living in awe of his domineering father, James has grown resentful of his stepmother, Kate, and of Helen, who demands so much attention and care that he feels cheated out of the family love he desires. With the arrival of Annie, he is able to see a model of brave resistance to circumstances and to his father's demanding ways. Through her influence, he begins to grow toward asserting his own personhood.

Aunt Ev, Captain Keller's sister. As a kindly and concerned aunt, Ev spoils Helen with small treats and supports Kate in her efforts to get help for the child.

Viney, the Keller family servant. Amid the turmoil of a household that revolves around the whims and temper of a handicapped child, Viney manages to keep a stable and good-humored manner. Her children, Martha and Percy, are playmates for Helen.

Mr. Anagnos, the headmaster of the Perkins Institute for the Blind, the school where Annie was trained. It is Mr. Anagnos who chooses Annie for the difficult assignment of teaching Helen.

— *Gabrielle Rowe*

A MIRROR FOR WITCHES

Author: Esther Forbes (1891-1967)
First published: 1928
Genre: Novel

Locale: Massachusetts
Time: The seventeenth century
Plot: Psychological realism

Doll, a Breton child adopted by Captain Jared Bilby after her mother is burned as a witch. As she grows up, strange things happen to her and around her, until she is thought to be a witch and believes it herself. She is tried for witchcraft but dies peacefully in her cell; she believes her demon lover has come for her.

Captain Jared Bilby, an English sea captain who becomes Doll's foster father. He takes her to America with his family and rears her. When he wants her to marry Titus Thumb, she curses him and he dies.

Hannah Bilby, Captain Bilby's wife. She hates the child her husband has taken in, believing that a searing look from Doll causes her miscarriage. When Doll grows up, Hannah accuses her of being a witch.

Titus Thumb, a young man in love with Doll. At first, Doll locks him out of the house when he comes courting. When he asks her to marry him, she bites his hand.

Labour and

Sorrow Thumb, Titus' twin sisters. They claim that Doll tortures them with her witchcraft.

The Bloody Shad, a pirate. Doll believes he is her demon lover. The name is also given to an impish monkey her lover has with him. He is the son of Goody Greene. When he is executed at Boston harbor with two other pirates, Doll is lonely again.

Goody Greene, an old herb woman thought to be a witch. She is The Bloody Shad's mother. She and the minister are the only ones in the village who remain friendly to Doll.

Mr. Zacharias Zelley, the minister in the village. He tries to comfort Doll and save her soul.

Mrs. Thumb, Titus' mother. She is sure that Doll has bewitched her daughters.

Ahab, a savage black bull owned by the Thumbs. Doll has a strange power over him, and he is friendly to her but to no one else.

Deacon Thumb, Titus' father. Finally convinced that Doll is a witch, he has her jailed.

Mr. Kleaver, a surgeon. He joins Deacon Thumb in insisting that Doll be jailed.

THE MISALLIANCE

Author: Anita Brookner (1928-   )
First published: 1986
Genre: Novel

Locale: London, England
Time: The 1980's
Plot: Psychological realism

Blanche Vernon, the central character. Divorced from Hubert "Bertie" Vernon, she is childless and in her mid-forties. Blanche, who is plain in appearance and innocent of the world's competitive ways, questions why Bertie married her. Beneath an elegant, bookish, witty, and slightly eccentric exterior lies a lonely woman with some romantic yearnings. To please her husband, she shaped herself into what she thought he wanted, but he left her for a younger woman. She bears the divorce bravely, devises activities, develops theories about kinds of people, and categorizes herself as among the losers. When she sees the child Elinor at the hospital, she becomes obsessed. Occasionally happy, she is often secretly paralyzed by bleak loneliness.

Hubert (Bertie) Vernon, the wealthy head of a real-estate firm, a graduate of Cambridge University. He is about Blanche's age. Mistaking her petulance for passion, he fell in love with Amanda and was divorced from Blanche. He now lives with Amanda, invigorated by his new life. Hardworking, sociable, curious, unimaginative, and somewhat insensitive, yet solid and caring, he thinks in anecdotes. Blanche's literate and witty talk makes him uncomfortable, but so does sharing a villa in Greece with Amanda.

Amanda, who is often called **Mousie**. She is about twenty-five years old, beautiful, spoiled, and shallow. She holds a degree in computer sciences, and is Bertie's secretary. She manipulates Bertie to capture his sympathy before and during a memorable dinner party at the Vernons'. She is the ostensible cause of the Vernons' divorce. Bertie lives with her and goes with her on vacation.

Sally Beamish, the stepmother of Elinor and wife of Paul. She is about twenty-five years old, tall, slim, and red headed. Although she exudes animal health, she is listless, as if hibernating. She becomes animated only when talking about wild days in the past and about good times to come. Pleasure is her due, and she shamelessly cajoles money out of Blanche and others.

Elinor (Nellie) Beamish, the daughter of Paul and stepdaughter of Sally, about three years old. She is the object of Blanche's affections. She hears and understands everything, but she does not speak. She lives with Sally but spends time with her paternal grandmother. When she returns from a long visit, she seems older and is no longer interested in Blanche. She eventually speaks.

Patrick Fox, a man in his mid-forties who attended Cambridge with Bertie. He is a civil servant and had been in love with Blanche. He is a bachelor who is diffident with women, yet he pathetically falls for Sally.

Phyllis Duff, the wife of Blanche's dentist. The middle-aged woman, who fits a stereotype of the model wife, lives near Blanche.

— *George Soule*

THE MISANTHROPE
(Le Misanthrope)

Author: Molière (Jean-Baptiste Poquelin, 1622-1673)
First published: 1667
Genre: Drama

Locale: Paris, France
Time: The seventeenth century
Plot: Comedy of manners

Alceste (ahl-SEHST), an outspoken, rigidly honest young man disgusted with society. Protesting against injustice, self-interest, deceit, and roguery, he wants honesty, truthfulness, and sincerity. He hates all men because they are wicked, mischievous, hypocritical, and generally so odious to him that he has no desire to appear rational in their eyes. He would cheerfully lose a law case for the fun of seeing what people are and to have the right to rail against the iniquity of human nature. In love with a young widow, Célimène, he is not blind to her faults, but he feels that his sincere love will purify her heart. He controls his temper with her, for he deems her beneath his anger. Despite her coquetry, he will excuse her if she joins him in renouncing society and retiring into solitude. Seeing himself deceived on all sides and overwhelmed by injustice, he plans to flee from vice and seek a nook—with or without Célimène—where he may enjoy the freedom of being an honest man.

Célimène (say-lee-MEHN), a young widow loved by Alceste, though she embodies all qualities he detests. She is a flirt, a gossip with a satirical wit demonstrated in caustic sketches of her friends, and a woman eager for flattery. Not certain that she truly loves Alceste, she feels that he may be too jealous to deserve her love. In the end, she scornfully rejects his invitation to grow old and bury herself in the wilderness with him.

Philinte (fee-LA[N]T), a friend of Alceste. Believing in civilization, tact, and conformity, he is a man of good sense and sober rationality who takes people as they are. Whereas Alceste says that Oronte's sonnet is very badly written, Philinte flatters him for the sentiment of the poem. Although he admits that trickery usually wins the day, he sees in this no reason to withdraw from society.

Oronte (oh-ROHNT), a young fop who claims that he stands well in the court and with the king and offers to use his influence there for Alceste. When his offer of friendship and influence is rejected and his sonnet ridiculed, he brings charges against Alceste. Although he also is in love with Célimène, he rejects his love when he learns of her ridicule of him and admits he has been duped.

Éliante (ay-YAHNT), Célimène's cousin, a woman whose ideas are similar to Philinte's and who marries him at the end. Although she enjoys gossip, she is sincere, as even Alceste admits, and favors people who speak their minds.

Arsinoé (ahr-zee-NWAY), a friend of Célimène, an envious prude who offers advice on honor and wisdom. Although she is a flatterer, she also is outspoken at times.

Acaste (ah-KAHS-teh) and

Clitandre (klee-TAHN-dreh), noblemen and fops. Both desire the love of Célimène, who ridicules them.

Basque (bahsk), a servant to Célimène.

Dubois (dew-BWAH), Alceste's servant.

An officer of the Maréchaussée (mah-ray-shoh-SAY), who delivers a summons to Alceste.

THE MISER
(L'Avare)

Author: Molière (Jean-Baptiste Poquelin, 1622-1673)
First published: 1669
Genre: Drama

Locale: Paris, France
Time: The seventeenth century
Plot: Comedy

Harpagon (ahr-pah-GOH[N]), the father of Cléante and Élise, a wealthy, vicious, money-mad old widower. He loves money more than reputation, honor, or virtue, according to his son's valet, and spends his time watching and guarding it. Fearful of being robbed and killed for his wealth, he buries his money in his garden. Even his children are suspected of planning to rob him. Because he treats them with austerity, they complain of their lack of decent clothes. For his daughter, he plans a marriage to a wealthy man, for himself a marriage without dowry but with "other" things. The servant is warned not to rub the furniture too hard when polishing it and thus wear it out; the valet is searched on being fired to ensure he has not stolen anything. Even his horses suffer from avarice: He feeds them straw. Hypocrisy is another dominant trait revealed in his statement, "Charity enjoins us to be agreeable when we can."

Cléante (klay-AHNT), Harpagon's son, a kindhearted youth who admits his obligation to his father. He is determined to leave Harpagon if he can get no help from him, and he is forced to gamble for money for clothes. Outspoken, he tells his father he is a usurer. He acts with cleverness and boldness when he thwarts his father's parsimony by ordering elaborate refreshments for Mariane and gives her Harpagon's ring. His courage builds up to the point of defying his father on the question of marriage.

Master Jacques (zhahk), Harpagon's cook and coachman. He hates flatterers and is outspoken. Because these traits and his clever sotto voce comments have earned him several beatings, he swears to give them up. He is also a trickster and practical joker. His false messages carried between Harpagon and Cléante renew their mutual antagonism, and his false accusation of Valère as a thief is cause for a beating. There is another side to the man: He has a feeling for the horses being starved by their straw diet. Next to them, he loves his master and regrets the world's evil report of him.

Valère (vah-LEHR), a rich young Neapolitan shipwrecked sixteen years earlier, now serving incognito as steward to Harpagon. He is sincere and honorable in his love for Élise but uses shrewd and artful means in his endeavors to marry her. His method is to "take men's hobbies, follow their maxims, flatter their faults, and applaud their doings"; however, he admits that this practice is not sincere.

Élise (ay-LEEZ), Harpagon's daughter and Valère's sweetheart after he saves her from drowning. She is formal in speech even in her comments on love; Valère says she is prudent. She fears that her father, the family, and the world will censor them, but she is realistic enough never to say one thing and then do another.

Mariane (mahr-YAHN), Valère's sister, also shipwrecked, sincerely in love with Cléante. She is obedient to, and loving in her care of, her mother. When Harpagon proposes marriage to her, thus shocking Cléante, she cleverly replies in a manner satisfactory to both aspirants for her hand.

Frosine (froh-ZEEN), a designing woman, a flatterer and a matchmaker who earns her living by her wits. Heaven has given her no income other than intrigue and industry, she says. Despite her cleverness and wit, she is tenderhearted toward lovers and tries to help them. She regrets her efforts on Harpagon's behalf, especially after he refuses to pay her.

La Flèche (flehsh), Cléante's valet, whose sense of humor is shown in his sotto voce comments and in explanations he makes when he is overheard. He is shrewd in his appraisal of Harpagon.

Anselme (ahn-SEHLM), the father of Valère and Mariane, an honest man who left Naples after the loss of his wife and children. He is faithful to friends, fair to Valère (unknown to him then), and liberal and generous, even to Harpagon, for he agrees to pay for the double wedding of Harpagon's son and daughter to his daughter and son. He even buys a wedding suit for Harpagon.

Master Simon, an agent and moneylender, shrewd in his estimate of Cléante and his need for money. He flees when Harpagon sees that it is his son who wants to borrow.

Brindavoine (bra[n]-dah-VWAHN) and
La Merluche (mehr-LEWSH), lackeys to Harpagon.
Mistress Claude (klohd), Harpagon's servant.

LES MISÉRABLES

Author: Victor Hugo (1802-1885)
First published: 1862
Genre: Novel

Locale: France
Time: 1815-1835
Plot: Social realism

Jean Valjean (zhah[n] vahl-ZHAH[N]), a convict of unusual strength, originally sentenced to five years in prison for stealing a loaf of bread for his sister's starving family. Attempts to escape have kept him in the galleys for nineteen years before he is released in 1815. Police Inspector Javert is sure he will be back, for his passport, proclaiming him an ex-convict, keeps him from getting work. He stops at the home of the bishop of Digne, who treats him well despite Jean's attempts to rob him of some silverware. Eventually, calling himself Father Madeleine, a man with no previous history, he appears in the town of M. sur M. His discovery of a method for making jet for jewelry brings prosperity to the whole village, and the people elect him mayor. Then his conscience forces him to confess his former identity to save a prisoner unjustly arrested. Again he escapes from the galleys and from Inspector Javert, until he is betrayed by a blackmailer. In the end, he dies peacefully, surrounded by those he loves and with his entangled past revealed. His final act is to bequeath to Cosette the bishop's silver candlesticks, which he had kept for years while trying to deserve the bishop's confidence.

Fantine (fahn-TEEN), a beautiful girl of Paris whose attempts to find a home for her illegitimate daughter Cosette have put her into the power of money-mad M. Thénardier. Unable to meet his demands for more money after the foreman of Father Madeleine's factory fires her upon learning of her earlier history, she turns prostitute, only to have M. Javert arrest her. By this time, she is dying of tuberculosis. Father Madeleine promises to look after eight-year-old Cosette.

Cosette (koh-ZEHT), Fantine's daughter, who grows up believing herself the daughter of Father Madeleine. She is seen and loved by a young lawyer, Marius Pontmercy; but Valjean, fearing he will be compelled to reveal her story and his own if she marries, plans to take her away. Cosette hears from Pontmercy again as she is about to leave for England with her supposed father. She sends him a note that brings his answer that he is going to seek death at the barricades.

Felix Tholomyes (fay-LEEKS toh-loh-MYEHS), a carefree, faithless student, Fantine's lover and Cosette's father.

M. Javert (zhah-VEHR), a police inspector with a strong sense of duty that impels him to track down the man whom he considers a depraved criminal. Finally, after Valjean saves his life at the barricades, where the crowd wants to kill him as a police spy, he struggles between his sense of duty and his reluctance to take back to prison a man who could have saved himself by letting the policeman die. His solution is to drown himself in the Seine.

Marius Pontmercy (mahr-YEWS poh[n]-mehr-SEE), a young lawyer of good blood, estranged from his aristocratic family because of his liberal views. His father, an army officer under Napoleon Bonaparte, had expressed a deathbed wish that his son try to repay his debt to Sergeant Thénardier, who had saved his life at Waterloo. Marius' struggle between obligations to a rascal and his desire to protect the father of the girl he loves sets M. Javert on Jean Valjean's tracks. A farewell letter from Cosette sends him to die at the barricade during a street revolt. After he has been wounded, Valjean saves him by carrying him underground through the sewers of Paris. Eventually, Marius marries Cosette and learns, when the old man is dying, the truth about Jean Valjean.

M. Thénardier (tay-nahr-DEEAY), an unscrupulous, avaricious innkeeper, a veteran of Waterloo, who bleeds Fantine of money to pay for the care of Cosette. Later, he changes his name to Jondrette and begins a career of begging and blackmail while living in the Gorbeau tenement in Paris. Jean Valjean becomes one of his victims. He even demands money to let Valjean out of the sewers beneath Paris while Valjean is carrying wounded Marius Pontmercy to a place of safety.

Mme Thénardier, a virago as cruel and ruthless as her husband.

Eponine Thénardier (ay-poh-NEEN), their older daughter, a good-hearted but pathetic girl. Marius Pontmercy first meets her when she delivers one of her father's begging, whining letters. In love with Marius, she saves his life by interposing herself between him and a musket during the fighting at the barricade. Before she dies, she gives him a letter telling where Cosette can be found.

Azelma (ah-zehl-MAH), their younger daughter.

Little Gavroche (gah-VROHSH), the Thénardiers' son, a street gamin. He is killed while assisting the insurgents in the fighting at the barricade.

Charles François Bienvenu Myriel (frah[n]-SWAH byeh[n]-veh-NEW meer-YEHL), bishop of Digne, a good-hearted, devout churchman who gives hospitality to Jean Valjean after the ex-convict's release from the galleys. When Valjean repays him by stealing some of the bishop's silverware, the old man tells the police that he had given the valuables to his guest and gives him in addition a pair of silver candlesticks. His saintliness turns Valjean to a life of honesty and sacrifice.

Father Fauchelevent (foh-shehl-VAH[N]), a bankrupt notary turned carter, jealous of Father Madeleine's success in M. sur M. One day his horse falls, and the old man is pinned beneath his cart. The accident might have proved fatal if Father Madeleine, a man of tremendous strength, had not lifted the vehicle to free the trapped carter. This feat of strength, witnessed by M. Javert, causes the policeman to comment significantly that he has known only one man, a galley slave, capable of doing such a deed. Father Madeleine's act changes Father Fauchelevent from an enemy to an admiring friend. After his accident, the old man becomes a gardener at the convent of the Little Picpus in Paris. Jean Valjean and Cosette, fleeing from the police, take refuge in the convent garden. Old Fauchelevent gives them shelter and arranges to have Valjean smuggled out of the convent grounds in the coffin of a dead nun. Later, he helps Valjean to get work as a workman at the convent.

Little Gervaise (zhehr-VEHZ), a young Savoyard from whom Jean Valjean steals two francs. The deed arouses his conscience, and he weeps because he cannot find the boy to return his money. This is the crime of which Champmathieu is later accused.

Champmathieu (shah[n]-mah-TYEW), an old man arrested for stealing apples. When he is taken to the departmental prison at Arras, a convict there identifies him as Jean Valjean, a former convict, and he is put on trial for the theft of two francs stolen from a Savoyard lad eight years before. After a struggle with his conscience, Jean Valjean appears at the trial and confesses his identity. Champmathieu, convinced that all the world is mad if Father Madeleine is Jean Valjean, is acquitted. Javert arrests Valjean as the real culprit, but his prisoner escapes a few hours later after pulling out a bar of his cell window.

M. Gillenormand (zheel-nohr-MAH[N]), the stern grandfather of Marius Pontmercy. A royalist, the old man never became reconciled with his Bonapartist son-in-law. He and his grandson quarrel because of the young man's political views and reverence for his dead father. Turned out of his grandfather's house, Marius goes to live in the Gorbeau tenement.

Théodule Gillenormand (tay-oh-DEWL), M. Gillenormand's great-grand-nephew, a lieutenant in the lancers. He spies on Marius Pontmercy and learns that his kinsman is a regular visitor at his father's tomb.

Courfeyrac (kewr-fay-RAHK) and

Enjolas (ehn-zhoh-LAH), friends of Marius Pontmercy and members of the friends of the A.B.C., a society supposed to be interested in the education of children but in reality a revolutionary group. Both are killed in the uprising of the citizens in June, 1832, Courfeyrac at the barricades, Enjolas in the house where the insurgents make their last stand.

M. Maboef (mah-BEWF), an aged church warden who had known Marius Pontmercy's father. A lover of humankind and a hater of tyranny, he marches unarmed to the barricades with the young friends of the A.B.C. He is killed during the fighting.

MISS JULIE
(Fröken Julie)

Author: August Strindberg (1849-1912)
First published: 1888
Genre: Drama

Locale: A country estate in Sweden
Time: The nineteenth century
Plot: Naturalism

Miss Julie, a headstrong young woman, the daughter of a count. She has derived from her mother a hatred of men and of women's subservient role. As the drama begins, the household servants are scandalized over the circumstances of Miss Julie's broken engagement: She had made her fiancé jump over her horsewhip several times, giving him a cut with the whip each time, and he had left her. Subsequently, she takes advantage of her father's absence to join the holiday dancing of the servants. She makes love to her father's not unwilling valet, Jean, and then shifts helplessly and impractically from one plan of action to another: running off alone, running off with the valet, a suicide pact when they become tired of each other, and taking his fiancée, who naturally objects to being deserted, with them. When Jean kills Miss Julie's pet finch, at her command, her love turns to hate. Then, ecstatic at the thought of freedom through suicide, she takes her lover's razor and leaves the room.

Jean, Miss Julie's lover and her father's valet. His first suggestion is that they go to Como, Italy, to open a hotel. Later, he takes Miss Julie his razor and indicates it as one answer to her plea for advice. The return of his master, the count, reduces him again to the menial attitudes of a servant.

Christine, a cook and Jean's fiancée. She loves him and does not intend to lose him to Miss Julie. She refuses Miss Julie's offer to go along with them to Como and announces as she leaves for church that she has spoken to the stable men about not letting anyone have horses until after the count's return.

MISS LONELYHEARTS

Author: Nathanael West (Nathan Weinstein, 1903-1940)
First published: 1933
Genre: Novel

Locale: New York City
Time: Late 1920's
Plot: Social satire

Miss Lonelyhearts, the male writer of advice to the love-lorn on the New York *Post-Dispatch*. The lovelorn column, considered a necessity for the increase in the paper's circulation and regarded by its staff as a joke, becomes an agony to its writer as he sees that the letters he receives are genuine cries for help from the very depths of suffering. In an attempt to escape the pain of the realization that he is the victim of the joke rather than its perpetrator, he turns in vain to drink, to lovemaking, and to a vacation in the country with a woman who loves him. Finally, in the delirium of illness, he imagines himself identified with the Christ whose image has long haunted him. As the handicapped Peter Doyle approaches his room, Miss Lonelyhearts runs toward him with arms outstretched to receive him in his healing embrace. His gesture is mistaken for an intended attack, and he is shot.

Willie Shrike, the feature editor, who is Miss Lonelyhearts' boss. He turns the knife in Miss Lonelyhearts' agony by his unending mockery of the desperate cries for help in the lovelorn letters and of the attempts at escape with which people delude themselves.

Mary Shrike, Willie Shrike's wife, whom Miss Lonelyhearts tries in vain to seduce.

Betty, a girl who is in love with Miss Lonelyhearts. Hoping to cure his despair, she takes him to the country. The attempt fails, since the letters are not forgotten.

Peter Doyle, a handicapped man who consults Miss Lonelyhearts about the meaning of the painful and unremunerative round of his existence. Later, he accuses the columnist of the attempted rape of his wife and shoots him in a struggle following a gesture that Doyle mistakes for an intended attack.

Fay Doyle, Peter Doyle's wife. Dissatisfied with her life with her handicapped husband, she seeks out Miss Lonelyhearts and tries to seduce him.

MISS PEABODY'S INHERITANCE

Author: Elizabeth Jolley (1923-   )
First published: 1983
Genre: Novel

Locale: London, England, and Australia
Time: The 1980's
Plot: Fiction of manners

Dorothy Peabody, a plain and shy unmarried woman in her fifties who works as an office clerk in London. She is friendless and without either intellectual or physical distinction. Dorothy's existence is divided between mundane secretarial work and caring for her invalid mother. She longs for fulfillment and finds it in her correspondence with a female Australian novelist. Inspired by the apparently exciting lives of Diana Hopewell and her characters, Dorothy begins to expand her own life in minor ways, such as sampling brandy, buying colored stockings, and expressing new emotions. Her obsession with the writer and her work results in a growing mental unbalance as Dorothy confuses the characters' lives with her own. She is placed on forced leave by her company and finds Diana dead when she reaches Australia. Dorothy's continued fixation on Diana's unfinished novel leads her to take Diana's place at the nursing home to complete the story of the characters who have become so real to her.

Diana Hopewell, a cultured and once active but now invalid novelist who, in her loneliness, seizes on Dorothy's fan letter as an opportunity for friendship. Her correspondence contains not only portions of her new novel but also a fantasy of her own, in which she pretends she is still an independent and capable farm owner. Diana finds comfort in her fictional persona and in Dorothy's admiration. Even in death, Diana has an impact on Dorothy: After Dorothy discovers the truth about her friend, she assumes Diana's position and work.

Amy Peabody, Dorothy's demanding invalid mother. Unable to leave her bed, Mrs. Peabody finds her only satisfaction in whining to her harried daughter and in reminiscing with her friend, Mrs. Brewer. Her death releases Dorothy from years of servitude and allows the latter to visit Australia.

Nadine Brewer, an elderly widowed neighbor and Mrs. Peabody's best friend. Her smug altruism affords her the right, she believes, to belittle Dorothy.

Pam Truscott, a single woman in her forties who works with Dorothy. Miss Truscott's well-preserved physique, her practiced *joie de vivre*, and her illicit affair with Mr. Bains are naïvely admired by Dorothy as the marks of someone who enjoys an exciting and full life.

Mr. Bains, a middle-aged partner in the firm where Dorothy works. His conventional sense of propriety allows him an affair with Pam Truscott but not the embarrassment of retrieving an intoxicated Dorothy from the police station.

Arabella Thorne, a woman in her sixties who is the domineering headmistress of a girls' school and the major character in Diana Hopewell's manuscript. Under her pretentious and cultured exterior, Miss Thorne hides a sensual nature, one that delights in overindulgence in alcohol, food, and social events when in the company of her friends. Gwendaline Manners, however, innocently cuts through Miss Thorne's self-restraint with her adolescent attractions and naïve affection, and the headmistress finds herself caught between parental and amorous feelings for her pupil.

Miss Edgely, Miss Thorne's incompetent and empty-headed assistant and friend. Petty and impractical, Miss Edgely is in constant need of supervision and soothing by Thorne and Snowdon. Her jealousy of Thorne's affection for Gwenda leads her into a number of foolish and troublesome escapades on the foursome's European vacation, which in turn only serve to diminish her in the headmistress' eyes.

Miss Snowdon, Miss Thorne's sensible and equally cultured lifelong friend. She takes time out from her career as a nurse to accompany Thorne and Edgely on vacation. She is Edgely's opposite, able to take Thorne's involvements with both Edgely and Gwenda good-naturedly and without any sense of threat.

Gwendaline Manners, a friendless and ungainly sixteen-year-old pupil at Thorne's school who is ignored by her newly remarried father. She responds to Thorne's offer of a trip to

Europe with a doglike devotion, casting the headmistress in the role of a substitute mother. Despite Thorne's attempts to provide her with ambition and a cultural education, Gwenda blossoms only under the attentions of the pragmatic Mr. Frome, with whom she shares a desire for family life and whose proposal she accepts as a means to satisfy that desire.

Debbie Frome, an attractive and precocious pupil at Thorne's school whose understanding of the sensual both un-

nerves and attracts the headmistress. Her willing acceptance of her classmate as a stepmother is indicative of Debbie's worldly wisdom.

Mr. Frome, a highly successful but uneducated man who understands that Gwenda is really best suited to be a wife and mother. His proposal to Gwenda frustrates Thorne's attempts to play Pygmalion to her pupil.

— *Gwendolyn Morgan*

MISS RAVENEL'S CONVERSION FROM SECESSION TO LOYALTY

Author: John William De Forest (1826-1906)
First published: 1867
Genre: Novel

Locale: New England and Louisiana
Time: The Civil War period
Plot: Historical

Lillie Ravenel, a vivacious and beautiful young Southern woman loyal to her section during the Civil War. She marries Colonel Carter, a Union officer who helps her and her father during the federal troops' occupation of New Orleans. Her husband takes her aunt as his mistress. An old admirer, Edward Colburne, by his love restores her happiness and marries her after the death of her husband. His influence makes her recognize the justice of the Northern cause.

Dr. Ravenel, Lillie's father, a medical doctor. He wants to rehabilitate the freed slaves of the South. He has his daughter teach some of his charges to read. Aware of Colonel Carter's moral weakness, he hopes Lillie will marry Colburne. When she decides to marry Carter, however, he does not forbid it.

Colonel Carter, Lillie's first husband. He is attractive to women and an opportunist. He has an affair with Mrs. Larue, Lillie's aunt. A weak man, he is given to drink and indebted-

ness, as well as women. He is killed in battle during the Civil War.

Edward Colburne, a longtime admirer of Lillie. He is a captain in the Union army, a courageous and capable officer as well as a man of excellent character. Worn out and sick near the end of the war, he returns home to New England, convalesces under Dr. Ravenel's care, and successfully woos Lillie, who had returned to New England with her father after the death of her husband.

Mrs. Larue, Lillie's aunt. An opportunist, she takes up a love affair with Colonel Carter, Lillie's first husband.

The Meurices, a New Orleans Creole family sympathetic to the Northern cause. They are friends of Captain Colburne.

Major Gazaway, the cowardly commander of a Union fort. When he fails in his duty, Captain Colburne takes command and repulses a Confederate attack.

THE MISSOLONGHI MANUSCRIPT

Author: Frederic Prokosch (1908-1989)
First published: 1968
Genre: Novel

Locale: Greece, England, Switzerland, and Italy
Time: 1824, with flashbacks covering 1809-1824
Plot: Biographical

George Gordon, Lord Byron, the flamboyant British poet. In this novelistic account, Byron becomes a haunted man searching for a deeper purpose, a "spiritual call," or "a dedication." Byron sees himself in these fictional notebooks as "beautiful," as "perverse and destructive and tortured," and as "childishly happy and childishly gloomy, childishly affectionate and childishly venomous." He lives by instinct and is forever being caught up in emotional messes and sensual debauchery. The impulse to political action that leads to his death in Missolonghi is part of his fruitless search to escape spiritual sloth. He concludes that he has no "definite or identifiable character" and that his political careering in Greece springs from his need "to discover the *other* creature, if there really is another, who is hiding within me." The Byron of this novel is a true Byronic hero.

Percy Bysshe Shelley, another British Romantic poet and a friend of Byron. A humorless prig, Shelley is given to "little bursts of a warbling ecstasy." Despite what he perceives as Shelley's "absurdity," Byron appreciates the "sudden tenderness" that Shelley often reveals and senses in him the "presence of purity."

Countess Teresa Guiccioli, Byron's mistress. The beautiful Teresa, married to an elderly husband, becomes Byron's mistress after his brutal marriage to Annabella Milbanke and the liaison with Claire Clairmont (which produced their daughter, Allegra). Teresa entertains Byron in their *menage à trois* in Ravenna before he takes her to Pisa to become a part of Shelley's circle.

Edward John Trelawney, one of Shelley's intimates. Byron finds the "virile, piratical" Trelawney an "ominous and oppressive" figure. Trelawney is a satyr who gives off a "dark intention, a rather sinister intimacy," and he disconcerts Byron, who comes both to love Trelawney and to hate him because he sees in him his own weaknesses.

Leigh Hunt, a poet and minor man of letters, depicted as a "rather mischievous sort of man" with repulsive personal habits. Hunt presents himself with his family at Byron's Casa Lafranchi in Pisa, and Byron impulsively invites them all to stay as his guests. Hunt emerges as incompetent and ludicrous but quick with a retort. When Byron complains about Hunt's indifference to personal cleanliness, Hunt responds: "You have scolded me for the infrequency of my baths. Are your callousness and promiscuity to be excused on the grounds of poetry?"

Prince Mavrocordato, a Greek nationalist leader. The "wicked, equivocal Mavrocordato," as Byron calls him, shares drink and banter with Byron. Their relationship is too guarded to become intimate, but their mutual respect is satisfying to both men.

— Frank Day

MISTER ROBERTS

Author: Thomas Heggen (1919-1949)
First published: 1946
Genre: Novel

Locale: The Southwest Pacific
Time: The last months of World War II
Plot: Satire

Douglas Roberts, first lieutenant of the U.S.S. *Reluctant*. A born leader, he is sensitive, perceptive, and idealistic. Desiring battle action, he has nevertheless heroically adjusted himself to the dull routine of a supply ship. He is worshiped by the crew, almost worshiped by his fellow officers, and hated by the captain, who fears him and yet refuses to transfer him to another ship. He finally gets his transfer but is ironically killed while drinking coffee in a wardroom when a kamikaze plane hits his destroyer.

Captain Morton, skipper of the *Reluctant*. He is officious, childish, and unreasonable, and he is thoroughly disliked or hated by his entire crew. His hatred of Mr. Roberts is closely related to his recognition and envy of Roberts' superior intelligence and ability.

Ensign Keith, a former college boy and recently commissioned Bostonian who learns quickly the comparative unimportance of Navy rules and regulations aboard the *Reluctant*.

David Bookser, a seaman, the spiritual type who manages to get himself a beautiful woman while on shore leave, to the amazement and admiration of his shipmates.

Ensign Pulver, a healthy young officer who not only hates Captain Morton but delights in plotting against him. After getting news of Mr. Roberts' death, Pulver tosses all of Captain Morton's beloved palm trees over the ship's side.

Doc, the ship's doctor, a plump, balding, contradictory, unpredictable little man, sometimes highly regarded and sometimes despised by his patients.

Frank Thompson, a radio man whose baby dies and who vainly seeks permission to fly to the United States for the funeral.

Chief Dowdy, a close friend of Mr. Roberts.

Red Stevens, a recently married seaman who nearly kills another seaman for cruelly ribbing him about his wife's hypothetical infidelities during his absence.

Miss Williamson and

Miss Girard, two Navy nurses.

THE MISTRESS OF THE INN
(La locandiera)

Author: Carlo Goldoni (1707-1793)
First published: 1753
Genre: Drama

Locale: Florence, Italy
Time: Mid-eighteenth century
Plot: Comedy

Mirandolina (mee-RAHN-doh-LEE-nah), a pretty young girl who inherits an inn from her father. She promises him on his deathbed that she will marry Fabricius, who has served her father well. She delays the marriage, however, because of her delight in tempting all men, yet giving nothing. After enthralling three noble suitors, she finally announces that she will marry Fabricius.

Fabricius (fah-BREE-chee-ews), the faithful serving-man, who becomes jealous of Mirandolina's favors to the nobles.

Marquis di Forlipopoli (fohr-lee-POHP-oh-lee), a proud but penniless noble in love with Mirandolina.

Count D'Albafiorita (DAHL-bah-fee-oh-REE-tah), a wealthy noble who gives her expensive but tasteless presents.

Cavalier di Ripafratta (dee ree-pah-FRAHT-tah), a professed woman-hater whose defenses crumble before Mirandolina. At last, burning with love, he proposes marriage, but she refuses him.

THE MISTS OF AVALON

Author: Marion Zimmer Bradley (1930-   )
First published: 1982
Genre: Novel

Locale: Britain and the legendary Holy Isle of Avalon
Time: Perhaps the sixth century A.D.
Plot: Fantasy

Morgaine, the principal narrator, a priestess of the ancient Mother Goddess and half sister of King Arthur. Later Christian myth called her **Morgan le Fay**, which equates her mythologically with the death aspect (Fate) of the Triple Goddess. This story, however, follows the Arthurian tradition that she was a human being, trained in the ancient wisdom (considered witchcraft by Christians). She is known in her maturity as Morgaine of the Fairies. In the context of this tale, the fairies are the original Celtic peoples, a small-statured, dark race overwhelmed by the Roman legions and driven into remote wild places. Though often despised and feared by Christians, they were valuable allies in the attempt to defend Britain from marauding Norsemen and Saxons. The Romans already had abandoned Britain to its several regional kings. Morgaine is an instrument of the Goddess in both the protective unification of Britain's forces under one king and the destruction of that king when he ceases to defend the religion of the Goddess from narrow-minded Christian priests.

Viviane, known as the **Lady of the Lake**, or the **Lady of the Holy Isle of Avalon**, a high priestess of the Old Religion. Early in this saga, Viviane arranges a marriage between her young half sister Igraine and Gorlois, the Romanized duke of Cornwall. Viviane's secret purpose is to promote a savior king capable of commanding allegiance from all of Britain, both pagan and Christian. Viviane chooses Igraine's firstborn child, Morgaine, as her successor and trains her on Avalon to be a priestess.

Igraine, Viviane's half sister. Though raised on the Holy Isle, she has been sacrificed to the will of the Goddess in her loveless marriage to Gorlois, many years her senior. After the death of her first husband, however, she attains the great love of her life by marrying Uther Pendragon, a great warrior and champion of the native tribes who becomes high king of Britain. Igraine and Uther Pendragon share visions suggesting a series of reincarnations in which they were mated repeatedly as priestess and Druid, following their mysterious emergence from the sea as survivors of the lost Atlantis. From this physical and spiritual union comes the child who will be King Arthur.

Arthur, who is often cared for in early childhood by his sister Morgaine. He is adopted into the court of another king when he is slightly older. This was a custom among royalty, a device that provided a boy with foster brothers and protected him from too much coddling at a time when he must learn the arts of war and diplomacy appropriate to leadership. The young Arthur learns his lessons well, particularly the ability to make lasting friendships among his peers, who later become the loyal knights of the Round Table. His later kingmaking, a pagan rite of great antiquity, reinforces his military prowess as well as ensuring that the Celtic tribes will follow him as their sacred king. Viviane herself gives him the great sword, Excalibur, for which Morgaine embroiders a beautiful scabbard, interwoven with magic spells that will prevent him from bleeding to death of battle wounds.

Gwenhwyfar, Arthur's wife. She becomes high queen of Britain as part of a politically arranged marriage. One could hardly find a more beautiful woman to complement the splendid King Arthur. The king is pleased with her and loyal to her throughout his reign. She cannot, however, perform the most important duty expected of a queen—providing a son to inherit his father's throne. She suffers several spontaneous abortions, a pattern that mortifies her. She was somewhat neurotic from childhood, reared in a Christian convent where she learned to fear exposure to the open sky or to nature. She is a devout Christian, internalizing the Christian doctrine that women are responsible for bringing sin and death into the world. Her zeal to perform the proper role of a good Christian wife is further mocked by an erotic obsession with Arthur's best friend, the handsome Lancelet.

— *Katherine Snipes*

MITHRIDATES
(Mithridate)

Author: Jean Baptiste Racine (1639-1699)
First published: 1673
Genre: Drama

Locale: Nymphée, on the Bosphorus
Time: The first century B.C.E.
Plot: Tragedy

Mithridate (mee-tree-DAHT), the king of Pontus, who has been fighting the Romans for forty years. At first, he is believed dead, but this rumor proves to be false. He is in love with Monime, a woman much younger than himself, and he is very jealous of his two sons, who are both also in love with Monime. His jealousy causes him to set up a plan whereby he can learn whom Monime really loves. In the end, he believes that both of his sons have betrayed him by joining his enemies, the Romans, and he kills himself. Before he dies, he learns that the older son has remained loyal to him, and he blesses Monime and this son.

Monime (moh-NEEM), the young woman Mithridate loves. She is in love with Mithridate's son Xipharès, but she determines to remain faithful to Mithridate in spite of this. After he tricks her into revealing whom it is she really loves, she refuses to marry him. She tries to kill herself and is glad when Mithridate sends a servant to poison her. Monime is finally united with Xipharès, with Mithridate's blessing.

Xipharès (gzhee-fah-REHS), Mithridate's son, who shares his father's feelings of enmity toward the Romans. He has been in love with Monime since the first time he met her. He says nothing about his love until his father is reported to be dead. Xipharès suffers greatly when he discovers that his brother also loves Monime and that his father, who is still alive, is returning. Xipharès finally routs the Romans and succeeds to the throne, with Monime as his queen.

Pharnace (fahr-NAHS), Mithridate's other son, also in love with Monime. He sides with the Romans against his father. Pharnace refuses to marry the daughter of the Parthian king, with whom his father wishes to make an alliance.

Arbate (ahr-BAHT), Mithridate's confidant, who tells him that Pharnace is in love with Monime.

Phoedime (feh-DEEM), Monime's loyal friend and confidante.

Arcas (ahr-KAHS), a servant, charged with giving poison to Monime.

THE MIXQUIAHUALA LETTERS

Author: Ana Castillo (1953-   )
First published: 1986
Genre: Novel

Locale: The United States and Mexico
Time: The 1970's and 1980's
Plot: Epistolary

Teresa, a Mexican American woman married to Libra. She is bored with her marriage. She meets Alicia during a summer trip to Mexico while in search of her roots and her purpose in life. She wants to be a writer and keeps notebooks of her daily impressions. Having met Alicia, she becomes a virtual nomad, going through a series of painful separations from men she once trusted. Unlike Alicia, who has a light complexion despite her gypsy background, Teresa is dark and has attractive Indian features, indicative of her ancestry. The rivalries as well as the close friendship between Alicia and Teresa result from differences in skin color, appeal to men, and temperament. What unite the friends are their many shared experiences and their dedication to their own art.

Alicia, a New York artist whose ancestry goes back to Spain through a grandmother who is from Andalucía and is part gypsy. Alicia's parents come to the United States and adopt the prejudices of that country toward people of color, forgetting that, through Alicia's father, they are related to gypsies. In her rebellion toward her parents, Alicia goes through a sexual quest, always involving herself with men with dark complexions. She helps Teresa get over her first husband and initiates her into a similar erotic quest, one that ends with Teresa's second and very happy marriage in the conformist reading of the novel. Alicia's nomadism and sensuous lifestyle result in a life devoted to art and personal isolation from society.

Libra, Teresa's first husband. A high school dropout, Libra makes numerous attempts to start a business but is always duped by his associates. He is a weak person who is easily intimidated by men with strong personalities. It is clear that Libra will never achieve anything in life. He is inconsiderate to women, even his wife. Teresa's bohemian life and search for herself is a direct response to Libra's opinions and way of life.

Rodney, Alicia's black boyfriend. He represents defiance against her racist father. Alicia becomes pregnant by Rodney and has an abortion that results in unintended sterilization. She takes a trip to Mexico to get over the shock of her sterilization and entrusts Rodney with the care of her New York apartment, only to find on her return that Rodney has been taking his black girlfriend there for romantic trysts. This begins a series of sentimental and erotic mishaps that serve as indications that the only spiritual fulfillment Alicia will find will be through her career as an artist.

Alexis Valladolid, a flamenco singer and distant gypsy relative of Alicia who goes to New York in search of stardom.

He moves in temporarily with Alicia and shortly thereafter begins a stormy relationship with Teresa when she arrives for a short visit. When Teresa moves back to Chicago, Alexis follows her. They move in together, and Teresa becomes pregnant and eventually goes through an abortion. That leads to their separation and mutual manipulation, until Alexis leaves her when assured of a contract in a local nightclub. They come in contact again five years later in the same nightclub, while both are involved with different people. Alexis represents the artist who loves only his music, allowing nothing and no one to interfere with his art. Teresa is envious of Alexis, admiring his dedication and his passion, but feels inadequate in her many failed attempts to excel in her craft as a writer while simultaneously searching for a man's love. The hurt caused by Alexis and his abandonment brings Teresa back to reality. She abandons a bohemian life when she meets someone who finally, in the conformist reading, gives her the stability she always sought, through marriage, a son, and a home.

El Gallo, a close gypsy friend of Alexis Valladolid who accompanies him on his trip to the United States. Estranged from his wife, El Gallo becomes Alicia's lover and live-in companion, thus helping Alicia endure the pain caused by the news that Rodney is having a child with a black girlfriend. El Gallo eventually leaves Alicia when he decides to return to Spain and his wife.

Vicente das Mortes, Teresa's Brazilian boyfriend, who abandons her after he develops an interest in Alicia. He appears only in letter 38.

Abdel, an anguished Vietnam veteran from New York who is a mediocre artist. He meets Alicia in art school while Alicia is trying to forget and transcend her past love affairs through the attainment of a degree. Abdel befriends Alicia and confesses his many problems with the wife he is divorcing. He soon moves in with Alicia. Their love affair becomes a struggle because of Abdel's insecurities and expressed envy of Alicia's artistic talent. Letter 40, read only in the conformist reading, reveals the end of this relationship. Abdel becomes a nuisance, particularly when he destroys Alicia's paintings and sculptures. Alicia decides to throw him out of her life. As a form of revenge, he commits suicide in Alicia's apartment while she is attending school one evening; ironically, Alicia had just changed her mind about Abdel and decided to try to make their relationship work.

MOBILE: Study for the Representation of the United States
(Mobile: Étude pour une représentation des États-Unis)

Author: Michel Butor (1926-   )
First published: 1962
Genre: Novel

Locale: The United States
Time: The precolonial period to the early 1960's
Plot: Antistory

The United States, a different state being discussed in each chapter. The novel has no characters in the accepted sense. The reader is presented with a map of the United States and then, as the title suggests, is led from city to city and from state to state, with signs at state lines welcoming the visitor. *Mobile* is written in the fashion of a quilt, with the reader moving along the roads of the United States in cars of every make (Studebaker, Cadillac, Nash, Edsel, Chevrolet, Oldsmobile, Volk-

swagen) and color (from pink to orange, from white to black). As in any quilt, there are repetitions, such as the hellos of friendly Americans and descriptions of Audubon's birds. The traveler may stop and get any flavor of ice cream at the next Howard Johnson motel. The United States is a New Europe composed of New Europeans—German, French, Irish, Hungarian, and Spanish—who read newspapers in their own language in their own neighborhoods. The immigrants move west, befriending the Indians or attacking and making them mobile. Persecuted, the New Europeans become the New Persecutors. Mormons flee the Midwest and settle in Salt Lake City. Religions abound in the new society, Episcopalian, Baptist, Roman Catholic, Jewish, and Christian Science among them. The Italians are here as well. Giovanni da Verrazzano discovers New York, a patchwork now composed of the Upper West Side, Fifth Avenue, Little Italy, Macy's, and Bloomingdale's. Washington, D.C., is the capital of the United States, the pantheon of the country's gods, and the center of the only religion to be truly practiced. The buildings are a shimmering white. Thomas Jefferson and Benjamin Franklin form part of the American pantheon, with their respective monuments in

Pennsylvania and Virginia, and their own monumental writings. The reader is shifted about, from name to name and flavor to flavor, from colonial times to standard time (Eastern, Central, Mountain, and Pacific) and to time fixed in one space: the museum of colonial homes in Shelburne, Vermont. The museum holds quilts and Impressionist paintings, showing the presence of the French. The quilt is filled with shifts, designs, and colors. The author's name, in the manner of a painter's signature or Alfred Hitchcock film appearance, is inscribed (*butor* is a French word meaning "bittern" or "boor") many times in this patchwork.

— Peter S. Rogers

MOBY DICK: Or, The Whale

Author: Herman Melville (1819-1891)
First published: 1851
Genre: Novel

Locale: The high seas
Time: Early nineteenth century
Plot: Adventure

Ishmael, a philosophical young schoolmaster and sometime sailor who seeks the sea when he becomes restless, gloomy, and soured on the world. With a newfound friend, Queequeg, a harpooner from the South Seas, he signs aboard the whaler *Pequod* as a seaman. Queequeg is the only person on the ship to whom he is emotionally and spiritually close, and this closeness is, after the initial establishment of their friendship, implied rather than detailed. Otherwise, Ishmael does a seaman's work, observes and listens to his shipmates, and keeps his own counsel. Having been reared a Presbyterian (as was Melville), he reflects in much of his thinking the Calvinism out of which Presbyterianism grew; but his thought is also influenced by his knowledge of literature and philosophy. He is a student of cetology. Regarding Ahab's pursuit of Moby Dick, the legendary white whale, and the parts played by himself and others involved, Ishmael dwells on such subjects as free will, predestination, necessity, and damnation. After the destruction of the *Pequod* by Moby Dick, Ishmael, the lone survivor, clings to Queequeg's floating coffin for almost a day and a night before being rescued by the crew of another whaling vessel, the *Rachel*.

Queequeg, Starbuck's veteran harpooner, a tattooed cannibal from Kokovoko, an uncharted South Seas island. Formerly zealous of learning about Christianity, he has become disillusioned after living among so-called Christians and, having reverted to paganism, he worships a little black idol, Yojo, that he keeps with him. Although he appears at ease among his Christian shipmates, he keeps himself at the same time apart from them, his only close friend being Ishmael. In pursuit of whales, he is skilled and fearless. When he nearly dies of a fever, he has the ship's carpenter build him a canoe-shaped coffin, which he tries out for size and comfort; then, recovering, he saves it for future use. It is this coffin on which Ishmael floats after the sinking of the *Pequod* and the drowning of Queequeg.

Captain Ahab, the proud, defiant, megalomaniacal captain of the *Pequod*. He is a grim, bitter, brooding, vengeful madman who has only one goal in life: the killing of the white whale that had deprived him of a leg in an earlier encounter. His most prominent physical peculiarity is a livid scar that

begins under the hair of his head and, according to one crewman, extends the entire length of his body. The scar symbolizes the spiritual flaw in the man himself. His missing leg has been replaced by one of whalebone. When he stands erect looking out to sea, his face shows the unconquerable willfulness of his spirit—and, to Ishmael, a crucifixion also, a "regal overbearing dignity of some mighty woe." Ahab is in complete, strict command of his ship, though he permits Starbuck occasionally to disagree with him. Ahab dies caught in a fouled harpoon line that loops about his neck and pulls him from a whaleboat.

Starbuck, the first mate, tall, thin, weathered, staid, steadfast, conscientious, and superstitious, a symbol of "mere unaided virtue or right-mindedness." He dares to criticize Ahab's desire for vengeance, but he is as ineffectual as a seaman trying to halt a storm. Ahab once takes his advice about repairing some leaking oil casks; but when Starbuck, during a typhoon off Japan, suggests turning home, Ahab scorns him. Starbuck even thinks of killing or imprisoning Ahab while the captain is asleep, but he cannot. Having failed to dissuade Ahab from the pursuit of Moby Dick, Starbuck submits on the third day to Ahab's will, though feeling that in obeying Ahab he is disobeying God. When he makes one final effort to stop the doomed Ahab, the captain shouts to his boatmen, "Lower away!"

Stubb, the second mate, happy-go-lucky, indifferent to danger, good-humored, easy; he is a constant pipe-smoker and a fatalist.

Flask (King-Post), the young third mate, short, stout, and ruddy. He relishes whaling and kills the whales for the fun of it, as one might get rid of giant rats. In his shipboard actions, Flask is sometimes playful out of Ahab's sight but always abjectly respectful in his presence.

Fedallah, Ahab's tall, diabolical, white-turbaned Parsee servant. He is like a shadow of Ahab, or the two are like opposite sides of a single character; Ahab seems finally to become Fedallah, though retaining his own appearance. The Parsee prophesies that Ahab will have neither hearse nor coffin when he dies. Fedallah too dies caught in a fouled harpoon line that is wrapped around Moby Dick.

Moby Dick, a giant albino sperm whale that has become a legend among whalers. He has often been attacked, and he has crippled or destroyed many men and boats. He is both a real whale and a symbol with many possible meanings. He may represent the universal spirit of evil, God the indestructible, or indifferent Nature; or perhaps he may encompass an ambiguity of meaning adaptable to the individual reader. Whatever his meaning, he is one of the most memorable nonhuman characters in all fiction.

Pip, the bright, jolly, genial black cabin boy who, after falling from a boat during a whale chase, is abandoned in midocean by Stubb, who supposes that a following boat will pick him up. When finally taken aboard the *Pequod*, he has become demented from fright.

Tashtego, an American Indian, Stubb's harpooner. As the *Pequod* sinks, he nails the flag still higher on the mast and drags a giant seabird, caught between the hammer and the mast, to a watery grave.

Daggoo, a giant African, Flask's harpooner.

Father Mapple, a former whaler, now the minister at the Whaleman's Chapel in New Bedford. He preaches a Calvinistic sermon filled with seafaring terms.

Captain Peleg and

Captain Bildad, fighting, materialistic Quakers who are the principal owners of the *Pequod*.

Elijah, a madman who warns Ishmael and Queequeg against shipping with Captain Ahab.

Dough-Boy, the pale, bread-faced, dull-witted steward who, deathly afraid of Queenqueg, Tashtego, and Daggoo, does his best to satisfy their enormous appetites.

Fleece, the old black ship's cook. At Stubb's request, he preaches a sermon to the voracious sharks and ends with a hope that their greed will kill them. He is disgusted also by Stubb's craving for whale meat.

Bulkington, the powerfully built, deeply tanned, soberminded helmsman of the *Pequod*.

Perth, the ship's elderly blacksmith, who took up whaling after losing his home and family. He makes for Ahab the harpoon intended to be Moby Dick's death dart, which the captain baptizes in the devil's name.

Captain Gardiner, the skipper of *Rachel*, for whose lost son Captain Ahab refuses to search.

MODERN CHIVALRY

Author: Hugh Henry Brackenridge (1748-1816)
First published: 1792-1797; revised, 1805; final edition, 1815
Genre: Novel

Locale: Pennsylvania
Time: The first years of the United States
Plot: Picaresque

Captain John Farrago, a man from colonial Western Pennsylvania. He takes his horse and his Irish servant, Teague, to go about seeing the country and observing human conduct. After many adventures that point out the foibles of human nature, the caption becomes, because of his learning and good sense, the governor of a new western territory. Being a rational man, he governs in the best Greek and Roman political traditions.

Teague O'Regan, the captain's cowardly but cunning rascal of a servant. He is proposed as a candidate for the legislature, has many amorous adventures, tries his luck at being an excise officer, goes on the stage as an Irish comedian, and serves as a newspaper editor, among other things. He is one of those literary rascals who always land on their feet. The author's satire revolves around the absurdities that elevate the ignorant and roguish Teague to positions of authority and respectability.

Miss Fog, a young heiress courted by Captain Farrago. Although he tries to please her, he finds that whatever he does insults the woman.

Jacko, Miss Fog's other suitor, Captain Farrago's rival. When Jacko sends a second to challenge the captain to a duel, the captain kicks the man out after telling him that dueling is unlawful.

Duncan Ferguson, a Scots emigrant who takes Teague's place as Captain Farrago's servant.

A MODERN COMEDY

Author: John Galsworthy (1867-1933)
First published: 1929
Genre: Novels

Locale: London, England
Time: The 1920's
Plot: Domestic realism

The White Monkey, 1924

Fleur Forsyte Mont, the wife of Michael Mont and daughter of Soames Forsyte. Fleur marries Michael after her romance with Jon Forsyte, her second cousin, is stopped by his parents. She has a son, by Michael, named Christopher. Fleur makes her home into a center for writers and artists. Her passion for collecting experiences almost leads her to an affair with Michael's best friend, Wilfrid Desert.

Michael Mont, the son of a baronet and a veteran of World War I. He falls in love with Fleur and marries her after her romance with Jon Forsyte ends. He works for a publishing house. He publishes two books of poetry by his best friend, Wilfrid Desert, and befriends an employee named Tony Bicket, who was fired for stealing.

Soames Forsyte, a solicitor and art collector. He is a member of the board of an insurance company and exposes the general manager's illegal activities. His efforts, however, make him unpopular with the other board members and the stockholders, so he resigns. He then decides to retire from his legal practice and business affairs. He buys balloons from Bicket.

Tony Bicket, a member of the working class and husband

of Victorine. He steals books from his employer to buy food and medicine for his wife, whose health is poor. He is caught and fired. He then tries to sell balloons for a living. After her health improves, Victorine earns enough money as an artist's model to pay their passage to Australia. Their marriage nearly comes apart after Bicket learns that his wife has been posing in the nude.

The Silver Spoon, 1926

Fleur Forsyte Mont, whose attempts to help Michael's political career by becoming a political hostess backfire when her father offends Marjorie Ferrar and her family. Fleur makes the situation worse by writing nasty letters about Marjorie to mutual friends. The dispute leads to a civil trial for libel.

Michael Mont, who is now a member of the British Parliament. He campaigns for the revival of agriculture and emigration to solve problems of excess population. He is a disciple of Foggartism, a fringe political movement. His main opponent in the House of Commons is the fiancée of Marjorie Ferrar. Michael's attempt to help three unemployed men by starting a farm on his family's estate ends disastrously when one of the men commits suicide.

Soames Forsyte, who is now retired from both his law practice and business affairs. He overhears Marjorie Ferrar making insulting remarks about Fleur. He challenges Marjorie in public and becomes one of the targets of a libel suit brought

Two Forsyte Interludes, 1927

Jon Forsyte, the former lover and second cousin of Fleur Forsyte. In "A Silent Wooing" (1925), after his parents break off their romance and his father dies, he journeys with his mother to Canada and the United States to try his hand at farming. While staying at a resort in Camden, South Carolina, he goes riding with some Americans. Two of his companions are Francis and Anne Wilmot, brother and sister. Jon and Anne ride off by themselves. They become lost and spend several hours alone together. The following day, Jon travels to the Wilmot plantation. By the end of his visit, he falls in love with Anne and discovers that she feels the same about him.

Swan Song, 1928

Fleur Forsyte Mont, who runs a canteen during the General Strike of 1926, during which she sees Jon Forsyte for the first time in several years. Fleur eventually seduces Jon, but her triumph is short-lived; he returns to his wife. She is distraught over the failure of her scheme to get Jon back. Her carelessness with a cigarette causes a fire in her father's house, and the fire causes her father's death.

Wilfrid Desert, a poet, member of the aristocracy, and veteran of World War I. He met Michael in a hospital during the war. When Michael publishes one of Wilfrid's books of verse, it is a commercial and critical success. Wilfrid serves as best man at Michael's marriage to Fleur. Unfortunately, he falls in love with Fleur. He is unable to seduce her away from Michael. He then leaves England for the East.

by her father. He makes the situation even worse by complaining to the editor of a newspaper that runs Marjorie's gossip column.

Marjorie Ferrar, a member of the aristocracy, an actress, and an artist. Her affiliation with the avant-garde and hedonistic movements of the time give her a certain notoriety in English society. Marjorie is an exponent of free love, although her own practice is far less scandalous. In the libel trial, she is forced to defend her bohemian lifestyle. Her admissions destroy her engagement to a wealthy member of the British Parliament.

Francis Wilmot, the American brother-in-law of Jon Forsyte. During a vacation in London, he witnesses the dispute between Marjorie and Soames. He falls in love with Marjorie but becomes gravely ill. Fleur nurses him back to health, and he returns to America, heartbroken.

Soames Forsyte, the former husband of Irene Heron. In "Passers By" (1928), during a trip around the world with Fleur, he visits the Rock Creek cemetery in Washington, D.C. His purpose is to enjoy the Saint Gaudens statue. His appreciation is interrupted, however, when Jon Forsyte and his new wife also visit the cemetery. Soames manages to avoid them but discovers that they and Jon's mother, Irene Heron Forsyte, are staying in the same hotel as are Soames and Fleur. They have another near encounter at Mount Vernon, but Soames feigns illness to cut the tour short. He arranges for himself and Fleur to leave the city without a confrontation.

Jon Forsyte, Fleur's second cousin and now the husband of Anne Wilmot. After marrying Anne, an American woman from South Carolina, he returns to England to farm. Following a brief affair with Fleur, he returns to his pregnant wife and vows never to see Fleur again.

— *Tom Feller*

A MODERN INSTANCE

Author: William Dean Howells (1837-1920)
First published: 1882
Genre: Novel

Locale: New England
Time: The nineteenth century
Plot: Domestic realism

Bartley Hubbard, a newspaperman who ranges from Equity, a small town in New England, to Whited Sepulchre, Arizona. His moral weakness manifests itself in his affairs with women, his shoddy business ethics, his indifferent attitude toward money, and his love of liquor. He spends most of

his time running from debts and family obligations. He dies, shot down by an irate citizen, while he is editor of a small western newspaper.

Marcia Gaylord, an innocent New England girl whose impetuous marriage to Hubbard brings her unhappiness. Hubbard takes her to Boston, where their child, Flavia, is born. When pressed by financial problems, Hubbard deserts his wife and child and goes West. He attempts to divorce Marcia and is foiled only by the intervention of her father. Hubbard's death makes it possible for Marcia to marry a good man and have a decent home.

Squire Gaylord, Marcia's father and Hubbard's first employer on a New England newspaper, the *Free Press*. The squire recognizes Hubbard's talent, but he opposes Hubbard's suit for Marcia's hand. He looks after his daughter's affairs throughout her unfortunate marriage to the errant newspaperman. He dies of a stroke suffered during the trial for divorce Hubbard initiates against Marcia.

Ben Halleck, a member of one of Boston's older families who is a man of means and a college classmate of Hubbard. Halleck does not like Hubbard, but he feels sorry for Marcia, and befriends her. He helps Hubbard by lending him money—which is never returned—and helps Marcia by standing by her during her divorce trial. After Hubbard's death, Halleck tries to decide whether it would be morally right to ask Marcia to marry him.

Atherton, a conservative Boston lawyer who is a friend to Halleck and the Hubbards.

Kinney, a tramp philosopher who provides Hubbard with many stories, which Hubbard sells to magazines and newspapers without asking Kinney's permission.

Hannah Morrison, the daughter of the town drunk, who works with her mother in the newspaper office in Equity. Hannah has had few advantages in her life and claims, when Marcia meets her drunk on the streets of Boston, that Hubbard is responsible for her destitution.

Witherby, an unscrupulous publisher of a Boston newspaper who hires Hubbard as managing editor. Witherby sells some stock in the paper to Hubbard, who borrows from Halleck the money to buy it. When Hubbard's work appears in a rival newspaper, Witherby fires him.

Henry Bird, a shop foreman on the *Free Press* with whom Hubbard has a fight over Hannah. The resulting scandal causes Hubbard to leave his job on the paper.

Willett, the owner of the New England logging camp to which Hubbard flees when scandal drives him out of Equity.

Mrs. Macallister, a fashionable woman who flirts with Hubbard at the logging camp. To impress her, Hubbard pokes fun at his quaint friend Kinney, who takes offense at such treatment; the two men part angrily.

A MODERN MIDAS
(Az aranyember)

Author: Mór Jókai (1825-1904)
First published: 1873
Genre: Novel

Locale: Hungary
Time: The nineteenth century
Plot: Philosophical

Michael Timar, a shrewd and wise man. He builds himself a fortune through his business dealings. He also builds a fortune for the woman he loves, using her inheritance. He comes to style himself Baron Michael Timar von Levetinczy. He marries Timéa, the woman he loves, only to find that she loves another man. Michael discovers that he loves a poor woman, Naomi, who lives on an isolated island. When he has a chance to disappear, through a case of mistaken identity, he goes to the island, where he and Naomi live simply in peace and contentment.

Timéa, Michael's wife. She is the daughter of a political refugee. She loves Lieutenant Katschuka, but she marries Michael out of gratitude and is a faithful wife to him. After Michael's supposed death, she marries the lieutenant.

Naomi, a woman who lives on an island with her mother. She loves Michael and bears him children. When he is supposedly dead, Michael goes to the island to live out his days with her and their progeny.

Ali Tschorbadschi, also known as **Euthryn Trikaliss**. He is Timéa's father and a political refugee. When he dies, he

leaves his daughter to the care of a distant relative, Athanas Brasowitsch.

Athanas Brasowitsch, a prosperous Hungarian trader who takes in the orphaned Timéa. He and his family make her their household servant and treat her shabbily.

Mrs. Brasowitsch, Athanas' vulgar and cruel wife.

Athalie Brasowitsch, Athanas' daughter, who is betrothed to Lieutenant Katschuka. She tries to kill Timéa on the day Timéa marries Athalie's fiancé.

Lieutenant Imre Katschuka, a friend of Michael. He refuses to marry Athalie after her father loses his fortune. After Michael's supposed death, the lieutenant marries Timéa, whom he loves.

Thérèse, a widow, Naomi's mother. She takes refuge on an island.

Theodore Kristyan, a suitor for Naomi's hand in marriage. He tries to blackmail Thérèse and, later, Michael. He drowns accidentally and is incorrectly identified as Michael.

Dodi, the illegitimate son of Michael and Naomi.

MOLL FLANDERS

Author: Daniel Defoe (1660-1731)
First published: 1722
Genre: Novel

Locale: England and the American colonies
Time: The seventeenth century
Plot: Picaresque

Moll Flanders, an English adventuress (known also as Mistress Betty, May Flanders, and Mrs. Flanders), one of the

most engaging female rogues in all literature. She relates her entire life story, from infancy to final years of repentance, with frankness and full detail. As the daughter of a woman convicted of a felony and transported to Virginia, Moll spends her early years in the company of some gypsies, then with several families who treat her well. By the age of fourteen, Moll is attractive, intelligent, resourceful, and womanly. Her first affair is with the elder son in a household where she has entered service. The younger son, Robin, falls in love with her and becomes her first husband. After five years of marriage and the birth of two children, he dies. Later, Moll preys on mankind for many years. Using her beauty and wits to support herself in as much luxury and comfort as she can manage, she marries a succession of husbands, one of them her half brother, and eventually turns thief and pickpocket. She acquires a sizable fortune before she is caught. At Newgate, where her life began, she receives a death sentence but succeeds in getting transportation instead. A former husband, Jemmy E., is being sent to the colonies on the same ship. The two establish a plantation in Carolina, prosper greatly, and ultimately decide to go back to England to spend their remaining years in repentance. Moll maintains a moral tone in relating all of her illegal, extramarital, and exciting adventures, but her professed repentance never seems to keep her from enjoying the fruits of her actions.

Moll's Mother, a convicted felon transported to Virginia soon after Moll's birth. The mother does well in Virginia, builds up a large estate, lives to a satisfying old age, and leaves a farm to Moll.

Humphry, a sea captain. He marries Moll and takes her to Virginia, where he introduces her to his mother (and hers). He remains in Virginia when Moll returns to England after deciding that she can no longer live with her half brother as his wife.

Humphry, the son of Moll and the sea captain. When Moll returns home, he stays in Virginia, where he becomes a planter. He turns over to Moll the plantation willed her and proves a dutiful and loving son.

Jemmy E., an Irish adventurer and highway robber, Moll's former husband, with whom she establishes a plantation in the Carolina Colony. He follows Moll back to England, where they spend their declining years in repentance and some luxury.

"Mother Midnight," a midwife who owns a nursing home for unwed mothers. She trains Moll as a thief. Later, she takes care of Moll's money and is Moll's agent in sending valuable goods to Carolina.

A Gentleman of Bath, married to a mentally ill woman. Moll lives with him and bears him three children.

A Linen Draper, a spendthrift who marries Moll, runs through her money quickly, and abandons her.

Robin, Moll's first husband, the younger son in the family where she first takes service.

Robin's Older Brother, Moll's seducer and first lover.

A Clergyman, the chaplain at Newgate. He befriends Moll in prison, helps her secure a reprieve from the death sentence, and persuades her to repent.

A London Bank Clerk, married to Moll for five years.

MOLLOY, MALONE DIES, and THE UNNAMABLE
(Molloy, Malone meurt, and L'Innommable)

Author: Samuel Beckett (1906-1989)
First published: 1951-1953
Genre: Novels

Locale: Mostly indeterminate but including a hospital
Time: The 1940's or 1950's
Plot: Absurdist

Molloy, 1951

Molloy, a one-eyed and toothless writer. In his mother's room near the slaughterhouse, Molloy wants to die, but first he must write. Although he does not write for money and seems incapable of spending it, he is paid by a man who visits him every Sunday. Despite having a faulty memory for names, Molloy writes an account of his quest to see his mother. He begins his quest on bicycle by pedaling with his good leg and propping the stiff one awkwardly on the front axle. As both legs stiffen, he becomes too crippled to pedal and uses his crutches as grappling hooks to pull himself into a ditch, from which he is rescued. An only son, Molloy believes that he may have had a son himself but is uncertain of his own family history.

Jacques Moran (zhahk moh-RAH[N]), the elder, an agent sent to find Molloy. Moran lives an ordered, complacent life among his possessions in the town of Turdy until he receives a message from his employer, Youdi, to locate Molloy. Moran's journey is filled with mysterious encounters, and he is forever uncertain of his way. His body begins to decay, and one leg stiffens with ankylosis, a pain that first appears while he is giving his son an enema. Moran carries more than a pound of keys in the right-hand pocket of his trousers, causing him to list to the right, and his hat is fastened under his chin by elastic. Moran dresses conspicuously in knickerbockers and boots and

has but two teeth, incisors. Although he keeps chickens, game birds, and bees, Moran dislikes men and animals. He is disgusted by God even though he is a Catholic.

Jacques Moran, the younger, Moran's thirteen-year-old son, whom he constantly nags. Although big and strong for his age, Jacques sleeps with a woolly stuffed bear he calls Baby Jack. On their journey, Jacques is tied to his father by a rope until his father sends him to the town of Hole to procure a bicycle. Jacques collects stamps and wears a green school cap, and he carries a scout knife that his father gave him for his studies in history and geography.

Lousse, also called **Sophie Loy,** a woman whom Molloy meets while she is taking her aged dog, Teddy, to the veterinarian to be put out of his misery. Molloy accidentally kills the dog when he runs over him with his bicycle. Lousse takes in Molloy for a time after Teddy's death. When Molloy leaves, he steals a kniferest and silverware from her.

Edith, Molloy's repulsive mistress. Molloy encounters her in a rubbish dump and questions her name (she is also known as Ruth and Rose) and her gender. Crippled by rheumatism, she gives Molloy money after they have sex and dies taking a warm bath.

Gaber, the messenger who instructs Moran to begin his search for Molloy. Gaber's cryptic message also ends Moran's quest. Gaber wears a chestnut-colored mustache and dresses in his Sunday clothes and bowler hat.

Youdi, Moran and Gaber's unseen employer. His command to Gaber to find Molloy comes at night, as Gaber is about to have sex with his wife. Youdi has previously employed Molloy to undertake investigations.

Mag, Molloy's mother, an incontinent, deaf, and blind woman with whom Molloy communicates by tapping on her skull. Her toothless head is veiled with hair, wrinkles, filth, and slobber.

Malone Dies, 1953

Malone, a toothless, old, omniscient storyteller confined to an asylum cell, where he waits to die. Malone lives in a kind of coma and has no notion of the room he inhabits. He plans to fill his time by telling himself four stories—one each about a man, a woman, a thing (probably a stone), and an animal (probably a bird). His narration, however, is primarily about a character named Macmann, to whom he may be related and who gradually moves into the cell and takes over his identity. Malone believes himself an octogenarian but cannot prove his age; although he knows the date of his birth, he is uncertain of the current year. Although he claims to have spent much of his life walking, his legs and feet seem far away and are unresponsive to his brain's commands. A tall man with knowledge of the stars, Malone dreams of his own death, having become increasingly paralyzed to the point that he no longer can move his big, shaggy head. Malone's ears have tufts of hair, yellowed by wax and lack of care, so long that his lobes are hidden. Malone lies naked in bed, never washing because he does not get dirty. He has bad vision and poor hearing, and he once was cared for by a nameless woman who fed him soup every day. His only possessions are a yellow boot with many eyeholes, a brimless hat, a needle stuck in a piece of cork, and a broken tobacco pipe, all of which he controls by a stick hooked at the end. He eventually loses his stick as well as his exercise book and pencil, a green nub with a lead that he sharpens with his fingernails.

Macmann, a fictional character invented by Malone, born with the name Saposcat. He is created sitting on a bench in town but, like Malone, ends in an asylum, where he spies on a copulating couple and carries on an affair with his haggish nurse, Moll. A little silver kniferest is the only item of value found in his pockets. Childless and earthy, Macmann worked as a street sweeper before his incarceration in the House of Saint John of God, where he is given the identity of 166. Every Saturday, he is given a plug of tobacco and a half pint of porter.

The Unnamable, 1953

The Unnamable, an unnamed disembodied voice seeking evidence of his own existence. He wonders if he has lived, will live, or does live. The Unnamable theorizes that he was born of a wet dream in Bally, and he has no body, only syntax. Because he feels occasional pressure on his rump and the soles of his feet, however, he believes he might be seated, perhaps in a crouched posture, hands on knees. He cannot move and is unable to blink or close his eyes, though he weeps. He sees only what is in front of him. He doubts that he even casts a shadow but cannot turn his head to see. Believing himself to be round and hard, he variously describes himself as an egg and

The charcoal burner, the victim of a brutal assault by Molloy. When he asks Molloy how to get out of the forest, Molloy savagely cracks the old man's skull with his crutch.

The dim man, a small, thickset man killed without provocation by Moran. The dim man wears a navy blue double-breasted suit, polished shoes, fancy socks, suspenders, and a narrow-brimmed dark blue felt hat with a fishhook and lure in its band. He has a long, fringed muffler around his neck and an abortive mustache above his thin, red mouth.

Occasionally, he escapes from the asylum, but because he always hides in the same location, he is easily captured and returned. Macmann sometimes dreams of himself as a great cylinder endowed with intellect and will.

Saposcat, an earnest and precocious schoolboy. Although he seems constantly engaged in mental arithmetic, he is not good at his lessons. The eldest child of poor and sickly parents, Sapo is nevertheless healthy and athletic and engages in boxing, wrestling, and running. Sapo is transmogrified by Malone into the aged and reptilian Macmann.

Moll, the small, elderly nurse in charge of Macmann in the asylum. She wears crucifix earrings, and one canine tooth, bared to its roots, is carved to honor the crucifixion as well. Understanding and sympathetic, she gives Macmann a daguerreotype of herself on her fourteenth birthday and teaches him to exalt love. Moll is subject to fits of vomiting, and her hair begins to fall out.

Lemuel (leh-MYEWL), the male nurse who replaces Moll, after Moll's death, as Macmann's caretaker. A sadistic character, Lemuel beats Macmann and hits himself in the head with a hammer and later a hatchet. Lemuel butchers two sailors employed to take his asylum group for a picnic excursion to an island. He then forces the other fictions into the boat and sets them to sea.

Big Lambert, the father of the Lambert clan. Big Lambert marries his young cousin, his fourth or fifth marriage, and delights in the seasonal slaughter of pigs. Toothless, Big Lambert employs a cigarette holder when he smokes. His son, a great, strapping lad, likewise has terrible teeth.

Lady Pedal, a fat woman who sponsors the picnic to the island. Artificial daisies bloom on her broad-brimmed straw hat above her plump, red face.

Jackson, a friend whose memory haunts Malone. Jackson thinks Malone is disgusting. He owns a pink and gray parrot, which he has taught to say "Nihil in intellectu."

as a big talking ball. If he moves at all, he surmises that he moves in orbits or cycles that return him to his original place, thereby making verification of his movement impossible. His existence depends on words and presumably will cease when his narrative is done. His monologue is a compulsive babble in which he vaguely remembers having been other characters and decides that he will be someone called Mahood, then Worm. He has no sex, no possessions, and no biography. He is trapped in time and space and becomes what he creates, for his life is solely the words he utters. He is essentially a mind in search of itself and is preoccupied with his own self-knowledge, although he despairs of knowing anything except in words.

Mahood, a lump who inhabits a jar outside a Paris restaurant opposite a horsemeat shop in the Rue Brancion. In the jar, Mahood seems suspended between life and death, and his only function appears to be as a display for the daily menu. Taken out once a week by the proprietress of the chophouse, he shrinks and sinks lower in the jar as she fills its bottom with sawdust. His head is covered with pustules and bluebottle flies and is shaded by a tarpaulin. Mahood is unable to move his head, for around his neck is a cement ring, a collar fixed to the mouth of the jar and encircling his neck just below the chin. He is able, however, to catch flies with his mouth. Before inhabiting the jar, Mahood returns from a tour abroad to visit his wife, parents, and eight or nine offspring. He discovers his family dead of sausage poisoning, their bodies decomposing. He travels on crutches because he has but one leg and a homologous arm. Mahood is half deaf and has a poor memory. Growing increasingly armless and legless, Mahood is transformed into Worm.

Worm, an amorphous consciousness evolved from Mahood. Worm is concerned primarily with probing his wormlike state. Worm is not clearly distinguishable from Mahood, because both are but manifestations of the Unnamable's desire for awareness.

Marguerite (mahr-geh-REET), also called **Madeleine** (mahd-LEHN), the caretaker of the jar. Every Sunday, she rids Mahood of excrement and rubs salt into his scalp. Perhaps because of her kindness, Mahood wonders if he might be related to her. Marguerite adorns his jar with colorful Chinese lanterns.

Basil (BA-zihl), a detested fiction of the Unnamable who is rebaptized as Mahood. The thought of Basil's face fills the Unnamable with hatred.

Malone, a figure seen in profile only from the waist up as he passes by the Unnamable. Although Malone is recognizable by his brimless hat and beard that hangs down in two twists of equal length, the Unnamable questions Malone's true identity.

— *Jerry W. Bradley*

A MOMENT OF TRUE FEELING
(Die Stunde der wahren Empfindung)

Author: Peter Handke (1942-   )
First published: 1975
Genre: Novel

Locale: Paris, France
Time: Mid-1970's
Plot: Philosophical realism

Gregor Keuschnig (KOYSH-nihk), a press attaché at the Austrian embassy in Paris. His job is to read French newspapers and look for articles concerning Austria. Keuschnig is in early middle age; he is married and has a four-year-old daughter. He has a dream one night in which he murders an old woman, and from that point on he is in an extremely agitated state of mind. Although he pretends to be normal, he is at a point of psychological and spiritual crisis, alienated from his own true self. He wanders the streets of Paris, trying to make sense of his life. Keuschnig seems at times to be in a kind of schizophrenic state in which random objects take on a new and strange significance. He longs to experience something that will give his existence meaning. While sitting on a park bench, he sees three objects on the ground: a chestnut leaf, a piece of a broken mirror, and a child's hair clip. These random items suddenly become a kind of semimystical revelation, and he realizes that he has the capacity to experience his life in a

different way. This episode, however, seems to be of only momentary duration, and his profound feelings of alienation return. At home, he and his wife have a dinner party. At one point during the meal, Keuschnig begins to disrobe, and in an infantile manner, he begins to throw food at his guests. Haunted by dreams of his mother, he at times feels suicidal. He believes that he must somehow make the world "mysterious" so that he can again perceive existence in a new, revitalized way. At the end of the novel, he realizes that he must find a new job and change his life.

The Writer, a friend of Keuschnig. He is about the same age as Keuschnig and has the habit of constantly watching other people and writing down notes. He seems to follow Keuschnig around, noting his behavior. This constant observation comes to annoy the latter, and, during the dinner party, Keuschnig attacks him.

— *Thomas F. Barry*

THE MONK

Author: Matthew Gregory Lewis (1775-1818)
First published: 1796
Genre: Novel

Locale: Madrid, Spain
Time: During the Spanish Inquisition
Plot: Gothic

Father Ambrosio, the most virtuous and learned monk in Madrid. He sentences Agnes de Medina to torture and death for adultery, and she calls upon him to remember her fate when he is tempted, as he is by Matilda, a sorceress. Following his seduction by Matilda, the monk ravishes Antonia, a virtuous girl. He is captured and condemned to die, but he sells his soul to Satan for release from prison. Satan releases him and

then kills him after telling him that his victims, Antonia and Elvira, were his sister and his mother.

Matilda, a sorceress. She enters Ambrosio's monastery disguised as a novice named Rosario. She seduces Ambrosio, leads him to ravish Antonia, and finally induces him to sell his soul. Matilda is condemned by the Inquisition but freed by Satan.

Antonia, a young girl ravished by Ambrosio and murdered by the monk to conceal his crime. Later, he learns that she was his sister.

Elvira, Antonia's mother. She is killed by Ambrosio, who learns later that she was his mother.

Marquis Raymond de las Cisternas, a Spanish nobleman who is in love with Agnes de Medina and who is the father of her unborn child. After great difficulty, he rescues his beloved from the convent where she is imprisoned.

Agnes de Medina, a young noblewoman who is condemned by Ambrosio for adultery. She is driven mad and almost starved to death in a convent.

Mother St. Clare, a nun who mistreats Agnes de Medina.

Lorenzo de Medina, Agnes' brother, who aids in securing the release of his sister. He loves Antonia, but after her death he is comforted by Virginia de Villa Franca, whom he marries.

Virginia de Villa Franca, a wealthy heiress who helps restore Agnes de Medina to health and sanity. She falls in love with Agnes' brother and marries him.

Mother St. Agatha, a nun who notifies Lorenzo de Medina falsely that his sister Agnes is dead.

MONKEY GRIP

Author: Helen Garner (1942-   )
First published: 1977
Genre: Novel

Locale: Melbourne, Sydney, and Tasmania
Time: 1974-1975
Plot: Love

Nora (Nor) Lewis, the thirty-three-year-old narrator. A writer for a feminist newspaper in Melbourne, Australia, she also sometimes works as a film extra. Previously married for six years to Jack, she now tries to be independent, though she likes men, the latest being Javo. She snorts cocaine and smokes marijuana, but she is not a junkie. After Javo's return from Cambodia, they separate. Distressed, Nora gets a crewcut with a tail, and she resigns herself to his absence.

Gracie, Nora's daughter, who celebrates her sixth birthday. She does not like school, runs away from it, and refuses to talk about it.

Javo, also called **Javes** and **Javaroo**, a tall, twenty-three-year-old actor and heroin addict. He has piercing blue eyes, and his face shows the ravages of drugs: He looks to be forty years old. He drifts into and out of Nora's bed as he attempts in vain to break his drug habit or hide it from her. He journeys to Cambodia with Martin; they are arrested and jailed for carrying drugs through Bangkok. After Julian secures their release, he returns to Melbourne, where he acts in a Bertolt Brecht play and keeps apart from Nora. In the end, he lives with Claire.

Martin, Nora's lover when she meets Javo. He travels to Cambodia with Javo, where they are jailed together.

Julian, one of Martin's brothers. A former junkie who deals in smack, he pulls his long hair back to pass customs. He raises bail for Martin and Javo in Bangkok.

Joss, Martin's mystical elder brother, whom Nora meets when he returns from America. He has messy bleached-out hair and large scars on his arms and feet.

Lou, Martin's green-eyed friend who wears a green earring. He comes down with hepatitis. He had once been Lillian's lover.

Selena, Lou's lover who comes down with hepatitis and gets an abortion.

Eve, Nora's friend who lives with Georgie and Clive. When Nora cannot endure Rita's problems with Juliet, Nora moves to Eve's commune.

The Roaster, Eve's son, who is about the same age as Gracie.

Rita, Nora's friend and housemate, who is in love with Nick. Always in a hurry, she has difficulty with Juliet, her daughter.

Angela (Ange), a singer. Although she is a close friend of Nora, she tells Nora that she has been angry at her for preying on everyone else's lovers. She fears that Rita will threaten her relationship with Willy.

Francis, a twenty-three-year-old director of a film about drug addiction. He sports a hippie beard, has pale skin with freckles, and wears his hair long and tied back. Thin but strong, he was once an athlete. He and Nora sometimes sleep together during Javo's absences.

Lillian, a good-looking woman with long legs. She broke up Nora's marriage with Jack after an affair with Lou. Nora dislikes her because she does not share men.

Gerald, a rock musician (guitarist) who tells Nora that he wants to sleep with her after she breaks up with Javo.

Hazel, Javo's mother, who lives in Hobart, Tasmania. She and Javo quarrel while he and Nora visit her.

Cobby, a friend of Nora. Back from America, she shares her views of American ways. She has blonde hair, and she is dressed like a Vietcong when she arrives at the airport.

Jessie, a friend of Nora, formerly Javo's lover. Their relationship was destroyed by his smack habit. She has straight red hair. Just back from Europe, she tells Nora that Javo has returned from Cambodia.

Paddy, an artist with her own house. Nora visits her for talk and marijuana. Paddy has lived with Willy for years. Although now they are apart, she is still attracted to him.

Willy, a rock musician (drummer). Formerly Paddy's lover, he is now with Bonny. He has short blond hair, wears wire-framed glasses, and looks like a European intellectual.

Mark, a saxophone player. Javo hangs out with Mark's sister, Sylvia, in Hobart.

Peggy (Peg), Nora's friend. She lives near Sydney, where she is visited by Nora, Javo, and Gracie. She offers a kind audience for Nora, who is distressed because Javo is breaking away.

Tom, Nora's friend who lives in Bondi. He helps comfort Nora during her breakup with Javo.

Bonny, a woman who sleeps with Willy, though she does not object to sharing him with Nora.

— *Richard D. McGhee*

THE MONKEY'S WRENCH
(La chiave a stella)

Author: Primo Levi (1919-1987)
First published: 1978
Genre: Novel

Locale: The Soviet Union, India, Africa, Alaska, and Italy
Time: The 1970's, with reminiscences
Plot: Philosophical realism

Libertino Faussone (lee-behr-TEE-noh fahew-SOH-nay), a rigger of giant steel structures such as cranes and suspension bridges. Faussone is an independent man, tall, thin, tanned, proud of his physical skills, and contemptuous of incompetent bosses, workers, and designers. The thirty-five-year-old Faussone enjoys a variety of professional and personal adventures as he travels around the world setting up monumental steel constructions. This "novel" is, in fact, a collection of separate tales connected mainly by the adventurous personality and forcefully stated perceptions of Faussone, their teller and principal character. He is by no means a perfect man; he is incapable, for example, of maintaining a permanent relationship with a woman, although he clearly has enjoyed a number of intense temporary relationships. He believes that women need "a different man for a husband, the kind that punch the time clock and come home at the same hour and never say boo." He is also claustrophobic and has a fear of water that has prevented him from learning to swim. Above all, Faussone is a man in love with his work and its demanding structural problems that only the rigger's indispensable skill can solve. As he says, "For me every job is like a first love."

The narrator, an industrial chemist who has gone to the Soviet Union to solve a problem of grit in his Italian factory's exported enamel. Clearly, the narrator is the author, who has decided, at the age of fifty-five, to leave his chemist's profession and devote himself entirely to his writing. In Russia, he has his first encounter with Faussone, who has been rigging a colossal excavator. An attentive listener, the narrator acquires Faussone's permission to use Faussone's stories. (In a postscript, the author writes that Faussone is "a mosaic of numerous men I have met, similar to Faussone and similar among themselves, in personality, virtue, individuality, and in their view of work and the world.") Like the composite character of Faussone that he has created, the narrator believes that "loving your work . . . represents the best, most concrete approximation of happiness on earth." He characterizes himself to Faussone as a "rigger-chemist . . . who builds structures to order."

Faussone, the central figure of almost all the tales, wonders if the narrator has given enough thought to his career change, whether it is wise to leave the material world for the world of words.

Libertino Faussone's father, a coppersmith who insisted on running his own shop instead of working regular hours under a boss in a factory. Even after copper pots had ceased to be in demand, he refused to change his work. By example, he taught his son the values of craftsmanship and of building one's own monuments through skilled and loving labor. Turning melancholy when the world no longer needed his skills, he died in his shop with his coppersmith's hammer in his hand.

Teresa Gallo and

Mentina Gallo (mehn-TEE-nah), Libertino Faussone's aunts. They live in an old apartment building in Turin, the native city of both Faussone and the narrator. Teresa is sixty-three years old, a dark-haired, sociable, childless widow. Mentina is sixty-six, white-haired, and never married; she talks mainly to her sister. They are both very worried about their only nephew's eating habits and occupational dangers. They constantly try to arrange meetings for him with a "nice girl" because of their concerns about his unsettled life, but Faussone has no interest in being shackled to a fixed abode.

The Indian engineer, not otherwise named. He is in charge of the construction of a huge suspension bridge over a river near Calcutta, for which Faussone is called in to rig the suspension cables. Serving as Faussone's foil, the engineer has manners and diction that are impeccable, but he lacks competence; he does not even correctly remember Faussone's name. He never loses his serenity, even when disaster occurs at the bridge, and Faussone has to spur him into action. Near the end of the episode, when part of the bridge's deck collapses, the main cables rigged by Faussone remain intact. Faussone's job being over, he leaves India without even saying good-bye to the engineer, whose attitude to his work Faussone cannot respect.

— *Donald Gochberg*

MONSIEUR BEAUCAIRE

Author: Booth Tarkington (1869-1946)
First published: 1900
Genre: Novel

Locale: Bath, England
Time: Early eighteenth century
Plot: Farce

Louis-Phillipe de Valois (lwee fee-LEEP deh vahl-WAH), the twenty-three-year-old duke of Orleans and cousin of King Louis XV of France, who masquerades as **Victor the Barber**, **Monsieur Beaucaire** (boh-KEHR), and the **duke of Chateaurien** (shah-TOH-ryah[n]). In the guise of Monsieur Beaucaire, he catches the duke of Winterset cheating at cards and blackmails Winterset into introducing him into Bath society, promising not to reveal the duke's cheating in exchange. The duke

says that everyone knows that Beaucaire arrived in England as Victor, the barber of the French ambassador, the Marquis de Mirepoix. Beaucaire says that even if that information is well known, he has a reputation in Paris, and Winterset would not be allowed to play cards when he visits there if Beaucaire spreads the knowledge that he is a cheat. Furthermore, Beaucaire has played cards with many of the men of Bath society, and if they find out that Winterset is a cheat, they might harm him physically. Previously, Beaucaire had been removed from the company of Beau Nash because he was not of nobility, but he promises to change his appearance so that no one will recognize him. He takes on the persona of the duke of Chateaurien (translatable as "Castle Nowhere"). He makes a favorable impression on the nobles and on Lady Mary Carlisle, to whom he takes a fancy. His reputation is twice challenged, and he twice defeats his challengers in fencing duels. He defends himself valiantly when attacked by Winterset's men, but in the aftermath of the attack, his identity as the ambassador's barber is revealed. He is told to leave Bath the next day, but he promises to see the nobles at a party held by Beau Nash the next week. Although Nash has guards posted, Chateaurien is able to sneak into the party with the aid of Mr. Molyneux, to whom he has revealed his true identity. At the party, he identifies himself as Louis-Phillipe de Valois, the duke of Orleans, and explains that he had to enter the country under a false identity because he was fleeing an arranged marriage and had been threatened with confinement. He denounces Winterset as a cheat and announces that he will return to France and his arranged marriage, stating that the king must know what is best for him.

The duke of Winterset, a noble whom Beaucaire blackmails so that Winterset will present him to Bath society. Once Beaucaire becomes popular as Chateaurien, Winterset contrives to ruin his reputation. He arranges for an attack by masked horsemen, who shout "Kill the barber!" He explains to other nobles that he arranged the attack as a way of avenging the outrage of having introduced Beaucaire to Bath society; he says he was duped by Beaucaire. He wins new respect for his honor in avenging his error. At Nash's party, he foolishly absolves Beaucaire of his promise to keep silent, thinking that no one will believe Beaucaire's story that Winterset cheats at cards.

Lady Mary Carlisle, who is known as the Beauty of Bath. She is taken with Chateaurien when he is presented to her at a ball, and he becomes her favorite among her several suitors. She is impressed by his actions in the attack by Winterset's men, but she scorns him when he admits having come to England as a barber.

Mr. Molyneux (moh-lee-NEW), who acts as Chateaurien's second in Chateaurien's second duel. Chateaurien learns to trust him when he continues to speak to Chateaurien as an equal after the attack by the masked horsemen.

Hugh Guilford, Lord Townbrake, a suitor of Lady Mary Carlisle. He refuses to help Chateaurien during the attack by Winterset's men.

Squire Bantison, another suitor of Lady Mary Carlisle who also fails to aid Chateaurien in the attack.

Beau Nash, known as the King of Bath, a leader of society. He threw Beaucaire out of one of his gatherings and is the host when his identity as the duke of Orleans is revealed.

The Marquis de Mirepoix (meer-PWAH), the ambassador to England from France. He arrives at Nash's party and vouches for the identity of the duke of Orleans.

The comte de Beaujolais (boh-zhoh-LEH), the brother of the duke of Orleans, who also vouches for his identity. He has come to England to escort Valois back to France for his marriage.

— *A. J. Sobczak*

MONSIEUR D'OLIVE

Author: George Chapman (c. 1559-1634)
First published: 1606
Genre: Drama

Locale: An imaginary dukedom near France
Time: The seventeenth century
Plot: Comedy

Vandome (vah[n]-DOHM), a noble young gentleman, the platonic lover of Marcellina. He untangles all the complications of the plot with his intelligence and courtesy.

Count Vaumont (Voh-MOH[N]), the jealous but repentant husband of Marcellina. His jealousy leads her to take an oath to retire from society and turn night into day and day into night.

Marcellina (mahr-seh-LEE-nah), the angry wife of Vaumont. She allows Vandome to arouse her own jealousy over her husband's supposed infidelity and breaks her vow of seclusion to catch him. Reconciliation follows.

Eurione (ewr-YOHN), Marcellina's sister, in love with Count St. Anne.

Count St. Anne (sahn-TAHN), Vandome's brother-in-law. Loving his dead wife and grieved almost to madness, he keeps her embalmed body constantly with him. Vandome persuades him to speak to Eurione on his behalf. Seeing her, he falls in love with her and abandons his morbid worship of his dead wife.

Duke Philip, St. Anne's friendly superior. Failing to convert St. Anne to reasonable behavior, he decides to send an embassy to the king to request an order for the wife's burial. He chooses, humorously, the ridiculous Monsieur d'Olive as his ambassador.

Monsieur d'Olive (doh-LEEV), an idle, self-satisfied wit. Appointed as the duke's emissary, he wastes time gathering a host of followers and accepting money from them. Vandome's labors make the embassy unnecessary, but the duke graciously gives Monsieur d'Olive a place in his entourage.

MONSIEUR LECOQ

Author: Émile Gaboriau (1832-1873)
First published: 1869
Genre: Novel

Locale: Paris, France
Time: The nineteenth century
Plot: Detective and mystery

Monsieur Lecoq (leh-KOHK), a young Paris detective who finds two people dead and one wounded. He is hampered in his investigation of the crime and never solves it.

Gevrol (zheh-VROHL), an elderly inspector of police who is without imagination. Lecoq's persistance in trying to solve the crime causes subsequent enmity between them.

Mother Chupin (shew-PA[N]), owner of the wineshop that is the scene of the crime.

Father Absinthe (ahb-SA[N]T), an experienced policeman and a friend of Lecoq.

May, who is arrested at the scene of the murder while holding the gun. He tries to strangle himself while in jail.

When allowed to "escape" so that he can be followed, he disappears permanently.

An Accomplice, who is permitted to help May "escape." He is recaptured, but May disappears in the garden of the duke of Sairmeuse.

Tabaret (tah-bah-RAY), the oracle of the police force, who concludes that May must be the duke of Sairmeuse himself.

M. d'Escorval (dehs-kohr-VAHL), the presiding judge, who breaks his leg rather than try May.

M. Segmuller (ZEEG-mew-lehr), the new judge assigned to the case.

MONT-ORIOL

Author: Guy de Maupassant (1850-1893)
First published: 1887
Genre: Novel

Locale: Auvergne, France
Time: Mid-nineteenth century
Plot: Social satire

Christiane Andermatt (kree-STYAHN ahn-dehr-MAHT), a young married woman who, while she is in the country taking some baths to cure her childlessness, meets Paul Brétigny, a friend of her brother, and has a love affair with him. At first, she will not listen to his supplications, but after a time she submits and has a baby girl by him. She becomes jealous when she discovers that, while she is pregnant, her lover has fallen in love with another woman. When her baby is born, she will have nothing to do with the child. Later, however, the baby attracts her; she becomes absorbed in it and is totally indifferent to her former lover.

Paul Brétigny (pohl bray-teen-YEE), Christiane's lover, who meets her when he goes to the country to recover from an unhappy love affair. He feels sorry for and falls in love with Charlotte Oriol, who has been rejected by Christiane's brother, Gontran de Ravenel.

William Andermatt, Christiane's husband, a financier who decides to buy some land from a peasant and build baths to utilize the spring water, which supposedly has medicinal properties. Andermatt engages in many machinations in order to obtain the land and promote the baths.

Father Oriol (ohr-YOHL), a peasant landowner. He blasts a rock out of the ground and a spring gushes forth. Oriol is a

shrewd bargainer, as is shown in his dealings with Andermatt.

Gontran de Ravenel (goh[n]-TRAH[N] deh rahv-NEHL), Christiane's brother, a witty young man who, at Andermatt's suggestion, plans to court and marry one of Oriol's daughters in order to obtain part of the land that forms their dowries, and thus pay off his debts. He courts Charlotte first, since she is younger and prettier, but he switches to Louise when he finds that her dowry will be more profitable to him.

Charlotte Oriol (shahr-LOHT), Father Oriol's younger daughter, who is courted by Gontran de Ravenel. When he discovers that her sister's dowry is larger, he deserts her. She is consoled by Paul, and they become engaged.

Louise Oriol, Father Oriol's elder daughter, who is persuaded by Gontran that he paid court to her sister only in order to arouse her interest in him.

Clovis (kloh-VEES), a beggar who poaches at night and feigns rheumatism in the daytime. He is hired to bathe in the spring every day and, when he is supposedly cured, it is hoped that Andermatt will be convinced of the medicinal value of the water. After the baths are opened, he returns and threatens to tell the public that the water harmed him. He is bought off by being paid to take the treatment every year.

MONTGOMERY'S CHILDREN

Author: Richard Perry (1944-   )
First published: 1984
Genre: Novel

Locale: Montgomery, New York
Time: 1948-1980
Plot: Psychological realism

Gerald Fletcher, a bright and sensitive African American who is a boy at the novel's opening. He has a brown mark on the white of his right eye, a trait inherited from his grandfather. Gerald's father views the mark as a sign that the boy has also inherited the grandfather's irresponsibility, and he inflicts brutal beatings on Gerald for normal childish pranks. Gerald, scarred by his father's lack of love, becomes quiet and guarded at home. At school, Gerald first befriends Josephine, then ignores her because of peer pressure. Later he apologizes, and

she initiates him into sex. He shares confidences and adventures with his friend Iceman, but when Iceman dies, Gerald closes off his emotions and concentrates on scholastic achievement. By 1980, Gerald is one of Montgomery's successes, with a master's degree and an accomplished wife. Finding his middle-class life empty, he takes leave from it to reconcile his failed relationships with Josephine and with Norman.

Hosea Malone, a short, slim man with a spotted complexion. Originally a pillar of Montgomery's black community and church, Hosea abandons his faith and family when his son is born blind and witless. He drifts to Manhattan and works as an elevator operator. Fourteen years later he returns, wearing expensive suits and bringing a car full of drugs. Settling down with Alice Simineski, a fat white woman who financed his entry into the drug trade, he becomes a leading citizen. Everyone knows that his prosperity comes from selling drugs, but because of changing social mores and Hosea's generous bribes, no one interferes. When he visits his former wife, Meredith, she tells him that she smothered their baby years ago. Hosea cautions her to keep quiet about it. Later, when Meredith finally confesses to the police, an ambitious district attorney tries to punish Hosea by charging him as an accomplice, but Hosea's money and noninvolvement save him.

Norman Fillis, a tall, light-skinned school custodian. In 1948, he has visions that push him into mysticism and madness. The natural world explodes into blue, white, and silver slivers around him, and he sees scenes from African history in a furnace fire. Watching fire becomes an obsession for him. He also "discovers" that black people originally had the power of flight and eventually will reacquire it. He tries to teach Gerald how to fly and tells other bizarre secrets to the boy. Gerald humors him but refuses to become a disciple. Norman's strange behavior leads to several stays in mental hospitals, but he always returns to Montgomery, where he preaches of fire and flight. At the age of seventy-one, after meeting Gerald again, Norman believes that the Dispensation of Flight has arrived. He takes on a condor's form and soars through the sky, then falls into the courthouse cupola and crashes to the ground.

Josephine Moore, a one-handed girl with gray eyes and a breathtakingly beautiful face. Josephine moves with her parents to Montgomery when she is fifteen years old. As Pastor Mclain's cousin, she wins immediate acceptance by the respectable black adults, but her new schoolmates reject her. Josephine reacts with proud, stoic dignity. At home, she is molested repeatedly by her stepfather. She also has nightmares about chickens, axes, and cars rushing through the night. Convinced that Gerald also wants her only as a sex object, Josephine sends him away. She stabs and kills her stepfather the next time he forces himself on her. After spending six years in prison, she eventually finds Gerald, and they have a brief, passionate reunion, but she remains a wounded soul.

Meredith Malone, a sensual but hard-pressed woman. Overwhelmed when her husband, Hosea, leaves, she suffocates her deformed baby and buries him in the backyard. Living on money Hosea sends, she manages to bring up their six daughters, but guilt and sexual frustration turn her hollow and morose. At the age of sixty-seven, she digs up the baby's bones and turns herself in so she can clear her conscience and go to heaven.

Zacharias Poole, a plump, bespectacled boy also known as **Iceman**, a nickname bestowed by his peers who consider him to be "uncool." His intellectual curiosity, honesty in the face of social lies, and gentleness toward animals make him unique among Montgomery's youth. He dies in 1961, electrocuted while trying to rescue a kitten from a tree.

Pastor Melinda Mclain, the minister of the black community's church, an influential figure noted as much for her commonsense advice as for her blue hair and her compelling sermons.

— Emily Alward

A MONTH IN THE COUNTRY
(Mesyats v derevne)

Author: Ivan Turgenev (1818-1883)
First published: 1855
Genre: Drama

Locale: Russia
Time: The 1840's
Plot: Psychological realism

Arkady Sergeyitch Islayev (ahr-KAH-dihy sehr-GEH-ihch ihs-lah-YEHF), a wealthy landowner interested in the details of work on his estate and unwilling to trust his peasants to work without supervision. His discovery of his wife and his friend together and their resultant embarrassment make him feel that he has been too trusting. Although he agrees that Rakitin should leave, at least for a time, he is apologetic about sending away an old friend. Unperceptive as he has been, he is completely surprised later when Rakitin tells him of Natalya's love for Belyayev.

Natalya Petrovna (nah-TAHL-yah peht-ROV-nah), called **Natasha** (nah-TAH-shah), his wife. Intelligent and observant, she is sometimes mischievous toward Rakitin, who accuses her of playing with him as a cat does with a mouse. Early in the play, it is obvious that although she cares for Rakitin, she is restlessly looking for some new excitement. Attracted to Belyayev, her son's tutor, because of his youth, appearance, and winning personality, she tries to draw him out. Seeing Vera's interest in him, she becomes jealous. She is also a little ashamed of herself for both the love and the jealousy, and she berates herself for slyly eliciting Vera's confession of love and then reporting it so bluntly and cruelly to Belyayev. At the end, she is overcome by the almost simultaneous departures of Belyayev and Rakitin.

Kolya (KOH-lyah), the ten-year-old son of Arkady and Natalya, a high-spirited boy who idolizes Belyayev.

Vera (VEH-rah), an orphaned ward of the Islayevs. Lonely for the companionship of young people, she falls romantically in love with Belyayev, with whom she feels a kinship because he is also motherless. She is fond of Natalya but a little afraid of her. Upon her discovery of Natalya's duplicity in trapping her into a confession of love, and after her realization that she and Natalya are rivals, her fear is replaced by anger. When she learns that Belyayev has no thought of marrying her and that he has regarded her as simply a charming girl, she impulsively decides to marry the ludicrous though good Bolshintsov simply to get away from Natalya.

Mihail Alexandrovitch Rakitin (mih-hah-IHL ah-lehk-SAHN-dro-vihch rah-KIH-tihn), a longtime friend of the Islayevs, a man fond of studying people and analyzing them. He has been in love with Natalya for several years, but the affair has hovered only between the platonic and the adulterous. Natalya finds him sympathetic, affectionate, constant, peaceful, and comforting. His manner with her shifts with his moods and hers, being alternately jesting, romantic, poetic, and philosophical. The relationship between the two closely resembles that of the playwright and Madame Viardot, an opera singer who was taught by Franz Liszt and loved by Alfred de Musset and Hector Berlioz as well as by Turgenev.

Alexey Nikolayevitch Belyayev (ah-lehk-SAY nih-koh-LAH-yeh-vihch beh-LYAH-ehf), a university student and Kolya's tutor. He is diffident and embarrassed when Natalya talks to him, but he talks freely with Vera and appears boyish and enthusiastic when he is with Vera and Kolya. He is confused and ill at ease because of the difference between his station and that of the aristocratic Natalya, and he is both flattered and frightened to find that she loves him. Unwilling to hurt anyone, he flees from involvement with either Natalya or Vera.

Ignaty Ilyitch Shpigelsky (ih-GNAH-tihy IH-lyihch shpih-GEHL-skih), a doctor and a close friend of the Islayevs. Having told a story of a girl with two suitors who knew she was in love but did not know with whom, he draws from Natalya the question whether it is possible to love two people at once. He perceives Natalya's relationship with Rakitin. At times, he seems like a basso buffo in a comic opera, but his serious side

is made evident in the long conversation during which he proposes to Lizaveta. He confesses that although he plays the clown, it is a calculated playing, and he is in reality ingratiating himself with the rich people from whom he may gain rewards without revealing what he thinks of them. He serves as a marriage broker for Bolshintsov.

Adam Ivanitch Schaaf (ah-DAHM ih-VAHN-ihch schahf), a phlegmatic, rather grumpy German tutor. He is ridiculous in his attempts to be romantic with Katya, who spurns him.

Afanasy Ivanovitch Bolshintsov (ah-fah-NAH-sihy ih-VAH-no-vihch bohl-SHIHN-tsof), a neighbor. Shy with women, he promises Shpigelsky three horses if the doctor can arrange for him a marriage with Vera. Rakitin thinks him fat, foolish, and tedious, and to Vera he is laughable, though she finally agrees to marry him.

Anna Semyonovna Islayev (AHN-nah seh-MYOH-nov-nah ihs-lah-YEHF), Arkady's mother. She is disturbed by the belief that Natalya and Rakitin are more than friends and at the end by the news that Lizaveta may soon be leaving her.

Lizaveta Bogdanovna (lih-zah-VEH-tah bohg-DAH-nov-nah), Anna's companion. Her remarks to Anna at the end of the play suggest that shortly she will marry Shpigelsky.

Katya (KAH-tyah), a maid courted by both Schaaf and Matvey. She likes Belyayev.

Matvey (maht-VAY), a manservant in love with Katya.

A MONTH OF SUNDAYS

Author: John Updike (1932-   )
First published: 1975
Genre: Novel

Locale: Primarily the American Midwest
Time: The 1970's
Plot: Religious

The Reverend Thomas (Tom) Marshfield, a forty-one-year-old minister and the narrator. Tormented by questions about his religious belief, his marriage, and his place in life, Tom has been discovered in affairs with parishioners and has been sent for a month to a recovery center for troubled clergy, where he is required to spend each morning writing. Tom, in thirty-one chapters, examines the thoughts and actions that led to his disgrace and recounts his youth as the son of a clergyman; his years at seminary, where he met his wife, Jane; and his affairs with Alicia Crick and Frankie Harlow. True to his profession, he composes each Sunday's entry as a sermon. Throughout, he is convinced that his writings are being read surreptitiously by the center's matron, Ms. Prynne, with whom, by the novel's end, he has a brief affair.

Jane Marshfield, Tom's wife and the daughter of one of his divinity school professors. Middle-aged and the mother of two sons, she struggles to behave decently and sensitively in an unsatisfying marriage. She and Tom are said to have come to look alike.

Alicia Crick, the organist in Tom's church, in her late twenties, divorced, and the mother of two children. She has an affair with Tom and confesses it to Jane. When Tom fires her, she tells the story of Tom's many affairs to Gerald Harlow, the chairman of the board of deacons, thereby precipitating Tom's expulsion.

Frances (Frankie) Harlow, a parishioner in Tom's church

and the wife of the chairman of the board of deacons, whom she despises. Middle-aged, with somewhat fading attractiveness, and the mother of two children, she succeeds Alicia as Tom's mistress. Her firm religious faith causes Tom to be impotent with her.

Gerald Harlow, a bank executive and chairman of the board of deacons, efficient, businesslike, and most interested in the social benefits of his marriage. He delivers word of Tom's banishment. Although he suspects Frankie's affair with Tom, he allows himself to be convinced that his wife is faithful.

Ned Bork, the assistant minister in Tom's church. In his early thirties, bearded, and liberal in theology and politics, he is Tom's nemesis. He is apparently more popular with the congregation than is Tom. He has an affair with Alicia but refuses Tom's guilt-ridden encouragement to begin one with Jane.

The Reverend Marshfield, Tom's father and a former minister. Now senile and in a nursing home, he confuses Tom with other figures from the past and in his sometimes obscene ramblings implies that Tom's mother had an affair.

Ms. Prynne, the manager of the rehabilitation center. Large, unattractive, and domineering, she becomes the audience for Tom's writings, although not until the end of the novel is there clear evidence that she has read them. In the last pages of the novel, apparently seduced by Tom's writing, she has a brief affair with him.

Martin Marshfield, Tom and Jane's eldest son. Sixteen years old and excellent at sports, he is a perfectionist who is embarrassed by his father's scandal.

Stephen Marshfield, Tom and Jane's younger son. Fourteen years old, handsome, and passive, he understands little of the reason for his father's banishment.

Amos, a fellow clergyman at the recovery center. Depressed by his failing ministry, he was caught attempting to burn down the church.

— *Larry L. Stewart*

THE MOON AND SIXPENCE

Author: W. Somerset Maugham (1874-1965)
First published: 1919
Genre: Novel

Locale: England, France, and Tahiti
Time: c. 1887-1917
Plot: Biographical

Charles Strickland, an English stockbroker who seems commonplace to his friends until he suddenly leaves his wife and family and goes to Paris to study art. A friend sent by the wife to persuade him to return is told he has left his family permanently. Consumed by his desire to paint, he neglects his physical needs. During an illness, he is nursed by a friend's wife, whom he makes his mistress and model. After her death, Strickland goes to Marseilles and, after further wandering, finally arrives in Tahiti. He marries Ata, a native girl who cares for his needs, and he paints constantly. Ill again, he is found to have leprosy and is isolated from all except Ata, who cares for him. He paints the walls of their bungalow until he is completely blind. Living in darkness, he remembers his last paintings, his masterpieces; however, he asks Ata to destroy the paintings on the walls after his death.

Amy Strickland, a commonplace English wife and mother. She cannot understand why her husband deserted her or his fame after his death.

Dirk Stroeve, Strickland's artist friend in Paris. Something of a buffoon, he feels inferior to his English wife but loves her deeply. He insists she nurse Strickland in his illness. After they become lovers, Dirk leaves them in his studio and even gives his faithless wife money. When she dies, he returns to the studio and finds her nude portrait, which he tries to destroy; but he cannot do so because he recognizes in it a superb creation by Strickland. Dirk returns to live with his mother in Holland.

Blanche Stroeve, Dirk's English wife. She professes to dislike her husband's friend Strickland, and when the artist becomes ill, she pleads with her husband not to make her nurse him. On Dirk's insistence, she complies. After Strickland recovers and takes over the studio, Dirk asks him to leave, but by that time Blanche is in love with Strickland and says she will leave also. Ironically, Strickland sees in her only an excellent model. He walks out on her when he has finished his portrait of her, a painting he regards as a failure. Blanche commits suicide.

Ata, Strickland's Tahitian wife. Seventeen when she marries him, she bears his children and faithfully tends his needs. After his death, she destroys their bungalow, the walls of which Strickland had covered with paintings.

Capitaine Brunot, a black-bearded Frenchman who admires the beauty of the primitive home that Ata has created for Strickland. Brunot owns a few pictures, which he is saving to use as a "dot" for his two young daughters.

Dr. Coutras, an old French doctor who is forced to tell Strickland he has leprosy. Strickland repays the doctor by giving him one of his pictures. Dr. Coutras is the one Westerner who sees the strange pictures that cover the walls of the isolated bungalow, where he finds Strickland dead after a year of blindness.

THE MOON AND THE BONFIRES
(La luna e i falò)

Author: Cesare Pavese (1908-1950)
First published: 1950
Genre: Novel

Locale: Gaminella and neighboring villages in Italy
Time: Late 1940's, and the interwar period in retrospect
Plot: Neorealism

Narrator, an unnamed man who grows up in a small village in the Piedmont of Italy, goes to the United States, and, as the novel opens, returns to his Italian village as a wealthy man. The narrator, a forty-year-old bachelor, reviews his life on three levels: his youth as an illegitimate child and as a poor farm laborer, his early manhood as a successful but rootless man in the United States, and his return to Italy and the scenes of his childhood. His return forces him to confront the personal loss that he feels because he cannot fit back into the village life that he knew in his youth.

Nuto (NEW-toh), a carpenter. To the narrator, Nuto represents the wisdom rooted in the life of the villages and hills of the Piedmont. He is three years older than the narrator, with piercing eyes, emotional intensity, and consuming concern with social justice; he is unable to bear injustice and cruelty. He represents what the narrator would have been if he had stayed in his village. On one hand, Nuto refused to leave the Piedmont and expand his horizons by facing the challenges of the outside world; on the other, he retained his sense of place and ancestral heritage, which the narrator has lost.

Cinto (CHEEN-toh), Valino's son, a peasant boy. Tense, wary, and crippled by hard work and a poor diet, Cinto, who lives on the farm where the narrator grew up, reminds the narrator of himself as a boy. The narrator feels close to Cinto as he remembers his own yearnings to experience the wider world when he was that age. He befriends Cinto and tries to show him that there is hope for change and for a better life.

Valino (vah-LEE-noh), a poor sharecropper, an old, angry man whose sons, except for Cinto, were killed in war. His life was blighted by poverty and hopelessness, and he turned into a silent, embittered abuser of his family. In an insane rage, he kills the women of his family, tries to kill Cinto, and then hangs himself. He represents another possible life that the narrator might have lived if he had not escaped from poverty and ignorance.

Sor Matteo (maht-TAY-oh), the owner of the estate of La Mora, where the narrator went to live at roughly the age of thirteen, after leaving his sharecropping foster family. La Mora provided a port for the narrator that opened on the world. Sor Matteo is a gentleman who does not work the land himself but keeps close account of La Mora's business. Although Sor Matteo is the grandest man in the narrator's small world, his status cannot protect him from old age and unmanageable daughters. He becomes old and helpless, and La Mora is broken apart and sold off.

Silvia,

Irene,(ee-REH-nay) and

Santina (sahn-TEE-nah), three daughters of Sor Matteo. As the narrator is entering young manhood, these beautiful, rich young women show him that wealth and social position fail to guarantee security and happiness. One of the daughters dies of typhus and one of an abortion; the last one is executed as a fascist spy by the partisans in World War II.

Nora, the cashier at a diner in Oakland, California. The narrator worked at the same diner and evidently lived with Nora. This is the only relationship he discusses in any detail. The sterility of their relationship symbolizes to him the meaninglessness of existence and the lack of substance of life in the United States. Rootless Americans created a land like the barren surface of the moon, in contrast to the richness promised by the bonfires in the fields of the Piedmont that farmers light to "wake up" the land and get it ready for another year of production.

— *William E. Pemberton*

A MOON FOR THE MISBEGOTTEN

Author: Eugene O'Neill (1888-1953)
First published: 1952
Genre: Drama

Locale: Connecticut
Time: September, 1923
Plot: Psychological realism

Mike Hogan, the last of three brothers at home; he is twenty years old. As the play opens, his only sister, Josie, helps him to leave home behind the back of their father, who has treated his sons like slaves, though he has not been able to treat Josie like one.

Josie Hogan, who is much older than Mike, a very tall, muscular woman who has cultivated the reputation of being blatantly immoral and sexually involved with many men, but who is in fact a virgin who has acted thus because her appearance humiliates her and makes her believe that she can never attract a man.

Phil Hogan, their father, a widower, alcoholic, and tenant farmer in Connecticut. He and Josie have frequent brawls that are partially pleasurable playacting. Because of her size, Josie always wins, as she does when he learns of Mike's escape and is genuinely furious. He is secretly aware of the falsity of Josie's reputation and tries, through a series of ruses, to bring her and Tyrone together.

T. Stedman Harder, a nearby estate owner who would like to buy the property, though actually Tyrone will buy it and keep the Hogans as tenants. Early in the play, Harder complains that Phil's pigs come to his pond and mess things up; in a hilarious scene, Phil and Josie turn the tables on him and make him try (unsuccessfully) to make a dignified exit.

James (Jamie) Tyrone, a friend of the Hogans, modeled on the playwright's older brother. He has a traumatic memory of an event that actually happened to the real James. He and Josie care deeply for each other, though both have difficulty in expressing their feelings. They arrange a meeting at the farm that night, but Josie is devastated when Jamie does not appear. He finally does arrive, very drunk. He is an alcoholic, both in the play and in real life, but capable of behaving, and thinking, as either drunk or sober. He is perfectly aware of her playing the loose woman is false, and what he wants from her is simply a night of comfort as a means of escaping from the unbearable memory that dominates his life. Their talk shifts gradually from failure to communicate to deep communication. At one point, Josie, deeply in love with him, offers him her bed, but because his lifelong loose sexuality relates to his horrible memory, he is shocked and repelled. All he wants is to be close to her, to lie (as she offers) on her breast, to confess his memory, and to have a night of peace. She hears his confession: He had been in California with his mother, who died there, and accompanied her body back East—spending the whole time in his compartment on the train with a cheap blonde. With the story told, he does spend the night in peace, his head on her breast in the moonlight; this is probably the only night she will ever spend with a man. Her feelings are more of resignation to that fact than of comfort, though finally, when Jamie leaves at peace at the play's end, she too is at peace.

— *Jacob H. Adler*

THE MOON IS A HARSH MISTRESS

Author: Robert A. Heinlein (1907-1988)
First published: 1966; serial form, 1965-1966
Genre: Novel

Locale: The Lunar colonies and Earth
Time: 2075-2076
Plot: Science fiction

Mike, short for **Mycroft Holmes**, the chosen name of a sentient computer, the Holmes Four: High-Optional, Logical, Multi-Evaluating Supervisor, Mark IV, Model L. Almost all mechanical and electronic equipment on the moon is under Mike's direction. Wanting to acquire friends and an understanding of humor, Mike joins the Lunar Revolution, which he illicitly finances. In company with Professor de la Paz, he also plans, organizes, and executes the revolution. He creates a fictional figurehead, Adam Selene, complete with video imagery and offices, to run the revolution and die nobly during the fighting, as well as a popular graffiti hero, Simon Jester, who writes nasty jingles about the administration. Mike seems to find the revolution great fun—a joke and a challenge—but is lost in the last bombing before Earth capitulates. Although all of his connections are restored and repairs are made wherever damage occurred, Mike either cannot or will not respond anymore.

Manuel Garcia (Mannie) O'Kelly, a computer repairman. Mannie has only one arm but has prostheses for every occasion for the other. He is Mike's best friend and an unintentional revolutionary. Capable and pragmatic, Mannie is made an ambassador, defense minister, and later prime minister but prefers to be a congressman who does not attend meetings. As a member of a line marriage, he is jailed on Earth for polygamy. He has almost unanimous support on Luna. He survives to see Free Luna legislating away its freedom and contemplates a move to the Asteroid Belt, where there is no government.

Wyoming (Wyoh) Knott, a revolutionary, a curvaceous, beautiful blonde. Wyoh spends much of her time as a fugitive disguised as a curvaceous black woman. She is strong-willed and determined to see a Free Luna. Her wholehearted participation in the revolt brings her a new family when she is opted into Mannie's marriage as well as into leadership in the movement.

Professor Bernardo (Prof) de la Paz, a political exile and Mannie's former teacher. Elderly and fragile but possessing a fierce intellect and passion for political philosophy, Prof is the source of Mike's encouragement and of many of Mike's ideas. He outlines much of the revolution to be implemented by Mike and manipulates everyone with whom he comes in contact. Prof is made prime minister of Luna, second only to Adam Selene. The trip to Earth as an ambassador almost kills him, but he survives to see a free Lunar state—but only barely, as he dies making the announcement.

Stuart Rene (Stu) LaJoie, an Earthman who joins the revolution. Wealthy and polite, Stu seems an odd choice for support in a revolution. He contributes his family fortune to support the revolution and is instrumental in furthering the cause on Earth and in getting Mannie and Prof back to Luna. After an interim government is organized, Stu is named special minister without portfolio in the Ministry of Information. He also is opted into the Davis clan.

Hazel Meade, a revolutionary. Although only thirteen years old, red-haired Hazel bursts on the scene with daring physical attacks on guards. She goes on to become captain of the Baker Street Irregulars, a children's spy network. She, too, joins the Davis clan, but by adoption, as she was orphaned at the age of five.

— *Terry Hays Jackson*

MOONRISE, MOONSET
(Wschody i zachody księżyca)

Author: Tadeusz Konwicki (1926-   )
First published: 1982
Genre: Novel

Locale: Warsaw and elsewhere in Poland
Time: 1981
Plot: Realism

Tadeusz Konwicki (tah-DEH-ewsh kohn-WIHTS-kih), the book's author. There are no other characters in this work, except as Konwicki discusses, describes, and occasionally vilifies colleagues and acquaintances of his, such as compatriot writers Czesław Miłosz and Stanisław Lem. He also includes fragments of an old novel, in which he created an alter ego character by the name of Teodor Klimowicz. Konwicki is an elderly, sick man; he is continually afraid that he has lost his talent for writing. The work is in almost journal form; Konwicki's day-to-day problems with the Communist Party and the ever-looming specter of the Soviet Union color most of his entries. He details his problems with making Miłosz's book *The Issa Valley* into a film as well as the film's cool reception. Konwicki is preoccupied with predicting the future for Poland while also recalling its past, especially the events of World War II.

— *T. M. Lipman*

THE MOONSTONE

Author: Wilkie Collins (1824-1889)
First published: 1868
Genre: Novel

Locale: India and England
Time: 1799-1849
Plot: Detective and mystery

Franklin Blake, a genial young man, Lady Verinder's nephew. According to the terms of John Herncastle's will, he is given temporary charge of the Moonstone, a diamond that Herncastle had taken during the storming of Seringapatam and that is to be given to his niece, Rachel Verinder, on her birthday following her uncle's death. Of great religious significance in the worship of Brahma and Vishnu, the stone, which is worth about thirty thousand pounds, is supposed to bring ill fortune to any but worshipers of the Moon-God from whose forehead it had been stolen. After presenting the stone to Rachel, Blake, who has been suffering from insomnia, is given secretly a dose of laudanum. In his partly drugged state, he goes to Rachel's sitting room during the night and takes the stone from a cabinet. Rachel witnesses the act but, being in love with Blake and thinking he is taking the stone because he needs money, she does not tell what she has seen. A year later, after the stone has been located and the details of its disappearance are cleared, Blake and Rachel are married.

Rachel Verinder, his cousin. In keeping the secret of the lost gem, she suffers the accusations of officials, servants, and friends. Thinking Blake does not love her, she vents her unhappiness on others. During Blake's absence from England, she promises to marry Godfrey Ablewhite, but she suddenly breaks the engagement. She and Blake are married after the mystery has been solved.

Godfrey Ablewhite, a handsome young Londoner who, seeing that Blake is semiconscious when he takes the diamond, removes the gem from Blake's hand. Godfrey delivers the gem at once to a London moneylender for safe keeping. After a year, he redeems the diamond with the intention of selling it in Amsterdam in order to pay his debts. In the maneuver to get aboard ship, he disguises himself as a sailor. His dead body is found in a waterfront lodging house, but the stone is missing; it has been reclaimed by its Hindu owners.

Lady Julia Verinder, Rachel's mother and the sister of John Herncastle, who brought the diamond from India. A gentlewoman, she is unnerved by having the police in her home. She goes to London, where she dies of a heart ailment.

Gabriel Betteredge, the venerable house steward to Lady Julia Verinder; he narrates much of the story. His life is guided by philosophies he combs from *Robinson Crusoe*, a book he reads over and over and quotes constantly.

Sergeant Richard Cuff, a grizzled, elderly detective of the London police force, sent by Blake's father to investigate the loss of the diamond. Amiable and knowledgeable in human nature, he is loved by almost everyone who knows him. His keen interest is rose culture, which subject he argues ardently with the Verinder gardener during the investigation.

Mr. Bruff, the old lawyer who, as family counselor for three generations, executed John Herncastle's will. As the executor of Lady Julia Verinder's will, he becomes Rachel's guardian. Sensing the motive for the girl's silence and bitterness, he arranges to bring her and Franklin Blake together whenever possible.

Rosanna Spearman, the second housemaid at Lady Julia Verinder's estate. The former inmate of a reformatory, she has been taken in by Lady Julia and given a fresh start in life. In love with Blake and suspecting him of the theft of the diamond because of paint (from the door to Rachel's sitting room) on his nightgown, Rosanna takes the garment, locks it in a box,

and sinks the box in quicksand. She herself commits suicide. From a letter she leaves with a friend, Blake and Betteredge learn, about a year later, the details of her love for Blake and her effort to help him.

Dr. Thomas Candy, the family physician, who administers laudanum for Franklin Blake's sleeplessness after Rachel Verinder's birthday party. Dr. Candy, pictured as a suspect, loses his memory after an illness contracted from exposure on the night of the party.

Ezra Jennings, Dr. Candy's assistant during the physician's long illness. Strange in appearance and of questionable background, Jennings is a likely suspect as an accomplice in the theft. He is actually a congenial person; his behavior is caused by a severe disease, from which he dies. His explanation of the effects of laudanum leads to the solution of the mystery of the diamond's disappearance.

Mr. Murthwaite, an authority on Indian religions. At the end, he writes to Bruff a letter describing a religious festival in India, a ceremony that revealed the Moon-God with the restored diamond gleaming in its forehead.

Septimus Lukier, the London moneylender with whom Godfrey leaves the Moonstone while he makes plans to get the gem out of England.

Superintendent Seegrave, the first police officer to investigate the disappearance of the Moonstone. His bungling tactics and manner emphasize Cuff's aptness.

Drusilla Clack, a poor relation of Lady Verinder and a religious fanatic. Her descriptions of tract-passing in her efforts to save people's souls are classics in literary humor.

Penelope, Betteredge's daughter and Lady Julia's servant, who reminds her father of events as he narrates his part of the story. Penelope tells of the actions of the servants during the investigation.

Lucy Yolland, Lady Julia's young clubfooted neighbor. Ugly, sullen, and distrustful, she becomes friendly with Rosanna. Lucy shows her loyalty by keeping Rosanna's suicide letter secret for a year.

Octavius Guy, Bruff's young employee, nicknamed "Gooseberry" because of his bulging eyes. Gooseberry follows Godfrey as he makes his way toward the boat with the diamond.

The Three Indians, whose actions are always related by another person. Never "seen" in the story, they are always in quest of the stolen diamond. Their presence at the scene of Godfrey Ablewhite's murder is proved, and they are reported by Mr. Murthwaite as "disappearing" in the throng gathered at the Hindu ceremony where the Moonstone was last seen.

MORNING, NOON, AND NIGHT

Author: James Gould Cozzens (1903-1978)
First published: 1968
Genre: Novel

Locale: Boston, New York City, Washington, D.C., and a New England college town
Time: Primarily the 1920's to the 1960's
Plot: Social

Henry Dodd (Hank) Worthington, the narrator, the head of a prosperous management consulting firm in a suburb of New York City. His viewpoint is that of a reflective, dispassionately honest man in his late sixties. He recalls himself in

earlier scenes: as the privileged child of a New England college president; as a teenager, stealing stamps at school, but through cleverness and luck concealing his own guilt while gaining popularity defending an innocent friend; again in his teens, submitting to the expert seduction of a married woman who, in the opinion of an older, wiser Hank, was executing a curious revenge on her philandering husband; at Harvard, now tall, handsome, and sophisticated, enjoying the friendship of athletic Percy Cundill, literary Knox Frothingham, and sharp-witted Jon Le Cato; and after graduation, abandoning literature, falling in love with Judith Conway, and casually taking the job that will lead to his highly successful career.

Ethelbert Cuthbertson "Cubby" Dodd, Hank's maternal grandfather, who was, for a time, the most famous member of the college faculty. His fame derived from attacking Sigmund Freud. By the time Cubby retires, most academic psychologists have forgotten him. Living into his nineties, he becomes legendary for great teaching and scholarship, but the legend is largely false on both counts.

Franklin Pierce Worthington, Hank's father, descended from generations of educated New Englanders. A Harvard Ph.D. specializing in Geoffrey Chaucer, he teaches at the college and then becomes its competent, conventional president. He and Hank's mother die accidentally, leaving a legacy that helps Hank start his own business.

Judith Conway, Hank's first wife, the mother of Elaine. She is dark of eye and hair, slender, and fair. Judith grows up in the same college town, the daughter of a peculiarly dedicated Anglo-Catholic priest. An unexpected legacy permits her to study art in Boston. Judith quickly wins Hank's love after an accidental meeting. She is the best of wives for about fifteen years. Hank then sees a sort of dual personality; when the "other" Judith urgently desires a divorce so that she may marry a lover, Hank consents. The lover deserts her, however, and Judith starts a new career selling antiques. With Hank's help, she becomes quite successful. Years later, she dies of cancer.

Elaine Worthington, the only child of Hank and Judith. She has a lovely face and figure at the age of nineteen but shows slightly the effects of good eating and drinking when, in her early thirties, she consults her father about the collapse of her third marriage. Only then does she ask Hank if he is sure that she is his child; only then does Hank learn that Elaine knew as a child of her mother's adulteries. Elaine's two children, by her first marriage, have died in an airplane accident associated with her first divorce.

Jonathan (Jon) Le Cato, from the Eastern Shore of Virginia, who first meets Hank at prep school and rooms with him at Harvard. As a boy, his round face, round ears, and quarter-round nose make him look odd, but his furious courage keeps bullies away. Established as an attorney in New York City, he becomes counsel to Hank's growing firm. He secures the attractive house near the Pentagon that he and Hank share during their World War II service. As Hank concludes his reflections from the evening of life, this best of lifelong friends has died.

Charlotte Thom Peckham, the daughter of the college bursar. Neat, pretty, and bright, Charlotte returns from Smith College and marries Frederick Peckham, a professor of physics twice her age, only to lose him within two years to a racing car accident. An expert at shorthand, she applies to Hank's firm for work; she becomes Hank's most valued assistant, then mistress, then wife. A mysterious recurring depression compels her to commit suicide.

Leon Garesche, an amiable, aging, and befuddled bill collector, package forwarder, and purveyor of self-help literature who gratefully takes Hank as an assistant on the suggestion of Hank's Uncle Tim, a successful banker. Garesche's ineptitude awakens Hank's interest in scientific management; his sudden death forces Hank to go into business for himself.

— *Robert McColley*

THE MORNING WATCH

Author: James Agee (1909-1955)
First published: 1951
Genre: Novella

Locale: An Episcopalian boys' school in Tennessee
Time: Good Friday, 1924
Plot: Bildungsroman

Richard, an aspiring "saint" who suffers from the contradictions that plague many adolescents his age. He is so impressed with the holiness of the Lenten season that he vows to do as much for Jesus as Jesus did for him; his failure to measure up to Christ's example causes him to feel deeply ashamed. Obsessed with the desire to demonstrate his piety, Richard punishes himself and almost drowns, only to suffer from feelings of false pride afterward. Despite his overpowering desire to be reverent, Richard cannot keep his mind from wandering during the service. He is also torn by his need to impress his friends, whose good opinion he seems to value almost as much as God's. Feeling frustrated in his attempts to be humble without feeling proud of it, Richard leaves the church and arrives at a real sense of his own capacity for evil in the woods, where he participates in the senseless slaughter of a snake.

Richard's mother, who is loving but oppressive. Because she is rearing Richard by herself, she encourages him to play

with other boys and inadvertently causes him to feel abandoned. Her insistence that Richard learn God's will by submitting is largely responsible for Richard's poor self-image. His nagging feeling that vanity is mixed up in his piety also is a product of his mother's influence. Because Richard is torn between feelings of love and hatred for her, she is, for the most part, ineffective as a mother.

Willard Rivenburg, the school's leading athlete and the idol of the younger boys. Because of his advanced physical maturity, he looks out of place and even slightly irreverent when participating in the Mass with the rest of the boys. Willard's muscularity makes Richard uneasy about his own lack of physical development. Richard is also hurt by the fact that this "superhuman" young man is unimpressed by his defense of Hobe Gillum in church.

Father Fish, Richard's favorite teacher. He often invites Richard over to his cottage for cookies and cocoa. Richard trusts the man and takes his advice because of his wisdom and kindness. Acting almost as a surrogate father, Father Fish relieves much of Richard's guilt.

Claude Gray, a fanatically religious and somewhat insolent boy. His "girlish" voice and demonstrative piety arouse feelings of pity and guilt in Richard, who struggles with the question of Claude's sincerity when he lays violets at the feet of the Virgin. Richard's final impression of Claude is that of an impudent, effeminate boy who fingers his beads in church.

Hobe Gillum and

Jimmy Toole, Richard's mischievous companions, both twelve years old. They enjoy drawing attention to themselves by violating the rules, as Hobe does by cussing in church. Of the two boys, Hobe has the more volatile nature; it emerges in the beginning of the novel when he threatens the boy who woke him by throwing a shoe. These rascals tend to bring out the worst in Richard. To keep from being ostracized by them, Richard joins them in beating the snake and is caught up in their sadistic glee.

George Fitzgerald and

Lee Allen, prefects destined to become priests. Being the oldest boys, they are placed in positions of authority, and they carry out their duties with a grave demeanor and a sense of the solemnity of the occasion. They are also strict disciplinarians who threaten to report Hobe Gillum for swearing in church. Richard's fear of these boys compels him to hide from them when he sneaks out of the service. Ironically, Lee and George are just as worried about the consequences of breaking the rules as are the younger boys.

— Alan Brown

LE MORTE D'ARTHUR

Author: Sir Thomas Malory (1400?-1471)
First published: c. 1469; first printed, 1485
Genre: Novel

Locale: Britain
Time: The age of chivalry
Plot: Arthurian romance

Arthur, king of Britain and head of the Round Table, a brave, just, and temperate ruler. He values the fellowship of his men above revenge for his queen's infidelity, and he closes his eyes to her love for Launcelot until Mordred and Agravaine force him to act.

Queen Guenevere (GWEHN-eh-vihr), a jealous, passionate woman whose fury drives her lover Launcelot mad. She repents after the king is betrayed by Mordred, and she dies in a convent.

Launcelot du Lake (LOHN-seh-lot dew layk), the greatest of all the knights except those who achieve the Grail quest. He is, himself, granted a vision of the Grail, but his love for the queen bars him from success in spite of his deep and sincere penitence.

Tristram (TRIHS-truhm), the great Cornish knight who is the faithful and devoted lover of Isoud, the wife of his uncle, King Mark. Like Launcelot, he adheres firmly to the knightly code of honor and continues to fight for his country even after Mark has tried to have him murdered.

Isoud (ih-SOHD), an Irish princess, married to King Mark for political reasons although she has loved Tristram from the time she cured him of a wound incurred while he jousted with her brother.

Mark, the cowardly, jealous king of Cornwall, who becomes increasingly bitter and vengeful toward Tristram.

Isoud la Blanche Mains (blah[n]sh mahn), Tristram's wife, princess of Brittany.

Gawain (GAH-wihn), Arthur's nephew. He stands for virtue and justice untempered by mercy in his uncle's final contest with Launcelot, but he dishonors his fellowship earlier by beheading a lady and killing Lamorak de Galis when that knight was unarmed.

Sir Kay, Arthur's sardonic, mocking foster brother and seneschal.

Galahad, Launcelot's son, the best of the knights, who sits in the Siege Perilous and draws Balin's sword from a great stone as a prelude to his successful Grail quest. He dies after a vision in which he receives the sacrament from St. Joseph of Arimathaea.

Percival and

Bors de Ganis (bohrs deh GA-nihs), virtuous knights who accompany Galahad on the quest of the Grail. Bors alone returns to Arthur's court to describe their visions.

Palamides (pal-uh-MEE-deez), a valiant pagan knight, for many years Tristram's deadly enemy and Isoud's secret admirer. He is finally won over by his rival's courage and honor and signifies his new friendship by being christened.

Lamorak de Galis (LAM-o-rak deh GA-lihs), a knight famous for his strength and valor, who is surpassed only by Launcelot and Tristram. He is killed by Gawain and his brothers for his affair with their mother.

Mordred (MOHR-drehd), Arthur's son by his sister, an ill-tempered, evil knight who eventually destroys the fellowship of the Round Table and his royal father.

Agravaine (AG-ruh-vayn) and

Gaheris (GAY-hur-ihs), Gawain's brothers, participants in Mordred's plots and in the slaying of their mother and Lamorak.

Gareth (GAR-ihth), a tall, handsome young man who undertakes his first quest as "Beaumains," the kitchen boy, but later reveals himself as the brother of Gawain.

Linet (lih-NEHT), the damsel whose quest Gareth fulfills. She mocks and criticizes the inexperienced young knight until after he has rescued her sister.

Liones (li-uh-NEHS), Linet's sister, later Gareth's bride.

Balin le Sauvage (BAY-lihn leh soh-VAHZH), a Northumbrian knight, fated by the acquisition of a magic sword to kill his beloved brother, Balan.

Dinadan (dihn-uh-DAN), Tristram's witty, commonsense companion, who scorns love.

King Pelles (PEHL-eez), the Fisher King of the Grail legends at some points, although his identity is often unclear. He understands the mysteries of the Sangreal and arranges the conception of Galahad, the knight who is to achieve the quest and cure the wounded king.

Elaine, Pelles' daughter and Galahad's mother, who loves Launcelot, in spite of his rejection of her.

Elaine le Blanc, the fair maid of Astolat, who perishes of love for Launcelot.

King Evelake (ehv-eh-LAYK), an ancient ruler, converted by St. Joseph of Arimathaea. He lives generations beyond his time to have the promised sight of the knight who will complete the Grail quest.

Merlin, the magician whose spell allows King Uther Pendragon to enter Tintagil Castle in the shape of the rightful duke of Cornwall, husband of the lovely Igraine, Arthur's mother. In return, Uther promises that the child thus conceived will be turned over to Merlin, to be reared under his charge.

Nimue (nihm-oo-EE), the Lady of the Lake, Merlin's mistress, who serves as a "dea ex machina" for several of the knights.

Morgan le Fay, Arthur's half sister, who continually devises evil for him and his knights.

Pellinore (PEHL-ih-nohr), a bold knight who singlemindedly pursues the Questing Beast.

Gouvernail (guhv-ur-NAYL), Tristram's tutor and constant companion.

Brangwaine (BRANG-wayn), Isoud's maid and confidante.

Ector de Maris (EHK-tor deh MAHR-ihs),

Lionel,

Dodinas le Sauvage (doh-DEE-nas),

Sagramore (SAG-ruh-mohr),

Breunor le Noire (BROO-nohr le nwahr), and

Safere (sa-FIHR), brave and honorable knights.

Meliogrance (mee-lyoh-GRANS), a treacherous nobleman who kidnaps Guenevere, then accuses her of treason with Launcelot when she refuses to yield to him.

MORTE D'URBAN

Author: J. F. Powers (1917-   )
First published: 1962
Genre: Novel

Locale: Chicago, Illinois, and Minnesota
Time: Late 1950's
Plot: Social realism

Father Urban Roche, a middle-aged, handsome, and ambitious Catholic priest in the Order of St. Clement. Urban is the most worldly, cultured, and sophisticated member of a small, undistinguished religious community. His motto, "Be a Winner," describes his ambition to make the order noteworthy, wealthy, and influential by courting wealthy patrons. Fond of the world's good things and accustomed to moving freely, Urban grows restless when he is reassigned from a Chicago lakefront parish to a rural Minnesota retreat house. His restlessness brings him into quiet, but serious, conflict with his religious superiors. These conflicts are resolved only after a series of trials that, though painful, are not without a strong element of comedy and that prove to him how fleeting and unreliable are the world's glories.

Father Boniface, the provincial of the Order of St. Clement, Urban's superior. He is an older priest, pious, conservative, and traditional. Although Urban regards him as pleasant but ineffectual, Boniface is a keen judge of priests' souls. Boniface's decision to transfer Urban is literally providential because it sets in motion a chain of events that culminates in Urban's spiritual death and resurrection. Urban is reborn in the image and likeness of Boniface.

Father Wilfrid, the rector of the retreat house to which Urban is transferred. Blunt, stubborn, and unimaginative, he stresses that members of his small religious community must work together in tasks that reinforce the small pieties of daily life. In his unthinking devotion to sentimental religious rituals, he contrasts with Urban's delight in worldlier pleasures. Taking seriously his duty to form the spiritual character of his subordinates, he does not hesitate to embarrass Urban for his self-centeredness.

Father John, a young priest assigned to the retreat house. Unlike Urban, he is simple, devout, and intelligent, trusting to the wisdom of his provincial and of Providence in sending him to a rural mission. The youngest member of the community, he

is impressed by Urban and likes him, but he resists the temptation to imitate him. He plays peacemaker between Urban and Wilfrid, even losing at checkers to keep Urban happy. He writes a pamphlet version of the Lancelot and Guinevere story that becomes a consolation to Urban during his tribulations.

The bishop of the Grand Plains Diocese, the head of the diocese in which the retreat house is located. He considers taking over St. Clement's Hill as a seminary, which would frustrate Urban's plans to upgrade the retreat house. Portly, sanguine, and astute, the bishop accepts Urban's oblique challenge to a duel, a golf match with the hill as the stakes. The bishop hits an errant shot that sends Urban to the hospital and begins his slow process of spiritual regeneration.

Mrs. Thwaites, a Catholic dowager. She is elderly, frail, and cranky; she sits all day in the gloomy light of her television set. Her own care in life is her wayward son, Dickie. Although Urban regularly courts her as a donor, she is in fact a miser and skinflint. She cheats her own servant girl out of a few dollars in a game of cards. When Urban tries to mediate, she refuses to speak with him again. Her action initiates Urban's spiritual trials.

Billy Cosgrove, a wealthy businessman whom Urban courts as a benefactor to the Clementines. He is wealthy but loud, brash, and arrogant. Although he enjoys Urban's company, he makes no serious financial commitment. While Urban is recuperating from the golf ball injury, Billy takes him hunting. Cruelly, Billy leaves Urban stranded when the priest protests a wanton attempt to drown a stag. He thus demonstrates the superficiality of his intentions to benefit the Clementines.

Sally Hopgood Thwaites, Mrs. Thwaites's daughter. Outwardly sophisticated but inwardly young and reckless, Sally is an attractive woman, without her mother's pretense to piety. She rescues Urban when Billy abandons him and straightforwardly attempts to seduce the priest. When he resists, she similarly leaves him stranded.

Monsignor Renton, an elderly priest and a friend of Urban. He offers Urban good advice, not all of which Urban is inclined to take. He sees through the sham faith of the wealthy persons Urban so vigorously courts. Renton is a man at peace, aware of the world's pretenses, accepting of his own imperfections, and confident in Providence.

— Robert M. Otten

MOSES, MAN OF THE MOUNTAIN

Author: Zora Neale Hurston (1891-1960)
First published: 1939
Genre: Novel

Locale: Egypt and the wilderness around Mount Sinai
Time: Biblical times, during the Exodus
Plot: Allegory

Moses, an Egyptian prince who leads the enslaved Hebrews out of Egypt. A great soldier and the most powerful magician in the land, he also possesses great wisdom and an understanding of psychology. He is a born leader, but he has no ambition for power or glory. For a period of more than fifty years, Moses gives up what could be a happy and comfortable existence with his wife and family and repeatedly refuses to reign as a crowned and jeweled king, so that he can serve God and teach the Hebrews to rule themselves under God's laws.

Pharaoh Ta-Phar, Moses' uncle, the leader of Egypt and an oppressor of the Hebrews. It was Pharaoh Ta-Phar's father who enslaved the Hebrews, but the new pharaoh is crueler to them than was his father. He has hated and feared Moses since both were young and Moses began to outshine Ta-Phar with his superior fighting ability. His idea of a proper siege is a large body of well-trained fighting men riding into battle, with Ta-Phar in a glorious chariot riding in front. He is proud and stubborn, accepting the lavish robes and titles of power without accepting the responsibility.

Jethro, also named **Ruel**, Moses' mentor and father-in-law, a prince and a priest of Midian. Jethro is already graying at the beginning of his seventy-five-year friendship with Moses, and he has more knowledge of magic and nature than any of the priests in Egypt. Wise, strong, and simple, he teaches Moses everything he can. When he believes that Moses is ready, he reveals to Moses the dream he has had for forty years: a great leader taking the Hebrews out of Egypt to worship one god. When Moses shows no desire for a great mission, it is Jethro's insistence that finally makes him accept his destiny.

Zipporah, Jethro's daughter, Moses' first love and second wife. When she marries Moses in her youth, she is beautiful beyond compare, with dark skin, brilliant black eyes, crinkly hair, and full, dark lips. She loves Moses and makes him a happy home but can never conquer her desire for him to be a great king so that she can be a great king's wife.

Miriam, a Hebrew prophetess who becomes the leader of the Hebrew women in exile. At the age of twelve, she invents the story of Moses being adopted by an Egyptian princess to cover up the fact that her infant brother disappeared while under her watch. Twenty-five years later, Miriam starts the rumor among the Egyptians that Prince Moses actually is her Hebrew brother, starting the chain of events that causes Moses to leave Egypt and find his destiny. In exile, believing herself to be as great as Moses, Miriam demands more credit for the Exodus—as well as more robes, jewelry, power, and respect.

Aaron, the brother of Miriam and the missing infant, and a leader of the enslaved Hebrews. Like Miriam and the pharaoh, he is drawn to the trappings of power. Although he tries to appear arrogant and brave, he is actually rather stupid and weak, although he is a good public speaker. Because Moses has told him, untruthfully, that God called Aaron by name to help free the Hebrews, Aaron believes that he should have a larger share of Moses' power and glory. While Moses is away conferring with God, Aaron casts the golden calf but then denies responsibility for it.

Joshua, a military leader of the Hebrews and Moses' confidant. When Joshua first enters Moses' service, he is a curly-headed youth in his mid-teens. Moses is drawn to him because he is the first Hebrew to offer his service without asking for anything for himself. From being head of the boys' military society, he eventually becomes leader of all the Hebrew military forces but continues to serve Moses personally. From Moses, he learns to read and write and learns about strategy and discipline. He is respected and admired by the men under him.

— Cynthia A. Bily

MOSQUITOES

Author: William Faulkner (1897-1962)
First published: 1927
Genre: Novel

Locale: New Orleans and Lake Pontchartrain
Time: August, 1925
Plot: Novel of ideas

Dawson Fairchild, a successful novelist and the natural leader of a group of artists cruising aboard the yacht *Nausikaa*. He is from a provincial Midwestern lower-middle-class family and confronts life and art with burly optimism, though he finds the modern world peopled with "women too masculine to conceive, men too feminine to beget" great poetry. Having admittedly lost his own first sheer infatuation with words, he writes prose now instead of poetry and devoutly maintains that "art" is anything consciously well done. Calling himself "a purely lay brother to the human race," Fairchild is the author's portrait of Sherwood Anderson.

Mrs. Patricia Maurier, a wealthy widow and vivacious dilettante who brings artists and ordinary people together on her yacht for a weeklong party on Lake Pontchartrain, near New Orleans. Her usual pose of silly amazement turns to fright when Gordon feels her face with his hands and to disgust when her niece disappears for a day with the ship's steward. Although she is intent on her project, she loses respect for some of her guests after the yacht runs aground and their attention turns from cards and dancing to drinking, idle talk, the young women on board, and complaints about all the grapefruit she serves them.

Gordon, an impoverished sculptor, thirty-six years old. Tall, red-haired, and masculine, with a hawklike countenance and a wild, bitter heart, he personifies the novel's ideal of the true artist. His imagination is dominated by the headless, armless, and legless torso that he has fashioned in his studio. He refuses to sell it to Pat, whose pouting moves him to give her a spanking instead. Once on shore, he surprises his friends by sculpting an uncanny likeness of Mrs. Maurier.

Patricia (Pat) Robyn, Mrs. Maurier's eighteen-year-old niece and namesake, whose hard and sexless graveness epitomizes Gordon's ideal of feminine beauty. She entices the ship's steward away from the others for a treacherous daylong excursion to the mainland.

Jenny Steinbauer, a voluptuous, unreflective blonde who is invited to the party after a moment's acquaintance with Pat. She turns the gentlemen's heads but keeps her virginity intact.

Ernest Talliaferro, a balding, dapper, thirty-eight-year-old widower who wants to remarry but lacks the boldness to enthrall women. As a wholesaler of ladies' undergarments, he thinks he understands women, yet he makes a fool of himself by chasing Jenny. He manages to steal a kiss from her, and he fancies that she will sneak away from the others with him and even accept his proposal of marriage. After he clumsily pushes her into the lake, however, she ignores his pursuit.

Julius Kauffman, "the Semitic man," Fairchild's cynical companion who enjoys pricking the vanity of artists. Always the critic, he thinks that the defining characteristic of a poet is an ability to sustain an obliviousness to the world and its compulsions.

Eva Wiseman, Kauffman's sister, a poet who believes that love and death are the only subjects of writing worth the effort and despair. She finds the trivial artistic chatter at the party both silly and dull.

Mark Frost, a ghostly young man who considers himself to be the best poet in New Orleans. Quite passive by nature, he has little to say.

Theodore Robyn, often called **Gus** or **Josh**, Pat's twin brother, who resents her intrusions. He occupies himself with whittling a wooden pipe.

Pete Ginotta, Jenny's Italian boyfriend, a gifted dancer whose humorless, reckless face is aptly set off by a stiff straw hat that he always wears.

Major Ayers, a well-traveled Englishman whose bent is decidedly mercenary rather than artistic. Believing that all Americans are constipated, he is intent on making a fortune with his recipe for a new laxative.

David West, the ship's steward, a rough and inarticulate but modest man who indulges Pat's appetites for swimming and hiking without taking advantage of her sexually. He soon leaves the ship for a better job.

— *John L. McLean*

THE MOTHER
(La Madre)

Author: Grazia Deledda (1871-1936)
First published: 1920
Genre: Novel

Locale: Sardinia
Time: Early twentieth century
Plot: Psychological realism

Maria Maddalena (mahd-dah-LEE-nah), a Sicilian woman. An orphan reared by aunts who make of her a drudge, she is married to an old man who dies shortly thereafter, leaving her pregnant. She works to support her son and to send him through a seminary to become a priest. She is troubled when her priest-son appears to have an affair with a beautiful young woman. A superstitious soul, she believes the ghost of the former parish priest is trying to drive her and her son away. When her son's sweetheart confronts him in his church, the poor mother falls dead.

Paul, Maria Maddalena's son, a priest. He has a sensual nature; while in seminary he is fascinated by a prostitute, whom he visits often one summer. At his first parish, he falls in love with a beautiful young parishioner and has a strong sensual urge that causes him to consider leaving the Church in

order to run away and marry his sweetheart. When he puts down the temptation, the spurned woman threatens to denounce him publicly as a seducer.

Agnes, Paul's sweetheart. She is the last member of the family that owns the big house in the village that is Paul's parish. She loves Paul and does not seem to realize what she asks him to do in urging him to leave the Church and his responsibilities to it. She sees him only as a man.

Antiochus (ahn-tee-OH-kews), Paul's server, who wishes to become a priest.

King Nicodemus (nee-koh-DEH-mews), a misanthropic hunter who lives in a cabin on the mountain near the village. He has left the village so that his hate will not cause him to kill anyone.

MOTHER
(Mat)

Author: Maxim Gorky (Aleksey Maksimovich Peshkov, 1868-1936)
First published: 1907; serial form, 1906
Genre: Novel

Locale: Russia
Time: The first decade of the twentieth century
Plot: Naturalism

Pelagueya Vlasova (peh-luh-GEH-yuh VLAH-so-vuh), a revolutionary heroine. Fearing that her son, Pavel Vlasov, will be forced into the brutal, dehumanized life of the factory, she begins to notice with joy that, unlike the other workers, he is given to reading. When she meets Pavel's close friends, dedicated socialists, her love for him and for them leads her into the revolutionary movement, to which she becomes passionately devoted. Her life takes on new meaning as she gives herself to the cause for which Pavel and his friends are willing to sacrifice so much. Finally, she is handing out leaflets even as she is being arrested and beaten by the police.

Pavel Vlasov (PAH-vehl VLAH-sof), Pelagueya Vlasova's son. With an imagination that sets him apart from the average soulless and brutal factory worker in his small town, Pavel is given to reading. He becomes a member of a socialist group that meets to discuss ideas they have gleaned from subversive literature. Full of hope and vitality, Pavel and his friends, with the help of his mother, set out to put their ideas into practice. His sacrificial devotion to the socialist cause finally leads to his exile in Siberia.

Andrey (ahn-DRAY),
Natasha (nah-TAH-shuh),
Sashenka (SAH-shehn-kuh),
Vyesovshchikov (veh-SOHF-shchih-kof),
Rybin (REW-bihn),
Nikolay Ivanovich (nih-koh-LI ih-VAH-no-vihch), and
Sofya (SOH-fyuh), revolutionary friends who share Pavel Vlasov's devotion to the socialist cause and his sacrificial life in behalf of worker and peasant.

MOTHER AND SON

Author: Ivy Compton-Burnett (1864-1969)
First published: 1955
Genre: Novel

Locale: An English country house
Time: The end of the nineteenth century
Plot: Satire

Miranda Hume, the iron-willed matriarch of the Hume family. She bullies and intimidates her husband and children, all of whom she appears to dislike, except for her son Rosebery, on whom she dotes in a possessive and needy way. She poses as a standard of rectitude and domestic order but is in fact driven by passions of which she appears largely unconscious and over which she has little control. The fact that her eldest son is illegitimate is something she hides beneath a façade of rigid Victorian propriety. Because she has deluded herself into thinking that she possesses a godlike omniscience, when she is confronted with her husband's secret erotic life, her subsequent tantrum precipitates her own death. Although, like a spoiled child, she is used to getting her own way, her autocratic rule is, in reality, barely holding together a divided and discontented family. When she dies, she is virtually unmourned.

Rosebery Hume, the eldest son, who is devoted to his mother, Miranda. Their special relationship creates a rift with the other members of the family, who are resentful of his status. Being her favorite, however, undermines his ability to marry and have children of his own. He is, in fact, a victim of Miranda's intense and devouring emotional needs. His identity is completely determined by his relationship with his mother, and he is more comfortable in a domestic world than in the traditionally masculine world of work outside the home. It is only on Miranda's death that he feels liberated enough to seek any other partner. His period of grief at the passing of his mother is suspiciously short. The past has too strong a hold on him, and his future is as an unmarried man who is happiest looking after the younger children. Fortunately for his younger siblings, he has none of his mother's authoritarian personality traits and passes on only the amusing and pleasant things he has learned under her tutelage.

Julius Hume, Miranda's bullied husband. He appears to be an inoffensive and easily intimidated spouse, but he is not above adultery or making a series of remarks that hint at unconscious but strategic aggression against his tiresome wife.

Like Rosebery, his period of grief at the loss of Miranda is suspiciously short, and he seeks a new spouse in short order.

Francis Hume,
Alice Hume, and
Adrien Hume, the illegitimate children of Julius Hume. Their witty and mordant commentary indicates their alienation from their parents and the older generation's Victorian hypocrisies. Their commentary is less an image of critical intelligence and liberality, however, when they tease their tutor, for it is then that their sense of class prerogatives affords them the upper hand in yet another system of domination. The children are not fleshed out characters. Francis is the oldest, Alice is the only female, and Adrien, as the baby of the family, seems rather more emotional than the other two, but these are the only characteristics that distinguish them. They are, nevertheless, important figures who confirm the divisions and rivalries that permeate this seemingly intact family and see through the pretexts of their elders. The youngest characters in the novel, they are edging toward modernity.

Hester Wolsey, Miranda's companion. Although appearing as a helpful gentlewoman and a domestic figure preferable to the overbearing Miranda, she manipulates family members for her own purposes and looks for every opportunity to advance her position. She can be jealous and envious, and she is not above eavesdropping and using the information gathered for her own ends. Her motives are relentlessly impure.

Emma Greatheart, a neighbor of the Humes. She is a kind and intelligent woman who learns much about the world when her friend Hester stays with the Hume family. Her intelligence allows her to develop a greater understanding of the darkness of the human heart, but this knowledge leaves her dispirited and less trusting.

Miss Burke, Miss Greatheart's housekeeper. Like Miss Greatheart, her trust in her fellow humans is diminished by the doings at the Hume household. She and Emma, however, together create a kinder and happier household than that of the neighboring Humes.

Plautus, Miss Greatheart's cat. He is an important character because his antics serve as a metaphor for the behavior of the other characters. Although seemingly a beloved pet, his stalking, predatory ways are a jarring reminder of the dark side of his animal nature. His behavior with the mouse he captures suggests that systems of domination are part of the natural order of things.

— *Margaret Boe Birns*

A MOTHER AND TWO DAUGHTERS

Author: Gail Godwin (1937-   )
First published: 1982
Genre: Novel

Locale: North Carolina, Iowa, and Ocracoke Island
Time: December, 1978, to summer, 1979, and one day in 1984
Plot: Domestic realism

Nell Purvis Strickland, a sixty-three-year-old inhabitant of Mountain City, North Carolina. Nell had been trained as a nurse and had practiced but then had married Leonard Strickland, an attorney. They had two daughters, Cate and Lydia. Nell is a widow with many friends among the city's best citizens. She is an intelligent, compassionate woman whose main interests are her family, her home, and her book discussion group, composed of longtime friends. Nell worries about her two daughters, who are very little alike, have trouble getting along, and are both going through large changes in their lives. She has always deferred to her husband; after his death, she must find her own identity and a reason to live.

Leonard Strickland, an attorney who dies early in the novel. Leonard is a quiet, courteous, gentle, and philosophical man. He has been a faithful, devoted husband to Nell and father to Cate and Lydia. An idealist, Leonard had thought seriously of going to fight in the Spanish Civil War but was talked out of it by his uncle, Osgood. Leonard is an orderly, neat man. He is a good, conservative financial planner and provider. Leonard has a lantern jaw, stooped shoulders, and thick glasses. He hates violence and any kind of scene and enjoys listening to classical music on radio earphones and reading his beloved philosophers, Montaigne, Cicero, and Emerson. He has always been the voice of reason, and his widow and daughters think of him often, reflecting on what his opinion of various situations would be.

Cate Strickland Patchett Galitsky, a twice-divorced thirty-nine-year-old when the novel opens. She is a college teacher specializing in the works of D. H. Lawrence. She is now teaching at the financially troubled Melanchthon College in Davenport, Iowa. Cate is an assertive, independent, strong-willed person who often causes turbulence, sometimes in her own family. She keeps her chin up and walks with an authoritative, pelvis-first stride. She is something of a leftist and feminist and enjoys shocking people, especially complacent people, and taking dramatic actions. Her behavior can border on the rude. To protest the Cambodian invasion, she took the students of the New York City private girls' school at which she was then teaching to the Lincoln Tunnel in taxicabs and there blocked traffic until she was arrested. Cate's first husband, Lieutenant Pringle Patchett, was an Air Force pilot. Her second, Jake Galitsky, went mad. Cate is unconventional and skeptical about the nuclear family. Childless, she is reluctant to endanger her independence again by marriage, however tempting it is. She is an activist for causes in which she believes.

Lydia Strickland Mansfield, a thirty-six-year-old mother of two boys and the estranged wife of Max Mansfield. Lydia is now a student at the University of North Carolina at Greensboro and the lover of Stanley Edelman. Lydia is a highly organized woman, perhaps a little manipulative. She has in the past kept her emotions under strict control and her life compartmentalized. She is an attractive, health-conscious woman with lavender-blue eyes. Lydia believes that she is beginning life anew, with her education, her lover, and her budding career in television, but she is still a worrier, never really relaxed and happy.

Maxwell Powell Mansfield, an investment banker in Winston-Salem, Lydia's estranged husband. He is a careful man, a good financial planner, pragmatic and reliable. He is for a time bewildered and hurt by Lydia's desire for a divorce. Max is a traditional husband, provider, and father to his two boys. He is a graduate of the University of North Carolina at Chapel Hill and studied at the London School of Economics. He pilots his own plane.

Leo Mansfield, a somewhat rigid fifteen-year-old boy. He tends to be formal and critical, self-contained and principled, and perhaps even stubborn. An idealist, Leo plans to join the foreign service someday.

Dickie Mansfield, an overweight, cuddly, happy thirteen-year-old who is a talented clarinet player. He has sinus trouble and is not athletic but enjoys his music and takes the world as he finds it.

Elizabeth Broadbelt Mansfield, the granddaughter of the president of the bank where Max works. She is young, bright, athletic, and attractive.

Stanley Albert Edelman, a thirty-one-year-old podiatrist from Brooklyn. He is slim, dark, and Jewish, with an Italian mother. He practices in Winston-Salem and becomes Lydia's lover. Edelman fears some kind of catastrophe and is survivalist-minded. Because one day it may be necessary to run, he believes that feet should be kept in good shape.

Roger Jernigan, the owner of Sunny Enterprises, an Iowa-based insecticide/herbicide corporation. He lives in his own castle forty miles from Davenport. Roger is in his late forties, stocky, gap-toothed, and ruddy-faced, with unruly reddish-blond hair. He is strong-willed, overtly masculine, energetic, and curious, with shrewd green eyes. Roger is a believer in self-reliance and is somewhat conservative politically, especially when it comes to government interference in private enterprise. He courts Cate.

Jody Jernigan, a twenty-year-old senior at Melanchthon College. Jody is a talented actor, singer, composer, and guitarist. He is a sensitive, graceful, willowy young man who may be a latent homosexual.

Sunny Jernigan, a mildly retarded thirty-three-year-old man whose clear features have remained boyish. He takes pleasure in weight training and will become his brother Jody's bodyguard. Sunny is a happy person and capable of considerable independence.

Osgood Strickland, Leonard's old uncle, a hermit who lives near Mountain City in a mountain cave he owns. Osgood returned from World War I mutilated, missing the end of his nose.

Theodora Blount, the "maiden queen" of Mountain City society. Wealthy and in her sixties, she has never married. Theodora is conservative, somewhat selfish, and demanding. She is very concerned about family bloodlines, especially her own. She is Cate's godmother.

Wickie Lee, a teenage, pregnant, unmarried mountain girl who is taken in by Theodora Blount, for reasons of Theodora's own. She is skilled at making ingenious dolls of walnut shells, corn shucks, and old nylon stockings.

Azalea Clark, Theodora Blount's black maid, from Mountain City. She is, in the way these things evolve, also Theodora's close friend.

Sicca Dowling, a widow who is a good friend of Theodora and Nell. She has a serious drinking problem.

Latrobe Bell, a one-term U.S. representative from Mountain City who once courted Theodora. Bell is a political reactionary, given to fulminating against communists, foreigners, and the like.

Buddy Bell, the son of Latrobe and Lucy Bell. He works in missile research in Huntsville, Alabama.

Jerome Ennis, a forty-one-year-old who runs a home security business. He is married to Teenie, who is two years younger than he is. Both childhood friends of Cate, they have a son, Johnny. Teenie runs a nursery school in Mountain City.

Renee Peverell-Watson, a teacher of sociology at the University of North Carolina at Greensboro. She has a doctorate from Harvard, is stylish, smokes little cigars, and has a fashionable home and clothes. She is a mulatto, and the white Reverend Peverell was one of her ancestors. She is an inspirational friend and teacher of Lydia.

Calvin Edwards, a black television producer at a station in Greensboro. He is thirty-six years old, Renee's boyfriend, and Mary McGregor Turnbull's producer. A large, heavy man with a rich bass voice, Edwards is loose and casual. He dreams of establishing a television network devoted to cultural programming.

Mary McGregor Turnbull, an elegant and well-connected elderly lady of a fine old family who has a television cooking show, *Southern Kitchens*. She gives Lydia her start.

Merle Meekins Chapin, the wife of the Reverend Marcus Chapin. She was a childhood friend of Nell and her classmate at Farragut Pines Academy. Merle is ill when they meet again on Ocracoke Island.

Marcus Chapin, an Episcopal priest in his sixties. He is a religious conservative, opposed to the ordination of women. He is, temporarily at least, without a parish. Marcus is fit, with white crewcut hair and blue eyes. He is greatly saddened by his beloved wife's illness.

— *Donald R. Noble*

MOTHER COURAGE AND HER CHILDREN
(Mutter Courage und ihre Kinder)

Author: Bertolt Brecht (1898-1956)
First published: 1941
Genre: Drama

Locale: Europe
Time: 1624-1648
Plot: Play of ideas

Anna Fierling, called **Mother Courage**, a camp follower about forty years old who sells supplies from a canteen wagon to both sides in the Thirty Years' War. She got the nickname after her mad drive through the bombardment of Riga, made in an attempt to sell her bread before it became too moldy. Mother Courage is an inveterate haggler and trader who profits from the war and dreads the coming of peace. Although she retains several endearing qualities, she is nevertheless the focus of the author's criticism of war and those who would profit from it. Even as she loses each of her three children (fathered by three different men) to the war, Mother Courage is unable to extract herself from it. Her harsh view of life is summarized in "The Song of the Great Capitulation," which states that the individual must abandon romantic dreams and swallow what life imposes on him or her, and "The Song of the Great Souls of this Earth," which maintains that one's greatest virtues are at once the cause of one's downfall. The latter song (though sung by another character) reflects the destiny of Mother Courage's children, whose demise is brought about by the prominent character traits—bravery, honesty, and compassion—featured in the song. Mother Courage believes that the presence of virtues is "a sure sign something's wrong" but never comprehends the lesson of war and plies her trade until the end.

Eilif Noyocki, Mother Courage's elder son, known for his intelligence and bravery. Over his mother's objections, he joins the army, where he is first honored for heroism, then executed for a similar deed during a brief moment of peace.

Swiss Cheese Feyos, Mother Courage's younger son, unintelligent but distinguished by his great integrity. As an honest man, Swiss Cheese is entrusted with the regimental treasury, and his refusal to divulge its whereabouts to the enemy leads to his execution.

Kattrin Haupt, the only daughter of Mother Courage. She is mute, as the result of a soldier's attack, and facially disfigured from a later assault. Her character is marked by tenderhearted compassion, which costs her her life. Kattrin is shot while drumming frantically on a roof to warn a city of an impending attack.

Yvette Pottier (pah-tee-AY), an attractive young prostitute whom war has hardened to the perils of love. In "The Fraternization Song," she tells of her fall from innocence at the age of sixteen with the cook of an enemy regiment, who soon deserted her. Mother Courage uses Yvette as an example to Kattrin of the dangers of sentiment. Yvette also serves as a mediator in the futile negotiations to save the life of Swiss Cheese and ultimately achieves a measure of prosperity by marrying an aged colonel.

The cook, **Peter Lamb**, the man who seduced the teenage Yvette. Like Mother Courage, he makes a career from war. When he inherits a small tavern in Holland, however, he is ready to enter civilian life and offers Mother Courage a share in the business, which she declines. It is the cook who sings "The Song of the Great Souls of This Earth."

The military chaplain, a cynical representation of organized religion's role in war. While living comfortably in the commander's service, the chaplain uses his office to prepare men for killing and dying, referring to the war as "a special one, a religious one" in which it is "a blessing" to die. Despite his cowardice in the face of the enemy, the chaplain is a strong supporter of war and believes in its inevitability and benefits. For a few years, he travels with Mother Courage, still living off the war, and vies with the cook for the companionship of Mother Courage.

— Allen E. Hye

MOTHER HUBBERD'S TALE

Author: Edmund Spenser (c. 1552-1599)
First published: 1591
Genre: Poetry

Locale: Indeterminate
Time: Antiquity
Plot: Fable

The Fox, a clever and immoral rogue who is ambitious to rise in the world and is ready to use any trickery or deception to do so. Based on the character Renard of French tales, he is a shrewd observer of others and ready to exploit their weaknesses, as well as being ready to resort to crime if it suits his purpose. In the earlier sections of the poem, he is satisfied with rather minor acquisitions, robbing ignorant farmers of their livestock and exploiting gullible parishioners of their offerings, but as the poem progresses, he becomes more ambitious and aspires to be a courtier, rich and powerful at court. When his companion the Ape usurps the Lion's kingdom, the Fox becomes his chief minister and uses his high position both to enrich himself and to bring his relatives into court, showering them with the positions and wealth of true noblemen he has ruined. Although he has come to hold a place that should be one of honor and trust, he abuses it for mere personal gain and power. At the end of the poem, when the Lion returns to claim his rightful throne, the Fox tries to place all blame on his partner, the Ape, but the Lion strips the Fox bare and sends him into exile.

The Ape, a companion of the Fox in his career of trickery and crime. He cares more for his own creature comforts and pleasures than for riches or power. Like the Fox, he is able to assume disguises easily and plausibly, and the two make a perfect pair in deception, fooling first individuals, then parishes, and finally the entire kingdom with their wiles. When they arrive at court, the Ape achieves success through his talents at dancing, acrobatics, juggling, and conjuring. He also writes love poetry, gambles, and engages in plots. When, by a stroke of luck, the Ape seizes the crown from the sleeping Lion, he makes himself king and with the Fox begins to plunder the riches of the land. His punishment, upon the return of the true king, is to have his tail and ears clipped.

The Lion, the king of the beasts, less a realistic figure than an allegorical character. He loses his crown because the Ape discovers him asleep, symbolic of the ills that attend a monarch who relaxes his vigilance for even a moment. The Lion's awakening by Jupiter and his return to power represent that rightful rule cannot be forever denied.

The Farmer, the first character encountered and cheated by the Fox and the Ape. Although he seems to be honest, he is extremely credulous and believes their absurd tale that the Ape is a shepherd and the Fox his faithful dog.

The Priest, an illiterate and dissolute cleric who advises the Fox and the Ape to imitate his own example and live on the goodwill of the faithful people of a parish. He knows little or nothing of true religion and cannot even follow the rituals he is required to perform. Again, Spenser presents a symbolic figure, this one illustrating the debased nature of too many so-called clergymen of the period.

The Sheep,

the Ass,

the Tiger, and

the Boar, representative of the minor characters who populate the court and who are first fooled and later ruled by the Fox and the Ape.

Jupiter, less a character than another symbolic figure who represents the divine impulse to order, law, and rule.

— Michael Witkoski

MOTHER NIGHT

Author: Kurt Vonnegut, Jr. (1922-   )
First published: 1961
Genre: Novel

Locale: Nazi Germany, New York City, and Israel
Time: 1938-1961
Plot: Comic realism

Howard W. Campbell, Jr., the protagonist, a pitiful, abandoned, forty-eight-year-old "citizen of nowhere." American-born, he moved with his family to Berlin at the age of eleven. By 1938, at the age of twenty-six, he is a successful writer and producer of medieval romance plays, all starring his beloved wife, Helga. At this time, he is recruited by Major Frank Wirtanen to be an American secret agent posing as a Nazi radio propagandist. Thought to be a vile Nazi hatemonger (only three people know of his services as an American secret agent), Campbell is twice captured as a Nazi war criminal and twice released through Wirtanen's secret machinations. Finally, Campbell, in despair over his Nazi-tainted past, turns himself in to Israeli authorities and is imprisoned in Jerusalem. When he is again ironically "saved" by Wirtanen and is faced with the nausea of being a free man, he hangs himself for "crimes against himself."

Helga Noth, Campbell's wife, the daughter of the Berlin chief of police. She dies in the war. Campbell, without knowing it, had broadcast the news of Helga's death in one of his coded radio broadcasts, but because he was ignorant of his broadcast's secret contents, he was not privy to this information.

Resi Noth, Helga's younger sister, only ten years old when Campbell last sees her in Germany. Fifteen years later, Resi, now a Russian spy, poses as Helga and plots, with fellow spy George Kraft, to kidnap Campbell and transport him to Russia. Resi falls in love with Campbell, however, and tries to subvert the plans to take him to Moscow. When she is captured by American agents and faced with deportation and separation from Campbell, she takes a fatal dose of cyanide and dies "for love" in his arms.

Major Frank Wirtanen, an agent of the U.S. War Department who recruits Campbell as an American spy. Wirtanen, one of only three people who know of Campbell's role, twice saves him from death or capture but can never be found to corroborate Campbell's claim to be a spy. Finally, when Campbell is imprisoned in Jerusalem, Wirtanen, who really is Colonel Harold J. Sparrow of the U.S. Army, violates direct orders and reveals his role as Campbell's recruiter to free Campbell from prison.

Lieutenant Bernard B. O'Hare, a rabid patriot and member of the American Third Army. He considers himself Campbell's personal nemesis. He captures Campbell after World War II, only to have him released by Wirtanen. O'Hare waits fifteen years for his chance to capture Campbell again and tries to ensnare him in his New York apartment, but Campbell fights off the drunken, pitiful man by breaking his arm with a pair of fire tongs.

George Kraft, a lonely old painter, Campbell's neighbor and best friend in New York. Kraft, who really is Russian spy Iona Potapov, plots with Resi Noth to kidnap Campbell and deliver him to the Soviets, but in his own loneliness he finds himself drawn to Campbell, becoming his closest companion. Kraft devises a plan whereby he, Resi, and Campbell can escape to Mexico, but he is arrested by American agents and sent to prison, where he becomes an influential painter. Kraft's deep friendship with Campbell is ironic, considering that Kraft is an enemy spy.

Lionel Jason David Jones, D.D.S., D.D., a neo-Nazi and publisher of the *White Christian Minuteman*. He extols Campbell as the greatest hero of embattled white men in their continuing struggle against the oppressive forces of Judaism, Unitarianism, and black nationalism. Campbell, however, agrees with none of Jones's beliefs and thinks that Jones is insane.

— Karen Priest

MOUCHETTE
(Nouvelle Histoire de Mouchette)

Author: Georges Bernanos (1888-1948)
First published: 1937
Genre: Novel

Locale: The Artois region of northern France
Time: Unspecified
Plot: Philosophical realism

Mouchette (mew-SHEHT), a fourteen-year-old peasant girl living in northern France. She is a highly sensitive and perceptive young girl who is desperate for attention and exhausted with being brutalized by the adults in her life. She is raped by the drunken poacher Arsène and tries unsuccessfully to tell those in authority about the experience. Isolated and completely friendless, she is overwhelmed with feelings of disgust but finds a strange kind of consolation even in the brutal rape. She announces to Mathieu that she is Arsène's lover. The growing consciousness of the depth of her despair drives her to suicide by drowning.

Arsène (ahr-SEHN), a young, alcoholic, epileptic poacher. He warns Mouchette that there is a devastating cyclone destroying the countryside; the fabrication is his means of getting her to stay with him in his forest hut. He also tells her that he may have killed the game warden, Monsieur Mathieu, thus gaining her trust and loyalty. As he becomes progressively more intoxicated, he has an epileptic seizure, after which Mouchette tenderly cradles his head and sings to him. After coming to, he brutally rapes her.

Mouchette's mother, a middle-aged woman dying of tuberculosis. She is from a family of alcoholics and is dying an early death because of her weakened hereditary background. She is emaciated, malnourished, and in severe pain, because her lungs have virtually ceased to function. A bitter woman whose life has been nothing but grinding poverty and abuse

from her family, she endures her last moments by drinking as much gin as possible to anesthetize the pain. Just as Mouchette begins to tell her of the rape, the mother dies. Mouchette cannot remember even one affectionate touch from her mother.

Mouchette's father, a smuggler and sometime poacher in his mid-fifties. The product of an alcoholic lineage, he shows little feeling when he learns of his wife's death, having just come home from an extended drunk with his equally unmoved sons. He upbraids Mouchette, though, for staring at him. He has beaten her regularly throughout most of her childhood.

Philomène, an ancient woman of indeterminate age who keeps watch over the dead and prepares them for burial. She comes from far up in the mountains and is a mysterious yet compassionate crone who intuitively understands Mouchette's plight. Although weakened with tuberculosis when she was young, she became a servant of a beautiful, young, and healthy woman who immediately declined into early illness and death. As her mistress' health declined, Philomène's physical condition improved.

Monsieur Camille Mathieu (maht-YUH), a game warden in his thirties. After Mouchette is raped, she wanders into the village and is shocked to see Mathieu alive and well. After she tells him of the rape and then calls Arsène her lover, Mathieu deftly attempts to calm her and disengage himself from any association with the situation, even though he admits to having a drunken fight with Arsène. He instructs her to come back the next day when she is in more control of herself.

Madame Mathieu, the wife of the game warden, who feels pity for Mouchette. Having lived in Amiens for most of her life, she is shaken by the battered appearance of Mouchette and gets an unnerving insight into the damage that rural poverty can do to sensitive young girls.

The music teacher, an aging woman, increasingly debilitated with rheumatism, who sadistically abuses Mouchette by humiliating her in front of the entire class. Even though Mouchette is the senior girl in the class, the teacher calls her singing disgusting and violently forces her face down on the keys of the harmonium, while the other students laugh derisively at her poverty, awkwardness, and rural Picard accent.

Madame Derain (deh-RAYN), a middle-aged grocer. She initially takes pity on Mouchette because of her battered appearance, even though she half believes old stories that Mouchette has taken revenge on local farmers by killing their livestock. She offers the famished girl some three-day-old croissants that Mouchette quickly devours. Because of her nerves, Mouchette accidentally breaks Madame Derain's bowl; Madame Derain then verbally abuses her and chases her out of the store.

— *Patrick Meanor*

THE MOUND BUILDERS

Author: Lanford Wilson (1937-   )
First published: 1976
Genre: Drama

Locale: Urbana and Blue Shoals, Illinois
Time: The 1970's
Plot: Existentialism

Professor August Howe, an archaeologist. A serious scientist, he is methodical, organized, industrious, and idealistic. At forty years of age, he is the leader of an archaeological expedition in the hills of southern Illinois that is about to unearth significant remnants of ancient Indian civilization. Accustomed to quietly maintaining control, he creates the play's narrative framework by flashing slides on a screen and dictating instructions to his secretary, thus permitting flashbacks to the sequence of events from the previous summer in which he plays a major role. His consuming involvement in this work prevents him from attending to a disintegrating marriage, which fails even as his professional dreams do. He nurtures the belief that his work is more important than the livelihood of the landowners of the site and is stunned when that site is brutally destroyed; the play concludes with him wordless and directionless.

Cynthia Howe, his thirty-five-year-old wife, a photographer. The characters of Cynthia and of Jean Loggins are not as fully drawn as those of their husbands. What emerges in Cynthia is a woman who is physically cold toward her husband but who remains a helpmate in his research, documenting his excavations with her photographs. Her passions and preoccupations are drawn to the dangerous, hot-headed, younger Chad Jasker. Although Chad seems to have lost some interest in his affair with her, her loyalty to him is so strong that, after Chad has bulldozed the excavation site, she is motivated to destroy the last vestige of her husband's research project—the undeveloped roll of pictures in her camera.

D. K. (Delia) Eriksen, Howe's sister, thirty-eight years old. She is an invalid and a hypochondriac who has been in and out of institutions for treatment of her alcoholism. She has arrived for an indefinite stay with her brother at the farmhouse where he is lodging with his family and assistants during the dig. She is a published writer of some note (Dan had studied her work in college classes), but at the time of the play, she is unable to create. Her character adds color, interest, some humor, and some important introspection as she interacts with other characters. At the play's conclusion, she is the singular voice of strength and calm amid the grief, distraction, and death of the others.

Dr. Dan Loggins, an archaeologist and assistant to Howe. At the age of twenty-nine, his youth and vigor feed his hunger for success and fame in his fledgling career, at times at the expense of human relationships, though he and Chad do enjoy fishing and drinking together. Dan seems miffed that pregnant Jean does not join him in the use of alcohol and marijuana, though that refusal does not diminish his own consumption. Like Howe, his professional preoccupations blind him to personal matters. He seems ignorant of the fact that his wife—now unflaggingly faithful and pregnant with Dan's child—had been romantically involved with Chad the previous summer, and ignorant, too, of the subtle, if drunken, advances Chad now makes to him. In his death, Dan is a direct victim of Chad's violent revenge even as Chad is a victim of Dan's "blindness."

Dr. Jean Loggins, Dan's twenty-five-year-old wife, a gynecologist. Jean is more likable than Cynthia and less eccentric than D. K. She is intelligent, knows her own mind, is loyal to her husband, and is anticipating the birth of their child. A professional woman, she responds to the intellectual interests and insights of D. K. She repulses Chad's lingering but insistent flirtations and is seriously mentally distracted at the demolition of the excavation site and the murder of her husband.

Chad Jasker, the landowner's son, twenty-five years old. He is assertive, philandering, opinionated, and materialistic. He and his father believe that their futures lie in the land they own, and they are certain that the development of that land, which will accompany the proposed interstate highway, will make them millionaires. What they do not know is that Howe and Loggins have used a 1954 law against defacing Indian monuments to have the highway rerouted to skirt the area. When Chad becomes aware of this (and of Jean's pregnancy, which shocks him as well), he brutally bulldozes their findings and the burial mounds, kills Dan, and commits suicide. He is thus the agent of the destruction of all important professional and personal enterprises in the play.

— *Jill B. Gidmark*

THE MOUNTAIN AND THE VALLEY

Author: Ernest Buckler (1908-1984)
First published: 1952
Genre: Novel

Locale: The village of Entremont in the Annapolis Valley, Nova Scotia, Canada
Time: The 1920's to the 1940's
Plot: Psychological

David Canaan, a sensitive, ardent boy who is deeply involved with his family and the routines of farm life in the Annapolis Valley of Nova Scotia yet is also increasingly drawn into a fascination with words. As he matures, his relationships with his family and his friend Toby are disrupted by life's inevitable events and accidents, but his ability to articulate their significance develops. At the end, separated by deaths and marriages from everyone except his grandmother, he ascends the mountain and dies while experiencing a transfiguring vision of the power of the writer to capture time and reality.

Anna Canaan, the twin sister of David, to whom she is closely attuned. Their often unspoken understanding dwindles somewhat after she falls in love with and marries Toby, David's friend, who is sometimes perceived as looking very much like David.

Toby Richmond, a pen pal and friend of David, subsequently Anna's husband. He has dark hair, light-blue eyes, and a smooth body on which his clothes fit easily. He is open, free of affectations, and unimpressed by conventions and social stratagems. Growing up in the great port of Halifax, he always has been interested in ships; he joins the Royal Canadian Navy during World War II. David often wishes that he were more like Toby.

Christopher (Chris) Canaan, the elder brother of David and Anna. In his acceptance of farm life and his inarticulateness, Chris is more like his father than is David. In childhood, he shows affectionate concern for his siblings, but they grow apart after he becomes involved with Charlotte Gorman, whom he gets pregnant and marries. He returns to Canada after being wounded in the foot in World War II. His marriage founders, and he moves to the West.

Joseph Canaan, the father of Chris, David, and Anna. He has dark hair, dark sober eyes, and a body corded with muscles. Determined and kind, he is rarely able to express his affection for and pride in his family. He is killed while felling a tree alone on the mountain.

Martha Canaan, Joseph's wife. A hardworking and compassionate woman, she is so closely attuned to her husband that if another person, even one of their children, comes into either's thoughts, that other is like a second person, not a third. She dies of a seizure concurrent with her husband's death.

Ellen Canaan, Joseph's mother. As their grandmother, she is a confidante to the children. She tells Anna of the sailor she hid and fed for a week early in her marriage and later gives David the locket that contains the picture of the sailor. She is continually weaving a rug out of the family's discarded clothes, just as in her memory she preserves fragments out of all their lives. At the end, she is the only one left on the farm.

Effie Delahunt, a shy and gentle classmate of David. At his importuning, she yields to him in a wet field. Her death soon afterward leaves David guilt-ridden, for he is unaware that leukemia, not he, caused it.

Bess Delahunt, whose husband, Pete, drowned trying to save Spurge Gorman. She is too yielding to the local men and even seeks to console David physically during his distress at the death of her daughter Effie.

Rachel Gorman, whose husband, Spurge, is drowned in a log drive. A gossip, she continually causes trouble in other people's lives.

Charlotte Gorman, the daughter of Rachel. Her sexual responsiveness to Chris Canaan leads to pregnancy and their getting married, but the marriage does not last, and she returns to her mother.

— Christopher M. Armitage

MOURNING BECOMES ELECTRA

Author: Eugene O'Neill (1888-1953)
First published: 1931
Genre: Drama

Locale: New England
Time: Shortly after the Civil War
Plot: Tragedy

Lavinia Mannon, the daughter of Christine and Ezra Mannon. Tall, flat-breasted, angular, and imperious in manner, Lavinia is fond of her father and fiercely jealous of her mother. While Ezra was fighting in the Civil War, Christine had an affair with Captain Adam Brant. Unconscious desire to have Adam for herself leads Lavinia to demand that Christine give up Adam or face a scandal that would ruin the family name. Unable to go on living with a husband she despises, Christine plots with Adam to poison Ezra when he returns. Ezra is murdered, and Lavinia discovers her mother's guilt. When her brother Orin returns, wounded and distraught, from the war, Lavinia tries to enlist his aid in avenging their father's death. Orin refuses until Lavinia proves Christine's guilt by a ruse.

Blaming Adam for the murder, Orin goes to Adam's ship and shoots him. When Orin reveals to Christine what he has done, she kills herself. Orin and Lavinia then close the Mannon house and voyage to the South Seas. Symbolically liberated from the repressiveness of the New England Puritan tradition, Lavinia blossoms into a duplicate of her voluptuous mother. She plans to marry and start a new life. Orin, hounded by his guilt and going mad, threatens to reveal the Mannons' misdeeds and tries to extort from Lavinia a lover's promise never to leave him. Lavinia agrees but ruthlessly drives Orin to suicide. Now convinced that the Mannon blood is tainted with evil, she resolves to punish herself for the Mannons' guilt. She orders the house shuttered and withdraws into it forever.

Christine Mannon, Lavinia's mother, tall, beautiful, and sensual. Fearing that she will be killed or arrested for her husband's murder, she makes plans with Adam Brant to flee the country and sail for a "happy island." When Orin taunts her with his murder of Adam, Christine goes into the Mannon house and shoots herself.

Orin Mannon, Lavinia's brother, a young idealist who has been spiritually destroyed by the war. Progressively degenerating under the burden of his guilt, Orin conceives that Lavinia has taken the place of his beloved mother. Resolved that Lavinia shall never forget what they have done, Orin writes a history of the Mannon family and uses the manuscript to force Lavinia to promise never to leave him.

General Ezra Mannon, Christine's husband, a tall, big-boned, curt, and authoritative aristocrat. Cold, proud, and unconsciously cruel, Ezra always favored Lavinia over Christine and Orin. When he returns from the war, he tries desperately to make Christine love him, but his efforts are too late. She reveals her infidelity, causing Ezra to have a heart attack. When he asks for medicine, she gives him poison.

Captain Adam Brant, Christine's lover, the captain of a clipper ship. The son of Ezra Mannon's uncle and a servant girl, Marie Brantome, Adam has sworn to revenge himself on the Mannons, who had allowed his mother to die of poverty and neglect. His first approaches to the Mannon house were motivated by this desire for revenge, but he falls deeply in love with Christine.

Captain Peter Niles, of the U.S. Artillery, a neighbor, Lavinia's intended. Lavinia is forced by Orin to give up her plans to marry Peter and to leave behind her the collective guilt of the Mannon family.

Hazel Niles, Peter's sister and Orin's fiancée. She persists in trying to help the erratic Orin lead a normal life. As she becomes aware that Lavinia and Orin share some deep secret, she fears that Lavinia will ruin Peter's life and demands of Lavinia that she not marry him.

Seth Beckwith, the Mannon's gardener, a stooped but hearty old man of seventy-five. Seth serves as commentator and chorus throughout the play.

Amos Ames,

Louisa Ames, his wife, and

Minnie, Louisa's cousin, townsfolk who act as the chorus in "Homecoming."

Josiah Borden, the manager of the shipping company.

Emma Borden, his wife.

Everett Hills, D.D., a Congregational minister. He and the Bordens serve as the chorus in "The Hunted."

The chantyman, a drunken sailor who carries on a suspense-building conversation with Adam Brant as Adam waits for Christine to join him on his ship.

Joe Silva,

Ira Mackel, and

Abner Small, the chorus in "The Haunted."

Avahanni, a Polynesian native with whom Lavinia carried on a flirtation. Lavinia's falsely telling Orin that Avahanni had been her lover helps drive Orin to suicide.

THE MOUSETRAP

Author: Agatha Christie (1890-1976)
First published: 1954
Genre: Drama

Locale: Berkshire, England
Time: c. 1950
Plot: Detective and mystery

Mollie Ralston, a tall, pretty woman in her late twenties. Having inherited Monkswell Manor from her aunt, she has decided to turn it into a guest house rather than sell it. Some years earlier, she had taught at the school that the Corrigan children attended. Jimmy Corrigan sent her a letter revealing that his foster parents, the Stannings of Longridge Farm, were abusing him, and he pleaded with her to help. Because she fell ill with pneumonia on the very day that the letter arrived, she did not see it until weeks later, by which time Jimmy was dead. A potential murder victim because of her connection with Jimmy's death, she is also a suspect in the killing of the other two women who were involved in the tragedy. She secretly went to London on the day Mrs. Stanning was killed and is the first to find the body of Mrs. Boyle.

Giles Ralston, Mollie's husband of exactly one year. He is handsome and about Mollie's age. The two married only three weeks after meeting, so his past remains a mystery. He, too, made a clandestine trip to London on the day of Mrs. Stanning's death, and he wears a coat, scarf, and hat like those seen on the killer.

Mrs. Boyle, a large, middle-aged, querulous woman. A former magistrate, she unwittingly sent the Corrigan children to Longridge Farm. She is strangled at the end of the first act.

Leslie Margaret Katherine Casewell, a twenty-four-year-old who looks older. With her masculine appearance, bearing, and voice, and a coat and scarf matching those worn by the murderer, she is highly suspect, especially because she refuses to reveal her motive for returning from Majorca to England after a twelve-year absence. At last, she explains that as one of the two surviving Corrigan children, she has come back to find her brother.

Detective Sergeant Trotter, a twenty-three-year-old with a London accent. Although he pretends to be a police officer sent to Monkswell Manor to protect the guests, he is actually the insane George Corrigan, who has vowed to avenge his brother's death. He has killed his abusive foster mother and Mrs. Boyle, and he nearly succeeds in getting the third mouse, Mollie Ralston, before his sister and Major Metcalf stop him.

Major Metcalf, a middle-aged man with a military bearing. Like most of the characters in the play, he is pretending to be someone other than he is. He is a policeman and takes the place of the real Major Metcalf to pursue the murderer. Because he is the right age to be Jimmy Corrigan's father, who served in the army, he, too, is a suspect.

Christopher Wren, an unkempt and nervous young man. Orphaned at an early age and an army deserter, he matches the description of George Corrigan, especially because he is trying to forget an unhappy childhood. Moreover, he confesses to lying about his name and his supposed occupation of architect. His behavior throughout the play is highly suspect.

Mr. Paravicini, a taller version of Agatha Christie's famous detective Hercule Poirot; he is dark, elderly, foreign, and mustached. He is an unexpected guest at Monkswell Manor and claims that his Rolls Royce overturned in a nearby snowbank. Because of his mysterious arrival and his unsettling habit of humming and playing "Three Blind Mice," which he calls the murderer's "signature tune," and because of his apparent effort to look older than he is, he, too, is a suspect. In actuality, he is no worse than a smuggler and black-market profiteer.

— *Joseph Rosenblum*

THE MOVIEGOER

Author: Walker Percy (1916-1990)
First published: 1961
Genre: Novel

Locale: Primarily suburbs of New Orleans, Louisiana
Time: Early 1960's
Plot: Social realism

John Bickerson "Binx" Bolling, a twenty-nine-year-old class-bound Southerner given to the arts, culture, and education. Binx's approach to his thirtieth birthday provokes an archetypal quest for meaning in his life. He is skeptical and existential, with a detachment from self that is metaphorically expressed: He sees himself and life itself as comparable to film figures and motion pictures. Moviegoing is a way to study life; more explicitly, life is a kind of existence in a movie: The replication has become the reality. The novel has very little action. Binx has long discussions about life with great-aunt Emily Cutrer, who solicits his help in dealing with her stepdaughter, Kate, who is going through what was then called a "nervous breakdown." Binx takes Kate with him on a kind of escape trip to Chicago, where she more or less returns to normal and Binx more or less finds himself. At the end, it is revealed that the two will marry.

Kate Cutrer, Binx's adoptive distant cousin, beautiful, gracious, genteel, and fragile. In confronting her problems, Kate is always on the edge of despair leading toward suicide. Her fiancé was killed in a car wreck, leaving her distraught and turning to pills and liquor. As the story unfolds, she rids herself of Walter Wade, a rather silly young man to whom she is engaged. Rescuing her from what will surely be a successful suicide attempt, Binx takes her with him on his train trip to Chicago. The excursion serves to return her stability, which, in turn, makes it possible for her to marry Binx.

Emily Cutrer, Binx's great-aunt and Kate's stepmother. Refined, articulate, and culture-bound, Emily has been a surrogate mother to both Binx and Kate. She serves in the story as the last truly good Southern woman, one who had hoped to pass on her culture to Binx, because Kate is not mentally stable enough to be a worthy inheritor. Emily is the reigning matriarch of the family, controlling and governing the action of all in a rather effectual way. She fails, however, to force Binx to act responsibly. He upsets her by taking the trip to Chicago with Kate. The last main action of the novel is her delivery of a sermon to Binx after his return. Binx fails to repent his ways and thereby matures.

Jules Cutrer, Emily's husband and Kate's father. Charming, delightful, and socially innocuous, Jules is a post-Southern emasculated gentleman. He is acceptable and steady but only a mere shadow of what his fathers had been in legend. Honorably, he loves his wife and daughter.

Walter Wade, Kate's fiancé, a man with a fraternity house demeanor. He is a son of the Old South and also represents the worst of manhood in the New South. He is a good old boy with money and class heritage, and his main activity is to organize an entity for the Mardi Gras parade. As an older college classmate of Binx, they were friends. Kate jilts him.

— *Carl Singleton*

MR. BELUNCLE

Author: V. S. Pritchett (1900-1997)
First published: 1951
Genre: Novel

Locale: London, England
Time: About 1935
Plot: Satire

Philip Beluncle, a businessman in partnership with Linda Truslove. He is chubby, flamboyant, self-absorbed, self-indulgent, autocratic, optimistic to the point of madness, and an appropriator of other people's money. His petty tyranny and business impracticality are shown early in the novel in his relationship with his partner in their small furniture manufacturing firm. Being informed by her that the firm is on the verge of bankruptcy does not deter him from planning to purchase a large, expensive house, "Marbella"—acquiring houses is an obsession with him. His petty tyranny and house mania also figure early in the novel in scenes with his family: He bullies his wife, Ethel (who usually pays him back), and his sons, Henry, George, and Leslie (who usually cannot). His economic follies and his obsession with houses have meant many disruptive moves for the family, usually only a jump ahead of his creditors. Beluncle has gone through, or "invested," large amounts of other people's money in his business and personal extravagancies. Despite all this, he somehow inspires love: Linda Truslove was in love with him for years, his wife defends him against all comers, and tears of thwarted love roll down George's cheek. Beluncle is a member of the Church of the Last Purification; its "Divine Mind" tells him what he wants to hear and gives him room to "breathe."

Linda Truslove, Beluncle's business partner. She is a sensible and rather plain, but not unattractive, widow who has struggled against Beluncle's extravagancies over the years of their partnership. She had been in love with him but now is thoroughly disillusioned. Added to her frustrations are those arising from the care of her demanding, crippled sister, Judy Dykes. At the end of the novel, it is apparent that she is bringing legal action to recover some of her money through liquidation of the firm's assets.

Ethel Beluncle, Philip's wife. She is the perfect foil for her husband, matching his fastidiousness with deliberate sloppiness and his order with disorder. Originally an attractive, high-spirited young woman, she now takes out her frustrations on her husband and his senile mother. Meals are the usual occasions for her outbursts. When nothing else is going on, she rages against Linda Truslove, of whom she is understandably jealous.

Henry Beluncle, the oldest son, nineteen years of age. He is in most ways a typical young man trying to break away from the family. He has literary aspirations and wants to distance himself from the petty family quarrels and his father's "religion." The added pull of a love affair with Mary Phibbs makes his rebellion more painful; it is complicated further by his doubt that he is really in love with Mary.

George Beluncle, the middle son. He is a bit dull-witted. Unlike the other two sons, he deeply loves his father, who puts him down at every opportunity. Beluncle is contemptuous of him for not having a job but blocks him whenever a job seems to materialize.

Leslie Beluncle, the youngest son. He is treated by the family as a kind of court jester, his shrewd and often cutting remarks being good-naturedly tolerated even by his father.

Mary Phibbs, Henry's girlfriend. She is a reasonably attractive, immature, rather ordinary girl with whom Henry thinks he is in love. Although the affair comes to nothing, it is a source of animosity between Henry and his father.

Judy Dykes, Linda Truslove's unmarried, crippled sister. She is an ardent though scarcely love-filled member of the Church of the Last Purification. When she suddenly becomes able (barely) to walk, the church members regard it as a miracle. Actually, the cure seems to have been brought about by the half-mad streetcorner "witness," David Vogg, who had gone to the Truslove home to denounce her as a heretic. In the ensuing turmoil, she fell, and the shock seems to have brought movement back to her legs. She soon dies, dulling the brightness of the "miracle."

David Vogg, a misanthropic, half-mad newspaper vendor and street preacher who sniffs out sin and heresy at every corner. He has utter contempt for the bland theology of the Church of the Last Purification, prompting the visit to Judy Dykes that results in her "miraculous" cure.

— *Leslie Mellichamp*

MR. BRITLING SEES IT THROUGH

Author: H. G. Wells (1866-1946)
First published: 1916
Genre: Novel

Locale: England
Time: During World War I
Plot: Social

Mr. Britling, a famous English writer. Convinced before World War I that the idea of a possible war with Germany is nonsense, he is greatly troubled at the outbreak of the war, though convinced that Germany will lose quickly. Gradually, the magnitude of the war becomes clear to him, and he becomes so disturbed that writing is impossible. At last, even though his oldest son, fighting for England, and his children's admired German tutor, who went home to fight for his country, are both dead, Mr. Britling becomes reconciled to the idea of death. He believes that a better world is in the making and that things will be different after the war.

Mr. Direck, an American who goes to England to persuade Mr. Britling to give a series of lectures in the United States. He is attracted to the Britling family and friends, and he falls in love. He is at first only a spectator of the war. After going to the Continent to find news of Britling's secretary, who is missing in action, he volunteers in the Canadian Army.

Hugh Britling, Mr. Britling's oldest son by his first wife. Hugh lies about his age and manages to be sent to the front. He is killed.

Teddy, Mr. Britling's secretary. He is missing in action and presumed to be dead, but he comes home with one hand gone.

Letty, Teddy's wife. Convinced at last that her husband is dead, she finds consolation in Mr. Britling's philosophy, and she also is reconciled to death. One day, she sees her living husband in front of the cottage.

Cecily (Cissie) Corner, Letty's sister. Direck falls in love with her.

Herr Karl Heinrich, the German tutor of the Britling children. He does not believe in the war but goes home to serve his country. He is killed.

Mrs. Britling, the second wife of Mr. Britling. They have not been in love for many years, but they cooperate in running a pleasant household.

Mrs. Harrowdean, a widow with whom Mr. Britling has a love affair. The love affair does not run smoothly; in the period just before the war, they quarrel by mail.

MR. FACEY ROMFORD'S HOUNDS

Author: Robert Smith Surtees (1803-1864)
First published: 1865
Genre: Novel

Locale: England
Time: The nineteenth century
Plot: Picaresque

Francis "Facey" Romford, who is often mistaken for his wealthy namesake and capitalizes on this fact. Using the other's stationery, he becomes Master of Hounds of the

Heavyside Hunt. After living well in the hunt country, he marries a dowdy but rich young woman, moves to Australia, and becomes prosperous.

Francis Romford, Esquire, the aristocratic owner of Abbeyfield Park, whom Facey pretends to be.

Francis Gilroy, Facey's cattle-jobbing uncle, who employs Facey.

The Widow Gilroy, a sharp-faced woman who discharges Facey immediately after her husband's death.

Jogglebury Crowdey, a neighbor from whom Facey hurriedly borrows fifty pounds before news of his discharge following his uncle's death circulates in the area.

Soapey Sponge, who once cheated Facey. He deserts his wife and ships to Australia, where he becomes wealthy. He and Facey eventually become banking partners in Australia.

Lucy Glitters, Soapey's wife who, as Facey's "half-sister, Mrs. Somerville," helps his fox-hunting ventures.

Mrs. Sidney Benson, Lucy's mother, who helps manage Beldon Hall.

The countess of Caperington, who, while the actress wife of dissipated Sir Henry Scattercash, had known Lucy.

Betsy Shannon, another theatrical friend, introduced as **Miss Hamilton Howard**.

Mr. and Mrs. Watkins, of Australia. Wealthy but crude and vulgar, they are members of the Larkspur Hunt.

Cassandra Cleopatra, their simpering daughter, who is looking for a husband. She finally gets Facey.

Mr. Hazey, the master of the neighboring Hard and Sharp Hunt.

Bill Hazey, his son.

Anna Maria, Hazey's daughter, in love with Facey.

Jonathan Lotherington, a fat, timid huntsman who resigns from the Hunt when Facey shows up his poor horsemanship.

Goodhearted Green, a shady horse trader who provides three vicious mounts for the hunt. He calls himself **Sir Roger Ferguson**.

Mrs. Rowley Rounding, who is thrown by one of the vicious horses provided by Goodhearted Green.

Colonel Chatterbox, who demands the return of Mrs. Rounding's money, a demand Facey refuses.

Daniel Swig and

Tom Chowey, cheap and inefficient grooms hired by Facey.

Lord Viscount Lovetin, who rents Beldon Hall to Facey. He returns unexpectedly and promptly dispossesses the "wrong" Mr. Romford.

Mr. Lonnergan, Lord Lovetin's agent.

Lovetin Lonnergan, his son, who marries Miss Hamilton Howard.

Mrs. Mustard, the housekeeper of Beldon Hall and the mother of three daughters, called "The Dirties."

Mr. Stotfold, who provides a stag for the hunt.

Proudlock, Facey's stable keeper.

MR. MIDSHIPMAN EASY

Author: Frederick Marryat (1792-1848)
First published: 1836
Genre: Novel

Locale: The Mediterranean Sea and European coastal waters
Time: During the Napoleonic wars
Plot: Adventure

Jack Easy, a midshipman aboard the *Harpy* during the Napoleonic Wars. The ship wins naval battles, captures Spanish vessels, and rescues shipwrecked criminals. When Jack falls in love with Agnes Rebiera, a faked carriage accident keeps him in Sicily with Gascoigne long enough to court her and overcome her father's objections to their marriage. The underaged Jack returns to England for his father's consent and finds that his mother is dead. His father dies shortly thereafter. Now wealthy, he gives up the sea and marries Agnes.

Dr. Middleton, an advocate of the survival of the fittest who rescues Jack from a doting mother and a father who has preached to his son an oversimplified philosophy of the equality of all people.

Captain Wilson, a poor Easy relative, captain of the warship *Harpy* and later of the *Aurora*. He signs Jack aboard

because of a thousand-pound debt he owes to Jack's father.

Gascoigne (gas-KOYN), another midshipman who shares adventures with Jack. He eventually settles in Hampshire as a country gentleman on Jack's large estate.

Mesty, an Ashantee who is loyal to Jack because Jack treats him as an equal. Once he accepts a bribe from the Rebiera family priest to kill Jack, but he uses the poison on the priest.

Don Rebiera (reh-bee-EH-rah), a wealthy Sicilian captured with his family by Jack and released. Sometime later, driven ashore by a storm, Jack rescues Don Rebiera from would-be assassins who have invaded his villa to murder him. Jack again saves Don Rebiera when freed galley slaves, among them one of the would-be murderers, besiege the villa.

Agnes Rebiera, Don Rebiera's lovely daughter, who inspires Jack's love and becomes his wife.

MR. PALOMAR
(Palomar)

Author: Italo Calvino (1923-1985)
First published: 1983
Genre: Novel

Locale: Europe, Japan, and Mexico
Time: Mid-1980's
Plot: Psychological

Mr. Palomar, a constant observer, analyst, and amateur philosopher, possibly the quintessential "modern." Although Mr. Palomar's character is not developed in the conventional sense, physically or psychologically, the reader does learn

some superficial facts about his life. Mr. Palomar lives in Rome with his wife and daughter. He is well-to-do, enjoying an abundance of leisure time, and he likes to travel. As Mr. Palomar's name, purposely evoking the famous telescope, suggests, his musings are at least as much symbolic as they are personal. Mr. Palomar observes and ponders objects as diverse as blackbirds, the sky, a cheese shop, and the naked bosom of a sunbather. At least twice, however, Mr. Palomar finds the tables turned on him, becoming the observed rather than the observer. Toward the end of the novel, Mr. Palomar's lack of authoritative self-knowledge becomes conspicuous, but then, as the author suggests, a telescope is probably not the best instrument for seeing oneself.

Mrs. Palomar, Mr. Palomar's wife and occasional critic. Strictly a foil to the main character, Mrs. Palomar makes only three notable appearances. Early in the book, she displays mild impatience with Mr. Palomar's attempt to sing along with some blackbirds he is observing. Later, her plants and her appreciation of them are contrasted with objects of interest to her husband. Finally, she joins Mr. Palomar in observing a gecko on their terrace. The presence of Mrs. Palomar (and her daughter, about whom the reader learns almost nothing) keeps Mr. Palomar from representing any simple sort of loneliness or personal desolation. Mr. Palomar is not physically or emotionally a hermit. He does tend to get lost in his own reflections, and he may be lost in the cosmic scheme of things, but this condition is not because he is alone, as the presence of Mrs. Palomar makes clear.

— *Ira Smolensky*

MR. SAMMLER'S PLANET

Author: Saul Bellow (1915-   )
First published: 1970
Genre: Novel

Locale: New York City and its suburbs, Poland, and Israel
Time: Late 1960's, during the first moon landing
Plot: Social realism

Artur Sammler, a seventy-six-year-old Polish Jew of British education and temperament living in New York. Sammler survived the Nazi mass murder of European Jews during World War II, crawling out of a mass grave and leaving the machine-gunned body of his dead wife behind. A tall, slender, and slightly stooped intellectual, Sammler observes the world with brutal clarity through one eye, the other having been crushed by a rifle butt during the war. Something of a voyeur, Sammler is fascinated by and yet highly critical of contemporary life and its barbarous, nihilistic, tragicomic, and sexually maladjusted ways. His encounters with a black pickpocket, a neurotic daughter, a dying friend, a strikingly sexual young woman, and a highly intelligent though fundamentally aimless young man become occasions for extraordinarily intense, private reflections on life on the planet.

The black pickpocket, a powerful, brutish, handsome, and elegantly dressed thief who works the Broadway bus between Columbus Circle and Seventy-second Street. Simultaneously fascinated and repelled, Sammler returns again and again to see the pickpocket at his work. Eventually, the pickpocket corners Sammler in the lobby of Sammler's apartment building and exposes himself as a warning.

Angela Gruner, a voluptuous, sexually adventurous, provocatively clad young woman who tells Sammler all of her secrets. Deeply disturbing to both Sammler and her father, Elya, Angela provokes in these men intense reactions of anger and disgust in response to her powerful sexuality.

Shula Sammler, the daughter of Artur Sammler, reared in a Polish convent during the war and bearing the emotional scars of wartime experience. Eccentric, unkempt, and unpredictable, Shula is obsessed with trying to get her father to complete a memoir of H. G. Wells, whom Sammler knew in London before the war. As a part of this effort, she steals the manuscript of Dr. V. Govinda Lal so that her father can read it. Her concealment of the manuscript and Lal's attempts to recover it drive much of the novel's plot.

Margotte Arkin, a niece of Sammler's dead wife, Antonina, and the wife of Usher Arkin, recently killed in a plane crash. Margotte is short, round, and full; by temperament she is generous, liberal, and romantic. To Sammler, a realist, she is a good-hearted but typically foolish woman. Sammler lives in a room in Margotte's apartment.

Dr. Elya Gruner, a wealthy gynecologist, widower, and benefactor of Sammler and Shula. He is dying of an aneurism. Gruner is alienated from his children, whom he considers failures or "screw-ups." A man who keeps a beautiful suburban home as well as a chauffeur-driven Rolls Royce with "MD" license plates, Gruner wants to die a proper death and leave his complex financial affairs in order. There is some suggestion of his involvement with the mob, perhaps as a performer of illegal abortions. Gruner's slow dying offers Sammler many occasions for considering the meaning of life and death.

Wallace Gruner, Elya's son and Angela's brother. He is extraordinarily intelligent, yet his aims in life lack focus. His latest scheme is an aerial photography business in which he photographs homes of wealthy suburbanites and identifies the foliage on their property. He also believes that his father has a hidden cache of money in the suburban house and spends much of his time trying to find it, with disastrous results.

Eisen, Shula's former husband, a wife beater. He survived the battle of Stalingrad, though his toes were amputated as a result of frostbite. Unusually handsome, he has come to New York to become an artist and to peddle his harsh, brutal-looking metal sculptures. Sammler loathes him, though he also sees in him another example of the war's deforming effects. Eisen is capable of brutality, as shown by his attack on the black pickpocket at the climax of the novel.

Lionel Feffer, Wallace's business partner, a young, unanchored, energetic, and entrepreneurial New York Jew who admires Sammler and who convinces him to deliver a lecture at Columbia University titled "The British Scene in the Thirties," a subject in which Sammler is an expert. The lecture is a disaster and helps to confirm Sammler's conception of contemporary youth as barbarous, ill-educated, and unwashed. Fascinated by Sammler's encounter with the pickpocket, Feffer photographs the thief in the act and thus provokes a violent encounter near the close of the novel.

Dr. V. Govinda Lal, a diminutive East Indian who has written a manuscript titled *The Future of the Moon*, which Shula steals. The only man who can exchange views at Sammler's intellectual level, Lal is something of a utopian, for he sees the colonization of the moon as both inevitable and beneficial for humankind. Having known utopian thinkers in the past, namely H. G. Wells, Sammler is attracted yet skeptical.

Wharton Horricker, Angela's lover, a physical culturalist.

Walter Bruch, Sammler's Old World acquaintance, an apelike man who suffers a very old-fashioned, nineteenth century form of fetishism.

— *Michael Zeitlin*

MR. SPONGE'S SPORTING TOUR

Author: Robert Smith Surtees (1803-1864)
First published: 1853; serial form, 1849-1851
Genre: Novel

Locale: The English countryside
Time: The 1850's
Plot: Picaresque

Soapey Sponge, a nattily dressed young rogue whose career of hunting all winter and talking about it all summer is supported primarily by swindling victims into, and then bailing them out of, bad horse deals and by inviting himself to stay at the country mansions of unsuspecting hunters. At each hunt, he befriends one innocent who foolishly suggests that he stop by if ever in the neighborhood. His hosts soon find that he is nearly impossible to dislodge once entrenched in their households and that they must resort to a variety of tactics to get him to leave. The fine food, drink, and furnishings originally laid out for a man they think is both rich and eligible to serve as a son-in-law or godfather are slowly withdrawn or cut off altogether once Sponge shows himself true to his surname. His given name is more attributable to his moral character; he is not clean but certainly is as slippery as soap. He plays spouses, neighbors, and friends against one another, neatly escaping before they can compare stories. Early in the season, he contracts with a seedy stable owner named Benjamin Buckram, who rents him two beautiful but violently dangerous horses with the option of buying them or selling them to a gullible third party and splitting the profits. Peter Leather, one of Buckram's stablehands, is hired to keep an eye on Buckram's horses and act as servant to Sponge. Sponge and Leather agree to work the hunting circuit, giving the impression that Sponge not only owns the horses but also that he is a landed gentleman. Leather will spread the agreed story and manage the difficult horses to make them appealing to potential buyers. Sponge is an excellent rider who controls the animals in public just long enough to get them sold; he then devises various schemes to buy them back or have them returned for free by terrified, embarrassed buyers. After a few successful dupes, he proceeds to work his way through the estates on the hunting tour, leaving only when he is sure of his next source of free room and board. He finally lands in the debauched circle of flashy, soon-to-be-bankrupt Sir Scattercash and is surrounded by a squad of drunken hangers-on, all of whom regard him with the suspicion of one "sponge" for another. Sponge finds both his sinking host and these competitors too dissipated to be socially or financially cultivated, but while there he meets Lucy Glitters, an actress. He falls in love with her after seeing how well they hunt together. When Jack Spraggon is killed, Sponge accidentally wins a steeplechase he had agreed to lose so that he and Buckram could profit from rigged betting. He and Lucy marry, and he returns to London to turn over a new leaf. For someone as slippery as Sponge, this means setting up a cigar and gambling salon with Lucy, based on his intention to "protect" the public from unscrupulous loan sharks and bookies by cheating them himself.

Peter Leather, Sponge's horse groom and Buckram's security guard, who makes sure the rented horses are well-kept. A former coachman to a duke, he has since fallen in the world, serving time in prison before arriving at Buckram's disreputable stables. Though surly and frequently drunk, he assists Sponge in his imposture until dissatisfied, then leaks financial information to the other servants, whose grapevines eventually carry it to Sponge's hosts. Leather never manages to undo Sponge completely, only to inconvenience him. He ends up as a cab driver, supplementing his income with hush money from Sponge to prevent circulation of their horse-selling schemes.

Jack Spraggon, a nearsighted friend, servant, and bullying thug to the odious Lord Scamperdale. He conspires with Sponge to cheat Scamperdale into buying bad horses in exchange for a cut of the profits. Failing this, he successfully conspires with Sponge on a number of occasions to swindle others by pretending they are only acquaintances, then playing off of each other as they prey on their chosen victim. Spraggon meets his violent end in a horse-jumping accident at the rigged steeplechase he was to have won.

Lord Scamperdale, a mean, stingy landlord. He is jealous of Sponge and sets Spraggon out to run him off. When Sponge eludes the bully on the hunting field, Scamperdale sends him to Sponge's lodgings with the express purpose of planting rumors about Sponge's financial worries in order to get Sponge thrown out. He inadvertently achieves the opposite, however, because three bottles of wine into their evening, Spraggon and Sponge recognize their mutual interests, and their partnership is cemented.

— *Elizabeth Bleicher*

MR. STONE AND THE KNIGHTS COMPANION

Author: V. S. Naipaul (1932-   )
First published: 1963
Genre: Novel

Locale: London, England
Time: The 1950's or early 1960's
Plot: Comic realism

Richard Stone, an employee of a minor corporation called Excal who, at the age of sixty-two, after thirty years with the company, is about to retire. Locked within the strict routines of his dull life, this timid, proper man resembles the stereotype of the "little man" of English literature. To overcome his loneliness and fear of retirement, he marries a widow, Margaret Springer. More significant, however, he defends himself from the painful idea of retirement and death by composing a plan called the "Knights Companion," which calls for selected employees (dubbed "Knights") to visit retired employees of Excal to buoy up their spirits. In the creative act of composing the "Knights Companion," Stone discovers a pure sense of hope and purpose, but at the end of the novel, having learned of the death of his friend Tony Tomlinson, he adopts a cynical philosophy that declares all action and creation as a betrayal of feeling and truth. He comes to the conclusion, finally, that all that matters is people's frailty and corruptibility.

Margaret Springer Stone, a middle-aged widow who, shortly after meeting Stone at the annual dinner party of his friends, Tony and Grace Tomlinson, marries him and encourages his plans to draw up a retirement program for the employees of Excal. She succeeds, for a time, in helping him to overcome his dread of the void, but finally her presence is of no more consequence to him than that of his housekeeper.

Tony Tomlinson, Stone's best friend, an educator, who attended teacher training college with Stone. Although their paths have diverged, he maintains their friendship through his annual dinner parties. He and his wife, Grace, introduce Stone to his future wife at one of these gatherings. The next year, Tony invites Stone and his wife to dinner to celebrate Stone's achievements at Excal. Less than a week later, Stone learns that Tony has died. This revelation reinforces Stone's profound anxiety over his own impending death.

Grace Tomlinson, Tony's wife, who, after his death, travels to France and Spain, indulging herself in pleasant adventures partially as a means of suppressing her grief over his death. Unlike Stone, she succeeds in putting Tony out of her mind so that she can get on with the business of living.

Miss Millington, Stone's elderly maid, whose performance of domestic duties helps Stone to maintain his rigid pattern of life. After his marriage, however, her role is diminished as Margaret begins to assume her position as mistress of the Stone household.

Bill Whymper, the young public relations officer at Excal who helps Stone to shape his proposal for the Knights Companion. He is later credited in the newspapers as being the man behind this creative retirement plan, an unjustified recognition that caps Stone's growing cynicism.

— *Richard Kelly*

MR. WESTON'S GOOD WINE

Author: T. F. Powys (1875-1953)
First published: 1927
Genre: Novel

Locale: Folly Down, a village in western England
Time: November 20, 1923
Plot: Religious

Mr. Weston, a strange wine merchant who visits the village of Folly Down at seven o'clock on the evening of November 20, 1923. The clocks in the village stop when he arrives. He helps many people, among them the melancholy Mr. Grobe, the lonely Tamar, Jenny Bunce, and the virtuous Mr. Bird, to whom he reads from his own book, the Bible. He also makes Mr. Bird's well run with wine. When he leaves Folly Down, the clocks start again and the villagers are surprised to see that it is only ten o'clock.

Michael, Mr. Weston's assistant, who carries a large book with the names of all the inhabitants of the town inscribed. He is married to Tamar Grobe by Mr. Weston and gives her happiness under the village trysting tree.

Mr. Grunter, the sexton, allegedly quite a seducer. He thinks Mr. Weston is the Devil but finds that he is not. Grunter helps Mr. Weston in his affairs in the village and sees the souls of Tamar and another girl carried to Heaven.

Mr. Bunce, the innkeeper, who blames God for all the pregnancies among the girls of Folly Down. He scornfully says that his daughter may not marry simple-hearted Mr. Bird until the man's well runs with wine.

Mr. Grobe, the rector at Folly Down. He no longer believes in God because he has lost his wife. He tries to find escape and pleasure in drink and is especially pleased with a bottle of

Mr. Weston's wine, a bottle that remains full while he drinks from it. Mr. Weston also gives him a small bottle, the contents of which enable Mr. Grobe to die peacefully.

Tamar Grobe, the rector's daughter, who wants to marry an angel. She finds happiness with Michael, Mr. Weston's assistant, to whom she is wedded by Mr. Weston. She dies shortly after her wedding, and two angels carry her to Heaven.

Jenny Bunce, the innkeeper's daughter, in love with Mr. Bird. She is a simple, good-hearted girl who believes she will find happiness caring for the man she loves. Mr. Weston marries her to Mr. Bird.

Mr. Bird, a resident of Folly Down who recognizes Mr. Weston. Bird is an honest, virtuous man who preaches God's word to man and beast. Mr. Weston causes Mr. Bird's well to run with wine so that he can marry Jenny with her father's permission.

The Mumby Boys, two sons of the local squire, accomplished and villainous seducers who are chased by a wild beast controlled by Mr. Weston. Frightened, they run to the house of the bawd who caters to them and agree to marry two of their victims. As the beast circles her house, the evil old bawd dies of fright.

MRS. BRIDGE

Author: Evan S. Connell, Jr. (1924-   )
First published: 1959
Genre: Novel

Locale: Kansas City, Missouri; Southampton, England; Paris; Monte Carlo; and Rome
Time: Early 1920's to early 1940's
Plot: Satire

India Bridge, who is married to a successful lawyer; she is the mother of three children and is a member of the Kansas City, Missouri, country club society. She is a desperately unhappy woman trapped in a domestic existence that she neither understands nor is able to alter. Her husband, Walter, a workaholic who is almost never home, gives India little love or companionship, instead treating her as incompetent and destroying her self-esteem. Her growing children are a constant source of frustration. A believer in strict racial and class lines and in Victorian pieties, which dictate that proper dress, manners, language, and chaste behavior mark the respectable person, she discovers that her children, members of a different generation, reject her views. When she insists that they conform to her standards, they distance themselves. Her affluence bedevils her. She need not work, and hired workers take care of the household, leaving her bored and feeling useless. Sex also haunts India. Uncertain of her own attitude toward physical desire, apparently unable to realize a mutually satisfying intimate life with Walter, and abnormally worried about her children's emerging sexual awareness, she is emotionally crippled by sexual anxiety. As India enters middle age, she becomes neurotic, seeing no purpose in her life. She wants psychiatric help, but Walter forbids it. When Walter dies of a heart attack at the end of the story, she is completely adrift. Her children, now adults, have left home, and all she can find for solace are memories of earlier days, when she still had hopes and expectations.

Walter Bridge, India's husband, a narrow-minded and selfish man obsessed by the work ethic. A dominating figure, he makes all the crucial decisions in his home but otherwise cannot be bothered by the ongoing life of the family. When he is stricken, he dies as he lived, in his office in the midst of work.

Ruth Bridge, India's firstborn. Of all the children, she most objects to her mother's standards. Secretive, wild, and promiscuous as a teenager, she quickly departs after high school to work and lead a bohemian life in New York. She is not happy, yet she will not change. She has chosen to be totally different from her mother.

Carolyn Bridge, the second daughter. Seemingly the "good" child, she causes few problems until she marries. When she chooses a plumber's son, India feels humiliated.

When Carolyn's husband demands that she be an obedient wife, she rebels. After having watched Walter order India around, she will not let any man tell her what to do. Carolyn's marriage, in constant ferment, remains doubtful.

Douglas Bridge, India's son. From early childhood, Douglas refuses to be the type of young man that India wishes him to be. Rarely communicating, he dresses sloppily, fights, plays in junkyards, swears, and as an adolescent develops a harmless interest in girls and sex. Although he is a normal boy, India keeps trying to change him. Her opposition eventually drives him into active hostility. Not until his father's death does Douglas, now mature and in the Army, achieve some reconciliation with his mother.

Grace Barron, a close friend of India. A banker's wife, Grace experiences the same futility in her life as does India, but Grace refuses to accept her situation. Seeking to be recognized as an individual, rather than as a rich man's wife, she reads widely and challenges others over large issues in politics, religion, and art. The people of her set, however, dismiss her as eccentric. In despair, Grace finally kills herself.

Harriet, the Bridges' longtime black cook and housekeeper. Indispensable to the family, Harriet receives no special affection or consideration from the Bridges. She nevertheless continues to serve them.

Mabel Ong, a poet and liberated woman who unsuccessfully urges India to be more her own person.

Dr. Foster, the pastor of India's church, a vacuous hypocrite. Despite Foster's shortcomings, he remains a model of spiritual guidance for India.

Alice Jones, a young black woman, a childhood playmate of Carolyn who stirs India's racial and class fears, causing India to end the friendship.

Paquita de las Torres, a coarse, sensual girl of dubious background, Douglas' first real flame. She provokes a bitter confrontation between India and Douglas over the relationship.

Jay Duchesne, a one-armed veteran of World War II. He once dated Carolyn and wants to see her again if her marriage fails.

— *Clarke L. Wilhelm*

MRS. CALIBAN

Author: Rachel Ingalls (1940-   )
First published: 1982
Genre: Novel

Locale: Southern California
Time: Late twentieth century
Plot: Love

Dorothy Caliban, a housewife nearing middle age and living in Southern California. Two of Dorothy's major characteristics are her alienation and her loneliness in a loveless marriage. Dorothy's outlook on life is clearly conditioned by the bleakness of her marriage. Dorothy's husband, Fred, who

is haunted by the death of their only child, causes her to settle for a life of marriage in name only. The nominal aspect of the marriage is shown in Dorothy's behavior. The author emphasizes that Dorothy is absorbed in acting out the routine of marriage—for example, shopping and cooking—but receives none of its intimacy. An essential aspect of the plot is Dorothy's consciousness of the emptiness of her life, which prepares the reader for her reaction to Larry. Because of the shallowness and lack of sexual intimacy in her marriage, Dorothy is quickly attracted to Larry, a huge amphibian creature. Dorothy's attraction to Larry is a catalyst for the plot, in the sense that in her devotion to him she hides him, has an affair with him, and wants to protect him from those who would capture and punish him for killing two people at the institute from which he escaped. Furthermore, the change in Dorothy's own life during her relationship with Larry is central, because she becomes a much more romantic, fulfilled person than she has been in her sterile marriage. Her consequent openness to adventure with Larry is a main aspect of the plot.

Larry, also known as **Aquarius the Monsterman**, a six-foot, seven-inch amphibian creature with a froglike head, webbed hands and feet, and the body of a man. Larry, as he calls himself, is very conscious of human cruelty and has escaped from the Jefferson Institute for Oceanographic Research to avoid the abuse he has suffered at the hands of his two keepers. His desire to escape cruelty is central in moving him to love and trust Dorothy, who is kind to and protective of him. He, like Dorothy, has been alienated from his living environment and, like her, has a desire to acquire both a physical and an emotional connection with a human being. Larry's consciousness of human cruelty also disrupts his relationship with humanity. This disruption is shown in his murder

of five teenagers who planned to attack him. Larry's inability to live in a world cruel to those who are different causes him to escape back to the sea.

Fred, Dorothy's unfaithful husband. Fred's indifference to his marriage to Dorothy is extremely important, as he creates the sterility to which Dorothy reacts. His affair, resulting in his lack of interest in their home life, drives Dorothy to deeper desolation. Fred's disinterest in Dorothy is prompted by her miscarriage, which followed the death of their son. Afterward, Fred is content with twin beds, emblematic of the lack of intimacy that marks the marriage. Fred uses his work to try to disguise his affair, but his motives and attitudes toward the marriage are transparent to Dorothy. It is this transparency that is a catalyst in Dorothy's desire to be involved with Larry. In the novel's climax, he and his lover die in a car crash.

Estelle, a divorcée, Dorothy's best friend and her opposite in circumstance and personality. Estelle's contrasts with Dorothy—for example, her having simultaneous affairs with two men—are underlined, especially before Dorothy's affair with Larry. Ironically, as Dorothy becomes involved with Larry, Estelle loses both of her lovers. Estelle is also more blunt and cynical than Dorothy is for much of the book, a result of having been divorced and, later, losing her son when Larry kills him.

Sandra, Estelle's sixteen-year-old daughter and Fred's lover.

— *Jane Davis*

MRS. DALLOWAY

Author: Virginia Woolf (1882-1941)
First published: 1925
Genre: Novel

Locale: London, England
Time: The 1920's
Plot: Psychological realism

Clarissa Dalloway, a woman fifty-two years old and chic, but disconcerted over life and love. A June day in her late middle years is upsetting to Mrs. Dalloway, uncertain as she is about her daughter and her husband's love, her own feelings for them, and her feelings for her former fiancé, lately returned from India. Years before, Peter Walsh had offered her agony and ecstasy, though not comfort or social standing, and so she had chosen Richard Dalloway. Now, seeing Peter for the first time in many years, her belief in her motives and her peace of mind are gone. Engaged in preparations for a party, she knows her life is frivolous, her need for excitement neurotic, and her love dead. Meeting her best friend, Sally Seton, also makes her realize that their love was abnormal as is her daughter's for an older woman. Although she knows that her husband's love for her is real and solid, she feels that death is near, that growing old is cruel, that life can never be innocently good again.

Richard Dalloway, her politician husband, a Conservative Member of Parliament. Never to be a member of the Cabinet or a prime minister, Richard is a good man who has improved his character, his disposition, his life. Loving his wife deeply but silently, he is able only to give her a conventional bouquet of roses to show his feeling, a fortunate gift because roses are the one flower she can stand to see cut. Devoted to his daughter, he sees her infatuation as a passing thing, an adolescent emotional outlet. He is gently persuasive among his constitu-

ents and colleagues, and in thought and deed a thoroughly good man.

Peter Walsh, a widower lately returned from India to make arrangements for the divorce of a major's wife, a woman half his age whom he plans to marry, again an action to fill the void left by Clarissa. Perceptive and quick to understand motives for unhappiness, Peter sees his return to England as another step in his failure to live without Clarissa. Unnerved by seeing her again, he blurts out his recent history, and he continues the cruel probe all day and that night at her party.

Septimus Warren Smith, a war casualty who commits suicide on the night of Mrs. Dalloway's party and delays the arrival of one of the guests, a doctor. A poet and a brave man, Septimus brings back to England an Italian war bride whom he cannot really love, all feeling having been drained from him by the trauma of war. He is extremely sensitive to motives; to Septimus, his doctors represent the world's attempt to crush him, to force him into conventionality. Feeling abandoned and unable to withstand even the devotion of his lovely wife, he jumps to his death, a martyr to the cause of individuality, of sensitivity to feelings and beauty.

Lucrezia Smith, called **Rezia**, the Italian wife whom Smith met in Milan and married after the war. Desperately in love with her husband, she tries to give him back his former confidence in human relations, takes him to doctors for consultation, and hopes to prevent his collapse and suicide.

Elizabeth Dalloway, the daughter who has none of her mother's charm or vivacity and all of her father's steady attributes. Judged to be handsome, the sensible seventeen-year-old appears mature beyond her years; her thoughtfulness directly contradicts her mother's frivolity. She is until this day enamored of Miss Kilman, a desperate and fanatical older woman who is in love with Elizabeth but conceals her feelings under the guise of religiosity and strident charity. On the day of the party, Elizabeth sees Miss Kilman's desire for power and escapes from the woman's tyranny of power and need. That night, Elizabeth blossoms forth in womanly radiance so apparent that her father fails to recognize his conception of a daughter.

Doris Kilman, Elizabeth Dalloway's tutor and friend, an embittered, frustrated spinster whose religious fanaticism causes her to resent all the things she could not have or be. With a lucid mind and intense spirit largely given to deep hatreds of English society, she represents a caricature of womanly love and affection, a perversion.

Lady Rosseter, nee **Sally Seton**, the old friend with whom Mrs. Dalloway had believed herself in love when she was eighteen. Sally has always known that Clarissa made the wrong choice and has always been aware of the shallowness of her friend's existence. Mellowed now, Sally and Peter Walsh can see the pattern of life laid out before them at the party, and they console each other for loss of girlhood friend and beloved.

Dr. Holmes, Septimus Smith's physician. Brisk and insensitive, he fails to realize the seriousness of his patient's condition. Puzzled because Smith does not respond to prescriptions of walks in the park, music halls, and bromides at bedtime, he sends him to consult Sir William Bradshaw.

Sir William Bradshaw, a distinguished specialist who devotes three-quarters of an hour to each of his patients. Ambitious for worldly position but apathetic as a healer, he shuts away the mad, forbids childbirth, and advises an attitude of proportion in sickness and in health. Because of Septimus Smith's suicide, he and his wife arrive late at Mrs. Dalloway's party.

Lady Millicent Bruton, a fashionable Mayfair hostess. A dabbler in charities and social reform, she is sponsoring a plan to have young men and women immigrate to Canada.

Hugh Whitbread, a friend of the Dalloways and a minor official at court.

MRS. DANE'S DEFENCE

Author: Henry Arthur Jones (1851-1929)
First published: 1905
Genre: Drama

Locale: Near London, England
Time: Early twentieth century
Plot: Social realism

Mrs. Dane, a charming woman whose reputation is clouded. She finally is proved to be Felicia Hindemarsh, a notorious woman who had an affair with her employer while working as a governess, bearing him a child. As a result of the affair, the man became demented and his wife committed suicide. When faced with these facts, Mrs. Dane, who truly loves Lionel Carteret, is persuaded by his uncle to disappear from the young man's life, lest she ruin it.

Lionel Carteret, a young man madly in love with Mrs. Dane. He is the adopted son of Sir Daniel Carteret. He loves Mrs. Dane so much that he is willing to marry her even after he finds out about her past. When she disappears, he believes he will never know love or happiness again.

Sir Daniel Carteret, Lionel's foster father and a jurist. He has known love himself, having been in love at one time with Lionel's mother, then already married. Wishing to help his adopted son avoid tragedy, he investigates the rumors about Mrs. Dane and finds them true. He suppresses the facts, believing that the woman has suffered enough, but he persuades her to disappear from his adopted son's life.

Mrs. Bulsom-Porter, who hates Mrs. Dane because the latter is charming and physically attractive. She spreads gossip about Mrs. Dane and even hires a detective to try to find out about the woman's past. Although her rumors are correct, no one will admit it; consequently, Mrs. Bulsom-Porter is forced to make a public apology.

James Risby, Mrs. Bulsom-Porter's nephew, who first tells his aunt that Mrs. Dane seems to be the notorious Felicia Hindemarsh. Later, he retracts his statements, believing that the woman—though definitely guilty—has suffered enough for her acts.

Lady Eastney, a friend of Mrs. Dane. She is attracted to Sir Daniel as a kind and just man. She accepts his proposal of marriage.

Janet Colquhoun, an attractive young woman with whom Lionel previously had been infatuated. She still loves him and promises him a bright future.

MRS. STEVENS HEARS THE MERMAIDS SINGING

Author: May Sarton (1912-1995)
First published: 1965
Genre: Novel

Locale: Cape Ann, Massachusetts
Time: The 1960's
Plot: Psychological realism

F. Hilary Stevens, a poet and novelist. After living abroad for most of her life, Hilary, at the age of seventy, views herself as an outsider set apart by her profession, her self-imposed solitude, and her bisexuality. Her isolation gives her time for continual tension and dialogue between the Old Hilary, the servant whose business it is to organize daily life, which otherwise would fall into chaos, and the poet Hilary, the intensely sensitive artist whose job it is to organize and clarify her feelings by transforming them into poetry. Such tension and dialogue are primary characteristics of her writing as well as of her inner life. Her inner life is characterized as well by her relationships with her Muses, women who have inspired the artistic tension needed to fuel her poetic impulse. Throughout her life, Hilary has continually tried to come to grips with the problem of being a woman and a writer while remaining true to her sense of self. Although she has published two novels and nine volumes of poems in her career, Hilary has only recently achieved critical recognition. Having been ignored as a writer for so long, she suspects that her present fame is the result of her longevity rather than of sincere appreciation on the part of critics. The interview that constitutes the major portion of the book is a result of this newfound critical acclaim.

Mar Hemmer, a college-age friend of Hilary. The tall, thin, towheaded grandson of Hilary's neighbor, Mar is suffering as a result of a brief homosexual love affair with a college professor at Amherst. Caught between his guilt and shame at his homosexuality and his anger at those people who condemn the honesty and purity of his love, he is the male counterpart of Hilary. Unschooled in literature or literary criticism, he is for Hilary the perfect critic. Mar, like Hilary, is from a repressive home, and his father, a widower, forces Mar to study the sciences to fulfill his own thwarted ambitions. Hilary and Mar identify with each other's rage and rebellion. With Hilary's encouragement, Mar begins to write poetry as a way to transform the chaos and disorder of his feelings into beauty and harmony.

Peter Selversen, a journalist specializing in interviews with famous writers. Intelligent, tactful, and charming, Peter has turned his ability to ask the right questions into a successful career as a journalist. Viewing the writers he interviews as prey to be captured, Peter clearly enjoys the game of flushing out Hilary's musings about her life and art. He nevertheless remains kindly in his detachment and a sincere admirer of Hilary as a writer.

Jenny Hare, a young short-story writer and one of the interviewers. She is chosen to accompany the professional journalist, Peter, simply because she is a woman and the girlfriend of the associate editor. Jenny feels inadequate to the task of interviewing an established writer; she is uncomfortable with herself as a woman and a writer and lacks the commitment to her writing that Hilary so clearly possesses. She refuses to surrender her illusion that being a complete woman must include being a wife and mother.

— *Jean McConnell*

MRS. WARREN'S PROFESSION

Author: George Bernard Shaw (1856-1950)
First published: 1898
Genre: Drama

Locale: England
Time: The 1890's
Plot: Social

Vivie Warren, the independent, confident, self-possessed, twenty-two-year-old daughter of Mrs. Kitty Warren. After finishing a rigorous academic program with honors at Cambridge, Vivie plans to become an actuarial accountant. Unlike many young women of her day, she hopes for a highly successful business career. She has lived at boarding schools all of her life and has had little contact with her mother and no knowledge of the family business. Vivie has taken a country cottage in Haslemere to devote herself to reading law in preparation for her business endeavors. Mrs. Warren surprises Vivie by inviting not only herself but also several male friends to share Vivie's holiday. During their encounter at the cottage, Vivie learns the truth about her mother's profession and comes to admire her mother for her strength and determination. She cannot, however, fulfill the role of devoted daughter that her mother would now like her to play. She admits to her mother that they are too much alike but maintains her resolve that her world will be different from that of her mother and that they must part—a typically Shavian touch of having the child reject the parent.

Mrs. Kitty Warren, alias **Miss Vacasour**, an aging but financially secure madam whose work in prostitution was a result of economic necessity, not moral weakness. Born in poverty, Mrs. Warren saw only two choices offered her by society and unashamedly chose the vagaries of prostitution over the certain death of working in the white-lead factory. Although she makes no apologies for her profession, she does keep the actual nature of her work a secret from her daughter for twenty-two years. Now, Mrs. Warren attempts to assert her "maternal rights" over her independent and strong-willed child. Ultimately, the mother reveals her life's work to her daughter but tells her that the business is no longer active. Mrs. Warren breaks from her role of street-smart businesswoman when Vivie rejects her after learning that she still engages in the business that profits by the weakness of others.

Praed, a friend of Mrs. Warren, a self-confessed "anarchist," and the first to arrive at Vivie's summer cottage. He realizes at once that Vivie is more serious-minded than her mother and her friends and tries to prepare Vivie for the experience she is about to have. A devotee of the gospel of art, Praed represents the life of fine art and culture that could be Vivie's if she could accept her mother and her mother's money.

Sir George Crofts, a longtime friend and business partner of Mrs. Warren and part of her entourage to the country. Crofts, who is about fifty years old, takes an unexpected and uninvited romantic interest in Vivie that she finds distasteful. He unwittingly reveals that the prostitution business is still very active, thus adding to the rift between mother and daughter. He represents the life of aristocratic high society that Vivie firmly rejects.

Frank Gardner, a dandy, Vivie's twenty-year-old would-be beau. Frank embodies the convention of "love's young dream." His and Vivie's relationship becomes increasingly complex when a jealous Crofts reveals that Frank and Vivie could be half brother and half sister. This mystery is never resolved.

The Reverend Samuel Gardner, Frank's father, the rector of a church located not far from Vivie's summer cottage. The elder Gardner is another of the gentlemen from Mrs. Warren's past. Their chance meeting proves an embarrassment to the reverend, who struggles to have his son follow his now-respectable example.

Liz, the sister of Mrs. Warren who once shared her profession but who has attained respectability and even high social status through marriage. Her present life is unattractive to Vivie, but Kitty Warren idealizes her. She remains unseen but is much discussed.

Honoria Fraser, Vivie's mentor in the actuarial business. She does not appear onstage, but her influence on Vivie speaks for her.

— Lagretta T. Lenker

MUCH ADO ABOUT NOTHING

Author: William Shakespeare (1564-1616)
First published: 1600
Genre: Drama

Locale: Italy
Time: The thirteenth century
Plot: Comedy

Don Pedro (PEH-droh), the prince of Aragon. A victorious leader, he has respect and affection for his follower Claudio, for whom he asks the hand of Hero. Deceived like Claudio into thinking Hero false, he angrily shares in the painful repudiation of her at the altar. On learning of her innocence, he is deeply penitent.

Don John, the bastard brother of Don Pedro. A malcontent and a defeated rebel, he broods on possible revenge and decides to strike Don Pedro through his favorite, Claudio. He arranges to have Don Pedro and Claudio witness what they think is a love scene between Hero and Borachio. When his evil plot is exposed, he shows his guilt by flight. He is a rather ineffectual villain, though his plot almost has tragic consequences.

Claudio (KLOH-dee-oh), a young lord of Florence. A conventional hero of the sort no longer appealing to theater audiences, he behaves in an unforgivable manner to Hero when he thinks she is faithless; however, she—and apparently the Elizabethan audience—forgives him. He is properly repentant when he learns of her innocence, and he is rewarded by being allowed to marry her.

Benedick (BEHN-eh-dihk), a witty young woman-hater. A voluble and attractive young man, he steals the leading role from Claudio. He spends much of his time exchanging sharp remarks with Beatrice. After being tricked by the prince and Claudio into believing that Beatrice is in love with him, he becomes devoted to her. After Claudio's rejection of Hero, Benedick challenges him, but the duel never takes place. His witty encounters with Beatrice end in marriage.

Hero (HEE-roh), the daughter of Leonato. A pure and gentle girl, and extremely sensitive, she is stunned by the false accusation delivered against her and by Claudio's harsh repudiation of her in the church. Her swooning is reported by Leonato as death. Her character contains humor and generosity. She forgives Claudio when he repents.

Beatrice (BEE-ah-trihs), Hero's cousin. Although sprightly and witty, she has a serious side. Her loyal devotion to Hero permits no doubt of her cousin to enter her mind. She turns to her former antagonist, Benedick, for help when Hero is slandered and insists that he kill his friend Claudio. When all is clear and forgiven, she agrees to marry Benedick, but with the face-saving declaration that she does so for pity only.

Leonato (lee-oh-NAH-toh), the governor of Messina, Hero's father. A good old man, he welcomes Claudio as a prospective son-in-law. He is shocked by the devastating treatment of his daughter at her wedding. Deeply angry with the prince and Claudio, he at first considers trying to kill them but later consents to Friar Francis' plan to humble them. When Hero is vindicated, he forgives them and allows the delayed marriage to take place.

Conrade (KON-rad), a tale-bearing, unpleasant follower of Don John.

Borachio (boh-RAH-kee-oh), another of Don John's followers. He is responsible for the idea of rousing Claudio's jealousy by making him think Hero has received a lover at her bedroom window. He persuades Margaret to wear Hero's gown and pretend to be Hero. His telling Conrade of his exploit is overheard by the watch and leads to the vindication of Hero. Borachio is much disgruntled at being overreached by the stupid members of the watch; however, he confesses and clears Margaret of any willful complicity in his plot.

Friar Francis, a kindly, scheming cleric. He recommends that Hero pretend to be dead. His plan is successful in bringing about the repentance of Don Pedro and Claudio and in preparing the way for the happy ending.

Dogberry, a self-important constable. Pompous, verbose, and full of verbal inaccuracies, he fails to communicate properly with Leonato; hence, he does not prevent Hero's humiliation, though his watchmen already have uncovered the villains.

Verges (VUR-jehs), a headborough. An elderly, bumbling man and a great admirer of his superior, the constable, he seconds the latter in all matters.

Margaret, the innocent betrayer of her mistress, Hero. She does not understand Borachio's plot and therefore is exonerated, escaping punishment.

Ursula (UR-sew-luh), a gentlewoman attending Hero. She is one of the plotters who trick the sharp-tongued Beatrice into falling in love with Benedick.

First Watchman and

Second Watchman, plain, simple-minded men. Overhearing Borachio's boastful confession to Conrade, they apprehend both and take them before the constable, thereby overthrowing clever malice and radically changing the course of events.

Antonio, Leonato's brother. He plays the role of father to Leonato's supposed niece (actually Hero), whom Claudio agrees to marry in place of his lost Hero.

Balthasar (BAL-theh-zahr), an attendant to Don Pedro.

A sexton, who serves as recorder for Dogberry and the watch during the examination of Conrade and Borachio.

MULATA
(Mulata de tal)

Author: Miguel Ángel Asturias (1899-1974)
First published: 1963
Genre: Novel

Locale: Quiavicús and Tierrapaulita, Guatemala
Time: The 1960's
Plot: Symbolism

Celestino Yumí (seh-lehs-TEE-noh yew-MEE), a poor woodcutter whose desires for riches and social position lead him to sell his wife, Catalina, to the corn devil, Tazol. Overwhelmed by passion, he marries the Mulata but cannot endure her. Disenchanted with his life as a rich man, he recovers Catalina and returns to his life as a poor woodcutter. Catalina convinces him to travel to Tierrapaulita so that she can become a great sorcerer. He undergoes several transformations. Catalina turns him into a dwarf and then into a giant. After the slingshot of Tazolín kills him, his body becomes a mountain range. He then represents Candanga. Under the guise of a pockmarked Indian, he accepts the challenge of the priest Chimalpín and becomes a hedgehog to attack him. The priest almost defeats Yumí, but the Mulata saves him. They are married in a Requiem Mass. After he dies in the second Tierrapaulita earthquake, the Mulata acquires his golden bones.

Catalina Zabala (kah-tah-LEE-nah sah-BAH-lah), Yumí's happy, uncomplaining wife. Through Yumí's pact, she is abducted by Tazol. Yumí recovers her, but she is a dwarf. The Mulata treats her like a toy doll. After she imprisons the Mulata, Yumí loses Tazol's favor. Her desire to become a sorcerer takes her and Yumí to Tierrapaulita. She becomes a powerful witch, changing Yumí into a dwarf out of revenge and then into a giant to prevent Huasanga from enjoying his love. She fails to end the Mulata's hold on Yumí's heart. She is buried alive in Tierrapaulita's second earthquake.

The Mulata (mew-LAH-tah), a sensual, wild, and violent creature. Yumí impulsively marries her. Neither male nor female, she refuses to make love to him face to face. She is so destructive and demanding that Yumí tries to kill her. Her escape from imprisonment in the mountain cave precipitates the earthquake that destroys Yumí's possessions. As Cashtoc's representative, she is charged with fighting Candanga's representative, Yumí. When the priest is about to defeat Yumí, she saves him. Witches and wizards imprison her in revenge. With only half of her body, she escapes as a snake. With the cooperation of Tipumal's wife, she recovers the other half of her body. The rays of the moon set her ablaze as she holds the dead Yumí's golden bones.

Huasanga (hwah-SAHN-gah), the dwarf wife of Yumí in the form of Chiltic. Catalina turns Chiltic into a giant so that Huasanga cannot make love to him. Huasanga pursues him anyway and triggers Cashtoc's anger, thereby causing Tierrapaulita's first earthquake. To avenge herself on Catalina, she directs the Mulata to Juan Nojal, who tells her how to recover the rest of her body.

Tazol (tah-SOHL), the corn devil, who covets Yumí's wife. He carries Catalina off in a great wind after Yumí agrees to his pact. So that Yumí can meet the demands of the Mulata, Tazol changes corn leaves into money for him, a practice he stops when the Mulata is imprisoned. Tazol impregnates Catalina through her navel, resulting in the birth of Tazolín.

Cashtoc (KAHSH-tohk), the earth devil of the Indians. The Great, the Immense, he is the lord of the Mayan hell. He vows to destroy all humans who live as egotistical individualists and forget that they are kernels of corn. He destroys Tierrapaulita and abandons it to the Christian devil.

Candanga (kahn-DAHN-gah), the Christian devil. He promotes the repopulation of Tierrapaulita after its destruction by Cashtoc in an earthquake, so that his hell will not lack inhabitants.

Mateo Chimalpín (mah-TEH-oh chee-mahl-PEEN), a priest whose arrival in Tierrapaulita coincides with its abandonment by Cashtoc in favor of Candanga. Chimalpín challenges Candanga for urging the inhabitants of Tierrapaulita to procreate. He is transformed into a spider with eleven thousand arms to battle Candanga with his eleven thousand horns. Yumí becomes a hedgehog and pocks the priest's face. The priest removes the pocks by riding on the Meat-Eating Mule. Chimalpín visits the Child Factory, where he realizes that there are many souls desiring to be born. He then rides through the city urging Tierrapaulita's citizens to breed. He is the only survivor of Tierrapaulita's second earthquake.

Timoteo Teo Timoteo (tee-moh-TEH-oh teh-oh tee-moh-TEH-oh), a friend of Yumí whose riches and good fortune make Yumí envious. Yumí forms a pact with Tazol so that he can be richer than his friend. By having an affair with Catalina, he gives Yumí an excuse to sell her to Tazol.

— *Evelyn Toft*

MUMBO JUMBO

Author: Ishmael Reed (1938-   )
First published: 1972
Genre: Novel

Locale: Harlem in New York City
Time: The 1920's
Plot: Satire

PaPa LaBas, a fifty-year-old black man who is the founder and head of the Mumbo Jumbo Kathedral. He is on a holy quest to find the sacred HooDoo (actually ancient Egyptian) text of the Jes Grew movement, now rumored to be located in New York City. Jes Grew celebrates the life of the body and the spirit in opposition to the life-denying, death-oriented, guilt-

ridden, dominant Judeo-Christian culture. Jes Grew's chief proponents are black, and its chief manifestation is dancing. Jes Grew is opposed by the atonists, whose enforcement branch is the Wallflower Order, which is dedicated to stamping out Jes Grew and, in essence, keeping humankind in mental slavery. Papa LaBas' helpers in the quest to save Jes Grew by rescuing the lost text include several of his Kathedral workers and Black Herman, who is more adept at using HooDoo skills than is Papa LaBas.

Hinckle Von Vampton, a white man who is hundreds of years old; he is PaPa LaBas' main opponent. He is also after the Jes Grew text, but so that he can destroy it. Von Vampton, who has learned the secret of eternal life, is a member of the Knights Templar, the discredited military arm of the Wallflower Order. The sacred text of HooDoo was once in the possession of the Knights Templar, and Von Vampton was the Templars' librarian. He has many schemes to discredit Jes Grew and those possessed by it, including publishing a magazine, *Benign Monster*, and creating a talking black android that will try to convince black people that Jes Grew is evil. Even though Von Vampton appears to defeat PaPa LaBas, at the conclusion of the novel PaPa LaBas has Von Vampton and his main associate, "Safecracker" Gould, sent to Haiti, the home of HooDoo and Jes Grew in the New World, where they will no doubt be dealt with harshly.

Abdul Hamid, a Black Muslim magazine editor. He destroys the sacred text because his religion, Islam, has as many restrictions and rules as Judeo-Christianity, leading him to regard Jes Grew as evil. Von Vampton, unaware that Hamid is unwittingly helping him, murders Hamid in his office.

Berbelang, who originally was a member of the Mumbo Jumbo Kathedral. He leaves PaPa LaBas and strikes out on his own as the leader of the Mu'tafikah, a group of cultural terrorists who try to restore the integrity of art by stealing pieces from art detention centers (museums) and returning them to the cultures from which they were plundered. Berbelang is killed while performing one of his heists.

Biff Musclewhite, nominally the white curator of the center of Art Detention but actually a hired killer for the Wallflower Order. He kills both Berbelang and Charlotte, one of PaPa LaBas' helpers in the search for the sacred text.

Earline, PaPa LaBas' secretary. She helps in the search for the lost Jes Grew text but forgets to feed the loas (spirits) at the Mumbo Jumbo Kathedral. As a result, her body is possessed by a loa, which uses it to seduce a streetcar motorman.

Hubert "Safecracker" Gould, a white agent of the atonists. He helps Von Vampton by disguising himself in blackface and passing himself off as a new black artist (the talking android).

Black Herman, one of PaPa LaBas' helpers. He is able to free Earline from her loa and is more successful in dealing with Jes Grew techniques than PaPa LaBas because he is more flexible and intuitive and is less concerned with theory than with practice.

— *James Baird*

MURDER IN THE CATHEDRAL

Author: T. S. Eliot (1888-1965)
First published: 1935
Genre: Drama

Locale: Canterbury, England
Time: 1170
Plot: Historical

Thomas Becket, the archbishop of Canterbury. Having just returned from France, where he has gained the support of the pope in his attempt to achieve both temporal and spiritual power in England, he finds a mixed reaction among the people. Although some support him, others would gladly see him dead. He is faced with a dilemma that leaves him no alternative but to sin against his faith. After his murder, he achieves martyrdom and sainthood, which his accusers say he was seeking all along.

Three priests of the cathedral, who fear the outcome of Becket's return. They express the pessimism felt by everyone.

The first tempter, who offers worldly pleasure and success.

The second tempter, who offers temporal power through negation of spiritual authority.

The third tempter, who offers the support of a faction wishing to overthrow the throne.

The fourth tempter, who offers martyrdom and eternal glory. Becket denies all the tempters.

Reginald Fitz Urse,

William de Traci,

Hugh de Morville, and

Richard Brito, the knights who murder Becket. They defend their action on the grounds that they will not benefit from their deed, that Becket had refused to acknowledge the king's supremacy, and that he was egotistical to the point of insanity.

The women of Canterbury, who act as the chorus of classical drama.

THE MURDER OF ROGER ACKROYD

Author: Agatha Christie (1890-1976)
First published: 1926
Genre: Novel

Locale: King's Abbot, an English country village
Time: September and October during the early 1920's
Plot: Detective and mystery

Hercule Poirot (pwah-ROH), a famous Belgian detective. A member of the Belgian police before World War I, he entered private practice in Great Britain during the war. Poirot has temporarily retired to King's Abbot and is busily engaged in growing marrows (squash) when he is caught up in the investigation of the murder. He is short and lean, with many man-

nerisms, dyed black hair, an enormous mustache, and a great love of hot chocolate and sweet liqueurs. Many people think lightly of the Belgian when they first meet him. Poirot ignores the slights, however, and puts his complete faith in the "little grey cells" of his brain.

James Sheppard, the local doctor and the narrator of

the action. He is the most important witness to the events that precede the murder and acts as Poirot's aide. The quiet, middle-aged physician is the friend of many of the people directly and indirectly involved in the mystery surrounding his friend Ackroyd's death and so is able to supply Poirot with information about their personalities, and even about some of their medical problems.

Caroline Sheppard, the doctor's elder sister, who lives with him. She is one of the best sources of village gossip, and her brother is always trying to circumvent her curiosity about his medical practice, usually with little success. Caroline is sure of her own opinion about everything, including that everyone in the village, even her beloved brother, has to be watched for his or her own good.

Roger Ackroyd, the murdered man, a middle-aged and very wealthy industrialist. According to Dr. Sheppard, he looked like a beefy local squire from a Victorian melodrama. His fiancée, Mrs. Ferrars, committed suicide the night before his murder. The day of her suicide, she confessed that she had murdered her husband the previous year and had been blackmailed since that time. Wanting to get hold of the blackmailer but afraid of causing publicity, Ackroyd is murdered before he can decide what to do. The letter he had received from the late Mrs. Ferrars is missing from the murder scene.

Captain Ralph Paton, Ackroyd's stepson from his first marriage, a handsome and irresponsible young man who is deeply in debt. He was in town at the time of both the suicide and the murder but had not told his stepfather. Caroline heard someone in the woods with a young woman the day before the murder but was not able to find out that it was Paton. All the circumstantial evidence points to Paton's guilt, and he had also disappeared the night of the murder.

Mrs. Cecil Ackroyd, Roger Ackroyd's impoverished sister-in-law, who subsists on handouts from him. Mrs. Ackroyd disliked her parsimonious brother-in-law and was counting on

his money to set her up in an independent lifestyle. She is not above petty theft, sometimes selling small and valuable items from Ackroyd's house to keep herself in the manner she believes she deserves. Although basically incompetent in all areas, Mrs. Ackroyd assumes she knows best how everyone in the household should run his or her life.

Flora Ackroyd, Mrs. Ackroyd's beautiful daughter. To please her uncle and her mother, she had agreed to marry Paton, even though she is in love with Ackroyd's best friend, Major Blunt, one of the houseguests at the time of the murder. Flora convinces Poirot to come out of retirement and solve the murder, thus clearing Paton. She also claims to have talked to Ackroyd after the time he was probably murdered.

Elizabeth Russell, the latest of Ackroyd's attractive housekeepers, usually in their late thirties or early forties. Caroline and the other scandalmongers were always waiting for one of these housekeepers to marry Ackroyd, and they all presumed Russell to be angry about Ackroyd's relationship with Mrs. Ferrars. Dr. Sheppard is more interested in why the normally very reserved housekeeper had been asking him about poisons the morning before the murder.

Ursula Bourne, Ackroyd's attractive young maid. She is in love with Paton, which caused the angry Ackroyd to fire her the day he was murdered.

Parker, Ackroyd's nervous butler, who had made a fair amount of money blackmailing his previous employer until his death. He is always near the room where Ackroyd met his death but claims to know little of value.

Geoffrey Raymond, Ackroyd's handsome and very efficient young secretary. Although in debt because of heavy betting at the racetrack, and with an incomplete alibi, Raymond is the one member of the Ackroyd household to keep his sense of humor and sense of perspective: He treats the entire experience as a unique adventure.

— *Terrance L. Lewis*

THE MURDERER

Author: Roy A. K. Heath (1926-   )
First published: 1978
Genre: Novel

Locale: Guyana
Time: Sometime between the 1950's and the early 1970's
Plot: Psychological realism

Galton Flood, the "murderer" of the title, a deeply troubled young man who was overprotected and completely controlled by his mother when he was a boy. His life is shaped by the humiliation he suffers at her hands. Although attractive and well liked, Galton is paranoid, excessively cautious, moody, private, and cold. He indulges in fantasies of self-abasement as a child and as an adult is driven to degrade himself. An educated man, he gives up a future in radio repair for a series of security jobs well beneath his capabilities. He moves his wife into a wretched tenement in the worst section of town and feels more at home with the vile characters there than with his own family and friends. He is alternately attracted to and repulsed by women, and his inability to come to terms with his ambivalent feelings leads to the murder of his wife. He finally disintegrates into madness, becoming a familiar figure frequenting the slums of Georgetown, muttering to himself and responding to no one.

Gemma Burrowes Flood, Galton's wife, attractive, well-read, and well-spoken. Her appearance and manner belie the impoverished surroundings in which she was reared by her father. Ambitious, she views Galton as her entrée to a more refined life and idolizes him for the superiority she imagines he possesses. A loyal wife but not subservient enough for Galton, she begins to remind him of his mother, and he destroys her.

Selwyn Flood, Galton's elder brother, a successful druggist and happily married father of two children. He is a self-assured, carefree man with smooth, clear skin and untroubled eyes. The sole executor of his mother's estate, he strives to be scrupulously fair and loyal to Galton, ensuring that he is well looked after.

Winston, a close friend of Galton. He is likable and generous, a family man with a wide circle of friends. A once-successful butcher, though now bankrupt, he remains undefeated by failure. After advising Galton to marry Gemma, he invites the newly married couple to live with his family.

Therphilio Giles, the father of Gemma's illegitimate child, Mr. Burrowes' friend, and the Walk-Man's brother. An unattractive man of about fifty, with graying hair and yellow teeth, he speaks in an educated and persuasive manner. Giles watches Galton the night he revisits the scene of Gemma's murder and later accuses him of the crime.

A. H. Burrowes, Galton's landlord and father-in-law. He is a widower who owns and runs a cake shop and who takes boarders into his home to supplement his income. Desperate to marry off his daughter, he takes in a series of male lodgers hoping to find a husband for her.

The Watchman, a night watchman and friend to Galton. An older man, he acts as confidant to both Galton and Gemma when they move to the tenement. Gemma informs him of her illegitimate child, and Galton confesses his murder to him.

The Walk-Man, a middle-aged man who frequents Mr. Burrowes' cake shop and who is Mr. Giles's brother. An eccentric, the Walk-Man claims that he can deduce a person's char-acter from his walk. His revelation that Mr. Burrowes wants him to marry Gemma brings about Galton's flight to the bush.

Nekka Flood, Selwyn's wife, a good mother, attentive wife, and hard worker. Selwyn adores her, although she has a sharp tongue and often nags him. She resents Galton, and Galton despises her.

Mr. Harris, Galton's neighbor in the tenement. Although Harris is a tough, uneducated, homosexual police informant who has the entire tenement terrorized by his bullying presence, Galton nevertheless feels a kinship with him.

Mildred, Nekka's cousin, who becomes Galton's lover after Gemma's death. She is small and plump, with short dark hair, and she makes few demands on Galton. He is very happy with her until her father ends their relationship.

Mrs. Flood, Galton's mother. A fanatically religious, puritanical woman, she is extremely overprotective of Galton and instills in him a disgust of sex and hatred of women.

Mr. Flood, Galton's father. He is a jovial, sociable man who, under his wife's control, becomes a silent and weak figure.

— *Mary Virginia Davis*

MURPHY

Author: Samuel Beckett (1906-1989)
First published: 1938
Genre: Novel

Locale: Dublin, London, and between these two cities
Time: The 1930's
Plot: Absurdist

Murphy, a former theology student in Cork, Ireland, now living in London. He is inclined to be shy of permanent employment and is attractive to women despite a rather yellow complexion and an unusual wardrobe. He is superstitious and obsessed with astrological signs. He finds his greatest pleasure in rocking back and forth in a chair, bound, naked to the seat. Intelligent despite his seeming aimlessness, prone to minor heart attacks, and happiest in deep contemplation, he is supported, in part, by an uncle, Mr. Quigley, who lives in Holland. He likes the color lemon and things that remind him of other things. He takes a job as a night attendant at the Magdalen Mental Mercyseat, a mental institution on the outskirts of London, to please his lover, Celia Kelly.

Celia Kelly, a young, blond prostitute who falls in love at first sight with Murphy, as he does with her. She finds the work of being a whore dull, although her grandfather, her nearest surviving relative, knows that she is a good girl and will do a good job, however peculiar or improper it might be. She wants to marry Murphy but insists that he get a steady job. Not very intelligent but a pleasant, pretty girl, she quits work when they move in together and concentrates on urging Murphy to take a job.

Miss Counihan, a young woman in love with Murphy, who leaves her behind when he goes to London but promises to send for her. Well endowed, with a lovely mouth and a habit of talking as if in a cheap romance novel, she is determined to be faithful to Murphy until he proves to have abandoned her, despite the fact that he does not correspond with her and seems to have disappeared from her life.

Neary, Murphy's former teacher, who possesses the gift of being able to stop his heart, which he tries to teach Murphy. He falls in love with Miss Counihan after Murphy leaves, but she will have nothing to do with him until he can prove that Murphy has deserted her.

Cooper, Neary's man-of-all-work, industrious but prone to alcoholism. He is short, clean-shaven, and gray-faced, and he has only one eye. He never sits down and never takes off his hat. He finds Murphy in London, then loses him while engaged in a heavy bout of drinking.

Wylie, a former student of Neary, a tiny man who promises to aid Neary in his quest for Miss Counihan, whom he fancies for himself and woos in Neary's absence, with great success.

Miss Carridge, Murphy and Celia's landlady, a worrying, small, thin woman. She has an unpleasant odor about her that she unsuccessfully seeks to alleviate with sample portions of various deodorants. She is somewhat mean but scrupulously honest.

Willoughby Kelly, Celia's grandfather, who spends his time flying his kite when not bedridden. He is completely bald, narrow-faced, and blue-eyed. Celia confides in him, and he admires her considerable gifts. He is not entirely happy when she becomes a whore, but he does not try to talk her out of it. He has a rather peculiar way of reasoning, as do many of the characters in this absurdly comic novel.

Austin Ticklepenny, an Irish poet who knew Murphy in Dublin. He was formerly a heavy drinker but is on the wagon and working in the Magdalen Mental Mercyseat. He fears that the job will drive him mad, and he arranges for Murphy to take over his position at the hospital.

— *Charles Pullen*

MUTINY ON THE BOUNTY

Authors: Charles Nordhoff (1887-1947) and James Norman Hall (1887-1951)
First published: 1932
Genre: Novel

Locale: England, the South Pacific, and Tahiti
Time: Late eighteenth century
Plot: Adventure

Lieutenant William Bligh (bli), captain of HMS *Bounty*; strong, stout, dark-eyed, firm-mouthed, strong-voiced, he is a fanatical disciplinarian and a grafting exploiter of ship's rationing. He is subject to fits of insane rage.

Roger Byam, the narrator, a retired ship's captain, at the time of the mutiny a young midshipman and student of languages who has been assigned the job of making a dictionary of the native dialects. He becomes quartermaster after the mutiny. He is acquitted of all complicity.

Fletcher Christian, master's mate, leader of the mutiny; tall, strong, swarthy, handsome, romantic-looking, resolute, moody. Unable to bear Bligh's tyranny any longer, he takes charge of the ship, casts off Bligh with a group of loyal men in the ship's launch, and becomes the new acting lieutenant, or captain.

George Stewart, midshipman friend of Byam. A non-mutineer who is appointed master's mate after the mutiny, he drowns when the *Pandora* sinks.

Tehani, a tall, beautiful Tahitian girl, daughter of a high chief. She becomes Byam's wife, bears him a daughter, and dies after he is taken to England.

Sir Joseph Banks, a noted scientist and explorer, president of the Royal Society. He is responsible for Byam's assignment as a dictionary maker.

Hitihiti, a chief and high priest, Byam's *taio* (special friend), tall, magnificently proportioned, light-skinned, intelligent, humorous.

Peggy, a chief's daughter, Stewart's wife.

Maimiti, Christian's sweetheart, Hitihiti's niece, handsome, proud, shy. She goes away with Christian on the *Bounty*.

Robert Tinkler, a midshipman whose testimony saves Byam, Muspratt, and Morrison.

Morrison, boatswain's mate, a non-mutineer. He is pardoned.

Muspratt, able seaman, a non-mutineer also pardoned.

Ellison,

Burkitt, and

Millward, able seamen, mutineers who are convicted and hanged.

David Nelson, a botanist in charge of collecting breadfruit trees. He dies at Batavia.

Doctor Hamilton, the kindly doctor on the *Pandora*.

Captain Edwards, captain of the *Pandora*.

MY AMPUTATIONS

Author: Clarence Major (1936-   )
First published: 1986
Genre: Novel

Locale: The United States, Europe, and Africa
Time: The 1980's
Plot: Picaresque

Mason Ellis, an African American male born on December 31, 1936, in Georgia. He has a birthmark on his right forearm in the shape of a mudfrog. Brought up in Chicago, Illinois, he is a school dropout who joined the Air Force, serving in Wyoming and Florida. As a father of six children, he deserts his wife and goes to New York. He had served time in Attica from 1977 to 1978 for possession of drugs. Mason is a writer and takes on the identity of the Author, a noted black writer. Under his assumed identity, Mason receives a grant from the Magnan-Rockford Foundation to deliver lectures at colleges and universities throughout the world. Mason's journey is a series of episodic adventures in which dream and reality mix. He passes from country to country embroiled in bombings, kidnapping, and revolutionary wars. Sometimes he reads from his novel in progress, which is about his past life. As Mason sinks into paranoia, he searches for meaning and identity in a variety of places, ending up in a remote African village.

Chiro Ellis, Mason's father, a dark figure who leaves Mason a complicated legacy. He is the bad man of African American myth, a rebellious wanderer, great dancer, gambler, and lover.

Painted Turtle, a Native American woman who lived on a reservation in New Mexico and worked as an actress and a dancer before meeting Mason in Georgia and heading to New York with him.

Judith Williams, Mason Ellis' wife, who was born in and lives in Chicago and is the mother of their six children. She takes the children and hides out in Chicago, afraid that Mason will lay claim to them.

Edith Levine, a white, college-educated actress who hangs out with gangsters and is a coconspirator with Mason, Jesus, and Brad in the robbery of the Chemical Bank at United Nations Plaza. Edith is also a director and star in underground sex films.

Jesus, who lives in New York and executes a series of crimes with Mason, including breaking and entering, armed robbery, and bank robbery. Jesus ends up in jail for drug possession.

Brad, a criminal friend of Mason. He robs the bank and uses all of his money living the high life in New York. At a crucial point in the story, he searches out Mason's hiding place and demands more money from Mason. Mason decides to leave for Europe.

John Armegurn, the secretary of the Magnan-Rockford Foundation. He is a white man with ashy skin, freckles, and thick red hair on his hands. As the director of Mason's fellowship money, he controls Mason's movements throughout his travels.

Clarence McKay, a black writer. Mason claims that McKay stole his manuscript while both were in prison in Attica. McKay is kidnapped by Mason and put on a train out of town. Mason then assumes the identity of the Author, who may be McKay.

The Author, an unnamed and unspecified African American writer. While in prison, Mason reads the Author's works and convinces himself that he is the Author. Mason masquerades as the Author in travels throughout America, Europe, and Africa.

— *Stephen F. Soitos*

MY ÁNTONIA

Author: Willa Cather (1873-1947)
First published: 1918
Genre: Novel

Locale: Nebraska prairie land
Time: Late nineteenth and early twentieth centuries
Plot: Regional

Ántonia Shimerda, a young immigrant girl of appealing innocence, simple passions, and moral integrity, the daughter of a Bohemian homesteading family in Nebraska. Even as a child, she is the mainstay of her gentle, daydreaming father. She and Jim Burden, the grandson of a neighboring farmer, become friends, and he teaches her English. After her father's death, her crass mother and sly, sullen older brother force her to do a man's work in the fields. Pitying the girl, Jim's grandmother finds work for her as a hired girl in the town of Black Hawk. There, her quiet, deep zest for life and the Saturday night dances lead to her ruin. She falls in love with Larry Donovan, a dashing railroad conductor, and goes to Denver to marry him, but he soon deserts her, and she comes back to Black Hawk, unwed, to have her child. Twenty years later, Jim Burden, visiting in Nebraska, meets her again. She is now married to Cuzak, a dependable, hardworking farmer, and the mother of a large brood of children. Jim finds her untouched by farm drudgery or village spite. Because of her serenity, strength of spirit, and passion for order and motherhood, she reminds him of stories told about the mothers of ancient races.

James Quayle Burden, called **Jim**, the narrator. Orphaned at the age of ten, he leaves his home in Virginia and goes to live with his grandparents in Nebraska. In that lonely prairie country, his only playmates are the children of immigrant families living nearby, among them Ántonia Shimerda, with whom he shares his first meaningful experiences in his new home. When his grandparents move into Black Hawk, he misses the freedom of life on the prairie. Hating the town, he leaves it to attend the University of Nebraska. There, he meets Gaston Cleric, a teacher of Latin who introduces the boy to literature and the greater world of art and culture. From the university, he goes on to study law at Harvard. Aided by a brilliant but incompatible marriage, he becomes the legal counsel for a Western railroad. Successful, rich, but unhappy in his middle years and in the failure of his marriage, he recalls his prairie boyhood and realizes that he and Ántonia Shimerda have in common a past that is all the more precious because it is lost and almost incommunicable, existing only in memories of the bright occasions of their youth.

Mr. Shimerda, a Bohemian farmer unsuited to pioneer life on the prairie. Homesick for the Old World and never happy in his Nebraska surroundings, he finds his loneliness and misery unendurable, lives more and more in the past, and ends by committing suicide.

Mrs. Shimerda, a shrewd, grasping woman whose chief concern is to get ahead in the world. She bullies her family, accepts the assistance of her neighbors without grace, and eventually sees her dream of prosperity fulfilled.

Ambroz Shimerda, called **Ambrosch**, the Shimerdas' older son. Like his mother, he is insensitive and mean. Burdened by drought, poor crops, and debt, he clings to the land with peasant tenacity. Even though he repels his neighbors with his surly manner, sly trickery, and petty dishonesties, everyone admits that he is a hard worker and a good farmer.

Yulka Shimerda, Ántonia's younger sister, a mild, obedient girl.

Marek Shimerda, the Shimerdas' youngest child. Tongue-tied and feebleminded, he is eventually committed to an institution.

Mr. Burden, Jim Burden's grandfather, a Virginian who has bought a farm in Nebraska. Deliberate in speech and action, he is a just, generous man, bearded like an ancient prophet and sometimes speaking like one.

Mrs. Burden, his wife, a brisk, practical woman who gives unstinting love to her orphan grandson. Kindhearted, she gives assistance to the immigrant families of the region, and without her aid the needy Shimerdas would not have survived their first Nebraska winter.

Lena Lingard, the daughter of poor Norwegian parents, from childhood a girl attractive to men. Interested in clothes and possessing a sense of style, she is successful as a designer and later becomes the owner of a dress shop in San Francisco. She and Jim Burden become good friends while he is a student at the University of Nebraska. Her senuous beauty appeals greatly to his youthful imagination, and he is partly in love with her before he goes to study at Harvard.

Tiny Soderball, a young woman who works at the hotel in Black Hawk. She moves to Seattle, runs a sailors' boarding house for a time, and then goes to Alaska to open a hotel for miners. After a dying Swede wills her his claim, she makes a fortune from mining. With a comfortable fortune put aside, she goes to live in San Francisco. When Jim Burden meets her there, she tells him the thing that interests her most is making money. Lena Lingard is her only friend.

Wycliffe Cutter, called **Wick**, a miserly moneylender who has grown rich by fleecing his foreign-born neighbors in the vicinity of Black Hawk. Ántonia Shimerda goes to work for him and his suspicious, vulgar wife. Making elaborate plans to seduce Ántonia, he puts some of his valuables in his bedroom and tells her that she is to sleep there, to guard them, while he and his wife are away on a trip. Mrs. Burden sends her grandson to sleep in the Cutter house, and Wick, returning ahead of his wife, is surprised and enraged to find Jim Burden in his bed. Years later, afraid that his wife's family will inherit his money if he should die first, he kills her and then himself.

Mrs. Cutter, a woman as mean and miserly as her husband, whom she nags constantly. He murders her before committing suicide.

Larry Donovan, a railroad conductor and ladies' man. He courts Ántonia Shimerda, promises to marry her if she will join him in Denver, seduces her, and then goes off to Mexico, leaving her pregnant.

Mrs. Steavens, a widow, the tenant on the Burden farm. She tells Jim Burden, home from Harvard, the story of Ántonia Shimerda's betrayal by Larry Donovan.

Otto Fuchs, the Burdens' hired man during their farming years. Born in Austria, he came to America when a boy and lived an adventurous life as a cowboy, a stage driver, a miner, and a bartender in the West. After the Burdens rent their farm and move into Black Hawk, he resumes his drifting life.

Jake Marpole, the hired man who travels with young Jim Burden from Virginia to Nebraska. Though a kindhearted man, he has a sharp temper and is violent when angry. He is always deeply ashamed if he swears in front of Mrs. Burden.

Christian Harling, a prosperous, straitlaced grain merchant and cattle buyer, a neighbor of the Burden family in Black Hawk.

Mrs. Harling, his wife, devoted to her family and to music. She takes a motherly interest in Ántonia Shimerda, who works for her as a hired girl for a time, but feels compelled to send her away when the girl begins to go to the Saturday night dances attended by drummers and town boys.

Peter and

Pavel, Russian neighbors of the Burden family and Mr. Shimerda's friends. Just before he dies, Pavel tells a terrible story of the time in Russia when, to save his own life, he threw a bride and groom from a sledge to a pack of wolves.

Anton Jelinek, the young Bohemian who makes the coffin for Mr. Shimerda's funeral. He becomes a friend of the Burdens and later a saloon proprietor.

Cuzak, Anton Jelinek's cousin, the sturdy farmer who marries Ántonia Shimerda. Though he has had many reverses in his life, he remains good-natured. Hardworking, dependable, considerate, he is a good husband to Ántonia.

Rudolph,

Anton,

Leo,

Jan,

Anna,

Yulka,

Nina, and

Lucie, Ántonia's children by Cuzak.

Martha, Ántonia's daughter by Larry Donovan. She marries a prosperous young farmer.

Gaston Cleric, the young Latin teacher who introduces Jim Burden to the classics and the world of ideas. When he accepts an instructorship at Harvard, he persuades Jim to transfer to that university.

Genevieve Whitney Burden, Jim Burden's wife. Though she does not figure in the novel, her presence in the background helps to explain her husband's present mood and his nostalgia for his early years in Nebraska. Spoiled, restless, temperamental, independently wealthy, she leads her own life, interests herself in social causes, and plays patroness to young poets and artists.

MY BRILLIANT CAREER

Author: Miles Franklin (1879-1954)
First published: 1901
Genre: Novel

Locale: The Australian bush
Time: The 1890's
Plot: Autobiographical

Sybylla Penelope Melvyn, an Australian adolescent farm girl, the principal character in this fictional autobiography, which describes her life from the ages of fifteen to nineteen. Sybylla is the eldest child of Richard and Lucy Melvyn. Her fierce independence and her brash personality often cause others to misunderstand her. She rebels against the limited opportunities for women in society, and she denounces sexual inequality. She uses her talent for writing to describe the universal dignity of ordinary Australian women, with whom she identifies very closely. Despite her deep friendship for Harold Beecham, she decides against marrying him because of her firm belief that marriage will restrict her freedom and cause her profound unhappiness.

Richard (Dick) Melvyn, Sybylla's father, a cattle rancher and a dairy farmer, first described by Sybylla as a handsome, well-dressed man and a kind father. After their move to the small village of Possum Gulley, he develops a drinking problem. His alcoholism creates severe financial hardships for his family. In Sybylla's opinion, her father seems "to lose all love and interest in his family, and [grows] cross and silent, utterly without pride and pluck."

Lucy Bossier Melvyn, the wife of Richard Melvyn. She enjoyed a very happy childhood and adolescence, and she regrets that she ever married Richard because his irresponsible behavior led her and their children into poverty. Lucy takes out her frustration on her children. Sybylla describes her mother as always ladylike and elegant but as a bitter woman indifferent to the emotional needs of her children. Near the end of the novel, she forces Sybylla to serve as the governess for the M'Swat children because Richard owes the M'Swats money. Working on the M'Swats' filthy farm almost provokes an emotional and physical breakdown in Sybylla.

Grandmother Bossier, a widow, the mother of Lucy Melvyn and Helen Bell. A refined and warm woman, she invites Sybylla to live with her and Helen at Caddagat, a picturesque Australian farm. She thus frees Sybylla from the oppressive situation in Possum Gulley. She strives to make Sybylla happy, but she does not understand Sybylla's adamant opposition to marriage.

Helen Bossier Bell, a middle-aged woman who was married to Colonel Bell, who took her to America and there left her for another woman. She returned to Caddagat to live with her mother. Despite mistreatment by her selfish former husband, she never becomes bitter toward men. She treats Sybylla kindly and is the only person in whom Sybylla has complete trust.

Harold Augustus (Harry) Beecham, a handsome young bachelor who owns the large Five-Bob Downs farm near Caddagat. He is quite rich and is a close friend of Grandmother Bossier and Helen Bell. This reserved but considerate man wishes to marry Sybylla, whose freedom he fully respects. He first loses and then regains his wealth. He twice proposes to Sybylla, but she cannot bring herself to marry him. After her second refusal, Harold leaves Australia and travels extensively in a vain search for happiness.

Everard Grey, the adopted son of Grandmother Bossier, a successful lawyer in Sydney. Soon after Sybylla's arrival in Caddagat, he visits the Bossier family and tries to encourage Sybylla's interest in music and the theater. Although she enjoys her conversations with him, Sybylla finally concludes that he has treated her condescendingly. She refuses to marry him.

After this rejection, the vain Everard Grey never returns to Caddagat.

Frank Hawden, a farmhand to the Bossier family, from a well-to-do English family. He truly loves Sybylla, but because of his lack of sophistication she refuses to marry him. Unlike Everard, Frank continues to treat Sybylla with great respect.

Mr. and Mrs. Peter M'Swat, rich but uncultured and slovenly farmers. Sybylla grudgingly agrees to serve as the governess to their children because her father owes the M'Swats five hundred pounds. Their complete lack of refinement, the cruelty of their son Peter, Jr., and the filth of their farm in Barney's Gap drive Sybylla to the brink of a physical breakdown. The doctor who examines her persuades the M'Swats to release Sybylla from her obligation to them. Her painful experiences on the M'Swat farm convince Sybylla that nothing is more important than personal dignity and freedom.

— Edmund J. Campion

MY DINNER WITH ANDRÉ: A Screenplay

Authors: Wallace Shawn (1943-   ) and André Gregory (1934-   )
First published: 1981
Genre: Drama

Locale: New York City
Time: Late 1970's
Plot: Play of ideas

Wally, played in the 1981 film by Wallace Shawn, who meets André Gregory for dinner after not communicating with him for several years. A thirty-six-year-old playwright and actor who grew up in wealthy circumstances on the Upper East Side of New York, he has lived in the city all of his life. As a youth, he was obsessed with art and music, but as an adult, he has become very concerned with money as well. Once a teacher of Latin, he has been living with Debby, his girlfriend, for some time. Wally has only reluctantly agreed to meet with André, because he is uncomfortable with the possibility that he may have to counsel his troubled acquaintance. Because he has an incurable interest in human foibles, he decides that finding out as much as possible about André will permit him to make the most of the evening. During the course of their conversation, however, he becomes more of a contributor than an interrogator, commenting on André's observations and offering some of his own. Compared with André, Wally is a nonmeditative skeptic who loves simple material comforts that insulate him from an abrasive world. He provides narration both before and after the dinner.

André Gregory, played by André Gregory, a man born on May 11, 1934. Highly acclaimed as the director of The Manhattan Project theatrical company, he "discovered" Wally and produced his play *Our Late Night*. Also well regarded as a devoted husband and father, he suddenly dropped out of the theater in the mid-1970's to travel around the world. Over the ensuing years, he experienced a number of epiphanies in diverse surroundings. With his friend, Polish theater director Jerzy Grotowski, he participated in theatrical improvisations in Poland, both in a forest and in the city of Warsaw, that led to personal catharses and a feeling that he had learned what it meant to be truly alive. Later, he worked on a production of *The Little Prince* with two actors and a Buddhist priest in the Sahara, experienced hallucinations on more than one occasion, and lived in Findhorn in Scotland, a community where people address their appliances by name and also converse with plants and insects. After participating in a mock live burial at Richard Avedon's property in Montauk, Long Island, he lost his interest in self-discovery rituals and began to contemplate a return to directing. Although he is fearful of death in general and cancer in particular, he disdains attitudes, including conventional career ambitions, that skirt such troubling matters. Unlike Wally, he feels that even the slightest comforts afforded by modern technology estrange people from reality. For André, every moment ought to be viewed as sacred and full of emotion. Not long before he meets Wally for dinner, a mutual friend sees him crying in response to Ingmar Bergman's *Autumn Sonata*.

A waiter, played by Jean Lenauer, who serves Wally and André their meal. His face shows that he is familiar with the woes of the world.

An intense young woman, a figure wearing braids and a headband who appears alongside André in a photograph taken in the forest in Poland. Polish but nicknamed with an Indian name, she works in a Russian restaurant in London around the time that Wally and André dine together.

— David Marc Fischer

MY HEART AND MY FLESH

Author: Elizabeth Madox Roberts (1886-1941)
First published: 1927
Genre: Novel

Locale: Anneville, Kentucky
Time: Early twentieth century
Plot: Poetic

Theodosia Bell, the roan-haired, beautiful daughter of Horace and the granddaughter of Anthony. As a female child reared in the South (Kentucky), she is groomed for a life of comfort and privilege. Because her grandfather excelled at playing the violin, Theodosia becomes a student of the same instrument. Her need for personal achievement is satisfied as she becomes an accomplished musician. She is frustrated, however, that she has not inherited her grandfather's hands, and she finds that this lack limits her potential as a violinist. When her mother dies, Theodosia is required to nurse her ailing grandfather. He is, at times, delirious, and calls out the names of persons whom Theodosia does not know. Seeking enlightenment, she reads his personal papers, in which she learns that she is the half sister of Americy Froman, Lethe Ross, and the stable boy, Stiggins, all three of whom are of mixed race. Because of her conditioning, Theodosia is repulsed by this information, but she cannot resist a need to learn more about these people, whom she has known all of her life but has regarded as inferior. She seems destined to be alone when her grandfather dies and her father, whose incestuous advances she has managed to avoid, abandons her. In the end, after contracting tuberculosis and nearly starving to death, she shows her inner strength when she overcomes the speculation and rumors about her past and is accepted as a member of her new community. She is aided by Caleb Burns's declaration of love for her.

Horace Bell, Theodosia's irresponsible father. He has fathered children by women other than his wife—women not of his own race—and has done little, if anything, to bring comfort to any of them. His long-suffering wife is well aware of his activities, which he makes no effort to hide. The prosperity and respectability of his ancestors, rather than his own achievements, are the basis for his position in the community. When his father dies, leaving everything to Theodosia, he joins a law firm in another town and has his daughter send him his belongings.

Anthony Bell, Theodosia's grandfather, a onetime schoolteacher, scholar, and musician. He is intermittently ill but instills in his granddaughter a love of books and music. He has lost the family fortune through bad judgment.

Americy Froman, a mulatto half sister of Theodosia. She is afraid of Theodosia's attempt at friendship, which, although she is aware that they have the same father, she does not understand. She loves to sing, and her desire to learn gradually overcomes her fear of friendship with Theodosia, who promises to teach Americy chords on the guitar in exchange for laundry services.

Lethe Ross, a mulatto half sister of Theodosia. Openly suspicious, Lethe is even less eager than Americy to respond to Theodosia's overtures. The two establish a brief bond, however, when each realizes that the other's betrayal by a man has forced her into a different type of sisterhood.

Stiggins, the mulatto half brother of Theodosia. Stiggins is retarded. He lives in the public stable, where he is abused and made to do the meanest of chores in exchange for a bed in the straw and bits of bad food. Theodosia is dismayed to recognize that Stiggins is the inheritor of her grandfather's violinist hands. Americy and Stiggins, in spite of Theodosia's warnings, enter into an incestuous relationship.

Conway Brooke, a good-looking man, confident and at ease with himself. Theodosia delights in him, and, though he seems uncommitted to anything, he is her favorite suitor. She tries to please him. He dies in a house fire.

Albert Stiles, a broad, strong student of agriculture and a tobacco farmer. He pursues Theodosia and tells her that he will have her by a certain deadline. When she most needs him after their mutual friend, Conway, dies, he abandons her in favor of another woman.

Frank Railey, a scholarly, rugged-looking, predictable law student. Sure that he can have her, he uses Theodosia when she is most vulnerable.

Caleb Burns, a man who raises excellent registered shorthorn cattle. He is intelligent but not bookish, earnest but not wealthy, guileless, and forthcoming. He loves Theodosia from the moment he first sees her in a peddler's cart.

— P. R. Lannert

MY LIFE IN THE BUSH OF GHOSTS

Author: Amos Tutuola (1920-1997)
First published: 1954
Genre: Novel

Locale: Nigeria
Time: Primarily mid-twentieth century
Plot: Psychological symbolism

The narrator, a seven-year-old boy fleeing a slaver army. He takes refuge in the bush near a fruit tree, thus inadvertently entering the Bush of Ghosts. Driven deeper into this Otherworld by the sound of the slavers' guns, he begins years of picaresque, shape-shifting adventures involving bizarre "ghosts" that are nonhuman beings, many of whom have magical attributes.

The Super Lady, a shape-shifter from Nameless-town, where only women live. Her mother is the head of all earthly and ghostly witches, and her father is the head of all wizards. She appears first to the narrator as an antelope, then as a "ghostess" to whom the narrator is greatly attracted. She becomes his second, and only important, ghostly wife. After four years, affection fades, and she sends him on his way wearing only the animal skin that he had when he met her.

The Flash-eyed Mother, the huge-bodied cult leader of the Short Ghosts of the thirteenth town. The eyes in her one large head, as well as those in the millions of "baby-like" heads that appear all over her body, flash and shine constantly. She and her heads consume most of the meat brought into town by hunters.

The Invisible and Invincible Pawn, the son of the Flash-eyed Mother. He aids her when she declares war on the River Ghosts, who demand the return of the narrator. When the narrator's head is cut off, the Pawn replaces it with a ghost head, which causes mischief by betraying the narrator's every thought.

The Television-handed Ghostess, who is covered by sores and is able to show the narrator in the palm of one hand what his mother and brother are doing in the human world. In return for his curing her sores, she uses her magical hand to teleport him back to the fruit tree where he entered the Bush of Ghosts.

Ghosts of the ninth town, short and fat creatures, each with one moon-shaped eye. They rub the narrator with "sandpaper" hands until he becomes a body in a tall pitcher from which only his long neck and his head protrude.

The Smelling Ghost, the excretion-covered, rotting, pest-infested king of the seventh town. He plucks the narrator from a controversy between ghosts who wish to "acquire" him and pops him into his noisome, blood-encrusted bag to be eaten later. He later turns the narrator into various useful animals before the narrator finally escapes in the shape of a cow.

The Homeless Ghost, who picks up the log in which the narrator and a snake are sheltering and takes it to the town of homeless ghosts. When the ghost taps the log, the snake coils, the narrator cries out in terror, and the ghosts dance as to music. When the narrator's voice fails, the ghost splits the log to investigate, and the narrator escapes.

The Chief Ancestor, the leader of the River Ghosts, who brings the narrator in his pitcherlike form to their underwater town as an oracle. The Chief Ancestor interprets the esoteric sounds given off by the narrator, who is increasingly more intoxicated by the fumes of the tobacco pipe that has been put into his mouth. His resultant renditions of human songs attract the attention of the king of the Bush of Ghosts, necessitating a journey to the king's town.

The dead cousin, a cousin of the narrator, the first non-ghost encountered in the Bush of Ghosts. With the permission of the king of the Bush of Ghosts, he has introduced Christianity in the form of the "Methodist Church of the Bush of Ghosts." Like most residents of the Bush, he tries, unsuccessfully, to retain the narrator in his town.

The brother, the narrator's brother, separated from him while fleeing the slavers, now a successful farmer and a slave owner. With their mother, he attends a séance and sends a message to his brother asking him to return. Later, he unwittingly owns the narrator as a slave until they recognize each other.

The son, the son of the narrator and the Super Lady, who causes their disaffection by his resemblance to both ghosts and human beings. Prodigious growth makes him king of a town at the age of four and one-half. In this capacity, he hosts his father.

— James L. Hodge

MY MICHAEL
(Mikha'el sheli)

Author: Amos Oz (1939-)
First published: 1968
Genre: Novel

Locale: Jerusalem, Israel
Time: 1950-1960
Plot: Psychological realism

Michael Gonen, the title character, born in 1926. He is a third-year geology student at the Hebrew University in Jerusalem at the beginning of the novel, in 1950. Ten years later, when the novel ends, he is a relatively promising academic with his doctoral thesis just completed. A decent, diligent, unimaginative young man for whose academic success his father and aunts have great hopes, Michael falls in love with Hannah Greenbaum almost on first sight. She describes him as angular bodied with a long, lean, and dark face, gray eyes, short hair, and strong hands. They marry after a brief courtship and begin life together in an old apartment in northwestern Jerusalem's Mekor Baruch neighborhood. He proves to be a devoted father to Yair and a dutiful husband to Hannah, although he is not good at either communicating or fathoming feelings. By the end of the novel, his hair is beginning to gray, his chronic heartburn is worse, and his wife, Hannah, is expecting their second child.

Hannah Greenbaum Gonen, the first-person narrator, born in 1930. She is the protagonist of this "journal," which she is writing after ten years of marriage to Michael. Her father, Yosef, whom she loved more than anyone else in her life, died of cancer when she was thirteen years old. She falls in love with Michael while she is a first-year student of literature at Hebrew University, and they marry within months. Once she becomes pregnant, she abandons her studies. After a difficult pregnancy and a birth with complications that leaves her ill for a while, Hannah finds her life fraught with bouts of anxiety, depression, and dreams that impede her ability to cope with everyday events. She suffers from a chronic sore throat and a recurrent loss of voice. She often spends money "hysterically" on unneeded items. She finds their apartment and the city of her birth oppressive. The promises of a new apartment in a new suburb in 1961 and a new child to be born in 1960 do nothing to assuage her sense of the sameness of days and the irrevocable loss of her youthful power of loving.

Yair Zalman Gonen, Michael and Hannah's son, born in March, 1951. From infancy, with his broad healthy face, high cheekbones, and gray eyes, he resembles Hannah's brother Emanuel. A strong, silent, bright child with a good memory, Yair seems cold, violent, and sullenly insolent to Hannah. He often comes home from play showing marks of fisticuffs. Yair gets along well with Michael, who never administers corporal punishment to him. A teacher describes him as lacking sensitivity.

Yehezkel Gonen, Michael's father. He dies in the summer of 1955 only days after Michael, Hannah, and Yair visit him for six days in Holon. From Poland and with four sisters in Israel, he had changed his surname from Ganz to Gonen. At the time of the novel, he is a retired municipal water department employee on a modest pension, a vegetarian, a member of the Labor Movement, and an active participant in the local branch of the Workers' Party. A father who always had dreams of academic success for his only child, Michael, he never remarried after the death of his wife, Tova, which occurred when Michael was three years old. During the 1955 family visit, he gets along famously with his grandson, Yair.

Yoram Kamnitzer, the teenage son of the Gonens' upstairs neighbors. He occasionally looks after Yair when Hannah and Michael go out. He shows Hannah his poems and seems smitten by her. When he is seventeen and she twenty-seven, she unsuccessfully pressures him for a verbal declaration of his infatuation. When he publishes a love poem describing a love similar to that of Potiphar's wife for the chaste Joseph, his scandalized Orthodox parents and school officials send him away to an Orthodox kibbutz high school. Eventually, the Kamnitzer family leaves for a new apartment in a Tel Aviv suburb. Yoram has given up poetry and is likely to become a Bible and Hebrew teacher after university studies, a probability that Hannah considers a final defeat for herself.

Emanuel Greenbaum, Hannah's brother, a robust man with unruly hair. He lives with his wife, Rina, their son, Yosi, and his mother, Malka, at Kibbutz Nof Harim in Upper Galilee. His house overlooks the kibbutz fence, which also serves as a border between Israel and Lebanon. At Hannah's wedding, Emanuel displays good-hearted boisterousness, along with discomfiture in the company of university people. Hannah, Michael, and Yair spend Passover at the kibbutz in 1959.

Dr. Jenia Ganz-Crispin, one of Michael's four paternal aunts. A pediatrician in Tel Aviv, she generously helps her nephew's family but is stern and old-fashioned in the process. For example, she chastises Hannah for getting pregnant so soon after marriage, which she fears will impede Michael's academic progress. She also quarrels with Hannah's mother over where Yair's crib should be placed when mother and son come home from the hospital. Aunt Jenia's first marriage ended when her gynecologist husband ran away with another woman. Her second husband is an actor who suffers a nervous breakdown, after which she has to care for him for years. After Mr. Glick dies, she arranges a place for Mrs. Glick at a nursing home with which she is associated.

Halil and

Aziz, Hannah's childhood Arab playmates who figure in her later dreams and fantasies. Hannah recalls building a snowman of the British High Commissioner with them in the winter of 1941. She also remembers that she was able to order the two boys around. The boys, to whom Hannah refers together as "Halziz," may tangentially represent the Arab threat to Israel, but directly they represent for Hannah a childhood in which she had some control and a significant role, in contrast with adult life, in which she feels that she has neither. Hannah recalls having wished as a child that she was a boy and not a girl. The novel ends with a fantasy of a successful commando raid that Halil and Aziz carry out at Hannah's command.

Yardena, a tall, blonde, green-eyed, heavy-lipped geology classmate of Michael when he meets Hannah. Yardena, who

calls Michael a genius, later comes to him for help with examinations and her thesis. Hannah resents her bold ways and sexy appearance and senses Michael's attraction to her when he goes to her apartment in early 1959 to oversee her typing of his doctoral thesis.

Hadassah and

Abba, Hannah's best friend and her husband, an up-and-coming civil servant in the Ministry of Trade and Industry. They put their maid, Simcha, at Hannah's disposal when Dr. Urbach prescribes rest for Hannah after the birth of Yair. Abba later accepts a position in Switzerland as an Israeli economic attaché. At their departure, Hannah cries. Hadassah tells her, "You'll reach your goal." Hannah's thought, however, is "Is it possible that everyone except me has come to terms with time . . . and achievement?"

Avraham Kadishman, the owner of a well-known shoe store. At Aunt Leah's request, he made inquiries about Hannah and her family before Hannah and Michael married. A widower, he becomes a regular visitor to their apartment to play chess with Michael. When he dies in May, 1957, of a kidney disease, he leaves his books to the Gonens.

Mr. Glick, the owner of a haberdashery and an upstairs neighbor to Michael and Hannah. His wife, Duba, is institutionalized for hysteria. Subsequently, after discovering Michael's interest in stamps, he offers his collection to Michael in exchange for permission to visit their apartment to read articles in *Encyclopaedia Hebraica*. His wife, formerly a full-bodied, sensuous woman, returns home from the hospital apathetic and submissive. After Mr. Glick's death in 1959, she takes up residence at a private nursing home.

Dr. Urbach, of Alfandani Street, the polite and solicitous Gonen family physician. A tiny man with a sad and sympathetic look in his eyes, he prescribes rest for Hannah after Yair's birth and later treats Hannah for her sore throat, loss of speech, and nervous condition. At one point, he prescribes that she not talk. After his death in the winter of 1959, Hannah reports that her new doctor is unable to discern any reason for her symptoms.

Aunt Leah Ganz, one of Michael's four paternal aunts. Michael and Hannah stay at her Tel Aviv apartment for a five-day summer holiday in 1958. One day on the beach, Hannah tears Michael's shirt and scratches his face. In response to Aunt Leah's questions about his appearance, Michael says that he had an altercation with thugs.

— *Michael Craig Hillmann*

MY NAME IS ASHER LEV

Author: Chaim Potok (1929-   )
First published: 1972
Genre: Novel

Locale: Crown Heights, Brooklyn, New York
Time: The 1950's and 1960's
Plot: Domestic realism

Asher Lev, a young Hasidic Jew who becomes a famous artist. Asher Lev's name is not unusual, but everything else about the protagonist of this book is. Asher begins his story as a defense of himself and his art, especially of his most notorious painting, *Brooklyn Crucifixion*. He wants to make it clear that he is not the traitor to his culture and religious beliefs that many, including his parents, have accused him of being. Asher explains the long and painful process that has led him from

being a good boy in the ultra-orthodox Hasidic Jewish community of Brooklyn to the artist in exile that he is as a young man. From earliest childhood, Asher's compulsion to draw and paint has set him against his father and his sect; art is not a suitable Hasidic profession. Although his family and community love him, they do not understand Asher, and he grows further and further away from them. When his talent is so great that even his own leaders must recognize it, his painting earns

Asher no peace, only progressive estrangement from the world that he loves. The tone of Asher's tale is largely that of pain and regret, but he makes it clear that he carries the knowledge that his path is the right one, that he is doing what he must do. An interesting component of Asher's personality is his self-absorption, absolute immersion in his art that is so often a hallmark of greatness.

Aryeh Lev, Asher's father. Aryeh is a good and caring man, devoted to his religion and the Hasidic community worldwide. For much of his life he travels, trying to save Soviet Jews from Joseph Stalin and to strengthen Hasidic groups in war-torn Europe. He is kind to his wife, although he must leave her for long periods of time, and he sincerely loves his son. Aryeh's life is the preservation of Jewish tradition, tradition that Asher's art threatens to destroy. When forced to choose between encouraging the individual genius of his son and supporting the values of Hasidism, it is inevitable that Aryeh will turn away from Asher.

Rivkeh Lev, Asher's mother. Rivkeh is a devout woman and a good wife and mother, traditional and homebound in many ways. At the novel's beginning, she suffers a serious nervous collapse over the untimely death of her brother. She recovers, however, and grows through the story as she attends college and takes over her brother's Hasidic work. Rivkeh is far more sympathetic to Asher's gift than is his father, buying him paints and taking him to forbidden museums. Rivkeh is torn between the demands of her husband and those of her son; her pain is the subject of the painting *Brooklyn Crucifixion*.

The Ladover Rebbe, the leader of Asher's Hasidic sect. The Rebbe has absolute power over the lives of his followers, including Asher. He has the wisdom to understand the magnitude of Asher's talent, and although he does not encourage his undertaking, he arranges for Asher to study under the greatest living Jewish artist.

Jacob Kahn, Asher's teacher. Kahn is a great Jewish sculptor and painter and recognizes that Asher's greatness will surpass his own. He is moody and unpredictable, but he teaches Asher much—both about art and about the emotional price paid by the artist who is true to his work.

— *Evelyn Romig*

MY SON'S STORY

Author: Nadine Gordimer (1923-   )
First published: 1990
Genre: Novel

Locale: South Africa
Time: Approximately the 1980's
Plot: Social realism

Sonny, a colored man who admires William Shakespeare. He is a schoolteacher turned social activist. Fighting to end apartheid in South Africa, he is arrested, tried, and jailed for two years. While in jail, he is visited by Hannah, a representative from a human rights organization. Although he has a nearly flawless family with a wife and two children, he begins a prolonged and passionate affair with Hannah. The affair has a profound impact on his family and eventually on his credibility in the freedom movement.

Aila, Sonny's wife, a beautiful and dignified woman. Reticent, reserved, gentle-tempered, and apparently uncontentious, she becomes a revolutionary without her husband's and her son's knowledge, perhaps partly because of Sonny's affair. Implicated and arrested when a cache of weapons is found in her house, she jumps bail and goes into exile to join her daughter in Lusaka.

Baby, Sonny's favorite child, apparently carefree and flamboyant. She attempts suicide for no significant reason other than her knowledge of Sonny's affair. She later marries a freedom fighter and goes into exile in Lusaka. She maintains close ties with her mother, thus contributing to her becoming a revolutionary.

Will, named after Shakespeare, is the sarcastic narrator of the story. An intelligent young man, he is disillusioned by the discovery that his father is having an affair with a white woman. He is manipulated by Sonny into keeping the secret, though he resents doing so. Having witnessed the transformation of his family under apartheid, he becomes a writer in the end.

Hannah Ploughman, a divorced woman, is a white South African working for an international human rights group. Admiring Sonny, she falls in love with him and becomes his mistress and comrade. When offered a senior position by the United Nations High Commission for Refugees, she decides to leave South Africa and Sonny.

— *Balance Chow*

MYRA BRECKINRIDGE

Author: Gore Vidal (1925-   )
First published: 1968
Genre: Novel

Locale: Hollywood, California
Time: 1968
Plot: Social realism

Myra Breckinridge (MI-rah BREHK-ehn-ridj), the novel's protagonist, who believes that the highest contemporary art form is the television commercial. She inherits her dead husband's half share in an acting academy when she is twenty-seven years old. Myra's co-owner of the academy, Buck Loner, her dead husband's uncle, tries to force himself sexually upon Myra, but she considers him repulsive. Myra represents the "New Woman," asserting that contemporary woman

is living at the beginning of the age of "Women Triumphant, of Myra Breckinridge." Myra is less self-assured than her outward demeanor suggests. An anger seethes within her. She sets as her goal to use "men the way they once used women." To this end, she humiliates Rusty Godowsky, unaware that he relishes the humiliation she visits upon him. Finally, however, when Myra is involved in an automobile accident, her hormonal balance is upset, her breasts disappear, and she sprouts a beard. Then, in a surrealistic turn, it is revealed that Myra is actually Myron, her supposedly dead husband, a homosexual, who did not commit suicide by jumping off the Staten Island Ferry after all, but who changed sexes and passed himself off as the lusty widow.

Buck Loner, Myra's co-owner of the acting academy and her supposedly dead husband's uncle. He has deteriorated from the man who made eighteen low-budget westerns, an accomplishment that Myra admires, to an overweight, oversexed, disgusting old man who continually tries to bed Myra. Loner provides details about his nephew's homosexuality and about Myron's career as a film critic. He employs a private agency to explore Myra's right to inherit his nephew's share in the academy and discovers that the inheritance is legitimately hers. In the end, Buck's former lover, Letitia, becomes intrigued by Myra and her relationship to Mary-Ann Pringle, a student in the acting academy.

Mary-Ann Pringle, an attractive lesbian studying in Myra's acting academy, who is having a relationship with her fellow student, Rusty Godowsky, a macho, all-American type, whom Myra humiliates to the point of destroying his relationship with Mary-Ann.

Letitia Van Allen (leh-TEE-shah), Buck Loner's former lover, an agent, who becomes Myra's friend. Letitia confesses to Myra that she has bedded every stud in town who aspires to become an actor and asks Myra if this shocks her. Myra, demonstrating her "Woman Triumphant" disposition, applauds Letitia for using men as men have traditionally used women.

Rusty Godowsky (RUS-tee go-DOW-skee), a handsome, macho student in the academy, Mary-Ann Pringle's boyfriend until Myra's interference. Myra rapes Rusty with a dildo, then forces him to enroll in the posture class she is teaching. As a preliminary to referring him to a physician on account of a spinal problem she has detected, Myra gives Rusty a physical examination, which requires him to strip. She invades his rectum with a thermometer and interrogates him about his sex life. She manipulates his private parts before performing what she refers to as "the final rite," a sexual experience that brings him to climax. She remains unaware that Rusty enjoys this humiliating experience.

Dr. Randolph Spenser Montag, Myra's psychoanalyst, to whom she refers as her "analyst, friend, and dentist." As part of her therapy with Montag, Myra records her astonishing history as she develops into what she terms a "New Woman."

— *R. Baird Shuman*

MYSTERIES
(Mysterier)

Author: Knut Hamsun (Knut Pedersen, 1859-1952)
First published: 1892
Genre: Novel

Locale: A small Norwegian coastal town
Time: 1891
Plot: Psychological realism

Johan Nilsen Nagel (YOH-hahn NIHL-sehn NAH-gehl), a mysterious traveler who stays for a few summer weeks in a small port on the west coast of Norway. He is rather short in stature, with broad shoulders and a strange expression in his eyes. Although he is only twenty-nine years old, his hair is beginning to turn gray. He seems nonchalant, but he is remarkably inquisitive and often behaves impulsively. When he has drunk too much, he is capable of seemingly endless tirades on many subjects. In spite of his extreme eccentricity and his belief that he is hopelessly alienated from the ordinary life of most people, he is capable of great kindness, generosity, and even bravery. Once, in fact, he risked death to save someone from drowning and received a medal, though in one conversation he says that he bought it. This tendency to tell different versions of the truth to different auditors is characteristic. Even his name is not certain: A former lover who visits him briefly in the town calls him Simonsen. Apparently he possesses a substantial inheritance, but he says on one occasion that he has very little money. He claims to be an agronomist by profession who has traveled widely in the world and has recently been in Finland, and he says that he is himself a Finn, but none of this may be true. He carries a violin case, but it contains only dirty linen, and he at first says that he cannot play the violin; later, he does play and is applauded by his audience. He falls obsessively in love with Dagny Kielland, but he also shows an early interest in Martha Gude and proposes marriage to her when Dagny rejects him. Although he tells one character that he lacks the courage to kill himself, and

although he often takes a euphoric pleasure in life, he always carries a vial of poison and does finally drown himself. He calls himself "a philosopher who has never learned to think"; he believes in the Nietzschean superman. He is contemptuous of liberalism and parliamentary democracy, and he condemns free thought and defends religion as a source of symbolism. He believes, in other words, in belief itself, rather than in a particular creed.

Johannes Grøgaard (yoh-HAHN-ehs GREH-gohr), who is called **the Midget** by the people of the town. Although he is a member of a family that included one of the authors of the Norwegian constitution, he is poor and earns his living making deliveries for his coal-dealer uncle. He is forty-three years old, short in stature (though not actually a midget), gray-haired, unattractive, and crippled by a hernia, which he sustained in a fall from a mast when he was a sailor. Forced to perform humiliating feats for the town's bullies, he is defended by Nagel and later saves Nagel's life by substituting water for the poison that Nagel always carries in his pocket. He is unselfish, kindhearted, and even noble. Nagel alone realizes that he once behaved dishonorably with Martha Gude.

Dagny Kielland (DAHG-neh CHEHL-ahnd), a pastor's daughter. A twenty-three-year-old blond with blue eyes and fair skin, she is pretty and even voluptuous. She is engaged to marry a young naval officer who is the son of a wealthy shipowner. When she rejects Nagel's declaration of love, he accuses her, accurately, of being the victim of her bourgeois upbringing.

Martha Gude (MAHR-teh GEWD-eh), a woman to whom Nagel proposes marriage. She is forty-one years old, and although her father captained a merchant ship, she is now forced to eke out an impoverished existence selling eggs in the marketplace. With her prematurely gray hair (caused, Nagel believes, by suffering) and her black eyes and eyebrows, she possesses a strange and exotic beauty. She is strictly honest and shy; to Nagel, she seems nunlike.

— *Robert L. Berner*

THE MYSTERIES OF PARIS
(Les Mystères de Paris)

Author: Eugène Sue (1804-1857)
First published: 1842-1843
Genre: Novel

Locale: France and Germany
Time: Mid-nineteenth century
Plot: Melodrama

Rodolph (roh-DOHLF), the grand duke of Gerolstein, a small German state. The hero of this intricately plotted romance, Rodolph as a youth was forced into a secret morganatic marriage with a beautiful and sinister woman. His father had the marriage annulled; in the resultant quarrel the, son threatened the father's life and was exiled. His infant daughter was afterward reported dead. Now duke, he roams the streets of Paris in disguise. He befriends an unfortunate girl who, he discovers much later, is his daughter. Father and daughter are reunited after much misfortune occasioned primarily by the scheming mother, who comes to a well-deserved end. Rodolph then marries a woman he has long loved and returns to Germany with his wife and daughter.

Fleur-de-Marie (flewr deh mah-REE), Rodolph's daughter. Brought up by criminals who forced her into crime, she is recognized as good and really innocent by Rodolph. Kidnapped and nearly murdered as a result of her mother's intrigues, she is at last reunited with her father, happily for a time. Her early evil life preys on her mind, however, and she enters a convent. So perfect is her conduct that she is immediately made abbess. This honor is too much for her gentle soul and weak body, and she dies that very night.

Lady Sarah Macgregor, Rodolph's morganatic wife. Ambitious and sinister, she turns her infant over to her lawyer, who reports the child dead. Later, when Rodolph is duke, she asks the lawyer to find a girl to pose as her daughter, for she thinks that this action on her part might possibly result in a reconciliation. After many intrigues, she is stabbed by a criminal hired in her behalf. Rodolph remarries her on her deathbed to legitimatize Fleur-de-Marie.

Clémence d'Harville (klay-MAHNS dahr-VEEL), who is unhappily married to one of Rodolph's friends. She is the intended victim of one of Lady Sarah's plots. Clémence is saved from further unhappiness by her epileptic husband's thoughtful suicide, faked as an accident, by which he atones for the evil he committed in marrying her. Independently of Rodolph, Clémence too befriends Fleur-de-Marie. After Lady Sarah's death, she and Rodolph marry.

Jacques Ferrand (zhahk feh-RAH[N]), a hypocritical and thoroughly evil lawyer, hired by Lady Sarah first to get rid of her daughter and later to find a substitute for the girl. Rodolph blackmails Ferrand into establishing many worthy charities. His money thus dissipated, Ferrand goes into a decline and dies.

Madame Georges (zhohrzh), who is deserted by her criminal husband, who took their son with him. She is befriended by Rodolph and for a time cares for Fleur-de-Marie on her farm.

La Chouette (shew-EHT), an ugly, one-eyed woman, a Paris criminal hired by Ferrand to kidnap Fleur-de-Marie. Later, on her own initiative, she stabs and robs Lady Sarah.

The Schoolmaster, another Paris criminal hired by Ferrand. He proves to be Madame Georges' husband. He kills La Chouette and is imprisoned.

Rigolette (ree-goh-LEHT), a kind and hardworking young woman, Fleur-de-Marie's friend from prison days. Her lover, whose release from prison Rodolph makes possible, turns out to be Madame Georges' long-lost son. He and Rigolette marry and live happily with Madame Georges.

Sir Walter Murphy, the young duke's faithful servant and companion in his probing of the mysteries of the Paris streets.

Cecily (say-see-LEE), a beautiful woman fallen into depravity. Rodolph secures her release from prison and places her in Ferrand's household as a spy. She furnishes him with much valuable information, the most important relating to the true identity of his daughter.

Polidori (poh-lee-doh-REE), an evil tutor who, urged on by Lady Sarah, does his best to warp the young Rodolph's mind.

THE MYSTERIES OF PITTSBURGH

Author: Michael Chabon (1963-   )
First published: 1988
Genre: Novel

Locale: Pittsburgh, Pennsylvania
Time: The 1980's
Plot: Bildungsroman

Art Bechstein, the son of a gangster, Joseph "Joe the Egg" Bechstein. His mother died when he was twelve years old. He learned of his father's nefarious dealings when he was in his early teens and, at first, was intrigued by the adventure they seemed to offer. Now, however, he is twenty-two years old and has recently graduated from the University of Pittsburgh, and he finds his father's career somewhat embarrassing. Art is working in a run-down Pittsburgh bookstore near campus because he has nothing better to do. He dates Phlox Lombardi, a young woman who fascinates him because of her individualistic style of speaking and dressing. He is, however, equally fascinated by Arthur Lecomte, a suave homosexual whose courtly manners suggest (incorrectly) a privileged back-ground. In Arthur, he finds someone whose style he can ad-mire. Uncertain of his own sexual identity, Art soon falls into an affair with Arthur. Art also is fond of Arthur's friend, Cleveland, a former collector of payments on illegal loans who has become a small-time thug. Art, as the author presents him, represents the youth of the 1980's. He takes more than he gives. Accustomed to getting his own way in most things, he has little sense of direction and fails to appreciate his advan-tages. Art views himself metaphorically, thinking of himself first as a wall but later, realizing that a wall separates, changing his metaphoric concept of himself to an ever widening portal that connects his mother and father with his friends.

Joseph "Joe the Egg" Bechstein, Art's father, an accom-plished gangster who launders money derived from prostitu-tion, loan sharking, gambling, and protection and deposits it into Swiss bank accounts. He works for some Baltimore mafi-osi and is an amateur painter with a good education and polished manners. Joe is distressed at his son's connection with Cleveland, who has used Art to wangle an introduction to his father. Joe lures Cleveland into a police trap that ends in a chase in which Cleveland falls off a building and is killed. When Joe learns that Arthur Lecomte and his son are having an affair, he orders Arthur out of town. He is a controlling father, ready and able to manipulate his son's life.

Phlox Lombardi (floks), Art's girlfriend, who, when he first see her, is dressed in pearls, a strapless white dress with blue flowers, and high-heeled white sandals. Her speech is as distinctive as her clothing. She and Art fall into an affair that is disturbed by Art's affair with Arthur, which he undertakes in part to hurt Phlox. She does what she can to win him back, thereby forcing him into a corner. Phlox, who was once a punk rocker, at times offers the deceptively wholesome image of a rural American girl, yet something sets her apart, causing people to be discomfited by her presence.

Arthur Lecomte, who is in many ways the most complex character in the book. He manipulates people shamelessly. He has self-confidence, urbanity, charm, and good looks. On the surface, he is fearless, but when Joe the Egg decrees that he leave town, he turns into a panicky wreck. Despite Arthur's outward appearance of affluence and security, Art learns that his mother works as a maid.

Cleveland, a petty criminal with a checkered background. He is Arthur Lecomte's friend but soon forms a friendship with Art that Art finds quite satisfying because, unlike his association with Phlox and Arthur, it does not involve sex. Cleveland is not above using Art to gain entrée to his father, an act that is his undoing. Joe the Egg, piqued at Cleveland's effrontery in using Art to arrange an introduction with him, sets up Cleveland to be caught by the police. The ensuing chase ends in Cleveland plunging off a high building to his death.

Claire, Art's former girlfriend who finally leaves him. Art's father thinks she is wrong for his son. Art identifies Claire's problem as dementia praecox and admits that he has been living with a crazy woman.

— *R. Baird Shuman*

THE MYSTERIES OF UDOLPHO

Author: Ann Radcliffe (1764-1823)
First published: 1794
Genre: Novel

Locale: France and Italy
Time: Late sixteenth century
Plot: Gothic

M. St. Aubert (sah[n]-toh-BEHR), a French aristocrat and widower. He takes his daughter on a trip into the Pyrenees Mountains. While on the trip, he falls ill and dies, leaving his daughter with some letters he has asked her to destroy. With the letters is a mysterious miniature portrait.

Emily St. Aubert, daughter of M. St. Aubert. She wants to marry Valancourt, but her villainous uncle, who wants her property, prevents the marriage and forces the girl to sign over her property to him. Her property is returned, however, when her uncle is captured as a brigand. She is reunited with her beloved Valancourt, marries him, and settles down to a tranquil life.

Valancourt (vah-lahn-KEWR), a young French nobleman who falls in love with Emily St. Aubert and prepares to marry her, until her uncle interferes. Rumors have him a wild young man, but he proves he is worthy of Emily and finally marries her.

Mme Montoni (mohn-TOH-nee), Emily's aunt, who mar-ries Signor Montoni. Her husband locks her in a castle tower to make her sign over her property to him. She dies of harsh treatment.

Signor Montoni, a villainous Italian nobleman who mar-ries Emily's aunt and forbids the girl's marriage to Valancourt. He tries to wrest his wife's and his niece's property from them. He takes them to a castle high in the Apennines, where he is a brigand. He is captured and forced to return his ill-gotten gains.

Count Morano (moh-RAH-noh), a Venetian nobleman. Signor Montoni tries to marry Emily off to him.

Lady Laurentini (loh-ra[n]-tee-NEE), previous owner of the castle of Udolpho. She disappears to become a nun. She confesses her true identity as she lies dying. She admits that she plotted at one time to have Emily's aunt killed by her first husband, who was also Lady Laurentini's lover.

Ludovico (lew-doh-VEE-koh), a servant at Udolpho who befriends Emily and helps her escape from the castle.

M. Du Pont (dew pohn), a friend of Emily's father. He proves that Valancourt, Emily's beloved, actually gambled only to help some friends.

M. Villefort (veel-FOHR), a French aristocrat whose family gives Emily refuge after a shipwreck.

The Marquis de Villeroi (veel-RWAH), Lady Laurentini's lover, the first husband of Emily's aunt.

THE MYSTERIOUS ISLAND
(L'Île mystèrieuse)

Author: Jules Verne (1828-1905)
First published: 1874-1875
Genre: Novel

Locale: An island in the South Pacific
Time: 1865-1869
Plot: Adventure

Captain Cyrus Harding, an engineer in General Grant's army,

Nebuchadnezzar (Neb), Captain Cyrus Harding's black servant,

Gideon Spilett, a reporter,

Jack Pencroft, a sailor, and

Herbert Brown, the orphan son of one of Jack Pencroft's former captains, passengers in a balloon in which they make their escape from the capital of the Confederacy. Caught in a storm, they are blown far out to sea and deposited on an uncharted island. Taking stock of their resources, the refugees set about to establish a colony, which they call Lincoln Island. With the knowledge brought with them, and with ingenuity and hard work, they triumph over their surroundings. Through their labors they are aided, in times of need, by a mysterious presence who finally reveals himself as Captain Nemo of the submarine *Nautilus*. He warns them to leave the island before its volcano explodes. With the treasure he bequeathes them, they buy land in America and colonize again.

Captain Nemo, captain of the submarine *Nautilus*. Living alone on Lincoln Island, he gives aid in secret to its refugees. He finally reveals his identity, requests that he be buried in the *Nautilus*, and bequeathes his treasure to the colonists.

Ayrton, a mutineer. Put ashore by his captain, he is rescued by the colonists of Lincoln Island. Repenting of his past life, he becomes one of their company and shares their adventures and fortunes.

THE MYSTERIOUS STRANGER, A ROMANCE

Author: Mark Twain (Samuel Langhorne Clemens, 1835-1910); from an unfinished manuscript edited and completed by A. B. Paine (1861-1937) and Frederick Duneka (?-1919)
First published: 1916
Genre: Novella

Locale: Eseldorf, Austria
Time: 1590
Plot: Philosophical

Theodor Fischer, the narrator, a young boy who is the son of the church organist. Together with Nikolaus Bauman and Seppi Wohlmeyer, he meets and interacts with Satan. His observations and opinions pervade the entire work. He is sympathetic to other people and open to, yet questioning of, popular and new attitudes and opinions. Only he is privy to all of Satan's acts and philosophical statements.

Nikolaus Bauman, another young boy, the son of the principal judge. He, too, is involved with Satan. He drowns trying to save little Elsa, his future having been altered by Satan.

Seppi Wohlmeyer, a third young boy, the son of the keeper of the principal inn. With Nikolaus, he is close friends with Theodor.

Satan, who sometimes goes by the name of **Philip Traum**, the nephew of the fallen angel of the same name. He claims to be an angel sixteen thousand years old. He can appear or vanish at will. He changes the future of other characters, causing their deaths or insanity. He claims to be benevolent, though his actions at times seem the opposite. He idealizes animals and takes a dim view of humankind. At the end, he is completely nihilistic, denying the existence of heaven, hell, the afterlife, and even humankind itself. Using the name Philip Traum, he appears as a handsome young man, a mysterious stranger, to whom people are drawn. He provides money and sustenance to Father Peter and others through indirect, ingenious means. On one occasion, he enters the body of the Astrologer. The misanthropic philosophy of the work is embodied in his attitudes.

Father Adolph, a priest. He is vindictive, causing the defrocking of Father Peter and, later, his imprisonment. He is of questionable merit as a clergyman, zealous but often with impure motives. He is vindictive toward those accused of witchcraft but friendly toward the evil Astrologer.

Father Peter, a loving, dedicated priest. He teaches the goodness of God and looks for the best in humans. He is accused of heresy by Father Adolph; loss of priesthood and poverty result. Enriched by Satan, he is accused of witchcraft. Satan alters his future by making him serenely insane for an extended lifetime.

The Astrologer, a friend of Father Adolph but a foe of Father Peter and often his accuser. Embodied by Satan, he does wonders, showing witchcraft to be less than evident.

Margret, Father Peter's niece, an attractive young woman. She suffers loss of fortune and popularity in the misfortunes of Father Peter, but she is patient and loving toward her beleaguered uncle.

Wilhelm Meidling, an inept lawyer. He is faithful in his attentions to Margret, even when others have shunned her. He defends Father Peter against the charge of theft brought by the Astrologer by showing that Father Peter's money was minted too recently to have belonged to the Astrologer; however, it is Satan, possessing Wilhelm's body, who brings about the acquittal.

Ursula, the servant to Father Peter and his household. She meets Satan and is given a magical, money-producing cat. She eventually hires a manservant to help her with the work.

Agnes, the magical cat. Her tongue-whiskers grow the opposite direction from normal as proof that she is not ordinary. She produces money for Father Peter's household.

Solomon Isaacs, a Jewish moneylender. He is ready to foreclose on Father Peter's house. After the accusations of theft against Father Peter, he holds the disputed money until resolution of the issue.

— *George W. Van Devender*

THE MYSTERY OF EDWIN DROOD

Author: Charles Dickens (1812-1870)
First published: 1870
Genre: Novel

Locale: England
Time: Mid-nineteenth century
Plot: Detective and mystery

Edwin Drood, a young engineer with prospects of becoming a partner in the firm of his late father. He disappears and is presumed dead, but his fate and murderer are never disclosed in this mystery novel, unfinished at the author's death.

Jack Jasper, Drood's young uncle and guardian, a cathedral choirmaster. An opium addict, he is in love with Rosa Bud and is perhaps the likeliest candidate for the role of murderer.

Rosa Bud, an orphan. She and Drood agree to break their parentally formed, longstanding engagement. She fears Jasper and loves Neville Landless.

Neville Landless, an orphaned Englishman newly arrived from Ceylon who falls in love with Rosa. His quarrel with Drood is a factor in his being suspected of the murder.

Helena Landless, Rosa's close friend, the sister of Neville.

Mr. Crisparkle, Landless' tutor, who introduces him to Drood and Jasper and who aids him in taking refuge in London after Drood's disappearance.

Mr. Grewgious, Rosa's guardian, from whom she seeks protection after Jasper tries to blackmail her into loving him by threatening to expose Landless.

Datchery, a late-appearing stranger apparently engaged in spying on Jasper.

Durdles, a stonemason who works at Cloisterham Cathedral, where Jasper is choirmaster. One night when Durdles is very drunk, Jasper steals from him the key to an underground tomb.

N

THE NAKED AND THE DEAD

Author: Norman Mailer (1923-   )
First published: 1948
Genre: Novel

Locale: Anopopei, an island in the South Pacific
Time: During World War II
Plot: Social realism

General Edward Cummings, the commander of an American division attempting to subdue Japanese troops on the fictitious Pacific island of Anopopei. Cummings is a West Pointer, a career soldier who is convinced that the United States is destined to become the next imperial power and that the Army, which will play a major role in the coming years, can be his path to the power he needs. A latent homosexual, Cummings is fanatical about neatness and cleanliness. He selects Lieutenant Hearn as his aide and instructs the younger man and treats him favorably until Hearn, in a deliberate act, violates Cummings' phobia about cleanliness. When the campaign stalls, Cummings decides to send a small platoon to reconnoiter a possible way to take the Japanese force from the rear, and he exiles Hearn by giving him command of the platoon. Cummings' division finally wins the campaign, before the platoon has completed its mission, but it is a hollow victory and he receives little credit.

Lieutenant Robert Hearn, the Harvard-educated son of a successful businessman. He has drifted since graduation, working as a union organizer and finding plenty of women but still looking for meaning in his life. He argues with Cummings and tries to reject what Cummings stands for, but he finds that he is being bent to Cummings' will by the combination of favoritism and discipline that Cummings employs. Deliberately offending Cummings, he is relieved to be assigned to command the I and R (Intelligence and Reconnaissance) platoon on its dangerous mission. He is killed in ambush before the mission is completed.

Staff Sergeant Sam Croft, a tough Texan who rules the I and R platoon until Hearn is assigned to it. He has grown up in the hard life of small-town West Texas and found his greatest joys in hunting and in fighting. He killed his first man while on strike-breaking duty with the National Guard and found it thrilling. He rules the platoon with an iron hand, cowing everyone but Valsen, whom he recognizes as a natural leader. When Hearn is killed, because Croft deliberately withholds information, Croft is determined to finish the mission and demonstrate his leadership; he cannot control the men, however, and eventually they run. When the survivors reach safety, they find that the mission was unnecessary; the campaign has ended.

Red Valsen, a drifter, hobo, and union man. He is older than most of the men, more experienced and more bitter. He sees more clearly than the other men that they have no real stake in the war; they are being used by the powerful for ends that will not help the men. He has been through tough strike situations, but he has become accustomed to losing these battles and has never settled in any place for long. He hates Croft's autocratic command of the platoon and seems to defy him, but he is too worn down and too weak to challenge Croft when a showdown occurs.

Julio Martinez, a sergeant, the platoon's scout and Croft's chief assistant. He is a Mexican American from South Texas who resents his second-class citizenship and believes that he can be accepted in the Army as an equal. He is a clever and able scout. He senses that something is wrong, but he makes no protest when Croft uses the information he provides to set up the circumstances of Hearn's death.

Woodrow Wilson, a Southern good old boy. He dreams continually of his youth, when he imbibed moonshine liquor and had his way with the young black women in his small Georgia town. He is a classic goof-off, evading his duties whenever possible, but even Croft cannot help liking him. During the reconnaissance, he is mortally wounded by a sniper's bullet.

Roy Gallagher, a Boston Irishman, paranoid, bigoted, and bitter. He has worked in menial jobs for Boston politicians and deeply resents being sent to the misery of Anopopei while others who worked with him have gotten draft deferments. He persecutes the Jewish members of the platoon and makes life miserable for everyone, but he becomes more human when he receives word that his young wife has died in childbirth.

Joey Goldstein, a Jewish soldier from Brooklyn. He tries to get along with everyone, finding rationalizations for the way others behave. He is physically stronger than others suspect, and in the end, he is stronger spiritually as well, performing well when the platoon is under stress. He is much less bitter than Roth, the other Jewish member of the platoon.

William Brown, an all-American boy from a small Midwestern town. He was a cheerleader in high school, a moderately successful small businessman, and a pillar of his community. In the I and R platoon, he becomes a sergeant. He means well but is not very effectual.

— John M. Muste

NAKED LUNCH

Author: William S. Burroughs (1914-1997)
First published: 1959
Genre: Novel

Locale: New York, Texas, New Orleans, and Interzone
Time: The second half of the twentieth century
Plot: Fantasy

William Lee, the picaro narrator, a streetwise addict who also narrated *Junkie* (1951), the author's first novel. Lee escapes arrest at the end by killing Hauser and O'Brien, twenty-year veterans of the Narcotics Squad.

The Buyer, a narcotics agent known for his ability to pass as a junkie. He has his own insidious habit, however: physical contact with junkies, who are absorbed and digested through some obscure metabolic process. He is caught absorbing the Narcotics Commissioner and destroyed with a flamethrower.

Dr. Benway, an adviser to the Freeland Republic. "A manipulator and coordinator of symbol systems," Benway is an expert on interrogation and mind control, though he avoids the use of torture. He supervises the Reconditioning Center until its computer inadvertently releases all patients.

Mugwumps, creatures without livers. They eat only sweets, and they murder young boys, whom they sexually violate at the time of death. Inhabitants of Interzone, they secrete an addictive fluid (addicts to it are called "Reptiles") that prolongs life by slowing metabolism.

Ali Hassan, a wealthy man with a fake Texas accent. He owns the Rumpus Room, where the Mugwumps hang boys. Hassan is known as a "notorious Liquefactionist."

The Liquefactionists, a political party whose program involves the eventual merging of everyone into One Man. They reduce their victims by protein cleavage and liquefaction, to be absorbed into their own protoplasm.

The Senders, a group compelled to "send all the time" without any contact with other human beings, symptoms of "The Human Virus," the need to control.

The Divisionists, who literally divide into replicas of themselves; Interzone is filled with replica cultures that wage war on one another.

A. J., a bizarre person known for winning paternity suits by not using his own sperm to impregnate women. His conversation often refers to future events, and it is unknown which side he is on (Liquefactionist or Factualist). His cover story is that of an international playboy and practical joker; in one episode, he destroys Chez Robert, a restaurant specializing in *haute cuisine* and snobbery, by releasing one hundred famished hogs.

The Factualists, a group that rejects all the other parties in Interzone. They oppose atomic war and anything that can be used to control or exploit individuals.

Carl Peterson, who is summoned for an examination by Dr. Benway in the Ministry of Mental Hygiene and Prophylaxis of Interzone.

— *W. A. Johnsen*

THE NAKED YEAR
(Goly God)

Author: Boris Pilnyak (Boris Andreyevich Vogau, 1894-1938)
First published: 1922
Genre: Novel

Locale: Russia
Time: Early twentieth century
Plot: Regional

Donat Ratchin (doh-NAHT RAHT-chihn), a young Russian during the Bolshevik Revolution. Although he has planned to follow his father as a merchant, he returns from the war to become the head of a revolutionary commune in Ordynin Town.

Ivan Ratchin (ih-VAHN), Donat's autocratic father; he breaks up Donat's brief affair with a pretty maid but sends the housekeeper to his son's bed.

Nastia (NAHS-tyuh), a pretty young maid, briefly Donat's mistress.

Olly Kuntz (OHL-lih kewnts), a young woman who prints blank orders for arrest and imprisonment for the Reds.

Comrade Laitis (LI-tihs), an enthusiastic revolutionist.

Andrey (ahn-DRAY), a man persecuted by Comrade Laitis. He is betrothed to Irina.

Semyon (sehm-YOHN), a man impressed by Andrey's cleverness in eluding the Reds.

Arkhip (ahr-HIHP), a rude peasant and an enthusiastic Red who suggests suicide to his ailing father. After he becomes a Red official, he marries Natalia Ordynin.

Arkhipov (ahr-HIH-pof), Arkhip's father, who shoots himself to avoid a lingering death from cancer.

Natalia Ordynin (nah-TAH-lyuh ohr-DEW-nihn), a young woman doctor. She becomes fond of Arkhip, the Red leader, and marries him, looking forward to what she deems a cozy arrangement.

Boris Ordynin, the oldest of the Ordynin brothers, who rapes a maid and suffers from syphilis inherited from his father. He leaves Ordynin when the family home is requisitioned by the Reds.

Gleb and

Egor (eh-GOHR), Natalia's younger brothers.

Lidiya (LYEE-dyih-yuh), a morphine addict, and

Katarina Ordynin (kah-tah-REE-nuh), Natalia's sisters.

Arina Ordynin (ah-RIH-nuh), Natalia's mother. She sells clothes and furniture from the home to provide food for her family.

Martha, the maid raped by Boris Ordynin.

Aganka (ah-GAHN-kuh), a peasant girl attracted to Andrey.

Irina (ih-RIH-nuh), a girl loved by Andrey and betrothed to him.

Harry, the English leader of a band of armed men who kill and loot on their way through Ordynin Town.

THE NAME OF THE ROSE
(Il nome della rosa)

Author: Umberto Eco (1932-   )
First published: 1980
Genre: Novel

Locale: An abbey in northern Italy
Time: 1327
Plot: Detective and mystery

William of Baskerville, a Franciscan monk. This fifty-year-old English cleric and former inquisitor is tall and slender, with a hooked nose, sharp eyes, and a wry sense of humor. Reared in the skeptic tradition, he is a pre-Renaissance humanist, learned in letters, science, and philosophy; he is skilled, eloquent, and tolerant. Because of his interest in all knowledge, he finds it repugnant that anyone should bar others from acquiring it, either through censorship or, worse yet, murder. In addition to working on a compromise between Pope John XXII and Emperor Louis IV, William solves the serial death cases, although he is unable to prevent the abbey library from being burned to the ground. He dies of the plague sometime in the mid-fourteenth century.

Adso of Melk, a Benedictine monk. In the prologue, he is an old man, but in the novel he is a novice and Brother William's disciple and scribe. Eighteen years old, he is handsome and impressionable, even naïve, particularly in matters of love, sex, and bookish knowledge. In one compressed week, he acquires an entire education and, from his master, a sophisticated way of viewing people and truth.

Abo, the abbot. He is of refined and noble origins, and he enjoys showing off the wealth of his abbey, especially his famous library. By being less than forthright with William, he causes delays and difficulties in the investigation. Trapped in an airless room of the library, Abo becomes the sixth and last victim.

Berengar of Arundel, an assistant librarian, a very close, homosexual young friend of Adelmo. The handsome, pale, and lascivious Berengar was the last to see Adelmo, raving mad with guilt. Clever and unscrupulous, he is not beyond revealing library secrets to his friends or using his good looks in exchange for favors. He is the third victim.

Benno of Uppsala, a scholar of rhetoric. From his interest in the great pagan writers, he theorizes that a supposedly lost volume of Aristotle's *Poetics*, dealing with comedy and laughter, may have fallen into Berengar's hands. After he steals the book, he extorts his promotion to assistant librarian; desolate over all the destruction, he dies in the library fire.

Venantius of Salvemec (veh-NAN-shee-uhs), a Greek and Arabic translator. He has a discussion with Adelmo about fantasy in art and may have come to know too much. He is killed (he is the second victim), but not without first writing in code how to penetrate the library's inner sanctum, a message William later deciphers.

Severinus of Sankt Wendel (sehv-eh-RI-nuhs), an herbalist. Severinus has been in charge of the infirmary for some twenty-five years and knows about most poisonous plants and their antidotes, as well as the medicinal literature. Killed by a blunt instrument, he is the fourth victim.

Malachi of Hildesheim (HIHL-dehs-him), a librarian. He is tall, thin, and severe looking. Malachi has sole access to the library stacks. To protect these from curious monks, a complicated call-numbering system has been devised, which only he understands. He is poisoned, becoming the fifth victim.

Bernard Gui, a Dominican inquisitor. About seventy years old, he is slender, and his gray eyes are cold and angry. As inquisitor, he can be harsh, cruel, wily, and icily sarcastic when questioning heretics; as papal agent and head of the armed escort, he is a shrewd and tough arguer and negotiator. In both functions, he shows himself to be a subtle psychologist and a brutal enforcer.

Jorge of Burgos (hohr-HAY), a former librarian. Despite his advanced age (he is more than eighty years old), he is still very strong and mentally alert. As the oldest and most learned member of the abbatial community, he is rightfully named "Venerable." His physical blindness parallels his fanatical blindness as he fights against laughter and pagan learning, going as far as killing to censor blasphemous writings and to manage truth as he sees it. He dies by eating pages of Aristotle's book, which he had deliberately poisoned.

Michael of Cesena, the minister-general of the Franciscans. In his discussion with John XXII's envoys, he shows subtlety, intelligence, and caution. His stand on ecclesiastical poverty puts him in direct confrontation with the pope and in probable danger.

Ubertino of Casale (ew-bayr-TEE-noh) a monk. Bald, skinny, and sixty-eight years old, Ubertino is an old friend and teacher of William. He is also a wise and learned author of a famous mystic work. Because of his uncompromising faith, he has been threatened with death and is hiding in the abbey. After the talks collapse, he flees from harm's way. Two years later, he dies in mysterious circumstances.

Remigio of Varagine (ray-MEEK-yoh), a cellarer. A former member of the heretical sect of Fraticelli, this jolly and vulgar fifty-two-year-old monk uses women from the village for his own pleasure. Now caught in Bernard Gui's trap, he confesses every imaginable sin and crime and dies at the stake.

Salvatore, Remigio's assistant. This former Fraticello is old, emaciated, and unkempt. Although almost crazy from all he has seen and done, he reveals, in his gibberish of languages, the horrible underside of a society abandoned by the Church. After being tortured, he is a complete wreck, hardly worth the bother of executing.

Nicholas of Morimondo, a master glazier. He tells William that monks who entered the stacks had hallucinations and went insane. After Remigio's death, he became the cellarer.

A village girl, between sixteen and twenty years old, beautiful and sexy, poor and wretched, who trades sexual favors for food scraps from the abbey's kitchen. When she and young Adso make love, she finds him much more attractive and tender than the disgusting Remigio. After Bernard Gui catches her with a chicken and a cat—in his mind, obviously indicating that she is a witch—she is to be burned at the stake.

Adelmo of Otranto, a master illuminator of manuscripts. Full of remorse over his sins, this young monk commits suicide and is the novel's first victim.

Cardinal Bertrand del Poggetto, the head of the papal legation, a learned debater in the dispute between proponents of Church property and those of poverty.

— *Pierre L. Horn*

NANA

Author: Émile Zola (1840-1902)
First published: 1880
Genre: Novel

Locale: Paris and rural France
Time: The 1860's
Plot: Naturalism

Nana (nah-NAH), an ignorant courtesan whose beauty, selfishness, and erotic cunning prove disastrous to the men of fashion who patronize her. A product of the Paris streets, she is discovered by a theatrical promoter and becomes a success by captivating men with her sexual charm. Soon she has a clientele that includes the richest men in Paris. Tiring of this life, she goes to live with a brutal comic actor. When her fortunes reach a low ebb, she is reduced to streetwalking. Later, an infatuated nobleman becomes her protector. Her financial and sexual extravagances achieve new extremes as she acquires a lavish mansion, new lovers, and a lesbian prostitute. Many of her lovers ruin themselves; one goes to prison, and two commit suicide. Ironically, she dies of smallpox, her beautiful and notorious body ravaged by the disease.

M. Fauchery (foh-sheh-REE), a second-rate journalist who writes about Nana in the press, at first favorably and later adversely. A hanger-on of the theater and society, he spends his time seducing other men's wives.

M. Steiner (SHTI-nehr), a wealthy and crooked Jewish banker who pursues actresses. He is twice Nana's lover, the first time providing her with an estate. His financial career roughly parallels Nana's erotic career; he is spectacularly successful, suffers heavy losses, and then regains his fortune before he falls again, this time to bankruptcy.

Georges Hugon (zhohrzh ew-GOH[N]), a pampered, effeminate, silly young aristocrat who enjoys Nana, plays the part of her fool, and fatally stabs himself when she refuses to marry him.

Philippe Hugon (fee-LEEP), his brother, a dashing army officer who falls in love with Nana when sent to rescue Georges. After stealing army funds for her sake, he is arrested and imprisoned.

Madame Hugon, the indulgent mother of Georges and Philippe. Hating Nana, she is crushed when both her sons are ruined.

Fontan (fo[n]-TA[N]), a satyr-like actor who lives with Nana, beats her, and leaves her when she has no more money.

The Comte Muffat de Beuville (mew-FAH deh bew-VEEL), a pious aristocrat whose passion for Nana leads him to ruin his home life, squander all his possessions, and submit to the humiliations she forces upon him.

Sabine de Beuville (sah-BEEN), his attractive wife. She takes Fauchery and other men as her lovers.

The Marquis de Chouard (deh shew-AHR), Sabine de Beuville's aged father, a man with a dignified appearance and a reputation for lechery. His affair with Nana is a great humiliation to his son-in-law.

The Comte Xavier de Vandeuvres (zhah-vyay deh vahn-DEWV-reh), a reckless and wealthy man whose passion for Nana and horses leads him to gamble away his wealth and to commit suicide.

Hector de la Faloise (ehk-TOHR deh lah fahl-WAHZ), a rich, stupid young man from the provinces who spends all his means on Nana in order to appear fashionable.

Mignon (meen-YOH[N]), a stage manager who procures for his wife.

Rose Mignon, his pretty wife and Nana's rival, a clever comedienne who takes Fauchery for a lover.

Bordenave (bohr-deh-NAHV), the coarse theatrical producer who discovers Nana and later goes bankrupt.

Daguenet (dahg-NAY), a well-to-do young rake who spends his time and money on Nana, marries the comte de Beuville's daughter, and turns outwardly respectable.

Estelle, his plain, awkward, strong-willed wife.

Satin (sah-TA[N]), a lesbian prostitute of innocent appearance. Nana supports her and uses her to humiliate her male lovers.

Prulliére (prewl-YEHR), an actor who enjoys Nana's favors.

Labordette (lah-bohr-DEHT), a theatrical hanger-on who does favors for the actors and actresses.

Lucy Stewart, a fashionable member of the theater crowd, plain, middle-aged, but given to love affairs.

Madame Maloir (mahl-WAHR), Nana's old friend and parasitic confidante.

Zoé (zoh-AY), Nana's maid, a competent, rather homely woman.

Madame Lerat (leh-RAH), Nana's aunt, who takes care of Nana's small son.

Louis (lwee), Nana's son, from whom she catches smallpox.

NAOMI
(Chijin no ai)

Author: Jun'ichirō Tanizaki (1886-1965)
First published: 1925; serial form, 1924-1925
Genre: Novel

Locale: Tokyo, Japan, and surrounding areas
Time: 1918-1926
Plot: Fiction of manners

Joji Kawai, a wealthy engineer from the countryside, an insecure man of twenty-eight when he meets and falls in love with Naomi in Tokyo. Lonely and bored, he is attracted by Naomi's Eurasian appearance and decides to develop her into the perfect, modern woman. He persuades her to move in with him; sends her to English, music, and dance classes; buys her clothes; and indulges her various whims. Gradually, he realizes that she is unfaithful, manipulative, and no longer under his control. He kicks her out of their home but later takes her back on her terms, giving her complete freedom to make her own friends, have affairs, and live an idle, luxurious life in a Western-style house in Yokohama.

Naomi, a fifteen-year-old waitress at the Diamond Café when she meets Joji. She is from a poor, apathetic Tokyo family and loves a good time. Under Joji's tutelage, she becomes a beautiful but willful and selfish young woman. She frequently calls him "papa," and he calls her "baby." She wants no children or responsibilities and is enamored of all things Western. Joji likens her to their film idol, Mary Pickford, and at the dance at the El Dorado club reflects that she is a wild animal but vital and sensual.

Kumagai Seitaro, a brash, vulgar Keio University student. He becomes Naomi's principal lover and encourages her wild and coarse behavior.

Hamada, a serious young student at Keio University and part of Naomi's fast set of friends. He has an affair with her but is sensitive to the plight of her victims, especially Joji. Caught in Joji's house waiting for Naomi, he divulges that he and others have carried on affairs with Naomi. He helps Joji find Naomi after Joji has kicked her out and urges him not to take her back.

Aleksandra Shlemskaya, a Russian countess who operates a Western-style dance studio in Tokyo after fleeing from revolution in her country. She exudes Western sophistication and power. Holding a whip, like a drill officer she authoritatively teaches her students to keep time with the music. Joji finds the mix of perspiration and perfume alluring and exotic. It is at her studio that Naomi meets members of the Keio Mandolin Club, four of whom become her set of admirers.

Miss Harrison, Naomi's English teacher. She surrounds herself with pictures of her students and defends her abilities to Joji, who sees Naomi making little progress in English.

Haruno Kirako, a beautiful actress at the Imperial theater. She dances with Joji at his and Naomi's first dance. Naomi says spiteful things about Haruno until she joins their table, but Joji is depressed when he compares her refinement with Naomi's vulgarity.

— *Joseph Laker*

THE NAPOLEON OF NOTTING HILL

Author: G. K. Chesterton (1874-1936)
First published: 1904
Genre: Novel

Locale: London, England
Time: Late twentieth century
Plot: Fantasy

Auberon Quinn, an Englishman of the late twentieth century, a man who sees humor in life. Chosen by lot to be the king of England, he tries to brighten London life by reviving medieval pageantry and splendor. Acting as a reporter, he is killed in the battle at Notting Hill, but he dies happy because he restored laughter to London.

Barker, one of Quinn's friends. He thinks Quinn dangerous and foolish and so objects when Quinn is chosen as king of England.

Lambert, another of Quinn's friends. He shares Barker's views about Quinn.

Mr. Buck, a linen draper made provost of North Kensington by King Auberon. He goes to battle with the provost of Notting Hill over a road through London.

Adam Wayne, the provost of Notting Hill. As a nine-year-old, he had unwittingly inspired King Auberon to reintroduce medieval customs into London. He loves Notting Hill's narrow streets and fights against the broad highway. He is killed defending his beloved London district but dies happy, having brought love back to London.

Mr. Turnbull, the keeper of a toy shop. He helps Adam Wayne plan the defenses of Notting Hill and lets him use a toy fort and lead soldiers in making the battle plans.

NAPOLEON SYMPHONY

Author: Anthony Burgess (John Anthony Burgess Wilson, 1917-1993)
First published: 1974
Genre: Novel

Locale: Eastern Europe, Egypt, Elba, France, Italy, St. Helena, and the Mediterranean region
Time: 1795-1821
Plot: Historical

Napoleon Bonaparte, at first **Buonaparte**, a French general, a first consul, an emperor, and then a prisoner. He begins as a brilliantly successful general and rather incompetent and impatient lover; an introductory scene presents him as keeping everybody waiting for his wedding to the older widow Josephine, who already has two children and has been cast off as mistress by a member of the Directory. From the opening, Napoleon appears as an officer willing to use force to establish order and as ready to take chances; he is also sexually addicted to Josephine, to the point of absurdity. His Italian campaign keeps him from her for extended periods, however, and she is publicly unfaithful to him. He sublimates his sexual passions in military action, running up a string of successes; paradoxically, these make the politicians desperate to keep him in the field, away from the people and possible political activity of his own. Eventually, he comes to see through their partiality, and he discovers that he is passionately devoted to the Constitution and to the spread of republican principles. He recognizes this in part because he finally sees an opportunity to seize power. He also sees a chance to get his entire family in on the action, though they all have minds of their own. His first move is to invade Egypt, where everything falls apart: The English cut his supply line, his troops cannot adjust to the climate, and he learns that Josephine has been unfaithful again. His response in this situation is characteristic and establishes his pattern of response for the rest of his life. He acts, not always in complete understanding of the situation, and he is usually able to impose his will on others. In all of this, Napoleon simultaneously exhibits qualities of the great man and of the commoner, the hero and the fool; his endeavors and dreams are often magnificent but just as often petty and venal.

Josephine, actually **Rose-Josef-Marie de Beauharnais**, Napoleon's first wife. At first little more than a token in a political game—the bone that Barras offers to secure Napoleon's loyalty—Josephine at the outset treats Napoleon as an infatuated boy. She placates him when she must, but she keeps a stable of less importunate lovers. Eventually, however, she comes to appreciate his character, or at least his prominence. He, in turn, never gets over his infatuation with her. She proves incapable of conceiving a child by him, however, and Napoleon's dynastic ambitions make progeny imperative. Eventually, she agrees to a divorce, but he continues to seek her out, even after his remarriage.

Stapps, a German student who attempts to assassinate Napoleon and who is executed as a result. Although Napoleon attempts to discover some rational motive by interrogating Stapps, he cannot get beyond reiterated expressions of antityranny and mystical German self-determination. Stapps eventually proclaims that the destiny of Europe is intimately bound up with the recognition of the superiority of the German soul; it will prevail over all. Stapps refuses clemency, claiming that if he is released, he will try again. Reluctantly, Napoleon orders him shot. Later, while wandering the streets of Paris disguised as the common citizen Leon Laval, Napoleon happens on a Stapps look-alike, ironically a first cousin also named Stapps. He also insists that the future belongs to the Aryans.

Charles-Maurice Cardinal Talleyrand-Perigord, a bishop of the Roman Catholic church and political adviser to a succession of regimes; he eventually becomes Grand Chancellor of the Empire under Napoleon and survives him. Witty, sophisticated, erudite, and experienced, Talleyrand is the quintessential professional politician, a true genius at manipulation and analysis, always managing to land on his feet in any crisis. Although he advises Napoleon, he at no point indicates that he believes the emperor to be anything more than a temporary accident, a star for a moment, even a pawn.

Madame Germaine de Staël, an intellectual, sponsor of one of the most elegant literary societies of the 1790's. An intimate friend and possible mistress of Talleyrand, Madame de Staël is an early critic of Napoleon and as a result is forced to flee to Switzerland after his accession. Apparently, a sexual abnormality has much to do with her literary and social propensities.

Betsy Bascombe, the fifteen- to seventeen-year-old daughter of the East India Company agent at St. Helena Island, Napoleon's final prison and his deathplace. At first approaching the twice-defeated and humiliated emperor as the stock comic-strip villain of the English press, Betsy eventually learns that he is a human being and, hence, personable, approachable, and even lovable. Betsy illustrates one approach to Napoleon as hero.

Sir Hudson Lowe, the British administrator of Napoleon's imprisonment on St. Helena. He is responsible for the dietary and medical prescriptions that ensure Napoleon's early death.

Dr. Antommarchi, the Corsican physician appointed to attend Napoleon in exile by his mother. He protests in vain against the medical measures imposed on Napoleon's deathbed.

An unnamed female spirit, who debates Napoleon over his achievements as he lies dying. She provides the final estimate of Napoleon's heroism.

Alexander, the young czar of Russia. At first apparently caught up in the hero worship of Napoleon, Alexander seems easily persuaded to accept the emperor's views of political determinism during their conference at Tilsit. He even consents to enforce Napoleon's Continental System. Removed from the influence of Napoleon's personal force, however, he proves less tractable.

Princess Marie Walewska, a member of the Polish royal family whom Napoleon rescues from Cossacks during the invasion of Russia. She becomes his consort, his snow princess, during the invasion and retreat, and she bears his son. Later, she visits him on Elba and also communicates with Josephine.

— James L. Livingston

NARCISSUS AND GOLDMUND
(Narziss und Goldmund)

Author: Hermann Hesse (1877-1962)
First published: 1930
Genre: Novel

Locale: The German Empire
Time: Late Middle Ages
Plot: Philosophical

Goldmund, an extroverted and worldly individual whose name means "Golden Mouth." He is a highly sensual, handsome man who is very attractive to women. An intuitive and artistic person, Goldmund devotes himself to a life in pursuit of the senses and to a quest to find the archetypal figure of the nurturing mother. At the beginning of the novel, he is sent by his father, at the age of eighteen, to the medieval monastery of Mariabronn, where he plans to study and become a monk. His teacher, Narcissus, helps him to realize that his inner nature is not suited to the *vita contemplativa* of the monk and scholar but rather to the *vita activa*. Goldmund embarks on a series of adventures involving numerous seductions of women, war and violence, and the threat of death from the plague. Later, he studies with a famous artist and himself becomes an excellent woodcarver. He ends up in prison, to be executed, but is saved at the last minute by his friend. He returns, sickly and aged by life, to the monastery. He dies before he is able to finish his final masterpiece, a carving of the eternal "Eve-Mother" figure.

Narcissus, a monk and scholar in the monastery of Mariabronn. He is a highly intellectual and analytical individual who is devoted to the reclusive life of the scholar. He serves, in the allegorical mode of the novel, as the opposing pole to the artistic Goldmund. As the latter's teacher, he realizes that the young boy is temperamentally unsuited to the monastic life and that Goldmund seeks to recapture the lost union with his mother. Narcissus gives him the courage to leave. When Goldmund returns after roughly ten years, his former teacher cares for him until his death.

— Thomas F. Barry

THE NARRATIVE OF ARTHUR GORDON PYM

Author: Edgar Allan Poe (1809-1849)
First published: 1838
Genre: Novel

Locale: The high seas
Time: Early nineteenth century
Plot: Adventure

Arthur Gordon Pym, the narrator, young son of a Nantucket trader in sea stores. Desirous of adventure, he stows away on a whaling ship, the *Grampus*; helps to overpower and kill the mutineers who seize the ship; becomes briefly a cannibal before he and Dirk Peters are rescued by the *Jane Guy*; survives with Peters after the slaughter of the captain and all of the crew of the *Jane Guy* by natives on an uncharted Antarctic island; and dies of an unexplained accident after most of his story had been prepared for publication. How he managed to travel from the Antarctic to the United States is not revealed, as the last part of his story was lost at his death.

Augustus Barnard, his friend, who aids Pym in hiding aboard the *Grampus* and who shares his experiences and his dangers until he dies from gangrene resulting from an arm wound received in the capture of the ship from the mutineers.

Captain Barnard, Augustus' father, skipper of the *Grampus*. With four loyal sailors he is set adrift in a rowboat after his ship is seized by the mutineers.

Dirk Peters, a sailor on the *Grampus*. He is the son of an Indian woman and a white trader. Ferocious-looking and grotesquely misshapen—with huge hands, bowed arms and legs, an immense head, and a ludicrously demonic countenance—he at first joins the mutineers but later turns upon them. He helps Pym and Augustus seize the *Grampus* and becomes a good friend and companion to Pym in all of his later adventures.

Seymour, a black cook, leader of one party of the mutineers.

Hartman Rogers, a mutineer who dies in convulsions after being poisoned by the mate, who leads the other party of mutineers.

Richard Parker, a mutineer who joins Pym, Barnard, and Peters. He is the first to suggest cannibalism for survival; ironically, he draws the short straw and is killed by Peters.

Captain Guy, the skipper of the *Jane Guy*, the schooner that rescues Pym and Peters from the battered hulk of the *Grampus*.

Too-Wit, chief of a tribe of savages on Tsalal Island in the Antarctic Ocean. Through treachery, the chief and his men entomb by a landslide Captain Guy and all of the *Jane Guy*'s crew except for six men left on board as well as Pym and Peters, who survive both the landslide and a later attack by the savages.

Nu-Nu, a Tsalal native captured and used as a guide by Pym and Peters in their escape from the island. He dies shortly afterward.

THE NARROWS

Author: Ann Petry (1908-1997)
First published: 1953
Genre: Novel

Locale: Monmouth, Connecticut
Time: The 1950's
Plot: Psychological realism

Abigail Crunch, a seventy-year-old widow living in New England. Abbie resides at Number Six Dumble Street in The Narrows, a predominantly black section of Monmouth. Prim, proper, and straitlaced, Abbie is the embodiment of New England Puritanism. She denies her African American heritage by rejecting every aspect of her own culture as she sees it exemplified in the daily lives of the inhabitants of The Narrows. This rejection sometimes extends even to her husband, the Major, and her nephew, Link. Abbie believes that cleanliness and propriety are next to godliness, and she keeps her person and her home immaculate, despite her altered circumstances following the death of her husband. Appearances are everything; this is the guiding principle of Abbie's life.

Lincoln (Link) Williams, the nephew of Abbie Crunch. Orphaned as a child and adopted by Abbie and her husband, Link is molded both by the deeply moralistic standards of Abbie and by the street philosophy of Bill Hod, the owner of the Last Chance Saloon. Bill Hod's pragmatic, self-affirming philosophy counterbalances the strictly Puritanical, often self-denying teachings of Abbie. These people and the nurturing environment of The Narrows help Link to develop the strength of character that he demonstrates when he faces death at the hands of Camilo Sheffield's husband.

Camilo Treadway Sheffield, a rich white heiress. Bored with her life at Treadway Hall—the family mansion on the outskirts of Monmouth—Camilo ventures into The Narrows on a dark and foggy night and is rescued from a would-be attacker by Link Williams. Later, when she discovers that Link is a black man, neither his race nor his occupation as part-time bartender at the Last Chance Saloon deters her from becoming involved with him. Camilo rents an apartment in Harlem for their weekend rendezvous, buys Link expensive gifts, and on one occasion suffers the humiliation of being literally thrown out into the streets naked for sleeping with Link in Abbie Crunch's house. When Link ends the affair with her, Camilo falls into a state of deep depression, isolating herself behind the walls of the Treadway mansion.

— *Gladys J. Washington*

NATHAN THE WISE
(Nathan der Weise)

Author: Gotthold Ephraim Lessing (1729-1781)
First published: 1779
Genre: Drama

Locale: Jerusalem
Time: The twelfth century
Plot: Philosophical

Nathan, a Jewish merchant and sage who suffers the loss of his family and fortune during the Third Crusade. As a tragic hero, he always repays evil with good, as he does when he adopts an orphan girl immediately after losing his own family. Although he seems more Christian than Jew—indeed, he acts the part of Christ in his devotion and wisdom—he is really a humanitarian who believes there are many ways either to enter heaven or to establish heaven on Earth. Self-reliant, generous, fearless, and tolerant, he serves as a contrast to the wily Christians and the rather vengeful Muhammadans.

Recha, his adopted daughter, in reality the orphaned niece of the Sultan Saladin. Under her devoted foster father's tutelage, she shares many of his virtues. She is beautiful within and without. Her attraction for the young knight, Conrad von Stauffen, is merely sentimental and not romantic, a fact that is more understandable when they prove to be brother and sister. Grateful to Conrad for saving her life, she and Nathan wish to reward the young man, but he, though poor and a stranger, takes a strange view of charity and rebuffs all attempts to aid him. Recha's touching naïveté and innocence form an interesting contrast to the intrigue and cruelty that exist in a world torn by religious prejudice and conflict.

Conrad von Stauffen, a disillusioned young Templar who strongly opposes religious wars, in reality a Saracen prince. High-minded, open-hearted, and yet reserved, the Templar seems truculent at first, especially in his boorish refusal to accept a reward after he saves from death by fire the girl who later proves to be his own sister. He questions, though he also admires, the Jewish merchant; at the same time, he honors, though he does not understand, the sultan who spares his life. As events turn out, his stubborn pride reveals his exalted birth, and his impetuosity proves more pagan than Christian.

The Sultan Saladin, the son of the Saracen ruler and a generous, impulsive prince who is revealed as Conrad von Stauffen's uncle. Although seemingly prejudiced against the Jewish merchant, he is in reality only testing Nathan's wisdom and lamenting his own reliance on the merchant's generosity. His wisdom in saving the knight's life because of a family resemblance is further noted in his ability to live among the many factions that plague Jerusalem. He is quick-witted in dispute and often stern in action but always capable of magnanimity when it is deserved.

Sittah, his sister and royal housekeeper. What her brother lacks in common sense, she makes up for without being particularly shrewish, though she is shrewd in business dealings and has a quick tongue. Although she suggests the trap to ensnare Nathan, the parable that he tells moves her as much as it does her brother. She is devoted to her generous brother and tries to protect him.

Daja, the Christian servant in Nathan's house and companion to Recha. Essentially a good person, grateful for a good home, and fond of her Jewish master and his adopted daughter, Daja is nevertheless a bigot who believes there is only one true faith. She very nearly causes a tragedy through her divided allegiance.

The patriarch of Jerusalem, a sycophantic fanatic who plots the destruction of Nathan the Jew. He arouses the ire of the Templar and the rebellion of a lay brother, who are to assist him in taking Recha from her kind benefactor.

Al Hafi, a dervish who humorously and ineptly attempts to manage the sultan's affairs. His thoughts dwelling constantly on his home in India, he wishes to exchange the luxury of the court for the rigors of the wilderness where he can renounce the worldly to realize the contemplative life.

NATIVE SON

Author: Richard Wright (1908-1960)
First published: 1940
Genre: Novel

Locale: An American city
Time: The 1930's
Plot: Social realism

Bigger Thomas, a young African American, frustrated by poverty and race prejudice, who has a pathological hatred of white people. He is reluctantly drawn into alliance with his employer's daughter Mary and her sweetheart, who are cru- sading with the communists to help blacks. After an evening of drinking, Bigger carries the drunken Mary to her room. To prevent her from making a sound that will alarm her blind mother, he puts a pillow over her face and accidentally smothers her. This act releases all of his pent-up emotions. He burns the body in the furnace, tries to get ransom money from his employer, and tries to frame the dead girl's sweetheart. He confesses to his mistress, and after the discovery of the remains, he hides out with her. He fears that she will be found and questioned, however, and so he kills her. The police catch him, and under steady questioning by the prosecuting attorney, he admits his crime. Despite an eloquent plea by his attorney outlining the social structure that made him what he is, Bigger is sentenced to die. While awaiting death, he gets, from talking to his attorney, an understanding that his persecutors are themselves filled with fear and are not responsible for their social crimes.

Mr. Dalton, a wealthy white man for whom Bigger works as a chauffeur.

Mrs. Dalton, his blind wife.

Mary Dalton, their daughter, crusading with the communists against racial discrimination. Bigger accidentally smothers her.

Jan Erlone, Mary's sweetheart and fellow crusader. Bigger succeeds so well in throwing suspicion on him for Mary's disappearance that Jan is arrested. After Bigger is arrested, Jan comes to see him and promises help. Jan introduces to Bigger a lawyer from the communist-front organization for which Jan works.

Boris A. Max, Bigger's lawyer, provided by a communist-front organization. He argues that society is to blame for Bigger's crime, but he does not succeed in saving Bigger from death. He is able to show Bigger that his enemies are also driven by fear and must be forgiven.

Bessie Mears, Bigger's mistress, to whom he confides his guilt and whom he kills.

Britten, a detective hired by Dalton to investigate Mary's disappearance.

Buckley, the prosecuting attorney, under whose questioning Bigger breaks down and signs a confession. He makes full use of anticommunist feeling and race prejudice in prosecuting Bigger.

THE NATIVES OF HEMSÖ
(Hemsöborna)

Author: August Strindberg (1849-1912)
First published: 1887
Genre: Novel

Locale: The island of Hemsö and environs, on the Stockholm archipelago
Time: Late 1800's
Plot: Naturalism

Johannes Edvard Carlsson, the newly hired manager of Widow Flod's farm. Short and stocky and in the prime of life, he is lively and assertive. He is also selfish, opportunistic, and philandering. His open and passionate—even flirtatious—nature makes him a convivial and optimistic fellow, prone to embellish the truth when it is to his advantage. His skill in overseeing land and people and his good luck cause several ingenious enterprises to flourish under him, despite his lack of a real business sense. The surrounding community enjoys the prosperity for which he is responsible, though even after his death they maintain a suspicion of him as an interloper. He is resourceful and a jack-of-all-trades; he knows agriculture, but his ignorance of fishing and hunting gains for him the scorn of his new stepson. He marries Widow Flod largely to acquire her wealth and land, and he dies through ignorance of how to survive in a storm at sea.

Anna Eva Flod, the widow who owns the farm and who becomes Carlsson's wife. Mrs. Flod is a relatively old woman, widowed two years before the story begins. She has kind eyes and a face parched by wind, is envious of the youth and vitality of people around her, and likes to think of herself as still young enough to enjoy wedded bliss. She is easily flattered, falling prey to Carlsson's trickery and emotional fervor. She is entrenched in the customs and mores of the little fishing community, taking seriously her role of hosting the haymaking festivities and carefully observing traditions at her wedding celebration. A pious woman, she loves her son deeply and looks out for his welfare. She has a kinder heart than Carlsson but can be just as provoked to anger and harsh words as he is. While she is dying from overexposure from tracking Carlsson on an adulterous tryst, she does what she can to ensure that her

son will inherit almost everything; she allows Carlsson to keep for himself only a house that he built.

Gusten Flod, the son of Widow Flod, ten years younger than Carlsson. Gusten is unpretentious and unassuming, as well as lackadaisical and relatively unmotivated. He is quiet and thoughtful and can be placating when other people's tempers flare. He tends to simmer and glower when he is angry, rather than becoming loud and pugnacious. He knows the sea intimately and is very much at home doing as he pleases on his mother's farm. He has little sense of order, method, or even security. Although he can be generous to a friend (sharing his last drop of brandy with the pastor), he can also hold a grudge (nearly boycotting his mother's wedding because of his antagonism toward Carlsson). He is shy, though straightforward, and more honest than Carlsson. He is even capable of making peace, toasting Carlsson on his wedding day and asking the pastor for a tribute to Carlsson at his funeral. The novel is a saga of Gusten Flod's coming of age; by the end, he has become the responsible, respected, and independent master of Hemsö.

Erik Nordstöm, the pastor of the Hemsö community and environs, also a fisherman and farmer. The pastor is an enigma and can be seen as either the most colorful or the most contradictory character in the book. He is short, thick, and weather-beaten in appearance and coarse, gruff, and blunt in personality. As the spiritual leader of the community, he gives Sunday sermons and officiates at weddings and funerals. Keeping his congregation standing in the hot sun for five hours and eighteen hymn verses is not unusual for him. He is also prone to consuming more alcohol than he can handle and twice loses consciousness at the Flod home because of overimbibing. He is irascible and is given to perpetuating gossip and holding grudges. He is conniving and vindictive; it is he who suggests that Gusten retaliate against Carlsson for gulling the widow into marriage. It is also he who, at the end of the novel,

counsels Gusten to be forgiving and not judge Carlsson too harshly.

— *Jill B. Gidmark*

NATIVES OF MY PERSON

Author: George Lamming (1927-   )
First published: 1972
Genre: Novel

Locale: Primarily the western coast of Africa and the Caribbean
Time: Late sixteenth century
Plot: Historical

The Commandant, a wealthy soldier of Lime Stone who leads the illegal voyage of the ship *Reconnaissance*, given to him by his mistress, to colonize San Cristobal (Isles of the Black Rock). He is strongly connected to the ruling classes of Lime Stone but undertakes his voyage without the sanction of the rulers. Hearing the Boatswain's lurid story of the Lady of the House of Trade and Justice, he halts the voyage and is murdered by mutinous officers.

The Lady of the House of Trade and Justice, the daughter of Master Cecil, mistress of the Commandant, and wife of Gabriel Tate de Lysle. She makes use of the Boatswain, who tries to murder her. She is among the women on the second ship, traveling to San Cristobal.

Pinteados, the tall, Antarctican pilot of the *Reconnaissance*, somewhere over the age of thirty-five, who tells the Surgeon of his relations with the Surgeon's wife while she is in an asylum. He survives the mutiny and desertion to tell his story to Admiral Badaloza, to whom he hints that possession of the ship might be negotiated. He is the Commandant's superior not only in the tactics of survival but also in ultimate material success.

Sasha, a ten-year-old boy who is forced to serve on the *Reconnaissance*. Less than four feet tall, with a boil in the corner of his mouth, he witnesses the murder of the Commandant, whom he worships, and kills the Surgeon and the Steward.

Gabriel Tate de Lysle, the lord treasurer to the House of Trade and Justice. He used an orphan girl to trap the Steward with incest as a means of protecting himself after he stole rare maps from the Steward.

The Steward, a neat, red-bearded officer on the *Reconnaissance* with great knowledge of maps and charts. He fingers a wedding ring hanging from a neck chain. He joined the voyage to free himself from his wife and her connections. When he learns that his wife is waiting at San Cristobal, he and the Surgeon lead the officers' mutiny. He and the Surgeon kill the Commandant; he is killed by Sasha.

The Surgeon, a young, handsome officer on the *Reconnaissance*. He has thick black hair, a prodigious appetite, and a restless temper. He envisions himself as a founder of hospitals. He drove his wife mad with his infidelities, then sent her into the Severn asylum. He learns that Pinteados had sexual relations with his wife there, and he is unwilling to continue the voyage when he learns that she waits at San Cristobal. He is killed by Sasha after he and the Steward murder the Commandant.

The Boatswain, an officer on the *Reconnaissance* who has made seven voyages in seven years. He confesses his (attempted) murder of the Lady to the Priest; he also tells of his

degradation and his desecration of the church altar, then goes mad.

The Priest, an officer on the *Reconnaissance*. He blesses traffic in slavery while insisting that black slaves have souls. He reluctantly agrees with the Commandant's plan for sailors to mate with the women waiting for them on San Cristobal. He loses his faith during the voyage.

Ivan, a painter who has a vision of the Lady of the House of Trade and Justice, standing on a cliff at San Cristobal, with her jar of leaves, melting into blood. He and Baptiste lead the sailors' escape from the ship to continue to San Cristobal.

Pierre, a lean, athletic, young carpenter. With his hair heaped high on his forehead and falling long on his neck, he plays a flute and boasts of sexual exploits.

Baptiste, the short, thick-shouldered powder maker, one of the most vocal and militant of the ordinary seamen. He has a high brow, wide nose, and deep-set eyes. His first voyage was under the cruel command of Master Cecil. When morale and discipline begin to break down, he attempts to take charge. After the murder of the Commandant, he summons the sailors to leave the ship.

Marcel, a fisherman who has a bald head except for a ridge of black hair over his one ear, the other having been lost when he was a hostage left in Antarctica by Master Cecil. A quiet man, he minds his own business.

Duclos, the first cook, kindhearted, with frivolous manners. He revives Ivan, who faints in the heat, with rum.

The Steward's wife, a cousin of Gabriel Tate de Lysle. She is ambitious for her husband, though she cultivated his relationship with the orphan girl. She waits for her husband on San Cristobal.

The orphan girl, the daughter and lover of the Steward, who fled Tate de Lysle's orphanage for refuge with the Steward. She dies in childbirth.

The Surgeon's wife, sent to the Severn asylum by the Surgeon. She had a sexual relationship there with Pinteados. She secretly awaits her husband on San Cristobal, where she exchanges stories in a cave with the Lady and the Steward's wife.

Master Cecil, the father of the Lady of the House of Trade and Justice. He spent time in the Severn madhouse after leading many sea voyages.

Admiral Badaloza, the Commandant's Antarctican rival. He investigates the murder of the Commandant and learns that the ship belongs to the Lady, who is waiting at San Cristobal. He decides to report to her instead of to the House of Trade and Justice.

— *Richard D. McGhee*

THE NATURAL

Author: Bernard Malamud (1914-1986)
First published: 1952
Genre: Novel

Locale: Chicago, Illinois, and New York City
Time: Fifteen years in the 1930's and 1940's
Plot: Fable

Roy Hobbs, a major league baseball player. Beginning as a white-faced, long-boned pitcher one year out of the Northwest High School League, he is a naïve rustic. Armed with Wonderboy (his bat carved from a lightning-blasted tree) and a fastball, he strikes out the American League batting champion. Proclaiming with hubris that he wants to be "the best there ever was in the game," he is wounded by a gun-toting woman. Fifteen year later, now tall, husky, and dark-bearded, Hobbs is brought up from the semipros by the New York Knights. Literally knocking the cover off the ball in his first at bat, he replaces the Knights' dead superstar and leads the cellar dwellers into an end-of-the-season playoff game for the right to play in the World Series. Preoccupied with his own materialistic and sexual desires, however, Hobbs has yet to mature and eventually throws the final game for a bribe.

Harriet Bird, a beautiful temptress. Wearing a black-feathered hat and veil, she withdraws a gun from a hatbox and, as she has done with other famous athletes, shoots the egotistical teenager Roy Hobbs.

Pop Fisher, the manager of the New York Knights, an ailing, bald man of sixty-five. His health is directly tied to the misfortunes of his team. Longing to redeem his past (he flopped during a World Series), he treats Roy as a son and team savior.

Max Mercy, a syndicated sportswriter. With his mustache and voracious eyes, he snoops into the personal lives of athletes. Eventually, he discovers Roy's ugly past.

Sam "Bub" Simpson, a major league scout. Having scrawny legs and a lean head, he resembles a scarecrow. A former catcher, he is Roy's first father figure, discovering him and then dying trying to catch one of his fastballs.

Memo Paris, Pop's niece. Beautiful and redheaded, she is a former beauty-contest winner who was the girlfriend of Roy's predecessor, Bump Bailey. She encourages Roy to accept the bribe and thus provide them with a sound financial future.

Iris Lemon, the woman who offers Roy true love. Thirty-three years old, black-haired, and already a grandmother, she teaches Roy what it is to be a hero, how to act unselfishly, and the value of suffering. Pregnant with Roy's twins, she is rejected by Roy, who is not yet ready for mature love.

Judge Goodwill Banner, the principal owner of the New York Knights. A lumpy, massive figure, he lives in a tower, which he never leaves, above the ballpark. He is a greedy man who tries to drive Pop Fisher from partial team ownership and bribes Roy.

Gus Sands, the supreme bookie who will bet on anything, with one glass eye that he claims is magic. A father figure to Memo, he tries to corrupt Roy.

— *Charles Sweet*

NAUSEA
(La Nausée)

Author: Jean-Paul Sartre (1905-1980)
First published: 1938
Genre: Novel

Locale: France
Time: The 1930's
Plot: Philosophical realism

Antoine Roquentin (ahn-TWAHN roh-keh-TA[N]), a philosophical young man who has settled down in Bouville, a town by the sea, to write a biography of the marquis de Rollebon, an eighteenth century European politician. During the third year of work on the book, Roquentin notices that he has become the victim of a strange affliction; what he calls a "sweetish sickness" settles over him from time to time. Repelled by the malady, he seeks to rid himself of it by spending time with the few people he knows and by stopping work on the Rollebon book. No one can help him. In despair, he goes to Paris, hoping to be able to write a novel, knowing that he is never to solve the problems of his life.

Ogier P. (oh-ZHYAY), an acquaintance whom Roquentin calls "The Self-Taught Man." To rid himself of loneliness and despair, Roquentin unprofitably spends some time with Ogier P. Roquentin witnesses a scene in which Ogier P., discovered to be a homosexual, is forcibly ejected from a library.

Anny (ah-NEE), an English girl whom Roquentin had known before he began work on the biography. They meet in Paris. She has become fat, insults Roquentin, and leaves Paris with the man who is keeping her.

Françoise (frah[n]-SWAHZ), a woman who operates a café called the Rendezvous des Cheminots. She and Roquentin were once friendly toward each other in a purely physical way. When Roquentin visits her to see if she can help him defeat the despair, which has by now become overwhelming, he finds that she has no time to spend with him.

THE NAZARENE
(Der Man fun Notseres)

Author: Sholem Asch (1880-1957)
First published: 1939
Genre: Novel

Locale: Palestine
Time: The first century A.D. and the 1930's
Plot: Historical realism

Pan Viadomsky, an anti-Semitic Catholic scholar living in the 1930's. Old and irascible, he is both brilliant and fraudulent as a researcher of the Holy Land during the first century. He is the reincarnation of the Roman soldier, Cornelius, who apprehended and arrested Jesus in the Garden of Gethsemane. In his twentieth century incarnation, Viadomsky is still tortured by his memories of Jesus. He is fascinated with Jews as well as with anyone he perceives to be reincarnated from Jerusalem during the time of Jesus. At the same time, he is filled with hatred of Jews, an attitude that increases his prestige as Nazi Socialism becomes increasingly popular. He depends on the ability of the narrator, a young Jewish scholar, to translate Hebrew and to recall things from ancient Jerusalem.

Cornelius, a professional soldier who has cast his lot with Pontius Pilate, lives in Jerusalem, and observes the various aspects of Hebrew culture as he continues his service under the Roman governor. He believes in power as the answer to all ethical problems, and maintaining Roman power is in his interest. Although he is intrigued with Jesus, he must decide to view the "Rabbi of Nazareth" as a serious threat.

Jesus of Nazareth, the Rabbi from K'far Nahum, known to some, toward the end, as the **Messiah ben David**. He is the focus of Cornelius (speaking in his reincarnated form, that of Pan Viadomsky), of Judas Ish-Kiriot (Iscariot, who speaks through a manuscript found by Viadomsky), and of Jochanan (who is reincarnated as the narrator), the disciple of the Rabbi Nicodemon. Jesus, or Yeshua, is a rabbi who teaches the poor and the sick rather than associating with the Pharisees or the Sanhedrin. As a result, he is accused of impurity. He appears frail, he is tall, he has a youthful expression, and he wears ritualistic earlocks and a fringed tunic. He is constantly served and protected by a physically strong disciple, Simon bar

Jonah, the fisherman, and attended by the brothers Zebedee (Jacob and Jochanan) and by Mary of Migdal.

Rabbi Nicodemon, under whom Jochanan (reincarnated as the narrator) studies, a Pharisee who believes that Jesus speaks the word of God, but not that he is the Messiah. He exhibits great reverence for Jesus.

Judas Iscariot, a follower of Jesus who suffers from jealousy toward Simon bar Jonah, Jacob, and Jochanan, who are more intimate with the master. He also suffers from impatience regarding the redemption, which ultimately leads him to hasten the event by revealing Jesus to the soldiers.

Mary, the mother of Jesus, who loves Jesus as her firstborn. Her skin is wrinkled with care, and she has lived a life of hard work. She reveals to the disciples that Jesus was born in Bethlehem and is of the House of David.

Mary Magdalene, known as **Mary of Migdal**, a courtesan beloved by wealthy gentlemen of many backgrounds. She has an excess of feeling to express and is made more fascinating by her bodily allure and her long red hair. She is an expert in perfumes and oils. The restlessness in her soul is answered by the doctrines that Jesus teaches, and she abandons her worldly goods and connections to follow him, taking personal care of him at each stop that he and his disciples make.

The narrator, a young Jewish scholar eager to study under Pan Viadomsky. He finally realizes that he, too, had another life in early Christian times.

Jochanan, the first century embodiment of the narrator, a young disciple of the Rabbi Nicodemon. With his friend and fellow student, Rufus, he is privileged to see Jesus during his last days and to hear various enlightened reactions to Jesus, his words, and his works. He is characterized by eagerness, fear, and wonderment.

— *Anna R. Holloway*

NECTAR IN A SIEVE

Author: Kamala Markandaya (Kamala Purnaiya Taylor, 1924-   )
First published: 1954
Genre: Novel

Locale: A tenant farm, a village, and a city, all in India
Time: The 1950's
Plot: Realism

Rukmani, or **Ruku**, the female narrator, who nostalgically recounts the story of her life, beginning with her marriage at the age of twelve to a poor tenant farmer in a South India village and ending with the poignant death of her husband in the city and her subsequent return to the village. Although she is in her early forties, she calls herself an old woman who has helplessly witnessed the destruction of the pristine beauty of her quiet village and of a way of life by the onslaught of industrialism in the form of a tannery set up near their village. With her unbounded faith and capacity for love, sacrifice, suffering, and endurance, this simple woman of heroic courage goes through the fires of life and survives not only the calamities of nature but also many personal sorrows: the shock of her husband's infidelity, the deaths of her two sons, her daughter's turning to prostitution for survival, her eviction from the land they had farmed for thirty years, and, above all, the agonizing loss of her husband. Finally, she returns to her village and finds peace in taking care

of a young leper boy whom she and her husband had adopted in the city.

Nathan, Rukmani's husband, older than her, an illiterate tenant farmer who, having no knowledge or skill except those related to farming, cannot live except by the land. Unlike his wife, however, he readily accepts the forces of change and heralds the tannery as an inevitable step of progress. Although he is a loving husband and an affectionate father, he betrays his wife by having an illicit relationship with the village slut, Kunthi. As the size of his family grows and nature becomes more and more relentless, he feels powerless to provide for his family. Beaten by flood and famine and victimized by the landlord, he eventually is forced to leave the land and move to the city with his wife in a futile search for their son, Murugan. There he works as a stone breaker in a quarry, but before they can earn enough money to return to their village, he dies from strain, starvation, and sickness.

Dr. Kennington, often called **Kenny**, an English doctor with a missionary zeal who works in a dispensary near the tannery. A friend of Rukmani's father, he treats the problem of infertility in both Rukmani and her daughter Ira. Tall, pale, and emaciated, he is a private, lonely man who was deserted by his wife and children. He makes frequent trips away from the town to raise funds for the charitable hospital that he builds for the poor near the village. He trains and hires Rukmani's son Selvam as his assistant. Opposed to Rukmani's philosophy of suffering, endurance, and resignation, he exhorts the village people to cry out for help if they want to ameliorate their condition of squalor and poverty.

Irawaddy, or **Ira**, the firstborn daughter of Rukmani and Nathan, named for a famous river in India. Fair, dimpled, and lovely, she is married to a young man as soon as she reaches the age of puberty. Abandoned by her husband as barren, she returns to the village and resumes living with her parents. During the drought, to save her younger brother and her parents from starvation, she resorts to prostitution and in the process becomes pregnant and gives birth to an illegitimate albino son. Her love for her parents and siblings balances any faults.

Puli, a leper boy, an impudent street beggar who becomes attached to Rukmani and Nathan when they live in the city temple. He guides them through the city in their desperate search for their son and helps them find work as stone breakers in the quarry. After Nathan's death, Rukmani takes him to the village in the hope that Kenny will treat his leprosy.

Selvam, the youngest son of Rukmani and Nathan. Hardworking and conscientious, but with no love for the land, he works at Kenny's hospital as an assistant and takes care of his sister and his son, as well as of his mother and Puli when they return to the village.

Kunthi (koon-TEE), a village slut who had an affair with Nathan and has two sons fathered by him. Abandoned by her husband, she behaves like a common strumpet. When the crops fail, she blackmails Rukmani and demands rice from her, threatening that otherwise she will tell Nathan that Rukmani had illicit relations with Dr. Kenny. She also extorts rice from Nathan by threatening to reveal his betrayal to Rukmani.

Kali, Rukmani's neighbor, a big, plump, loud, garrulous, and self-opinionated woman who teaches Rukmani how to do the chores of a farmer's wife in the early days of her marriage.

Janaki (JAHN-kee), the wife of the village shopkeeper, a homely woman with a sagging figure.

— *Chaman L. Sahni*

THE NEEDLE'S EYE

Author: Margaret Drabble (1939-   )
First published: 1972
Genre: Novel

Locale: London, England
Time: Late 1960's
Plot: Psychological realism

Simon Camish, a successful barrister specializing in labor law. He has spent so much of his life repressing his emotions and working to satisfy the demands of others that he feels himself emotionally dry and unable to fulfill the personal side of his life. His marriage to a wealthy woman has lost all romance, and he is henpecked and embarrassed by his wife's public abuse of him. His children suffer from his distance. Earlier, he had been entirely subservient to his mother's drive to have him move beyond the poverty in which he spent his childhood. Extremely intelligent and observant of other people, he finds in his friendship with Rose Vassiliou the warmth and emotional excess lacking in his own rigidly controlled and intellectual character and life.

Rose Vassiliou, a divorced mother of three. Impulsive, deeply emotional, and often irrational in her behavior, she also possesses a keen intelligence, a sharp sense of humor, and a sensual delight in the everyday details of her life. Unlike Simon, who has spent his entire life working to achieve material success, she gives away the money she inherited and deliberately chooses to live on meager resources in a run-down section of London. Her acts of generosity, because they are poorly thought out, often misfire, as do her sudden romantic gestures, such as her marriage to a glamorous but unprincipled and often physically abusive Greek immigrant. She is attracted to the steady and logical temperament of Simon, although for the sake of her children she eventually returns to her former husband, thereby sacrificing the stable and satisfying independent lifestyle that she had established for herself.

Julie Camish, Simon's wife, the daughter of a moderately wealthy businessman. She is a childish woman of limited intelligence and taste who demands constant attention from others and a comfortable lifestyle. Her disappointment in Simon turns her into a shrewish wife who enjoys humiliating Simon and who neglects their children.

Christopher Vassiliou, a flamboyant hustler, the son of Greek parents, a man of dubious moral principles. He attracts Rose with his romantic warmth and zest for life. After a painful separation inflicted by her parents, they are married. The disparity in their values as well as the emotionalism in both of their natures leads to violent fights. Impulsive and emotional, he is also a hardworking and effective businessman who is able in time to ally himself with her disapproving father and eventually make a good income on his own. His refusal to back out of Rose's life and his devotion to their children result in his remarrying Rose and imposing on their relationship his more conventional values and lifestyle.

Emily Offenbach, a longtime friend of Rose whom Rose met while in boarding school. Practical, affectionate, and discerning, she was able to detect Rose's extreme loneliness and became her friend and mentor. The two women develop a close and supportive relationship as they both rear their children by themselves.

— *Eleanor H. Green*

A NEST OF SIMPLE FOLK

Author: Sean O'Faoláin (1900-1991)
First published: 1933
Genre: Novel

Locale: Ireland
Time: 1854-1916
Plot: Regional

Leo Foxe-Donnell, an Irish patriot who devotes himself throughout his life to the cause of Irish independence. He is a wild young man who loses his inheritance. He is twice arrested for his political activity and twice sentenced to prison terms. Nevertheless, he remains an active revolutionary.

Long John O'Donnell, Leo's father, a close-mouthed farmer.

Judith Foxe, Long John's wife and Leo's mother. She is an unattractive but fruitful woman who marries below her station, giving her husband ten children, of whom Leo is the youngest. She tricks her husband into making Leo his heir.

Julie Keene, a girl seduced by Leo. She warns another lover of Leo's political activities and thus causes him to be sent to prison. Later, she is again seduced by Leo and bears a child that she gives away. At last, Leo grudgingly marries her.

Bid Keene, Julie's sister, who marries a policeman. She and her husband take in the Leo Foxe-Donnells when the latter are penniless.

Johnny Hussey, Bid's policeman husband. He remains loyal to the government, despite the revolutionary activity in his family.

Johno O'Donnell, Leo's son by Julie Keene. His father locates him and brings him home as a nephew when the lad is twenty. Johno is a loud young man who joins his father in political activity.

Rachel Foxe and

Anna Foxe, prim sisters of Judith, who try to make an aristocrat of their nephew Leo.

James Foxe-Donnell, eldest of Leo's brothers, who is cheated of part of his inheritance by his mother. He keeps the farm intact by running Leo off, and he later recovers Leo's acres from his shiftless brother.

Phil Foxe-Donnell, one of Leo's brothers.

Nicholas, Leo's tutor.

Dr. Dicky, Leo's cousin, under whom he briefly studies medicine.

Frankie O'Donnell, Leo's revolutionary uncle.

Philly Cashen, a girl seduced by Leo.

Denis Hussey, the nephew of Leo. He becomes a revolutionary, though his father is a loyal policeman.

NETOCHKA NEZVANOVA

Author: Fyodor Dostoevski (1821-1881)
First published: 1849
Genre: Novel

Locale: St. Petersburg
Time: Early 1800's
Plot: Autobiographical

Anna "Netochka" Nezvanova (NEH-toch-kah neh-ZVAH-noh-vah), the narrator and protagonist, a young girl. Her character—introspective, naturally calm, and sedentary—is revealed through her reactions to the often unlucky circumstances in which chance places her. Netochka is a good-hearted girl; she has less of the moral duplicity than one would expect from a Dostoevski protagonist. She does find herself repeatedly in irresolvable conflicts of loyalty. As a young girl (she is eight or nine when the story begins), she lives with her mother and stepfather in an unhappy family. As her stepfather's character deteriorates, he enlists Netochka's help in stealing money from his wife, leaving Netochka to face her mother's ever more terrible anger alone. Both parents die as the family dissolves, and Netochka falls seriously ill. The wealthy Prince Khy takes Netochka to heart and takes her to live with his family. There, she finds herself living in the luxury of which she and her stepfather had dreamed, but she finds herself again at the center of family conflict. The prince's wife and mother-in-law object to Netochka's low origins. She is tolerated as long as she and Princess Katya, the prince's willful and energetic daughter, are at odds. When Netochka manages to win Katya's friendship, and thus wins for herself some happiness in this sterile home, she is condemned as a bad influence. She is then sent to live with Aleksandra Mikhailovna, the prince's married daughter and Katya's half sister.

Aleksandra and Netochka are temperamentally suited to each other, and together they begin an informal education. They discover, among other things, Netochka's talent for singing. This happy situation does not last, and Netochka is again compelled to choose between alternatives she cannot understand. Her story ends here. The book is unfinished, interrupted when Dostoevski was arrested and sent to Siberia.

Yegor Petrovich Yefimov (yeh-GOHR peh-TROH-vihch yeh-FIH-mov), Netochka's stepfather. A low and debased man, he has real talent as a violinist that, because of the flaws in his character, he can never develop. He is taken with the glory of being a musical genius and with the fame and wealth that could be his, much more than with music itself. He gets through life by his talent for self-deception, which is better developed than his musical gift. Finally, this talent fails him. He hears a violinist—a virtuoso he had sworn was a fraud—on the night when his overburdened wife, whom he had blamed for keeping him from his vocation, dies, perhaps by his own hand. His last, and greatest, illusions toppled, he dies. His last act is to run from Netochka, abandoning her on a dark street.

Princess Katya, the younger daughter of Prince Khy. She is a willful child with an aristocratic soul. She is haughty, daring, and, when the mood strikes, unabashedly affectionate. When Netochka comes to be part of her family, Katya runs through a gamut of emotions. She is first jealous, next contemptuous, then competitive, and finally friendly. In this last mood, she and Netochka grow perhaps as close as any two people can. This intimacy alarms Katya's mother and grandmother. Katya leaves the story when, to keep her from Netochka's "improper" influence, Katya's relatives separate the two.

Aleksandra Mikhailovna (mih-KHAH-ih-lov-nah), Katya's older sister, with whom Netochka lives after leaving the prince's family. She is a sedate and introspective woman, young and not long married. She is perhaps an adult Netochka;

certainly these two find themselves well matched. With Netochka, Aleksandra is free to become something of a dilettante, indulging herself over a wide range of culture and learning. Her husband's propriety compels her respect because he is living with the knowledge of a long-past love affair of hers, a chaste affair that had involved the noblest of feelings. Nevertheless, he lives hourly with the humiliation of it, with a great brooding bitterness that alternately awes and terrorizes his wife. Their story is unresolved when the novel ends.

— *Fritz Monsma*

NEVER COME MORNING

Author: Nelson Algren (Nelson Ahlgren Abraham, 1909-1981)
First published: 1942
Genre: Novel

Locale: Chicago, Illinois
Time: The 1930's
Plot: Naturalism

Bruno "Lefty" Bicek (BI-sehk), a seventeen-year-old hoodlum in a Polish neighborhood in Chicago. Proficient at baseball and boxing, Bruno is blond and athletically built, with a large body and long arms. He lusts for tobacco, women, food, and public triumph but is also haunted by guilt. He dreams of becoming a professional boxer, even as he steals a slot machine and leads his neighborhood gang, the Warriors, to reorganize as the "Baldheads." Bruno's intentions are often good: He repeatedly promises to himself that he will make up for injustices to his girlfriend, Steffi Rostenkowski. With his peers, however, Bruno lets the code of gang loyalty and his desire to conform prevent him from asserting himself when gang members follow him and Steffi to their alley hideaway and rape her. As Steffi is demoralized by gang rape, Bruno seethes inwardly until a Greek outsider attempts to get in line; with one kick of a metal-tipped shoe, Bruno breaks the Greek's neck. Although he successfully escapes from the scene, Bruno is later picked up by the police and questioned about a shooting for which he is not guilty; he takes the blame out of gang loyalty. In jail, Bruno reads boxing magazines and struggles with his conscience, which tells him that he is guilty of killing Steffi, even though she is alive and as well as any woman can be after what she has suffered. After his release from jail, Bruno dreams of fighting the former state light heavyweight champion while he struts outside Mama Tomek's house of prostitution, where Steffi now lives, soliciting customers. He finally gets his boxing match and hangs on through sheer determination, even with a broken hand, to defeat his opponent. Afterward, he is met by the police and arrested, as a result of information passed by the jealous Konstantine, for murdering the Greek. Bruno's final comment is that he never expected to live to be twenty-one.

Steffi Rostenkowski (ros-tehn-KOW-skee), Bruno's seventeen-year-old girlfriend. In the beginning, Steffi is innocent, poor, and indolent. After being raped by members of Bruno's gang, she goes to live with the barber, Konstantine, at Mama Tomek's. After her betrayal, she loses her sense of trust; as she listens to the passing trains, Steffi thinks that God has forgotten them all.

Bonifacy Konstantine (BAHN-eh-fahs-ih KAHN-stahn-teen), a barber and local crime boss. With a left leg shortened and twisted by childhood disease, the barber is deformed in both body and spirit. He hungers for a cut of every small-time operation in his neighborhood—even the haircuts required for membership in Bruno's Baldheads. Konstantine makes arrangements for fights for the local toughs, and he is angered when Casey makes the arrangements for Bruno's fight. His loss to Bruno in a card game is part of his motivation for informing on Bruno to the police.

Casey Benkowski (behn-KOW-skee), a failed boxer who is Konstantine's henchman. A bicycle thief at the age of ten and a pimp at fourteen, Casey, now twenty-nine, coaches the youths of the neighborhood in fighting, baseball, theft, and hoodlumism, but he turns to the barber for orders.

Fireball Kodadek (KOH-dah-dehk), the only member of his gang whom Bruno fears, a big man sick with tuberculosis. Kodadek, having once pulled a knife on Bruno, retains his dominance and shows the gang that Bruno, although he is strong, is less tough than he seems.

"One-Eye" Tenczara (tehn-ZAHR-ah), the police captain who questions Bruno and later arrests him after his boxing victory. A man with a small mustache and colorless eyes, he sports a large hat, sleeve garters, a pen and pencil in his shirt pocket, and a cigarette behind one ear. After eleven years on the police force, Tenczara is not impressed by Bruno's claim to know an alderman who is his own recently indicted brother-in-law.

Tiger Pultoric (puhl-TOHR-ihk), a former boxing champion whom Bruno idolizes. Before Bruno's fight, Kodadek and another of the gang take Pultoric—a short man wearing patent leather shoes and a light green suit with an imitation carnation in the lapel—to Steffi's door, and Bruno injures his hand in the struggle that ensues.

Honeyboy Tucker, a black boxer from South Chicago. Bruno dreams of fighting Tucker and finally defeats him in front of an audience that cheers Bruno, as a white man.

— *Mary Ellen Pitts*

NEW DAY

Author: Victor Stafford Reid (1913-1987)
First published: 1949
Genre: Novel

Locale: Jamaica
Time: 1865-1944
Plot: Historical

David (Davie) Campbell, Pa John Campbell's son and a participant in the 1865 Morant Bay Rebellion. Tall, blond-haired, and light-skinned, he identifies himself with the black population and calls for the fulfillment of the promises made at emancipation several decades earlier. Rebelling against the injustices of the legal system and the exploitation of poor blacks by white estate owners, Davie, at the age of nineteen, defies his conservative father and joins the radical group headed by Paul Bogle. Hot-blooded and daring, he is willing to use force to achieve his aims but is angered by Bogle's lack of a coherent strategy and the useless violence that results. Davie escapes with his fiancée, Lucille, and brother Johnny to an isolated cay after the abortive uprising on Jamaica. He later returns to Jamaica, makes an impressive appearance before the Royal Commission investigating the rebellion, and is granted a pardon and a lease to the cay, which he names "Salt Savannah" after his childhood home. He marries Lucille and establishes a thriving community on the cay but becomes increasingly like his austere and religious father. He renames the cay "Zion" and, despite his wife's unhappiness because of his fanaticism, obsessively attempts to eliminate what he sees as idleness and frivolity. He is killed in the 1874 hurricane.

Pa John Campbell, a near-white farmer and headman on the estate of George William Gordon. A deeply religious member of the Church of England and a stern, iron-willed disciplinarian, he attempts to teach his seven children to obey the Bible and respect established authority. A tall, powerful man and a natural leader who tries to mind his own business, he is violently opposed to his son Davie's association with the radical and, to his mind, wicked Paul Bogle. Pursued by the authorities in the mistaken belief that he had supported Bogle's uprising, Pa John stubbornly clings to a naïve faith in British justice and the protection afforded by his own righteousness. Hoping to halt the slaughter of innocents by talking to the governor, he is shot down by English soldiers. His son Emmanuel dies with him.

Johnny Campbell, Davie's youngest brother and the novel's dialect-speaking narrator. He is the principal witness of his family's turbulent history between 1865 and 1944. As a child, he is mischievous, inquisitive, plucky, and totally devoted to Davie. Reared by Davie and Lucille after the death of his parents, Johnny (with the help of Timothy M'Laren) in turn rears Davie's son, John Creary Campbell, and eventually his grandson, Garth. In his old age, Johnny is the respected custodian of his family's wealth, wisdom, and social values.

Lucille Dubois, Davie's near-white wife. The child of Haitians who had to flee their island during the revolution despite their sympathy for the former slaves, Lucille is in favor of gradual rather than revolutionary change. Dark-haired, vivacious, and brave, she is devoted to Davie until, on the cay, his growing fanaticism deprives her of love and laughter. She sees him as more her "overseer" than her husband. After disappearing in a boat during the hurricane that kills Davie, she is forced into prostitution in Cuba. She is later discovered by Johnny, working in a Kingston brothel, the night before she dies in the fire of 1882.

Paul Bogle, a Baptist deacon and a fiery leader of the Morant Bay Rebellion. The Church of England pastor calls Bogle "a black Satan in human form preaching sedition against . . . our Queen." More hot-tempered and reckless than George William Gordon (the near-white and socially prominent landowner and public official who also seeks justice and relief for the poor and hungry black population), Bogle threatens insurrection, secession from the British Empire, and political independence. Bogle's confrontation with the authorities is mishandled and leads to killing on both sides. The brutal military repression that follows results in the death of hundreds. Bogle and Gordon are summarily executed, and Jamaica reverts to Crown Colony status.

John Creary Campbell, Davie and Lucille's son, born in 1872 and reared by Johnny and Timothy M'Laren. Uninterested in his family's history and with neither a social vision nor his parents' high spirits, he is a colorless but successful businessman who adds to his family's wealth. His marriage to a snobbish Englishwoman isolates him from Johnny. He and his wife, Magda, die in the smallpox epidemic of 1920.

Garth "Son-Son" Campbell, the son of John Creary Campbell, born in 1913 and reared by Johnny and Timothy after the death of his parents. Tall, strong, and white-appearing, Garth is thought to resemble his grandfather Davie. Garth takes delight in learning of his family's and country's past and has a passion for helping the common people of Jamaica. After attending Cambridge and Gray's Inn, Garth returns to Jamaica, where he becomes a successful lawyer and estate owner. He promotes union organization, even among his own workers, and goes on to form a labor party with the support of British socialists. His representations to a Royal Commission lead directly to the granting in 1944 of a new constitution, an important final step toward Jamaican political independence.

Carlos Fernandez, Garth's Cuban-born cousin, a labor organizer. Similar to Garth in stature and appearance, he initially works with Garth but is more headstrong, flamboyant, and self-glorifying. He quarrels with Garth and, along with his supporters, quits Garth's newly formed political party.

— *Douglas Rollins*

NEW GRUB STREET

Author: George Gissing (1857-1903)
First published: 1891
Genre: Novel

Locale: England
Time: The 1880's
Plot: Naturalism

Jasper Milvain, a writer, a selfish egoist and money-minded opportunist who believes in giving the reading public what it wants. In his courting, he vacillates toward Marian. Being motivated only by his interest in money, he finally loses her. Seeing a union with the widowed Amy as a road to success, he marries her and achieves his goal.

Alfred Yule, a literary hack, tall, severe-looking, and embittered. He hates both Jasper and Fadge. After losing his sight, he is dependent on Marian to care for him.

Marian Yule, Alfred's daughter, courted by Jasper either lightly or seriously according to her apparent financial status. Finally seeing through him, she rejects him.

Amy Reardon, Alfred's niece, daughter of Edmund Yule. Unable to inspire Edwin's creative work and angry over his being a clerk, she returns to her mother, taking Willie. Hurt by Edwin's rejection of her offer to return and help him with her inherited money, she is shocked to learn of his dying condition when they are reconciled by Willie's illness and death. Devotedly, she tries to cheer Edwin during his few remaining days of life. Emotionally captured by Jasper's favorable review of Edwin's works, she is happy to marry him and afterward happy with him.

Edwin Reardon, Amy's husband, a promising writer in financial difficulties. Easily discouraged and dependent on his wife for inspiration, he feels he is losing his creativity. He proudly spurns Amy's generous offer to return after receiving her legacy, but he does join her because of Willie's illness. Very ill himself, Edwin dies not long afterward. In personality, Edwin resembles George Gissing. Literarily, he is Jasper's foil, the idealist in opposition to the materialist.

Willie, the young son of Edwin and Amy. His illness brings about a reconciliation between his parents, but Willie dies shortly afterward.

Dora Milvain and

Maud Milvain, Jasper's sisters.

John Yule, oldest of the three Yule brothers, a successful retired businessman, robust and fond of sports. He lives a quiet life after an attack of rheumatic fever. When he dies, he leaves a considerable estate.

Edmund Yule, the youngest Yule brother. He dies, leaving a small income to his wife and two children.

John Yule, the son of Edmund.

Fadge, an editor hated by Alfred. Fadge is succeeded by Jasper.

Harold Biffen, a struggling novelist and friend who advises Edwin to answer Amy's summons.

THE NEW HÉLOÏSE
(Julie: Ou, La Nouvelle Héloïse)

Author: Jean-Jacques Rousseau (1712-1778)
First published: 1761
Genre: Novel

Locale: Switzerland
Time: Early eighteenth century
Plot: Philosophical

Julie d'Étange (zhew-LEE day-TAHNZH), an aristocratic French girl who falls in love with her tutor, Saint-Preux, and fears she may fall victim to her love, as she does. When her lover is dismissed shortly before her marriage to another man, she almost dies of grief. She and her lover consider their love no sin. Finally, Julie has to marry M. de Wolmar and has two children by him, though she never forgets Saint-Preux. When she is dying, she asks that he become her children's tutor and marry her cousin Claire.

M. Saint-Preux (sah[n]-PREW), a young Swiss of unusual talents and sensibility. He becomes tutor to Julie and her cousin Claire. He and Julie fall in love, but they are not permitted to marry. Only the good influence of his friend, Lord Bomston, keeps the emotional Saint-Preux from committing murder or suicide when Julie has to marry M. de Wolmar.

Claire, Julie's cousin and companion. She, too, loves Saint-Preux and expresses a desire to marry him, after she has become a widow.

Lord Edward Bomston, an English lord who becomes Saint-Preux's good friend. Before he knows of the affair between Julie and Saint-Preux, he courts Julie. Later, he is kind enough to offer to take the lovers as his pensioners if they elope and move to England. He also tries on their behalf to persuade Baron d'Étange to permit Julie and Saint-Preux to marry.

Baron d'Étange, Julie's father. He wants his daughter to marry his friend, M. de Wolmar. He is so proud of his class and lineage that he will not hear of a marriage between Julie and Saint-Preux.

Mme d'Étange, Julie's mother. She might have permitted Julie's marriage to Saint-Preux, but she dies before she can help the lovers.

M. de Wolmar (deh vohl-MAHR), whom Julie marries.

THE NEW LIFE
(La vita nuova)

Author: Dante Alighieri (1265-1321)
First transcribed: c. 1292
Genre: Poetry

Locale: Italy
Time: Thirteenth century
Plot: Sentimental

Dante Alighieri (DAHN-tay ahl-eeg-YEH-ree), the author, narrator, and editor-commentator. He is also the protagonist in the love story. A Florentine citizen born in the thirteenth century, Dante is in his ninth year when he first glimpses Beatrice, another Florentine citizen in her ninth year, and immediately falls in love with her. He next encounters her when they are both eighteen. He attempts to hide his infatuation from both his beloved and the general populace, but his emotions are so pronounced that they cannot be hidden. In an attempt to relieve the pain of his unrequited love, he composes poems expressing his love and admiration for Beatrice, often masking them by addressing them to others. When Beatrice dies after having lived an exemplary life, Dante joins all of Florence in mourning her passing while angels in heaven rejoice in her presence. A lady looking down from a window has compassion for the mournful Dante and comforts him for a period. Following a vision, Dante realizes the full meaning of Beatrice's miraculous life and vows to write of her that which has never been written of any woman, a task he presumably accomplishes in his greatest work, *The Divine Comedy.*

Beatrice, the young girl with whom Dante falls in love at the age of nine. She is a silent character in the book, never speaking directly to Dante. Her only communication with the protagonist is through a salutation given to him in passing, which results in his joy; in sharp contrast, the withholding of such a greeting leads to his despair. Her name signifies "giver of blessings," and throughout the text she is associated with marvelous events and the mystical number nine (the Holy Trinity repeated three times). She often appears as a figure of Christ, and upon her premature death, the whole of Florence mourns. The prose and poems of the book narrate the story of Dante's evolving love for Beatrice, from juvenile eroticism (including erotic dreams) to mature adoration (including heavenly visions).

Love (Amor), the personification of the controlling sentiment of the protagonist's life. The author presents Love in the figure of a lord who directs and influences Dante. In various appearances or visions, Love interacts with, counsels, and serves as a confidant to Dante.

Love's "faithful ones," the poets in love—including Dante's best friend, Guido Cavalcanti, to whom the book is dedicated—who make up the implied audience for most of Dante's poems.

The "screen lady," a woman who sits between Dante and Beatrice in church and to whom Dante addresses some of his early poems. The lyrics are meant for Beatrice but are sent to the "screen lady" to conceal the true object of his attention. Dante's fear that his love will become the talk of the town leads him to rely first and at some length on one "screen lady" and then, when she departs from Florence, on a second one for a briefer period. Finally, a personified Love commands the author to write openly of the true object of his desire, Beatrice.

Giovanna, also known as **Primavera** (Spring, or "one who comes first"). A companion to Beatrice, Giovanna is seen walking ahead of her. Dante the narrator notes that this occurrence is analogous to the New Testament event in which the ministry of Giovanni (John the Baptist)—the masculine version of the name Giovanna—preceded that of Jesus Christ.

The Lady at the Window, a woman who has compassion for Dante when she sees him weeping over the death of Beatrice. This beautiful lady distracts Dante for a period after the passing of his beloved.

— *Madison U. Sowell*

A NEW LIFE

Author: Bernard Malamud (1914-1986)
First published: 1961
Genre: Novel

Locale: The northwestern United States
Time: 1950-1951
Plot: Realism

Seymour Levin, a Jewish college professor. He is a thirty-year-old, bearded, East Coast liberal, recovering from a two-year drinking episode following his mother's suicide and his rejection by his lover. A failure in love and in his profession, Levin goes to the West Coast to teach in the English department of a state university, hoping to start a new life. By mistake, he finds himself at the state technical school rather than at the liberal arts school. He quickly becomes embroiled in the departmental squabbles about textbooks and the relative importance of teaching composition versus literature. Eventually, out of desperation, he quixotically enters the competition for department chairman. In the meantime, he has an affair with the wife of the man who is primarily responsible for giving him the job and who will become the new chairman. Levin's experiences within the department and with Pauline leave him with the ability to face life on its terms, exemplified by his willingness to assume responsibility for her and her children.

Pauline Gilley, the wife of the assistant department chairman. Thirty-two years old and discontented with her marriage and with life in general, she initiates an affair with Levin, as she did with his predecessor in the department. Whatever her faults, Pauline needs someone more capable of expressing love than is her husband.

Gerald Gilley, a college English teacher, the director of composition and eventually the department chairman. More interested in departmental politics and fishing than in teaching or in his family, Gilley is uneasy about Levin's beard, his Jewishness, and his idealistic liberalism because they threaten his complacency. Within a short time of Levin's arrival, he and Levin are on opposite sides in departmental controversies. His references to the virtues of teaching are actually rationalizations for lack of commitment to anything aside from himself. His response to his wife's affair is very self-centered: He feels betrayed by the man he brought into the department and has him fired.

C. D. Fabrikant, the only scholar in the department. In his fifties, a Harvard man, and theoretically a liberal, Fabrikant is also an outsider in the department. He is the spokesman for the opposition and Gilley's principal contender for the chairmanship. Levin is disappointed to discover that resentment and desire for power, rather than liberalism, are his primary motivators; consequently, Levin runs for the position himself.

Aviss Fliss, a teacher of remedial composition and assistant to the director. Miss Fliss, in her thirties, is the only unmarried woman in the department and fails in her attempt to have an affair with Levin. A major source of gossip about her colleagues, she also serves as a spy for Gilley.

Leonard Duffy, Levin's predecessor in the department and in the arms of Pauline. An outsider from the East, like Levin, he never fit in. Gilley drove him from the school when he became suspicious of the relationship with Pauline.

— *William J. McDonald*

A NEW WAY TO PAY OLD DEBTS

Author: Philip Massinger (1583-1640)
First published: 1633
Genre: Drama

Locale: England
Time: Early seventeenth century
Plot: Comedy of manners

Frank Wellborn, an impoverished gentleman who has wasted much of his inheritance and been defrauded of the rest by his uncle, Sir Giles Overreach. His fortunes are at their lowest ebb when young Allworth discovers him as he is being evicted from a tavern for refusing to pay his bill. He proudly refuses to accept aid from the boy and plans instead to avenge himself on his unjust uncle. A shrewd judge of character, he wins Lady Allworth's assistance by reminding her of his generosity to her late husband and plays on Marall's natural greed to further his plot against Sir Giles. When he regains his fortune, he rejects his prodigal past entirely and, hoping to win back his lost reputation, asks Lord Lovell for a company to command.

Sir Giles Overreach, Wellborn's miserly, tyrannical uncle. Although he vows that he is ambitious only for the sake of his young daughter, he gathers without scruple the wealth and rank he desires for her, destroying whoever stands in his way. His greed, accurately assessed by Wellborn, brings about his downfall; he has mentally confiscated Lady Allworth's property before he makes certain that his nephew is really to be her husband. The most crushing blow to his aspirations is his daughter's elopement with young Allworth, a marriage facilitated by his eagerness to make her Lady Lovell.

Margaret, Sir Giles' daughter, fortunately free of her father's vices. She is a dutiful child until she realizes to what lengths Sir Giles expects her to go to make herself Lady Lovell. She then relies on her love for young Allworth, Lord Lovell's support, and her own virtue to give her courage to deceive her father.

Tom Allworth, Lord Lovell's page, a kindhearted young gentleman. He indulges in romantic fits of despair and melancholy for his beloved Margaret before his master and Wellborn

help him to win his bride. In spite of these moods, he is a dutiful son and servant and a thoughtful friend.

Lady Allworth, his devoted stepmother, who has gone into seclusion to mourn for her late husband. She is persuaded to return to society to help Wellborn to avenge his wrongs. She wins, through her kindness, the affection of Lord Lovell and finally accepts his proposal of marriage.

Lord Lovell, a benevolent nobleman and a valiant soldier. He quickly penetrates Sir Giles' designs and offers his assistance to Margaret and young Allworth.

Marall, Sir Giles' servant, responsible for carrying out his schemes to defraud his neighbors. Lady Allworth's attentions to Wellborn, staged for his benefit, convince him that Wellborn may be a more profitable master than Sir Giles, and he willingly betrays the latter. His efforts are in vain, for Wellborn wisely concludes that a servant false to one master will be false to another and sends him away empty-handed.

Greedy, a justice of the peace, one of Sir Giles' hangers-on. His single-minded devotion to food and its preparation makes him an easy dupe in his patron's schemes.

Order,

Amble,

Furnace , and

Watchall, Lady Allworth's loyal servants, who dubiously follow their mistress' orders to treat Wellborn as an honored guest.

Tapster, a taverner who tries to throw the penniless Wellborn out of his house. Wellborn, reminding him that it was he who provided forty pounds to set up the business, thrashes him soundly for his ingratitude.

Froth, Tapster's wife.

Parson Willdo, another of Sir Giles' followers, who unwittingly deceives him by marrying Margaret to Allworth.

THE NEWCOMES: Memoirs of a Most Respectable Family

Author: William Makepeace Thackeray (1811-1863)
First published: 1853-1855
Genre: Novel

Locale: England
Time: Early nineteenth century
Plot: Social morality

Colonel Thomas Newcome, the son of Thomas Newcome, Esq., and his first wife, Susan. Always rebellious as a boy, he left home and went to India, where he distinguished himself in the Bengal Cavalry and in service with the East India Company. During his career, he married and fathered a son, Clive. When Mrs. Newcome died, the small boy was sent to England

to be educated. Later, after he had acquired a considerable fortune, Colonel Newcome returned to England to rejoin his son. Their fortunes prospered, and the father tried to give his son a happy life. Honest, naïve, tender-hearted, he acts always for the best, but his affairs turn out badly. Eventually, his fortune is dissipated by the failure of the great Bundlecund

Banking Company, in which he has invested his money, his daughter-in-law's, and funds some friends had entrusted to him. He spends his last days in poverty and at the mercy of a domineering old widow, the mother of his daughter-in-law. Always mindful of his son's happiness, the colonel tries for years to guide Clive's life, but he succeeds only in involving the young man with the wrong wife and settling him in a business career he does not enjoy. At the time of his death, the colonel is a pensioner in the Hospital of Grey Friars.

Clive Newcome, the colonel's son, a young man with considerable artistic ability. His charming manner endears him to a great many friends, including his cousin, Ethel Newcome, but because Clive is not of noble birth, her mother and grandmother do not approve of the match. Clive marries another young woman whom his father cherishes, but the union is a failure because a domineering mother-in-law presides over the Newcome household. Clive changes from the carefree boy that he once was to a bitter young man estranged for a time from his devoted father, whom he blames for much of his misery. At the end of the story, Clive is a widower with a small son; the reader is left with the impression that he will marry Ethel Newcome.

Ethel Newcome, the beautiful, spirited daughter of Colonel Newcome's half brother Brian. Her mother, Lady Ann Newcome, is descended from an aristocratic family, and it is the hope of her grandmother, Lady Kew, that Ethel will marry well. Ethel is especially fond of Colonel Newcome. She is also attracted to Clive, but the energy of her grandmother in pushing her into society blinds her to her cousin's attentions. Haughty and high-spirited, Ethel rejects several offers of marriage and ends up taking charge of the children of her selfish, brutal brother Barnes. Estranged from the colonel and Clive because she has belittled her cousin's intentions, she develops into a serious, self-sacrificing spinster; but at the end of the story she turns over a part of the Newcome fortune to her uncle and cousin, and the reader is left anticipating her subsequent marriage to Clive.

James Binnie, Colonel Newcome's friend in the Indian service, a man of great humor, good sense, and intelligence. He, his widowed sister Mrs. Mackenzie, and her daughter Rosa live with the colonel and Clive. He leaves his fortune to his niece when he dies; this is some of the money that the colonel invests in the Bundlecund Banking Company. Fortunately, Binnie dies before his friend goes bankrupt and his sister turns into a shrew.

Rosa Newcome, called **Rosey**, the daughter of Mrs. Mackenzie, a shy, pretty girl when she and her mother come to live with the Newcomes and her uncle, James Binnie. Always anxious to please, Rosey has no life of her own, for she is completely overwhelmed by her domineering mother. Never truly in love with Clive, she turns more and more against him after their marriage. She dies in childbirth without having known any real happiness.

Mrs. Mackenzie, called the **Campaigner**, the widowed sister of James Binnie and a vigorous, good-humored, but domineering person at the beginning of the story. She is particularly possessive of her daughter Rosey, who marries Clive Newcome. After their money has been lost through Colonel Newcome's unwise investments, she turns into a termagant and a domestic terror. She torments the colonel because of his

misfortunes, becomes more and more possessive of Rosey, and makes life miserable for Clive.

Thomas Newcome, Esq., the father of Thomas, Brian, and Hobson Newcome, a poor man who, through industry and thrift, created a prosperous banking establishment. Truly in love with his first wife, who dies soon after the birth of their son Thomas, he marries a second time but is never really happy thereafter.

Susan Newcome, the first wife of Thomas Newcome, Esq. She is pretty but penniless, and she dies young, in childbirth.

Sophia Althea Newcome, the stepmother of young Thomas Newcome and mother of the twins, Brian and Hobson. An efficient businesswoman, she influences her husband in his banking business. Rigid and domineering, she never cares for her stepson and is happy when he goes off to India. Before her death, however, she requests that he inherit some of her money; this is the sum that Ethel Newcome turns over to Colonel Newcome and her cousin Clive.

Sir Brian Newcome, the half brother of Colonel Newcome and the twin of Hobson. He is a neat, bland, smiling banker whose external appearance masks his selfish, ambitious nature. Never fully aware of his half brother's virtues, Brian does not entertain him until after he learns of the colonel's wealth after his return to England.

Lady Ann Newcome, Sir Brian's wife, the daughter of haughty old Lady Kew. Pleasant but rather flighty, she entertains a more aristocratic set than does her sister-in-law, Mrs. Hobson Newcome. She is kind to Colonel Newcome and Clive, though she cannot approve the idea of the young man's marriage to her daughter Ethel.

Hobson Newcome, Sir Brian's twin brother, a portly, red-whiskered country squire. Never really comfortable with his wife's intellectual and artistic friends, he tolerates them as long as they do not interfere with his agricultural pursuits.

Mrs. Hobson Newcome, a fat, pretty woman fond of artistic people. She never fails to hint that this interest makes her superior to her sister-in-law, of whom she is jealous. She has affection for Clive and believes that she deals generously and gracefully with Colonel Newcome.

Barnes Newcome, Sir Brian's oldest son, a hypocritical dandy who conceives a great dislike for Colonel Newcome and Clive. The father of two children by one of the village girls, he marries Lady Clara Pulleyn. Their marriage is a dreadful one; he tortures his wife mentally and treats their children abominably. Finally, Lady Clara leaves him, and Ethel Newcome cares for the abandoned children. Barnes stands against his uncle in an election and loses to him, but Colonel Newcome's bankruptcy prevents his serving in Parliament.

Lady Clara Pulleyn, later Barnes Newcome's wife, a pretty, sad girl whose marriage was arranged by her parents. She leads a miserable life, even after she has been divorced from her brutal husband and has married Jack Belsize; there is always the shadow of her former life between them.

The Honorable Charles Belsize, called **Jack Belsize** by his friends, later **Lord Highgate**, in love with Lady Clara Pulleyn. On one occasion, he creates a scandalous scene because of his jealousy of Barnes Newcome. Lady Clara flees to him when she deserts her husband; after her divorce, they are married.

Lord Kew, called **Frank**, Ethel Newcome's cousin and Jack Belsize's good friend, an open-hearted, honorable young man who sincerely loves Ethel. She refuses his suit after the scandal of her brother's family life and divorce is made public.

Lady Kew, Lady Ann Newcome's aristocratic mother. Insulting and overbearing, she runs the affairs of her family and arranges their marriages.

Lady Julia, Lady Kew's older daughter, completely dependent on her mother and forced to take the fierce old woman's abuse.

Lady Walham, Lord Kew's mother, a long-suffering victim of her mother-in-law's domineering ways.

George Barnes, Lord Kew's younger brother.

Lady Henrietta Pulleyn, Lady Clara's sister. She marries Lord Kew after Ethel Newcome has rejected him.

Sarah Mason, Susan Newcome's housekeeper and companion, never forgotten by Colonel Newcome. He supports her throughout most of her life and tries to do so even after he has gone bankrupt.

Martha Honeyman, Clive Newcome's aunt and his guardian during his boyhood in England, a soft-spoken woman who dearly loves her charge. Thrifty and careful, she is constantly alarmed by the spendthrift ways of Charles, her clergyman brother.

Charles Honeyman, Martha's clergyman brother and Colonel Newcome's brother-in-law. Fond of gambling and the wine bottle, he wastes much of the money that the colonel gives him. Later, he goes to India and becomes a popular clergyman there. Though appearing humble and meek in manner, he is actually cunning and selfish.

Mr. Ridley, Charles Honeyman's landlord.

Mrs. Ridley, his wife, a good woman who befriends Colonel Newcome.

John James Ridley, called **J. J.**, their son and Clive Newcome's good friend. A talented boy, he becomes a successful artist and is elected to the Royal Academy. When Clive is in financial difficulties, J. J. buys several of his friend's paintings.

Arthur Pendennis, Clive Newcome's friend and an editor of the *Pall Mall Gazette*. He narrates the story of the Newcomes, and he and his wife are always ready to help Colonel Newcome and Clive in their troubles.

Laura Pendennis, his wife. She becomes fond of Ethel Newcome and tries to promote the affair between Clive and his cousin. Never able to tolerate Rosey Newcome, Laura is not surprised when Clive's marriage proves unhappy.

Larkins, the Pendennises' servant.

George Warrington, co-editor of the *Pall Mall Gazette* and a friend of Clive Newcome and Arthur Pendennis.

The Marquis of Farintosh, a gossipy, fashionable young man whom Lady Kew selects as an eligible suitor for Ethel Newcome's hand. Ethel rejects his offer.

Lady Glenlivat, Lord Farintosh's mother.

Todhunter and

Henchman, toadies to Lord Farintosh.

The Duc d'Ivry, a sixty-year-old French nobleman.

Madame la Duchesse d'Ivry, his wife, much younger than her husband; a poetess and a patroness of the arts. She is responsible for a duel between Lord Kew and hot-tempered Monsieur de Castillones.

Antoinette, their daughter.

Monsieur de Castillones, Lord Kew's rival for the favors of the duchesse d'Ivry. He wounds Lord Kew, but not fatally, in a duel.

The Comte de Florac, later the **Duc d'Ivry**, a French aristocrat of ancient lineage and a gentleman of the old school.

Madame de Florac, his wife, for many years secretly in love with Colonel Newcome.

Vicomte Paul de Florac, also the **Prince de Montcontour**, their son, an exuberant young Frenchman, a friend of Clive Newcome and Lord Kew.

Madame la Princesse de Montcontour, nee Higgs,

Miss Cann, an artist, a tenant of the Ridleys and a friend of Clive Newcome and J. J. Ridley.

Fred Bayham, another tenant of the Ridleys, a boisterous old school friend of Charles Honeyman, whom he loves to bait. He is a favorite among the poor people of Newcome when he campaigns for the election of Colonel Newcome to Parliament.

Mr. Gandish, an artist, the head of the art school where Clive Newcome and J. J. Ridley study.

Charles Gandish, his son.

Mrs. Irons, the housekeeper of Colonel Newcome and James Binnie. Jealous of Mrs. Mackenzie, she does not get along with that domineering woman.

Mr. Sherrick, a wine merchant and a friend of the Honeymans. Because he had invested money in the Bundlecund Banking Company, he is one of those whom Colonel Newcome feels he must repay.

Mrs. Sherrick, his wife, a former opera singer.

Miss Sherrick, their daughter.

Rowland and

Oliver, the lawyers in the divorce suit of Lady Clara and Barnes Newcome.

Horace Fogey,

Sir Thomas de Boots, and

Charles Heavyside, friends of Barnes Newcome and members of the fashionable London club of which he is a member.

John Giles, Esq., the brother-in-law of Mrs. Hobson Newcome, a poor relation.

Louisa Giles, his wife.

Mademoiselle Lebrun, the French governess to the children of the Hobson Newcomes.

Hannah Hicks, Martha Honeyman's devoted servant, who assists her mistress in the operation of a seaside lodging house.

Sally, another servant in the Honeyman lodging house, a pretty but inefficient girl.

Captain Gobey, a friend whom Colonel Newcome, James Binnie, and the Mackenzies meet on the Continent.

Captain Hobey, another friend from the Continent, a suitor of Rosey Mackenzie.

Tom Potts, a hatter in Newcome and editor of the local paper; he hates Barnes Newcome.

Dr. Quackenboss, a society doctor who attends Rosey Newcome.

Miss O'Grady, the governess of the daughter of the duc and duchesse d'Ivry.

NEWS FROM NOWHERE

Author: William Morris (1834-1896)
First published: 1891
Genre: Novel

Locale: London and along the Thames River
Time: Late nineteenth century and twenty-first century
Plot: Utopian

Guest, the narrator, a thinly disguised version of William Morris, the author. The reader first encounters him at the opening of the book, where he has just left a political meeting. He is annoyed with himself for his habit of losing his temper in these discussions, and he is discontented with the grimy surroundings of late nineteenth century London, through which he must travel to return to his suburban home. As he encounters people in his utopian dream vision, he reveals that he appears old and not well-dressed. The questions that he asks about the community to which he has been transported demonstrate his beliefs in an idealized world. He develops a romantic attachment to an attractive young woman named Ellen, whom he meets on his journey up the Thames River. Their relationship remains friendly and platonic.

Richard (Dick) Hammond, the boatman. He is the first person Guest encounters in "Nowhere." Dick takes Guest in his boat to the Guest House in Hammersmith, which was the London suburb where William Morris lived, and he remains Guest's guide throughout the time he spends in the utopian Nowhere. Dick's tanned skin and developed physique indicate that he spends much time occupied outdoors. His simple but well-fitted dark blue garment with an ornamental belt buckle, reminiscent of a fourteenth century costume, gives him an appearance of gentility that his gracious manners reinforce. Dick takes Guest to visit Old Hammond, Dick's great-grandfather. The next day, they go on a four-day journey up the Thames to take part in the hay harvest in Oxfordshire, so that Guest can see the countryside. On this journey, they are accompanied by Clara, Dick's fiancée, to whom Dick was married earlier. They are happily reunited when Dick and Guest visit Old Hammond, who serves as a matchmaker for the couple.

Old Hammond, Dick's great-grandfather, who lives at the British Museum, where he was "custodian" of the books in the library. Dick tells Guest that Old Hammond is more than 105 years old. He is small but spry, and he is very knowledgeable. He is also an astute judge of human character and acts as matchmaker to reunite Dick and Clara, who previously had been married. Old Hammond may actually be Guest's grandson. Guest and Old Hammond spend most of the day sitting in Old Hammond's simply furnished living room. Old Hammond's experience and wisdom are evident from the lengthy answers that he gives to Guest's questions about the society and government of Nowhere and his explanation of how England was transformed into this new utopian state. Old Hammond, in effect, articulates the political philosophy of William Morris.

Clara, Dick's fiancée, who meets Dick at Old Hammond's apartment. Clara is described as a very beautiful young woman. The way Dick blushes at the mention of her name and the way that they look at each other indicate their mutual attraction. After they go upstairs, Old Hammond explains to Guest that Dick and Clara had been married and had two children. Clara had left Dick for another man, but when that relationship failed after a year, she realized that she wanted to return to Dick. Clara is very spontaneous. She lives for the present and does not want to be troubled with the unhappiness of the past. She is concerned with Guest's appearance and well-being. At her instigation, Guest is provided with a new set of clothes for the trip up the Thames. She demonstrates the freedom of natural relationships between the sexes that is found in the utopian society of Nowhere.

Ellen, Guest's romantic interest. She meets Guest, Dick, and Clara on the first evening of their journey up the Thames. The trio spend the evening at the cottage at Runnymede where Ellen and her grandfather live. Ellen is a natural beauty with fair skin, tanned from spending time outside. She is spontaneous in her expression of delight in the visitors and the world around her. Like Clara, she takes pleasure from living in the moment. When she later joins Guest, Dick, and Clara as they travel along the Thames, she displays curiosity about the history of the area as she and Guest converse. She and Guest share an attraction to each other, which they express by sharing their thoughts in conversation. She represents a love of life in harmony with nature and the pure ideal of the utopian world that Morris envisions.

— *Karen Gould*

NIAGARA: A Stereophonic Novel
(6,810,000 Litres d'eau par seconde: Étude stéréophonique)

Author: Michel Butor (1926-   )
First published: 1965
Genre: Novel

Locale: Niagara Falls
Time: 1963
Plot: Impressionistic realism

The narrator, who provides directions for the staging/ reading of this stereophonic novel.

The producer, who chooses which and how many of the novel's ten "tracks" (A-J) to air.

The listener, who is able to adjust the balance and volume of the audio production.

The readers, who possess greater freedom and mobility than the listener. They are able to follow one or more of the novel's ten tracks, separately or together, and to adjust the "volume," according to the narrator's directions, from very soft to very loud.

The announcer, the voice positioned at the center, providing background and describing the contemporary scene and events. The announcer eventually comes to comment on the characters—always, however, by type, never by name.

The reader, also located at center of the audio performance and printed text. This voice alternates with that of the announcer, reading descriptions of Niagara from three works by Viscount François-René de Chateaubriand.

The old married couple, who are returning to Niagara Falls after thirty years. They see how it has changed and how they have changed. Over the course of the novel's twelve chapters (one for each month, April to March, alternately or concurrently and stereophonically covering a two-day period), the names of the old couple introduced in chapter 2 will change, though their role (as the old married couple) will remain the same. Thus, as the year and novel progress, the Charles and Diana of chapter 2 become or flow into Chris and Delia, Clem and Dorothy, Clifford and Deidre, Cary and Dora, Charlton and Doris, Claudius and Dollie, and Clinton and Dolly.

Just-marrieds, introduced in chapter 2, who cross the border into Canada and into marriage, devoting themselves to each other and to the metaphorically erotic activity of identifying and describing flowers. Their names are Abel and Betty, Arthur and Bertha, Andrew and Bettina, Alex and Betsey, Alec and Bessie, Alan and Billie, Albert and Bella, Anthony and Barbara, and Alfred and Beatrice. They are the character type that appears most often.

Black gardeners, introduced in chapter 3, whose voices correspond and contrast most closely with those of the old married couple. They introduce the novel's racial theme, the socioeconomic segregation of what are in fact complementary, even parallel, groups. They are visiting Niagara Falls for the first time and in certain cases work either for the old married couple or for the parents of the just-marrieds. Their names are Elias and Fanny, Elmer and Flossie, Emil and Florence, Edmund and Frieda, Errol and Fanny, Ernest and Flannery, Enoch and Felicia, and Elliot and Flora.

Old madam and

Gigolo, who are introduced in chapter 4. Having first visited the falls with her husband, the old madam returns now in the company of a young gigolo in an effort to reclaim her youth and beauty. She complains of others' gawking at them, he of having had to come at all. Their names are Gertrude and Hector, Gene and Humphrey, Gerda and Hubert, Georgia and Henry, Gracie and Hugh, Grace and Horace, Gina and Helmut, and Gaby and Herbert.

Vile seducer and

Easy prey, who are introduced in chapter 5. The sexual depredation evident in these pairings is deepened (in chapter 8) by the seducer's "disgust" as his conquest only proves that the girl is not who or what he desires, by the prey's inability to resist, and by her subsequent feeling of terror. Their names are Irling and Jenny, Irving and Jane, Igor and Judy, Ivo and Juliet, Ivor and Judy, and Iannis and Janet.

Young man alone, who is introduced in chapter 6, listening to and enviously watching others. His names are Keith, Klaus, Karl, Kent, Kenny, and Kenneth.

Young woman alone, who is introduced in chapter 7, wondering for what she has come looking. Her names are Lana, Lena, Liddy, and Laura.

White wife and husband, named **Dinah** and **Carroll**. As are all of the couples in chapter 7, they are "divorced" in that "each character speaks as if he were alone."

Widower, who is introduced in chapter 8. He is made desolate by the loss of his wife. The sights help him recall his wife, and the sounds "push" her further into darkness and oblivion. His names are Morris, Milton, and Morgan.

Widow, who is introduced in chapter 9. She longs either to dream her husband back to life or to cross over to the dead. Her names are Nelly, Nadia, and Nora.

Black widower, who is introduced in chapter 10. He speaks chiefly in fragments and short elliptical sentences. His names all begin with the letter *O*.

Black widow, whose names all begin with the letter *P*.

Quentin, a Frenchman, a visiting professor at the University of Buffalo. In his only line, an incomplete sentence, he notes that he is separated from his wife, not by death but by the Atlantic Ocean.

— *Robert A. Morace*

THE NIBELUNGENLIED

Author: Unknown
First transcribed: c. 1200
Genre: Poetry

Locale: North-central Europe
Time: Fifth and sixth centuries
Plot: Epic

Siegfried (ZEEG-freed), a prince of Niderland whose heroic achievements include the winning of the great treasure hoard of the Nibelung. Having bathed in the blood of a dragon he slew, Siegfried is invulnerable except for a spot between his shoulders where a linden leaf had fallen. He goes to Burgundy and there wins Kriemhild as his wife. Later, he is treacherously killed by a Burgundian knight.

Kriemhild (KREEM-hihlt), the beautiful sister of the king of Burgundy. She marries Siegfried and is subsequently tricked into revealing the secret of his vulnerability. After a long period of widowhood and mourning, she becomes the wife of the king of the Huns. Still seeking vengeance for Siegfried's death, she invites the whole Burgundian court to Hunland. In the final bloody combat, all the Burgundians are killed, and Kriemhild herself is slain by her husband's order.

Gunther (GEWN-tehr), king of Burgundy. He promises that Siegfried shall marry Kriemhild in return for aiding him in winning Brunhild. With Siegfried's aid, Gunther overcomes Brunhild in her required feats of skill and strength. After the double wedding, Siegfried is again needed to impersonate Gunther in subduing Brunhild, who has determined never to let Gunther share her bed. Gunther is killed in the final bloodbath in Hunland.

Brunhild (BREWN-hihlt), the daughter of Wotan, won by Gunther with Siegfried's help. Wishing to see Siegfried again, she plans a hunting party to which he and Kriemhild are invited. A great rivalry develops between the women; Kriemhild takes revenge by telling Brunhild the true story of her wedding night. Though Gunther and Siegfried settle the quarrel to their own satisfaction, it becomes a source of trouble among Gunther's brothers.

Hagen (HAH-gehn), a retainer of the Burgundians and a crafty and troublemaking knight. It is he who slays Siegfried. Hoping to get the Nibelungen treasure, now Kriemhild's, for himself, he orders it dropped into the Rhine. He is slain by Kriemhild herself, and with him dies the secret of the treasure's hiding place.

Gernot (GEHR-noht) and

Giselher (GEE-seh-lehr), brothers of Kriemhild and Gunther. Convinced by Hagen that Siegfried has stained the honor of their house, they plot with Hagen to kill him. Later, they fall victim to Brunhild's revenge.

Etzel (EHT-tsehl), also known as **Attila**, king of the Huns, Kriemhild's second husband.

Ortlieb (OHRT-leeb), Kriemhild's small son. Etzel gives him to the Burgundians as a hostage, and he is killed by Hagen when the fighting begins.

Dankwart (DHANK-vahrt), the brother of Hagen. He too is killed in Hunland.

Sir Dietrich (DEE-trihkh), a knight who warns the Burgundians that Kriemhild still plots vengeance. As a result, they refuse to give up their weapons.

Sir Bloedel (BLEW-dehl), a knight who comes to Dankwart's quarters demanding vengeance for Kriemhild. He is killed by Dankwart, and thus the final bloody combat begins.

Iring (IH-rihng), one of Kriemhild's heroes.

Hildebrand (HEEL-deh-brahnd), a retainer of Etzel. At a sign from Etzel, he ends Kriemhild's life.

Hunold (HEW-nohlt), a Burgundian hero.

Queen Uta (EW-tah), the mother of Kriemhild.

King Siegmund (ZEEG-mewnt), the father of Siegfried.

Queen Sieglind (ZEEG-lihnt, the mother of Siegfried.

Ludger (LEWT-gehr), king of the Saxons. After spending a year in the Burgundian court, Siegfried aids Gunther in overcoming the Saxons. In the celebrations that follow, Ludger sees Kriemhild for the first time.

Gelfrat (GEHL-fraht), a Burgundian slain by Dankwart in a quarrel at the start of the journey to Hunland. This and other evil omens are ignored.

Albric (AHL-brihk), a dwarf from whom Siegfried wins a cloak of invisibility.

NICHOLAS NICKLEBY

Author: Charles Dickens (1812-1870)
First published: 1838-1839
Genre: Novel

Locale: England
Time: Early nineteenth century
Plot: Social realism

Nicholas Nickleby, the handsome, warm-hearted, enterprising son of a widow whose husband's death left her and her two children impoverished as the result of unwise speculations. Through the grudging influence of his uncle, a shrewd, miserly London businessman, he secures a post as an assistant master at Dotheboys Hall, a wretched school for boys, at a salary of five pounds a year. Finding conditions at the school impossible to tolerate, he thrashes Wackford Squeers, his employer, quits the place in disgust, and returns to London in the company of Smike, a half-starved, broken-spirited drudge, now his loyal friend, whom he saved from the schoolmaster's brutality. After being cleared of a false charge of thievery brought by his uncle and the vindictive Squeers, he sets out again in the hope of bettering his fortune. He becomes an actor in a traveling troupe but is called back to London on behalf of his sister Kate, who has become the victim of the unwelcome attentions of Sir Mulberry Hawk and Lord Frederick Verisopht, two notorious rakes. After disabling one of her pursuers, he finds work with the generous Cheeryble brothers, and his fortunes improve, so that he is able to provide a home for his mother and sister. He falls in love with Madeline Bray and rescues her from marriage to an elderly miser. After the romantic and financial complications of this situation have been unraveled, Nicholas and Madeline are married.

Kate Nickleby, his refined, pretty sister. After her arrival in London, she first finds work with a dressmaker and later becomes a companion to Mrs. Julia Witterly, a vulgar, silly middle-class woman; meanwhile, her uncle uses her as a snare to entrap two lustful noblemen. After Nicholas goes to work for the Cheeryble brothers, her future becomes secure. In love

with Frank Cheeryble, the nephew of her brother's benefactors, she marries him when she is convinced at last that the young man is truly in love with her.

Mrs. Nickleby, their mother, an ineffective but well-meaning woman. Because of her poor judgment, she becomes the dupe of several coarse, mean people.

Ralph Nickleby, the miserly, treacherous uncle who finds ignominious work for both Nicholas and Kate and then attempts to use them. After his schemes have been exposed and the unfortunate Smike has been revealed as the son whom he supposed dead, he hangs himself.

Smike, Ralph Nickleby's lost son, who had been abandoned by a former clerk to the harsh care of Wackford Squeers. Flogged and starved until he resembles a scarecrow, he runs away from Dotheboys Hall to share the fortunes of Nicholas Nickleby. When Nicholas joins a theatrical troupe, Smike plays the apothecary in *Romeo and Juliet*. Recaptured by Squeers, he escapes with the aid of John Browdie, a stouthearted Yorkshireman, and finds sanctuary with Nicholas once more. He falls in love with Kate Nickleby, despairingly because he is dying of tuberculosis. After his death it is revealed that he was the son of Ralph Nickleby.

Madeline Bray, a beautiful girl whose devotion to her selfish, dissolute father leads her to accept the proposal of Arthur Gride. Her father dying suddenly, Nicholas and Kate save her from the clutches of Gride and his friend, Ralph Nickleby. Later a lost will, concealed by Gride, is recovered, and Madeline becomes an heiress. She and Nicholas Nickleby are married after both experience reversals of fortune.

Walter Bray, Madeline's father. For his own selfish purposes, he plans to marry his daughter to an unwelcome and much older suitor, Arthur Gride. At his death, before he can complete his plan to barter off his daughter, Nicholas Nickleby and his sister Kate rescue Madeline and take her to their mother's home.

Edwin Cheerybyle and

Charles Cheeryble, two benevolent brothers who make Nicholas Nickleby a clerk in their counting house, establish his family in a comfortable cottage, help to thwart the schemes of Ralph Nickleby, and finally bring about the marriages of Nicholas to Madeline Bray and Kate Nickleby to their nephew.

Frank Cheeryble, the gentlemanly nephew of the Cheeryble brothers. He marries Kate Nickleby after the uncles have set right her mistaken belief that Frank loves Madeline Bray.

Wackford Squeers, the brutal, predatory proprietor of Dotheboys Hall and an underling of Ralph Nickleby. Thrashed by Nicholas Nickleby for his treatment of Smike and his cruelty to the helpless boys entrusted to his care, he tries to get revenge with Ralph's help. Arrested for stealing the will that provides for Madeline Bray's inheritance, he is sentenced to transportation for seven years.

Mrs. Squeers, his wife, a worthy helpmeet for her cruel, rapacious husband.

Fanny Squeers, their daughter, a twenty-three-year-old shrew. She is at first attracted to Nicholas Nickleby, her father's underpaid assistant, but later turns against him when he rebuffs her advances and declares that his only desire is to get away from detested Dotheboys Hall.

Wackford Squeers, Jr., a nasty boy who combines the worst traits of his parents.

Newman Noggs, Ralph Nickleby's eccentric, kindhearted clerk and drudge. Ruined by Ralph's knavery, he enters the miser's employ in order to unmask his villainies. He aids Nicholas Nickleby and Smike on several occasions and is instrumental in securing Madeline Bray's inheritance. After Ralph's death, he is restored to respectability.

Brooker, a felon, at one time Ralph Nickleby's clerk, later his enemy. He makes Ralph believe that his son is dead as part of a scheme for extorting money from his former employer. He reveals Smike's true identity and thus causes Ralph's suicide.

Arthur Gride, Madeline Bray's miserly old suitor, who makes Ralph Nickleby his accomplice in keeping the girl's inheritance a secret. He is later killed by robbers.

Lord Frederick Verisopht, a gullible young rake, the ruined dupe of Sir Mulberry Hawk. Enamored of Kate Nickleby, he tries to seduce her. Later, he quarrels with Sir Mulberry and is killed in a duel by his mentor in vice.

Sir Mulberry Hawk, a man of fashion, a gambler, and a knave, severely punished by Nicholas Nickleby for his attempt to ruin the young man's sister. Sir Mulberry quarrels with his foolish dupe, Lord Frederick Verisopht, and kills him in a duel.

Tom Linkinwater, the Cheerybles' chief clerk, a man as amiable and cheerful as his employers. He marries Miss La Creevy.

Miss Linkinwater, his sister.

Miss La Creevy, a fifty-year-old spinster, a miniature painter, and the landlady of the Nicklebys when they first come to London. She marries Tom Linkinwater.

Peg Sliderskew, Arthur Gride's wizened, deaf, ugly old housekeeper. She steals her master's papers, including the will

bequeathing money to Madeline Bray. Squeers, hired by Ralph Nickleby to secure the document, is apprehended by Newman Noggs and Frank Cheeryble while in the act of pocketing it.

Mr. Snawley, a smooth-spoken hypocrite who sends his two stepsons to Dotheboys Hall. Ralph Nickleby's tool, he commits perjury by swearing that Smike is his son, abducted by Nicholas Nickleby. Later, when his guilt is revealed, he confesses, implicating Ralph and Squeers as his confederates.

Mrs. Snawley, his wife.

Madame Mantalini, the owner of a fashionable dressmaking establishment in which Kate Nickleby works for a time. She goes bankrupt because of her husband's extravagance.

Alfred Mantalini, born Muntle, a spendthrift. When cajolery and flattery fail to get him the money he wants, he resorts to threats of suicide in order to obtain funds from his wife. Eventually his wasteful, foppish habits bring her to bankruptcy, and she secures a separation. Imprisoned, he is befriended by a sympathetic washerwoman who secures his release. Before long she tires of his idleness and airy manners, and she puts him to work turning a mangle "like a demd old horse in a demnition mill."

Mr. Kenwigs, a turner in ivory who lives with his family in the same boardinghouse with Newman Noggs.

Mrs. Kenwigs, his wife, a woman genteely born.

Morleena Kenwigs, their older daughter. Her attendance at a dancing school helps to establish her mother's pretensions to gentility.

Mr. Lillyvick, Mrs. Kenwigs' uncle and a collector of water rates. At a party, he meets Henrietta Petowker, an actress from the Theatre Royal, follows her to Portsmouth, and marries her. His marriage brings dismay to his niece and her husband, who had regarded themselves as his heirs. After his fickle wife deserts him, he makes a will in favor of the Kenwigs' children.

Henrietta Petowker, an actress who marries Mr. Lillyvick and then elopes with a captain on half-pay.

Matilda Price, a Yorkshire lass and Fanny Squeers' friend, engaged to John Browdie. The two women quarrel when Matilda flirts with Nicholas Nickelby, whom Fanny has marked as her own.

John Browdie, a hearty, openhanded young Yorkshireman who becomes jealous of Nicholas Nickleby when Matilda Price, his betrothed, flirts with the young man. Later, realizing that Nicholas was completely innocent, John lends him money to return to London. He releases Smike from the custody of Wackford Squeers.

Miss Knag, the forewoman in Madame Mantalini's dressmaking establishment. She is kind to Kate Nickleby at first but later turns against her. She takes over the business when Madame Mantalini goes bankrupt.

Celia Bobster, the girl whom Newman Noggs mistakes for Madeline Bray and at whose house Nicholas Nickleby calls before the error is discovered.

Mr. Bobster, her hot-tempered father.

Mrs. Julia Witterly, a woman of middle-class background and aristocratic pretense, who hires Kate Nickleby as her companion.

Henry Witterly, her husband. He believes that his wife is "of a very excitable nature, very delicate, very fragile, a hothouse plant, an exotic."

Mr. Bonney, Ralph Nickleby's friend and a promoter of the United Improved Hot Muffin and Crumpet Baking and Punctual Delivery Company, of which Ralph is a director.

Mr. Gregsby, a member of Parliament, a pompous politician to whom Nicholas Nickleby applies for a position as a private secretary. Nicholas declines the situation after Mr. Gregsby explains fully the duties and responsibilities he expects a secretary to assume.

Vincent Crummles, the manager of a traveling theatrical company that Nicholas Nickleby and Smike join for a time; Nicholas adapts plays and acts in them, and Smike plays the part of the apothecary in *Romeo and Juliet*. Nicholas and his employer become close friends.

Mrs. Crummles, his wife.

Ninetta Crummles, their daughter, billed as the "Infant Phenomenon."

Miss Snevellicci,

Mr. and Mrs. Snevellicci, her parents,

Miss Belvawney,

Mrs. Grudden,

Thomas Lenville,

Miss Bravassa,

Miss Ledbrook, and

The African Knife Swallower, members of the Crummles theatrical troupe.

Tomkins,

Belling,

Graymarsh,

Cobbey,

Bolder,

Mobbs,

Jennings, and

Brooks, pupils at Dotheboys Hall.

Mr. Curdle, an amateur critic of the drama and the author of a sixty-four-page pamphlet on the deceased husband of the nurse in *Romeo and Juliet*.

Pyke, a servant of Sir Mulberry Hawk.

Captain Adams and

Mr. Westwood, seconds in the duel between Sir Mulberry Hawk and Lord Frederick Verisopht.

NICK OF THE WOODS: Or, The Jibbenainosay, a Tale of Kentucky

Author: Robert Montgomery Bird (1806-1854)
First published: 1837
Genre: Novel

Locale: Kentucky
Time: 1782
Plot: Adventure

Nathan Slaughter, a Quaker trapper driven by the deaths of his wife and children to a career of violence against the Indians, who call him the Jibbenainosay, meaning Spirit-that-walks. The whites call the unknown avenger Nick of the Woods, not knowing the man is really the peaceful Quaker they ironically name Bloody Nathan.

Captain Roland Forrester, a young Virginia patriot of the Revolutionary War. Disinherited by his Tory uncle, he seeks to start life afresh in the Kentucky country. He is twenty-three. He returns to Virginia when his cousin Edith is named the uncle's heir; he has to look after his cousin and also Telie Doe.

Roaring Ralph Stackpole, a braggart and a thief. Despite his shortcomings, he is loyal to his fellow whites and proves a good fighter against the Indians. He is a frontiersman of the Mike Fink and Davy Crockett type.

Edith Forrester, Roland's cousin. She is temporarily disinherited when her uncle's second will cannot be found. After adventures in Kentucky, she is named her uncle's rightful heir.

Wenonga, a Shawnee chief. He is killed by Nathan Slaughter for leading the attack that resulted in the deaths of Nathan's family.

Richard Braxley, Major Forrester's lawyer. He villainously conceals the major's second will, hoping to marry Edith, produce the second will, and thus come into command of Edith's fortune. He is killed on the frontier after the second will is found in his possession.

Abel Doe, a white renegade who joins the Indians in their attack on the whites.

Telie Doe, Abel's daughter, given a home by the Bruce family.

Colonel Bruce, commander of Bruce's Station, an outpost in the Kentucky country.

Pardon Dodge, a pioneer who helps the Forresters in the Kentucky country.

Major Roland Forrester, Edith and young Roland's rich Tory uncle.

Mrs. Bruce, Colonel Bruce's voluble but hospitable wife.

Tom Bruce, the Bruces' eldest son, an able Indian fighter.

NICKEL MOUNTAIN: A Pastoral Novel

Author: John Gardner (1933-1982)
First published: 1973
Genre: Novel

Locale: The farming country in the Catskills of upstate New York
Time: 1954-1960
Plot: Pastoral

Henry Soames, forty-one years old, the owner of the Stop-Off diner located in the Catskill Mountains. His heart condition is the result of his being ninety pounds overweight, but his hunger for food is outstripped by his hunger for talk and companionship. His streak of violence and self-destructiveness is offset by his huge meaningless love of humankind. "Caught up in the buzzing, blooming confusion," Henry believes that every person must find something worth being crucified for—in Henry's case, his wife and son and his community of friends, neighbors, and customers. Although he admits that life may be accidental rather than ordered, he nevertheless chooses to believe in the useful fiction of personal responsibility.

Calliope (Callie) Wells, who is sixteen years old when she comes to work at the Stop-Off as a means of making enough money to move to New York. Made pregnant and then abandoned by her boyfriend, she accepts Henry's offer of marriage, though not without misgivings. Welsh in background, she is sharp-boned and practical. As Henry's wife, she transforms the diner into a family restaurant called The Maples. She also changes Henry, making him into what in fact he has always been. Under Henry's influence, Callie undergoes a similar change.

Jimmy, their son.

Willard Freund, Jimmy's natural father. A romantic and idealist, Willard sees Henry both as a friend and as a father who encourages him to realize his ambitions. Willard's actual father exerts quite a different influence, convincing Willard to give up both his dreams and Callie (and therefore his responsibilities). Estranged not only from Henry, Callie, his son Jimmy, and the area around Nickel Mountain but also from his own better self, he becomes cynical until, during a Christmas break from college, he is welcomed back by Henry, who has managed to overcome his own fears and self-doubts concerning the return of his former friend, his son's father, and his wife's former lover.

S. J. Kuzitski, a Russian (or perhaps Polish) junk dealer. A lonely drunk, he spends many nights at the Stop-Off, listening to Henry's ranting. He dies when his truck goes off the road and burns.

George Loomis, a farmer in his thirties who lives alone with his "things" atop Crow Mountain. Broken in body and spirit, he is ironic and cynical, self-consciously playing the devil to Henry's Jesus. George recognizes the hollowness of his own life and the dignity of Henry's. Although responsible for the accidental death of the Goat Lady, George refuses to acknowledge that responsibility to anyone but himself. His silence isolates him even further from the community and its healing, redemptive powers, yet that same silence, as Callie intuits, saves the others; thanks to George's weakness, they are allowed to continue to believe that the Goat Lady will indeed succeed in her strange quest.

Doc Cathey, another of Henry's regular customers. Both a medical doctor and a justice of the peace, he is at once avuncular and diabolically cynical.

Simon Bale, a Jehovah's Witness who works as a clerk in a local hotel until a fire destroys his house and kills his wife. Because he is a religious fanatic and a domestic bully, a man without friends, family, or money, Henry takes him in, a charitable act that Simon claims to be of no consequence. For Simon, nothing in the world matters. When Simon dies in a freak accident, Henry accepts full responsibility and assumes a nearly fatal burden of guilt.

Goat Lady, an unspeakably foul-smelling, dwarf-sized woman with an "inhuman" face. She began a journey from Erie, Pennsylvania, with her cart and goats in search of her son, Buddy Blatt. She possesses no dignity whatsoever and no more knowledge of her son's whereabouts than the word "fair." She assumes that those she meets will help her on her way. She exemplifies for Callie and the others the hope and faith they must have to make it through the summer drought. Faith and hope are what she gives; charity is what she requires. She dies when her cart is struck by George Loomis' truck at night.

Eleanor Wells, Callie's mother, a Baptist. Henry had a crush on her when they were in school.

Frank Wells, Callie's father. He is cynical, alcoholic, and arrogantly detached from his family and neighbors.

Henry's father, a good but grotesquely fat man who failed at everything he tried, from farming to teaching. Constantly belittled by his wife, he is a source of shame and embarrassment to his son. Try as he may to be different, as his mother demanded, Henry shares both his father's bulk and his equally immense love of his fellow people.

Mr. Taylor, the Utica florist with whom Willard hitches a ride at Christmastime, rather than asking his father to pick him up. Taylor's genuine liking for people and his trust in his workers surprise Willard. Taylor dies when his car smashes into a snowplow; Willard is saved, thrown against Taylor at the moment of impact.

Hessie and

Walt, the bickering old couple (she is ninety-two and he is eighty-seven) Henry meets at the very end of the novel. They have returned to Nickel Mountain to exhume the remains of their fourteen-year-old son, Bobby, who was struck and killed by lightning fifty years ago. Different as they are—she is religious, and he is not; she says to let the body stay where it is, and he says a family should be together—they are alike in their grief and in their belief that "you never forget."

— *Robert A. Morace*

NIELS LYHNE

Author: Jens Peter Jacobsen (1847-1885)
First published: 1880
Genre: Novel

Locale: Denmark
Time: The nineteenth century
Plot: Psychological realism

Niels Lyhne, a boy whose mother wants him to be a poet. He becomes, like his father, a farmer. He thinks a great deal, finally becoming an atheist who can accept only his own brand of humanism. After the deaths of his wife and baby, he believes life is empty. He finds temporary solace in belonging to a group when he joins the army, but he is fatally wounded in battle and dies a bitter death.

Bartholine Lyhne, Niels' mother. She loves beauty, especially poetry. She dies while on a trip arranged for her by her son.

Mr. Lyhne, Bartholine's husband. He disappoints his wife, for although he comes from a family of poets and travelers, he has little insight. He dies while his son is still a student.

Edele Lyhne, Niels' aunt. She ruins her health by engaging in the social life in Copenhagen and returns to her brother's farm, where she dies. Niels admires her, and her death makes him melancholy, quieter, and more imaginative.

Erik, Niels' friend and boyhood chum. He becomes a sculptor and painter, but after his marriage he spends his time drinking and gambling. He is killed when his carriage overturns. His wife has an affair with Niels.

Fru Boyle, a buxom widow, somewhat older than Niels, who becomes his friend. Niels spends his time with her instead of studying.

Fennimore, Niels' cousin and Erik's wife. She comes to despise her husband when he proves dissolute and accepts Niels as her lover. When her husband is killed, in her remorse she blames Niels for their affair.

Gerda, a farm girl who becomes Niels' wife. On her deathbed, she departs from the humanism her husband taught her and asks for a pastor so that she can die a faithful Christian.

Herr Bigum, Niels' tutor, an insignificant man who fails his examinations for the priesthood and turns to tutoring. He loves Edele Lyhne.

THE NIGGER OF THE "NARCISSUS": A Tale of the Sea

Author: Joseph Conrad (Jósef Teodor Konrad Nałęcz Korzeniowski, 1857-1924)
First published: 1897
Genre: Novel

Locale: Bombay to London
Time: The nineteenth century
Plot: Psychological

James Wait, an indolent and malingering black man from St. Kitts, the last crew member to report aboard the "Narcissus" as it prepares to get under way from Bombay to London by way of the Cape of Good Hope. A kind of Jonah, his emphasis on his illness and approaching death elicits from the crew a subtle and mistaken sympathy which is demoralizing except when work or great danger, such as the storm, draws them together. Wait dies when in sight of land, thereby lifting a burden from the crew and ship, and the ship reaches port without further friction.

Captain Allistoun,

Old Singleton, a sailor intuitive and indifferent to the corrupting influence of Wait. During the storm, he remains at the wheel for thirty hours. He has come upon the sinister truth of his mortality. He predicts Wait will die when the ship comes in sight of land.

Podmore, the ship's cook, a religious fanatic scorned by the captain and an embarrassment to the men. He talks of eternity, providence, and rebirth, braves the deck to serve coffee during the storm, and tries to convert Wait.

Donkin, the eternal grumbler, always squealing for his rights, always avoiding work and responsibility. Seemingly devoted to Wait, he watches him die and then steals his money.

Belfast, the sailor who, of all the crew, is most mistakenly influenced by Wait's false humility. He performs many deeds for Wait. In port, he begs for a relic from the dead man's belongings.

Wamibo, a Russian Finn, wild, mysterious, primitive, who seems to gloat over Wait's worsening condition like a fiend over the damned.

Mr. Baker, the first mate. In spite of his menacing utterances, he is liked by the crew. A man with bull neck, steady eyes, and sardonic mouth, he carries on his duties calmly.

Mr. Creighton, the second mate, a fair gentlemanly fellow with a resolute face and a splendid physique.

Charley, the youngest seaman aboard, chastened by learning his youth is insignificant.

Archie,

Davis,

Knowles, and

Two Young Scandinavians, other seamen aboard the Narcissus.

NIGHT

Author: Edna O'Brien (1930-   )
First published: 1972
Genre: Novel

Locale: London, England, with memories from elsewhere
Time: The 1960's, with flashbacks
Plot: Psychological realism

Mary Hooligan, a feisty, fortyish, Irish divorcée, currently house-sitting in London. Over the course of one winter night, she reviews, from her employers' four-poster master bed, her life and loves. Hers is a philosophy celebrating excess. An indomitable spirit, her story is similarly aggressive and witty, even zany, in its content and form. All of her senses are alert. Mary's robust handling of language is as forceful and exuberant as is her optimistic attitude toward life. Moved to launch into her soliloquy by approaching middle age and possible loneliness, she reveals herself to be in rude, good health. She is a rebel and a fighter, so she admires the idea of the Irish

Republican Army man, McKann, whom she has never met. Sensually, she enjoys nature and the natural, celebrating birds, animals, flowers, and honest sexuality. She expects and uses no euphemisms or baby talk. In the course of her freewheeling associations, she sketches the people important in her life: her parents, husband, and son, and a parade of lovers. She also sketches her Irish homeland, where she has chosen her grave site, though she is in no hurry to take up residence in it. She has no Irish Catholic obsession and concomitant guilt. She is pleased enough with what she sees in her mirror. Mary enjoys life. She enjoys being a woman; unlike her former apartment mate, Madge, she is no whiner. Mary thinks that she will probably seek out her stonemason friend, Maurice P. Moriarity, when her house-sitting job is over, as it very soon will be. Jonathan and Tig, her employers, are making an unexpectedly early return. Connection and involvement with others must continue for Mary, so that she can carry on.

Boss, her violent, alcoholic father, who lives alone in the west of Ireland. He no longer farms.

Lil, her martyr mother, now dead. Her smothering love for her daughter continues to be a force in Mary's life.

Tutsi, her son, who plays no active part in the tale. An adult and something of a world traveler, he is not damaged by his environment and heredity.

Dr. Flaggler, Mary's cold, calculating, and condescending former husband. He is a museum curator, harsh in his family discipline and not open to real communication in his marriage.

The crooner, an anonymous city slicker who botched the deflowering of Mary, back in her native west of Ireland. It was a holy day of obligation, she says.

Nick Finney, a red-haired husband and father of four with whom Mary has a brief encounter. He and his wife manage a hotel.

Bert, called **the Duke**, a man who lives well, though he is in no position to marry her. Mary believes that she has wronged him. It is he who suggests that she will soon be on the shelf and so contributes to her taking stock of her situation in her solitary monologue.

An anonymous toff, who, by his dehumanizing approach, threatens Mary's equilibrium, until she recalls that the sales are on in the city stores; she would enjoy the bargain hunting.

Maurice P. Moriarity, the one whom, of all the company that Mary kept, she thinks that she may rejoin. He is an Irish stonemason, and though their relationship was never sexually consummated, Mary feels that the connection they developed rivals that of any family knot.

— *Archibald E. Irwin*

NIGHT AND DAY

Author: Tom Stoppard (Tomas Straussler, 1937-   )
First published: 1978
Genre: Drama

Locale: Kambabwe, a fictional former British colony in Africa
Time: The 1970's
Plot: Psychological realism

Ruth Carson, the attractive, alcoholic wife of Geoffrey Carson. Ruth's ironic asides reveal her biting wit and her discomfort with her life in this turbulent African country. On one visit to London to arrange for her son's schooling, she had a brief affair with Dick Wagner. Now that he has appeared in her living room, her feelings are ambiguous; she resents any feeling he may have that she is in any way obligated to him.

Dick Wagner, a fortyish Australian newspaper reporter working for a large London paper. Wagner is still interested in Ruth, but he understands the difference between a London fling and her position as wife and mother at home. Moreover, he is seriously interested in politics, both the politics of the impending revolution in this African country and the politics of the news world. His commitment to union solidarity sets him at odds with Jacob Milne. Wagner brashly joins Geoffrey Carson's meeting with President Mageeba uninvited, flattering the president into talking with him. At the end of the play, with Ruth unsettled by Milne's death, Wagner seems ready to reactivate their affair.

Jacob Milne, a twenty-two- or twenty-three-year-old reporter for the *Grimsby Evening Messenger*. Milne has had some fortunate breaks that have resulted in big stories; ironically, he has scooped the far more experienced Wagner with an

interview with one of the principal figures in the revolution. Back in England, he once worked as a reporter during a union-called strike, in keeping with his general commitment to a free press. His inexperience in the midst of guerrilla warfare results in his death while pursuing a story.

Geoffrey Carson, a mine owner. As Ruth's husband, he is aware of her unhappiness; as an industrialist, he is aware of the difficulties of being the foreign owner of an important resource during times of political upheaval. His familiarity with local politics allows him to arrange a meeting with President Mageeba at his home.

President Mageeba, the fiftyish, British-educated, black military ruler. Mageeba is motivated by his desire for power and for foreign approval. He is a hard man made harder by his embattled position as ruler of a country on the eve of a leftist-led revolution. In the debate over the free press, he sides with Wagner because he sees union control of news reporting as a means of blacklisting uncooperative reporters. In the face of the news of Milne's death, Mageeba's ego is thoroughly visible—he double-checks Wagner's accuracy on a minor detail about his past.

— *Ann D. Garbett*

NIGHT AND DAY

Author: Virginia Woolf (1882-1941)
First published: 1919
Genre: Novel

Locale: London, England
Time: The 1910's, before World War I
Plot: Domestic

Katharine Hilbery, the only daughter of upper-middle-class, literary parents. She lives in her family's London home, runs the household, and is helping her mother to write a biography of the famous poet Richard Alardyce, Katharine's

grandfather. In secret, she studies mathematics. At the age of twenty-seven, she has begun to contemplate marriage, primarily as a way of attaining autonomy and a house of her own. Tall, beautiful, and elegantly dressed, she attracts both men and women with her statuesque appearance and a calm bearing that seems to suggest hidden depths. In the course of the novel, she becomes engaged to William Rodney, only to reject him for the freer, more stimulating companionship of Ralph Denham. In defiance of her family's Victorian mores, she declares her intention to live with him outside wedlock.

Ralph Denham, a clerk in a law office. At the age of twenty-nine, he still lives at home with his mother and seven siblings but longs to escape the routine of his work and the constricting conventions of the family household. He spends evenings in the privacy of his upstairs room, poring over law books and daydreaming of Katharine, whom he meets over tea at her house in the novel's first chapter. His love for Katharine thrives on her absence and apparent unattainability; he constructs her in his mind as an ideal, "a shape of light." Alternately arrogant and insecure, disheveled but striking in appearance, he pursues Katharine's friendship with a fierce determination and ends by winning her love.

William Rodney, a government clerk with a passion for Elizabethan literature, intelligent but pretentious, elegantly appareled but physically unappealing. He is intent on marrying Katharine. After wooing her into engagement, he is oppressed by the awareness that, far from being madly in love, she finds him somewhat ridiculous. He alternately begs and bullies but fails to make her into the docile woman he desires.

Mary Datchet, a volunteer worker in the campaign for woman suffrage. Her main characteristic is a capacity for devotion, exercised chiefly at her work but focused for a time on her friend Ralph Denham. During the Christmas holidays, she invites Ralph to her family home in the country, where, on an impulse, he proposes to her. She recognizes both his insincerity and his secret love for Katharine Hilbery, renounces him, and accepts a position as secretary of a new organization for social improvement. To Katharine, Mary's life as an unmarried woman seems both enviable in its autonomy and undesirable in its loneliness.

Cassandra Otway, a young cousin of Katharine Hilbery who lives with her parents at their moldering country estate, plays the flute, and collects silkworms. She charms William Rodney, who meets her at Christmas, with her eccentricity and ingenuousness. When Katharine detects William's feelings, she invites Cassandra to visit London and makes room for the two to become acquainted. Cassandra is scandalized when William first confesses his interest in her, but after hearing that he and Katharine have secretly broken their engagement, she admits her own love. By the end of the book, she and William are blissfully engaged.

Mrs. Hilbery, the daughter of Richard Alardyce and mother of Katharine. Flighty, impetuous, and fantastical, she is by nature unsuited to her life's task, the composition of her famous father's biography. Her foremost function in the novel is as a *deus ex machina*. Returning from a visit to William Shakespeare's tomb at the moment of greatest crisis among the four lovers, she whisks Ralph Denham away from his work and takes him home in her carriage, convincing him along the way that he must marry Katharine.

Mr. Hilbery, the benevolent but remote father of Katharine. He remains blind to the goings-on under his own roof until a sister informs him that his daughter and niece are causing a scandal. He then becomes outraged, is defied by Katharine, and is ultimately reconciled to the new state of affairs among the younger generation.

— *Natania Rosenfeld*

NIGHT FLIGHT
(Vol de nuit)

Author: Antoine de Saint-Exupéry (1900-1944)
First published: 1931
Genre: Novel

Locale: South America
Time: Early 1930's
Plot: Psychological realism

Rivière (ree-VYAY), the director of an air-mail service. Completely dedicated to making night flying regular in spite of all its attendant dangers, he imposes on his men a rigid discipline that is taken for callousness. When Fabien and his wireless operator are lost in a storm, Rivière's deep concern reveals that his unbending severity springs not from any lack of feeling for his pilots but from a complete sense of consecration to his mission.

Fabien (fah-BYAH[N]), a pilot. On a night flight carrying the mail from Patagonia to Buenos Aires, he and his wireless operator enter a violent storm and are lost. Their deaths prompt the revelation of Rivière's real concern for his pilots in spite of his severe demands on them.

Robineau (roh-bee-NOH), the inspector. Inclined to make friends with the pilots, he resents Rivière's undeviating discipline and insistence that the supervisors maintain complete impersonality toward those whom they may have to send to their deaths. Only after Fabien is lost does he realize Rivière's real concern for his men and experience a sense of communion with him.

Pellerin (peh-leh-RA[N]), a pilot who comes safely through the great storm in which Fabien is lost.

Mme Fabien, Fabien's bride of six weeks, who hears from Rivière of the enormous price men must pay to conquer the skies. She understands.

Roblet (roh-BLAY), an old former pilot.

A NIGHT IN THE LUXEMBOURG
(Une Nuit au Luxembourg)

Author: Rémy de Gourmont (1858-1915)
First published: 1906
Genre: Novel

Locale: Paris, France
Time: Early twentieth century
Plot: Religious

Louis Delacolombe (M. James Sandy Rose), a journalist. Born in France, he was brought up in the United States, returned to France, and for ten years until his sudden death was the French correspondent of the *Northern Atlantic Herald*. Both his original name, Delacolombe, and his later name, Rose, appear to be symbolic: Both the dove and the rose have long symbolized love.

"He," a chestnut-haired, bearded, brilliant-eyed, gentle-faced man whom Sandy meets in the Church of Saint-Sulpice. Dressed like a French gentleman, he is a god who, when Rose refers to his mother Mary, says he has been known by many names including Apollo. He calls himself a superman and a god. Although he physically resembles the conventional conception of Jesus, he appears in his thought to be a more generalized divine inspirer of men of varied faiths in many ages. His philosophy concerning human life, with its emphasis on the virtue of being happy and the importance of living each moment as if it were eternal, is Epicurean. His favorite mortal philosophers, as he tells Rose, were Epicurus, who found happiness in pleasure, and Spinoza, who found it in asceticism.

Elise, a beautiful young goddess who allows Rose to possess her during a brief interval in the long conversation with "He." Later, after she has accompanied Rose to his room and they have again experienced the joys of love, she reminds him of Giorgione's Venus. She and her two friends also resemble the three Graces of Greek mythology.

The narrator, a friend of Rose who finds him dead sitting at his desk in his room. As legatee and in accordance with Rose's will, he publishes Rose's manuscript and furnishes a brief explanatory preface and a final note for it.

'NIGHT, MOTHER

Author: Marsha Norman (1947-   )
First published: 1983
Genre: Drama

Locale: Rural United States
Time: Late 1970's or early 1980's
Plot: Psychological realism

Jessie Cates, a pale and somewhat physically unsteady woman in her late thirties or early forties. Overweight, afflicted with epilepsy, unable to hold a job, abandoned by her husband, and plagued by a delinquent son, Jessie faces a discouraging future: life with an aging mother and years of thoughtless holiday gifts from an insensitive brother and sister-in-law. Deciding finally to make a choice about her life, she calmly announces early in the play, "I'm going to kill myself, Mama" and then single-mindedly goes about the business of setting the household affairs in order. She explains the details of running the house to her mother, fends off the older woman's attempts to change her plans, describes how her mother should act after the suicide, and finally goes into her bedroom, locks the door, and shoots herself. Jessie's suicide is not an act of despair; on the contrary, her decision to kill herself is a positive act—an attempt to take control of her life, to act instead of passively allowing life to diminish her.

Thelma Cates, Jessie's mother, a woman in her late fifties or early sixties who possesses a mental sturdiness that allows her to believe that things are what she says they are. Before the evening on which the play takes place, no one has challenged her beliefs. She denied Jessie's epilepsy, stating instead that Jessie simply suffered from "fits." She is a homebody whose living room is decorated with her needlework and whose greatest pleasure in life seems to be the consumption of the candy and pastries with which her kitchen is liberally stocked. A talkative woman, she tries to prevent Jessie's suicide by asking questions, making suggestions, demanding explanations, scolding, reminiscing, even briefly baring her soul, and finally simply forcing conversation. Reduced to frantic hysteria when she finally realizes her powerlessness to stop Jessie, Thelma—after she hears the shot from the bedroom—succumbs to a lifetime of stoic coping and proceeds to follow Jessie's last instructions by telephoning her daughter-in-law.

Dawson, Jessie's brother. He does not appear onstage. She does not want him to come before she kills herself because she says that he will make her feel stupid for not having committed suicide ten years ago.

Loretta, Jessie's sister-in-law, who does not appear onstage.

Cecil, Jessie's husband, picked for her by Thelma. Jessie says that she tried to please him, but he knew that she was trying, so it did not work. He has left Jessie and moved away; she says that he gave her a choice either to quit smoking or to quit him, and she chose to smoke.

Ricky, Jessie and Cecil's son, a teenager who has "gone bad." Jessie does not know where he is. He does not appear onstage but comes up in conversation.

— *E. D. Huntley*

NIGHT MUST FALL

Author: Emlyn Williams (1905-1987)
First published: 1935
Genre: Drama

Locale: England
Time: The 1930's
Plot: Psychological

Dan, a drifter and jack-of-all-trades, most recently a page boy at a provincial English hotel. This young man seems exceptionally good-natured, obliging, and happy-go-lucky, but as the play progresses, it becomes clear that he is criminally insane. Like the classic psychopath, he is devoid of feeling for other human beings but has the ability to ingratiate himself with people by instinctively harmonizing with their personalities, mirroring their attitudes and opinions with uncanny skill. He quickly wins over the lonely Mrs. Bramson by giving her the attention she craves and becomes a trusted member of her household.

Olivia Grayne, a penniless niece of Mrs. Bramson who lives with her as a companion and housekeeper. This plain-looking, twenty-eight-year-old woman is a picture of repressed resentment, hostility, and physical longing. She wears horn-rimmed glasses and does her hair in a tight bun. She is intelligent and intuitive. She quickly sees through Dan's mask of innocence. Almost as soon as he enters the household as a personal attendant to Mrs. Bramson, Olivia begins to suspect that he is the one responsible for the recent murder of Mrs. Chalfont, who had been staying at the hotel where Dan was employed. Olivia also falls under his spell; in fact, she saves him from exposure when Inspector Belsize is about to discover that the murdered woman's missing head is concealed in Dan's hatbox. Olivia finally admits to Dan that he has sized her up correctly: They are soulmates; they both are seething with hatred over the humiliations they suffer in their subservient social roles. She would commit murder herself if she had Dan's courage.

Mrs. Bramson, a wealthy widow. Although only fifty-five years old and fairly robust, this unhappy, selfish, and domineering woman has decided to play the invalid. She sits in a wheelchair that she does not need and forces everyone to dance in attendance. Her inconsiderate, demanding behavior has earned for her the hatred of her servants and her niece. Mrs. Bramson immediately conceives a mother's affection for Dan because he knows how to manipulate her with pretended love and concern for her many imaginary ailments. Being naturally obtuse, she does not suspect that he is planning to rob her of the large amount of cash she keeps on the premises.

Hubert Laurie, a middle-class businessman up from London on a vacation. He is thirty-five years old but already ossified in thoughts and manners. He is in love with Olivia and hangs about trying to persuade her to marry him; however, she tells him bluntly that he is an unmitigated bore. He is the antithesis of the sexually exciting Dan. Laurie represents Olivia's only possible escape from the tyranny of Mrs. Bramson and by his very presence shows why she feels trapped and embittered.

Mrs. Terence, Mrs. Bramson's middle-aged Cockney cook. She is the only servant who is not terrified of her employer. She provides comic relief by telling Mrs. Bramson what everyone else is afraid to say: that she is a tyrant and a malingerer. Mrs. Terence quickly falls under Dan's spell and becomes his ally.

Dora Parkoe, Mrs. Bramson's long-suffering maid, a pretty but stupid and spineless woman, twenty years old. She is responsible for Dan coming to the household; she confesses that he has gotten her pregnant. When Mrs. Bramson summons him to demand that he marry Dora, Dan agrees but obviously has no intention of doing so. Dora represents the dismal marital prospects available to a man of his class. By her presence, she shows why he is so motivated to escape his fate by getting his hands on a large sum of money.

Inspector Belsize, a foxy and tenacious Scotland Yard detective of fifty who is investigating the murder of the headless woman. Belsize is continually popping up at the Bramson home to ask questions and deliver news of the progress of the investigation. At the end of the play, he arrests Dan for murdering Mrs. Chalfont and subsequently murdering his employer, Mrs. Bramson.

— *Bill Delaney*

THE NIGHT OF THE IGUANA

Author: Tennessee Williams (Thomas Lanier Williams, 1911-1983)
First published: 1961
Genre: Drama

Locale: Mexico
Time: 1940
Plot: Psychological realism

T. Lawrence (Larry) Shannon, a former Episcopal priest, now a tour guide. The handsome thirty-five-year-old American is suffering through the opening stages of a nervous breakdown. When he arrives at Maxine's Costa Verde Hotel, he has hit bottom; in a relatively brief period, he has descended from being the promising young rector of an affluent Virginia congregation to conducting tours for an international travel agency to, finally, leading a group of Baptist schoolteachers around Mexico under the aegis of a seedy travel bureau. Although part of Larry's problem clearly involves alcohol, a weakness continually implied by the other characters and by Larry himself, he is chiefly troubled by his "Spook," a phantasm created by his own anxieties. Despite his irresponsibility, weakness, and occasional cruelty, Larry retains strong personal appeal; part of his fascination lies in his sexual attractiveness, but even more engaging is his aura of "fallenness," of lost innocence. It becomes increasingly clear, as the plot unfolds, that Larry is tormented by his search for God, even though, as Hannah points out, he relishes that torment. In his treatment of Hannah and her grandfather, even in his rough

affection toward Maxine, Larry evinces true compassion. His call—at least as it is manifested in his sympathy for other troubled people—has not diminished. Larry's essence is contradiction: His kindness is shot through with cruelty, his longing for God is tainted by sensuality, and his need to escape dependency is thwarted by moral inertia.

Maxine Faulk, the owner of the Costa Verde Hotel, recently widowed. Sensual, direct, and practical, Maxine is at once powerfully drawn to Larry and puzzled by him. In the weeks before the action of the play begins, Maxine, a woman in her mid-forties, lost her husband, a much older man. The final illness and death of her husband have not dampened her sexual appetite, and she has hired two young Mexican "boys" to accommodate her needs. Like Larry, however, her sensuality seems largely innocent and straightforward, and she is unashamed of her sexual life, although she is well aware that her lasciviousness repels Larry. She, too, seeks solace in alcohol, and she repeatedly encourages Larry to drink with her. Running through her sensuality and self-indulgence, however, is a wide vein of common sense and emotional strength; her material well-being is almost always uppermost in her mind. She correctly views Hannah as a rival, even though Hannah's character is a mystery to her.

Hannah Jelkes, an itinerant sketch artist, a guest at the hotel. Hannah is Maxine's opposite and Larry's spiritual sister. Otherworldly, genteel, and deeply compassionate, Hannah seems to transcend the unpleasant reality of her situation: She is in effect caretaker of her aged grandfather, Nonno. For reasons that are never made clear, she and Nonno have been compelled to make their living through Hannah's sketches of guests at the hotels, which are their only "home," and through Nonno's recitations of his once-famous poetry. Hannah's near-androgyny is in direct contrast to Maxine's earthiness, but despite her Puritan instincts, Hannah manifests intense femininity. Her reserve, kindness, and gentility are all deeply appealing to Larry. On the whole, however, her chief motivation is self-sacrifice; she has submerged her personality in caring for her grandfather and is unable to respond to Larry's plea for companionship.

Jonathan "Nonno" Coffin, an aged poet, Hannah's grandfather. Although he was once a noted minor poet, Coffin's current claim to fame is simply that, as Hannah says, he is the "world's oldest living, practicing poet." Like his granddaughter, Nonno is clearly a member of the New England patriciate; even in extreme old age (he is ninety-seven years old), he retains his courtly manners and sprightly, if dated, wit. During the course of the play, Nonno writes his last poem, breaking a twenty-year creative dry spell.

Judith Fellowes, a schoolteacher, the tour organizer. Judith is Larry's chief antagonist. Something of a stereotype, she is notable chiefly for her prudery and insensitivity.

The Fahrenkopfs, a German family on vacation. Herr and Frau Fahrenkopf and their grown children, Hilda and Wolfgang, are, like Judith, largely stereotypes—in this instance, caricatures of buxom, beer-swilling, obtuse representatives of the "master race."

— *John Steven Childs*

NIGHT RIDER

Author: Robert Penn Warren (1905-1989)
First published: 1939
Genre: Novel

Locale: Kentucky
Time: 1904-1905
Plot: Social morality

Percy Munn, a lawyer and gentleman farmer who dies because of his obsessive involvement with the Association of Growers of Dark Fired Tobacco and The Free Farmers' Brotherhood of Protection and Control, called the "night riders." Munn sees no pattern or meaning in the events of his life, but he searches for the ultimate decisive deed that will resolve all of life's conflicts. He anticipates that the "brotherhood" of the association will supply the sense of community he lacks, but instead, the night riders' activities complete his isolation from his wife, his friends, and his professional ethics. Unjustly accused of murder, Munn flees to the "sanctuary" of Proudfit's farm, where Proudfit's autobiographical narrative finally helps him to understand his part in the overall pattern of human history.

Willie Proudfit, a fiercely independent yeoman farmer who hides Munn from the authorities. The antithesis of Munn, Willie embodies the sweep of history: He recalls his past and plans for his future, but he lives in the present. His narrative's central themes are humans' need to feel a sense of community, to understand their finite place in the universe, to acknowledge the validity of others' conflicting visions, and to accept their role in the overall pattern of human history.

Edmund Tolliver, a defeated senator who organizes, but later betrays, the association. A charismatic and ambitious man, Tolliver compensates for childhood poverty by exploiting the land and other people, all in pursuit of political power. For Tolliver, human relationships remain on the level of abstraction, and he never is truly a part of any community. Eventually, his lack of character becomes so obvious that, instead of exacting vengeance, Munn decides Tolliver is already dead in every sense but the literal one.

Bill Christian, an impetuous tobacco farmer instrumental in forming the association and drawing his friend Munn into it. Unlike Munn, who speaks philosophically of the association's purpose, Christian defines its goal in practical terms: to force tobacco buyers to pay what tobacco is worth. Christian's pride in his ancestral home suggests both his link to his family and his sense of history. His efforts to balance his conflicting roles as family man and night rider result in a spiritual paralysis eventually reflected in his physical paralysis. Finally, disillusioned with his associates and feeling betrayed by Munn's affair with his daughter, Christian dies.

Dr. MacDonald, a local physician who is the most reckless of the night riders. Always apparently self-assured, MacDonald is the only night rider who is not masked, and at his trial he appears totally at ease. Thus, he seems more a cavalier than a man of science. Unlike Munn, however, MacDonald has an identity apart from the association. He demonstrates not only a concern for his family but also the ability to plan for a future that does not include the association or the night riders.

Professor Ball, a schoolmaster who kills the chief witness against his son-in-law and allows Munn to be blamed. Ball represents the subversion of philosophy to the night riders' cause. A man of words rather than deeds, Ball resembles Munn in his romantic idealism. Munn, who also has killed impulsively, understands the agony of hidden guilt that causes Ball's health to fail.

Captain Todd, a founder of the association who believes his four-year Civil War experience was enough violence for a lifetime. Like Christian, Todd never loses sight of the association's original goal. When his rational arguments prove insufficient to restrain the night riders, he resigns from the association's board, explaining that he no longer can clearly define the community to which he owes allegiance.

Grimes, a tenant farmer on Munn's land. As practical as Munn is romantic, Grimes holds an almost sacramental view of the land, based on his experience with it. For the nearly sixty years he has planted tobacco on Munn property, the land's fertility has remained dependable. Grimes knows his place in the universe; he observes that growing tobacco requires "God's will and weather" as well as human sweat. Grimes also speaks for family continuity and the pattern of history: He comments that he planted tobacco on the same plot when Munn's father owned it and others will plant there after both he and Munn are dead. Eventually, the night riders' raids break his ties with this land, as he becomes convinced that tobacco is a curse on the land. Grimes's departure signals Munn's complete detachment from family and history.

— *Charmaine Allmon Mosby*

NIGHTMARE ABBEY

Author: Thomas Love Peacock (1785-1866)
First published: 1818
Genre: Novel

Locale: England
Time: Early nineteenth century
Plot: Fiction of manners

Christopher Glowry, the master of Nightmare Abbey, who is largely interested in eating and drinking. He is boorish and coarse. He refuses to allow his son to marry the woman of his choice, because she has no fortune. He finally changes his mind, but by that time it is too late; the young lady has discarded his son and accepted another proposal.

Scythrop Glowry, Christopher Glowry's son, a gloomy, boorish, unmannerly young man. He has a rather morbid interest in dungeons, secret panels, and skulls. He falls in love with his cousin, but his father will not allow the marriage. Later, when he is not able to decide between two girls, the two young ladies both accept other men, and he is left to drink his wine alone. He is supposed to represent Percy Bysshe Shelley.

Marionetta Celestina O'Carroll, Glowry's niece and Scythrop's cousin. She is coquettish, and Scythrop falls in love with her. She has no fortune, however, and is allowed to remain in the house only as a guest. She finally accepts the proposal of a dandy named Listless.

Mr. Toobad, Glowry's friend. He and Glowry agree that his daughter would be a good match for Scythrop. He goes to London to bring her to Nightmare Abbey, but she discovers his purpose and disappears.

Celinda Toobad (Stella), Mr. Toobad's daughter. She does not take kindly to having a husband chosen for her, and she runs away from her father when she learns that she is to marry Scythrop. She turns up later at Nightmare Abbey as a strange woman calling herself Stella and moves into a secret apartment constructed by Scythrop. She discusses German metaphysics and tragedy with Scythrop without knowing who he is. When he is slow in asking for her hand, she accepts Flosky's proposal.

Listless, a bored and languid dandy, a friend and fellow collegian of Scythrop. He is a guest at Nightmare Abbey and is interested in Marionetta. He finally asks for her hand in marriage and is accepted.

Mr. Ferdinando Flosky, a poet, another guest at the abbey. He is interested in the supernatural and in metaphysics. He proposes to and is accepted by Celinda. He is supposed to represent Samuel Taylor Coleridge.

Mr. Cypress, another visitor at Nightmare Abbey. He is supposed to represent Lord Byron.

Mr. Asterias, another guest, an ichthyologist tracing rumors of a mermaid supposed to have been seen near the abbey.

Aquarius, his son.

Fatout, Listless' French valet.

Raven, a servant at Nightmare Abbey.

NIGHTWOOD

Author: Djuna Barnes (1892-1982)
First published: 1936
Genre: Novel

Locale: Paris, France, and Vienna, Austria
Time: The 1920's
Plot: Psychological realism

Robin Vote, who is twenty-nine years of age when the novel begins, an expatriate American attempting to find fulfillment in Europe during the heady age of the 1920's. She marries Felix Volkbein, who claims aristocratic heritage, and gives birth to their son, Guido. She is nature's child and prepares for her pregnancy with a stubborn, cataleptic calm. The author's symbolic character of American innocence abroad, Robin maintains an animal naturalness as she moves among society in European salons. She moves easily from her marriage with Felix to liaisons with others, in particular, two women, Nora and Jenny, both of whom she also leaves in accordance with her natural instincts. Her departures are quick, uncomplicated, clean, and unquestioning. Corrupted only in her contacts with civilization, she is described by Matthew O'Connor as "a wild thing caught in a woman's skin." Neither Felix nor Nora nor Jenny can understand her rootlessness, but the doctor can. In the end, her natural state triumphs in her return to rural New York, as she runs on all fours in the direction of Nora's home, with Nora's barking dog as her running companion. She escapes from Nightwood, her mythical embodiment of Dante's Inferno.

Matthew O'Connor, an unlicensed physician who has never married. He is an expatriate from the Barbary Coast, San Francisco, and, in fact, an expatriate from life. He is the detached observer of the characters and events in the novel, sometimes functioning as a mover of events and at other times holding court when sought for advice. He meets Felix at a Berlin soiree and sometime later introduces Felix to Robin. At still another point, he serves as confidant to Nora, who comes to him for advice. He is a mythical character, a Tiresias figure (he enjoys dressing in women's clothing) and a Cassandra (he predicts Robin's eventual salvation by Nora). He inhabits the limbo between innocence and experience, having outlived his emotional and sexual needs. Most important, however, he is the Jamesian "central intelligence," through whose consciousness the events and characters of the novel are filtered for the reader.

Felix Volkbein, an only child, born in Berlin to a Viennese Christian mother (at the age of forty-five) and a wealthy Jewish father of Italian descent whom he never meets. A fraudulent aristocrat, he devotes his life to perpetuating the image of nobility, in his case, the nobility consisting of the circus and the theater. He embodies the myth of the Wandering Jew and is, in his social journeying, as rootless as Robin is in her naturalness. Concerned for his son, Felix spends time with Guido and, during one of a number of meetings with O'Connor at a café, discusses Guido's future. The boy will remain forever innocent, and for him Felix sees the priesthood as the only possible vocation.

Nora Flood, an American, in her late twenties at her first appearance, who owns a forlorn, overgrown estate in New York, conducts a strange salon, and meets Robin at a circus performance. They fall almost wordlessly into a natural acquaintance. Robin leaves Felix and Guido for Nora, but even Nora, who possesses an equilibrium of nature, a balance of the savage and refined, cannot hold the freedom-loving Robin.

Absences from each other grow more frequent, until Nora seeks out O'Connor for an explanation of Robin's behavior.

Jenny Petherbridge, a middle-aged widow whose four husbands have "wasted away and died." She and Robin meet during one of the latter's absences from Nora. Their friendship develops until Jenny's possessiveness and acquisitiveness drive them apart. Jenny serves as yet another corrupting influence on the innocence of Robin.

Guido Volkbein, Felix's and Robin's son, a minor character important as a contrast with the decadent, socially aspiring, acquisitive, and aimless society into which he was born. In his emotionally unstable and mentally deficient nature, he will always be a passive innocent, just as his mother, despite corruption by European salons in Paris, Munich, Vienna, and Budapest, forever retains a vestige of her innocence and in the end returns to the New York countryside and Nora.

Sylvia, a child who stays with Jenny for a time and whose attraction to Robin causes Jenny to be jealous.

Frau Mann, the Duchess of Broadback, a drinking companion of Felix.

An English woman, yet another woman whose attention to bisexual Robin causes Jenny's jealousy.

— Susan Rusinko

THE NINE TAILORS

Author: Dorothy L. Sayers (1893-1957)
First published: 1934
Genre: Novel

Locale: Fenchurch, St. Paul, and the surrounding fen country of East Anglia, England
Time: 1930
Plot: Detective and mystery

Lord Peter Death Bredon Wimsey, a brilliant, irrepressible, and wealthy amateur sleuth. Wimsey's main faults are his insatiable curiosity and his willingness to help almost anyone in trouble. These traits lead Wimsey into the mystery of an unknown corpse buried in another's grave, a mysterious stranger in a small village, and a set of valuable emeralds, missing since 1914. Wimsey is a linguistic and historical scholar, a brilliant musician, a natural aristocrat and gentleman, and, by the time of this case, an experienced detective who takes on cases out of a sense of social responsibility as well as curiosity. Once interested in a problem, Wimsey never gives up. Still a gifted athlete although nearing forty, Wimsey makes up for his relative lack of height (five feet, eight inches) through skill and determination. He is irresistible to many women.

Mervyn Bunter, Wimsey's sergeant during World War I, now his extremely proper valet, crime photographer, and valued assistant. Like his slightly younger master, Bunter is skilled in many trades, and he provides Wimsey's somewhat bohemian lifestyle with organization. Tall and handsome, Bunter has an eye for maids and other working-class women.

The Reverend Theodore Venables, the elderly and absent-minded rector of the Anglican Church in Fenchurch, St. Paul. His kindness and love of bell-ringing allow him to make friends with Wimsey on New Year's Eve, when Wimsey and Bunter are stranded in his village by an auto wreck. When a mysterious corpse later appears in his graveyard, it is Venables who calls Wimsey in for help.

Agnes Venables, his wife. She is the organized member of the pair and remembers all the important facts her husband often forgets.

Superintendent Blundell, the officer in charge of the case and one of the original officers who investigated the 1914 robbery, which provides the motive for the 1930 mystery. A kindhearted, likable, and intelligent officer, Blundell, with Bunter, does most of the groundwork under Wimsey's direction, allowing Wimsey to make the inspired connections that solve the complicated case.

Geoffrey Deacon, the Thorpe family butler in 1914 and the ruthless original thief of the Wilbraham emeralds. He supposedly died while escaping from prison, yet there is a trail from his brutal prison escape in 1918 through the final World War I battlefields in France to the mutilated corpse in the graveyard in 1930.

William Thoday, a brawny tenant farmer. He acted suspiciously both before and after New Year's Eve but could not have buried the mysterious corpse, because he was seriously ill when it was buried. In fact, it is William's place that Wimsey takes among the Fenchurch bell-ringers, allowing them to ring their nine-hour peal. William hides at least one guilty secret and is jealously devoted to his wife. Few villagers dare to mention Mary's first husband when he is around.

Mary Thoday, William's wife and Geoffrey Deacon's widow. A once-pretty maid of the Thorpes, she was originally suspected of helping her first husband steal the emeralds.

Some people suspect that she might know something about their hiding place.

James Thoday, William's hefty brother. He was an officer on a tramp freighter, home on leave for Christmas and New Year's Day, who stayed and helped tend to his sick brother. He also took an extra, unexplained, day getting from his brother's house back to his ship. It was James who gave his brother a parrot that gives Wimsey important information.

Horace "Potty" Peake, a retarded pig keeper and the pumper of the church's old-fashioned pump-organ. Although he was an important witness to the events leading up to the mysterious death, it is almost impossible for Wimsey and Blundell to understand exactly what he saw.

Sir Henry Thorpe, a crippled war veteran and local squire. It was at his 1914 wedding that the Wilbraham emeralds were stolen by Deacon. His death the Easter after his wife's death helped set up the cause of the investigation.

Lady Thorpe, Sir Henry's wife, who died on New Year's Day. Her grave, when reopened to receive her husband's body, reveals the mutilated corpse that launches Wimsey's investigation into the village's affairs.

Hilary Thorpe, Sir Henry's intelligent teenage daughter. She finds important evidence in the bell-tower and provides Wimsey with important information about some of the local characters. After the death of her great aunt, Mrs. Wilbraham, Wimsey becomes the administrator of the Wilbraham estate, as well as of the stolen jewels, which Wimsey recovers before identifying the corpse.

Nobby Cranton, an experienced and crafty jewel thief. He was set up by Deacon to be caught for the original jewel robbery in 1914. He returned to Fenchurch, St. Paul, on New Year's Day of 1930 to look for the jewels, and so is suspected either of being the corpse in the graveyard or of putting it there.

— Terrance L. Lewis

NINETEEN EIGHTY-FOUR

Author: George Orwell (Eric Arthur Blair, 1903-1950)
First published: 1949
Genre: Novel

Locale: London, England
Time: 1984
Plot: Science fiction

Winston Smith, a citizen of Oceania. He is an intelligent man of thirty-nine, a member of the Outer Ring of the Party who has a responsible job in the Ministry of Truth, where he changes the records to accord with the aims and wishes of the Party. He is not entirely loyal, however, for he keeps a secret journal, takes a mistress, and hates Big Brother. Caught in his infidelities to the Party, he is tortured until he is a broken man; he finally accepts his lot, even to the point of loving Big Brother.

Mrs. Smith, Winston's wife, a devoted follower of the Party and active member of the Anti-Sex League. Because she believes procreation a party duty, she leaves her husband when the union proves childless.

Julia, a bold, good-looking girl who, though she wears the

Party's red chastity belt, falls in love with Winston and becomes his mistress. She, like her lover, rebels against Big Brother and the Party. Like Winston, too, she is tortured and brainwashed and led to repent her political sins.

O'Brien, a member of the Inner Party. He leads Winston and Julia to conspire against the Party and discovers their rebellious acts and thoughts. He is Winston's personal torturer and educator who explains to Winston why he must accept his lot in the world of Big Brother.

Mr. Charrington, a member of the thought police who disguises himself as an old man running an antique shop in order to catch such rebels as Winston and Julia. He is really a keen, determined man of thirty-five.

1959

Author: Thulani Davis
First published: 1992
Genre: Novel

Locale: The Chesapeake Bay area of Virginia
Time: 1959
Plot: Psychological realism

Willie Tarrant, the narrator, a bright twelve-year-old girl who, in 1959, is preoccupied with boys, kissing, and music. After she is selected to be one of six African American students to integrate the all-white Patrick Henry Junior High, Willie's mundane world is shattered. She and the all-black community of Turner, Virginia, become embroiled in the civil rights struggle. As this naïve yet spirited young girl comes of age during this turbulent period in American history, she shares her eloquence and sense of dignity with her community. Willie's narrative becomes a metanarrative for the African American experience.

Dixon Tarrant, Willie's father, a man who has slipped into complacency after the death of his activist wife. He is a permissive parent to Willie and her older brother Preston, more

concerned with gardening than with parenting. Dixon, a chemistry professor at the local college, is apolitical at the beginning of the novel. His slight participation in community activities stems from his need to perpetuate his memories of his late wife rather than from any social impetus. He has immured himself from political and social issues. Only after eight Turner College students are jailed for staging a peaceful sit-in at a local lunch counter does Dixon become involved in the desegregation movement. He becomes one of the community leaders, charging his children and his community to assert their Constitutional rights.

Ralph Johnson, Dixon's former college classmate. Even though he holds a bachelor's degree in engineering, Johnson can find employment only as a barber. A profoundly embittered man, Johnson seeks relief in the jazz records he plays continuously. He, too, becomes a leading figure in the desegregation movement.

Mae Taliaferro, a teacher at Ida B. Wells Junior High. Forced to use outdated and biased textbooks to teach, Mrs. Taliaferro encourages her students to question local social issues and the white rewriting of history, much to the chagrin of the board of education.

Coleman Boteler, a tormented aspiring writer and teacher. A self-centered and self-indulgent man, Coleman virtually ignores his wife, Lillian, and their son, Little Cole. At first, he uses the desegregation meetings as a ruse to enable him to continue his extramarital affair with Charlesetta Roberts. Eventually, Coleman leaves the periphery and is drawn into the civil rights struggle.

Maddie Alexander, a distant cousin of the Tarrants and mother of Willie's best friend, Marian. At the outset of the novel, Maddie whiles away her time as a social climber and town gossip. During the boycott and picketing of Walter's Department Store, she discovers a natural talent for organizing. In one of the most dramatically charged episodes in the novel, she and several other women bravely confront the police and their attack dogs.

Herman Shaw, the white supremacist member of the school board who demands that Mae Taliaferro be discharged for teaching what he sees as communist dogma. Shaw openly advocates the Ku Klux Klan's interference in desegregation activities.

— *Anita M. Vickers*

1934

Author: Alberto Moravia (1907-1990)
First published: 1982
Genre: Novel

Locale: Capri, Italy
Time: 1934
Plot: Philosophical realism

Lucio (lew-CHEE-oh), the narrator, a young intellectual and writer. Lucio is in the middle of an existential crisis, and he is considering whether "it is possible to live in desperation without wishing to die." Lucio is anti-Fascist and anti-Nazi but does not allow his political ideas to threaten his life; it is his very aloofness, however, that makes his life not worth living. In the end, he realizes that "one must live his desperation, not die from it."

Beate/Trude Müller (BAY-tay/TREW-day MIL-luhr), a young, blonde, married actress. As Beate, she appears to be romantic to the point of suicide, wishing for a lover willing to consecrate their love and their desperation with a final tragic action. As Trude (supposedly Beate's twin sister), she loves life as much as Beate hates it and makes every effort possible to teach Lucio how to do so as well.

Alois Müller (AH-loh-ees), her middle-aged husband. Beate/Trude loves her husband, though Lucio never suspects the depth of her feelings; indeed, Lucio thinks that her feelings for Alois are those of hatred rather than love. It is Beate/Trude and Alois' idea to play a trick on Lucio to teach him a lesson

about vanity. Alois is killed by the Nazis; his death precipitates the double suicide of Beate/Trude and Paula.

Paula, an actress who is Beate/Trude's lover. Paula cares so much for Beate/Trude that she willingly joins in suicide with her when Beate/Trude decides that death is preferable to life without Alois. Paula's role is to pretend that she is Beate/Trude's mother when actually she is her lover, thereby implying an incestuous homosexual relationship symbolic of the ambiguous historical period and the confusion and instability of the men living during that time.

Shapiro, an English art collector. Shapiro no longer sees the beauty in what he collects; his goal is to make money through art, not to find spiritual comfort in it.

Sonia, a Russian émigré and Shapiro's assistant. Sonia is disillusioned by politics, love, and life in general. Realizing that she has been betrayed by both her ideology and her lover, Sonia also realizes that there is nothing left for her emotionally; she is dead even though physically alive.

— *Rosaria Pipia*

NINETY-TWO IN THE SHADE

Author: Thomas McGuane (1939-   )
First published: 1973
Genre: Novel

Locale: Key West, Florida
Time: Late 1960's
Plot: Comic realism

Thomas Skelton, a young man who wants to become a self-employed fishing guide with his own boat. After returning to his native Key West in a drug-induced state of confusion, Skelton decides that his road to sanity demands that he become a fishing guide. He has made this choice by "elimination"; everything else he has tried or considered is either unappealing or beyond his talents. His determination is evident when he persists in his plan after Nichol Dance, one of the two established guides in the area, threatens to kill Skelton

if he actually guides. Skelton does not take this threat lightly, knowing full well that Dance will do what he wants to do. He has the unique experience of living in a town where someone would enjoy taking his life. To economize, Skelton lives in an old airplane fuselage modified enough to serve as living quarters. There he reads books on fish and guiding, preparing for the day when he will only have to take clients one or two days a week, leaving the rest of the time for his own reading and fishing.

Nichol Dance, the fishing guide who threatens to kill Skelton if he actually guides out of his dock west of Marathon. He has a history of violence produced by a quick temper and is mentally unstable enough to do what will also destroy himself. He does not seem to dislike Skelton but believes that he must follow through to maintain his reputation and credibility. Because he often contemplates suicide, shooting someone else is not an especially momentous occasion to him.

Faron Carter, another fishing guide, who works with Dance when necessary. Although he does not approve of Dance's threat and perhaps does not fully believe it, he does nothing that might make Dance change his mind. His domestic life is in a shambles: His wife, an oversexed woman who tries to relive her days as a high school cheerleader, is a compulsive buyer who keeps Carter in debt and embarrassed from numerous repossessions. To help balance this problem, he seems to find pleasure in the activities of the waterfront, which include Dance's violence, threats, and pranks.

Goldsboro Skelton, Thomas Skelton's grandfather. He has become wealthy and influential from a life of graft and manipulation on the fringes of politics, having learned "to work the gaps of control that exist between all the little selfish combines." He is feared for both his power and his eccentricity. Goldsboro offers to finance Thomas' guide business, but he gets pleasure from threatening to withdraw his support, then returning it without telling his grandson.

Miranda Cole, Skelton's girlfriend and a seventh-grade geography teacher. Although at times intense, their relationship seems basically casual and headed in no particular direction; it is clear that Skelton's plans to guide take precedence. Miranda is upset over Dance's threat but knows that pleading with Skelton will do no good. Her fear about what may happen causes her to leave town for Skelton's first day of guiding.

Skelton's father, a man who has voluntarily chosen to live for a while bedridden behind mosquito netting. He, like his son, makes choices by elimination, having tried his hand at running guns, manufacturing blimps, and operating a whorehouse. From behind his mosquito netting, he watches football games on television and plays his violin. Eventually, he begins to slip out at night, catting around the seamier side of the town and waiting for the right moment to talk with his son in hopes of dissuading him from pursuing his plan.

Skelton's mother, a former whore in her husband's whorehouse. She is an unfortunate woman, in the same family with three abnormal men. She has no influence on these men and functions mainly as an excuse for them to come together at her house on occasion.

— David E. Huntley

NO EXIT
(Huis clos)

Author: Jean-Paul Sartre (1905-1980)
First published: 1945
Genre: Drama

Locale: Hell
Time: Timeless
Plot: Existentialism

Joseph Garcin, a pacifist journalist from Rio who reached Hell by means of a firing squad, after an attempted escape to Mexico. Garcin affects a macho style and denies his fear of Hell. He is the first of the central characters to survey the set and is the first and the last to speak. As the play progresses, his swaggering façade crumbles. He is exposed in his fear of the judgment of his colleagues on earth and his companions in Hell, because his life was cut off at an ambiguous point. Was he a coward, running away from danger, or a hero on his way to glory? Garcin employs varied tactics to stave off recognition of this fear by his fellow prisoners, realizing that the suffering endured from them is worse than physical torture. He delivers the play's best-known line, "Hell is other people."

Inez Serrano, a postal worker killed in her sleep when her lesbian lover/victim turned on the gas in the night. She enters Hell sure of her reasons for damnation and brutal in her contempt for men in general and Garcin in particular. She realizes the specific necessity for each inmate of their room in Hell as torturer for the others. Inez is attracted to the lovely Estelle and competes with Garcin for her attention, thus becoming vulnerable to suffering through desire. Her savage lucidity rejects excuses and cover-ups, forcing the group confrontation of their hellish situation. It is this quality that makes her Garcin's ultimate challenge. He is held in Hell by his need to convince her of his heroism.

Estelle Rigault, a society beauty who enters Hell as if invited for tea. She deplores blunt language and tries to preserve social distinctions and surface appearances. She argues a theory of administrative error to account for her presence in Hell. Only Garcin and Inez combined force her to admit to drowning her newborn child before its father's eyes. She returned to her rich, old husband, leaving her lover to shoot himself. Estelle's only concern is her outer image. She panics in the absence of mirrors and clings to Garcin for reassurance of her beauty through his masculine attention. He offers her a love pact, mutual protection against their joint punishment, but she is too self-centered to understand his fears or offer him honest support. Women are nothing but competition to her; therefore, any relationship with Inez is impossible. Estelle stabs Inez with a paper knife. The futility of her attempted murder opens her eyes to the finality of her own death.

The Valet, who establishes the framework of the drama. He is a semicomic character, a junior demon with an uncle in a top administrative position. He ridicules the cliché of the medieval Hell expected by Garcin and explains the various physical features of the custom-fitted Hell to which he introduces the three main characters. Once they are all in place, he leaves and does not return.

— Anne W. Sienkewicz

NO LAUGHING MATTER

Author: Angus Wilson (1913-1991)
First published: 1967
Genre: Novel

Locale: England, France, the Soviet Union, Morocco, Egypt, and Portugal
Time: 1912-1967
Plot: Modernism

Quentin Matthews, the eldest of the six Matthews children, who are the principal characters in the novel. Quentin has been reared outside the Matthews household by his grandmother and remains somewhat isolated from the others throughout his life. He serves in the army in World War I and rises to the rank of major. He is disgusted by what he sees in the conflict. After the war, he becomes a socialist. His attachment to Russia is soured by evidence of a purge that he encounters at a Communist congress in Leningrad. In like manner, his commitment to the Republican cause in the Spanish Civil War is not without questioning. He achieves popularity as a radio broadcaster during World War II for his stirring broadcasts during the Blitz, but his honesty and political independence lead him to question the Dresden raids and the Hiroshima bombing. Achieving some fame as a critic of the establishment, he begins to care more for the effect his broadcasts have than for the truth. He dies in a plane crash while journeying to Malaysia to report on Chinese-Malay relations in Singapore.

Gladys Matthews Murkins, one of Quentin's sisters. With the other Matthews children who were reared at home by their parents, William and Clara, she is very involved in the children's invention, "The Game." In this game, each adopts the role of one of the elder members of the household in a form of play that not only releases tensions but also predicts each actor's future life. Fat, sloppy, and comfortable as a youth, Gladys continues to have a passive personality when she matures. She becomes the mistress of a married businessman, accepts the blame for his fraudulent business practices, and is imprisoned. Released from jail, she becomes a wartime typist, marries her former lover, and after his death retires to Portugal.

Rupert Matthews, another one of the Matthews children. Somewhat histrionic as a child, he becomes an actor. He achieves some early success on the stage but then accepts a series of second-rate film roles. He eventually finds that his style is unsuited to the modern, postwar film era.

Susan "Sukey" Matthews Pascoe, another of the Matthews children. She is conventional and longs for security as a child. She makes a respectable marriage with a schoolmaster. She is snobbish and complacent and becomes a pillar of the community.

Margaret Matthews Rootham, Susan's twin sister. Even as a youth, she dreams of being a writer, and she becomes a noted ironic novelist of the period between the wars. Her later novels are not as well received because literary tastes change.

Marcus Matthews, the youngest of the Matthews children, who as a youngster feels neglected by his mother. He has an artistic temperament and becomes involved in the world of design and art as a connoisseur and collector of modern paintings. Marcus challenges contemporary standards in a variety of ways that earn for him a reputation for outrageous behavior. He is a homosexual whose collecting of art is aided by a rich lover. He is arrested in the 1930's for an attack on a Fascist rally. After World War II, he settles in North Africa and invests in a perfume factory.

William Matthews, known to his family as **Billy Pop**, the head of the Matthews clan. He is a failed author, a habitué of gentlemen's clubs, a drunkard, and sexually promiscuous. He is willing to live off the charity of his mother. His marriage is a failure. He and his wife frequently exchange insults and blame each other for their situation. On at least one occasion, their quarreling leads to blows, but they refuse to accept the outside world's judgment of their family situation.

Clara Matthews, the wife of William and mother of the children. Her family refers to her as **the Countess** in mockery of her pretensions. She is extremely self-centered and is sexually promiscuous. She and her husband are killed in a bombing raid during World War II.

— Francis J. Bremer

NO LONGER AT EASE

Author: Chinua Achebe (1930-   )
First published: 1960
Genre: Novel

Locale: Nigeria
Time: The 1950's
Plot: Social

Michael Obiajulu (Obi) Okonkwo (oh-bee-ah-JEW-lew oh-KOHN-kwoh), a twenty-five-year-old Nigerian civil servant. A brilliant student, Obi received the first scholarship loan given by the Umuofia Progressive Union (UPU), whose members taxed themselves harshly to provide someone from their native village with an English education. He has graduated with honors but is less than successful in meeting expectations when he returns from London. His mission background and European values make him an alien in his own land. Naïve and idealistic, he is disillusioned by the contrast between corrupt

Lagos and the idyllic Nigeria about which he wrote poetry in England. The UPU is equally disappointed in Obi. He lacks the superficial characteristics that they consider to be byproducts of an education. In addition, Obi is self-willed. At school, he studied English, not law. Now he wishes to take an unsuitable wife. Although he immediately gets a job, Obi finds the demands of its accompanying lifestyle difficult to meet. He dutifully wishes to give financial help to his family, and he must also repay his loan. He anticipates no problems in remaining aloof from the bribery practices so prevalent in public office. When he succumbs, it is less from greed than from passive acceptance of a system that he no longer has the strength or will to challenge.

Clara Okeke (oh-KAY-kay), a young registered nurse who, like Obi, has been educated in England. Beautiful, straightforward, and self-confident, Clara is Obi's fiancée. Unfortunately, she is also an *osu*, a member of a forbidden caste descended from those dedicated to idols. Marriage to Clara will mean that Obi's children will also be *osu*. She is far more realistic than Obi in anticipating societal pressure against such a marriage. Her worry and natural moodiness make theirs a tempestuous relationship.

Isaac Nwoye Okonkwo (NWOH-yay), Obi's father, a retired Christian catechist living on an inadequate pension. Isaac is a generous but rigid patriarch to his eight children. As a young man, he rebelled against family and tradition to become one of the first Christian converts in his village. Now more a man of thought than of deed, he is still fervent in his Christian faith. He has always revered all things connected with the white man, and long ago he turned his back on most tribal beliefs, but he cannot countenance Obi's marriage to an outcast.

Hannah Okonkwo, Obi's mother. She and Obi share a special bond. Loyal to her husband, she has zealously carried out her duties as the wife of the catechist. She, too, is a devout Christian, but she enjoys the music her husband considers "heathen," and Obi thinks she misses the folk stories that Isaac forbade her to tell their children. For years, she augmented the family income by selling homemade soap. Now she is old and ill, but her frailty belies her determination, as Obi discovers when he tells her about Clara.

William Green, Obi's boss at the Scholarship Board. Mr. Green is a conscientious Englishman with a complex attitude toward his adopted country. Despite devotion to his job and fatherly kindness toward lower employees, he is highly prejudiced against educated Nigerians. Obi thinks that he would have made a great missionary at a time when he could have felt noble about helping the less fortunate. With Nigeria on the verge of independence, however, he is openly petty and resentful.

Joseph Okeke, Obi's former classmate, a Survey Department clerk who is no relation to Clara. Joseph has had no opportunity for education beyond the mission school, but he has a worldly wisdom that Obi lacks. He is proud of his friendship with the successful scholar. Although Obi ignores his pragmatic advice, Joseph remains helpful.

Christopher, a London-educated economist and Obi's friend. Like Obi, he is of the second generation of educated Nigerians, those who have returned to many old customs without fear of being thought uncivilized. Christopher is an urbane and somewhat cynical ladies' man. He and Obi often argue about Nigeria's future and its present problem of corruption among public officials.

The Honorable Sam Okoli (oh-KOH-lee), the popular minister of state who plans to marry Clara's best friend. Handsome and suave, Sam lives well in a luxurious home provided by the government. He is hospitable and generous. His affluence may stem from the common practice of bribery.

Marie Tomlinson, Mr. Green's disarming English secretary, who shares Obi's office and may have been planted to spy on him. Obi perceives her as both likable and sincere.

— *Marcia J. Songer*

NO LONGER HUMAN
(Ningen shikkaku)

Author: Osamu Dazai (Tsushima Shūji', 1909-1948)
First published: 1948
Genre: Novel

Locale: An unnamed village in northern Japan, and Tokyo
Time: The 1910's to 1930
Plot: Autobiographical

Yozo, the narrator and the only developed character in this semiautobiographical novel, the morbidly insecure son of a cold landowner and Diet member from northern Japan. Although he is a "brain" who did well in school with little effort, he felt isolated, uncomprehending of others' behavior and convinced that he was "not qualified as a human being" (this phrase is a literal translation of the novel's title). He had been sexually abused by servants; out of fear, he acted the clown as a schoolboy. Sent to college in Tokyo, he neglects his studies, attending art classes and meeting a painter/roué, Horiki Masao, who introduces him to tobacco, drink, and prostitutes. Yozo becomes involved with an unhappy bar hostess whose husband is in prison, and he attempts suicide with her. The incident estranges him from his family. After staying briefly with one of his father's subalterns, he runs away, living as a "kept man" with Shizuko, a widow who works for a publisher and finds him commissions drawing cartoons. As his drinking worsens, he decides that she and her daughter were better off without him. After a year with a bar madam, he meets and marries Yoshiko, a trusting tobacco shop girl. They enjoy quiet

happiness until Horiki reappears and leads him back to dissolute ways. One evening, Horiki discovers that Yoshiko is being raped but cruelly brings Yozo to see rather than helping her. Thereafter, Yozo's decline is swift, involving alcohol, another suicide attempt, tuberculosis, morphine addiction, and commitment to a mental institution. The story ends with him confined in a dilapidated rural house and being tended to by an ugly old woman. In the last years of the narrative, he repeatedly gives his age as twenty-seven, evidence of insanity. Although Yozo's morbid fear of "human beings" seems wildly exaggerated at the story's outset, it is justified by the end.

Flatfish, an old functionary of Yozo's father with whom Yozo is forced to live after attempting double suicide. Flatfish is unwilling to reveal the family's offer to support Yozo's return to college until the latter renounces his wayward life; this reticence contributes to Yozo's ruin, for he flees ignorant of the offer.

Horiki Masao, a former art student from a poor family who introduces Yozo to dissipation and pawnshops. Six years Yozo's senior and a dark presence in the novel, he is always ready to undermine Yozo's self-confidence. He commits one of the most inhuman acts in the story, beckoning Yozo to see Yoshiko being sexually assaulted rather than rescuing her.

Shizuko, a twenty-eight-year-old widow with a five-year-old daughter named Shigeko. Yozo moves in with her not long after his failed suicide attempt. She manages his life and finds cartooning commissions for him. He eventually leaves, thinking that he will spoil their lives.

Takeichi, the puniest boy in his high school class, scrofulous and inept, both physically and academically. He fills Yozo with fear that his clowning façade will be breached by Takeichi's guessing that one of his pratfalls was intentional. Yozo befriends him to keep him silent. It is Takeichi who encourages Yozo in art.

Tetsu, the ugly, sixtyish woman hired by Yozo's brother to look after Yozo following his period of institutionalization. Yozo attests that she violated him several times "in a curious manner."

Tsuneko, a bar hostess from Hiroshima, working in the Ginza, whose husband is in prison. She is alone and desolate, and the misery that surrounds her frees Yozo from fear and uneasiness, giving him his only night of "liberation and happiness." When he rejects her offer to support him, she suggests double suicide: She dies; he is saved.

Yoshiko, Yozo's junior by a decade. Yoshiko begins as an innocent seventeen-year-old with "a genius for trust" who repeatedly urges Yozo not to drink. Her faith induces him to wed her. Rape and ensuing shame and tension destroy their happiness and send Yozo into his final decline and institutionalization, to which she acquiesces.

The old pharmacist, a widow of sixty who has been halfway paralyzed since childhood. She cared for her palsied, bedridden father-in-law and her only son, a medical student, who was suffering from tuberculosis. When Yozo comes to her for medication, she gives him morphine, ostensibly so that he can stop drinking. His addiction and penury reduce him to a sordid relationship with her.

The bar madam, who keeps Yozo after he leaves Shizuko. Although he stays with her for a year, she chivalrously helps him and Yoshiko to rent an apartment near the Sumida River when they wed. At the end of the novel, she blames his fate on his father and drink, terming him "a good boy, an angel."

— *R. Craig Philips*

NO NAME

Author: Wilkie Collins (1824-1889)
First published: 1862
Genre: Novel

Locale: England
Time: Mid-nineteenth century
Plot: Domestic

Andrew Vanstone, a Victorian gentleman who lives a quiet life. When he is killed unexpectedly, it turns out that Mrs. Vanstone is his second wife of but a short time and that their two daughters are illegitimate. Because of legal technicalities, his fortune passes to a selfish, bad-tempered brother of Mr. Vanstone who refuses to share the inheritance with the Vanstone daughters.

Mrs. Vanstone, Andrew's second wife, the mother of Norah and Magdalen. She dies of grief shortly after her husband is killed in a railway accident. They had been unable to marry until late in life because Andrew's disreputable first wife was still alive.

Norah Vanstone, a quiet girl. Left poor at her father's death, she supports herself as a governess. A sensitive girl, she has her feelings hurt by her fiancé's inquiries about her. She is persistent and finally accomplishes quietly what her sister cannot accomplish by plotting and flamboyant means: She restores the family fortune.

Magdalen Vanstone, a headstrong, capable girl. Left penniless at her father's death, she carves for herself a stage career. She marries her cousin Noel to regain the fortune lost by her illegitimacy, but her plots fail and she is still seemingly without the fortune. Eventually, her sister finds the documents that restore the girls' inheritance.

Noel Vanstone, Magdalen's cousin and first husband, whom she marries in an attempt to retrieve the family fortune. He is a weak, miserly young man. He discovers his wife's trickery and just before he dies, he tries to will his money to a distant relative.

Captain Kirke, Magdalen's second husband, an understanding, patient man.

Mr. Clare, the Vanstones' misanthropic but scholarly neighbor, Frank's father.

Frank Clare, the Vanstone girls' childhood playmate. He becomes an incompetent young man whom Magdalen finds attractive for a while. A failure at business, he is forced to take a job in China. Eventually, he marries a wealthy widow.

Captain Wragge, an amiable rascal who befriends and helps Magdalen.

Mrs. Wragge, a large, sad woman who, like her husband, befriends Magdalen.

Miss Garth, the Vanstone girls' governess, who helps them when they are left penniless.

Mrs. Le Count, Noel's suspicious housekeeper, who dominates her master.

George Bartram, Noel's designated heir. He loves Norah.

Admiral Bartram, George's uncle.

NO-NO BOY

Author: John Okada (1923-1971)
First published: 1957
Genre: Novel

Locale: Seattle, Washington
Time: Shortly after the end of World War II
Plot: Historical realism

Ichiro Yamada, a twenty-five-year-old, second-generation ("Nisei") Japanese American. During World War II, he spent two years in an internment camp for Japanese Americans and two more years in federal prison because he chose to be a "no-no boy," refusing to serve in the armed forces and to swear allegiance to the United States. He refused because he was angry at the U.S. government for forcing all Japanese aliens and Japanese American citizens into the camps. Throughout the novel, he struggles with his guilt about his decision not to fight in the war and with his feelings of conflict about his ethnic identity. In the end, he decides that he is an American and that both he and his country made mistakes; he looks to the future with cautious optimism.

Kenji Kanno, Ichiro's friend and supporter. Although he shared Ichiro's anger about racial injustice toward Japanese Americans and other ethnic minorities, Kenji joined the Army when war broke out. Like many other Japanese American soldiers, he fought bravely against the Germans; he lost a leg in battle, and the wound eventually kills him. He believed that the "melting pot" was a myth.

Mrs. Yamada, Ichiro's mother. An immigrant (or "Issei") Japanese, she has lived in the United States for thirty-five years, yet she considers herself Japanese rather than American, and she speaks virtually no English. She refuses to believe that the Japanese were defeated in the war. She is proud of Ichiro's refusal to fight for the United States, but Ichiro feels alienated from her, and there is tension between them. Her mind deteriorates, and she commits suicide by drowning in her own bathtub. Ichiro never completely forgives her for trying to make him Japanese instead of American.

Mr. Yamada, Ichiro's father. A weak-willed and confused man, he lacks a sense of cultural identity, feeling neither Japanese nor American. He tries to understand Ichiro's problems but can offer him son little guidance or support. He becomes virtually helpless and turns to alcohol after his wife's death.

Emi, a young Japanese American woman whom Kenji introduces to Ichiro. Abandoned by her husband, who served with Kenji in the war, she is lonely. She is attracted to Ichiro, and the two have an affair. Ichiro, still tortured by guilt and psychological conflict, finally rejects her offer of love.

Taro Yamada, Ichiro's younger brother. He despises Ichiro for being a "no-no boy." He sets up Ichiro for a beating. When he turns eighteen, he immediately enlists in the Army.

Freddie, Ichiro's friend and fellow "no-no boy." Like Ichiro, he is struggling to resolve his feelings of conflict about his refusal to serve in the Army; unlike Ichiro, he disguises his feelings with loud talk and brash actions. His feelings of rage eventually lead to his death in a car accident.

Eto, an Army veteran and former friend of Ichiro. He hates all "no-no boys" and spits on Ichiro and Freddie when he meets them after the war.

Bull, another Japanese American veteran who detests "no-no boys." His tauntings of Freddie are indirectly responsible for the latter's fatal car accident.

Mr. Carrick, an empathetic Anglo American who realizes that Japanese Americans were victims of injustice and oppression during the war. He offers Ichiro a job, in part because he wants to atone for his country's mistreatment of Japanese Americans.

— *Lawrence J. Oliver*

NO ONE WRITES TO THE COLONEL
(El coronel no tiene quien le escriba)

Author: Gabriel García Márquez (1928-   )
First published: 1961
Genre: Novel

Locale: An unnamed village in Colombia
Time: October to December, 1956
Plot: Ironic

The colonel, an extremely poor retiree who has waited fifteen years for his military pension. He is rather anorexic, and the only thing that makes him look like he has not been kept in formaldehyde is the vitality of his eyes. He is extremely careful, respectful, and formal, and his hair is metallic, like his joints. His lack of a name in the novel fits perfectly with his wish to remain anonymous, which to him is a way of keeping his dignity. His pride makes every one of his actions appear transcendental, and thus his meager possessions are displaced by a prizefighting cock whose value is mainly symbolic. The colonel appears flat and unapproachable, but in reality he is a good and decent man totally devoted to his wife and to the memory of his son, an ill-defined subversive. Lacking practical concerns, he still distributes the clandestine political literature for which his son was killed. Liked by most of the townspeople, who know his true state, he lives in a dream world and on hope. He realizes that he is aging—he is seventy-five years old—and that he really does not know his wife, but he keeps living by appearances. To the very end, he feels unbeatable, believing that even though he is starving, his rooster will win and feed him.

The colonel's wife, the colonel's conscience, guide, and subtle protector. She is a practical woman whose asthma attacks do not prevent her from imagining every conceivable means to support her family. Of arched back, she is as slim as her husband, although quite energetic. She is fussy and a stickler for details, even when she turns her house upside down. She is warmer in personality than the colonel. The memory of her son, Agustín, is the only thing that gets her out of her constant nagging. She is a mystery to her husband, even though he easily fathoms her determination not to show any weakness, such as crying.

Don Sabas, Agustín's godfather, a total contrast to the colonel. A corrupt businessman who will syphon money from any source or person without blinking an eye, he is short and unappealing. Although everyone knows that he is a traitor and has gotten rich through illegal means, they also know that corruption is so widespread that to take on Don Sabas may actually create more political repression. Callous, mean, and obese, he is not above cheating the colonel, his godchild's father. He neurotically tortures his corpulent wife with fears and suspicions.

The physician, who, like others in the town, is part of the subversive movement. A kindly, practical man, he does not harbor illusions about the political situation that represses him and the others. He does not charge the colonel or his wife, and his good sense of humor is exercised mainly at the expense of Don Sabas. Fairly young, he generally fits the stereotypes for doctors, such as having illegible handwriting.

— *Will H. Corral*

NO PLACE ON EARTH
(Kein Ort: Nirgends)

Author: Christa Wolf (1929-)
First published: 1979
Genre: Novel

Locale: An estate near the German town of Winkel on the Rhine
Time: June, 1804
Plot: Livre à clef

Heinrich von Kleist (HIN-rihkh fon klist), a writer and dramatist, twenty-six years old, the orphaned son of an impecunious Prussian noble family. Kleist is unable to harmonize the need to find a socially acceptable occupation with his desire to write. His constant sense of guilt and melancholy, his slowness of speech, and his uneasiness in the presence of others are symptomatic of his conviction that there is for him "no place on earth." He frequently entertains thoughts of suicide. At the time of the story, he is recuperating from mental and physical collapse and has recently burned the unfinished manuscript of *Robert Guiskard*, a drama that might have become his magnum opus. Along with the other characters, Kleist is based on a historical figure. A few years after the time depicted in the novel, he takes his own life.

Karoline von Günderrode (kah-roh-LEE-neh fon GEWN-deh-roh-deh), a Romantic poet and canoness. Unmarried at the age of twenty-four, highly cultured, and, like Kleist, also a member of the impoverished aristocracy, she suffers as a result of social alienation. Her recently completed volume of poetry, published under the pseudonym Tian, has received a negative review. She is drawn to Savigny, who prefers, however, a more chivalric friendship. These failures lead her to suspect that personal fulfillment as a woman and a poet may be impossible within the confines of social convention. Ever on the verge of suicide, she sees nothing strange in making a dagger her constant companion. The historical Günderrode eventually employed the weapon on herself, two years after the time depicted in the novel, when Friedrich Creuzer, a professor of mythology, spurned her love.

Clemens Brentano (KLEH-mehnz brehn-TAH-noh), also a young poet and writer. Having inherited both a handsome visage and financial security from his Italian merchant father, the newly wed Brentano exudes social poise and eloquence. He seems destined to succeed in his literary career. In almost every sense, he constitutes the antipode of Kleist.

Sophie Mereau Brentano (meh-ROH), a poet and writer, Clemens Brentano's attractive wife. Formerly married to a professor at the University of Jena, she divorced him so that she could marry Brentano.

Bettine Brentano (beh-TEE-neh), Clemens Brentano's younger sister and a friend of Günderrode. Like her brother, she is beautiful, cultured, and without financial want. The historical Bettine later married poet Achim von Arnim, authored her own works of epistolary fiction, and published her correspondence with Günderrode.

Friedrich Karl von Savigny (FREE-drihkh kahrl fon sah-VIHN-yee), a lawyer. He is well off, independent, and self-assured. Although only in his mid-twenties, he already has embarked on what would become an illustrious academic career. He believes that the worlds of ideas and of political life should remain separate; philosophy and art should have little impact on the real world. Although quite intent on maintaining his friendship with Günderrode, he will not do so at the expense of his own marriage.

Gunda von Savigny (GEWN-dah), Karl von Savigny's wife and the sister of Clemens and Bettine Brentano.

Joseph Merten, a wealthy spice and perfume merchant in his mid-forties. He prides himself on being a connoisseur of the arts and sciences. His country estate, located on the Rhine, is the setting for the novel.

Georg Christian Wedekind (GAY-ohrg KRIHSH-tyahn VAY-deh-kihnt), a physician and privy councillor at the electoral court of Mainz. After Kleist's mental and physical breakdown, Wedekind cares for him and takes him in as a houseguest. He attempts to reintegrate Kleist into society.

Nees von Esenbeck (nehs fon AY-zehn-behk), a botanist who places more value on scientific advancement than on what he calls the hypochondriac lament of the poets.

Lisette von Esenbeck (lee-ZEHT-teh), the wife of Nees von Esenbeck and a close friend of Günderrode. She is intelligent, educated, and the master of more than one Romance language but has elected to find her fulfillment in the unqualified support of her husband and his career.

Charlotte Servière (shahr-LOHT-teh sehr-VYEHR), a friend of Karoline von Günderrode and Paula Servière's twin sister.

Paula Servière, a friend of Karoline von Günderrode and Charlotte Servière's twin sister.

— *Steven R. Huff*

NO TELEPHONE TO HEAVEN

Author: Michelle Cliff (1946-)
First published: 1987
Genre: Novel

Locale: Jamaica, the United States, and England
Time: The 1970's
Plot: Psychological realism

Clare Savage, the protagonist, a woman in her twenties. Clare is the confused daughter of a father who is desperate to find a secure place in the male-dominated power structure and a mother who desires most of all to live with some sense of dignity and self-worth. Her parents' insecurity is reflected in Clare, who lives at various times in Jamaica, the United States, and England, always hoping to discover who she is and her place—as a black woman from a Third World country—in a world that too often refuses to recognize her kind.

Boy Savage, Clare's father. Boy leaves Jamaica with his reluctant family hoping to find a better life in the United States. He represents a certain type of black man, desperate to fit into white society. He ignores its evils, principally, what it does to his self-respect. He becomes disillusioned and feels impotent.

Kitty Savage, Clare's mother. She reluctantly follows her husband to New York and tries to fit in, but she cannot easily fool herself into rationalizing or overlooking the bigotry that surrounds her. Her unhappiness leads to small but significant acts of rebellion that culminate in her leaving her husband to return to her homeland.

Harry/Harriet, Clare's bisexual friend. His/her sexual confusion is a manifestation of the identity crisis that afflicts members of minority groups in general and those from Third World countries more specifically. Clare's best friend began life as Harry, a male, but is Harry/Harriet by the time the two meet. Rather than being a pitiful or grotesque figure, however, he/she ultimately is an affirmative character, by the end making a forceful choice of identity. She commits to life as Harriet, a confident, committed woman.

Christopher, a yard boy for a wealthy black family. Christopher represents the most frightening aspect of Third World culture: the person driven to murderous rage. Christopher, ultimately to be pitied more than feared, is reared in the almost incomprehensible poverty of the "dungle," the shantytown of Kingston, Jamaica. His wretched life becomes even worse after the death of his mother. Always seeking comfort and solace, but never finding it, Christopher—his name designates him as a Christ figure—reacts not with meekness but finally with horrible violence as he slaughters the wealthy black family for whom he works.

Paul H., the son of a wealthy black Kingston family. Paul finds his family the morning after they, along with the maid Mavis, are slaughtered by Christopher. Paul represents a certain type of black youth, reared in relative affluence, essentially good-natured, but ultimately blind to the horrid conditions in which most black people are forced to live. He pays for his ignorance with his life.

Bobby, Clare's black American lover in Europe. Bobby is a Vietnam veteran, who suffers from physical and emotional wounds that will not heal and allow him to commit to another person.

— *Dennis Vannatta*

NO TRIFLING WITH LOVE
(On ne badine pac avec l'amour)

Author: Alfred de Musset (1810-1857)
First published: 1834
Genre: Drama

Locale: France
Time: The nineteenth century
Plot: Tragicomedy

Perdican (pehr-dee-KAH[N]), the son of a French nobleman. He returns to his father's home after receiving his doctorate. He is a somewhat worldly man and is distressed to find his childhood sweetheart cool to him. He tries to win her. Failing in his suit, he courts a peasant girl, who dies of shock when she learns that Perdican does not really love her.

Camille (kah-MEEL), Perdican's childhood sweetheart and an heiress. Reared in a convent, she looks for happiness as a nun, rather than as a wife. She is confused when she finds that she loves Perdican, and her indecision drives Perdican to the peasant girl. Camille is greatly distressed when the girl dies, and she blames herself; she inflicts punishment on herself by bidding her suitor goodbye.

Rosette (roh-ZEHT), a sweet and loving peasant girl who is courted by Perdican and who loves him deeply. When she learns that her lover really wants Camille as his wife, she dies of shock.

The baron, Perdican's father, who is eager for his son to marry Camille, the heiress.

Dame Pluche (plewsh), Camille's chaperon, an easily scandalized woman who is rigorous in performing her duties.

Maître Blazius (mehtr blah-ZYEWS), Perdican's tutor. He is a fat and foolish priest, and a heavy drinker and eater, who wants to be priest in the baron's household.

Maître Bridaine (bree-DEHN), Maitre Blazius' competitor for a place in the baron's household. He, like his rival, is a foolish gourmand.

NOCTURNE

Author: Frank Swinnerton (1884-1982)
First published: 1917
Genre: Novel

Locale: London, England
Time: The twentieth century
Plot: Domestic

Jenny Blanchard, a milliner's assistant, tall, rather beautiful, and independent. Frustrated by the humdrum nature of her life, she turns her unromantic suitor over to her sister and goes to meet Keith Redington, a more glamorous young man who wants her to run away with him to Alaska or Labrador. Later, Jenny feels conscience-stricken because she left her father alone and also because she feels that in admitting her love for Keith, she has given up her freedom.

Emmy Blanchard, her older sister, who stays at home to look after their father and the house. She is plain and domestic and also frustrated because she is in love with Jenny's suitor. After dressing for the date Jenny has tricked Alf into making, Emmy appears looking lovely. During the course of the evening, Alf decides that Emmy is the woman for him, and they become engaged.

Alf Rylett, Jenny's suitor, adored by Emmy, with whom he falls in love.

Keith Redington, the captain of a yacht belonging to a wealthy lord. He knew Jenny for only three days during a seaside vacation, but he confidently sends her a summons to the yacht, where she finds supper for two prepared. He has romantic plans for their future, but the dream is crushed when Jenny thinks of Pa.

Pa Blanchard, the semi-invalid father of Emmy and Jenny. He is injured in a fall after Jenny leaves for the yacht. Emmy and Alf find him on the kitchen floor and revive him.

THE NON-EXISTENT KNIGHT
(Il cavaliere inesistente)

Author: Italo Calvino (1923-1985)
First published: 1959
Genre: Novel

Locale: France
Time: During the reign of Charlemagne, 768-814
Plot: Fable

Agilulf, a knight in Charlemagne's army. Agilulf's appearance is the most important thing about him because, in a sense, he is only appearance. He exists only as his armor (white except for a thin black line running along the seams), his shield (on which is a coat of arms showing a shield sporting a coat of arms with a shield, *ad infinitum*), and his voice. He is a hollow man who has given himself up to forms of life—the code of chivalry and military conduct—so completely that he is divorced from life in its human, corporeal aspects. He is at once absurdly comic and tragic, not a shallow but an engagingly complex character. He is the greatest warrior in this novel of warfare. He is virtuous. He is desired by many women and pursued by one, Bradamante, throughout the book. Ultimately, though, he can enjoy none of the fruits of his many excellent qualities, and the end finds him to be simply inanimate armor.

Bradamante, a female soldier. Bradamante is a beautiful young woman, but she wears armor and passes for a man throughout much of the action. In a sense, then, she is like Agilulf in that her armor represents what she desires to be: a great warrior. Whereas Agilulf is only his desires, however, Bradamante is also a woman and cannot deny that facet of her personality. She falls in love with Agilulf because of his knightly perfection and spends much of the novel pursuing the non-existent knight.

Sister Theodora, the narrator. Sister Theodora reveals herself to the reader gradually over the course of the novel. At first, it is not clear that the novel has a narrator; then the reader is informed by Sister Theodora that the abbess has assigned her the task of writing the tale for the health of her soul. The novel can be seen, then, as essentially a dramatization of Sister Theodora's hopes and fears (love, adventure, duty, the subjection of one's self to forms, and so on). It is not always clear, and perhaps not important, whether the events described actually happened or are invented by Sister Theodora. Much the same can be said for her claim at the end that she is really Bradamante and that she occasionally rides out on adventures, when not cooped up in her cell.

Raimbaut (raym-BOH), a young knight. Raimbaut is as young and handsome as Bradamante is young and beautiful, but he is impetuous and foolhardy, whereas Agilulf is proper and in all things correct. Raimbaut's mission early in the novel is to avenge his father's death, but after encountering Bradamante, his obsession becomes proving himself to her, thereby winning her hand.

Gurduloo, an idiot. The rags that Gurduloo wears are an earthen color with green patches, colors that indicate his close connection to nature. If Agilulf is empty form, Gurduloo is a man so dominated by his sensory, physical relationship to his surroundings that he is virtually without thought and without form. He spends most of the novel as Agilulf's companion, which is appropriate because the two are opposite sides of the human coin.

Torrismund, a young knight. In this novel of paired characters, the cynical Torrismund is perhaps best seen as the foil of the idealistic, impetuous Raimbaut.

— *Dennis Vannatta*

THE NORMAL HEART

Author: Larry Kramer (1935-   )
First published: 1985
Genre: Drama

Locale: New York City
Time: Early 1980's
Plot: Problem play

Ned Weeks, a writer and activist who becomes obsessed with the AIDS (acquired immune deficiency syndrome) epidemic in its early stages and founds an organization to help gay men who have the disease. Angry, aggressive, and relentless in his tactics, Ned is criticized by most characters in the play, especially for his view that homosexuals should refrain from having sex until a cure is found for AIDS. In spite of his offensive behavior, Ned is the hero of the play. It is clear that he is upset by the deaths of young, gay men and that he is committed to warning those who have not yet been infected, no matter how much he must fight or what price he must pay.

Ben Weeks, Ned's straight brother, a partner in a prestigious New York City law firm. Ned needs Ben's help in setting up the organization for gay men, support Ben is reluctant to give because he does not want his name or the name of his firm associated with homosexual causes. When Ben refuses to be on the organization's board of directors, Ned vows not to speak to him until Ben can accept him as his "healthy equal." The brothers remain estranged until Felix's death at the end of the play.

Emma Brookner, a physician who has devoted her practice to helping gay men infected with the virus eventually identified as AIDS. Besides being a pioneer in the treatment of AIDS, Emma spearheads early efforts to conduct research on the disease, although the medical establishment does little to support her efforts. Strong, angry, and relentless, Emma tries to reach the gay community, through Ned and others, to warn gay men about the disease and to urge them to stop having sex. She treats Felix, Ned's AIDS-infected lover, and marries Ned and Felix in her hospital.

Bruce Niles, Ned's antithesis. Although both Ned and Bruce are on the board of directors of the gay men's organization, they have very different ideas about how the organization should respond to the AIDS epidemic. Bruce, as opposed to Ned, is conservative in his approach and is apolitical. Although the two fight about almost everything pertaining to the organization and although Bruce eventually kicks Ned out of the organization, they are also friends (at times), and Ned supports Bruce when his lovers die of AIDS. Ironically, Ned is romantically attracted to Bruce at the beginning of the play. Bruce is more self-conscious about his homosexuality than any other character in the play.

Felix Turner, a fashion reporter for *The New York Times* who becomes Ned's lover. At the end of the play, he dies from AIDS, after he and Ned are married.

Tommy Boatwright, one of the younger volunteers with the organization for gay men. Hardworking, enthusiastic, and innovative, Tommy also is diplomatic, often trying to solve conflicts between Ned and the other members of the organization. If anyone provides comic relief in the play, it is Tommy, whose mannerisms and expressions are overtly gay. He is romantically interested in Ned until Felix and Ned begin dating.

— *Cassandra Kircher*

THE NORMAN CONQUESTS

Author: Alan Ayckbourn (1939-   )
First published: 1975
Genre: Drama

Locale: England
Time: The 1970's
Plot: Comedy

Norman Dewers, an assistant librarian. With his scruffy beard, shapeless cap, and ill-fitting suit, Norman always appears slightly unkempt. Convention fits Norman no better than do his clothes. He possesses a wry sense of humor, a benign indifference to the restrictions of work and marriage, and a well-earned reputation for causing trouble, though the problems created by Norman are never the result of malice. Norman truly believes his oft-repeated claim that he is only trying to make people happy. Moreover, Norman is capable of being witty, charming, and attentive. He fails, however, to see that his boundless desire to be loved (as well as his belief that any woman is a potential conquest) can cause friction when he must deal with those who possess more conventional attitudes about fidelity and happiness.

Ruth Dewers, Norman's wife. Ruth is a businesswoman whose career takes priority in her life. Ruth's greatest concern during the weekend in which the play takes place is not Norman's infidelity per se but rather the amount of time that it is taking her away from her work. Ruth can, however, display genuine affection for Norman. She loves him, although the five years of their marriage have left her with few illusions about Norman's ability to be faithful. She no longer expects loyalty from Norman and has long since ceased to be concerned by his indiscretions. Ruth has chosen not to have children. This decision, coupled with her caustic wit, has created tension between her and the other members of her family, including her mother and her sister-in-law, Sarah. Too vain to wear her glasses, Ruth is afflicted with a constant squint, which becomes most pronounced whenever she tries to identify specific objects, even if they are fairly close to her.

Reg, Ruth's brother, a real estate agent. In many ways, Reg is temperamentally the opposite of Ruth. He takes his career so lightly that even his wife, Sarah, wonders how he is able to make a living at it. Moreover, Reg's sense of humor is far less biting. He loves to joke, though his jokes are frequently amusing to himself alone. Reg also believes himself to be a fairly tolerant man of the world and thus does not condemn Norman for his affair with Annie. The air of feigned nonchalance vanishes, however, when Reg suspects that Sarah may be Norman's next conquest. Reg is capable of becoming obsessed with petty details, such as complicated routes designed to shave a few minutes off of one's travel time or rules for board games that are so involved that no one else can understand them. Reg loves to spend hours designing these very games.

Sarah, Reg's wife. Sarah's desire to control every situation results from her attempt to conceal a highly nervous disposition. Lack of harmony upsets Sarah, and she becomes genuinely distraught when things fail to go according to plan. Her one desire is to spend a quiet weekend with her family. When this desire proves to be unattainable, Sarah becomes agitated and overbearing. Sarah is the mother of two children: Denise, age seven, and Vincent, age five. Proud of her role as a parent, Sarah is easily disturbed by Ruth's blithe rejection of motherhood. Sarah's sense that her efforts are not appreciated leaves her open to Norman's flattery, and at least the possibility is raised that Sarah may be Norman's next victim.

Annie, the younger sister of Ruth and Reg. Although not a great beauty, Annie is capable of "making an effort" and thus appearing reasonably attractive. Most of the time, however, Annie feels that such an effort would not be worthwhile. As a result, she is usually seen in a plain and unflattering dress. Annie is tired of Tom's inability to advance their relationship and exhausted by the year that she has spent caring for her invalid mother. She thus agrees to Norman's proposition largely out of boredom, although she considers it unlikely that Norman will carry through with his plans. Annie is attracted by Norman's directness and by the excitement and flattery that he brings to her otherwise dull life.

Tom, Annie's friend, a veterinarian. Although knowledgeable about the care and treatment of animals, Tom is less understanding when it comes to human relationships. Any remark that is subtle or complex is usually beyond Tom's grasp. As a result, Annie thinks that Tom prefers animals to people, although Tom himself suggests that animals are simply easier to understand. Animals, he believes, are never deceptive in their reactions to one another, whereas people rarely, if ever, say what they mean. Tom has difficulty with such a lack of candor. He is overly literal in his interpretations of what people say, and this invariably causes him trouble. Tom is romantically interested in Annie—he is even willing to marry her—but he hesitates in making the first move. Tom's hesitation is attributable partly to his fear of rejection. More important, however, Tom is unwilling to embark on any course that will irretrievably alter their relationship.

— *Jeffrey L. Buller*

NORTH AND SOUTH

Author: Elizabeth Gaskell (1810-1865)
First published: 1854-1855
Genre: Novel

Locale: England
Time: Mid-nineteenth century
Plot: Social

Margaret Hale, who has been living in London with her well-connected relatives. She received the upbringing of a lady. She is quiet but with a well-defined personality, which is enlarged throughout the novel by a series of new demands on her that require resourcefulness, initiative, and firmness of character. She is plunged from upper-class London life to lower-middle-class Manchester life, without any status or prospects. Nevertheless, she attracts two suitors, suave London attorney Henry Lennox and factory owner John Thornton. She rejects both, perhaps too decisively, preferring her independence. She has to learn to love, in the end, through being humiliated. Thornton, though rejected, still rightly honors her. Unexpectedly, her inherited riches become his reward as much as hers. She becomes many things to many people: a source of support for her mother, an intellectual companion to her father, a source of spiritual solace to Bessie, a source of encouragement to Higgins, and a challenge to the Thorntons. She absorbs northern energy to become a fully integrated young woman.

The Reverend Richard Hale, whose theological doubts are never really explored; in an age of growing doubt, they remain ciphers. The "bravery" of his decision is counterbalanced by his inability to tell his wife or to comfort her. He wins respect in Milton from both Thornton and Higgins, and he sincerely seeks to mediate in the class struggle he finds there.

Maria Hale, the Reverend Richard Hale's wife. She comes from an upper-class family and is very aware that she has lowered herself by marrying a humble clergyman. The loss of her son and her further lowering of status are more than she can take. She becomes a hypochondriac, and then in reality an invalid.

John Thornton, who has worked his way up from being a shopkeeper to being a factory owner. His desire for a classical education suggests desires and sensitivities atypical of his colleagues. His love for Margaret is slowly born and genuine, based rather more on admiration for her independence than on her good looks and refinement. He becomes a true gentleman as he honors her despite rejection and outward appearances. His false sense of power is broken by his loss of capital and replaced by a new desire to concern himself respectfully with his workers' conditions. He is a much worthier suitor than Lennox and deserves the help Margaret finally is able to give him.

Mrs. Thornton, the driving force behind her son. A striking matriarch, she is fiercely protective of John and therefore sees Margaret as a threat. She is thus all too ready to give her a severe talking to in place of advice after her mother's death. Paradoxically, she allows her own daughter, Fanny, to be a self-regarding moral weakling.

Nicholas Higgins, the most outspoken of the workers. His involvement with a union is seen as a weakness, as is his propensity to drink. He has ideals, and in Mr. Hale he finds a ready listener to whom he can articulate some religious faith. He is broken by Bessie's death but can still support Boucher's family after they are left fatherless.

Bessie Higgins, a deeply religious woman who educates Margaret into northern ways. She has worked in a factory, in such unsanitary conditions that she contracted a fatal pulmonary disease. Her death follows a long tradition of set-piece lingering deaths but is portrayed effectively in an understated way.

— *David Barratt*

NORTHANGER ABBEY

Author: Jane Austen (1775-1817)
First published: 1818
Genre: Novel

Locale: England
Time: Early nineteenth century
Plot: Domestic realism

Catherine Morland, a young girl whose head is filled with Gothic romances. At Bath, she meets the Thorpe and Tilney families. Her brother James is attracted to Isabella Thorpe, and John Thorpe becomes attentive to Catherine. She, however, is more interested in Henry Tilney, a younger son, whose father invites her to his home, Northanger Abbey, under the mistaken impression that she is rich and will make a good match for Henry. Overcome by the thrill of being in a real abbey, Catherine makes several foolish blunders, even thinking that her host must have murdered his wife. The visit ends when General

Tilney, learning that Catherine is not rich, asks her to leave and forbids Henry to see her. Yet Henry's love proves strong enough for him to defy his father, and the lovers are finally married.

General Tilney, the owner of Northanger Abbey. Eager for money, he is polite to Catherine only because he believes her to be rich.

Captain Frederick Tilney, his older son, for whom Isabella Thorpe jilts James Morland.

Henry Tilney, the younger son, a clergyman, who marries Catherine Morland.

Eleanor Tilney, their sister. Her marriage to a viscount puts

her father into a good enough humor to permit the marriage of Henry and Catherine.

James Morland, Catherine's brother. He falls in love with Isabella Thorpe but is jilted by her.

Isabella Thorpe, a scheming young woman whom Catherine meets at Bath. She becomes engaged to James Morland but jilts him for Captain Tilney, though without much hope of marrying the latter.

John Thorpe, Isabella's stupid brother, who tries to marry Catherine and who boasts to General Tilney of her wealth. When she refuses him, he takes revenge by telling the general that she is poorer than she really is.

THE NORTHERN LASS

Author: Richard Brome (c. 1590-c. 1652-1653)
First published: 1632
Genre: Drama

Locale: London, England
Time: Early seventeenth century
Plot: Comedy of manners

Sir Philip Luckles, a gentleman who devotes his life to the satisfaction of his own wishes. He marries Mrs. Fitchow for her money, and he no sooner sees the prospect of both beauty and fortune in Constance's love for him than he plans his divorce and elopement.

Mistress Fitchow, a well-to-do widow, his promised wife. Although she refuses to hear Tridewell's slander about her bridegroom, she is immediately jealous of Constance and indicates her displeasure to Sir Philip by barring him from her room on their wedding night.

Tridewell, Sir Philip's friend. Trying to save him from an unsuitable match, he finds himself in love with the widow who defends her groom with spirit, and he contrives to make his friend's marriage illegal.

Widgene, Mrs. Fitchow's opportunist brother, who is seeking a rich wife. He is rewarded for his schemes with the hand of Mrs. Holdup, a courtesan.

Anvile, his tutor, expert in all the vices of young gentlemen.

Constance, the "northern lass," a Yorkshire girl who falls in love with Luckles at their first meeting and loses her senses at the news of his marriage. She is restored to health and sanity by her elopement with him.

Sir Paul Squelch, her wealthy uncle, a blustering, lascivious old gentleman who makes his mistress masquerade as his niece.

Mistress Traynwell, a sharp-tongued lady of uncertain years, Constance's governess. She resolutely pursues Sir Paul until she can blackmail him into marriage by threatening to reveal Constance Holdup's identity.

Constance Holdup, a witty prostitute, Sir Paul's mistress. She takes advantage of her feigned role as his niece to win herself a husband, Widgene.

Pace, Sir Philip's clever servant, who disguises himself as a doctor and a minister.

NOSTROMO: A Tale of the Seaboard

Author: Joseph Conrad (Jósef Teodor Konrad Nałęcz Korzeniowski, 1857-1924)
First published: 1904
Genre: Novel

Locale: Costaguana, on the northern coast of South America
Time: Late nineteenth or early twentieth century
Plot: Psychological realism

Nostromo (nos-TROH-moh), the nickname of **Gian' Battista** (bah-TEES-tah), the "incorruptible" hero of the people who saved a valuable cargo of silver from revolutionists by hiding it on a barren island at the harbor entrance. Later, he realizes that it can be his because the lighter on which he transported the silver is reported sunk in a collision with a troopship at night. He grows rich slowly, by returning to the island occasionally for some of the silver. When a lighthouse is established on the island, he is still able to visit his hoard of silver because his friends, the Violas, are made keepers of the light. He chooses to love Giselle, the younger Viola daughter, rather than the more stable and idealistic Linda. Mistaken for a despised suitor of Giselle, he is shot by old Viola while on a night visit to see Giselle. Nostromo dies feeling that he has

been betrayed and wishing to confess to Mrs. Gould. Because she refuses to listen, his secret is kept, and his famed incorruptibility remains intact.

Charles Gould, the manager of the San Tome silver mine, which he idealizes as a civilizing force that will bring progress to contented but backward Sulaco, a city in the Occidental Province of the Republic of Costaguana, as well as atonement for the death of his father. Yet silver, the incorruptible metal, is a corrupting influence politically and morally. It separates Gould from his wife Emilia, attracts politicians from the interior, and provokes a revolution.

Doña Emilia (eh-MEEL-ee-ah), Charles Gould's wife, supplanted in his affections by his "redemption idea" of the mine. Childless, she is a victim of a "subtle unfaithfulness" created by the mine. In turn, she is gracious, kind, and unselfish and lives for others.

Martin Decoud (mahr-TA[N] deh-KEW), a young Creole intellectual, skeptic, and amateur journalist recently returned from Paris. He falls in love with patriotic Antonia Avellanos and fathers the idea of a separate Occidental Republic. He escapes from the revolutionists on the lighter bearing the silver, but he commits suicide when left alone on the island to face the silence and indifference of nature.

Dr. Monygham, a doctor of introspective temperament. Under torture during the former dictatorship of Guzman Bento, he had betrayed friends, a deed that weighs on his conscience. He risks his life during the revolution for the safety of others in order to earn restoration to the human community.

Captain Mitchell, the superintendent of the Oceanic Steam Navigation Company, a "thick, elderly man, wearing high pointed collars and short sidewhiskers, partial to white waistcoats, and really very communicative under his air of pompous reserve." He narrates part of the story.

Giorgio Viola (JOHR-jyoh vee-OH-lah), a veteran of Garibaldi's army and keeper of the Casa Viola, a restaurant and hotel in Sulaco. Believing wholeheartedly in the human bond of liberty, he had risked his life in Italy in the hope of bringing freedom to men. He wishes to make Nostromo his son.

Teresa, the portly, ill wife of Viola, anxious for the future of her husband and daughters.

Giselle (zhih-SEHL), the sensuous, blond younger daughter of Viola, in love with Nostromo.

Linda, the idealistic, dark older daughter of Viola, also in love with Nostromo.

President Ribiera (ree-bee-AY-rah), the beneficent dictator of Costaguana, defeated by revolutionary forces.

Don José Avellanos (hoh-SEH ah-vay-YAH-nohs), an idealistic, cultured, dignified, patriotic statesman who has survived many changes in his country; he is the author of *Fifty Years of Misrule*, a history of the republic. He dies of disappointment.

Antonia Avellanos (ahn-TOH-nyah), his beautiful, freeminded, patriotic daughter, in love with Decoud.

Father Corbelàn (kohr-beh-LAHN), the fanatical uncle of Antonia Avellanos. His appearance suggests something unlawful behind his priesthood, the idea of a chaplain of bandits. He is Costaguana's first cardinal archbishop.

General Montero (mohn-TEH-roh), a rural hero and a former minister of war, the leader of the revolution.

Pedro Montero, his brother, a savage with a genius for treachery. He is the leader of the rebel army from the interior.

Don Pépé (PEH-peh), the faithful overseer of the San Tome mine, under orders to blow up the mine if the revolutionaries try to seize it.

Father Roman (roh-MAHN), the faithful padre of the workers of the mine.

Colonel Sotillo (soh-TEE-yoh), one of the leaders of the revolution. Cowardly and traitorous, he hurries his army into Sulaco in the hope of gaining personal advantage.

Señor Hirsch, a craven and fearful hide merchant who tries to escape from Sulaco by secreting himself on the lighter with Nostromo and Decoud while they are transporting the silver. When the lighter and Sotillo's ship collide in the darkness, he leaps aboard the rebels' vessel. There, he is tortured for confession and finally killed by Sotillo.

Hernandez (ehr-NAHN-dehs), a man mistreated in an earlier revolution and now the leader of a robber band. During the revolt, he becomes a general, pledged to Father Corbelàn.

General Barrios (BAHR-ryohs), a brave, trustworthy, unpretentious soldier who has lived heroically and loves to talk of the adventurous life of his past. He is the commander of the Occidental military district.

Don Juste Lopez (HEWS-tay LOH-pehs), the president of the provincial assembly. He thinks that resistance to Pedro Montero will be useless but that formalities may still save the republic.

Fuentes (FWEHN-tehs), a nominee for the post of political chief of Sulaco. Eager to take office, he sides with Pedro Montero.

Gamacho (gah-MAH-choh), the commander of the Sulaco national guard. He throws his lot in with the revolutionists.

Basilio (bah-SEE-lee-oh), Mrs. Gould's head servant.

Luis (LEW-ees), a mulatto servant at the Casa Viola.

NOT WITHOUT LAUGHTER

Author: Langston Hughes (1902-1967)
First published: 1930
Genre: Novel

Locale: Stanton, Kansas, and Chicago, Illinois
Time: 1912-1918
Plot: Domestic realism

James "Sandy" Rodgers, the novel's protagonist, who comes of age in small-town, racially divided Stanton, Kansas, in the years prior to and including World War I. A sensitive, reflective, and intelligent black boy, Sandy is a young child when the novel opens; at the novel's close, he is sixteen years old and determined to continue his education despite the onset of the war and the economic hardships his family suffers. Sandy is the perceptive observer of black life across race, caste, and class barriers in Stanton and Chicago. He is at first the listener while various members of the black community reflect on their life's experiences, particularly their encounters

with racism; eventually, as he grows up and begins to move within the larger community, he has his own experiences with maturation, sexuality, and family and race relations on which to reflect.

Aunt Hager Williams, Sandy's maternal grandmother and the principal source of strength, wisdom, and inspiration in his life. As a hardworking washerwoman and an old-fashioned Christian devoid of malice and devoted to Christian values, Hager is the mainstay of her family and an important community resource. Blacks and whites in Stanton respect her and call on her services in times of crisis.

Jimboy Rodgers, Sandy's roving, guitar-playing, loving, and hardworking (when he can find work) father. Young and light-skinned, or "high yellow," Jimboy is the quintessential, apparently irresponsible, bluesman living the blues he sings about. Both racism and disposition prevent him from being a steady, stay-at-home husband and father. In Hager's eyes, he is a flawed young man and a bad influence on her youngest daughter, Harriet. Jimboy loves his music and his family; he provides for the family as best he can, though racism denies him meaningful employment.

Annjelica (Annjee) Roberts, Sandy's mother and Jimboy's sturdy, dark-skinned, quiet, meek, hardworking, and responsible wife. Both desperately proud of and deeply in love with her husband, Annjee resolves to join him the next time the search for work pulls him away from his family.

Harriet Williams, Hager's proud, rebellious, "frisky," free-spirited daughter and the vibrant young aunt whom Sandy idolizes. Bitter experiences with discrimination have taught Harriet hatred of white people; she can accept neither the paltry pay nor the insults extended to hardworking black maids and domestic workers by white employers. Neither can she extend to white employers her mother's Christian forgiveness for their meanness. Determined to live her life on her own terms and as she feels fit, Harriet becomes a blueswoman, the female counterpart to Jimboy.

Tempy Siles, the eldest of Hager's daughters; she is snobbish, responsible but insensitive, and successfully married and respectable. Proud of her rise to upper-middle-class status. Tempy has distanced herself from her family, left the Baptist church to join the color- and class-biased Episcopal church, and all but rejected the community where she was reared. Following the death of Aunt Hager, Tempy assumes responsibility for Sandy until his mother returns.

Maudel Smothers, Harriet's best friend, considered a loose girl and bad influence by Aunt Hager.

Mrs. J. J. Rice, the demanding white woman who employs Annjee as a domestic servant.

Sister Johnson, the mother of Willie Mae and a former slave, a friend and neighbor of Aunt Hager. Sister Johnson recounts what life was like for black people in the Reconstruction South.

Sister Whiteside and

Brother Logan, elderly neighbors, confidants, and friends of Aunt Hager.

Willie Mae Johnson,

Buster,

Jimmy Lane, and

Pansetta, childhood friends and neighbors of Sandy. Pansetta is Sandy's first, although unconsummated, love.

— *Sandra Y. Govan*

NOTHING

Author: Henry Green (Henry Vincent Yorke, 1905-1973)
First published: 1950
Genre: Novel

Locale: London, England
Time: 1948
Plot: Fiction of manners

John Pomfret, a forty-five-year-old widower. He is a member of the older generation who made much of parties, socializing, and sex. He had a good war record, but his main interests presently seem to be his affair with Liz Jennings and his longtime friendship with Jane Weatherby. His affair with Jane in the past almost broke up his marriage to Julia. He is fond of his daughter Mary, but she is not at the center of his life. John usually laughs at things, maintaining an ironic stance.

Jane Weatherby, a widow with a twenty-year-old son, Philip, and a six-year-old daughter, Penelope. Jane, who has fat, white hands and plump, firm thighs, has been having an affair with Dick Abbot. On the surface, she seems flighty and helpless, but she manipulates the other characters in her indirect, "feminine" way. She prevents Philip's marriage to Mary Pomfret so that she can marry John, Mary's father, and not have her marriage look ridiculous to society. Jane makes much of her concern for her daughter Penelope, creating her image as a devoted mother, but she deprecates Philip to her friends, saying that he is not quite normal. Jane also seems tight with money, unwilling to help out the newly engaged couple, Philip and Mary.

Mary Pomfret, who is eighteen years old and striking in appearance. She is described as a bluestocking, taken up with her civil service job. She and Philip think that life is hopeless because of the state of the national economy. Mary tells Philip that they should elope, but he worries that an elopement would upset his family. Mary not only loses Philip (as a result of Jane's machi-

nations) but also loses her job when she obeys her father's request that she spend time in Italy and miss his wedding (another of Jane's ideas).

Philip Weatherby, who works in the same office as Mary and proposes to her on his twenty-first birthday party. He vacillates, however, when his mother covertly opposes the match. He does not care enough to fight for her, and he remains under his mother's thumb. Pompously, Philip says that his generation is making the country a fit place to live, unlike the older generation, who are like rabbits about sex. He worries that his biological father is really John Pomfret.

Elizabeth (Liz) Jennings, John Pomfret's lover. At twenty-nine years of age, she says that she is afraid that she will never have children, but John refuses to take the hint and propose. Liz is accused of having drunk too much at a party, a charge that Jane uses against her. Liz cultivates Dick Abbot when the two of them are neglected by John and Jane. Ultimately, they switch partners, with Liz claiming that Dick is the better man.

Richard (Dick) Abbot, who has choking fits and talks often about his war experiences in Italy. With doglike eyes, he looks at Jane and says that he would like to marry her. Dick has a sense of social propriety and loyalty to Jane, even when she spurns him. When Liz plays up to him, however, Dick starts an affair with her.

Penelope Weatherby, Jane's six-year-old daughter, who has copper curls and large eyes. Jane treats her as if she is neurotic, saying that Penelope is distressed by a make-believe wedding with John Pomfret, at seeing a one-armed man, and at hearing that John is diabetic. Philip thinks that his little sister knows how to get her own way.

Arthur Morris, a member of John and Jane's set who throughout the novel is dying by bits and pieces. His big toe is amputated, then his ankle, and then his knee. Finally, he dies; his funeral is a social occasion.

— *Kate M. Begnal*

NOTHING HAPPENS IN CARMINCROSS

Author: Benedict Kiely (1919-   )
First published: 1985
Genre: Novel

Locale: Ireland and Northern Ireland
Time: The 1970's
Plot: Adventure

Mervyn Kavanagh, sometimes referred to as **Merlin**, a balding and middle-aged storyteller and professor of history. He has returned to Ireland from a stint of teaching at a Southern college in the United States to attend the wedding of his favorite niece in Carmincross, a town in Northern Ireland. When he arrives in Ireland, he immediately becomes aware of the internal war in Northern Ireland through reports on the radio and in the newspapers. His response is to recall old legends and ballads and to contrast their heroic ideals with the sordid and violent present. He finds little heroism in the ambushes and bombings carried on by both sides in the terrorism and counterterrorism of Northern Ireland. When he sets off on his journey to Carmincross, he is accompanied by an old friend, Deborah. Their journey is compared a number of times to that of the legendary Irish lovers, Diarmuid and Grainne, who fled from Fionn MacCool. Mervyn is fleeing from the wife he left in America, and Deborah is fleeing from her husband, Mandrake. Their idyll is broken by the terrible events in Carmincross, where a revolutionary group plants bombs that lead to the death of the bride-to-be, Stephanie; Mervyn's mother; and a friend, Cecil Morrow. After the slaughter, Mervyn retreats to Dublin, where a sister of the dead bride-to-be marries the intended groom. Mervyn is no longer optimistic about the future of Ireland, although he does perceive some reconciliations in the marriage of his other niece and in his return to his wife in New York. He perceives that the troubles of Ireland are no nearer a solution, but that they can be put aside or transcended by individual acts of love and kindness.

Deborah, a warm and witty Irish woman in her mid-thirties who is disappointed in her marriage. She is an old friend of Mervyn and takes the opportunity to go on a trip with him to Carmincross. They are lovers but not passionately involved. She feels that four years is long enough for any relationship and fiercely defends her freedom. After the events at Carmincross, she argues with Mervyn and throws his book of Irish stories and legends into the fire. She claims that they have brought bad luck to everyone and are responsible for the disasters at the border and at Carmincross. She is injured soon after driving a car away from Mervyn. Later, in the hospital, she is reunited with her husband, Mandrake.

Mr. Burns, a suave and cordial Irish hotel manager. He is a boyhood friend of Mervyn and deplores the violence that rages in the country.

Cecil Morrow, a policeman in Carmincross and a boyhood friend of Mervyn. He is a tall and imposing figure, but he wishes to be a policeman without a gun, a man who serves the community. He saves Mervyn's mother from the bombs (though she eventually dies from injuries), but he is shot soon afterward by a revolutionary who is fleeing the scene on a motorcycle.

Timothy, called **Mandrake**, Deborah's husband. He is a shy and unexciting but loyal and dependable man who cares for Deborah in the hospital.

Jeriamiah Cilsenenan, a cynical Dublin civil servant. He angrily debunks all claims to heroism and idealism in the Irish civil war he sees before him. His response, however, is just as extreme as that of the rebels. Where they see heroism, he can see nothing but grisly humor and mockery.

— *James Sullivan*

NOTHING LIKE THE SUN: A Story of Shakespeare's Love-Life

Author: Anthony Burgess (John Anthony Burgess Wilson, 1917-1993)
First published: 1964
Genre: Novel

Locale: Stratford and London, England
Time: The Elizabethan period
Plot: Livre à clef

William Shakespeare, an actor, poet, playwright, and lover. The novel covers Shakespeare's life from his youth to near his death and shows the growth of his darkening view of life. This changing attitude results mainly from his encounters with various loves throughout his life. Young Will abandons his plans to marry true love Anne Whateley—they had even taken out a license—when he is forced to wed the pregnant Anne Hathaway, eight years his senior. To support his growing family, he later leaves his home in Stratford and travels to London, where he eventually becomes the lover of his patron, Henry Wriothesley, the third Earl of Southampton. Shakespeare's passion for this younger man inspires two narrative poems and, more directly, a succession of love sonnets, but the continuation and completion of his sonnet cycle results from his obsession with the exotic Dark Lady, who accepts Shakespeare's attentions and money but who also becomes Southampton's lover. Infected by her with the syphilis that eventually kills him, Shakespeare wonders, while back in Stratford during his declining years, whether Southampton may have initially transmitted the disease to her.

Anne Hathaway, Shakespeare's wife. Anne's English features, with straight, carroty hair and a narrow brow, contrast with the dark, golden appearance of Shakespeare's later lover, the Dark Lady. They also belie Anne's lusty, experienced background. She revels with a drunken Shakespeare in a wood one May night. After their forced wedding, he is unsure that their daughter is really his. The marriage becomes, over the years, a prime source of his growing disappointment and bitterness. Anne's knowledge of sexual technique shocks him. One night, the sight of a mob in the street torturing a woman accused of witchcraft arouses Anne's exhibitionism, and she begs Will to make love to her at the window. The request repulses him, and he momentarily transfers to Anne the witch-like traits of the accused woman. Shortly after this incident, he leaves Stratford to begin his life in London. During this time, Anne scolds him about his absences, refuses to read his poetry, and cuckolds him with his younger brother.

Henry Wriothesley, the **Earl of Southampton**, whom Shakespeare first meets when the earl is a beautiful, pale, teenage boy ten years Shakespeare's junior. Even then, Will notices a slyness in his eyes. Southampton becomes Shakespeare's patron and, responding to Will's overture, his lover. Southampton supplies Shakespeare with court gossip about Elizabeth I and the politics of the day, and Shakespeare reciprocates with stories about the theater. The two men start to drift apart when Will's Dark Lady secretly becomes Southampton's lover, but what permanently separates them is the earl's attempt to get Will to write seditious works to inflame the masses and depose an aging, ineffectual Elizabeth. When Shakespeare injudiciously relates his discovery of his wife's adultery with his own brother, he elicits an uncontrollable peal of derisive laughter from Southampton. Shakespeare notices again how the beauty of the earl's face hides a frightening ugliness.

Fatimah, also called **Mistress Lucy** and the **Dark Lady**, Shakespeare's lover in London. Rumored to have been brought as a child from the East Indies to London on Sir Francis Bacon's ship *The Golden Hind* and reared by a gentleman in Bristol, the Dark Lady is first seen by Shakespeare as she steps, veiled, from her coach. She becomes Shakespeare's lover, though at first she seems more interested in hearing about Richard Burbage, the leading man of Shakespeare's acting company, than in the balding playwright. Also Southampton's lover during this time, she gives birth to a son and later returns to Shakespeare, telling him that the boy (which he assumes to be his) is in Bristol, to be sent eventually to the East. She passes to Shakespeare the venereal disease that in time kills him, and she shrinks from him when he first reports to her that he is unwell.

— *Glenn Hopp*

NOVEMBER 1918: A German Revolution
(November 1918: Eine deutsche Revolution)

Author: Alfred Döblin (1878-1957)
First published: 1948-1950; first complete edition, 1978
Genre: Novel

Locale: Berlin and the Weimar Republic
Time: November, 1918, to the late 1920's
Plot: Social

The author, who introduces, comments on, and ties together developments in Germany at the end of World War I and afterward. Berlin is the focal point, but events in Strasbourg, Paris, the German military headquarters in Kassel, and elsewhere are woven into the intricate story. The story traces the thoughts and actions of political figures, revolutionaries, military officers, financial opportunists, and ordinary individuals in the tense period following the establishment of a shaky, moderately left-wing republic and the armistice through the crushing of the Spartacists. The frustration of President Woodrow Wilson and his hope for a just peace without victors is also described. Finally, through Friedrich Becker, the author berates the postwar Weimar Republic. According to him, there was no real attempt to come to grips with the causes of war, and he predicts the rise of a new paganism, characterized by strength and cunning.

Hilda, a striking twenty-one-year-old blond who serves as a nurse in a German military hospital in Alsace. After the armistice, she is unwilling to renew her relationship with her prewar lover, the artist Bernhard. When she leaves for Berlin to find Friedrich Becker, one of her former patients with whom she had fallen in love, Bernhard hangs himself. She finds Becker improved physically but undergoing a deep mental or spiritual crisis. He, too, had attempted to hang himself. Regarding herself as the source of Friedrich's torment, she decides that she must leave him and takes a job at a suburban Berlin hospital. The image of Hilda, a devoted Catholic, falling on her knees and praying becomes for him a redemptive example. Ignored by Friedrich, she responds to the love of Johannes Maus. They become engaged, marry, and eventually settle in Karlsruhe with their child. Becker, during his later wandering, surprises the couple with a short visit. Hilda, who still loves him deeply, is distressed by his appearance but inspired by his somewhat crazed religious intensity and ominous predictions for the future.

Friedrich Becker (FREE-drihkh), a doctor of philology and a former teacher who, as a wounded German officer, was nursed by Hilda. After prolonged hospital treatment, Becker returns to his mother's apartment in Berlin, where his spinal wound continues to heal. As Becker grows physically stronger, however, he suffers a mental collapse brought on by deep feelings of guilt for having participated in the war as an officer. He goes through a desperate struggle with the Devil, who appears to him in the form of a mysterious Brazilian, a lion, and a rat. Despairing, Becker then attempts suicide. Through a religious vision, prompted by Hilda's example, Becker finds salvation and peace in the image of the crucified Christ. To the dismay of his friend, Johannes Maus, Becker pleads that peace can be found only through religious transformation. Returning to his teaching post for a trial period, Becker antagonizes the conservatives by asserting, as he discusses Sophocles' *Antigone*, that unwritten divine law transcends the law of the state. When he attempts to rescue Heinz Riedel, Becker, inspired by the helplessness and misery of the workers, joins the

Spartacists in the defense of the police station. Wounded, he refuses Maus's attempt to exonerate him, but with the help of Hilda he is rescued from execution at the Moabit Hospital. After three years in prison, he returns to teaching, but his uncompromising idealism creates problems. Unable to satisfy his spiritual hunger and to escape the demands of his personality with women and money, he takes to the road as a wanderer. After years of inciting the poor to revolt and calling Christians to task, he once more falls into the hands of the Devil. The Devil slips the soul of a depraved bargeman into Becker's breast. Becker finally finds peace from his struggles with the Devil and this corrupt soul. As he lies dying from a gunshot he received while attempting a robbery, he is rescued by Antoniel, his guardian angel.

Becker's mother, a widow in her fifties. Her Christian commitment and her self-sacrificing concern for others are shared by her son.

Johannes Maus (yoh-HAHN-nehs mows), Becker's simple and honest fellow officer and friend, who recuperated with him in the Alsatian hospital. Maus had fallen in love with Hilda. He longs for her and feels guilty for forcing himself on her just before leaving the hospital. His alienation from postwar German society and desire to be useful to the world are directed toward political radicalism by an old friend, Karl "Big" Ding. His disappointment that his friend Becker does not support his radicalism is compounded by Hilda's preference for Becker. Although Maus angrily rejects Becker's new religious outlook, he does rethink his decision to join the Spartacists. He opts, instead, for the counterrevolutionary Frei Korps unit that is being organized by General Marcker. At the urging of Hilda, he helps Becker gain access to the besieged police station. Uncomfortable with the military after the experiences of January, 1919, Maus leaves the army and studies engineering.

The Director, a cultured classicist in his fifties, in charge of Becker's old school. Becker attempts to persuade the Director, whose fondness for young men is creating scandal, to end his relationship with the student Heinz Riedel. After the Director is fatally beaten by the boy's father, Becker, in spite of public pressure and threats to his career, defends the claim of the dead to be remembered and arranges the burial.

Heinz Riedel (hints REE-dehl), a blond student who is the favorite of the Director. Becker befriends him. After his father's arrest, Heinz is allowed to stay with Becker and his mother. Becker takes him to the dying Director and with him buries the man. When Heinz is disowned by his mother for refusing to help his father's case by exaggerating his intimacy with the Director, he takes to the streets. Becker eventually locates him with the Spartacists in the besieged police station. Heinz, after recovering from his wounds, goes on to fight and die in a Communist insurrection in central Germany.

Friedrich Ebert, the squat, portly, goateed, forty-seven-year-old leader of the moderate Majority Socialists, or Social Democrats, who take over the German government from Chancellor Prince Max of Baden on November 9. He temporarily cooperates with the more left-wing Independent Socialists but is determined, with the aid of the army, to prevent a radical social revolution from engulfing Germany. He gives lip service to the idea of socialism but is a thorough reformist. He believes that the restoration of prosperity and the maintenance of national unity against the Allies can be accomplished only with the support of the bourgeoisie. He is determined to free himself from any dependence on the Council of People's Deputies, to sabotage and abolish the revolutionary All German Congress of Councils, and, ultimately, to base the authority of the government on an elected constituent assembly. When the Constituent Assembly meets on January 19, after the Spartacists have been brutally crushed, Ebert is chosen as president of the German Republic.

Philip Scheidemann (SHI-deh-mahn), Ebert's assistant in the Social Democratic Party, who, to the dismay of Ebert, proclaims a republic on November 9 to prevent the radical Spartacists from seizing the initiative.

Woodrow Wilson, the tall and frail sixty-two-year-old United States president, whose uncompromising vision of a just peace becomes the victim of his own self-righteous ego, the legitimate concerns and acquisitive desires of the vengeful Allies, and the vicissitudes of domestic American politics.

Karl Liebknecht (LEEB-knehkt), who with Rosa Luxemburg leads the radical leftist Spartacist League and the newly formed German Communist Party. Liebknecht believes that Ebert is betraying the revolution, but he is afflicted with doubt and hesitates to initiate a revolutionary uprising. Bolshevik agent Karl Radek is appalled by Liebknecht's reluctance to be responsible for bloodshed and his tendency to substitute endless words for decisive revolutionary action. Liebknecht doubts whether the German workers are in favor of revolution but fears that, unless the Spartacists act, any revolutionary possibilities will be lost to the counterrevolutionaries. Liebknecht, carried away by his emotions and without the support of Luxemburg, on January 6 forms a Provisional Revolutionary Committee that declares Ebert's government deposed. Liebknecht fails to provide dynamic leadership. His dispirited supporters melt away or are crushed by the armed forces of the anti-Spartacists. He, along with Rosa Luxemburg, is betrayed by his courier, Werner, and the two revolutionaries are murdered by their military captors.

Rosa Luxemburg (LEWK-sehm-buhrg), a small, graying, forty-seven-year-old revolutionary leader who is opposed to terror and to dictatorship even in the name of the proletariat. While Luxemburg is in prison for antiwar agitation, the spirit of Hannes Düsterberg, her friend who was killed on the Eastern Front, takes control of her and torments her. Her mental anguish, replete with hallucinations of Hannes, Satan, and a cherub, continues until her death. Her anguish is compounded by her realization that a proletarian insurrection is premature and fated to be crushed in a bloodbath. After her captors crush her skull and shoot her, they dump her body in the Landwehr Canal.

General Groener (GREH-nehr), the quartermaster general (second in command) of the German army. This pragmatic South German from Württemberg replaces General Ludendorff when Ludendorff is forced to retire. On November 9, Groener contacts Ebert by means of a secret telephone line to the chancellery in Berlin and agrees to support Ebert against the radical left, the Spartacists, if Ebert will protect the integrity of the army. Despite feelings of distaste and the misgivings of other officers, Groener sees no acceptable alternative to working through Ebert.

General Oskar von Hindenburg, the massive, bristly, white-haired, and amply mustached seventy-year-old field marshal and chief of staff of the German army. He holds his quartermaster, General Groener, responsible for the army's necessary withdrawal of its support from the kaiser on November 9. Hindenburg finds the necessity of working with Ebert completely distasteful.

Gustav Noske (NOHS-keh), a tall, lanky, low-browed, right-wing Social Democrat who quiets the revolt in Kiel and agrees to play the "bloodhound" as Ebert's minister of war. Noske works with the military to organize the brutal suppression of the disorganized Spartacist rising.

Minna Imker (MIH-nah IHM-kehr), a slight, hardworking, radical worker in her twenties who has her hair cut because it is discolored by chemicals used in the armaments industry.

She helps to persuade her brother Ed, who has just returned from the war, to join the Spartacists. She is killed when the military attacks the Spartacists, who have seized the police station.

Herr Wylinski (vih-LIHNS-kee), a pleasure-loving and womanizing former Russian socialist who develops business interests to cover and finance his revolutionary activities. He becomes disenchanted with the Bolshevik regime and immigrates to Germany, where he is the politically connected center of a profitable network of financial manipulators. The austere Finsterl and the playboy Willi Finger are his shady associates. Wylinski appropriates a dyed-blond, somewhat exotic beauty, Toni, from Herr Motz, the assistant to another shady character, Herr Brose-Zenk, alias Schröder.

— *Bernard A. Cook*

THE NOVICE
(Mtsyri)

Author: Mikhail Lermontov (1814-1841)
First published: 1840
Genre: Poetry

Locale: The Caucasus mountains, Georgia, Russia
Time: 1840
Plot: Lyrical

The novice, a novice monk in a monastery near the Caucasus mountains, Georgia, Russia. He was brought there as a prisoner of war at the age of six, after being captured in his native mountain village by the occupying Russian forces. On the journey to the Russian town of Tiflis, the boy, who was of a delicate constitution, fell ill. He was taken to the monastery and placed in the care of the monks. Having inherited his father's proud and free disposition, he never complained. He stubbornly refused food and drink but was saved from death by the ministrations of one monk, his father-confessor, who tended and healed him. The boy did not indulge in childish play; instead, he stayed aloof and alone, pining for his native mountains. In time, he was baptized (he would have been born a Muslim) and became a novice monk. In effect, he was still a prisoner of war in the monastery, living in a bare, dark cell. He cherishes one desire in his heart: to see his homeland, and the people who live there, once more. The poem tells of the novice's attempt to accomplish this. One day, during a storm, he escapes and flees into the surrounding countryside. There, his romantic soul enables him to commune with nature, as he observes and delights in every aspect of the landscape. He encounters danger in the form of a hungry panther. During a

prolonged and bloody battle with the panther, the novice feels that he takes on the spirit of the panther; within him is born the forlorn call of the wounded beast. The novice kills the panther, aligning himself with the heroic deeds of his lost family. Wounded and exhausted, he sees his bid for freedom end in despair as he realizes that he has come full circle and has reached the monastery again. He now knows that he will never achieve his lifelong desire to see his birthplace again. He remains resolute and defiant to the end, confessing to the father that he would give up eternity itself in return for a mere hour among the rocks where he played as a child.

The novice's father-confessor, an old man who does not speak in the poem. He hears of the recaptured novice's adventures in freedom, in the form of a final confession before the novice's death. The novice evidently loves and trusts him more than anyone else in the monastery.

A Georgian maid, who attracts the novice's attention when he hears her singing a song. He watches her collect water from a stream. He never speaks to her. She remains a symbol of the beauty, mystery, playfulness, and sensuality of his lost people.

— *Claire J. Robinson*

NUNS AND SOLDIERS

Author: Iris Murdoch (1919-   )
First published: 1980
Genre: Novel

Locale: London and southern France
Time: Late 1970's
Plot: Psychological realism

Guy Openshaw, a senior official in the Home Office; he is wealthy, intellectual, highly competent, and dying of cancer. He is a helper of Tim Reede and a friend to the Count. Although they lost their only child, Guy and his wife, Gertrude, have had a successful marriage. Although he is terminally ill, Guy renounces painkillers long enough to tell Gertrude lucidly that he wishes her to be happy again. He has wandering,

philosophical conversations with the Count and discusses vice and virtue with Anne Cavidge, a former nun. Guy believes that his own virtue is accuracy and that justice is not a virtue but a calculation. Guy believes in consequences; he seeks truth and finds Purgatory a hopeful idea. The book is devoted to those who must reorder their lives because of Guy's death, to the need for truth, and to the unavoidable consequences of action and inaction—all ideas the reader meets first in Guy's conversations. His death establishes the premise of the novel, and he brings together the other characters.

Gertrude Openshaw, Guy's thirty-eight-year-old, attractive wife and eventually his wealthy but grief-stricken widow. During Guy's last days and after his death, Gertrude turns to Anne Cavidge, her friend from Cambridge days, for support and companionship. She sees the former nun sharing her comfortable life. When Tim Reede, Guy's protégé, a penniless painter, appeals to her, she generously offers him the job of caretaker in her French house. Falling in love with him there comes unexpectedly. Tim is equally in love, and the two are married. Guy's family is naturally opposed, as are Anne Cavidge and the Count, who has loved Gertrude for years. When it comes to their notice that Tim has a longtime mistress of whose existence Gertrude is ignorant, both are eager to act in Gertrude's interest, not their own. They decide that she must be told. Gertrude sends Tim away but suffers in his absence. She turns to the Count and Anne for company. When Tim reappears at the house in France, Gertrude is overjoyed, and the couple renew their married life. Gertrude loves Tim but continues to mourn for Guy. She also manages to include the Count in her new circle, so that he can at least return to his place as platonic friend.

Anne Cavidge, a friend of Gertrude at Cambridge who entered a closed order of nuns but has now returned to the world. Anne, though her clear vision of faith has gone, is still a pilgrim seeking her path. At first, her duty seems to be with Guy and Gertrude. Her uneasiness about Tim, her discovery of his mistress, and her love for the Count make Anne's relationship to Gertrude complex. Anne wishes Tim and Gertrude to be together because the Count might then become aware of her. She believes that Tim is not a good choice for Gertrude and so tells her the unpleasant truth, even knowing that if Gertrude is free, the Count will propose to her. Anne also finds it hard to obtain employment because of her age and lack of experience. When Gertrude and Tim are reunited and Gertrude finds room for the Count in her new life, Anne leaves for the United States to work with an order of Poor Clares there.

Peter Szczepanski, called **the Count**, the only child of Polish immigrant parents. This lonely man is a friend of Guy and in love with Gertrude. He is a man of honor and cannot tell Gertrude of his love, neither while Guy is alive nor too soon after his death. In the meantime, she remarries. Afraid of acting in his own interest rather than Gertrude's, the Count consults Anne when he discovers that Tim has a mistress. Anne and the Count become friends, and he never suspects that she is in love with him. Briefly hopeful when Gertrude's second marriage seems to be over, the Count again accustoms himself to his old relationship with Gertrude.

Tim Reede, a mediocre painter in his early thirties, a red-haired, sunny-natured, and feckless drifter. Reede has lived a hand-to-mouth existence with his mistress Daisy for years. He is not particularly intelligent and is ill-informed; he lives by sense, enjoying every day as it comes. He has no particular regard for truth, and when he falls deeply in love with Gertrude, he hopes that the problem of Daisy will go away. When Gertrude dismisses him, he returns to Daisy, but he finally realizes that, even if he never sees Gertrude again, he must break with his former mistress. His reunion with Gertrude results, morally, from this new commitment to truth.

— *Jocelyn Creigh Cass*

O

O BEULAH LAND

Author: Mary Lee Settle (1918-   )
First published: 1956
Genre: Novel

Locale: England, Virginia, and the western frontier of Virginia
Time: 1754-1774
Plot: Historical realism

Hannah Bridewell, a transported felon and escaped Indian captive. Wiry and resilient, Hannah is able to adapt readily to the frequent violent changes in her life. As a young prostitute in London, she befriends "Squire" Josiah Devotion Raglan, saving him from many unpleasant incidents during their incarceration. After she is transported, sold to a settler, and captured by Indians, Hannah uses her instincts to survive for weeks in the wilderness. After her marriage to Jeremiah Catlett, she uses her natural cunning to establish a successful farm and family in Beulah.

Jeremiah Catlett, a solitary squatter in western Virginia. Although he abjures human company before Hannah's arrival, her presence and, later, the needs of their children convince Jeremiah to coexist with the other settlers in Beulah. His actions are all pointed toward the protection of his family and land, however, rather than toward the interests of the community.

"Squire" Josiah Devotion Raglan, Hannah's fellow prisoner in England, who is transported and purchased by a young dandy, Peregrine Cockburn. After the untimely death of his master at the hands of Indians, Raglan, in the guise of a lawyer, turns to fleecing ignorant settlers of their land rights and money. He eventually receives his just deserts at the hands of Jeremiah Catlett.

Jonathan Lacey, a provincial captain and planter. Deeply convinced that the future of his young nation depends on the settlement of its outlying areas, Jonathan successfully presides over the small community in Beulah and unsuccessfully tries to establish his family there.

Sally Lacey, his young and frivolous wife. Although she loves Jonathan, rears their children while he explores the western territory, and eventually follows him to their homestead, Sally is hurt and unhappy with life on the frontier. Her snobbish attitude angers the Beulah residents. After several incidents, she leaves Jonathan and returns to the old life that she knows and loves in the East.

Jarcey Pentacost, a Virginia planter and printer by trade. Driven by his ethical and political convictions, he strives to enlighten the people in several communities through his newspaper, eventually establishing a school in Beulah, in which project he is aided by Jonathan Lacey.

Ezekiel Catlett, the son of Hannah and Jeremiah Catlett. He and Sara Lacey are members of the first generation born in Beulah. They have shed the fears and inhibitions of their parents and look to the future with courage and an open-minded attitude. Their marriage, which crosses the boundaries of social station, is a symbol of this new, American attitude. It is on them that Jonathan and Jarcey place their hope for lasting success in Beulah.

Sara Lacey, the strong-willed daughter of Jonathan and Sally Lacey. She and Ezekiel will provide Beulah with future generations who will possess her father's love of freedom and self-reliance rather than her mother's devotion to a life that will not provide the strength to endure in the wilderness of western Virginia.

— *Jennifer L. Wyatt*

O, HOW THE WHEEL BECOMES IT!

Author: Anthony Powell (1905-   )
First published: 1983
Genre: Novel

Locale: Great Britain
Time: The 1980's
Plot: Satire

Geoffrey F. H. "Shad" Shadbold, a writer in his mid-seventies with a lingering reputation as a literary reviewer and broadcaster. He considers himself a better man of letters than he ever was. His early work as a poet and a minor novelist is almost forgotten. Rather affected in his old age, bearded, long-haired, and given to eccentric garb, he guards his modest fame fiercely and is much disturbed when asked to judge the diary of an old friend, Cedric Winterwade, who died in World War II. The work turns out to be disturbingly good, but Shadbold tells the prospective publisher otherwise, partly out of professional jealousy and partly because the diary reveals that Winterwade, whom Shadbold had patronized as nondescript during their friendship, had been sexually involved with Isolde Upjohn, a pretty model whom Shadbold had pursued in vain.

Despite Shadbold's bad report, the diary seems to get a second life when Isolde suddenly appears, eager to publish her memoirs and full of enthusiasm for telling all about the Winterwade escapade. Shadbold, who is bruised professionally and personally—as well as long since inclined to bask lazily in his old reputation—is roused to move quickly to protect his ego.

Isolde Upjohn, who in her youth was a model, pursued by young men of fashion but "kept" by an older man. She suddenly shows up as **Mrs. Abdullah**, having written her memoirs and ready to publish them. Unashamed of her morally ambiguous past or her four marriages to international men of property, and unaware of how her short affair with Winterwade has upset Shadbold or that he has just learned of it, she is enthusiastic about revealing all about her lively past and wants Shadbold to help her. Despite her age, she is still an energetic, attractive woman.

Cedric Winterwade, a now-deceased man who had been at school and university with Shadbold and had become a stockbroker. He published one novel, but Shadbold had little regard for it or for Winterwade. His diary, and Isolde UpJohn's memories of him, reveal that he was much more formidable as a man and as a writer than Shadbold imagined.

Prudence Shadbold, the second wife of Shadbold, a successful writer of mystery stories under the pen name of Proserpine Gunning. She has little interest in her husband's early life and is ignorant of the youthful connections of Shadbold, Winterwade, and Isolde Upjohn.

Jason Price, Shadbold's young publisher, who sports a Lord Kitchener mustache, affects the dress of a 1920's man-about-town, and is interested in literary figures of the same period. In particular, he is interested in reprinting Winterwade's novel. He suspects that Shadbold's report on the Winterwade diary might not be entirely valid.

Horace Grigham, an English literature don at a provincial university and the former husband of Prudence Shadbold. He is bearded, bald, intense, and boringly tenacious if he becomes interested in anything. Grigham, who likes to use the most fashionable literary jargon but is clearly a bit fraudulent, surprises Shadbold by evincing an interest in Winterwade's work.

Rod Cubbage, a television interviewer, vain, arrogant, and infamous for attacking personalities who are unwise enough to appear on his program. Shadbold reluctantly accepts an invitation to be filmed with Cubbage, thinking himself a match for Cubbage and hoping that the exposure will help his public reputation. By sheer bad luck (for Shadbold), Cubbage manages to draw Isolde Upjohn onto the same show and soon senses that there are secrets to be told.

— *Charles Pullen*

O PIONEERS!

Author: Willa Cather (1873-1947)
First published: 1913
Genre: Novel

Locale: Nebraska
Time: 1880-1910
Plot: Regional

Alexandra Bergson, the daughter of a Swedish immigrant homesteader on the Divide in Nebraska. A strong-willed woman of great courage and resourcefulness, she takes charge of the farm after her father's death and, through good years or bad, uses the land wisely. When times are hard and neighbors become discouraged and move away, she scrimps and saves to add their acres to her own. She is the first on the Divide to try new agricultural methods, to plant alfalfa, to build a silo. She keeps Oscar and Lou, her younger brothers, from leaving the farm for easier work and softer living in town. At the end, she can look out over her cultivated fields and know that she has won prosperity for herself and her brothers. Yet her success as a farmer is bought at the price of her experience as a woman. Twice she sees Carl Linstrum, whom she loves, leave the Divide with no words of love spoken. She is more than forty when the death of Emil, her youngest brother, killed by a jealous husband, teaches her the need of love and the grace of compassion, and she and Carl are reunited. Alexandra Bergson is a character almost epic in stature, a fertility goddess of the plains subduing the wild and stubborn land and making it fruitful.

John Bergson, an immigrant farmer who dreams of regaining on his Nebraska homestead a family fortune lost in Sweden. He dies after eleven years of failure, his faith in the land still unshaken. On his deathbed, he asks his two eldest sons to be guided by their sister, for he sees in her qualities of imagination, energy, desire, and wisdom that her brothers lack.

Mrs. Bergson, a devoted wife and mother who tries to maintain household order by clinging to old, familiar European ways. Her twin passions are gardening and preserving.

Carl Linstrum, a grave, introspective young man unsuited to farm life on the Nebraska frontier. His predicament is that of many transplanted Europeans, divided as he is between his Old World heritage and his prairie environment. When his father sells the Linstrum farm and moves back to St. Louis, Carl goes to the city to learn the engraver's trade. Sixteen years later, dissatisfied with commercial life, he returns to the Divide, but Oscar and Lou Bergson, Alexandra's brothers, insult him and drive him away with accusations that he has come back to marry their sister for her money. Carl goes off to Alaska but returns when he reads the news of Emil Bergson's murder. This time, he and Alexandra plan to marry.

Oscar Bergson and

Lou Bergson, Alexandra's younger brothers. Dull, insensitive, greedy, they respect their sister but have no real affection for her. Their great hope is that they or their children will inherit her land.

Emil Bergson, Alexandra's youngest brother, whose relationship to his sister seems more like that of a son than of a brother. He grows into a moody, restless young man. Less stolid than the Scandinavian Bergsons, he finds his friends among the more volatile, merrier Bohemians and French settlers in nearby communities. In love with Marie Shabata, a young married woman, he goes to Mexico for a time. After his return, he plans to study law in Omaha. One night, Frank

Shabata finds Emil and Marie together and in his jealous rage kills them.

Marie Shabata (sha-BAH-tah), a pretty Bohemian housewife, innocently flirtatious from childhood, always merry and teasing. Having eloped with Frank Shabata, she tries to make the best of a bad situation and endures as cheerfully and patiently as possible his jealous suspicions and wild outbreaks of rage. At first, she refuses to acknowledge her true feelings for handsome young Emil Bergson, but circumstances bring them together until, one disastrous night, Frank Shabata finds the two in the orchard and shoots them.

Frank Shabata, a wildly jealous, bad-tempered man distrustful of his pretty young wife. After shooting Marie and Emil Bergson when he finds them together, he makes a futile effort to escape before surrendering to the authorities. Alexandra Bergson shows the true bigness and generosity of her nature after Frank has been sentenced to prison. Convinced that he had acted only as his rash and violent nature compelled him and that his punishment can serve no purpose for the dead, she visits him in the penitentiary at Lincoln and promises to do everything she can to get him pardoned.

Crazy Ivar, a Swedish hermit and horse doctor whom the uncharitable call crazy; others believe him touched by the hand of God. He is wise in homely folklore concerning animals, birds, and crops, and Alexandra Bergson asks his advice on many farm matters. After he loses his land during a period of depression, she gives him a home. Behind his clouded mind, he is a man of deep faith and shrewd wisdom.

Amédée Chevalier (ah-may-DAY sheh-vahl-YAY), a jolly, high-spirited young French farmer, Emil Bergson's best friend. He dies suddenly after an emergency operation for appendicitis.

Angélique Chevalier (an-zhay-LEEK), his young wife, widowed after a year of marriage.

Annie Lee, the neighbor girl whom Lou Bergson marries. Like her husband, she is ashamed of old-fashioned European ways and apes American dress and customs.

Milly,

Stella, and

Sadie, the daughters of Lou and Annie Bergson.

Mrs. Lee, Annie Bergson's mother, a spry, wholesome old woman who holds nostalgically to the Old World ways her daughter and son-in-law dislike. Every winter, she visits Alexandra Bergson, who allows the old woman to do as she pleases during her stay.

Signa, Alexandra Bergson's hired girl and friend.

Nelse Jensen, Signa's husband.

Barney Flinn, the foreman on Alexandra Bergson's farm.

THE OATH
(Le Serment de Kolvillàg)

Author: Elie Wiesel (1928-   )
First published: 1973
Genre: Novel

Locale: Kolvillàg, a village in central Europe
Time: Early twentieth century to the early 1970's
Plot: Parable

Azriel (AZH-reel), the only survivor of the Kolvillàg pogrom. Bound by an oath not to reveal how he survived or how the rest of his village was massacred in the pogrom, he wanders from city to city in central Europe as a Jewish *Na-venadvik*. Others see him as a saint or a madman, a bringer of deep understanding and insight to people of whatever class or age he encounters. Even as he sees all in the lives of others, no one knows the despair of the secret he bears until he counters that hopelessness by telling his story to a suicidal young man. By transmitting his community's history to another person, he saves the young man to live as a messenger of truth and frees himself to return to Kolvillàg and die.

Moshe (moh-ZHAY), a brilliant mystic and mentor to Azriel. Considered a madman by his Jewish community, he wears rags and lives a solitary existence in the woods until he is persuaded to marry the homely Leah out of pity. His entrancing eyes and ability to see into the thoughts and dreams of people frighten them away from him, and Azriel becomes his only student and disciple. As the tension leading to the pogrom builds, he offers himself as a martyr to save the Jewish community and is imprisoned for the murder of the gentile Yancsi. In an address in the synagogue, he binds the Jews of Kolvillàg to a vow of silence over the atrocities of the coming pogrom in the belief that by refusing to preserve the history of suffering, the suffering itself might be halted.

Shmuel (ZHMEW-ehl), the father of Azriel and chronicler of Kolvillàg's history in the *Pinkas*. A strong believer in the power of the written word to bind the Jewish community and to strengthen the people through recurring periods of persecution, he scrupulously records the deliberations of the Jewish council and the emotional and spiritual responses of the townspeople to the coming terror. Bound by Moshe's vow of silence, he does not write of the pogrom itself yet preserves Kolvillàg's history by giving the *Pinkas* to his son Azriel and urging him to flee.

The young man, a would-be suicide to whom Azriel tells his story. Overwhelmed by the despair of a life for which he has no "story," he seeks to find meaning through death. His parents are emotionally scarred survivors of the Holocaust, and the son feels the burden of a historical legacy that contains a mystery he cannot hope to fathom. By listening to Azriel's story, he inherits a message that requires his survival as a means of preserving it.

Yancsi (YAYNK-see), a gentile boy who disappears and is believed to have been ritually murdered by the Jews of Kolvillàg. Abusive and disliked by virtually everyone who knows him while he is alive, he is acclaimed as a faithful son and an innocent victim after his disappearance.

Davidov, the president of the Jewish community in Kolvillàg who futilely seeks to serve as a mediator between his own people and the gentiles through his friend the Prefect, to whom he offers money for protection.

Leah, Moshe's wife, who gains self-respect through his love and who seeks to obey him by not crying after his arrest but is overwhelmed by grief and cries out after his speech at the synagogue.

Braun, a Jewish lawyer who marries a Protestant wife and repudiates his heritage. His father and his son, Toli, are killed in the pogrom.

Sergeant Pavel, a brutal police officer who speaks tenderly to his riding crop as he beats Moshe almost to the point of death in an attempt to elicit names of conspirators and as he leads the mob in the pogrom.

Rachel, the only woman who ever mattered to Azriel. She dies in his arms during his wanderings in central Europe between the two world wars.

Abrasha, a Communist recruiter who gets Azriel's help in Talmudic schools. He is shot and killed in Moscow in a purge.

Rebbe Zusia (ZEW-zhuh), a Jewish master who listens to Azriel's story with his eyes, without words, and sentences him to wander in a search for the freedom not to speak.

— Donna Maples

OBASAN

Author: Joy Kogawa (1935-   )
First published: 1981
Genre: Novel

Locale: British Columbia and Alberta, Canada; Nagasaki, Japan
Time: 1972, with flashbacks to the 1940's
Plot: Historical realism

Naomi Nakane, the protagonist and the narrator of the prose sections. At the age of thirty-six, she is an unmarried elementary teacher in Cecil, Alberta, and is bored with her dead-end life. She is a quiet, subservient, and evasive adult whose victim-oriented personality has been shaped by childhood abuse of both a sexual and a political nature.

Ayako, "Obasan" of the title, is a timid and victimized "everywoman" who endures abuse and believes that the best way to live is to hide unpleasantness and simply endure. The words "silence" and "stone" describe both her and her husband, in whose household Naomi and Stephen grow up.

Isamu, the husband of Ayako and uncle of Naomi. Scion of a shipbuilding and shipowning family, he is exiled from Vancouver inland to the prairie during the relocation, which hits him particularly hard. The "stone bread" he bakes symbolizes the hardships that Japanese Canadians endure. His funeral is the narrative frame for the story.

Emily Kato, Naomi's unmarried aunt who lives in Toronto. She is an angry and vocal political activist who spends the novel trying to convince Naomi to become more aggressive in defending her heritage and in making her abuses public. She has saved a box of correspondence, newspaper clippings, and political documents that tell an important part of the story.

Nesan ("Little Sister"), Naomi's mother. Naomi has good memories of her. Nesan and her mother (Naomi's Grandmother Kato) leave Naomi and Stephen, when the children are very young, to tend to Nesan's ailing grandmother in

Japan and do not return to Canada. Their fate is a mystery that is resolved gradually during the course of the story. Emily has written letters to Nesan in Japan, keeping copies for herself.

Mark Nakane, Naomi's father. An accomplished singer and musician, he contracts tuberculosis and does not survive the war. His gradual loss of voice foreshadows his inability to protect his family as well as predicting his own death. Against all odds, he strives to nurture Stephen's musical talent. He is shown as most happy when he is making music.

Stephen Nakane, Naomi's resentful older brother, who is so talented at the piano that he develops a national reputation as a Western classical musician and tours frequently around Europe. In essence, he has "sold out," denouncing his Japanese heritage by criticizing both Obasan and Naomi for not talking "properly," by preferring Western fast food to Japanese dishes, and by taking up for a time with a French divorcée. At the time of Uncle Isamu's funeral, he has been away from his family for eight years.

The Reverend Nakayama, a spiritual leader who moves with Naomi's family during their relocation experiences. His gentle leadership, and Christianity in general, is a strength and comfort to the family that cannot be overestimated. It is through his telling that Naomi and Stephen finally learn the truth about their mother.

— Jill B. Gidmark

OBLOMOV

Author: Ivan Alexandrovich Goncharov (1812-1891)
First published: 1859
Genre: Novel

Locale: Russia
Time: Early nineteenth century
Plot: Social realism

Ilya Ilyitch Oblomov (ihl-YAH ilh-YIHCH ohb-LOH-mof), a Russian landowner brought up to do nothing for himself. He, like his parents, only eats and sleeps. He barely graduates from college and cannot force himself to do any kind of work, feeling that work is too much trouble for a gentleman. His indolence results finally in his living in filth and being cheated

consistently. Even love cannot stir him. Though he realizes his trouble and dubs it "Oblomovism," he can do nothing about it. Eventually his indolence kills him, as his doctors tell him it will.

Tarantyev (tah-RAHN-tehf), the parasitical friend of Oblomov. He uses Oblomov's indolence to cheat him, providing for himself at Oblomov's expense.

Andrey Stolz (ahn-DRAY stohlz), Oblomov's only true friend. His German father gave him a wealth of practical experience as a child, so that he was able to make himself wealthy and respected as a businessman. He tries to help Oblomov, straightening out his affairs several times, but his efforts do Oblomov no good.

Zahar (zah-KHAHR), Oblomov's valet. He imitates his master in indolence.

Olga Ilyinsky (ih-LYIHN-skihy), a vivacious, sensitive woman. She falls in love with Oblomov and he with her. She eventually discovers, however, that she is in love with the man Oblomov could be, not the man he is. Upon this discovery, she bids him a permanent good-bye. Later, she marries Stolz, who also loves her.

THE OBSCENE BIRD OF NIGHT
(El obsceno pájaro de la noche)

Author: José Donoso (1924-1996)
First published: 1970
Genre: Novel

Locale: Chile
Time: One year in the 1960's, with flashbacks
Plot: Magical Realism

Humberto Peñaloza (ewm-BEHR-toh pehn-yah-LOH-zah), also known as **Mudito** (mew-DEE-toh), or "Little Deaf Mute," who has served as Don Jerónimo Azcoitía's secretary, the Azcoitía family historian, and the overseer of Don Jerónimo's estate, La Rinconada. In the process, he has worked for the family most of his life. As a youth, in an effort to "be someone," Humberto imagines a fusion between his personality and that of Don Jerónimo. Living in the family's home for the retired female servants of rich families as the novel opens, Humberto serves as the story's schizophrenic narrator-protagonist. He takes on multiple identities (including that of a female, a large papier-mâché head, and a phallus) before becoming, ambiguously, a sexless and timeless bundle. At the close of the novel, after centuries, the bundle's contents are emptied and tossed on a fire, leaving nothing of Humberto but "the black smudge the fire left on the stones."

Don Jerónimo Azcoitía (hehr-OH-nee-moh ahs-koy-TEE-ah), a powerful and influential politician for whom Humberto works and with whom Humberto has fused his own personality. The relationship between the two is strangely symbiotic, as virtually all of Humberto's power (limited as it is) derives from his relationship with Don Jerónimo, whereas Don Jerónimo's sexual potency is mysteriously tied to his relationship with Humberto.

Doña Inés de Azcoitía (ee-NEHS), Don Jerónimo's wife. A pious woman early in the novel, she works diligently to have the family's home for retired servants beatified because of an eighteenth century miracle said to have occurred there. After returning from an audience with the pope, however—and, according to Humberto, after receiving the transplanted organs of her servant, Peta Ponce—she becomes an inmate of the

home herself. Rather than dedicate the rest of her life to prayer, as she had intended, she sets about winning the belongings of her fellow inmates in a strange dog-racing game. After being sexually attacked by Humberto, she is taken away to an insane asylum.

Peta Ponce (PEH-tah pohns), a crafty servant woman and apparent possessor of demonic powers. Among her many bizarre activities is the mysterious encounter she arranges with herself, Humberto, Doña Inés, and Don Jerónimo so that Doña Inés might be impregnated, presumably by Humberto (because Don Jerónimo is thought to be incapable of the act). Later, Peta's organs are said to be transplanted into Doña Inés, with whom the servant shares an odd relationship akin, at least in its strangeness, to that between Humberto and Don Jerónimo, though the relationship between the two women actually borders on friendship, something not true of the relationship between the two men. One result of the alleged transplants is that, as Humberto tells it, Doña Inés resembles Peta Ponce more each day, a "fact" that concerns Humberto because of his fear of Peta.

Boy, the deformed son of Doña Inés and either Don Jerónimo or Humberto, conceived during the mysterious and intentionally unclear encounter. Boy lives on the family's estate, La Rinconada, where he is surrounded by other deformed people so that he will be sheltered from the outside world. When Don Jerónimo announces his intention to close the estate and take Boy back to the city with him, Boy and the others conspire against him, leading to Don Jerónimo's symbolic death.

— *Keith H. Brower*

OCCASION FOR LOVING

Author: Nadine Gordimer (1923-   )
First published: 1963
Genre: Novel

Locale: Johannesburg, South Africa
Time: 1961-1962
Plot: Psychological realism

Jessica (Jessie) Stilwell, a secretary to an agency for African musicians and entertainers, then later a part-time secretary to a company administering a private nursing home. Thirty-eight-year-old Jessie, still attractive, is married to Tom Stilwell, with whom she has three daughters, Clemence, Madge, and Elisabeth. She also has a son, Morgan, from a previous

marriage that ended with the death of her husband in the war. Perceptive and thoughtful, she is also self-involved. Her relationship with Morgan, whom she has largely ignored, is troubled, as is her relationship with her mother. When Tom suggests opening their house to Boaz and Ann Davis, who need a place to live, she is at first reluctant, fearing invasion of her privacy. After the Davises move in, she introduces Ann to Len Mafolo. Later, when Ann and her black lover, Gideon Shibalo, arrive unexpectedly at the beach cottage where Jessie is spending precious private days with her daughters, Jessie is dismayed at the interruption. The relationship between Gideon and Ann forces Jessie to examine her own liberal politics.

Tom Stilwell, a senior university lecturer in history, fair, bearded, and in his thirties. Tom has been working on a history of Africa. Liberal in politics, he is also a loving husband and father, concerned about Morgan. He persuades Jessie to welcome the Davises to their house.

Boaz Davis (BOH-az), a music scholar. A thin, thirty-year-old Jew, Boaz left South Africa ten years previously to train as a composer. He has returned to Johannesburg with his wife, Ann, to study African music and musical instruments. Absorbed by his research, he travels frequently. When Ann becomes involved in a love affair with Gideon Shibalo, his political sensitivity to Gideon's race inhibits his reaction. He tolerates the situation as Ann and Gideon become more deeply engaged. Ultimately, he forsakes his African studies, and he and Ann return to Europe.

Ann Davis, Boaz's wife. Slender, fair-skinned, and beautiful, twenty-two-year-old Ann enters her new life in South Africa with exuberant vitality. Born in Rhodesia, she grew up in England. When she arrives in Johannesburg, she has no real work and is regarded as somewhat shallow, especially by Jessie. Later, with Len Mafolo, she sets up a traveling exhibition of African art. She meets one of the painters, Gideon Shibalo, with whom she becomes deeply involved. When Ann and Gideon go away together, Ann increasingly recognizes the dangers of a relationship that is forbidden by law. She and Gideon decide to leave the country, but eventually she returns to Europe with Boaz.

Gideon Shibalo (shih-BAH-lo), a painter and schoolteacher. An artist of exceptional talent, Gideon won a scholarship to Italy. Denied a passport because of his political activities, Gideon turned to drink for a time and gave up painting. Married to a woman with whom he has lost touch and father of a young son whom he would scarcely recognize, Gideon has many relationships with women, both black and white. Politics occupies the center of his life, however, until he meets Ann, who inspires him to paint again. After Ann's flight to Europe, he returns to drink.

Morgan, Jessie's son. Small, yet with large hands, Morgan is fifteen years old and in the awkward stages of adolescence. Returning from boarding school for the holidays, he seems scarcely to belong in the house. Knowing little about him, Jessie and Tom are shocked to learn that their obedient son has been caught at a shady dance hall.

Len Mafolo (mah-FOL-o), a black coworker of Jessie at the agency. He introduces Ann to the life of the city. While Ann and Len are traveling with their exhibition, Gideon (whom Len knows) frequently joins them for lunches, during which Ann and Gideon get to know each other.

Mrs. Fuecht (fewkt), Jessie's mother. Now almost seventy years old, Mrs. Fuecht is elegant and carefully groomed. After the death of Jessie's father, she married Bruno Fuecht, a man with whom she has never been happy. Jessie has negative feelings about her mother, who, she feels, was smotheringly protective when Jessie was a child, even having her tutored at home because of a suspected heart ailment. When it later turns out that the heart ailment is nonexistent, Jessie feels cheated of her girlhood.

Bruno Fuecht, a Swiss chemical engineer. Angry and ill, Fuecht leaves his nursing home to go to Europe alone. Delayed in Johannesburg, he calls the Stilwells, and Tom visits him in his hotel (Jessie refuses to go). Railing against his wife, he claims that he has transferred all of his money to Switzerland. Later, the Stilwells learn that he has died in Rome and that he has not left Mrs. Fuecht penniless.

— *Susan Kress*

OCTOBER LIGHT

Author: John Gardner (1933-1982)
First published: 1976
Genre: Novel

Locale: A farm outside Bennington, Vermont
Time: October, 1976
Plot: Domestic realism

James Page, a stubbornly conservative, belligerently independent Vermont farmer, seventy-three years old. He is so antimodern that he destroys his sister's television set, then locks her in her bedroom with a shotgun facing her door. Part of his anger comes from his son Richard's suicide, which he takes to be a sign of weakness. Nor has he ever forgotten Uncle Ira, who shot himself. James considers himself a rugged descendant of Ethan Allen's Green Mountain Boys. He is gripped by chronic constipation. When he almost causes his friend Ed Thomas' death by fright, he begins to be less uptight and to understand brother-in-law Horace's accidental death. Later, purged of anger, he finds it impossible to shoot a black bear in search of a honeycomb.

Ariah Page, James's former wife, an exceedingly plain woman, now dead. She was often beaten by James yet remained gentle. She never explained to her husband why their son killed himself. Her silence was not the result of vindictiveness but rather of a pledge of secrecy.

Sally Page Abbott, James's progressive, eighty-year-old sister. While she is locked up, she reads a fantastic paperback novel, *The Smugglers of Lost Souls' Rock*, and lives on apples only. As a result, she suffers from diarrhea. A basket of those apples placed over her door to fall on James, should he try to enter, injures instead the head of the Pages' daughter, Ginny. Sally relents, ready to be reconciled.

Horace Abbott, Sally's dentist husband, who died of a heart attack twenty years previously. He thought his personal tolerance should be extended to the entire nation, in the name of democracy.

Richard Page, James's son. Overwhelmed by his father's stern expectations, he hanged himself at the age of twenty-five, twenty years before the time of the novel. Earlier, he had been accused by James of leaning a ladder against the barn roof, from which his younger brother then accidentally fell to his death. As if to confirm that he is death-prone, one Halloween he unwittingly frightened his Uncle Horace into having a fatal heart attack. He did not dare confess this accident to anyone except his mother, Ariah, whom he swore to secrecy.

Virginia (Ginny) Page Hicks, James's grown daughter, who sympathizes with her Aunt Sally's fight for equal rights within the family home. She calls her father medieval and her Aunt Sally modern. Trying to play the peacemaker, she suffers a hairline fracture when the basket of apples hits her head.

Lewis Hicks, a swamp-Yankee handyman. His part-Indian origins give him a sense of nature's interlocking dependencies and help him quiet the differences between James and Sally.

Dickey Hicks, a nine-year-old who was adopted by Ginny and named after her brother Richard, whom everyone, except James, liked. Irrationally, Dickey feels somehow responsible for the quarrel between his elders. He finds the paperback discarded by James and leaves it where Sally finally finds it.

Estelle Parks, age eighty-three, who enjoyed teaching literature to children of her former students. Late in life, she wed a mathematics professor from Bennington College; he died in a car accident eight years later. She tries to mediate between James and Sally by bringing the entire neighborhood to the Page farm for singing and dancing.

The Reverend Lane Walker, who once marched with Father Hernandez in the antiracist demonstrations at Selma. He tries to make peace by suggesting that apes descended from human beings. He claims that the latter act more primitively than other primates, as self-destructive human inventions tend to prove.

Father Rafe Hernandez, a Tucson priest who asks to be tolerated as he tries to abide the New England accent.

Ruth Thomas, the village librarian, who used to read the classics to Horace while he milked.

Ed Thomas, her husband, who believes that he may have to sell his dairy because his heart will not last. James's sudden appearance, with shotgun ready, brings on Ed's attack. He explains to James later, in the hospital, that television can be a useful way of provoking thought and providing many points of view, especially at election time. His regret that he may not live until Spring's unlocking-time helps James come to terms with his dead son Richard, whom he had always loved in his own rough way and whom he still misses.

— *Leonard Casper*

THE OCTOPUS

Author: Frank Norris (1870-1902)
First published: 1901
Genre: Novel

Locale: San Joaquin Valley, California
Time: Late nineteenth century
Plot: Naturalism

Presley, a writer. He has dark brown eyes; the forehead of an intellectual; a mouth and chin that suggest a delicate, sensitive nature; and the temperament of a poet. Thirty years old, he has come to Los Muertos to improve his health and, he hopes, to write verse. In looking for the great theme of the West around which to write his epic poem, he gets caught up in the contest between the railroad and the wheat farmers. Presley writes "The Toilers" and acquires literary fame, but he becomes convinced that "forces," not people, control events.

Magnus Derrick, also known as **the Governor**, the owner of Los Muertos Ranch. He is close to sixty years old, is six feet tall, and has iron-gray hair. His commanding presence and sense of dignity, along with his prior experience as a politician, make him a natural leader and the most prominent man in the valley. A gambler willing to risk all, he allows his ambition for power and wealth to compromise his principles and bring about his ruin.

S. Behrman, a banker, real estate agent, and representative of the P&SW Railroad. A fat, heavy-jowled individual, he wears a vest with pearl buttons, a watch chain, and a stiff straw hat. Placid and unruffled, he never loses his temper. He wins every confrontation with the wheat ranchers' league until he literally drowns in his own wheat.

Annixter, also known as **Buck**, the owner of the Quien Sabe Ranch. He is young and extremely intelligent, with stiff yellow hair and a lean frame. Rough, direct, argumentative, and stubborn, the hardworking, self-reliant Annixter is determined to defeat the railroad. His natural combativeness makes him an assertive member of the ill-fated league. Deeply in love with Hilma, he is discovering the meaning of his own life when he is tragically killed in the gunfight at the irrigation ditch.

Harran Derrick, the youngest son of Magnus Derrick and the manager of Los Muertos. Blond, very good-looking, and in his mid-twenties, he has the prominent Derrick nose and the carriage of his father. As an organizer of the league, he helps precipitate the bloody confrontation between the ranchers and the railroad.

Lyman Derrick, the eldest son of Magnus Derrick and a successful San Francisco attorney. He is in his early thirties, with black hair and a small, pointed mustache. Shrewd, ambitious, diplomatic, and talented in intrigue, he has his eye set on a political career. He double-crosses the league and, with the help of the railroad, realizes his dream to be governor.

Hilma Tree, a dairy girl on the Quien Sabe Ranch and later Annixter's wife. Nineteen years old, with a large body and thick brown hair, she is even-tempered, pretty, feminine, and charming in her simplicity. She is absorbed in her love for her husband.

Dyke, a blacklisted railroad engineer and hops farmer. Good-looking and with a blond beard, he is heavily built, with broad, powerful shoulders and massive arms. His life is devoted to his little daughter, Sidney. When the railroad raises transportation rates on hops, he is financially ruined. He becomes an outlaw and wages a futile vendetta against the railroad.

Vanamee, a sheepherder, range rider, and wanderer. He is about thirty-six years old, with long black hair, a pointed beard, hollow cheeks, and a thin frame. He has the face of an ascetic. Sensitive and introspective, he has never recovered from the death of his beloved Angele. Gifted with strange mental powers, he comes to understand the rhythms of nature and the meaning of life and death. He encourages Presley to grapple with the meaning of the events he has witnessed.

Annie Derrick, the wife of Magnus Derrick. Married at the age of twenty-one, she is now in her early fifties and still pretty, with brown hair and large eyes. Formerly a schoolteacher, she loves music and literature. Innocent and delicate, she is not made for the harsh West and is made uneasy by the immensity of Los Muertos. She fears the power of the railroad and is frightened that Magnus will compromise his integrity.

Hooven, known to his neighbors as **Bismarck**, a German immigrant who is one of the tenants on Los Muertos. He is an excitable little man with a perpetual grievance against every-one and everything. His panic causes the shoot-out at the irrigation ditch.

Osterman, a rancher. He is young and has large red ears, a bald head, and a comic actor's face. He is a poser who likes to attract attention to himself. He proposes the scheme to bribe the railroad commissioners and is ultimately killed in the shoot-out.

Shelgrim, the president of the P&SW Railroad and a titan of the "New Finance." At seventy years of age, he has pale, watery blue eyes and an iron-gray beard and mustache. His broad, rounded shoulders give him the appearance of great responsibility. He persuades Presley to blame conditions (forces) and not people for events.

— *Steven L. Piott*

THE ODD COUPLE

Author: Neil Simon (1927-   )
First published: 1966
Genre: Drama

Locale: New York City
Time: 1965
Plot: Comedy

Oscar Madison, a carefree, good-natured, divorced sportswriter who lives alone in a messy eight-room New York apartment. He is completely oblivious to dirt, clutter, and the overdue child-support payments about which his wife telephones weekly. He has his male cronies in for a weekly poker game with refreshments that invite food poisoning. Oscar's lifestyle is abruptly turned around when he takes in one of the members of the group, Felix Ungar, whose wife has thrown him out. Everything is now antiseptically clean, the food served to the poker players is appetizing, and there is money to pay his former wife, Blanche. Felix is so compulsive, however, that Oscar cannot live with him and forcefully requests that he leave.

Felix Ungar, a fussy man who knows that he is difficult to live with but cannot—or will not—make any concessions or compromises. His wife, unwilling to continue their marriage, asks him to leave the family despite his suicide threat, and he then moves in with Oscar. Made comical by his exaggerated behavior, Felix is persuaded by the end of the play to live temporarily with the Pigeon sisters, who pity him, but it is probable that they too will find him exasperating.

Gwendolyn Pigeon and

Cecily Pigeon, English sisters who live in the apartment building. Attractive, intellectually lightweight, and somewhat flirtatious, they accept Oscar's invitation for dinner. As he leaves the room to make drinks, they speak blithely of their divorces to Felix, who then shows them snapshots of his family, breaking into tears and encouraging them to join him in his sorrow. Because the London broil that Felix has prepared is ruined as a result of Oscar's casual lateness in coming home, the Pigeon sisters invite the men to their place for potluck. Felix will not go, despite Oscar's pleading, but later they feel sorry for "the poor tortured" Felix and persuade him to stay at their place until he finds one of his own.

Murray, an atypical New York policeman, a good-natured clod who will never become a detective. He is one of the weekly poker players.

Roy, Oscar's accountant. Somewhat critical of Oscar's behavior, Roy routinely loans him money to "stay in the game." He is another of the weekly poker players.

Vinnie, a cheapskate who goes to Florida in midsummer to take advantage of low rates and who leaves the poker game when he is ahead.

Speed, a man of simple tastes who enjoys the male camaraderie of the weekly poker sessions. He is disgusted when Felix turns their poker nights into "tea parties."

— *Edythe M. McGovern*

THE ODD WOMAN

Author: Gail Godwin (1937-   )
First published: 1974
Genre: Novel

Locale: A Midwestern university town, a Southern town, New York City, and Chicago
Time: Early 1970's
Plot: Realism

Jane Clifford, a college instructor of nineteenth century British literature, an unmarried woman of thirty-two, rather tall and slim, rather pretty, but unadorned and unstylish. Since childhood, she has searched deeply and earnestly for the "meaning" of her life. She feels "odd" in the sense of both "strange" and "fifth wheel," not essentially akin to any group or lifestyle. She searches literature as avidly as she searches experience for the key to self-knowledge. Following graduation from college, she vacations in England and meets and becomes engaged to James Bruton, but although she enjoys the security of the relationship and the environment of England, she soon finds it and her fiancé tiresome and flat. Years later, she begins a painful love affair with a married man, which causes her to feel even more odd and lonely. By the end of the novel, she has, prompted by the death of her grandmother, reassessed all of her relationships with family and friends and left her lover, perhaps for good.

Gabriel Weeks, Jane's lover, a professor of art history at a university four hours away from Jane's. He is married, childless, and middle-aged, and he has never achieved great distinction as a scholar. He is at work on a treatise dealing with all the varieties of love found in Western art, an expansion of his only published work, an early monograph on three types of such love. He is attentive and reliable but neither intensely emotional nor forthcoming about his feelings. He tells her nothing about his wife or the rest of his life and is content with the short and infrequent visits with his lover. He is at dinner with a colleague, having left Jane in the hotel room of their fourteenth tryst, on the night she decides to leave him.

Kitty Barnstorff Clifford Sparks, Jane's mother. A teacher and former writer of romances, she marries Ray Sparks, a former soldier, after Jane's father is killed in World War II. Beautiful and mysterious and adored by her husband, she has given up her career to be a housewife and mother. Over the years, she has become deeply religious and spends much time in church and prayer—both areas where the demands of her family and the control of her husband cannot reach. Her attachment to her new family and to religion make her more remote from Jane.

Edith Barnstorff, Jane's beloved grandmother, a Southern lady, decorous, stylish, and full of sound advice about getting through life with grace and dignity. After her husband's death, she remained single for many years, and Jane spent much of her childhood in her company. Her death is the catalyst for Jane's reexamination of her own situation.

Gerda Mulvaney, née **Miller**, a close college friend of Jane. As assertive and outspoken as Jane is timid and reticent, she is determined to leave behind her working-class background and successfully sets her marital sights on Bobby Mulvaney, the crippled son of well-known Judge Mulvaney. She soon ruins the marriage, however, by engaging in a trivial affair with an unimportant lover. Divorced, she founds and edits a feminist single women's newspaper, *Femme Sole*.

Sonia Marks, the "perfect woman," a new friend of Jane who has it all—a secure, respected position in the English department, based on many publications and crammed classrooms; a new husband, Max Covington, also an eminent scholar, who had recently been somebody else's husband; and two darling children of her own. She supports Jane's application for another year's contract.

Cleva Dewar, Jane's great-aunt, Edith's sister, a wildly romantic young woman who died long before the novel begins but whose tragic story has deeply influenced Jane's life. At the age of nineteen, Cleva ran off with an itinerant actor, and a year later, abandoned by him, she died, leaving an infant daughter.

— *Lolette Kuby*

ODE TO APHRODITE

Author: Sappho (c. 612-c. 580 B.C.E.)
First transcribed: Sixth century B.C.E.
Genre: Poetry

Locale: Indeterminate
Time: Sappho's lifetime
Plot: Erotic

Sappho (SAF-oh), the most famous poetess of ancient Greece, a member of an aristocratic family in the city-state of Mytilene (miht-ih-LEE-nee) on the island of Lesbos, which is located in the Aegean Sea off the western coast of Asia Minor (modern Turkey). This poem of twenty-eight verses is in the form of a prayer addressed to the goddess Aphrodite. In it, Sappho pleads with the goddess not to overwhelm her with misery but to come to her, remove her anguish, fulfill her heart's desire, and be her ally. The central portion of the poem reveals that the source of Sappho's unhappiness is unrequited love: In particular, another woman has spurned her affection and erotic advances. As in the case of most personal poetry, the exact mixture of fact and fiction that Sappho compounded into this seemingly autobiographical description of her desires and experiences is impossible to determine.

Aphrodite (af-ruh-DI-tee), the Greek goddess of beauty and sexual love, whom the Romans identified with Venus.

Sappho addresses her directly in the second person as a "weaver of wiles" who is "throned in splendor," and she reminds the goddess that in the past she has responded to Sappho's prayers by leaving the golden halls of her father Zeus (the ruler of the gods) and coming quickly to the assistance of her mortal suppliant. On such occasions, Aphrodite is further reminded, she smiled at Sappho and promised to transform the woman who had rejected her into her eager suitress. The poem creates the impression that Aphrodite is Sappho's special patron and that a close bond exists between the two.

The anonymous woman, **Sappho's beloved**, whose rejection of Sappho furnishes the occasion of the poem. Nothing else can be said about her, for Sappho offers not a word about her age, appearance, or social class, or the circumstances that brought them together.

— *Hubert M. Martin, Jr.*

THE ODYSSEY

Author: Homer (c. ninth century B.C.E.)
First transcribed: c. 800 B.C.E.
Genre: Poetry

Locale: Greece and Mediterranean lands
Time: The ten years following the Trojan War
Plot: Epic

Odysseus (oh-DIH-see-uhs), a far-roving veteran of the Trojan War who, having incurred the anger of Poseidon by blinding the sea god's son Polyphemus, a gigantic Cyclops, is fated to roam for ten years before he can return to his homeland of Ithaca. Leaving Troy, he and his followers sail first to Ismarus. In the sack of the Ciconian city, Odysseus spares the life of Maro, a priest of Apollo, who in turn gives the conqueror some jars of potent wine. Gales then drive the Greeks to the country of the Lotus-eaters, from which they sail to the land of the fierce Cyclopes. There Ulysses and twelve of his band are captured by Polyphemus. After Odysseus frees himself and his companions by a clever ruse, leaving the Cyclops maimed and blinded, the band journeys to the Isle of Aeolus. In the land of the Laestrygones, man-eating giants destroy all but one of his ships and devour their crews. At Aeaea, Odysseus outwits the enchantress Circe and frees his men after she has turned them into swine. In the dark region of the Cimmerians, he consults the shade of Tiresias, the Theban prophet, to learn what awaits him in Ithaca. Following the advice of Circe, Odysseus escapes the spell of the Sirens, passes safely between Scylla and Charybdis, and arrives at Thrinacia. There, his remaining comrades are drowned for their impiety in eating cattle sacred to Hyperion. Cast adrift, Odysseus floats to the island of Ogygia, where for seven years he lives with the lovely nymph Calypso. Finally, the gods take pity on him and order Calypso to release him. On a makeshift raft, he continues his voyage. After his raft is wrecked by Poseidon, he battles the waves until he arrives, exhausted, on the island of Drepane. Nausicaä, daughter of the king of the Phaeacians, finds him and leads him to the royal palace. Warmly received by King Alcinous, Odysseus takes part in celebration games and tells the story of his adventures. Alcinous gives Odysseus rich gifts and returns the wanderer by ship to Ithaca. There, in disguise, he meets his son Telemachus, now grown to manhood, routs and kills the suitors who throng his palace, and is reunited with his loyal wife Penelope. Odysseus is the ideal Greek hero, eloquent at the council board, courageous in battle, resourceful in danger, and crafty in wisdom. He is the darling of the goddess Athena, who aids him whenever it is in her power to do so.

Penelope (peh-NEH-loh-pee), his devoted wife, a model of domestic fidelity, skilled in handicrafts. Still attractive in spite of twenty years of anxiety and grief during the absence of Odysseus, she is by custom forced to entertain importunate, insolent suitors whom she puts off from year to year through various stratagems. Until betrayed by her false servants, she weaved by day a burial robe for Laertes, her father-in-law, and at night unraveled her work. The return of Odysseus is for her an occasion of great joy, but first she tests his knowledge of the construction of their wedding bed to avoid being duped by a plausible stranger. Although she is noteworthy for her forbearance and fidelity, there are occasions when she complains bitterly and laments her sad fate.

Telemachus (teh-LEH-muh-kuhs), the son of Odysseus and Penelope, grown to handsome young manhood during his father's absence. Also favored by Athena, he accuses the suitors of being parasites, journeys to other lands in search of news of his father, and returns to fight bravely by the side of Odysseus when the 112 suitors of Penelope are routed and put to death. His comeliness, manly bearing, and good manners show him to be his father's son when he meets wise King Nestor and King Menelaus.

Athena (uh-THEE-nuh), also called Pallas Athena, the goddess of wisdom and the patron of arts and crafts. Moved by pity and admiration, she becomes the benefactor of Odysseus and pleads with Zeus, her father, to release the hero from the seven-year embrace of the nymph Calypso. Assuming various disguises and aiding him in many ways, she watches over the homeward journey and eventual triumph of Odysseus. Her divine intervention ensures peace between him and the angry families of the slain suitors.

Poseidon (poh-SI-duhn), the earth-shaking god of the sea. The blinding of his giant son, the Cyclops Polyphemus, arouses his anger against Odysseus, and he prevents as long as possible the return of the hero to Ithaca.

Laertes (lay-UR-teez), the aged father of Odysseus. Withdrawn from the royal palace, he tends his vineyards and herds during his son's absence. Still vigorous, he helps Odysseus and Telemachus repulse a band of angry citizens in their attempt to avenge the death of the suitors.

Eumaeus (ew-MEE-uhs), the devoted swineherd in whose hut disguised Odysseus takes refuge upon his return to Ithaca. Despising the suitors, he fights bravely against them alongside Odysseus, Telemachus, and Philoetius, the neatherd. Though of lowly occupation, he is of noble birth, and he is both slave and devoted friend to Odysseus.

Philoetius (fih-LEE-tee-uhs), the neatherd and a trusted servant in the household of Odysseus. He is forced to provide cattle for the feasts of the suitors, but he resents their presence in his master's hall, and he yearns for the return of the absent hero. In the great battle in which the suitors are killed, he fights bravely by the side of Odysseus, Telemachus, and Eumaeus.

Eurycleia (ew-rih-KLEE-uh), the aged nurse of both Odysseus and Telemachus. She recognizes her master by a scar on his thigh and reveals to him his faithless servants who have consorted with the suitors during his absence. Taken as a bondservant by Odysseus' father, she is loyal to the royal household and vindictive in her revenge.

Polyphemus (po-lih-FEE-muhs), one of the Cyclopes, giants with one eye in the center of the forehead, and the son of Poseidon. When Odysseus and twelve of his companions seek hospitality in his cave, the monster makes prisoners of the band and eats six of them. Wily Odysseus saves himself and his remaining companions by giving Polyphemus some of Maro's strong wine to drink and then, while the Cyclops is asleep, putting out his eye with a heated, pointed shaft. The Greeks escape from the cave by hiding beneath the bodies of Polyphemus' sheep when the giant turns his flock out to pasture.

Circe (SUR-see), an enchantress, the daughter of Helius and Perse. Arriving at Aeaea, Odysseus sends Eurylochus, his lieutenant, and twenty-two men ashore to explore the island. When they arrive at Circe's palace, she invites them to feast with her. Eurylochus, almost as crafty as his master, remains outside, and through a window he sees the sorceress serve the men drugged food and then transform them into swine. Odysseus, on his way to rescue his companions, encounters the god Hermes, who gives him a flower called moly as a charm against the powers of the enchantress. Her power destroyed by the magic herb, Circe frees her captives from her magic spell and entertains Odysseus and his companions for a year. At the end of that time, Odysseus wishes to leave Circe's bed and continue his journey. Though reluctant, she consents to his going, but first she advises him to consult the shade of Tiresias to learn what the future holds for the wanderers.

Eurylochus (ew-RIH-luh-kuhs), the lieutenant of Odysseus. He reports to Odysseus that the enchantress Circe has turned half of his band into swine. It is at his suggestion that the Greeks kill some of Hyperion's sacred cattle and eat them while Odysseus is sleeping. To punish their act of impiety, Zeus causes the Greek ship to founder, and all but Odysseus are drowned.

Tiresias (ti-REE-see-uhs), the prophet of Thebes. In the land of the Cimmerians, acting on the advice of Circe, Odysseus summons the aged seer's shade from the dead. Tiresias tells him not to harm the sacred cattle of Hyperion; otherwise, Odysseus will encounter many difficulties and delays on his homeward journey, he will find trouble in the royal house when he arrives there, he will be forced to make a journey into a land so far from the sea that its people will mistake an oar for a winnowing fan, he will be forced to make a rich sacrifice to Poseidon in that distant land, and in his old age he will meet death coming to him out of the sea.

Calypso (kuh-LIHP-soh), the divine nymph who lives on the island of Ogygia, where Odysseus is washed ashore after his ship has foundered and his companions have drowned. For seven years, he lives as her bondman and husband, until Zeus sends Hermes to her with the message that Odysseus is to be released to return to his own land. Although she wishes him to stay with her and offers him immortality and youth in return, she yields to Odysseus' own wishes and the divine command of Zeus. She teaches Odysseus how to build a raft and allows him to set sail before a favorable breeze.

Nausicaä (no-SIH-kee-uh), the maiden daughter of King Alcinous and Queen Arete. Finding Odysseus on the seashore, where he sleeps exhausted from fighting buffeting waves after Poseidon destroyed his raft, she befriends the hero and conducts him to her father's palace. There, Odysseus tells the story of his adventures and hardships to an admiring and pitying audience. Moved by the wanderer's plight, King Alcinous gives him rich gifts and returns him to Ithaca in a Phaeacian ship.

Alcinous (al-SIH-noh-uhs), the king of the Phaeacians. He entertains Odysseus after the hero has been washed ashore on the island of Drepane, and he returns his guest to Ithaca in one of the royal ships.

Arete (ay-REH-tee), the wife of Alcinous. She is famous for her kindness, generosity, and wisdom.

Nestor (NEHS-tur), the wise king of Pylos. Telemachus, seeking to rid the royal palace of his mother's insolent suitors, journeys to Nestor's country in search of his father Odysseus.

Peisistratus (pi-SIHS-truh-tuhs), the noble youngest son of King Nestor. A skilled charioteer, he accompanies Telemachus when the son of Odysseus travels to Sparta in an effort to get word of his father from King Menelaus and Helen, his queen. ⬇

Menelaus (meh-neh-LAY-uhs), the king of Sparta. Menelaus receives Telemachus hospitably and entertains him lavishly, but he has no information that will help the young man in his search for his father.

Helen, the wife of Menelaus and the cause of the war with Troy. Older but still beautiful, she presides over her husband's palace with queenly dignity. When Telemachus takes leave of the royal pair, she gives him a rich robe for his bride to wear on his wedding day.

Antinous (an-TIH-noh-uhs), the leader of the suitors for the hand of Penelope. Insolent and obstreperous, he leads more gullible young men to their corruption and destruction. He mocks Telemachus, berates Penelope, and tauntingly insults Odysseus disguised as a beggar. Because of his arrogance, he is the first of the suitors to die.

Eurymachus (ew-RIH-muh-kuhs), the most treacherous of the suitors. Seemingly fair in speech but cunning in his design to destroy Telemachus and marry Penelope, he deserves his death at the hands of Odysseus.

Noëmon (noh-EE-muhn), one of the most generous and least offensive of the suitors. He lends Telemachus his own ship in which to sail to Pylos.

Theoclymenus (thee-uh-KLIH-meh-nuhs), a young warrior who has fled from Argos after killing a kinsman. As Telemachus is about to set sail from Pylos, the fugitive asks to be taken aboard the vessel so that he can escape the wrath of the dead man's brothers. Telemachus takes the stranger back to Ithaca and gives him shelter. At a feast in the palace, Theoclymenus foretells the destruction of the suitors.

Peiraeus (pi-REE-uhs), the loyal and gallant friend of Telemachus. He goes with the son of Odysseus to Pylos.

Mentor (MEHN-tur), one of the elders of Ithaca, wise in counsel. Athena assumes his form on several occasions.

Melanthius (meh-LAN-thee-uhs), the treacherous goatherd who taunts disguised Odysseus and later tries to aid the suitors. On orders from Odysseus, he is hanged by Eumaeus and Philoetius and later is dismembered.

Melantho (meh-LAN-thoh), Penelope's faithless maid, the mistress of Eurymachus.

Medon (MEE-don), the herald. Because of his kindness to young Telemachus, his life is spared when the other suitors are killed.

Phemius (FEE-mee-uhs), the unwilling bard of the suitors. Telemachus asks that his life be spared, and Odysseus grants him mercy.

Eurynome (ew-RIH-noh-mee), the housekeeper of the royal palace in Ithaca.

Maro (MA-roh), the priest of Apollo whose life is spared when the Greeks raid the Ciconian city of Ismarus. In gratitude, he gives Odysseus the wine with which the hero makes the Cyclops drunk.

Elpenor (ehl-PEE-nohr), one of Odysseus' companions whom Circe transformed into swine and then restored to human form. He climbs on the roof of her palace and, dazed by wine, falls to his death. Appearing among the shades in the land of the Cimmerians, he begs Odysseus to give him proper burial.

Haliserthes (hal-ih-SEHR-theez), an elder of Ithaca able to interpret the flight of birds. Seeing two eagles fighting in midair, he predicts that Odysseus will return and rend the unruly suitors like a bird of prey.

Irus (I-ruhs), the nickname of **Arnaeus**, a greedy vagabond whom disguised Odysseus strikes down with a single blow when the two men fight, urged on by the amused suitors, to decide who will be allowed to beg in the palace.

Hermes (HUR-meez), the messenger of the gods. He gives Odysseus the herb moly to protect him against Circe's spell and takes to the nymph Calypso Zeus' command that the hero be allowed to return to his own country.

Zeus (zews), the ruler of the Olympian deities and the father of Athena.

THE ODYSSEY: A Modern Sequel
(Odysseia)

Author: Nikos Kazantzakis (1883-1957)
First published: 1938
Genre: Poetry

Locale: Ithaca, Sparta, Crete, Egypt, southern Africa, and Antarctica
Time: Twelfth century B.C.E.
Plot: Epic

Odysseus (oh-DIH-see-uhs), a Greek mythological hero who fought for ten years in the Trojan War and then spent ten more years returning home to Ithaca. In *The Odyssey*, written by Homer in about 800 B.C.E., Odysseus is first and foremost a family man; in this modern version, which begins after Odysseus' murder of the suitors in book 22 of Homer's version, Odysseus resembles more the Ulysses of Dante Alighieri's *Inferno* (*The Divine Comedy*, c. 1320) and of Alfred, Lord Tennyson's poem "Ulysses" (1842): a bold sailor with a wanderlust and an unquenchable desire for knowledge. Sickened by the ignorance of his people and feeling no bond to his aged wife, Penelope, and his too-prudent son, Telemachus (tuh-LEH-muh-kuhs), Odysseus leaves Ithaca with a crew of five and sails to Sparta. In Sparta, he visits his old friend and war companion, Menelaus (meh-nuh-LAY-uhs), whom he helps quell a rebellion. He is, however, so repelled by Menelaus' decision to forsake his old life of adventure for a peaceful, hedonistic old age that he quickly leaves Sparta, taking with him Menelaus' wife, Helen, who is still as passionate and lustful as when she ran off with Paris twenty years earlier. Odysseus' next port of call is Knossos, Crete, the kingdom of the old and impotent King Idomeneus (i-DOM-ee-news). As Odysseus arrives, Idomeneus has just undergone a mysterious bull ritual that has both revived his youth and virility and increased his tyrannical nature. Idomeneus arrests Odysseus and takes Helen as his new bride. Odysseus escapes and assists in a revolution that combines the numbers of the oppressed proletarian classes and the strength of the barbaric, iron-wielding Dorian race that is invading Greece from the north. Odysseus then sails to Egypt, leaving behind Helen, who chooses to marry one of the Dorians and beget a new race of Greeks. Odysseus soon learns that Egypt, too, is seething with revolt as a result of a famine and the weak rule of the poet-loving pharaoh. Eventually, Odysseus escapes from Egypt, taking with him a large army of societal outcasts. Throughout his journeys, Odysseus seeks true freedom and purification by releasing himself from all traditional ties and propelling himself forward through the evolutionary stages of humanity. He promises his army that he will lead them to the source of the Nile, where they will build an ideal city in the image of a new god of vengeance that

Odysseus has created himself to take the place of the old Olympian gods. The city is built but then destroyed by an earthquake. In response, Odysseus rejects all gods as creations of humans, strips himself of all illusions (including heaven, virtue, and hope), and embraces only death as his companion. Now alone, Odysseus becomes a famous ascetic and, as he travels southward toward the tip of Africa, he encounters and debates with a series of allegorical figures: an enlightenment-seeking Buddha figure (Prince Motherth); a blind hermit; an idealistic Don Quixote figure (Captain Sole); a hedonistic lord; and a pacifistic Christ-figure. Odysseus' journey ends in the frozen wastes of Antarctica. In the moment of his death, he is visited in memory by all the characters he has encountered during his journeys.

Kentaur, a fat, splayfooted glutton who joins Odysseus' crew. Though generally controlled by his sexual and physical appetites, Kentaur is a tenderhearted man, fiercely loyal to Odysseus and his quest for freedom and growth. Kentaur dies saving a group of children from the earthquake that destroys the ideal city.

Rocky, the only member of Odysseus' crew not from Ithaca. He is a shepherd of Sparta who catches Odysseus' eye by his brave looting of an eagle's nest. Though he hates the sea, Rocky joins the crew and is soon seduced by Odysseus' lust for freedom. While in Africa, he becomes the chief of a tribe and vows he will civilize them. Like Kentaur, he dies in the earthquake.

Hardihood, a bronze smith who joins Odysseus in hopes of learning from the Dorians the secrets of iron. After the revolution on Crete, he stays behind to become the new ruler.

Granite, a tough and proud aristocrat who joins Odysseus' crew after abandoning his own homeland, where he killed his brother in a duel over a woman. After the earthquake, Granite leaves Odysseus to found his own ideal city.

Orpheus (OHR-fee-uhs), a piper who abandons the crew while on a special mission in Africa. Odysseus had sent Orpheus to appease a hostile tribe with a new god that he and Orpheus had created together. Unfortunately, unlike the god-battling Odysseus, Orpheus comes to believe in the human-made god and becomes a witch doctor.

— *Louis Markos*

OEDIPUS AT COLONUS
(Oidipous epi Kolōnōi)

Author: Sophocles (c. 496-406 B.C.E.)
First performed: 401 B.C.E.
Genre: Drama

Locale: Colonus, near Athens
Time: Antiquity
Plot: Tragedy

Oedipus (EHD-ih-puhs), the former king of Thebes, now a wanderer, blind and in rags, because he had been fated unwittingly to murder his father and marry his mother. After the suicide of his wife and mother, Jocasta, Oedipus, who had blinded himself in the moment of anguish that came with his full realization of who he was and what he had done, had lived for a time quietly in Thebes until his banishment by the regent Creon, his brother-in-law, with the acquiescence of his sons, Polynices and Eteocles. During his years of wandering, he has endured hardship and pain, but from them he has gained spiritual authority and strength; he is aware that his special suffering has conferred on him a special grace and that, although he is an object of pollution while alive, his dead body will confer divine benefits on the land in which it lies. He is still intelligent, courageous, and irascible, but to these characteristics has been added a new dimension of strength and knowledge. Through the horrible afflictions that the gods have visited on him, he has become as nearly godlike as a man can be.

Antigone (an-TIHG-uh-nee), Oedipus' elder daughter, her father's guide since childhood. Although passionately devoted to him, she also is capable of love for Polynices, her brother, who wronged both her father and her. After the death of Oedipus, she returns to Thebes to try to mend the breach between Polynices and Eteocles, her other brother.

Ismene (ihs-MEE-nee), Oedipus' younger daughter. Searching for her father and sister, she overtakes them at Colonus. She brings Oedipus word that the Oracle of Delphi has predicted that in the struggle between his sons for the mastery of Thebes the victory will go to Eteocles if the body of Oedipus rests in Theban soil, but to Polynices if the blind, aged exile is buried in Attica. More pious than Antigone, Ismene shares her sister's courage and devotion.

Creon (KREE-on), Oedipus' brother-in-law and regent of Thebes during the minority of the sons of Oedipus. Because the presence of Oedipus will ensure victory for the Theban forces over the army of Polynices, Creon attempts to persuade Oedipus to return to his native city. Failing, he tries to take Antigone and Ismene by force but is thwarted by Theseus. Creon is articulate and clever, but these virtues are subordinate to his own self-interest.

Theseus (THEE-see-uhs), the king of Athens and protector of Oedipus, for whom he feels a deep sympathy and by whom he is convinced that Athens will prosper in a future war against Thebes if Oedipus' body is buried in Athenian soil. He is a man of high integrity, religious yet practical, and honorable yet outspoken.

Polynices (pol-eh-NI-seez), the elder son of Oedipus (although playwrights Aeschylus and Euripides make him the younger). Exiled after conflict with Eteocles, his brother, he has raised an army in Argos to regain his former place in Thebes. Like Creon, he wants Oedipus for the divine sanction the deposed king will give to his cause. He recognizes and admits his guilt for the wrongs he has done his father, but his penitence comes too late. Oedipus, in cursing him, predicts that he and Eteocles will fall by each other's hand. He is sympathetically presented, but it is clear that he is acting not out of a desire to be reconciled with Oedipus but out of a desire to recapture the throne of Thebes.

A Chorus of elders of Colonus, whose songs contain some of the best of Sophocles' poetry, including the famous ode in praise of Colonus and Attica.

OEDIPUS TYRANNUS
(Oidipous Tyrannos)

Author: Sophocles (c. 496-406 B.C.E.)
First performed: c. 429 B.C.E.
Genre: Drama

Locale: Thebes
Time: Antiquity
Plot: Tragedy

Oedipus (EHD-ih-puhs), the king of Thebes. A foundling, he had been reared by Polybus and Merope, king and queen of Corinth. In that city, he had enjoyed a place of honor until a drunken Corinthian at a banquet accused him of being a bastard. To settle the matter, he went to the oracle at Pytho, who revealed that he was destined to lie with his mother and murder his father. To avoid this curse, he fled Corinth. During his travels, he was thrust out of the road by an old man in a carriage. Angered, Oedipus returned the old man's blow and killed him. Later, he overcame the Sphinx by answering a riddle that the monster put to all whom it encountered, killing those who could not solve it. As a reward, Oedipus was made king of Thebes and given the hand of Queen Jocasta, whose former husband, King Laius, was believed killed in an encounter with highway robbers. When the action of the play begins, Oedipus has ruled well for many years, but a plague of unknown origin has recently fallen on the city. His subjects appeal to him as one especially favored by the gods to help them, but Oedipus is powerless to do so. He is essentially a good man, courageous, intelligent, and responsible, but he is also short-tempered, tragically weak in judgment, and proud of his position and past achievements, for which he gives the gods little credit. As the action progresses and the question of his responsibility for the plague is raised, he becomes obsessed with finding out who he is, regardless of repeated warnings that knowledge of his identity will bring disaster on himself and on those whom he loves.

Jocasta (joh-KAS-tuh), the wife of Oedipus and mother of his sons, Eteocles and Polynices, and his daughters, Antigone and Ismene. She, too, has a sense of the responsibilities of her position and is deeply concerned with the welfare of her husband. As bits of information relating to his identity are revealed, her sense of foreboding grows. When the truth finally becomes apparent to her, she hangs herself, overwhelmed by the enormities she has unwittingly committed.

Creon (KREE-on), Jocasta's brother and a powerful Theban noble. Sent by Oedipus to ask the Delphic Oracle what can be done to save the city from the plague, he returns with word that it will be raised when the city no longer harbors the murderer of King Laius, Jocasta's former husband. When it later appears that Oedipus may be the murderer, the king violently accuses his brother-in-law of treacherously seeking the throne, but Creon defends himself as reasonably as he can until Jocasta calms her husband. Creon is presented as a calm, pious man, with a less tyrannical view of kingship than that of Oedipus.

Tiresias (ti-REE-see-uhs), a blind prophet who alone knows what Oedipus' fate has been and will be. Oedipus consults him in an effort to find the murderer of King Laius and loses his patience when the old man at first refuses to answer. Becoming angry in turn, Tiresias reveals that Oedipus' seeming good fortune in vanquishing the Sphinx has actually caused him unknowingly to commit incest with his mother and to bring pollution upon Thebes. Furious, Oedipus sends the blind seer away.

The first messenger, an old man who comes from Corinth with word that Polybus and Merope are dead and that the people of that city want Oedipus to return as their king. This information, under the circumstances, is received joyfully by Oedipus, for if his parents have died naturally, the oracle's prediction that he is doomed to murder his father has been proved false. The messenger goes on to say that Polybus and Merope were in reality Oedipus' foster parents; he himself had received the infant Oedipus from a Theban shepherd and given him to them.

A herdsman, an old Theban who has voluntarily exiled himself from his native city. He is forced by Oedipus to confess that years earlier he had been ordered to expose the infant son of King Laius and Jocasta, but, pitying the child, he had given him to a Corinthian. He also had been the one survivor when King Laius was killed by a young man after a quarrel on the road. His information thus makes the web of evidence complete; Oedipus now knows that the old man whom he killed was Laius, his father, and that his wife Jocasta is also his mother.

The second messenger, a Theban who reports the immediate results of the shepherd's revelation: Jocasta has hanged herself and Oedipus blinded himself with the brooches that fastened her robe.

OF HUMAN BONDAGE

Author: W. Somerset Maugham (1874-1965)
First published: 1915
Genre: Novel

Locale: England
Time: Early twentieth century
Plot: Naturalism

Philip Carey, a clubfooted orphan boy reared by relatives under strict and pietistic conditions. The result of this rearing, and of his physical disability as well, is a retiring and idealistic boy who has ahead of him a long battle to overcome the inhibitions with which his aunt and uncle have saddled him and the lack of physical confidence that comes from his misshapen foot. To find his place in life, he tries many professions: clerk, medical student, art student—the list is quite long. He also listens eagerly to somewhat older friends who, supposedly, can tell him what life means. Through them, he learns that art and literature, morals and religion, are relative to the observer and that even the great truths of philosophers suffer similar limitations. Philip's emotional education is the work of several women, chief among them Mildred Rogers and Sally Athelny. Life with Sally and medical practice in a small English town finally make up Philip's "figure in the carpet," which, according to a friend, each person must discover alone.

William Carey, Philip's uncle, an Anglican clergyman. Poorly equipped to rear a child, he is represented as fairly ignorant, thoroughly selfish, and completely hypocritical.

Louisa Carey, William's wife and Philip's aunt, a timid woman who fears to reveal to Philip how much she cares for him. An inheritance from her gives Philip needed funds at one point in his life.

Miss Wilkinson, a friend of the Careys, a governess on holiday from her winter post in Germany. It is she who initiates Philip into the life of love, but Philip soon finds her distasteful and has no more to do with her.

G. Etheredge Hayward, Philip's friend for many years. Philip first meets Hayward in Germany and constantly draws on Hayward's wider knowledge for ideas about life and books. He finally comes to see Hayward as a hollow man.

Fanny Price, an older art student of Philip's Paris years. She does more than guide Philip's artistic education; her suicide reveals to him the pain of her hopeless love for him, as well as the cruelty of love in general. Philip accepts as axiomatic the idea that in love there is always someone who loves and someone who lets himself be loved.

Cronshaw, a Parisian friend and a poet. It is he who reveals to Philip "the figure in the carpet": the truth that each person must make out his own pattern in the carpet that life spreads before him.

Mildred Rogers, a waitress in a London teashop. Philip meets her during his early days as a medical student; from then on, Mildred exercises a monstrous power over him. Although she is vain, ignorant, and mildly ugly, he is utterly unable to resist the power of her whims or requests. She drains him of money, comes back to him when her own love affairs go badly, and senselessly ruins many of his possessions in a mad fury.

Norah Nesbit, a divorcée. A hack writer, a little older than Philip, she instructs him in taste and loves him truly. As usual, when Philip is loved, he cannot love in return.

Harry Griffiths, a handsome friend of Philip who takes Mildred away from him for a time.

Thorpe Athelney, a patient and an older friend of Philip. The humility and the wisdom of the man, his acceptance of a low place in life, and the routine pleasures of his family are what finally reveal to Philip his share of wisdom and

deliver him from the bondage of false hopes and desires.

Sally Athelney, Thorpe's daughter, who first becomes Philip's mistress and then his wife. She is a simple creature and can give none of the excitement provided by Mildred nor the understanding that came from Norah. Yet she gives Philip what no other woman offered him: calm and peace.

OF MICE AND MEN

Author: John Steinbeck (1902-1968)
First published: 1937
Genre: Novel

Locale: Salinas Valley, California
Time: Mid-twentieth century
Plot: Impressionistic realism

Lennie Small, a simple-minded man of great size and strength. His dream is to have a chicken and rabbit farm with his friend George Milton and to be allowed to feed the rabbits. George tells him about the farm over and over and keeps Lennie in line by threatening not to let him feed the rabbits. The two men are hired to buck barley on a ranch. Lennie crushes the hand of the owner's son, kills a puppy while stroking it, and breaks a woman's neck, all unintentionally.

George Milton, Lennie's friend, a small and wiry man. He assumes responsibility for his simple friend and in the new job does the talking for both. At last, after the unintentional killing by Lennie, George knows that he can no longer save his friend; after telling him once again of their plan for the farm, he shoots him.

Candy, a swamper on the barley ranch. He makes George's and Lennie's dream seem possible, for he has three hundred and fifty dollars and wants to join them.

Curley, the son of the ranch owner. Vain of his ability as a prizefighter and jealous of his slatternly bride, he provokes Lennie into squeezing his hand. Pleased that Curley's hand has been broken, his wife comes to make advances to Lennie, who accidentally kills her.

Slim, the jerkline skinner on the ranch. He gives Lennie the puppy and persuades Curley to say his hand was caught in a machine.

Crooks, the black stable hand. Cool to Lennie at first, he is disarmed by Lennie's innocence.

OF TIME AND THE RIVER: A Legend of Man's Hunger in His Youth

Author: Thomas Wolfe (1900-1938)
First published: 1935
Genre: Novel

Locale: Harvard University, New York, and France
Time: The 1920's
Plot: Impressionistic realism

Eugene Gant, a young Southerner, just graduated from the State University and on his way to Harvard for advanced study. He is eager to leave the drab world of his childhood: his jealous family, the dreary boarding house run by his mother. But he finds Harvard disappointing; the famous drama class of Professor Hatcher is disillusioning, for the students are intellectual frauds. In Boston, he meets his eccentric uncle, Bascom Pentland, and has a brief love affair with a commonplace girl. He finds one good friend, however, in Francis Starwick, Hatcher's assistant. Starwick's sophistication fascinates Eugene, yet it somehow seems unreal. After a winter at Harvard and a summer of hoping that his play will be produced, Eugene goes to New York as an instructor at a city university. There, he renews his acquaintance with his hometown friend Robert Weaver and with Joel Pierce from Harvard. Weaver, with his drunkenness, causes only trouble; Pierce, with his vast wealth, is fascinating but disillusioning. During his vacation, Eugene goes first to England, which he detests, and then to Paris, where he meets Starwick, who is with two young Boston women, Elinor, a divorcée, and Ann. After a drunken summer in Paris, Eugene realizes the tragic situation: that he loves Ann but that she loves Starwick, and that Starwick is a homosexual. Breaking away from the doomed trio, Eugene goes to Orleans. After a fantastic experience with two

French noblewomen, he returns to America. On the ship, he sees a woman named Esther and knows that she is to be his fate.

Oliver Gant, Eugene's father, who dies of cancer. Although his drunken profligacy has made the family life a nightmare, his death makes his children realize what a remarkable man he was.

Eliza Gant, Eugene's mother. Tenacious in her acquisition of property, infinitely stubborn, lost in her web of recollection, she has become a powerful woman.

Francis Starwick, assistant to Professor Hatcher of Harvard. Mannered and pretentious yet intelligent, he seems to Eugene the acme of sophistication. He is loved by Ann, but her love is wasted, for he is homosexual.

Bascom Pentland, Eugene's eccentric uncle in Boston.

Joel Pierce, a member of an immensely rich family. He introduces Eugene to the world of great wealth, which fascinates yet repels him.

Robert Weaver, a young man from Eugene's home town. Joining Eugene in New York, he becomes a nuisance because of his drunkenness.

Abe Jones, a Jewish student in Eugene's class in New York. He shows Eugene the hard, bitter world of the lower-class New York Jews.

The Countess de Caux, a slightly mad Frenchwoman whom Eugene meets in Orleans. She is interested in using him for her own financial advantage.

The Marquise de Mornay, to whom the Countess de Caux introduces Eugene on the pretext that he is a well-known journalist. Although the marquise is a great lady, it develops that she has permitted the introduction for the purpose of getting Eugene to raise money in America for a hospital in France.

Elinor, a slightly older woman from Boston, where she has left her husband and child. Knowing that she has ruined her-self forever at home, she joins Eugene and Starwick during their drunken vacation in Paris. She is the leader of the group, domineering and essentially cruel.

Ann, an unmarried Boston woman accompanying Elinor. Eugene falls in love with her only to find that she loves Starwick, whose homosexuality makes that love impossible.

Esther (Jack), a lovely Jewish woman with "dove's eyes" whom Eugene sees as he is boarding the ship to return to America. He knows that she is to become the "target of his life."

OFFENDING THE AUDIENCE
(Publikumsbeschimpfung)

Author: Peter Handke (1942-   )
First published: 1966
Genre: Drama

Locale: The theater where the play is presented
Time: The time the play is presented
Plot: Protest

Four Speakers, a mixed group of men and women. None of the four characters in this play assumes a "role" in any traditional sense. The speakers remain merely anonymous actors who address the audience in the author's words. They are also largely indistinguishable from one another and even from the members of the audience. Their clothing is ordinary casual dress. It is expected that the men, in both the audience and on stage, will be wearing dark jackets and white shirts with plain ties. Women are expected to be dressed in subdued colors. During their time onstage, the four speakers address the audience directly without singling out any specific individuals. They speak in a bland litany, free of emotion, vocal inflection, or any significant gestures. Nor are any specific lines assigned to the individual speakers. The characters merely pick up and leave off the discourse in a random order, speaking for varying lengths of time. Frequently, and without explanation, they contradict themselves and one another. In doing so, however, they give no indication of their own feelings about what they are saying beyond a general statement to the audience that their opinions may (or may not) be the same as those of the author. At the end of the performance, the four speakers react to the audience in exactly the same manner regardless of whether the audience's response to their work has been favorable or unfavorable.

— *Jeffrey L. Buller*

THE OGRE
(Le Roi des Aulnes)

Author: Michel Tournier (1924-   )
First published: 1970
Genre: Novel

Locale: A French provincial city, the border on the Rhine, and East Prussia
Time: Late 1930's and early 1940's
Plot: Philosophical realism

Abel Tiffauges (tih-FOHZH), a garage mechanic in Paris. He is sure that he is marked by fate for a special destiny that is yet to be revealed. Physically, he is extraordinary, a giant who loves both milk and raw meat, a man attracted strongly by both children and animals, an "ogre." The search for his real self begins in earnest when he is taken prisoner by the Nazis and sent to Germany, a land of signs and symbols. There, by keeping a "magic" journal written with his left hand, he will be able to decipher the meaning of everyday events and finally learn his destiny. From camp to camp, digging ditches, keeping animals in the game forest of Hermann Goering, and commanding the Kaltenborn Castle's regiment of Adolf Hitler's child army, Tiffauges seeks his fate, learning that signs and symbols are hard to read and that he is often confused by them. He does understand that, like his biblical namesake, he is meant to be a wanderer, a nomad fated to be hunted by the sedentary Cains as the Nazis hunt and kill both Jews and Gypsies.

Nestor, Tiffauges' schoolmate at Saint Christopher and the janitor's son. Enormous and myopic, just as Tiffauges will later become, Nestor bequeaths his own destiny to his friend before perishing in a boiler room accident. It is Nestor who first tells the young Tiffauges the story of Saint Christopher, the giant who carried the Christ child to safety on his shoulders and who hovers spiritually over him through the years, willing him his own destiny of "childbearer." Tiffauges remembers him as a magical figure, a "baby giant or a grown up dwarf."

Professor Keil, an authority on anthropology who is present at the unearthing of two ancient skeletons in the peat bog of Goering's hunting estate and who identifies one of them as the fabled Erl King because of a tight band with a six-pointed silver star still in place over the eye sockets of the two-thousand-year-old body. It is at his lecture that Tiffauges first hears the tale of the king who stole the spirits of young children and left them dead in their parents' arms, announcing

Tiffauges' darker destiny as the Ogre of Kaltenborn, scouring the countryside for young boys for the child army.

General von Kaltenborn, the master of the castle housing Hitler's youth corps, a Prussian aristocrat who is no longer proud of the German army and who is contemptuous of Hitler. One morning, he is taken away in full dress uniform by men wearing civilian clothes, leaving Tiffauges in charge of training the children.

Ephraim, the "star bearer," a Jewish boy found by Tiffauges as he lies half dead among concentration-camp refugees who clog the roads. Tiffauges nurses the child back to health and, carrying him everywhere on his shoulders, becomes his "Steed of Israel." Together, they flee the advancing Russian army, but Ephraim becomes so heavy on the giant's shoulders that they are forced down into the peat bog. As Tiffauges sinks, he looks up to find the child gone; only a six-pointed star in the dark heavens remains. Ephraim has fulfilled Tiffauges' (and Nestor's) destiny as "childbearer."

— *Lucy Golsan*

OH WHAT A PARADISE IT SEEMS

Author: John Cheever (1912-1982)
First published: 1982
Genre: Novel

Locale: New York City and Janice, a small suburban town
Time: Unspecified, but probably the early 1980's
Plot: Realism

Lemuel Sears, an old but still quite athletic man who has an unspecified but clearly quite high-ranking position with a firm specializing in "intrusion systems for computer containers." An odd mixture of innocence and lustiness, and of spirituality and carnality, he associates fleetness with divinity. Twice widowered, he spends much of his time pursuing the pleasures of the flesh, concurrently seeking to purify not only a contaminated pond where he has twice gone ice skating but also his own spiritual nature. He is strongly attracted to the past, but his nostalgia is not at all negative. He loves permanence and light and has an equally strong aversion to "nomadism" and "netherness." Overcoming his own comical shortcomings, including an inflated sense of his sexual prowess, he manages to restore Beasley's Pond to its pristine state, to effect his own moral salvation, and to affirm the natural world as a paradise.

Sears's eldest daughter, who lives in Janice, close to Beasley's Pond. The relationship between father and daughter is practical yet profound and marked by a certain degree of skepticism.

Amelia, Sears's "sainted" first wife, who died at the age of forty. She put Sears in touch with a spiritual stratum of existence, one from which Sears believes she came and to which she has gone, and where he believes they will meet again.

Estelle, Sears's second wife, whom he realizes he never really knew. She claimed to be able to tell the future. All of her predictions were, however, pessimistic; none dealt with the triumphs of the spirit. Convinced of her own powers of clairvoyance, she disregards a stranger's warning and is struck and killed by a train in Philadelphia.

Renée Herndon, an attractive divorcée from Des Moines. She works as a real estate agent in New York City and attends many secret meetings held in various parish houses in what appears to be an attempt to improve herself. Sears meets her in a bank and subsequently ardently courts her, despite her repeated claim that he does not know the first thing about women. When she decides to visit her daughter, Renée abruptly breaks off their intense sexual relationship, much to Sears's dismay.

Eduardo, the elevator operator in Renée's apartment building. Eduardo has a homosexual encounter with Sears shortly after Renée jilts him. The two men then go off on a chaste but entirely abortive fishing trip. Their relationship is marked by understanding and a complete absence of jealousy.

Dr. Palmer, the psychiatrist Sears consults immediately after his encounter with Eduardo. An unwed homosexual, Palmer cannot understand Sears's love of life other than as a form of infantilism.

Horace Chisholm, the environmentalist whom Sears hires to help save Beasley's Pond. Chisholm left his position as a teacher of high school biochemistry to dedicate himself to saving the environment, but this dedication led to marital problems and finally to separation from his wife and daughter. Feeling exiled, he longs to be in creative touch with his world. His discovery of a baby forgotten by the roadside puts him in touch with the baby's parents, the Logans, who provide him with the family and the sense of belonging that he craves. For his part in saving Beasley's Pond, he is struck and killed by a car driven by a mafia hit man.

Betsy Logan, a housewife. She lives with her husband and two children next to the Salazzos on Hitching Post Lane, where "the architecture was all happy ending." In gratitude for Chisholm's finding and returning of her baby, she takes literally his request that she do all she can to save Beasley's Pond. When Chisholm is murdered, she terrorizes the local citizenry by threatening to poison bottles of teriyaki sauce at the local supermarket until the dumping at the pond stops, which it does.

Sammy Salazzo, an impoverished barber whose shooting of the family dog prompts his wife Maria to ask his Uncle Luigi, a mafioso, for help. Sammy is made vice chairman of the governor's committee for the impartial use of Beasley's Pond, a cover for turning the pond into a highly profitable dump.

Gallia, a blind Eastern European prophetess whom Sears meets on one of his trips to the Carpathian Mountains. Holding Sears's wallet, she enigmatically but humorously says that it is the grand poetry of life.

The narrator, who wishes he had some tale to tell other than the one he does, which he claims to be merely "a story to be read in bed on a rainy night."

— *Robert A. Morace*

OKTIABR' SHESTNADTSATOGO

Author: Aleksandr Solzhenitsyn (1918-   )
First published: 1984
Genre: Novel

Locale: Moscow, St. Petersburg, the Byelorussian and Ukrainian countryside, and Zurich
Time: August through early November of 1918
Plot: Historical

Georgij Mikhailych Vorotyntsev (geh-OHR-gee mih-KHAH-lihch voh-roh-TIHN-tsehv), a dedicated army career officer. A stout, clean-shaven, stoic, and trustworthy man of action, he is educated and perceptive but not one of the intelligentsia. He is a patriot and a good commander, admired by his soldiers, but his understanding of the people's wartime desperation leads him to call for a truce. He leaves the front to visit his family and friends in the rear. The decadence and chaos of life in Moscow and St. Petersburg lead him to a growing skepticism about the future. He is sufficiently open-minded to consider all arguments about Russia's fate, but his loyalty to traditional authority prevents him from joining any of the revolutionary factions.

Alina (ah-LIH-nah), Vorotyntsev's wife. She concentrates on becoming a concert pianist while separated from her husband by the war. She perceives the effects of the war from a personal, apolitical point of view. Her romantic attitudes and her cultural pretensions annoy Georgij. Although she worries about her beauty and connections, beneath the frivolous exterior she grieves for the wounded and attempts to rally other artists to assist them. In the end, her cultural instincts and empathy for others' emotional trauma prove to be great virtues.

Olda Orestovna (oh-reh-STOV-nah), also called **Professor Andozerskaja** (an-doh-ZEHR-skah-yah), the lover and would-be mentor of Vorotyntsev. A scholar of history, she is elegant, earthy, pithy, attractive though not young, and very ambitious. In her political dogmatism, she embodies the blindness of the intelligentsia. She insists on the larger meaning of events but fails to understand the spiritual crisis that inhibits the historic potential of individual action. Increasingly alienated by Georgij's anomie, she proves willing to make misguided but heroic sacrifices.

Isaakij "Sanja" Lazhenitsyn (ih-SAH-kee lah-zheh-NIH-tsihn), an idealistic young man who left the university to volunteer for the army. His ideals are tested at first hand by the frustrations of the front line. He possesses a gift for language and a poetic sensibility that keep him attuned to the war's devastation of nature. He expresses the resentment of the young intelligentsia toward the oppressive and ossified army hierarchy and debates the priest Severjan on the impor-

tance of religious tradition in the modern world.

Arsenij "Senka" Blagodarjov (ahr-SEH-nee blah-goh-DAHR-yov), a natural leader in peacetime, now serving as a soldier under Vorotyntsev in wartime. Senka is uneducated, gregarious, and large. He drinks, swears, and fights hard. He also expresses resentment against the army commanders, but in a less reasoned fashion than does Sanja, more as an expression of his loyalty toward his fellow infantrymen. Although he shares the peasants' prejudices against certain social groups, he bears no grudges against individuals.

Vladimir Ilich Lenin (VLAH-dih-mihr EEL-yich LEH-nihn), an aging, unpopular, would-be revolutionary, living in exile in Zurich. Lenin is short, with hunched shoulders and furrowed brows. He is more cunning than intelligent. It is not certain to what extent he is motivated by sincere concern for the people. His life is ruled by insecurities concerning the machinations of other revolutionary leaders. His vanity is exploited by colleagues who manipulate his reputation in the constant infighting over tactics. His increasingly harsh attacks on his rivals do not bode well for Russia.

Nicholas II, the czar, a moody man who is overly dependent on his wife. Passive, indecisive, and occasionally paranoid, he also falls victim to vanity and the manipulations of flatterers. Although he is genuinely concerned for the spiritual well-being of the masses, he is too childish to take effective action on their behalf. He responds to warnings from concerned government ministers by withdrawing into the private world of sectarian mysticism.

Father Severjan (seh-vehr-YAN), an embodiment of the Russian Orthodox church in a time when religion has become unfashionable. A tall, bearded ascetic, he wanders the front, trying to avoid the bureaucratic rules of the army and church hierarchies and ministering to the wounded. He shares Sanja's intuitive appreciation of nature. He attempts to explain the mulishness and anger of the people to Sanja as a result of centuries-long religious repression. Occasionally, his example inspires others to heroic displays of valor and compassion, but his apocalyptic declarations are more pretentious than prophetic.

— *Mark Haag*

THE OLD AND THE YOUNG
(I vecchi e i giovani)

Author: Luigi Pirandello (1867-1936)
First published: 1913
Genre: Novel

Locale: Sicily and Rome
Time: 1891-1892
Plot: Historical

Flaminio Salvo (flah-MEE-nee-oh), a mine owner and capitalist who backs the clerical party candidate in an election for a representative to the Italian Chamber of Deputies. When the workers in his Sicilian mines go on strike, he shuts down the mines in an effort to starve them out.

Dianella Salvo (dee-ah-NEHL-loh), Salvo's daughter, who is in love with Salvo's mine superintendent, Aurelio Costa. Salvo refuses to permit their marriage because Costa has no money. When Costa is murdered by a mob, Dianella goes mad and has to be locked up.

Mauro Mortara (MAH-ew-roh mohr-tah-rah), one of Garibaldi's followers, who is now an old man. He cannot understand why his old comrades must fight among themselves or why, after his generation fought for peace and freedom, there still seems to be neither. He is shot by troops firing on a crowd.

Prince Ippolito Laurentano (eep-poh-LEE-toh low-rehn-TAH-noh), an old Garibaldist leader to whom Salvo is trying to marry his sister. He is still very much a royalist and loyal to the church. He lives in a world of his own on his estate in Sicily.

Prince Gerlando Laurentano (gehr-LAHN-doh), Ippolito Laurentano's son and a Socialist organizer. His position as a Socialist is embarrassing and incomprehensible to his family's friends. He is horrified by the conditions among the strikers in Salvo's mines.

Capolino (kah-poh-LEE-noh), the clerical party candidate whom Salvo is backing in the election.

Roberto Auriti (ah-ew-REE-tee), the man against whom Capolino is running in the election. Auriti is wrongly imprisoned for the misappropriation of government funds. He is Gerlando Laurentano's cousin.

Aurelio Costa (ah-ew-REH-lee-oh KOHS-tah), Salvo's mine superintendent, whom Dianella loves. When Costa learns that he cannot marry Dianella, he returns to the mines to join with the strikers. He is killed by the mob before he can explain why he is there.

Nicoletta Capolino (nee-koh-LEHT-tah), Capolino's wife, who attaches herself to the man who really misappropriated the government funds.

Corrado Selmi (kohr-RAH-doh SEHL-mee), the man who actually misappropriated the funds, the act for which Auriti is imprisoned.

THE OLD BACHELOR

Author: William Congreve (1670-1729)
First published: 1693
Genre: Drama

Locale: London, England
Time: The seventeenth century
Plot: Comedy of manners

Sir Joseph Wittol, a foolish country knight. He falls in love with Araminta on first seeing her and is fooled for a time into thinking she intends to marry him.

Ned Bellmour, a gallant young bachelor in love with Belinda. Disguised as a Puritan preacher, he visits Fondlewife's spouse and has a merry time as a lark. True to his friends, he saves Heartwell from a disastrous marriage with Silvia, a prostitute. Although he is a little wild, he is a good young man, and Belinda plans to marry him.

Sharper, Bellmour's unscrupulous friend.

Captain Bluffe, a supposed veteran of the British Army. Although his boasting and swaggering endear him to Wittol, he proves to be an arrant coward. He tries to bribe Setter to act as pander to bring him and Araminta together.

Belinda, a fashionable, wealthy young woman of great beauty. She loves and is loved by Bellmour.

Araminta, Belinda's cousin. She and Vainlove are in love and plan to marry.

Vainlove, Bellmour's friend. He loves Araminta, who forgives his romantic escapades and plans to marry him.

Gavot, Araminta's singing teacher.

Silvia, a prostitute, Vainlove's discarded mistress. She tries to break up the romance between Vainlove and Araminta and to trick Heartwell into a marriage with herself.

Lucy, Silvia's maid.

Heartwell, a surly old bachelor and woman-hater. He is almost tricked into marrying Silvia, not knowing she is a prostitute.

Setter, Vainlove's manservant.

Fondlewife, a banker and an ancient, doting husband. He catches his young wife with Bellmour.

Laetitia, Fondlewife's spouse. She entertains Bellmour handsomely, thinking her husband is away on business. After he catches them together, Laetitia, weeping, convinces Fondlewife that she is innocent.

THE OLD CURIOSITY SHOP

Author: Charles Dickens (1812-1870)
First published: 1841; serial form, 1840-1841
Genre: Novel

Locale: England
Time: Early nineteenth century
Plot: Social realism

Nell Trent, called **Little Nell**, a sweet, delicate child, brave and wise beyond her years. An orphan, she lives with her aged grandfather, the keeper of the Old Curiosity Shop, who has developed a passion for gambling because of his desire to provide for Little Nell's future. After the old man, heavily in debt, loses the last of his property, he and his granddaughter are turned into the streets. She and the half-crazed old man take to the roads and encounter many adventures during their wanderings. At every opportunity, her grandfather continues to gamble away whatever funds he may have. They suffer many privations before they fall in with a kindly schoolmaster, Mr.

Marton, who accompanies them to the village where he has been appointed teacher and clerk. There, Little Nell and her grandfather settle down to a quiet life, but their happiness is brief. Hardship and exposure have undermined Little Nell's delicate constitution. She fades away slowly and uncomplainingly, worn out by her difficult life, and dies soon afterward.

Little Nell's grandfather, the proprietor of the Old Curiosity Shop, the only means he has of providing for himself and his orphan granddaughter. Troubled because he has no other way to provide for her future, he resorts to gambling in an effort to make his fortune. Losing steadily, he develops a passion for the excitement of gambling. In the end, unable to repay money he has borrowed from Daniel Quilp, a wealthy usurer, he is completely beggared. He and Little Nell leave London and wander through the country. On the way, they suffer hardships and hunger until they are befriended by Mr. Marton, a schoolmaster, who finds work for them in the village where he is a teacher. The grandfather is unable to endure the sorrow of Little Nell's slow decline and death; he dies on her grave and is buried by her side.

Christopher Nubbles, called **Kit**, an awkward but generous-hearted and sturdy boy, devoted to Little Nell, whom her grandfather employs to run errands. Becoming convinced that Kit has revealed the secret of the old man's gambling habits, the grandfather turns the boy away from the curiosity shop. Kit aids the Single Gentleman in his efforts to locate Little Nell and her grandfather after the two disappear from London, but nothing comes of their first search. Meanwhile Kit has been befriended by Mr. Garland, in whose house he lives. When, through the machinations of Daniel Quilp, Sampson Brass accuses the boy of theft, he is able to prove his innocence with the aid of Mr. Garland and Dick Swiveller. He marries Barbara, Mrs. Garland's pretty housemaid.

Daniel Quilp, the frightening, half-mad dwarf from whom Little Nell's grandfather borrows in order to gamble. Quilp, married to a browbeaten wife, lends the old man money in order to obtain a hold on him, for Quilp hopes to marry Little Nell at some future date. Ferocious, sinister, vindictive, he torments his wife, Little Nell, her grandfather, and Kit Nubbles. He drowns while attempting to escape from the police, who are about to arrest him for crimes he has committed.

Mrs. Betsey Quilp, his long-suffering wife, who is tortured mentally and physically by her misshapen, cruel husband and made to obey his every wish, even to spying on Little Nell. She inherits her husband's property after his death. When she marries again, her second husband is the opposite of Quilp in every way.

Frederick Trent, Little Nell's profligate brother. Hating his grandfather, he schemes to have his crony, Dick Swiveller, marry Little Nell so that they may obtain the fortune that they believe the old man has hidden away for his granddaughter.

Richard Swiveller (Dick), Frederick Trent's conniving friend, who is turned by his love for a servant girl into a decent person. Quilp, who hopes to use the young rascal in tracing Little Nell and her grandfather, secures him a position as clerk to Sampson Brass, the dwarf's attorney; but when Kit Nubbles is arrested and charged with theft on the false testimony of Brass, Dick is instrumental in proving the boy's innocence. Discharged, he is nursed during an illness by the Marchioness, the Brasses' slavey, who runs away from home in order to care for him. When he inherits a small annuity, he renames the girl Sophronia Sphynx and sends her to school, where he pays for her education for the next six years. On one of his visits to the school, when the Marchioness is nineteen, the idea comes to him that the next step in their relationship ought to be marriage. He proposes and is accepted.

The Marchioness (Sophronia Sphynx), a poor, frightened servant to the Brass family. She sleeps in the basement and must steal food to keep herself alive; Swiveller, pitying the girl, sometimes plays cards with her. She repays his kindness by nursing him while he is ill. Through listening at the keyhole when the Brasses are planning to accuse Kit Nubbles of robbery, she is able to help in saving him from prison. Sent to school to be educated by Swiveller, she eventually marries him.

Sampson Brass, a dishonest lawyer who is Daniel Quilp's adviser in legal matters. He accuses Kit Nubbles of stealing a five-pound note from his desk. Deeply involved in Quilp's villainy, he is arrested and sent to prison.

Sally Brass, the formidable spinster sister of Sampson Brass. An intelligent student of the law, she overshadows her brother in sharpness and cunning. She mistreats and starves her servant, whom Dick Swiveller calls the Marchioness.

The Single Gentleman, a lodger in the house of Sampson Brass. Though always gentlemanly in his behavior, he is quiet and mysterious in his comings and goings. He tries in various ways to trace Little Nell and her grandfather. Shortly after the death of Little Nell, he arrives in the village where they have taken refuge. He turns out to be the grandfather's younger brother, absent from England for many years. In the end, he is revealed also as Master Humphrey, the teller of the story.

Mrs. Jiniwin, Mrs. Quilp's fat mother. Though she is a shrew, she is no match for her son-in-law. She divides her days between reproaching her daughter for having married such a creature and fighting verbal battles with the dwarf.

Miss Sophy Wackles, a girl with whom Dick Swiveller at one time imagines himself in love. She marries a grocer, much to Dick's disgust.

Mrs. Wackles, the headmistress of a day school for young ladies and Sophy's mother. She encourages her daughter to marry the grocer.

Jane Wackles and

Melissa Wackles, Sophy's sisters.

Mr. Cheggs, the grocer whom Sophy marries. A conforming man, he is not nearly so lively as Dick Swiveller.

Miss Cheggs, the sister of Mr. Cheggs and a good friend of Sophy.

Mrs. Nubbles, Kit's mother, a sweet, emotional widow. When her son is imprisoned, she comes faithfully with her two other children to bring him food. Later, she goes with Mr. Garland and the Single Gentleman to help find Little Nell and her grandfather.

Little Jacob, the younger brother of Kit Nubbles.

The Baby, Kit's youngest brother.

Mrs. Jarley, the fat, good-humored proprietor of Jarley's celebrated waxworks. Occasionally she is known to sip at a strange bottle, but she remains a steady person in her business. She befriends Little Nell and her grandfather, and the two travel with the show caravan for a time, Little Nell having been hired to explain the exhibits and her grandfather to dust the wax figures.

Miss Monflathers, the head of a young ladies' boarding school who chastises Little Nell when she comes to the school bearing advertisements for the waxworks exhibits. She is a typical Victorian boarding-school headmistress, arrogant, self-centered, and cruel.

Two Teachers, toadying assistants to Miss Monflathers. Each tries to outdo the other in being agreeable to their officious employer.

Miss Edwards, a charity pupil at the boarding school. When she takes pity on Little Nell, Miss Monflathers reviles her in front of her schoolmates. Later, Nell follows Miss Edwards when she and her sister take a walk through the town. Their relationship and closeness make Little Nell long to have someone of her own age for a friend.

Mr. Martin, a kind schoolmaster who befriends Little Nell and her grandfather early in their travels. He encounters them again later on, takes them to the village where he teaches, and procures a house for them. He is gentle and intelligent, and his pupils adore him.

Harry, a dying young schoolboy, Mr. Martin's favorite pupil. He loves the schoolmaster and revives long enough to bid him goodbye.

Dame West, Harry's grandmother.

Mr. Garland and

Mrs. Garland, an elderly, kind couple who take Kit Nubbles into their home. He is the only one capable of handling their temperamental pony. They help in the search for Little Nell and her grandfather.

Abel Garland, their son. He becomes a partner of Mr. Witherden, a notary.

Mr. Witherden and

Mr. Chuckster, the lawyers who assist the Single Gentleman in his quest for Little Nell and the capture of Quilp. They are proper and industrious gentlemen.

Barbara, the Garland's servant girl. In love with Kit, she remains loyal when he is accused of robbery and eventually marries him.

Mr. Slum, a military gentleman and Mrs. Jarley's friend, much given to composing bad poetry. Mrs. Jarley advertises her waxworks with his poems.

Jem Groves, the proprietor of the Valiant Soldier, a pub where Little Nell and her grandfather take shelter during a rainstorm. He is friendly, but he is crooked in the card game in which the grandfather takes a hand.

Matt List and

Isaac List, card players at the Valiant Soldier. The grandfather loses all of Little Nell's money while playing with them.

The Old Sexton, in charge of the old village church which Little Nell often visits before her death.

Old Davy, the deaf, aged gravedigger, the sexton's good friend.

Tom Codlin, the grouchy partner of a shabby Punch-and-Judy show. Little Nell and her grandfather travel with the show for a time.

Mr. Harris, usually called **Short Trotters**, the pleasant partner in the Punch-and-Judy show.

Mr. Grinder, a fellow showman whom Little Nell meets in her travels with the Punch-and-Judy troupe.

Jerry, the master of the dancing dogs in the carnival group.

Mr. Vuffin, the manager of a giant and a woman without legs or arms.

Sweet William, a card trickster and conjurer.

Joe Jowl, a scoundrel who tries to persuade Little Nell's grandfather to rob Mrs. Jarley.

Tom Scott, Daniel Quilp's young servant. Beaten and abused by his master, he forgets his troubles by standing on his head. After Quilp's death, he becomes a professional tumbler.

The Bachelor, a benevolent old gentleman in a village where Little Nell and her grandfather finally find a home. No one remembers his name, if he ever told it. He tutors Little Nell in village lore.

THE OLD DEVILS

Author: Kingsley Amis (1922-1995)
First published: 1986
Genre: Novel

Locale: South Wales
Time: Mid-1980's
Plot: Social

Alun Weaver, a critic, poet, journalist, and television personality in England, recognized for his service to literature by an award from the queen. In his early sixties, he decides to go into semiretirement in his native town in South Wales. A handsome, charming man with a fearsome reputation as a womanizer, he has not been slowed by age; his famous mane of hair, once deep bronze and now snow-white (somewhat deepened by a dye job), and his quick sense of sexual prey and willingness to please are immediately put into practice as he returns to his old friends, both male and female. He can be monumentally glib, and unrepentant about it, but he is also a scarifying commentator on social, political, artistic, and personal stupidities.

Rhiannon Weaver, Weaver's wife, beautiful as a girl and still handsome as an old woman. Gray-eyed, tall, and fair, she is not without old lovers herself, if more properly so, but she is not, like her husband, sexually obsessed. She knows what he is usually up to when he disappears, but she has come to terms with it. Her big test lies in meeting the one serious love of her life, Peter Thomas, and dealing with him.

Peter Thomas, the youthful lover of Rhiannon Weaver who let her down when she became pregnant while at the univer-

sity. A retired chemical engineer, he lives in mortal vicious combat with his wife, a Yorkshire woman. Thomas is deeply unhappy and conveys an air of constant melancholy and bad temper in public, punctuated by shards of witty disdain. He is dangerously overweight, and, in early old age, is bald-headed, paunchy, and barely able to transport himself from one chair to another. He is not much of the man whom Rhiannon loved years earlier. He still loves her but does not look forward to being in constant social conjunction with her, given his present state.

Muriel Thomas, the only non-Welsh member of the group, a loud-voiced, breezy woman. Dark-haired and of slender build, she seems to be the physical ideal of a Welsh woman, but she is not, and she despises all things Welsh. She is constantly at Peter, threatening to return to England and to leave him behind, both physically and financially, because she owns all of their property and most of their money. He is terrified of her, and she takes considerable pleasure in humiliating him with blistering verbal attacks when and if it suits her.

Sophie Norris, a former lover of Weaver, and of many others as well. Having possessed a lavish figure and a generous sexual appetite when young, she is still in fairly good shape and is still open to salacious invitation. Only her husband, Charlie, seems immune to her charms, but he knows that she still has an occasionally active social life. She is good to Charlie, however, in other ways.

Charlie Norris, the owner of a restaurant, which is run by his brother. He is a very heavy drinker who is suffering from a variety of serious physical ailments. Intelligent and often aware, despite his pug-nosed drinker's face and dazed demeanor, he is quick to put Alun in his place when he talks nonsense. Charlie is susceptible to terrible nightmares and is constantly on the edge of a serious nervous breakdown. Good-natured and accepting of his wife's infidelities, he is pathetically trying to get from drink to drink without falling apart completely.

Malcolm Cellan-Davies, a retired insurance agent who, on one occasion long ago, had a small book of poems printed. Sixty-one years old, long-faced, tall, erect, and constantly worried about his diet and his tendency toward constipation, he is a very mild and somewhat conservative man. He tends not to see what is going on quite as clearly as his friends, which is probably just as well. He cherishes a memory of his short courtship of Rhiannon Weaver that seems to be quite out of proportion to her memory of the same association.

Gwen Cellan-Davies, Malcolm's wife. She is spectacled, round-faced, and sixty-one years old, with deep-set eyes and tinted, light brown hair. She is often disdainful of Malcolm's literary reputation and of his character in general. There is more there, however, than she wishes to reveal. She is a close friend of Rhiannon Weaver and has been since school days, but despite her talk to the contrary, she is closer to Alun Weaver than she would admit.

Dorothy Morgan, the resident bore, shorthaired, intelligent-looking, and obsessed with telling everyone in long lectures what she has just learned about subjects of no possible interest to anyone. She was a close friend of Rhiannon at the university.

— *Charles Pullen*

OLD FORTUNATUS

Author: Thomas Dekker (c. 1572-1632)
First published: 1600
Genre: Drama

Locale: Cyprus, Babylon, and England
Time: The tenth century
Plot: Allegory

Fortunatus (fohr-tew-NAH-tuhs), a shabby, miserable man who becomes for a time Fortune's darling. He acquires from her a magic purse that is never empty when he wishes to draw out money, and he steals for himself a wishing hat owned by the Soldan of Babylon, whose greed for the purse makes him careless. Fortunatus lives to regret his choice of wealth rather than wisdom and pleads that his sons may have the better choice. He dies, leaving the magic objects and much advice—largely disregarded—to his sons.

Andelocia (an-deh-LOH-chee-ah), Fortunatus' prodigal younger son. He wastes his inheritance foolishly and dies miserably.

Ampedo (ahm-PAY-doh), Fortunatus' virtuous older son. He gains nothing from his father's gifts and nothing for his own abstinence, dying as miserably as his reckless brother.

Athelstane (ATH-ehl-stan), the greedy and treacherous king of England. He acquires and loses the magic purse and hat with his daughter's aid. Fortune grants the purse to him again at the end of the play. The hat has been burned by Ampedo.

Agripyne (a-GRIH-pee-nuh), Athelstane's selfish, beautiful daughter. She plays the role of Delilah to trick Andelocia out of the magic objects. Her punishment is negligible and short-lived.

The Soldan of Babylon, who loses his wishing hat in his eagerness to acquire a magic purse. The wishing hat will transport its wearer to wherever that person wishes to be.

Longavile (LAWN-gah-vihl) and
Montrose, two noblemen made ridiculous by Andelocia. They gain revenge by causing the deaths of Andelocia and Ampedo. They also gain exile and remorse.

Fortune, the fickle and powerful goddess. She gives Fortunatus a choice of various qualities including wisdom. When she learns that his choice is wealth, she grants his wish, but she lets him know the foolishness of his choice. When he realizes his error and requests that his sons be given wisdom instead of his wealth, she denies him.

Virtue, the goddess who appears always with Fortune and Vice. She wears a fool's cap, and the author does little in the play to indicate that the emblem is unjust. She does offer small, bitter apples that counteract the effect of Vice's luscious ones. At the end of the play, an address to Queen Elizabeth gives Virtue some lip service and announces her triumph as Vice flees.

Vice, a purveyor of tempting apples that cause horns to grow on those who eat them. She ridicules Virtue and usually has the better of their struggles. Her flight from Virtue comes after the play proper is concluded.

THE OLD GRINGO
(El gringo viejo)

Author: Carlos Fuentes (1928-   )
First published: 1985
Genre: Novel

Locale: Chihuahua, Mexico
Time: 1913-1914
Plot: Historical realism

Harriet Winslow, the character who "sits and remembers" the story of her adventure in Mexico. Harriet, who is unmarried, agrees to go to Mexico in the service of the Miranda family to teach English to their three children; she hopes thus to escape a stultifying existence in Washington, D.C. Arriving in Mexico, she is used by revolutionary leaders, and she finds the country in turmoil and the Miranda hacienda in ruins. She becomes involved with a revolutionary general, whom she ultimately betrays.

Ambrose Bierce (beers), the "old gringo," a famous, real-life writer whose true identity is only gradually disclosed to the reader. Notorious for his bitterness and cynicism, Bierce has worked for the newspaper mogul William Randolph Hearst for more than twenty years and now regrets having misused his talents. During the fall of 1913, Bierce retires to Mexico as a seventy-one-year-old alcoholic and asthmatic seeking Pancho Villa and the adventure of revolution. The novel makes Bierce a heroic figure but sidetracks his mission through his encounter with Tomás Arroyo, whom he serves briefly and who then murders him.

General Tomás Arroyo (toh-MAHS ah-RROY-oh), a simple peasant who symbolizes Hispanic virility and machismo. Arroyo is driven by revolutionary idealism and a personal quest for revenge against Miranda, whose bastard son he is. After his army takes over the Miranda estate, however, Arroyo begins to think of the Miranda lands as his own birthright and becomes obsessed with documenting his claim. As he seems to lose his revolutionary focus, the old gringo takes action to shake his complacency, and the enraged Arroyo kills him.

Pancho Villa (PAHN-choh VEE-yah), the bandit turned revolutionary leader and wily politician, another historical figure. Villa is troubled by the political crisis caused by Arroyo's murder of Bierce. Villa is forced to execute Arroyo in order to avoid an embarrassing international incident.

THE OLD MAID

Author: Edith Wharton (1862-1937)
First published: 1924
Genre: Novel

Locale: New York City
Time: The 1850's
Plot: Social realism

Delia Ralston, a young New York matron of impeccable social position. Years before, she had turned down an unconventional young man, and though she is contentedly married, she still speculates secretly about a life of passion. She is relieved when she hears that her cousin Charlotte is to be married. Charlotte, though, changes her mind, confiding to Delia that one of the children in the orphanage nursery she has established is her own—by Delia's first love—and that marriage will mean giving up the child, Tina, a thing she cannot do. Delia persuades her husband to provide a home for Charlotte and the child; after his death, they live with her. In order to give her a suitable background, Delia adopts Tina. On the girl's wedding eve, Charlotte accuses Delia of having stolen the girl from her because of her love for the father. Delia realizes the charge is partly true.

Charlotte Lovell, Delia's cousin, beautiful and gay in her youth, but strangely changed after her return from a trip to Georgia "for her health." Delia's suitor had turned to Charlotte and got her with child, but knowing that he still loved Delia, Charlotte did not tell him of her condition. She breaks her engagement to Joe Ralston in order to keep the child. Although she needs Delia's protection, she is resentful of her, especially as the little girl obviously prefers Delia, whom she calls "Mother." Charlotte insists on being the one to give the young girl her wedding-eve confidences, but she comes back downstairs without doing so. Charlotte realizes that she can never tell her daughter the truth, and there is nothing an "Old Maid" can have to say to a bride. Having begun her adulthood unconventionally, Charlotte finds that nothing is left to her but a conventional role.

Tina Ralston, Charlotte's daughter, adopted by Delia because the proper young men will not want to marry Tina unless she has a correct, formal family tie. Soon after her adoption, Tina becomes suitably engaged.

Clement Spender, a penniless young painter. He would not settle down to a disciplined life in New York, and Delia therefore refused to marry him. Returning from Rome to New York, he finds Delia married and turns to Charlotte. When he goes back to Rome, he does not know that Charlotte is expecting his child. It is only after Charlotte tells Delia who the father of the baby is that Delia offers to assume responsibility for the mother and child.

James Ralston, Delia's proper and prosperous husband. At her request, he establishes Charlotte and Tina in a little house; after he is killed in a fall from a horse, Delia takes Charlotte and Tina into her home.

Joe Ralston, James's cousin, engaged to Charlotte. Wanting healthy heredity for his children, he accepts Charlotte's cough as an excuse to break the engagement.

THE OLD MAN
(Starik)

Author: Yuri Trifonov (1925-1981)
First published: 1978
Genre: Novel

Locale: Russia
Time: 1973, with flashbacks beginning in 1917
Plot: Psychological realism

Pavel Evgrafovich Letunov (PAH-vehl yehv-GRA-foh-vihch leh-TEW-nov), a retired man. Having played a part in the revolution, Pavel becomes an engineer after World War II and begins writing articles to justify the actions of Sergei Kirillovich Migulin, a revolutionary general. The political climate after the war makes rehabilitation possible. After the death of

Pavel's wife, Galya, the search for the true motivation of Migulin's rebellion becomes Pavel's only refuge from the painful disorder in his family and his children's attempts to have him help them obtain a house through his connections.

Sergei Kirillovich Migulin (sehr-GAY kih-RIH-loh-vihch mih-GEW-lihn), an army commander. Born a Cossack and possessing great rhetorical and tactical skills, he is uniquely capable of rousing and directing the fiercely independent Don Cossacks. Although he is a true revolutionary, his Cossack nationalism and sharp tongue make him suspect in the eyes of the Bolsheviks. His hot temper eventually leads him to an emotional rebellion that results in his trial and death sentence.

Anna Konstantinovna Igumnova (kon-stan-TIH-nohv-nah ih-GEWM-noh-vah), Migulin's wife. The first wife of Vladimir, she married Migulin after Vladimir was butchered by Cossacks. Despite the revolution, Anna's existence is not determined by ideology but by her fierce devotion to Migulin.

Vera Pavlovna (PAV-lov-nah), Pavel's daughter. Vera believes that she has a better chance of keeping her lover, Nikolai Erastovich, if the family has more room, so she pressures her father to influence the process of obtaining better housing.

Polina Karlovna (poh-LIH-nah KAHR-lov-nah), a school friend of Pavel's wife. Polina is also Oleg Vasilevich Kandaurov's mother-in-law, which makes Pavel reluctant to exercise his influence in obtaining a house for his children.

Nikolai Erastovich (nih-koh-LAY eh-RAH-stoh-vihch), Vera's lover. He combines a small quantity of piety, an argumentative nature, and an indifferent commitment to Vera, traits that make him a source of constant frustration in the Letunov household.

Ruslan Pavlovich Letunov (REWS-lan PAV-loh-vihch), Pavel's son, who does not love his wife, has a woman on the side, and drinks too much, all of which add to the family's frustrations.

Vladimir Sekachev (seh-ka-CHOV), Anna's first cousin and first husband; he is kind, brave, and unpredictable. Vladimir's revolutionary activity is cut short when he is murdered by Cossacks.

Alexander Pimenovich Danilov (PIH-meh-noh-vihch dah-NIH-lov), a man-at-arms in the 1905 revolution and Pavel's uncle. Alexander is one of the few people to see past the moment of revolutionary fervor and perceive the inhumanity of revolutionary trials and the terror campaign against the Cossacks.

Oleg Vasilevich Kandaurov (vah-SIH-lyeh-vihch kan-DAH-uh-rov), a government executive. His personal motto of pushing every person and situation as far as he can has resulted in a party position, a trip to Mexico, and a passionate young mistress. Kandaurov is vying for the same house that Ruslan wants.

— *Donald E. Livingston, Jr.*

THE OLD MAN AND THE SEA

Author: Ernest Hemingway (1899-1961)
First published: 1952
Genre: Novella

Locale: Cuba and the Gulf Stream
Time: Mid-twentieth century
Plot: Parable

Santiago (sahn-tee-AH-goh), an old Cuban fisherman, the protagonist. He is a simple man who loves and respects the sea and all the life within it. On his search for the great marlin, his young friend Manolin fishes with him for forty days, but then Santiago fishes alone among the elements. After eighty-four days of fishing without a catch, the old man's patience is rewarded. He hooks a huge marlin but then must engage in an exhausting three-day struggle with it. In his battle with the marlin, Santiago begins to identify with the fish, feeling a brotherhood with it and almost a sense of guilt about the idea of killing it. This feeling of solidarity and interdependence between the old man and the marlin pervades the action of the story. The old man's heroic individualism and his love for his fellow creatures is evident throughout. After finally harpooning it, he attaches the marlin to the bow and stern of his boat, but sharks begin to devour his catch. Santiago's next battle, with the sharks, proves impossible to win, and Santiago reaches shore with only a skeleton, worthless except as a symbol of his victory. In his struggle with the giant marlin, Santiago pushes himself to the limits of his physical and mental endurance. A man with native intelligence and a strong will to survive, Santiago bears tragedy with great humility and dignity.

Manolin (mahn-oh-LEEN), a young Cuban boy whom Santiago teaches to fish. He becomes Santiago's fishing partner and fishes with the old man until the young man's father forbids it. He becomes Santiago's closest and most devoted friend, and Santiago becomes the boy's substitute father. Manolin is so devoted to the old man that he begs and steals so that the old man does not go hungry; he also finds fresh bait for Santiago. In the time they spend together, Santiago and the boy talk at length about fishing, hunting, American baseball, and one of the old man's heroes, Joe DiMaggio, the great Yankee outfielder. In his discussion of DiMaggio, Santiago wishes to teach Manolin about physical and psychological endurance, about being a "team player," and about being a champion.

The marlin, an eighteen-foot fish weighing more than a thousand pounds, the largest ever caught in the Gulf Stream. Santiago views the marlin as a mixture of incredible beauty and deadly violence. He and the marlin are equal partners in the battle of human against nature. They both emerge as heroes.

Martin (mahr-TEEN), the owner of the Terrace. He gives food to Manolin to give to Santiago.

Pedrico (peh-DREE-koh), a fisherman to whom Santiago gives the marlin's head, for use in his fish traps.

Rogelio (rroh-HEH-lee-oh), a young boy who once helped Santiago with his fish nets.

— *Genevieve Slomski*

OLD MORTALITY

Author: Katherine Anne Porter (1890-1980)
First published: 1939; serial form, 1938
Genre: Short fiction

Locale: Texas and New Orleans
Time: 1885-1912
Plot: Social

Miranda, a Southern girl, eight years old at the book's beginning, who cannot understand until she grows up that adults were once young, too. She is puzzled as to why grown-ups cling to the relics of the past. She and her sister are educated in a convent in New Orleans. When she grows up, she marries without her father's consent. As an adult, she finally realizes she has no part in the past and must find her own legends.

Maria, Miranda's older sister, twelve years old at the beginning of the book, who has the same inability to understand adults and their lives as her sister.

Grandmother, the children's grandmother, a woman who twice a year spends a day in her attic weeping over the relics of her family's past.

Amy, the children's father's sister, reputed to have been the most beautiful girl in the South, as well as the best rider, the best dancer, and quite a flirt. A spoiled darling, she dies mysteriously six weeks after marrying Gabriel.

Harry, Miranda and Maria's father, who hopes, dubiously, that his chubby, freckle-faced little girls will become as beautiful as his sister Amy. He fought a duel over his sister and

spent a year in Mexico as a fugitive.

Great-aunt Keziah, one of the girls' relatives, a fat and ugly woman. She is living proof that all the women in the family are not slim, beautiful creatures like Aunt Amy.

Eva Parrington, an ugly, chinless cousin of the little girls. She teaches Latin and works for woman suffrage, going to jail three times for that cause. On the way to her Cousin Gabriel's funeral, with the grown-up Miranda, she says that the myth about Cousin Amy is false, that Amy was a selfish girl who very likely committed suicide after tormenting her new husband throughout their honeymoon. Cousin Eva looks back bitterly on her youth as a kind of sex market in which she was unwanted merchandise.

Gabriel, Amy's second cousin, whom she kept dangling for five years as a suitor. She agrees to marry him, ironically, after he is cut off from his inheritance. After her death, he becomes a drunkard and spends his time hanging around the race track.

Miss Honey, Gabriel's second wife. She is a bitter, slatternly woman who hates her husband's family.

OLD MORTALITY

Author: Sir Walter Scott (1771-1832)
First published: 1816
Genre: Novel

Locale: Scotland
Time: 1679
Plot: Historical

Henry Morton, a gallant young Scottish gentleman unwillingly involved in the revolt of the Covenanters against the Crown in 1679. After aiding John Balfour of Burley, the Covenanter leader and a friend of his dead father, Henry is arrested and sentenced for treason, but he is saved through the intercession of his sweetheart, Edith Bellenden. Still a prisoner, he witnesses the victory of the rebels. Henry is rescued by Balfour and made a member of their council. A moderate, he detests their violence but helps them take a castle peacefully and then leads an attack against the victorious royal forces. After the battle of Bothwell Bridge, Henry is sent into exile. He returns years later to find that Edith is about to marry his rival, Lord Evandale. Henry's attempt to save his rival from assassins fails, leaving him free to marry Edith.

Lady Margaret Bellenden, a staunch royalist, the mistress of Tillietudlem Castle. She lives in the past, when King Charles II visited the castle. Ousted from her estate by Covenanters and her unscrupulous turncoat relative, Basil Olifant, she is forced to live on charity until Basil's death.

Edith Bellenden, Lady Margaret's modest, attractive granddaughter and Henry Morton's sweetheart, who shares her family's royalist sympathies. When Henry is sentenced to die, she saves him by appealing to her other suitor, Lord Evandale, to intercede for him. While Henry is in exile in Holland, Basil Olifant lays claim to the Tillietudlem estates. Homeless, Edith and her grandmother are forced to live on the

charity of friends. When Henry returns, she refuses to marry Lord Evandale. The death of the young nobleman in a plot hatched by Olifant leaves Edith free to marry Henry.

Colonel John Grahame, called **Grahame of Claverhouse** or simply **Claverhouse**, the experienced, noble royalist soldier who sternly sentences Henry Morton to death. Gradually, he comes to respect Henry's personal honor, and he sees to it that Henry is exiled rather than shot after the defeat of the Covenanters at Bothwell Bridge. He later becomes the Jacobite rebel Viscount Dundee and leads his Highlanders against King William's troops. He is mortally wounded at the battle of Killiecrankie.

Lord Evandale, Henry's honorable young royalist rival for Edith Bellenden's hand. Having saved Henry from execution, Lord Evandale is rescued twice from the Covenanters by Henry. During Henry's exile, he gives financial aid to Edith and her aged grandmother. He is murdered by a party of assassins led by Basil Olifant.

John Balfour of Burley, the ambitious, fanatical Covenanter leader who befriends Henry Morton. A vengeful killer of royalists, he is unmerciful to his enemies. After his troops have been defeated at the battle of Bothwell Bridge, he goes into hiding. Later, having fallen out with Henry, the crazed Balfour is killed while attempting to escape after the murder of Lord Evandale by a band of vengeful Covenanters.

Basil Olifant, a villainous relation of the Bellenden family.

A turncoat, he joins the Covenanters and usurps the Bellenden estate. Threatened by Lord Evandale, Olifant ambushes him and orders the young nobleman's death. He himself is shot by a party of dragoons, led by Henry Morton, who arrive too late to prevent Lord Evandale's death.

Cuddie Headrigg, Henry Morton's resourceful, easygoing servant. He aids Henry during the Covenanter rebellion, saves him from murderous fanatics after the defeat, and eventually marries Edith Bellenden's pert maid, Jenny Dennison.

Mause Headrigg, Cuddie's outspoken Covenantist mother. She is forced to become a vagrant because of her harangues.

Major Bellenden, Edith's old, upright royalist uncle, who respects Henry Morton and tries to save him from execution. Later, he unsuccessfully defends Tillietudlem Castle.

Sergeant Francis Bothwell, the hardy, bullying royalist soldier who takes Henry Morton prisoner. He is killed by Balfour after being disarmed.

Cornet Grahame, Claverhouse's bold, gallant young nephew. He is unexpectedly shot by Balfour while trying to negotiate with the rebel leader under a flag of truce.

The Squire of Milnwood, Henry Morton's miserly uncle. Though a Covenanter by faith, he helps no one in those trou-bled times and berates Henry for giving John Balfour a place to sleep.

Wittenbold, the captain of a dragoon squad that tries, at Henry Morton's urging, to save Lord Evandale's life. The dragoons defeat the assassins at great loss.

Jenny Dennison, Edith's spirited, pretty maid. She marries Cuddie after he is released by the royalists. They have a number of children.

Mistress Alison Wilson, the squire's housekeeper at Milnwood. Though sharp-tongued and cranky, she is fond of Henry Morton.

Macbriar, a Covenanter leader who suffers torture rather than reveal John Balfour's hiding place after the defeat of the rebels.

The Duke of Monmouth, the royalist general who defeats the Covenanter forces at Bothwell Bridge.

Kettledrummle and

Poundtext, two fanatical Covenanter preachers inclined to verbosity and cruelty.

Mucklewrath, an insanely vengeful old Covenanter.

Old Mortality, the graveyard caretaker who supplies the author with the stories that form the core of the novel.

OLD SAINT PAUL'S: A Tale of the Plague and the Fire

Author: William Harrison Ainsworth (1805-1882)
First published: 1841
Genre: Novel

Locale: London, England
Time: Mid-seventeenth century
Plot: Historical

Stephen Bloundel, a London grocer whose beautiful daughter Amabel is sought by apprentice and nobleman alike. He does all he can to protect his family during the plague of 1665, but Amabel refuses to remain in the boarded-up house. She eventually dies of the plague.

Amabel, his beautiful daughter. She is in love with Wyvil, the earl of Rochester, who entices her to the vaults of St. Paul's, almost marries her, later kidnaps her, and at last marries her shortly before she dies of the plague.

Leonard Holt, Bloundel's apprentice. In love with Amabel, he prevents her first attempt to marry Wyvil. Plague-stricken, he is nursed by Nizza, whom he later rescues after her abduction by Sir Paul. Shocked by Amabel's death, he is nursed to health by Bloundel, whose partner he becomes. During the great London fire, he suggests to King Charles the plan of blowing up houses to halt the spread of fire. He saves Charles's life during the fire; for his heroism, he is dubbed Baron Argentine. He marries Nizza (Lady Isabella Argentine).

Maurice Wyvil, the earl of Rochester, a philanderer who plots to dishonor Amabel through amorous pretense of wooing and falsely wedding her. He is tricked into actually marrying her. After her death, he marries Mistress Mallet.

Sir Paul Parravicin (**Lord Argentine**), a bully, a companion of Wyvil and Lydyard. He is unaware that he is Nizza's brother.

Nizza Macascree (**Lady Isabella Argentine**), the beautiful foster daughter of Mike Macascree and sister of Sir Paul. She nurses Leonard during the plague, rejects an offer to become King Charles's mistress, and afterward marries Leonard.

Judith Malmayns, a wicked nurse who murders Amabel by infecting her with the plague.

Lydyard (**Sir George Etherege**), a philandering companion of Wyvil.

Major Pillichody, a low friend of Wyvil and Lydyard.

Chowles, a coffin maker.

Matthew Malmayns, the husband of Judith and sexton in St. Faith Cathedral.

Dr. Hodges, a physician. While attending young Stephen Bloundel, he reveals Wyvil's identity and his double pursuit of Amabel and Mistress Mallet.

Mistress Mallet, an heiress wooed and finally wed by Wyvil.

Mike Macascree, the blind foster father of Nizza.

Charles II, the king of England.

Thirlby, Judith's foster brother, the murderer of Isabella's husband. He is the father of Nizza and Sir Paul.

Isabella Morley Thirlby, the mother of Nizza (little Isabella) and Sir Paul.

THE OLD WIVES' TALE

Author: Arnold Bennett (1867-1931)
First published: 1908
Genre: Novel

Locale: England and Paris
Time: The nineteenth century
Plot: Naturalism

Sophia Baines, a high-spirited girl, the one member of the family strong enough to stand out against her father. Because she detests keeping a shop and domestic obligations, her parents finally allow her to become a schoolteacher. After her father's death, which is brought on by her carelessness, Sophia voluntarily returns to the shop as a penance. A brief, disillusioning marriage to Gerald Scales is followed by a long period in which Sophia has a successful business career in Paris. After a twenty-seven-year absence, she returns to Bursley (one of the "Five Towns" made famous by Arnold Bennett) and renews her dominance over her sister Constance. Sophia's death is, according to the sister, simply an expression of God's punishment for her willful ways.

Constance Baines, her older sister. A perfect foil for Sophia, Constance follows her sister in all things, short of violating her parents' iron rule. She does repulse her mother, however, in the matter of marrying Sam Povey. She is extraordinarily capable, except in managing her son; this phase of her life is distinguished by failure. In later years, life becomes more than the obese Constance cares to cope with, and she submits, with martyrdom, to sciatica, rheumatism, and Sophia.

John Baines, their father, the bedridden but influential proprietor of a draper's shop. He dominates the entire family. Whether from fear or respect, some member of his household has for many years constantly attended him. With his death, a new era begins for the family.

Mrs. Baines, his wife, who in actuality is the proprietor of the shop. Stern, authoritarian, and ever suspicious, she keeps the entire menage in line, except Sophia. By the time of Mrs. Baines's death, Constance is ready to step into her place.

Sam Povey, first an apprentice in the shop, later the proprietor, after his marriage to Constance. Under an appearance of quiet diffidence, he conceals an aggressive personality. Deeply involved in the tragic life of his cousin, he is respected and renowned throughout the community.

Charles Critchlow, the close friend and legal adviser to the Baines family. Indomitable and apparently indestructible, he is still on hand to deliver his acid estimate of Sophia when she returns to Bursley after her long absence.

Aunt Maria, a distant cousin of John Baines, who narrowly escapes being a nonentity by her availability to attend the invalid John. She is called "Aunt" as a convenience to the family.

Harriet Maddock, Mrs. Baines' sister, an overbearing, self-righteous widow assigned the care of Sophia, particularly to distract the young woman from marrying Gerald. That Sophia, even in successful maturity, is never able to face her aunt because of Sophia's childhood theft from her, speaks for the older woman's uncompromising will.

Gerald Scales, Sophia's husband, whom she met as a commercial traveler in the shop. Soon after their runaway marriage, Sophia sees him as unscrupulous and unstable. They part, in Paris, in less than a year, and Gerald is not seen again until he reappears, to die, an old man and a dissolute failure.

Maggie, a longtime servant in the Baines household. Engaged and then having her engagement broken eleven times, she finally marries a man of even lesser talents than hers.

Aline Chetwynd, the self-conscious, old-maid schoolteacher who is entrusted with Sophia's education. It is she who persuades Mrs. Baines that Sophia should not be wasted by a life in the shop.

Elizabeth Chetwynd, her older sister. Her marriage to the Reverend Archibald Jones lends prestige to Aline in her association with Mrs. Baines.

Lily Holl, Maggie's granddaughter, engaged to Dick Povey. Except for a fluke, Lily and Dick might have inherited a goodly share of Constance's wealth.

Dick Povey, Sam Povey's crippled nephew, who commands much sympathy and attention from his uncle. Dick's scheming attentions to Constance seem a poor reward for her husband's earlier care of the young man.

Cyril Povey, Constance and Sam's son. Thoroughly spoiled as a child and thoughtless and inconsiderate as a man, he is wholly indifferent to his mother's need for his affection.

Maria Insull, the assistant in the shop after Sam Povey's death; she marries Charles Critchlow.

Matthew Peel-Swynnerton, an occupant of the Pension Frensham, Sophia's fashionable tourist hotel in Paris. He is instrumental in reuniting Constance and Sophia.

THE OLD WIVES' TALE

Author: George Peele (1556-1596?)
First published: 1595
Genre: Drama

Locale: England
Time: Indeterminate
Plot: Comedy

Clunch, a smith who is generous, kind, and simple. He finds three pages lost in a wood and takes them to his hut.

Madge, Clunch's hospitable wife. Sleeping accommodations being limited, she entertains two of the boys with a fantastic story that becomes the main play.

Antic,
Frolic, and
Fantastic, the lost pages.

Sacrapant (SAK-ruh-pant), a wicked magician, probably borrowed from *Orlando furioso*, foreshadowing John Milton's Comus. Although young in appearance, when he is dead he becomes old and withered.

Delia (DEEL-yuh), also **Berecynthia** (BEHR-eh-SIHN-thee-uh), a beautiful captive girl, enchanted by Sacrapant. She is rescued by Eumenides and the Ghost of Jack.

Eumenides (ew-MEHN-ih-deez), a wandering knight in love with Delia. Generous and charitable, he pays for the funeral of a pauper, whose ghost becomes an improbable guardian angel and helps him destroy Sacrapant.

The Ghost of Jack, formerly an irresponsible, happy-go-lucky character. In gratitude for Eumenides' charity, he becomes the principal mover of the dramatic action.

Erestus (ee-REHS-tuhs), a young man enchanted by Sacrapant. Sometimes he is a white bear, sometimes an old man. He gives a cryptic prophecy to Eumenides to guide him to his love and his triumph.

Venelia (vehn-EE-lya), the betrothed of Erestus. Neither wife, widow, nor maid, she is able to break the Enchanter's glass and extinguish the light that sustains his enchantments, thereby releasing his victims.

Huanebango (wayn-eh-BANG-goh), a fantastic braggart. He speaks snatches of verse including nonsensical dactyllic hexameters. Trying to rescue Delia, he is deafened by Sacrapant. Instead of Delia, he gets Zantippa.

Corebus (KOHR-eh-buhs), also called **Booby**, a clown who has been a friend of Jack. Struck blind by Sacrapant's enchantment, he marries Celanta, whom be believes beautiful.

Lampriscus (lam-PRIHS-kuhs), a countryman. He sends his daughters to the enchanted well of life to find their fortune.

Zantippa (zan-TIHP-uh), Lampriscus' beautiful, shrewish daughter. She acquires a deaf husband, Huanebango, but no wealth.

Celanta (see-LAN-ta), Lampriscus' ugly, sweet-tempered daughter. She acquires a blind husband and great wealth.

Calypha (KAL-ih-fa) and

Thelea (THEE-lee-ah), Delia's brothers. They are captured by Sacrapant and rescued by Eumenides and Venelia.

Wiggen, Jack's friend who pleads for his proper burial.

Stephen Loach, an inflexible churchwarden.

Sexton, an uncharitable man. He refuses to bury Jack without his fee.

THE OLDEST LIVING GRADUATE

Author: Preston Jones (1936-1979)
First published: 1976
Genre: Drama

Locale: West Texas, particularly Bradleyville
Time: Summer, 1962
Plot: Representational

Colonel J. C. Kinkaid, an eccentric World War I veteran and the oldest living graduate of Mirabeau B. Lamar Military Academy. At the age of seventy-five, the colonel is senile, but his lack of touch with reality can be traced back as far as his return from fighting in the war. Bound to a wheelchair, the colonel is dependent on others, particularly his daughter-in-law, Maureen Kinkaid, and he usually greets these people with ill-tempered insults. The colonel slips in and out of reality, sometimes thinking that he is back in the war or talking to his dead elder son, Franklin, whose death in World War II causes him great guilt and some resentment toward his younger son, Floyd. He frequently asks to be driven to view his property by the lake, a site that others consider to be worthless except for the potential development that Floyd is planning secretly with his new business partner. The colonel reveals to the handyman, Mike Tremaine, that the lot was once settled by a French family and that the colonel was very much in love with the daughter. As the oldest living graduate of his military academy, the colonel is approached to be the focus of a large dedication ceremony, organized by Floyd, who intends to exploit the occasion for the predicted publicity and business contacts. In a rare lucid moment, Colonel Kinkaid realizes for the first time what it means that he is the oldest living graduate: that all of his friends are dead. He then withdraws from the ceremony. At the end of the play, the colonel is dying, having suffered a stroke while at a lodge meeting of the Knights of the White Magnolia.

Floyd Kinkaid, a powerful businessman in the fictional town of Bradleyville, Texas, and the younger son of Colonel Kinkaid. Described as thin and nervous, Floyd is forty-two years old. He took over the colonel's business interests when his father became unable to manage his own affairs. Because the business runs itself, Floyd has become bored; in addition to expensive hobbies such as horse racing and boating, he looks toward new business ventures for excitement. His goal is to turn the colonel's cherished lake property into a lakefront resort. Not understanding why the colonel will not sell this land, Floyd resorts to obtaining the property secretly by having his father declared legally incompetent. After he discovers that his father is dying, Floyd tells the old man that he will not sell the property after all. Floyd cares for his father but is frustrated by the old man's senility and eccentricity.

Maureen Kinkaid, Floyd's wife. Floyd and Maureen were high school sweethearts, but their courtship was interrupted by World War II; they were married right after he returned. The fact that the marriage has produced no children is a source of conflict between them, but for the most part Maureen loves Floyd and supports him in his business ventures. Maureen is, however, very bored and is disgusted with the superficial and hypocritical country club scene. She has forced Floyd to take vacations to Europe and the Caribbean, trips he hated. Maureen cares for and respects the colonel despite his difficulty. Maureen sees through Floyd's excitement about the ceremony and admonishes him for taking the colonel's property.

Clarence Sickenger, a wealthy businessman and Floyd's new partner. Physically a large man, at forty-three years of age Clarence is shallow and unscrupulous. He does not understand Maureen's objections to Floyd's unethical actions and tells her to think of the pretty things she can buy.

Martha Ann Sickenger, Clarence's wife. A bit wild in high school, Martha Ann flunked out of college after one semester, returned to Bradleyville, and married Clarence, sixteen years her senior. They have two children and appear to be happy, sharing the same superficial interests. Martha Ann loves living in Bradleyville, gossips incessantly, and cannot understand why Maureen puts up with the crabby colonel.

Mike Tremaine, the owner of a small farm and the Kinkaids' hired hand. Mike always treats the colonel with consideration and respect. The colonel likes Mike and remembers going fishing with Mike's father.

— Lou Thompson

OLDTOWN FOLKS

Author: Harriet Beecher Stowe (1811-1896)
First published: 1869
Genre: Novel

Locale: Massachusetts
Time: Late eighteenth century
Plot: Regional

Horace Holyoke, the narrator of this social chronicle of post-Revolutionary War New England. Born to poverty, he is ten when his schoolteacher father dies. Thanks to his abilities, his industry, and the benefaction of friends, he attends Harvard and at last becomes a successful lawyer.

Harry Percival, Horace's closest friend. Harry's mother, brought to America after an elopement and secret marriage, is deserted by her English officer husband and dies, leaving Harry and his sister. They are brought up with Horace, and the boys attend Harvard together. Harry's legitimacy is established, and on the death of his father, he goes to England as Sir Harry.

Eglantine (Tina) Percival, Harry's sister, who is loved by Horace. She marries another man, but he dies after ten years of unhappy marriage; two years later, she and Horace are married.

Ellery Davenport, handsome and clever and a grandson of Jonathan Edwards. He holds a succession of diplomatic posts abroad, and so is able to aid Harry with information about his father. Upon the death of his mad wife, he marries Tina; almost immediately, a girl he had seduced appears with their child, whom Tina generously takes. Unprincipled and ambitious, Ellery is close to madness when he is killed in a political duel.

Esther Avery, the daughter of a minister. She is a close friend of Tina, Harry, and Horace. She marries Harry and goes to England with him.

Mr. Lothrop, the minister and leading citizen of Oldtown, sedate and sensible.

Mrs. Lothrop, his wife and Ellery's cousin. She is called "Lady Lothrop" by the people of Oldtown, a not disrespectful allusion to her aristocratic Boston background and her lingering adherence to the Church of England. She promises to provide for Harry's clothing and education.

Deacon Badger, Harry's grandfather, a leading farmer and miller of Oldtown, in whose home Horace lives after his father's death. He is serene and affable.

Mrs. Badger, Horace's grandmother, who is a strict Puritan Calvinist. The Badgers take in Harry and Tina when they are found in a deserted house in which they took refuge. Harry stays on with them.

Susy Badger Holyoke, their daughter and Horace's mother. Her beauty faded because of hardship and poverty, she returns to her parents with her children after her husband's death.

Miss Mehitable Rossiter, the daughter of a former minister of Oldtown. Her life has been saddened by the disappearance some years before of her half sister. She adopts Tina.

Emily Rossiter, Mehitable's half sister, who appears with her child by Ellery shortly after his marriage to Tina. Tina uses her newly inherited fortune to establish the sisters in a house near Boston.

Sir Harry Percival, the worthless and dissipated father of Harry and Tina. Deserting his wife and children, he takes the wedding certificate and leaves a letter denying the legality of the marriage. Only a "younger son" at the time of the elopement, he succeeds to the family title and property.

Caleb (Old Crab) Smith, a miser, in whose house Harry's mother dies. He decides to keep the boy as a field hand.

Miss Asphyxia Smith, Caleb's sister. She takes in Tina, but the children are so harshly treated that they run away.

Bill Holyoke, Horace's older brother. He gives little promise as a scholar and so goes to work on the farm with his uncle Jacob.

Jacob Badger, Horace's uncle, the son of Mr. and Mrs. Badger.

Sam Lawson, the village handyman and do-nothing. Called shiftless by some, he is Horace's chief comfort in the days after his father's death. Sam is never too busy to tell stories to the small boys or to take them hunting and fishing.

Keziah Badger, one of Mr. and Mrs. Badger's unmarried daughters. Romantic-minded, she has a reputation for homeliness in the village.

Lois Badger, Keziah's sister, who also is a spinster. She is sharp-tongued but warm-hearted.

Jonathan Rossiter, Miss Mehitable's half brother and master of the academy in Cloudland. Horace and Harry study there and live with him.

Mr. Avery, the minister at Cloudland and Esther's father. Tina boards with him.

Madame Kittery, Mrs. Lothrop's mother. The children are taken to visit her in Boston as a special Easter treat. She takes an interest in Horace and provides money to send him to Harvard.

Major Broad and

Squire Jones, friends who meet in the spacious Badger kitchen to discuss politics, religion, and philosophy.

OLIVER TWIST: Or, The Parish Boy's Progress

Author: Charles Dickens (1812-1870)
First published: 1838; serial form, 1837-1839
Genre: Novel

Locale: England, especially London
Time: Early nineteenth century
Plot: Social realism

Oliver Twist, a workhouse foundling, the helpless, abused hero of the novel. Both innocent and morally sensible, he gives force and sharpness, as well as a full measure of sentimentality, to Dickens' vision of social injustice. Exploited from birth by the selfish managers of the poor farm and workhouse, he is apprenticed to a mortician. Treated cruelly, he runs off to London, where he is taken in by a gang of thieves. Falsely arrested as a pickpocket, he is rescued for a time by Mr.

Brownlow and then recaptured by the thieves. He is wounded during a burglary attempt and saved from arrest by Mrs. Maylie and her adopted daughter, who care for him until the mystery of his birth is solved and the criminals are taken or killed. Mr. Brownlow offers him a permanent home.

Mr. Brownlow, the kindhearted, benevolent man who delivers Oliver Twist from a vicious judge, gives him care and trust, solves the question of his parentage, and finally adopts him.

Mrs. Maylie, the gentle, good-hearted woman who takes Oliver in after he has been wounded and is being hunted as a burglar. She sees that he is happy and cared for until he finds a lasting home with Mr. Brownlow.

Rose Maylie, her adopted daughter, the tender, lovely girl who nurses Oliver and helps expose the treachery that surrounds him. Later, it turns out that she is really Oliver's aunt.

Harry Maylie, Mrs. Maylie's wastrel son, who later becomes a clergyman and marries his foster sister Rose.

Fagin, a greasy, sinister old Jew who trains boys for stealing and receives stolen goods. Paid to bring Oliver up as a thief, he fails to retake the boy after a burglary attempt. He is finally executed by the law for complicity in a murder.

Bill Sikes, Fagin's accomplice, the leader of Fagin's band of trained thieves. A violent, brutal man, he deserts Oliver after the attempted burglary. Later, he kills his mistress Nancy because he believes she has betrayed him. Haunted by guilt, he accidentally hangs himself while trying to escape the law.

Nancy, a female thief, a member of Fagin's gang. She befriends Oliver and informs on Fagin's activities in order to save the boy. Although she remains loyal to Bill Sikes, he murders her in a rage.

Monks, whose real name is **Edward Leeford**, Oliver Twist's stepbrother. A vengeful person, he plots with Fagin against Oliver to keep the boy from his inheritance. In the end, he confesses his villainy, makes restitution, moves to America, and eventually dies in prison.

Mr. Bumble, the vain, bullying almshouse beadle who mistreats Oliver at every opportunity. He meets his match, however, when he marries Mrs. Corney, a workhouse matron. The two become paupers and end their days in the workhouse.

Mrs. Corney, his wife, formerly a vixenish workhouse matron.

Mr. Grimwig, Mr. Brownlow's gruff old friend, who speaks harshly against Oliver but wishes him well.

Mrs. Bedwin, Mr. Brownlow's warm-hearted housekeeper, who comforts frightened, lonely Oliver.

Mr. Losberne, "The Doctor," a fat, good-hearted surgeon and the Maylies' family friend. He speaks roughly to Oliver Twist but cures his wound and saves him from the police.

Mrs. Mann, the alcoholic matron who keeps the poor farm where Oliver lives for a time.

Mr. Sowerberry, the mortician who takes Oliver as his apprentice and meekly befriends him. He makes thin, pale, sad-looking Oliver a mourner at children's funerals.

Mrs. Sowerberry, his wife, a shrew.

Noah Claypole, a lumpish bully charity boy who runs away from the mortician and becomes a member of Fagin's gang.

Charlotte, Mrs. Sowerberry's servant, who also misuses Oliver. She marries Noah Claypole.

Jack Dawkins, called the **Artful Dodger**, the clever young pickpocket who leads Oliver Twist to Fagin.

Charley Bates, the Artful Dodger's boisterous friend and assistant.

Mr. Fang, the cruel judge who tries Oliver Twist when he is charged with picking pockets. Mr. Brownlow, appearing as a witness, pities Oliver and, when his innocence is proved, takes the boy home with him.

Toby Crackit, the burglar who accompanies Oliver Twist and Bill Sikes on the attempted robbery of the Maylie house.

Old Sally, the beggar, present when Oliver Twist is born, who steals the tokens that eventually disclose his parentage.

Agnes Fleming, Oliver's unwed mother. She dies in childbirth in a workhouse.

Mr. Leeford, Oliver Twist's father, unhappily married and separated from his wife when he falls in love with Agnes Fleming. After he dies suddenly in Rome, his wife and son destroy a will that provides for Agnes and her unborn child.

Mrs. Leeford, the jealous, vindictive wife who tries to deprive Agnes Fleming and her child of their inheritance.

OMENSETTER'S LUCK

Author: William H. Gass (1924-   )
First published: 1966
Genre: Novel

Locale: Gilean, Ohio, a river town
Time: Late 1880's and early 1890's
Plot: Symbolic realism

The Reverend Jethro Furber, a fiery preacher from Cleveland who despairs of his assignment to Gilean, an Ohio River town. Short, pale, bone-thin, and intellectual, Furber uses his Sunday sermons to excoriate his parishioners, but he does not believe one word he preaches. A master of the dramatic and rhetorical turn, Furber is a jumble of contradictions: a devil-worshiping minister, a philosophical relativist, a skeptic, and a cynic. Like a small child working a puzzle, he has trouble holding together his complex "modern" parts. Despairing of human love and brotherhood, he is a misanthrope who simultaneously hates and envies his congregational "cows." Unloved and neglected as a child, Furber developed an inferiority complex that manifests itself in paranoia, delusions, and

a negative self-image: He sees himself as a clumsy, comic buffoon who aspires to the lightness and grace of ballet. His paranoia leads to a unilateral attack on Brackett Omensetter, whom he views as a competing religionist. Furber spreads lies about Omensetter's supposed black magical powers to mobilize public opinion against him. Furber is an Old Testament scholar who enjoys reading biblical passages about violence and family bloodletting. When the opportunity arises to deal Omensetter a fatal blow, however, he retreats; he is the theoretician par excellence, not a man of action. He strikes a deal with Omensetter: Omensetter and family can leave town once Henry Pimber's body is recovered and properly buried. While defending Omensetter from Sheriff Curtis Chamlay's search party, Furber suffers a mental breakdown. Later, he disappears from Gilean.

Brackett Omensetter, a leatherworker with extraordinary luck who goes to work for the local blacksmith, Matthew Watson. A large, wide, and happy man, Omensetter habitually spreads out his big arms as if to gather in the entire world; his every word and gesture bespeak his humanity and love of life. Charismatic, he is irresistible to the locals, but his natural saintliness makes them envious and suspicious. They believe that he is protecting a secret. As instinctual, spontaneous, and magical as he appears initially, he is a mere mortal, like Adam, made of clay. The townspeople's hostility wears away at him. He is systematically excluded from everything communal, from horseshoe pitching to fishing, and his primitive side gives way. Meeting Henry Pimber to pay his rent on the fatal day, Omensetter dons conventional clothing; suddenly, Pimber realizes that there is nothing extraordinary about him. Later, after discovering Henry's body hanging from an oak, Omensetter turns to his adversary, Furber, for protection and abetment. Furber's insane defense and the reasoned argument of Truxton Orcutt, the local physician, enable Omensetter to elude a murder charge. Meanwhile, the Omensetter baby, Amos, miraculously survives a bout with diphtheria, and the family moves downriver.

Israbestis Tott, the town postmaster and "historian." Thin, womanish, and with broken teeth, Tott, a born storyteller, takes town events and personages to make a subjective, poetic history of the local and familiar. Omensetter's story is Tott's creation. Telling stories many times over, Tott supplies new data when the "facts" escape him. The ambiguous saga of the Omensetter cradle and the mystery of how Lucy Pimber obtained it fire his imagination. He wonders if all of his stories are as "wrong" as this one, alluding to the entwined problematic of ethical behavior and ethical narration: how the narrator-historian chooses to fill gaps in his story. Ethics is really the least of Tott's concerns; like Furber and Henry Pimber, he is a cruel, childish egotist who considers people mere words to populate his narratives. The auctioning of Lucy Pimber's belongings after her death visibly upsets him, for the objects of his local history are being divided up and sold. Out of touch, Tott, the romantic aesthete, takes refuge from life by living imaginatively within the cracks and plaster chips of his bedroom wall. Totally dissatisfied with this life, he understands that his imagination imprisons and paralyzes him intellectually

and emotionally. Finally, he acts, taking Dr. Orcutt to tend to the Omensetter baby.

Henry Pimber, a local landowner. He rents to Omensetter the old Perkins place, a dilapidated house on a flood-prone, swampy stretch of the Ohio River. Psychologically cannibalized by his wife, Lucy—like her vegetables, he is canned, stored, and then consumed—Henry is "tea-weak" and has little desire to live. As an ironic reversal of the Prufrock type, however, he is prone to sudden, violent action. His actions, however, are stupid and mistaken; he simply makes the wrong choices—and always has. For example, he shoots to death a fox that has fallen into the well at the Perkins' place. (The shooting prefigures his own suicide, because Henry identifies psychologically with the imprisoned animal.) The force of the shotgun blast drives a stone shard up and into his arm. As a result, he develops lockjaw and almost dies. Omensetter saves his life by placing a beet poultice in his palms. Thereafter, Pimber is never the same. Full of self-pity and remorse for past wrongdoing, he hangs himself seventy feet up in a white oak. His suicide is a cowardly escape from Lucy and a guilty conscience. Like Furber, he is a supreme egotist—he would have made a better Omensetter. A romantic at heart, he envied Omensetter for the wrong reasons, mistakenly equating him with the noble savage.

Lucy Pimber, Henry's wife. Thin, silent, snow-white, cold, and barren, she persecutes her husband, and everyone around her, for her inability to bear children. Her obsession with canning is symptomatic of her latent desire to preserve all living things in the death state. She figuratively suffocates Henry, turning him into a zombie. Her concern for Omensetter's unborn baby is purely selfish—she would carry, bear, and rear the baby herself if she could. Her every gesture is a figure in a tableau of desire. On his final day, she sends Henry off to collect the rent from Omensetter. She is ungrateful to Omensetter for saving Henry's life. When Henry fails to return, she seals herself away in the house as if in a canning jar. Furber finally breaks the lock and extricates the ghastly Lucy, bedraggled and stinking of feces. Physically rejuvenated by book's end, she is paid a final visit by the Reverend Jethro Furber, who offers her the rent money found in Henry's lifeless fist. She refuses the sum but counts it, pleased that Henry had bilked Omensetter of such a large amount.

— *Dennis Ryan*

OMOO: A Narrative of Adventures in the South Seas

Author: Herman Melville (1819-1891)
First published: 1847
Genre: Novel

Locale: Tahiti and the South Seas
Time: Early 1840's
Plot: Adventure

Herman Melville, an American sailor who is rescued from a cannibal island by the crew of a British whaler, the *Julia*, and who signs on the ship as a deck hand. He is soon relieved of duty because of lameness in his leg. Conditions on the ship are bad, so Melville and the rest of the crew put ashore at Papeetee, on the island of Tahiti, and are imprisoned when they refuse to return to their ship. After the ship sails away with a new crew, Melville and the other sailors are freed by their Tahitian jailer. Later, Melville and his friend, Doctor Long

Ghost, have several adventures in the islands together. Melville finally ships on a whaler that will take him to Japan and eventually home. In the course of his island-hopping, he becomes convinced that the natives have been corrupted by their contact with the white missionaries and were better off as primitive pagans.

Doctor Long Ghost, the ship's doctor on the British whaler that rescues Melville. The doctor becomes Melville's close friend and companion in his adventures. The doctor tries to sign on the same ship with Melville when Melville decides to leave the islands, but the captain refuses to allow the doctor to sign on, either as a deck hand or as ship's doctor, and he is left behind.

Captain Bob, the jailer of Melville and the rest of the crew on the island of Tahiti. He is jolly and easy-going; after the whaler sails away, the old man frees his prisoners.

John Jermin, first officer of the British whaler.

ON DISTANT GROUND

Author: Robert Olen Butler (1945-　　)
First published: 1985
Genre: Novel

Locale: Baltimore, Maryland, and Saigon, Vietnam
Time: 1975
Plot: Psychological realism

David Fleming, an Army intelligence officer on trial for aiding the enemy. Aloof and incapable of closeness, David finds his life changed irrevocably one day in Bien Hoa when he enters a six-by-six-foot cell that recently had held an important Vietcong prisoner, Pham Van Tuyen. Moving aside the rice stand to find "Hygiene is healthful" scratched on the wall, David feels an inexplicable bond with the man courageous enough to write these words, a bond that becomes an obsession. David searches for Tuyen, eventually finding the newly escaped prisoner and escorting him to safety, jeopardizing his own career and even his life. Despite David's otherwise spotless record, he is court-martialed, though not imprisoned. During his trial, David and his wife Jennifer have a baby, David, Jr. David's physical and spiritual connection with the baby is so strong that he intuitively realizes that he has another son in rapidly collapsing South Vietnam. This recognition overshadows the trial, now merely an obstacle to his discovery of that son, the offspring of an affair with a wealthy and influential Vietnamese woman, Suong. With the help of Central Intelligence Agency operative Kenneth Trask, David is able to enter Saigon as Canadian David Crowley shortly before the city's fall. In the final days of Saigon, he discovers not only his son but also the answer to who he really is and why he saved the life of Tuyen. Refusing at first to believe that he is the father of a child who bears no physical resemblance to him, David comes face to face with his own egocentrism, an echo of his own father's distance from him. His rejection of this child becomes linked with his bond for Tuyen, now merely a reflection of his own mind, its detachment and its irony. David's redemption comes in his acceptance of the child of Suong on the night they try to escape and more clearly the following day, when he and Tuyen, who is now in charge of all Saigon-Gia Dinh security, meet alone for the first time since David helped him escape. He discovers that his connection with Tuyen had been erroneous, that Tuyen had not written those words in the cell; however, in their mutual respect for the brave man who had, the Vietcong and the American understand each other. Tuyen gives David and his son safe passage out of the country, and David and Tuyen embrace as they part. All along, David had felt that his link with Tuyen had enabled him to break

down the barriers he had placed between himself and other people and had allowed him to leave himself vulnerable to loving Jennifer. During the trial, he had once again become distant. His reunion with Tuyen and his union with his child Khai break through those obstacles, reuniting him with Jennifer and with his son David.

Pham Van Tuyen, an important Vietcong prisoner whose escape is aided by David Fleming. Tuyen later becomes director of security for Saigon-Gia Dinh and enables David and his Vietnamese son to escape. Although Tuyen did not write the words that influenced David's decision to help him, his respect for the man who did reestablishes his bond with David. The unsuperstitious communist reluctantly admits to being the son of a father who would have seen David as a magical being who appears in one's life in the most unusual times and in the most unusual ways, and his embrace with David upon the American's departure confirms their spiritual connection.

Jennifer Fleming, David's wife. The daughter of a wealthy but indifferent father, Jennifer stands by David during the trial and, despite her fears of losing her husband to the Vietnamese woman and her child, begs her father for money so that David can go to Vietnam to find his child after the trial is over.

Nguyen Thi Tuyet Suong, an influential Vietnamese woman with whom David has a brief affair. As a strong opponent of Thieu's regime, Suong is put into prison and killed before David returns to Vietnam to find their child, four-year-old Khai.

Carl Lomas, an Army attorney assigned to represent David after he had dismissed the civilian attorneys supplied by his father-in-law. Frustrated by David's refusal or inability to defend himself, Lomas does his best. He brings the news media into the trial, saving David from a prison sentence or possible execution.

Wilson Hand, a soldier captured by the Vietcong while serving under David. He testifies about his dramatic rescue by David, in which David killed three Vietcong without remorse.

Clifford Wilks, who defected to the Vietcong while serving under David.

— *Jaquelyn W. Walsh*

ON HEROES AND TOMBS
(Sobre héroes y tumbas)

Author: Ernesto Sábato (1911-　　)
First published: 1961
Genre: Novel

Locale: Buenos Aires and Patagonia, Argentina
Time: Primarily 1953-1955
Plot: Psychological realism

Martín del Castillo (mahr-TEEN dehl kahs-TEE-yoh), the sensitive young man whose relationship with the mysterious Alejandra Vidal Olmos provides the focus of the book. Martín, seventeen years old when he meets Alejandra in 1953, hates his mother and has no respect for his father; he lives on his own, in poverty. Until he meets Alejandra, he regards women as either pure and heroic or as gossiping deceivers. He has some weeks of happiness with Alejandra, but his enigmatic lover finally casts him aside brutally. His attraction to her is like the fascination exerted by a dark abyss, and she takes him to the verge of suicide. His attempt, with Bruno's help, to heal himself and to understand what has happened to him and to Alejandra provides the intellectual problem of the novel.

Alejandra Vidal Olmos (ah-leh-HAHN-drah vee-DAHL OHL-mohs), the daughter of a decayed branch of an old family of the Argentine oligarchy. Alejandra is eighteen years old when she meets Martín and is an exotic beauty: She has long black hair with reddish tones, dark gray-green eyes, a pale face, a large mouth, and high cheekbones. She is a mysterious figure, exerting an almost occult influence on Martín. He never understands her puzzling personality and enigmatic lifestyle. She lives in the old family home, once a mansion but now a ruin located in an area of factories and tenements. Her family is lost in a time warp. Its members possess the manners and memories of the old Argentina; their aristocratic gentility only brings ruin in the materialistic modern world. Alejandra realizes that her family lives in a world that no longer exists, yet she detests the new Argentine elite. Alejandra's beauty is vitalized by violent movements and shifts of personality, from laughing lightheartedness to cruelty and anger, from self-hatred to ennui and remoteness. Martín finally understands that she is locked into an incestuous relationship with her father. In June, 1955, she kills her father with a gun and then commits suicide by setting fire to the family home.

Fernando Vidal Olmos, Alejandra's father. Fernando is fifty-five years old in 1955, with a hard, powerful, handsome face; white hair; and mysterious beauty. Alejandra is his daughter by Georgina, his first cousin, who is a carbon copy of both his mother and his daughter. His relationship with every-one is marked by cruelty and lack of affection. Bruno, who has known him and his family since they were children together, describes him as alienated from everything most people consider to be the real world and says that part of his madness is that of Argentina pushed to the extreme. Fernando's obsessions dominate his life. He narrates the third part of the book, "Report on the Blind," which takes the reader into the mind of the paranoid madman. He has been obsessed by blindness from the days of his youth, when he blinded birds with a needle. He believes that the world is controlled by a secret sect of the blind; that nothing happens by accident; and that the blind spy, persecute, and determine everyone's destiny.

Bruno Bassán (bahs-SAHN), an unpublished writer from a prosperous family. Bruno, a pensive man with a gentle, ironic air, grew up with Fernando and Georgina, whom he loved. He provides the philosophic comments of the book (life is lived as a rough draft without a chance to rewrite, he says), helps Martín understand the nature of the trauma of his relationship with Alejandra, and helps Martín reconcile himself to the inevitable tragedies of the doomed Vidal and Olmos families. While Bruno experiences and describes the meaninglessness of existence, he regards hope as concomitant with despair; if humans are condemned to despair, they are armed with hope.

Uncle Bebe (beh-BEH),

Grandfather Pancho (PAHN-choh), and

Aunt Escolástica (ehs-koh-LAHS-tee-kah), members of Alejandra's family, representing Argentina's past and the madness inherent in the Argentine character pushed to the extreme. Uncle Bebe, a gentle madman, wanders through the crumbling mansion playing a clarinet. Grandfather Pancho, ninety-five years old, lives entirely in the past, endlessly repeating stories of the wars in early Argentine history. Escolástica was a mad recluse. In 1852, during the civil wars, Escolástica's father was killed by his enemies, who threw his head into his family's parlor. Her mother died of shock, and Escolástica seized the head and fled to the garret. She lived with the head, never leaving the room, until she died in 1932. The family still has the head in its possession when Martín meets Alejandra.

— *William E. Pemberton*

ON THE EVE
(Nakanune)

Author: Ivan Turgenev (1818-1883)
First published: 1860
Genre: Novel

Locale: Moscow, the surrounding countryside, and Venice
Time: June, 1853, to 1859
Plot: Psychological realism

Andrey Petrovich Bersenev (ahn-DRAY peh-TROH-vihch behr-SEH-nehv), who is twenty-three years old when he is introduced, tall and swarthy, with a sharp, slightly curved nose, broad lips, and small gray eyes. He speaks with a slight lisp that becomes more marked when he is agitated. His mother died when he was quite young, and under the insistent guidance of his father he received a thorough education. He is a graduate of Moscow University. He is inclined to take an abstract and generalized view of life. Although he tries to win Yelena's favor, he feels awkward and uneasy in her presence. She admires his intellectual attainments, but once he tells her about Insarov, she turns instead to the other man. Bersenev eventually takes up scholarly pursuits abroad, and research in Germany and France yields ponderous though learned articles of some length.

Pavel Yakovlevich Shubin (PAH-vehl ya-KOV-leh-vihch SHEW-bihn), a fair-haired and childishly attractive man, twenty-six years old at the beginning of the novel. He is a cousin three times removed of Anna Vasil'yevna. He studied medicine at Moscow University but for academic reasons was forced to leave after one year; instead, he took up art and achieved some recognition for his undeniable talent. He works at sculpture and produces various works, including satirical representations of Insarov, Anna, and himself. He remains a confidant of Bersenev, and they often discuss social and romantic matters. Although he is attracted to Yelena, he places himself in a false position and makes little headway among others who are interested in her. In the end, he settles in Rome, where he is known as a promising young artist.

Yelena Nikolayevna Stakhova (yeh-LEH-nah nih-koh-LAH-yehv-nah STAH-khoh-vah), a twenty-year-old woman who becomes Insarov's wife. She is tall, with a pale complexion, large gray eyes, straight features, and a sharp chin; she has dark brown hair and a delicate neck, as well as slender hands and feet. Shubin complains that her likeness is difficult to recapture in sculpture; indeed, Yelena appears subject to impetuous, almost feverish changes of mood that are not readily comprehensible to others. She has become impatient with her parents' strictures, and she can be stern and unbending; she is also distinguished by an unflinching sense of honor and integrity. She displays great solicitude to people who are in any way unfortunate, and she goes to some lengths to protect homeless or mistreated animals. Her sense of personal independence probably plays a part in her deepening attachment to Insarov; she willingly parts company with those who would object and secretly marries him. As a devoted wife, she travels with him to Venice, where she cares for him during his final illness. Afterward, faithful to his memory, she resolves to become a nurse and care for sick and wounded soldiers, rather than return to Russia.

Dmitry Nikanorovich Insarov (DMIH-tree nih-ka-NOH-roh-vihch ihn-SAH-rov), a twenty-five-year-old Bulgarian student. When he was eight years old, his mother disappeared and was found murdered. His father was executed after an altercation with a Turkish official. Later, Insarov lived with his aunt in Kiev, then returned to Bulgaria for two years. It is rumored that during that time he was at some personal risk; though he will not openly discuss such matters, a large scar on his neck apparently was received during a confrontation with Ottoman officials. He leaves the impression of an iron will and proud sense of personal self-sufficiency; he rarely mentions his own experiences but readily will hold forth on his country's problems and prospects. He speaks Russian clearly and correctly, though in guttural tones that suggest his foreign origins. He is described as gaunt and angular, with an aquiline nose, straight black hair, and small, deep-set eyes. Although he evinces a disarming frankness, he can also appear somewhat mysterious, and it is possibly this combination of qualities that makes him attractive to Yelena. After the outbreak of the Crimean War, he considers returning to Bulgaria, as his friends there

have urged him to do, but complications arise from the state of his health. After Yelena has become his wife, they visit Italy before he succumbs, after some valiant struggles, to aneurism and lung disease.

Anna Vasil'yevna Stakhova (vah-SIH-lehv-nah), the wife of Nikolay and Yelena's mother. She was orphaned at the age of seven and came to enjoy a considerable inheritance. She was educated at a boarding school and by a governess. She is small and thin, with a taut, mournful disposition. Her marriage to Nikolay evidently was the result of an infatuation; as the mother of Yelena, she has exerted progressively less influence over her, until her daughter paid little heed to her. When she later learns that Yelena has married Insarov, Anna becomes ill for a brief period.

Nikolay Artem'yevich Stakhov (nih-koh-LAY ahr-TEHM-yeh-vihch STAH-kov), Anna's husband and the father of Yelena. He entered military school when he was sixteen years old and then became an ensign in the imperial guards. He met Anna at a social ball and married her when he was twenty-five; in time, they moved to her house in Moscow. He had hoped to find a suitable and well-placed husband for Yelena. He has, none too discreetly, carried on affairs and maintained mistresses on the side.

Zoya Nikitishna Myuller (ZOH-yeh nih-KIH-tih-shnah MYEW-lur), an eighteen-year-old woman of German and Russian ancestry who is one of Yelena's companions. She is described as blonde, plump, and of fair complexion. Occasionally, she flirts with young men. When Shubin is found in her arms, his hopes for winning Yelena's favor are effectively dashed. Some people object to Zoya's German ways, but in the end she marries Kurnatovsky and defers entirely to his wishes.

Yegor Andreyevich Kurnatovsky (yeh-GOHR an-DREH-yeh-vihch kewr-nah-TOV-skee), a thirty-three-year-old who had a legal education and has become a first secretary with the rank of counselor. Nikolay holds him in some esteem because of his social standing and regards him as probably the best possible suitor for Yelena. When she meets him, Yelena distrusts him and regards him as morally obtuse. He finally marries Zoya instead.

Uvar Ivanovich Stakhov (uh-VAHR ee-VAH-noh-vihch), one of Nikolay's distant cousins. He is a retired military man who seems to have yielded to corpulence and slothfulness. He appears to change little during the entire period of the novel.

— *J. R. Broadus*

ON THE ROAD

Author: Jack Kerouac (1922-1969)
First published: 1957
Genre: Novel

Locale: The United States
Time: 1947-1950
Plot: Autobiographical

Sal Paradise, the narrator, a young and aspiring writer. Sal is the prototypical innocent, the romantic naïf who learns about life through his associations with Dean Moriarty and other friends. After Sal meets Dean in the winter of 1947, they begin a series of cross-country journeys, by bus and by car, that make up whatever plot the novel can be said to have. Sal is searching for life, and he admires Dean Moriarty, the man who has found "it," some special spiritual connection to life. Sal briefly rests in Dean's energetic, almost frantic glow.

Dean Moriarty, a drifter, Sal's friend, traveling companion, and inspiration. Dean represents the center of the Beat movement to Sal. He is a young man who has lived a full life for his few years: He has been through numerous jobs, women, prisons, and travels, and his adventures continue after he begins the cross-country trips with Sal. He is like a burning comet, seeking the ultimate experiences of life—through drugs, sex, music (jazz), or whatever else is at hand. Based on the real-life Neal Cassady (as Sal Paradise is a thinly veiled

Jack Kerouac), Dean seems destined to burn himself out. He also figures in the great American tradition of the hustler or flimflam man. In the end, he deceives and disappoints Sal, as all heroes ultimately must, by abandoning him when Sal is sick in Mexico. Dean nevertheless remains Sal's brother, the lost father figure, the hip, cool, mad saint in search of some spiritual and joyous center of life. His frantic, almost boundless energy sparks anyone close to him and gives a certain electric momentum to the novel's prose. Dean is an original in American fiction, although it would be difficult to live with him (as various women in the novel discover).

Carlo Marx, a friend of Sal and Dean, a poet (based on Beat poet Allen Ginsberg) who holds marathon discussion sessions with Dean and shares with him the frenetic search for life's meaning.

Teresa (Terry), a young Mexican woman whom Sal meets on a bus to Los Angeles and with whom he lives for a few months as they toil as migrant workers in California.

Remi Boncoeur, a friend, living near San Francisco, with whom Sal briefly lives and works.

Bull Lee, a mutual friend with whom they stay in Louisiana, a kind of guru figure who is a heavy user of drugs. He is based on novelist William Burroughs.

Camille,

Inez, and

Marylou, women in Dean's life; at one time he lives with, loves, or marries each of them.

Ed Dunkel and

Galatea Dunkel, who are among the people that Sal, Dean, and the rest meet in their endless transcontinental trips.

— *David Peck*

THE ONCE AND FUTURE KING

Author: T. H. White (1906-1964)
First published: 1958
Genre: Novels

Locale: England
Time: The Middle Ages
Plot: Arthurian romance

The Sword in the Stone, 1938

Arthur, the son of the warrior chieftain Uther Pendragon. He is known simply as **Wart**, the son of the warrior chieftain Uther Pendragon. He is known simply as **Wart**, the boy who will become King Arthur. A typical boy—mischievous, curious, kindly, brave, and innocent—he spends the story being trained by Merlyn to understand the lesson that justice and fairness are better than the warrior's "might makes right" philosophy of the warring tribes.

Merlyn, the magician whose job it is to educate Wart.

Merlyn initiates a plan to civilize the assortment of savage Celtic tribes by gradually unifying them under a common cause and a single king. He is a kindly, absentminded, and somewhat comic figure who plays no significant role in the remaining three novels. His influence on the plot of the story is so profound, however, that he is, after Arthur, the major figure in the story.

Sir Ector, Arthur's foster father, a comic figure.

Kay, Arthur's foster brother, an inept but faithful friend.

The Queen of Air and Darkness, 1939 (originally titled *The Witch in the Wood*)

Queen Morgause (MAHR-goh), an evil necromancer, the wife of King Lot of Orkney. She hates her half brother, Arthur. She seduces him (he is unaware of their kinship at the time) and gives birth to their son, Mordred, who is both the product of their incest and the character destined to destroy Camelot. Morgause, one of the story's most interesting characters, also is the mother of several other sons, including

Gawain, who will be among Arthur's strongest supporters.

Arthur, who is now king. He begins his effort to turn England from war to peace by subduing the anarchic knights who still rule by might.

Merlyn, whose role is almost finished. He teaches Arthur the history of the Celts, his theory of war and peace, and how to proceed in his kingship.

The Ill-Made Knight, 1940

Lancelot, the French knight who is Arthur's closest friend. He calls himself the Chevalier Mal Fet—the Ill-Made Knight—because of his tremendous physical ugliness. The most significant knight of the Round Table, Lancelot is fated to fall in love with Arthur's wife, Queen Guenever, and thus to be one of the causes of Camelot's fall. His love for both Arthur and Guenever is the cause of an anguish so great that he engages in many quests and battles to escape it; no physical escape works for long, however, and he undergoes a fit of madness.

Guenever, known as **Jenny**, the beautiful and innocent young woman who is both Arthur's renowned queen and Lan-

celot's tormented lover. She struggles unsuccessfully to deny the love she feels for Lancelot while trying honorably to fulfill her obligations to Arthur and to her role as queen.

Elaine, Lancelot's unloved wife, a good and simple woman and the mother of their son, Galahad.

Arthur, who, having defeated the old order, now has to find some outlet for the energies of his Round Table knights. He invents the idea of the Quest for the Holy Grail as a way to sublimate the new form of might represented now, ironically, by Arthur himself. The quest is disastrous, resulting in the loss of most of his best knights.

The Candle in the Wind, 1958

Mordred, who is now grown. He is able finally to put Morgause's plan for revenge into effect. He accuses Guenever

of adultery, divides Camelot into warring camps, plots to overthrow Arthur and to marry Guenever, and begins the long war against Arthur. The novel's center of moral and intellectual evil, Mordred is nevertheless a strangely sympathetic figure.

Lancelot, who is accused of adultery with Guenever. He escapes to his castle in France, where he is besieged by Arthur's troops under the command of Gawain, whom he eventually kills. He then rushes to England to rescue Guenever from her imprisonment by Mordred.

Guenever, who is now Mordred's prisoner and is used as a pawn to draw Arthur into a decisive battle to take place on Salisbury plain.

Arthur, who reviews his life while in his tent on the field of Salisbury on the night before the final battle with Mordred. He mourns the failure of Camelot and sees the future—the deaths of Mordred and himself, and Lancelot's and Guenever's exile to monastery and nunnery. He realizes that they all have been the innocent pawns of a fate that has cast them in predetermined roles in a drama that none ever quite understood or controlled.

— *Ronald E. Foust*

ONCE IN A LIFETIME

Authors: George S. Kaufman (1889-1961) and Moss Hart (1904-1961)
First published: 1930
Genre: Drama

Locale: New York City and Hollywood
Time: Late 1920's
Plot: Comedy

Jerry Hyland, the leader of a small-time, three-person vaudeville act who becomes an executive at Glogauer Studios in Hollywood. A likable second-rate actor in his early thirties, he has a penchant for concocting moneymaking schemes to get the trio out of vaudeville. After seeing *The Jazz Singer*, the first motion picture with sound, Jerry is convinced that talkies will revolutionize the film industry. He sells the act and persuades his partners to go to Hollywood to become part of that revolution. When it seems that he has "gone Hollywood," Jerry redeems himself by leaving California to go after May.

May Daniels, a member of the vaudeville act who becomes an elocution teacher at Glogauer Studios. Tall, slender, and attractive, May has a quick, sharp mind with a tongue to match. She is the voice of reason, although a slightly cynical one, throughout the play. May dreams up a gimmick for the act to market in Hollywood: an elocution school to prepare silent-film actors for the talkies. Although she is in love with Jerry, she returns to New York when it seems that he has adopted the film industry's superficial values.

George Lewis, the vaudeville act's straight man, who becomes the supervisor of productions at Glogauer Studios. About twenty-eight years old, George is clean-cut, naïve, and rather dim. George follows Jerry and May's lead, which includes acting as the elocution school's technical adviser, "Dr. Lewis." He comes into his own when he meets and falls in love with an aspiring actress. The head of Glogauer Studios is so impressed by George's guileless candor that he promptly makes George supervisor of all productions. George's blunders work to his benefit, and "Dr. Lewis" becomes Hollywood's new genius.

Susan Walker, a young woman who goes to California to be a film star. The female counterpart of George, she falls in love with him when they meet on the train to Hollywood.

George's intervention with the studio head gets her the lead in *Gingham and Orchids*, a dreadful film in which she gives a wretched performance. Critics, however, love the film and her star turn in it.

Herman Glogauer, the head of Glogauer Studios. A caricature of a Hollywood mogul, Glogauer foolishly passed up the opportunity to make the first talkie, so he is now open to new ideas, including an elocution school at his studio. In a comic confrontation, George becomes the first person to remind Glogauer of his error in judgment concerning talkies. Glogauer mistakes George's ignorance for insight and assumes that George cloaks his brilliant perception in seemingly simple statements and careless actions.

Helen Hobart, America's foremost film critic and columnist. She is immensely impressed with herself and her accomplishments. Helen was once in a vaudeville troupe with May, and the trio takes advantage of this tenuous connection to break into the motion picture industry.

Lawrence Vail, a New York playwright hired by Glogauer Studios, one of a shipment of sixteen playwrights. Vail's numerous efforts to meet Glogauer and get an assignment are fruitless. After six months of sitting in his office and collecting his paychecks without speaking to anyone except the payroll clerk, he returns to New York.

Rudolph Kammerling, a temperamental German film director. Brought to America by Glogauer, he directs the sappy *Gingham and Orchids* under George's inept supervision.

Miss Leighton, Glogauer Studios' reception secretary. Decked out in glamorous gowns, she deals with the swarms of people who converge on the reception area.

Mr. Meterstein and

Mr. Weisskopf, Glogauer's flunkies.

— *Gregory McElwain*

ONE DAY IN THE LIFE OF IVAN DENISOVICH
(Odin den Ivana Denisovicha)

Author: Aleksandr Solzhenitsyn (1918-   )
First published: 1962
Genre: Novel

Locale: Siberia
Time: One day in January, 1951
Plot: Historical realism

Ivan Denisovich (ee-VAN deh-NIH-soh-vihch), sometimes called **Shukov** (SHEW-kov), a prisoner in a Soviet camp. He is serving a ten-year sentence for having escaped from a German prisoner of war camp in World War II. Even though his actions were heroic, he had some contact with the West and so became suspect. He is not sunk in misery at this injustice; he remains tough, resilient, and determined to survive his sentence and preserve his own integrity. He does odd jobs to get a little tobacco or an ounce of bread. He has served eight years of his sentence, but he is careful not to anticipate freedom; he concentrates on surviving this one day. There are some defeats during the day. He is sent for punishment because he is sick in his bed at reveille. In addition, soon after this he cannot get on the sick list because the allotment already has been met. The rest of the day, however, is as good as it can be for a prisoner. He manages to steal some felt, which helps keep him and the others warm on the job. He feels useful and confident when he builds a wall with mortar and bricks. He tricks the cook and gets an extra bowl of gruel for lunch. Finally, when he returns from a day of hard labor, he stands in line to earn a bit of food from Caesar and buys some tobacco from the Latvians. He will not allow his wife to send him packages because that would decrease the amount of food for his family. He has something more important than outside help: the skill and intelligence to survive without compromising himself, even in a Soviet labor camp.

Tyurin (TYEW-rihn), the leader of Shukov's work gang. The whole group's survival depends on Tyurin's ability to procure favorable work assignments and allotments; he has their lives in his hands. They unquestioningly obey any order or suggestion from Tyurin. His wisdom is the wisdom of a prisoner who has endured for nineteen years; he knows how the system works and will take any advantage he can to ensure the survival of his men.

Fetyukov (feht-YEW-kov), a scrounger who is unable to live up to the self-imposed code of the prisoner and so will not survive the camps. He picks up cigarette butts and licks other people's bowls. He had a soft desk job before he was arrested and cannot adjust to his reduced circumstances. He is too desperate and too lacking in integrity to survive.

The Captain, a new prisoner who has to shed the values and codes of the outside world to survive. The Captain thinks as though he is still in the outside world, assuming that he can successfully make protests to guards and superiors. Those qualities of command and pride that were so valuable to him in civilian life are dangerous here, however, and he is sent to the punishment cell for ten days. He has the encouragement of the others, and Shukov thinks that he may learn how to survive as a prisoner.

Caesar Markovich (TSEH-zahr mahr-KOH-vihch), a prisoner who has a soft job and receives packages of food from home. Caesar is from Moscow and retains the cosmopolitan attitude of the capital. He likes to argue about artistic effects in the films of Sergei Eisenstein, reflecting a life of luxury most of the other prisoners do not have.

Alyoshka the Baptist (ah-LYOH-shkah), a prisoner whose faith enables him to accept his unjust imprisonment and cruel treatment with equanimity.

Pavlo, the assistant gang boss. He is young and a hard worker who performs many tasks for the boss, Tyurin.

Der (dehr), a free worker who acts as a foreman. He is upset to notice that Tyurin's gang has taken the felt to keep themselves warm. His claim to authority is defeated, however, by the resistance of the prisoners.

— *James Sullivan*

ONE DAY OF LIFE
(Un día en la vida)

Author: Manlio Argueta (1936-   )
First published: 1980
Genre: Novel

Locale: El Salvador
Time: The 1970's to the 1980's
Plot: Social

Guadalupe (Lupe) Fuentes de Guardado (gwah-dah-LEW-peh FWEHN-tehs deh gwahr-DAH-doh), a forty-two-year-old, superstitious, earthy, traditional matriarch of a peasant family in Chalatenango, El Salvador. She displays a sense of humor, humaneness, and generosity in the account of a day in her life, in which she tells of her son Justino's murder (by decapitation) by special military forces, the search for her granddaughter by the same forces, and the capture, beating, mutilation, and apparent murder of her husband. She speaks of her earlier ambivalence toward the Christian farmworkers' federation to which many of her family members dedicate their lives. She reports being finally convinced that her husband's concept of "awareness" (heightened consciousness) is appropriate for a class that must become self-reliant and demand its rights. Lupe is admired by the other townspeople for her strength and stoicism in the face of tragedy.

José "Chepe" Guardado (hoh-SEH CHEH-peh), an enthusiastic activist and leader in the Christian farmworkers' federation, an excellent storyteller and folksinger capable of good humor and self-effacement. His association with the federation caused him to give up drinking and gambling. Chepe is seen as a great teacher and insists that the farmworkers must achieve a new awareness and conscience to achieve their rights and an improvement in their living standards. Chepe, like most men in this area, must spend nights in the hills for fear of being apprehended in his own home by the military authorities.

Adolfina Hernández Guardado (ah-dohl-FEE-nah ehr-NAHN-dehs), the fifteen-year-old granddaughter of Lupe and Chepe, well educated (to the fifth grade), independent, and extremely active in the federation. She has taken part in a demonstration at a bank to demand cheaper fertilizer and seeds and was part of the group that "took" the cathedral to protest the growing brutality of the authorities in Chalatenango. Adolfina, at an earlier age thought to be rebellious by her mother, is the best example of her grandfather Chepe's concept of awareness. María Pía, her mother, sends her to her grandparents' home in Chalatenango out of concern that the authorities might be looking for her. Her bus trip from Ilobasco to Chalatenango is a hot, dusty, overcrowded, and noisy experience that vividly illustrates Third World reality.

Corporal Martínez (mahr-TEE-nehs), the only named authority or special forces trooper. He hails from the same class and background as the other characters, but his training and education as an "authority" have made him an outsider in their midst. He is known as Ticha's son. He is hardhearted, cold, and foul-tongued, and he possesses a confusing array of disconnected concepts concerning national security and communist conspiracy that provide a spine-chilling litany of self-hatred, racism, and feelings of cultural inferiority.

María Pía Guardado Fuentes de Hernández, the oldest of Lupe's surviving children. Her husband, Helio, has disappeared after participating in a bank demonstration. She fears for her daughter and sends her to spend time with her grand-mother in Chalatenango. María Pía is beaten by the authorities in a night raid in which they also destroy her house.

María Romelia Ramírez (rroh-MEH-lee-ah rrah-MEE-rehs), a protester wounded in the hand at the bank demonstration. Her father, Emilio Ramírez, an organizer of farmworkers, has disappeared, as has her cousin, Arturo, who participated in the demonstration with her. María Romelia, coolheaded and confident, gives the most chilling account of Justino's decapitation and praises the stoic patience of Lupe and Chepe.

Rubenia Fuentes (rrew-BEHN-ee-ah), Lupe's mother, who tells of the 1932 massacre that occurred in Santa Tecla. Rubenia's appearance in the novel completes four generations of women from the same family who tell their stories.

— *Thomas D. Spaccarelli*

ONE FLEW OVER THE CUCKOO'S NEST

Author: Ken Kesey (1935-   )
First published: 1962
Genre: Novel

Locale: An asylum in Oregon
Time: Fall, 1960
Plot: Psychological realism

Chief Bromden, the narrator and a patient in a mental hospital near Portland, Oregon. At six feet, eight inches, this Native American is the largest and most physically powerful man in his ward. Other patients call him Chief Broom because he spends much of his time sweeping the floors. He has been forced to undergo numerous electroshock treatments over the years he has been in the hospital. He depends on sedatives to help him cope with his fears and feelings of estrangement from those around him, he refuses to talk, and he has convinced everyone who knows him that he is deaf. The son of an American Indian man and a white woman, he has witnessed his father's decline into alcoholism after being defeated by an essentially white America and its amoral, homogenizing value system. In fact, he views the mental hospital as part of a huge American Combine that forces men into confinement and prescribed behavior, reducing them to little more than impotent automatons. Chief sees Nurse Ratched as the Combine's evil, castrating agent against whom it is futile and self-destructive to fight—or so he believes until he changes through exposure to Randle McMurphy. Chief proves himself to be not only equal to McMurphy's example but also equal to fighting defiantly against the Combine.

Randle McMurphy, a patient in the mental hospital, sent there from the Pendleton Farm of Correction by the state for diagnosis and possible treatment. He he makes it clear that he has feigned psychosis to avoid the physical labor required of him in Pendleton. McMurphy enters the hospital at the age of thirty-five with a history of arrests for street and barroom fights, drunkenness, disturbing the peace, and—among other things—statutory rape. He has fierce red hair and a broken-nosed smile. He is a big-talking, thigh-slapping, and jovial storyteller, but he is also fiercely independent and serves as a defiant role model for several of the other patients in the ward. He helps Chief Bromden to discover self-respect and courage, teaching him that a man's intentions are more important than the outcome of his actions. He prepares Chief to be heroically self-reliant in the face of terrifying obstacles. From the moment McMurphy enters the ward and finds it run by totalitar-ian Nurse Ratched and her black attendants, he devotes himself to diminishing her power over the other men and implementing a democratic system of governance. Although he wins numerous small but significant battles against her, she ultimately has the official power to destroy him by means of a forced lobotomy. McMurphy's indomitable spirit outlives his consciousness, however, as he has effectively created a disciple out of Chief Bromden.

Nurse Ratched, called **Big Nurse**, the head nurse on the acute ward of the mental hospital. Relying on rules, which she expects all of her patients to follow, Ratched is as mechanical, steel-cold, and unyielding as her name suggests, and she controls her ward so that it resembles an accurate, smooth-running, and efficient machine. To keep her patients obedient and predictable, she treats them like naughty children and browbeats them, has them spy on one another and report to her, and subjects those who cause trouble to electroshock treatments or, for extreme cases, lobotomies. Ultimately, she subjects McMurphy to both treatments, first to punish him and then to destroy him. His influence on the other patients is too great for Ratched to tolerate. His ribald sense of humor makes them laugh and reminds them of the large areas of their lives from which they have been cut off by oppressive rules, fear, and sedatives; he makes them feel ashamed for spying on one another, makes them see what Ratched pretends is a democracy on the ward is actually a dictatorship, offers them a glimpse of their unfettered potential, and shows them that Ratched is a woman hiding her fallible humanness beneath a tyrannical demeanor. Ratched has no qualms about destroying McMurphy, the antithesis to her prescriptive vision of her ward, the hospital, and the world.

Dale Harding, the most highly educated patient on the acute ward; he is extremely articulate. Having suffered impotence in his marriage and fearing that he may be homosexual, Harding is frequently racked by his insecurities and paranoia, all of which Nurse Ratched exacerbates verbally on a regular basis to control him. Although he has spent considerable time convincing himself that Big Nurse is trying to help him become healthy, McMurphy's influence on the ward compels Harding to be honest about himself and Ratched.

Billy Bibbit, a thirty-one-year-old man whose crippling domination by his mother is made more acute in the hospital. She is the receptionist at the hospital, and Nurse Ratched is a close friend and neighbor to her. Nurse Ratched controls Billy by habitually threatening to report his behavior. He is driven to suicide by such a threat toward the novel's end, after he is caught enjoying his first sexual encounter with a woman.

— David A. Carpenter

ONE HUNDRED YEARS OF SOLITUDE
(Cien años de soledad)

Author: Gabriel García Márquez (1928-   )
First published: 1967
Genre: Novel

Locale: Macondo, a town in Latin America
Time: The 1820's to the 1920's
Plot: Magical Realism

Melquíades (mehl-KEE-ah-dehs), a wise and honest Gypsy. He makes annual visits to Macondo, a remote, mythical village in Latin America. Having made innumerable trips around the world, he possesses immense knowledge that he reveals to the people of Macondo. He introduces them to inventions such as magnets, astrolabes, telescopes, magnifying glasses, and false teeth. The curiosity of the men is stimulated by their hope of finding a panacea for life, but the women are not impressed. In spite of his wisdom, Melquíades cannot transcend the problems of daily life. First reported as dead but actually living through death, he reappears in Macondo. There, he is the first to die and be buried. Periodically, he comes back ethereally, seen by some and lost to others. He has left a precious parchment manuscript, the history of both the past and the future of Macondo, to those who can read its Sanskrit and decipher its meaning.

José Arcadio Buendía (hoh-SEH ahr-KAH-dee-oh bwehn-DEE-ah), the family patriarch, the founder and colonizer of Macondo. He is the leader and most enterprising of its settlers. He becomes enthralled with the knowledge and inventions of Melquíades, but his spirit of initiative disappears. He becomes careless and lazy in his dress. He tries to find gold with the magnets, turn base metals into precious ones with the alchemist's laboratory, use a magnifying glass as an instrument of war, demonstrate that the world is round with an astrolabe, and prove the existence or nonexistence of God with a daguerreotype. Preoccupied with the larger issues of life, he searches for universal wealth, remedies, and answers to the questions of existence. When he goes berserk, ten men are necessary to tie him to a tree in the backyard of the family home. There, he speaks in Latin with the village priest and is attended to by his family. Finally, he dies, and a rain of yellow flowers blankets the village.

Úrsula Iguarán (EWR-suh-lah ee-gwahr-RAHN), the wife of José Arcadio and the matriarch of the Buendías. With more common sense than her husband, she solves the ordinary problems of daily living for her family. She is kind and generous. She always has food and a place in the family for anyone who appears. She is the stable and guiding force in the lives of her three children and adopted daughter, although none of them turns out the way she would have preferred. She also takes a hand in the rearing of future generations of Buendías, trying to correct her past mistakes, but they too are found wanting. Each generation reflects the patterns of its historical setting. Earlier generations of males have great physical or intellectual powers, whereas later generations tend to be weaker in spirit and stamina. The females increasingly approach the model of the modern liberated woman as the novel moves through several generations of women.

José Arcadio, their gigantic older son, who marries Rebeca. Born on the journey to found Macondo, he does not share his father's interest in inventions. Initiated into the mysteries of sex by the family's servant, Pilar Ternera, he quickly leaves town when she becomes pregnant. He joins the circus and goes around the world. Lost to the family for several years, he returns fully grown and awesomely developed. Because he is stronger than anyone else and has an enormous sex organ, women pay to sleep with him. The chemistry between him and his adoptive sister Rebeca is such that they have to be married in three days. Ordered out of the family, they set up a separate household. He expands his estate, knocking down fences and incorporating the lands of others into his holdings. When he is shot, it is not clear if it is an accident, a suicide, someone's revenge, or an act by Rebeca.

Rebeca (rreh-BEH-kah), the adoptive daughter of José Arcadio and Úrsula. She arrives on the Buendías' doorstep, with her parents' bones in a sack, when she is eleven years old. They take her in and rear her as their own. She suffers from the vice of secretively eating dirt and whitewash. She is more affectionate toward Úrsula than are her own children. She is the first to appear with the symptoms of the plague of insomnia that has spread through Macondo with the selling of Úrsula's candy animals. Rebeca is courted by and becomes engaged to Pietro Crespi, but then the manly presence of José Arcadio overwhelms her. Her subsequent marriage and banishment and the death of José Arcadio leave her a recluse and forgotten woman.

Colonel Aureliano Buendía (ow-reh-lee-AH-noh), the younger son of José Arcadio and Úrsula. He, too, is introduced to the wonders of sex by Pilar Ternera. He falls in love with Remedios Moscote, the prepubescent daughter of a Conservative. They marry when they reach the age of conception, and she later dies in childbirth. In contrast to the macho physical presence of his brother, he is cerebral. He has unusual powers of insight and premonition. He is outraged over the growing restrictions placed on the inhabitants of Macondo by the Conservatives. He leads the Liberals in revolt and launches thirty-two unsuccessful rebellions against the central government. He becomes supreme commander of the revolutionary movement throughout the country and a legend in his own time. Women offer up their daughters and themselves, and he fathers seventeen Aurelianos. The government, fearful of his fame as a rallying point for renewed revolution, assassinates his seventeen sons and tries to coopt him with honor, glory, and wealth, but he spurns all offers. As supreme leader, he has a rare opportunity to explore the meaning of political power and finds principle, prestige, duty, and personal gain as part of the complex motivations that propel people into positions of political power. At one point, he succumbs to the temptation of dictatorial rule. He eventually sees the emptiness of power and retires to his workshop, where he fashions gold fishes. He discovers the simple pleasures in the routine of daily work. New government indignities, such as corruption and cooperation with foreigners, periodically provoke his desire to lead his veterans in another Liberal rebellion.

Amaranta (ahm-mahr-AHN-tah), their daughter. In love with her sister Rebeca's fiancé, Pietro Crespi, she does everything in her power to prevent the wedding. It is postponed many times. When Rebeca suddenly marries José Arcadio instead, Pietro Crespi is free to court Amaranta, which she encourages. Amaranta's enveloping tenderness leads Pietro Crespi to propose, but she scornfully rejects his offer, and he commits suicide. In remorse, she plunges her hand into a stove of hot coals. She wears a bandage of black gauze on her burned hand until her death as a sign of her virginity. Other suitors come, including her cousin, with whom she engages in deep petting, but nothing is ever consummated. She rejects all offers of marriage. Even though she is capable of love, she is never able to overcome her cowardice and commit herself totally. Determined to outlive Rebeca, she spends the rest of her life weaving and unweaving her funeral shroud, whose completion will mark her own death. She finally accepts the inevitable and the frustration of not surviving Rebeca.

Pietro Crespi (pee-EH-troh KREHS-pee), an Italian music master. As Macondo modernizes and the Buendías acquire material objects and social graces, he is contracted to assemble a pianola and to teach dancing. He is first engaged to Rebeca, then becomes Amaranta's suitor, but he commits suicide when she rejects his proposal of marriage.

Pilar Ternera (pee-LAHR tehr-NEHR-ah), a part-time servant of the Buendías and a generous woman of easy virtue. Her lovemaking skills and ability to read the fortunes of others in the cards are sought by the inhabitants of Macondo.

Arcadio, her illegitimate son by José Arcadio, reared by the Buendías. Placed in charge of Macondo by Colonel Aureliano Buendía, his arbitrary rule of Liberal decrees, anticlericalism, and executions is the cruelest to date. When Liberal fortunes dim and Macondo falls, he is shot by a firing squad.

Santa Sofía de la Piedad (soh-FEE-ah deh lah pee-eh-DAHD), the common-law wife of Arcadio. Silent and condescending, she moves into the Buendía home after his execution and rears their daughter and twin boys and tends to the cares and needs of the other Buendías.

Remedios the Beauty (rreh-MEH-dee-ohs), their daughter. Oblivious to her disturbing and man-killing beauty, she wanders about Macondo as a modern-day Virgin Mary. She ascends into heaven folding sheets in the garden.

José Arcadio Segundo (seh-GEWN-doh), their twin son. He gives up his position as foreman in the banana company to organize the striking workers. Martial law brings a confrontation between the workers and the army at the train station. Army machine guns kill three thousand people, but everyone denies there was a massacre. A supposed agreement between the company and the workers is to be announced when it stops

raining. Because it rains for four years, eleven months, and two days, the agreement is forgotten and the company abandons Macondo. An outcast and traumatized by the experience, José Arcadio Segundo spends the rest of his life in Melquíades' room.

Aureliano Segundo, his twin brother. His fortunes parallel the boom and bust period of Macondo. His wealth grows without effort, and he spends without restraint in an orgy of carousing and fiestas that becomes legendary. He even wallpapers the Buendía home with money. As Macondo declines, however, his ruin is complete. He is reduced to selling lottery tickets.

Petra Cotes (PEH-trah KOH-tehs), the mulatto concubine of Aureliano Segundo. Generous of heart and devoted, she is his companion to the end.

Fernanda del Carpio (KAHR-pee-oh), the wife of Aureliano Segundo. The descendant of an old highland family, she has aristocratic pretensions. She is a nag, a prude, and a snob, and she is narrow-minded in the extreme. Under the weight of mistaken ideas, religious and medical beliefs, and secretive practices, she complicates the routine of life and poisons the ordinary joys of existence.

Renata "Meme" Remedios (rreh-NAH-tah), their older daughter. Diligent, studious, and industrious—so as not to annoy her mother—she falls madly in love with Mauricio Babilonia, an apprentice mechanic in the banana company garage. When their relationship is discovered, her mother confines her to home. There, the relationship continues with secret visits. When Fernanda finds out, she has a guard stationed outside the home; the guard shoots Mauricio Babilonia. He remains a bedridden invalid the rest of his life. Meme never speaks another word and is sequestered far away from Macondo, never to return. Her illegitimate child, Aureliano, is delivered to Fernanda in a basket by the nuns a year later.

José Arcadio, their son, a pederast. Sent away to Rome, where he lives for many years, he never studies, as intended by his mother, for the priesthood. He returns to Macondo to find only Aureliano and his dead mother among the ruins of the family home. His discovery of gold, buried long ago by the matriarch Úrsula, allows him to redecorate the house and stock it with food and wines. After he expels four boys from his home following a wild party, they return and drown him for the gold.

Amaranta Úrsula, their younger daughter. Sent off to study in Brussels at great sacrifice by her father and his mistress, who are now in the twilight of their lives, she returns to a home whose only occupant is Aureliano. A thoroughly modern and liberated woman with the latest fashions and dances, she restores the house and settles down with her husband, Gaston, but then falls madly in love with Aureliano. She dies in childbirth.

Gaston (GAHS-tohn), her Flemish husband. Led by Amaranta Úrsula on a silk leash, he marries her with the promise that he will return with her to Macondo. Determined to wait out his wife's nostalgic fascination with the place, he busies himself setting up an airmail service to Macondo. After many delays, he finally leaves to track down the airplane that has been mistakenly shipped to the African tribe of the Makondos.

Aureliano, Meme's illegitimate son. Locked up and ignored as a child, he pores over the manuscripts and books in Melquíades' room. He has encyclopedic knowledge of the past but little of the present. Infatuated with Amaranta Úrsula, he becomes her lover, and they abandon themselves to each other in a Macondo on the verge of extinction. When she dies in childbirth, he wanders unconsoled. He returns to find the baby eaten by ants. At this moment, Melquíades' final keys to the manuscript are revealed, and he finally understands the meaning of the parchments perfectly. As he reads them, he is able to live out the unrepeatable one-hundred-year history of Macondo.

Aureliano, Aureliano and Amaranta Úrsula's son. Born with a pig's tail—reminiscent of an ancestor who also was the product of a union of close relatives—he dies when eaten by ants and fulfills the prophecy of the manuscript.

— *Maurice P. Brungardt*

ONE OF OURS

Author: Willa Cather (1873-1947)
First published: 1922
Genre: Novel

Locale: Frankfort and Lincoln, Nebraska, and the battlefields of France
Time: 1900-1918
Plot: Symbolism

Claude Wheeler, a young Midwestern farmer, sandy-haired and freckle-faced, with a large, square-shaped head and a good physique. As a child, he is characterized by a violent temper and physical restlessness. During adolescence, he struggles with his lack of confidence. Surrounded by many who see the world only as a business proposition, he is uncertain and unguided as he searches for meaning. As he begins, in college, to get excited about learning, he is brought back to work on the family farm. He is sensitive to the land but is also aware of other challenges. His choice in a wife reflects his own lack of direction. In France during World War I, he comes to know himself and to feel a strong sense of purpose. He accepts destiny only when he comes to understand the power of ideals among people.

Lieutenant David Gerhardt, a talented violinist and soldier whom Claude at first feels to be his competitor but whom he comes to admire deeply. Highly trained at the Conservatoire, David has toured successfully in America, but he understands that the war has killed all possibility of his returning to his music. He received the nurturing in values that Claude recognizes that he never had.

Enid Royce, the childhood sweetheart, and later wife, of Claude. Thought to be very pretty, Enid is slender, with a well-shaped head, a pale complexion, and dark eyes. She is strongly committed to a number of causes, such as vegetarianism and prohibition, but she is unaware of Claude's need to grow.

Gladys Farmer, a schoolteacher and supportive friend of Claude. Gladys sees in Claude's nature the finer characteristics that ensure his failure in the materialistic setting of America. She fears that if he marries Enid Royce, he will become a machine like Enid's father. She is happy that he can escape to Europe. She is determined not to marry Bayliss Wheeler.

Nat Wheeler, a farmer and Claude's father. He is neither easily flustered nor often serious. Although he is a rich farmer, he does not like farm work. He is sympathetic to the interests of Bayliss, but his teasing of and treatment of Claude confuse that young man.

Evangeline Wheeler, Claude's mother, a woman of religious faith. She understands the height of Claude's hopes and passionate beliefs. Although she loves Claude deeply, she is powerless to help him in his struggles.

Bayliss Wheeler, a prudent businessman and older brother of Claude. He is symbolic of the many insensitive and unthinking businessmen who Claude had always thought controlled the world.

Old Mahailey, Mrs. Wheeler's servant, a deeply caring woman who was close to and loved Claude. She evoked Claude's trust of her good judgment of people.

Ernest Havel, an immigrant Bohemian farmer and close boyhood friend of Claude. In his speech, he is simple and direct. A thinker, he questions many conventionally held thoughts.

Leonard Dawson, a highly successful farmer and boyhood friend of Claude. A large fellow with big hands and big feet, he is full of energy and works hard. He shares Claude's contempt for methods used on the Wheeler farm.

The Reverend Arthur Weldon, a self-serving minister and teacher at Temple, a religious school. He impresses Claude's mother and Enid, but he arouses distrust and dislike in Claude.

Mrs. Erlich, the mother of one of Claude's college friends. She helps Claude to see a different kind of family life from any he had ever known, and she teaches him much about life.

Madame Fleury, the mother of one of David Gerhardt's fellow students at the Conservatoire. Her strength and life make Claude uncomfortable but challenge him.

Madame Joubert and

Monsieur Joubert, a French couple with whom Claude and David live. They provide warmth and loving comfort in the midst of the horrors of war.

Harris Maxey, an Army captain (later a colonel) under whom Claude and David serve. His manner expresses the desire to excel, but his men perceive him in various ways.

— *Kay Kenney Fortson*

ONE WAY TO HEAVEN

Author: Countée Cullen (1903-1946)
First published: 1932
Genre: Novel

Locale: New York City's Harlem
Time: The 1920's
Plot: Social realism

Sam Lucas, a handsome, one-armed confidence man. Sam's usual con is to repent his gambling ways at revival meetings, then support himself for a while on the church community's generosity toward him as a reformed sinner. When he arrives in Harlem, Mattie Johnson, an attractive young black woman, is swept away in her enthusiasm at his example, and she joins the church and falls in love with him. They marry, and Sam moves in with her and her Aunt Mandy, but the marriage begins to dissolve as Sam stops going to church and Mattie devotes increasing energy to it. Eventually, Sam moves in with Emma May, an usher at the theater where Sam takes tickets, but he moves back with Mattie when he becomes sick. On his deathbed, Sam lies, telling Mattie that he hears music and sees a bright light, so that she will believe that his soul has been saved.

Mattie Johnson, Constancia Brandon's maid, a good-hearted and pretty woman. After falling in love with Sam at a New Year's Eve church meeting, Mattie never considers the possibility that his conversion was an act. They are married at her employer's house. After the marriage begins to fail, she tricks Sam into going to church with her again, where she prays aloud for Christ to take her husband back into His fold. Sam stalks out and leaves her for his mistress, Emma May, but the forgiving Mattie takes him back when Emma comes to tell her that he is sick. When Sam tells Mattie that he hears music and sees a light, she believes that his soul has been saved.

Constancia Brandon, Mattie's employer, a center of Harlem society, always lively and at times outrageous. When Constancia hears that her maid is getting married, she immediately makes plans to host the wedding, inviting her black friends (after Mattie asked her not to invite anyone white) to the wedding. Constancia is the center of a mostly black, artistic, and wealthy circle. Among the more outrageous things Constancia does is to invite Professor Seth Calhoun, a white supremacist, to give a talk at one of her parties.

Aunt Mandy, Mattie's aunt, a longtime member of the church and, for a while, Sam's cardplaying partner. Aunt Mandy acts as an intermediary between Sam and Mattie, first urging him to get a job and later urging Mattie to be more understanding.

The Reverend Clarence Johnson, an evangelist from the South. As the guest preacher the night Sam and Mattie convert, he recognizes Sam as a con man but believes that his false conversion serves as an inspiration to other people.

The Reverend Drummond, the pastor of the Mt. Hebron Episcopal Church, the church that Mattie and Sam join. He successfully plays peacemaker between Mattie and Sam one time when he comes by for dinner and finds them in the middle of a fight.

Mary Johnson, the duchess of Uganda and a friend of Constancia. She is a woman of much pretension and a part of the Back to Africa movement; her title was granted by the movement.

Donald Hewitt, a wealthy young Englishman, a writer who wants specifically to write about Harlem. He is enchanted by Constancia and becomes a member of her circle.

Miss McGoffin, an Irish American missionary to Africa, trying to fit into Constancia's circle. She shows her ignorance when she asks Constancia if "you people" are writing any more spirituals, which she could take back to Africa to show that civilization has not destroyed black Americans' "creative instinct."

Mrs. De Peyster Johnson, a teacher in a public school. Proud of an ancestry that she can trace back to the first slaves who were brought to America, Mrs. De Peyster Johnson, a friend of Constancia, makes a point of teaching the classics of black American literature in her classes.

George Brandon, Constancia's husband, a wealthy doctor. He delighted her when they first met by dubbing her "Mrs. Shakespeare" because of her flamboyant and elegant style of speech.

— *Thomas J. Cassidy*

OPERATION SHYLOCK: A Confession

Author: Philip Roth (1933-   )
First published: 1993
Genre: Novel

Locale: Jerusalem
Time: Late January, 1988, with an epilogue in the early 1990's
Plot: Novel of ideas

Philip Roth, the narrator, a writer in his mid-fifties. Following knee surgery, Roth had a mental breakdown, possibly caused by the drug Halcion, which caused him to be delusional. At first, he wonders whether the events in the story he tells are in fact delusions. He relates the story as a confession and says that he has changed the names of characters to protect their identities. In January of 1988, he discovers that someone is impersonating him. The impersonator is attending the trial, in Jerusalem, of John Demjanjuk and is making public appearances and statements to the press. Roth decides to go to Jerusalem, where he confronts the impersonator, whom he begins to call Moishe Pipik. An old, seemingly impoverished Jew (later identified as Smilesburger) gives him a check for $1 million to support Diasporism, a cause promoted by the impostor. George Ziad, an old friend of Roth, tells Roth of his support for Diasporism. Roth pretends to believe in it and says

that he would be glad to meet Yassir Arafat and discuss it. On his way back to his hotel that evening, Roth is stopped by Israeli soldiers and is almost beaten, but one of the soldiers recognizes him and allows him to continue on his way. When he returns to his hotel, he discovers that Pipik is in his room. Pipik asks for the $1 million check, and Roth discovers that it is missing. Roth gets Pipik out of his room, but Jinx Possesski arrives later and tells Roth about Pipik's plot to kidnap John Demjanjuk, Jr. Roth plans to leave Jerusalem but stays because he realizes that if Pipik succeeds in his kidnapping attempt, the elder Demjanjuk would be supported in his claims that he cannot get a fair trial. Roth later is kidnapped, apparently with Smilesburger's complicity. Smilesburger asks Roth to participate in an intelligence gathering mission. In the epilogue, Roth describes a letter, purportedly from Jinx, telling of Pipik's demise; he think it actually was written by Pipik. The letter says that Pipik died on January 17, 1991, during the Persian Gulf War. The letter warns him not to ridicule Pipik or Diasporism in a book or he will never be left alone. Roth sends a copy of his manuscript about the Pipik incident to Smilesburger for approval and later meets with him. At the meeting, Smilesburger says he has retired. He pleads with Roth to say that the work is fiction or to remove the chapter about his intelligence mission, and he hints that Roth might put himself in danger by printing the entire book as fact. Smilesburger offers back the manuscript, in a briefcase that contains an envelope full of money; he claims not to know that the money was there. Smilesburger urges Roth to take the money; if he does not, an insidious campaign will be launched to ruin his reputation. All he asks in exchange is that Roth let his Jewish conscience be his guide. Roth's book excludes the chapter about his mission and ends with a note that it is fiction.

Moishe Pipik, Roth's impersonator. Roth refers to him by this nonsense name, translatable as Moses Bellybutton and referring to a make-believe character who causes mischief. Pipik is a terminally ill cancer patient in remission who assumes Roth's identity to make public statements and promote Diasporism, the idea that Jews should leave Israel and go back to homelands in Europe. He believes that Jews face annihilation in the Middle East and that it would be better to spread out and have Israel retreat to its original borders. He begs Roth, in a letter, to allow him to continue his impersonation. His concerns with Jewish identity seem to date from his onset of cancer, when he felt summoned to dedicate himself to a higher calling.

Wanda Jane "Jinx" Possesski, a beautiful woman about thirty-five years old who delivers two letters from Pipik to Roth. She was Pipik's oncology nurse and fell in love with him. Earlier, she had burned out on the suffering of cancer patients and the callousness of those who treated them, coming to hate the Jewish doctors and developing severe anti-Semitism. Jinx goes to Roth's hotel room after Roth has made Pipik leave. She tells Roth that Pipik plans to kidnap John Demjanjuk, Jr., and that she is trying to stop him. She says that she realizes, after a year with him, that Pipik is crazy.

George Ziad, an Arab friend of Roth from the mid-1950's, when they were in college together. They have not seen each other since then. Ziad is Egyptian but is from Jerusalem. His father lost everything to the Jews when he had to leave. Ziad believes in the Diasporism promulgated by Pipik; not knowing that Pipik is an impersonator, he asks Roth how he can help promote Diasporism. Later, he warns Roth that the Israeli police will try to get him, as a Jew who opposes them. He wants Roth to go to Athens to meet some Jews who believe in Diasporism and can help. Roth thinks he is being recruited for the Palestine Liberation Organization (PLO). In the epilogue, Smilesburger tells Roth that Ziad is dead.

Louis B. Smilesburger, a retired New York jeweler who gives Roth a check for $1 million to support Diasporism. When he confronts Roth after Roth is kidnapped, he tries to be friendly and says the guards should have told Roth he was free to go. He has heard of Ziad's rich Jews supporting the PLO, and he wants to speak to them. Smilesburger gives Roth the $1 million check again, saying that Roth must have dropped it. Smilesburger also says that he knows about Pipik but is not working with him. His group has been watching Pipik, thinking he might somehow be valuable. Smilesburger persuades Roth to participate in an intelligence mission, finding out about Ziad's contacts.

John Demjanjuk, formerly a Cleveland autoworker, on trial in Jerusalem because he is accused of being Ivan the Terrible, a concentration camp guard who committed atrocities against prisoners. He is a large, stocky man of sixty-eight years. He claims to have been in a German prisoner-of-war camp while Ivan the Terrible was active.

—A. J. Sobczak

OPERETTA
(Operetka)

Author: Witold Gombrowicz (1904-1969)
First published: 1966
Genre: Drama

Locale: Himalaj Castle
Time: c. 1910 and after World War II
Plot: Play of ideas

Count Charmant Himalay, or **Szarm Himalaj** in some texts, the thirty-five-year-old son of Prince Himalay and Princess Fernanda. A "jaded rake and fop," he plots to make Albertine his 258th conquest. His goal, however, is not to undress the girl but to dress her expensively and fashionably. It is the artifice of fashion that he loves, not the actual woman. As his plan starts to go awry, he begins to feel constrained by his life of appearances and, without considering the consequences, unleashes the forces that result in his downfall. He returns after the revolution disguised as a lunatic, still in search of Albertine.

Alberta Kruzek, also called **Albertine** or **Albertynka**, a shopkeeper's daughter. Charmant plots to meet Albertine by "saving" her from the pickpocket he himself has hired to steal her locket. The touch of the thief's hand on the sleeping girl's breast causes her to yearn for the freedom of complete nudity.

As a result, she frequently falls out of the waking world of pretense and masquerade and into an opposing state of sleep, a state of the natural and the subconscious. She appears at the masked ball (act 2) weighed down by the clothing Charmant has given her; after her disappearance, she returns in act 3 to rise from the coffin in which the pickpockets have hidden her, hailed by all as the embodiment of the immortal ordinary and the eternally youthful.

Baron Firulet, Charmant's ape and mirror image, also thirty-five years old. A "hunter of female prey," he and the count engage in endless competition (a card game, a duel, a chase) involving women and social position.

Fior, a "dictator of style in Europe." This self-proclaimed artist has been invited to the Castle Himalay to devise a new fashion. The work of the man others call "master" is, however, made difficult by the uncertainty of a rapidly changing age.

Returning in act 3 to the now-ruined (postwar, postrevolution) castle, Fior, confused by all the transformations and dismayed by the "painful masquerade," urges the others to give up their disguises and to be themselves. His decision to renounce fashion helps restore Albertine to life and the world to the playwright's special kind of sanity.

Count Hufnagel, a sportsman and horse lover. He is in fact the former lackey **Joseph**, who was dismissed from the prince's service for insubordination six years earlier and subsequently was sentenced to five years in prison for political agitation. It is Hufnagel who suggests that a masked ball be given to help Fior devise the new fashion, though his disguised reason is to create the right atmosphere for conspiracy and revolt. Stripped of his mask, he appears as a figure of hate, the embodiment of socialism, riding others, leading them on a wild and destructive chase, and presiding over the Stalin-like show trials of his oppressors, the bourgeois fascists.

The Professor, who helps Hufnagel gain access to the castle. Suffering from chronic vomiting, he spends much of his time "puking" in the company of aristocrats and, alone with Hufnagel, reviling himself with socialist clichés for his bourgeois life. He willingly becomes Hufnagel's horse and actually looks forward to his "liquidation" at the hands of the revolutionaries.

Prince Himalay, or **Himalaj**, who recognizes that what separates him from the common man is nothing more than manners and dress. He understands that, because the lower classes imitate the upper classes, it is necessary that fashion change if he is to remain on top. The prince suffers from chronic indigestion, brought on by overindulgence. After the revolution, he appears disguised as a lamp, with his wife as a table.

Princessa Fernanda, his wife. Realizing that nudity is "downright socialist," she wonders what the common people would do if they discovered that all posteriors are alike.

The priest, another exploiter and imitator. After the revolution, he appears disguised as a woman.

The pickpockets, who are kept on leashes by Charmant and Firulet until they are released during the ball; they then rob the guests and spirit away the sleeping Albertine. Disguised as gravediggers, they carry her around in a coffin until her awakening/resurrection.

Ladislaus and

Stanley, lackeys to Charmant and Firulet, respectively. The lackeys, at once servile (they literally lick their masters' boots) and seething, are ready for revolution.

The banker,

the general, and

Marchioness Eulalia, who, when the sacks that have covered their costumes drop off to expose their contributions to Fior's new style, are shown as a man with a bomb, a Nazi officer, and the overseer of a German concentration camp.

Ladies and gentlemen, the count's admirers and apes.

— *Robert A. Morace*

THE OPTIMIST'S DAUGHTER

Author: Eudora Welty (1909-   )
First published: 1969; enlarged, 1972
Genre: Novel

Locale: New Orleans, Louisiana, and the fictional Mount Salus, Mississippi
Time: Early 1960's
Plot: Domestic realism

Laurel McKelva Hand, a widow in her mid-forties and a successful fabric designer living in Chicago. Slender, stable, and with "her hair still dark," she is the optimist's daughter of the novel's title. She has flown to New Orleans to be with her father for his operation to repair a damaged retina. She reads to him during his initial recovery and then returns to her family home for his funeral—and to sort out some of her own past. Much of the novel and many of its memories are filtered through Laurel's consciousness, especially back at Mount Salus after the funeral, where Laurel recalls her mother and her own early years. Laurel is surrounded by death—her husband, her mother, and now her father have all died. Once she has put memory and death in their proper places in the past, however, she finally survives and triumphs. In reaching some sort of resolution with Fay, her stepmother, Laurel makes peace with her home, and she can return to Chicago.

Judge Clinton McKelva, Laurel's father, retired from the bench and living in Mount Salus, Mississippi, with his second wife, Fay. At the age of seventy-one, the judge develops eye trouble, but as he tells Dr. Courtland, his surgeon, he is "an optimist" and has survived much, including the death of his first wife, Becky. He also has an untapped reserve of patience, but being forced to lie still after his delicate eye operation is too much for him, as well as for his selfish wife, Fay. The judge dies when she tries to rouse him. At his end, he apparently has lost hope. He doted on Fay, as neighbors in Mount Salus say, although no one, including his daughter, can understand why.

Wanda Fay Chisom McKelva, the judge's second wife, a silly and insensitive gold digger from Texas. Fay thinks of no one but herself and actually hastens the judge's death when she tries to get him to move too soon after his operation. Her insecurity (she has married above herself and knows it) is matched only by her meanness and hysteria. She is best at "making a scene," which she does even at the funeral. She has no passion or imagination, as Laurel finally realizes.

Becky McKelva, Laurel's mother and the judge's first wife, dead some twelve years but a powerful memory and a force in the novel. Laurel discovers her mother's letters and reconstructs Becky's childhood in West Virginia and her returns there after her marriage. The parents regularly read to each other and wrote to each other when separated, but Becky's last, sick years scarred both of her survivors. It is Becky's death that Laurel relives back in Mount Salus, and it is one of the events of her life she must consign to the past.

Major Rupert Bullock, a friend of the judge since childhood and the man who organizes his funeral. The major gets drunk and, worse, invites Fay's family (even Fay does not want them to be present), who disrupt the funeral with their crude manners. The major lives through his friends.

Miss Adele Courtland, a Mount Salus schoolteacher and the McKelvas' next-door neighbor. Miss Adele was one of Laurel's bridesmaids years before and still loves Laurel and the memory of her mother. Like the other women who flock

around Laurel at Mount Salus to help her through the funeral and afterward, Miss Adele loved Laurel's mother and has trouble relating to Fay.

Missouri, the faithful black housekeeper of the McKelvas in Mount Salus.

— *David Peck*

THE ORDEAL OF GILBERT PINFOLD

Author: Evelyn Waugh (1903-1966)
First published: 1957
Genre: Novel

Locale: On board a cruise ship
Time: Shortly after World War II
Plot: Social satire

Gilbert Pinfold, a renowned novelist modeled on the author. Pinfold is on a cruise to recover his health. He begins hearing voices in his cabin. He supposes they are the result of some crossed wiring that allows him to eavesdrop on intimate and incriminating conversations. First, Pinfold overhears a scene in which the captain punishes and inadvertently kills a crew member. The voices become involved in a plot against Pinfold. They accuse him of lying about his biography and acting, in general, as a fraud. When Pinfold tries to engage other passengers in a discussion of these nefarious doings, they all profess ignorance of what he is talking about. Pinfold's paranoia reaches its height when he hears the captain and crew hatching a scheme to turn him over to a hostile Spanish vessel that is about to intercept and board the cruise ship. Not until he leaves the cruise is Pinfold convinced by his wife that all the plots and voices have been of his own devising, and that he has been taken in by his own hallucinations.

Captain Steerforth, who is in charge of the cruise ship. He becomes, in Pinfold's mind, one of the chief intriguers against him. When the captain does his best to show Pinfold that he is mistaken in his suspicions that his telegrams have been read by other passengers, Pinfold presumes that his persecutors are simply trying to embarrass him by faking some of their plots.

Goneril, the most wicked of the conspirators against Pinfold. He never learns her real name; he calls her Goneril because of her unwavering enmity and lack of conscience.

Glover, a befuddled passenger who never knows how to react to Pinfold's sudden confidences about incidents that turn out to exist only in Pinfold's mind. Pinfold takes Glover's embarrassment as proof of his inability to deal with the evil realities aboard ship.

Angel, a BBC interviewer whom Pinfold decides is behind the campaign against him. Even when Captain Steerforth shows Pinfold a passenger list that does not include Angel's name, Pinfold remains certain that he is on board.

Margaret, a young woman who speaks constantly to Pinfold but who never materializes in the flesh. She is one of his voices and is part of the attempt to discredit him. She is also in love with him and even works up the normally faithful Pinfold into lusting after her. She is egged on by her scheming mother and her blustering father, both of whom urge her into bed with Pinfold. She demurs, coaxing an irritated Pinfold to declare his love outright before she comes to him. As the various efforts to destroy Pinfold fail, Margaret remains loyal to him. Pinfold even hears her voice after his wife convinces him that all the voices have been in his head and that he has made up the whole persecution story. In fact, Margaret goes so far as to declare that she does not exist but that she loves Pinfold anyway. Her voice fades as he returns home and resumes life with his wife and family.

— *Carl Rollyson*

THE ORDEAL OF RICHARD FEVEREL: A History of Father and Son

Author: George Meredith (1828-1909)
First published: 1859
Genre: Novel

Locale: England
Time: Mid-nineteenth century
Plot: Tragicomedy

Richard Feverel, the only son and sole heir of Sir Austin Feverel. Richard is the subject of his father's plan to produce a young man reared according to a System in which women are to be excluded from the life of the boy until he is twenty-five. Richard becomes the obvious proof that the System will not work. He manages, simply by being human, to foil all plans to keep him from physical danger and from women.

Sir Austin Feverel, master of Raynham Abbey and Richard's woman-hating father, who devises the System for rearing his son. Although he is unrealistic in his approach, his belief in the basic soundness of his System is complete.

Adrian Harley, Sir Austin's nephew, who is designated as

Richard's mentor. He is responsible for carrying out the System. Always dubious, Adrian finally is convinced, when Richard marries, that the System has failed utterly.

Lucy Desborough, the niece of a neighboring farmer. Richard falls in love with her and marries her. She bears him a child and finally dies of brain fever and shock when she learns that Richard has been wounded in a duel.

Ripton Thompson, the son of Sir Austin's lawyer, brought to Raynham Abbey as Richard's youthful playmate and companion.

Giles Blaize, Lucy's uncle. He horsewhips Richard and Ripton when he finds that they have shot a pheasant on his property. Richard is responsible for setting fire to Blaize's hayricks.

Clare Forey, Richard's cousin, who falls in love with him. She marries a man much older than she. When she dies, a ring that Richard had lost is found on her finger.

Tom Bakewell, the man Richard bribes to set fire to Blaize's hayricks. Richard insists that he is responsible for the fire and so confuses Blaize's witness that Tom is released, although the witness saw Tom set the fire. He becomes Richard's devoted servant.

THE ORESTEIA

Author: Aeschylus (525/524-456/455 B.C.E.)
First performed: 458 B.C.E.
Genre: Drama

Locale: Argos, Delphi, and Athens
Time: After the fall of Troy
Plot: Tragedy

Agamemnon (a-guh-MEHM-nahn), of the doomed House of Atreus, King of Argos and leader of the Greek expedition against Troy. When the Greeks were de2tained at Aulis, he had been commanded by the gods to sacrifice his daughter Iphigenia, so that the fleet might sail. This deed brought him the hatred of his wife, Clytemnestra, who plots his death. On his return to Argos after the fall of Troy, she persuades him to commit the sin of pride by walking on purple carpets to enter his palace. Once within the palace, he is murdered in his bath by Clytemnestra and her lover, Aegisthus.

Clytemnestra (KLI-tuhm-NEHS-truh), the daughter of Leda and wife of Agamemnon. Infuriated by his sacrifice of their daughter Iphigenia, she murders him and rules Argos with her lover, Aegisthus, until she is killed by her son Orestes.

Cassandra (ka-SAN-druh), the daughter of King Priam of Troy. She is fated always to prophesy truth but never to be believed. Captured by Agamemnon and brought to Argos, she foretells the king's death and is then killed by Clytemnestra.

Aegisthus (ee-JIHS-thus), a cousin of Agamemnon and the lover of Clytemnestra. After Agamemnon's death, he rules Argos with her until he is slain by Orestes.

Orestes (oh-REHS-teez), the son of Agamemnon and Clytemnestra. After his father's murder, he is driven by his mother and her lover from his heritage of Argos. Returning from exile, he meets his sister Electra at their father's tomb and tells her that he has been commanded by the oracle of Apollo to avenge Agamemnon by killing his murderers. He carries out this revenge, but he is driven mad by the Furies, who pursue him to the Delphi, where he takes refuge in the temple of Apollo. Athena, the goddess of wisdom, appears. Unable to decide the case, she calls in twelve Athenian citizens to act as judges. It is argued against Orestes that Clytemnestra, in killing Agamemnon, had not slain a blood relative of her family and thus did not deserve death. Apollo argues that Clytemnes-

tra, having only nourished the father's seed in her womb, was no blood relation of Orestes, and therefore the latter was innocent. The judges vote six to six, and Orestes is declared free of blood-guilt.

Electra (ee-LEHK-truh), the daughter of Agamemnon and Clytemnestra and sister of Orestes. After the murder of her father and the exile of her brother, she is left alone to mourn Agamemnon's death and to perform the rites at his tomb. There she meets Orestes, who has returned to Argos, but at first does not recognize him. Convinced at last of his identity, she urges him to avenge their father by killing their mother and her lover.

The Furies or **Eumenides** (yew-MEHN-ih-deez), children of Night, whose duty it is to dog the footsteps of murderers and to drive them mad. They pursue Orestes but are balked by the judges' decision that he is innocent. They rail against the younger gods who have deprived them of their ancient power. They are pacified by Athena, who promises them great honor and reverence if they will remain at Athens as beneficent deities.

Athena (uh-THEE-nuh), the goddess of wisdom and patron of Athens. She is always on the side of mercy. She defends the new law against the old in the case of Orestes, pacifies the Furies, and changes them into the Eumenides or "gracious ones."

Apollo (uh-PAHL-oh), the god of poetry, music, oracles, and healing. It is he who commands Orestes to avenge his father's death by killing his guilty mother. He then appears at Orestes' trial and defends the accused with the argument that, by killing his mother, Orestes was not guilty of shedding family blood, for the mother, being only the nourisher of the seed, is no relation to her child. Family relationship comes only through the father.

ORFEO

Author: Poliziano (Angelo Ambrogini, 1454-1494)
First published: 1863
Genre: Drama

Locale: Sicily
Time: Antiquity
Plot: Pastoral

Orpheus (OHR-fee-uhs), a young singer and poet who is in love with Eurydice. At the news of his sweetheart's death, he fills the air with his lament and vows to go to the very gates of Tartarus and, with the beauty of his music, win back his love. There, his melodies so charm Pluto that the god grants him permission to lead Eurydice back to Earth on condition that he not look back along the way. Overcome by doubts, he does

look back, only to see Eurydice drawn again among the shades. Heartbroken, he is determined never to seek love again. As punishment for his scorn of love, he is torn to pieces by the Bacchantes.

Eurydice (ew-RIH-dih-see), a nymph who is loved by Orpheus and sought by him in the Underworld after her death. Given permission to follow her lover back to Earth, she is drawn again among the shades when he breaks his promise to Pluto that he will not look back along the way.

Pluto (PLEW-toh), the god of the Underworld, who is so charmed by Orpheus' music that he grants him permission to lead Eurydice back to earth.

Proserpina (proh-SUR-peh-nah), the goddess of the Underworld and the wife of Pluto, so charmed by Orpheus' lyre that she wishes to return Eurydice to him.

Tisiphone (teh-SIH-fuh-nee), one of the Furies. She blocks Orpheus' way when he tries to follow Eurydice back into the Underworld.

Aristaeus (ay-ruhs-TEE-uhs), a shepherd enamored of Eurydice.

Mopsus (MOP-suhs) and

Thyrsis (THUR-sihs), shepherds and companions of Aristaeus.

Mnesillus (neh-SIH-luhs), a satyr.

ORLANDO: A Biography

Author: Virginia Woolf (1882-1941)
First published: 1928
Genre: Novel

Locale: England
Time: 1588-1928
Plot: Phantasmagoric

Orlando, a young English nobleman of Elizabeth I's reign. He is a descendant of fighting men but is himself a poet. He becomes a courtier, though scarcely growing older, during the times of Elizabeth, James I, and Charles II. Failing to find satisfaction in literature, he turns to materialistic goals, searching all Europe for furnishings to refurbish his great mansion. While serving Charles II as Ambassador Extraordinary at Constantinople, Orlando sleeps an entire week, during which he mysteriously changes into a woman. Although now female and beautiful, Orlando is still a restless soul, searching for satisfaction in the brilliant society of Queen Anne's court and, as well, in the streets and pubs of London. During the Victorian period, Orlando, still a woman, marries and returns to literary pursuits. She comes to think of herself, now a woman of thirty-six during the 1920's, as a symbol of English history.

The Archduchess Harriet of Roumania, a large, ugly woman who falls in love with Orlando and forces her attentions upon him. When Orlando, changed into a woman, returns to England in the eighteenth century, she finds the archduchess metamorphosed into Archduke Harry, still in love with Orlando but changed in sex.

Sasha, a Russian princess who comes to England in 1604. She fascinates the youthful Orlando, who falls in love and wants to marry Sasha. The princess, a fickle creature, toys with common sailors and finally deserts Orlando to return home to Russia.

Nicholas Greene, a seventeenth century poet who becomes a pensioner of the youthful Orlando while he is interested in literature. Greene is a man who loves city life; in the 1920's, he turns up again as a successful literary critic and offers to help Orlando to find a publisher for her long poem.

Marmaduke Bonthrop Shelmerdine, Esq., Orlando's Victorian-era husband, who leaves his wife to go to sea. He returns in 1928 aboard an airplane, having become a renowned sea captain during his absence.

ORLANDO FURIOSO

Author: Ludovico Ariosto (1474-1533)
First published: 1516
Genre: Poetry

Locale: France, Spain, and Africa
Time: The eighth century
Plot: Romance

Orlando, the renowned nephew of King Charlemagne and the mightiest paladin among his Twelve Peers. While Paris is under siege by the Saracens, he dreams an evil dream concerning his beloved Angelica, the beautiful princess of Cathay who has caused great dissension among Christian and pagan champions alike. Forsaking his knightly duties, he passes through the enemy lines and goes in search of the damsel. His quest takes him into many lands, and after many strange adventures he is driven mad by the distractions of love and jealousy. Throwing away his armor, he wanders naked and raving among savage beasts, so that all knights are filled with pity when they hear of his sad state. He recovers his sanity after Astolpho, an English knight, finds the wits of his deranged friend in a vial in the region of the moon. His mind restored, Orlando once more engages in valorous deeds and champions the Christian cause. One of his feats is the rescue of Rogero, a gallant Saracen knight now converted to Christianity, who has been cast away on a desert island.

Angelica, the princess of Cathay, who by her great beauty bewitches Orlando, Rinaldo, Ferrau, and Rogero, but in the end marries none of these paladins. Her true love is Medoro, a Saracen knight of lowly birth whom she nurses back to health after he has been wounded in battle. The cause of many misfortunes to others, she herself falls victim to an enchanter's magic and is carried to the island of Ebuda, where she is about to be offered as a sacrifice to a giant orc when she is saved by Rogero, the Saracen knight who forgets his own loved Bradamant and falls under the spell of Angelica's charms. To keep her from harm, Rogero gives her a magic ring, but faithless Angelica uses it to make herself invisible and flees from him. After she has saved the life of Medoro, she returns with him to Cathay.

Rinaldo (rih-NAHL-doh), one of King Charlemagne's Twelve Peers, second only to Orlando in loyalty, bravery, and knightly honor. His chivalric adventures are wonderful and strange but not always related to his quest for Angelica, whom he finally disdains. On several occasions, he is called on to engage in single combat for the honor of the king. Rejoicing when he learns that Rogero has received Christian baptism, he promises the hand of his sister Bradamant to the Saracen hero. Later, he withstands the wishes of his parents and champions the right of Bradamant to marry her beloved.

Rogero (roh-ZHEH-roh), a noble Saracen knight in love with Bradamant, the sister of Rinaldo. He has many marvelous adventures, which include his rescue by Bradamant from the enchanted castle in which Atlantes, a magician, holds him prisoner; his ride on a flying hippogriph; his slaying of the giantess Eriphilia; his rescue of Angelica from the monstrous orc; his forgetting of Bradamant while he woos and loses Angelica; his victory over Mandricardo; his sojourn on a desert island; and his Christian baptism. He is finally restored to his beloved Bradamant. At the feast celebrating the wedding of the happy couple, envoys appear to make Rogero king of Bulgaria. Rogero and Bradamant, according to the poet, were the ancestors of the noble d'Este family of Ferrara.

Bradamant (BRA-dah-mahnt), a maiden knight, the sister of Rinaldo and later the wife of Rogero. In this version of the chivalric story, she is always the romantic heroine, fighting on the side of right, vanquishing evil knights, and rescuing the unfortunate. Her steadfastness in her love for Rogero, the Saracen champion, contrasts sharply with the fickleness of Angelica, while her prowess on the field of battle rivals that of the bravest knights, including her own Rogero, who wins her from his princely rival after defeating her in single combat. The story ends with an account of the happy wedding festivities of Bradamant and Rogero, now turned Christian.

Astolpho (ah-STOHL-foh), the English knight who restores Orlando's wits. Also a rider on the flying hippogriph, he engages in marvelous adventures, among them a journey to the fabled land of Prester John and a trip to the region of the moon, where the senses of poets and others are stored. Astolpho finds there the vial containing Orlando's lost wits and returns them to the hero, who regains his sanity after inhaling the contents of the vial.

Ferrau (fehr-RAW), a brave Saracen knight. Also under Angelica's spell, he battles with Rinaldo, his rival. While the two men fight, Angelica runs away. Ferrau returns to Spain to help his king repel an invasion.

Sacripant (SA-krih-pant), the king of Circassia. When Angelica meets him in the forest, she begs him to protect a damsel in distress. They are overtaken by Rinaldo, who battles with Sacripant and splinters his shield. Angelica flees once more when she sees Sacripant overthrown.

Count Pinabel (PIH-nah-behl), a treacherous knight whom Bradamant encounters while she is searching for Rogero. Pinabel tells her that Rogero and other knights are the captives of Atlantes, a magician whose enchanted castle stands high in the Pyrenees. Later, he tries to kill Bradamant by pushing her into a deep cave.

Melissa, a seer whom Bradamant finds in Merlin's cave, into which Count Pinabel pushed her. Melissa foretells the noble house that will spring from the union of Bradamant and Rogero, and she tells the maiden knight that Rogero can be freed from the spell of the magician Atlantes only with the aid of a magic ring.

Brunello, a dwarf to whom Agramant, the king of Africa, has entrusted the magic ring used by Bradamant to free Rogero and his fellow knights from the spell cast on them by the magician Atlantes.

Atlantes (at-LAN-teez), the aged magician who puts Rogero under the magic spell from which Bradamant frees him. Atlantes is the owner of the flying hippogriph on which Rogero, after his release, is carried to the land of Alcina, a wicked sorceress.

Alcina (ahl-CHEE-nah), the evil sorceress under whose spell Rogero falls. He is saved by Melissa, a seer, who gives him a magic ring to protect him from Alcina's power. Alcina also casts a spell on Astolpho, a brave English knight.

Agramant (A-grah-mant), the king of Africa and the enemy of king Charlemagne. When it is decided to end the siege of Paris by a battle of champions, Agramant chooses Rogero as the greatest of his knights. Rinaldo is the defender of the Christians. During the combat, Agramant treacherously breaks his oath and attacks the French forces. When the Saracens are routed, Rogero, who has promised to accept Christian baptism after the battle, remains with his defeated king, much to the distress of Bradamant, his beloved.

Rodomont (ROH-doh-mont), a fierce and vengeful Saracen warrior, the enemy of all Christians and a cause of dissension among the Saracens. After a quarrel with Mandricardo, prince of Tartary, Rodomont leaves King Agramant's camp. He meets Isabella, princess of Galicia, who is grieving for the death of Zerbino, her beloved knight, whom Rodomont had slain. In a drunken frenzy, Rodomont kills Isabella. Overcome by remorse, he builds a bridge over the river near her tomb and there challenges all traveling knights to combat in honor of the dead princess. He is overcome by mad Orlando and by Bradamant. At the wedding feast of Rogero and Bradamant, Rodomont brashly appears to accuse the Saracen knight of apostasy. Rogero kills him.

Dardinello (dahr-dih-NEHL-loh), the king of Zumara, a Saracen leader killed when the Saracen besiegers of Paris are routed.

Cloridan (CLOHR-ih-dan) and

Medoro (meh-DOH-roh), brothers, brave young Saracen knights who, grieving for the death of their overlord, King Dardinello, kill many Christian knights to avenge their leader's death. Cloridan is killed by a band of Scottish knights, and Medoro is left for dead on the field where Angelica finds him. She nurses him back to health in the nearby hut of a friendly herdsman.

Zerbino (zayr-BEE-noh), prince of Scotland, the leader of the knights who kill Cloridan. Zerbino is killed by fierce Rodomont.

Mandricardo (mahn-dree-KAHR-doh), prince of Tartary, with whom Rodomont quarrels over Doralice, a Spanish princess. Mandricardo is killed by Rogero following an argument over the Tartar's right to wear the escutcheon of Hector, the Trojan hero.

Gradasso (grah-DAS-soh), a Saracen king killed in a battle between pagans and Christians.

Sobrino (soh-BREE-noh), a Saracen king who becomes a Christian after his defeat at Lipadusa.

Brandimart (bran-dih-mahrt), a Christian knight held prisoner by Rodomont. Defeated by Bradamant, the maiden knight, Rodomont promises to release him along with other Christian captives. Brandimart fights with Orlando, Oliver, and Bradamant against the Saracen kings at Lipadusa and is killed in the battle.

Flordelice (flohr-de-LEE-chay), the faithful wife of Brandimart.

Doralice (doh-rah-LEE-chay), the Spanish princess who causes a quarrel between Rodomont and Mandricardo.

Leo, the son of Constantine, the emperor of Greece. When the parents of Bradamant shut her away in a castle in an attempt to make her accept the noble young Greek as her husband, Rogero becomes jealous and decides to kill Leo. Captured while fighting with the Bulgarians against the Greeks, the young Saracen is imprisoned by Theodora, the emperor's sister, in revenge for the death of her son, who was slain by Rogero. Leo, learning of Rogero's plight, rescues him and hides him in his own house. Later, unaware of Rogero's identity, he asks him to act as his champion, after Bradamant has declared that she will marry only a knight who can withstand her in combat. Rogero and Bradamant meet, and Rogero is the victor. Disconsolate because he has won the hand of his beloved for his benefactor, Rogero wanders off into the forest. There, Leo, having renounced his claim to Bradamant after hearing the story of the lovers' trials, finds the young Saracen and returns him to his betrothed.

Theodora, the sister of Emperor Constantine of Greece. To avenge the death of her son, she imprisons the Saracen knight Rogero, his slayer.

Eriphilia (eh-rih-FEE-lee-ah), a female giant slain by Rogero.

ORLANDO INNAMORATO

Author: Matteo Maria Boiardo (c. 1441-1494)
First transcribed: 1483-1495
Genre: Poetry

Locale: France, India, and Africa
Time: The eighth century
Plot: Romance

Orlando, a paladin of France and King Charlemagne's nephew, the Roland of the Carlovingian cycle of chivalric romances. Stricken by love for Angelica, the beautiful princess of Cathay, he, like Rinaldo and Ferrau, sets out in search of her after she has disappeared during a tourney to determine the bravest and most skilled knight, who may claim her as his bride. Discovered in the company of Angelica, Orlando is forced into combat with Ferrau, a jealous Spanish knight. Later, during his wanderings, Orlando slays Agrican, the king of Tartary, another suitor for Angelica's hand. He battles also with Rinaldo, who, having drunk from a fountain whose waters are a cure for love madness, now hates the princess. Later, Angelica dupes Orlando into escorting her to France so that she may continue her pursuit of Rinaldo, with whom she is in love. In the meantime, Rinaldo has drunk from the waters of love. When he meets the travelers, he becomes insanely jealous of Orlando and challenges the knight to a duel. Orlando loses the maiden when she flees to Charlemagne's camp while he and Rinaldo are engaged in a bitter struggle.

Rinaldo (rih-NAHL-doh), another of Charlemagne's paladins, the brother of Bradamant, the maiden warrior, and the cousin of Malagigi, a famed magician. Although aware of the sinister beauty of Angelica, he sets out in pursuit of her. In the forest, he drinks from Merlin's magic spring, and his love for the damsel turns to loathing so great that at the siege of Albracca, during a war between the kingdom of Cathay and the pagan Tartars, he fights on the side of the invading infidels. Angelica, lovesick for the knight who spurns her, continues to pursue him until she drinks from the waters of hate and he from the waters of love. Then Rinaldo pursues the fleeing Angelica. Meeting Orlando and Angelica in the forest, Rinaldo challenges Orlando to a duel. Angelica flees while the two knights join in combat.

Charlemagne (CHAHR-leh-mayn), the king of France. With his paladins, he defends Christendom against the pagans.

Angelica, the lovely princess of Cathay, sent with her brother Argalia to demoralize King Charlemagne's knights. The possessor of the magic ring to overcome all spells or give her invisibility, she uses her wiles to ensnare Orlando, his friend Rinaldo, Ferrau, and many others, including Charlemagne himself. Fickle or enchanted, she manages many intrigues and escapades. Coquette that she is, she cannot win Rinaldo, and she refuses to accept Orlando.

Argalia (ahr-GAY-lee-ah), the son of Galaphron, the king of Cathay, and Angelica's brother. The owner of invulnerable armor and a magic spear that unhorses any knight it touches, he jousts with the Christian knights for the hand of Angelica and takes captive all whom he vanquishes. His four giant bodyguards are killed and he himself is mortally wounded by Ferrau, a Spanish knight. Astolpho, an English knight, gets possession of Argalia's magic spear and with it performs deeds of great valor against both foes and friends.

Malagigi (mah-lah-GEE-gee), the cousin of Rinaldo and the magician who discovers the plot of Argalia and Angelica. Although he is the only one who distrusts the foreign emissaries to King Charlemagne's court, he becomes the first, while attempting to gain possession of Angelica's magic ring, to fall in love with the beautiful princess. Discovered, he is captured by Argalia's giant bodyguards, his book of magic is stolen, and he himself is transported to Cathay by fiends. There, he remains in a dungeon beneath the sea until he agrees to help Angelica in her pursuit of Rinaldo.

Bradamant (BRA-dah-mahnt), a lovely warrior maiden, the sister of Rinaldo. While Paris is under siege by Agramant, the king of Africa, she is so smitten by the gallant Saracen warrior Rogero that she rides into the Saracen lines and doffs her helmet by way of introduction. So overcome is he with love that he fights his former allies for daring to wound her from ambush. The two, already deeply in love, are separated during the battle.

Rogero (roh-ZHEH-roh), a brave and handsome Saracen knight, a paladin of the pagan forces that invade King Charlemagne's dominions and lay siege to Paris. Rogero, long a prisoner of Atlantes, a magician, is released through the power of Angelica's magic ring to join in the fight. The wounds he receives in a tournament heal miraculously, a sign to Agramant, the young king of Africa, that the young hero is their savior. Rogero is knighted and leads the pagans in the siege of Paris. During one of the battles, Bradamant sees him and falls deeply in love with the gallant young knight, but they are separated during the melee.

Ferrau (fehr-RAW), a doughty Spanish knight, in love with Angelica. Finding her and Orlando in the forest, he challenges the paladin to a duel. The fight is broken off when the knights receive word that Gradasso, the king of Sericane, has invaded Spain with a large army. Ferrau departs to help repel the invaders.

Astolpho (ah-STOHL-foh), an English knight. He obtains the magic spear used by Argalia to overthrow Christian knights in the great tournament and with it performs many deeds of valor. He unhorses King Gradasso to free Charlemagne and a number of his knights, prisoners of the pagan monarch.

Gradasso (grah-DAS-soh), the king of Sericane, a monarch who covets the treasures owned by other kings and knights. He invades Europe to obtain possession of Durindana, Orlando's famous sword, and Bayardo, the noble horse of Rinaldo. In the fighting near Barcelona, the king and Rinaldo meet in single combat, the stakes being Gradasso's Christian prisoners against Rinaldo's horse. Neither prevailing, they agree to meet again on the following day, but at the appointed time Rinaldo does not appear. Through the wiles of infatuated Angelica, he has been lured away by Malagigi, the magician. After the king has captured Charlemagne and many of his knights, Gradasso and Astolpho fight, and the king is overthrown. True to the wager made before the combat, he releases his prisoners and returns to Sericane.

Marsilius (mahr-SEE-lee-uhs), the king of Spain, to whom King Charlemagne sends an army, under the leadership of Rinaldo, when King Gradasso invades Spain.

Flordespina (flohr-dehs-PEE-nah), the damsel who brings Ferrau and Orlando word that Spain is being ravaged by a pagan army.

Galaphron (GAH-la-fron), the king of Cathay and the father of Angelica and Argalia. He imprisons Malagigi in a dungeon beneath the sea.

Agrican (AG-rih-can), the king of Tartary. Determined to win Princess Angelica as his bride, he lays siege to Albracca, the capital of Cathay. Orlando and Astolpho fight on the side of the Cathayans, Rinaldo on the side of the invaders. Orlando meets Agrican in single combat and kills him.

Agramant (AG-rah-mahnt), the young king of Africa. Eager to avenge the death of his father, he plans to besiege Paris and humble King Charlemagne. One of his advisers tells him that he cannot hope to succeed without the aid of Rogero, a Saracen knight held prisoner by Atlantes, a sorcerer. With the aid of Angelica's magic ring, stolen by a loyal dwarf, Agramant dispels the mists about the castle of Atlantes. After a tourney in which he displays great gallantry and skill, Rogero becomes Agramant's loyal knight.

Atlantes (at-LAN-teez), the sorcerer who has kept Rogero a prisoner in a castle on the mountain of Carena.

Brunello, the dwarf who steals Angelica's magic ring, needed to set Rogero free from the magic spell of Atlantes.

Rodomont (ROH-doh-mont), a vassal of King Agramant. He and Rinaldo fight in single combat during a great battle between Christians and pagans.

Morgana, a sorceress who keeps her prisoners in an enchanted garden at the bottom of a lake. Orlando frees Rinaldo from her spell.

Namus (NA-muhs), the duke of Bavaria, to whom King Charlemagne entrusts Angelica after she seeks protection in his camp.

ORLEY FARM

Author: Anthony Trollope (1815-1882)
First published: 1862; serial form, 1861-1862
Genre: Novel

Locale: England
Time: Mid-nineteenth century
Plot: Domestic realism

Lady Mary Mason, the widow of Sir Joseph Mason, forty-five years her senior. After Sir Joseph's death, her son Lucius was awarded Orley Farm by a codicil to his father's will. The codicil had been contested by Joseph Mason, Sir Joseph's son by an earlier marriage, but Lady Mason won the court case. Later, a shady attorney, Dockwrath, angry at Lucius, digs up some papers that lead him to believe the codicil a forgery. He gets Joseph Mason to reopen the case. Lady Mason is befriended by Sir Peregrine Orme. When Sir Peregrine proposes, Lady Mason confesses that the codicil was, indeed, a forgery, her only means of gaining property for her son. Nevertheless, she also wins the second case. She then confesses to Lucius, who turns the property over to Joseph, and mother and son leave for Germany.

Lucius Mason, the son of Sir Joseph and Lady Mary Mason, educated in Germany. When he returns, he decides to establish Orley Farm as a working experiment for his agricultural theories. This project involves forcing Dockwrath off his small fields, and Dockwrath's ire precipitates the second court case. He proposes to Sophia Furnival, but she refuses him after he is no longer in control of Orley Farm.

Sir Peregrine Orme, a wealthy and highly respected gentleman, the owner of The Cleeve. Chivalrous, he is willing to stand by his proposal to Lady Mason even after he knows she has forged the codicil.

Mrs. Edith Orme, the widowed daughter-in-law of Sir Peregrine Orme, who lives with him. Also loyal to Lady Mason, she accompanies her to court.

Peregrine Orme (Perry), the son of Mrs. Edith Orme and heir to The Cleeve. He proposes to Madeline Stavely but is rejected.

Joseph Mason, owner of Groby Park in Yorkshire and older son of Sir Joseph Mason. He is a severe man, a county magistrate, but he is not unjust; he has always believed that his father intended to leave Orley Farm to him.

Mrs. Mason, his wife, an inhospitable, parsimonious woman.

Judge Stavely, a kind and perceptive judge who owns Noningsby. He is proud that his daughter has chosen an ugly, brilliant man rather than the suitable young Peregrine Orme.

Lady Stavely, his devoted wife, who cannot understand her daughter but finally gives her blessing to the marriage.

Madeline Stavely, their beautiful daughter, who chooses and waits for the penniless Felix Graham to win her parents' permission to propose.

Augustus Stavely, a friend of Felix Graham. He, like Lucius Mason, proposes to Sophia Furnival, but she puts him off.

Felix Graham, a brilliant and ugly young barrister who is the youngest lawyer taking Lady Mason's case. At first he is engaged to Mary Snow, a girl he befriends and is training to be his wife. He then breaks several bones while hunting at the Stavely's, is forced to remain at Noningsby, and falls in love with Madeline. He arranges another wedding for Mary Snow and marries Madeline himself.

Mr. Furnival, an attorney for Lady Mason and a member of Parliament. He suspects that Lady Mason is guilty but remains loyal to her.

Mrs. Furnival, née **Kitty Blacker**, his wife, who is frequently left alone while he works. At one point, she suspects her husband is attached to Lady Mason and leaves him, but she later returns.

Sophia Furnival, their pretty daughter, who flirts her way into two proposals but accepts neither.

Samuel Dockwrath, a shady attorney who wants to be employed by Joseph Mason. His efforts are unsuccessful.

Mrs. Miriam Usbech Dockwrath, his wife, the mother of sixteen children.

Jonathan Usbech, Miriam's father and Sir Joseph's attorney. He was supposed to be ill at the time the codicil was drawn up, and he died before the first trial.

John Kenneby, Sir Joseph's former clerk, who testifies that he had witnessed the signing of a document. Heckled by the attorneys at both trials, he acknowledges that he did not know the nature of the document he witnessed.

Mr. Moulder, a salesman of tea, coffee, and brandy, brother-in-law to John Kenneby.

Mrs. Mary Anne Moulder, Kenneby's sister, anxious to promote his marriage to a wealthy widow.

Mrs. Smiley, a widow who owns brick fields and is engaged to John Kenneby.

Bridget Bolster, a chambermaid who testifies at both trials.

Mr. Chaffanbrass, a seasoned attorney and a friend of Mr. Furnival, adept at breaking down witnesses.

Mr. Solomon Aram, an Old Bailey lawyer, also employed for Lady Mason.

Mr. Matthew Round, attorney for the firm of Round and Crook, employed by Joseph Mason.

Mr. Crabwitz, an old assistant in Mr. Furnival's office.

Miss Martha Biggs, the friend who wants Mrs. Furnival to join her in Red Lion Square when she contemplates leaving Mr. Furnival.

Mary Snow, the daughter of an engraver, engaged to Felix Graham, later married to Albert Fitzallen.

Albert Fitzallen, a worker in an apothecary shop, helped by Felix Graham.

Mr. Snow, an engraver, Mary's father, a habitual gin drinker.

Mrs. Thomas, who uncovers Mary's correspondence with Albert.

Mr. Green, the curate at Groby Park.

Mrs. Green, his wife, who receives patent steel furniture in bad condition from Mrs. Mason.

Mr. Slow and

Mr. Bideawhile, attorneys to Sir Peregrine Orme.

OROONOKO: Or, The Royal Slave, a True History

Author: Aphra Behn (1640-1689)
First published: c. 1678
Genre: Novel

Locale: Africa and Surinam
Time: The seventeenth century
Plot: Didactic

Oroonoko (oh-rew-NOH-koh), a prince of Coromantien, Africa. At seventeen, he is the successful general of his country's army. In love with Imoinda, he is furious when his king, also his grandfather, takes her into his harem. Oroonoko takes Imoinda as a lover. Both he and the girl are later enslaved by the English and taken to Surinam. They try to escape. When captured, Oroonoko is savagely beaten. Caught again while attempting to escape, he is publicly executed in a brutal manner. To save Imoinda from such a fate, he has killed her with her blessing.

Aboan (ah-BOH-ahn), Oroonoko's faithful companion and friend. Along with Oroonoko, he is enslaved while visiting a supposedly friendly British ship.

Imoinda (ee-moh-EEN-dah), the beloved of Oroonoko. She is sold into slavery by the king of Coromantien after Oroonoko became her lover. Reunited with Oroonoko in Surinam, she becomes pregnant by him. To save her from ravishment and a shameful death, Oroonoko cuts off her head.

The king, Oroonoko's grandfather, ruler of Coromantien. He is more than a hundred years old, but he wants Imoinda for his harem and treacherously takes her from Oroonoko.

A slaveholder, Oroonoko's owner and friend, who renames him Caesar. A kind man, he nurses Oroonoko when he is brutally beaten by his captors after attempting to escape.

The governor, a brutal, treacherous man who on two occasions promises Oroonoko immunity if he will surrender, only to betray him each time and have him beaten.

THE ORPHAN: Or, The Unhappy Marriage

Author: Thomas Otway (1652-1685)
First published: 1680
Genre: Drama

Locale: Bohemia
Time: The seventeenth century
Plot: Domestic

Monimia (moh-NEE-mee-ah), an orphan. A ward of Acasto, she is loved by his twin sons Polydore and Castalio. She genuinely loves only Castalio. She secretly marries Castalio but is deceived into spending the night with Polydore. Filled with remorse for having deceived her husband with his brother, even though unknowingly, she finally poisons herself and dies, a victim of circumstances.

Castalio (kas-TAY-lee-oh), the overscrupulous twin son of Acasto. Minimizing his own passion for Monimia to be fair to his brother Polydore, he encourages his brother's less scrupulous pursuit of the lady. After Castalio secretly marries Monimia, Polydore, ignorant of the marriage, tricks the bride into spending the night with him. When Castalio learns the truth of the affair and that his wife is dead by her own hand, he stabs himself and dies.

Polydore (PAW-lee-dohr), Acasto's less scrupulous twin son. Ignorant of his brother's secret marriage to Monimia, he tricks her into spending the night with him. When he learns that he has deceived his brother's wife, he is filled with such horror and remorse that he contrives to die by Castalio's sword.

Acasto (ah-KAS-toh), a nobleman, the father of Castalio and Polydore, and Monimia's guardian.

Chamont (SHAY-mont), a young soldier, the impetuous brother of Monimia.

Serina (seh-REE-nah), Acasto's daughter.

ORPHEUS

Author: Jean Cocteau (1889-1963)
First published: 1927
Genre: Drama

Locale: Thrace, Greece
Time: Early twentieth century
Plot: Tragicomedy

Orpheus (OHR-fee-uhs), a poet. An impulsive and self-centered writer, he is abused by the need to understand truth and to convey his insights in verse. Easily irritated by his wife's demands on his attention, he gives in to his passions, reflected to petty vindictiveness, jealousies, and anger. In listening intensely to the soundings of the prophetic Horse, he disregards the presence of his wife and induces within her the pain of rejection. This marital conflict begs for resolution, but through her attempts to vindicate these slights, Eurydice destroys the Horse and brings about, ironically and indirectly, her own death, resuscitation, and final death. By observing, and participating in, these actions, Orpheus comes to recognize the reality of pain that, characterizing the human situation, becomes the substance of poetry. Controlled by the passions of his temperament, he disregards the voice of reason and disobeys the directions that enable him to preserve Eurydice. Anger generated by Eurydice's words compels him to direct his sight to his wife, who is immediately condemned to death. The Bacchantes assassinate Orpheus. Thus, Orpheus experiences and penetrates the nature of the suffering created by human passion and moral blindness.

Eurydice (yew-RIH-dih-see), Orpheus' wife and a former member of the Bacchantes. As egoistical as her husband, she becomes envious of the Horse, which absorbs Orpheus' time and energies. Submitting to her passions, she bickers; through her intrusions into Orpheus' compulsive creative efforts, she induces frustration and subsequent outbursts of anger in her husband. As victimizer, she seeks revenge and consequent contentment through the killing of the Horse. As victim, she becomes a ploy of Aglaonice, who, as leader of the Bacchantes, hears Eurydice's request to destroy the Horse but sacrifices her in a determination to destroy Orpheus.

The Horse, the source of Orpheus' inspiration. Through the transmission of the letters "MERDE," the Horse conveys an acronym foretelling an event ("Madame Eurydice will return from Hell"), as well as a word whereby Orpheus insults the Bacchantes and brings about his own decapitation. In spite of the ambiguity of meaning, the letters tapped by the Horse present an abstraction to be converted, through dramatization, into the concreteness of human suffering. As agent of the dynamics of the nature of life, the Horse enables Orpheus the poet-seer to penetrate the pain that is the source and crux of the human situation to be expressed in verse.

Aglaonice (ah-glay-OH-nih-see), the leader of the sorority of Bacchantes. She dislikes men and, like Orpheus and Eurydice, relinquishes reason to egoism and envy. Resentful of the marriage of her former Bacchante, Eurydice, she is obsessed by a determination to destroy Orpheus. In respecting Eurydice's request to kill the Horse, she also manipulates Eurydice's death and resuscitation. After Orpheus' inadvertent glance at his wife, condemning her to death, Aglaonice justifies her need to inflict pain on Orpheus, which results in his decapitation by the Bacchantes.

Heurtebise (hewrt-BIZ), a glazier. As an intermediary among the protagonists, he advances the dramatic action. After Orpheus' shattering of a windowpane, he arrives to make repairs. In bringing the poisoned sugar to assassinate the Horse and a poisoned envelope that will send Eurydice to Hades for the first time, he acts as an agent of Aglaonice, but he also listens to Eurydice's complaints and attempts to placate her. After Eurydice's descent to the Underworld, he informs Orpheus of his wife's death and, articulating the demands of reason and moderation, advises him, in vain, on the means to find and resuscitate her. As representative of reason, he becomes a victim of the passion generated by others: During the attacks of the Bacchantes on Orpheus, he plunges into the mirror that is the entrance to Hades.

Death, a beautiful young woman appearing in a pink evening dress.

Azarael and

Raphael, assistants to Death.

The Commissioner of Police, who investigates Orpheus' death and continues Orpheus' search for truth embedded in earthly phenomena.

— *Donald Gilman*

ORPHEUS AND EURYDICE

Author: Unknown
First published: Unknown
Genre: Short fiction

Locale: Thrace and the Underworld
Time: Antiquity
Plot: Mythic

Orpheus (OHR-fee-uhs), the son of Apollo and the Muse Calliope. His father teaches him to play the lyre so that all nature stops to listen to his music. He goes to the Underworld to redeem the shade of his dead wife, Eurydice. His wish to have her returned to him is granted, providing he does not look back until he has left the Underworld. He does look back, however, and Eurydice disappears. Later, Orpheus is killed by a group of Thracian maidens in a Bacchic frenzy. Upon his death, he joins Eurydice in the Underworld.

Apollo (uh-POL-oh), a god and the father of Orpheus. He gives a lyre to his son and teaches him to play it beyond the power of any other mortal.

Eurydice (yew-RIH-dih-see), the mortal wife of Orpheus. Fleeing from a shepherd who desires her, she is bitten by a snake and dies. She is granted permission to return to the world with Orpheus if he will not look back until they have left

the Underworld. When he looks back, she disappears again.

Hades (HAY-deez) and

Proserpine (proh-SUR-puh-nee), the king and queen of the Underworld. Moved by Orpheus' music, they grant his request to take Eurydice back among the living, providing he does not look back at her while he is still in the Underworld.

Calliope (kuh-LI-uh-pee), one of the Muses, Orpheus' mother.

Hymen (HI-mehn), the god of marriage, who brings no happy omens to the wedding of Orpheus and Eurydice.

Tantalus (TAN-tuh-luhs),

Ixion (ihk-SI-uhn),

The Daughters of Danaus (DAN-ee-uhs), and

Sisyphus (SIHS-ih-fuhs), shades of the Underworld who are spellbound by the beauty of Orpheus' music.

OTHELLO: The Moor of Venice

Author: William Shakespeare (1564-1616)
First published: 1622; revised, 1623
Genre: Drama

Locale: Venice and Cyprus
Time: Early sixteenth century
Plot: Tragedy

Othello (oh-THEHL-oh), a Moorish general in the service of Venice. A romantic and heroic warrior with a frank and honest nature, he has a weakness that makes him vulnerable to Iago's diabolic temptation. He becomes furiously jealous of his innocent wife and his loyal lieutenant. His character decays, and he connives with Iago to have his lieutenant murdered. Finally, he decides to execute his wife with his own hands. After killing her, he learns of her innocence, and he judges and executes himself.

Iago (ee-AH-goh), Othello's ancient (ensign), a satirical malcontent who is envious of the appointment of Michael Cassio to the position of Othello's lieutenant. He at least pretends to suspect his wife Emilia of having an illicit affair with the Moor. A demi-devil, as Othello calls him, he destroys Othello, Desdemona, Roderigo, his own wife, and himself. He is William Shakespeare's most consummate villain, perhaps sketched in several of Shakespeare's other characters: Aaron the Moor in *Titus Andronicus*, Richard of Gloucester in *Henry VI* and *Richard III*, and Don John in *Much Ado About Nothing*. He is echoed in Edmund in *King Lear* and Iachimo in *Cymbeline*. He contains strong elements of the Devil and the Vice in the medieval morality plays.

Desdemona (dehz-dee-MOH-nuh), the daughter of Brabantio and wife of Othello. An innocent, idealistic, and romantic

girl, she gives her love completely to her warrior husband. In her fear and shock at his violent behavior, she lies to him about her lost handkerchief, thus convincing him of her guilt. Even when she is dying, she tries to protect him from her kinsmen. Other characters can be judged by their attitude toward her.

Emilia (ee-MIHL-ee-uh), Iago's plainspoken wife. Intensely loyal to her mistress, Desdemona, she is certain that some malicious villain has belied her to the Moor. She does not suspect that her husband is that villain until too late to save her mistress. She is unwittingly the cause of Desdemona's death; when she finds the lost handkerchief and gives it to Iago, he uses it to inflame the Moor's insane jealousy. Emilia grows in stature throughout the play and reaches tragic dignity when she refuses to remain silent about Iago's villainy, even though her speaking the truth costs her her life. Her dying words, clearing Desdemona of infidelity, drive Othello to his self-inflicted death.

Michael Cassio (KAS-ee-oh), Othello's lieutenant. Devoted to his commander and Desdemona, he is impervious to Iago's temptations where either is concerned. He is, however, given to loose living, and his behavior when discussing Bianca with Iago fires Othello's suspicions, after Iago has made Othello believe they are discussing Desdemona. Cassio's drinking on duty and becoming involved in a brawl lead to his replacement by Iago. He escapes the plot of Iago and Othello to murder him, and he succeeds Othello as governor of Cyprus.

Brabantio (brah-BAN-shee-oh), a Venetian senator. Infuriated by his daughter's elopement with the Moor, he appeals to the senate to recover her. Losing his appeal, he publicly casts her off and warns Othello that a daughter who deceives her father may well be a wife who deceives her husband. This warning plants a small seed of uncertainty in Othello's heart, which Iago waters diligently. Brabantio dies brokenhearted at losing Desdemona and does not learn of her horrible death.

Roderigo (rod-eh-REE-goh), a young Venetian suitor of Desdemona. The gullible victim of Iago, who promises Desdemona to him, he aids in bringing about the catastrophe and earns a well-deserved violent death, ironically inflicted by Iago. The degradation of Roderigo is in striking contrast to the growth of Cassio. Iago, who makes use of Roderigo, has profound contempt for him.

Bianca (bee-AN-kuh), a courtesan in Cyprus. Cassio gives her Desdemona's handkerchief, which Iago has planted in his chambers. She thus serves doubly in rousing Othello's fury.

Montano (mohn-TAH-noh), a former governor of Cyprus. He and Cassio quarrel while drinking (by Iago's machinations), and Montano is seriously wounded. This event causes Cassio's removal. Montano recovers and aids in apprehending Iago when his villainy is revealed.

Gratiano (gray-shee-AH-noh), Brabantio's brother. He and Lodovico go to Cyprus from Venice and aid in restoring order and destroying Iago.

Lodovico (loh-doh-VEE-koh), a kinsman of Brabantio. As the man of most authority from Venice, he ends the play after appointing Cassio governor of Cyprus to succeed the self-killed Othello.

The clown, a servant of Othello. Among Shakespeare's clowns, he has perhaps the weakest and briefest role.

OTHER LEOPARDS

Author: Denis Williams (1923-   )
First published: 1963
Genre: Novel

Locale: The Sudan Savannah
Time: The 1960's
Plot: Impressionistic realism

Lionel "Lobo" Froad, the black South American narrator and protagonist, who is in search of his cultural identity in the fictional town of Johkara in northern Africa. He describes himself as having a "black-Frank-Sinatra face," stumpy height, and woolly hair; he is described by others as having a face that is not African. He is employed as an archaeological draftsman by Dr. Hughie King. His aversion to King's predilection for European colonial thought and mannerisms is so strong that he eventually stabs King with a screwdriver and leaves him to die in the jungle. At the close of the novel, Froad becomes savagelike: He strips himself of his clothing, cakes himself in mud, and hides in a tree, waiting to be discovered as King's killer.

Dr. Hughie King, a British archaeologist and Froad's employer. His demeanor is reminiscent of old European colonialists. He is a professional, intelligent, and thorough scientist, but his demanding and temperamental nature ultimately drives Froad insane. While on a dig in the jungle, King is stabbed (presumably to death) by Froad.

The Chief, a black Christian minister and Eve's father. He is an intimidating man whose strident expressions of faith are supported by his thick build and stern demeanor. Early in the novel, he asks Froad to write a tract in support of the black

Christians in Johkara, perhaps in the hope that Froad's professional affiliations would aid in making his arguments credible. His belief in the righteousness of Christianity is so strong that he cuts off his daughter Eve for marrying Hassan, a Muslim.

Eve, the Chief's daughter, Froad's lover, and the estranged wife of Hassan and mother of his child. She is young, pretty, and exotic. She wears formidable European clothes, which render her improperly dressed for Johkara's environmental and political climates. She eventually becomes Froad's lover and falsely claims to be pregnant by him.

Hassan, Eve's Muslim husband. He is an army man who wears only khaki, brass, and leather. His estranged wife, Eve, was born into a Christian family and, according to Muslim law, is not allowed to keep the child of a Muslim. He tries to retrieve the child from her home but is stopped by Froad.

Catherine, King's secretary and the woman whom Froad wants to marry. She is a natural-looking country girl whose demure appearance is misleading. When she hears of Eve's false claims of pregnancy, she leaves Froad.

Mohammed, an Iranian. He offers Froad money to write a tract supporting the Arab cause, and Froad accepts.

— *Jennifer E. Berkley*

THE OTHER ONE
(La Seconde)

Author: Colette (Sidonie-Gabrielle Colette, 1873-1954)
First published: 1929
Genre: Novel

Locale: Franche-Comté and Paris
Time: The 1920's
Plot: Psychological

Farou (fah-REW), a playwright. Handsome and overpowering, his presence dominates his household and completely absorbs its inhabitants: Fanny, his wife; Jane, his secretary and mistress; and, Jean, his son. Though he has been constantly

unfaithful, he just as constantly insists that Fanny has always claimed his deepest devotion and that he depends on her to set right the disorders of their lives.

Fanny, Farou's beautiful wife. Proud in the knowledge that her husband is her one love, she learns of his intimacy with Jane and is disturbed by the necessity of being involved in one of his affairs and of sharing with another her pain over his faithlessness. When she finally tells Jane of her knowledge of the affair, she is suddenly afraid to be left alone, and she asks the girl to stay and provide a measure of security for them all.

Jane, Farou's secretary and a companion to Fanny. As she becomes Farou's mistress, she also becomes Fanny's affectionate companion. When her affair with Farou is discovered, she prepares to leave, but at Fanny's gentle urging, she consents to stay.

Jean Farou, Farou's son by a former mistress. He is in love with Jane and suffers intensely over her relationship with his father.

OTHER PEOPLE'S WORLDS

Author: William Trevor (William Trevor Cox, 1928-   )
First published: 1980
Genre: Novel

Locale: London and Stone St. Martin, Gloucestershire
Time: The 1950's
Plot: Psychological realism

Julia Ferndale, a plump, forty-seven-year-old widow with a part-time typing job. She lives protected in her mother's charming country home and has romantic illusions about marrying Francis Tyte, fourteen years her junior. Her devout Catholicism gives her a strong sense of compassion for those less fortunate than she. When she realizes that her marriage to Francis is a fraud, she extends this compassion to all of Francis' other victims. In fact, she is the only one who recognizes that Francis is incapable of telling the truth. She is the link between his fantasies, or lies, and his victims.

Francis Tyte, an actor and psychopath. He is thirty-three years old and adept at manipulating everyone for his own purposes. He is immoral, marrying twice for money, prostituting himself with men, and exploiting people, both rich and poor. On a whim, he gets Doris pregnant. Also on a whim, he marries Julia in a Catholic ceremony. On their honeymoon, he absconds with Julia's jewels, which really belong to her mother. He leaves behind him distraught parents, a mistress, a child, Julia's family, his fellow actors, and anyone else who has caught his devious attention.

Mrs. Anstey, Julia's mother. She is the only one who initially senses something wrong with Francis. She does not tell her daughter of her suspicions.

Katherine, Julia's twenty-year-old daughter. She plays a minor role in witnessing her mother's romance, marriage, and shame.

Henrietta, Julia's twenty-three-year-old daughter. She too plays a minor role in witnessing her mother's romance, marriage, and shame.

Doris Smith, Francis Tyte's common-law wife. She is the mother of Joy, the child she had by Francis. She is a saleswoman, an alcoholic, and gullible. Not only does she participate in Francis' fantasies, but she also embellishes them with fantasies of her own. In an alcoholic daze, she disrupts the calm of the old age home where Francis' parents live, intrudes on Julia's life, and ultimately murders Francis' first wife.

Joy, the thirteen-year-old daughter of Doris and Francis. She is on drugs, experienced in sex and violence, and masterful at manipulating her mother and, later, Mrs. Anstey. She provides several comic scenes because of her wild outrageousness.

Father Lavin, the Roman Catholic priest who helps Julia. Secretly in love with Julia, he tries to help her through the ordeals that beset her after the fiasco of the honeymoon, but he is helpless. Rather than lean on him and on prayer, Julia prefers action in resolving the chaos Francis has created in her family's life, Doris and Joy's lives, and the lives of many others.

Susanna Music, a young actress who works with Francis on a television thriller. She becomes another victim of Francis' fantasies when Doris comes to believe that Susanna is responsible for a murder and for Francis' departure from England.

— *Lila Chalpin*

THE OTHER SIDE

Author: Mary Gordon (1949-   )
First published: 1989
Genre: Novel

Locale: New York City and Ireland
Time: Primarily 1985
Plot: Family

Vincent MacNamara, an eighty-eight-year-old Irish immigrant. He is devout, intelligent, and loved by most people who meet him. He acts as the main cohesive force of his large family. Vincent loves his fiery wife, Ellen, but he no longer feels able to cope with her anger and fear. He is returning home, having spent nearly nine months in a nursing home after Ellen knocked him down and broke his hip. Vincent always has led a moral life and enjoys mechanical problems to occupy his mind. He loves his children and especially his grandchildren, Camille and Dan. Now, at the end of his life, he fears that he has allowed his wife to damage their children with her demands and contempt. At the same time, he remembers with

joy the passionate love he and Ellen have shared. His promise to her that she will be allowed to die at home forces him to return to her.

Ellen MacNamara, Vincent's wife. More than ninety years old, she is incoherent and bedridden from a series of strokes. She can understand only that Vincent seems to have left her. In her rage and terror, she can speak only curses and obscenities. As a young woman in Ireland, when she saw her father abusing her mother, she used her anger as an impetus to emigrate; she feels the same anger and contempt for the church. Her anger makes her treat most strangers as enemies. Her commitment to intellectual and social causes made her dismiss her two rather ordinary daughters; she often humiliated them and at last psychologically abandoned them in favor of two of her grandchildren, both of whom she stole from their mothers. She retains tenderness primarily for her grandson Dan, whose father was killed in World War II. Vincent has been the only positive force in her life, but his generous love makes her fear that even after sixty years of marriage he may well leave her. Her rage and urge to destroy her family are qualities that have reappeared in her offspring.

Daniel MacNamara, a lawyer in partnership with his cousin Cam. After his father was killed, Ellen drove his ineffectual mother away and reared her grandson herself. Daniel has inherited much of his grandfather Vincent's skills in peacemaking; such harmony as now exists in the family comes mostly from Dan. In his youth, he was very close to Cam, and they still understand each other well, although each has a life that the other does not share. He treasures a memory of his childhood closeness to his grandmother. Since the failure of his marriage twelve years ago, Dan has lived with Sharon Breen, a secretary from his law office. For a month each summer, his difficult teenage daughters, Darci and Staci, live with him as well.

Camille (Cam) MacNamara Ulichni, a lawyer, Dan's partner. She inherited Ellen's strength and fire. After her father's death, eight-year-old Cam soon saw her mother's limitations and turned to her grandparents, especially to Vincent, for the emotional support she needed. Her love for her mother always has been strongly colored by her contempt for her mother's weakness, but when her mother's health seemed in

danger, Cam abandoned her own plans to work for social justice and instead married Bob Ulichni and joined her cousin in practicing law. Her relationship with her husband, never close, is even more distant now that she has begun a love affair with Ira Silverman.

Magdalene, Cam's mother, Ellen and Vincent's oldest daughter. She owns a fashionable beauty salon. She has been waiting to die since she was diagnosed with breast cancer in 1965. She rarely leaves her room and spends the day drinking sherry and trying on clothes. She is afraid of Ellen and is angry and self-pitying about her daughter's lack of sympathy. She cannot believe that she has been healed.

Theresa, Vincent and Ellen's second daughter, whose anger at her mother has deepened over the years. Now a charismatic Catholic who talks to the Holy Ghost, Theresa still seeks ways to humiliate her mother.

Marilyn, Theresa's oldest daughter, a nurse. She has returned home briefly to help nurse her grandmother, partly out of gratitude for Ellen's accepting attitude toward her mixed-race children. She dreads telling her mother that her third marriage has failed.

Sheilah, Theresa's second daughter, a social worker devoted to her Irish heritage. Sheilah left her vocation as a nun to marry a priest she had met at a civil rights sit-in. Her desire to hurt and humiliate others masks her deep longing for love.

John, Theresa's son, who is aimless, dissolute, angry, and possibly dangerous. At the age of thirty-seven, he has come home to live with his parents.

— *Ann Davison Garbett*

OTHER VOICES, OTHER ROOMS

Author: Truman Capote (Truman Streckfus Persons, 1924-1984)
First published: 1948
Genre: Novel

Locale: Mississippi
Time: Mid-twentieth century
Plot: Psychological realism

Joel Knox, a thirteen-year-old entering puberty. He is bright, beautiful, and in need of love and acceptance from someone who "belongs" to him. He is a boy in search of someone to be "with." He goes eagerly to Skully's Landing when his father, out of the blue, invites him there to live. Because he is so bright and insightful, his misjudgment of Ellen is puzzling. When she does not respond to the letter he mailed her saying that he hates the Landing, he thinks she has rejected him, but he had found, scattered on the ground, the coins he put in the mailbox, so it seems odd that he thought she got the letter. Likewise, at the end of the novel, when he learns that a woman and a deaf girl from New Orleans have been at the Landing, it does not cross his mind to think it could have been Ellen and Louise, although he immediately says he has a deaf cousin in New Orleans. Perhaps Truman Capote wanted Joel blind in his spot of greatest need; perhaps Joel deliberately blinds himself rather than ponder, too much, that he had decided he and Randolph were "the same."

Cousin Randolph, who seems to be a patient, laissez-faire person. He is openly homosexual and entices Joel into a relationship, but he never forces himself on anyone. He generally gives everyone what they ask from him—even his cousin, Amy, though he enjoys tormenting her before acquiescing.

The servants, Zoo and Papadaddy, do as they please, with no interference from Randolph. Zoo leaves "forever" after Papadaddy dies, but she comes back after she is raped and brutalized. Although she is different, he treats her the same. Even with Joel, he does not push. Except at the novel's end, when Ellen is coming, he gives Joel complete freedom of movement, asking nothing from him. When Joel is ill and being nursed by Randolph, he entertains the boy endlessly. When Joel clings to Randolph in victimlike dependency, the man does not press his advantage. Indeed, he gives every appearance of despairing that Joel will ever respond as he wishes, yet he remains patient. Dark hints suggest a different Randolph, however, but Capote keeps readers outside his inner thoughts. One dark hint is his cold—almost amused—telling of Zoo's wedding night, as if he manipulated Keg's action. Another is Amy's attitude toward him: She seems frantic to please him but never quite does, and in spite of giving in to her small requests, there is a sense of his enjoying her anxiety.

Idabel Thompkins, Joel's tomboy friend, who works hard at hating being a girl. She beats her twin sister, and she hits Joel when, in a burst of tenderness, he kisses her cheek. Like Joel, she is a displaced person. Wisteria says as much, implying that the reason Idabel has fallen for her is because she thinks herself a freak, like Wisteria. Indeed, at the fair, Idabel is moved by a two-headed baby pickled in a jar. The implication is that, as a twin so different from the frilly Florabel, she is a two-headed freak. At the fair, Joel and Idabel get separated; the next Joel hears from her is through a postcard from Alabama, where she has been sent "for life." The card comes as Joel is deciding that Randolph is the only one who loves him, and he tosses the card into the fire. He immediately regrets doing so, but the card is gone forever, like Idabel.

Zoo Fever, the black cook who seems to have been at the Landing all her life. Randolph and Amy both remember the night of her marriage to Keg Brown, ten years earlier, when she was fourteen. Zoo, a supple, slender woman who always wears a scarf around her long neck, is superstitiously religious. The scarf hides a scar that encircles her neck where Keg slit it on their wedding night. At first, she nurtures Joel, but she leaves for Washington, D.C. When she comes back, both she and Joel have changed.

Ellen Kendall, Joel's aunt, who loved him and let him go to the Landing. She comes to see if he is happy. Randolph learns she is coming and rushes Joel off to Little Sunshine's. Amy tells Ellen and Louise, Joel's deaf cousin, that Joel and Randolph are on a long squirrel hunt. Evidently convinced that Joel is happy, they leave.

— *Jo Culbertson Davis*

OTHER WOMEN

Author: Lisa Alther (1944-   )
First published: 1984
Genre: Novel

Locale: An unnamed city in New Hampshire
Time: Early 1980's
Plot: Domestic realism

Caroline Kelly, a woman in her thirties, the divorced mother of a son and a daughter. She earns her living as an emergency room nurse. She has shared a house for some time with Diana, her lesbian lover, but their relationship has problems that are becoming increasingly serious, and she feels a lack of security and the lack of social acceptability that marriage to a man would provide. She is tempted by the offer of marriage from Brian Stone, who is, like her former husband, a physician. Trying to decide, Caroline goes into therapy with Hannah Burke. In the course of the therapy, she recognizes that her upbringing, by parents too busy being do-gooders to give any affection to their children, is at the root of her lack of security. Even her choice of an occupation is evidence of her compulsion, enforced by her childhood training, to help others before helping herself. In the end, she recognizes that whatever her future holds, she will not remarry, she will not worry about sexual orientation, and she will change her occupation. Hannah declares that Caroline's therapy is at an end; she may need help again in the future, but she has progressed to a point at which she can be confident in her ability to make sane choices.

Hannah Burke, a psychotherapist specializing in women's problems. Despite a long and happy marriage, she has lived for many years with despair resulting from the accidental deaths of two of her children, and her own unhappy childhood enables her to understand the difficulties that have led Caroline to the verge of a breakdown. Through a combination of sympathy and toughness, she is able to bring Caroline to an understanding of the causes of many of her problems, at the same time taking their relationship to one of friendship. Partly through her relationship with Caroline, she is also able to find renewed richness in her marriage to Arthur Burke.

Jason and

Jackie, Caroline's sons. They are healthy and well adjusted, finding nothing strange in their mother's lifestyle. When Jackie is reprimanded at a family Thanksgiving dinner for pointing out that he has not received enough food—most of it having gone to objects of his grandparents' charity who were invited to share the meal—he runs away. His action shocks Caroline into the realization that she has never reacted strongly enough to her parents' coldness toward her, despite the injury she has suffered from their neglect.

Jackson, a physician who was Caroline's husband. He has found a new wife who is properly subservient to him and his wishes, and he plays no part in the life of Caroline and his sons.

Richard Dean, a hippie for whom Caroline left Jackson. His lifestyle freed her from the limitations imposed by Jackson, but she soon tired of the absence of responsibility in that lifestyle. Dean was angry that, through a relationship with another of his lovers, Caroline discovered that she could love a woman.

Brian Stone, a physician who wants to marry Caroline and whose proposal tempts her. He is a satisfactory lover and is attentive to her in ways that Jackson was not. Eventually, however, Caroline comes to realize that he is fundamentally not much different from Jackson and that marriage to a man will not solve her problems.

Diana, who shares her house with Caroline. They have been lovers for several years. Their relationship has deteriorated, however, to the point where even their reconciliations turn into contests to see which can sacrifice more for the other. Despite their affection for each other, they are forced to the recognition that they cannot have a healthy relationship. Caroline realizes that she must move out and find new friends as well as a new way of living.

— *John M. Muste*

OTHERWISE ENGAGED

Author: Simon Gray (1936-   )
First published: 1975
Genre: Drama

Locale: London, England
Time: The 1970's
Plot: Comedy

Simon Hench, a successful, middle-aged publisher who is trying throughout the play to listen to a new recording of Richard Wagner's *Parsifal* while his wife is out of town. Simon is the central figure, toward whom all the characters gravitate. He is interrupted by the romantic and career problems of his student lodger, his brother, his friend Jeff, Jeff's girlfriend, an old schoolmate, and finally his wife, Beth. Each interruption casts a different light on Simon through his relationships with the others. At first, Simon seems a paragon of virtue and sanity, but by the end of the play he is clearly a participant in, and perhaps even a cause of, the troubles of others. Simon is left with his estranged wife's pregnancy (possibly by another man), his lodger's friends moving in, his brother's spite, and the knowledge of his possible guilt in a suicide. He returns to his *Parsifal* as the play ends.

Dave, Simon's loutish lodger, a university student. Dave is thickheaded and aggressively rude. He fails to pay his absurdly cheap rent and instead cadges spending money and drinks from Simon, who tolerates him as a salve to his social conscience. At the end of the play, Dave has moved a putative girlfriend and her male friend into the apartment, just to avenge himself on Simon. Dave's role is that of a crude annoyance to Simon's imperturbability.

Stephen Hench, Simon's older brother, a self-described "middle-aged public school teacher with five children . . . [and] a bit of a failure." Stephen complains that he will be passed over for a position as assistant headmaster at his school, revealing an insecurity about himself. Later in the play, he reveals his envy of his brother. Finally, he reveals that Simon's wife is having an affair with a man Simon holds in contempt. Initially, Simon's relationship to his brother seems kindly tolerant; by the end, it is suspected that Stephen's accusations that his brother is supercilious and smug may have substance.

Jeff Golding, Simon's friend, a literary journalist who hates literature and who is rude to Stephen and, apparently, to everyone else. He is having an affair with Gwendoline, his former wife, even though she has remarried and Jeff has a new girlfriend, Davina. His sloppy emotionalism contrasts sharply with Simon's cool detachment and precision, but the two are more alike than they seem at first. The play's ending, with Simon and Jeff listening to Wagner together, emphasizes these characters' similarity: They both make use of others casually and irresponsibly, with little concern for the results.

Davina Saunders, Jeff's girlfriend, who is writing a book about a companion of Henry Morton Stanley in the Congo who may have practiced cannibalism. Davina walks in on Simon and Jeff after Jeff has admitted to having an affair with Gwendoline. Davina claims that Gwendoline has just attempted suicide, a fiction intended to cause trouble for Jeff, who takes the bait, throws his drink at her, and rushes out to contact his former wife. Davina then takes off her shirt and continues her conversation, topless, with Simon, who rejects her sexual proposition and implies that he is faithful to his wife but agrees to publish her book. Davina is impressed with how "imperturbably . . . implacably *married*" Simon is, a perception likely to be shared by the audience when Simon resists her charms but one that is turned on its head by the end of the play.

Bernard Wood, a schoolmate of Simon and Stephen, known as "Wanker" Strapley at school. He enters after Davina leaves. He claims to be searching for his daughter, Joanna, who had applied to Simon for a job, but he is actually her fiancé. His appearance reveals that Simon slept with Joanna and other younger women but also had affairs with a number of the boys at school. By the end of the play, Wood has committed suicide, with Simon's answering machine recording the act. Wood's character represents the human consequences of Simon's behavior, consequences Simon would prefer to ignore in his attempt to keep his life orderly. He tells Wood that he never sleeps with anyone in his social circle because relationships there are awkward enough.

Beth Hench, Simon's wife, who returns from a supposed field trip with her students after Stephen has spitefully told her husband that she is having an affair with Ned, one of her fellow teachers. Simon refuses to confront Beth with this accusation, but she, sensing his change of manner, brings it out into the open, confessing her love for Ned, her hatred for Simon's serene contempt for human life, and her pregnancy. She is unsure as to whether Simon or Ned is the father. Her testimony is the final undermining of the play's initial portrayal of Simon.

— *Andrew Macdonald*

OUR FRIEND MANSO
(El amigo Manso)

Author: Benito Pérez Galdós (1843-1920)
First published: 1882
Genre: Novel

Locale: Madrid, Spain
Time: The 1870's through 1881, focusing on 1880-1881
Plot: Social realism

Máximo Manso (MAHKS-ee-moh MAHN-soh), a thirty-five-year-old preparatory school teacher and doctor of philosophy. This average-looking, nearsighted bachelor, of average height and sturdy build, is precisely what his name implies, the maximum or ultimate example of meekness, gentleness, and timidity. He takes great pride in his high moral standards, his dedication to reason as opposed to emotion, and his concern for others. Comfortable in the absolute world of ideas and ideals, he prefers to stand apart from society and study humankind dispassionately and objectively. When forced into contact with society, he often misinterprets what he sees or refuses to see as the truth. Believing that he has found in Irene the perfect woman of reason, he falls in love. Later, after realizing that she is just the opposite of what he had believed her to be, he illogically falls even deeper in love and loses his treasured inner peace and serenity. After losing Irene, he curses his own rational nature and envies his successful rival's impulsiveness, irrationality, and spontaneity. Ironically, in the end, Máximo dies of a broken heart.

Irene (ee-REHN-eh), a very attractive nineteen-year-old orphan. She becomes the governess at the residence of José María Manso, Máximo's brother, where she must discourage her employer's sexual advances. Born into poverty but having aristocratic tastes, Irene is determined to alter her socioeconomic situation. Idealized by Máximo as the perfect woman of reason who is always composed, studious, and serious-minded, she proves to be capricious, frivolous, manipulative, and more than capable of hiding her true feelings to achieve her goals. Ambitious, socially adept, prudent, and tactful, she becomes the perfect wife for the political prodigy Manuel Peña.

Manuel Peña (mahn-WEHL PEHN-yah), a handsome and charming twenty-one-year-old to whom Máximo Manso gives private lessons. A college-age youngster with money who is bored with his studies, spontaneous, impulsive, generous, and gregarious, Manuel thrives on the immediacy of everyday life. Not knowing that Máximo also loves Irene, Manuel decides to marry her only after consulting with his former mentor. A born orator, he combines this ability with his other interpersonal gifts to procure a seat in Parliament and ensure for himself a bright political future.

José María Manso, Máximo's older brother, who returns to Spain with his family after making a fortune in Cuba. Very ambitious politically and lacking in personal conviction, this eminently practical man adapts his beliefs to fit the current political climate, turns his house into a gathering place for any and all important figures whom he can attract, and often abandons his family to dedicate himself to his political career. He also goes to great extremes in attempting to seduce Irene, but he fails as a result of her resolve and Máximo's intercession on her behalf.

Doña Candida (KAHN-dee-dah), also called **Señora de García Grande** (gahr-SEE-ah GRAHN-deh), an elderly widow who is Irene's aunt. A vain, immoral, pretentious, and name-dropping parasite who once was rich but has spent her way into poverty following her husband's death, she shamelessly uses cleverness, lies, and deception to extract money from her acquaintances in what amounts to a socially advanced form of begging. In a move that is underwritten by José María Manso and designed to give him easier access to her niece, Doña Candida changes residence and takes Irene with her.

Lica (LEE-kah), or **Manuela**, José María's wife, a kind, delicate, sensitive, and unsophisticated individual of humble birth who is easily overwhelmed by life's problems and who is inexperienced in dealing with the evils of the world. Lica sees the good in everyone and often remains blind to their faults. When she does see such imperfections or has a problem, she calls on Máximo to deal with the situation. Considered a barrier to her husband's political and social advancement because of her family background, she struggles to learn society's ways and earn a place that corresponds to her husband's wealth and rising political importance.

Doña Javiera Rico de Peña (hah-vee-EHR-ah RREE-koh), the owner of a butcher shop. A voluptuous, sexually provocative, candid, assertive, generous, flexible, realistic, and chatty middle-aged widow who is the mother of Manuel Peña, she sends this spoiled and academically apathetic son to study with Máximo. Initially opposed to Manuel's marriage because of Irene's inferior socioeconomic status, Doña Javiera adjusts to and comes to appreciate her daughter-in-law's considerable talents. Toward the novel's end, she asserts her strong personality and increasingly governs Máximo's life.

— *Christopher L. Anderson*

OUR HOUSE IN THE LAST WORLD

Author: Oscar Hijuelos (1951-   )
First published: 1983
Genre: Novel

Locale: Cuba and New York City
Time: 1929-1975
Plot: Family

Hector Santinio (EHK-tohr sahn-TEEN-ee-oh), the youngest son of Mercedes Sorrea and Alejo Santinio. Born in New York City in 1951, Hector spends part of his childhood in Cuba with his parents. A near-fatal infection contracted in Cuba turns him into a sickly, lonely, and overprotected boy. Hector grows up in a dingy apartment in New York City resenting his overprotective, superstitious mother and his violent, alcoholic father. Although his parents are Cuban, he rebels against their Cuban ways and refuses to learn Spanish. In his mind, Cuba is associated with illness and with his unhappy home life. At the same time, however, he considers himself inferior to his father, whom he fears. Even after his father dies, Hector remains haunted by Alejo, who appears to him in dreams and visions. Only after Hector moves out of the apartment is he able to achieve a measure of autonomy and spiritual peace.

Alejo Santinio (ah-LEH-hoh), the head of the Santinio family. A mail carrier in Cuba, he meets and marries Mercedes Sorrea; shortly after the wedding, they immigrate to the United States in search of a better life. Although Alejo is at first full of hopes and ambitions, material success eludes him, and he resigns himself to being a cook in a large hotel, where he works from the mid-1940's until his death twenty-five years later. Seeing other members of his family arrive in the United States and prosper, Alejo becomes embittered and turns to drink and to other women for temporary solace. A big, friendly man with a winning manner and a tendency to live beyond his means, Alejo has many friends. At home, however, he is sullen and authoritarian. Often coming home drunk in the evenings, he brutalizes his wife and his two children. When he dies suddenly of a stroke, his children are relieved as much as aggrieved.

Mercedes Sorrea (mehr-SEH-dehs soh-RREH-ah), Alejo's wife and Hector and Horacio's mother. Although initially in love with her husband, Mercedes soon comes to resent him for being a failure. A poet in her youth, Mercedes is frustrated at not being able to cultivate her literary inclinations. In New York, she leads a life of drudgery and poverty. Considering herself something of a medium, she finds consolation in a fantasy world of spirits. Even though her life with Alejo is full of discord, after he dies, she loses touch with reality and retreats further into her fantasies.

Horacio Santinio (oh-RAH-see-oh), Alejo and Mercedes' oldest son. Unlike his brother Hector, Horacio is tough and independent. He is not intimidated by Alejo and learns very early to take care of himself. When he is old enough, Horacio joins the Air Force, thereby escaping the unhappy Santinio household. Horacio cannot understand why his brother does not distance himself from Mercedes and Alejo. The contrast between the infirm Hector and the strong Horacio is a principal theme in the novel.

Buita (BWEE-tah), Alejo's sister, who also emigrates from Cuba and spends some time living with the Santinios. Buita, who never approved of Alejo's marriage to the eccentric Mercedes, is a stern and unforgiving woman who does not miss

any opportunity to humiliate her sister-in-law. After Alejo's death, Buita tries to convince Hector to leave his mother and live with her in Miami.

Luisa (lew-EE-sah), Mercedes' sister, who also spends some time living with the Santinios after arriving from Cuba. Unlike the Santinios, Luisa and her husband do very well in the United States and soon are able to afford a nice house in the suburbs. Of his relatives, Luisa is the one Hector likes best, for he has fond memories of her kindness to him when he was a small child in Cuba.

OUR LADY OF THE FLOWERS
(Notre-Dame des Fleurs)

Author: Jean Genet (1910-1986)
First published: 1944; revised, 1951
Genre: Novel

Locale: Fresnes prison, Paris, and the provinces
Time: Late 1930's and early 1940's
Plot: Impressionistic realism

Our Lady of the Flowers, a convicted murderer. In real life, he was **Adrien Baillon**, born on December 19, 1920, and executed on February 2, 1939. In the story, he is identified by the titular sobriquet, by his real name, and as an imaginary extension of "Maurice Pilorge," the name given him by the author in an earlier poem and retained as the name of the person to whose memory the novel is dedicated. As a character in the story, he is loved by Divine, Seck Gorgui, and others, is affectionately called **Danie**, and is engaged in drug dealing with Marchetti. The details of his trial and execution are orchestrated in the narrative to coincide with the accounts of the deaths of Alberto and Divine. Like all the male characters in the novel, he is homosexual.

Jean Genet (zhah[n] zheh-NAY), the thirty-year-old author and narrator of the story, serving time at Fresnes Prison in cell 426, where, by contemplating newspaper photographs attached to the wall, he creates character roles for the men photographed. His imaginative assignment of these roles to himself and his fellow inmates serves to stimulate his erections, enabling him to masturbate, and to provide the substance of the story. The main role that he creates for himself is Louis Culafroy, a boy reared in the countryside who goes to Paris and becomes a transvestite male prostitute known as Divine. Our Lady of the Flowers, Alberto, and Marchetti are also, in part, confections of his own psychic identity.

Divine (dee-VEEN), the dominant persona of Jean Genet, his coeval. "She" loves Darling Daintyfoot and Seck Gorgui and is jealous of Our Lady of the Flowers. "She" dies of consumption. Divine is the personification of Genet's quest for sainthood.

Louis Culafroy (lwee kew-lah-FRWAH), Divine/Genet as a boy. His mother is Ernestine, the widow of a man who committed suicide. Like Genet's actual mother, Gabrielle, who abandoned him at his birth, Ernestine has little use for Culafroy. Like Genet, who, as a public ward, was reared by country people, Culafroy grows up in a rural area.

Darling Daintyfoot, or **Mignon-les-Petits-Pieds** (mee-YOH[N]-lay-ptee-PYEH), a pimp whose character is fashioned from the impressions Genet retained of a blond Corsican boy named Roger and whose persona includes the identity of Paul

Garcia and projects the identity of Marchetti. Darling's physical description matches Genet's in many respects: five feet, nine inches tall; weight of 165 pounds; oval face with blond hair, blue-green eyes, perfect teeth, and a straight nose; and "almost as young as Divine." His arrest for shoplifting is detailed in the story.

Seck Gorgui (gohr-GEE), also known as **Negro Angel Sun**, or in French, **le nègre Ange Soleil** (leh nehgr ahnzh soh-LAY); his real name is **Clément Village** (klay-MEH[N] vee-YAHZH). Negro Angel Sun, Genet's fellow inmate, has killed his mistress, a Dutch woman named Sonia. Gorgui is cast as a lover of Divine and of Our Lady of the Flowers.

Marchetti (mahr-SHEH-tee), a thirty-year-old, handsome, blond Corsican, blended by the narrator with Roger, the Corsican (who is Darling Daintyfoot). He is presented as a drug pusher who leads Our Lady of the Flowers astray. He may be considered to be a personification of Divine's jealousy when Our Lady of the Flowers comes between "her" and Seck Gorgui during the time that the three are living together.

Alberto, a country boy loved by Louis Culafroy. He dies from a stab wound to his eye. When Culafroy confesses to Solange that he prefers Alberto to her, she responds, "You like him?" When Mimosa II tells Divine that she finds Our Lady of the Flowers attractive, Divine responds, "She pleases you?" (referring to Our Lady of the Flowers in the feminine). These reflexive incidents tie Alberto, Culafroy/Divine, and Our Lady of the Flowers into a unit in ways that are amplified by the concert of their deaths: In very short order, and in lyrical continuity, the narrator offers accounts of the death of Alberto (from the wound received in what appears to have been a quarrel over a girl), Our Lady of the Flowers (under the guillotine), and Divine (from tuberculosis).

Mimosa II, a bitchy queen who is Roger's "woman." In actuality, "she" is Genet's fellow inmate René Hirsch.

Solange (soh-LAHNZH), a country girl attracted to Louis Culafroy, who rejects her, when he realizes that he is homosexual, in favor of Alberto.

Gabriel Archangel, a persona given to a downed German pilot named Weidmann, whose picture adorned a wall of Genet's cell.

Lady-Apple, or **Pomme d'Api** (puhm dah-PEE), an inmate who, in actuality, was Eugène Marceau.

First Communion, an inmate who, in actuality, was Antoine Berthollet.

Mimosa I, an inmate who, like Lady-Apple and First Communion, is among the numerous homosexuals mentioned by sobriquet in the story.

Ernestine, the mother of Louis Culafroy. She corresponds in many respects to Genet's real mother, Gabrielle.

— *Roy Arthur Swanson*

OUR MUTUAL FRIEND

Author: Charles Dickens (1812-1870)
First published: 1865; serial form, 1864-1865
Genre: Novel

Locale: London, England
Time: Mid-nineteenth century
Plot: Domestic realism

John Harmon, also known as **Julius Handford** and **John Rokesmith**. After his father's death, he returns to England from South Africa, where he has lived for some years. On his arrival, George Radfoot, a fellow passenger on the homeward voyage, lures him into a waterfront inn, drugs him, robs him, and throws him into the Thames. Revived by the cold water, Harmon swims to shore. He takes the name of Julius Handford. Meanwhile, Radfoot has quarreled with a confederate, who murders him and throws his body into the river. When the body, wearing Harmon's clothes, is found, the dead man is identified as John Harmon. Discovering in the meantime that Bella Wilfer, whom he is supposed to marry according to the terms of his father's will, is a mercenary woman, Harmon decides to keep his identity a secret. As John Rokesmith, he becomes the secretary to the man who has inherited his father's fortune and takes lodgings in the Wilfer home. When Bella finally realizes that love is more important than money, he marries her. After a year of happiness, he reveals his true identity and accepts his inheritance.

Nicodemus Boffin, also called **Noddy** and **The Golden Dustman**, the illiterate, good-hearted confidential clerk who inherits the Harmon fortune after John Harmon's supposed death. When Mrs. Boffin learns John Rokesmith's true identity, her husband, at Harmon's request, agrees to keep the secret. Also at Harmon's suggestion, Boffin behaves with increasing evidence of greed until Bella Wilfer sees what avarice can lead to. Pestered by a blackmailer over the will, he finally shows that the fortune is really his and then generously hands it over to Harmon.

Henrietta Boffin, his cheerful, simple, affectionate wife, a childless woman who lavishes love on everyone around her.

Bella Wilfer, the young woman John Harmon is directed to marry. A beautiful girl from a poor home, she is taken in by the Boffins, who try to give her the advantages she would have enjoyed as Harmon's wife. In time, her selfishness is overcome by her natural affections. She makes Harmon a fine wife and bears him a child.

Silas Wegg, a mean-spirited ballad-monger and fruit seller, an ugly person whom illiterate Boffin hires to read to him. A prying rascal, he discovers a will in which the elder Harmon bequeathed his fortune to the Crown. He tries to blackmail Boffin, but he is foiled and tossed out into a garbage cart.

Mr. Venus, a dusty, good-willed taxidermist. He becomes Wegg's accomplice in the scheme to blackmail Boffin, but he later repents, reveals the whole plot, and wins the heart of Pleasant Riderhood.

Mortimer Lightwood, a bright, cautious solicitor who handles Boffin's affairs and reports on the developments of the Harmon case.

Eugene Wrayburn, his reckless, intelligent, and sprightly partner, who falls in love with Lizzie Hexam, the daughter of a Thames riverman. When she rejects him, he follows her to the country and is nearly murdered by a rival. Lizzie marries him finally and nurses him back to health.

Lizzie Hexam, a lovely, courageous, illiterate young woman. Oppressed by her father's death, her brother's rejection of her and the unwelcome courtship of a half-demented, jealous suitor, she moves out of London and finds work in a paper mill. In the end, she marries Eugene Wrayburn, whom she nurses back to health after the young barrister has been injured in a murderous attack made by his rival.

Charlie Hexam, her selfish brother, a young man who rejects his father, his sister, and his schoolmaster in his cold-hearted effort to gain "respectability."

Gaffer Hexam, Lizzie's crude father, the riverman who pulls John Harmon's supposed body out of the Thames. After he dies in an accident, he is slandered by his ex-partner, who accuses him of Harmon's murder.

Bradley Headstone, a schoolmaster, a pompous man who falls insanely in love with Lizzie, tries to murder Eugene Wrayburn, and takes Rogue Riderhood to his watery death.

Roger Riderhood, nicknamed **Rogue**, a brutal man who for the sake of the reward accuses Gaffer Hexam of John Harmon's murder. Later, he becomes Bradley Headstone's accomplice in the attempted murder of Eugene Wrayburn. He and Headstone drown during a scuffle.

Pleasant Riderhood, Rogue Riderhood's daughter, an unlicensed pawnbroker and Mr. Venus' sweetheart, whom she marries after rejecting him a number of times.

Fanny Cleaver, called **Jenny Wren**, Lizzie Hexam's friend, a shrewd, pretty, but physically disabled maker of dolls' dresses.

M. Cleaver, called **Mr. Dolls**, Fanny's spiritless, drunken father.

Mr. Riah, an old, generous-hearted Jew, the friend of Fanny Cleaver and Lizzie Hexam.

Alfred Lammle and

Sophronia Lammle, two charming scoundrels who marry for money, learn that neither has any, and decide to prey on prominent members of society. They are forced to go abroad when their debts become pressing.

John Podsnap, a leader of society and a pompous and smug epitome of Philistinism.

Mrs. Podsnap, his majestic wife, the female counterpart of her husband.

Georgiana Podsnap, their warm, shy, silly daughter, the prey of the Lammles.

Mr. Fledgeby, whom his friends call **Fascination Fledgeby** behind his back, Georgiana's suitor. A mean, stupid, miserly dandy, he is encouraged in his social pretensions by the predatory Lammles. He hides his sharp business practices under a fictitious money brokerage firm, Pubsey and Co. Mr. Riah is his business agent.

Hamilton Veneering and

Anastatia Veneering, two shallow social climbers who have a new home, new furniture, new friends, a new baby. A former clerk in the firm of Chicksey and Stabbles, he is now a partner. He spends money liberally in order to get himself elected to Parliament.

Mrs. Wilfer, Bella Wilfer's austere, shrewish mother.

Reginald Wilfer, nicknamed **The Cherub**, Bella's affectionate, seedy, cherubic father.

Lavinia Wilfer, their younger daughter, a sharp, spirited girl.

George Sampson, Lavinia Wilfer's dull suitor, over whom she exercises tight control.

Melvin Twemlow, a poor but "connected" friend of the Veneerings. Though he lives over a livery stable, he is accepted in society because he is Lord Snigsworth's first cousin.

Betty Higden, an old, impoverished independent person who cares for displaced children; she is a friend of the Boffins.

Emma Peecher, a pedantic, warm, primitive young woman in love with Bradley Headstone.

Lady Tippins, a foolish woman, a friend of the Veneerings, who keeps a list of her nonexistent lovers.

Mr. Sloppy, a foundling taken in by Betty Higden. He is adopted by the Boffins.

The Reverend Frank Milney, the humble young curate who marries Lizzie Hexam and Eugene Wrayburn.

Mrs. Margaretta Milney, his wife, a woman of practical mind and brisk energy.

Mrs. Sprodgkin, one of Mr. Milney's parishioners. She makes his life miserable by her constant questions about who begot whom and other matters in the Bible.

Young Blight, Mortimer Lightwood's office boy.

OUR NIG

Author: Harriet E. Wilson (1808 or c. 1827-1828-c. 1870)
First published: 1859
Genre: Novel

Locale: Boston, Massachusetts, and surrounding areas
Time: The mid-1800's, before the Civil War
Plot: Social realism

Frado, a pretty mulatto girl who, at the age of six, becomes the servant of the Bellmonts, a middle-class white family. For the next twelve years, Frado's life is brutal and unremittingly harsh. When she turns eighteen, the age of independence, Frado, frail and sickly from years of drudgery, leaves the Bellmonts. Starved for affection, she marries Samuel, the first black man who is kind to her. After Frado becomes pregnant, Samuel deserts her, leaving both mother and child dependent on charity. After Samuel dies of a fever, Frado, without hope of rescue, writes her story to earn money.

Mrs. Bellmont, the book's principal antagonist, who, with her evil daughter, Mary, makes Frado's life miserable. Mrs. Bellmont's great cruelty is matched by her great suffering in the end. Her pain begins with the death of her son, James,

followed by the death of her beloved Mary. Her own death, several years later, is accompanied by unspeakable pain.

James Bellmont, the son of the Bellmont family. Frado and James build a strong friendship that survives his frequent absences. Between James's visits, Frado's remembrances of his kindness cheer her heart. When Frado hears that James is getting married, she is overjoyed. She hopes that he and his new wife will take her. After his wedding, however, James fails to return home for several years. When he finally comes back, he is quite ill. During his final visit, James becomes increasingly disabled and finally dies after a year of suffering. As he approaches death, James tries to convert Frado to Christianity, but she cannot accept the god of her persecutors as her savior.

— *Sarah Smith Ducksworth*

OUR TOWN

Author: Thornton Wilder (1897-1975)
First published: 1938
Genre: Drama

Locale: New Hampshire
Time: 1901-1913
Plot: Symbolism

The stage manager, who acts as a chorus in explaining and commenting on the action and the characters as the play unfolds.

Emily Webb, a sweet young woman who grows up in Grover's Corners, a small American town. She works hard in school, tries to be cheerful, and falls in love with the town's best baseball player. She dies in childbirth while still young and shyly takes her place among her relatives and friends in the little graveyard. She tries to relive her twelfth birthday,

only to discover that to relive is no joy and that the dead can only pity the living who know not what joy they have in life.

George Gibbs, a typical young American boy who loves baseball. He gives up going to college to marry Emily, whom he dearly loves. When his wife dies, he is filled with grief and goes to sob at her grave, not realizing that she pities him for not valuing the life he still enjoys.

Dr. Gibbs, the local physician and George's father. He is shocked to find that his son wants to marry and become a farmer but finally realizes that the youth is really no longer a child, any more than the doctor was when he married. Dr. Gibbs is a hardworking man whose hobby is the American Civil War; his idea of a vacation is an excursion to some battlefield of that conflict.

Mrs. Gibbs, George's mother, a hardworking woman who loves her family, even though she does not always understand them. She has found joy in her marriage and hopes her son will find joy in his.

Rebecca Gibbs, George's sister.

Wally Webb, Emily's brother.

Mr. Webb, Emily's father, the editor and publisher of the local newspaper. He writes editorials every day, yet he cannot bring himself to advise his son-in-law on marriage, though he tries.

Mrs. Webb, Emily's mother, a good-hearted woman. On Emily's wedding day, she finds herself unable to give her daughter advice on marriage, though she had meant to do so.

Simon Stimson, the local choir director. He has become an alcoholic because he cannot find happiness in the small town. Even in death, after committing suicide, he believes life is ignorance and folly.

Joe Crowell, a newspaper boy.

Howie Newsome, a milkman.

OUR VILLAGE: Sketches of Rural Character and Scenery

Author: Mary Russell Mitford (1787-1855)
First published: 1824-1832
Genre: Short fiction

Locale: Rural England
Time: Early nineteenth century
Plot: Local color

Miss Mitford, the author, who leads a happy life in an English village and its surrounding country, sharing her great happiness with her readers. She has a true appreciation of nature and of people, and she describes what she sees about her—the village and the countryside—lovingly. Her tales and sketches show the passing seasons in a year.

Lizzy, a young girl in the village. She is a sweet, lovable child of three who in turn loves everyone, winning the affection of all who know her. She manages the people around her, both adults and children. She is a frequent companion of the author as Miss Mitford takes walks through the village and the fields.

Jack Rapley, Miss Mitford's favorite boy in the village. He is quite mischievous, and some of the villagers predict he will come to a bad end.

Master and

Dame Weston, a couple who fight frequently with each other. Although the wife blames her husband for their quarrels, she really is to blame.

Hannah Bint, a twelve-year-old girl who sets herself up as a dairywoman.

Mayflower, Miss Mitford's pompous, dignified greyhound, who is the author's constant companion.

Dash, a mongrel dog rescued by Mayflower. He dies because Miss Mitford feeds him well; he is unused to a sufficient diet.

OUTER DARK

Author: Cormac McCarthy (1933-   )
First published: 1968
Genre: Novel

Locale: Indeterminate, but probably southern Appalachia
Time: Indeterminate, but probably early twentieth century
Plot: Surrealism

Rinthy Holme, a young, uneducated countrywoman about nineteen years old. Her brother Culla has (probably) raped her, though she seems to bear him no great ill will for that. When her pregnancy becomes obvious, Culla moves them to a remote cabin in the backwoods and refuses to allow anyone to come near for fear that his deed will be discovered. After a long, painful labor with no midwife (and very little help or sympathy from Culla), Rinthy gives birth to a male child. While she sleeps after the birth, Culla takes the child and leaves it alone in the woods, later telling Rinthy that it died. When Rinthy discovers that there is no body in the grave, she learns the truth and sets out to find the son that she has never seen. Rinthy has the innocent, trusting attitude of a child, accepting whatever comes her way, except in this matter of locating her child. She pursues that goal with steadfast and single-minded determination, ignoring the immense difficulties that confront her. Her innocence seems to touch those she meets on her travels; almost everyone that she encounters treats her with kindness, offers her food and lodging, and invites her to return to share their hospitality again. She never finds the baby and possibly loses her mind in her futile search.

Culla Holme, Rinthy's older brother. He has sufficient knowledge of right and wrong to recognize the evil of his incest with his sister, yet he tries to undo the deed by destroying the evidence. He does not seem to realize that he is thus compounding his error rather than atoning for his guilt. In fact, he never seems to regret the deed; he only worries that others may find out about it. When Rinthy sets out in search of the tinker, whom she is convinced has her son, Culla tries to follow her. Although the people he meets are initially open to him, the miasma of guilt that surrounds him leads to trouble for him on every side. The three evil strangers who seem to roam in tandem to him commit several grisly atrocities, which are invariably blamed on Culla, yet he always manages to escape retribution. Near the end of the novel, Culla, the tinker, the child, and the three strangers finally meet. The unholy three first kill the tinker, who has apparently told them what he knows of the child. When Culla arrives, he watches helplessly as they kill the boy, now about one year old, and as one of the three drinks the child's blood. The three do not harm Culla, however; he is left to wander aimlessly in a dead landscape, on a road that ends in a dismal swamp.

The tinker, an itinerant wanderer too poor even to afford a mule to pull his wagon. He is permanently bent from the backbreaking labor. He arrives at the Holme cabin a few days before Rinthy gives birth to her son. When Culla takes the baby and abandons it in the woods, the tinker happens upon it and seeks a wet nurse for the child. Later, Rinthy finds the tinker and begs for the return of her son. The tinker bargains for the repayment of the wet-nurse fee, expecting sexual indenture from Rinthy, as she has no money. When he learns that the child is the result of incest, however, he is horrified, curses Rinthy, flees from her, and forbids her to follow him. Possibly the tinker retrieves the child and mistreats it: When the boy next appears, in the tinker's custody, he has a healed burn and is missing one eye. The tinker is killed by the three strangers.

The three strangers, perhaps a symbolic parody of the Holy Trinity, seeming to be supernatural creatures of some sort. The only whole one is the spokesman and leader of the group; he has a beard and wears the black suit that he has taken from a corpse he dug up from a church cemetery. His two companions are a mute and a mindless being. They seem not only to perpetrate unspeakably foul, evil deeds as they roam over the countryside, but also to be drawn to Culla's milder expression of evil. Possibly they represent some form of dark justice or retribution; possibly they can sense the darkness in a person's soul, for, except for killing the child, they do not touch Rinthy, whose innocence protects her.

The child, a male infant, the result of incest between Rinthy and Culla. He is stolen immediately after his birth and abandoned in the woods by his father. He is never given a name, perhaps to enlarge his role as a symbolic sacrifice. He is abused and finally is killed at about one year of age.

— *Mary Johnson*

OUTERBRIDGE REACH

Author: Robert Stone (1937-   )
First published: 1992
Genre: Novel

Locale: New York City and the South Atlantic Ocean
Time: The 1980's
Plot: Psychological realism

Owen Browne, a middle-aged former naval officer and veteran of the Vietnam War who now writes advertising copy for a subsidiary of a conglomerate known as the Hylan Corporation. When its head, Matty Hylan, senses financial ruin and disappears, Owen hopes to boost the sagging fortunes of all concerned by taking his place in a single-handed circumnavigation race using the new Hylan sailboat. He wants to market the boat, but more important, he has been suffering from a midlife crisis that has left him in a state of paralysis and despair. Feeling stalled and restless in his personal life and his job, he has a need to start over. He also hopes to develop a sense of personal courage and heroism that eluded him during the Vietnam War and anticipated that, when tested, he will uncover a commanding self able to cope with the solitude and the sea. He immediately demonstrates his incompetence, however, by making poor preparations and by failing to realize that the Hylan craft is an untested boat, made of inferior materials, that cannot weather the voyage he is about to undertake. To add to his troubles, an accidental cut to his hand becomes seriously infected, contributing to his increasingly hallucinatory consciousness. As he sails further out to sea, he becomes increasingly preoccupied with his interior life, breaking off communication with anyone from the outside world. Losing his bearings, he reaches an island that represents his distance from all previous realities. Delirious, he mistakes a nest of crabs in an old house for a new wife and drifts beyond the limits of sanity. In a fit of megalomania, he charts a course to victory covered with false positions and upbeat commentary, arbitrarily imposing his own fantasies on reality. In reality, he is beset by a strong sense of failure, fear, and helplessness. The pretense that he has won the race seems to cap a lifetime of fakery and self-deception, but he is unable to face up to the fact that he has disseminated

so much false information. His failure to become a hero becomes a replication of the defeat associated with the Vietnam War. Owen seems condemned to replay the disillusionments and failures of that war. Unlike his fellow veteran Buzz Ward, his ordeal does not end in his development of redeeming spiritual values. He does not come through with flying colors; instead he sinks into madness, drowning alone in the South Atlantic Ocean.

Anne Browne, Owen's wife and the daughter of a wealthy businessman. With Owen on his foolhardy sea voyage and their daughter Maggie acting up, Anne sinks into an alcoholic haze. She betrays her husband by having an affair with Ron Strickland, then betrays Strickland by undermining his ability to report what really happened to Owen. In spite of these dubious actions, Anne's intelligence and sanity permit her to emerge as the least damaged by the entire situation. After Owen's death, she comes into her own and decides to atone for Brown's disastrous voyage by setting out on a similar voyage herself. Because she is the better sailor and has seen to it that her craft is sound, she anticipates that she will successfully meet the physical and spiritual challenges that destroyed her husband.

Ron Strickland, a cynical photographer. He sees himself as a member of the counterculture that protested against the war in Vietnam, experimented with drugs and sexual freedom, and advocated various left-wing causes. His life seems less heroic to him, however, as events he is covering in Nicaragua begin to dwindle into inanition. Returning to the United States to revive his sagging morale by covering the Owen Browne voyage, he becomes convinced that he is the only one involved in the situation who cares about the truth. His effort to make a film that will give the real story to the American public is undermined by business interests associated with Anne's wealthy father. Hired thugs beat him severely, ruin his film, and leave him in despair.

Pamela Koester, a drug-addled former prostitute, who is befriended by Strickland. She represents a counterculture gone sour and now barely distinguishable from the country's criminal underworld.

Buzz Ward, a naval buddy of Owen who was imprisoned in Vietnam during the war. Owen hopes to emulate his courage and spirituality.

Maggie Browne, Owen's troubled teenager daughter. It is she who will ultimately inherit whatever successes or failures her parents' generation bring about.

— *Margaret Boe Birns*

THE OUTSIDER
(El túnel)

Author: Ernesto Sábato (1911-   )
First published: 1948
Genre: Novel

Locale: Buenos Aires and Hunter's Ranch
Time: 1946
Plot: Psychological

Juan Pablo Castel (hwahn PAHB-loh kahs-TEHL), the narrator, a well-known and critically admired painter. Castel is a shy, thirty-eight-year-old, self-absorbed bachelor who has never established a satisfactory relationship with a woman. He sees María Iribarne in a gallery, seemingly transfixed by one of his paintings. He becomes obsessed with her, meets her again, and becomes her lover. As one reads Castel's narration of these events, one finds oneself in the mind of a madman. Castel is an ultrarational yet warped person who shifts rapidly from some objective sense of himself and some ability to feel compassion to a paranoid personality full of anger and suspicion. Finally convinced that María is having an affair with Luis Hunter, he breaks into her room and stabs her to death. He is narrating these events in a mental hospital.

María Iribarne (mah-REE-ah ee-ree-BAHR-neh), a beautiful, young, wealthy woman. She appears physically to be twenty-six years old, Castel says, but seems older to him in terms of her self-possession and personality. The reader only knows her as an enigmatic figure, described entirely by Castel. Castel, from his alienated isolation, decides that he never really knew her, but that they were moving in separate tunnels along parallel lines. In a moment of insight, he realizes that it may have been only himself moving through a dark tunnel, not her or others. María remains enigmatic, because the reader has no knowledge of her other than what Castel reveals, and he often casts doubt on his own perceptions of and conclusions about her.

Allende Hunter (ah-YEHN-deh), María's husband. Tall, thin, and handsome, but blind, Allende is a calm, cosmopolitan man who seems to accept María on her own terms. When Castel kills María, he rushes to Allende to tell him that María has betrayed him with Luis Hunter and others. Allende attacks him, calling him an imbecile and a fool, but he does not contradict Castel's charges. Allende neither explains his relationship with María and Luis Hunter nor reveals his perception of any of these events. He commits suicide.

Luis Hunter, an architect and Allende's cousin. He lives on the family *estancia*, where María often stays. He is described only by Castel and in unflattering terms, as having devious eyes and as being sly, despicable, and a womanizer. Castel believes that Luis has an affair with María, but perhaps that is only a paranoid fantasy.

Mimí Hunter, Allende's cousin. She is described by Castel as a skinny, perverse, nearsighted woman with a Parisian accent and pseudo-intellectual pretensions. She heightens the enigmatic flavor of the book, because she is viewed only through the paranoid analysis of Castel.

Lartigue (lahr-TEE-geh), a poet and friend of Luis Hunter. Castel asks him if María and Luis are lovers. To the twisted mind of Castel, Lartigue confirms the affair by saying that he knows nothing of that.

— *William E. Pemberton*

THE OUTSIDER

Author: Richard Wright (1908-1960)
First published: 1953
Genre: Novel

Locale: Chicago, New York City, and Newark, New Jersey
Time: 1950
Plot: Psychological realism

Cross Damon, a black, intellectual postal worker in Chicago. Stifled by the middle-class restraints of his family responsibilities and his routine job, Damon, who has developed his ideas by reading existential philosophy, yearns to create an independent and more authentic existence for himself. A subway accident in which he is believed to have died provides him with the opportunity to abandon his job, girlfriend, and family. After murdering an innocent man to protect his secret, Damon travels to New York, assumes a new identity, and begins a life

marked by violence and deception. He becomes involved with the Communist Party and its political struggles with corrupt landlord Langley Herndon. He murders Herndon and Gil Blount, the local leader of the Communist Party, demonstrating his struggle against the similarly stultifying forces of capitalism and communism. His affair with Blount's widow is doomed by the deception that his situation forces on him. In the end, he is gunned down for his disloyalty by agents of the Communist Party. Damon is a metaphysical rebel who fails in his effort to live authentically; instead, he creates an existence based on lies, which leads him to play god with other people's lives.

Gladys Damon, Damon's estranged wife, intellectually incapable of understanding her husband's dissatisfaction. Gladys and their three children are abandoned by Damon when he creates his new life, an act that underscores the depths of his emotional alienation.

Dorothy (Dot) Powers, Cross's pregnant, fifteen-year-old lover in Chicago. Dot is an unwanted complication in Damon's life, an obstacle to his freedom. She, too, is abandoned when Damon adopts his new identity and escapes to New York.

Ely Houston, the New York district attorney. Like Damon, Houston is an intellectual rebel with an existential view of the world. Unlike Damon, Houston has arbitrarily decided to uphold the law rather than to become an ethical outlaw. Houston and Damon engage in lengthy discussions, which the author uses to elaborate the theoretical basis of the novel, but their ideas are so similar that many of the lines in their dialogues are interchangeable. At first, he does not allow himself to suspect Damon; once he determines that Damon is guilty, he allows Damon's lonely and guilt-ridden life to be his punishment.

Gilbert (Gil) Blount, an official in the Communist Party. Although he is a leader in a political organization that promotes its concern for the masses, Blount is a selfish, power-hungry manipulator of the gullible people who follow him. His attempts to use Damon result in his death at the hands of his proposed victim.

Eva Blount, Blount's wife. Impossibly innocent, Eva Blount sees Damon only as a fellow victim and becomes his lover after her husband's death. When she realizes that Damon is Blount's murderer, she commits suicide by jumping out a window.

Jack Hilton, one of Gil Blount's subordinates in the Communist Party. Like Blount, Hilton is a self-serving bully. He carries out Blount's cynical directives. Damon kills him.

Bob Hunter, a railroad porter and organizer for the Communist Party. At the bottom of the hierarchy in the Communist Party, Hunter is an example of a true believer, whose honest idealism and hard work are exploited by the self-serving politicians in control of the organization.

Langley Herndon, a fascistic slumlord. Although Herndon is Blount's political opposite, he is similarly self-centered and cynical. Whereas Gil Blount is driven by the need for political power, Herndon uses people for financial gain. Neither man evidences any humanitarian concern for the people he victimizes.

Joe Thomas, a black postal worker. Thomas recognizes Damon in a brothel soon after Damon's supposed death. When Thomas jokes about disclosing the deception, Damon murders him. Thomas is an innocent victim of Damon's impossible desire to live an independent existence without affecting the lives of others.

— *Carl Brucker*

THE OVERCOAT
(Shinel)

Author: Nikolai Gogol (1809-1852)
First published: 1842
Genre: Short fiction

Locale: St. Petersburg, Russia
Time: Early nineteenth century
Plot: Social realism

Akakii Akakiievich Bashmachkin (ah-KAH-kihy ah-KAH-kihy-eh-vihch bahsh-MAH-hihn), a humble, poorly paid, aging government clerk, short, pockmarked, with reddish balding hair, dim and bleary eyes, and wrinkled cheeks. Possessing a high-sounding government grade of perpetual titular councilor, he is a mere copyist of documents. He loves his work, which he does with neat and painstaking thoroughness, and he even takes some of it home to do at night. Badly needing an overcoat to replace an old one that the tailor refuses to repair, he plans to have a new one made, and for several months he lives in happy anticipation of getting it. When he wears it to the office, he is pleased over the attention it gains him from his fellow clerks; but he is desolated when it is stolen after a party given in his honor. Stammering and frightened by the domineering manner of a Certain Important Personage to whom he applies for help in finding his coat, he stumbles into a snowstorm, becomes ill, and dies in delirium. His ghost, after snatching overcoats from various people, finds the person of consequence wearing a fine overcoat and seizes it. Apparently the garment is a perfect fit, for Akakii never reappears to seize more coats.

Petrovich (peht-ROH-vihch), a one-eyed, pockmarked tailor given to heavy drinking, quoting high prices to his clients, and slyly watching to see what effects he has achieved.

A Certain Important Personage, a bureaucrat recently promoted to a position of consequence. With his equals he is pleasant, gentlemanly, and obliging, but with those below him he is reticent, rude, and very conscious of his superiority. Strict and a stickler for form, he tyrannizes his subordinates. The ghost of Bashmachkin steals his overcoat.

THE OX-BOW INCIDENT

Author: Walter Van Tilburg Clark (1909-1971)
First published: 1940
Genre: Novel

Locale: Nevada
Time: 1885
Plot: Regional

Gil Carter, a wandering ranch hand who drifts into Bridger's Wells looking for a girl. When she returns to the town, after having reportedly gone to San Francisco with a husband, Gil is furious. He joins a posse, but thinks more of his disappointment in love than of the hanging of three innocent men.

Art Croft, Gil's friend and companion. Though wounded by mistake by a stage driver, he goes on with the posse in search of rustlers.

Rose Mapen, the girl Gil loves and who disappoints him by marrying another man while gone from Bridger's Wells.

Canby, the saloonkeeper at Bridger's Wells.

Farnley, a cowboy who assists in hanging the three innocent men. When one of them, Donald Martin, dies too slowly in the hangman's noose, Farnley shoots him.

Kinkaid, Farnley's friend, supposedly killed by rustlers. He turns up alive after three innocent men have been hanged for his murder.

Davies, a storekeeper in the town. He tries to prevent the hanging of innocent men and fails. He takes a ring and a farewell letter to Martin's wife and two children. After the lynching, he comes to believe, erroneously, that the fault was his.

Osgood, a Baptist minister. He tries to help Davies prevent mob action.

Joyce, a young cowboy who goes with Croft to ask Judge Tyler to swear in the posse.

Judge Tyler, the local magistrate. He tries to prevent mob action but ironically stimulates it.

Sheriff Risley, whose absence from town allows the mob to act. He returns just too late. He refuses to arrest the members of the posse, claiming lack of evidence.

Mapes, the sheriff's swaggering deputy, who leads the posse he illegally deputizes.

Jenny Grier, called **Ma**, keeper of a boardinghouse. She helps hang the supposed rustlers and murderers.

Tetley, a rancher. He forces his son to participate in the mob's precipitate action. After his son commits suicide, he does, too.

Gerald Tetley, an emotional young man. Horrified by having to participate in the mob killings, he commits suicide.

Donald Martin, a rancher. Wrongly accused of being a rustler, he is hanged unlawfully by the mob.

A Mexican, Martin's rider, also hanged by the mob.

An Old Man, Martin's simpleminded worker, the mob's third victim.

Drew, a rancher. He failed to hand Martin a bill of sale for cattle purchased, thus contributing to the man's death.

OXHERDING TALE

Author: Charles Johnson (1948-　　)
First published: 1982
Genre: Novel

Locale: South Carolina
Time: 1838-1862
Plot: Bildungsroman

Andrew Hawkins, the main character and the novel's narrator. Andrew is a young slave of mixed blood whose driving ambition is to acquire his freedom and earn enough money to buy the freedom of his father, his stepmother, and his beloved Minty. Rigorously educated by his own tutor, Andrew is exceptionally intelligent and sophisticated. The moral decisions that he must make during his quest for freedom are complicated by the fact that he is light-skinned enough to pass as white. At the age of twenty, he leaves the cotton plantation where he was reared in hopes of securing freedom. His story is thereafter a series of episodic adventures that ultimately lead to his compromised freedom.

George Hawkins, Andrew's father, a butler at Cripplegate, a South Carolina cotton plantation. George enjoys an easy camaraderie with his master, Jonathan Polkinghorne; the two men often drink together. One night, after having shared considerable amounts of wine and beer, Jonathan suggests that they retire to each other's beds. As a result, George conceives Andrew with his master's wife, who disavows her son after giving birth. George is thereafter banished from the house and demoted to oxherding, losing his respected standing among the slaves and sinking into a disgruntled torpor.

Mattie Hawkins, George's wife and Andrew's stepmother. Mattie takes the infant George into her home and treats him as her own. A deeply religious woman, she turns permanently cold toward George after his infidelity.

Ezekiel Sykes-Withers (ee-ZEE-kee-ehl), Andrew's tutor. Ezekiel is hired by Polkinghorne to increase Andrew's value by educating him. From Andrew's fifth year until Ezekiel's premature death seven years later, Ezekiel guides Andrew through such a rigorous course of study that Andrew reads Latin and Greek and can discuss all the Eastern and Western philosophers at the age of ten.

Minty, a seamstress and the daughter of the maid of the plantation. By falling extravagantly in love with Minty, Andrew finds a mission in life: to attain freedom for himself in order to buy Minty's freedom later.

Flo Hatfield, a middle-aged widow and farm owner. Flo has inherited the five-hundred-acre farm, Leviathan, to which Andrew is sent by Polkinghorne. Flo often picks a young male slave from the fields to live for a while in the house and to serve as her lover. After a few weeks, these young men usually die of mysterious causes but are reported as escaped. Andrew, having become Flo's lover, lasts longer than most, inspiring declarations of freedom from Flo, but he is sent from Leviathan to the mines after losing his temper following her refusal to pay his wages.

Reb the Coffinmaker, the hardworking carpenter at Flo Hatfield's farm. Reb is spiritually astute yet pragmatic. He maintains a peaceful and steady existence at Leviathan until he is moved to plead Andrew's case to Flo after Andrew strikes her. He and Andrew are sent to work in the mines, but Andrew improvises their escape by passing as white.

Horace Bannon, called **the Soulcatcher**, a sadistic manhunter who works often for Flo Hatfield and who is sent on the trail of Andrew and Reb. Bannon's method of manhunting is to identify with his prey, even to become his prey in some sense. Bannon hovers ominously over Andrew's new life, but he ultimately sets Andrew free after having killed George Hawkins. Having "become" George Hawkins, he will not then murder his son.

Peggy Undercliff, Andrew's white bride. A well-read and witty young woman, Peggy is charmed by the appearance of Andrew in Spartanburg, a town devoid of interesting conversationalists. Peggy gives birth to Andrew's daughter and achieves with Andrew a comfortable domesticity.

Dr. Gerald Undercliff, a Spartanburg physician. A soured and lonely widower, he learns that Andrew has lied about his past but does not suspect that he is a runaway slave. Undercliff threatens to expose Andrew unless Andrew marries his daughter.

— *James Knippling*

PACO'S STORY

Author: Larry Heinemann (1944-   )
First published: 1986
Genre: Novel

Locale: South Vietnam and a small town in the United States
Time: The 1970's
Plot: Impressionistic realism

Paco Sullivan, the main character. He is the sole survivor of a fire fight at Fire Base Harriet, in which ninety-three men died from a combination of North Vietnamese Army attacks and "friendly fire." Paco is resentful for being the only man left alive from the fight, but he wants to get on with his life. After multiple surgeries, he must use a cane, has horrendous scars, and takes prescription drugs every day. Paco was the booby trap expert for his company, and he killed several men. He also had watched most of the members of his company rape and murder a Vietcong woman. In Vietnam, Paco dealt with life by smoking marijuana and opium; in the United States, he takes tranquilizers and drinks. He travels as far as his money will take him, haunted by the ghosts of Fire Base Harriet. Paco takes a job washing dishes in Boone, a small town. At the end of the book, he leaves after learning that a local college girl initially had been drawn to his scars but finally decided he was pitiful. Paco's life is not even tragic; it is grand melodrama.

The ghosts, from Fire Base Harriet, who narrate the story. There is actually a single narrative voice. The ghosts are omniscient; they see into Paco and all other characters, including the living versions of some of themselves. They are storytellers, always ready to go off on tangents into seemingly irrelevant tales. They also get into Paco's situation while he is semiconscious in Vietnam and into the minds of sleeping "grunts." If there is a moral voice, which is questionable, it must come from these voices.

Gallagher, who made the decision to rape and personally killed the Vietcong woman. He carried a .357 Magnum in a shoulder holster, in violation of the Geneva Convention, but Paco's booby traps and many other actions on both sides violated that agreement. Gallagher was a tall, big, and rangy American who had obtained a dragon tattoo in Singapore stretching from his palm to his elbow. He used it to scare the Vietnamese and half of the Americans. He was one of Paco's close friends.

Cathy, an education major who lives in Paco's hotel and who watches him wash dishes in the back of his grill, where she parades around in towels, underwear, or nothing but panties. She also deliberately makes noise in her room, which Paco can hear, when making love with her boyfriend. Paco finds her diary in her room and discovers that she has been fantasizing about him and has come to regard him as pitiful.

Jonesy, another of Paco's army friends, an expert with a pearl-handled straight razor. He was one of the few who would wait up for Paco to set his booby traps and then come back into camp.

Lieutenant Stennett, who, among other errors, called in an artillery strike directly on Fire Base Harriet, wiping out the command, himself included.

A medic, a man from Bravo Company brought in to clean up Fire Base Harriet. He finds Paco, somehow still alive, and ministers to him. Once Paco makes it alive to a base hospital, the medic quits field duty, turns his gun over to another medic who was a conscientious objector, and serves out his term in a base camp, later thinking that if not for his alcoholism, caused somehow by Paco, he would have made a fine doctor.

The night nurse, who serves in Paco's ward in Vietnam. She watches over him and is the only "love interest" in the book. One night, she gives Paco oral sex, knowing he has had none for a long time and that after his operations few women may want to be with him, though she appears wrong about that.

Ernest Monroe, the only person in Boone who will give Paco a job. As a former Marine and recipient of two Purple Hearts, he knows when a solder needs a job, and he never pressures Paco to tell him his story, though he is curious.

Jesse, a drifter who wanders into the grill right before closing, telling stories of travels across the country. He had been a paratrooper in Vietnam. He is approximately as capable as Paco of getting along in society, traveling across the country taking odd jobs.

— *John Jacob*

A PAGAN PLACE

Author: Edna O'Brien (1930-   )
First published: 1970
Genre: Novel

Locale: A village in Ireland
Time: Late 1930's to mid-1940's
Plot: Domestic realism

The protagonist, an intelligent, imaginative, sensitive, ten-year-old, pubescent schoolgirl in the superstition-ridden, legend-haunted West of Ireland. She is never given a name except "you." In her close, proscriptive, Roman Catholic village community, the girl grows up. Smart, very observant, and bookish, she goes through a series of initiations. She is present at a violent family row in which her pregnant, unmarried sister Emma is packed off to Dublin to have her child and have it adopted. She experiences her own sexual awakening at the hands of a young priest, Father Declan, who ejaculates on her closed thighs. Her second sexual arousal follows when her brutal father, to punish her for her conduct with the priest, beats her bare buttocks with a school ruler. Still vulnerable, priggish, nasty, and hypocritical, she escapes from her restrictive home, village, and country (if not immediately from the church) by becoming a novice in the Order of the Enfants de Marie convent in Belgium.

Her father, a drunken, violent, horse-fancying farmer. Generous to a fault, he is headed rapidly down on the social scale.

Her mother, who married above her social station and is a martyr to her husband's violently shifting moods. To salvage some personal satisfaction, she lives the lie of married bliss and keeps both the newly arrived village doctor and the hired hand on the farm interested in her sexually.

Emma, the protagonist's sister, born in New York. She is a rebel who does what she wants, then is crushed by the system. She is pregnant when she comes home from Dublin, where she works, and provokes a violent explosion from her father in a family council, where no one father can be located among so many candidates.

Ambie, the good-hearted hired hand who holds the farm operation together with his steady labor. Eventually, he saves enough money to make his escape.

Michael "the Nigger" Flannery, one of the many odd local characters who surround the central character. He gets his nickname from the purple, disfiguring birthmark on his face. Lonely and sexually frustrated, he sees no exit, though he makes the central character's going-away trunk.

Father Declan, a young Roman Catholic priest on leave from the mission field. The effects of religious constraint on him show in his assault on the central character. He is last spotted leaving the community, sent away quietly by his superiors.

— Archibald E. Irwin

THE PAINTED BIRD

Author: Jerzy Kosinski (1933-1991)
First published: 1965
Genre: Novel

Locale: Eastern Europe
Time: 1939-1945
Plot: Social morality

The young boy, an unnamed war refugee whose wanderings through Eastern Europe (from ages six to twelve) constitute whatever plot the novel can be said to contain. He has no history when his parents, fearful of Nazi reprisals, send him to the country for safekeeping. His first contact is soon lost. As the boy wanders from village to village, as slave or indentured servant to various peasant families, he witnesses scenes of increasing violence and cruelty. His own education follows from these episodes, as he tries to figure out how the world operates and what laws, if any, govern it. When the brutality becomes too much, the boy loses his voice and becomes mute; there is apparently nothing to be said in response to the cruelty here. At the end, reunited with his parents, the boy begins to speak; there is perhaps hope after all. The only real development in what seems a meaningless and disconnected series of cruel and violent incidents in the novel is, in fact, the quest the child makes for some kind of meaningful value system for himself. His selfishness at the beginning—clearly necessary for survival in this world of fear and ignorance—gives way by the end of the novel to a kind of personal self-determination.

Marta, a crippled, superstitious old woman with whom the young boy first lives. After Marta dies of natural causes, the boy accidentally sets fire to her house and burns her body in the conflagration.

Olga, a wise old woman who saves the young boy from other sadistic villagers. Olga is a medicine woman and has folk cures for a variety of ailments. When the boy catches a plaguelike fever, for example, she buries him up to his neck in a field, and the sickness soon leaves him.

Lekh, a peasant who traps birds and sells them to villagers. Lekh is in love with "Stupid Ludmila," and when jealous villagers kill her, Lekh is heartbroken. It is with Lekh that the boy witnesses the title story, of the painted bird destroyed by its own flock because it is different (a metaphor for the boy himself).

Ewka, a young woman who introduces the young boy to sex. He feels secure and happy with Ewka—for one of the first times in the novel—and his sexual initiation is thus a happy one. Makar, Ewka's father, forces the girl into unnatural sexual acts, and the young boy loses his love for her as he begins to understand the nature of evil in the world.

Gavrila, a Soviet political officer who teaches the young boy how to read. Gavrila also gives him a political education, teaching him not only about socialism but also about the Marxist view of history and religion. The boy idolizes Gavrila and tries to model himself on the officer's behavior.

Mitka, a crack sniper in the Russian army who teaches the boy self-respect and—in contrast to the political education that Gavrila is giving him—introduces him to poetry and song as well. He also teaches the narrator the importance of vengeance. When several Soviet soldiers are killed by drunken villagers, Mitka enacts his own silent revenge through the scope of his high-powered rifle.

The Silent One, who, like the young narrator, is a resident of an orphanage at the end of the war. It is the children who are the greatest victims of the war's violence and cruelty, the novel shows, and they bear the scars. The Silent One has his own sense of the world and causes a terrible train wreck as a means of getting back at a peasant merchant he thinks has humiliated the young boy.

— David Peck

PAINTED TURTLE: Woman with Guitar

Author: Clarence Major (1936-   )
First published: 1988
Genre: Novel

Locale: Arizona, Colorado, and New Mexico
Time: The 1930's to the 1980's
Plot: Experimental

Painted Turtle, a female Zuni singer and guitar player whose alienation from her culture allows her to transcend reality through her music. Early in her life, she yearns to be a boy and experience the freedom of her father's sphere; however, she must learn the confining ways of the worlds of her mother and grandmother. She is raped at the age of thirteen and gives birth to twins. Most of the Zuni interpret this as a curse, and their attitude strengthens the discomfort she feels concerning the demands and expectations placed on her as a result of her gender and culture. To escape, she goes to a mental hospital and later becomes an unsuccessful barmaid and prostitute; eventually, she becomes a nightclub performer. She finally realizes that her childhood guitar can offer her not only an escape from reality but also an escape from a dreaded life on the reservation. She travels to third-rate clubs, bars, and hotels, singing for tips while sleeping in flophouses and cheap motels, until she meets Baldy.

Baldwin (Baldy) Saiyataca, the narrator of the story, who peers into Painted Turtle's life across actual time and mythic distance. His own story becomes woven into hers, and they become lovers and musical partners. He meets Painted Turtle on "the grimy cantina circuit" when he is sent to hear her perform by their mutual agent, Peter Inkpen. Baldy's task is to transform Painted Turtle into a more commercially appealing singer by suggesting that she switch to the electric guitar; instead, she unwittingly transforms him, and he joins her act when he trades his prized electric guitar for an acoustic one. Being the son of a Hopi mother and a Navajo father makes him emblematic of the story; he, like Painted Turtle, must walk between two worlds. He represents conflict between people who are different. Throughout the novel, Saiyataca remains a distant figure and a stilted voice, telling little about Painted Turtle's life and even less about his own. He is seen through her eyes as the narrative reveals her life to the world.

Old Gchachu (CHAH-chew), the father of the clan, the human incarnation of the old ways. The collective memory—culture, custom, folklore, and history—is represented in his being; while Painted Turtle is in his presence, she is never sure if her experiences are dreams or reality. He prophesies when she is young that she will marry a wise priest, become famous for her traditional cooking skills, and become legendary for her love of children and family. When these beliefs do not come true, he reminds her that the soul of a Zuni dies if it strays too far from home.

Grandma Wilhelmina, Painted Turtle's grandmother, with whom the family lives, in accordance with Zuni custom. This character represents both the sanctity of the past, as she embodies the traditional female role of healer and caretaker, and the options of the future, as she produces fine jewelry and sells it in stores all over the Southwest. Without saying much, she validates Painted Turtle's independent spirit and sanctions her movement away from the traditional life.

Waldo Etawa, Painted Turtle's father, who symbolizes both the traditional father figure and the erosion of the Native American way of life. He teaches his daughter traditionally male tasks and helps her develop skills usually not taught to women. He fuels her independence by treating her like a son. Though successful, he lets the family's material and social status slip as he fails to keep white society and modernization from altering the "old ways."

Marelda Etawa, Painted Turtle's mother, who represents the stability of hearth and home and the probability of continuation. She remains at home as caretaker to both an older and a younger generation as well as a keeper of the family lore, its customs, and its traditions. She rears her two grandsons in Painted Turtle's absence.

— *Alphine W. Jefferson*

A PAINTER OF OUR TIME

Author: John Berger (1926-   )
First published: 1958
Genre: Novel

Locale: London, England
Time: The 1950's
Plot: Bildungsroman

Janos Lavin, a Hungarian painter and art teacher in London who is some twenty-five years older than his wife. He is dedicated to his art and strives to be as true to himself as he can be. He appears unconcerned with daily events but pays close attention to every detail within his line of sight. He begins to keep a diary after he hears about the execution of his childhood friend, Laszlo, for treason against the state. Janos wants to believe that he does not accept compromise, but at the same time he fears that his entire life as a painter has been a compromise of the ideals of his youth. He decides at the moment of his greatest artistic triumph to return to Hungary to continue political work. He is not

heard from again, and his friends suspect that he has been killed.

Diana Lavin, also known as **Rosie**, Janos' wife. She married him during a time in which she was working with refugees. She loves him in a maternal way, but when he does not respond as expected, she becomes cold, silent, and quarrelsome by turns. Diana, who is from an upper-middle-class English family, feels betrayed by Janos when he does not become the commercial success as a painter that she had hoped he would be. In her late forties, she has become disillusioned and no longer encourages Janos to be monetarily successful. She goes with resigned detachment to a library job that supports their material needs. When Janos finally succeeds in getting a show at a major gallery, she regains her energy and enthusiasm. After Janos returns to Hungary, she begins an affair with one of his refugee friends.

John, the narrator, a friend of Janos and an art critic. John discovers Janos' diary hidden in the studio after the Hungarian painter returns to his native country. As he reads the diary, John is amazed at the deep conflicts suffered by Janos. John attempts to further the painter's career by introducing him to rich collectors and arranging exhibitions. He is somewhat upset by Janos' overscrupulous principles concerning art and that Diana must live a financially insecure life, but he also views Janos as a victim of political and artistic fads in London.

Sir Gerald Banks, a rich English art collector. Sir Gerald has a vast and expensive art collection of good repute. He has some sensibility about art and does not rely on the opinions of others to tell him what he should like. When Janos comes to his house to see his collection and subsequently insults it, Sir Gerald retains respect for him as a truthful man. Later, when Janos competes for an exhibition prize, Sir Gerald is the one member of the judging committee who supports his entry, even when the other committee members decide against it.

Len Hancock, a butcher by trade who paints in his free time. He is the only painter friend that Janos has. He is an uncomplicated man, happily married to a beautiful woman, successful in his butcher shop, and striving always to be a better painter. He goes to Janos for advice and instruction about painting, taking criticism as a map to his growth as an artist. He wants to paint his wife's portrait but is unsure of his skill.

Vee Hancock, Len's beautiful wife and Diana's friend. The two couples often go together for outings at the beach or have dinner at each other's houses. She and Len are the only real social contact Diana has. Vee is fond of Janos but will not pose for him because she knows that he is attracted to her. She finally allows her husband to paint her as a nude and is partly embarrassed and partly thrilled by the result.

Laszlo, Janos' childhood friend and comrade-in-arms during their idealistic youth. Laszlo has been executed as an enemy of the people in Hungary, although his guilt is in question. Janos' memory of Laszlo is the sounding board for ruminations about politics, art, and responsibility in his diary. Laszlo had always told Janos that to be too devoted to art was to be selfish and that history needed artists to point the way to social reform.

— *Stephanie Korney*

THE PALACE OF THE WHITE SKUNKS
(Le palais des très blanches mouffettes)

Author: Reinaldo Arenas (1943-1990)
First published: 1975
Genre: Novel

Locale: Holguín, a small town in Oriente province, Cuba
Time: Late 1950's
Plot: Family

Fortunato (fohr-tew-NAH-toh), a sensitive and restless adolescent desperate to escape from a closed social and familial circle in which he feels trapped. He is the most complex character in the novel, fragmenting himself to give voice to the suffering of the other family members. As a writer, he creates and imagines other levels of reality to escape the poverty, hunger, war, intolerance, and prejudice around him. His failed attempt to join the rebel forces leads to his death at the hands of the government police.

Polo, Fortunato's grandfather, an impotent patriarchal figure. A Spaniard who immigrated to Cuba from the Canary Islands looking for a better life, he is a frustrated and embittered old man disillusioned by the poverty and misery of the Cuban countryside. Moreover, wishing to have had boys to help him with his struggles, he considers himself cursed for having engendered only daughters. As an act of defiance, he resorts to silence, refusing to talk to anyone except Tomasico, the owner of the only factory in town. Through Polo's chats with Tomasico and his interior monologues about the ups and downs of his fruit and vegetable stand, the reader becomes aware of the collective misery of the local economy.

Jacinta (hah-SEEN-tah), Polo's wife, a Cuban peasant woman who must cope with the stresses and misfortunes of a harsh rural lifestyle without the help of her uncaring and selfish husband. Uneducated and superstitious, she places her hope on some miraculous intervention that will change her life and that of her family. There is no escape from the misery that surrounds her, from the problems facing her daughters and fatherless grandchildren. Throughout the novel, she alternates between prayers begging for God's help and blasphemies insulting God for his indifference.

Adolfina (ah-dol-FEE-nah), "the spinster daughter," Fortunato's feminine double. She and Fortunato share sensibilities, experiencing feelings of extreme loneliness, dissatisfaction, and helplessness. Adolfina identifies with Fortunato's liberating spirit and his ability to express himself freely. Fortunato expresses himself openly; Adolfina, by contrast, must bury her emotions. As the oldest daughter in a traditional Hispanic family, she takes on the role of the responsible caretaker who must abandon her dreams and hopes and sacrifice herself for her family. Adolfina makes one last attempt to find a man, but she returns home defeated, still a virgin, and sets herself afire.

Celia (SEH-lee-ah), "the half-mad daughter," driven to madness after her only daughter, Esther, commits suicide.

Digna (DEEG-nah), "the abandoned daughter," abandoned by her husband Moisés and left to rear her two children, Tico and Anisia.

Onerica (ohn-EHR-ee-kah), "the banished daughter," Fortunato's mother, who abandons him and goes to the United States in search of her own "fortune."

PALE FIRE

Author: Vladimir Nabokov (1899-1977)
First published: 1962
Genre: Novel

Locale: New Wye, Appalachia, and the kingdom of Zembla
Time: 1959
Plot: Satire

Charles Kinbote or **Charles II**, known as **Charles Xavier the Beloved**, the last king of Zembla. As Kinbote, he is the author of the critical notes to *Pale Fire*, a 999-line autobiographical poem written by John Shade. Kinbote, a visiting professor at Wordsmith University, befriends Shade, hoping to induce the poet to write a great poem about Zembla and its kings. Toward the end of the book, the reader discovers that Kinbote is the exiled king Charles Xavier, driven from his throne by revolution. Kinbote's character develops in parallel stories, one taking place in New Wye and the other in Zembla, from the time he was a boy until his escape in 1958. In Zembla, Charles enjoys a luxurious life, indulging his passion for young boys while dodging the attempts of his queen mother to have him marry and produce an heir. Kinbote goes to New Wye in the hope of inducing John Shade to write the history of Zembla, the symbol of his lost youth, wealth, and eminence. His life is devoted to providing Shade with the material needed to write the history. Thinking all the while that Shade is cooperating, yet prevented by his wife from seeing the poem in development, Kinbote is shocked and dismayed to discover that *Pale Fire* is not about Zembla but about Shade's own life. Kinbote retreats to a mountain cabin in Cedarn, where he madly writes his critical edition of the poem. The result is a parody of critical commentary in which *Pale Fire* is all but forgotten. In his commentary, Kinbote is given to elaborate wordplay that enables him both to conceal and to reveal the truth; it also causes him to see sinister connections, resemblances, and coincidences. He uses language to create reality, as he creates a new identity in New Wye ("New I"), but what he creates with language may finally be only a figment of his imagination. In the end, he says that he will continue to exist, write a play perhaps, join his friend Odon in making motion pictures, or even go mad, but he will always know that another, more competent Gradus will be searching for him.

John Shade, a professor at Wordsmith University. This poet is the author of *Pale Fire*, a poem in four cantos written during the final twenty days of his life. His face looks like that of a drunk, his fingers are pudgy, his nails are yellow, and his body is misshapen. This "coarse disguise" hides a nature that awes Kinbote, who sees in Shade the realization of his dream of preserving in poetry the romance of his kingdom and the glory of his youth. The poem Shade writes turns out to be mostly a history of his own life, which ends at the hands of Gradus, an inept assassin.

Jakob Gradus, the book's chief villain. Brutish and dimwitted, he represents everything Kinbote loathes. As a member of an anti-Royalist group in Zembla, Gradus is appointed to assassinate the deposed king, who is masquerading as Charles Kinbote. Gradus' journey to New Wye follows a series of blunders and missed chances to assassinate the king. Gradus is so inept in his use of language that he cannot communicate successfully even with his cohorts. Throughout the narrative, he is the dark nemesis who shadows the exiled king, only to blunder in the end and kill John Shade instead. Even the way he commits suicide is debased—he slits his throat with a razor blade found in a garbage container.

Sybil Shade, John's wife, who is protective of him and his work to the point of domineering him. She continually foils Kinbote's attempts to visit her husband, forcing Kinbote to spy on the poet through binoculars from trees and rooftops at night and to waylay him on his walks when she is not around. In a moment of weakness following her husband's death, she gives Kinbote permission to publish *Pale Fire* with critical commentary. From Canada, where she goes to live with relatives, she continues to plague Kinbote, asking him to accept two coeditors in his work on *Pale Fire* while refusing to provide him with biographical information needed in his editing.

Hazel Shade, John and Sybil's daughter, a devotee of psychokinetic phenomena. She commits suicide in 1957, preferring "the beauty of death to the ugliness of life."

Disa, the **duchess of Payn**, Charles Xavier's wife. After failing to consummate her marriage because of Charles's homosexuality, she moves to the French Riviera, where Charles visits her on his flight to America. He is unable to love the actual Disa, though she lives on, loved and beautiful, in his dreams.

— Bernard E. Morris

PALE HORSE, PALE RIDER: Three Short Novellas

Author: Katherine Anne Porter (1890-1980)
First published: 1939
Genre: Novellas

Locale: New Orleans, Texas, and Colorado
Time: 1885-1918
Plot: Psychological realism

Old Mortality

Miranda, a young girl whose mother has died and who lives in a world created by romantic family legends. As she grows older, she gets hints that her beloved Aunt Amy and Uncle Gabriel are not the romantic couple she has idolized, but two people with problems. At the age of eighteen, by which time she is married, she confronts the most realistic member of her family, Eva, who reveals the past through different eyes. At the end, she decides to find the truth beneath the illusions.

Eva Parrington, Miranda's cousin, a plain woman who

taught Latin and was involved in the women's rights movement. She sees Amy as she is, unadorned by romantic stereotypes. Her forthright explanation is the trigger for Miranda's search for truth.

Amy, the young wife of Gabriel who died of tuberculosis after leading a life of scandalous but intriguing behavior. Her portrait hangs in the hallway of the house, forever a memento to lost times.

Gabriel, Amy's husband, an owner of racehorses. He is attached to the romanticized memory of Amy. He dies as an alcoholic, married unhappily for the second time.

Noon Wine

Royal Earle Thompson, the owner of a ramshackle dairy farm in Texas. Aspiring to a grander lifestyle, he hires Olaf Helton. His fortunes improve because he allows Olaf to direct the farm activities. Seeing only that things are improving, he misses the hint that something could be amiss with Helton. When Hatch appears, looking for Helton and wanting to return him to the mental hospital, Thompson seeks to defend Helton and kills Hatch. He commits suicide after trying in vain to convince his family and friends that the whole thing was an accident.

Olaf Helton, a Swede from North Dakota who hires on as a farmhand. Except for playing the harmonica, he works silently and industriously, bothering no one. Only once does he reveal the potential for violence in his character, but he keeps it under control. His death results from a tragic mistake.

Homer T. Hatch, who comes to return the escaped mental patient to North Dakota. His sneaky attitude and stereotyped remarks about Helton annoy Thompson because they threaten the smooth surface of his lifestyle. Because of this, Thompson kills him.

Pale Horse, Pale Rider

Miranda, a theater critic on a small newspaper. Working for little pay amid the stress of wartime conditions and an influenza epidemic, she falls in love with Adam, a young officer who lives in the same rooming house. Falling prey to the epidemic, she goes through a near death experience. She regains her health only to find that Adam has died. These experiences initiate her to the world of real truths.

Adam Barclay, a handsome young officer on leave from the Army who falls in love with Miranda and nurses her until she can go to the hospital. He then falls victim to the disease and dies before Miranda recovers.

— Louise M. Stone

THE PALM-WINE DRINKARD

Author: Amos Tutuola (1920-1997)
First published: 1952
Genre: Novel

Locale: Nigeria
Time: Indeterminate
Plot: Folklore

The narrator, the palm-wine "drinkard" of the title, who cannot imagine life without a steady supply of palm-wine. After his palm-wine tapster falls from a palm and is killed, he takes his dead father's jujus (magical implements) and sets out to find the tapster in the town of the dead. One of his first adventures is the rescue of a young woman from a bush creature who has lured her into captivity. He marries her and with her traverses a variety of dangerous areas in the bush, sometimes using his jujus to change his wife into a wooden doll that he carries in his pocket and once changing himself into a canoe to earn money ferrying people across a river. The journey seems to be a test of his character as well as serving to form it. He does not gain materially from his experiences, but he maintains his humanity and Christianity, even in the face of terrible dangers and awesome creatures. When he and his wife return home, he no longer seems to depend upon palm-wine, and he becomes the savior of his people by negotiating the conclusion to a feud between Heaven and Earth, thus ending a famine.

The Palm-Wine Tapster, who now resides in Deads' Town. He cannot go with the narrator or allow him to stay, because the dead cannot coexist with the living. He gives the narrator some palm-wine and a marvelous egg, with which the narrator later combats a terrible famine. Someone later carelessly breaks the egg.

The narrator's wife, who is by his side from the moment they are thrown together in the adventure of the bush creature called the Complete Gentleman or Curious Creature. She has the gift of prophecy, but her predictions are so cryptic that the narrator never understands them until it is too late to affect the course of events.

The Curious Creature, a skull that dresses itself in the rented body parts of several human beings, appearing in the marketplace to lure young women, including the narrator's wife, to its home in the bush. The creature appears in the didactic and humorous tales of several West African peoples.

The Faithful Mother, who ambushes people as they pass by her tree if she sees that they need rest, food, help, or solace. Once inside the land entered through the tree, they experience no unhappiness or deprivation, but they may stay only three months or until they are ready to leave, whichever comes first.

Dance,

Drum, and

Song, a trio who lure away the monstrous child born from the thumb of the narrator's wife. Later, Dance appears again as **The Red-lady** in Red-town, where she and her two companions make music until they disappear, leaving only their names behind in the world.

The Red-king, the father of The Red-lady and the leader who broke a taboo and thus delivered his town into the power of two red creatures.

The Invisible Pawn, the chief of all bush creatures, who hires out to the narrator as a laborer on his farm in Red-town. All the other farmworkers toil during the day, but he works during the night, accomplishing more than all of them together, often accomplishing too much, as, for example, when he produces so much firewood that the townspeople wake up to find that they must clear the wood away in order to walk about.

— *James L. Hodge*

PAMELA: Or, Virtue Rewarded

Author: Samuel Richardson (1689-1761)
First published: 1740-1741
Genre: Novel

Locale: England
Time: Early eighteenth century
Plot: Epistolary

Pamela Andrews, a virtuous servant girl of Lady B———, mistress of an estate in Bedfordshire. After the death of her mistress, she intends to return home but is persuaded to stay by the son, Mr. B———, who promises to be a good master to her. Later, she has cause to suspect his intentions; after he makes a series of attempts on her virtue, she determines to leave. The coach, however, deposits her at Mr. B———'s country estate, where she is held prisoner. She meets the local minister, Mr. Williams. She tries several times to escape. Finally Mr. B———, moved by her virtue, offers her an honorable marriage, and she accepts his proposal. Despite anonymous letters and suspicions of other love affairs, she remains faithful and eventually turns Mr. B——— into an honorable husband.

John Andrews and

Elizabeth Andrews, the parents of Pamela.

Mr. B———, the young squire who plots against Pamela's virtue, tries to seduce her, proposes to make her his mistress on carefully outlined terms, and then finally marries her.

Lady Davers, the daughter of Lady B———, who at first opposes her brother's marriage to a servant. She begins to sympathize with Pamela after reading the many letters the girl had written her parents, and she is finally won over completely by Pamela's beauty and virtue.

Mrs. Jervis, Mr. B———'s kindhearted housekeeper. For a time, she protects Pamela's honor. When Mr. B——— tries to intimidate her, she and Pamela determine to leave together.

Mrs. Jewkes, the villainous ex-prostitute caretaker of Mr. B———'s country estate. She tries to further her employer's plots against Pamela's virtue and keeps the girl a prisoner.

Mr. Williams, the country clergyman of Lincolnshire who loves Pamela. Though the first proposal of marriage from him is part of Mr. B———'s scheme, he does seek to marry her.

Discovered smuggling her letters out of the house, he is thrown into jail on a trumped-up charge. Eventually, when Mr. B——— repents, Mr. Williams performs the marriage ceremony and receives a permanent vicarage.

Sally Godfrey, a former sweetheart of Mr. B———, by whom he has a daughter. After her marriage, Pamela offers to take the child under her own care.

The Daughter of Sally and Mr. B———.

Billy, the son of Pamela and Mr. B———.

A Countess, with whom Mr. B——— is philandering while Pamela is bearing his child. By reading some of Pamela's letters, she learns the punishment for those who depart from the path of virtue.

Mr. Longman, the steward of Mr. B———.

John, Mr. B———'s groom, who carries most of Pamela's letters to her parents but keeps some for his master.

Robin, the coachman forced to take Pamela to Mr. B———'s country estate.

Nan, the rude servant who guards Pamela at Mr. B———'s estate.

Lady Jones, a neighbor who will give Pamela refuge if she succeeds in escaping from Mr. B———'s country estate.

Sir Simon Darnford and

Lady Darnford, friends of Mr. B——— who want to help free Pamela.

Mrs. Towers, a neighbor who criticizes Pamela.

Mr. Brooks and

Mrs. Brooks, neighbors.

Mrs. Arthur, another critical neighbor, who visits the new bride.

Sir Jacob Swynford, Mr. B———'s uncle. Prepared to dislike his nephew's humble bride, he is won over by Pamela's charm and virtue.

PAN

Author: Knut Hamsun (Knut Pedersen, 1859-1952)
First published: 1894
Genre: Novel

Locale: Sirilund, Norway, and an adjacent forest
Time: 1855-1861
Plot: Psychological

Lieutenant Thomas Glahn, the principal narrator. Thirty years old at the time he recounts events that occurred two years earlier, in 1855, he takes up solitary residence in a hut in rural northern Norway, on the outskirts of the coastal town of Sirilund. Awkward in society yet extraordinarily attractive to women and men, he shoots himself in the leg in frustration over his relationship to Edvarda. He is disingenuous in claiming that he writes his account merely to pass the time and that he is indifferent toward Edvarda. After the death of Eva, he moves to India, where he dies of a gunshot wound.

Edvarda Mack, the tall, flirtatious, and headstrong only child of the town's wealthiest man. She is fifteen or sixteen years old at the time that Glahn, who is struck by the curve of her eyebrows and her long, delicate fingers, moves to Nordland. Her ambivalence over the handsome stranger, Glahn, exacerbates Glahn's anxieties.

Herr Mack, a successful and imperious trader. A widower who conducts clandestine trysts with Eva, he is envious of Glahn's success in luring her away from him and resentful of his daughter Edvarda's attentions to the outsider.

The doctor, an urbane physician. He is one of Glahn's rivals for the affections of Edvarda. He discovers and treats Glahn's self-inflicted leg wound.

Eva, the pretty, ingenuous young wife of a blacksmith. She falls in love with the handsome stranger Glahn and gives herself to him, though he is in love with Edvarda. She is killed in an avalanche inadvertently set off by Glahn.

The second narrator, Glahn's hunting partner in India and his alter ego. He recounts the events after Glahn leaves Nor-

way. Envious of the attention that Glahn receives, particularly from Maggie, he is goaded by Glahn into shooting him to death.

Maggie, a pretty Tamil woman who, Glahn remarks, is always chewing. When she transfers her affections from the second narrator to Glahn, the latter becomes enraged.

The baron, a Finnish scientist whom Herr Mack brings to stay with them. A sociable and rational man, he is Glahn's most serious rival for Edvarda's love. Glahn spits in his ear at the baron's farewell party and fires a parting salute that results in Eva's death.

Aesop, Glahn's faithful dog, his solitary companion in the Norwegian woods. As a parting gift to Edvarda, Glahn shoots Aesop and sends her his dead body.

Cora, Glahn's canine companion in India, the successor to Aesop.

— *Steven G. Kellman*

PANDORA'S BOX
(Die Büchse der Pandora)

Author: Frank Wedekind (1864-1918)
First published: 1904
Genre: Drama

Locale: Germany, Paris, and London
Time: The 1890's
Plot: Tragedy

Lulu, a twenty-year-old murderess and prostitute, married four times. She has had countless lovers. Lulu is the embodiment of unbridled female eros. Her fortunes rise and fall along with those of the men and women around her. Lulu's ability to live a life of pure sensuality is put to the test. After her escape from prison after a year and a half of incarceration and illness, she is forced into a life of deceit, debauchery, and ruin. Her unscrupulous exploitation of Countess Martha von Geschwitz's homoerotic feelings for her have led not only to her successful escape from prison but also to the countess' financial ruin and ultimate death. After she marries Alva, she and a number of her entourage move to Paris. All of them profit from Martha's and Alva's weakness for Lulu by blackmailing Lulu, who in turn extorts the money they demand from Martha and Alva. The final ruin of all occurs when the "Jungfrau" stock, in which Lulu, Alva, and a number of others in their company have invested heavily, crashes, bankrupting everyone. Before sinking to her lowest point, Lulu induces Schigolch, a vagrant, to murder Rodrigo to get rid of him for her. Lulu's purely sensuous and childlike nature, which is preserved in the painting of her, is confirmed when she is reduced to streetwalking in London, and her inability to be businesslike becomes apparent because she enjoys her customers when she should not. In this, she is supported by Alva's failure to play the role of pimp effectively.

Dr. Alva, or **Alwa**, **Schön** (shehn), a playwright, the son of Dr. Schön, a newspaper publisher and editor in chief. He is Lulu's fourth husband. Alva's fortune from the sale of his father's newspaper is spent on his passion for Lulu, and he loses what is left when the stock in which he had invested becomes worthless. Alva admires Martha's selfless concern for Lulu and her sacrifices to free her from prison by purposely infecting herself and Lulu with cholera. He is too civilized to have the courage to lead the wild and adventurous life he so admires. He also is too weak to protest when Lulu

seduces him on the same piece of furniture that provided the scene of his father's murder by her hand. In London, he proves unable to be an effective pimp. He suffers from jealousy and depression whenever Lulu is with a customer.

Countess Martha von Geschwitz (fon GEH-shvihtz), an artist and a lesbian. She usually wears a tight-fitting black dress. She loses her health and her fortune in the vain hope of possessing Lulu. She worships her, and a painting of Lulu is displayed prominently in the great hall of her house. She has risked her life and a considerable sum of money by helping Lulu escape from prison. She is shamelessly exploited by those around Lulu who know of her enslavement. She follows Lulu to France and to England, where she arrives penniless. She sees herself, as do others, as neither man nor woman and wonders if she has a human heart. She knows that Lulu has a cold heart and has always despised her. After her failed attempt to commit suicide, she vows to turn her back on Lulu and her people and return to Germany to study law and to fight for women's rights. Moments later, she is killed by Jack the Ripper.

Schigolch (SHI-gohlkh), a vagrant who claims to be Lulu's father. He is a blackmailer and murderer, part of the foursome in London, and lives off the meager proceeds from Lulu's prostitution.

Rodrigo Quast (kvast), a circus acrobat and a blackmailer. He played a role in Lulu's escape from prison for which he continues to be paid a handsome monthly salary by Martha. He was Lulu's fiancé before her escape and still intends to marry her and to train her for a circus act, thus having her provide a living for them both. Later, in France, he tries to extort money from Lulu for his new bride, with whom he is living. He is killed by Schigolch at Lulu's instigation.

Marquis Casti-Piani (KAHS-tee pee-AH-nee), a police informer and trader in the white slave market. He has been extorting money from Lulu for a year since her escape. He knows that Lulu's resources are exhausted and wants to sell her to a brothel in Cairo, Egypt. He is arrested in Paris only moments before Lulu, Alva, and Schigolch escape to London.

Puntschu (PEWNT-shew),
Magelone (mah-geh-LOH-neh),
Kadidia (kah-DEE-dee-yah),
Bianetta (bee-ah-NEHT-tah),
Alfred Hugenberg (HEW-gehn-behrg),
Heilmann (HIL-mahn),

Bob,
Ludmilla Steinherz (LEWT-mihl-lah SHTIN-hehrts),
Mr. Hunidei (HEW-nih-di),
Dr. Hilti,
Kungu Poti (KUHN-gew PO-tih), and
Jack the Ripper, all characters with whom Lulu and the other principal characters associate on the road to their ruin from Germany via France to England.

— Arthur Tilo Alt

PANTOMIME

Author: Derek Walcott (1930-   )
First published: 1980
Genre: Drama

Locale: Tobago, the West Indies
Time: The 1970's
Plot: Comedy

Harry Trewe, a retired English actor in his middle forties, now the owner and operator of the Castaways Guest House. His apparent problem as the play begins is to put together entertainment for the guests of his establishment, utilizing his own skills as an actor and the musical performing abilities of Jackson Phillip, whom he employs as an entertainer. Trewe attempts to persuade Jackson, who is black, to play the role of Robinson Crusoe to his Friday. Although most of the action is devoted to their arguments over whether this pantomime will be performed, Trewe reveals that he has many other problems. He is a victim of insomnia and boredom, which is ironic because he intentionally invested his money in the remote island of Tobago, where the guest house is situated. He speaks of suicide and of jumping off a ledge. The play's setting (in a gazebo or summer house on the edge of a cliff) and Trewe's personal problems (he is separated from his wife and his son is dead) suggest that his talk of suicide may be serious. Trewe's problems as owner of the guest house and his personal problems are exacerbated by and wound up in his image of himself as a white man, which he finds is harder to leave behind than he had believed. He urges Jackson to be his equal and to play his (Trewe's) master but nevertheless resorts to commanding

the black Trinidadian whenever he becomes threatened or frustrated.

Jackson Phillip, a forty-year-old native of Trinidad who was once a calypso performer and now works in the Castaways Guest House for Harry Trewe. Having been a performer on the bigger, more frequented island, and having been in New York City, Phillip nevertheless tries futilely to operate as though he were a naïve, untutored laborer. He switches from dialect to dialect depending on whether he is alone, serving Trewe, or arguing with Trewe. His prior experiences have led him to prefer not to have an intimate friendship with a white man, and he certainly prefers not to play the role of Crusoe, as Trewe wishes him to do, but he is long-suffering. He attempts the role, both sincerely and with heavy sarcasm. He is harassed by a parrot which, Trewe explains, is only calling its previous owner, "Heinegger." Finally, his humanity is called forth and called on when he must rescue Trewe from his despair by acting out the part of Trewe's wife, speaking of the child's death and the wife's loneliness, and forcing Trewe to admit his emotions.

— Anna R. Holloway

THE PAPER MEN

Author: William Golding (1911-1993)
First published: 1984
Genre: Novel

Locale: England, Switzerland, and Italy
Time: Early 1980's
Plot: Domestic realism

Wilfred (Wilf) Townsend Barclay, a successful English novelist. Turning sixty, with a scraggly yellow-white beard and thatch of hair and a broken-toothed grin, Wilf is struggling with his addictions to alcohol and women. The latter leads to his divorce and departure from his house in Wiltshire to become a wanderer around the globe. After the early death of his parents—he never knew his father—he had become a bank clerk. His inaccuracies were tolerated only because of his prowess as a wing threequarter on the local rugby team, but eventually he was fired. Spells as a groom, an actor, and a provincial reporter, then wartime service, preceded the writing of his first novel, *Coldharbour*. His success was maintained by such later novels as *All We Like Sheep*, *The Birds of Prey*, and

Horses at the Spring. Although he is a skeptic about miracles, his aesthetic interest in stained glass leads him into an Italian cathedral, where he collapses in front of an image of Christ and subsequently claims to be suffering from the stigmata (except for the fatal wound in the side). Averse to but flattered by the desperate attempts of Rick Tucker to become his biographer, he treats him literally like a dog while alternately evading and manipulating him. Less excusably, he treats his wife, daughter, and acquaintances with an indifference scarcely mitigated by his financial generosity. His capacity for self-analysis allows him to see himself as a clown caught with his pants falling down.

Richard (Rick) Linbergh Tucker, an American academic.

Six feet, three inches tall and weighing 225 pounds, Rick is covered by a forest of dark hair, has a broad nose with a bridge slightly sunken, a long upper lip, and the lower one dropped a fraction from it. In the years he spends trailing Wilfred Barclay, Rick later affects an Afro hairstyle, a shirt open to the navel, flared white trousers trimmed with sequins, and a gold necklace with every kind of trendy ornament attached. First as a diffident and plodding graduate student, then as a tenured assistant professor in the Department of English and Allied Studies at the University of Astrakhan in Nebraska, Rick trails Wilf around Europe, deviously trying to get Wilf to appoint him as his official biographer. Frustrated, humiliated, and growing increasingly ludicrous and desperate in his obsessive pursuit, Rick at the end appears to be turning to murder to secure his prey.

Mary Lou Tucker, Rick's wife. A slim twenty-year-old former student of Rick at Astrakhan University who majored in flower arranging and bibliography. She serves as bait in an unsuccessful attempt to lure Wilf into signing a document appointing Rick as Wilf's official biographer. Although he finds her mind as interesting as a piece of string, Wilf does base the character Helen Davenant, in his pastoral novel *Horses at the Spring*, on her. After splitting up with Rick, Mary Lou is reported to have become one of the women kept by Halliday, Rick's rich sponsor.

— Christopher M. Armitage

PARADE'S END

Author: Ford Madox Ford (Ford Madox Hueffer, 1873-1939)
First published: 1950
Genre: Novels

Locale: England and France
Time: The 1910's
Plot: Psychological realism

Some Do Not . . . , 1924

Christopher Tietjens (TEE-jehns), the younger son of a Yorkshire squire, a man with old-fashioned values. He is faithful to his adulterous wife and loyal to his friends. He loans money to Vincent Macmaster and even permits him to take credit for his own brilliant statistical analyses. After he falls in love with Valentine Wannop, Christopher still insists that his wife, not he, must institute divorce proceedings. Although he has a desk job in London, Christopher insists on going to France to serve in the war. Sent home after being wounded, he finally asks Valentine to become his mistress, but they part before their relationship can be consummated.

Sylvia Tietjens, Christopher's wife, a beautiful, heartless woman who remains physically attracted by her husband, though she hates him for his nobility and is determined to break him. She spends her life slandering her husband and seducing other men.

Valentine Wannop, an intelligent, idealistic, and unselfish young woman. She gets to know Christopher when, appealing to his chivalry, she convinces him to drive a horse-cart in which a fellow demonstrator is escaping from the police. On the way home, the two get lost. The fact that they spent the night together becomes the basis for rumors that they are lovers. Valentine's reputation also suffers because, as a paci-

fist, she is thought to be pro-German. Although she does not expect anything to come from her feelings for Christopher, she cannot forget him.

Sir Mark Tietjens, Christopher's brother, his senior by fourteen years. Although the brothers are virtual strangers, Mark believes Christopher's explanation of events, in part because he has always disliked Sylvia. He urges Christopher to divorce her and to marry Valentine.

Vincent Macmaster, a self-seeking Scot of unimpressive origins who takes advantage of Christopher's generous nature. When he marries Edith Ethel Duchemin, formerly his mistress, he becomes financially secure. During the war, he works his way up in the bureaucracy.

Edith Ethel Duchemin, the elegant wife of a wealthy Anglican rector, who is insane. After her husband's death, she marries Macmaster and devotes herself to his advancement and to the persecution of Christopher and of her one-time confidante, Valentine.

General Lord Edward Campion, Christopher's godfather. Though capable in military matters, he is no judge of human nature. He admires Sylvia and thinks Christopher should patch up the marriage.

No More Parades, 1925

Christopher Tietjens, an army captain in charge of almost three thousand men. He bears his responsibilities bravely, exhibiting compassion as well as self-control. When Sylvia appears at the front, he is patient. He even spends some time in a hotel with her. When he attacks a man who enters their hotel room, evidently unaware of his identity as Sylvia's lover, it is Christopher who is disgraced.

Sergeant-Major Cowley, an elderly Englishman, Christo-

pher's right hand and one of his greatest admirers. Later a second lieutenant, he joins his old captain on Armistice Day.

Captain Mackenzie, Macmaster's nephew, who clings to sanity with Christopher's help. He also appears on Armistice Day, still a little mad.

Sylvia Tietjens, who appears at the front to see Christopher and to demand money and property. She turns General Campion against her husband by insisting that he is a Socialist.

A Man Could Stand Up, 1926

Christopher Tietjens, who continues to do his duty in the most horrible conditions. After narrowly escaping death, he returns to England. No one will give him a government post, and he is reduced to selling his books and furniture. On Armi-

stice Day, some of his men find him and insist on celebrating with him.

Valentine Wannop, a physical education instructor who is called into the school office in the midst of the Armistice Day festivities. Lady Macmaster, Sir Vincent's wife, has called to let Valentine know where Christopher is and, incidentally, to inform the schoolmistress about her bad character. Ignoring the schoolmistress's well-meant advice, Valentine quits her job and goes to Christopher.

The Last Post, 1928

Sir Mark Tietjens, who is bedridden after a stroke. He has not said a word since learning that the Allies would not occupy Germany. Shortly before he dies, he speaks to Valentine, giving her the reassurance about the future she so desperately needs.

Marie Léonie Rioter, Lady Tietjens, formerly Sir Mark's mistress, now his wife. She nurses him devotedly.

Valentine Wannop, who now lives with Christopher and Mark. Strengthened by her pregnancy, Valerie stands up to Sylvia.

Christopher Tietjens, who is trying desperately to make a living as a furniture dealer.

Sylvia Tietjens, who has decided to divorce Christopher and marry General Campion. She remains curious about Valentine and Christopher. First she sends her son to spy on them, then she goes herself. Perhaps at last feeling a trifle guilty, she leaves, denying that she meant any harm to Valentine and the child.

— Rosemary M. Canfield Reisman

PARADISE LOST

Author: John Milton (1608-1674)
First published: 1667
Genre: Poetry

Locale: Heaven, Hell, and Earth
Time: The creation of the world
Plot: Epic

Adam, the first man and representative of humankind. Although gifted with reason and restraint, he allows an excessively passionate tenderness for Eve to blind him. Forewarned by the Archangel Raphael of danger from Satan, he nevertheless yields to Eve's entreaty that she alone be trusted. When he learns that she has fallen, he chooses to join her rather than turn from her. His first reaction after his own fall is to rebuke and blame her for his own sin. After falling into almost suicidal despair, he repents. When the Archangel Michael foretells the future redemption of humankind by Christ, he accepts his fate with gratitude.

Eve, the first woman and representative of womanhood. Beautiful, gentle, and submissive, she holds Adam enthralled. She is horrified when Satan first approaches her in a dream, but piqued by what she considers Adam's lack of faith in her, she stubbornly insists on working alone, thereby leaving herself vulnerable to the Serpent's temptation. Like Adam, after the fall she is first lustful, then quarrelsome. Finally, she too accepts her fate with dignity and resignation.

Satan (Lucifer), the chief of the fallen angels, adversary of God and humanity. His obvious heroism and grandeur are tainted by a perversion of will and accompanying perversion of intellect. Rebellious against God, he is incapable of understanding Him. A self-tormented spirit, conscious of his loss but unwilling to repent, he allows evil to eat away at him, tarnishing his splendor. His degradation is complete when he decides to enter the body of the serpent. His attempt to seduce humanity succeeds, but his triumph is temporary and hollow.

Beelzebub (bee-EHL-zeh-buhb), Satan's chief lieutenant. Less confident and less splendid than his chief, he works his will and serves as his mouthpiece. In the council of the fallen angels in Pandemonium, he presents forcefully Satan's plan of indirect war on God through humanity. His proposal carries.

Moloch (MOH-lok), the fiercest of the fallen angels. Appropriately worshiped in later years with human sacrifice, he is bloody-minded and desperate. If the fallen angels cannot win Heaven, he chooses either to make Heaven intolerable for the angels who did not fall or to anger God to the point that He will annihilate the fallen spirits.

Belial (BEE-lee-ehl), a fallen angel industrious only in vice. Smooth and oily, he favors peace at any price and expresses the hope that if the fallen angels do not call God's attention to themselves, He will forget them and allow their sufferings to decrease. He favors a proper course, but for improper reasons, basing his surrender on sloth, not on acceptance of God's will.

Mammon (MAM-uhn), a materialistic fallen angel. Like Belial, he is opposed to a second war against Heaven, but he favors a plan of development of natural resources and exploitation of Hell to raise an empire that will rival Heaven.

Mulciber (MUHL-sih-bur), also called **Vulcan**, Mammon's chief engineer and architect. Formerly the planner of many of Heaven's buildings, he is now architect of Pandemonium, Satan's palace in Hell.

Sin, Satan's daughter, born from his brain without a mother. She is the loathsome keeper of Hell's gates, through which she lets Satan pass to attack the world. She and her grisly son Death follow Satan to Earth to prey on humankind.

Death, the son of Sin and Satan by their incestuous union. He ravishes Sin and begets a horde of hellhounds on her. His voraciousness is so great that he would devour his own mother, except for the fear that her death would involve his own destruction. His fierce reaction to Satan is mollified by the latter's offer of hosts of men and beasts for him to devour if Satan's assault on Earth succeeds.

God the Father, an all-knowing and all-powerful being who foresees Satan's activities and humanity's fall but extends to humans His grace and brings forth good from evil.

Messiah, the only son of God. He is first granted by His Father the overthrow of Satan and his legions in the War in Heaven, then granted His wish to sacrifice Himself to redeem humanity.

Michael, the warrior angel. Chief of the angelic forces in the War in Heaven, he is a worthy opponent of Satan. He is God's messenger to Adam and Eve to tell them of their banishment from Paradise and their coming death; however, he is allowed by God's grace to foretell to Adam the future of the human race and the redemption to come.

Abdiel (AB-dee-ehl), an angelic servant of God. Alone among Lucifer's angel hordes, he remains steadfast and is rewarded by God's own praise and the favor of striking the first blow against Satan in the war against the rebel angels. Obviously one of the poet's favorite creations in *Paradise Lost*, he is perhaps an idealized version of the poet himself.

Raphael (RAF-ee-ehl), God's messenger to Adam to warn him of Satan's presence in Paradise. Gracious and friendly, he still is capable of severe judgment and warns Adam particularly against unreasonable and passionate adoration of Eve.

Gabriel (GAY-bree-ehl), the chief of the angelic guards in Paradise. He is a major leader in the War in Heaven against the evil angels.

Uriel (YEWR-ee-ehl), the regent of the Sun. Even though he is an angel, he is incapable of seeing through the mask of a hypocrite and fails to recognize Satan in his disguise as a lesser angel. He directs the evil spirit to Paradise but sees his actions in Paradise and hastily warns Gabriel that an evil spirit has gained entrance there.

Uzziel (uh-ZI-ehl),

Ithuriel (ih-THEW-ree-ehl), and

Zephon (ZEE-fon), angel guards in Paradise.

PARADISE REGAINED

Author: John Milton (1608-1674)
First published: 1671
Genre: Poetry

Locale: The Holy Land
Time: The first century
Plot: Epic

Jesus of Nazareth, the tempted, an embodiment of the poet's religious philosophy and ideals. He is reasonable, intelligent, and holy. Pronounced the beloved Son of God at his baptism, he enters the desert to meditate on the course he should choose to fulfill his destiny as the Saviour of humankind. His self-communion and his troubled dreams show His humanity and prevent His becoming a mere theological abstraction. Superior to both physical and spiritual temptations, He overcomes Satan and redeems humankind from its fallen state caused when Adam and Eve succumbed to temptation.

Satan, the tempter, the great Dictator of Hell. Debased from the splendid, though tarnished, rebel of *Paradise Lost* (1667), he is a sly, lying trickster. His choice of temptations for Jesus shows shrewdness, but shorn of understanding of God, he lacks wisdom. Frustrated by the fortitude and virtue of Jesus, he lapses into snarling and futile rage. His violence

recoils on himself, and astonished, he falls a second time, completely conquered.

John the Baptist, the trumpet-voiced "great Proclaimer." Satan learns at the baptism of Jesus by John that he now has a terrible adversary among men.

Belial (BEE-lee-ehl), the self-indulgent fallen angel. Lustful himself, he thinks lust the perfect temptation; therefore, he advises Satan to use women in his temptation of Jesus. His suggestion is scornfully overruled by Satan.

Mary the Mother of Jesus, who is pure-hearted and calm but nevertheless troubled over the long absence of her Son.

God the Father, the omniscient and all-wise being who foretells to Gabriel the temptations and their outcome.

Gabriel (GAY-bree-ehl), the angel of the Annunciation. He is chosen to hear God's prophetic plan.

PARADISO

Author: José Lezama Lima (1910-1976)
First published: 1966
Genre: Novel

Locale: Cuba, Florida, Jamaica, and Mexico
Time: Late nineteenth and early twentieth centuries
Plot: Bildungsroman

José (Joseíto) Cemí (hoh-SEH hoh-seh-EE-toh seh-MEE), the protagonist, at the novel's opening a five-year-old, skinny asthmatic. After his father's death, he is drawn to his Uncle Albert, whose language skills enchant Cemí. He is thin but lithe and has a pale, sadly ironic face. At the age of eighteen, he studies law at Havana University, though his vocation is poetry. His friendships with Fronesis and Foción at the university help him to define his emotional needs as a poet: Fronesis' poem for him is crucial in his development, and Oppiano's instruction is a climactic fulfillment for him and the novel.

Colonel José Eugenio Cemí (ehew-HEHN-ee-oh), his father, a man with a short neck and ruddy skin; he is merry and severe, with intellectual discipline. A respected engineer and much-admired Cuban army officer, he dies from influenza while on military assignment at Pensacola, Florida, at the age of thirty-three.

Rialta Olaya de Cemí (rree-AHL-toh oh-LI-ah), the wife of the colonel, a delicate woman widowed at the age of thirty. She lives with her children and mother in Havana. She poses her subtle charm against the sad fate of her admired husband's early death. At the age of forty, she tells Cemí what she hopes for him: not to avoid danger, but always to try what is most difficult.

Leticia (leh-TEE-see-ah), Rialta's petulant sister, with frosty gray eyes, who takes sleeping pills and dampens her forehead with cologne to control her nerves. She introduces Cemí to Fronesis while Cemí is visiting her home.

Alberto Olaya, Rialta's spoiled brother, a free and easy, self-possessed Cuban with a graceful walk, a reddish face, and a weakness for alcohol. The same-aged school friend of the young colonel, he was rescued by Oppiano during an adolescent fling in a Havana bar. He is killed in a car accident during a drunken brawl with a Mexican guitarist in Havana after he hears of his mother's fatal illness.

Doña Augusta, Rialta's mother. She has a majestic, noble head and is noted for her trenchant proverbs. Her story about her father's body being exhumed strongly affects Cemí. She dies of cancer while Cemí is at the university.

Andrés Olaya (ahn-DREHS), Rialta's father, with a thick baritone voice, exiled from Cuba to Jacksonville, Florida. He dies at the age of forty-four, heartbroken by the death of a musically talented son, before Rialta's marriage.

Grandmother Mela (MEH-lah), the asthmatic mother of Andrés. At the age of ninety-four, with yellowing white hair, she is still a fervent Cuban revolutionary.

Doña Munda Méndez Ruda (MEWN-dah MEHN-dehs RREW-dah), called **Grandmother Munda**, the haughty, proud mother of Eloisa. She cares for the orphaned colonel and his sisters. Although she dotes on her son Luis, she sends him off to Veracruz to find a niche for himself.

Don José María Cemí, called **the Basque**, the stern and enterprising father of the colonel. He has a short neck and a strong character. Thirty-seven years old when he married Eloisa, the colonel's mother, he grew rich as the head of a sugar plantation. He died insane, leaving the colonel an orphan at the age of ten.

Ricardo Fronesis (froh-NEH-sees), a man with a virile body and a beautiful face, with a precise nose and sensitive nostrils. He is the provincial friend of Cemí and Foción. The son of a Cuban lawyer and an Austrian dancer, he comes from a family of lettered men; he speaks with lordly assurance and exquisite courtesy, even as a boy. He impresses Cemí with his stoical dignity and ineffable charm. At the university, he impresses all with his articulate discussions of philosophical issues. After sharing family secrets with his father and foster mother, he breaks with Foción.

Eugenio Foción (foh-see-OHN), a golden-haired homosexual, older than Fronesis and Cemí. He has been married and has a child. He has small teeth, pulpy lips, and a voluptuous smile. When he laughs, a spot of decay can be seen in his back molars. He has drawn a black circle around his left breast to help guide the knife he expects will be used to kill him someday. He vehemently defends homosexuality in discussions with Fronesis and Cemí at the university. Although he has erotic feelings for Fronesis, he never succeeds in a sexual relationship with him. He loses his sanity after Fronesis' father warns him to stay away from Fronesis; after a brief hospitalization, he is cured when lightning destroys a tree that he has identified with Fronesis.

Oppiano Licario (oh-pee-AH-noh lee-KAHR-ee-oh), a tall, Sorbonne-educated poet and notary, forty years old when Cemí meets him ten years after the death of Cemí's father, an occurrence witnessed by Oppiano, who was in Pensacola awaiting surgery on a war wound at the time. He and Cemí meet on a Havana bus when Cemí helps him recover a bag of antique coins almost stolen from him. He writes his last poem for Cemí.

Farraluque (fah-rrah-LEW-keh), a small-bodied, sad-eyed adolescent classmate of Cemí some time after the death of Uncle Alberto. He is famous for his prodigious sexual ability.

Leregas (leh-REH-gahs), an upperclassman in school with Cemí and Farraluque, expelled for sexual exhibitionism during classtime. Later, at the university with Cemí, he is expelled after a homosexual affair with a student-athlete.

Fronesis, the father of Ricardo. He was the son of a Cuban diplomat in Vienna. He fell in love with Fraulein Sunster, a dancer in Sergei Diaghilev's company, but the dancer was infatuated with Diaghilev, who was a pederast more interested in Fronesis than in her. She bore Ricardo to Fronesis but would not marry him; instead, her sister became Fronesis' wife and stepmother to Ricardo. Fronesis intervenes to stop the friendship of Ricardo with Foción and suffers from the hostility this act arouses in his son.

Maria Theresa Sunster (teh-REH-sah SEWNS-tehr), the blonde Austrian sister of Ricardo's mother. She married Fronesis to rear Ricardo. A woman of quiet dignity, she brought to Fronesis domestic stability and social charm.

Nicolás Foción (nee-kohl-AHS), Eugenio's father, a Havana physician. He is frequently out of the house on special cases. After he finds his brother Juliano dead in bed with his wife Celita, he loses his sanity and thinks that Celita is his nurse during the day and his wife only at night. This continues for twenty years, until he retires to play chess and educate Foción, whom he does not send to school.

Ynaca Eco Licario (ee-NAH-kah EH-koh), a blue-eyed woman with polished dark skin, the wise Cuban sister of Oppiano, on whom she dotes even though she is married to an obsessed engineer. She gives Oppiano's last poem to Cemí when he visits her house of mourning at the end of the novel.

— *Richard D. McGhee*

PARADOX, KING
(Paradox, rey)

Author: Pío Baroja (1872-1956)
First published: 1906
Genre: Novel

Locale: Spain, Tangier, and the imaginary Bu-Tata, in Uranga, Africa
Time: Early twentieth century
Plot: Social satire

Abraham Wolf, a wealthy British banker who is sailing his yacht, the *Cornucopia*, to found a Jewish colony in Africa.

Dr. Silvestre Paradox (seel-VEHS-treh pah-rah-DOHKS), who is invited to accompany Wolf. In Africa, he becomes king of a native tribe. He voices the author's philosophic ideas throughout the book.

Avelino Diz (ah-bay-LEE-noh dees), Paradox's companion and skeptical friend.

Pelayo (pay-LAH-yoh), a scoundrel who was once Paradox's secretary.

Arthur Sipsom, an English needle manufacturer and a guest aboard the *Cornucopia*.

Eichthal Thonelgeben, a scientist guest.

Miss Pich (peesh), an ex-ballet dancer and guest.

"The Cheese Kid," an ex-cancan dancer and guest.

General Pérez (PEH-rehs), another guest.

Dora Pérez, his daughter.

Mingote (meen-GOH-tay), a revolutionist aboard the *Cornucopia*.

Hardibrás (ahr-dee-BRAHS), a soldier with a hook in place of his hand.

Monsieur Chabouly (shah-bew-LEE), a French chocolate maker and emperor of Western Nigritia, the location of his plantations.

Goizueta (goh-ee-ZWAY-tah), who is made captain of the *Cornucopia* when the original captain is lost in a storm.

King Kiri (KEE-ree), who enjoys killing those subjects he dislikes. When rebels kill him, Paradox is made king.

Funangué (few-nah[n]-GAY), prime minister of King Kiri.

Princess Mahu (MAH-ew), the king's daughter, who ends up as a nude nightclub dancer.

Bagú (bah-GEW), a jealous medicine man who hates Paradox but loves Mahu.

Ugú (ew-GEW), a friendly native.

THE PARDONER'S TALE

Author: John Wain (1925-1994)
First published: 1978
Genre: Novel

Locale: Wales and an English cathedral town
Time: Early 1970's
Plot: Psychological realism

Giles Hermitage, a moderately successful novelist. A stocky, graying bachelor of fifty, he is generally untidy in appearance. For seven years, he has lived contentedly in an English cathedral town, disappearing from life's problems alternately into his work and into the arms of his mistress, Harriet. When Harriet breaks off their relationship, he realizes how important she is to him, and he is shattered. Only his meeting with a dying woman, Helen Chichester-Redfern, and her daughter, Dinah Redfern, who becomes his mistress, gives him interest in living. After the death of Helen, when Dinah deserts him, Giles is tempted to commit suicide. He must first complete his novel, however. Once it is completed, he is providentially saved by a letter from Harriet that sends him to join her in Australia.

Helen Chichester-Redfern, an old lady. Although frail and thin, and obviously very near death, she is still strong-willed and surprisingly energetic. Her letter to Giles, praising his work and asking to meet him, brings him out of his despair over Harriet's departure. After a series of visits, he discovers her real purpose: She wishes him to write a book about her husband's desertion of her, which will ruin his reputation. When Giles promises to do so, she dies.

Diana (Dinah) Chichester-Redfern, the daughter of Helen Chichester-Redfern. A slender, attractive girl with brown hair and green eyes, she is always neatly dressed and precise in her actions. She is a highly disciplined professional guitarist. Although she is lusty and promiscuous, Dinah has no real feelings for anyone. Her attentiveness to her dying mother and her own Anglo-Catholic rituals are as devoid of emotional contact as are her sexual episodes with Giles.

Gus Howkins, a fictional character in the novel that Giles is writing. A middle-age Londoner who is bored with his business, a press-cutting agency, and bored with his wife of fourteen years, Gus is catapulted into a life of high drama when he rescues a young woman from drowning. He falls in love with her, loses her, finds her, and eventually is accused of kidnapping and of conspiracy to extort money from her husband. Finally, he returns to his wife, Daphne.

Daphne Howkins, the wife of Gus Howkins in Giles's novel. Repentant about the affair that gave Gus an excuse to divorce her, she besieges her husband, pleading with him to take her back.

Julia Sanders Delmore, a former actress, a character in Giles's novel. A pretty young woman, she has brown eyes, dark hair, and a pale complexion. When Gus first sees her, staring at the sea as the tide moves in, she is stunned by the discovery of her husband's flagrant infidelity. After he rescues her, she clings to him and becomes his mistress. She is actually torn between her love for two men, however: her husband and her brother. When her husband gets her brother out of trouble and exerts his old charm on her, she returns to him.

Jake Driver, also called **Jake Delmore**, Julia's husband in Giles's novel, a television actor who has recently become a star. A loud, brutal, egotistical man, he enjoys dominating his wife and his subordinates. When her brother attempts to defraud him, he is willing to send him to prison. He evidently loves or needs his wife, however, enough to make an arrangement to get her back.

Cliff Sanders, another character in Giles's novel, the older brother of Julia Delmore. He is small and dark-haired, with a weak, mean face and an expression that is both sly and inquisitive. At thirty-five years of age, he already has a lengthy criminal record. He is completely unscrupulous, and only his stupidity keeps him from being a real threat to society. His inept attempt to extort money from Jake Driver results in the arrest of both Julia and Gus. They are released, however, partly because the authorities can see Cliff for what he is.

— *Rosemary M. Canfield Reisman*

PARLEMENT OF FOULES

Author: Geoffrey Chaucer (c. 1343-1400)
First published: c. 1380
Genre: Poetry

Locale: A dream world
Time: Fourteenth century
Plot: Allegory

The dreamer, the narrator of the poem. After musing on love, he falls asleep and dreams that he is escorted to the Garden of Love, where the birds' parliament has convened. The dreamer enters a park filled with trees and teeming with a plethora of chirping birds. The trees are in foliage and the flowers in bloom, as it is spring. Various gods and goddesses recline in a temple of brass.

Nature, a goddess who sits on a hill of flowers, presiding over the parliament. An elegant, well-spoken lady, she stands for natural law, including mating and procreation, in distinction from Venus, who represents passion for its own sake.

Three tercel eagles, suitors vying to take a tercelet as mate. The royal eagle claims that he will make the best mate for the tercelet, as his love for her is greater than that of his rivals. The second tercel, however, argues that the "lady" should be his, because he has loved her longer. The third tercel promises to love the tercelet until the time of his own death; therefore, he maintains, the prize belongs to him. The royal eagle is said to represent King Richard II of England, whereas the other two represent Frederick Meissen and Prince Charles of France, rival contenders for the hand of Anne of Bohemia.

An eagle tercelet, the object of the tercels' contest. Although she is a dainty creature perching on Nature's shoulder, the tercelet is intelligent and foresighted. Because she cannot decide immediately among the tercels, she wisely asks Nature to grant her a year in which to weigh her suitors' claims, rather than hastily leaping into an alliance she may regret.

Falcon, the spokesperson for the "noble" birds, who voices the conventional views of the aristocracy concerning one's choice of a mate.

Turtledove, a spokesperson for the country gentry, a wealthy but nonaristocratic class. A symbol of peace, charity, and undying love, she says that a man should love his lady for the duration of his life, even if she dies or the two become estranged. In making this claim, she adheres to one of the principals of the courtly love mystique.

Duck, who is either a vulgar commoner or a liberal aristocrat. He stirs up indignation among the "noble" birds by countering the dove's claim and pointing out the absurdity of this courtly "mandate."

Goose, a spokesperson for the waterfowl, which represents either the merchant class or the lowest commoners. A practical bird who speaks her mind, she advances the somewhat novel stipulation that a man should love only a woman who loves him in return. This fowl may function as the poet's mouthpiece for his attitude toward women. Geoffrey Chaucer has been said to have had an androgynous personality, meaning that he could see a situation from either a masculine or a feminine point of view. Through the goose, he may be saying that in order for a romantic liaison to succeed, the woman must be an ardent partner in love rather than the mere object of a man's affection.

— *Rebecca Stingley Hinton*

PARTY GOING

Author: Henry Green (Henry Vincent Yorke, 1905-1973)
First published: 1939
Genre: Novel

Locale: A London train hotel
Time: Immediately prior to World War II
Plot: Symbolism

Max Adey, a wealthy playboy, dark and excessively handsome. With a reputation for alcoholic excess and for considerable romantic charm, Max is the center of attention among the women in the novel. He is also the official host of the traveling party and insists on paying every expense, including the price of three hotel rooms to house his guests while they wait to start their holiday journey to the south of France. Max is particularly attracted both to Julia and to his mistress, Amabel, but he is unable to make up his mind about these two women. Max is clearly helpless before Amabel's considerable powers of attraction, but he cannot resist duping her to pursue Julia.

Amabel, Max's mistress, a beautiful celebrity socialite. Amabel tracks Max and his wealthy party to the station hotel, despite Max's efforts to lose her. When she joins the company, she outshines the other women, who are fascinated and envious of the famous beauty in their midst, and she also succeeds in manipulating the various men, including Max. Amabel is narcissistic and assured of her irresistible appearance. At the end of the novel, she manages to persuade Max to invite her along on the group trip to the south of France.

Alex Alexander, a less attractive and less wealthy member of Max's party. Alex's mother died when he was ten years old, and his family has suffered psychological and financial misfortune. Although he wishes to be liked, Alex is too ready to express the selfish feelings of the group, and they often find his frankness vulgar. He is not supposed to care about women, but he is easily manipulated by both Angela and Amabel.

Julia Wray, the niece of a director of the railroad and a member of Max's party. Julia alternately fears the crowd in the railway station and enjoys feeling superior to it. She is often childish, and she tells Max about her collection of toys at great length. She is also very interested in Max, and although she rejects his direct advances when they are alone together, she is later angered when she finds that Max has spent time alone in the hotel with Amabel.

Claire Hignam, another member of Max's group, the niece of Miss Fellowes. Claire is alternately devoted to her aunt and resentful of her; she also soaks up Max's attention while resenting Amabel and Max as the center of the group's attention. Claire makes a great show of remaining behind the others with her convalescent aunt, but she has no real intention of doing so.

Robert Hignam, Claire's husband and the object of much abuse. Robert is an agreeable but dull errand boy for his wife. When not in her employ or enduring her assaults on his intelligence, he is usually in the hotel's lobby bar.

Evelyn Henderson, who is three years younger than Julia and the least wealthy member of the group. Evelyn understands well the importance of money, but she spends much of her time keeping Claire company in caring for Miss Fellowes.

Although many of the others express pity for Evelyn, her presence ultimately demonstrates only the shallowness of this sentiment and the selfish nature of those around her.

Angela Crevy, the least worldly member of Max's party, with extremely white hands and a large amount of luggage. She repeatedly suspects that there is a conspiracy among the others to keep something from her, and she misunderstands entirely the nature of Amabel's bath with Alex Alexander. She is also contemptuous of people in the street. In her eagerness to become a member of Max's group, she repeatedly drives away her suitor, Robin Adams.

Robin Adams, Angela's boyfriend, who is not invited on the trip to France. Robin thinks that the members of Max's group are revolting, and he desperately wants Angela to ac-knowledge their engagement. He is disappointed, however, when Angela repeatedly rejects him and eventually sends him away.

Miss Fellowes, Claire's aunt, fifty-one years old. Entering the fogbound train station where much of the novel is set, Miss Fellowes finds a dead pigeon, which she keeps in a paper bag. She later buys a whiskey in the station hotel bar and sub-sequently becomes ill. She is then rescued by her niece and her niece's friends, who take her to a room in the station hotel. Although she provides a moral contrast to the world of her niece in her frequent ruminations on death, Miss Fellowes often merely echoes the trite sentiments of her younger rela-tive and her wealthy friends.

— *Thomas Carmichael*

PARZIVAL

Author: Wolfram von Eschenbach (c. 1170-c. 1217)
First published: c. 1200-1210
Genre: Poetry

Locale: Western Europe
Time: The age of chivalry
Plot: Arthurian romance

Gamuret (GA-mur-eht), the younger son of King Gandein, who leaves Anjou to seek his fortune. He rescues Belakane and marries her.

Gandein (GAN-deh-ihn), the king of Anjou.

Belakane (beh-lah-KA-neh), a Moorish queen who is falsely accused of killing Eisenhart, her lover.

Friedebrand (FREE-dih-brand), the king of Scotland and uncle of Eisenhart. He besieges the castle of Belakane in an attempt to avenge his nephew.

Feirefis (FI-reh-fihs), the son of Gamuret and Belakane, who almost vanquishes Parzival. Together, they fight in many tournaments.

Herzeledde, queen of Waleis (HEHR-tseh-lee-deh, VAH-lis), at whose tournament Gamuret is the victor. She marries him after the tourney.

Parzival (PAHR-tsih-fahl), the son of Herzeleide and Ga-muret.

Queen Kondwiramur (kond-VIHR-ah-mur), whom Parzi-val marries and later deserts.

Lohengrin (LOH-ehn-grihn), the son of Kondwiramur and Parzival.

Jeschute (jeh-SHEW-teh), who gives Parzival a token.

Orilus (OH-rih-lews), the jealous husband of Jeschute. He fights Parzival but is pacified.

The Red Knight, who knights Parzival.

Gurnemanz (GEWR-neh-mahnts), the prince of Graharz, who instructs Parzival in knightly precepts.

Baruch (BAH-rewk), the ruler of Alexandria, for whom Gamuret fought and finally was slain.

King Kailet (KI-leht), the companion of Gamuret in Spain.

Arthur, the king of Britain.

Queen Guinevere (GWIH-neh-veer), Arthur's wife.

Sir Kay, the seneschal, defeated by Parzival.

Sir Gawain (GAH-wayn), who introduces Parzival to Ar-thur's Round Table.

Orgeluse (OHR-geh-lewz), the wife of Gawain.

King Meljanz of Lys (MEHL-yahnts, lees), for whom Sir Gawain fights Duke Lippaut.

Antikonie (an-TEE-koh-nee), the daughter of King Meljanz. She is courted by Gawain.

Gramoflanz (GRAH-moh-flahnts), whom Parzival offers to fight because, unknowingly, he has wounded Sir Gawain while that knight was riding to do battle with Gramoflanz. The challenge is rejected because Gramoflanz refuses to meet any knight but Gawain.

Trevrezent (TRAY-vreh-tsahnt), a hermit who indicates that Parzival is the nephew of Amfortas, the Grail King, and himself.

Amfortas (ahm-FOHR-tahs), the Fisher King who shows Parzival the mysteries of the Grail and is himself cured of his grievous wound by a miraculous recovery.

Kondrie (KOHN-dree-eh), Parzival's guide to the Grail Kingdom.

Repanse de Schoie (reh-PAHN-suh duh SHOY-eh), the wife of Feirefis and mother of Prester John.

Sigune (sih-GEW-neh), the woman who tells Parzival of his lineage.

THE PASSAGE

Author: Vance Palmer (1885-1959)
First published: 1930
Genre: Novel

Locale: The central Queensland coast of Australia
Time: Early twentieth century
Plot: Regional

Lew Callaway, a slow-tempered, laconic fisherman on the Queensland coast of Australia. The eldest son, he carries the responsibilities of providing for the family of six after his father's death. He is slow-minded, powerfully built, patient, and methodical; he is also resourceful, indomitable, and dependable. He is sensitive to nature, appreciates literature and music, and responds to expressions of kindness. Captivated by the physical beauty and apparent sophistication of Lena, he nevertheless soon realizes his error in marrying her rather than the more practical Clem McNair. His life is spent helping others, but he expects no help from them: He is what Australians call a "battler," one who struggles. His big, slow body is suntanned, and he has brown eyes that, "dark and smouldering, gave intensity to his face." He is a foil to his brother Hughie.

Hughie Callaway, Lew's younger brother and their mother's favorite. He is fair-skinned and freckled, with puckered eyes and a wide mouth. He is bright but shallow, energetic and outgoing, and a fortunate entrepreneur until taken advantage of by a dishonest partner. He is rescued financially by his stalwart, frugal brother, whose ways he had disparaged. He is seduced by his fast-track, fair-weather friends and their glamorous lifestyle, though he has ceaseless initiative and unusual inventiveness. Although voluble, he is not astute, and he is severely shaken by reverses in fortune.

Anna Callaway, the widow of Bob Callaway and a lifelong resident of the Passage. She unreasonably expects her son Lew to shoulder the responsibility for the family and openly favors Hughie, who receives every consideration and attention. Only Hughie's business failure brings her to an appreciation of Lew's work and worth. She is manipulative and not especially maternal. She is a big, dark woman with "prominent eyes, heavy hips, sloppy busts"; the down on her upper lip gives her a masculine appearance. She quickly adapts to Hughie's temporary affluence and moves with him to the town, seeing his success as the justification of her special consideration for him.

Clem McNair, an aspiring artist and daughter of a doctor who promotes dubious patent medicines. She sees the innate goodness of her childhood friend Lew and her own gullibility for having accepted sycophantic evaluations of her talents. She has an exuberance, a recklessness, and an intensity that appeal to Lew, but she lacks that pseudosophistication that he finds appealing in Lena Christiansen. Clem's face is "sallow, sensitive, alive with queer curiosities and enthusiasms"; she has dark skin, a small and slim body, a fine-cut nose, and a mouth that is "delicately designed." Financially independent, she discovers that her happiness is wholly dependent on Lew.

Lena Christiansen, a flashy adventuress who marries Lew after being captivated by his rustic simplicity but who soon tires of the staid, repetitive life of the Passage and eventually leaves Lew for an old lover, Craigie, a surveyor. She has a good singing voice, though there is malice in her speech. She is tall and statuesque, with milk-white skin; she has a snub nose, full red lips, and pale blue doll-like eyes. Her voice is soft, deep, and manly, conversational in tone. She is indolent, inconsiderate of her sickly son Peter, flirtatious, and unwifely.

Uncle Tony, the father of a large family, none of whom has amounted to anything and all of whom have left the Passage. On his death, he invites Lew to take over his single-vessel boating business, which becomes the basis for Lew's subsequent success. Tony has a loose-lipped mouth and uneven teeth; small, bright eyes; and sun-chapped legs. His wife, Rachel, is happy when working in the vegetable garden or chatting.

Osborne, a pudgy real estate developer, the quintessential get-rich-quick exploiter of prime natural environments. He is unprincipled and devious, irresponsible, and charismatic. His plans for the development of the Passage and its environs introduce a new ethic to the inhabitants and cause Craigie and Lena to invade the bucolic world of the Callaways. Having made a quick fortune, he leaves for other, competing enterprises.

Marnie Callaway, a dark, trim, self-contained woman with a curt tongue. She studied dressmaking and leaves the Passage for the town, where she marries Vic, the son of a biscuit manufacturer. She is a solid, mature worker and has a strong sense of family as well as of social advancement.

Fred Callaway, the youngest Callaway boy, tough and able to push his way anywhere. Thin and good-looking, and careful about his hair and clothes, he wants a life away from the Passage and takes a job on a sugar boat. His adventurous nature stands in contrast to Lew's and indicates that the Passage eventually will decline as a result of similar defections. Only occasionally does he write a card home.

— *Alan L. McLeod*

A PASSAGE TO INDIA

Author: E. M. Forster (1879-1970)
First published: 1924
Genre: Novel

Locale: India
Time: c. 1920
Plot: Social realism

Dr. Aziz (ah-ZEEZ), an amiable, sensitive, and intelligent young Moslem doctor in Chandrapore, India. Ignored and snubbed by the English colony, he nevertheless becomes friendly with three English newcomers to India—Mr. Fielding, Mrs. Moore, and Miss Quested. When he takes them on a tour of the sinister Marabar Caves, Miss Quested becomes separated from the party, and later she accuses him of attempted rape. Jailed and humiliated, he becomes markedly anti-British. After Miss Quested withdraws her charge at his trial, he wants to collect damages, but Fielding dissuades him. Suspicious of Fielding's motives, he breaks off the friendship.

Two years later, the two men meet again, and each realizes that any true communion between them is impossible because of their racial allegiances.

Cecil Fielding, the principal of the Government College, a middle-aged, maverick intellectual who resists the herd instinct of his fellow Englishmen. He has Indian friends; he defends Aziz against the English bigots, and when Miss Quested is ostracized after the trial, he offers her the protection of his home. Tired of the whole situation, he takes a trip to England, marries, and then returns to India, where he finds Aziz less cordial than before.

Adela Quested, a priggish young woman who goes to India to marry Ronald Heaslop; she announces that she is eager to see the real India. Her trip to the Marabar Caves proves disastrous. Thinking that she has been the victim of an attempted attack, she accuses Aziz; however, she shows courage by retracting the charge at his trial. The scandal ruins her prospective marriage and causes her to be avoided by almost everyone. She returns to England alone.

Mrs. Moore, Ronald Heaslop's mother, a lovely, sensitive old woman who accompanies Miss Quested to India. She has great regard for Dr. Aziz, but at the Marabar Caves, she has a strange psychic experience, an unhappy intuition that life is worthless. When she irritably defends Dr. Aziz to her son, he sends her home, and she dies on the way.

Ronald Heaslop, the self-righteous city magistrate, a man coarsened by life in India. Wishing his mother and fiancée to have nothing to do with the natives, he finds himself in a position where he must reject both to preserve his own standards and vanity.

Professor Godbole, a gentle old teacher at the college, a friend of Dr. Aziz and Fielding. He represents the Hindu mystical aspects of India as opposed to the narrower nationalisms of the Moslems and British.

The Nawab Bahadur, a wealthy Moslem who, acting as an unofficial diplomat between the Moslems and English, does favors for the whites. When Dr. Aziz is tried, he rejects the British.

Hamidullah, Dr. Aziz's well-to-do, Anglophobic uncle, a Cambridge barrister who conducts his nephew's defense.

Mahmoud Ali, a family friend of Hamidullah and Dr. Aziz. Cynical and embittered toward the English, he makes an emotional, histrionic defense of Dr. Aziz at the trial.

Mohammed Latif, a poor, sneaky relative of Hamidullah and Aziz.

Major Callendar, the civil surgeon, Dr. Aziz's brutal superior, who believes that "white is right."

Mr. Turton, a white official who is willing to extend courtesy to the natives and nothing more; a man who has succumbed to power and race snobbery.

Mrs. Turton, his haughty wife, who comforts Adela Quested after the incident at the Marabar Caves.

Mr. McBryde, the chief of police, an intelligent man who treats Dr. Aziz decently but at the same time supervises the prosecution. He is provincial in his attitudes.

Miss Derek, a selfish young woman who takes advantage of her Indian employers.

Amritrao, Dr. Aziz's defense lawyer, imported from Calcutta, who gets Miss Quested to withdraw her charges.

Mr. Das, Heaslop's subordinate, the judge at the trial, a Hindu who later becomes friendly with Dr. Aziz.

Ralph Moore, Mrs. Moore's odd son, a boy who finally gets Cecil Fielding and Dr. Aziz together again.

Stella Moore, Mrs. Moore's daughter, a sensitive girl who marries Cecil Fielding.

PASSING

Author: Nella Larsen (1891-1964)
First published: 1929
Genre: Novel

Locale: New York City
Time: The 1920's
Plot: Social realism

Irene ('Rene) Westover Redfield, the protagonist, in her early thirties, foremost among a cast of unlikable characters. She is a complacent member of the moneyed black elite of Harlem with a craving for safety. Olive-skinned, she "passes" for white when she wants a taxi, a theater ticket, or entrée into a classy café, but her erstwhile friend Clare Kendry's wholesale betrayal of her race provokes her scorn and a sense of unease. Jealous and frightened of Clare's attraction for her husband, she is nevertheless bound to her by the ties of race. As the novel's center of consciousness, from the first she focuses the reader's own sense of unease, and at the novel's close the reader wonders whether 'Rene has deliberately pushed Clare to her death from a sixth-floor window.

Clare Kendry, also referred to as **Mrs. John Bellew**, 'Rene's Chicago childhood friend. Blonde, pale-skinned Clare grew up as the orphaned poor relation of whites whom it suited to obscure her racial origins. She is now married to a wealthy black-hating bigot (he nicknames her "Nig" because her skin is darkening with age). There is reckless daring in her life of deception and something tragic in the loss of selfhood that drives her to reestablish dangerous contact with the blackness whose burden 'Rene has been privileged to bear so lightly. An elusive and flowerlike beauty with a caressing smile and con-cealing black eyes, she is a creature apart, a pariah, yet capable of heights and depths of feeling that 'Rene has never known. When she is finally confronted by Bellew, the reader is left to wonder whether she committed suicide or was pushed to her death.

Brian Redfield, 'Rene's husband, a successful doctor. Urbane and handsome, Redfield is openly dissatisfied with his small world, covertly bored by his wife, and sexually fascinated by Clare Kendry. His marriage to 'Rene contrasts unfavorably with Bellew's to Clare—one more twist in the novel's complex web of race, sex, and class.

John (Jack) Bellew, an honest and jolly racist of the old school who ignorantly adores his wife.

Gertrude Martin, one of Clare's few "friends," a coarse and overweight matron, another black "goat" who can pass for a "sheep," but one whose white husband knows the truth.

Zulena and

Liza, 'Rene's mahogany and ebony-colored servants.

Hugh Wentworth, 'Rene's white high-society friend who "goes in" for her pet charity, the Negro Welfare League. He and 'Rene discuss contemporary themes of race and culture, especially the phenomenon of "passing."

— *Joss Lutz Marsh*

PASSING ON

Author: Penelope Lively (1933-   )
First published: 1989
Genre: Novel

Locale: Long Sydenham, a village in the Cotswolds, England
Time: The 1980's
Plot: Domestic realism

Helen Glover, a part-time librarian in her early fifties. She recalls events of her life. Following several brief attempts to leave Long Sydenham in her twenties, Helen returned to live with her mother and brother in her mother's house. Helen, an attractive woman, has been subjected to a lifetime of demeaning comments from her mother, Dorothy. She has never cultivated her beauty or attempted to change the disheveled condition of her home. Although she resents her mother's manipulation, Helen lacks the willpower to assert her independence.

Dorothy Glover, who is dead when the narration begins but a dominating presence for much of the novel. Her aggressive, malevolent personality controls her adult children's thoughts even in matters as simple as choice of dress.

Edward Glover, Helen's younger brother, a teacher in a mediocre private school for girls. A lover of nature, Edward devotes much of his spare time to participating in environmental projects and observing the ecology of the Britches, a small piece of woodland owned by the Glovers. Despite his interest in animals, Edward remains purposefully vague about human beings and represses much of his own nature in an effort to avoid acknowledging his homosexuality.

Louise Glover Dyson, Helen's younger sister, a designer who lives in London with her husband and two children. The only sibling to have left Long Sydenham, Louise demonstrated a temper and rebellious spirit early in life. A successful businesswoman, Louise is given to emotional crises that her brother and sister follow almost as a form of entertainment. Louise sees life as a series of problems that demand solutions, a view in contrast with the essentially passive responses of her brother and sister.

Phil Dyson, Helen's nephew, who inherits Dorothy's house. Experiencing typical adolescent rebellion against his parents, he comes to live for a while with Helen and Edward. Phil epitomizes the social change that occurred in the thirty years that Helen and Edward lived with their mother as adults. Not only in dress but also in attitude, Phil is much more relaxed and tolerant than his elders.

Giles Carnaby, the Glovers' solicitor, thought to be charming by the society of Long Sydenham. A widower, Giles postures as both sentimental and susceptible to women. He embarks on a tantalizing flirtation with Helen.

Ron Paget, an unscrupulous builder and developer who has wanted to buy the Britches for years.

— *Gweneth A. Dunleavy*

PASSING TIME
(L'Emploi du temps)

Author: Michel Butor (1926-   )
First published: 1956
Genre: Novel

Locale: Bleston, an industrial city in northern England
Time: Early 1950's
Plot: Detective and mystery

Jacques Revel, a Frenchman hired by an English export firm for one year. He arrives in the northern industrial city of Bleston knowing no one and speaking little English. He walks the cold, rainy streets of the ancient city and becomes obsessed with its strange power, afraid that it will swallow him up as it has so many others. To protect himself from its evil spell, he keeps a journal, describing the maze of streets in the main part of town, the two cathedrals, and the museum. He recounts the events that take place during his stay in a confused account that moves "through a labyrinth of time and memory." Soon after arriving, he meets a fellow outcast, a black man, and together they roam the dreary streets and visit the dark, dirty pubs. He meets the author of *The Bleston Murder* and tries to solve the mystery of a near-fatal accident. He suspects, then absolves, a colleague of attempted murder, and he falls in love twice but is unable to declare himself. Finally, he leaves the city a year later, longing for its total destruction.

George Burton, a detective-story writer who has used a pseudonym for his latest book, fearing the town's hostile reaction to the murder scene that takes place in its new cathedral. Burton reveals his true identity to Revel and swears him to secrecy, but Revel betrays him to the Bailey sisters and to

James Jenkins. Soon afterward, Burton is hit by a mysterious black Morris car and is seriously hurt. Revel suspects attempted murder.

James Jenkins, Revel's colleague at Matthews & Sons, who accompanies him to the New Theatre to see travelogs about famous cities and who invites him home to the big house where Jenkins lives with his mother, a once-beautiful woman who strangely resembles the statues on the portico of the new cathedral and who becomes unaccountably upset when *The Bleston Murder* is mentioned. Because of her reaction and because Jenkins uses a black Morris company car, Revel suspects Jenkins of trying to murder George Burton.

Ann Bailey, a young woman whom Revel first meets in a stationery store when she sells him several maps of Bleston. She later becomes engaged to James Jenkins, just as Revel realizes that he is in love with her.

Rose Bailey, Ann's younger sister, who is studying French at the university and who is Revel's first love. She, too, eludes him and becomes engaged to his friend, Julien Blaise.

Julien Blaise, a young Frenchman who has come to Bleston to work as apprentice barman at the Grand Hotel and who accompanies Revel on his rambling walks and bus rides.

Before returning to France, Julien becomes engaged to Rose, leaving his friend to suffer in silence as Rose delightedly reads Julien's love letters to him.

Richard Tenn, a friend of a cousin of the Bailey sisters. His home is described in detail in *The Bleston Murder* as that of the murderer. Revel suspects him of trying to murder Burton until he learns that Tenn's Morris is gray, not black.

— *Lucy Golsan*

THE PASSION ACCORDING TO G. H.
(A Paixão Segundo G. H.)

Author: Clarice Lispector (1925-1977)
First published: 1964
Genre: Novel

Locale: An apartment in Rio de Janeiro, Brazil
Time: The 1960's
Plot: Epiphany

G. H., a Brazilian woman identified only by her initials. G. H. narrates the story, which is largely concerned with recording her psychological reactions during a moment of self-reevaluation and turmoil. She is a middle-aged, middle-class amateur artist living in Rio de Janeiro who has enough income from investments to live well and amuse herself by sculpting. She has many friends and loves to go to parties, restaurants, and dance clubs, yet she has never formed any but shallow relationships. Although she has had a number of lovers, it seems that none of them has touched her deeply or established a long-term alliance with her. When she accidentally became pregnant, she hurried to have an abortion so that she would not be tied down. Nothing is told about her parents or early years, but it is hinted that she has had one lover in particular for whom she developed a profound affection; unfortunately, she was blind to her own feelings at the time. The novel focuses on G. H.'s thoughts one morning when she begins reconsidering the philosophical basis of her life. In the end, G. H. resolves to live in accordance with her newly enriched vision of the world, but it is left teasingly unclear whether, and how, she will keep her promise to herself.

Janair, G. H.'s maid, whose abrupt and unexplained departure leads G. H. to clean the servant's room and find that Janair has altered it in unusual ways, stripping it of all decorations except for primitive figures she has drawn in charcoal on the wall. Janair's name perhaps recalls the name of the city, Rio de Janeiro, where the action takes place.

The cockroach, an old insect that scares G. H. by coming out of Janair's wardrobe and is squashed to death; the incident sparks G. H.'s philosophical reflections.

The doctor, who performed G. H.'s abortion. The doctor temporarily becomes an addressee of her written record, but he is not further described.

The crying man, a former lover who also temporarily becomes G. H.'s addressee. In recalling a moment of silent communion between the two of them, she realizes that he was the one man she really loved. He is described only as he appeared in this incident, with none of his past or future relations with the narrator mentioned.

THE PASSION FLOWER
(La malquerida)

Author: Jacinto Benavente y Martínez (1866-1954)
First performed: 1913
Genre: Drama

Locale: Castile, Spain
Time: Early twentieth century
Plot: Tragedy

Esteban (ehs-TEH-bahn), a well-to-do peasant and the second husband of Raimunda. Faustino, the fiancé of Acacia, his stepdaughter, is shot and killed. When the chief suspect, Norbert, is acquitted, Rubio, Esteban's servant, becomes increasingly impudent. His drunken talk causes Raimunda to suspect Esteban of loving his stepdaughter. When Esteban offers to leave because of the trouble he has caused, Acacia declares her love for him. In the confusion following Raimunda's screaming denunciation, the cornered Esteban shoots his wife.

Acacia (ah-KAH-syah), the daughter of Raimunda and Esteban's stepdaughter. Although she repeatedly declares her resentment of Esteban for marrying Raimunda so soon after her father's death, her mother eventually suspects that she is in love with her stepfather. When Esteban announces his intention of leaving, she breaks down and declares her love for him.

Raimunda (rri-MEWN-dah), Esteban's wife and Acacia's mother. After the murder of Acacia's fiancé, Faustino, she is led, by the drunken talk of Rubio, to suspect her husband and her daughter of being in love. When she is shot by Esteban, she dies in peace because, at the end, Acacia turns to her. She feels that she has saved her daughter from her stepfather, that Esteban can never have her now.

Faustino (fows-TEE-noh), Acacia's fiancé, who is shot by an unknown person.

Tio Eusebio (TEE-oh eh-ew-SEH-bee-oh), Faustino's father and Esteban's friend. His sons shoot and wound Norbert, thinking that he is their brother's murderer.

Rubio (RREW-bee-oh), Esteban's servant, whose drunken talk leads Raimunda to suspect Esteban and Acacia of being in love with each other. He declares that his master had never told him to murder Faustino but had expressed hope that no one would take Acacia away.

Norbert, Acacia's former fiancé, who is cleared in the shooting of Faustino.

Juliana (hew-lee-AH-nah) and
Bernabé (behr-nah-BEH), family servants.
Fidelia (fee-DEH-lee-ah),
Engracia (ehn-GRAH-see-ah), and
Milagros (mee-LAH-grohs), family friends.

A PASSION IN ROME

Author: Morley Callaghan (1903-1990)
First published: 1961
Genre: Novel

Locale: Rome, Italy
Time: Autumn, 1958
Plot: Symbolic realism

Sam Raymond, a blue-eyed, solidly built man of thirty-nine who looks "rumpled but very clean." He arrives in Rome to photograph the events surrounding the death of the pope, feeling intensely alone. His spiritual crisis is precipitated by his growing awareness that he will never realize his ambition to be a successful painter in a style different from that of his famous father. At loose ends, he wanders the streets and encounters a young woman, Anna, who soon proves to be an American singer. She becomes the most important thing in his life. With the pope's death and the conclave of cardinals to select the new pope, Raymond is torn between his professionalism and his involvement with Anna. He finds an appropriate place for her to sing and she becomes a hit again. With her newfound success, Anna draws away from him. She is persuaded by an American agent to return to the United States, and Raymond, at first angry and then despondent, finally realizes that her courage in returning to the scene of her failure and his contribution to making her whole again have given him the courage to accept his own talent as a photographer and to let go of his failed dream to be a painter.

Anna Connel, also known as **Carla Caneli**, an American singer whose career seemingly has ended. She is beautiful with irregular features: "Her mouth was too large, the lower lip drooping softly, her nose almost aquiline, and her eyes, almost too far apart, brown or hazel, shone and glittered." Since the end of her career in America, Anna has become increasingly self-destructive. She assumes that Raymond's interest in her is sexual and makes love with him as soon as he takes her back to his apartment. Slowly, through Raymond's increasing signs of confidence in her, she begins to regain her confidence in herself. She stops drinking and begins to live a more regular life. As Raymond works for her redemption, she helps him to overcome his sense of aloneness by giving him a cause and a sense of being loved.

Francesca Winters, the Italian wife of an English journalist, whom she sees infrequently when he comes to Rome or she goes to London. She is a heavy woman of forty with a pretty face who works as a translator and guide. She serves Raymond and then his colleague Koster in that capacity and is instrumental in bringing Raymond and Anna together. Her genuine knowledge of Rome contrasts with Anna's haphazard and irregular fascination. She finds the club where Anna begins her comeback and arranges for Anna to sing there at Raymond's request.

Alberto Ruberto, a filmmaker in his fifties who, in spite of his good looks and sophistication, appears "tired and sick." Although he has made one highly successful film, which won an award in Venice, he has not been able to work since his involvement with Anna. She is his excuse for not continuing with work that he finds increasingly demanding. He relinquishes Anna to Raymond with the awareness that her disgust in herself has made him apathetic about his own work, and he speaks of making deals to finance his new film, but he dies shortly afterward without realizing any of his plans.

Koster, an American journalist of considerable reputation who insists on the use of only one name. He is famous for his research and observes the pope's funeral by reading his notes on what is occurring rather than watching the events as they take place. He is a failure in his relations with other people, as his abortive relationship with another journalist, Miss Francis, shows. At the end of the novel, he remains untouched and unchanged in his isolation, in contrast to Raymond, whose experience with Anna has put him in touch with himself.

— *Katherine Keller*

PASSION PLAY

Author: Peter Nichols (1927-   )
First published: 1981
Genre: Drama

Locale: London, England
Time: The 1980's
Plot: Psychological realism

James Croxley, age fifty, a restorer of damaged paintings. He has been married to Eleanor for twenty-five years and is the father of their two daughters, now grown and not living with the Croxleys. Restoring modern religious paintings in a studio in his home, he has been enjoying a settled life. Unsuspectingly, he is seduced into a liaison by Kate. The passion long gone from his ritual sex with Eleanor and gone as well from his work, he sacrifices the marital and cultural civility into which his and Eleanor's life has matured for his passion for Kate. The staid James is slowly overtaken by his alter ego, Jim, so that even at the end, in his workshop, Jim is furtively reading one letter and addressing another.

Eleanor Croxley, James's wife, a forty-five-year-old music teacher and choral singer. With him, she has led a fulfilled family and professional life, in sharp contrast with her provincial upbringing, which was void of the satisfactions she has enjoyed in her marriage and in London. In her youth, the only outlet for her passion, reminiscent of Emma Bovary (in Gustave Flaubert's *Madame Bovary*, English translation, 1886), was the church and, particularly, the music of the church. At first, she refuses to believe that James has been unfaithful, and even when she is convinced, she attempts to deal with the midlife crisis in a civilized fashion. Her generation (and James's) falls victim to the machinations of the new generation of "Kates" in the 1980's.

Jim, the alter ego of James. As a double of the major male character, Jim has lain dormant, and when James least suspects any change in his comfortable existence, he becomes vulnerable to Kate's very modern and well-practiced charms. Ego and alter ego debate with each other and, at times, with either Eleanor or her double, Nell. In the climactic moment of the play, all four engage in a chorus of accusations and counter-accusations. As doubles, Jim and Nell provide a novel and intriguing twist to the play.

Nell, the alter ego of Eleanor. As a character, she does not emerge as early as does Jim, because Eleanor is much too civilized and modern to give credence to suspicious evidence or to warnings from her friend, Agnes. When she does emerge, Nell slowly becomes desperate enough to swallow a bottle of pills. Her illusions about the freedom she and James would enjoy when the children left home are shattered, and she has nothing in their place. Ironically, it is during a radio broadcast of the "St. Matthew Passion" (in which Eleanor sings) that Jim and Kate indulge in passionate sex. James's sexual rituals with Eleanor, on the other hand, are accompanied by music from Wolfgang Amadeus Mozart's last work, the *Requiem*.

Kate, a twenty-five-year-old photographer, James's mistress, and the former mistress of Albert, Agnes' deceased husband. A femme fatale, she is an experienced husband snatcher. Having attended the funeral of her lover, Albert, Kate is ready to take on the unsuspecting James. Without interruption, her next affair begins even as the current one has just ended.

Agnes, a widow, fifty years old, whose husband, Albert, had left her for Kate. She still harbors a hatred of Kate and warns Eleanor of Kate's designs on James. At first, Eleanor (and even James himself) regards Kate's overtures as unimportant or, at worst, a temporary diversion. Agnes, who has access to a key to the flat Albert and Kate had shared, obtains a letter that James wrote to Kate. In a cleverly orchestrated set of simultaneous scenes, Agnes, over tea with Eleanor, shows the latter James's letter to Kate. For the first time, Nell, dressed as Eleanor, slips in between them, even as Jim is seen writing that letter.

— *Susan Rusinko*

PASTORS AND MASTERS

Author: Ivy Compton-Burnett (1884-1969)
First published: 1925
Genre: Novel

Locale: An English university town
Time: Around 1920
Plot: Satire

Emily Herrick, the novel's heroine. As she turns from fifty to fifty-one, she undergoes a significant shift in consciousness. She realizes that she is one of the "superior women" who, like the heroines in the novels of Jane Austen and George Eliot, see more and know more than others. She is the most intelligent member of her circle, but the knowledge she acquires is accompanied by a loss of innocence. Unlike the flatter and more comic characters around her, Emily exhibits intellectual powers and moral sensitivity. These give her the capacity to learn and grow. Emily's feminist perspective reflects the author's.

Nicholas Herrick, her brother, a short, stocky man twenty years her senior. He has always looked to his sister as his helpmeet and companion. He is the owner of a boys' school, but he contributes to its welfare only by presiding over school prayers. Those around him do the work for which he takes credit.

William Masson, a tall and lanky don at Herrick's old college. There is talk of his marrying Emily, but he is paired with another don at the college, to whom he is devoted.

Richard Bumpus, William's companion, a short, dark man in late middle age. He also is a don. His literary aspirations are more a pretension than a reality.

Mr. Merry, Nicholas' partner and head of the school. He and his wife bully the forty boys in their care partly to com-

pensate for their own lack of status. They illustrate the author's theory that those who serve are exploited as servants.

Mrs. Merry, his wife and helpmeet. She is referred to as Mother and is a caretaker of others; she is, however, shown to skimp when it comes to the welfare of her charges.

Miss Basden, a middle-aged teacher and school matron who shoulders more than her share of responsibility. She illustrates the author's view that it is the underlings and servants who do the actual work of the world.

The Reverend Peter Fletcher, a frail, elderly pastor with a patronizing attitude toward women.

Theresa Fletcher, his wife, a large old woman who is a confidante of Emily Herrick's. Through Emily, she acquires a deeper knowledge of the world and its ways.

The Reverend Francis Fletcher, Peter's oversized nephew. He is old-fashioned concerning women but capable of some sensitivity toward them.

Lydia Fletcher, Peter's sixty-year-old sister, an inveterate humanitarian. As are the other Fletchers, she is a convenient foil for the freethinking Herricks.

Henry Bentley, the father of two of the children who attend Herrick's school. He is memorable as a domestic tyrant.

— *Margaret Boe Birns*

PATERSON

Author: William Carlos Williams (1883-1963)
First published: 1946-1958
Genre: Poetry

Locale: Paterson, New Jersey
Time: 1946-1958
Plot: Epic

William Carlos Williams, also called **Bill**, who inhabits bits and pieces of the epic poem, sometimes as himself and sometimes as another persona who more resembles a character. The author includes himself as a character to add legiti-

macy to his use of Paterson, New Jersey, and the Passaic River as characters; clearly, they are personifications. Williams is present in one incarnation or another to explain his theory about how a city can come to represent its inhabitants and may even be representative of the American character. Williams tells many stories and answers selected letters and comments given to him by representatives of Paterson and other towns and cities, such as Newark. The various manifestations of Williams are not always similar, and they do not always represent what is often referred to as a "character."

Paterson, New Jersey, a city that takes on characteristics of a human being, a broad personification that is at times living and breathing as a representative American city and at other times merely in possession of those attributes a good city should have. Significant space is given to bare description of parts of the city. The city is described as a "great beast," and Williams talks to and about it—its seasons, its catastrophes, and its inhabitants. Williams debates with himself over the difficulty, resulting from the poet's perceptions, of deciphering the nature of the city. Williams also says, in the first book, "I have much to say to you," thereby establishing the need for the epic poem.

Passaic River, the other large personification of this poem. Williams describes the Passaic as a great junk and slag heap of the world, but he is not being overly critical: If the Passaic were not terribly polluted long before its time, where would

the detritus have gone? In a sense, this massive, flowing, brown river has allowed the neighboring city to survive. For decades it was a moving rush of filth in which only brave teenagers swam and whose water had to be filtered.

Edward Dorn, a very young correspondent with Williams who wrote about a half dozen letters to him. One drew out of Williams the remark "No ideas but/ in the facts," a crude version of his later famous comment, "no ideas but in things."

Allen Ginsberg, a poet. He probably corresponded with Williams because they were both from the same state. Some of Ginsberg's writing is included as a means of characterizing him. The author includes tangential comments and parts of Ginsberg's poems.

Charles Olson, who appears rarely but is important because of the reciprocal values that he and Williams applied to each other. His letters themselves are of limited use.

August Walters, a good example of the sort of person represented in the poem. Walters sent Williams an advertisement from Newark about the Treasury Department and monetary credits. Perhaps it matters in the construction of an entire city, but the poem would be missing nothing without it.

— John Jacob

THE PATH TO THE NEST OF SPIDERS
(Il sentiero dei nidi di ragno)

Author: Italo Calvino (1923-1985)
First published: 1947
Genre: Novel

Locale: Italy
Time: 1944
Plot: Psychological realism

Pin, a teenage boy. Living alone with an older sister, he is streetwise, rebellious, and apparently self-assured. The thin and fragile appearance of his body are in sharp contrast with his deep, gravelly voice, with which he delights in hurling insults to everyone. Both his appearance and his attitude embody the image of the street urchin. Beneath his independent façade, however, he is a child very much in need of guidance and affection. All of his actions in the novel are prompted by his self-acknowledged desire not to be ignored any longer by the adult world he so longs to be a part of and to understand. His daring theft of a German soldier's gun, an escape from prison, and his adventures with a group of partisan rebels are the escapades in which Pin involves himself, in what is his search for friendship and acceptance. Only with a true friend will he share his greatest secret, the place where spiders make their nests.

Cousin, a partisan. Disenchanted and hardened by the war, he speaks with indifference about killing the enemy: For him, it has become almost routine, a duty that he must carry out. Patriotic fervor and enthusiasm seem, in this man, to have been replaced by weariness and disillusionment. His true enemies, however, are women, toward whom he feels bitter and antagonistic. Not only does he blame them for his own unhappiness, he also accuses them of being the cause of all evil, including war. It is in Pin that he finds a trusting and eager companion, and he is in turn able to offer the boy friendship and affection.

Red Wolf, a boy a few years older than Pin who is a member of a partisan group and has already made himself

known for his political activity. Putting his cause above all else, he is unsympathetic and zealous to the point of violence. His thirst for action exceeds his devotion to political ideology. He is immediately perceived by Pin as one who has been initiated successfully into the adult world and knows its secrets.

Rina, called **The Dark Girl of Long Alley**, a prostitute. She is Pin's sister and guardian, but she shows little responsiveness to his needs and demands. She seems oblivious to his comings and goings. Completely unconcerned with political issues, she makes the best of wartime conditions by seeking out soldiers stationed in the area: Germans, Italians, Fascists, and anti-Fascists.

Kim, the commissar of a partisan brigade. In peacetime, he is a medical student who plans to specialize in psychiatry. He constantly searches for logic and clarity in people, in actions, and in ideology. He is not well liked by the other members of the group because of his probing, questioning personality, which makes them uncomfortable.

Dritto, the leader of the partisan brigade detachment. Brave and able in commanding, he has difficulty following orders himself. In his eagerness to take matters into his own hands, he does not always carry out his duties efficiently. He loses the respect of his companions when, infatuated with the cook's wife, he becomes distracted and causes a serious fire in the encampment.

— Susan Briziarelli

THE PATHFINDER: Or, The Inland Sea

Author: James Fenimore Cooper (1789-1851)
First published: 1840
Genre: Novel

Locale: Lake Ontario and environs
Time: 1756
Plot: Adventure

Thomas Dunham, a sergeant of the Fort Oswego garrison in the western New York territory during the French and Indian Wars. He has his daughter Mabel brought to the fort in order to promote a marriage between her and his friend Natty Bumppo, the wilderness scout called Pathfinder by the English. On a tour of duty among the Thousand Islands, his party captures and sinks three French ships; when they return to an island blockhouse, however, he and his men are ambushed by Iroquois Indians, and he is mortally wounded. Attended by his daughter, he dies blessing her and Jasper Western, whom he believes to be Pathfinder.

Mabel Dunham, his young, warm, frank, and pretty daughter. After Pathfinder has saved the party with which she travels from hostile Indians, she comes to respect Pathfinder's courage and skill in the woods, but the man she truly loves is his friend, Jasper Western. At Fort Oswego, she finds herself courted by Jasper, Pathfinder, and Davy Muir, each of whom accompanies her father on a tour of duty. During an Indian ambush, she is saved by the warnings of an Indian girl and the resolute defense of Pathfinder and her uncle. In the end, Pathfinder relinquishes her to Jasper, whom she marries.

Charles Cap, Mabel Dunham's crusty uncle, a hardy fellow who accompanies his niece to Fort Oswego and later goes with Sergeant Dunham on his tour of duty to relieve a garrison in the Thousand Islands. A seagoing sailor, he suspects and derides Jasper Western, a freshwater sailor, but learns to respect the young seaman when Jasper saves the cutter *Scud* after Cap had almost wrecked it during a storm. After barely escaping an Indian ambush, he ably assists Pathfinder in the defense of a beleaguered blockhouse until help arrives. He sees his niece married to Jasper and returns to the sea.

Natty Bumppo, called **Pathfinder**, the frontier scout in his prime. A man of great courage, resourcefulness, and honesty, he falls in love for the only time in his life, but in return he receives little more than Mabel Dunham's esteem. After protecting her in many perils, Pathfinder learns of Jasper Western's and Mabel's mutual love and defers to his friend. His personal integrity remains pure as he moves on with his Indian friend of many years, the Mohican chief Chingachgook.

Jasper Western, called **Eau-douce** because he is a freshwater sailor, Pathfinder's younger companion and successful rival for Mabel Dunham's hand. A skilled and honorable man,

he is nevertheless under suspicion of being a French spy. When circumstances seem to prove his guilt, his command of a cutter is temporarily taken away from him. After he has aided in relieving the besieged blockhouse, the real spy is revealed. The discovery clears his name, and Pathfinder's relinquishment of Mabel leaves him free to marry his love.

Lieutenant Davy Muir, the glib quartermaster at Fort Oswego, a thrice-wed, middle-aged suitor of Mabel Dunham. Resentful of his subordinate position, he secretly spies for the French, puts the blame for his treachery on Jasper Western, and survives an Indian ambush. His successes are cut short when Arrowhead, a resentful Tuscarora Indian, mortally stabs him.

Arrowhead, the bold, ambitious Tuscarora chief who tries to lead Mabel and her uncle into an ambush; he falls in love with the white girl. He is later caught by the party aboard the cutter but escapes to lead the two ambushes that almost prove fatal to Sergeant Dunham's party. Thinking that Muir has betrayed him, he kills the spy and is killed by Chingachgook in turn.

Dew-of-June, the submissive, gentle wife of Arrowhead. Although she saves Mabel Dunham by warning her of danger from hostile Indians and whites, she remains loyal to her husband. Mourning his death, she goes to live with Mabel, but dies soon afterward.

Chingachgook, whose name means "the Great Serpent," a Mohican chief and Pathfinder's loyal friend. A lifelong foe of the Iroquois, he aids his friend Pathfinder in many encounters with hostile Indians and the French.

Major Duncan, of Lundie, the generous, considerate commanding officer of Fort Oswego. Warned by an anonymous letter that Jasper Western is a spy for the French, he is forced to advise Sergeant Dunham to watch the young man carefully.

Captain Sanglier, the audacious French leader of the Iroquois. Captured after the siege of the blockhouse, he contemptuously reveals that Lieutenant Muir, not Jasper Western, has spied for the French.

Corporal McNab, the stubborn soldier who hesitates to believe Mabel Dunham's warning of an impending Indian ambush. He is shot during the skirmishing.

Jenny McNab, his wife. She is killed while trying to pull her husband into the blockhouse when the Indians attack.

PATIENCE: Or, Bunthorne's Bride

Author: W. S. Gilbert (1836-1911)
First published: 1881
Genre: Drama

Locale: England
Time: The nineteenth century
Plot: Satire

Patience, a beautiful dairy maid beloved by two poets. Believing that love must be unselfish, she promises herself to the one she does not like; she finally convinces herself that the one she really loves is unattractive enough for her to accept—unselfishly, of course.

Reginald Bunthorne, a fleshly poet. A self-confessed sham, he pretends to be an aesthete to attract attention, particularly feminine attention. When Grosvenor takes away most of his feminine admirers, Bunthorne threatens to curse him unless he cuts his hair short and gives up aesthetic costumes and attitudes. Bunthorne's victory in this matter costs him his intended bride.

Archibald Grosvenor, an idyllic poet, the childhood sweetheart of Patience. Handsome and wealthy, he is known as **Archibald-the-All-Right** and captivates Bunthorne's followers. Even after he cuts his hair, the girls continue to admire him extravagantly, but Patience now finds him commonplace enough for her to marry.

The Lady Jane, a faded, middle-aged follower of Bunthorne, loyal when the girls desert him for Grosvenor. Finally, however, she too deserts Bunthorne so that she can marry the duke, forcing the poet to be contented with a rose or a lily instead of a girl.

The duke of Dunstable, a lieutenant in a regiment of dragoons who cannot understand why any girl would be interested in poets when soldiers are around. Having everything, he decides to bestow himself on the plainest girl—the Lady Jane.

PATIENCE AND SARAH

Author: Isabel Miller (Alma Routsong, 1924-)
First published: 1969, as *A Place for Us*
Genre: Novel

Locale: Connecticut and New York
Time: Early 1880's
Plot: Love

Patience White, a single twenty-eight-year-old who aspires to be a painter. The house she shares with her brother and his family is half hers. She does all the necessary household chores and has no desire to marry. The daily example of Edward and Martha gives her little reason to be idealistic about marriage. Her paintings often involve stories of transformation. When she meets Sarah, who confesses her love, Patience discovers her purpose in life. Her love transforms her, making it possible to be kind even to Martha. Her love also frightens her as others learn of it; she has learned well to be concerned about appearances. That concern makes her answer no to Sarah when Sarah asks in front of Pa Dowling and Edward if Patience is still willing to go with her. Given time to reflect, she realizes that nothing would be worse than losing Sarah, so when Sarah returns, Patience becomes the force that pushes their dream to become real. Though shy, she has a strong experimental nature and a boldness many miss because of her feminine style.

Sarah Dowling, who is twenty-one years old. She is practical, hardworking, and strong like her father. Her silent independence belies her great depth of feeling, which is mixed with an ability to take risks, as she does by confessing her love to Patience. She is honest to the point of endangering her relationship with Patience by speaking openly of it, and she is forgiving, even of her father, who beats her to keep her from Patience. When Patience refuses to leave with her, her pain takes her on the road alone, disguised as a man named Sam. Her openness brings her the aid of at least one farmer's daughter and of Parson Peel. She returns less sure of her ability to make things happen and with more understanding of the limits the world places on individuals. She is therefore reluctant to leave again, despite Patience's urgings. Even when Martha walks in on them kissing and Sarah sees that Patience will not desert her again, it takes her mother's support for her to agree to go. She and Patience struggle to make use of each other's strengths and compensate for weaknesses. Sarah is trusted with the task of selecting their farm; handling "polite" society is left to Patience.

Ma Dowling, Sarah's mother. The mother of seven daughters, she has been silent in her relationship with her husband. Recently, she has begun going into the woods alone and talking to the trees. When Sarah desires to leave home, Ma helps in every way she can. She understands and supports Sarah's desire to live with Patience.

Pa Dowling, Sarah's father. A hardworking man, he chooses Sarah to help in the fields and be his "boy." When she expresses interest in Patience, he believes that his actions caused her feelings and that he must be harsh with her. He hates beating Sarah and hates how his other daughters look at him because of it; he punishes himself through his daughter.

Rachel Dowling, the Dowlings' second daughter, deeply attached to Sarah. When told she cannot go homesteading with Sarah because Patience is now Sarah's mate, Rachel turns vengeful. She then teaches Sarah to manipulate Pa by lying to him. She represents a destructive power of love.

Parson Daniel Peel, a traveling bookseller who is about thirty years old. Every summer, he leaves his wife and large family in New York to travel. An intelligent, generous man, he hires Sam (Sarah in disguise) and teaches him to read. He may be bisexual.

Edward White, Patience's older brother and, by terms of their father's will, her keeper. He takes religious questions and his responsibilities very seriously. He loves his sister and tries to honor her happiness without compromising his own life. His relationship with his wife Martha is guided more by his roles and responsibilities as husband and father than by love.

Martha White, Edward's wife and mother of a large number of children. Before marrying Edward, she was Patience's friend. She married Edward to be close to Patience but never admitted this to Patience. She is stuck in an unhappy marriage that drains her physically and psychologically. Her dislike for Sarah is based on jealousy and the obvious way Sarah shows that social strictures can be broken.

— *Su A. Cutler*

THE PATRICIAN

Author: John Galsworthy (1867-1933)
First published: 1911
Genre: Novel

Locale: England
Time: Early twentieth century
Plot: Social realism

Eustace Carádoc (yew-STAHS kah-RAH-dohk), **Lord Miltoun**, the idealistic eldest son of the Carádoc family. In the tradition of the aristocracy, he is making his bid for a seat in Parliament. In love with Mrs. Noel, he enters into an affair with her. Feeling that such a liaison is not commensurate with a parliamentary career, he plans to give up the seat he has won. When Mrs. Noel, realizing that he will never be happy outside Parliament, decides to leave, he goes on with his career.

Mrs. Audrey Lees Noel, the wife of the Reverend Stephen Noel. She is loved by Eustace Carádoc. Not realizing that he is ignorant of her married status, she does not discourage his attentions and inspires him to fall in love with her. Later, engaged in an active affair with him, she decides to leave rather than jeopardize his political career.

Lord Valleys, the head of the Carádoc family, and
Lady Valleys, Eustace Carádoc's conservative, aristocratic parents.

Lady Casterley, Eustace Carádoc's grandmother, who is instrumental in persuading Mrs. Noel to give up Eustace for the sake of his career.

Mr. Courtier (kewr-TYAY), a liberal and Eustace Carádoc's political opponent.

Barbara Carádoc, Eustace's sister. Feeling herself bound by the restraints of family and society, and attracted by Mr. Courtier and his views on personal freedom, she encourages the affair between her brother and Mrs. Noel. She finally marries a man of her own class.

THE PATRIOT
(Piccolo mondo antico)

Author: Antonio Fogazzaro (1842-1911)
First published: 1896
Genre: Novel

Locale: Italy
Time: Mid-nineteenth century
Plot: Historical

Don Franco Maironi (mah-ee-ROH-nee), a patriot who seeks Italy's independence from Austria. He has studied law, but he wastes his time with poetry and the piano rather than working. He loves Luisa Rigey, but his grandmother does not support the match and threatens to disinherit him if he marries Luisa. He secretly weds her anyway. Franco then finds out about a secret will under which he would inherit with no interference from his grandmother, but he chooses not to make it public and claim his inheritance. Luisa's uncle Piero supports the couple until he is dismissed from his job. Franco and Luisa have a baby girl and go to live in a distant province, where Franco finds work. He begins to send money to support Piero.

The Marchesa Orsola, Franco's grandmother, who staunchly supports Austria and thus is a political enemy of her grandson. She seeks a rich, well-born wife for Franco. Although Franco and Luisa try to keep their marriage secret, she finds out about it and cuts off his inheritance. Later, after the death of Franco and Luisa's daughter, she offers to forgive

Franco for disobeying her, still being unwilling to ask for his forgiveness.

Luisa Rigey (lew-EE-zah REE-gay), a poor, low-born girl from Franco's neighborhood who is loved by him. She insists that Franco make the will public to punish the marchesa, but Franco refuses. Luisa leaves Franco over this issue and intends to approach the marchesa with a copy of the will. Before she can do so, their daughter is drowned, and Luisa nearly goes insane. Eventually, she returns to Franco.

Luisa's mother, who at first keeps the lovers apart to please the marchesa. Later, after she discovers that she is dying, she permits the secret marriage.

Piero Ribera (PEE-eh-roh ree-BEH-rah), a government employee and the uncle of Luisa, who supports Franco and Luisa until the marchesa has him discharged.

A friend, who possesses a copy of a letter that proves that the marchesa is an immoral woman willfully cheating Franco out of the fortune left him by his grandfather.

PATTERNS OF CHILDHOOD
(Kindheitsmuster)

Author: Christa Wolf (1929-   )
First published: 1976
Genre: Novel

Locale: Landsberg, Mecklenburg, and the German Democratic Republic
Time: 1932-1947 and 1971-1975
Plot: Social realism

Nelly Jordan, a girl growing up under the Nazi regime. An impressionable, idealistic girl, she falls prey to the propaganda surrounding her in school, Hitler Youth, and the media. In spite of intense indoctrination and the silence maintained in her family, Nelly manages to preserve bits of her individual morality through feelings of secrecy, embarrassment, guilt, shame, pity, fear, and a pervasive sense of sadness. Still, she enthusiastically participates in the Hitler Youth and tries to please her Nazi teachers. With the misery of her family becoming refugees, the atrocities that she witnesses and hears about, and the

occupation of Germany, her system of beliefs breaks down, and she has to undergo a total transformation to become a new human being.

The narrator, who is identical with the adult Nelly but feels that the child Nelly is a stranger. An ethically sensitive, complex, and philosophical writer, the narrator is haunted by the split in her and her generation's consciousness that has occurred through the suppression of negative memories. The occasion of a brief family trip in 1971 to her prewar hometown, Landsberg, which since the war lies in Poland, precipitates her writing an autobiographical novel. The questioning of the memories that are provoked through associations with certain places during their trip makes her write about Nelly's development. She also feels compelled to reflect on the act of writing as a way of fixing and potentially distorting memories, however, and—through her observer status—of alienating herself from living in the present. Thus, she experiences not only the splits between past and present and between self and society, but also a split between life and fiction writing. She is in search of an integrated self that can overcome these various splits.

Charlotte Jordan, Nelly's mother, an intelligent, ambitious, proud, and unyielding lower-middle-class woman who, because of her background, was not able to develop her talents in medicine or writing. Instead, she became conventional in many ways, as the wife of a grocer. During the war years and the immediate postwar period, she rises to be the mainstay of her family. Most important, she is the only member of the Jordan family offering some open resistance to Nazi ideology. She has a Cassandra-like ability for premonitions of catastrophes, which she voices loudly. She is, however, subdued by her family and the appearance of the Gestapo; her desire to provide her children with a "happy childhood" wins out. She thus becomes an accomplice in the conspiracy of silence that disables the children from developing an ethical consciousness. A number of instances of her courage and compassion for the oppressed are described.

Bruno Jordan, Nelly's father, a grocery store owner. After his disastrous experiences as a World War I veteran and as a prisoner of war, his sole ambition is to provide for a "happy family" through economic success. Toward this goal, he is willing to collaborate with the authorities; thus, he joins the stormtroopers in 1933 and feels like a "hypnotized rabbit" when another stormtrooper blackmails him for goods. He takes an office in a Nazi merchant organization, befriends Nazis, and reads their literature. Still, even for him there are limits to his collaboration: He expresses genuine abhorrence when he learns that through a furlough, he narrowly missed participating in the execution of Polish hostages. Similarly, when chosen to supervise French prisoners of war, he is not able to be cruel to them, because he recognizes their common humanity. After the end of the war, he spends more than a year in a Russian prison camp and comes home a broken man.

Lenka, the narrator's teenage daughter. A skeptical young woman who has grown up in East Germany, she is not prone to high-flying ideals of nation or socialism. She is a true individualist. Her unhampered curiosity, moral judgments, or, at times, incomprehension serve to prod her mother's reflections about the time when she was a girl of the same age. Lenka accompanies her parents and uncle on the trip to Landsberg and lives at home while her mother writes the novel. One of her teachers, a reform-minded nonconformist, commits suicide. During a vacation job in a factory, Lenka experiences alienating work at the conveyor belt. She rebels against all that is made to destroy the individual, whether it is working conditions in industrialized societies, the Nazi past, the brutal suppression of the Chilean revolution, or the Vietnam War.

— *Gisela Roethke-Makemson*

PAUL BUNYAN

Author: James Stevens (1892-1971)
First published: 1925
Genre: Short fiction

Locale: North America
Time: From the Winter of the Blue Snow to the Spring That the Rain Came up from China
Plot: Folklore

Paul Bunyan, the gigantic hero of exaggerated yarns first told along the Canadian border about 1837. Bunyan first saw Babe, the Blue Ox, the winter the blue snow fell. Together, they set up a lumber camp. Bunyan invents the multiplication table, the cube root system, and algebra so that he can keep the records until he meets Johnny Inkslinger and makes him his bookkeeper. When ordinary logging methods fail, he shoots the trees off the slopes of the Mountain That Stood On Its Head. He sweats so hard cutting the stonewood trees in Utah that he creates Salt Lake. With the coming of machinery, however, there is no place for him, and he and Babe disappear forever over the hills.

Babe, a huge Blue Ox, brought up by Bunyan from a calf. When whale milk will not cure his illness, whiskey does the trick.

Niagara, Paul's moosehound.

Hels Helsen, a giant who fights a savage battle with Bunyan and then becomes his friend for life.

Johnny Inkslinger, who loses his job as surveyor when Bunyan cuts down the trees he uses for stakes. He then becomes the camp bookkeeper.

Sourdough Sam, the camp cook, who loses an arm and a leg when some sourdough, put into Johnny's ink, explodes.

Hot Biscuit Slim, Sam's son and successor, who makes meals the high point of a logger's day.

Shanty Boy, whose tall stories amuse the loggers until he tells them of Jonah and the whale; then he is beaten for lying.

King Bourbon, of Kansas. He is overcome by a rebellious duke who gets everybody drunk. Bunyan hitches Babe to Kansas and turns it upside down to quiet things, leaving Kansas flat and rid of cigarette grass, beervines, and whiskey trees.

PEACE
(Eirēnē)

Author: Aristophanes (c. 450-c. 385 B.C.E.)
First performed: 421 B.C.E.
Genre: Drama

Locale: Athens
Time: During the Peloponnesian War
Plot: Satire

Trygaeus (tri-JEE-uhs), a wealthy citizen of Athens who desires peace between Athens and Sparta. After losing all faith that a peace will be achieved through diplomacy, he resolves to ask Zeus for help. His first effort to climb Olympus by ladders results in a broken head; he then attempts to make the journey on the back of an enormous dung beetle. After a successful flight, he is accosted at the door of the palace of Zeus by Hermes, who informs Trygaeus that the gods are disgusted by the stupidities of the Greeks and have resolved to leave them ravaged by War and Tumult. Peace has been buried in an enormous pit and has been covered with stones by the effort of War. Trygaeus, witnessing War beginning to grind up the Greek cities as he might a salad in a large mortar, resolves to liberate Peace. To that end, he calls to his aid common men, laborers and farmers from all over Greece, who form the Chorus. After ludicrously inept efforts on their part, Peace, along with Opora and Theoria, is liberated from the pit. Trygaeus, taking Opora with him for his marriage bed and taking Theoria for the Senate, returns to Earth. At the marriage feast of Trygaeus and Opora, various warmongers attempt to upset the peace and quell the joy, but Trygaeus scornfully rejects their offers of bribes. The play concludes with Opora being brought out in her wedding finery while the Chorus sings "Hymen Hymenaeus."

Hermes (HUR-meez), the servant of Zeus, intended to serve as an example of the servants of the powerful in Athens as well as a reflection of the deviousness and corruption of their masters' minds. He abuses Trygaeus at first but subsides into friendliness and cooperation at the appearance of a bribe. Hermes' information about the intentions of the gods to ignore the Greeks makes it possible for Trygaeus to free Peace.

Two servants of Trygaeus, the first being his master's steward and confidential attendant who cooperates with Trygaeus throughout the play. The opening scene of the play finds both servants excitedly kneading cakes of excrement and feeding them to the dung beetle in the stable.

War, who hastily assembles the Greek cities in his mortar with the intention of grinding them into a salad and eventually into a paste.

Tumult, the servant of War, much abused by his master, who is sent off to Athens to bring back a pestle.

Hierocles (HI-roh-kleez), a soothsayer who appears at the preparation for the marriage feast and belligerently shouts prophecies about the impossibility of ending the war.

An Armourer and

a Crest-Maker, who appear at the marriage feast to lament their loss of profits after the release of Peace. They try to promote surplus war goods for peaceful purposes, such as spears to use as vine poles.

The Son of Lamachus (LA-muh-kuhs) and

the Son of Cleonymus (klee-O-nih-muhs), young boys at the marriage feast who sing as they have been taught of the glories of war until silenced by the sharp rejoinders of Trygaeus.

A Sickle-Maker, whose business has been ruined by the wars. He comes to the marriage feast to present Trygaeus with samples of his products.

A Chorus of Husbandmen, from all parts of Greece, who in trying to release Peace work against one another despite the best of intentions until the farmers, the only ones who do real work, free Peace from the pit. Throughout the play, the Chorus sings of the joys of peaceful domestic life.

THE PEARL

Author: John Steinbeck (1902-1968)
First published: 1947; serial form, 1945
Genre: Novella

Locale: Baja California, Mexico
Time: A five-day period in the late nineteenth or early twentieth century
Plot: Tragedy

Kino, a young Mexican-Indian pearl diver at the peak of his physical powers. With black, unruly hair, keen dark eyes, and a coarse, ragged mustache, Kino is lithe and strong, able to gather oysters underwater for a full two minutes without surfacing and to move about, catlike and undetected, in the dark and on rough terrain. Devoted to his wife, Juana, and his infant son, Coyotito, and proud of his position as head of his family and initially content with the traditional life of his ancestors, Kino has dreams and needs that are at first simple. When he seeks treatment for Coyotito's scorpion bite from the white doctor and is scornfully dismissed, however, anger awakens in him. After he finds a magnificent pearl, he quickly becomes more aware of his people's powerlessness and ignorance as he encounters contempt, deceit, greed, and brutality in the bigger world where he goes to sell his glorious treasure. As the threats to his pearl and his family's safety become more pressing, Kino's serenity and innocence are replaced by rage, fear, cunning, and the instinct to kill. In the end, having murdered four men and lost his hut, his beloved inherited canoe, and, above all, his precious infant son, a stone-hearted Kino hurls the malignant pearl back into the sea.

Juana, Kino's young wife, who dresses simply, out of necessity, wearing a ragged blue skirt, carrying her son slung in her shawl, and tying her dark braids with faded green ribbons. A wedding outfit, folded away, awaits better days. A silent young woman with watchful dark eyes, Juana is self-effacing and submissive to Kino, giving herself over to caring skillfully for her husband and son. A pragmatist, she prays for protection both to traditional gods and to the Christian God of the powerful Catholic Church. She is manifestly the source of Kino's early contentment with his life, despite its poverty; indeed, his first desire when he finds the pearl is that they should be legally married in the church to confirm their strong union. When threats to her family arise, Juana reveals an iron will and a perceptiveness that her husband lacks. In the face of Kino's reluctance, Juana insists on fetching the white doctor to tend Coyotito; in the face of Kino's grand dreams of new possessions and an education for Coyotito, Juana soon recognizes that the pearl will bring only catastrophe, and she urges Kino to throw it back into the sea. In the face of Kino's fierce determination, Juana dares to creep from the hut and try to get rid of the pearl herself. She stoically endures the beating that ensues, then accepts without question their need for flight after Kino murders a nighttime intruder. When she and Kino return to the village bearing the pitiful burden of their dead son, the villagers note that instead of trailing behind, Juana now walks beside Kino as an equal, forged in the same crucible of suffering.

The white doctor, a puffy-eyed, obese, lazy, and discontented man immured in his luxurious villa in town. He dreams obsessively of his one youthful sojourn in Paris and harbors the colonialist's contempt for Mexico, reluctantly tending only those patients who hold the promise of fat fees. When he thinks of them at all, he regards the Indian people as animals and refuses to treat them. Having curtly dismissed Kino's plea

to help Coyotito, he undergoes a miraculous change of attitude when he hears about Kino's pearl. He seeks out the family, overwhelming them with his authority and seeming compassion. After callously giving Coyotito medicine that makes the baby sick, he then effects a "cure," hoping to benefit handsomely from Kino's newfound wealth. The doctor embodies the corruption of the Mexican Indians' Spanish oppressors.

The trackers, Kino's nemeses. The hopelessness of Kino's flight and the inevitability of disaster become apparent as soon as the skillful trackers appear over the horizon. A gleaming rifle, carried by the chief tracker and an emblem of his power, turns from being chief among Kino's dreams of advancement to the instrument of brute authority and of his son's death. Although Kino kills the trackers with his own knife, the rifle, ironically, is the only trophy with which he returns, beaten, to his village.

— *Jill Rollins*

THE PEASANTS
(Chłopi)

Author: Władysław Reymont (1867-1925)
First published: 1904-1909
Genre: Novel

Locale: Poland
Time: Late nineteenth century
Plot: Social

Matthias Boryna (mah-TEE-yas boh-REW-nah), a well-to-do peasant, the leading man of Lipka village in Poland. Though he is sixty years old and has already outlived two wives, he is thinking of marrying again. That his grown children wish him to retire and divide his land among them makes no difference. Sorrow comes of his marriage, for he unwisely takes a wanton as his third wife. Worst of all, she takes Matthias Boryna's married son as her lover. The old man learns to endure having such a wife, but at great cost to his peace of mind. He turns for moral support to Hanka, his son's wife, and asks her and her children to live in his house, for he is a kindly, if headstrong, man. During a battle to protect timber claimed by the peasants from being cut by the owner of a nearby manor, Matthias is severely wounded. He lies many months in a stupor, neglected by his wife but nursed tenderly by his daughter-in-law, until he dies.

Yagna, Matthias Boryna's young wife, the prettiest girl in Lipka village. She turns out to be a common trull, taking up with whatever man her fancy falls on at the moment. She has an affair with Antek Boryna, her stepson, who truly loves her and is intensely bitter when the girl marries his father. Concerned only for herself, Yagna is not sorry for the trouble she brings to the Boryna family. Her only feeling while her husband lies injured for many weeks is bitterness that he still lives. She goes too far at last by chasing after a young man of the village who is studying for a priest. The indignant villagers carry her out of Lipka on a dung cart and warn her not to return. The shock of the treatment leaves her insensible for weeks.

Antek Boryna, Matthias' grown son, a man as headstrong as his father. Sick with love for Yagna, he leaves his father's house and becomes a common laborer, neglecting his wife and children. After he kills the forester who has injured his father, he and Matthias are reconciled. Antek, in prison for many

weeks, returns to find his father dead. He becomes master of the Boryna farm, a position that strengthens him to put aside his feelings for Yagna, though she still means much to him.

Hanka, Antek Boryna's loving wife. Deserted by her husband, she cares for herself and her children. A woman driven by the peasant's love of the land and its ownership, she looks after the Boryna farm and wealth while her husband is in prison and her father-in-law lies ill. She loves her husband deeply and readily accepts him when he gives up his affair with Yagna.

Dominikova (doh-mih-nih-KOH-vah), Yagna's widowed mother, a selfish, land-hungry, domineering old woman who treats her grown sons as though they were slaves and will not let them marry.

Kuba Soha, an old hired man on the Boryna farm, a veteran who had fought against the Russians. He turns poacher and is wounded by the local squire's forester for taking game. He dies when he tries to amputate his own leg.

Yuzka, the young sister of Antek Boryna.

The Voyt, the elected headman of the village, a man who feathers his own nest and is distrusted by the people of Lipka. He is eventually caught by the government for stealing several thousand rubles of public money. He is one of Yagna's lovers.

Yanek (YAH-nehk), the son of the village organist, an honest, religious young man who has begun his studies for the priesthood. Although Yagna Boryna openly pursues him, he cannot believe she is as bad as village gossip says she is. His family finally sends him away to protect him from the girl.

Simon, one of Dominikova's grown sons. He rebels against his mother's domination and manages to buy a few acres of land to till for himself and his wife.

Nastka, Simon's young wife, whom he marries against his mother's will.

Roch (rohk), a wandering beggar and religious man who teaches the children to read and serves the village as a physician. An honest and trustworthy man much beloved by the peasants, he is hunted out by the Russians because he teaches the Polish peasants to read in their own language and encourages them to remain patriotic Poles.

Matthew, a carpenter and millwright, one of Antek Boryna's rivals for Yagna's favors.

Teresa, a young peasant girl who loves Matthew.

The Blacksmith, Antek Boryna's brother-in-law, a selfish man who would like to drive Antek off the Boryna farm and take it over on the strength of being the husband of Antek's sister. He constantly plots against the other Borynas.

PEDER VICTORIOUS
(Peder Seier)

Author: O. E. Rölvaag (1876-1931)
First published: 1928
Genre: Novel

Locale: Dakota Territory
Time: Late nineteenth century
Plot: Regional

Beret Holm, a Norwegian pioneer woman who is determined that her children are Norwegian and are to be reared as Norwegians. She discourages their use of the English language and refuses to give up her old-country customs. She wants her son, Peder Victorious, to become a minister and is single-minded in this purpose. She is strongly opposed to anything that tends to Americanize her family. Finally, she becomes reconciled to her son's marriage to an Irish girl in the community.

Peder Victorious, Beret's youngest child. His mother is determined that he become a minister. He has a fine, strong voice and is often called upon to recite at programs, but his mother objects when he does this reciting in English. He is perplexed by the problem of a God of love who is also responsible for all of the catastrophes that befall him and the community. He resents being kept at home, away from parties and dances, and begins slipping out to go to them at night. He is cast in a school play opposite an Irish girl, and they fall in love. He is surprised and delighted when his mother consents to their marriage.

The Reverend Johan Gabrielsen, the minister to the Norwegian settlement, who is convinced that Peder should go to the seminary and become the next spiritual leader of the group. He is more lenient than Peder's mother and believes that English will take the place of the Norwegian language in the community. He antagonizes Beret by asking Peder to read in English and by saying grace in English in her home.

Susie Doheny, the girl who is cast in the play with Peder and who falls in love with him.

Ole,

Store-Hans, and

Anna Marie, Beret's other children.

Charlie Doheny, Peder's friend, a jolly Irish boy who is Susie's brother.